D0729742

KIBBLE AND TIDBITS FROM

Vacationing With Your Pet

WHERE TO STAY

A comprehensive guide to pet-friendly accommodations, Eileen's award-winning directory includes more than 25,000 hotels, motels, inns and B&Bs in the United States and Canada that welcome you and your pet.

- Fluff Fido's pillow at the Four Seasons Hotel in Beverly Hills (page 140).

- Do the River Walk with Rover when you stay at the Plaza San Antonio in Texas (page 555).

- Fill your eyes with starry skies in Tucson at the Westward Look Resort (page 123).

- Window shop till you drop and then rest your weary paws at the Hotel Plaza Athenee in New York City (page 427).

- Fall hard for autumn colors with furface in Vermont at the award-winning Topnotch at Stowe Resort (page 575).

- Take your sun-loving pet on a journey to the Amerisuites in Tampa (page 227).

WHERE TO STAY

- Let your Sandy have her way on the sandy shores of Cannon Beach, Oregon when you stay at the Tolovana Inn (page 471).

- Enjoy a winter wonderland with your snow-sniffing wagalong at the The Little Nell in Aspen, Colorado (page 181).

- Go for the gold with Digger in Knoxville and get your money's worth at the Quality Inn (page 520).

- Better than an igloo, cozy into Alaska Auntie's B&B (Bed & Biscuit?) in Anchorage (page 106).

- Don't be sleepless in Seattle, hightail it to The Alexis Hotel (page 605).

- People and pooch watch under the famous clock at San Francisco's historic Westin St. Francis Hotel (page 170).

- Give Bowser something to bark home about from the Four Seasons Hotel in Toronto, Ontario (page 695).

- Have a howl of a good time at a Holiday Inn in Montreal, Quebec (page 699).

HOW TO DO IT

Increase your travel know-how with some handy traveling tips.

- How to Pack For Your Pet (page 38).
- 29 Tips For Travel Safety (page 57).
- 27 "On-the-Road Tips" (page 61).

Old dogs can learn new tricks.

- Training Do's and Don'ts (page 33).
- Prevent Aggression in Your Dog (page 36).
- Get Crate Smart (page 34).

Make a night of it.

- Hotel and Motel Policies (page 17).
- Travel by Car (page 42).
- Travel by Plane (page 49).

Kitty comes along.

- What About Cats (page 25).
- Cat Travel Tips (page 27).

Directories by Eileen Barish

DOIN' ARIZONA WITH YOUR POOCH

DOIN' CALIFORNIA WITH YOUR POOCH

DOIN' NEW YORK WITH YOUR POOCH

DOIN' TEXAS WITH YOUR POOCH

DOIN' THE NORTHWEST WITH YOUR POOCH

VACATIONING WITH YOUR PET

THE GUIDE TO LODGING IN ITALY'S MONASTERIES

THE GUIDE TO LODGING IN SPAIN'S MONASTERIES

Novels by Eileen Barish

ARIZONA TERRITORY
AS TIME GOES BY

EILEEN'S DIRECTORY OF PET-FRIENDLY LODGING IN THE UNITED STATES & CANADA

VACATIONING WITH YOUR PET

Over 25,000 Listings of
Hotels, Motels, Inns, Ranches
and B&Bs that Welcome
Guests with Pets

Pet-Friendly Publications
P.O. Box 8459, Scottsdale, AZ 85252

Copyright © 2003, 2001, 2000, 1999, 1998, 1997, 1996, 1995, 1994
Eileen Barish
All rights reserved.

No part of this book may be reproduced or
transmitted in any form or by any means now known or
which will become known, without written permission from
the publisher. Permission is granted for reviewers and others
to quote brief passages for use in newspapers, periodicals, or
broadcasts provided credit is given to:

VACATIONING WITH YOUR PET
by Eileen Barish

Pet-Friendly Publications
P.O. Box 8459, Scottsdale, AZ 85252
Tel: (800) 638-3637

ISBN # 1-884465-15-3
Library of Congress Catalog Card Number: 2001-130277
Printed and bound in the United States of America.
Fifth Edition - Second Printing

While due care has been exercised in the compilation
of this directory, we are not responsible for errors or omis-
sions. We are sorry for any inconvenience. Inclusion in this
directory does not constitute endorsement or recommendation
by the author or publisher. It is intended as a guide to assist in
providing information to the public and the listings are
offered as an aid to travelers.

S P E C I A L   E D I T I O N S

Eileen's directories are available at special discounts when purchased in
bulk for premiums and special sales promotions as well as for fund-
raising or educational use. Special editions or book excerpts can also be
created to specification. For details, call 1-800-638-3637.

CREDITS

Author & Managing Editor — Eileen Barish

Associate Editor — Harvey Barish

Lodging & Research Editor — Phyllis Holmes

Research/Writing Staff — Alison Dufner
Tiffany Geoghegan
Courtney Mechling

Illustrator — Gregg Myers

Graphic Designer — Tawni Hensley

Photographer — Ken Friedman

ACKNOWLEDGEMENTS

Phyllis, I am grateful for your tireless dedication and extraordinary thoroughness. Your efforts meant the difference between good and great.

For Nona, Kenny and Chris for being so supportive and especially for Harvey who makes it all come together, who's always up for the often demanding challenge and more than ready for the next adventure.

In memory of Sam, the "best friend" who started it all.

Cover photo
COOPER

TABLE OF CONTENTS

TRAVELING BY PLANE (cont.)

How will my pet feel about a kennel?
What about identification?
How can I make plane travel comfortable for my pet?
Will there automatically be room on board for my pet?
What will pet travel cost?
What about food and water?
What about tranquilizers?
What about after we land?
Pets who shouldn't fly.
Health certificates - will I need one?

Allergies.
Bites and stings.
Bleeding.
Burns.
Earache.
Eye scratches or inflammation.
Falls or impact injuries.
Fleas.
Heatstroke.

UNITED STATES DIRECTORY OF PET-FRIENDLY LODGING

CANADIAN DIRECTORY OF
PET-FRIENDLY LODGING

Traveling With Your Pet Can Be A Rewarding Experience

You never have to leave your best friend home or kenneled in a small cage while you vacation. Bring your four-legged buddy along. Double your enjoyment and increase your safety. If your pet is a great companion at home, he can be just as companionable when you travel.

HOW TO USE THIS DIRECTORY
No more sneaking Snoopy

Whether you're a seasoned pet traveler or a first-time explorer, *Vacationing With Your Pet* will make traveling with your pet easier and more enjoyable.

At a glance, you'll locate thousands of accommodations in the United States and Canada that welcome people traveling with their pets.

Choose lodging from hotels, B&Bs (aka Bed & Biscuits), motels, resorts, inns and ranches that welcome you and your pet *through the front door*. Arranged in an easy-to-use alphabetical format, *Vacationing With Your Pet* covers the United States and Canada. Within each state or province, cities are also arranged in alphabetical order. Each listing includes the name of the lodging, address, zip code and phone number. Wherever available, the high/low range of room rates and toll-free 800-numbers are provided.

Do hotel and motel policies differ regarding pets?

Yes, but all the accommodations in *Vacationing With Your Pet* allow pets. Policies can vary on charges and sometimes on pet size or type. Some might require a damage deposit while some combine their deposit with a daily and/or one-time charge. Others may restrict pets to specific rooms, perhaps cabins or cottages.

Residence-type inns which cater to long-term guests often charge a long-term fee. Some also require advance notice. But most accommodations do not charge a fee or have restrictive policies. As with all travel arrangements, it is recommended that you call in advance to confirm policies and room availability. Be aware that hotel policies may change. At the time your reservations are made, determine the pet-policy of your lodging choice.

Not just for vacationers, this is a "must-have" reference for anyone who has a pet.

Increase your travel horizons and give your best friend a new leash on life. Owning a copy of *Vacationing With Your Pet* means you won't have to leave your trusted companion at home when you travel. Containing a comprehensive overview of practical, hands-on information, this directory to make your travel experiences safer and more pleasurable. Training do's and don'ts, crate use and selection, driving tips, pet etiquette, travel manners, what and how to pack for your pet, first-aid advice and a pet identification form are just some of the topics covered. See the Table of Contents for a complete listing of travel, training and pet care information.

A word about area codes.

Area codes keep changing all over the country and every attempt has been made to keep up with these changes. To help you, we have included toll-free numbers wherever available. If a local phone number doesn't go through, check for a new area code.

Lodging Guidelines For You and Your Pet

Conduct yourself in a courteous manner and you'll continue to be welcome anywhere you travel. Never do anything on vacation with your pet that you wouldn't do at home. Some quick tips follow that can make traveling with your pet more pleasurable.

1. If your pet is accustomed to sleeping on the bed with you, take along a sheet or favorite blanket and put that on top of the bedding provided by your lodging.

2. Place a towel or small mat under your pet's food and water dishes and feed your pet in the bathroom where clean-up is easier should an accident occur.

3. Try to keep your pet off the furniture. Pack a lint and hair remover to eliminate unwanted hairs.

4. Always keep your dog on a leash on the hotel and motel grounds and carry plastic bags and/or paper towels for clean-up.

5. Keep your cat's litter box in the bathroom. Clean it often, flushing away waste.

Can my dog be left alone in the room?

Only you know the answer to that. If your dog isn't destructive, if he doesn't bark incessantly and if the hotel allows unattended dogs, try leaving him in the room for short periods of time — say when you dine out. Hang the "Do Not Disturb" sign on your door to alert the chambermaid or hotel staff members that your room shouldn't be entered.

Before leaving your dog unattended, the following suggestions might prove helpful:

1. Walk or otherwise exercise your pooch. An exercised dog will fall asleep more easily.

2. Provide a favorite toy as a distraction.

3. Turn on the TV or radio for audio/ visual companionship.

4. Be certain that there is an ample supply of fresh water available.

5. Calm your dog with a reassuring goodbye and a stroke of your hand.

Pooch Rules & Regulations

BE A RESPONSIBLE DOG OWNER AND OBEY THE RULES.

- Clean up after your dog even if no one has seen him do his business.
- Leash your dog in areas that require leashing.
- Train your dog to be well behaved.
- Control your dog in public places so that he's not a nuisance to others.

Note: When leashes are required, they must be six feet or less in length. Leashes should be carried at all times. They are prudent safety measures .

<u>FIDO FACT:</u>

- *Problems with dogs in many recreation areas have increased in recent years. The few rules that apply to dogs are meant to assure that you and other visitors have enjoyable outdoor experiences.*

INTRODUCTION

Vacationing with your pet can be a fun-filled adventure. It doesn't require special training or expertise. Just a little planning and a little patience. This directory is filled with information to make traveling with your pet easier and more satisfying. From training tips to what to take along, to the do's and don'ts of travel, virtually all of your questions will be answered.

Vacationing with pets.

Not something I thought I'd ever do. But as the adage goes, necessity is the mother of invention. What began as a necessity turned into a lifestyle. A lifestyle that has improved every aspect of my vacation and travel time.

Although my family had dogs on and off during my childhood, it wasn't until my early thirties that I decided it was time to bring another dog into my life. And the lives of my young children. I wanted them to grow up with a dog; to know what it was like to have a canine companion, a playmate, a friend who would always be there, to love you, no questions asked. A four-legged pal who would be the first to lick a teary face or a bloody knee. Enter Samson, our family's first Golden Retriever.

Samson.

For nearly fifteen years, Sammy was everything a family could want from their dog. Loyal, forgiving, sweet, funny, neurotic, playful, sensitive, smart, too smart, puddle loving, fearless, strong and cuddly. He could melt your heart with a woebegone expression or make your hair stand on end with one of his pranks. Like the time he methodically opened the seam on a bean bag chair and then cheerfully spread the beans everywhere. Or when he followed a jogger and ended up in a shelter more than 20 miles from home.

As the years passed, Sam's face turned white and one by one our kids headed off to college. Preparing for the inevitable, my husband Harvey and I decided that when Sam died, no other dog would take his place. We wanted our freedom, not the responsibility of another dog.

Sammy left us one sunny June morning with so little fanfare that we couldn't believe he was actually gone. Little did we realize the void that would remain when our white-faced Golden Boy was no longer with us.

Life goes on...Rosie and Maxwell.

After planning a two-week vacation through California, with an ultimate destination of Lake Tahoe, Harvey and I had our hearts stolen by two Golden Retriever puppies, Rosie and Maxwell. Two little balls of fur that would help to fill the emptiness Sam's death had created. The puppies were ready to leave their mom and come home with us only weeks before our scheduled departure. What to do? Kennel them? Hire a pet sitter? Neither felt right.

Sooo...we took them along.

Oh, the fun we had. And the friends we made. Both the two-legged and four-legged variety. Having dogs on our trip made us more a part of the places we visited. We learned that dogs are natural conversation starters. Rosie and Maxwell were the prime movers in some lasting friendships we made during that first trip together. Now when we revisit Lake Tahoe, we have old friends to see as well as new ones to make. The locals we met made us feel at home, offering insider information on little known hikes, wonderful restaurants and quiet neighborhood parks. This knowledge enhanced our vacation and filled every day with wonder.

Since that first trip, our travels have taken us to many places. We've visited national forests, mountain resorts, seaside villages, island retreats, big cities and tiny hamlets. We've shared everything from luxury hotel rooms to rustic cabin getaways. We've experienced good times together and always come home with wonderful memories. I can't imagine travel that doesn't include our dogs.

When I watch Rosie and Maxwell frolic in a lake or when they accompany us on a hike, I stop and think of Sammy and remember the legacy of love and friendship he left behind. So for those of you who regularly take your pet along and those who would if you knew how, come share my travel knowledge. And happy trails and tails to you.

Is my pet vacation-friendly?

Most pets can be excellent traveling companions. It stands to reason that if you accustom your pet to travel at an early age, he will adapt more quickly. That doesn't mean that an older pet won't love vacationing with you. And it doesn't mean that the training period has to be a difficult one.

Even if your dog hasn't traveled with you in the past, chances are he'll make a wonderful companion. And chances are that this unique time will result in a closer relationship with your animal and fill your travels with memories to last a lifetime.

A socialized pooch is a sophisticated traveler.

Of course, every dog is different. And you know yours better than anyone. To be sure that he will travel like a pro, accustom him to different situations. Take him for long walks around your neighborhood. Let him accompany you while you do errands. If your chores include stair climbing or using an elevator, take him with you. The more exposure to people, places and things, the better. Make your wagger worldly. The sophistication will pay off in a better behaved, less frightened pet. It won't be long until he will happily share travel and vacation times with you.

Just ordinary dogs.

Rosie and Maxwell, my traveling companions, are not exceptional dogs to anyone but me. Their training was neither intensive nor professionally rendered. They were trained with kindness, praise, consistency and love. And not all of their training came about when they were puppies. I too had a lot to learn. And as I learned what I wanted of them, their training continued. It was a sharing and growing experience. Old dogs (and humans too) can learn new tricks. Rosie and Maxwell never fail to surprise me. Their ability to adapt to new situations has never stopped. So don't think you have to start with a puppy. Every dog, young and old, can be taught to be travel friendly.

Rosie and Maxwell know when I begin putting their things together that another holiday is about to begin. Their excitement mounts with every phase of preparation. They stick like glue - remaining at my side as I organize their belongings. By the time I've finished, they can barely contain their joy. Rosie grabs her leash and prances about the kitchen holding it in her mouth while Max sits on his haunches and howls. If they could talk, they'd tell you how much they enjoy traveling. But since they can't, trust this directory to lead you to a different kind of experience. One that's filled with lots of love and an opportunity for shared adventure. So with an open mind and an open heart, pack your bags and pack your pooch. Slip this handy book into your suitcase or the glove compartment of your car and let the fun begin.

WHAT ABOUT CATS?

When people learn about my book and the fact that I travel with my two Golden Retrievers, they often say, "well, you travel with dogs, but I have cats."

Well cat lovers, rejoice! You too can enjoy the companionship of your feline when you vacation or travel. Of course, not every cat is going to adapt to travel. That's a decision only you can make. But if you'd like to give it a try, the following should prove helpful.

A walk in the park!

Perhaps one of the biggest obstacles cat owners face when they think of taking their cats along is what to do with them; how to include a feline friend on something as simple as a walk in the park. Although you don't often see people walking cats, it's not because it can't be done. It can. According to my cat-loving friends, it's not that difficult and they maintain it's worth the effort; not to mention the novelty of the sight and the friendly encounters it can provoke.

One step at a time.

Walking your kitty is not something that can be hurried. Before you begin, you'll need a well-made, lightweight harness and leash. Don't even think of using a collar with just a piece of rope. Too tight and your cat will be uncomfortable and dread her walks. Too loose and she might squirm away. A properly fitted harness is a necessity. As a rule of thumb, if you can slip the width of two fingers between the harness and your cat's neck and between the harness and her belly, you've got a good fit.

Begin slowly…as you would with a baby. Once you buy the harness and leash, let her sniff it. Leave it next to her until she becomes accustomed to its sight and smell. When she appears relaxed, gently slip on the harness. Let her wear it. You'll know when she's feeling comfortable. At that point, attach the leash and again wait for her to feel at ease. Let her walk around with it, feel the weight trailing behind. During these times, remain with your cat to supervise her. You know her better than anyone. When you sense she's ready, pick up the leash and walk around the house. Take along a handful of treats. As you walk, talk reassuringly to her, stopping every so often to praise her efforts. Give her a treat to reinforce your pleasure. Let her know how happy you are with her progress. Continue this "practice walking" until you feel confident she's up to the next step…the great outdoors. Remember she is apt to feel ill at ease and somewhat vulnerable. She'll look to you for protection. Once you're outdoors, be alert to your surroundings. If you sense anything that might frighten your cat, scoop her up in your arms. Reinforce the sense of security that being with you provides.

Follow the leader.

Make your outings fun. Praise your feline and reward her with a treat as she follows your lead. Or if you prefer, let her choose the direction and pace of your walk. Or try a combination of both approaches.

Training kitty to walk can be the first step to more shared times and a closer relationship. Not only will you be getting exercise and fresh air, but you'll be spending unique, quality time together. And don't overlook the social benefits that having your cat with you can mean. You're bound to attract other cat lovers who share the same interests.

Once you make the decision to try, proceed slowly and be generous with praise. Patience, love and a treat or two can mean success as well as a new way of life for you and your furry friend.

CAT TRAVEL TIP #1:
Several weeks before your journey, have your cat examined by your vet. If shots are due, have them done early and avoid the possibility of side effects at the time of your trip. If your cat has a tendency to carsickness, ask your vet about sedatives.

CAT TRAVEL TIP #2:
Cats should always be confined to a kennel when in a car — for their safety and yours. Cats love to jump and perch and a kennel will eliminate the potential for accidents. Make your cat's kennel as comfortable as you can by including a small scratch post or a favorite toy. Put some soft bedding on the floor of the kennel as well. Shortly before you plan to leave on your vacation, fill your cat's home litter box with fresh litter. Generally this will prompt your cat to answer nature's call before your departure. You can then begin your trip knowing your cat has already voided.

CAT TRAVEL TIP #3:
If you have more than one cat and they're companionable, buy a larger carrier and let them share the accommodations. At home or on the road, it's comforting for friendly felines to curl up together. Being in the same crate also means that your cats can continue to groom one another, a sure antidote to anxiety.

TRAVEL TRAINING

A well-trained, well-behaved dog is easy to live with and especially easy to travel with. There are basics other than sit, down and stay which you might want to incorporate into your training routine. Whenever you begin a training session, remember that your patience and your dog's attention span are the key elements to success. Training sessions should be 5-10 minutes each. Even if the results are initially disappointing, don't become discouraged. Stick with it. After just a few lessons, your canine will respond. Dogs love to learn, to feel productive and accomplished. Training isn't punishment. It's a gift. A gift of love. You'll quickly see the difference training can make in your animal. Most of all, keep a sense of humor. It's not punishment for you either.

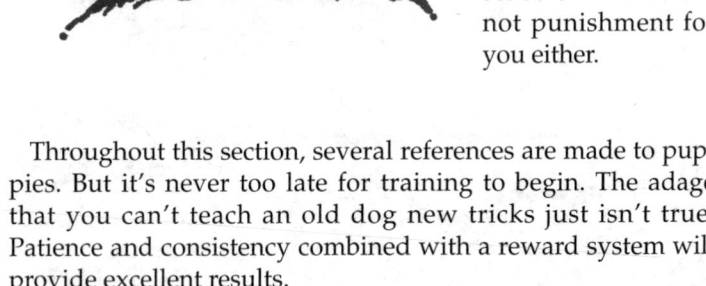

Throughout this section, several references are made to puppies. But it's never too late for training to begin. The adage that you can't teach an old dog new tricks just isn't true. Patience and consistency combined with a reward system will provide excellent results.

Let's get social.

When it comes to travel training, not enough can be said about the benefits of socialization. The lessons of socialization are the foundation of a well-trained, well-behaved dog.

Socialize your dog at an early age. Allow your puppy to be handled by different people. Include men and children since puppies are inherently more fearful of both. When your puppy is three months old, join an obedience/training class. These classes are important because they provide puppies with the experience of being with other dogs. Your puppy will have the opportunity of putting down other dogs without inflicting harm and he'll also learn how to bounce back after being put down himself. Socialization can continue with walks around your neighborhood, visits to parks frequented by other dogs and children and by working with friends who have dogs they want to socialize.

FIDO FACT:

- *Dog ownership is a common bond and the basis of impromptu conversations as well as lasting friendships.*

Walking on a leash.

It's very natural for a puppy to pull at his leash. Instead of just pulling back, stop walking. Hold the leash to your chest. If your dog lets the leash slacken, say GOOD DOG. If he sits, say GOOD SIT. Then begin your walk again. Stop every ten feet or so and tell your dog to sit. Knowing he'll only be told to sit if he pulls, he'll eventually learn to pay attention to the next command. It makes sense to continue your training while on walks because your dog will learn to heed your commands under varying conditions. This will prove especially important when traveling together. Eliminating the "tug of war" factor can mean the difference between enjoying or disliking the company of your pooch at home or away.

Chewing.

Most dogs chew out of boredom. Eliminate destructive chewing by teaching your dog to chew on chew toys. An easy way to interest him in chewing is to stuff a hollow, nonconsumable chew toy with treats such as peanut butter, kibble or a piece of hard cheese. Once the toy is stuffed, attach a string to it and tempt your dog's interest by pulling the toy along. He'll take it from there.

Until you're satisfied that he won't be destructive, consider confining your pooch to one room or to his crate with a selection of chew toys. This is a particularly important training tool for dogs who must be left alone for long periods of time, and for dogs who travel with their owners. If your pooch knows not to chew destructively at home, those same good habits will remain with him on the road.

Bite inhibition.

The trick here is to keep a puppy from biting in the first place, not break the bad habit after it's formed, although that too can be accomplished. Your puppy should be taught to develop a soft mouth by inhibiting the force of his bites. As your dog grows into adolescence, he should continue to be taught to soften his bite and as an adult dog should learn never to mouth at all.

Allow your puppy to bite but whenever force is exhibited, say OUCH! If he continues to bite, say OUCH louder and then leave the room. When you return to the room, let the puppy come to you. Your pup will begin to associate the bite and OUCH with the cessation of playtime and will learn to mouth more softly. Even when your puppy's bites no longer hurt, pretend they do. Once this training is finished, you'll have a dog that will not mouth. A dog who will not accidentally injure people you meet during your travels.

Jumping dogs.

Dogs usually jump on people to get their attention. A fairly simple way to correct this habit is to teach your dog to sit and stay until released. When your dog is about to meet new people, put him in the sit/stay position. Be sure to praise your dog for obeying the command and then pet him to provide the attention he craves. Ask friends and visitors to help reinforce the command.

Come.

The secret to this command is to begin training at an early age. But older dogs can also learn. It might just take a little longer. From the time your pup's brought home, call him by name and say COME every time you're going to feed him. The association will be simple. He'll soon realize that goodies await if he responds to your call. Try another approach as well. During training sessions, call to your dog every few minutes. Reward him with praise and sometimes with a treat. And take advantage of normally occurring circumstances, such as your dog approaching you. Whenever you can anticipate that your dog is coming toward you, command COME as he nears you. Then reward him with praise for doing what came naturally.

NEVER order your dog to COME for punishment. If he's caught in the act of negative behavior, walk to him to reprimand.

Pay attention.

Train your dog to listen to you. For example, when your dog is at play in the yard, call him to you. When he comes, have him sit and praise him. Then release him to play again. Your dog will soon understand that obeying does not mean the end of playtime. Instead it means that he'll be petted and praised and then allowed to resume play.

Communication - talking to your dog.

Training isn't just about teaching your dog to sit or give his paw. Training is about teaching your pooch to become an integral part of your life. To fit into your daily routine and into your leisure time. Take notice of how your dog studies you, anticipates your next move. Incorporate his natural desire to please into your training. Let him know what you're thinking, how you're feeling. Talk to him as you go about your daily chores. He'll eventually recognize and understand changes in your voice, facial expressions, hand movements and body language. He'll know when you're happy or angry with him or with anyone else. If you want him to do something, get his attention and then speak to him. For example, if you want him to fetch his ball, ask him in an emphatic way, stressing the word ball. He won't understand at first, so fetch it yourself and tell him ball. Put the ball down and then repeat the command. This training method can be used in both play related activities and general obedience. It won't be long until you increase your dog's vocabulary and his understanding of numerous commands.

Training do's & don'ts.

- Never hit your dog.

- Praise and reward your dog for good behavior. Don't be embarrassed to lavish praise upon a dog who's earned it.

- Unless you catch your dog in a mischievous act, don't punish him. He will not understand what he did wrong. And when you do punish, go to your dog. Never use the command COME for punishment.

- Don't repeat a command. Dogs have excellent hearing. Say the command once in a firm voice. If he doesn't obey it's not because he hasn't heard you. Return to the training method for the disobeyed command.

- Don't be too eager or too reticent to punish. Most of all, be consistent.

- Don't encourage fearfulness. If your dog has a fear of people or places, work with him to overcome this fear rather than ignoring it, or believing it can't be changed.

- Don't ignore or encourage aggression.

- Don't use food excessively as a reward.

- Don't become discouraged if your initial attempts at training are unsuccessful. Try other approaches. Every dog can be trained.

CRATE TRAINING IS GREAT TRAINING

Many people erroneously equate the crate to jail. But that's only a human perspective. To a dog who's been properly crate trained, the crate represents a private place where your dog will feel safe and secure. It is much better to prevent behavioral problems by crate training than to give up on an unruly dog.

4 reasons why crate training is good for you.

1. You can relax when you leave your dog home alone. You'll know that he is safe, comfortable and incapable of destructive behavior.

2. You can housebreak your pooch faster. Confinement to a crate encourages control and helps establish a regular walk time routine.

3. You can safely confine your dog to prevent unforeseen situations. For example, if he's sick, if you have workers or guests that are either afraid of or allergic to dogs, or if your canine becomes easily excited or confused when new people enter the scene, the crate provides a reasonable method of containment.

4. You can travel with your pooch. Use of a crate in your automobile eliminates the potential for distraction. It also assures that your dog will not get loose during your trip.

FIDO FACT:

- *Want to register your puppy or locate a breeder? The American Kennel Club's customer service line is (919) 233-9767.*

5 reasons why crate training is good for your dog.

1. He'll have an area for rest when he's tired, stressed or sick.

2. He'll be exposed to fewer bad behavior temptations which can result in punishment.

3. He'll have an easier time learning to control calls of nature.

4. He'll feel more secure when left alone.

5. He'll be able to join you in your travels.

Some do's and don'ts.

- DO exercise your dog before and after crating.

- DO place the crate in a well-used, well-ventilated area of your home.

- DO make sure that you can always approach your dog while he is in his crate. This will insure that he does not become overly protective of his space.

- DON'T punish your dog in his crate or banish him to the crate.

- DON'T leave your pooch in the crate for more than four hours at a time.

- DON'T let curious kids invade his private place. This is his special area.

- DON'T confine your dog to a crate if he becomes frantic or completely miserable.

- DON'T use a crate without proper training.

10

Ways To Prevent Aggression in Your Dog

1. Socialize him at an early age.

2. Set rules and stick to them.

3. Under your supervision, expose him to children and other animals.

4. Never be abusive towards your dog by hitting or yelling at him.

5. Offer plenty of praise when he's behaving himself.

6. Be consistent with training. Make sure your dog responds to your commands before you do anything for him.

7. Don't handle your dog roughly or play aggressively with him.

8. Neuter your dog.

9. Contact your veterinarian to deal with persistent behavior problems.

10. Your dog is a member of the family. Treat him that way. Tied to a pole is not a life.

Take your dog's temperament into account.

- Is he a pleaser?
- Is he the playful sort?
- Does he love having tasks to perform?
- Does he like to retrieve? To carry?

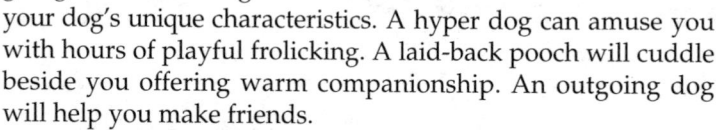

Dogs, like people, have distinct personalities...mellow, hyper, shy or outgoing. Take advantage of your dog's unique characteristics. A hyper dog can amuse you with hours of playful frolicking. A laid-back pooch will cuddle beside you offering warm companionship. An outgoing dog will help you make friends.

If you can combine what you know of your dog's personality with what you want to teach, your dog will train more easily. Together you will achieve a fulfilling compatibility.

<u>FIDO FACT:</u>

- ***Staying at a hotel for a few days or more? Here's an easy way to identify your pet's temporary home. Staple one of the hotel's matchbook covers to your pet's collar. Be sure to remove the matches first.***

WHAT AND HOW TO PACK FOR YOUR POOCH

Be prepared.

Dogs enjoy the adventure of travel. If your dog is basically well behaved and physically fit, he should make an excellent traveling companion. But traveling times will be more successful with just a little common sense and preparation.

Just as many children (and adults I might add) travel with their own pillow, your pooch will also enjoy having his favorites with him. Perhaps you'll want to include the blanket he sleeps with or his favorite toy. Not only will a familiar item or toy make him feel more at ease, but it will keep him occupied as well.

I restock Max and Rosie's travel bags at the end of each trip. That way I'm always prepared for our next adventure. "My Pooch's Packing List" is found on page 41. Consider including some or all of the items that follow.

- A blanket to cover the back seat of your vehicle.
- Two or three old towels for emergencies.
- Two bowls, one for water, the other for food.
- Plastic clean-up bags (supermarket produce bags work well).
- Paper towels — for spills, clean-up and everything in between.
- A long line of rope. You'll be surprised how often you'll use this very handy item.
- An extra collar and lead.
- Can opener and spoon.
- Flashlight.
- An extra flea and tick collar.
- Dog brush.
- Small scissors.
- Blunt end tweezers — great for removing thorns and cactus needles.
- Chew toys, balls, frisbees, treats — whatever your pooch prefers.
- Nightlight.
- A room deodorizer.
- A handful of zip-lock bags in several sizes.
- Pre-moistened towelettes. Take along two packs. Put one in your suitcase, the other in the glove compartment of your car.
- Dog food, enough for a couple of days. Although most brands are available throughout the country, either at pet stores, supermarkets or veterinary offices, you'll want to pack enough and eliminate having to find dog food the first night or two of your vacation.
- Water — a full container from home. Top off as needed and gradually accustom your dog to his new water supply.

People packing made easy...12 tips.

No matter where your travels take you, whether it's to the local park or on a cross-country trip, never leave home without your dog's leash and a handful of plastic bags or pooper scooper. I clearly remember those awful moments when I ended up without one or both.

1. Consolidate. Even if you're traveling as a family, one tube of toothpaste and one hair dryer should suffice.

2. Avoid potential spills by wrapping perfume, shampoo and other liquids together and placing them in large zip-lock plastic bags.

3. When packing, layer your clothing using interlocking patterns. You'll fit more into your suitcase and have less shifting and wrinkling.

4. Write out your itinerary, including flight info, car rental confirmation numbers, travel agent telephone numbers and lodging info. Keep one copy with you and put a duplicate in a safe place.

5. Take along a night light, especially if you're traveling with a child. A flashlight always comes in handy too.

6. Stash a supply of zip-lock plastic bags, moist towelettes, trash bags, an extra leash (or rope) and a plastic container in an accessible place.

7. If you plan to hike with children, give each a whistle; they're great for signaling help.

8. Include a can opener and some plastic utensils.

9. Comfortable walking shoes are a must. If you plan on hiking, invest in a sturdy pair of hiking boots, but be sure to break them in before your trip. Take an extra pair of socks with you whenever you hike.

10. Don't forget to include first aid-kits. One for dogs and one for people.

11. Pack an extra pair of glasses or contact lenses.

12. Keep medications in separate, clearly marked containers.

MY POOCH'S PACKING LIST

1 _____

2 _____

3 _____

4 _____

5 _____

6 _____

7 _____

8 _____

9 _____

10 _____

11 _____

12 _____

13 _____

14 _____

15 _____

16 _____

17 _____

18 _____

19 _____

20 _____

21 _____

22 _____

23 _____

24 _____

25 _____

26 _____

27 _____

28 _____

29 _____

30 _____

TRAVEL BY CAR

"Kennel Up"…the magical, all-purpose command.

When Rosie's and Maxwell's training began, I used a metal kennel which they were taught to regard as their spot, their sleeping place. Whenever they were left at home and then again when they were put to bed at night, I used the simple command, "Kennel Up," as I pointed to and tapped their kennel. They quickly learned the command. As they outgrew the kennel, the laundry room became their "kennel up" place. As full-grown dogs, the entire kitchen became their "kennel up" area. Likewise, when they began accompanying me on trips, I reinforced the command each time I told them to jump into the car. They soon understood that being in their "kennel up" place meant that I expected them to behave, whether they were at home, in the car or in a hotel room. Teaching your dog the "kennel up" command will make travel times easier and more pleasurable.

Old dogs can learn new tricks.

When we first began vacationing with Rosie and Max, some friends decided to join us on a few of our local jaunts. Their dog Brandy, a ten year-old Cocker Spaniel, had never traveled with them. Other than trips to the vet and the groomer, she'd never been in the car. The question remained… would Brandy adjust? We needn't have worried. She took to the car immediately. Despite her small size, she quickly learned to jump in and out of the rear of the station wagon. She ran through the forests with Rosie and Max, playing and exploring as if she'd always had free run. To her owners and to Brandy, the world took on new meaning. Nature as seen through the eyes of their dog became a more exciting place of discovery.

Can my dog be trained to travel?

Dogs are quite adaptable and responsive and patience will definitely have its rewards. Your pooch loves nothing more than to be with you. If it means behaving to have that privilege, he'll respond.

Now that you've decided to travel and vacation with your dog, it's probably a good idea to get him started with short trips. Before you go anywhere, remember two of the most important items for happy dog travel, a leash for safety and the proper paraphernalia for clean-up. There's nothing more frustrating or scary than a loose, uncontrolled dog. And nothing more embarrassing than being without clean-up essentials when your dog unexpectedly decides to relieve himself.

Make traveling a pleasant experience. Stop every so often and do fun things. But when you do stop to let him out, leash him before you open the car doors. When the walk or playtime is over, remember the "Kennel Up" command when you tell your pooch to get into the car or into his kennel. And use lots of praise when he obeys.

You'll find that your dog will most likely be lulled to sleep by the motion of the car. Rosie and Maxwell fall asleep after less than fifteen minutes. I stop every few hours, give them water and let them "stretch their legs." They've become accustomed to these short stops and anticipate them. The moment the car is turned off and the hatch-back popped open, they anxiously await their leashes. When our romping time is over and we're back at the car, a simple "kennel up" gets them into their travel area.

To kennel or not to kennel.

Whether or not you use a kennel for car travel is a personal choice. Safety should be your primary concern. Yours and your dog's. Whatever method of travel you choose, be certain that your dog will not interfere with your driving. If you plan to use a kennel, line the bottom with an old blanket, towel or shredded newspaper and include a favorite toy. When you're vacationing by car and not using a kennel, consider a car harness.

If you're not going to use a kennel or harness, consider confining your dog to the back seat and commanding him to "kennel up." Protect your upholstery by covering the seat with an old blanket. This will make clean-up easier at the end of your trip. To keep my car fresh smelling and free from doggie odors, I stash a deodorizer under the front seat.

How often should I stop?

Many people think that when their dogs are in the car, they have to "go" more often. Not true. Whenever you stop for yourself, let your pooch have a drink and take a walk. It's not necessary to make extra stops along the way unless your dog has a physical problem and must be walked more often. Always pull your car out of the flow of traffic so you can safely care for your pooch. Never let your dog run free. Use a leash at all times.

Can my pet be left alone in the car?

Weather is the main factor to consider in this situation. Even if you think you'll only be gone a few minutes, that's all it takes for an animal to become dehydrated in warm weather. Even if all the windows are open, even if your car is parked in the shade, even when the outside temperature is only 85°, the temperature in a parked car can reach 100° to 120° in just minutes. Exposure to high temperatures, even for short periods, can cause your pet's body temperature to skyrocket.

NEVER LEAVE YOUR DOG UNATTENDED IN WARM WEATHER.

During the winter months, be aware of hypothermia, a life threatening condition when an animal's body temperature falls below normal. In particular, short-haired dogs and toys are very susceptible to illness in extremely cold weather.

What about carsickness?

Just like people, some dogs are queasier than others. And for some reason, puppies suffer more frequently from motion sickness. It's best to wait a couple of hours after your dog has eaten before beginning your trip. Or better yet, feed your dog after you arrive at your destination. Keep the windows open enough to allow in fresh air. If your pooch has a tendency to be carsick, sugar can help. Give your dog a tablespoon of honey or a small piece of candy before beginning your trip (**NO CHOCOLATE**). That should help settle his stomach. If you notice that he still looks sickly, stop and allow him some additional fresh air or take him for a short walk. In time most dogs will outgrow carsickness.

What about identification if my dog runs off?

As far as identification, traveling time is no different than staying at home. Never allow your pooch to be anywhere without proper identification. ID tags should provide your dog's name, your name, address and phone number. Most states require dog owners to purchase a license every year. The tag usually includes a license number that is registered with your state. If you attach the license tag to your dog's collar and you become separated, your dog can be traced. There are also local organizations that help reunite lost pets and owners. The phone numbers of these organizations can be obtained from local police authorities.

Use the form on the following page to record your pooch's description so that the information will be handy should the need arise.

MY POOCH'S IDENTIFICATION

In the event that your dog is lost or stolen, the following information will help describe your pooch. Before leaving on your first trip, take a few minutes to fill out this form, make a duplicate, and then keep them separate but handy.

Answers to the name of: _____

Breed or mix: _____

Sex: _____ Age: _____ Tag ID#: _____

Description of hair (color, length and texture): _____

_____

Indicate unusual markings or scars: _____

_____

_____

TAIL: ❑ Short ❑ Screw-type ❑ Bushy ❑ Cut

EARS: ❑ Clipped ❑ Erect ❑ Floppy

Weight: _____ Height: _____

If you have a recent photo of your pet, attach it here.

TRAVEL BY PLANE

Quick takes:

- Always travel on the same flight as your pet. Personally ascertain that your pet has been put on board before you board the plane.

- Book direct, nonstop flights.

- Upon boarding, inform a flight attendant that your pet is traveling in the cargo hold.

- Early morning or late evening flights are best in the summer, while afternoon flights are best in the winter.

- Fill the water tray of your pet's travel carrier with ice cubes rather than water. This will prevent spillage during loading.

- Clip your pet's nails to prevent them from hooking in the crate's door, holes or other openings.

Carriers/kennels.

Most airlines require pets to be in specific carriers. Airline regulations vary and arrangements should be made well in advance of travel. Some airlines allow small pets to accompany their owners in the passenger cabins. The carrier must fit under the seat and the pet must remain in the carrier for the duration of the flight. These regulations also vary and prior arrangements should be made.

Airlines run hot and cold on pet travel.

Many airlines won't allow pets to travel in the cargo hold if the departure or destination temperatures are over 80°. The same holds true if the weather is too cold. Check with the airlines to ascertain specific policies.

What about the size of the carrier?

Your pet should have enough room to stand, lie down, sit and turn around comfortably. Larger doesn't equate to more comfort. If anything, larger quarters only increase the chances of your pet being hurt because of too much movement. Just as your pet's favorite place is under your desk, a cozy, compact kennel will suit him much better than a spacious one.

Should anything else be in the carrier?

Cover the bottom with newspaper sheets and cover that with shredded newspaper. This will absorb accidents and provide a soft, warm cushion for your pet. Include a blanket or an old flannel shirt of yours; some article that will remind your pet of home and engender a feeling of security. You might want to include a hard rubber chew, but forget toys, they increase the risk of accidents.

How will my pet feel about a kennel?

Training and familiarization are the key elements in this area. If possible, buy the kennel (airlines and pet stores sell them) several weeks before your trip. Leave it in your home in the area where your animal spends most of his time. Let him become accustomed to its smell, feel and look. After a few days, your pet will become comfortable around the kennel. You might even try feeding him in the kennel to make it more like home. Keep all the associations friendly. Never use the kennel for punishment. Taking the time to accustom your pet to his traveling quarters will alleviate possible problems and make vacationing more fun.

What about identification?

The kennel should contain a tag identifying your pet and provide all pertinent information including the pet's name, age, feeding and water requirements, your name, address and phone number and your final destination. In addition, it should include the name and phone number of your pet's vet. A "luggage-type" ID card will function well. Use a waterproof marker. Securely fasten the ID tag to the kennel. Your pet should also wear his state ID tag. Should he somehow become separated from his kennel, the information will travel with him. Using a waterproof pen, mark the kennel "LIVE ANI-MAL" in large letters of at least an inch or more. Indicate which is the top and bottom with arrows and more large lettering of "THIS END UP."

How can I make plane travel comfortable for my pet?

If feasible make your travel plans for weekday rather than weekend travel. Travel during off hours. Direct and nonstop flights reduce the potential for problems and delays. Check with your airline to determine how much time they require for check in. Limiting the amount of time your pet will be in the hold section will make travel time that much more comfortable. Personally ascertain that your pet has been put on board your flight before you board the aircraft.

Will there automatically be room on board for my pet?

Not always. Airline space for pets is normally provided on a first-come, first-served basis. As soon as your travel plans are decided, contact the airline and confirm your arrangements.

What will pet travel cost?

Prices vary depending on whether your pet travels in the cabin or whether a kennel must be provided in the hold. Contact the airlines to determine pricing policies.

What about food and water?

It's best not to feed your pet at least six hours before departure; water two hours.

What about tranquilizers?

Opinions vary on the subject. Discuss this with your vet. But don't give your pet any medication not prescribed by a vet. And be aware that dosages for animals and humans are not the same.

What about after we land?

If your pooch has not flown in the passenger cabin with you, you will be able to pick him up in the baggage claim area. Since traveling in a kennel aboard a plane is an unusual experience, your dog may react strangely. Leash him before you let him out of the kennel to avoid mishaps. Once he's leashed, provide a cool drink of water and walk him ASAP. Cats should remain in their kennel until you arrive at your destination, but provide water upon landing.

Pets who shouldn't fly.

In general, very young puppies, females in heat, sickly, frail or pregnant pets should not be flown. In addition to the stress of flying, changes in altitude and cabin pressure might adversely effect your animal. Also, pug-nosed pets are definite "no flys" in the cargo section. These pets have short nasal passages and the noxious fumes in the cargo area can severely limit their supply of oxygen, leaving them highly susceptible to illness.

Health certificates - will I need one?

Although you may never be asked to present a health certificate, it's a good idea to have one with you. Your vet can supply a certificate listing the inoculations your pet has received, including rabies. Keep this information with your travel papers.

Airlines have specific regulations regarding animal flying rights. Make certain you know your pet's rights.

37
WAYS TO HAVE A BETTER VACATION WITH YOUR PET

Some tips and suggestions to increase your enjoyment when you and your pet hit the road.

1. Don't feed or water your animal just before starting on your trip. Feed and water your pet at least two hours before you plan to depart. Better still, if it's a short trip, wait until you arrive at your destination.

2. Exercise your dog before you leave. A tired pet will fall off to sleep more easily and adapt more readily to new surroundings.

3. Take a large container of water to avoid potential stomach upset. Your pet will do better drinking from his own water supply for the first few days. Having water along also means you can stop wherever you like and not worry about finding water. Gradually accustom your pet to the new water source by topping off the container with local water.

4. Plan stops along the way. Just like you, your animal will enjoy stretching his legs. As you travel, you'll find many areas conducive to a leisurely walk or a bit of playtime. If you make the car ride an agreeable part of the journey, your vacation will begin the moment you leave home - not just when you reach your ultimate destination.

5. While driving, keep windows open enough to allow the circulation of fresh air but not enough for your dog to jump out. If you have air conditioning, that will keep your pet cool enough.

6. Don't let your dog hang his head out of the window. Eyes, ears and throats can become inflamed.

7. Use a short leash when walking your pooch through public areas — he'll be easier to control.

8. Pack your pet's favorite toy or chew. If it entertains him at home, it'll entertain him on the road.

9. Before any trip, allow your pooch to relieve himself.

10. Cover your back seat with an old blanket or towel to protect the upholstery.

11. A room freshener under the seat of your car will keep it smelling fresh. Take an extra one for your room.

12. If your dog has a tendency to be carsick, keep a packet of honey in the glove compartment or carry a roll of hard candy like Lifesavers. Either remedy might help offset queasiness.

13. Use a flea and tick collar on your pet.

14. When traveling in warm weather months, drape a damp towel over your pet's crate. Adding moisture to the air will reduce the heat.

15. Before you begin a trip, expose your animal to experiences he will encounter while traveling; such as crowds, noise, people, elevators, walks along busy streets and stairs (especially those with open risers).

16. Shade moves. If you must leave your pet in the car for a short period of time, make sure the shade that protects him when you park will be there by the time you return. As a general rule though, it's best not to leave your pet in a parked car. <u>NEVER LEAVE YOUR PET IN THE CAR DURING THE WARM SUMMER MONTHS</u>. In the colder months, beware of hypothermia, a life threatening condition that occurs when an animal's body temperature falls below normal. Short-haired dogs and toys are very susceptible to illness in extremely cold weather.

17. Pack a clip-on minifan for airless hotel rooms.

18. When packing, include a heating pad, ice pack and a few safety pins.

19. A handful of clothespins will serve a dozen purposes, from clamping together motel curtains to sealing a bag of potato chips.

20. A night light will help you find the bathroom in the dark.

21. Don't forget that book you've been meaning to read.

22. Include a journal and record your travel memories.

23. Pack a roll of duct tape. Use it to repair shoes, patch suitcases or strap lunch onto the back of a rented bicycle.

24. Never begin a vacation with a new pair of shoes.

25. Pooper scoopers make clean-up simple and sanitary. Plastic vegetable bags from the supermarket are great too.

26. FYI, in drier climates, many lodging accommodations have room humidifiers available for guest use. Arrange for one when you make your reservation.

27. Use unbreakable bowls and storage containers for your pet's food and water.

28. Don't do anything on the road with your pet that you wouldn't do at home.

29. Brown and grey tinted sun lenses are the most effective for screening bright light. Polarized lenses reduce the blinding glare of the sun.

30. Before you leave on vacation, safeguard your home. Ask a neighbor to take in your mail and newspapers, or arrange with your mail carrier to hold your mail and stop newspaper delivery. Use timers so that a couple of lights go on and off. Unplug small appliances and electronics. Lock all doors and windows. Place steel bars or wooden dowels in the tracks of sliding glass doors and windows. Ladders or other objects that can be used to gain entry into your home should be stored in your garage or inside your home. Arrange to have your lawn mowed. And don't forget to take out the garbage.

31. Pack some snacks and drinks in a small cooler.

32. As a precaution when traveling, once you arrive at your final destination, check the yellow pages for the nearest vet and determine emergency hours and location.

33. It is unsafe for your dog to travel in the bed of a pickup truck. If you must use this means of transportation, there are safety straps available at auto supply stores that can offset the danger to your animal. Never use a choke chain, rope or leash around your dog's neck to secure him in the bed of a pickup.

34. Pack a spray bottle of water. A squirt in your dog's mouth will temporarily relieve his thirst.

35. Heavy duty zip-lock type bags make terrific traveling water bowls. Just roll down the edges to form a bowl and fill with water. They fold up into practically nothing. Keep one in your purse, jacket pocket or fanny pack and another in your glove compartment.

36. Arrange with housekeeping at your lodging choice to have your room cleaned either while you're in the room to supervise your pet or while you're out with your pet.

37. Traveling with children too? Keep them occupied with colored pencils and markers. Avoid crayons — they can melt in the sun. Question cards from trivia games as well as a pack of playing cards are handy amusements. Travel size magnetic games like checkers and chess are also good diversions. Don't forget those battery operated electronic games either. Include a book of crossword puzzles, a pair of dice and a favorite stuffed animal for cuddling time. In the car, games can include finding license plates from different states, spotting various makes or colors of cars, saying the alphabet backwards, or completing the alphabet from roadsigns.

29
TIPS FOR TRAVEL SAFETY

Whether you're just running errands at home or on a travel adventure, practice travel safety. A healthy dose of common sense can go a long way towards preventing you from becoming a statistic, no matter where you are.

1. When returning to your room late at night, use the main entrance of your hotel.

2. Don't leave your room key within sight in public areas, particularly if it's numbered instead of coded.

3. Store valuables in your room safe or in a safety-deposit box at the front desk.

4. Don't carry large amounts of cash, use traveler's checks and credit cards instead.

5. Avoid flaunting expensive watches and jewelry.

6. When visiting a public attraction like a museum or amusement park, decide where to meet should you become separated from your traveling companions.

7. Use a fanny pack and not a purse when touring.

8. Make use of the locks provided in your room. In addition to your room door, be certain all sliding glass doors, windows and connecting doors are locked.

9. If someone comes to your room, the American Hotel and Motel Association advises guests to ascertain the identity of the caller before opening the door. If you haven't arranged for room service or requested a delivery, call the front desk and determine if someone has been sent to your room before opening the door.

10. Carry your money (or preferably traveler's checks) separately from credit cards.

11. Use your business address on luggage tags, not your home address.

12. Be alert in parking lots and underground garages.

13. Check the back seat of your car before getting inside.

14. In your car, always buckle up. Seatbelts save lives.

15. Keep car doors locked.

16. When you stop at traffic lights, leave enough room (one car length) between your vehicle and the one in front so you can quickly pull away.

17. AAA recommends that if you're hit from behind by another vehicle, motion the other driver to a public place before getting out of your car.

18. When driving at night, stay on main roads.

19. Fill your tank during daylight hours. If you must fill up at night, do so at a busy, well-lit service station.

20. If your vehicle breaks down, tie a white cloth to the antenna or the raised hood of your car to signal other motorists. Turn on your hazard lights. Remain in your locked car until police or road service arrive.

21. Don't pull over for flashing headlights. Police cars have red or blue lights.

22. Lock video cameras, car phones and other expensive equipment in your trunk. Don't leave them in sight.

23. Have car keys ready as you approach your car.

24. At an airport, allow only uniformed airport personnel to carry your bags or carry them yourself. Refuse offers of transportation from strangers. Use the airport's ground transportation center or a uniformed taxi dispatcher.

25. Walk purposefully.

26. When using an ATM, choose one in a well-lit area with heavy foot traffic. Look for machines inside establishments - they're the safest.

27. Avoid poorly lit areas, shrubbery or dark doorways.

28. When ordering food from an outside source, have it delivered to the front desk rather than to your room.

29. Trust your instincts. If a situation doesn't feel right - it probably isn't.

11
WAYS TO TAKE THE STRESS OUT OF VACATIONS

Vacations are intended to be restful occasions but sometimes the preparations involved in "getting away from it all" can prove stressful. The tips on the following page are proven stress reducers to help you cope before, during and after your trip.

1. Awaken fifteen minutes earlier each day for a couple of weeks before your trip and use that extra time to plan your day and do vacation chores.

2. Write down errands to be done. Don't rely on your memory. The anticipation of forgetting something important can be stressful.

3. Don't procrastinate. Whatever has to be done tomorrow, do today. Whatever needs doing today, do now.

4. Take stock of your car. Get car repairs done. Have your car washed, your journey will be more pleasant in a clean car. Fill up with gas the day before your departure and check your tires and oil gauge. Summertime travel, check your air conditioning. In the winter, be certain your heater and defroster work. Make sure wiper blades are also in good working condition.

5. Learn to be more flexible. Not everything has to be perfect. Compromise, you'll have a happier life.

6. If you have an unpleasant task to do, take care of it early in the day.

7. Ask for help. Delegating responsibility relieves pressure and stress. It also makes others feel productive and needed.

8. Accept that we are all part of this imperfect world. An ounce of forgiveness will take you far.

9. Don't assume responsibility for more tasks than you can readily accomplish.

10. Think positive thoughts and eliminate negativism, like, "I'm too fat, I'm too old, I'm not smart enough."

11. Take 5-10 minutes to stretch before you begin your day or before bedtime. Breathe deeply and slowly, clearing your mind as you do.

27

ON-THE-ROAD TIPS

1. Keep your pet confined with either a crate, barrier or harness.

2. To avoid sliding in the event of sharp turns or sudden stops, be certain that your luggage, as well as your pet's crate are securely stored or fastened.

3. Ascertain that your vehicle is in good working order. Check brakelights, turn signals, hazard and headlights. Clean the windshield and top off washer fluid whenever you fill up. Since you'll be driving in unfamiliar territory, so keep an eye on the gas gauge. Fill up during daylight hours or at well-lit service stations.

4. When packing, include a flashlight, tool kit, paper towels, an extra leash, waterproof matches, a first-aid kit, blanket and a supply of plastic bags. During the winter months, keep an ice scraper, snow brush and small shovel in your trunk.

5. Never drive tired. Keep the music on and the windows open. Fresh air can help you remain alert.

6. Keep your windshield clean, inside and out.

7. Avoid using sedatives or tranquilizers when driving.

8. Don't drink and drive.

9. Never drive and read a map at the same time. If you're driving alone, pull off at a well-lit gas station or roadside restaurant and check the map. If you're unsure of directions, ask for assistance from a safe source.

10. Wear your seatbelt, they save lives.

11. Keep car doors locked.

12. Good posture is especially important when driving. Do your back a favor and sit up straight. For lower back pain, wedge a small pillow between your back and the seat.

13. If you're the driver, eat frequent small snacks rather than large meals. You'll be less tired that way.

14. Don't use high beams in fog. The light will bounce back into your eyes as it reflects off the moisture.

15. When pulling off to the side of the road, use your flashers to warn away other cars.

16. Before beginning your drive each day, do a car check. Tire pressure okay? Leakage under car? Windows clean? Signals working? Mirrors properly adjusted? Gas tank full?

17. Roads can become particularly slippery at the onset of rain, the result of water mixing with dust and oil on the pavement. Slow down and exercise caution in wet weather.

18. Every so often, turn off your cruise control. Overuse can lull you into inattention.

19. If you'll be doing a lot of driving into the sun, put a towel over the dashboard. It will provide some relief from the heat and brightness.

20. Even during the cooler months, your car can become stuffy. Keep the windows or sun roof open and let fresh air circulate.

21. Kids coming along? A small tape or CD player can amuse youngsters. Hand-held video games are also entertaining. And action figures are a good source for imaginary games. Put together a travel container and include markers or colored pencils, stamps, stickers, blunt safety scissors, and some pads of paper, both colored and lined.

22. If your car trip requires an overnight stay on route to your destination, pack a change of clothing and other necessities in a separate bag. Keep it in an accessible location.

23. When visiting wet and/or humid climates, take along insect repellent.

24. Guard against temperature extremes. Protect your skin from the effects of the sun. Hazy days are just as dangerous to your skin as sunny ones. Pack plenty of sunscreen. Apply in the morning and then again in the early afternoon. The sun is strongest midday so avoid overexposure at that time. To remain comfortable in warm weather, wear lightweight, loose fitting cotton clothing. Choose light colors, dark ones attract the sun. In dry climates, remember to drink lots of liquids. Because the evaporation process speeds up in arid areas, you won't be aware of how much you're perspiring.

25. In cold climes, protect yourself from frostbite. If the temperature falls below 32° fahrenheit and the wind chill factor is also low, frostbite can occur in a matter of minutes. Layer your clothing. Cotton next to your skin and wool over that is the best insulator. Wear a hat to keep warm - body heat escapes very quickly through your head.

26. Changes in altitude can cause altitude sickness. Whenever possible, slowly accustom yourself to an altitude change. Don't overexert yourself either. Symptoms of high altitude sickness occur more frequently over 8,000 feet and include dizziness, shortness of breath and headaches.

27. Store your maps, itinerary and related travel information in a clear plastic container (shoe box storage type with a lid works best). Keep it in the front of your vehicle in an easy-to-reach location.

FIDO FACT:

• *If your pooch is becoming too aggressive or is misbehaving, try startling him. Dogs dislike loud, grating noises. Load an empty soda can with pebbles or coins and keep it handy. When your pooch starts to act up, a firm "No" and a vigorous shaking of the can should prove to be an excellent deterrent to bad behavior. Be firm but not terrifying. And remember, corrective training must be administered immediately following the offending act.*

WHAT YOU SHOULD KNOW ABOUT DRIVING IN THE DESERT

Water: Check your radiator before journeying into the desert. Other than metropolitan areas, service stations are few and far between, even on major roads. Always carry extra water.

Gasoline: Since you'll be traveling through sparsely populated areas, fill up before beginning any desert adventure. When your vehicle has half a tank or less, refuel at the first service station.

Flash floods: Summer thunderstorms in the desert can wreak havoc, especially where roads dip into washes. The runoff quickly fills the washes, creating hazardous driving conditions and impassable roads. Heed the warning signs which pinpoint flash flood areas.

Dust storms: When a dust storm approaches, pull your vehicle off the road as far as possible, switch off your headlights and wait until the storm passes.

Breakdowns: Use your hazard lights or raise the hood. Remain in your vehicle until help arrives. Keep doors locked and do not open doors except for police officers. If you break down on a secluded back road and must seek help, retrace your route. Don't take any short cuts.

<u>FIDO FACT:</u>

- ***Never leave your dog unattended in the car during very warm or very cold weather.***

Desert survival.

Anyone can end up lost or stranded in the desert. All it takes is a flat tire or a wrong turn and suddenly you're faced with a dire situation which requires survival skills. Remain calm. Think through your options. Use common sense and keep focused. Survivalists recommend that you stay with your vehicle. Do not attempt to walk through the desert. Dehydration, exposure and exhaustion are killers.

Prepare yourself before traveling into a desert environment by considering the following:

- Plan your excursion and familiarize yourself with the area.
- Know where water sources exist.
- Determine local weather conditions and forecasts before hand.
- If you're hiking, carry a topographical map of the area and avoid the intense desert heat with an early morning outing.
- Never overestimate your hiking abilities - know your limits.
- Don't take sidetrips, they may cause you to lose your bearings.
- Carry as much drinking water as possible, it can save your life.
- If you're planning an overnight, establish camp near water.
- Inform a third party of your plans and when you'll be home. Contact that person upon your return.

Heat Stroke / Exhaustion.

Early heat exhaustion indicators include weakness, pale skin, dizziness, nausea, dehydration, muscle cramping and profuse sweating. Heat stroke symptoms include the preceding as well as hot, dry, red skin. In either case, seek shade, cool off by fanning yourself and apply damp cloths to face, neck and ears. Cases of heat stroke demand immediate medical attention.

Hypothermia.

Although hypothermia is a serious medical condition most commonly associated with mountain hiking, desert hikers and campers are also susceptible. Temperatures do not have to dip below freezing for exposure to occur. In fact, hypothermia strikes most often in the 30-50° temperature range - a common temperature for winter nights in the desert. Damp clothing and a cool breeze can sometimes be enough to cause the body to lose heat faster than it can be replaced - causing cold shivers. If you experience unstoppable shivering, it's imperative that you put on dry clothes, wrap yourself in a blanket and drink hot liquids. Without these precautions, you can lapse into the second, and sometimes fatal stage of hypothermia. When that occurs, there is little chance of the body rewarming itself without the aid of conventional heating methods and immediate medical attention.

Keep your cool.

- When traveling with your animal, it's a good idea to keep a cooler of cold towels in the car. Cold towels can help to bring down a dog's body temperature after a long afternoon of hiking.

- A wet bandana wrapped around your neck, and another around your dog's neck, can keep you both comfortably cool while hiking.

FIRST-AID EMERGENCY TREATMENT

Having a bit of the Girl Scout in me, I like being prepared. Over the years, I've accumulated information regarding animal emergency treatment. Although I've had only one occasion to use this information, once was enough. I'd like to share my knowledge with you.

Whether you're the stay-at-home type who rarely travels with your pet, or a gadabout who can't sit still, every pet owner should know these simple, but potentially lifesaving procedures.

The following are only guidelines to assist you during emergencies. Whenever possible, seek treatment from a vet if your animal becomes injured and you are unprepared to administer first aid.

Allergies: One in five pets suffers from some form of allergy. Sneezing and watery eyes can be an allergic reaction caused by pollen and smoke. Inflamed skin can indicate a sensitivity to grass or to chemicals used in carpet cleaning. See your vet.

Bites and stings: Use ice to reduce swelling. If your animal has been stung in the mouth, immediately take him to the vet. Swelling can close the throat. If your pet experiences an allergic reaction, an antihistamine may be needed. For fast relief from a wasp or bee sting, dab the spot with plain vinegar and then apply baking soda. If you're in the middle of nowhere, a small mud pie plastered over the sting will provide relief. Snake bites, seek veterinary attention ASAP.

Bleeding: If the cut is small, use tweezers to remove hair from the wound. Gently wash with soap and water and then bandage (not too tightly). Severe bleeding, apply direct pressure and seek medical attention ASAP.

Burns: First degree burns: Use an ice cube or apply ice water until the pain is alleviated. Then apply vitamin E, swab with honey or cover with a freshly brewed teabag.

Minor burns: Use antibiotic ointment.

Acid: Apply dampened baking soda.

Scalds: Douse with cold water. After treatment, bandage all burns for protection.

Earache: A drop of warm eucalyptus oil in your pet's ear can help relieve the pain.

Eye scratches or inflammation: Make a solution of boric acid and bathe eyes with soft cotton.

Falls or impact injuries: Limping, pain, grey gums or prostration need immediate veterinary attention. The cause could be a fracture or internal bleeding.

Fleas: Patches of hair loss, itching and redness are common signs of fleas, particularly during warm months. Use a flea bath and a flea collar to eliminate and prevent infestation. Ask your vet about new oral medication now available for flea control.

Heatstroke: Signs include lying prone, rapid or difficult breathing and heartbeat, rolling eyes, panting, high fever, a staggering gait. Quick response is essential. Move your animal into the shade. Generously douse with cold water or if possible, partially fill a tub with cold water and immerse your pet. Remain with him and check his temperature. Normal for dogs and cats: 100°-102°. Don't let your pet's temperature drop below that.

Prevent common heatstroke by limiting outdoor exercise in hot or humid weather and providing plenty of fresh, cool water and access to shade. Never leave your pet in a car on a warm day, even for "just a few minutes."

Heartworm: Mosquitos can be more than pests when it comes to the health of your dog. They are the carriers of heartworm disease, which can be life threatening to your furry friend. There is no vaccine. However, daily or monthly pills can protect your pet from infection. In areas with high mosquito populations, use a heartworm preventative. Contact your local veterinarian about testing and medication. In the case of heartworm, "an ounce of prevention equals a pound of cure."

Poisons: Gasoline products, antifreeze, disinfectants, and insecticides are all poisonous. Keep these products tightly closed and out of reach. Vomiting, trembling and convulsions can be symptoms of poisoning. If your pet suffers from any of these symptoms, get veterinary attention. (See listings on Poison Control Centers in section "Everything You Want to Know About Pet Care...")

Poison ivy: Poison ivy or oak on your pet's coat will not bother him. But the poison can be passed on to you. If you believe your pet has come in contact with poison ivy or oak, use rubber gloves before handling your animal. Rinse him in salt water, then follow with a clear water rinse. Shampoo and rinse again.

Shock: Shock can occur after an accident or severe fright. Your animal might experience shallow breathing, pale gums, nervousness or prostration. Keep him still, quiet and warm and have someone drive you to a vet.

FIDO FACT:

- *Got a fussy eater?*

Although missing a meal isn't unhealthy, you don't want meal times to become problem times. Never beg your dog to eat. Put the food down and leave the area. If the food hasn't been eaten in an hour, pick it up and save it for the next feeding. Your dog will eventually get the message. And no table scraps, they only encourage bad eating habits.

Skunks: The following might help you avoid a smelly encounter.

1. Don't try to scare the skunk away. Your actions might provoke a spray.

2. Keep your dog quiet. Skunks have an unforgettable way of displaying their dislike of barking.

3. Begin an immediate retreat.

If you still end up in a stinky situation, try one of these three home remedies.

1. Saturate your pet's coat with tomato juice. Allow to dry, then brush out and shampoo.

2. Combine 5 parts water with one part vinegar. Pour solution over your pet's coat. Let soak 10-15 minutes. Rinse with clear water and then shampoo.

3. Combine 1 quart of 3% hydrogen peroxide with 1/4 cup of baking soda and a squirt of liquid soap. Pour solution over your pet's coat. Let soak 10-15 minutes. Rinse with clear water and then shampoo.

Snake bites: Immobilization and prompt medical attention are the key elements in handling a poisonous snake bite. Immediate veterinary care (within 2 hours) is essential to recovery. If the bite occurs in a remote area, immediately immobilize the bitten area and carry your pet to the vehicle. Don't allow your pet to walk, the venom will spread more quickly. Most snake bites will be to the head or neck area, particularly the nose. The second most common place will be a pet's front leg.

Severe swelling within 30 to 60 minutes of the bite is the first indication that your pet is suffering from a venomous snake bite. Excessive pain and slow, steady bleeding are other indicators. Hemotoxins in the venom of certain snakes prevent blood from clotting. If your pet goes into shock or stops breathing, begin CPR. Cardiopulmonary resuscitation for pets is the same as for humans. Push on your pet's chest to compress his heart and force blood to the brain. Then hold his mouth closed and breathe into his nose.

When treating a snake bite:

- DO NOT apply ice to the bite - venom constricts the blood vessels and ice only compounds the constriction.

- DO NOT use a tourniquet - the body's natural immune system fights off the venom. By cutting off the blood flow, you'll either minimize or completely eliminate the body's natural defenses.

- DO NOT try to clean the bite or administer medication.

Ticks: Use lighter fluid (or other alcohol) and loosen by soaking. Then gently tweeze out. Make sure you get the tick's head.

Winter woes: Rock salt and other commercial chemicals used to melt ice can be very harmful to your animal. Not only can they burn your pet's pads, but ingestion by licking can result in poisoning or dehydration. Upon returning from a walk through snow or ice, wash your pet's feet with a mild soap and then rinse. Before an outdoor excursion, spray your pet's paws with cooking oil to deter adherence.

FITNESS FOR FIDO

A daily dose of exercise is as important for the pooch's health as it is for yours. A 15-30 minute walk twice daily is a perfect way to build muscles and stamina and get you and the dogster in shape for more aerobic workouts. In the summertime, beat the heat by walking in the early hours of the morning or after sundown. Keep in mind that dogs don't sweat, so if you notice your pooch panting excessively or lagging behind, stop in a cool shaded area for a water break.

If your dog is overweight or still a puppy, consult with your vet to determine an appropriate exercise program. Overweight canines may have other health problems which must be considered. Young dogs are still developing their bone structure and may not be ready for a rigorous program.

FIDO FACT:

- *Fido's fitness counts towards insuring a longer, healthier life. The most common cause of ill health in canines is obesity. About 60% of all adult dogs are or will become overweight due to lack of physical activity and overfeeding.*

MASSAGE, PETTING WITH A PURPOSE

Treat your dog to some special quality time. Give him the attention he craves while also doing something healthful for him. The simple procedures that follow require only 10 to 15 minutes of your time.

1. Gently stroke your animal's head.
2. Caress around his ears in a circular fashion.
3. Rub down both his neck and shoulders, first on one side of the spine, and then the other, continuing down to the rump.
4. Turn your dog over and gently knead his abdominal area.
5. Rub his legs.
6. Caress the area between his paw pads.

After the massage, offer your pooch plenty of fresh, cool water which will flush out the toxins released from the muscles.

Massages are also therapeutic for dogs recovering from surgery and/or suffering from hip dysplasia, circulatory disorders, sprains, chronic illness and old age. Timid and hyperactive pooches can benefit as well.

FIDO FACT:
- *Is your pooch pudgy? Place both thumbs on your dog's backbone and then run your fingers along his rib cage. If the bony part of each rib cannot be easily felt, your dog may be overweight. Another quickie test - stand directly over your dog while he's standing. If you can't see a clearly defined waist behind his rib cage, he's probably too portly.*

6

STEPS TO BETTER GROOMING

Grooming is another way of saying "I love you" to your pooch. As pack animals, dogs love grooming rituals. Make grooming time an extension of your caring relationship. Other than some breeds which require professional grooming, most canines can be kept well-groomed in about 10 minutes a day.

1. Designate a grooming place, preferably one that is not on the floor. If possible, use a grooming table. Your dog will learn to remain still and you won't trade a well-groomed pooch for an aching back.

2. End every grooming session with a small treat. When your dog understands that grooming ends with a goodie, he'll behave better.

3. Brush out your dog's coat before washing. Wetting a matted coat only tightens the tangles and makes removal more difficult.

4. Using a soft tissue, wipe around your dog's eyes daily, especially if his eyes tend to be teary.

5. When bathing a long-haired dog, squeeze the coat, don't rub. Rubbing can result in snarls.

6. To gently clean your dog's teeth, slip your hand into a soft sock and go over each tooth.

FIDO FACT:
- *Stroke a dog instead of patting it. Stroking is soothing. Patting can make a dog nervous.*

Grooming tips...sticky problems

Chewing gum: There are two methods you can try. Ice the gum for a minimum of ten minutes to make it more manageable and easier to remove. Or use peanut butter. Apply and let the oil in the peanut butter loosen the gum from the hair shaft. Leave on about 20 minutes before working out the gum.

Tar: This is a tough one. Try soaking the tarred area in vegetable or baby oil. Leave on for an hour or more and then bathe your dog. The oil should cause the tar to slide off the hair shaft. Since this method can be messy, shampoo your dog with Dawn dishwashing soap to remove the oil. Follow with pet shampoo to restore the pH balance.

Oil: Apply baby powder or cornstarch to the oily area. Leave on 20 minutes. Shampoo with warm water and Dawn. Follow with pet shampoo to restore the pH balance.

Burrs:

1. Burrs in your dog's coat may be easier to remove if you first crush the burrs with pliers.

2. Slip a kitchen fork under the burr to remove.

3. Soften the burrs with vegetable or baby oil before working them out.

Keep cleaning sessions as short as possible. Your dog will not want to sit for hours. If your dog's skin is sensitive, you might want to simply remove the offending matter with a scissors. If you don't feel competent to do the removal yourself, contact a grooming service in your area and have them do the job for you.

FIDO FACT:
- *Inflamed skin can indicate a sensitivity to grass or chemicals used in carpet cleaning. Patches of hair loss, itching and redness are common signs of fleas, particularly during warm months.*

12
TIPS ON MOVING WITH YOUR PET

Every year, one out of five Americans will move. Of those, nearly half will be moving with their pets. If you're part of the "pet half", be aware that your pet can experience the same anxiety as you. The following tips can make moving less stressful for you and your animal.

1. Although moving companies provide information on how to move your pet, they are not permitted to transport animals. Plan to do so on your own.

2. Begin with a visit to your vet. Your vet can provide a copy of your pet's medical records and possibly recommend a vet in the city where you'll be moving.

3. If you'll be traveling by plane, contact the airlines ASAP. Many airlines offer in-cabin boarding for small pets but only on a first-come, first-served basis. The earlier you make your reservations, the better chance you'll have of securing space.

4. If you'll be driving to your new home, *Vacationing With Your Pet* will assist you with your lodging reservations. By planning ahead, your move will proceed more smoothly .

5. Buy a special toy or a favorite chew that's only given to your pet when you're busy packing.

6. Don't feed or water your animal for several hours before your departure. The motion of the ride might cause stomach upset.

7. Keep your pet kenneled up on moving day to avoid disasters. Never allow your pet to run free when you're in unfamiliar territory.

8. Pack your pet's dishes, food, water, treats, toys, leash and bedding in an easy-to-reach location. Take water and food from home. Drinking unfamiliar water or eating a different brand of food can cause digestion problems. And don't forget those plastic bags for clean-up.

9. Once you're moved in and unpacked, be patient. Your animal may misbehave. Like a child, he may resent change and begin acting up. Deal with problems in a gentle and reassuring manner. Spend some extra time with your pet during this upheaval period and understand that it will pass.

10. If your pet requires medication or prescription diet, pack plenty for your journey and keep a copy of your pet's medical records with you.

11. Always carry your current veterinarian's phone number. You never know when an emergency may arise or when your new veterinarian will need additional health information

12. Learn as much as you can about your new area, including common diseases, local laws and required vaccinations.

10
REASONS WHY PETS
ARE GOOD FOR YOUR HEALTH

Adding a pet to your household can improve your health and that of your family. In particular, pets seem to help the very young and seniors. The following is based on various studies.

1. People over 40 who own pets have lower blood pressure. 20% have lower triglyceride levels. Talking to pets has been shown to lower blood pressure as well.

2. People who own pets see their doctor less than those who don't.

3. Pets have been shown to reduce depression, particularly in seniors.

4. It's easier to make friends when you have a pet. Life is more social with them.

5. It's healthier too. Seniors with pets are generally more active because they walk more.

6. Pets are friends. Here again, seniors seem to benefit most.

7. Pets can help older people deal with the loss of a spouse. Seniors are less likely to experience the deterioration in health that often follows the stressful loss of a mate.

8. Pets ease loneliness.

9. Perhaps because of the responsibility of pet ownership, seniors take better care of themselves.

10. Pets provide a sense of security to people of all ages.

FIDO FACTS

The following facts, tidbits and data will enhance your knowledge of our canine companions.

- Gain the confidence of a worried dog by avoiding direct eye contact or by turning away, exposing your back or side to the dog.

- When dogs first meet, it's uncommon for them to approach each other head on. Most will approach in curving lines. They'll walk beyond each other's noses sniffing at rear ends while standing side by side.

- Dog ownership is a common bond and the basis of impromptu conversations as well as lasting friendships.

- Chemical salt makes sidewalks less slippery but can be harmful to your dog's footpads. Wash your dog's paws after walks to remove salt. Don't let him lick the salt either, it's poisonous.

- Vets warn that removing tar with over-the-counter petroleum products can be highly toxic.

- Although a dog's vision is better than humans in the dark, bright red and green are the easiest colors for them to see.

- Puppies are born blind. Their eyes open and they begin to see at 10 to 14 days.

- The best time to separate a pup from his mother is seven to ten weeks after birth.

- It's a sign of submission when a dog's ears are held back close to his head.

- Hot pavement can damage your dog's sensitive footpads. In the summer months, walk your pooch in the morning or evening or on grassy areas and other cool surfaces.

- Never leave your dog unattended in the car during the warm weather months or extremely cold ones.

- Always walk your dog on a leash on hotel/motel grounds.

- Want to register your puppy, or locate a breeder in your area? The American Kennel Club has a new customer service line at (919) 233-9767. Their interactive voice processing telephone system is open twenty-four hours a day, seven days a week. Information is available on dog and litter registrations. You can also use the number to order registration materials, certified pedigrees, books and videos. If you want to speak with a customer service rep, call during business hours.

- Stroke a dog instead of patting it. Stroking is soothing. Patting can make some dogs nervous.

- If your dog is lonely for you when he's left alone, try leaving your voice on a tape and let it play during your absence.

- When a dog licks you with a straight tongue, he's saying "I Love You."

- Don't do anything on the road with your dog that you wouldn't do at home.

- Never put your dog in the bed of a pickup truck as a means of transportation.

- Black dogs and dark colored ones are more susceptible to the heat.

- When traveling, take a spray bottle of water with you. A squirt in your dog's mouth will temporarily relieve his thirst.

- Changing your dog's water supply too quickly can cause stomach upset. Take along a container of water from home and replenish with local water, providing a gradual change.

- One in five dogs suffers from some form of allergy. Sneezing and watery eyes can be an allergic reaction caused by pollen or smoke.

- Inflamed skin can indicate a sensitivity to grass or chemicals used in carpet cleaning.

- Patches of hair loss, itching and redness are common signs of fleas, particularly during warm months.

- Normal temperature for dogs: 100° to 102°.

- No matter how much your dog begs, do not overfeed him.

- Housebreaking problems can sometimes be attributed to diet. Consult with your vet about one good dog food and be consistent in feeding. A change in your dog's diet can lead to digestive problems.

- Spay/neuter your dog to prevent health problems and illnesses that plague the intact animal. Contrary to popular belief, spaying/neutering your canine will not result in weight gain. Only overfeeding and lack of exercise can do that.

- Spend ample quality time with your canine every day. Satisfy his need for social contact.

- Obedience train your dog; it's good for his mental well being and yours.

- If you make training fun, your dog will learn faster.

- Always provide cool fresh drinking water for your dog.

- If your pooch lives outdoors, make sure he has easy access to shade and plenty of water.

- If your pooch lives indoors, he'll need access to cool moving air and ample fresh water.

- In the summertime, avoid exercising your dog during the hottest parts of the day.

- Never tie your dog or let him run free while he's wearing a choke collar. Choke collars can easily hook on something and strangle him.

- The Chinese Shar-Pei and the Chow have blue-black tongues instead of pink ones.

- The smallest breed of dog is the Chihuahua.

- Poodles, Bedlington Terriers, Bichon Frises, Schnauzers and Soft-Coated Wheaten Terriers don't shed.

- Terriers and toy breeds usually bark the most.

- The Basenji is often called the barkless dog.

- Labs and Golden Retrievers are fast learners, making them easy to train.

- Climate counts when deciding on a breed. Collies and Pugs will be unhappy in hot, humid climates. But the Italian Greyhound and Chihuahua originated in hot climes. The heat won't bother them, but winter will. They'll need insulation in the form of dog apparel to protect them from the cold. And as you might think, heavy-coated dogs like the Saint Bernard, Siberian Husky and the Newfy thrive in cooler weather.

- Apartment dwellers, consider the Dachshund and Cairn Terrier. Both can be content in small quarters.

- Fido's fitness counts towards insuring a longer, healthier life. In this arena, you're the one in control. The most common cause of ill health in canines is obesity. Approximately 60% of all adult dogs are overweight or will become overweight due to lack of physical activity and overfeeding. Much like humans, the medical consequences of obesity include liver, heart and orthopedic problems. As little as a few extra pounds on a small dog can lead to health-related complications.

- Is your pooch pudgy? Place both thumbs on your dog's backbone and then run your fingers along his rib cage. If the bony part of each rib cannot be easily felt, your dog may be overweight. Another quickie test - stand directly over your dog while he's standing. If you can't see a clearly defined waist behind his rib cage, he's probably too portly.

- The infamous Red Baron owned a Great Dane named Moritz who lived on the military base with the pilot. The Red Baron fondly referred to Moritz as his "little lapdog."

- Frederick the Great owned an estimated 30 Greyhounds. His love of these animals led him to coin the saying: "The more I see of men, the more I love my dogs."

- It's easier than you might think to help your dog lose those extra pounds. Begin by eliminating unnecessary table scraps. Cut back a small amount on the kibble or canned dog food you normally feed your pooch. If he's accustomed to two full cups each day, reduce that amount to 1 3/4 cups instead. If you normally give your pooch biscuits every day, cut the amount in half. And don't feel guilty. Stick with the program and you'll eventually see a reduction in weight. Slow and steady is the best approach. And don't let yourself imagine that your dog is being deprived of anything. Even when he looks at you with a woebegone expression, remember you're doing him a favor by helping him reduce and you're adding years of good health to his life.

- Exercise. Not enough can be said about the benefits. Establish a daily exercise routine. Awaken twenty minutes earlier every morning and take a brisk mile walk. Instead of watching TV after dinner, walk off some calories. Your pooch's overall good health, as well as your own, will be greatly enhanced.

- According to a survey, 90% of dog owners speak to their dogs like humans, walk or run with their dogs and take pictures of them; 72% take their pups for car rides; 51% hang Christmas stockings for their dogs; 41% watch movies and TV with their pooches; 29% sign Rover's name to greeting cards and more than 20% buy homes with their dogs in mind, carry photos of Fido with them and arrange the furniture so FiFi can see outside.

- Lewis and Clark traveled with a 150-pound Newfoundland named "Seamen." The pooch was a respected member of the expedition and his antics were included in the extensive diaries of these famous explorers.

- The English have a saying: The virtues of a dog are its own, its vices those of its master.

- Lord Byron, in his eulogy to his dog Boatswain, wrote, "One who possessed beauty without vanity, strength without insolence, courage without ferocity, and all the virtues of man without his vices."

- "Be Kind To Animals Week" (May 7-13) was established in 1915. Recognized by Congress, it is the oldest week of its kind in the nation.

- The "Always Faithful" Memorial, which honors Dogs of War, was unveiled on June 20, 1994. It now stands on the US Naval Base in Orote Point, Guam.

- During WWII, Dobermans were official members of the US Marine Corps combat force.

- The domestic dog dates back more than 50,000 years.

- Ghandi once said, "The greatness of a nation and its moral progress can be judged by the way its animals are treated."

- England's Dickin Medal is specifically awarded to dogs for bravery and outstanding behavior in wartime.

- Napoleon's wife, Josephine, had a Pug named Fortune. She relied on the animal to carry secret messages under his collar to Napoleon while she was imprisoned at Les Carnes.

- Former First Lady Barbara Bush said: "An old dog that has served you long and well is like an old painting. The patina of age softens and beautifies, and like a master's work, can never be replaced by exactly the same thing, ever again."

- Dogs and Halloween don't mix. Even the mellowest of pooches can become frightened and overexcited by all the commotion. Save the candy collecting and chocolate for the kids and leave the dog at home.

- Most outdoor dogs suffer from unnoticed parasites like fleas.

- In winter, the water in an outdoor dog dish can freeze within an hour.

- In summer, dogs consume large quantities of water. Bowls need frequent refilling.

EVERYTHING YOU WANT TO KNOW ABOUT PET CARE AND WHO TO ASK

Whether you've always had a pet or you're starting out with your first, the following organizations and hotlines can provide information on the care, feeding and protection of your loyal companion.

Pet behavior information.

Tree House Animal Foundation: If you are concerned with canine aggression, nipping, biting, housebreaking or other behavioral problems, the Tree House Animal Foundation will try to help. But don't wait until the last minute. Call for advice early on and your animal's problems will be easier to correct. Consultation is free, except for applicable long distance charges. Call (773) 784-5488, 9AM to 5PM CST, seven days a week.

Pet Loss Helpline - 630-603-3994: The Chicago Veterinary Medical Association is a non-profit organization that promotes the health and well being of animals through veterinary care. Veterinarians, by their concern for and knowledge of animal health and behavior, help pet owners and their pets enjoy long and rewarding relationships.There is no charge. These services are funded primarily by donation. If you wish to make a donation in the name of your pet it would be greatly appreciated. We would also be interested in poems, drawings, prose or any creative expression of the love for your pet. CVMA, 120 East Ogden Avenue, Suite 22, Hinsdale, IL 60521, 630-325-1231.

Animal Behavior Helpline: This organization is sponsored by the San Francisco Society for the Prevention of Cruelty to Animals. It will assist you in solving canine behavioral problems. Staffed by volunteers, you may reach a recorded message. However, calls are returned within 48 hours by volunteers trained in animal behavior. Problems such as chewing, digging and barking are cited as the most common reasons dog owners call. Housebreaking tips, how to deal with aggression and other topics are covered. Callers are first asked to speak about the problem and describe what steps have been taken to correct inappropriate behavior. After evaluating the information, specific advice is given to callers. The consultation is free, except for applicable long distance charges or collect call charges when a counselor returns your call. Messages can be left any time. Call (415) 554-3075.

Poison Control Center: There are two telephone numbers for this organization. The 800 number is an emergency line for both veterinarians and pet owners for poisoning control information. Calls are taken by the veterinarian-staffed National Animal Poison Control Center at the University of Illinois. When calling the 800 number, there is a charge of $30 per case. Every call made to the 800 number is followed up by the NAPCC. The 900 number is for non-emergency questions and there is no follow up. Callers to the 900 line pay $20 for the first 5 minutes and $2.95 for every minute thereafter with a minimum charge of $20 and a maximum of $30.

When calling the NAPCC, be prepared to provide your name and address and the name of the suspected poison (be specific). If the product is manufactured by a company that is a member of the Animal Product Safety Service - the company may pay the charge.

In all other cases, you pay for the consultation. You must also provide the animal species, breed, sex, and weight. You will be asked to describe symptoms as well as unusual behavior. This detailed information is critical - it can mean the difference between life or death for your animal.

For emergencies only, call (800) 548-2423. Major credit cards are accepted. For non-emergency questions, call (900) 680-0000. The Poison Control Center offers poison control information by veterinarians 24 hours a day, 7 days a week.

Poinsettias and other toxic plants... pretty but deadly.

During the Christmas holidays, the risk of poisoning and injury is greater for your pet. If eaten, poinsettias and holly berries for example, can be fatal. Although there are conflicting reports on the effects of mistletoe, play it safe and keep your pet away from this plant. Be alert - swallowed tree ornaments, like ribbon and tinsel can cause choking and/or intestinal problems.

Christmas wiring is another potential problem. Your pet can be electrocuted by chewing on it. And don't forget about the dangers of poultry bones. The same goes for aluminum foil including the disposable pans that are used at holiday time.

Keep your trash inaccessible. And remember that the holidays are a source of excitement and stress to both people and animals. Maintain your pet's feeding and walking schedules and provide plenty of TLC and playtime. Then everyone, including your animal, will find the holidays more enjoyable.

FYI...

common plants* that are toxic to pets

Amaryllis (bulbs)
Appleseeds (cyanide)
Azalea
Boxwood
Caladium
Cherry Pits (cyanide)
Climbing Lily
Daffodil (bulb)
Delphinium
Dumb Cane
English Ivy
Foxglove
Holly
Hydrangea
Japanese Yew
Jerusalem Cherry
Laburnum
Laurel
Marigold
Mistletoe (berries)
Mushrooms
Nightshade
Peach
Poinsettia
Privet
Rhubarb
Stinging Nettie
Tobacco
Walnuts
Yew

Andromeda
Arrowgrass
Bittersweet
Buttercup
Castor Bean
Chokecherry
Crown of Thorns
Daphne
Dieffenbachia
Elephant Ear
Elderberry
Hemlock
Hyacinth (bulbs)
Iris (bulb)
Jasmine (berries)
Jimsonweed
Larkspur
Locoweed
Marijuana
Monkshood
Narcissus (bulb)
Oleander
Philodendron
Poison Ivy
Rhododendron
Snow on the Mountain
Toadstool
Tulip (bulb)
Wisteria

NOTE: This is only a partial list.

PET POEMS, PROCLAMATIONS, PRAYERS...& DOG BISCUITS

Ode to Travel with Pets

We're all set to roam

Going far from home

With doggies in tow

Off shall we go

To wander and gadabout

Since travel we're mad about

With Rosie and Max by my side

We'll all go for a ride

As we travel for miles

And bring about smiles

Rosie will grin

Max will chime in

Driving into the sunset

Odometers all set

But enough of these word rhymes

Let's roll with the good times!

— Eileen Barish, November 1994

Alone Again

I wish someone would tell me what it is
      That I've done wrong.
Why I have to stay chained up and
      Left alone so long.
They seemed so glad to have me
      When I came here as a pup.
There were so many things we'd do
      While I was growing up.
They couldn't wait to train me as a
      Companion and a friend.
And told me how they'd never fear
      Being left alone again.
The children said they'd feed me and
      Brush me every day.
They'd play with me and walk me
      If only I could stay.
But now the family "Hasn't time,"
      They often say I shed.
They do not even want me in the house
      Not even to be fed.
The children never walk me.
      They always say "Not now!"
I wish that I could please them.
      Won't someone tell me how?
All I had, you see, was love.
      I wish they would explain
Why they said they wanted me
      Then left me on a chain?

— Anonymous

A Dog's Bill of Rights

I have the right to give and receive
        unconditional love.
I have the right to a life that is beyond
        mere survival.
I have the right to be trained so I do not become
        the prisoner of my own misbehavior.
I have the right to adequate food and
        medical care.
I have the right to fresh air and green grass.
I have the right to socialize with people
        and dogs outside my family.
I have the right to have my needs
        and wants respected.
I have the right to a special time with
        my people .
I have the right to only be bred
        responsibly if at all.
I have the right to be foolish and silly, and
        to make my person laugh.
I have the right to earn my person's trust
        and be trusted in return.
I have the right to be forgiven.
I have the right to die with dignity.
I have the right to be remembered well.

A Dog's Prayer

Treat me kindly, my beloved master, for no heart in all the world is more grateful for kindness, than the loving heart of mine.

Do not break my spirit with a stick, for though I should lick your hand between the blows, your patience and understanding will more quickly teach me the things you would have me do.

Speak to me often, for your voice is the world's sweetest music as you must know by the fierce wagging of my tail when your footstep falls up on my waiting ear.

When it is cold and wet, please take me inside...for I am now a domesticated animal, no longer used to bitter elements...and I ask no greater glory than the privilege of sitting at your feet beside the hearth...though had you no home, I would rather follow you through ice and snow, than rest upon the softest pillow in the warmest home in all the land...for you are my God...and I am your devoted worshipper.

Keep my pan filled with fresh water, for although I should not reproach you were it dry, I cannot tell you when I suffer thirst. Feed me clean food, that I may stay well, to romp and play and do your bidding, to walk by your side, and stand ready willing and able to protect you with my life, should your life be in danger.

And beloved master, should the Great Master see fit to deprive me of my health or sight, do not turn away from me. Rather hold me gently in your arms, as skilled hands grant me the merciful boon of eternal rest...and I will leave you knowing with the last breath I draw, my fate was ever safest in your hands.

Rainbow Bridge

There is a bridge connecting Heaven and Earth. It is called the Rainbow Bridge because of its many colors. Just this side of the Rainbow Bridge there is a land of meadows, hills and valleys with lush green grass.

When a beloved pet dies, the pet goes to this place. There is always food and water and warm spring weather. The old and frail animals are young again. Those who are maimed are made whole again. They play all day with each other.

There is only one thing missing. They are not with their special person who loved them on Earth. So each day they run and play until the day comes when one suddenly stops playing and looks up! The nose twitches! The ears are up! The eyes are staring! And this one suddenly runs from the group!

You have been seen, and when you and your special friend meet, you take him or her in your arms and embrace. Your face is kissed again and again, and you look once more into the eyes of your trusting pet.

Then you cross Rainbow Bridge together, never again to be separated.

— Anonymous

<u>FIDO FACT</u>:
- *Lord Byron, in his eulogy to his dog Boatswain, wrote, "One who possessed beauty without vanity, strength without insolence, courage without ferocity, and all the virtues of man without his vices."*

Homemade dog biscuits

(Makes about 8 dozen biscuits)

Ingredients

3 1/2 cups all-purpose flour

2 cups whole wheat flour

1 cup rye flour

1 cup cornmeal

2 cups cracked wheat bulgur

1/2 cup nonfat dry milk

4 tsp. salt

1 package dry yeast

2 cups chicken stock or other liquid

1 egg and 1 tbsp. milk (to brush on top)

Combine all the dry ingredients except the yeast. In a separate bowl, dissolve the yeast in 1/4 cup warm water. To this, add the chicken stock. (You can use bouillon, pan drippings or water from cooking vegetables.) Add the liquid to the dry ingredients. Knead mixture for about 3 minutes. Dough will be quite stiff. If too stiff, add extra liquid or an egg. Preheat oven to 300 degrees. Roll the dough out on a floured board to 1/4" thickness, then immediately cut into shapes with cookie cutters. Place on an ungreased cookie sheet and brush with a wash of egg and milk. Place in oven. After 45 minutes, turn off the heat and leave biscuits overnight in the oven to get bone hard.

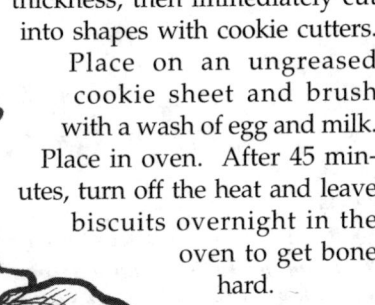

In Memory of Max and Rosie

It seemed like it was just yesterday...

MAXWELL
MAY 1991 - July 2000

ROSIE
MAY 1991 - MARCH 2001

UNITED STATES DIRECTORY OF PET-FRIENDLY LODGING

ALABAMA

ABBEVILLE

BEST WESTERN
Hwy 431 S (36310)
Rates: $40-$100
(334) 585-5060
(800) 528-1234

ALABASTER

**SHELBY
MOTOR LODGE**
Hwy 31 S (35007)
Rates: $35-$40
(205) 663-1070

ALBERTVILLE

**KINGS INN
MOTOR MOTEL**
7080 Hwy 431 N
(35950)
Rates: $32-$50
(256) 878-6550
(800) 490-8589

TWIN HOUSE B&B
705 Baltimore Ave
(35950)
Rates: $70-$90
(256) 878-7499

ANDALUSIA

**BEST WESTERN
OF ANDALUSIA**
305 W Bypass
(36420)
Rates: $42-$60
(334) 222-9999
(800) 528-1234

CHARTER HOUSE
US 84 Bypass E
(36420)
Rates: $31-$49
(334) 222-7511
(800) 443-9110

DAYS INN
1604 E Bypass
(36420)
Rates: $46-$90
(334) 427-0050
(800) 329-7466

TOWN LINE MOTEL
1106 US 29
Bypass W (36420)
Rates: $32-$35
(334) 222-3191

ANNISTON

RAMADA INN
300 Quintard Ave
(36201)
Rates: $46-$150
(256) 237-9777
(800) 272-6232

ARDMORE

ECONO LODGE
28555 Boyds
Chapel Rd (35620)
Rates: $37-$47
(205) 423-6699
(800) 553-2666

ATHENS

BEST WESTERN
1329 Hwy 72 East
(35611)
Rates: $49-$89
(256) 233-4030
(800) 321-0122

BOMAR INN
1101 Hwy 31 S
(35611)
Rates: $34-$41
(256) 233-6944
(800) 824-6834

BUDGET INN
606 Hwy 31 S
(35611)
Rates: $30-$37
(256) 232-0131

DAYS INN
1322 Hwy 72 E
(35611)
Rates: $36-$68
(256) 233-7500
(800) 329-7466

HAMPTON INN
1488 Thrasher
Blvd (35611)
Rates: $54-$78
(256) 232-0030
(800) 426-7866

THE MARK MOTEL
210 Hwy 31 St
(35611)
Rates: $30-$40
(256) 232-6200

ATTALLA

ECONO LODGE
507 Cherry St
(35954)
Rates: $35-$115
(256) 538-9925
(800) 553-2666

**HOLIDAY INN
EXPRESS**
801 Cleveland Ave
(35954)
Rates: $52-$58
(256) 538-7861
(800) 465-4329

AUBURN

**AUBURN
UNIVERSITY
HOTEL &
CONFERENCE
CENTER**
241 S College St
(36830)
Rates: $69-$129
(334) 821-8200
(800) 228-2876

**BEST INN &
SUITES**
1577 S College
(36830)
Rates: $44-$84
(334) 821-7001
(800) 282-8763

COMFORT INN
2283 S College
(36830)
Rates: $52-$78
(334) 821-6699
(800) 228-5150

ECONO LODGE
2145 S College
(36830)
Rates: $44-$130
(334) 826-8900
(800) 553-2666

HEART OF
AUBURN INN
333 South College
(36830)
Rates: $41-$55
(334) 887-3462
(800) 843-5634

**QUALITY INN
UNIVERSITY
CENTER**
1577 S College St
(36830)
Rates: $59-$150
(334) 821-7001
(800) 228-5151

BAY MINETTE

DAYS INN
1819 Hwy 31 S
(36507)
Rates: $69-$109
(334) 580-8111
(800) 329-7466

QUALITY INN
1402 US 31 S
(36507)
Rates: $42-$75
(334) 937-9521
(800) 228-5151

BESSEMER

BEST WESTERN
5041 Academy Dr
(35022)
Rates: $64-$125
(205) 481-1950
(800) 528-1234
(877) 741-3232

DAYS INN
1121 9th Ave SW
(35022)
Rates: $56-$89
(205) 424-6078
(800) 329-7466

**MASTERS
ECONOMY INN**
1113 9th Ave SW
(35022)
Rates: $34
(205) 424-9690
(800) 633-3434

MOTEL 6
1000 Shiloh Ln
(35020)
Rates: $33-$39
(205) 426-9646
(800) 466-8356

TRAVELODGE
1098 9th Ave SW
(35020)
Rates: $47-$63
(205) 424-0880
(800) 578-7878

BIRMINGHAM

ADAM'S INN
300 10th St N
(35203)
Rates: $45-$50
(205) 328-8560

**AMERISUITES
INVERNESS**
4686 Hwy 280 E
(35242)
Rates: $79-$99
(205) 995-9242
(800) 333-1516

**BAYMONT INN
& SUITES**
513 Cahaba Park
Circle (35203)
Rates: $56+
(205) 995-9990
(800) 301-0200

**BEST SUITES
OF AMERICA**
140 State Farm
Pkwy (35209)
Rates: $69-$139
(205) 940-9990
(800) 237-8466

**BEST WESTERN
CIVIC CENTER**
2230 Civic Center
Blvd (35203)
Rates: $64-$125
(205) 328-6320
(800) 528-1234
(800) 636-4669

AREA CODES - If the local number doesn't connect, check for a new area code.

EMBASSY SUITES
2300 Woodcrest
Place (35203)
Rates: $119-$149
(205) 879-7400
(800) 362-2779

HAMPTON INN
1466 Montgomery
Hwy (35216)
Rates: $66-$77
(205) 822-2224
(800) 426-7866

**HAWTHORN
SUITES**
5320 Beacon Dr
(35210)
Rates: $60-$140
(205) 951-1200
(800) 527-1133

**HOLIDAY INN
SOUTH ON
THE LAKE**
1548 Montgomery
Hwy (35216)
Rates: $69-$79
(205) 822-4350
(800) 465-4329

**HOMESTEAD
VILLAGE**
12 Perimeter Park
South (35243)
Rates: $64-$80
(205) 967-3800
(888) 782-9473

**HOWARD
JOHNSON**
275 Oxmoor Rd
(35209)
Rates: $49-$69
(205) 942-0919
(800) 446-4656

**KEY WEST INN
& SUITES**
4400 Colonnade
Pkwy (35243)
Rates: $59-$89
(205) 968-3700
(800) 831-8485

LA QUINTA INN
905 11th Ct W
(35204)
Rates: $67-$89
(205) 324-4510
(800) 687-6667

**LA QUINTA INN
& SUITES
HOMEWOOD**
60 State Farm
Pkwy (35209)
Rates: $79-$99
(205) 290-0150
(800) 687-6667

**MOTEL
BIRMINGHAM**
7905 Crestwood
Blvd (35210)
Rates: $59-$110
(205) 956-4440
(800) 338-9275

PICKWICK HOTEL
1023 20th St S
(35205)
Rates: $94-$129
(205) 933-9555
(800) 255-7304

REDMONT HOTEL
2101 Fifth Ave N
(35212)
Rates: $129
(205) 324-2101

RELAX INN
6101 1st Ave N
(35212)
Rates: n/a
(205) 591-5575

**RESIDENCE INN
BY MARRIOTT**
50 State Farm
Pkwy (35209)
Rates: $139
(205) 943-0044
(800) 331-3131

**RESIDENCE INN
BY MARRIOTT**
3 Green Hill Pkwy
(35242)
Rates: $89-$195
(205) 991-8686
(800) 331-3131

**ROEBUCK
PARKWAY INN**
9225 Parkway E
(35206)
Rates: $48-$56
(205) 836-5400
(800) 545-1734

SUPER 8 MOTEL
1813 Crestwood
Blvd (35210)
Rates: $40+
(205) 956-3650
(800) 800-8000

SUPER 8-NORTH
624 Decatur Hwy
(35068)
Rates: $39-$89
(205) 841-2200
(800) 800-8000

**THE TUTWILER-
A WYNDHAM
GRAND HOTEL**
2021 Park Place N
(35205)
Rates: $140-$204
(205) 322-2100
(800) 845-1787

BOAZ

**BEST WESTERN
BOAZ OUTLET
CENTER**
751 US 431 S
(35957)
Rates: $43-$55
(256) 593-8410
(800) 528-1234

KEY WEST INN
10535 Alabama
Hwy (35957)
Rates: $50-$65
(256) 593-0800
(800) 833-0555

BREMEN

**BREMEN
LAKEVIEW
RESORT**
1940 CR 143
(35033)
Rates: $44
(256) 287-0023

BREWTON

**COLONIAL
MANOR MOTEL**
643 South Blvd
(36427)
Rates: $31-$33
(334) 867-5421

CALERA

**BEST WESTERN
SUITE LIFE**
11960 Hwy 28
(35040)
Rates: $59-$79
(205) 668-0222
(800) 528-1234
(800) 254-1267

DAYS INN
11691 Hwy 25
& I-65 (35040)
Rates: $35-$60
(205) 668-0560
(800) 329-7466

CAMDEN

DAYS INN
39 Camden
Bypass (36726)
Rates: $47-$57
(334) 682-4555
(800) 329-7466

CEDAR BLUFF

**CEDAR BLUFF
MOTEL**
3775 Hwy 9
(35959)
Rates: $35-$40
(256) 779-6868

**JR'S MARINA &
MOTEL**
CR 102 (35959)
Rates: n/a
(256) 779-6461

RIVERSIDE MOTEL
1210 CR 131
(35959)
Rates: $30-$60
(256) 779-6117
(800) 292-9324

CHICKASAW

**HOWARD
JOHNSON
EXPRESS**
370 W Lee St
(36611)
Rates: $39-$89
(334) 457-4006
(800) 446-4656

CHILDERSBURG

DAYS INN
33669 US Hwy 280
(35044)
Rates: $40-$55
(256) 378-6007
(800) 329-7466

CLANTON

BEST WESTERN
801 Bradberry Ln
(35046)
Rates: $48-$70
(205) 280-1006
(800) 528-1234

DAYS INN
2000 Holiday Inn
Dr (35046)
Rates: $40-$60
(205) 755-0510
(800) 329-7466

KEY WEST INN
2045 7th St (35045)
Rates: $44-$70
(205) 755-8500
(800) 833-0555

SCOTTISH INNS
2301 7th St S
(35046)
Rates: n/a
(205) 755-4049
(800) 251-1962

SHONEY'S INN
946 Lake Mitchell
Rd (35045)
Rates: $41-$55
(205) 280-0306
(800) 222-2222

COLLINSVILLE

**HOWARD
JOHNSON INN**
Hwy 68 W (35961)
Rates: $29-$130
(256) 524-2114
(800) 446-4656

CULLMAN

**BEST WESTERN
FAIRWINDS INN**
1917 Commerce
Ave NW (35055)
Rates: $49-$125
(256) 737-5009
(800) 528-1234
(888) 559-0549

DAYS INN
1841 4th St SW
(35055)
Rates: $38-$56
(256) 739-3800
(800) 329-7466

ECONOMY INN
1834 Second Ave
NW (35055)
Rates: $35+
(256) 734-0122

MOTEL I-65
14466 Hwy 91
(35077)
Rates: $26
(256) 287-1114

SMITH LAKE FISHING RESORT
175 CR 312
(35057)
Rates: $55
(256) 734-1598

SUPER 8 MOTEL
Hwy 157 & I-65
Exit 310 (35057)
Rates: $40-$60
(256) 734-8854
(800) 800-8000

DADEVILLE

HEART OF DIXIE MOTEL
1775 E South St
(36853)
Rates: $36-$40
(256) 825-4236

STILLWATERS RESORT
1816 Stillwaters Dr (36853)
Rates: $139-$179
(256) 825-7021
(800) 687-3732

DALEVILLE

DALEVILLE INN
108 N Daleville Ave (36322)
Rates: $30-$50
(334) 598-4451

ECONO LODGE
444 N Daleville Ave (36322)
Rates: $36-$53
(334) 598-6304
(800) 553-2666

GREEN HOUSE INN & LODGE
761 S Daleville Ave (36322)
Rates: $33-$40
(334) 598-1475

DAPHNE

EASTERN SHORE MOTEL
29070 Hwy 98 (36526)
Rates: $41
(334) 626-6601

ECONO LODGE
29546 N Main St (36526)
Rates: $44-$94
(334) 625-0020
(800) 553-2666

LEGACY INN
70 Hwy 90 (36526)
Rates: $41-$48
(334) 626-3500

DAUPHIN ISLAND

GULF BREEZE MOTEL
1512 Cadillac Ave (36528)
Rates: $42-$67
(334) 861-7344
(800) 286-0296

DECATUR

DAYS INN
810 6th Ave NE (35602)
Rates: $48-$65
(256) 355-3520
(800) 329-7466

KEY WEST INN & SUITES
2212 Danville Rd SW (35601)
Rates: $79-$105
(256) 355-1999
(888) 568-1999

RAMADA LIMITED
1317 E Hwy 67 (35602)
Rates: $44-$70
(256) 353-0333
(800) 272-6232

SUPER 8 MOTEL
125 6th Ave, SE (35601)
Rates: $39-$59
(256) 355-8504
(800) 800-8000

DEMOPOLIS

DAYS INN
1005 Hwy 80E (36732)
Rates: $51-$70
(334) 289-2500
(800) 329-7466

HERITAGE MOTEL
1324 Hwy 80 (36732)
Rates: $27-$32
(334) 289-1175

RIVERVIEW INN
Hwy 45 N (36732)
Rates: $45-$60
(334) 289-0690
(888) 427-9271

DOTHAN

BEE LINE MOTEL
733 N Oates St (36303)
Rates: $30
(334) 794-8631

COMFORT INN
3595 Ross Clark Cir, NW (36303)
Rates: $66-$95
(334) 793-9090
(800) 228-5150

DAYS INN
2841 Ross Clark Cir (36301)
Rates: $40-$48
(334) 793-2550
(800) 329-7466

EASTGATE INN
1885 E Main St (36302)
Rates: $27-$42
(334) 794-6643

HAMPTON INN
3071 Ross Clark Cir (36301)
Rates: $55-$70
(334) 671-3700
(800) 426-7866

HOLIDAY INN SOUTH
2195 Ross Clark Cir (36301)
Rates: $61-$76
(334) 794-8711
(800) 465-4329

MOTEL 6
2907 Ross Clark Cir SW (36301)
Rates: $30-$36
(334) 793-6013
(800) 466-8356

SUBURBAN LODGE
2880 Ross Clark Cir (36301)
Rates: $48-$55
(334) 673-9111
(800) 951-7829

TOWN TERRACE MOTEL
251 N Oates St (36303)
Rates: $25-$35
(334) 792-1135

ELBA

RIVIERA MOTEL
154 Yelverton (36323)
Rates: $27-$36
(334) 897-2204

ENTERPRISE

COMFORT INN
615 Boll Weevil Cir. (36330)
Rates: $63-$139
(334) 393-2304
(800) 228-5150

RAMADA INN
630 Glover Ave (36330)
Rates: $52-$65
(334) 347-6262
(800) 272-6232

EQUALITY

REAL ISLAND MARINA
2700 Real Island Rd (36026)
Rates: $69
(334) 857-2741

EUFAULA

BEST WESTERN EUFAULA INN
1375 Hwy 431S (36027)
Rates: $39-$65
(334) 687-3900
(800) 528-1234

COMFORT SUITES
12 Paulee Pkwy (36027)
Rates: $45-$80
(800) 228-5150

DAYS INN
1521 Eufaula Ave (36027)
Rates: $39-$99
(334) 687-1000
(800) 329-7466

RAMADA INN
631 E Barbour St (36027)
Rates: $49-$65
(334) 687-2021
(800) 272-6232

EUTAW

SPINN ON ASHBY BED & BREAKFAST
108 Ashby Circle (35462)
Rates: $75
(205) 372-3516

EVERGREEN

COMFORT INN
Bates Rd (36401)
Rates: $42-$78
(334) 578-4701
(800) 228-5150

DAYS INN
901 Liberty Hill Dr (36401)
Rates: $35-$85
(334) 578-2100
(800) 329-7466

FAIRHOPE

BARONS ON THE BAY INN
701 S Mobile Ave (36532)
Rates: $34-$65
(334) 928-8000

BEAULIEU
50 Fairhope Ave (36532)
Rates: $85-$125
(334) 928-4196

KEY WEST INN
231 S Greeno Rd (36532)
Rates: $39-$90
(334) 990-7373
(800) 833-0555

MARCELLA'S TEA ROOM & INN B&B
114 Fairhope Ave (36532)
Rates: $85
(334) 990-8520

AREA CODES - If the local number doesn't connect, check for a new area code.

OAK HAVEN COTTAGES
355 S Mobile St
(36532)
Rates: $50-$60
(334) 928-5431

THE PARKER HOUSE
411 N Section St
(36532)
Rates: $21-$65
(334) 928-8472

FAYETTE

JOURNEY'S INN
2502 Temple Ave N (35555)
Rates: $34-$54
(205) 932-6727

FLORENCE

DAYS INN
1915 Florence Blvd (35630)
Rates: $45-$65
(256) 766-2620
(800) 329-7466

DOUBLEHEAD RESORT
145 CR 134, Town Creek (35672)
Rates: $145-$275
(256) 685-9267
(800) 685-9267

HOMESTEAD EXECUTIVE INN
504 S Court St (35630)
Rates: $38-$59
(256) 766-2331
(800) 248-5336

SUPER 8 MOTEL
101 Hwy 72 (35631)
Rates: $42-$58
(256) 757-2167
(800) 800-8000

FOLEY

HOLIDAY INN EXPRESS
2682 S McKenzie St (36535)
Rates: $55-$80
(334) 943-9100
(800) 465-4329
(800) 962-1833

KEY WEST INN
2520 S McKenzie St (36535)
Rates: $80-$100
(334) 943-1241
(800) 833-0555

RIVIERA LODGE
126 CR 20 W (36535)
Rates: $35-$80
(334) 943-3339
(800) 572-4225

FORESTDALE

TRAVELER'S REST MOTEL
1066 Forestdale Blvd (35214)
Rates: n/a
(205) 798-3831

FORT PAYNE

ADAMS OUTDOORS
6102 Mitchell Rd NE (35967)
Rates: $20-$60
(256) 845-2988

TRAVELODGE
1828 Gault Ave N Fort (35967)
Rates: $29-$59
(245) 845-0481
(800) 578-7878

FULTONDALE

DAYS INN
616 Decatur Hwy (35068)
Rates: $51-$89
(205) 849-0111
(800) 329-7466

GADSDEN

DAYS INN
1612 W Grand Ave (35901)
Rates: $50-$125
(256) 442-7913
(800) 329-7466

GADSDEN INN & SUITES
200 Albert Rains Blvd (35901)
Rates: $44-$59
(256) 543-7240
(800) 637-5678

RED ROOF INN
1600 Rainbow Dr (35901)
Rates: $51-$100
(256) 543-1105
(800) 843-7663

RODEWAY INN
3909 W Meighan Blvd (35904)
Rates: $42-$100
(256) 543-0323
(800) 228-2000

SUPER 8 MOTEL
2110 Rainbow Dr (35901)
Rates: $35-$45
(256) 547-9033
(800) 800-8000

GAYLESVILLE

THE LIGHTHOUSE MOTEL
Hwy 68 (35973)
Rates: $40-$55
(256) 779-8400

GREENVILLE

BEST WESTERN
106 Cahaba Rd (36037)
Rates: $40-$70
(334) 382-9200
(800) 528-1234

COMFORT INN
1029 Fort Dale Rd (36037)
Rates: $45-$78
(334) 383-9595
(800) 228-5150

ECONO LODGE
946 Fort Dale Rd (36037)
Rates: $45-$55
(334) 382-3118
(800) 553-2666

HAMPTON INN
219 Interstate Dr (36037)
Rates: $60-$72
(334) 382-9631
(800) 426-7866

RAMADA INN
941 Fort Dale Rd (36037)
Rates: $48-$55
(334) 382-2651
(800) 272-6232

THRIFTY INN
105 Bypass (36037)
Rates: $38+
(334) 382-6671

GULF SHORES

BON SECOUR LODGE
16730 Oyster Bay Pl (36542)
Rates: $60-$85
(334) 968-7814

COMFORT INN
3049 W 1st St (36542)
Rates: $29-$284
(334) 968-8604
(800) 228-5150

GULF PINES MOTEL
245 E 22nd Ave (36542)
Rates: $29-$78
(334) 968-7911
(888) 878-9575

LIGHTHOUSE MOTEL
455 E Beach Blvd (36542)
Rates: $35-$150
(334) 948-6188

RIVERSIDE INN
5587 CR 6 (36542)
Rates: $45-$70
(334) 968-7478

ROGERS' CASTLE BY THE SEA
809 W Beach Blvd (36547)
Rates: $115-$150
(334) 948-6954

SUNSET SHORES DUPLEX RENTAL
515-B W 1st Ave (36547)
Rates: $45-$95
(334) 948-6986

GUNTERSVILLE

DAYS INN
14040 Hwy 431 S (35976)
Rates: $54-$80
(256) 582-3200
(800) 329-7466

MAC'S LANDING MOTEL /MARINA
7001 Val-Monte Dr (35976)
Rates: $55-$150
(256) 582-1000

RIVER HOUSE VACATION RENTAL
71 Signal Point Dr, Lake Guntersville (35976)
Rates: $100-$175
(256) 582-2003
(205) 951-3548
(800) 239-2100

HALEYVILLE

HALEYVILLE MOTEL
3800 Beech Grove Rd (35565)
Rates: $28-$33
(205) 486-2263

HAMILTON

DAYS INN
1849 Military St S (35570)
Rates: $45-$99
(205) 921-1790
(800) 329-7466

HANCEVILLE

MOTEL I-65
14466 Hwy 91 (35077)
Rates: $30-$50
(256) 287-1114

HEFLIN

HOWARD JOHNSON EXPRESS
1957 Almon St (36264)
Rates: $35-$55
(256) 463-2900
(800) 446-4656

HOMEWOOD

HOLIDAY INN
260 Oxmoor Rd (35209)
Rates: $70-$85
(205) 942-2041
(800) 465-4329

MICROTEL
251 Summit Pkwy
(35209)
Rates: $38-$52
(205) 945-5550
(888) 771-7171
(800) 275-8047

**THE MOUNTAIN
BROOK INN**
2800 Hwy 280
(35223)
Rates: $115
(205) 870-3100
(800) 523-7771

RED ROOF INN
151 Vulcan Rd
(35209)
Rates: $46-$64
(205) 942-9414
(800) 843-7663

HOOVER

AMERISUITES
2980 Hwy 150
(35244)
Rates: $94-$114
(205) 988-8444
(800) 833-1516

DAYS INN
1535 Montgomery
Hwy (35216)
Rates: $40-$75
(205) 822-6030
(800) 329-7466

**LA QUINTA INN
& SUITES**
120 Riverchase
Pkwy E (35244)
Rates: $69-$99
(205) 403-0096
(800) 687-6667

HOPE HULL

RODEWAY INN
7725 Mobile Hwy
(36043)
Rates: $28-$79
(334) 281-7151
(800) 228-2000

HUNTSVILLE

**BAYMONT INN
& SUITES**
4890 University
Dr NW (35816)
Rates: $54-$65
(256) 830-8999
(800) 301-0200

**EXECUTIVE
LODGE
SUITE HOTEL**
1535 Sparkman Dr
(35816)
Rates: $65-$120
(256) 830-8600
(800) 248-4772

**GUESTHOUSE
SUITES PLUS**
4020
Independence Dr
(35816)
Rates: $63-$100
(256) 837-8907
(800) 214-8378

HILTON HOTEL
401 Williams Ave
(35801)
Rates: $99-$129
(256) 533-1400
(800) 445-8667

**HOLIDAY INN
EXPRESS**
3808 Univeristy
Dr (35816)
Rates: $59-$69
(256) 721-1000
(800) 465-4329

**HOLIDAY INN
SPACE CENTER**
3810 University
Dr (35816)
Rates: $62-$71
(256) 837-7171
(800) 465-4329

**LA QUINTA INN
RESEARCH PARK**
4870 Univeristy
Dr (35816)
Rates: $56-$79
(256) 830-2070
(800) 687-6667

**LA QUINTA INN
SPACE CENTER**
3141 Univeristy
Dr (35816)
Rates: $65-$79
(256) 533-0756
(800) 687-6667

MOTEL 6
3200 University
Dr (35816)
Rates: $30-$36
(256) 539-8448
(800) 466-8356

MOTEL 6
8995 Hwy 20 W
(35824)
Rates: $35-$43
(256) 772-7479
(800) 466-8356

JASPER

TRAVEL-RITE INN
200 Mallway Dr
(35501)
Rates: $26-$39
(205) 221-1161

**UNCLE MORT'S
WARRIOR RIVER
MOTEL**
30 Hwy 78 Loop
(35501)
Rates: $38
(205) 483-9212

LAFAYETTE

**HILL-WARE-
DOWDELL
MANSION**
203 2nd Ave SW
(36862)
Rates: n/a
(205) 864-7861

LEEDS

DAYS INN
1835 Ashville Rd
(35094)
Rates: $50-$100
(205) 699-9833
(800) 329-7466

LEESBURG

LEESBURG LODGE
5915 Weiss Lake
Blvd (35983)
Rates: $33-$52
(256) 526-7378
(800) 209-3219

LINDEN

COUNTRY INN
705 S Main St
(36748)
Rates: $37-$48
(334) 295-8704

LIVINGSTON

COMFORT INN
141 Trucker Blvd
(35479)
Rates: $68-$100
(205) 652-4839
(800) 228-5150

**LIVINGSTON
MOTEL**
Hwy 11 (35479)
Rates: $32
(205) 652-9621

LOXLEY

LOXLEY MOTEL
Hwy 59 S (36551)
Rates: $30-$75
(334) 964-5094
(334) 964-5095

RUTH'S MOTEL
Hwy 59 S (36551)
Rates: $25-$45
(334) 964-5094
(334) 964-5516

WIND CHASE INN
13156 N Hickory
(36551)
Rates: $50
(334) 964-4444
(800) 401-4181

MADISON

**DAYS INN
AIRPORT**
102 Arlington Dr
(35758)
Rates: $42-$95
(256) 772-9550
(800) 329-7466

**FEDERAL SQUARE
MOTEL & SUITES**
8781 Hwy 20 W
(35758)
Rates: $40-$88
(256) 772-8470
(800) 458-1639

MOTEL 6
8995 Hwy 20
(35758)
Rates: $32-$38
(256) 772-7479
(800) 466-8356

MAGNOLIA
SPRINGS

**MAGNOLIA
SPRINGS BED
& BREAKFAST**
14469 Oak St
(36555)
Rates: $94+
(334) 965-7321
(800) 965-7321

MENTONE

**MENTONE
SPRINGS
HISTORICAL
HOTEL**
6114 Hwy 117
(35984)
Rates: $54-$125
(256) 634-4040
(800) 404-0100

MOBILE

**BEST INNS
OF AMERICA**
156 Beltline Hwy
S (36608)
Rates: $49-$79
(334) 343-4911
(800) 237-8466

**BEST SUITES
OF AMERICA**
150 Beltline Hwy
S (36608)
Rates: $67-$129
(334) 343-4949
(800) 237-8466

**BEST WESTERN
BATTLESHIP INN**
2701 Battleship
Pkwy (36601)
Rates: $61-$66
(334) 432-2703
(800) 528-1234

**THE CLARION
HOTEL-BEL AIR**
3101 Airport Blvd
(36606)
Rates: $50-$99
(334) 476-6400
(800) 982-9822

COMFORT SUITES
70 Springdale
Blvd (36606)
Rates: $55-$85
(334) 471-1515
(800) 228-5150

DAYS INN
5480 Inn Dr
(36619)
Rates: $39-$55
(334) 661-8181
(800) 329-7466

**DAYS INN
AIRPORT**
3650 Airport Blvd
(36608)
Rates: $40-$90
(334) 344-3410
(800) 329-7466

DRURY INN
824 Beltline Hwy
S (36609)
Rates: $59-$76
(334) 344-7700
(800) 378-7946

ECONO LODGE-MIDTOWN
1 Beltline Hwy S
(36606)
Rates: $36-$46
(334) 479-5333
(800) 553-2666

GUESTHOUSE INN
3132 Government
Blvd (36606)
Rates: $40-$65
(334) 471-2402
(800) 535-8029

HOLIDAY INN
6527Hwy 90 N
(36619)
Rates: $59-$85
(334) 666-5600
(800) 465-4329

HOLIDAY INN DOWNTOWN
301 Government
St (36602)
Rates: $135-$155
(334) 694-0100
(800) 465-4329

HOLIDAY INN I-65
850 S Beltline
(36616)
Rates: $62-$80
(334) 342-3220
(800) 465-4329

LA QUINTA INN
816 Beltline Hwy
S (36609)
Rates: $62-$82
(334) 343-4051
(800) 687-6667

MOTEL 6-AIRPORT
400 Beltline Hwy
S (36608)
Rates: $38-$48
(334) 343-8448
(800) 466-8356

MOTEL 6-TILLMANS CORNER
5488 Inn Rd
(36619)
Rates: $33-$40
(334) 660-1483
(800) 466-8356

OLSSON'S MOTEL
4137 Government
Blvd (36693)
Rates: $29-$35
(334) 661-5331
(800) 332-1004
(800) 351-1023

RADISSON ADMIRAL SEMMES HOTEL
251 Government
St (36602)
Rates: $140-$260
(334) 432-8000
(800) 333-3333

RAMADA INN ON THE BAY
1525 Battleship
Pkwy (36633)
Rates: $45-$81
(334) 626-7200
(800) 272-6232

RED ROOF INN-N.
33 Beltline Hwy S
(36606)
Rates: $47-$68
(334) 476-2004
(800) 843-7663

RED ROOF INN-S.
5450 Coca Cola Rd
(36619)
Rates: $38-$50
(334) 666-1044
(800) 843-7663

RESIDENCE INN BY MARRIOTT
950 S Beltline
Hwy (36609)
Rates: $97-$124
(334) 304-0570
(800) 331-3131

RIVERHOUSE B&B
13285 Rebel Rd
(Theodore 36590)
Rates: $90-$130
(334) 973-2233
(800) 552-9791

SHONEY'S INN
5472-A Inn Rd
(36619)
Rates: $52-$65
(334) 660-1520
(800) 222-2222

MONROEVILLE

BEST WESTERN
4419 S Alabama
Ave (36460)
Rates: $48-$90
(334) 575-9999
(800) 528-1234

BUDGET INN
605 S Alabama
Ave (36460)
Rates: $20-$32
(334) 575-3101

MONTGOMERY

BAYMONT INN & SUITES
5225 Carmichael
Rd (36106)
Rates: $47-$65
(334) 277-6000
(800) 301-0200

BEST INNS OF AMERICA
5135 Carmichael
Rd (36106)
Rates: $49-$62
(334) 270-9199
(800) 237-8466

BEST SUITES OF AMERICA
5155 Carmichael
Rd (36106)
Rates: $49-$79
(334) 270-3223
(800) 237-8466

BEST WESTERN MONTGOMERY LODGE
977 W South Blvd
(36105)
Rates: $40-$65
(334) 288-5740
(800) 528-1234

BEST WESTERN MONTICELLO INN
5837 Monticello
Dr (36117)
Rates: $50-$60
(334) 277-4442
(800) 528-1234

COLISEUM INN
1550 Federal Dr
(36107)
Rates: $31-$39
(334) 265-0586
(800) 876-6835

COLONEL'S REST B&B
11091 Atlanta
Hwy (36117)
Rates: $60+
(334) 215-0380
(800) 461-3758

DAYS INN
2625 Zelda Rd
(36107)
Rates: $54-$69
(334) 269-9611
(800) 329-7466

DAYS INN-SOUTH
1150 South Blvd
(36105)
Rates: $42-$140
(334) 281-8000
(800) 329-7466

DAYS SUITES
4470 Northchase
Blvd (36109)
Rates: $50-$100
(800) 329-7466

ECONO LODGE
4135 Troy Hwy
(36116)
Rates: $42-$55
(334) 284-3400
(800) 553-2666

GOVERNORS HOUSE HOTEL & CONF CENTER
2705 E South Blvd
(36116)
Rates: $55-$65
(334) 288-2800
(800) 334-8459

HOLIDAY INN EAST HOLIDOME
1185 Eastern Blvd
(36117)
Rates: $69-$119
(334) 272-0370
(800) 465-4329

LA QUINTA INN
1280 East Blvd
(36117)
Rates: $59-$79
(334) 271-1620
(800) 687-6667

MOTEL 6
1051 Eastern
Bypass (36117)
Rates: $40-$46
(334) 277-6748
(800) 466-8356

RAMADA INN-STATEHOUSE
924 Madison Ave
(36104)
Rates: $56-$74
(334) 265-0741
(800) 272-6232

REGENCY INN
1771 Cong.
Dickinson Dr
(36109)
Rates: $53-$57
(334) 260-0444
(800) 824-0737
(888) 301-2992

RESIDENCE INN BY MARRIOTT
1200 Hilmar Ct
(36117)
Rates: $99-$144
(334) 270-3300
(800) 331-3131

TRAVEL INN
970 W South Blvd
(36105)
Rates: $24-$28
(334) 288-2600

TRAVELODGE
4231 Mobile Hwy
(36108)
Rates: $30-$55
(334) 288-0610
(800) 578-7878

MOODY

SUPER 8 MOTEL
2451 Moody Pkwy
(35004)
Rates: $40-$49
(205) 640-7091
(800) 800-8000

NATURAL BRIDGE

BUDGET INN
Hwy 278 & 5
(35577)
Rates: $30-$33
(205) 486-5261

NORTHPORT

BEST WESTERN CATALINA INN
2015 McFarland Blvd (35476)
Rates: $40-$60
(205) 339-5200
(800) 528-1234

ONEONTA

SANDSTONE MOTEL
605 2nd Ave E (35121)
Rates: $30-$40
(205) 274-2007

OPELIKA

BEST WESTERN MARINER INN
1002 Columbus Pkwy (36801)
Rates: $35-$99
(334) 749-1461
(800) 528-1234

DAYS INN
1014 Anand Ave (36801)
Rates: $45-$200
(334) 749-5080
(800) 329-7466

MOTEL 6
1015 Columbus Pkwy (36804)
Rates: $30-$36
(334) 745-0988
(800) 466-8356

SHONEY'S INN
1520 Columbus Pkwy (36801)
Rates: $45
(334) 742-0270
(800) 222-2222

OPP

OPP MOTOR LODGE
Hwy 331S (36467)
Rates: $42
(334) 493-3551

OXFORD

DAYS INN
#1 Recreation Dr (36203)
Rates: $55-$85
(256) 835-0300
(800) 329-7466
(800) 266-8694

ECONO LODGE
25 Elm St (36203)
Rates: $32-$59
(256) 831-9480
(800) 553-2666

HOLIDAY INN
Hwy 78 & 21 South (36203)
Rates: $59-$69
(256) 831-3410
(800) 465-4329

HOWARD JOHNSON EXPRESS
Hwy 78 & 21 South (36203)
Rates: $38-$46
(256) 835-3988
(800) 446-4656

MOTEL 6
202 Grace St (36203)
Rates: $36-$44
(256) 831-5463
(800) 466-8356

SLEEP INN
88 Colonial Dr (36203)
Rates: $49-$150
(256) 831-2191
(800) 753-3746

TRAVELODGE
1207 Hwy 21 S (36203)
Rates: $35-$125
(256) 835-0185
(800) 578-7878

OZARK

BAYWOOD SUITES
401 Newton Ave (36360)
Rates: $30
(334) 774-4470

BEST WESTERN OZARK INN
Hwy 231 S & Deese Rd (36361)
Rates: $44-$52
(334) 774-5166
(800) 528-1234

BUDGET INN
1610 Hwy 231S (36360)
Rates: $25-$35
(334) 774-5105

HOLIDAY INN
151 US 231 N (36360)
Rates: $56-$61
(334) 774-7300
(800) 465-4329

PELHAM

BEST WESTERN OAK MOUNTAIN INN
100 Bishop Cir (35124)
Rates: $49-$59
(205) 982-1113
(800) 528-1234

COMFORT INN
110 Cahaba Valley Pkwy (35124)
Rates: $56-$135
(205) 444-9200
(800) 228-5150

SLEEP INN
200 Southgate Dr (35124)
Rates: $59-$99
(205) 982-9800
(800) 753-3746

PELL CITY

BEST WESTERN RIVERSIDE INN
11900 Hwy 78 (35135)
Rates: $59-$79
(205) 338-3381
(800) 528-1234

PIEDMONT

LAMONT MOTEL
Hwy 278 E (36272)
Rates: $35-$41
(256) 447-6002

PIKE ROAD

SCOTTISH INNS
7237 Troy Hwy (36064)
Rates: n/a
(334) 288-1501
(800) 251-1962

PINE APPLE

TURKEY HOLLOW "MAN" HUNTING LODGE
Rt 2, Box 57 (36768)
Rates: n/a
(334) 746-2159

PRATTVILLE

COMFORT INN
797 Business Park Dr (36067)
Rates: $49-$80
(334) 365-6003
(800) 228-5150

DAYS INN
I-65 & Hwy 31 N (36067)
Rates: $44-$110
(334) 365-3311
(800) 329-7466

HOLIDAY INN
2598 Cobbs Ford Rd (36066)
Rates: $57-$66
(334) 285-3420
(800) 465-4329

JUPITER INN
1940 Hwy 82 W (36067)
Rates: $30-$45
(334) 361-0499

ROGERSVILLE

ECONOMY INN
Hwy 72 (35652)
Rates: $30-$40
(256) 247-5416

SARALAND

BAMBOO MOTEL
1113 Hwy 43 (36571)
Rates: $33-$47
(334) 675-5691

PLANTATION MOTEL
1010 Hwy 43 (36571)
Rates: $32-$45
(334) 675-5511

SCOTTSBORO

DAYS INN
1106 John T Reid Pkwy (35768)
Rates: $39-$65
(256) 574-1212
(800) 329-7466

RAINBOW INN
1401 E Willow St (35768)
Rates: $33-$39
(256) 574-1115

SELMA

GRACE HALL B&B
506 Lauderdale St (36701)
Rates: $79-$99
(334) 875-5744

GRAYSTONE MOTEL
1200 W Highland Ave (36701)
Rates: $33-$45
(334) 874-6681

HOLIDAY INN
1806 US 80W (36701)
Rates: $55-$65
(334) 872-0461
(800) 465-4329

TRAVELERS INN OF SELMA
2006 W Highland Ave (36701)
Rates: $33-$54
(334) 875-1200

SHEFFIELD

CLARION HOTEL
4205 Hatch Blvd (35660)
Rates: $69-$99
(256) 381-3743
(800) 252-7466

HOLIDAY INN
4900 Hatch Blvd (35660)
Rates: $58-$72
(256) 381-4710
(800) 465-4329

SHORTER

DAYS INN
450 Main St (36075)
Rates: $40-$70
(334) 727-6034
(800) 329-7466

STEVENSON

BUDGET INN
42973 Hwy 72 (35772)
Rates: $40-$45
(256) 437-2215

AREA CODES - If the local number doesn't connect, check for a new area code.

SYLACAUGA

TOWNE INN
Hwy 280 (35150)
Rates: $32-$50
(256) 249-3821

THOMASVILLE

BEST WESTERN
1200 Mosely Dr
(36784)
Rates: $42-$60
(334) 636-0614
(800) 528-1234

DAYS INN
424 Hwy 43 N
(36784)
Rates: $34-$42
(334) 636-5467
(800) 329-7466

TROY

DAYS INN
1260 US Hwy 231
S (36081)
Rates: $30-$99
(334) 566-1630
(800) 329-7466

ECONO LODGE
1013 Hwy 231
(36081)
Rates: $40-$70
(334) 566-4960
(800) 553-2666

HOLIDAY INN
Hwy 231 N &
Hwy 29 (36081)
Rates: $53-$64
(334) 566-1150
(800) 465-4329

**HOLIDAY INN
EXPRESS**
Hwy 231 &
Hwy 29 (36081)
Rates: $50-$55
(334) 670-0012
(800) 465-4329

SCOTTISH INNS
186 Hwy 231 N
(36081)
Rates: $32-$42
(334) 566-4090
(800) 251-1962

TUSCALOOSA

KEY WEST INN
4700 Doris Pate Dr
(35405)
Rates: $55
(205) 556-3232
(800) 833-0555

LA QUINTA INN
4122 McFarland
Blvd E (35405)
Rates: $49-$79
(205) 349-3270
(800) 687-6667

**MASTERS
ECONOMY INN**
3600 McFarland
Blvd (35405)
Rates: $34-$48
(205) 556-2010

MOTEL 6
4700 McFarland
Blvd E (35405)
Rates: $32-$44
(205) 759-4942
(800) 466-8356

RAMADA INN
631 Skyland Blvd
E (35405)
Rates: $45-$68
(205) 759-4431
(800) 272-6232

TUSCUMBIA

KEY WEST INN
1800 Hwy 72 W
(35674)
Rates: $43-$50
(256) 383-0700
(800) 833-0555

WETUMPKA

KEY WEST INN
4225 Hwy 231 N
(36093)
Rates: $47-$65
(334) 567-2227
(800) 833-0555

WETUMPKA INN
8534 Hwy 231 N
(36092)
Rates: $25
(334) 567-9316

YORK

DAYS INN
17700 Hwy 17
(36925)
Rates: $50-$79
(205) 392-9675
(800) 329-7466

AREA CODES - If the local number doesn't connect, check for a new area code.

ALASKA

ANCHOR POINT

ANCHOR RIVER INN
P. O. Box 154 (99556)
Rates: $50-$85
(800) 435-8531

ANCHORAGE

A COMFORT B&B
8501 Brookridge Dr (99504)
Rates: n/a
(907) 338-0453

A COUSIN OF MINE
4406 Forest Rd (99517)
Rates: n/a
(907) 248-3462

ADAMS PLACE BED & BREAKFAST
5701 E 97th Ave (99516)
Rates: n/a
(907) 346-3604

ALASKA AUNTIE'S BED & BREAKFST
1206 W 47th Ave (99503)
Rates: n/a
(907) 562-7626

ANCHORAGE EAGLE NEST HOTEL
4110 Spenard Rd (99517)
Rates: $40-$170
(907) 243-3433
(800) 848-7852

ARCTIC INN MOTEL
842 W Int'l Airport Rd (99518)
Rates: n/a
(907) 561-1328

AURORA WINDS B&B RESORT
7501 Upper O'Malley (99516)
Rates: $105-$250
(907) 346-2533

BEAR DEN B&B
3002 154th St (99516)
Rates: n/a
(907) 345-4012

BEST WESTERN BARRATT INN
4616 Spenard Rd (99517)
Rates: $139-$167
(907) 243-3131
(800) 528-1234
(800) 221-7550

BIG TIMBER MOTEL
2037 E 5th Ave (99501)
Rates: n/a
(907) 272-2541

DAYS INN DOWNTOWN
321 E 5th Ave (99501)
Rates: $155-$250
(907) 276-7226
(800) 329-7466

DUKES 8TH AVENUE HOTEL
630 W 8th Ave (99520)
Rates: $55-$165
(907) 274-6213
(800) 478-4837

EXECUTIVE SUITE HOTEL
4360 Spenard Rd (99517)
Rates: $89-$289
(907) 243-6366
(800) 770-6366

FERNBROOK BED & BREAKFAST
8120 Rabbit Creek Rd (99516)
Rates: $75-$95
(907) 345-1954

HILLSIDE ON GAMBELL
2150 Gambell St (99503)
Rates: $46-$100
(907) 258-6006
(800) 478-6008

HILTON HOTEL
500 W 3rd Ave (99501)
Rates: $209-$229
(907) 272-7411
(800) 445-8667

HOLIDAY INN EXPRESS
4411 Spenard Rd (99517)
Rates: $129
(907) 248-8848
(800) 465-4329

LONG HOUSE ALASKAN HOTEL
4335 Wisconsin St (99517)
Rates: $69-$199
(907) 243-2133
(888) 243-2133

MERRILL FIELD INN
420 Sitka St (99501)
Rates: $100-$125
(907) 276-4547
(800) 898-4547

MICROTEL INN & SUITES
5205 Northwood Dr (99517)
Rates: $129-$149
(907) 245-5002
(888) 771-7171

MUSH INN MOTEL
333 Concrete St (99501)
Rates: n/a
(907) 277-4554
(800) 478-4554

PARKWOOD INN
4455 Juneau St (99503)
Rates: $115
(907) 563-3590

POPPY SEED B&B
616 E 72nd Ave (99518)
Rates: $50-$85
(907) 344-2286

PUFFIN INN
4400 Spenard Rd (99517)
Rates: $60-$209
(907) 243-4044
(800) 478-3346

QUPQUIGIAQ BED & BREAKFAST
3801 Spenard Rd (99517)
Rates: n/a
(907) 562-5681

REGAL ALASKAN HOTEL
4800 Spenard Rd (99517)
Rates: $119-$310
(907) 243-2300
(800) 544-0553

RODEWAY INN
1104 E 5th Ave (99501)
Rates: $49-$120
(907) 274-1650
(800) 228-2000

6 BAR E RANCH BED & BREAKFAST
11401 Totem Rd (99516)
Rates: n/a
(907) 346-2665

SIXTH & B BED & BREAKFAST
145 W Sixth Ave (99501)
Rates: $38-$105
(907) 279-5293

SOURDOUGH VISITORS LODGE
801 E Erickson St (99520)
Rates: $69-$125
(907) 279-4148
(800) 777-3716

SUPER 8 MOTEL
3501 Minnesota Dr (99503)
Rates: $60-$147
(907) 276-8884
(800) 800-8000

12TH & L B&B
1134 L St (99501)
Rates: $45
(907) 276-1225

VALARIAN VISIT BED & BREAKFAST
1536 Valarian St (99508)
Rates: $50-$75
(907) 274-5760

WESTMARK INN
115 E Third Ave (99501)
Rates: $109-$119
(907) 272-7561
(800) 544-0970

ANGOON

KOOTZENAHOO INLET LODGE
P. O. Box 91 (99820)
Rates: $55-$65
(907) 788-3615

BETTLES

BETTLES LODGE WILDERNESS TRIPS & CABINS
P. O. Box 27-VP (99726)
Rates: $95-$145
(907) 692-5111
(800) 770-5111

BIG LAKE

BIG LAKE MOTEL
P. O. Box 520728 (99652)
Rates: $65-$75
(907) 892-7976

AREA CODES - If the local number doesn't connect, check for a new area code.

CANTWELL

BACKWOODS LODGE
MP 210 George Parks Hwy (99729)
Rates: $110-$120
(907) 768-2232

REINDEER MOUNTAIN LODGE
MP 210 George Parks Hwy (99729)
Rates: n/a
(907) 768-2420

CIRCLE SPRINGS

CIRCLE HOT SPRINGS RESORT
P. O. Box 254 (99730)
Rates: n/a
(907) 520-5113

COOK INLET WEST SIDE

CHINITNA BAY LODGE
P. O. Box 233032 (Anchorage 99523)
Rates: $1100/ Three days
(907) 522-2715

COOPER LANDING

SUNRISE INN MOTEL
MP 45-A, Sterling Hwy (99572)
Rates: $39-$99
(907) 595-1222

DELTA JUNCTION

ALASKA 7 MOTEL
3548 Richardson Hwy (99737)
Rates: $60-$70
(907) 895-4848

BLACK SPRUCE LODGE
2740 Old Richardson Hwy (99737)
Rates: n/a
(907) 895-4668

DELTA INTERNATIONAL HOSTEL
Main St. USA North (99737)
Rates: n/a
(907) 895-5074

SUMMIT LAKE LODGE
Mile 195 Richardson Hwy (99737)
Rates: n/a
(907) 822-3969

DENALI NATL. PARK & PRESERVE

DENALI GRIZZLY BEAR CABINS & CAMPGROUND
P. O. Box 7 (99755)
Rates: $49-$160
(907) 683-2696

DENALI RV PARK & MOTEL
MP 245, George Parks Hwy (99755)
Rates: $54-$119
(800) 478-1501

DENALI WEST LODGE
Box 40VP (Lake Minchumina 99757)
Rates: Package
(907) 674-3112

EARTHSONG LODGE
P. O. Box 89 (Healy 99743)
Rates: $95-$115
(907) 683-2863

MCKINLEY/DENALI PRIVATE CABINS
P. O. Box 90 (99755)
Rates: $65-$115
(907) 683-2733

MT. MCKINLEY MOTOR LODGE
P. O. Box 77 (99755)
Rates: $98
(907) 683-1240

SOURDOUGH CABINS
P. O. Box 118 (99755)
Rates: $80-$144
(907) 683-2773

VALLEY VISTA BED & BREAKFAST
P. O. Box 395 (Healy 99743)
Rates: $89-$129
(877) 683-2841

EAGLE RIVER

EAGLE RIVER MOTEL
11111 Old Eagle River Rd (99577)
Rates: $75-$89
(907) 694-5000

MOUNTAIN AIR BED & BREAKFAST
HC83, Box 1652 (99577)
Rates: $40-$60
(907) 696-3116

SHOOTING STAR BED & BREAKFAST
19211 Upper Skyline Dr (99577)
Rates: n/a
(907) 696-1748

ELFIN COVE

TANAKU LODGE
P. O. Box 72 (99825)
Rates: n/a
(800) 482-6258

FAIRBANKS

AAAA CARE B&B
557 Fairbanks St (99709)
Rates: $65-$150
(907) 479-2447
(800) 478-2705

A PIONEER B&B
1119 Second Ave (99701)
Rates: $55-$85
(907) 452-5393

ALASKA MOTEL
1546 Cushman St (99701)
Rates: $45-$70
(907) 456-6393

CAPTAIN BARTLETT
1411 Airport Way (99701)
Rates: $130-$139
(907) 452-1888
(800) 544-7528

CHENA RIVER BED & BREAKFAST
1001 Dolly Varden Ln (99709)
Rates: $50-$100
(907) 479-2532

COMFORT INN
1908 Chena Landings Lp (99701)
Rates: $79-$209
(907) 479-8080
(800) 228-5150

FOX CREEK B&B
2498 Elliott Hwy (99712)
Rates: $54-$70
(907) 457-5494

GOLDEN NORTH HOTEL
4888 Old Airport Rd (99709)
Rates: $45-$119
(907) 479-6201
(800) 447-1910

HILLSIDE B&B
310 Rambling Road (99712)
Rates: $35-$55
(907) 457-2664

NORTH WOODS LODGE & CABINS
P. O. Box 83615 (99708)
Rates: $20-$87
(907) 479-5300
(800) 478-5305

OLD F. E. GOLD CAMP
5550 Old Steese Hwy N (99712)
Rates: n/a
(907) 389-2414

REGENCY FAIRBANKS HOTEL
95 Tenth Ave (99701)
Rates: $70-$250
(907) 452-3200
(800) 348-1340

SOURDOUGH BED & BREAKFAST
1146 Gilmore Tr. (99708)
Rates: $75-$90
(907) 457-6684

SUCH A DEAL BED & BREAKFAST
P. O . Box 82527 (99708)
Rates: $45-$65
(907) 474-8159

SUPER 8 MOTEL
1909 Airport Way (99701)
Rates: $68-$147
(907) 451-8888
(800) 800-8000

WESTMARK INN
1521 S Cushman (99701)
Rates: $99-$139
(907) 456-6602
(800) 544-0970

GAKONA

GAKONA JUNCTION VILLAGE
P. O. Box 222 (99586)
Rates: $55-$98
(800) 962-1933

GIRDWOOD

THE RESORT INN
NHN Crystal Ave (99587)
Rates: $75
(907) 783-2492

GLENNALLEN

THE NEW CARIBOU HOTEL
P. O. Box 329 (99588)
Rates: $79-$115
(907) 822-3302
(800) 478-3302

GUSTAVUS

BEAR TRACK INN
255 Rink Creek Rd (99826)
Rates: $328-$1125 Weekly
(907) 697-3017
(888) 697-2284

AREA CODES - If the local number doesn't connect, check for a new area code.

A PUFFIN'S B&B
(1/4 Mile Logging
Rd) Box 3 (99826)
Rates: $85-$125
(907) 697-2260

**TRI BED &
BREAKFAST**
P. O. Box 214
(99826)
Rates: $90
(907) 697-2425

HAINES

**CAPTAIN'S
CHOICE MOTEL**
108 2nd Ave
(99827)
Rates: $76-$145
(907) 766-3111
(800) 478-2345

**EAGLE'S NEST
MOTEL**
1069 Haines Hwy
(99827)
Rates: $60-$95
(907) 766-2891
(800) 354-6009

**FORT SEWARD
LODGE &
SALOON**
P. O. Box 307
(99827)
Rates: $50-$95
(907) 766-2009
(800) 478-7772

**FORT WM. H.
SEWARD B&B**
House #1, Box 5
(99827)
Rates: $58-$125
(907) 766-2856
(800) 615-6676

**MOUNTAIN VIEW
MOTEL**
P. O. Box 62
(99827)
Rates: $59-$85
(907) 766-2900
(800) 478-2902

**THUNDERBIRD
MOTEL**
242 Dalton St
(99827)
Rates: $58-$68
(800) 327-2556

HATCHER PASS

**HATCHER PASS
LODGE**
P. O. Box 763
(Palmer 99645)
Rates: $95-$115
(907) 745-5897

HOMER

**ANNA'S GUEST
HOUSE**
460 Bonanza Ave
(99603)
Rates: $55-$99
(907) 235-2716
(877) 374-2716

**BEST WESTERN
BIDARKA INN**
575 Sterling Hwy
(99603)
Rates: $125-$146
(907) 235-8148
(800) 528-1234

**BRIGITTE'S
BAVARIAN B&B**
P. O. Box 2391
(99603)
Rates: $105
(907) 235-6620

DRIFTWOOD INN
135 W Bunnell
Ave (99603)
Rates: $40-$128
(907) 235-8019
(800) 478-8019

**HERITAGE HOTEL
& LODGE**
147 E. Pioneer Ave
(99603)
Rates: $50-$80
(907) 235-7787

**HOME B&B/
SEEKINS**
P. O. Box 1264
(99603)
Rates: $50-$80
(907) 235-8996

LAKEWOOD INN
984 Ocean Dr #1
(99603)
Rates: n/a
(907) 235-6144

**LAND'S END
RESORT**
4786 Homer Spit
Rd (99603)
Rates: $46-$140
(907) 235-2500

**OCEAN SHORES
MOTEL**
3500 Crittenden
Dr (99603)
Rates: $65-$165
(907) 235-7775
(800) 770-7775

**PATCHWORK
FARM B&B**
P. O. Box 1654
(99603)
Rates: n/a
(907) 235-7368

**SEASIDE FARM
HOSTEL &
CABINS**
58335 E End Rd
(99603)
Rates: $65
(907) 235-7850

SUNDMARKS B&B
East Hill Rd
(99603)
Rates: n/a
(907) 235-5188

HOPE

**BEAR CREEK
CABINS**
P O Box 64 (99605)
Rates: $75-$95
(907) 782-3730
(800) 360-8498

INDIAN

**CABIN COMFORT
BED & BREAKFAST**
HC 52, Box 8802
(99540)
Rates: n/a
(907) 653-7726

JUNEAU

**BEST WESTERN
COUNTRY LANE
INN**
9300 Glacier Hwy
(99801)
Rates: $80-$140
(907) 789-5005
(800) 528-1234
(888) 781-5005

**THE DRIFTWOOD
LODGE**
435 Willoughby
Ave (99801)
Rates: $62-$108
(907) 586-2280
(800) 544-2239

**FRONTIER SUITES
AIRPORT HOTEL**
9400 Glacier Hwy
(99801))
Rates: $119-$159
(800) 544-2250

GOLDBELT HOTEL
51 Egan Dr
(99801)
Rates: $89-$179
(888) 478-6809

JAN'S VIEW B&B
P. O. Box 32245
(99803)
Rates: $40-$65
(907) 463-5897

**PROSPECTOR
HOTEL**
375 Whittier St
(99801)
Rates: $75-$145
(907) 586-3737
(800) 331-2711

SUPER 8 MOTEL
2295 Trout St
(99801)
Rates: $68-$143
(907) 789-4858
(800) 800-8000

**WATERFRONT
BREAKWATER INN**
1711 Glacier Ave
(99801)
Rates: $99-$119
(800) 544-2250

KENAI

**CAPT. BLIGH'S
BEAVER CREEK
LODGE & GUIDES**
P. O.Box 4300
(Soldotna 99669)
Rates: Package
(907) 262-7919
(907) 283-7550

**THE FISH HUT
CHARTERS &
LODGING**
1125 Angler Dr
(99611)
Rates: $100-$200
(877) 827-2675

KENAI KINGS INN
P. O. Box 1080
(99611)
Rates: $74-$104
(907) 283-6060

MERIT INN
260 S Willow
(99611)
Rates: $50-$90
(907) 283-6131
(800) 227-6131

KENAI PENINSULA

**ALASKA
MOUNTAIN VIEW
CABINS**
P. O. Box 423
(Sterling 99672)
Rates: $50-$155
(907) 262-4827

**ANGLER'S LODGE
& FISH CAMP**
P. O. Box 508-VG
(Sterling 99672)
Rates: $49-$150
(907) 262-1747

**KENAI MAGIC
LODGE &
FISHING**
2440 E Tudor Rd
#205
(Anchorage 99507)
Rates: $99-$158
(888) 262-6644

**KENAI
PENINSULA
CONDOS**
P. O. Box 3416
(Soldotna 99669)
Rates: $79-$99
(800) 362-1383

**KENAI
WILDERNESS
LODGE**
3074 Commercial
Dr
(Anchorage 99501)
Rates: $40+
(907) 262-4390

**MORGAN'S
LANDING
CABIN RENTALS**
P. O. Box 422
(Sterling 99672)
Rates: $85-$140
(907) 262-8343

AREA CODES - If the local number doesn't connect, check for a new area code.

KETCHIKAN

BEST WESTERN THE LANDING
3434 Tongass Ave (99901)
Rates: $85-$160
(907) 225-5166
(800) 528-1234
(800) 428-8304

THE GILMORE HOTEL
P. O. Box 6814 (99901)
Rates: $65-$110
(907) 225-9423
(800) 275-9423

INGERSOLL HOTEL
303 Mission St (99901)
Rates: $57-$99
(907) 225-2124
(800) 478-2124

MILLAR STREET HOUSE B&B
P. O. Box 7281 (99901)
Rates: $55-$80
(907) 225-1258
(800) 287-1607

SUPER 8 MOTEL
2151 Sea Level Dr (99901)
Rates: $66-$119
(907) 225-9088
(800) 800-8000

KING SALMON

KING SALMON GUIDES B&B
P O Box 602 (99613)
Rates: $180
(800) 976-2202

KODIAK

BEST WESTERN KODIAK INN
236 Rezanof Dr, W (99615)
Rates: $74-$199
(907) 486-5712
(800) 528-1234
(888) 563-4254

BUSKIN RIVER INN
1395 Airport Way (99615)
Rates: $125-$135
(907) 487-2700
(800) 544-2202

KALSIN BAY INN
P. O. Box 1696 (99615)
Rates: n/a
(907) 486-2659

KODIAK B&B
308 Cope St (99615)
Rates: $70-$82
(907) 486-5367

NORTHLAND RANCH RESORT
P. O. Box 2376 (99615)
Rates: Package
(907) 486-5578

SHELIKOF LODGE
211 Thorsheim Ave (99615)
Rates: $55-$65
(907) 486-4141

LAKE LOUISE

LAKE LOUISE LODGE
(HC01 Box 1716, Glenallen 99588)
Rates: $45-$105
(907) 822-3311

PALMER

HATCHER PASS BED & BREAKFAST
HC01, Box 6797-D (99645)
Rates: $55
(907) 745-4210

PETERSBURG

NARROWS INN
P. O. Box 1048 (99833)
Rates: $70
(907) 772-4284

SCANDIA HOUSE HOTEL
P. O. Box 689 (99833)
Rates: $90-$175
(907) 772-4281

SALCHA

SALCHA RIVER LODGE
P. O. Box 111 (99714)
Rates: n/a
(907) 488-2233

SEWARD

NEW SEWARD HOTEL
P. O. Box 670C (99664)
Rates: $35-$96
(907) 224-8001
(800) 478-1774 (AK)

TAROKA INN
P. O. Box 2448 (99664)
Rates: $45-$105
(907) 224-8975

"THE FARM" B&B
P. O. Box 305 (99664)
Rates: $65-$100
(907) 224-2300

SITKA

BARANOF WILDERNESS LODGE
P. O. Box 2187-VP (99835)
Rates: $2850-$3850 Package
(800) 613-6551

SUPER 8 MOTEL
404 Sawmill Creek Rd (99835)
Rates: $78-$118
(907) 747-8804
(800) 800-8000

SKAGWAY

SARGEANT PRESTONS LODGE
6th Ave & State St (99840)
Rates: $70+
(907) 983-2521

WESTMARK INN
3rd & Spring Sts (99840)
Rates: $99-$119
(907) 983-2291
(800) 544-0970

SOLDOTNA

BED & BREAKFST COTTAGES
General Del (99669)
Rates: $60-$80
(800) 582-7829

KENAI PENINSULA CONDOS
P. O. Box 3416A (99669)
Rates: $89-$109
(888) 811-6433
(800) 362-1383

RAVEN MTN FARM B&B
P. O. Box 344 (Kasilof 99610)
Rates: $45-$76
(907) 262-9186

SOARING EAGLE LODGE
HC01, Box 1203 (99669)
Rates: $50-$100
(907) 337-1223

TALKEETNA

ALASKA LOG CABIN B&B
#1A Beaver Rd (99676)
Rates: $55-$85
(907) 733-2668

LATITUDE 62 LODGE
P. O. Box 478 (99676)
Rates: n/a
(907) 733-2262

TOK

CLEFT OF THE ROCK B&B
5 Sundog Trail (99780)
Rates: $80-$125
(907) 883-4219
(800) 478-5646

SNOWSHOE MOTEL
P. O. Box 559 (99780)
Rates: $42-$78
(907) 883-4511
(800) 478-4511

STAGE STOP B&B
P. O. Box 69 (99780)
Rates: $40-$85
(907) 883-5338

TOK LODGE
P. O. Box 135 (99780)
Rates: $50-$80
(907) 883-2851

WESTMARK INN
P. O. Box 130 (99780)
Rates: $99-$129
(907) 883-5174
(800) 544-0970

YOUNG'S MOTEL
Mile 1313,
Box 482,
Alaska Hwy (99780)
Rates: $55-$78
(907) 883-4411

TRAPPER CREEK

MCKINLEY FOOTHILLS B&B
P. O. Box 13089 (99683)
Rates: $80+
(907) 773-1454

VALDEZ

TIEKEL RIVER LODGE
Richardson Hwy
Mile 56, (99686)
Rates: $45-$85
(907) 822-3259

TOTEM INN
P. O. Box 648 (99686)
Rates: $69-$154
(907) 835-4443

WASILLA

KOZEY CABINS
351 E Spruce Ave (99654)
Rates: $85-$100
(907) 376-3190

AREA CODES - If the local number doesn't connect, check for a new area code.

WILLOW

**SHEEP CREEK
LODGE**
Mile 88, Parks
Hwy (99688)
Rates: n/a
(907) 495-6227

WOOD-
TIKCHIK
STATE PARK

**MAURICE'S
FLOATING
LODGE**
P. O. Box 1261
(Dillingham
99576)
Rates: Package
(800) 356-2844

WRANGELL

**HARDING'S OLD
SOURDOUGH
LODGE**
P. O. Box 1062
(99929)
Rates: $75-$195
(800) 874-3613

AREA CODES - If the local number doesn't connect, check for a new area code.

ARIZONA

AHWATUKEE

HOLIDAY INN EXPRESS & SUITES
15221 S 50th St (85044)
Rates: $99-$119
(480) 785-8500
(800) 465-4329

HOMEGATE STUDIOS & SUITES
5035 E Chandler Blvd (85044)
Rates: n/a
(480) 753-6700

QUALITY INN SOUTH MOUNTAIN
5121 E La Puente Ave (85044)
Rates: $99-$139
(480) 893-3900
(800) 228-5151 (US)
(800) 562-3332 (AZ)

AJO

LA SIESTA MOTEL
2561 N Ajo-Gila Bend Hwy (85321)
Rates: $36-$58
(520) 387-6569

MARINE MOTEL
1966 N 2nd Ave (85321)
Rates: $44-$69
(520) 387-7626

ALPINE

CORONADO TRAILS CABINS & RV PARK
25302 Hwy 191 (85920)
Rates: $45+
(520) 339-4772

TAL-WI-WI LODGE
40 County Road 2220 (85920)
Rates: $61-$95
(520) 339-4319

APACHE JUNCTION

APACHE JUNCTION MOTEL
1680 W Apache Trail (85219)
Rates: $54-$66
(480) 982-7702

SUPER 8 MOTEL
251 E 29th Ave (85219)
Rates: $74-$88
(480) 288-8888
(800) 800-8000

APACHE LAKE

APACHE LAKE MARINA & RESORT
Hwy 88 (Tortilla Flat 85290)
Rates: $50-$60
(520) 467-2511

ASH FORK

ASH FORK INN
1137 W Hwy 66 (86320)
Rates: $22-$39
(520) 637-2514

STAGECOACH MOTEL
823 Park Ave (86320)
Rates: $20-$30
(520) 637-2278

BENSON

BEST WESTERN QUAIL HOLLOW INN
699 N Ocotillo St (85602)
Rates: $38-$70
(520) 586-3646
(800) 528-1234
(800) 822-1850

HOLIDAY INN EXPRESS
630 S Village Loop (85602)
Rates: $56-$89
(520) 586-8800
(800) 465-4329

MOTEL 6
637 S Whetstone Commerce Dr (85602)
Rates: $32-$56
(520) 586-0066
(800) 466-8356

SUPER 8 MOTEL
855 N Ocotillo Rd (85602)
Rates: $42-$59
(520) 586-1530
(800) 800-8000

BISBEE

THE BISBEE INN BED & BREAKFAST
45 OK St (85603)
Rates: $29-$45
(520) 432-5131

MAIN STREET INN
26 Main St (85603)
Rates: $40-$95
(520) 432-5237
(800) 467-5237

MILE HIGH COURT TRAVEL LODGE
901 Tombstone Canyon (85603)
Rates: $35-$50
(520) 432-4636

PARK PLACE B&B
200 E Vista in Warren (85603)
Rates: $40-$60
(520) 990-0682
(800) 456-0682

SAN JOSE LODGE
1002 Naco Hwy (85603)
Rates: $49-$75
(520) 432-5761

BUCKEYE

DAYS INN
25205 W Yuma Rd (85326)
Rates: $79-$159
(623) 386-5400
(800) 329-7466

BULLHEAD CITY

(Also see Laughlin, NV)

ARIZONA BLUFFS
2220 Karis Dr (86442)
Rates: $192 Wkly
(520) 763-3839

BEST WESTERN BULLHEAD CITY
1124 Hwy 95 (86429)
Rates: $39-$99
(520) 754-3000
(800) 528-1204
(800) 634-4463

COLORADO RIVER RESORT
434 Riverglen Dr (86440)
Rates: $33-$65
(520) 754-4101

DAYS INN & SUITES
2200 Rancho Colorado Blvd (86442)
Rates: $35-$200
(520) 758-1711
(800) 329-7466

DESERT RANCHO MOTEL
1041 Hwy 95 (86430)
Rates: $30-$45
(520) 754-2578

LA PLAZA INN
1978 Hwy 95 (86442)
Rates: $26-$35
(520) 763-8080

LAKE MOHAVE RESORT & MARINA

At Katherine Landing (86430)
Rates: $70-$100
(520) 754-3245
(800) 752-9669

LODGE ON THE RIVER MOTEL
1717 Hwy 95 (86442)
Rates: n/a
(520) 758-8080

RIVER QUEEN RESORT
125 Long Ave (86430)
Rates: $35-$53
(520) 754-3214

SHANGRI-LA LODGE/VILLAGER LODGE
1767 Georgia Ln (86442)
Rates: $30-$60
(520) 758-1117

SUNRIDGE HOTEL & CONF CENTER
839 Landon Dr (86429)
Rates: $49-$89
(520) 754-4700
(800) 977-4242

SUPER 8 MOTEL
1616 Hwy 95 (86442)
Rates: $30-$40
(520) 763-1002
(800) 800-8000

CAMERON

CAMERON TRADING POST
Hwy 89, P. O. Box 83 (86020)
Rates: $49-$79
(520) 679-2231

AREA CODES - If the local number doesn't connect, check for a new area code.

CAMP VERDE

COMFORT INN
340 N Industrial
Dr (86322)
Rates: $29-$99
(520) 567-9000
(800) 228-5150

**FORT VERDE
MOTEL**
628 S Main St
(86322)
Rates: $35+
(520) 567-3486

**MICROTEL INN
& SUITES**
504 Industrial Dr
(86322)
Rates: $39-$74
(520) 567-3700
(888) 771-7171

CAREFREE

THE BOULDERS
34631 N Tom
Darlington Rd
(85377)
Rates: $175-$545
(480) 488-9009
(800) 553-1717

CAREFREE INN
37220 Mule Train
Rd (85377)
Rates: $75-$700
(480) 488-5300
(800) 949-1994

CASA GRANDE

**BEST WESTERN
CASA GRANDE
SUITES**
665 Via Del Cielo
(85222)
Rates: $50-$145
(520) 836-1600
(800) 528-1234

**FRANCISCO
GRANDE RESORT
& GOLF CLUB**
26000 Gila Bend
Hwy (85222)
Rates: $59-$196
(520) 836-6444
(800) 237-4238

HOLIDAY INN
777 N Pinal Ave
(85222)
Rates: $74-$87
(520) 426-3500
(800) 858-4499 (AZ)
(800) 465-4329 (US)

MOTEL 6
4965 N Sunland
Gin Rd (85222)
Rates: $44-$60
(520) 836-3323
(800) 466-8356

SE-TAY MOTEL
901 N Pinal Ave
(85222)
Rates: $29-$40
(520) 836-7489

SUNLAND INN
7190 S Sunland
Gin Rd (85222)
Rates: $32-$38
(520) 836-5000

SUPER 8 MOTEL
2066 E Florence
Blvd (85222)
Rates: $49-$130
(520) 836-8800
(800) 800-8000

CHAMBERS

**BEST WESTERN
CHIEFTAIN INN**
I-40 & Jct US 191,
Exit 333 (86502)
Rates: $48-$65
(520) 688-2611
(800) 528-1234
(800) 657-7632

CHANDLER

ALOHA MOTEL
445 N Arizona
Ave (85224)
Rates: $79-$200
(480) 963-3403

**HAWTHORN
SUITES**
5858 W Chandler
Blvd (85226)
Rates: $99-$109
(480) 705-8881
(800) 527-1133

**HOMEWOOD
SUITES**
7337 W Detroit St
(85226)
Rates: $159-$209
(480) 753-6200
(800) 225-5466

**LA QUINTA INN
& SUITES**
15241 S 50th St
(85224)
Rates: $85-$134
(480) 961-7700
(800) 687-6667

MICROTEL INN
255 N Kyrene
(85226)
Rates: $59-$159
(480) 705-8882
(888) 771-7171

RED ROOF INN
7400 W Boston St
(85226)
Rates: $50-$85
(480) 857-4969
(800) 843-7663

**SHERATON SAN
MARCOS GOLF
& CONFERENCE
RESORT**
1 San Marcos
Place (85224)
Rates: $99-$255
(480) 963-6655
(800) 325-3535

**SOUTHGATE
MOTEL**
7445 W Chandler
Blvd (85226)
Rates: $59-$99
(480) 940-0308
(800) 286-7991

SUPER 8 MOTEL
7171 W Chandler
Blvd (85226)
Rates: $60-$85
(480) 961-3888
(800) 800-8000

**WELLESLEY INN
& SUITES**
5035 E Chandler
Blvd (85226)
Rates: $99-$109
(480) 753-6700
(800) 444-8888

WINDMILL INN
3535 W Chandler
Blvd (85226)
Rates: $116-$149
(480) 812-9600
(800) 547-4747

CLARKDALE

**BIRD'S EYE VIEW
B&B / GUEST
COTTAGES**
Hwy 89A (86324)
Rates: $55-$75
Monthly: $600
(480) 990-0682
(800) 456-0682

COTTON-WOOD

**BEST WESTERN
COTTONWOOD
INN**
993 S Main St
(86326)
Rates: 59-$119
(520) 634-5575
(800) 528-1234 (US)
(800) 350-0025 (AZ)

**COTTONWOOD
PINES MOTEL**
920 S Camino
(86326)
Rates: $36-$52
(520) 634-9975

**LITTLE DAISY
MOTEL**
34 S Main St
(86326)
Rates: $36-$40
(520) 634-7865

SUPER 8 MOTEL
800 S Main St
(86326)
Rates: $48-$66
(520) 639-1888
(800) 800-8000

THE VIEW MOTEL
818 S Main St
(86326)
Rates: $34-$48
(520) 634-7581

DOUGLAS

MOTEL 6
111 16th St (85607)
Rates: $33-$42
(520) 364-2457
(800) 466-8356

**PRICE CANYON
GUEST RANCH**
P. O. Box 1065
(85607)
Rates: $85-$170
(520) 558-2383

DRAGOON

**KELLY'S
WHISTLESTOP
BED & BREAKFAST**
I-10 & Hwy 191
(85609)
Rates: $50-$60
(480) 990-0682
(800) 456-0682

EAGAR

**BEST WESTERN
SUNRISE INN**
128 N Main St
(85925)
Rates: $53-$99
(520) 333-2540
(800) 528-1234

EHRENBERG

**BEST WESTERN
FLYING J MOTEL**
I-10 Exit 1, South
Frontage Rd
(85334)
Rates: $79-$109
(520) 923-9711
(800) 528-1234 (US)
(800) 292-9711 (AZ)

ELOY

SUPER 8 MOTEL
3945 W Houser
Rd (85231)
Rates: $55-$73
(520) 466-7804
(800) 800-8000

FLAGSTAFF

AMERISUITES
2455 S Beulah
Blvd (86001)
Rates: $89-$159
(520) 774-8042
(800) 833-1516

**ARIZONA
MOUNTAIN INN**
685 Lake Mary Rd
(86001)
Rates: $65-$100
(520) 774-8959
(800) 239-5236

AREA CODES - If the local number doesn't connect, check for a new area code.

BEST WESTERN KINGS HOUSE MOTEL
1560 E Rt 66
(86001)
Rates: $39-$89
(520) 774-7186
(800) 528-1234

CANYON INN
510 S Milton Rd
(86001)
Rates: $60-$100
(520) 774-7301
(888) 822-6966

COMFORT INN
914 S Milton Rd
(86001)
Rates: $49-$109
(520) 774-7326
(800) 228-5150

CRYSTAL INN
602 W Rt 66
(86001)
Rates: $60-$96
(520) 774-4581
(800) 654-4667

DAYS INN HWY 66
1000 W Rt 66
(86001)
Rates: $59-$119
(520) 774-5221
(800) 329-7466

ECONO LODGE
2355 S Beulah
Blvd (86001)
Rates: $60-$119
(520) 774-2225
(800) 553-2666

EMBASSY SUITES
706 S Milton Rd
(86001)
Rates: $114-$209
(520) 774-4333
(800) 362-2779

FRONTIER MOTEL
1700 E Rt 66
(86001)
Rates: $18-$80
(520) 774-8993

HALEY'S HIDEAWAY B&B
5705 Townsend-
Winona Rd
(86004)
Rates: $85
(800) 526-1780

HIGHLAND COUNTRY INN
223 S Milton Rd
(86001)
Rates: $46-$93
(520) 774-5041
(800) 642-4186

HOLIDAY INN
2320 E Lucky Ln
(86004)
Rates: $69-$129
(520) 526-1150
(800) 465-4329

HOWARD JOHNSON
2200 E Butler Ave
(86004)
Rates: $69-$129
(520) 779-6944
(800) 446-4656

HOWARD JOHNSON INN
3300 E Rt 66
(86004)
Rates: $49-$79
(520) 526-1826
(800) 446-4656
(800) 437-7137

INNSUITES HOTEL
1008 E Rt 66
(86001)
Rates: $67-$195
(520) 774-7356
(888) 235-2478

LA QUINTA INN & SUITES
2015 S Beulah
Blvd (86001)
Rates: $65-$99
(520) 556-8666
(800) 687-6777

MASTER HOST FIVE FLAGS INN
2610 E Rt 66
(86004)
Rates: $42-$65
(520) 526-1399
(800) 251-1962
(800) 535-2466

MOTEL 6
2010 E Butler Ave
(86004)
Rates: $33-$56
(520) 774-1801
(800) 466-8356

MOTEL 6
2440 E Lucky Ln
(86004)
Rates: $30-$52
(520) 774-8756
(800) 466-8356

MOTEL 6
2745 S Woodlands
Village Blvd
(86001)
Rates: $34-$56
(520) 779-3757
(800) 466-8356

MOTEL 6
2500 E Lucky Ln
(86004)
Rates: $30-$52
(520) 779-6184
(800) 466-8356

PINECREST MOTEL
2818 E Rt 66
(86001)
Rates: $24-$54
(520) 526-1950

RAMADA LIMITED
2350 E Lucky Ln
(86004)
Rates: $59-$79
(520) 779-3614
(800) 272-6232

RED ROOF INN
2520 E Lucky Ln
(86004)
Rates: $39-$74
(520) 779-5121
(800) 843-7663
(800) 545-5525

RELAX INN MOTEL
1416 E Santa Fe
(86001)
Rates: $35-$44
(520) 774-5123

RESIDENCE INN BY MARRIOTT
3440 N Country
Club Dr (86004)
Rates: $160
(520) 526-5555
(800) 331-3131

RODEWAY INN
2650 E Rt 66
(86004)
Rates: $29-$88
(520) 526-2200
(800) 228-2000

ROYAL INN
2140 E Rt 66
(86001)
Rates: $52-$120
(520) 774-7308

SUPER 8 MOTEL
2285 E Butler Ave
(86004)
Rates: $27-$45
(520) 774-1821
(800) 800-8000

SUPER 8 MOTEL
3725 Kasper Ave
(86004)
Rates: $54-$74
(520) 526-0818
(800) 800-8000

TOWN HOUSE MOTEL
122 W Route 66
(86001)
Rates: $24-$49
(520) 774-5081

TRAVELODGE
2610 E Rt 66
(86004)
Rates: $39-$75
(520) 526-1399
(800) 578-7878

TRAVELODGE UNIVERSITY
801 W Rt 66
(86001)
Rates: $45-$80
(520) 774-3381
(800) 578-7878

WESTERN HILLS MOTEL
1580 E Rt 66
(86001)
Rates: $20-$65
(520) 774-6633

FLORENCE

RANCHO SONORA INN
9198 N Hwy 79
(85232)
Rates: $69-$74
(520) 868-8000

FOREST LAKES

FOREST LAKES LODGE
SR 260 (85931)
Rates: $41-$69
(520) 535-4727

FOUNTAIN HILLS

ARIZONA TRAILS BED & BREAKFAST RESERVATION SERVICE
P. O. Box 18998
(85269)
Rates: $65-$575
(480) 837-4284
(888) 799-4284

FREDONIA

CRAZY JUG MOTEL
465 S Main (86022)
Rates: $38-$49
(520) 643-7752

GILA BEND

BEST WESTERN SPACE AGE LODGE
401 E Pima St
(85337)
Rates: $45-$85
(520) 683-2273
(800) 528-1234

YUCCA MOTEL
836 E Pima St
(85337)
Rates: $28-$48
(520) 683-2211

GLENDALE

HOLIDAY INN EXPRESS
7885 W
Arrowhead
Towne Center Dr
(85308)
Rates: $89-$109
(623) 412-2000
(800) 465-4329

LA QUINTA INN
16321 N 83rd St
(85308)
Rates: $49-$99
(623) 487-1900
(800) 687-6667

GLOBE

CLOUD NINE MOTEL
1649 E Ash St
(85501)
Rates: $47-$89
(520) 425-5741

AREA CODES - If the local number doesn't connect, check for a new area code.

COMFORT INN
1515 South St
(85501)
Rates: $49-$90
(520) 425-7575
(800) 228-5150

EL REY MOTEL
1201 E Ash St
(85501)
Rates: $25-$37
(520) 425-4427

HOLIDAY INN EXPRESS
2119 Hwy 60
(85501)
Rates: $60-$68
(520) 425-7008
(800) 465-4329

RAMADA LIMITED
1699 E Ash St
(85501)
Rates: $47-$78
(520) 425-5741
(800) 272-6232

GOODYEAR

BEST WESTERN
1100 N Litchfield
Rd (85338)
Rates: $89-$159
(623) 932-3210
(800) 528-1234

COMFORT INN
1770 N Dysart Rd
(85338)
Rates: $32-$99
(623) 932-9191
(800) 228-5150

HAMPTON INN & SUITES
2000 N Litchfield
Rd (85338)
Rates: $99-$129
(623) 536-1313
(800) 426-7866

HOLIDAY INN EXPRESS
1313 Litchfield Rd
(85338)
Rates: $89-$149
(623) 535-1313
(800) 465-4329

SUPER 8 MOTEL
1710 N Dysart Rd
(85338)
Rates: $38-$65
(623) 932-9622
(800) 800-8000

GRAND CANYON NAT'L PARK (SOUTH RIM)
(Canyon hotels & lodges provide kennels.)

BRIGHT ANGEL LODGE & CABINS
P. O. Box 699
(86023)
Rates: $60-$115
(520) 638-2631
(303) 297-2757

EL TOVAR HISTORIC HOTEL
P. O. Box 699
(86023)
Rates: $120-$300
(520) 638-2631
(303) 297-2757

KACHINA LODGE
P. O. Box 699
(86023)
Rates: $124
(520) 638-2631
(303) 297-2757

MASWIK LODGE
P. O. Box 699
(86023)
Rates: $94-$118
(520) 638-2631
(303) 297-2757

QUALITY INN & SUITES
Hwy 64
(Tusayan 86023)
Rates: $73-$175
(520) 638-2673
(800) 228-5151

RODEWAY RED FEATHER LODGE
Hwy 64,US 80
(Tusayan 86023)
Rates: $79-$119
(520) 638-2414
(800) 228-2000
(800) 538-2345

THUNDERBIRD LODGE
P. O. Box 699
(86023)
Rates: $124
(520) 638-2631
(303) 297-2757

YAVAPAI LODGE
P. O. Box 699
(86023)
Rates: $63-$100
(520) 638-2631
(303) 297-2757

GREEN VALLEY

BEST WESTERN GREEN VALLEY INN
111 S La Canada
Dr (85614)
Rates: $59-$135
(520) 625-2250
(800) 528-1234
(800) 344-1441

HOLIDAY INN EXPRESS
19200 Frontage Rd
(85614)
Rates: $59-$139
(520) 625-0900
(800) 465-4329

GREER

MOLLY BUTLER LODGE & CABINS
109 Main St
(85927)
Rates: $30-$90
(520) 735-7232

HEBER

BEST WESTERN SAWMILL INN
1877 Hwy 260
(85928)
Rates: $45-$75
(520) 535-5053
(800) 528-1234
(800) 372-9564

HOLBROOK

BEST INN
2211 E Navajo
Blvd (85026)
Rates: $41-$57
(520) 524-2654
(800) 237-8466

BEST WESTERN ADOBE INN
615 W Hopi Dr
(86025)
Rates: $40-$58
(520) 524-3948
(800) 528 1234

BEST WESTERN ARIZONAN INN
2508 E Navajo
Blvd (86025)
Rates: $39-$70
(520) 524-2611
(800) 528-1234
(877) 280-7300

BUDGET HOST INN
235 W Hopi Dr
(86025)
Rates: $22-$34
(520) 524-3809
(800) 283-4678

COMFORT INN
2602 E Navajo
Blvd (86025)
Rates: $46-$70
(520) 524-6131
(800) 228-5150

ECONO LODGE
2596 E Navajo
Blvd (86025)
Rates: $30-$55
(520) 524-1448
(800) 553-2666

HOLIDAY INN EXPRESS
1308 E Navajo
Blvd (86025)
Rates: $67
(520) 524-1466
(800) 465-4329

MOTEL 6
2514 E Navajo
Blvd (86025)
Rates: $29-$34
(520) 524-6101
(800) 466-8356

RAMADA LIMITED
2608 E Navajo
Blvd (86025)
Rates: $50-$99
(520) 524-2566
(800) 272-6232

RELAX INN
2418 E Navajo
Blvd (86025)
Rates: $35-$40
(520) 524-6815

JEROME

THE SURGEON'S HOUSE B&B
101 Hill St (86331)
Rates: $75-$110
(480) 990-0682
(800) 456-0682

KAYENTA

HAMPTON INN
Hwy 160 (86033)
Rates: $60-$105
(520) 697-3170
(800) 426-7866

KEARNY

GENERAL KEARNY INN
301 Alden Rd
(85237)
Rates: $29-$39
(520) 363-5505

KINGMAN

BEST WESTERN WAYFARER'S INN
2815 E Andy
Devine (86401)
Rates: $49-$99
(520) 753-6271
(800) 528-1234
(800) 548-5695

BEST WESTERN KING'S INN & SUITES
2930 E Andy
Devine (86401)
Rates: $51-$92
(520) 753-6101
(800) 528-1234
(800) 750-6101

BRUNSWICK HOTEL
315 E Andy
Devine (86401)
Rates: $25-$60
(520) 718-1800

DAYS INN EAST
3381 E Andy
Devine (86401)
Rates: $36-$75
(520) 757-7337
(800) 329-7466

DAYS INN WEST
3023 E Andy
Devine (86401)
Rates: $45-$75
(520) 753-7500
(800) 329-7466

HIGH DESERT INN
2803 E Andy
Devine (86401)
Rates: $25-$75
(520) 753-2935

AREA CODES - If the local number doesn't connect, check for a new area code.

HILL TOP MOTEL
1901 E Andy
Devine (86401)
Rates: $24-$48
(520) 753-2198

HOLIDAY INN
3100 E Andy
Devine (86401)
Rates: $39-$99
(520) 753-6262
(800) 465-4329

MOTEL 6 EAST
3351 W Andy
Devine (86401)
Rates: $31-$36
(520) 757-7151
(800) 466-8356

MOTEL 6 WEST
424 W Beale St
(86401)
Rates: $42-$58
(520) 753-9222
(800) 466-8356

QUALITY INN
1400 E Andy
Devine (86401)
Rates: $50-$90
(520) 753-4747
(800) 228-5151
(800) 869-3252

SUPER 8 MOTEL
3401 E Andy
Devine (86401)
Rates: $35-$59
(520) 757-4808
(800) 800-8000

LAKE HAVASU CITY

BEST WESTERN LAKE PLACE INN
31 Wing's Loop
(86403)
Rates: $46-$99
(520) 855-2146
(800) 528-1234 (US)
(800) 258-8558 (AZ)

BRIDGEVIEW MOTEL
101 London
Bridge Rd (86403)
Rates: $35-$110
(520) 855-5559

EZ-8 MOTEL
41 S Acoma Blvd
(86403)
Rates: $25-$40
(520) 855-4023

HAVASU MOTEL ALL-SUITE INN
2035 Acoma Blvd
(86403)
Rates: $20-$45
(520) 855-2311

HOLIDAY INN
245 London
Bridge Rd (86403)
Rates: $60-$80
(520) 855-4071
(800) 465-4329

ISLAND INN HOTEL
1300 W
McCulloch Blvd
(86403)
Rates: $65-$90
(520) 680-0606
(800) 243-9955

LAKEVIEW MOTEL
440 London
Bridge Rd (86403)
Rates: $25-$45
(520) 855-3605

MOTEL 6
111 London
Bridge Rd (86403)
Rates: $35-$52
(520) 855-3200
(800) 466-8356

PECOS II CONDOMINIUMS
451 N Lake
Havasu Ave
(86403)
Rates: $385 Wk
(520) 855-7444

SANDMAN INN
1700 N McCulloch
Blvd (86403)
Rates: $30-$90
(520) 855-7841
(800) 835-2410

SUPER 8 MOTEL
305 London
Bridge Rd (86403)
Rates: $36-$95
(520) 855-8844
(800) 800-8000

WINDSOR INN
451 London
Bridge Rd (86403)
Rates: $26-$49
(520) 855-4135
(800) 245-4135

LAKESIDE

FOREST HOUSE MOTEL
2990 W White Mtn
Blvd (85929)
Rates: $30-$55
(520) 368-6628
(888) 440-2220

LAKE OF THE WOODS
2244 W White Mtn
Blvd (85929)
Rates: $43-$83
(520) 368-5353

LAZY OAKS RESORT COTTAGES
1075 Larson Rd
(85929)
Rates: $62-$78
(520) 368-6203

MOONRIDGE LODGE & CABINS
P. O. Box 1058
(85929)
Rates: $35-$135
(520) 367-1906

THE PLACE RESORT CABINS
Rt 3, Box 2675
(85929)
Rates: $66-$74
(520) 368-6777

LITCHFIELD PARK

THE WIGWAM RESORT
300 Wigwam Blvd
(85340)
Rates: $330-$475+
(623) 935-3811
(800) 327-0396

MARANA

DAYS INN & SUITES
Cortaro Rd & I-10
(85741)
Rates: $49-$129
(800) 329-7466

MARBLE CANYON

LEES FERRY LODGE
HC67, Box 1
(Vermillion
Cliffs 86036)
Rates: $47+
(520) 355-2231

MARBLE CANYON LODGE
Hwy 89A (86036)
Rates: $50-$65
(520) 355-2225
(800) 726-1789

MESA

ARIZONA GOLF RESORT & CONF CENTER
425 S Power Rd
(85206)
Rates: $149-$180
(480) 832-3202
(800) 528-8282

BEST WESTERN MESA INN
1625 E Main St
(85203)
Rates: $43-$115
(480) 964-8000
(800) 528-1234

BEST WESTERN SUPERSTITION SPRINGS INN
1342 S Power Rd
(85206)
Rates: $49-$139
(480) 641-1164
(800) 528-1234

BUDGET SUITES MOTEL
537 S Country
Club Dr (85210)
Rates: n/a
(480) 969-5248

DAYS INN
333 W Juanita Ave
(85210)
Rates: $86-$126
(480) 844-8900
(800) 329-7466

HOLIDAY INN HOTEL & SUITES
1600 S Country
Club Dr (85210)
Rates: $99-$159
(480) 964-7000
(800) 465-4329

HOMESTEAD VILLAGE EXTENDED STAY
1920 W Isabella
Ave (85202)
Rates: $59
(480) 752-2266
(888) 782-9473

LA QUINTA INN & SUITES
902 W Grove Ave
(85210)
Rates: $95-$134
(480) 844-8747
(800) 687-6777

LA QUINTA INN & SUITES
6530 E
Superstition Spgs
Blvd (85208)
Rates: $95-$134
(480) 654-1970
(800) 687-6777

MOTEL 6 MAIN
630 W Main St
(85201)
Rates: $37-$52
(480) 969-8111
(800) 466-8356

MOTEL 6 NORTH
336 W Hampton
Ave (85210)
Rates: $37-$52
(480) 844-8899
(800) 466-8356

MOTEL 6 SOUTH
1511 S Country
Club Dr (85210)
Rates: $42-$61
(480) 834-0066
(800) 466-8356

RAMADA LIMITED
1750 E Main St
(85203)
Rates: $49-$99
(480) 969-3600
(800) 272-6232

RESIDENCE INN BY MARRIOTT
941 W Grove Ave
(85210)
Rates: $149
(480) 610-0100
(800) 331-3131

AREA CODES - If the local number doesn't connect, check for a new area code.

SAN DEE MOTEL
6649 E Apache Tr
(85205)
Rates: $45-$58
(480) 985-1912

**SHERATON MESA
HOTEL &
CONVENTION
CENTER**
200 N Centennial
Way (85201)
Rates: $59-$159
(480) 898-8300
(800) 456-6372

SLEEP INN
6347 E Southern
Ave (85206)
Rates: $39-$129
(480) 807-7760
(800) 753-3746

SUPER 8 MOTEL
1550 S Gilbert Rd
(85204)
Rates: $39-$76
(480) 545-0888
(800) 800-8000

**TRAVELODGE
SUITES**
4244 E Main
(85205)
Rates: $84-$124
(480) 832-5961
(800) 578-7878

MIAMI

**TRAVELODGE
COPPER HILLS
INN**
4805 E Hwy 60
(85539)
Rates: $57-$84
(520) 425-7151
(800) 578-7878
(800) 825-7151

MUNDS PARK

**MOTEL IN THE
PINES**
80 W Pinewood
Rd (86017)
Rates: $40-$65
(520) 286-9699
(800) 574-5080

NOGALES

**AMERICANA
MOTOR HOTEL**
639 N Grand Ave
(85621)
Rates: $45-$65
(520) 287-7211
(800) 874-8079

**BEST WESTERN
SIESTA MOTEL**
673 N Grand Ave
(85621)
Rates: $48-$80
(520) 287-4671
(800) 528-1234
(888) 215-4783

MOTEL 6
141 W Mariposa
Rd (85621)
Rates: $38-$44
(520) 281-2951
(800) 466-8356

SUPER 8 MOTEL
547 W Mariposa
Rd (85621)
Rates: $55-$79
(520) 281-2242
(800) 800-8000

TRAVELODGE
921 N Grand Ave
(85621)
Rates: $40-$54
(520) 287-4627
(800) 578-7878

ORACLE

**VILLA CARDINALE
BED & BREAKFAST**
1315 W Oracle
Ranch Rd (85623)
Rates: $45-$60
(520) 896-2516

PAGE

**BEST WESTERN
ARIZONAINN**
716 Rimview Dr
(86040)
Rates: $47-$140
(520) 645-2466
(800) 528-1234
(800) 826-2718

**BEST WESTERN
WESTON INN
& SUITES**
207 N Lake Powell
Blvd (86040)
Rates: $42-$185
(520) 645-2451
(800) 528-1234 (US)
(800) 637-9183 (AZ)

**DAYS INN
& SUITES**
961 N Hwy 89
(86040)
Rates: $79-$99
(520) 645-2800
(800) 329-7466

ECONO LODGE
121 S Lake Powell
Blvd (86040)
Rates: $55-$69
(520) 645-2488
(800) 553-2666

**EMPIRE HOUSE
MOTEL**
100 S Lake Powell
Blvd (86040)
Rates: $50-$62
(520) 645-2406

**LAKE POWELL
MOTEL**
Hwy 89 N (86040)
Rates: $79-$99
(520) 645-2433

**LINDA'S LAKE
POWELL CONDOS**
1019 Tower Butte
(86040)
Rates: $68-$115
(520) 645-3222

**MOTEL 6 PAGE/
LAKE POWELL**
637 S Lake Powell
Blvd (86040)
Rates: $55-$70
(520) 645-5888
(800) 466-8356

**RAMADA INN
PAGE /LK POWELL**
287 N Lake Powell
Blvd (86040)
Rates: $69-$125
(520) 645-8851
(800) 272-6232

**WAHWEAP
LODGE/LAKE
POWELL RESORTS
& MARINA**
100 Lake Shore Dr
(86040)
Rates: $169-$189
(520) 645-2433
(602) 331-5226
(800) 528-6154

PARADISE VALLEY

**DOUBLETREE
LA POSADA
RESORT**
4949 E Lincoln Dr
(85253)
Rates: $210-$265
(480) 952-0420
(800) 222-8733

**MARRIOTT'S
CAMELBACK INN
RESORT/GOLF
CLUB & SPA**
5402 E Lincoln Dr
(85253)
Rates: $255-$469
(480) 948-1700
(800) 242-2635

**MARRIOTT'S
MOUNTAIN
SHADOWS
RESORT &
GOLF CLUB**
5641 E Lincoln Dr
(85253)
Rates: $199-$325
(480) 948-7111
(800) 228-9290 (US)
(800) 782-2123

PARKER

**BEST WESTERN
PARKER INN**
1012 Geronimo
Ave (85344)
Rates: $45-$99
(520) 669-6060
(800) 528-1234
(888) 889-6808

**EL RANCHO
MOTEL**
709 California Ave
(85344)
Rates: $35+
(520) 669-2231

**HAVASU SPRINGS
RESORT**
2581 Hwy 95
(85344)
Rates: $75-$85
(520) 667-3361

**HOLIDAY
KASBAH**
604 California Ave
(85344)
Rates: $39-$63
(520) 669-2133

PATAGONIA

STAGE STOP INN
Box 777 (85624)
Rates: $49-$95
(520) 394-2211

PAYSON

**CHRISTOPHER
CREEK LODGE
& MOTEL**
Star Rt Box 119
(85541)
Rates: $40-$75
(520) 478-4300

**DAYS INN &
SUITES**
215 S Beeline Hwy
(85547)
Rates: $69-$149
(520) 474-9800
(800) 329-7466

**GREY HACKLE
LODGE**
Star Rt Box 145
(85541)
Rates: $40-$95
(520) 478-4392

**HOLIDAY INN
EXPRESS**
206 S Beeline Hwy
(85547)
Rates: $79-$149
(520) 472-7484
(800) 465-4329

INN OF PAYSON
801 N Beeline
Hwy (85541)
Rates: $89-$149
(520) 474-3241
(800) 247-9477

KOHL'S RANCH LODGE
E Hwy 260 (85541)
Rates: $75-$250
(520) 478-4211
(800) 331-5645

MAJESTIC MOUNTAIN INN
602 E Hwy 260 (85541)
Rates: $56-$140
(520) 474-0185
(800) 408-2442

PUEBLO INN
809 E Hwy 260 (85541)
Rates: $54-$159
(520) 474-5241
(800) 888-9828

RIM COUNTRY INN
101 W Phoenix St (85541)
Rates: $39-$89
(520) 474-4526

TRAILS END MOTEL
811 S Beeline Hwy (85541)
Rates: $39-$99
(520) 474-2283

PEARCE

SUNGLOW GUEST RANCH
Turkey Creek Rd (85625)
Rates: n/a
(520) 824-3334

PEORIA

BUDGETEL INN
16771 N 84th Ave (85345)
Rates: n/a
(800) 428-3438

COMFORT SUITES
8473 W Paradise Ln (85382)
Rates: $99-$145
(623) 334-3992
(800) 228-5150

LA QUINTA INN & SUITES
16321 N 83rd Ave (85345)
Rates: $99-$134
(623) 487-1900
(800) 687-6777

RESIDENCE INN BY MARRIOTT
8435 W Paradise Ln (85382)
Rates: $79-$219
(623) 979-2074
(800) 331-3131

PHOENIX
(and Vicinity)

AMERISUITES METRO CENTER
10838 N 25th Ave (85029)
Rates: $89-$126
(602) 997-8800
(800) 833-1516

ARIZONA BILTMORE RESORT & SPA
2400 E Missouri (85016)
Rates: $165-$520
(602) 955-6600
(800) 950-0086

BEST WESTERN AIRPORT INN
2425 S 24th St (85034)
Rates: $99-$120
(602) 273-7251
(800) 528-1234
(800) 528-8199

BEST WESTERN BELL HOTEL
17211 N Black Cnyn Hwy (85023)
Rates: $93-$109
(602) 993-8300
(800) 528-1234
(877) 263-1290

BUDGETEL INN DEER VALLEY
21605 N 26th Ave (85027)
Rates: n/a
(800) 428-3438

BUDGETEL INN
1525 N 51st Ave (85043)
Rates: n/a
(800) 428-3438

COMFORT INN
5050 N Black Canyon Hwy (85017)
Rates: $76-$109
(602) 242-8011
(800) 228-5150

COMFORT INN TURF PARADISE
1711 W Bell Rd (85023)
Rates: $45-$139
(602) 866-2089
(800) 228-5150

COMFORT SUITES
10210 N 26th Dr (85021)
Rates: $99-$109
(602) 861-3900
(800) 228-5150

CROWNE PLAZA METRO CENTER
2532 W Peoria Ave (85029)
Rates: $119-$159
(602) 943-2341
(800) 227-6963

DAYS INN AIRPORT
3333 E Van Buren St (85008)
Rates: $72-$129
(602) 244-8244
(800) 329-7466

DAYS INN I-17 & THOMAS
2420 W Thomas Rd (85015)
Rates: $73-$99
(602) 257-0801
(800) 329-7466

EMBASSY SUITES AIRPORT WEST
2333 E Thomas Rd (85016)
Rates: $149-$180
(602) 957-1910
(800) 362-2779

EMBASSY SUITES BILTMORE
2630 E Camelback St (85016)
Rates: $120-$265
(602) 955-3992
(800) 362-2779

E-Z 8 MOTEL
1820 S 7th St (85034)
Rates: $26-$33
(602) 254-9787

HAMPTON INN I-17
8101 N Black Canyon Hwy (85021)
Rates: $94
(602) 864-6233
(800) 426-7866

HAWTHORN SUITES
24th St & University Dr (85040)
Rates: n/a
(800) 527-1133

HILTON SUITES PHOENIX PLAZA
10 E Thomas Rd (85012)
Rates: $157-$176
(602) 222-1111
(800) 445-8667

HOLIDAY INN EXPRESS & SUITES
620 N 6th St (85004)
Rates: $149-$199
(602) 452-2020
(800) 465-4329

HOLIDAY INN EXPRESS & SUITES
3401 E University Dr (85034)
Rates: $109-$189
(602) 453-9900
(800) 465-4329

HOLIDAY INN SELECT AIRPORT
4300 E Washington St (85034)
Rates: $99-$149
(602) 273-7778
(800) 465-4329

HOLIDAY INN WEST
1500 N 51st Ave (85043)
Rates: $99-$129
(602) 484-9009
(800) 465-4329

HOMEGATE STUDIOS & SUITES-AIRPORT
4357 E Oak St (85008)
Rates: $35-$135
(602) 225-2998

HOMESTEAD VILLAGE GUEST SUITES-METRO
2102 W Dunlap Ave (85021)
Rates: $39-$59
(602) 944-7828
(888) 782-9473

HOMESTEAD VILLAGE-DEER VALLEY
18405 N 27th Ave (85023)
Rates: $39-$59
(602) 843-1151
(888) 782-9473

HOMEWOOD SUITES BILTMORE
2001 E Highland Ave (85016)
Rates: n/a
(602) 508-0937
(800) 225-5466

HOMEWOOD SUITES HOTEL
2536 W Beryl Ave (85021)
Rates: $49-$99
(602) 674-8900
(800) 225-5466

HOWARD JOHNSON
3400 NW Grand Ave (85017)
Rates: $109
(602) 264-9164
(800) 446-4656

LA QUINTA INN COLISEUM
2725 N Black Canyon Hwy (85009)
Rates: $69-$100
(602) 258-6271
(800) 687-6667

LA QUINTA PHOENIX NORTH
2510 W Greenway Rd (85023)
Rates: $79-$109
(602) 993-0800
(800) 687-6667

LES JARDINS HOTEL & SUITES
401 W Clarendon Ave (85013)
Rates: $79-$139
(602) 234-2464
(800) 527-3467

AREA CODES - If the local number doesn't connect, check for a new area code.

LEXINGTON HOTEL & CITY SQUARE SPORTS CLUB
100 W Clarendon (85013)
Rates: $99-$159
(602) 279-9811
(800) 537-8483

LOS OLIVOS HOTEL & SUITES
202 E McDowell Rd (85004)
Rates: $99-$149
(602) 528-9100
(800) 776-5560

MOTEL 6 AIRPORT
214 S 24th St (85034)
Rates: $39-$54
(602) 244-1155
(800) 466-8356

MOTEL 6
2323 E Van Buren St (85006)
Rates: $30-$41
(602) 267-7511
(800) 466-8356

MOTEL 6
5315 E Van Buren St (85008)
Rates: $38-$52
(602) 267-8555
(800) 466-8356

MOTEL 6
1530 N 52nd Dr (85043)
Rates: $38-$54
(602) 272-0220
(800) 466-8356

MOTEL 6
8152 N Black Canyon Hwy (85051)
Rates: $39-$52
(602) 995-7592
(800) 466-8356

MOTEL 6
4130 N Black Canyon Hwy (85017)
Rates: $38-$49
(602) 277-5501
(800) 466-8356

MOTEL 6
2330 W Bell Rd (85023)
Rates: $40-$54
(602) 993-2353
(800) 466-8356

MOTEL 6
2735 W Sweetwater Ave (85029)
Rates: $39-$52
(602) 942-5030
(800) 466-8356

PARKWAY INN-METROCENTER
8617 N Black Canyon Hwy (85021)
Rates: $39-$89
(602) 995-9500

PHOENIX SUNRISE MOTEL
3644 E Van Buren St (85008)
Rates: $29-$46
(602) 275-7661
(800) 432-6483

PREMIER INNS
10402 N Black Canyon Hwy (85051)
Rates: $50-$100
(602) 943-2371
(800) 786-6835

QUALITY HOTEL & RESORT
3600 N 2nd Ave (85013)
Rates: $109-$129
(602) 248-0222
(800) 228-5151

RED ROOF INN NORTH
17222 N Black Canyon Hwy (85023)
Rates: $50-$85
(602) 866-1049
(800) 843-7663

RED ROOF INN WEST
5215 W Willetta (85043)
Rates: $50-$85
(602) 233-8004
(800) 843-7663

RESIDENCE INN BY MARRIOTT
8242 N Black Canyon Fwy (85051)
Rates: $119-$199
(602) 864-1900
(800) 331-3131

ROYAL PALMS HOTEL & CASITAS
5200 E Camelback Rd (85018)
Rates: $115-$315
(602) 840-3610
(888) 654-8655

SHERATON CRESCENT HOTEL
2620 W Dunlap Ave (85021)
Rates: $119-$250
(602) 943-8200
(800) 423-4126

SLEEP INN AIRPORT
2621 S 47th Place (85023)
Rates: $89-$119
(480) 967-7100
(800) 753-3746

SUPER 8 MOTEL
1242 N 53rd Ave (85043)
Rates: $42-$85
(602) 415-0888
(800) 800-8000

SUPER 8 MOTEL
3401 E Van Buren (85008)
Rates: $89
(602) 244-1627
(800) 800-8000

TOWNPLACE SUITES
9425 N Black Canyon Hwy (85021)
Rates: $39-$85
(602) 943-9510
(800) 257-3000

TRAVELODGE
1624 N Black Canyon Hwy (85008)
Rates: $50-$80
(602) 269-6281
(800) 578-7878

TRAVELODGE
3541 E Van Buren (85008)
Rates: $59-$85
(602) 273-7121
(800) 578-7878

UPTOWN B&B
7th Ave & Thomas Rd (85007)
Rates: $60-$75
(602) 990-0682
(800) 456-0682

WELLESLEY INN & SUITES AIRPORT
4357 E Oak St (85008)
Rates: $80-$100
(602) 225-2998
(800) 444-8888

WELLESLEY INN & SUITES METROCENTER
11211 N Black Cnyn Hwy (85029)
Rates: $65-$110
(602) 870-2999
(800) 444-8888

WELLESLEY INN & SUITES PARK CENTRAL
217 W Osborn Rd (85013)
Rates: $65-$100
(602) 279-9000
(800) 444-8888

PINETOP

BEST WESTERN
404 S White Mtn Blvd (85935)
Rates: $59-$109
(520) 367-6667
(800) 528-1234

BUCK SPRINGS RESORT COTTAGES
P. O. Box 130 (85935)
Rates: $65-$145
(520) 369-3554

COMFORT INN
1637 SR 260 (85935)
Rates: $55-$116
(520) 368-6600
(800) 228-5150

DOUBLE B LODGE & CABINS
P. O. Box 747 (85935)
Rates: $34-$62
(520) 367-2747

HOLIDAY INN EXPRESS
431 E White Mtn Blvd (85935)
Rates: $79-$109
(520) 367-6077
(800) 465-4329

MEADOW VIEW LODGE
P. O. Box 325 (85935)
Rates: $48+
(520) 367-4642

MOUNTAIN HACIENDA LODGE
1023 E White Mtn Blvd (85935)
Rates: $35-$79
(520) 367-4146
(888) 567-4148

NORTHWOODS RESORT
165 E White Mtn Blvd (85935)
Rates: $69-$139
(520) 367-2966
(800) 813-2966

WHISPERING PINES RESORT CABINS
PO Box 1043 (85935)
Rates: n/a
(520) 367-4386
(800) 840-3867

WOODLAND INN & SUITES
458 E White Mtn Blvd (85935)
Rates: $55-$109
(520) 367-3636

PRESCOTT

ANTELOPE RESORT ESTATES
6200 N Hwy 89 (86301)
Rates: 2 month rental/$2950
(520) 776-2600

APACHE MOTEL
1130 E Gurley St
(86301)
Rates: $39-$59
(520) 445-1422

**BEST WESTERN
PRESCOTTONIAN**
1317 E Gurley St
(86301)
Rates: $59-$125
(520) 445-3096
(800) 528-1234

CASCADE MOTEL
805 White Spar Rd
(86303)
Rates: $30-$80
(520) 445-1232

HERITAGE HOUSE
819 E Gurley St
(86301)
Rates: $36-$85
(520) 445-9091

HI-ACRE RESORT
1001 White Spar
Rd (86303)
Rates: $29-$110
(520) 445-0588

**LYNX CREEK FARM
BED & BREAKFST**
5555 Onyx Dr
(86302)
Rates: $85-$155
(520) 778-9573

MOTEL 6
1111 E Sheldon St
(86301)
Rates: $42-$58
(520) 776-0160
(800) 466-8356

9 PINES COTTAGE
P. O. Box 2099
(86302)
Rates: $55-$85
(520) 778-3620

PINE VIEW MOTEL
500 Copper Basin
Rd (86303)
Rates: $20-$60
(520) 445-4660

**PRESCOTT SIERRA
INN**
809 White Spar Rd
(86303)
Rates: $34-$95
(520) 445-1250

SENATOR INN
1117 E Gurley St
(86301)
Rates: $35-$145
(520) 445-1440

SKYLINE MOTEL
523 E Gurley St
(86301)
Rates: $32-$65
(520) 445-9963

**SPRINGHILL
SUITES BY
MARRIOTT**
200 E Sheldon St
(86301)
Rates: $48-$69
(520) 776-1282

SUPER 8 MOTEL
1105 E Sheldon St
(86301)
Rates: $49-$69
(520) 776-1282
(800) 800-8000

PRESCOTT VALLEY

DAYS INN
7875 E Hwy 69
(86314)
Rates: $59-$109
(520) 772-8600
(800) 329-7466

MOTEL 6
8383 E Hwy 69
(86314)
Rates: $45-$72
(520) 772-2200
(800) 466-8356

**PRESCOTT VALLEY
MOTEL**
8350 E Hwy 69
(86314)
Rates: $35-$85
(520) 772-9412

RIO RICO

**RIO RICO RESORT
& COUNTRY CLUB**
1069 Camino
Caralampi (85648)
Rates: $165-$185
(520) 281-1901
(800) 288-4746

SAFFORD

**BEST WESTERN
DESERT INN**
1391 W Thatcher
Blvd (85546)
Rates: $59-$75
(520) 428-0521
(800) 528-1234
(800) 707-2331

COMFORT INN
1578 W Thatcher
Blvd (85546)
Rates: $46-$76
(520) 428-5851
(800) 228-5150

DAYS INN
520 E Hwy 70
(85546)
Rates: $55-$165
(520) 428-5000
(800) 329-7466

ECONO LODGE
225 E Hwy 70
(85546)
Rates: $40-$65
(520) 348-0011
(800) 553-2666

ST. JOHNS

DAYS INN
125 E Commercial
St (85936)
Rates: $34-$48
(520) 337-4422
(800) 329-7466

SUPER 8 MOTEL
75 E Commercial
St (85936)
Rates: $35-$44
(520) 337-2990
(800) 800-8000

SCOTTSDALE

**ADOBE APT
HOTEL**
3635 N 68th St
(85251)
Rates: $54-$89
(480) 945-3544

**AMERISUITES
CIVIC CENTER**
7300 E 3rd Ave
(85251)
Rates: $125-$179
(480) 423-9944
(800) 833-7576

**CHAPARRAL
SUITES**
5001 N Scottsdale
Rd (85250)
Rates: $155+
(480) 949-1414
(800) 528-1456

**COUNTRY INN
& SUITES BY
CARLSON**
10801 N 89th Pl
(85260)
Rates: $109-$169
(480) 314-1200
(800) 456-4000

**FOUR SEASONS
RESORT
SCOTTSDALE AT
TROON NORTH**
10600 E Crescent
Moon Dr (85255)
Rates: $250-$625
(480) 515-5700
(800) 332-3442

**GAINEY SUITES
HOTEL-GAINEY
RANCH**
7300 E Gainey
Suites Dr (85258)
Rates: $139-$212
(480) 922-6969
(800) 970-4666

**HAMPTON INN
OLD TOWN
SCOTTSDALE**
4415 N Civic
Center Blvd
(85251)
Rates: $48-$145
(480) 941-9400
(800) 426-7866

**HOLIDAY INN
HOTEL & SUITES
MUNICIPAL
AIRPORT**
7515 E Butherus
Dr (85260)
Rates: $59-$169
(480) 951-4000
(800) 465-4329

**HOLIDAY INN
OLD TOWN
SCOTTSDALE**
7353 E Indian
School Rd (85251)
Rates: $130-$149
(480) 994-9203
(800) 465-4329 (US)
(800) 695-6995 (AZ)

**HOMESTEAD
VILLAGE
EXTENDED STAY**
3560 N Marshall
Way (85251)
Rates: $85-$100
(480) 994-0297
(888) 782-9473

**HOMEWOOD
SUITES**
9880 N Scottsdale
Rd (85253)
Rates: $69-$130
(480) 368-8705
(800) 255-5466

**HOSPITALITY
SUITE RESORT**
409 N Scottsdale
Rd (85257)
Rates: $129-$299
(480) 949-5115
(800) 445-5115

**INN AT THE
CITADEL**
8700 E Pinnacle
Peak Rd (85255)
Rates: $89-$265
(480) 585-6133
(800) 927-8367

**INNSUITES OF
SCOTTSDALE AT
EL DORADO PARK**
7707 E McDowell
Rd (85257)
Rates: $79-$139
(480) 941-1202
(800) 238-8851

**IVY AT THE
WATERFRONT-
A HAWTHORN
SUITE HOTEL**
7445 E Chaparral
Rd (85250)
Rates: $99-$425
(480) 994-5282
(877) 284-3489

**LA QUINTA INN
& SUITES**
8888 E Shea Blvd
(85260)
Rates: $99-$144
(480) 614-5300
(800) 687-6667

MOTEL 6
6848 E Camelback
Rd (85251)
Rates: $40-$65
(480) 946-2280
(800) 466-8356

THE PHOENICIAN RESORT
6000 E Camelback Rd (85251)
Rates: $185-$3500
(480) 941-8200
(800) 888-8234

QUALITY INN & SUITES
3131 N Scottsdale Rd (85251)
Rates: $59-$199
(480) 675-7665
(800) 228-5151

RAMADA VALLEY HO RESORT
6850 E Main St (85251)
Rates: $99-$179
(480) 945-6321
(800) 272-6232
(800) 321-4952

RENAISSANCE SCOTTSDALE RESORT
6160 N Scottsdale Rd (85253)
Rates: $149-$349
(480) 991-1414

RESIDENCE INN BY MARRIOTT
6040 N Scottsdale Rd (85253)
Rates: $149-$269
(480) 948-8666
(800) 331-3131

SAN ANTIQUA IN MCCORMICK RANCH CONDOS
8311 E Via de Ventura (85258)
Rates: n/a
(480) 948-1997

SCOTTSDALE DESERT CASITAS
1251 N Miller Rd (85257)
Rates: $59-$189
(480) 949-8637
(800) 786-9329

SCOTTSDALE PIMA INN & SUITES
7330 N Pima Rd (85258)
Rates: $99-$229
(480) 948-3800
(800) 344-0262

SCOTTSDALE PRINCESS RESORT
7575 E Princess Dr (85255)
Rates: $159-$569
(480) 585-4848
(800) 344-4758

SCOTTSDALE RESORT ACCOMMODATIONS
7025 E Greenway Pkwy, Ste 250 (85254)
Rates: n/a
(480) 515-2300
(888) 868-4378

SCOTTSDALE SIESTA SUITES
7601 E 2nd St (85251)
Rates: $50-$110
(480) 947-7244
(888) 990-1326
(800) 346-6663

SLEEP INN
16630 N Scottsdale Rd (85254)
Rates: $85-$109
(480) 998-9211
(800) 753-3746

SUMMERFIELD SUITES HOTEL
4245 N Civic Center Blvd (85251)
Rates: $159-$189
(480) 946-7700
(800) 833-4353

SUN DESTINATIONS SCOTTSDALE RENTALS
7552 E Camelback Rd (85251)
Rates: n/a
(480) 946-2384
(800) 527-4059

SEDONA

BEST WESTERN INN OF SEDONA
1200 Hwy 89A (86336)
Rates: $90-$160
(520) 282-3072
(800) 528-1234 (US)
(800) 292-6344 (AZ)

CANYON MESA COUNTRY CLUB
500 Jacks Canyon Rd (86351)
Rates: $125-$200
(520) 284-2176

COURTHOUSE BUTTE VILLA B&B
2451 Red Rock Loop Rd (86336)
Rates: $70-$95
(520) 204-1505

DESERT QUAIL INN
6626 Hwy 179 (86336)
Rates: $64-$150
(520) 284-1433
(800) 385-0927

FOREST HOUSES-ON THE CREEK IN OAK CREEK CANYON
9275 N Hwy 89A (86336)
Rates: $75-$120
(520) 282-2999

GREYFIRE FARM BED & BREAKFAST
1240 Jacks Canyon Rd (86351)
Rates: $80-$200
(520) 284-2340
(800) 579-2340

HAWTHORN SUITES-BELL ROCK INN
6426 Hwy 179 (86351)
Rates: $59-$139
(520) 282-4161
(800) 527-1133
(800) 881-7625

HOLIDAY INN EXPRESS-OAK CREEK
6175 Hwy 179 (86351)
Rates: $89-$129
(520) 284-0711
(800) 465-4329
(888) 236-6075

MATTERHORN MOTOR LODGE
230 Apple Ave (86336)
Rates: $74-$104
(520) 282-7176

OAK CREEK TERRACE RESORT
4548 N Hwy 89A (86336)
Rates: $72-$165
(520) 282-3562
(800) 224-2229

QUAIL RIDGE RESORT
120 Canyon Circle Dr (86351)
Rates: $69-$136
(520) 284-9327

QUALITY INN-KING'S RANSOM MOTOR HOTEL
771 Hwy 179 (86339)
Rates: $79-$159
(520) 282-7151
(800) 228-5151

RAILROAD INN AT SEDONA
2545 W Hwy 89A (86336)
Rates: $45-$66
(520) 282-1533
(800) 858-7245

SKY RANCH LODGE MOTEL
SR 89A, Airport Rd (86336)
Rates: $75-$180
(520) 282-6400
(888) 708-6400

SUGAR LOAF LODGE
1870 W Hwy 89A (86340)
Rates: $36-$60
(520) 282-9451

VILLAGE LODGE
78 Bell Rock Blvd (86336)
Rates: $45-$49
(520) 284-3626

WHITE HOUSE INN
2986 W Hwy 89A (86336)
Rates: $38-$95
(520) 282-6680

SELIGMAN

CANYON SHADOWS MOTEL
114 E Chino (86337)
Rates: $35+
(520) 422-3255

HISTORIC ROUTE 66 MOTEL
500 W Hwy 66 (86337)
Rates: $47-$67
(520) 422-3204

SUPAI MOTEL
134 W Chino (86337)
Rates: $35+
(520) 422-3663

SHOW LOW

DAYS INN
480 W Deuce of Clubs Ave (85901)
Rates: $54-$69
(520) 537-4356
(800) 329-7466

KIVA MOTEL
261 E Deuce of Clubs Ave (85901)
Rates: $40-$59
(520) 537-4542

MOTEL 6
1941 E Deuce of Clubs Ave (85901)
Rates: $46-$62
(520) 537-7694
(800) 466-8356

SNOWY RIVER MOTEL
13640 E Deuce of Clubs Ave (85901)
Rates: $34-$43
(520) 537-2926

SIERRA VISTA

BELLA VISTA MOTEL
1101 E Fry Blvd (85635)
Rates: $30-$40
(520) 458-6737

AREA CODES - If the local number doesn't connect, check for a new area code.

**BEST WESTERN
MISSION INN**
3460 E Fry Blvd
(85635)
Rates: $50-$70
(520) 458-8500
(800) 528-1234

MOTEL 6
1551 E Fry Blvd
(85635)
Rates: $30-$36
(520) 459-5035
(800) 466-8356

SIERRA SUITES
391 E Fry Blvd
(85635)
Rates: $79
(520) 459-4221

SUPER 8 MOTEL
100 Fab Ave
(85635)
Rates: $49-$69
(520) 459-5380
(800) 800-8000

**THUNDER
MOUNTAIN INN**
1631 S Hwy 92
(85635)
Rates: $55-$75
(520) 458-7900
(800) 222-5811

VISTA INN
201 W Fry Blvd
(85635)
Rates: $29+
(520) 458-6711

**WINDMERE
HOTEL**
2047 S Hwy 92
(85635)
Rates: $78-$195
(520) 459-5900
(800) 825-4656

SPRINGERVILLE

**EL-JO MOTOR
INN**
425 E Main St
(85938)
Rates: $24-$36
(520) 333-4314

**REED'S
MOTOR LODGE**
514 E Main St
(85938)
Rates: $24-$40
(520) 333-4323

SUPER 8 MOTEL
138 W Main
(85938)
Rates: $45-$60
(520) 333-2655
(800) 800-8000

STAR VALLEY

**OPAL RANCH INN
BED & BRKFAST**
2160 Moonlight
Dr (85541)
Rates: $55-$90
(520) 472-6193

STRAWBERRY

**STRAWBERRY
LODGE**
HCR 1, Box 331
(85544)
Rates: $42-$52
(520) 476-3333

SUMMER-HAVEN

**SUMMERHAVEN
SUITES & SWEETS**
P. O. Box 757
(85619)
Rates: $135
(520) 576-1542

SUN CITY/

**BEST WESTERN
INN & SUITES**
11201 Grand Ave
(85363)
Rates: $80-$115
(623) 933-8211
(800) 528-1234
(800) 253-2168

SURPRISE

**DEL WEBB'S
VACATION
GETAWAY**
19606 N Desert
Garden Dr (85374)
Rates: n/a
(623) 546-7200
(800) 528-2604

**THE HOTEL
LODGE AT SUN
RIDGE**
12129 W Bell Rd
(85374)
Rates: $44-$138
(623) 583-0993
(800) 337-6667

**QUALITY INN
& SUITES**
16741 N
Greasewood St
(85374)
Rates: $59-$119
(623) 583-3500
(800) 228-5151

**WINDMILL INN AT
SUN CITY WEST**
12545 W Bell Rd
(85374)
Rates: $85-$149
(623) 583-0133
(800) 547-4747

TAYLOR

SILVER CREEK INN
825 N Hwy 77
(85939)
Rates: $46-$69
(520) 536-2600
(888) 246-5440

TEMPE

**AMERISUITES
ARIZONA
MILLS MALL**
1520 W Baseline
Rd (85283)
Rates: $99-$129
(480) 831-9800
(800) 833-1518

**BEST WESTERN
INN OF TEMPE**
670 N Scottsdale
Rd (85282)
Rates: $62-$132
(480) 784-2233
(800) 528-1234

**BRIDGESTREET
ACCOMMODA-
TIONS RENTALS**
1445 E Guadalupe
Rd, Ste 107 (85283)
Rates: n/a
(480) 345-9061
(800) 645-9061

**THE BUTTES-
A WYNDHAM
RESORT**
2000 Westcourt
Way (85282)
Rates: $99-$448
(480) 225-9000
(800) 996-3429

COMFORT SUITES
1625 S 52nd
(85281)
Rates: $49-$149
(480) 446-9500
(800) 228-5150

**COUNTRY INN
& SUITES
BY CARLSON**
1660 W Elliot Rd
(85283)
Rates: $69-$125
(480) 345-8585
(800) 456-4000

**COUNTRY INN
& SUITES
BY CARLSON**
808 N Scottsdale
Rd (85281)
Rates: $65-$109
(480) 858-9898
(800) 456-4000

**FIESTA INN
RESORT**
2100 S Priest Dr
(85282)
Rates: $88-$185
(480) 967-1441
(800) 528-6481

**HAMPTON INN
& SUITES**
1429 N Scottsdale
Rd (85281)
Rates: $105-$155
(480) 675-9799
(800) 426-7866

**HOLIDAY INN
EXPRESS**
5300 S Priest Dr
(85283)
Rates: $99-$129
(480) 820-7500
(800) 465-4329

**HOLIDAY INN
TEMPE / ASU**
915 E Apache
Blvd (85281)
Rates: $154-$164
(480) 968-3451
(800) 465-4329
(800) 553-1826

**HOMESTEAD
VILLAGE**
4909 S Wendler Dr
(85282)
Rates: $39-$59
(480) 414-4470
(888) 782-9473

KNIGHTS INN
1915 E Apache
Blvd (85281)
Rates: $80-$90
(480) 736-1700
(800) 843-5644

**INNSUITES HOTEL
AIRPORT**
1651 W Baseline
Rd (85283)
Rates: $99-$139
(480) 897-7900
(800) 841-4242

LA QUINTA INN
911 S 48th St
(85281)
Rates: $89-$109
(480) 967-4465
(800) 687-6667

MAINSTAY SUITES
2165 W 15th St
(85281)
Rates: $60-$129
(480) 557-8880
(800) 660 6246

**MICROTEL INN
& SUITES**
1375 E University
(85281)
Rates: $59-$89
(480) 774-2500
(888) 771-7171

MOTEL 6
513 W Broadway
Rd (85282)
Rates: $38-$52
(480) 967-8696
(800) 466-8356

MOTEL 6
1720 S Priest Dr
(85281)
Rates: $38-$52
(480) 968-4401
(800) 466-8356

MOTEL 6
1612 N Scottsdale
Rd (85281)
Rates: $38-$52
(480) 945-9506
(800) 466-8356

RED ROOF INN
1701 W Baseline
Rd (85283)
Rates: $38-$82
(480) 413-1188
(800) 843-7663

AREA CODES - If the local number doesn't connect, check for a new area code.

RED ROOF INN AIRPORT
2135 W 15th St
(85281)
Rates: $49-$84
(480) 449-3205
(800) 843-7663

RESIDENCE INN BY MARRIOTT
5075 S Priest Dr
(85282)
Rates: $145-$210
(480) 756-2122
(800) 331-3131

RODEWAY INN AIRPORT EAST
1550 S 52nd St
(85281)
Rates: $59-$105
(480) 967-3000
(800) 228-2000

SUPER 8 MOTEL
1020 E Apache
Blvd (85281)
Rates: $69-$99
(480) 967-8891
(800) 800-8000

TEMPE MISSION PALMS HOTEL-OLD TOWN/ASU
60 E 5th St (85281)
Rates: $209-$399
(480) 894-1400
(800) 547-8705

TRAVELODGE UNIVERSITY
1005 E Apache
Blvd (85281)
Rates: $69-$99
(480) 968-7871
(800) 578-7878

TOLLESON

ECONO LODGE
1520 N 84th Dr
(85353)
Rates: $39-$95
(623) 936-4667
(800) 553-2666

TOMBSTONE

BEST WESTERN LOOKOUT LODGE
Hwy 80 W (85638)
Rates: $65-$85
(520) 457-2223
(800) 528-1234
(877) 652-6772

LARIAN MOTEL
410 Fremont St
(85638)
Rates: $32-$55
(520) 457-2272

TOMBSTONE MOTEL
502 E Fremont St
(85638)
Rates: $45-$70
(520) 457-3478

TRAIL RIDERS INN
13 N 7th St (85638)
Rates: $35-$45
(520) 457-3573

TUBA CITY

QUALITY INN
Main & Moenave
(86045)
Rates: $70-$140
(520) 283-4545
(800) 228-5151
(800) 644-8383

TUBAC

TUBAC GOLF RESORT
1 Otero Rd (85646)
Rates: $75-$177
(520) 398-2211
(800) 848-7893

TUCSON

BAYMONT INN
1560 W Grant Rd
(85745)
Rates: $84-$90
(520) 624-3200
(800) 789-4103
(800) 301-0200

BAYMONT INN & SUITES TUCSON AIRPORT
2548 E Medina Rd
(85706)
Rates: $70-$110
(520) 889-6600
(800) 789-4103
(800) 301-0200

BEST WESTERN EXECUTIVE INN
333 W Drachman
(85705)
Rates: $40-$115
(520) 791-7551
(800) 528-1234 (US)
(800) 255-3371 (AZ)

BEST WESTERN INNSUITES CATALINA FOOTHILLS
6201 N Oracle Rd
(85704)
Rates: $119-$189
(520) 297-8111
(800) 528-1234
(800) 554-4535

CANDLELIGHT SUITES
1440 S Craycroft
Rd (85711)
Rates: $65-$70
(520) 747-1440
(800) 223-1440

THE CAT AND THE WHISTLE B&B
22nd St & Kolb Rd
(85710)
Rates: $65-$75
Monthly:
$850-$1000
(602) 990-0682
(800) 456-0682

CHATEAU SONATA
550 S Camino Seco
(85710)
Rates: $59-$239
(520) 886-2468
(800) 597-8483

CLARION SANTA RITA HOTEL
88 E Broadway
(85701)
Rates: $99-$159
(520) 622-4000
(877) 526-7737

COMFORT SUITES
515 W Auto Mall
Dr (85705)
Rates: $57-$130
(520) 888-6676
(800) 228-5150

THE COVE B&B
Tucson Blvd &
Norton (85713)
Rates: $60-$80
Weekly: $350-$400
(602) 990-0682
(800) 456-0682

DOUBLETREE GUEST SUITES
6555 E Speedway
Blvd (85710)
Rates: $127-$175
(520) 721-7100
(800) 222-8733

DOUBLETREE HOTEL AT REID PARK
445 S Alvernon
Way (85711)
Rates: $119-$215
(520) 881-4200
(800) 222-8733

EMBASSY SUITES HOTEL
5335 E Broadway
(85711)
Rates: $100-$169
(520) 745-2700
(800) 362-2779

FOUR POINTS HOTEL BY SHERATON
350 S Freeway
(85745)
Rates: $89-$99
(520) 622-6611

GHOST RANCH LODGE
801 W Miracle
Mile (85705)
Rates: $69-$99
(520) 791-7565
(800) 456-7565

THE GOLF VILLAS AT ORO VALLEY
10950 N La
Canada Dr (85737)
Rates: $99-$489
(520) 498-0098
(888) 388-0098

HAMPTON INN
1375 W Grant Rd
(85745)
Rates: $69-$130
(520) 206-0602
(800) 426-7866

HAWTHORN SUITES
7007 E Tanque
Verde Rd (85715)
Rates: $99-$139
(520) 298-2300
(800) 527-1133

HOTEL CONGRESS
311 E Congress
(85701)
Rates: $29-$58
(520) 622-8848
(800) 722-8848

HOWARD JOHNSON EXPRESS
1010 S Freeway
(85745)
Rates: $39-$119
(520) 622-5871
(800) 446-4656

INN SUITES HOTEL & RESORT
475 N Granada
Ave (85701)
Rates: $75-$125
(520) 622-3000
(800) 446-6589

KNIGHTS INN
720 W 29th St
(85713)
Rates: $99-$119
(520) 624-8291
(800) 843-5644

LA QUINTA INN EAST
6404 E Broadway
(85710)
Rates: $75-$109
(520) 747-1414
(800) 687-6667

LA QUINTA INN & SUITES AIRPORT
7001 S Tucson
Blvd (85706)
Rates: $78-$119
(520) 573-3333
(800) 687-6667

LA QUINTA INN WEST
665 N Frwy
(85706)
Rates: $79-$99
(520) 622-6491
(800) 687-6667

THE LODGE ON THE DESERT
306 N Alvernon
Way (85711)
Rates: $88-$175
(520) 325-3366
(800) 456-5634

LOEWS VENTANA CANYON RESORT
7000 N Resort Dr
(85750)
Rates: $99-$320
(520) 299-2020
(800) 234-5117

AREA CODES - If the local number doesn't connect, check for a new area code.

MOTEL 6
1031 E Benson
Hwy (85713)
Rates: $30-$48
(520) 628-1264
(800) 466-8356

MOTEL 6
755 E Benson
Hwy (85713)
Rates: $30-$48
(520) 622-4614
(800) 466-8356

MOTEL 6
960 S Freeway
(85745)
Rates: $32-$51
(520) 628-1339
(800) 466-8356

MOTEL 6
4630 W Ina Rd
(85741)
Rates: $35-$56
(520) 744-9300
(800) 466-8356

MOTEL 6
1222 S Freeway
(85713)
Rates: $32-$51
(520) 624-2516
(800) 466-8356

**MOUNTAIN
VIEWS B&B**
E Tanque Verde
Rd (85749)
Rates: $65-$75
Weekly: $390-$450
(520) 990-0682
(800) 456-0682

**RED ROOF INN
NORTH**
4940 N Ina Rd
(85743)
Rates: $66-$110
(520) 744-8199
(800) 843-7663

**RED ROOF INN
SOUTH**
3700 E Irvington
Rd (85714)
Rates: $66-$91
(520) 571-1400
(800) 843-7663

**RESIDENCE INN
BY MARRIOTT**
6477 E Speedway
Blvd (85710)
Rates: $149-$300
(520) 721-0991
(800) 331-3131

RODEWAY INN
810 E Benson
Hwy (85713)
Rates: $99-$120
(520) 884-5800
(800) 228-2000

RODEWAY INN
1365 W Grant Rd
(85745)
Rates: $50-$89
(520) 622-7791
(800) 228-2000

**SHERATON EL
CONQUISTADOR
GOLF & TENNIS
RESORT**
10000 N Oracle Rd
(85737)
Rates: $354-$469
(520) 544-5000
(800) 325-7832

STUDIO 6
4950 S Outlet
Center Rd (85706)
Rates: n/a
(520) 746-0030
(800) 466-8356

SUPER 8 MOTEL
1248 N Stone St
(85705)
Rates: $39-$99
(520) 622-6446
(800) 800-8000

**THE TILLINGHAST
PLACE B&B**
N Oracle Rd
& Rt 89 (85705)
Rates: $65-$105
(520) 990-0682
(800) 456-0682

**TRAVELODGE
FLAMINGO**
1300 N Stone Ave
(85705)
Rates: $44-$142
(520) 770-1910
(800) 578-7878 (US)
(800) 300-3533 (AZ)

**TRAVELODGE
SUITES**
401 W Lavery Ln
(85704)
Rates: $39-$145
(520) 797-1710
(800) 578-7878

UNIVERSITY INN
950 N Stone Ave
(85705)
Rates: $32-$59
(520) 791-7503

**WAYWARD WINDS
LODGE**
707 W Miracle
Mile (85705)
Rates: $69-$99
(520) 791-7526
(800) 791-9503

**WESTWARD
LOOK RESORT**
245 E Ina Rd
(85704)
Rates: $200-$399
(520) 297-1151
(800) 722-2500

**WINDMILL INN
AT ST. PHILLIP'S
PLAZA**
4250 N Campbell
Ave (85718)
Rates: $65-$145
(520) 577-0007
(800) 547-4747

WICKENBURG

**BEST WESTERN
RANCHO GRANDE
MOTOR HOTEL**
293 E Wickenburg
Way (85390)
Rates: $66-$110
(520) 684-5445
(800) 528-1234
(800) 854-7235

SUPER 8 MOTEL
975 N Tegner
(85930)
Rates: $55-$75
(520) 684-0808
(800) 800-8000

**WESTERNER
MOTEL**
680 W
Wickenburg Way
(85358)
Rates: $35-$50
(520) 684-2493

WILLCOX

**BEST WESTERN
PLAZA INN**
1100 W Rex Allen
Dr (85643)
Rates: $69-$99
(520) 384-3556
(800) 528-1234
(800) 262-2645

DAYS INN
724 N Bisbee Ave
(85643)
Rates: $40-$65
(520) 384-4222
(800) 329-7466

MOTEL 6
921 N Bisbee Ave
(85643)
Rates: $33-$42
(520) 384-2201
(800) 466-8356

**ROYAL WESTERN
LODGE**
590 S Haskell Ave
(85643)
Rates: $24-$38
(520) 384-2266

WILLIAMS

**ARIZONA
WELCOME INN
& SUITES**
750 N Grand
Cnyn Rd (86046)
Rates: $45-$59
(520) 639-9127
(888) 895-0997

BIG SIX MOTEL
134 E Bill Williams
Ave (86046)
Rates: $25+
(520) 635-4591

**BUDGET HOST
INN**
620 W Bill
Williams Ave
(86046)
Rates: $30-$59
(520) 635-4415
(800) 283-4678
(800) 745-4415

CANYON MOTEL
Old E Hwy 66
(86046)
Rates: $20-$45
(520) 635-9371

**DOWNTOWNER
HOTEL**
201 E Bill Williams
Ave (86046)
Rates: $30+
(520) 635-4041

**EL RANCHO
MOTEL**
617 E Rt 66 (86046)
Rates: $52-$72
(520) 635-2552
(800) 228-2370

FAMILY INN
200 E Bill Williams
Ave (86046)
Rates: $17-$50
(520) 635-2562

GATEWAY MOTEL
219 E Bill Williams
Ave (86046)
Rates: $25-$40
(520) 635-4601

GRAND MOTEL
234 E Bill Williams
Ave (86046)
Rates: $24-$40
(520) 635-4601

**HIGHLANDER
MOTEL**
533 W Bill
Williams Ave
(86046)
Rates: $40-$48
(520) 635-2541
(800) 800-8288

HOLIDAY INN
950 N Grand
Canyon Blvd
(86046)
Rates: $79-$119
(520) 635-4114
(800) 465-4329

MOTEL 6
710 E Rt 66 (86046)
Rates: $36-$67
(520) 635-4464
(800) 466-8356

MOTEL 6
831 W Bill
Williams Ave
(86046)
Rates: $38-$69
(520) 636-9000
(800) 466-8356

AREA CODES - If the local number doesn't connect, check for a new area code.

MOUNTAINSIDE INN-GATEWAY TO THE GRAND CANYON
642 E Rt 66 (86046)
Rates: $76-$86
(520) 635-4431
(800) 462-9381

QUALITY INN MOUNTAIN RANCH & RESORT
6701 E Mtn Ranch Rd (86046)
Rates: $89-$109
(520) 635-2693
(800) 228-5151

ROUTE 66 INN
128 E Rt 66 (86046)
Rates: $40-$70
(520) 635-4791
(888) 786-6956

SUPER 8 MOTEL
911 W Rt 66 (86046)
Rates: $59-$89
(520) 635-4045
(800) 800-8000

TRAVELODGE
430 E Rt 66 (86046)
Rates: $49-$169
(520) 635-2651
(800) 578-7878

WESTERNER MOTEL
530 W Bill Williams Ave (86046)
Rates: $38-$48
(520) 635-4312
(800) 385-8608

WINDOW ROCK

DAYS INN
392 W Hwy 264 (86515)
Rates: $45-$110
(520) 871-5690
(800) 329-7466

NAVAJO NATION INN
48 W Hwy 264 (86515)
Rates: $57-$77
(520) 871-4108
(800) 662-6189

WINSLOW

BEST WESTERN ADOBE INN
1701 N Park Dr (86047)
Rates: $50-$69
(520) 289-4638
(800) 528-1234

DAYS INN
2035 W Third St (86047)
Rates: $39-$95
(520) 289-1010
(800) 329-7466

ECONO LODGE
1706 N Park Dr (86047)
Rates: $45-$79
(520) 289-4687
(800) 553-2666

HOLIDAY INN EXPRESS
816 Transcon Ln (86047)
Rates: n/a
(520) 289-2960
(800) 465-4329

LA POSADA HISTORIC HOTEL
303 E 2nd st (86047)
Rates: $69-$99
(520) 289-4366

MOTEL 6
520 W Desmond St (86047)
Rates: $40-$50
(520) 289-9581
(800) 466-8356

MOTEL 10
725 W Third St (86047)
Rates: $29-$40
(520) 289-3211
(800) 675-7478

SUPER 8 MOTEL
1916 W Third St (86047)
Rates: $46-$58
(520) 289-4606
(800) 800-8000

TRAVELODGE
1914 W Third St (86047)
Rates: $42-$67
(520) 289-4611
(800) 578-7878

YOUNGSTOWN

MOTEL 6
11133 Grand Ave (85363)
Rates: $56-$72
(623) 977-1318
(800) 466-8356

YUMA

BEST WESTERN CORONADO MOTOR HOTEL
233 4th Ave (85364)
Rates: $99-$145
(520) 783-4453
(800) 528-1234
(877) 234-5667

BEST WESTERN INNSUITES HOTEL
1450 S Castle Dome Ave (85365)
Rates: $99-$109
(520) 783-8341
(800) 528-1234 (US)
(800) 922-2034 (AZ)

CARAVAN OASIS MOTEL
10574 Fortuna Rd (85365)
Rates: $25-$43
(520) 342-1292

COMFORT INN
1691 S Riley (85365)
Rates: $70-$115
(520) 782-1200
(800) 228-5150

HOLIDAY INN EXPRESS
3181 S 4th Ave (85364)
Rates: $72-$85
(520) 344-1420
(800) 465-4329

INTERSTATE 8 INN
2730 S 4th Ave (85364)
Rates: $33+
(520) 726-6110
(800) 821-7465

MOTEL 6
1640 S Arizona Ave (85364)
Rates: $29-$43
(520) 782-6561
(800) 466-8356

MOTEL 6
1445 E 16th St (85365)
Rates: $32-$46
(520) 782-9521
(800) 466-8356

OAK TREE INN & PENNY'S DINER
1731 S Sunridge Dr (85365)
Rates: $49-$55
(520) 539-9000
(888) 897-9647

RADISSON SUITES
2600 S 4th Ave (85364)
Rates: $119-$179
(520) 726-4830
(800) 333-3333

RAMADA INN CHILTON CONF CENTER
300 E 32nd St (85364)
Rates: $49-$105
(520) 344-1050
(800) 272-6232

ROYAL MOTOR INN
2941 S 4th Ave (85364)
Rates: $40-$110
(520) 344-0550
(800) 729-0550

SHILO CONFERENCE HOTEL
1550 S Castle Dome Ave (85365)
Rates: $79-$150
(520) 782-9511
(800) 222-2244

SUPER 8 MOTEL
1688 S Riley Ave (85365)
Rates: $73-$93
(520) 782-2000
(800) 800-8000

TRAVELODGE AIRPORT
711 E 32nd St (85365)
Rates: $54-$84
(520) 726-4721
(800) 578-7878
(800) 835-1132

YUMA CABANA MOTEL
2151 S 4th Ave (85364)
Rates: $56-$74
(520) 783-8311
(800) 874-0811

AREA CODES - If the local number doesn't connect, check for a new area code.

ARKANSAS

ALMA

DAYS INN
250 N US Hwy 71
(72921)
Rates: $35-$50
(501) 632-4595
(800) 329-7466

ARKADELPHIA

**BEST WESTERN
CONTINENTAL
INN**
136 Valley Rd
(71923)
Rates: $39-$75
(870) 246-5592
(800) 528-1234

COLLEGE INN
1015 Pine (71923)
Rates: n/a
(870) 246-2404

DAYS INN
137 Valley Dr
(71923)
Rates: $48-$56
(870) 246-3031
(800) 329-7466

ECONO LODGE
106 Crystal Palace
Dr (71923)
Rates: $45-$57
(870) 246-8026
(800) 553-2666

HOLIDAY INN
150 Valley St
(71923)
Rates: $65-$75
(870) 230-1506
(800) 465-4329

QUALITY INN
I-30 &SR 7 (71923)
Rates: $49-$68
(870) 246-5855
(800) 228-5151

ASHDOWN

BUDGET INN
Hwy 71 (71822)
Rates: n/a
(501) 898-3357

BALD KNOB

SCOTTISH INNS
3505 US Hwy 167
(72010)
Rates: n/a
(501) 724-3204
(800) 251-1962

BATESVILLE

ECONOMY INN
Hwy 233 N
(72501)
Rates: n/a
(870) 793-3871
(800) 826-0778

RAMADA INN
1325 N St. Louis St
(72501)
Rates: $62-$69
(870) 698-1800
(800) 272-6232

BEEBE

ADAMS MOTEL
2110 Devil Hive
(72012)
Rates: n/a
(501) 882-6473

BENTON

**BEST WESTERN
INN**
17036 I-30 (72015)
Rates: $46-$70
(501) 778-9695
(800) 528-1234

CAPRI MOTEL
15631 I-30 (72015)
Rates: n/a
(501) 778-8216

DAYS INN
17701 I-30 (72015)
Rates: $50-$55
(501) 776-3200
(800) 329-7466

ECONO LODGE
1221 Hot Springs
Rd (72015)
Rates: $32-$49
(501) 776-1515
(800) 553-2666

RAMADA INN
16732 I-30 (72015)
Rates: $44-$80
(501) 776-1900
(800) 272-6232

SLEEP CHEAP
Cedarwood I-30,
Exit 117 (72015)
Rates: n/a
(501) 778-2305

TROUTT MOTEL
15348 I-30 (72015)
Rates: $27-$38
(501) 778-3633

BENTONVILLE

**BEST WESTERN
INN**
2307 SE Walton
Blvd (72712)
Rates: $40-$55
(501) 273-9727
(800) 528-1234

CLARION HOTEL
211 SE Walton
Blvd (72712)
Rates: $69-$169
(501) 464-4600
(800) 252-7466

DAYS INN
3408 S Moberly Ln
(72712)
Rates: $55-$105
(501) 271-7900
(800) 329-7466

BISMARCK

**DEGRAY
LAKEVIEW
COTTAGES**
Rt 3, Box 450
(71929)
Rates: n/a
(501) 865-3389

**MORRISON'S
COTTAGES**
Rt 3 (71929)
Rates: n/a
(501) 865-4872

BLYTHEVILLE

BEST BUDGET INN
357 S Division
(72315)
Rates: n/a
(870) 763-4588

COMFORT INN
I-55 & SR 18E
(72316)
Rates: $60-$66
(870) 763-7081
(800) 228-5150

DAYS INN
I-55 & SR 18 E
(72316)
Rates: $41-$65
(870) 763-1241
(800) 329-7466

DELTA K MOTEL
P. O. Box 1472
(72316)
Rates: $25-$36
(870) 763-1410

DRURY INN
201 N I-55 (72315)
Rates: $55-$71
(870) 763-2300
(800) 378-7946

HOLIDAY INN
112 E Main
(72316)
Rates: $68-$85
(870) 763-5800
(800) 465-4329

BOLES

**Y-C MOUNTAIN INN
& CAMPGROUND**
HCR 69, Box 199
(72926)
Rates: n/a
(501) 577-2211

BRINKLEY

BEST WESTERN
1306 Hwy 17 N
(72021)
Rates: $46-$69
(870) 734-1650
(800) 528-1234

BRINKLEY INN

1124 S Main
(72021)
Rates: n/a
(870) 734-3141

ECONO LODGE
I-40 & Hwy 49 NE
(72021)
Rates: $36-$70
(870) 734-2035
(800) 553-2666

HERITAGE INN
1507 Hwy 17 N
(72021)
Rates: $29-$42
(870) 734-2121

SUPER 8 MOTEL
I-40 & Hwy 49 N
(72021)
Rates: $44-$54
(870) 734-4680
(800) 800-8000

BULL SHOALS

**BULL SHOALS
WHITE RIVER
LANDING**
P. O. Box 748
(72619)
Rates: n/a
(501) 445-4166

**DOGWOOD
LODGE**
505 Shorecrest Dr
(72619)
Rates: n/a
(501) 445-4311
(800) 883-4311

**DRIFTWOOD
RESORT**
P. O. Box 75
(72619)
Rates: n/a
(501) 445-4455
(800) 424-1129

**MAR-MAR
RESORT**
Shorecrest Dr &
Hwy 178 (72619)
Rates: n/a
(501) 445-4444
(800) 332-2855

CABOT

DAYS INN
1114 W Main
(72023)
Rates: $45-$65
(501) 843-0145
(800) 329-7466

SUPER 8 MOTEL
15 Ryeland Dr
(72023)
Rates: $47-$70
(501) 941-3748
(800) 800-8000

CADDO GAP

ARROWHEAD CABINS
HC 65, Box 2
(71935)
Rates: n/a
(501) 356-2944

CALICO ROCK

FOREST HOME LODGE & LOG CABINS
HC 61, Box 72
(72519)
Rates: n/a
(501) 297-8211

JENKINS MOTEL
605 Hwy 56 E
(72519)
Rates: n/a
(501) 297-8987

WISEMAN MOTEL
Box 546, Hwy 5
(72519)
Rates: n/a
(501) 297-3733

CAMDEN

AIRPORT INN
2115 Hwy 79 N
(71701)
Rates: n/a
(870) 574-0400

AMERICAN FAMILY INN
Hwy 7 S &
Goodgame
(71701)
Rates: n/a
(870) 231-6661

CARLISLE

BEST WESTERN INTERSTATE INN
I-40 & Hwy 13
(72024)
Rates: $45-$70
(870) 552-7566
(800) 528-1234

CLARKRIDGE

TREASURE COVE RESORT
902 County Rd
470 (72623)
Rates: n/a
(501) 425-4325

CLARKSVILLE

BEST WESTERN SHERWOOD MOTOR INN
1200 S Rogers St
(72830)
Rates: $40-$60
(501) 754-7900
(800) 528-1234

COMFORT INN
1167 S Rogers Ave
(72830)
Rates: $47-$80
(501) 754-3000
(800) 228-5150

DAYS INN
2600 W Main St
(72830)
Rates: $36-$99
(501) 754-8555
(800) 329-7466

TAYLOR MOTEL
Hwy 64 E (72830)
Rates: n/a
(501) 754-2106

CLINTON

BEST WESTERN HILLSIDE INN
Hwy 65 & 65 B
(72031)
Rates: $29-$69
(501) 745-4700
(800) 528-1234

SUPER 8 MOTEL
Hwy 65 S (72031)
Rates: $40-$52
(501) 745-8810
(800) 800-8000

CONWAY

BEST WESTERN
I-40 & US 64 East
(72032)
Rates: $49-$69
(501) 329-9855
(800) 528-1234
(800) 800-6298

COMFORT INN
150 Hwy 65 N
(72033)
Rates: $45-$70
(501) 329-0300
(800) 228-5150

CONTINENTAL MOTEL
134 Harkrider St
(72032)
Rates: n/a
(501) 327-7736

ECONOMY INN
P. O. Box 606
(72033)
Rates: $32-$46
(501) 327-4800
(800) 826-0778

HOWARD JOHNSON
I-40 & Hwy 65 N
(72033)
Rates: $54-$75
(501) 329-2961
(800) 446-4656

MOTEL 6
1105 Hwy 65 N
(72032)
Rates: $35-$48
(501) 327-6623
(800) 466-8356

RAMADA INN
815 E Oak St
(72032)
Rates: $52-$65
(501) 329-8392
(800) 272-6232

COTTER

CHAMBERLAIN'S TROUT DOCK
Denton Ferry Rd,
Rt 1, Box 620
(72626)
Rates: n/a
(501) 435-6535

RAINBOW DRIVE RESORT
Rainbow Dr,
Rt 1, Box 1185
(72626)
Rates: n/a
(501) 430-5217

WHITE SANDS MOTEL
P. O. Box 116
(72626)
Rates: n/a
(501) 435-2244

CROSSETT

THE ASHLEY INN
Hwy 72 E (71635)
Rates: n/a
(501) 364-4911
(800) 276-7738

DARDANELLE

WESTERN FRONTIER MOTEL
I-40, Exit 81
(72834)
Rates: $36-$46
(501) 229-4118

DEER

THE PINEY INN
Hwy 7, P. O. Box
10 (72628)
Rates: n/a
(501) 428-5878

DERMOTT

ECONOMY INN
Rt 1, Box 60,
Hwy 65 N (71638)
Rates: n/a
(501) 222-4017

DEQUEEN

SCOTTISH INNS
1314 US Hwy 71
W (71832)
Rates: $22-$32
(501) 642-2721
(800) 251-1962

DEVALLS BLUFF

PALAVER PLACE BED & BREAKFAST
Rt 1, Box 29-A
(72041)
Rates: n/a
(501) 998-7206

DEWITT

SAHARA MOTEL
Hwy 1, Box 309
(72042)
Rates: n/a
(870) 946-3581

DOGPATCH

ERBIE LODGE
HCR 73, Box 145
(72648)
Rates: $90+
(501) 446-5851

DOVER

MACK'S PINES
22816 SR 7 N
(72837)
Rates: n/a
(501) 331-3261

DRASCO

TANNEBAUM RESORT & GOLF CLUB
1329 Tannebaum
(72530)
Rates: n/a
(501) 362-3075

DUMAS

EXECUTIVE INN
310 Hwy 65 S
(71639)
Rates: n/a
(501) 382-5115

PENDLETON INN
Rt 1 (71639)
Rates: n/a
(501) 382-4215

EL DORADO

COMFORT INN
2303 Junction City
Rd (71730)
Rates: $64-$74
(870) 863-6677
(800) 228-5150

EL DORADO INN MOTEL
3019 N West Ave
(71730)
Rates: n/a
(870) 862-6676

FLAMINGO MOTEL
420 S West Ave
(71730)
Rates: n/a
(870) 862-4201

WHITEHALL MOTEL
840 W Hillsboro
(71730)
Rates: n/a
(870) 863-4136

ELIZABETH

HOLIDAY HILLS RESORT
Rt 1, Box 22
(72531)
Rates: n/a
(501) 488-5303

KELLER'S KOVE RESORT
Rt 1, Box 45
(72531)
Rates: n/a
(501) 488-5360

EUREKA SPRINGS

A CLIFF COTTAGE, THE PLACE NEXT DOOR-A B&B INN
42 Armstrong Dr
(72632)
Rates: $120-$195
(501) 253-7409

ALPEN-DORF MOTEL
Rt 4, Box 580
(72632)
Rates: $48-$89
(501) 253-9475
(800) 776-9865

BASIN PARK HOTEL
12 Spring St
(72632)
Rates: $72-$109
(501) 253-7837
(800) 643-4972

BEST WESTERN INN OF THE OZARKS
Hwy 62 W (72632)
Rates: $49-$139
(501) 253-9768
(800) 528-1234
(800) 552-3785

BEST WESTERN SWISS HOLIDAY
Hwy 62 East
(72632)
Rates: $39-$129
(501) 253-9501
(800) 528-1234
(888) 582-2220

BRACKENRIDGE LODGE
Rt 4, Box 60
(72632)
Rates: n/a
(501) 253-6803

CARRIAGE HOUSE
75 Lookout Ln
(72632)
Rates: n/a
(501) 253-5259

CHALET INN
Rt 6, Box 156
(72632)
Rates: $32-$48
(501) 253-9687

COLONIAL MANSION INN
154 Huntsville
(72632)
Rates: $32-$68
(501) 253-7300

COTTAGE INN BED & BREAKFAST
Rt 6, Box 115
(72632)
Rates: $65
(501) 253-5282

DAYS INN
120 W Van Buren
(72632)
Rates: $59-$120
(501) 253-8863
(800) 329-7466

DOGWOOD COTTAGES
RR 1, Box 168
(72632)
Rates: n/a
(501) 253-8897

DOGWOOD INN
170 Huntsville Rd
(72632)
Rates: $48-$58
(501) 253-7200

1876 INN
Rt 6, Box 247
(72632)
Rates: $30-$71
(501) 253-7183
(800) 643-3030

EUREKA SUNSET COTTAGES
10 Dogwood
Ridge (72632)
Rates: n/a
(501) 253-9565
(888) 253-9565

FOUR RUNNERS INN
RR 4, Box 306
(72632)
Rates: n/a
(501) 253-6000

HARVEST HOUSE BED & BREAKFST
104 Wall (72632)
Rates: n/a
(501) 253-9363
(800) 293-5665

HIDDEN VALLEY GUEST RANCH
777 Hidden Valley
Ranch (72632)
Rates: n/a
(501) 253-9777

HILLSIDE COTTAGE BED & BREAKFAST
23 Hillside (72632)
Rates: n/a
(501) 253-8688

INDIAN MOUNTAIN LODGE & CABINS
Rt 4, Box 570
(72632)
Rates: n/a
(501) 253-5221

KATIE WILLOW COTTAGES
Rt 6, Box 354
(72632)
Rates: n/a
(501) 253-8199

KINGS HI-WAY INN
92 Kings Hwy
(72632)
Rates: n/a
(501) 253-7311

LAKE LEATHER-WOOD PARK
Hwy 62 W (72632)
Rates: n/a
(501) 253-8624

LAKE LUCERNE RESORT
P. O. Box 441
(72632)
Rates: n/a
(501) 253-8085

LAZEE DAZE LOG CABIN RESORT
5432 Hwy 23
South (72632)
Rates: $105-$135
(501) 253-7026
(800) 760-7413

LOG CABIN INN MOTEL
42 Kings Hwy
(72632)
Rates: n/a
(501) 253-9400
(800) 254-9411

MARIPOSA INN
3 Echols (72632)
Rates: n/a
(501) 253-9169

OAK CREST COTTAGES
Rt 6, Box 126
(72632)
Rates: $30-$45
(501) 253-9493
(800) 262-6255

OLD HOMESTEAD
82 Armstrong St
(72632)
Rates: n/a
(501) 253-7501

PINE LODGE
Rt 2, Box 18
(72632)
Rates: n/a
(501) 253-8065

PINE TOP LODGE
Rt 6, Box 265
(72632)
Rates: $24-$56
(501) 253-7331
(800) 643-2233

POINTE WEST RESORT
Rt 2, Box 87 (72632)
Rates: n/a
(501) 253-9050

POTTER'S HOUSE MOTEL
Passion Play Rd
(72632)
Rates: n/a
(501) 253-7398

PURPLE IRIS INN
RR 6, Box 339
(72632)
Rates: n/a
(800) 831-4747

REGENCY 7
62E Passion Play
Rd (72632)
Rates: n/a
(800) 470-5959

ROADRUNNER INN
3034 Mundell Rd
(72632)
Rates: $33-$44
(501) 253-8166
(888) 253-8166

ROGUE'S MANOR AT SWEET SPRINGS BED & BREAKFAST
124 Spring St
(72632)
Rates: n/a
(501) 253-4911
(800) 764-8376

SCANDIA INN BED & BREAKFAST
33 Ave, Hwy 62 W
(72632)
Rates: n/a
(501) 253-8922
(800) 523-8922

SHERWOOD COURT
27 Glenn Ave
(72632)
Rates: n/a
(501) 253-8920
(800) 268-8920

SOUTHERN COUNTRY INN
Rt 1, Box 460 (72632)
Rates: n/a
(501) 253-5600
(800) 264-9565

STATUE ROAD INN MOTEL
Rt 1, Box 965
(72632)
Rates: n/a
(501) 253-9163
(800) 501-7666

AREA CODES - If the local number doesn't connect, check for a new area code.

STUDIO GUEST HOUSE
120 N Main (72632)
Rates: n/a
(501) 253-8773

SWISS VILLAGE INN
Rt 6, Box 5 (72632)
Rates: $44-$65
(501) 253-9541
(800) 447-6525

TAYLOR-PAGE INN B&B
33 Benton St
(72632)
Rates: n/a
(501) 253-7315

TRADEWINDS MOTEL
77 Kings Hwy
(72632)
Rates: $26-$80
(501) 253-9774
(800) 242-1615

TRAVELERS INN
2044 E Van Buren
(72632)
Rates: $38-$58
(501) 253-8386
(800) 643-5566

WHISPERING OAKS MOTEL
Rt 6, Box 338
(72632)
Rates: n/a
(501) 253-9459

WHITE DOVER MANOR B&B
8 Washington St
(72632)
Rates: n/a
(501) 253-6151
(800) 261-6151

WILDFLOWER COTTAGES
22 Hale St (72632)
Rates: n/a
(501) 253-9173

EVENING SHADE

THE TURMAN HOUSE B&B
P. O. Box 146
(72532)
Rates: n/a
(870) 266-3405
(800) 257-3405

FAYETTEVILLE

BEST WESTERN WINDSOR SUITES
1122 S Futrail Dr
(72701)
Rates: $59-$89
(501) 587-1400
(800) 528-1234

CHIEF MOTEL
1818 N College
Ave (72703)
Rates: n/a
(501) 442-7326

DAYS INN
2402 N College
Ave (72703)
Rates: $69-$125
(501) 443-4323
(800) 329-7466

HILTON HOTEL
70 N East Ave
(72701)
Rates: $80-$160
(501) 442-5555
(800) 445-8667

HOLIDAY INN EXPRESS
1251 N Shiloh Dr
(72701)
Rates: $70-$95
(501) 444-6006
(800) 465-4329

THE INN OF FAYETTEVILLE
1000 Hwy 71 (72701)
Rates: $38-$44
(501) 442-3041
(800) 290-3041

MOTEL 6
2980 N College
Ave (72703)
Rates: $34-$39
(501) 443-4351
(800) 466-8356

QUALITY INN
523 S Shiloh Dr
(72704)
Rates: $60-$100
(501) 444-9800
(800) 228-5151

RAMADA INN
3901 N College
Ave (72703)
Rates: $55-$78
(501) 443-3431
(800) 272-6232

SLEEP INN
728 Millsap Rd
(72703)
Rates: $54-$99
(501) 587-8700
(800) 753-3746

TWIN ARCH MOTEL
521 N College Ave
(72701)
Rates: n/a
(501) 521-9452

FLIPPIN

SEAWRIGHT'S MOTEL
1st & Sunset Sts
(72634)
Rates: n/a
(870) 453-2555

SHADY OAKS COTTAGES
HC 62, Box 128
(72634)
Rates: $50-$65
(870) 626-5474
(800) 467-6257

SPORTSMAN'S RESORT
HCR 62, Box 96
(72634)
Rates: n/a
(870) 453-2424
(800) 626-5474

WHITE HOLE RESORT
HCR 62, Box 100
(72634)
Rates: n/a
(870) 453-2913

WILDCAT SHOALS RESORT
P. O. Box 1032
(72634)
Rates: n/a
(870) 453-2321

FORDYCE

A-OK MOTEL
2403 Hwy 167 &
79 (71742)
Rates: n/a
(501) 352-3197

ANTLERS INN MOTEL
2400 Bypass
(71742)
Rates: n/a
(501) 352-5174

FORREST CITY

BEST WESTERN COLONY INN
2333 N
Washington
(72335)
Rates: $70-$100
(870) 633-0870
(800) 528-1234

ECONO LODGE
204 Holiday Dr
(72335)
Rates: $40-$52
(870) 633-6900
(800) 553-2666

HOLIDAY INN
200 Holiday Dr
(72335)
Rates: $65-$68
(870) 633-6300
(800) 465-4329

LUXURY INN
315 Barrow Wheel
Rd (72335)
Rates: $33-$39
(870) 633-8990

REGENCY INN
907 E Broadway
(72335)
Rates: n/a
(870) 633-4433

SAVE INN
105 NW St, Hwy
70 W (72335)
Rates: n/a
(870) 633-3214

FORT SMITH

BAYMONT INN & SUITES
2123 Burnham Rd
(72903)
Rates: $46-$53
(501) 484-5770
(800) 301-0200

BEST WESTERN FORT SMITH
101 N 11th St
(72901)
Rates: $48-$61
(501) 785-4121
(800) 528-1234
(888) 765-9467

BEST WESTERN KINGS ROW INN
5801 Rogers Ave
(72903)
Rates: $42-$73
(501) 452-4200
(800) 528-1234
(800) 531-5464

COMFORT INN
2120 Burnham Rd
(72903)
Rates: $51-$65
(501) 474-2223
(800) 228-5150

DAYS INN
1021 Garrison Ave
(72901)
Rates: $36-$50
(501) 783-0548
(800) 329-7466

DENNIS MOTEL
5100 Midland
Blvd (72904)
Rates: n/a
(501) 782-4064

FIFTH SEASON MOTOR INN
2219 S Waldron
Rd (72903)
Rates: $59-$79
(501) 452-4880
(800) 643-4567

HOLIDAY INN CIVIC CENTER
700 Rogers Ave
(72901)
Rates: $89-$109
(501) 783-1000
(800) 465-4329

MOTEL 6
6001 Rogers Ave
(72903)
Rates: $31-$40
(501) 484-0576
(800) 466-8356

QUALITY INN
2301 Towson Ave
(72901)
Rates: $42-$95
(501) 785-1401
(800) 228-5151

SHERATON INN
5711 Rogers Ave
(72901)
Rates: $55-$65
(501) 452-4110
(800) 356-7046

AREA CODES - If the local number doesn't connect, check for a new area code.

GAMALIEL

BAYOU RESORT
HC 66, Box 390
(72537)
Rates: n/a
(501) 467-5277

CASTAWAYS RESORT & CAFE
Hwy 101 (72537)
Rates: n/a
(501) 467-5348

DRIFTWOOD RESORT
HC 66, Box 6000
(72537)
Rates: n/a
(501) 467-5330

LAKESIDE RESORT
Koeller Rd, CR 801 (72537)
Rates: n/a
(501) 467-5196

LUCKY 7 RESORT
HC 66, Box 1345
(72537)
Rates: n/a
(501) 467-5451

SHADY VALLEY RESORT
HC 66, Box 220
(72537)
Rates: n/a
(501) 467-5350

TWIN GABLES RESORT
HC 66, Box 1385
(72537)
Rates: n/a
(501) 467-5686

GASSVILLE

RED BUD DOCK MOTEL
Rt 2, Box 541
(72635)
Rates: n/a
(501) 435-6303

GATEWAY

HOLIDAY HILL MOTEL
Hwy 62 E
Gateway (72733)
Rates: n/a
(501) 656-3395

GENTRY

GENTRY MOTEL
P. O. Box 177
(72734)
Rates: n/a
(501) 736-8006

GILBERT

BUFFALO CAMPING & CANOEING
P. O. Box 45
(72636)
Rates: n/a
(870) 439-2888

GENERAL STORE CABINS
1 Frost St (72636)
Rates: n/a
(501) 439-2386

GILLETT

RICE PADDY MOTEL
P. O. Box 536
(72055)
Rates: n/a
(501) 548-2223

GLENWOOD

CADDO RIVER MOTEL
Rt 2, Box 786
(71943)
Rates: n/a
(501) 356-4117

OUACHITA MTN INN
Box 32, Hwy 70
Bypass (71943)
Rates: n/a
(501) 356-3737

GREERS FERRY

COLE'S OZARK MOTEL
7650 Edgemont
Rd (72067)
Rates: n/a
(501) 825-6607

NARROW'S INN
7910 Edgemont
Rd (72067)
Rates: n/a
(501) 825-6246

RED BIRD INN
9174 Edgemont
Rd (72067)
Rates: n/a
(501) 825-6256

HAMPTON

SMITH'S MOTEL
P. O. Box 823
(71744)
Rates: n/a
(501) 798-2755

HARDY

FRONTIER MOTOR LODGE
Rt 1, Box 62
(72542)
Rates: n/a
(501) 966-3377

HIDEAWAY INN B&B
Rt 1, Box 199
(72542)
Rates: n/a
(501) 966-4770
(888) 966-4770

MOTOR CENTER MOTEL
Rt 1, Box 57-A
(72542)
Rates: n/a
(501) 856-3282

RAZORBACK MOTEL
Rt 1, Box 234
(72542)
Rates: n/a
(501) 856-2465

WEAVER MOTEL
Rt 1, Box 2 (72542)
Rates: n/a
(501) 856-3224

HARRISON

AIRPORT MOTEL
1605 Hwy 62-65 N
(72601)
Rates: n/a
(870) 741-5900

CRESTHAVEN INN
825 N Main
(72601)
Rates: n/a
(870) 741-9522

FAMILY BUDGET INN
401 S Main Hwy
65B (72601)
Rates: $30-$37
(870) 743-1000

HARRISON HOTEL & SUITES
816 N Main
(72601)
Rates: $52-$61
(870) 741-2391

HOLIDAY INN EXPRESS
117 Hwy 43E
(72601)
Rates: n/a
(870) 741-3636
(800) 465-4329

LITTLE SWITZERLAND
Jasper Star Rt,
Hwy 7 (72601)
Rates: n/a
(870) 446-2693
(800) 510-0691

MERRY OTTER BED & BREAKFAST
103 W South St
(72601)
Rates: n/a
(870) 743-9010

ROCK CANDY MTN
Hwy 7 South
(72601)
Rates: n/a
(870) 743-1531

SCENIC 7 MOTEL
Rt 1, Box 16
(72601)
Rates: n/a
(870) 741-9648

SUPER 8 MOTEL
1330 Hwy 62/65
N (72601)
Rates: $45-$75
(870) 741-1741
(800) 800-8000

HEBER SPRINGS

ARKANSAS INN
2233 Hwy 25 NB
(72543)
Rates: n/a
(501) 362-2500
(800) 530-7740

BARNETT MOTEL
616 W Main St
(72543)
Rates: $36-$47
(501) 362-8111

LAKE & RIVER INN
2322 Hwy 25B
(72543)
Rates: $35-$45
(501) 362-3161

LAKESHORE RESORT MOTEL
801 Case Ford Rd
(72543)
Rates: $42+
(501) 362-2315

OZARK TRAIL MOTEL
1631 Hwy 25 B
(72543)
Rates: n/a
(501) 362-3102

PINES MOTEL
1819 25 B (72543)
Rates: n/a
(501) 362-3176

HELENA

RIVERBLUFF HOTEL
Box 730 (72342)
Rates: $40-$75
(501) 338-6431
(800) 543-5352

HENDERSON

CRYSTAL COVE RESORT
HC 66, Box 845
(72544)
Rates: n/a
(501) 488-5373

RODEWAY INN
US 62 E (72544)
Rates: $35-$74
(501) 488-5144
(800) 228-2000

HETH

BEST WESTERN LAKE SIDE INN
I-40 & St 149, Exit
260 (72346)
Rates: $40-$50
(870) 657-2101
(800) 528-1234

AREA CODES - If the local number doesn't connect, check for a new area code.

HINDSVILLE

FOXFIRE CAMP RESORT
Rt 1, Box 198
(72738)
Rates: n/a
(501) 789-2122

HOPE

BEST WESTERN INN OF HOPE
Jct I-30 & SR 4,
Exit 30 (71801)
Rates: $50-$69
(870) 777-9222
(800) 528-1234
(800) 429-4494

DAYS INN
1500 N Hervey
(71801)
Rates: $38-$65
(870) 722-1904
(800) 329-7466

FRIENDLY INN
P. O. Box 930
(71801)
Rates: n/a
(870) 777-4665

HOLIDAY INN EXPRESS
2600 N Hervey
(71801)
Rates: $61-$70
(870) 722-6262
(800) 465-4329

QUALITY INN
I-30 & Hwy 29
(71801)
Rates: $40-$55
(870) 777-0777
(800) 228-5151

SUPER 8 MOTEL
I-30 & Hwy 4
(71801)
Rates: $29-$39
(870) 777-8601
(800) 800-8000

HORSESHOE BEND

BOXHOUND RESORT, MARINA & RV PARK
1313 Tri-Lake Dr
(72512)
Rates: n/a
(870) 670-4496

HOT SPRINGS

APPLE TREE INN
805 E Grand
(71901)
Rates: n/a
(501) 624-4672
(800) 782-7753

CLARION RESORT ON THE LAKE
4813 Central Ave
(71913)
Rates: $70-$149
(501) 525-1391
(800) 252-7466

EL RANCHO MOTEL
1611 Central Ave
(71901)
Rates: n/a
(501) 624-1273

FOUNTAIN MOTEL
1622 Central Ave
(71901)
Rates: n/a
(501) 624-1262

HOT SPRINGS RESORT
1871 E Grand
(71901)
Rates: n/a
(501) 623-8824
(800) 238-4891

HOWARD JOHNSON
400 W Grand Ave
(71901)
Rates: $40-$80
(501) 624-4441
(800) 446-4656

KING'S INN MOTEL
2101 Central Ave
(71901)
Rates: n/a
(501) 623-8824
(800) 235-8824

MAJESTIC HOTEL
Park & Central
Ave (71901)
Rates: $45-$65
(501) 623-5511

MTN SPRINGS INN
1127 Central Ave
(71901)
Rates: n/a
(501) 624-7131

PARK HOTEL
211 Fountain St
(71901)
Rates: $65-$125
(501) 624-5323

PATTON'S LAKE RESORT
100 San Carlos
Point (71913)
Rates: n/a
(501) 525-1678

QUALITY INN
1125 E Grand Ave
(71901)
Rates: $64-$89
(501) 624-3321
(800) 228-5151

ROYALE VISTA INN
2204 Central Ave
(71901)
Rates: n/a
(501) 624-5551

SHAMROCK MOTEL
508 Albert Pike
(71913)
Rates: n/a
(501) 624-3833

SUPER 8 MOTEL
4726 Central Ave
(71913)
Rates: $56-$74
(501) 525-0188
(800) 800-8000
(888) 526-0188

TAYLOR ROSAMOND MOTEL
316 Park Ave
(71901)
Rates: n/a
(501) 624-1255

TOWN HOUSE MOTEL
100 Cove (71901)
Rates: n/a
(501) 624-9271

TRAVELIER MOTOR LODGE
1045 E Grand Ave
(71901)
Rates: n/a
(501) 624-4681

VAGABOND MOTEL
4708 Central Ave
(71913)
Rates: n/a
(501) 525-2769

WILLOW BEACH RESORT
260 Lake
Hamilton (71913)
Rates: n/a
(501) 525-1362
(800) 874-1385

WOODBINE HOLLOW B&B
213 Woodbine
(71901)
Rates: n/a
(501) 624-3646

HOT SPRINGS NATIONAL PARK

AVANELLE MOTOR LODGE
1204 Central Ave
(71901)
Rates: $44-$70
(501) 321-1332

BUENA VISTA RESORT
201 Abernia
(71913)
Rates: $45-$120
(800) 255-9030

HAMILTON INN RESORT
106 Lookout Point
(71913)
Rates: $45-$58
(501) 525-5666

HOLIDAY INN LAKE HAMILTON
4813 Central Ave
(71902)
Rates: $56-$95
(501) 525-1391
(800) 465-4329

LAKE HAMILTON RESORT
2803 Albert Pike
Rd (71913)
Rates: $99-$150
(501) 767-5511

MARGARETE MOTEL
217 Fountain St
(71901)
Rates: $33-$48
(501) 623-1192

SHORECREST RESORT
360 Lakeland Dr
(71901)
Rates: $41-$52
(800) 447-9914

TRAVELIER INN
1045 E Grand Ave
(719019)
Rates: $29-$52
(501) 624-4681

HUTTIG

TRACKS INN MOTEL
1141 K Ave (71747)
Rates: n/a
(501) 943-2943

JACKSONVILLE

DAYS INN
1414 John Harden
Dr (72076)
Rates: $46-$60
(501) 982-1543
(800) 329-7466

OXFORD INN
920 Hwy 161
(72076)
Rates: n/a
(501) 982-1976

RAMADA INN
200 Hwy 67N
(72076)
Rates: $45-$62
(501) 982-2183
(800) 272-6232

SANDS MOTEL
1008 S Hwy 161
(72076)
Rates: n/a
(501) 985-0266

JASPER

LOOKOUT MTN LOG CABINS
HCR 31, Box 90
(72641)
Rates: n/a
(870) 446-6224
(800) 596-5409

MOCKINGBIRD MOTEL
HCR 31, Box 64-B (72641)
Rates: n/a
(870) 446-2643

JESSIEVILLE

OUACHITA MOTEL
6127 N Hwy 7 (71949)
Rates: n/a
(501) 984-5363

JONESBORO

BEST WESTERN
2901 Phillips Dr (72401)
Rates: $49-$69
(870) 932-6600
(800) 528-1234

COMFORT INN
2904 Phillips Dr (72401)
Rates: $50-$70
(870) 972-8686
(800) 228-5150

DAYS INN
2406 Phillips Dr (72401)
Rates: $43-$89
(870) 932-9339
(800) 329-7466

HOLIDAY INN
3006 S Caraway Rd (72401)
Rates: $40-$95
(870) 935-2030
(800) 465-4329

HOLIDAY INN EXPRESS
2407 Phillips Dr (72401)
Rates: n/a
(870) 932-5554
(800) 465-4329

JAMI BEE MOTEL
3423 E Nettleton Ave (72401)
Rates: n/a
(870) 932-1611

JONESBORO MOTEL
403 S Gee St (72401)
Rates: n/a
(870) 932-6615

MOTEL 6
2300 S Caraway Rd (72401)
Rates: $30-$48
(870) 932-1050
(800) 466-8356

PARK PLACE INN
1421 S Caraway Rd (72401)
Rates: n/a
(870) 935-8400

QUALITY SUITES
Kazi St (72401)
Rates: $60-$90
(800) 228-5151

RAMADA LIMITED
3000 Apache Dr (72401)
Rates: $54-$82
(870) 932-5757
(800) 272-6232

SCOTTISH INNS
3116 Mead Dr (72401)
Rates: $30-$35
(870) 972-8300
(800) 251-1962

SUPER 8 MOTEL
2500 S Caraway Rd (72401)
Rates: $33-$54
(870) 972-0849
(800) 800-8000

WILSON INN
2911 Gilmore Dr (72401)
Rates: $35-$55
(870) 972-9000

KIRBY

DAISY MOTEL
HC 71, Box 255 (71950)
Rates: n/a
(501) 398-5173

LAKESIDE GROCERY & MOTEL
HC 71, Box 67 (71950)
Rates: n/a
(501) 398-5304

LAKE VILLAGE

LA VILLA MOTEL
Hwys 65 & 82 (71653)
Rates: n/a
(870) 265-2277

LAKE SHORE MOTEL
P. O. Box 231 (71653)
Rates: n/a
(870) 265-2238

PLAZA MOTEL
Hwys 65 & 82 S (71653)
Rates: n/a
(870) 265-5341

LAKEVIEW

BAY BREEZE RESORT
Box 185, Hwy 178 (72642)
Rates: n/a
(870) 431-5261

CEDAR OAKS RESORT
Rt 1, Box 694 (72642)
Rates: $45-$75
(870) 431-5351

GASTON'S WHITE RIVER RESORT
1 River Rd (72642)
Rates: $57-$105
(870) 431-5202

LAST RESORT
P. O. Box 144 (72642)
Rates: n/a
(870) 431-5681
(800) 799-5253

NEWLAND FLOAT TRIPS & LODGE
Rt 1, River Rd (72642)
Rates: n/a
(870) 431-8620
(800) 334-5604

TWIN FIN RESORT
P. O. Box 218 (72642)
Rates: n/a
(870) 431-5377
(800) 622-6291

LEAD HILL

BON TERRE INN
Hwy 281 N (72644)
Rates: n/a
(501) 436-7318

HILL TOP COTTAGES
Rt 1, Box 280 (72644)
Rates: n/a
(501) 436-5365

LITTLE ROCK

AMERISUITES
10920 Financial Center Pkwy (72209)
Rates: $89-$119
(501) 225-1075
(800) 833-1516

BAYMONT INN & SUITES
1010 Breckenridge Rd (72205)
Rates: $56-$63
(501) 225-7007
(800) 301-0200

BUDGET INN
9351 I-30 (72209)
Rates: n/a
(501) 565-0111

CIMARRON INN
10200 I-30 (72209)
Rates: n/a
(501) 565-1181

DAYS INN SOUTH
2600 W 65th St (72209)
Rates: $32-$60
(501) 562-1122
(800) 329-7466

DOUBLETREE HOTEL
424 W Markham (72201)
Rates: n/a
(501) 372-4371
(800) 937-2789

HAMPTON INN
6100 Mitchell Dr (72209)
Rates: $57-$75
(501) 562-6667
(800) 426-7866

HOLIDAY INN EXPRESS
3121 Bankhead Dr (72206)
Rates: $58-$68
(501) 490-4000
(800) 465-4329

HOLIDAY INN SELECT
201 S Shackelford (72211)
Rates: $98
(501) 223-3000
(800) 465-4329

JACK'S MOTEL
9515 Hwy 365 (72206)
Rates: n/a
(501) 897-4951

KNIGHTS INN
9709 I-30 (72209)
Rates: $33-$40
(501) 568-6800
(800) 843-5644

LA QUINTA INN
11701 I-30 (72209)
Rates: $65-$82
(501) 455-2300
(800) 687-6667

LA QUINTA INN
901 Fair Park Blvd (72204)
Rates: $59-$75
(501) 664-7000
(800) 687-6667

LA QUINTA INN
2401 W 65th St (72209)
Rates: $59-$76
(501) 568-1030
(800) 687-6667

LEGACY HOTEL
625 W Capitol (72201)
Rates: n/a
(501) 374-0100

MARKHAM INN
5120 W Markham (72205)
Rates: n/a
(501) 666-0161
(800) 654-0161

MOTEL 6-S EAST
7501 I-30 (72209)
Rates: $33-$40
(501) 568-8888
(800) 466-8356

AREA CODES - If the local number doesn't connect, check for a new area code.

MOTEL 6-WEST
10524 Markham St
(72205)
Rates: $39-$46
(501) 225-7366
(800) 466-8356

RED ROOF INN
7900 Scott
Hamilton Dr
(72209)
Rates: $38-$47
(501) 562-2694
(800) 843-7663

RESIDENCE INN BY MARRIOTT
1401 S Shackeford
Rd (72211)
Rates: $139
(501) 312-0200
(800) 331-3131

WILSON INN
4301 E Roosevelt
(72206)
Rates: $34-$54
(501) 376-2466

LONOKE

ECONOMY INN
Hwy 31 N & I-40
(72086)
Rates: n/a
(501) 676-3116
(800) 826-0778

PERRY'S MOTEL
200 Nathan Dr
(72086)
Rates: n/a
(501) 676-3181

MAGNOLIA

BEST WESTERN COACHMAN'S INN
420 E Main (71753)
Rates: $55-$60
(870) 234-6122
(800) 528-1234
(800) 237-6122

CASTLE INN MOTEL
912 E Main
(71753)
Rates: n/a
(501) 234-2262

FLAMINGO MOTEL
100 N Vine (71753)
Rates: n/a
(501) 234-4752

MALVERN

ECONOMY INN
Hwy 270 N
(71204)
Rates: n/a
(501) 332-2487
(800) 826-0778

TOWN HOUSE MOTEL
304 E Page Ave
(72104)
Rates: n/a
(501) 332-5437

MAMMOTH SPRING

RIVERVIEW MOTEL
P. O. Box 281
(72554)
Rates: n/a
(870) 625-3218

MARBLE FALLS

ERBIE LODGE
HCR 73, Box 145
(72648)
Rates: $90+
(870) 446-5851

MARION

BEST WESTERN REGENCY MOTOR INN
3635 I-55 (72364)
Rates: $48-$65
(870) 739-3278
(800) 528-1234

MARSHALL

ROSE MOTEL
P. O. Box 913
(72650)
Rates: n/a
(501) 448-2596

SUNSET MOTEL
P. O. Box 205
(72650)
Rates: n/a
(501) 448-3348

MAUMELLE

SUPER 8 MOTEL
14325 Frontier Dr
(72113)
Rates: $45-$65
(501) 851-3500
(800) 800-8000

MCGEHEE

BEST WESTERN
225 Hwy 65 N
(71654)
Rates: $44-$57
(800) 528-1234

SENATOR MOTEL
222 Hwy 65
(71654)
Rates: n/a
(501) 222-5511

MENA

AERIE B&B
Hwy 375 (71953)
Rates: n/a
(501) 394-6473

HOLIDAY MOTEL
1162 US 71 S
(71953)
Rates: n/a
(501) 394-2611

NANA'S COUNTRY INN
203 US 71 N
(71953)
Rates: n/a
(501) 394-6433

OZARK INN
2102 US 71 S
(71953)
Rates: $28-$35
(501) 394-1100

MIDWAY

HOLIDAY SHORES RESORT
943 Howard
Creek Rd (72651)
Rates: n/a
(870) 431-5370
(800) 365-4089

HOWARD CREEK RESORT
RR 1, Box 282
(72651)
Rates: n/a
(870) 431-5371

RED ARROW RESORT
Rt 1, Box 281
(72651)
Rates: n/a
(870) 431-5375
(800) 548-8724

SUNSET POINT RESORT
354 Westview Rd
(72651)
Rates: n/a
(870) 431-5372
(800) 336-8113

MONTICELLO

BEST WESTERN MONTICELLO INN
306 Hwy 425 N
(71655)
Rates: $43-$53
(870) 367-6771
(800) 528-1234

HIWAY HOST INN
617 W Gaines
(71655)
Rates: n/a
(501) 367-8555

MORRILTON

DAYS INN
1506 N SR 95
(72110)
Rates: $34-$52
(501) 354-5101
(800) 329-7466

SCOTTISH INNS
356 Hwy 95 & I-40
(72110)
Rates: n/a
(501) 354-0181
(800) 251-1962

MOUNT IDA

COLONIAL MOTEL
HC 63, Box 306
(71957)
Rates: n/a
(501) 867-2431

DENBY POINT LODGE & MARINA
SR 1, Box 241
(71957)
Rates: $35-$90
(501) 867-3651

MOUNT IDA MOTEL
HC 67, Box 67-X
(71957)
Rates: n/a
(501) 867-3456

MOUNTAIN HOME

BEST WESTERN CARRIAGE INN
963 US 62 E
(72653)
Rates: $45-$85
(870) 425-6001
(800) 528-1234

BLACKBURNS RESORT
Rt 6, Box 280
(72653)
Rates: n/a
(870) 492-5115

BLUE PARADISE RESORT
Rt 6, Box 379-CC
(72653)
Rates: $29-$46
(870) 492-5113

BUNGALOW RESORT
Rt 4, Box 439
(72653)
Rates: n/a
(870) 492-5105

BUZZARD ROOST INN
4271 Buzzard
Roost Rd (72653)
Rates: $39
(870) 492-5187

CHIT-CHAT-CHAW RESORT
9476 Promise
Land Rd (72653)
Rates: n/a
(870) 431-5584

DURBON'S NOE CREEK RESORT
Rt 1, Box 128
(72653)
Rates: n/a
(870) 431-5574
(800) 264-5574

EDGEWATER RESORT & LODGE
10108 Promise
Land Rd (72653)
Rates: n/a
(870) 431-5222

FISH & FIDDLE RESORT
Rt 10, Box 430
(72653)
Rates: n/a
(870) 491-5161

AREA CODES - If the local number doesn't connect, check for a new area code.

GENE'S TROUT FISHING RESORT
Rt 3, Box 348
(72653)
Rates: n/a
(870) 499-5381
(800) 256-3625

HOLIDAY INN
1350 Hwy 62 SW
(72653)
Rates: $42-$56
(870) 425-5101
(800) 465-4329

LASALLE RESORT
Rt 4, Box 485-C
(72653)
Rates: n/a
(870) 492-5133

MOCKINGBIRD BAY RESORT
Rt 3, Box 183-MH
(72653)
Rates: n/a
(870) 491-5112

MT HOME MOTEL
411 S Main (72653)
Rates: n/a
(870) 425-2171
(800) 413-2171

OZARKS OAKS MOTEL
147 S Main (72653)
Rates: n/a
(870) 425-4881

PEAL'S RESORT
Rt 3, Box 252
(72653)
Rates: n/a
(870) 499-5215

PROMISE LAND RESORT
323 CR 107
(72653)
Rates: n/a
(870) 431-5576
(888) 730-3799

RIM SHOALS TROUT RESORT
Rt 2, Box 594
(72653)
Rates: n/a
(870) 435-6695

ROCKING CHAIR RANCH
Rt 6, Box 445
(72653)
Rates: $39-$95
(870) 492-5157

ROCKY RIDGE RESORT
Rt 10, Box 610
(72653)
Rates: n/a
(501) 491-5665

ROYAL MOTEL RESORT
Rt 6, Box 500
(72653)
Rates: $33-$80
(870) 492-5288

SCOTT VALLEY RESORT & GUEST RANCH
P. O. Box 1447
(72653)
Rates: $77-$175
(870) 425-5136
(888) 855-7747

SILVER SADDLE APARTMENTS & MOTEL
128 N College St
(72653)
Rates: n/a
(870) 425-9998

SISTER CREEK RESORT
9833 Promise
Land Rd (72653)
Rates: n/a
(870) 531-5587

SPRING VALLEY MOTEL
548 Hwy 62 NE
(72653)
Rates: n/a
(870) 425-3717

SUNRISE POINT RESORT
Rt 10, Box 620-CC
(72653)
Rates: n/a
(870) 491-5188

TEAL POINT RESORT
715 Teal Point Rd
(72653)
Rates: $66-$90
(870) 492-5145

WATERTREE INN
Rt 4, Box 495
(72653)
Rates: n/a
(870) 492-6477

Y CABINS
Hwy 5 S & Hwy
177 (72653)
Rates: n/a
(870) 499-5294

MOUNTAIN VIEW

DAYS INN
Hwys 5, 9 & 14
(72560)
Rates: $35-$85
(870) 269-3287
(800) 329-7466

ECONO LODGE
619 Sylamor Ave
(72560)
Rates: $50-$75
(870) 269-3775
(800) 553-2666

HIDDEN VALLEY CABINS
P. O. Box 740
(72560)
Rates: n/a
(870) 269-2655

JACK'S FISHING RESORT & MOTEL
Hwy 5 N (72560)
Rates: n/a
(870) 585-2211

SYLAMORE LODGES
P. O. Box 1378
(72560)
Rates: n/a
(870) 585-2221
(800) 538-2221

MURFREES-BORO

AMERICAN HERITAGE INN
705 N Washington
(71958)
Rates: n/a
(501) 285-2131

LITTLE SHAMROCK MOTEL
919 N Washington
(71958)
Rates: n/a
(501) 285-2342

RIVERSIDE COTTAGE MOTEL
RFD 1 (71958)
Rates: n/a
(501) 285-2255

NASHVILLE

HOLIDAY MOTOR LODGE
Hwy 27-B S
(71852)
Rates: n/a
(501) 845-2953

NEWPORT

DAYS INN
101 Olivia Dr
(72112)
Rates: $50-$65
(501) 523-6411
(800) 329-7466

LAKESIDE INN
203 Malcolm Ave
(72112)
Rates: n/a
(501) 523-2787

NEWPORT MOTEL
1504 Hwy 67 N
(72112)
Rates: n/a
(501) 523-2768

PARK INN INTL
901 Hwy 67 N
(72112)
Rates: $47-$62
(501) 523-5851
(800) 437-7275

NORFOLK

WOODSMAN'S MOTEL
HC 61, Box 461
(82658)
Rates: n/a
(501) 499-7454

NORTH LITTLE ROCK

BAYMONT INN & SUITES
4311 Warden Rd
(72116)
Rates: $59-$66
(501) 758-8888
(800) 301-0200

DAYS INN
5800 Pritchard Dr
N (72117)
Rates: $40-$95
(501) 945-4100
(800) 329-7466

DAYS INN
7200 Bicentennial
Rd (72118)
Rates: $45-$110
(501) 851-3297
(800) 329-7466

HAMPTON INN
500 W 29th St
(72114)
Rates: $59-$70
(501) 771-2090
(800) 426-7866

HOWARD JOHNSON INN
111 W Pershing
Blvd (72114)
Rates: $59-$69
(501) 758-1440
(800) 446-4656

LA QUINTA INN
4100 E McCain
Blvd (72117)
Rates: $62-$82
(501) 945-0808
(800) 687-6667

MASTERS INN
2508 Jacksonville
Hwy (72117)
Rates: $30-$34
(501) 945-4167

MOTEL 6-NORTH
400 W 29th St
(72114)
Rates: $39-$46
(501) 758-5100
(800) 466-8356

RED ROOF INN
5571 Pritchard Dr
(72117)
Rates: n/a
(501) 945-0080
(800) 843-7663

SUPER 8 MOTEL
1 Grey Rd (72117)
Rates: $40-$49
(501) 945-0141
(800) 800-8000

TRAVELODGE
3100 N Main
(72116)
Rates: $50-$65
(501) 758-8110
(800) 578-7878

AREA CODES - If the local number doesn't connect, check for a new area code.

OAKLAND

BLACK OAK RESORT
P. O. Box 100 (72661)
Rates: n/a
(870) 431-8363

FIN 'N' FEATHER RESORT
Rt 1, Box 14 (72661)
Rates: n/a
(870) 431-5621

HENRY'S RESORT
Rt 1, Box 16 (72661)
Rates: n/a
(870) 431-5626

HIDDEN BAY RESORT
Rt 1, Box 320 (72661)
Rates: n/a
(870) 431-8121

PERSIMMON POINT RESORT
Rt 1, Box 169 (72661)
Rates: n/a
(870) 431-8877

SOUTHERN COMFORT RESORT
Rt 1, Box 40 (72661)
Rates: n/a
(870) 431-8470

OLA

MIMA'S MOTEL
P. O. Box 157 (72853)
Rates: n/a
(501) 489-5611

OMAHA

AUNT SHIRLEY'S SLEEPING LOFT
Rt 1, Box 84-D (72662)
Rates: n/a
(501) 426-5408

OSCEOLA

BEST WESTERN INN
I-55 & Hwy 140 (72370)
Rates: $50-$66
(870) 563-3222
(800) 528-1234

OZARK

BUDGET HOST MOTEL
1711 W Commercial (72949)
Rates: $28-$34
(501) 667-2166

OXFORD INN
305 N 18th St (72949)
Rates: $34-$41
(501) 667-1131

PARAGOULD

LINWOOD MOTEL
1611 Linwood Dr (72450)
Rates: n/a
(870) 236-7671

PARIS

BLAKELY INN
2010 E Walnut St (72855)
Rates: n/a
(501) 963-2400

PARTHENON

A CABIN IN THE WOODS
HCR 72, Box 134 (72666)
Rates: n/a
(501) 446-2293

PEA RIDGE

BATTLEFIELD INN MOTEL & RV PARK
14753 Hwy 62 E (72751)
Rates: n/a
(501) 451-1188

PERRYVILLE

COFFEE CREEK MOTEL
Harrisbrake (72126)
Rates: n/a
(501) 889-2745

PIGGOTT

OPEN ROADS MOTEL
148 Independent St (72454)
Rates: n/a
(501) 598-5941

PINE BLUFF

ADMIRAL BENBOW MOTEL
Box 5009 (71611)
Rates: $35-$48
(870) 535-8300

BEST WESTERN PINES
2700 E Harding (71601)
Rates: $53-$63
(870) 535-8640
(800) 528-1234

CLASSIC INN
4125 Rhinehart Rd (71601)
Rates: n/a
(870) 535-1200

DAYS INN
8006 Sheridan Rd (White Hall, 71602)
Rates: $47-$64
(870) 247-1339
(800) 329-7466

HAMPTON INN
3103 E Market St (71601)
Rates: $60-$70
(870) 850-0444
(800) 426-7866

POCAHONTAS

SCOTTISH INNS
1501 Hwy 67 N (72455)
Rates: $30-$38
(870) 892-4527
(800) 251-1962

PONCA

LOST VALLEY CANOE & LODGING
Hwy 43, Buffalo National River (72670)
Rates: n/a
(870) 861-5522

PRESCOTT

BROADWAY HOTEL
123 W 1st (71857)
Rates: n/a
(870) 887-5446

ECONO LODGE
1703 Hwy 371 W (71857)
Rates: $40-$60
(870) 887-6641
(800) 553-2666

ROGERS

BEAVER LAKE LODGE
14733 Dutchman Dr (72756)
Rates: $50-$56
(501) 925-2313
(800) 367-4513

DAYS INN
2102 S 8th St (72756)
Rates: $40-$125
(501) 636-3820
(800) 329-7466

HARTLAND LODGE
2931 W Walnut (72756)
Rates: n/a
(501) 631-6000
(800) 451-1588

HIWAY HOST INN
915 S 8th (72756)
Rates: n/a
(501) 636-9400

JAN-LIN MOTOR INN
1601 71-B S (72756)
Rates: n/a
(501) 636-1733

PARK INN INTERNATIONAL
3714 W Walnut (72756)
Rates: n/a
(501) 631-7000
(800) 437-7275

SECOND HOME BEAVER LAKE
100 W Locust (72756)
Rates: n/a
(501) 530-1773

SUPER 8 MOTEL
915 S 8th St (72756)
Rates: $37-$45
(501) 636-9600
(800) 800-8000

TANGLEWOOD LODGE
Rt 6 (72756)
Rates: n/a
(501) 925-2100

RUSSELLVILLE

BEST WESTERN
2326 N Arkansas Ave (72801)
Rates: $44-$58
(501) 967-1000
(800) 528-1234

HOLIDAY INN
2407 N Arkansas Ave (72801)
Rates: $65-$70
(501) 968-4300
(800) 465-4329

HOLLEY JOHNSON MOTEL
1206 E Main St (72801)
Rates: n/a
(501) 968-4959
(800) 465-4329

LAKESIDE RESORT MOTEL
3320 N Arkansas Ave (72801)
Rates: n/a
(501) 968-9715

MERRICK MOTEL
1320 E Main St (72801)
Rates: n/a
(501) 968-6332

MOTEL 6
215 W Birch St
(72801)
Rates: $27-$34
(501) 968-3666
(800) 466-8356

PARK MOTEL
2615 W Main St
(72801)
Rates: $26-$36
(501) 968-4862

SUNRISE INN
154 E Aspen Rd
(72801)
Rates: n/a
(501) 968-7200

SUPER 8 MOTEL
2404 N Arkansas
(72811)
Rates: $46-$59
(501) 968-8898
(800) 800-8000

TRAVELODGE
2200 N Arkansas
(72802)
Rates: $35-$50
(501) 968-4400
(800) 578-7878

**WOODY'S
CLASSIC INN**
1522 E Main St
(72801)
Rates: n/a
(501) 968-7774

SEARCY

COMFORT INN
107 S Rand Dr
(72143)
Rates: $45-$70
(501) 279-9100
(800) 228-5150

HAMPTON INN
3204 E Race Ave
(72143)
Rates: $59-$74
(501) 268-0654
(800) 426-7866

ROYAL INN
2203 E Race Ave
(72143)
Rates: $30-$45
(501) 268-3511

SILOAM SPRINGS

**EASTGATE
MOTOR LODGE**
1951 Hwy 412
(72761)
Rates: n/a
(501) 524-5157

SUPER 8 MOTEL
1800 Hwy 412 W
(72761)
Rates: $60-$65
(501) 524-8898
(800) 800-8000

SPRINGDALE

**BAYMONT INN
& SUITES**
1300 S 48th
(72764)
Rates: $51-$57
(501) 751-2626
(800) 301-0200

EXECUTIVE INN
2005 Hwy 71-B S
(72764)
Rates: $44-$49
(501) 756-6101

**HAMPTON INN
& SUITES**
1700 S 48th
(72762)
Rates: $79-$106
(501) 756-3500
(800) 426-7866

ST. JOE

**MAPLEWOOD
MOTEL**
P. O. Box 1 (72675)
Rates: n/a
(501) 439-2525

STAMPS

**LAFAYETTE
MOTEL**
Hwy 72 E (71860)
Rates: n/a
(501) 533-4333

STORY

AQUA MOTEL
HC 64, Box 105
(71970)
Rates: n/a
(501) 867-2123

STUTTGART

**BEST WESTERN
DUCK INN**
704 W Michigan
(72160)
Rates: $56-$100
(870) 673-2575
(800) 528-1234

SUPER 8 MOTEL
701 W Michigan
(72160)
Rates: $47-$55
(870) 673-2611
(800) 800-8000

**WALKER
MOTOR INN**
405 E Michigan
(72160)
Rates: n/a
(501) 673-2671

TEXARKANA

**BAYMONT INN
& SUITES**
5012 N State Line
Ave (75502)
Rates: $50-$55
(870) 773-1000
(800) 301-0200

**BEST WESTERN
KINGS ROW INN**
4200 N State Line
Ave (71854)
Rates: $50-$58
(870) 774-3851
(800) 528-1234
(800) 643-5464

FOUR STATES INN
4300 N State Line
Ave (75502)
Rates: $34-$42
(870) 773-3144

HOLIDAY INN
5100 N State Line
Ave (75503)
Rates: $68-$78
(870) 774-3521
(800) 465-4329

LA QUINTA INN
5201 N State Line
Ave (75503)
Rates: $46-$59
(870) 794-1900
(800) 687-6667

MOTEL 6-EAST
900 Realtor Ave
(71854)
Rates: $27-$34
(870) 772-0678
(800) 466-8356

**SHERATON
BUSINESS HOTEL**
5301 N State Line
Ave (75503)
Rates: $49-$71
(870) 792-3222

SHONEY'S INN
5210 N State Line
Ave (75504)
Rates: $65-$75
(870) 772-0070
(800) 222-2222

SUPER 8 MOTEL
325 E 51st St
(75502)
Rates: $35-$50
(870) 774-8888
(800) 800-8000

TRUMANN

WEEM'S MOTEL
404 Hwy 63 N
(72472)
Rates: n/a
(501) 483-6331

VAN BUREN

COMFORT INN
3131 Cloverleaf St
(72956)
Rates: $50-$89
(501) 474-2223
(800) 228-5150

MOTEL 6
1716 Fayetteville
Rd (72956)
Rates: $36-$52
(501) 474-8001
(800) 466-8356

SUPER 8 MOTEL
106 N Plaza Ct
(72956)
Rates: $49-$60
(501) 471-8888
(800) 800-8000

WALNUT RIDGE

**ALAMO COURT
MOTEL**
Hwy 67 S (72476)
Rates: $30-$95
(501) 886-2441
(800) 633-9575

PHILLIPS MOTEL
501 Hwy 67 N
(72476)
Rates: n/a
(501) 886-6767

WARREN

ECONOMY INN
108 E Church St
(71671)
Rates: n/a
(870) 226-5881

SUPER 8 MOTEL
1408 E Curch St
(71671)
Rates: $44-$59
(870) 226-9888
(800) 800-8000

**TOWN HOUSE
MOTEL**
201 E Church St
(71671)
Rates: n/a
(870) 226-5822

WEST HELENA

BEST WESTERN
1053 Hwy 49 W
(72390)
Rates: $50-$65
(870) 572-2592
(800) 528-1234
(800) 884-8632

**HARBOR INN
MOTEL**
Hwy 49-B (72390)
Rates: n/a
(870) 572-2597

SANDS MOTEL
Hwy 49-B (72390)
Rates: n/a
(870) 572-6774

WEST MEMPHIS

**BEST WESTERN
WEST MEMPHIS
INN**
3401 Service Loop
Rd (72302)
Rates: $43-$95
(870) 735-7185
(800) 528-1234

ECONO LODGE
2315 S Service Rd
(72303)
Rates: $45-$59
(870) 732-2830
(800) 553-2666

EXPRESS INN
3700 E Service Rd
(72301)
Rates: n/a
(870) 732-5688

MOTEL 6
2501 S Service Rd
(72301)
Rates: $36-$46
(870) 735-0100
(800) 466-8356

RED ROOF INN
1401 N Ingram
Blvd (72301)
Rates: n/a
(870) 735-7100
(800) 843-7663

SUPER 8 MOTEL
901 Martin Luther
King Jr. (72301)
Rates: $59-$68
(870) 735-8818
(800) 800-8000

WHEATLEY

RAMADA LIMITED
129 Lawson Rd
(72392)
Rates: $46-$55
(870) 457-2202
(800) 272-6232

WOOSTER

**PATTON HOUSE
BED & BREAKFAST**
Hwy 25, P. O. Box
61 (72181)
Rates: n/a
(501) 679-2975

WYNNE

**NATION WIDE 9
MOTEL**
706 Hwy 64 E
(72396)
Rates: n/a
(501) 238-9399

YELLVILLE

**SILVER RUN
CABINS**
14 Silver Run
Lane (72687)
Rates: n/a
(870) 449-6355
(800) 741-2022

**WILD BILL'S
OUTFITTERS-
MOTEL & CABINS**
23 Hwy 268E
(72687)
Rates: n/a
(870) 449-6235
(800) 554-8657

CALIFORNIA

ADELANTO

DAYS INN
11628 Bartlett Ave (92301)
Rates: $39-$89
(760) 246-8777
(800) 329-7466

AGOURA HILLS

RADISSON HOTEL
30100 Agoura Rd (91301)
Rates: $79+
(818) 707-1220
(800) 333-3333

AHWAHNEE

SILVER SPUR B&B
44625 Silver Spur Tr (93601)
Rates: $45-$60
(209) 683-2896

ALAMEDA

ISLANDER LODGE MOTEL
2428 Central Ave (94501)
Rates: $44-$59
(510) 865-2121

ALTURAS

BEST WESTERN TRAILSIDE INN
343 N Main St (96101)
Rates: $55-$65
(530) 233-4111
(800) 528-1234

DRIFTERS INN
395 Lake View Rd (96101)
Rates: $40+
(530) 233-2428

ESSEX MOTEL
1216 N Main St (96101)
Rates: $36-$42
(530) 233-2821

FRONTIER MOTEL
1033 N Main St (96101)
Rates: $28-$43
(530) 233-3383

HACIENDA MOTEL
201 E 12th St (96101)
Rates: $26-$45
(530) 233-3459

ANAHEIM

ANAHEIM HARBOR INN
2171 S Harbor Blvd (92802)
Rates: $44-$59
(714) 750-3100

ANAHEIM INN AT THE PARK
1855 S Harbor Blvd (92802)
Rates: $87-$97
(714) 750-1811
(800) 421-6662

BEST WESTERN ANAHEIM STARDUST
1057 W Ball Rd (92802)
Rates: $48-$115
(714) 774-7600
(800) 222-3639

BEST WESTERN RAFFLES INN & SUITES
2040 S Harbor Blvd (92802)
Rates: $59-$120
(714) 750-6100
(800) 528-1234
(800) 654-0196

CAVALIER INN & SUITES
11811 S Harbor Blvd (92802)
Rates: $35-$65
(714) 750-1000
(800) 821-2768

ECONO LODGE
1126 W Katella Ave (92802)
Rates: $35-$55
(714) 533-4505
(800) 553-2666

ECONO LODGE NORTH
2691 W La Palma Ave (92801)
Rates: $39-$69
(714) 826-8100
(800) 553-2666

HAWTHORN SUITES
1752 S Clementine St (92802)
Rates: $79-$89
(714) 535-7773
(800) 527-1133

HILTON & TOWERS
777 Convention Way (92802)
Rates: $88-$325
(714) 750-4321
(800) 233-6904

MARRIOTT HOTEL
700 W Convention Way (92802)
Rates: $125-$270
(714) 750-8000
(800) 228-9290

MOTEL 6-DISNEYLAND
100 W Freedman Way (92802)
Rates: $37-$56
(714) 520-9696
(800) 466-8356

MOTEL 6-FULLERTON EAST
1440 N State College (92806)
Rates: $36-$48
(714) 956-9690
(800) 466-8356

THE PAN PACIFIC
1717 South West St (92802)
Rates: $135-$175
(714) 999-0990
(800) 321-8976

PORTOFINO INN & SUITES
1831 S Harbor Blvd (92802)
Rates: $69-$169
(714) 491-2400
(88)8 296-5863

QUALITY HOTEL-MAINGATE
616 Convention Way (92802)
Rates: $99-$170
(714) 750-3131
(800) 228-5151
(800) 231-6215

RED ROOF INN
1251 N Harbor Blvd (92801)
Rates: $51-$80
(714) 635-6461
(800) 843-7663

RESIDENCE INN BY MARRIOTT
1700 S Clementine St (92801)
Rates: $178-$239
(714) 533-3555
(800) 331-3131

STATION INN & SUITES
989 W Ball Rd (92802)
Rates: $35-$65
(800) 874-6265

TRAVELODGE AT THE PARK
1166 W Katella Ave (92802)
Rates: $54-$105
(714) 774-7817
(800) 578-7878

ANAHEIM HILLS

BEST WESTERN ANAHEIM HILLS INN
5710 E La Palma (92807)
Rates: $89-$129
(714) 779-0252
(800) 528-1234
(800) 346-6662

ANDERSON

AMERIHOST INN
2040 Deschutes Rd (96007)
Rates: $59-$139
(530) 365-6100
(800) 434-5800

ANDERSON VALLEY INN
2861 McMurry Dr (96007)
Rates: $45-$65
(530) 365-2566

BEST WESTERN KNIGHTS INN
2688 Gateway Dr (96007)
Rates: $50-$60
(530) 365-2753
(800) 528-1234

ANGELS CAMP

ANGELS INN MOTEL
600 N Main St (95221)
Rates: $65-$120
(209) 736-4242
(888) 753-0226

ANTIOCH

BEST WESTERN HERITAGE INN
3210 Delta Fair Blvd (94509)
Rates: $64-$84
(925) 778-2000
(800) 528-1234

RAMADA INN
2436 Mahogany Way (94509)
Rates: $89-$125
(925) 754-6600
(800) 272-6232

APPLEGATE

ORIGINAL FIREHOUSE MOTEL
17855 Lake Arthur Rd (95703)
Rates: $34-$43
(916) 878-7770

APTOS

**APPLE LANE INN
BED & BREAKFAST**
6265 Soquel Dr
(95003)
Rates: $70-$175
(831) 475-6868
(800) 649-8988

**MANGELS HOUSE
BED & BREAKFAST**
570 Aptos Creek
Rd (95003)
Rates: $105-$135
(831) 688-7982

ARCADIA

MOTEL 6
225 Colorado Place
(91007)
Rates: $37-$51
(626) 446-2660
(800) 466-8356

**RESIDENCE INN
BY MARRIOTT**
321 E Huntington
Dr (91006)
Rates: $139-$169
(626) 446-6500
(800) 331-3131

ARCATA

**BEST WESTERN
ARCATA INN**
4827 Valley West
Blvd (95521)
Rates: $83-$87
(707) 826-0313
(800) 528-1234
(888) 646-6514

COMFORT INN
4701 Valley West
Blvd (95521)
Rates: $65-$170
(707) 826-2827
(800) 228-5150

HOTEL ARCATA
708 9th St (95521)
Rates: $72-$138
(707) 826-0217
(800) 344-1221

MOTEL 6
4755 Valley West
Blvd (95521)
Rates: $39-$54
(707) 822-7061
(800) 466-8356

**NORTH COAST
INN**
4975 Valley West
Blvd (95521)
Rates: $105-$140
(707) 822-4861

SUPER 8 MOTEL
4887 Valley West
Blvd (95521)
Rates: $49-$60
(707) 822-8888
(800) 800-8000

ARNOLD

**EBBETT'S PASS
LODGE**
1173 Hwy 4, PO
Box 2591 (95223)
Rates: $42-$59
(209) 795-1563
(800) 225-3764

**RELIABLE
VACATION
RENTALS**
P. O. Box 869
(95223)
Rates: $140-$200
(209) 795-4111

**SIERRA
VACATION
RENTALS**
P. O. Box 1080
(95223)
Rates: $130-$170
(800) 225-3764

**WEHE'S
MEADOWMONT
LODGE**
2011 Hwy 4
(95223)
Rates: $47-$58
(209) 795-1394
(800) 225-3764

ARROYO
GRANDE

ECONO LODGE
611 El Camino
Real (93420)
Rates: $55-$125
(805) 489-9300
(800) 553-2666

ATASCADERO

**LAKEVIEW BED
& BREAKFAST**
9065 Lakeview Dr
(93422)
Rates: $90
(805) 466-5665

MOTEL 6
9400 El Camino
Real (93422)
Rates: $31-$42
(805) 466-6701
(800) 466-8356

SUPER 8 MOTEL
6505 Morro Rd
(93422)
Rates: $49-$125
(805) 466-0794
(800) 800-8000

AUBURN

**BEST INN
& SUITES**
1875 Auburn
Ravine Rd (95603)
Rates: $64-$120
(530) 885-1800
(800) 237-8466

**BEST WESTERN
GOLDEN KEY
MOTEL**
13450 Lincoln
Way (95603)
Rates: $68-$82
(530) 885-8611
(800) 528-1234
(800) 201-0121

HOLIDAY INN
120 Grass Valley
Hwy (95603)
Rates: $109
(530) 887-8787
(800) 465-4329
(800) 814-8787

TRAVELODGE
13480 Lincoln
Way (95603)
Rates: $49-$79
(530) 885-7025
(800) 478-7878

AVALON
(Catalina Island)

**BEST WESTERN
CATALINA
CANYON RESORT
& SPA**
888 Country Club
Dr (90704)
Rates: $159-$250
(310) 510-0325
(800) 528-1234
(888) 478-7829

BADGER

**BADGER INN
MOTEL**
49496 Hwy 245
(93603)
Rates: $75-$85
(559) 337-0022
(800) 223-4374

BAKER

BUN BOY MOTEL
I-15 & SR 127
(92309)
Rates: $30-$53
(760) 733-4363

BAKERSFIELD

BEST INN
200 Trask St
(93312)
Rates: $40-$54
(661) 764-5221
(800) 237-8466

**BEST WESTERN
HERITAGE INN**
253 Trask (93312)
Rates: $50-$65
(661) 764-6268
(800 528-1234

**BEST WESTERN
HILL HOUSE INN**
700 Truxtun Ave
(93301)
Rates: $54-$89
(661) 327-4064
(800) 528-1234

**BEST WESTERN
INN**
2620 Buck Owens
Blvd (93308)
Rates: $49-$79
(661) 327-9651
(800) 528-1234

CALIFORNIA INN
1030 Wible Road
(93304)
Rates: $36-$42
(661) 834-3377

COMFORT INN
830 Wible Rd
(93304)
Rates: $36-$89
(661) 831-1922
(800) 228-5150

**DAYS INN
& SUITES**
2700 White Ln
(93304)
Rates: $49-$79
(661) 396-8417
(800) 329-7466

**DOUBLETREE
HOTEL**
3100 Camino Del
Rio Ct (93308)
Rates: $99-$175
(661) 323-7111
(800) 222-8733

**ECONOMY INNS
OF AMERICA**
6100 Knudsen Dr
(93308)
Rates: $30+
(661) 392-1800
(800) 826-0778

**ECONOMY INNS
OF AMERICA**
6501 Colony St
(93307)
Rates: $26-$45
(661) 831-9200
(800) 826-0778

LA QUINTA INN
3232 Riverside Dr
(93308)
Rates: $59-$79
(661) 325-7400
(800) 687-6667

LONE OAK INN
10614 Rosedale
Hwy (93312)
Rates: $39-$49
(661) 589-6600

**MOTEL 6
AIRPORT**
5241 Olive Tree Ct
(93308)
Rates: $30-$40
(661) 392-9700
(800) 466-8356

**MOTEL 6
CONV CENTER**
1350 Easton Dr
(93309)
Rates: $32-$44
(661) 327-1686
(800) 466-8356

MOTEL 6 EAST
8223 E Brundage
Ln (93307)
Rates: $31-$42
(661) 366-7231
(800) 466-8356

MOTEL 6 SOUTH
2727 White Lane
(93304)
Rates: $31-$42
(661) 834-2828
(800) 466-8356

OXFORD INN & SUITES
4500 Pierce Rd
(93308)
Rates: $44-$60
(661) 324-5555

PARKWAY INN
3535 Rosedale
Hwy (93304)
Rates: $45-$75
(661) 327-0681

QUALITY INN
1011 Oak St
(93304)
Rates: $46-$66
(661) 325-0772
(800) 228-5151

RESIDENCE INN BY MARRIOTT
4241 Chester Ln
(93309)
Rates: $115-$165
(661) 321-9800
(800) 331-3131

RIO BRAVO RESORT
11200 Lake Ming
Rd (93306)
Rates: $65-$108
(661) 872-5000
(800) 282-5000

ROYAL OAK INN
889 Oak St (93304)
Rates: $38-$52
(661) 324-9686

TRAVELODGE
818 Real Rd
(93309)
Rates: $47-$69
(661) 324-6666
(800) 578-7878

BALDWIN PARK

MOTEL 6
14510 Garvey Ave
(91706)
Rates: $33-$44
(626) 960-5011
(800) 466-8356

RADISSON HOTEL-SAN GABRIEL VALLEY
14635 Baldwin
Park Towne Ctr
(91706)
Rates: $94-$109
(626) 962-6000
(800) 333-3333

BANNING

DAYS INN
2320 W Ramsey St
(92220)
Rates: $55-$75
(909) 849-0509
(800) 329-7466

SUPER 8 MOTEL
1690 W Ramsey St
(92220)
Rates: $44-$59
(909) 849-6887
(800) 800-8000

BARSTOW

ASTRO BUDGET MOTEL
1271 E Main St
(92311)
Rates: $22-$38
(760) 256-2204

BEST MOTEL
1281 E Main St
(92311)
Rates: $30-$38
(760) 256-6836

BEST WESTERN DESERT VILLA INN
1984 E Main St
(92311)
Rates: $70-$85
(760) 256-1781
(800) 528-1234
(877) 498-1652

BUDGET INN
1111 E Main St
(92311)
Rates: $20-$40
(760) 256-1063

DAYS INN
1590 Coolwater
Ln (92311)
Rates: $30-$50
(760) 256-1737
(800) 329-7466

DESERT INN MOTEL
1100 E Main St
(92311)
Rates: $28-$38
(760) 256-2146

ECONO LODGE
1230 E Main St
(92311)
Rates: $26-$55
(760) 256-2133
(800) 553-2666

EL RANCHO MOTEL
112 E Main St
(92311)
Rates: $19-$31
(760) 256-2401

EXECUTIVE INN
1261 E Main St
(923118
Rates: $25-$50
(760) 256-7581

GATEWAY MOTEL
1630 E Main St
(92311)
Rates: $22-$52
(760) 256-8931

GOOD NITE INN
2551 Commerce
Pkwy (92311)
Rates: $51-$85
(760) 253-2121
(800) 648-3466

HOLIDAY INN EXP
1861 W Main St
(92311)
Rates: 69-$109
(760) 256-1300
(800) 465-4329

MOTEL 6
150 N Yucca Ave
(92311)
Rates: $30-$38
(760) 256-1752
(800) 466-8356

QUALITY INN
1520 E Main St
(92311)
Rates: $49-$64
(760) 256-6891
(800) 228-5151

RODEWAY INN
31951 E Main
(92311)
Rates: $29-$36
(760) 252-2055
(800) 228-2000

SAGE MOTEL
220 W Main St
(92311)
Rates: $18-$24
(760) 256-2116

STARDUST INN
901 E Main St
(92311)
Rates: $30-$50
(760) 256-7116

SUNSET INN
1350 W Main St
(92311)
Rates: $24-$35
(760) 256-8921

SUPER 8 MOTEL
170 Coolwater Ln
(92311)
Rates: $52-$59
(760) 256-8443
(800) 800-8000

BASS LAKE

FORK'S RESORT
39150 Rd 222
(93604)
Rates: $75-$125
(209) 642-3737

THE LAKEHOUSE BED & BREAKFAST
39131 Lake Dr
(93604)
Rates: $115-$195
(209) 683-8220

BEAUMONT

BEST WESTERN EL RANCHO MOTOR INN
480 E 5th St
(92223)
Rates: $32-$105
(909) 834-2176
(800) 528-1234

BUDGET HOST INN
625 E 5th St
(92223)
Rates: $36-$50
(909) 845-2185
(800) 283-4678

WINDSOR MOTEL
1265 E 6th St
(92223)
Rates: $34-$44
(909) 845-1436

BELLFLOWER

MOTEL 6
17220 Downey
Ave (90706)
Rates: $37-$48
(562) 531-3933
(800) 466-8356

BELMONT

MOTEL 6
1101 Shoreway Rd
(94002)
Rates: $60-$86
(650) 591-1471
(800) 466-8356

BEN LOMOND

CHATEAU DES FLEAURS B&B
7995 Hwy 9
(95005)
Rates: $95-$120
(831) 336-8943
(800) 596-1133

TYROLEAN INN & COTTAGES
9600 Hwy 9
(95005)
Rates: $43-$60
(831) 336-5188

BENICIA

BEST WESTERN HERITAGE INN
1955 E 2nd St
(94510)
Rates: $70-$105
(707) 746-0401
(800) 528-1234

THE PAINTED LADY B&B
141 East F St
(94510)
Rates: $70-$85
(707) 746-1646

BERKELEY

BEAU SKY HOTEL
2520 Durant Ave
(94704)
Rates: $60-$85
(510) 540-7688

GOLDEN BEAR MOTEL
1620 San Pablo
Ave (94702)
Rates: $54-$175
(510) 525-6770
(800) 252-6770

RAMADA INN
920 University
Ave (94710)
Rates: $69-$89
(510) 849-1121
(800) 272-6232

BERRY CREEK

**LAKE OROVILLE
BED & BREAKFST**
240 Sunday Dr
(95916)
Rates: $105-$155
(530) 589-0700

BEVERLY HILLS

**BEVERLY HILTON
HOTEL**
9876 Wilshire Blvd
(90210)
Rates: $270-$330
(310) 274-7777
(800) 922-5432

**FOUR SEASONS
BEVERLY HLLS**
300 S Doheny Dr
(90048)
Rates: $345-$1300
(310) 273-2222
(800) 332-3442

**HOTEL NIKKO AT
BEVERLY HILLS**
465 S La Cienega
Blvd (90048)
Rates: $270-$700
(310) 247-0400
(800) 645-5687

**HOTEL SOFITEL
MA MAISON**
8555 Beverly Blvd
(90048)
Rates: $229-$344
(310) 278-5444
(800) 521-7772

**L'ERMITAGE
BEVERLY HILLS**
9291 Burton Way
(90210)
Rates: $418-$448
(310) 278-3344

**THE REGENT
BEVERLY
WILSHIRE**
9500 Wilshire Blvd
(90212)
Rates: $350-$770
(310) 275-5200
(800) 421-4354

BIG BEAR LAKE

**ALPINE VILLAGE
SUITES LODGE**
546 Pine Knot Ave
(92315)
Rates: $109-$145
(909) 866-5460

**BEAR CLAW
CABINS**
586 Main St
(92315)
Rates: $55-$94
(909) 866-7633

**BEAR VALLEY
MTN HOMES**
1301 E Big Bear
Blvd (92314)
Rates: $45+
(909) 585-0500

BIG BEAR CABINS
39774 Big Bear
Blvd (92315)
Rates: $59-$149
(909) 866-2723

**BIG BEAR LAKE
INN**
39471 Big Bear
Lake Blvd (92315)
Rates: $79-$99
(909) 866-3477

**BLACK FOREST
LODGE**
P. O. Box 156
(92315)
Rates: $38-$110
(909) 866-2166
(800) 255-4378

**BOULDER CREEK
RESORT**
Box 92 (92315)
Rates: $45-$300
(909) 866-2665
(800) 244-2327

CAL-PINE CABINS
41545 Big Bear
Blvd (92315)
Rates: $59-$175
(909) 866-2574

**COZY HOLLOW
LODGE**
40409 Big Bear
Blvd (92315)
Rates: $79-$139
(909) 866-8886
(800) 882-4480

**CREEK RUNNER'S
LODGE**
374 Gerogia St
(92315)
Rates: $50-$200
(909) 866-7473

**EAGLE'S NEST
BED & BREAKFAST**
41675 Big Bear
Blvd (92315)
Rates: $85-$150
(909) 866-6465
(888) 866-6465

EDGEWATER INN
40570 Simonds Dr
(92315)
Rates: $89-$99
(909) 866-4161

**FRONTIER LODGE
& MOTEL**
40472 Big Bear
Blvd (92315)
Rates: $79-$290
(909) 866-5888
(800) 457-6401

**GOLD MOUNTAIN
VACATION
RENTAL**
1117 Anita St
(92314)
Rates: $75-$180
(909) 585-6997
(800) 509-2604

**GOLDEN BEAR
COTTAGES**
39367 Big Bear
Blvd (92315)
Rates: $69-$119
(909) 866-2010

**GREY SQUIRREL
RESORT**
39372 Big Bear
Blvd (92315)
Rates: $68-$155
(909) 866-4335

THE GRIZZLY INN
39756 Big Bear
Blvd (92315)
Rates: $55+
(800) 423-2742

**HAPPY BEAR
VACATION RNTLS**
42000 Big Bear
Blvd (92315)
Rates: n/a
(909) 866-7744
(800) 766-9766

**HAPPY BEAR
VILLAGE RESORT**
40154 Big Bear
Blvd (92315)
Rates: $65-$165
(909) 866-2415
(800) 352-8581

**HONEY BEAR
LODGE**
40994 Pennsylvania
(92315)
Rates: $49-$259
(909) 866-7825
(800) 628-8714

MOTEL 6
42899 Big Bear
Blvd (92315)
Rates: $37-$60
(909) 585-6666
(800) 466-8356

**THE MOUNTAIN
INN**
P. O. Box 3706
(92315)
Rates: $39-$199
(909) 866-7444
(800) 544-7454

**QUAIL COVE
LODGE**
39117 N Shore Dr
(92315)
Rates: $89-$229
(909) 866-5957
(800) 595-3683

ROBINHOOD INN
40797 Lakeview
Dr (92315)
Rates: $54-$279
(909) 866-4643

**SHORE ACRES
LODGE**
40090 Lakeview
Dr (92315)
Rates: $95-$350
(909) 866-8200
(800) 524-6600

**SMOKETREE
RESORT**
40210 Big Bear
Blvd (92315)
Rates: $49-$167
(909) 866-2415
(800) 352-8581

**SNUGGLE CREEK
LODGE**
40440 Big Bear
Blvd (92315)
Rates: $79-$109
(909) 866-2555

**STAGE COACH
LODGE
COTTAGES**
652 Jeffries (92315)
Rates: $84-$300
(909) 878-3088
(800) 756-9871

**TIMBER HAVEN
LODGE**
877 Tulip Ln
(92315)
Rates: $49-$179
(909) 866-3568

**TIMBERLINE
LODGE**
39921 Big Bear
Blvd (92315)
Rates: $71-$200
(909) 866-4141
(800) 352-8581

**WILDWOOD
RESORT
COTTAGES**
40210 Big Bear
Blvd (92315)
Rates: $66-$148
(909) 876-2178

**WISHING WELL
MOTEL**
540 Pine Knot
(92315)
Rates: $69-$99
(909) 866-3505
(800) 541-3505

BIG PINE

BIG PINE MOTEL
370 S Main (93515)
Rates: $30-$46
(760) 938-2282

**BRISTLECONE
MOTEL**
101 N Main
(93513)
Rates: $34-$48
(760) 938-2067

BISHOP

**BEST WESTERN
CREEKSIDE INN**
725 N Main St
(93514)
Rates: $99-$151
(760) 872-3044
(800) 528-1234
(800) 273-34550

BEST WESTERN HOLIDAY SPA LODGE
1025 N Main St
(93514)
Rates: $65-$99
(760) 873-3543
(800) 528-1234
(800) 576-3543

COMFORT INN
805 N Main St
(93514)
Rates: $59-$99
(760) 873-4284
(800) 576-4080
(800) 228-5150

DAYS INN
724 W Line St
(93514)
Rates: $49-$119
(760) 872-1095
(800) 329-7466

MOTEL 6
1005 N Main St
(93514)
Rates: $39-$89
(760) 873-8426
(800) 466-8356

RODEWAY INN
150 E Elm St
(93514)
Rates: $60-$90
(760) 873-3564
(800) 228-2000

SIERRA FOOTHILLS MOTEL
535 S Main (93514)
Rates: $43-$55
(760) 872-1386

SPORTSMAN'S LODGE
636 N Main St
(93514)
Rates: $25-$70
(760) 872-2423

SUNRISE MOTEL
262 W Grove St
(93514)
Rates: $33+
(760) 873-3656

SUPER 8 MOTEL
535 S Main St
(93514)
Rates: $60-$70
(760) 872-1386
(800) 800-8000

THUNDERBIRD MOTEL
190 W Pine St
(93514)
Rates: $50-$99
(760) 873-4215

VAGABOND INN
1030 N Main St
(93514)
Rates: $67-$78
(760) 873-6351
(800) 522-1555

VILLAGE MOTEL
286 W Elm St
(93514)
Rates: $35+
(760) 873-3545

BLAIRSDEN

FEATHER RIVER PARK RESORT
Hwy 89, Box 37
(96103)
Rates: $82-$182
(530) 836-2328

LAYMAN RESORT
Hwy 70, Box 8
(96103)
Rates: $48-$55
(530) 836-2511
(800) 635-8788

RIVER PINES RESORT
8296 Hwy 89
(96103)
Rates: $50-$75
(530) 836-2552
(800) 696-2551

BLYTHE

ASTRO MOTEL
801 E Hobsonway
(92225)
Rates: $25-$42
(760) 922-6101

BEST WESTERN SAHARA MOTEL
825 W Hobsonway
(92225)
Rates: $75-$119
(760) 922-7105
(800) 528-1234

COMFORT INN
903 W Hobsonway
(92225)
Rates: $75-$110
(760) 922-4146
(800) 228-5150

ECONO LODGE
1020 W Hobsonway
(92225)
Rates: $45-$100
(760) 922-3161
(800) 553-2666

HOLIDAY INN EXPRESS
600 W Donlon St
(92225)
Rates: $85-$139
(760) 921-2300
(800) 465-4329

MOTEL 6
500 W Donlon St
(92225)
Rates: $35-$42
(760) 922-6666
(800) 466-8356

SUPER 8 MOTEL
550 W Donlon St
(92225)
Rates: $42-$78
(760) 922-8881
(800) 800-8000

TROPICS INN & SUITES
9274 E Hobsonway
(92225)
Rates: $50-$85
(760) 922-5101

BOLINAS

PARROT'S COVE VACATION RENTALS
P O Box 86 (94924)
Rates: $100-$150
(415) 868-9588
(888) 844-8255

BOONVILLE

ANDERSON CREEK INN B&B
12050 Anderson
Valley Way
(95415)
Rates: $110-$170
(707) 895-3091
(800) 552-6202

BORREGO SPRINGS

STANLUNDS DESERT MOTEL
2771 Borrego
Springs Rd
(92004)
Rates: $50-$65
(760) 767-5501

BRAWLEY

TOWN HOUSE LODGE
135 Main St
(92227)
Rates: $49-$55
(760) 344-5120

BREA

HOMESTEAD VILLAGE EXTENDED STAY
3050 E Imperial
Blvd (92621)
Rates: $59-$94
(714) 528-2500
(888) 782-9473

HYLAND MOTEL
727 S Brea Blvd
(92621)
Rates: $45-$50
(714) 990-6867

WOODFIN SUITE HOTEL
3100 E Imperial
Hwy (92621)
Rates: $159-$199
(714) 579-3200
(800) 237-8811

BRIDGEPORT

BEST WESTERN RUBY INN
333 Main St
(93517)
Rates: $85-$175
(760) 932-7241
(800) 528-1234

REDWOOD MOTEL
425 Main St
(93517)
Rates: $60-$90
(760) 932-7060
(888) 932-3292

SILVER MAPLE INN
310 Main St
(93517)
Rates: $55-$80
(760) 932-7383

WALKER RIVER LODGE
100 Main St
(93517)
Rates: $70-$140
(760) 932-7021
(800) 688-3351

BROOKDALE

BROOKDALE LODGE
11570 Hwy 9
(95007)
Rates: $44-$60
(408) 338-6433

BUELLTON

ECONO LODGE
630 Ave of Flags
(93427)
Rates: $45-$99
(805) 688-0022
(800) 553-2666

MOTEL 6
333 McMurray Rd
(93427)
Rates: $40-$66
(805) 688-7797
(800) 466-8356

RANCHO SANTA BARBARA MARRIOTT
555 McMurray Rd
(93427)
Rates: $125+
(805) 688-1000
(800) 638-8882

BUENA PARK

BEST WESTERN BUENA PARK INN
8580 Stanton Ave
(90620)
Rates: $42-$69
(714) 828-5211
(800) 528-1234
(800) 646-1629

COLONY INN
7800 Crescent Ave
(90620)
Rates: $32-$55
(714) 527-2201
(800) 982-6566

COVERED WAGON MOTEL
7830 Crescent Ave
(90620)
Rates: $28-$32
(714) 995-0033

DAYS INN
7640 Beach Blvd
(90620)
Rates: $40-$85
(714) 522-8461
(800) 329-7466

GUESTHOUSE INN
7878 Crescent Ave (90620)
Rates: n/a
(714) 527-1515

INN SUITES HOTEL
7555 Beach Blvd (90620)
Rates: $99-$109
(714) 522-7360
(888) 522-5885

MOTEL 6-KNOTTS BERRY FARM/ DISNEYLAND
7051 Valley View (90620)
Rates: $33-$46
(714) 522-1200
(800) 466-8356

BURBANK

HILTON HOTEL & CC/AIRPORT
2500 Hollywood Way (91505)
Rates: $110-$270
(818) 843-6000
(800) 445-8667

HOLIDAY INN
150 E Angeleno (91510)
Rates: $123-$133
(818) 841-4770
(800) 465-4329

BURLINGAME

EMBASSY SUITES
150 Anza Blvd. (94010)
Rates: $139-$234
(650) 342-4600
(800) 362-2779

MARRIOTT SF AIRPORT
1800 Old Bayshore Hwy (94010)
Rates: $199-$249
(650) 692-9100
(800) 228-9290

RED ROOF INN
777 Airport Blvd (94010)
Rates: $110-$150
(650) 342-7772
(800) 843-7663

VAGABOND INN SF AIRPORT
1640 Old Bayshore Hwy (94010)
Rates: $89-$115
(650) 692-4040
(800) 522-1555

BURNEY

CHARM MOTEL
37363 Main St (96013)
Rates: $47-$64
(530) 335-2254

GREEN GABLES MOTEL
37385 Main St (96013)
Rates: $47-$65
(530) 335-2264

SHASTA PINES MOTEL
37386 Main St (96013)
Rates: $35-$69
(530) 335-2201

SLEEPY HOLLOW LODGE
36898 Main St (96013)
Rates: $30-$60
(530) 335-2285

BUTTONWILLOW

GOOD NITE INN
20645 Tracy Ave (93206)
Rates: $27-$39
(661) 764-5121
(800) 648-3466

MOTEL 6
20638 Tracy Ave (93206)
Rates: $29-$38
(661) 764-5153
(800) 466-8356

SUPER 8 MOTEL
20681 Tracy Ave (93206)
Rates: $37-$52
(661) 764-5117
(800) 800-8000

CAJON PASS

ECONOMY INNS OF AMERICA
8317 Hwy 138 (92371)
Rates: $48-$57
(619) 249-6777
(800) 826-0778

CALABASAS

GOOD NITE INN
26557 Agoura Rd (91302)
Rates: $55-$70
(818) 880-6000
(800) 648-3466

CALIMESA

CALIMESA INN MOTEL
1205 Calimesa Blvd (92320)
Rates: $45-$60
(909) 795-2536

CALIPATRIA

CALIPATRIA INN
700 N Sorenson (92233)
Rates: $59-$74
(760) 348-7348

CALISTOGA

MEADOWLARK COUNTRY HOUSE
601 Petrified Forest Rd (94515)
Rates: $125-$150
(707) 942-5651

PINK MANSION
1415 Foothill Blvd (94515)
Rates: $85-$160
(707) 942-0558

TRIPLE "S" RANCH
4600 Mtn Home Ranch Rd (94515)
Rates: $42-$59
(707) 942-6730

WASHINGTON STREET LODGING
1605 Washington St (94515)
Rates: $90-$105
(707) 942-6968

CALPINE

SIERRA VALLEY LODGE
Box 115 (96124)
Rates: $38-$42
(530) 994-3367
(800) 858-0322

CAMARILLO

GOOD NITE INN
1100 Ventura Blvd (93010)
Rates: $45-$50
(805) 388-5644
(800) 648-3466

MOTEL 6
1641 E Daily Dr (93010)
Rates: $34-$51
(805) 388-3467
(800) 466-8356

CAMBRIA

CAMBRIA PINES LODGE
2905 Burton Dr (93428)
Rates: $60-$120
(805) 927-4200
(800) 445-6868

CAMBRIA SHORES INN
6276 Moonstone Beach Dr (93428)
Rates: $65-$135
(805) 927-8644
(800) 433-9179

CAMERON PARK

BEST WESTERN CAMERON PARK
3361 Coach Ln (95682)
Rates: $62-$74
(530) 677-2203
(800) 528-1234
(800) 601-1234

CAMPBELL

MOTEL 6
1240 Camden Ave (95008)
Rates: $64-$76
(408) 371-8870
(800) 466-8356

RESIDENCE INN BY MARRIOTT
2761 S Bascom Ave (95008)
Rates: $79-$159
(408) 559-1551
(800) 331-3131

CANOGA PARK

SUPER 8 MOTEL
7631 Topanga Canyon Blvd (91304)
Rates: $49-$73
(818) 883-8888
(800) 800-8000

CAPITOLA

CAPITOLA INN
822 Bay Ave (95010)
Rates: $75-$175
(831) 462-3004

EL SALTO BY THE SEA B&B
620 El Salto Dr (95010)
Rates: $100-$185
(831) 462-6365

SUMMER HOUSE BED & BREAKFST
216 Monterey Ave (95010)
Rates: $75
(831) 475-8474

CARLSBAD

FOUR SEASONS RESORT AVIARA
7100 Four Seasons Point (92009)
Rates: $415-$525
(760) 603-6800

INNS OF AMERICA
751 Raintree Dr (92009)
Rates: $80-$90
(760) 931-1185
(800) 826-0778

MOTEL 6
1006 Carlsbad Vllge Dr (92008)
Rates: $40-$61
(760) 434-7135
(800) 466-8356

MOTEL 6 EAST
6117 Paseo del
Norte (92009)
Rates: $37-$52
(760) 438-1242
(800) 466-8356

MOTEL 6 SOUTH
750 Raintree Dr
(92009)
Rates: $37-$50
(760) 431-0745
(800) 466-8356

CARMEL

**BEST WESTERN
CARMEL MISSION
INN**
3665 Rio Rd
(93922)
Rates: $129-$239
(831) 624-1841
(800) 528-1234
(800) 348-9090

BRIARWOOD INN
San Carlos
between 4th & 5th
(93921)
Rates: $150-$295
(831) 626-9056
(800) 999-8788

**CARMEL
COUNTRY INN
BED & BREAKFST**
Dolores & 3rd Ave
(93921)
Rates: $95-$205
(831) 625-3263

**CARMEL GARDEN
COURT B&B**
4th Ave & Torres
St (93921)
Rates: $150-$265
(831) 624-6926

**CARMEL RIVER
INN COMPLEX**
Carmel River
Bridge at Oliver
Rd (93921)
Rates: $100-$180
(831) 624-1575
(800) 882-8142

**CARMEL
TRADEWINDS INN**
Mission & 3rd Ave
(93921)
Rates: $99-$250
(831) 624-2776
(800) 624-6665

**CASA DE CARMEL
INN**
Ocean & 7th Ave
(93921)
Rates: $115-$125
(831) 624-2429
(800) 262-1262

**COACHMAN'S
INN**
San Carlos St &
7th Ave (93921)
Rates: $95-$275
(831) 624-6421
(800) 336-6421

CYPRESS INN
Lincoln St & 7th
Ave (93921)
Rates: $125-$350
(831) 624-3871
(800) 443-7443

**FOREST LODGE
BED & BREAKFAST**
P. O. Box 1316
(93921)
Rates: $149-$300
(831) 624-7023

**HIGHLANDS INN-
A PARK HYATT
HOTEL**
Hwy 1 in Carmel
Highlands (93921)
Rates: $200-$850
(831) 624-3801
(800) 2331234
(800) 682-4811

**LAMPLIGHTER'S
INN**
Ocean & Camino
Real (93921)
Rates: $119-$259
(831) 624-7372

**LINCOLN GREEN
INN**
Carmelo between
15th/16th (93921)
Rates: $185
(831) 624-7738
(831) 624-1880
(800) 262-1262

**SUNSET HOUSE
BED & BREAKFAST**
Ocean on Camino
Real (93921)
Rates: $190-$230
(831) 624-4884

**VAGABOND
HOUSE INN B&B**
Dolores & 4th Ave
(93921)
Rates: $95-$205
(831) 624-7738
(800) 262-1262

WAYSIDE INN
Mission & 7th Ave
(93921)
Rates: $99-$259
(831) 624-5336
(800) 433-4732

CARMEL VALLEY

BLUE SKY LODGE
Flight Rd (93924)
Rates: $55-$109
(831) 659-2935
(800) 733-2160

**CARMEL
COUNTRY SPA**
10 Country Club
Way (93923)
Rates: $85+
(831) 659-5466

**CARMEL VALLEY
LODGE**
8 Ford Rd (93924)
Rates: $139-$309
(831) 659-2261
(800) 641-4646

**CARMEL VALLEY
RANCH**
1 Old Ranch Rd
(93923)
Rates: $265-$750
(831) 625-9500
(800) 541-3113

**QUAIL LODGE
RESORT & GOLF**
8205 Valley
Greens Dr (93923)
Rates: $295-$1350
(831) 624-2888
(888) 828-8787
(800) 538-9516

CARPTINERIA

**BEST WESTERN
CARPINTERIA INN**
4558 Carpinteria
Ave (93013)
Rates: $89-$135
(805) 684-0473
(800) 528-1234
(888) 769-5611

COMFORT SUITES
5606 Carpinteria
Ave (93013)
Rates: $75-$124
(805) 566-9499
(800) 228-5150
(888) 409-8300

MOTEL 6-NORTH
4200 Via Real
(93013)
Rates: $36-$46
(805) 684-6921
(800) 466-8356

MOTEL 6-SOUTH
5550 Carpinteria
Ave (93013)
Rates: $39-$56
(805) 684-8602
(800) 466-8356

CASTAIC

COMFORT INN
31558 Castaic Rd
(91384)
Rates: $64-$89
(661) 295-1100
(800) 228-5150

CASTROVILLE

**CASTROVILLE
MOTEL**
11656 Merritt St
(95012)
Rates: $36-$48
(831) 633-2502

CATALINA
ISLAND
(See Avalon)

CATHEDRAL
CITY

**CHARLEENE APTS
MOTEL**
37-112 Palo Verde
Dr (92234)
Rates: $40-$65
(760) 328-5427

DAYS INN SUITES
69-151 E Palm
Canyon Dr
(92234)
Rates: $220
(760) 324-5939
(800) 329-7466

**DORAL PALM
SPRINGS RESORT**
67-967 Vista Chino
(92234)
Rates: $169-$330
(760) 322-7000
(888) 337-0996

**EMERALD COURT
HOTEL**
69-375 Ramon Rd
(92234)
Rates: $35-$70
(760) 324-4521

CAYUCOS

**CYPRESS TREE
MOTEL**
125 S Ocean Ave
(93430)
Rates: $50-$90
(805) 995-3917
(800) 241-4289

DOLPHIN INN
399 S Ocean Ave
(93430)
Rates: $45-$140
(805) 995-3810
(800) 540-4726

**ESTERO BAY
MOTEL**
25 S Ocean Ave
(93430)
Rates: $72-$125
(805) 995-3614
(800) 736-1292

SHORELINE INN
1 N. Ocean Ave
(93430)
Rates: $80-$160
(805) 995-3681

CAZADERO

**CAZANOMA
LODGE**
100 Kid Creek Rd
(95421)
Rates: $80-$115
(707) 632-5255

CEDARVILLE

SUNRISE MOTEL
54889 Hwy 299
(96104)
Rates: $35-$50
(530) 279-2161

CERES

HOWARD JOHNSON EXP
1672 Herndon Rd
(95307)
Rates: $55-$80
(209) 537-4821
(800) 446-4656

CERRITOS

SHERATON HOTEL TOWNE CENTER
12725 Center
Court Dr (90703)
Rates: $85-$300
(562) 809-1500
(800) 325-3535

CHATSWORTH

RAMADA INN
21340 Devonshire
St (91311)
Rates: $65-$79
(818) 998-5289
(800) 272-6239

SUMMERFIELD SUITES HOTEL
21902 Lassen St
(91311)
Rates: $130-$160
(818) 773-0707
(800) 833-4353

CHESTER

CEDAR LODGE MOTEL
Hwy 36, Box 677
(96020)
Rates: $29-$53
(530) 258-2904

SENECA MOTEL
Cedar & Martin
Box 504 (96020)
Rates: $35-$47
(530) 258-2815

TIMBER HOUSE LODGE
First & Main
Box 1010 (96020)
Rates: $35-$60
(530) 258-2729

CHICO

DELUXE INN
2507 Esplanada
(95926)
Rates: $39-$53
(530) 342-8386

THE ESPLANADE BED & BREAKFST
620 Esplanade
(95926)
Rates: $45-$60
(530) 345-8084

HOLIDAY INN
685 Manzanita Ct
(95926)
Rates: $59-$85
(530) 345-2491
(800) 465-4329

MATADOR MOTEL
1934 Esplanade
(95926)
Rates: $30-$50
(530) 342-7543

MOTEL 6
665 Manzanita Ct
(95926)
Rates: $35-$46
(530) 345-5500
(800) 466-8356

O'FLAHERTY HOUSE B&B
1462 Arcadian
(95926)
Rates: $65+
(530) 893-5494

OXFORD SUITES
2035 Business
Lane (95928)
Rates: $85-$159
(530) 899-9090
(800) 870-7848

SAFARI GARDEN MOTEL
2352 Esplanade
(95926)
Rates: $45-$50
(530) 343-3201

SUPER 8 MOTEL
655 Manzanita Ct
(95926)
Rates: $45-$75
(530) 345-2533
(800) 800-8000

VAGABOND INN
630 Main St
(95928)
Rates: $40-$65
(530) 895-1323
(800) 522-1555

CHINO

MOTEL 6
12266 Central Ave
(91710)
Rates: $34-$43
(909) 591-3877
(800) 466-8356

CHOWCHILLA

DAYS INN
220 E Robertson
Blvd (93610)
Rates: $40-$57
(559) 665-4821
(800) 329-7466

CHULA VISTA

GOOD NITE INN
225 Bay Blvd
(91910)
Rates: $49-$79
(619) 425-8200
(800) 648-3466

LA QUINTA INN
150 Bonita Rd
(91910)
Rates: $79-$99
(619) 691-1211
(800) 687-6667

MOTEL 6
745 "E" St (91910)
Rates: $35-$52
(619) 422-4200
(800) 466-8356

PALOMAR INN
801 Palomar St
(91911)
Rates: $69-$149
(619) 423-8889

TRAVEL INN
394 Broadway
(91910)
Rates: $45-$89
(619) 420-6600

VAGABOND INN
230 Broadway
(91910)
Rates: $36-$55
(619) 422-8305
(800) 522-1555

CITRUS HEIGHTS

OLIVE GROVE SUITES
6143 Auburn Blvd
(95621)
Rates: $85-$125
(916) 725-0100

CLAREMONT

RAMADA INN & TENNIS CLUB
840 S Indian Hill
Blvd (91711)
Rates: $59-$80
(909) 621-4831
(800) 272-6232

CLEAR CREEK

CLEAR CREEK MOTEL
667-150 Hwy 147
(96137)
Rates: $35-$45
(916) 256-3166

CLEARLAKE

SHIP 'N SHORE RESORT
13885 Lakeshore
Dr (95422)
Rates: $30-$75
(707) 994-2248

SUNSET LODGE
13961 Lakeshore
Dr (95422)
Rates: $40-$85
(707) 994-6642

CLEARLAKE OAKS

BLUE FISH COVE RESORT
10573 E Hwy
(95423)
Rates: $35-$95
(707) 998-1769

LAKE HAVEN MOTEL
100 Short St
(95423)
Rates: $36-$53
(707) 998-3908

LAKE POINT LODGE
13440 E Hwy 20
(95423)
Rates: $54-$91
(707) 998-4350

TWENTY OAKS COURT
10503 E Hwy 20
(95423)
Rates: $40
(707) 998-3012

CLIO

WHITE SULPHUR SPGS RCH B&B
2200 Hwy 89, PO
Box 136 (96106)
Rates: $85-$140
(530) 836-2387
(800) 854-1797

CLOVERDALE

ABRAMS HOUSE INN B&B
314 N Main St
(95425)
Rates: $60-$125
(707) 894-2412
(800) 764-4466

CLOVERDALE KOA CAMPING RESORT
26460 River Rd
PO Bx 600 (95425)
Rates: $37
(707) 894-3337
(800) 368-4558

COALINGA

BIG COUNTRY INN
25020 W Dorris
Ave (93210)
Rates: $52-$86
(559) 935-0866
(800) 836-6835

THE INN AT HARRIS RANCH
24505 W Dorris
Ave (93210)
Rates: $100-$110
(559) 935-0717
(800) 942-2333

MOTEL 6-EAST
25008 W Dorris
Ave (93210)
Rates: $35-$44
(559) 935-1536
(800) 466-8356

COFFEE CREEK

BONANZA KING RESORT
Rt 2, Box 4790
(96091)
Rates: $65-$70
(530) 266-3305

AREA CODES - If the local number doesn't connect, check for a new area code.

COLEVILLE

ANDRUSS MOTEL
Walker Rte, Box 64
(96107)
Rates: $36-$42
(530) 495-2216

MEADOWCLIFF MOTEL
Rte 1, Box 126
(96107)
Rates: $32-$45
(530) 495-2255

COLTON

DAYS INN
2830 Iowa St
(92324)
Rates: $46-$119
(909) 788-9900
(800) 329-7466

COLUMBIA

COLUMBIA GEM MOTEL
22131 Parrotts
Ferry Rd (95310)
Rates: $50-$150
(209) 532-4508

COMMERCE

RAMADA INN
7272 Gage Ave
(90040)
Rates: $59-$70
(562) 806-4777
(800) 272-6232

WYNDHAM GARDEN HOTEL
5757 Telegraph Rd
(90040)
Rates: $79-$129
(323) 887-8100
(800) 996-3426

CONCORD

CONCORD INN
1050 Burnett Ave
(94520)
Rates: $99-$109
(925) 687-5500

SHERATON CONCORD HOTEL
45 John Glen Dr
(94520)
Rates: $89-$139
(925) 825-7700
(800) 325-3535

CORNING

AMERIHOST INN
910 Hwy 99 W
(96021)
Rates: $55-$75
(530) 824-5200
(800) 434-5800

BEST WESTERN
2165 Solano St
(96021)
Rates: $54-$79
(530) 824-2468
(800) 528-1234
(800) 221 2230

DAYS INN
3475 Hwy 99 W
(96021)
Rates: $42-$50
(530) 824-2000
(800) 329-7466

SHILO INN
3350 Sunrise Way
(96021)
Rates: $55-$109
(530) 824-2940
(800) 222-2244

CORONA

DYNASTY SUITES MOTEL
1805 W 6th St
(91720)
Rates: $48-$54
(909) 371-7185
(800) 842-7899

MOTEL 6
200 N Lincoln
(91719)
Rates: $33-$41
(909) 735-6408
(800) 466-8356

TRAVELODGE
1701 W 6th St
(91720)
Rates: $48-$95
(909) 735-5500
(800) 578-7878

CORONADO

CORONADO INN
266 Orange Ave
(92118)
Rates: $59-$85
(619) 435-4121
(800) 598-6624

CROWN CITY INN
520 Orange Ave
(92118)
Rates: $105-$175
(619) 435-3116
(800) 442-1173

EL CORDOVA MOTEL
1351 Orange Ave
(92118)
Rates: $70-$148
(619) 435-4131
(800) 229-2032

LOEWS CORONADO BAY RESORT
4000 Coronado
Bay Rd (92118)
Rates: $195-$425
(619) 424-4000
(800) 815-6397

COSTA MESA

BEST WESTERN NEWPORT MESA INN
2642 Newport
Blvd (92627)
Rates: $49-$129
(949) 650-3020
(800) 825-1234
(800) 554-2378

DOUBLETREE HOTEL/AIRPORT
3050 Bristol St
(92626)
Rates: $89-$154
(949) 540-7000
(800) 222-8733

LA QUINTA INN
1515 S Coast Dr
(92626)
Rates: $59-$79
(949) 957-5841
(800) 687-6667

MOTEL 6
1441 Gisler Ave
(92626)
Rates: $40-$56
(949) 957-3063
(800) 466-8356

RAMADA LIMITED
1680 Superior Ave
(92626)
Rates: $82-$112
(949) 645-2221
(800) 272-6232

RESIDENCE INN BY MARRIOTT
881 W Baker St
(92626)
Rates: $129
(949) 241-8800
(800) 331-3131

VAGABOND INN
3205 Harbor Blvd
(92626)
Rates: $60-$70
(949) 557-8360
(800) 522-1555

WESTIN SOUTH COAST PLAZA
686 Anton Blvd
(92626)
Rates: $115-$175
(949) 540-2500
(800) 937-8461

WYNDHAM GARDEN HOTEL
3350 Ave of the
Arts (92626)
Rates: $79-$125
(949) 751-5100
(800) 996-3426

COULTERVILLE

YOSEMITE GOLD COUNTRY MOTEL
10407 Hwy 49
(95311)
Rates: $43-$59
(209) 878-3400

COVELO

WAGON WHEEL MOTEL
75860 Covelo Rd
(95428)
Rates: $32-$39
(707) 983-6717

CRESCENT CITY

ANCHOR BEACH INN
880 Hwy 101 S
(95531)
Rates: $49-$95
(707) 464-2600

BEST VALUE PACIFIC MOTOR HOTEL
440 Hwy 101 N
(95531)
Rates: $39-$65
(707) 464-4141
(800) 323-7917

CRESCENT CITY REDWOODS KOA CABINS
4241 Hwy 101 N
(95531)
Rates: $22
(707) 464-5744

ECONO LODGE
119 L St (95531)
Rates: $30-$60
(707) 464-2181
(800) 553-2666

JADE RIVER LODGE
180 Oak St (95531)
Rates: $60-$70
(707) 464-4003

RIVER RETREAT VACATION RENTALS
4901 North Bank
Rd (95531)
Rates: $100+
(707) 458-3231

ROYAL INN MOTEL
102 L St. (95531)
Rates: $33-$70
(707) 464-4113

SUPER 8 MOTEL
685 Hwy 101 S
(95531)
Rates: $56-$79
(707) 464-4111
(800) 800-8000

CRESTLINE

CREST LODGE MTN RESORT
23508 Lake Dr
(92325)
Rates: $55-$150
(909) 338-2418

CULVER CITY

RADISSON HOTEL-LA WESTSIDE
6161 Centinela
Ave (90230)
Rates: $99-$119
(310) 649-1776
(800) 333-3333

CYPRESS

WOODFIN SUITE HOTEL
5905 Corporate Ave (90630)
Rates: $89-$179
(714) 828-4000
(800) 237-8811

DANA POINT

HOLIDAY INN EXPRESS DANA POINT EDGEWATER
34744 Pacific Coast Hwy (92624)
Rates: n/a
(949) 240-0150
(800) 465-4329

DANVILLE

DANVILLE INN
803 Camino Ramon (94526)
Rates: $65-$80
(925) 838-8080
(800) 654-1050

DARDANELLE

DARDANELLE RESORT
Hwy 108 (95314)
Rates: $49-$65
(209) 965-4355

DAVIS

BEST WESTERN UNIVERSITY LODGE
123 "B" St (95616)
Rates: $79-$119
(530) 756-7890
(800) 528-1234

ECONO LODGE
221 "D" St (95616)
Rates: $50-$65
(530) 756-1040
(800) 553-2666

HOWARD JOHNSON
4100 Chiles Rd (95616)
Rates: $79-$129
(530) 792-0800
(800) 446-4656

MOTEL 6
4835 Chiles Rd (95616)
Rates: $35-$46
(530) 753-3777
(800) 466-8356

DEATH VALLEY NATIONAL MONUMENT

STOVE PIPE WELLS VILLAGE
SR 190 (92328)
Rates: $53-$76
(760) 786-2387

DEL MAR

DEL MAR INN-A CLARION CARRIAGE HOUSE MOTEL
720 Camino Del Mar (92014)
Rates: $109-$189
(858) 755-9765

HAMPTON INN
I-5 & Hwy 56 (92110)
Rates: $59-$79
(800) 426-7866

DELANO

COMFORT INN
2211 Girard St (93215)
Rates: $52-$60
(661) 725-1022
(800) 228-5150

SHILO INNS
2231 Girard St (93215)
Rates: $45-$69
(661) 725-7551
(800) 222-2244

DESERT HOT SPRINGS

ATLAS HI LODGE
18-336 Avenida Hermosa (92240)
Rates: $28-$39
(760) 329-5446

BROADVIEW LODGE
12-672 Eliseo Rd (92240)
Rates: $25-$45
(760) 329-8006

CARAVAN SPA
66-810 E 4th St (92240)
Rates: $38+
(760) 329-7124

EL REPOSO MOTEL
66-334 W 5th St (92240)
Rates: $35-$75
(760) 329-6632

KISMET LODGE
13-340 Mountain View Rd (92240)
Rates: $45-$65
(760) 329-6451

LAS PRIMAVERAS RESORT SPA
66-659 6th St (92240)
Rates: $45-$75
(760) 251-1677
(800) 400-1677

MINERAL SPRINGS RESORT
11-000 Palm Dr (92240)
Rates: $29-$125
(760) 329-6484

MIRACLE MANOR
12-589 Reposo Way (92240)
Rates: $45-$50
(760) 329-6641

MOTEL 6-NORTH
63-950 20th Ave (92258)
Rates: $34-$41
(760) 251-1425
(800) 466-8356

ROYAL PALMS INN B&B
12-885 Eliseo Rd (92240)
Rates: $45-$65
(760) 329-7975
(800) 755-9538

SAN MARCUS INN
66-540 San Marcus Rd (92240)
Rates: $32-$64
(760) 329-5304

STARDUST SPA MOTEL
66-634 5th St (92240)
Rates: $48-$63
(760) 329-5443
(800) 482-7835

SUNSET INN
67-585 Hacienda Ave (92240)
Rates: $45-$125
(760) 329-4488

TAMARIX SPA
66-185 Acoma (92240)
Rates: $25-$60
(760) 329-6615

DIAMOND BAR

BEST WESTERN DIAMOND BAR
259 Gentle Spring Lane (91765)
Rates: $60-$80
(909) 860-3700
(800) 528-1234

DINUBA

BEST WESTERN AMERICANA INN
1450 S Alta Ave (93618)
Rates: $50-$88
(559) 595-8401
(800) 528-1234
(800) 900-7550

DIXON

BEST WESTERN DIXON INN
1345 Commercial Way (95620)
Rates: $68-$99
(707) 678-1400
(800) 528-1234

DOUGLAS CITY

INDIAN CREEK LODGE
Hwy 299 E., PO Box 100 (96024)
Rates: $28-$75
(530) 623-6294

DOWNEY

EMBASSY SUITES
8425 Firestone Blvd (90241)
Rates: $144-$154
(562) 861-1900
(800) 362-2779

DOWNIEVILLE

DOWNIEVILLE RIVER INN RESORT
121 River St (95936)
Rates: $70-$165
(530) 289-3308
(800) 696-3308

DOYLE

7W CAFE & MOTEL
434-455 Doyle Loop (96109)
Rates: $22-$33
(530) 827-3331

MIDWAY MOTEL
Doyle Loop (96109)
Rates: $28+
(530) 827-2208

DUNNIGAN

BEST WESTERN COUNTRY INN
3930 Rd 89 (95937)
Rates: $52-$79
(530) 724-3471
(800) 528-1234

VALUE LODGE-IMA
39309 County Rd 89 (95937)
Rates: $46-$58
(530) 724-3333
(800) 341-8000

DUNSMUIR

BEST CHOICE INN
4221 Siskiyou Ave (96025)
Rates: $30-$80
(530) 235-0930

CAVE SPRINGS RESORT
4727 Dunsmuir Ave (96025)
Rates: $37-$49
(530) 235-2721

CEDAR LODGE MOTEL
4201 Dunsmuir Ave (96025)
Rates: $36-$50
(530) 235-4331

AREA CODES - If the local number doesn't connect, check for a new area code.

OAK TREE INN MOTEL
6604 Dunsmuir Ave (96025)
Rates: $48-$96
(530) 235-2884
(877) 235-2884

RIVERWALK INN BED & BREAKFST
4300 Dunsmuir Ave (96025)
Rates: $49-$71
(530) 235-4300
(800) 954-4300

EL CAJON

BEST WESTERN COURTESY INN
1355 E Main St (92021)
Rates: $48-$68
(619) 440-7378
(800) 528-1234

MOTEL 6
550 Montrose Ct (92020)
Rates: $34-$46
(619) 588-6100
(800) 466-8356

THRIFTLODGE
1220 W Main St (92020)
Rates: $39-$55
(619) 442-2576
(800) 578-7878

VILLA EMBASADORA
1556 E Main St (92020)
Rates: $25-$42
(619) 442-9617

EL CENTRO

BARBARA WORTH GOLF COURSE & CONV CENTER
2050 Country Club Dr (Holtville 92250)
Rates: $64-$80
(760) 356-2806
(800) 356-3806

BRUNNER'S MOTEL
215 N Imperial Ave (92243)
Rates: $65-$73
(760) 352-6431

EXECUTIVE INN
725 State St (92243)
Rates: $27-$44
(760) 352-8500

RAMADA INN
1455 Ocotillo Dr (92243)
Rates: $56-$67
(760) 352-5152
(800) 282-6232
(800) 805-4000

SUPER 8 MOTEL
611 N Imperial Ave (92243)
Rates: $50-$70
(760) 352-0715
(800) 800-8000

EL CERRITO

FREEWAY MOTEL
11645 San Pablo Ave (95430)
Rates: $38-$58
(510) 234-5581

EL MONTE

MOTEL 6
3429 Peck Rd (91731)
Rates: $33-$44
(626) 448-6660
(800) 466-8356

SUPER 8 MOTEL
12040 Garvey Ave (91732)
Rates: $49-$66
(626) 442-8354
(800) 800-8000

EL PORTAL

YOSEMITE VIEW LODGE
11156 Hwy 140 (95318)
Rates: $109-$159
(209) 379-2681
(800) 321-5261

EL SEGUNDO

EMBASSY SUITES HOTEL LAX
1440 E Imperial Ave (90245)
Rates: $164
(310) 640-3600
(800) 362-2779

HOMESTEAD VILLAGE EXTENDED STAY
1910 E Mariposa Ave (90245)
Rates: $413-$453/ Weekly
(310) 607-4000
(888) 782-9473

SUMMERFIELD SUITES LAX
810 S Douglas Ave (90245)
Rates: $220-$260
(310) 725-0100
(800) 833-4353

ELK

GREENWOOD PIER INN
5938 Hwy One (95432)
Rates: $120-$235
(707) 877-9997

ENCINITAS

DAYS INN
133 Encinitas Blvd (92024)
Rates: $69-$99
(760) 944-0260
(800) 329-7466

ECONO LODGE
410 N US 101 (92024)
Rates: $55-$135
(760) 436-4999
(800) 553-2666

ESCONDIDO

HOWARD JOHNSON EXP
555 N Centre City Pkwy (92025)
Rates: $39-$89
(760) 743-3700
(800) 446-4656

MOTEL MEDITERRANEAN
2336 S Escondido Blvd (92025)
Rates: $34-$75
(760) 743-1061

MOTEL 6
900 N Quince St (92025)
Rates: $34-$46
(760) 745-9252
(800) 466-8356

PALMS INN MOTEL
2650 S Escondido Blvd (92025)
Rates: $34-$47
(760) 743-9733

PINE TREE LODGE
425 W Mission (92025)
Rates: $44
(760) 740-7613

THE SHERIDAN INN
1341 N Escondido Blvd (92026)
Rates: $59-$99
(760) 743-8338
(800) 258-8527

SUNSHINE MOTEL
1107 S Escondido Blvd (92025)
Rates: $29-$95
(760) 743-3111

SUPER 7 MOTEL
515 W Washington Ave (92025)
Rates: $21-$72
(760) 743-7979

LAWRENCE WELK RESORT CENTER
8860 Lawrence Welk Drive (92026)
Rates: $139-$525
(760) 749-3000
(800) 932-9355

ETNA

BRADLEYS' ALDERBROOK MANOR
836 Main St (96027)
Rates: $20-$60
(530) 467-3917

MOTEL ETNA
317 Collier Way (96027)
Rates: $30-$38
(530) 467-5330

EUREKA

A WEAVER'S INN BED & BREAKFAST
1440 B St (95501)
Rates: $75-$125
(707) 443-8119
(800) 992-8119

BEST WESTERN BAY SHORE INN
3500 Broadway (95501)
Rates: $70-$175
(707) 268-8005
(800) 528-1234
(888) 268-8005

BAYVIEW MOTEL
2844 Fairfield St (95501)
Rates: $50-$125
(707) 442-1673

BUDGET MOTEL
1140 4th St (95501)
Rates: $30-$45
(707) 443-7321

ECONO LODGE
1830 4th St (95501)
Rates: $38-$62
(707) 443-8041
(800) 553-2666

EUREKA INN HISTORIC HOTEL
518 7th St (95501)
Rates: $88-$250
(707) 442-6441
(800) 862-4906

FIRESIDE INN
5th & R Sts (95501)
Rates: $30-$55
(707) 443-6312

LAMPLIGHTER MOTEL
4033 S Broadway (95501)
Rates: $35-$50
(707) 443-5001

MOTEL 6
1934 Broadway (95501)
Rates: $35-$54
(707) 445-9631
(800) 466-8356

PINE MOTEL
2411 Broadway (95501)
Rates: $25-$45
(707) 441-9204

QUALITY INN
1209 4th St (95501)
Rates: $68-$120
(707) 443-1601
(800) 228-5151

AREA CODES - If the local number doesn't connect, check for a new area code.

RAMADA LIMITED
270 5th St (95501)
Rates: $65-$85
(707) 443-2206
(800) 272-6232

RED LION INN
1929 4th St (95501)
Rates: $82-$92
(707) 445-0844
(800) 733-5466

ROYAL INN
1137 5th St (95501)
Rates: $30-$42
(707) 442-2114

**SAFARI
BUDGET 6 MOTEL**
801 Broadway
(95501)
Rates: $30-$58
(707) 443-4891

**SANDPIPER
MOTEL**
4055 Broadway
(95501)
Rates: $34-$45
(707) 443-7394

**SUNRISE INN
& SUITES**
129 4th St (95501)
Rates: $45-$59
(707) 443-4751

**TOWN HOUSE
MOTEL**
933 4th St (95501)
Rates: $42-$58
(707) 443-4536
(800) 445-6888

TRAVELODGE
4 Fourth St (95501)
Rates: $39-$70
(707) 443-6345
(800) 578-7878

FAIRFIELD

**BEST WESTERN
CORDELIA INN**
4373 Central Place
(94533)
Rates: $60-$80
(707) 864-2029
(800) 528-1234
(800) 422-7575

MOTEL 6
1473 Holiday Ln
(94533)
Rates: $39-$51
(707) 425-4565
(800) 466-8356

FALL RIVER MILLS

HI-MONT MOTEL
43021 Hwy 299
(96028)
Rates: $50-$71
(530) 336-5541

LAVA CREEK LODGE
One Island Rd
(96028)
Rates: $75-$135
(530) 336-6288

FALLBROOK

**BEST WESTERN
FRANCISCAN INN**
1635 S Mission Rd
(92028)
Rates: $62-$82
(760) 728-6174
(800) 528-1234

LA ESTANCIA INN
3135 S Old Hwy
395 (92028)
Rates: $65-$106
(760) 723-2888

FIREBAUGH

**APRICO INN/
SHILO INNS**
46290 W Panoche
Rd (93622)
Rates: $42-$58
(209) 659-1444
(800) 222-2244

FISH CAMP

**THE NARROW
GAUGE INN**
48571 Hwy 41
(93623)
Rates: $95-$140
(559) 683-7720
(888) 644-9050

**TENAYA LODGE
AT YOSEMITE**
1122 Hwy 41
(93623)
Rates: $169-$294
(559) 683-6555
(800) 322-2547
(800) 332-3135

FONTANA

MOTEL 6
10195 Sierra Ave
(92335)
Rates: $35-$42
(909) 823-8686
(800) 466-8356

FORT BIDWELL

FT. BIDWELL HOTEL
Main St, PO Box
100 (96112)
Rates: $35-$45
(916) 279-2050

FORT BRAGG

**BEACHCOMBER
MOTEL**
1111 N Main St
(95437)
Rates: $79-$119
(707) 964-2402
(800) 440-7873

**CEDAR RUN
VACATION
RENTAL**
26700 Hwy 1
(95437)
Rates: $110-$150
(800) 710-4825

**CLEONE
GARDENS INN**
24600 N Hwy 1
(95437)
Rates: $77-$150
(707) 964-2788
(800) 400-2189 (CA)

COAST MOTEL
18661 Hwy 1
(95437)
Rates: $38-$64
(707) 964-2852

**DELAMERE SEASIDE
COTTAGE**
16821 Ocean Dr
(95437)
Rates: $125
(707) 964-9188

EBB TIDE LODGE
250 S Main St
(95437)
Rates: $45-$75
(707) 964-5321
(800) 974-6730

**OLD STEWART
HOUSE INN**
511 Stewart St
(95437)
Rates: $75-$115
(707) 961-0775
(800) 287-8392

RENDEZVOUS INN
647 N Main St
(95437)
Rates: $55-$95
(800) 491-8142

**RIVERVIEW
HOUSES
VACATION
HOMES**
220 Riverview Dr
(95437)
Rates: $95-$125
(707) 964-5236
(800) 742-7620

**SHORELINE
VACATION
RENTALS**
18200 Old Coast
Hwy (95437)
Rates: $100-$400
(707) 964-1444
(800) 942-8288

**WISHING WELL
COTTAGES**
31430 Hwy 20
(95437)
Rates: $65-$75
(707) 961-5450

FORTUNA

**BEST WESTERN
COUNTRY INN**
2025 River Walk
Dr (95540)
Rates: $78-$83
(707) 725-6822
(800) 528-1234
(800) 679-7511

**FORTUNA
MOTOR LODGE**
275 12th St (95540)
Rates: $36-$57
(707) 725-6993

**NATIONAL 9
MOTEL**
819 Main St
(95540)
Rates: $30-$52
(707) 725-5136

6 RIVERS MOTEL
531 S Fortuna
Blvd (95540)
Rates: $30-$58
(707) 725-1181

SUPER 8 MOTEL
1805 Alamar Way
(95540)
Rates: $54-$79
(707) 725-2888
(800) 800-8000

FOUNTAIN VALLEY

RAMADA LIMITED
9125 Recreation
Circle (92708)
Rates: $79
(714) 847-3388
(800) 272-6232

**RESIDENCE INN
BY MARRIOTT**
9930 Slater Ave
(92708)
Rates: $94-$169
(714) 965-8000
(800) 331-3131

FREESTONE

GREEN APPLE INN
520 Bohemian
Hwy (95472)
Rates: $85-$92
(707) 874-2526

FREMONT

**BEST WESTERN
GARDEN COURT**
5400 Mowry Ave
(94538)
Rates: $139-$149
(510) 792-4300
(800) 528-1234
(800) 541-4909

GOOD NITE INN
4135 Cushing
Pkwy (94538)
Rates: $42-$49
(510) 656-9307
(800) 648-3466

**HOMESTEAD
VILLAGE GUEST
STUDIOS**
46080 Fremont
Blvd (94538)
Rates: $109-$134
(510) 353-1664
(888) 782-9473

ISLANDER MOTEL
4101 Mowry Ave
(94538)
Rates: $35-$53
(510) 796-8200

LA QUINTA INN
46200 Landing
Pkwy (94538)
Rates: $109-$139
(510) 445-0808
(800) 687-6667

AREA CODES - If the local number doesn't connect, check for a new area code.

LORD BRADLEY'S INN B&B
43344 Mission Blvd (94539)
Rates: $65-$75
(510) 490-0520

MISSION PEAK LODGE
43643 Mission Blvd (94539)
Rates: $29-$50
(510) 656-2366

MOTEL 6-NORTH
34047 Fremont Blvd (94536)
Rates: $39-$54
(510) 793-4848
(800) 466-8356

MOTEL 6-SOUTH
46101 Research Ave (94539)
Rates: $39-$54
(510) 490-4528
(800) 466-8356

RESIDENCE INN BY MARRIOTT
5400 Farwell Pl (94536)
Rates: $189-$209
(510) 794-5900
(800) 331-3131

FRESNO

BEST WESTERN GARDEN COURT INN
2141 N Parkway Dr (93705)
Rates: $49-$89
(559) 237-1881
(800) 528-1234
(800) 437-3766

DAYS INN
1101 N Parkway Dr (93728)
Rates: $39-$69
(559) 268-6211
(800) 329-7466

DAYS INN
2640 S Second St (93706)
Rates: $38-$53
(559) 237-0705
(800) 329-7466

ECONO LODGE
445 N Parkway Dr (93706)
Rates: $35-$45
(559) 485-5019
(800) 553-2666

ECONOMY INNS OF AMERICA
2570 S East St (93706)
Rates: $28-$35
(559) 486-1188
(800) 826-0778

EXECUTIVE SUITES
P.O. Box 42 (93707)
Rates: $650-$1495 Monthly
(559) 237-7444

HILTON HOTEL
1055 Van Ness Ave (93721)
Rates: $79-$129
(559) 485-9000
(800) 445-8667

KNIGHTS INN
3093 N Parkway Dr (93722)
Rates: $49-$69
(559) 275-7766
(800) 843-5644

LA QUINTA INN
2926 Tulare St (93721)
Rates: $59-$79
(559) 442-1110
(800) 687-6667

MOTEL 6
1240 Crystal Ave (93728)
Rates: $32-$42
(559) 237-0855
(800) 466-8356

MOTEL 6 NORTH
4245 N Blackstone Ave (93726)
Rates: $31-$44
(559) 221-0800
(800) 466-8356

MOTEL 6 SOUTH
4080 N Blackstone Ave (93726)
Rates: $31-$44
(559) 222-2431
(800) 466-8356

RADISSON HOTEL
2233 Ventura St (93722)
Rates: $90
(559) 268-1000
(800) 333-3333

RAMADA INN
4270 W Ashlan (93722)
Rates: $59-$85
(559) 275-2727
(800) 672-6232

RAMADA LIMITED
1804 W Olive Ave (93722)
Rates: $45-$60
(559) 442-1082
(800) 672-6232

RED ROOF INN
5021 N Barcus Ave (93722)
Rates: n/a
(559) 276-1910
(800) 843-7663

RESIDENCE INN BY MARRIOTT
5322 N Diana Ave (93710)
Rates: $124
(559) 222-8900
(800) 331-3131

RODEWAY INN
949 N Parkway Dr (93728)
Rates: $32-$85
(559) 268-0363
(800) 228-2000

SUPER 8 MOTEL
1087 N Parkway Dr (93728)
Rates: $49-$89
(559) 268-0741
(800) 800-8000

SUPER 8 MOTEL
2127 Inyo St (93721)
Rates: $45-$55
(559) 268-0621
(800) 800-8000

SUPER 8 MOTEL UNIVERSITY
2655 E Shaw Ave (93710)
Rates: $52-$61
(559) 294-0224
(800) 800-8000

TRAVELODGE
3093 N Parkway Dr (93722)
Rates: $49-$69
(559) 276-7745
(800) 578-7878

TRAVELODGE
3876 Blackstone Ave (93726)
Rates: $45
(559) 229-9840
(800) 578-7878

FULLERTON

FULLERTON INN
2601 W Orange-thorpe Ave (92633)
Rates: $45-$55
(714) 773-4900

MARRIOTT HOTEL CAL STATE
2701 E Nutwood Ave (92831)
Rates: $124-$164
(714) 738-7300
(800) 228-9290

MOTEL 6-WEST
1415 S Euclid St (92632)
Rates: $32-$38
(714) 992-0660
(800) 466-8356

GARBERVILLE

BEST WESTERN HUMBOLDT HOUSE INN
701 Redwood Dr (95542)
Rates: $85-$95
(707) 923-2771
(800) 528-1234

GARBERVILLE MOTEL
948 Redwood Dr (95542)
Rates: $49-$69
(707) 923-2422

HARTSOOK INN
900 Hwy 101 (95542)
Rates: $49-$79
(707) 247-3305

SHERWOOD FOREST MOTEL
814 Redwood Dr (95542)
Rates: $60-$94
(707) 923-2721

GARDEN GROVE

CANDLEWOOD SUITES ANAHEIM SOUTH
12901 Garden Grove Blvd (92843)
Rates: $69
(714) 539-4200
(888) 226-3539

HIDDEN VILLAGE BED & BREAKFAST
9582 Halekulani Dr (92641)
Rates: $55
(714) 636-8312

GARDENA

CARSON PLAZA HOTEL
111 W Albertoni St (90248)
Rates: $32-$50
(310) 329-0651

GEORGETOWN

AMERICAN RIVER INN B&B
Main & Orlean Sts (95643)
Rates: $89-$105
(530) 333-4499
(800) 245-6566

GILROY

LEAVESLEY INN
8430 Murray Ave (95020)
Rates: $50-$73
(408) 847-5500
(800) 624-8225

MOTEL 6 EXTENDED STAY
6110 Monterey Hwy (95020)
Rates: $42-$56
(408) 842-6061
(800) 466-8356

GLEN AVON

CIRCLE INN MOTEL
9220 Granite Hill Dr (92509)
Rates: $29-$36
(909) 360-1132

AREA CODES - If the local number doesn't connect, check for a new area code.

GLEN ELLEN

BIG DOG INN B&B
15244 Arnold Dr
(95442)
Rates: $125-$175
(707) 996-4319

GLENDALE

DAYS INN
600 N Pacific Ave
(91203)
Rates: $84-$149
(818) 956-0202
(800) 329-7466

VAGABOND INN
120 W Colorado St
(91204)
Rates: $72-$81
(818) 240-1700
(800) 522-1555

GLENHAVEN

**INDIAN BEACH
RESORT**
9945 E Hwy 20
(95443)
Rates: $35-$100
(707) 998-3760

GLENNVILLE

**THE BUNKHOUSE
MOTEL**
12044 Hwy 15 S
(93226)
Rates: $65-$95
(661) 536-9100

GOLETA

HOLIDAY INN
5650 Calle Real
(93117)
Rates: $90-$160
(661) 964-6241
(800) 465-4329

MOTEL 6
5897 Calle Real
(93117)
Rates: $49-$76
(661) 964-3596
(800) 466-8356

GRASS VALLEY

**ALTA SIERRA
VILLAGE INN**
11858 Tammy Way
(95949)
Rates: $49-$160
(530) 273-9102
(800) 992-5300

**BEST WESTERN
GOLD COUNTRY**
11972 Sutton Way
(95945)
Rates: $70-$99
(530) 273-1393
(800) 528-1234

**COACH N' FOUR
MOTEL**
628 S Auburn St
(95945)
Rates: $48-$80
(530) 273-8009

**GOLDEN CHAIN
RESORT MOTEL**
13363 SR 49
(95949)
Rates: $44-$88
(530) 273-7279

HOLIDAY LODGE
1221 E Main St
(959448
Rates: $48-$60
(530) 273-4406
(800) 742-7125

GRAYEAGLE

**GRAYEAGLE
LODGE**
Gold Lake Rd
Box 38 (96103)
Rates: $155+
(530) 836-2511
(800) 635-8778

GREEN VALLEY LAKE

**LODGE AT GREEN
VALLEY B&B**
33655 Green
Valley Lk Rd
(92341)
Rates: $65-$95
(909) 867-4281

GREENVILLE

**HIDEAWAY
RESORT MOTEL**
101 Hideaway Rd
(95947)
Rates: $42-$45
(530) 284-7915

**OAK GROVE
MOTOR LODGE**
700 Hwy 89
(95947)
Rates: $40-$47
(530) 284-4671

SIERRA LODGE
303 Main St, Box
578 (95947)
Rates: $24-$40
(530) 284-6565

**SPRING MEADOW
RESORT MOTEL**
18964 Hwy 89
(95947)
Rates: $53+
(530) 284-6768

GRIDLEY

PACIFIC MOTEL
1308 Hwy 99
(95948)
Rates: $37-$58
(530) 846-4580

GROVELAND

**GROVELAND
HOTEL HISTORIC
COUNTRY INN**
18767 Main St
(95321)
Rates: $125-$200
(209) 962-4000
(800) 273-3314

**MOUNTAIN RIVER
MOTEL**
12655 Jacksonville
Rd (95321)
Rates: $35
(209) 984-5071

YOSEMITE INN
31191 Hardin Flat
Rd (95321)
Rates: $28-$55
(209) 962-0103

**YOSEMITE
WESTGATE
MOTEL**
7633 Hwy 120
(95321)
Rates: $69-$149
(209) 962-5281
(800) 253-9673

GUALALA

**GUALALA
COUNTRY INN**
47955 Center St
(95445)
Rates: $89-$165
(707) 884-4343
(800) 564-4466

SURF MOTEL
39170 Hwy 1
(95445)
Rates: $89-$175
(707) 884-3571
(888) 451-7873

GUERNEVILLE

AVALON INN
16484 4th St
(95446)
Rates: $50-$125
(707) 869-9566

**CREEKSIDE INN
& RESORT**
16180 Neeley Rd
(95446)
Rates: $70-$200
(707) 869-3623
(800) 776-6586

HACIENDA HEIGHTS

MOTEL 6
1154 S 7th Ave
(91745)
Rates: $33-$46
(626) 968-9462
(800) 466-8356

HALF MOON BAY

RAMADA LIMITED
3020 N Cabrillo
Hwy (94019)
Rates: $65-$210
(650) 726-9700
(800) 350-9888
(800) 272-6232

**ZABALLA HOUSE
INN B&B**
324 Main St
(94019)
Rates: $75-$250
(650) 726-9123

HANFORD

**DOWNTOWN
MOTEL**
101 N Redington
St (92320)
Rates: $30-$42
(559) 582-9036

**SEQUOIA INN
MOTEL**
1655 Mall Dr
(92320)
Rates: $66-$76
(559) 582-0338

HAPPY CAMP

**FOREST LODGE
MOTEL**
63712 Hwy 96
(96039)
Rates: $40-$55
(530) 493-5424

HARBOR CITY

MOTEL 6
820 W Sepulveda
Blvd (90710)
Rates: $30-$56
(310) 549-9560
(800) 466-8356

HAWTHORNE

**HOWARD
JOHNSON PLAZA**
114306 S
Hawthorne Blvd
(90250)
Rates: $89-$169
(310) 675-0001
(800) 446-4656

HAYFORK

**BIG CREEK
LODGE**
Big Creek Rd
(96041)
Rates: $25-$65
(916) 628-5521

HAYWARD

MOTEL 6
30155 Industrial
Pkwy SW (94544)
Rates: $39-$56
(510) 489-8333
(800) 466-8356

SUPER 8 MOTEL
2460 Whipple Rd
(94544)
Rates: $47-$67
(510) 489-3888
(800) 800-8000

VAGABOND INN
20455 Hesperian
Blvd (94541)
Rates: $49-$64
(510) 785-5480
(800) 522-1555

HEALDSBURG

**BEST WESTERN
DRY CREEK INN**
198 Dry Creek Rd
(95448)
Rates: $84-$159
(707) 433-0300
(800) 528-1234
(800) 222-5784

FAIRVIEW MOTEL
74 Healdsburg
Ave (95448)
Rates: $65-$95
(707) 433-5548

HEMET

**BEST WESTERN
HEMET MOTOR
INN**
2625 W Florida
Ave (92545)
Rates: $40-$78
(909) 925-6605
(800) 528-1234
(800) 605-0001

**COACH LIGHT
MOTEL**
1640 W Florida
Ave (92545)
Rates: $32-$44
(909) 658-3237
(800) 678-0124

HEMET INN
800 W Florida Ave
(92543)
Rates: $36-$46
(909) 929-6366
(800) 909-6366

RAMADA INN
3885 W Florida
Ave (92545)
Rates: $46-$54
(909) 929-8900
(800) 272-6232

TRAVELODGE
1201 W Florida
Ave (92543)
Rates: $75-$85
(909) 766-1902
(800) 578-7878

HESPERIA

DAYS INN SUITES
14865 Bear Valley
Rd (92345)
Rates: $55-$64
(760) 948-0600
(800) 329-7746

HOLLISTER

**CINDERELLA
MOTEL-IMA**
110 San Felipe Rd
(95023)
Rates: $42-$95
(831) 637-5761
(800) 341-8000

HOLLYWOOD

**BEST WESTERN
HOLLYWOOD
HILLS**
6141 Franklin Ave
(90028)
Rates: $89-$159
(323) 464-5181
(800) 528-1234
(800) 287-1700

**HOWARD
JOHNSON EXP**
1615 N Western
Ave (90027)
Rates: $45-$75
(213) 469-2700
(800) 446-4656

MOTEL 6
1738 N Whitley
Ave (90028)
Rates: $40-$62
(323) 464-6006
(800) 466-8356

OBAN HOTEL
6364 Yucca St
(90028)
Rates: $25-$45
(323) 466-0524

HOMEWOOD

HOMESIDE MOTEL
5205 W Lake Blvd
(96141)
Rates: $55-$85
(530) 525-9990
(800) 824-6348

HOPE VALLEY

**SORENSON'S
RESORT**
14255 Hwy 88
(96120)
Rates: $80-$450
(530) 694-2203

HUNTINGTON LAKE

**LAKEVIEW
COTTAGES**
58374 Huntington
Lodge Rd (93634)
Rates: $45-$93
(559) 893-2330

HYAMPOM

**ZIEGLER'S
TRAILS' END**
1 Main St (96046)
Rates: $50-$80
(530) 628-4929
(800) 566-5266

IDYLLWILD

FIRESIDE INN
54540 N Circle Dr
(92549)
Rates: $55-$110
(909) 659-2966

IDYLLWILD INN
P. O. Box 515
(92549)
Rates: $47-$124
(909) 659-2552

**KNOTTY PINE
CABINS**
54340 Pine Crest
Dr (92549)
Rates: $42-$120
(909) 659-2933

TAHQUITZ MOTEL
25840 Hwy 243
(92549)
Rates: $55-$85
(909) 659-4554

**WOODLAND
PARK MANOR /
CEDAR CORNER
CABINS**
PO Bx 86 (92549)
Rates: $105
(909) 659-2657

IMPERIAL

**BEST WESTERN
IMPERIAL VALLEY
INN**
1093 Airport Blvd
(92251)
Rates: $48-$100
(760) 355-4500
(800) 528-1234
(800) 232-2378

IMPERIAL BEACH

**BEACH FRONT
VACATION
RENTALS**
716 Ocean Lane
(91932)
Rates: n/a
(619) 423-9958

**HAWAIIAN
GARDENS
SUITE-HOTEL**
1031 Imperial
Beach Blvd
(91932)
Rates: $79-$175
(619) 429-5303
(800) 334-3071

INDEPENDENCE

RAY'S DEN MOTEL
405 N Edwards
(93526)
Rates: $43-$56
(760) 878-2122

INDIAN WELLS

**MIRAMONTE
RESORT HOTEL**
76-477 Hwy 111
(92210)
Rates: $259-$339
(760) 341-2200

INDIO

**BEST WESTERN
DATE TREE HOTEL**
81-909 Indio Blvd
(92201)
Rates: $59-$159
(760) 347-3421
(800) 528-1234
(800) 292-5599

COMFORT INN
43-505 Monroe St
(92201)
Rates: $59-$129
(760) 347-4044
(800) 228-5150

HOLIDAY MOTEL
44-301 Sungold St
(92201)
Rates: $45-$65
(760) 347-6105

MOTEL 6
82-195 Indio Blvd
(92201)
Rates: $34-$41
(760) 342-6311
(800) 466-8356

PALM SHADOW INN

80-761 Hwy 111
(92201)
Rates: $84-$144
(760) 347-3476

**ROYAL PLAZA
INN**
82-347 Hwy 111
(92201)
Rates: $79-$104
(760) 347-0911
(800) 228-9559

SUPER 8 MOTEL
81-753 Hwy 111
(92201)
Rates: $59-$109
(760) 342-0264
(800) 800-8000

TRAVELODGE
84115 Indio Blvd
(92201)
Rates: $35-$55
(760) 342-4747
(800) 578-7878

INGLEWOOD

ECONO LODGE
439 W Manchester
Blvd (90301)
Rates: $45-$70
(310) 674-8596
(800) 553-2666

**HAMPTON INN
INT'L AIRPORT**
10300 La Cienega
Blvd (90304)
Rates: $75-$99
(310) 337-1000
(800) 426-7866

**MOTEL 6
INT'L AIRPORT**
5101 W Century
Blvd (90304)
Rates: $49-$72
(310) 419-1234
(800) 466-8356

INVERNESS

**COTTAGES ON
THE BEACH**
12790 Sir Frances
Drake (94937)
Rates: n/a
(415) 663-9696

AREA CODES - If the local number doesn't connect, check for a new area code.

MANKA'S INVERNESS LODGE
P. O. Box 1110 (94937)
Rates: $65-$160
(415) 669-1034

ROSEMARY COTTAGE B&B
75 Balboa Ave (94937)
Rates: $152-$256
(415) 663-9338
(800) 878-9338

INYOKERN

THREE FLAGS INN
1233 Brown Rd (93527)
Rates: $30-$120
(760) 377-3300

IRVINE

ATRIUM MARQUIS HOTEL
18700 MacArthur Blvd (92612)
Rates: $148-$179
(949) 833-2770
(800) 854-3012

HILTON HOTEL-AIRPORT
18800 MacArthur Blvd (92612)
Rates: $169-$224
(949) 833-9999
(800) 445-8667

HOLIDAY INN-ORANGE COUNTY AIRPORT
17941 Von Karman Ave (92614)
Rates: $79-$170
(949) 863-1999
(800) 854-3012

HOMESTEAVE VILLAGE EXTENDED STAY
30 Technology Dr (92618)
Rates: $69-$79
(949) 727-4228

LA QUINTA INN-IRVINE SPECTRUM
14972 Sand Canyon Ave (92618)
Rates: $69-$109
(949) 551-0909
(800) 687-6667

MARRIOTT HOTEL
18000 Van Karman Ave (92612)
Rates: $100-$200
(949) 553-0100
(800) 228-9290

MOTEL 6-ORANGE CNTY AIRPORT
1717 E Dyer Rd (92705)
Rates: $44-$58
(949) 261-1515
(800) 466-8356

RESIDENCE INN BY MARRIOTT
10 Morgan St (92618)
Rates: $79-$159
(949) 380-3000
(800) 331-3131

ISLETON

HOTEL DEL RIO & CASINO
207-11 2nd St (95641)
Rates: $35-$75
(916) 777-6033

JACKSON

AMADOR MOTEL
12408 Kennedy Flat Rd (95642)
Rates: $35-$65
(209) 223-0970

EL CAMPO CASA RESORT MOTEL
12548 Kennedy Flat Rd (95642)
Rates: $46-$85
(209) 223-0100

JACKSON GOLD LODGE
850 N Hwy 49 (95642)
Rates: $54-$80
(209) 223-0486
(888) 777-0380

LINDA VISTA MOTEL
10708 N Hwy 49 (95642)
Rates: $40-$60
(209) 223-1096

JAMESTOWN

HISTORIC NATL HOTEL B&B
77 Main St (95327)
Rates: $80-$120
(209) 984-3446
(800) 894-3446

QUALITY INN
18730 SR 108 (95327)
Rates: $54-$89
(209) 984-0315
(800) 228-5151

SONORA COUNTRY INN
18755 Charbroullian Ln (95327)
Rates: $54-$69
(209) 984-0315
(800) 847-2211

JENNER

JENNER INN & COTTAGES
10400 Hwy 1 (95450)
Rates: $75-$235
(707) 865-2377
(800) 732-2377

STILLWATER COVE RANCH
22555 Coast Hwy 1 (95450)
Rates: $55-$80
(707) 847-3227

TIMBER COVE INN
21780 Coast Hwy 1 (95450)
Rates: $68-$110
(707) 847-3231

JOSHUA TREE

HIGH DESERT MOTEL
61310 29 Palms Hwy (92252)
Rates: $45+
(760) 366-1978

JOSHUA TREE INN B&B
61259 29 Palms Hwy (92252)
Rates: $95-$150
(760) 366-1188

MOJAVE ROCK RANCH LODGE & CABINS
P. O. Box 552 (92252)
Rates: n/a
(760) 366-8455

JULIAN

APPLE TREE INN
4360 Hwy 78 (92070)
Rates: $77-$87
(760) 765-0222
(800) 410-8683

JUNCTION CITY

BIGFOOT CAMPGROUND
Hwy 299 (96048)
Rates: $69
(530) 623-6088
(800) 422-5219

STEELHEAD COTTAGES
Hwy 299 W (96048)
Rates: $43-$76
(530) 623-6325

JUNE LAKE

DOUBLE EAGLE RESORT & SPA
5587 Hwy 158 (93529)
Rates: $167-$236
(760) 648-7004

GULL LAKE LODGE
132 Leonard Ave (93529)
Rates: $50-$125
(760) 648-7516
(800) 631-9081

JUNE LAKE MOTEL & CABINS
2716 Boulder Dr (93529)
Rates: $60-$150
(760) 648-7547
(800) 648-6835

JUNE LAKE VILLAGER MOTEL
85 Boulder Dr (93529)
Rates: $35-$75
(760) 648-7712

REVERSE CREEK LODGE
4479 Hwy 158 (93529)
Rates: $45-$100
(760) 648-7535
(800) 762-6440

KELSEYVILLE

BELL HAVEN RESORT APT COTTAGES
3415 White Oak Way (95451)
Rates: $470 Wkly
(707) 279-4329

CREEKSIDE LODGE
7990 Hwy 29 (95451)
Rates: $39-$59
(707) 279-1380
(800) 279-1380

EDGEWATER RESORT/SODA BAY
6420 Soda Bay Rd (95451)
Rates: $25-$85
(707) 279-0208
(800) 396-6224

JIM'S SODA BAY RESORT
6380 Soda Bay Rd (95451)
Rates: $40-$59
(707) 279-4837

KENWOOD

THE LITTLE HOUSE B&B
255 Adobe Canyon Rd (95452)
Rates: $160-$175
(707) 833-2536

KERNVILLE

HI-HO RESORT LODGE
11901 Sierra Way (93238)
Rates: $65-$85
(760) 376-2671

LAZY RIVER LODGE
15729 Sierra Way (93238)
Rates: $36-$65
(760) 376-2242

AREA CODES - If the local number doesn't connect, check for a new area code.

RIVER VIEW LODGE
2 Sirretta St
(93238)
Rates: $55-$95
(760) 376-6019

KETTLEMAN CTY

BEST WESTERN OLIVE TREE INN
33410 Powers Dr
(93239)
Rates: $61-$100
(559) 386-0804
(800) 528-1234

SUPER 8 MOTEL
33415 Powers Dr
(93239)
Rates: $43-$69
(559) 386-9530
(800) 800-8000

KING CITY

COURTESY INN
4 Broadway Circle
(93930)
Rates: $42-$150
(831) 385-4646
(800) 350-5616

DAYS INN
1130 Broadway St
(93930)
Rates: $35-$100
(831) 385-6508
(800) 329-7466

MOTEL 6
3 Broadway Circle
(93930)
Rates: $31-$40
(831) 385-5000
(800) 466-8356

PALM MOTEL
640 Broadway
(93930)
Rates: $27-$49
(831) 385-3248

SAGE MOTEL
633 Broadway
(93930)
Rates: $29+
(831) 385-3274

KINGS BEACH

FALCON LODGE & SUITES
8258 N Lake Blvd
(96143)
Rates: $69-$129
(530) 546-2583
(800) 682-4631

NORTH LAKE LODGE
8716 N Lake Blvd
(96143)
Rates: $70+
(530) 546-2731
(800) 824-6348

NORTH SHORE LODGE
8755 N Lake Blvd
(96143)
Rates: $60+
(530) 546-4833

STEVENSON'S HOLIDAY INN
8742 N Lake Blvd
(96143)
Rates: $55-$95
(530) 546-2269
(800) 634-9141

KINGSBURG

SWEDISH INN
401 Conejo St
(93631)
Rates: $48-$58
(559) 897-1022
(800) 834-1022

KLAMATH

CAMP MARIGOLD GARDEN CTGS
16101 Hwy 101
(95548)
Rates: $42-$165
(707) 482-3585
(800) 621-8513

KNIGHTS FERRY

KNIGHTS FERRY RESORT COTTAGE
17525 Sonora Rd
(95361)
Rates: $95
(209) 881-3349

LA HABRA

LA HABRA INN
700 N Beach Blvd
(90631)
Rates: $42-$50
(562) 694-1991

LA JOLLA

ANDREA VILLA INN
2402 Torrey Pines Rd (92037)
Rates: $109-$155
(858) 459-3311

HYATT REGENCY
3777 La Jolla Village Dr (92122)
Rates: $189-$225
(858) 552-1234
(800) 233-1234

MARRIOTT HOTEL
4240 La Jolla Village Dr (92037)
Rates: $219
(858) 587-1414
(800) 228-9290

RESIDENCE INN BY MARRIOTT
8901 Gilman Dr (92037)
Rates: $189
(858) 587-1770
(800) 331-3131

LA MESA

E-Z 8 MOTEL
7851 Fletcher Pkwy (92041)
Rates: $35-$50
(619) 698-9444

MOTEL 6
7621 Alvarado Rd (91941)
Rates: $36-$52
(619) 464-7151
(800) 466-8356

LA MIRADA

RESIDENCE INN BY MARRIOTT
14419 Firestone Blvd (90638)
Rates: $119-$149
(714) 523-2800
(800) 331-3131

LA QUINTA

LA QUINTA RESORT & CLUB
49-499 Eisenhower Dr (92253)
Rates: $199-$229
(760) 564-4111
(800) 854-1271

LAGUNA BEACH

TRADE WINDS MOTOR LODGE
2020 S Coast Hwy (92651)
Rates: $35-$120
(949) 494-5450

VACATION VILLAGE
647 S Coast Hwy (92651)
Rates: $80-$285
(949) 494-8566
(800) 843-6895

LAKE ALMANOR

ALMANOR LAKESIDE LODGE
3747 Eastshore Dr (96137)
Rates: $70
(530) 284-7376
(800) 238-3924

KNOTTY PINE RESORT
430 Peninsula Dr (96137)
Rates: n/a
(530) 596-3348

LAKE ALMANOR RESORT
2706 Big Springs Rd (96137)
Rates: $47-$90
(530) 596-3337

LASSEN VIEW RESORT
7457 Eastshore Dr (96137)
Rates: $42-$92
(530) 596-3437

LITTLE NORWAY RESORT
432 Peninsula Dr (96137)
Rates: $50-$100
(530) 596-3225

LAKE ARROWHEAD

ARROWHEAD SADDLEBACK HISTORIC COUNTRY INN
SR 173 & 189 (92352)
Rates: $79-$170
(909) 336-3571

ARROWHEAD TREE TOP LODGE
27992 Rainbow Dr (92352)
Rates: $59-$173
(909) 337-2311
(800) 358-8733

PROPHETS' PARADISE B&B
26845 Modoc Ln (92352)
Rates: $90-$160
(909) 336-1969
(800) 987-2231

LAKE SAN MARCOS

QUAIL INN HOTEL
1025 La Bonita Dr (92069)
Rates: $99-$299
(760) 744-0120
(800) 447-6556

LAKE TAHOE AREA

(Kings Beach)

FALCON LODGE & SUITES
8258 N Lake Blvd (96143)
Rates: $69-$129
(530) 546-2583
(800) 682-4631

NORTH LAKE LODGE
8716 N Lake Blvd (96143)
Rates: $70+
(530) 546-2731
(800) 824-6348

NORTH SHORE LODGE
8755 N Lake Blvd (96143)
Rates: $60+
(530) 546-4833

STEVENSON'S HOLLIDAY INN
8742 N Lake Blvd (96143)
Rates: $59-$129
(530) 546-2269
(800) 634-9141

(Lake Tahoe Area-South Lake Tahoe)

ALDER INN
1072 Ski Run Blvd (96150)
Rates: $42-$125
(530) 544-4485
(800) 544-0056

ALPENROSE INN
4074 Pine Blvd (95729)
Rates: $49-$99
(530) 544-2985

BEACHSIDE INN & SUITES & SPA
930 Park Ave (96150)
Rates: $35-$79
(530) 544-2400
(800) 884-4920

BLUE JAY LODGE
4133 Cedar Ave (96150)
Rates: $59-$129
(530) 544-5232
(800) 258-3529

BLUE LAKE MOTEL
1055 Ski Run Blvd (96150)
Rates: $50-$80
(530) 541-2399

CARNEY'S CABINS
P. O. Box 601748 (96153)
Rates: $70-$100
(530) 542-3361

DAYS INN-CASINO AREA-STATELINE
968 Park Ave (96150)
Rates: $67-$115
(530) 541-4800
(800) 329-7466

ECHO CREEK RANCH
P. O. Box 20088 (96151)
Rates: $100+
(530) 544-5397
(800) 462-5397

HARRAH'S LAKE TAHOE HOTEL & CASINO
15 Hwy 50 (Stateline, NV 89449)
Rates: $179-$269
(775) 588-6611
(800) 427-7247
(Kennels provided)

HIGH COUNTRY LODGE
1227 Emerald Bay Rd (96150)
Rates: $25-$150
(530) 541-0508

INN AT HEAVENLY VALLEY B&B
1261 Ski Run Blvd (96150)
Rates: $75-$395
(530) 544-4244
(800) 692-2246

LA BAER INN
4133 Lake Tahoe Blvd (96150)
Rates: $49-$109
(530) 544-2139
(800) 544-5575

LAKEPARK LODGE
4081 Cedar Ave (96150)
Rates: $45-$85
(530) 541-5004

LAMPLITER MOTEL
4143 Cedar Ave (96150)
Rates: $45-$100
(530) 544-2936

MATTERHORN MOTEL
2187 Lake Tahoe Blvd (96157)
Rates: $40-$185
(530) 541-0367

MONTGOMERY INN
966 Modesto Ave (96151)
Rates: $49-$69
(530) 544-3871
(800) 624-8224

MOTEL 6
2375 Lake Tahoe Blvd (96150)
Rates: $34-$70
(530) 542-1400
(800) 466-8356

PARK AVENUE/ MEADOWOOD LODGE
904 Park Ave (96150)
Rates: $70-$100
(530) 544-3503

RAVEN WOOD HOTEL
4075 Manzanita Ave (96150)
Rates: $52-$169
(800) 659-4185

RIDGEWOOD INN MOTEL
1341 Emerald Bay Rd (96150)
Rates: $40-$78
(530) 541-8595

RODEWAY INN
4082 Lake Tahoe Blvd (96150)
Rates: $29-$99
(530) 541-7900
(800) 228-2000

SAFARI MOTEL
966 LaSalle St (96150)
Rates: $70-$100
(530) 544-2912

SLEEPY RACCOON MOTEL
1180 Ski Run Blvd (96150)
Rates: $40-$70
(530) 544-5890

SOUTH LAKE TAHOE CABIN RENTAL
4 Miles South at Hwy 89 & 50 Jct (96150)
Rates: $120-$250
(619) 246-0678
(888) 818-3283

SUPER 8 MOTEL
3600 Lake Tahoe Blvd (96150)
Rates: $44-$118
(530) 544-3476
(800) 237-8882
(800) 800-8000

TAHOE COLONY INN
3794 Montreal (96150)
Rates: $48-$110
(530) 655-6481
(800) 338-5552

TAHOE HACIENDA MOTEL
3820 Lake Tahoe Blvd (96150)
Rates: $35-$85
(530) 541-3805

TAHOE KEYS RESORT
599 Tahoe Keys Blvd (96150)
Rates: $108-$440
(530) 544-5397
(800) 438-8246

TAHOE LAKESHORE LODGE & SPA
930 Bal Bijou Rd (96150)
Rates: $129-$500
(530) 541-2180
(800) 448-4577

TAHOE QUEEN MOTEL
932 Poplar St (96157)
Rates: $40-$70
(530) 544-2291

TAHOE SUNDOWNER MOTEL
1211 Emerald Bay (96150)
Rates: $30-$140
(530) 541-2282

TAHOE SUNSET LODGE
1171 Emerald Bay (96150)
Rates: $25-$110
(530) 541-2940

TAHOE TROPICANA LODGE
4132 Cedar Ave (96154)
Rates: $40-$70
(530) 541-3911

TAHOE VALLEY LODGE
2241 Lake Tahoe Blvd (96150)
Rates: $95-$195
(530) 541-0353
(800) 669-7544

TRADE WINDS MOTEL
944 Friday Ave (96150)
Rates: $35-$125
(530) 544-6459
(800) 628-1829

(Lake Tahoe Area -Tahoe City)

THREE BUCK INN
135 Alpine Meadows Rd #34 (96146)
Rates: $95-$175
(530) 550-8600

(Lake Tahoe Area -Tahoe Vista)

BEESLEY'S COTTAGES
6674 N Lake Blvd (96148)
Rates: $70-$140
(530) 546-2448

HOLIDAY HOUSE
7276 N Lake Blvd (96148)
Rates: $95-$145
(530) 546-2369
(800) 294-6378 (CA)

RUSTIC COTTAGES
7449 N Lake Blvd (96148)
Rates: $49-$139
(530) 546-3523

(Lake Tahoe Area -Tahoma)

NORFOLK WOODS COUNTRY INN
6941 W Lake Blvd (96142)
Rates: $100-$170
(530) 525-5000

TAHOE LAKE COTTAGES
7030 W Lake Blvd (96142)
Rates: $125-$185
(530) 525-4411
(800) 824-6348

AREA CODES - If the local number doesn't connect, check for a new area code.

TAHOMA LODGE
7018 W Lake Blvd
(96142)
Rates: $45-$115
(530) 525-7721
(800) 824-6348

(Lake Tahoe Area -Truckee)

ALPINE VILLAGE MOTEL
12660 Deerfield
Dr (96161)
Rates: $50-$79
(530) 587-3801
(800) 933-1787

THE INN AT TRUCKEE
11506 Deerfield Dr
(96161)
Rates: $89-$139
(530) 587-8888
(888) 773-6888

RICHARDS MOTEL
15758 Donner
Pass Rd (96160)
Rates: $60-$110
(530) 587-3662

LAKEHEAD

ANTLERS RESORT & MARINA
P. O. Box 140
(96051)
Rates: $90-$170
(800) 238-3924

SUGARLOAF COTTAGES
19667 Lakeshore
Dr (96051)
Rates: $64-$218
(530) 238-2448
(800) 953-4432

TSASDI RESORT
19990 Lakeshore
Dr (96051)
Rates: $47-$175
(530) 238-2575
(800) 995-0291

LAKEPORT

CHALET MOTEL
2802 Lakeshore
Blvd (95453)
Rates: $34-$45
(707) 263-5040

COVE RESORT
2812 Lakeshore
Blvd (95453)
Rates: $50-$85
(707) 263-6833

LAKE VACATION RENTALS
1855 S Main St
(95453)
Rates: $125-$325
(707) 263-7188

RAINBOW MOTEL
2569 Lakeshore
Blvd (95453)
Rates: $34-$55
(707) 263-4309

LAKESHORE

LAKEVIEW COTTAGES
58374 Huntington
Ldge Rd (93634)
Rates: $45-$80
(310) 697-6556

LAKEWOOD

CRAZY 8 MOTEL
11535 E Carson St
(90715)
Rates: $34-$42
(562) 860-0546

LANCASTER

BEST WESTERN ANTELOPE VALLEY INN
44055 N Sierra
Hwy (93534)
Rates: $69-$91
(661) 948-4651
(800) 528-1234
(800) 810-9430

MOTEL 6
43540 17th St W
(93534)
Rates: $30-$42
(661) 948-0435
(800) 466-8356

OXFORD INN & SUITES
1651 W Ave K
(93534)
Rates: $55-$70
(661) 949-3423

LASSEN VOLCANIC NATIONAL PARK

DRAKESBAD GUEST RANCH RESORT
CR Chester-
Warner Valley
(96020)
Rates: $119-$230
(530) 529-1512

LATHROP

DAYS INN
14750 S Harlan Rd
(95350)
Rates: $58-$68
(209) 982-1959
(800) 329-7466

LAYTONVILLE

THE RANCH MOTEL
P. O. Box 1535
(95454)
Rates: $26-$45
(707) 984-8456

LEBEC

BEST REST FLYING J INN
42810 Frazier Mtn
Park Rd (93243)
Rates: $49-$59
(661) 248-2700
(800) 766-9009

LEE VINING

MURPHEY'S MOTEL
US 395 (93541)
Rates: $68-$98
(760) 647-6316
(800) 334-6316

LEGGETT

BIG BEND LODGE
P. O. Box 111 (95585)
Rates: n/a
(707) 984-6321

LEMOORE

BEST WESTERN VINEYARD INN
877 East D St
(93245)
Rates: $60-$75
(559) 924-1261
(800) 528-1234
(888) 924-7384

LEWISTON

LAKEVIEW TERRACE RESORT
HC01, Box 250
(96052)
Rates: $50-$100
(530) 778-3803
(800) 291-0308

LEWISTON VALLEY MOTEL
Trinity Dam Blvd
(96052)
Rates: $35-$43
(530) 778-3942

OLD LEWISTON INN B&B
Deadwood Rd
(96052)
Rates: $75-$85
(530) 778-3385

LINDSAY

OLIVE TREE INN
390 N Hwy 65
(93247)
Rates: $47-$57
(559) 562-5188
(800) 366-4469

LITTLE RIVER

THE INN AT SCHOOLHOUSE CREEK B&B
7051 N Hwy 1
(95456)
Rates: $110-$225
(707) 937-5525
(800) 731-5525

S S SEAFOAM LODGE
6751 N Hwy 1
(95456)
Rates: $95-$150
(707) 937-1827
(800) 606-1827

LIVERMORE

HAMPTON INN
2850 Constitution
Dr (94550)
Rates: $94-$114
(925) 606-6400
(800) 426-7866

MOTEL 6
4673 Lassen Rd
(94550)
Rates: $45-$58
(925) 443-5300
(800) 466-8356

RESIDENCE INN BY MARRIOTT
1000 Airway Blvd
(94550)
Rates: $89-$174
(925) 373-1800
(800) 331-3131

SPRINGTOWN MOTEL
933 Bluebell Dr
(94550)
Rates: $37+
(925) 449-2211

LODI

COMFORT INN
118 N Cherokee
Ln (95240)
Rates: $65-$69
(209) 367-4848
(800) 228-5150

LOMITA

ELDORADO COAST HOTEL
2037 Pacific Coast
Hwy (90717)
Rates: $44-$58
(310) 534-0700
(800) 536-7236

LOMPOC

BEST WESTERN VANDENBERG INN
940 E Ocean Ave
(93436)
Rates: $70-$105
(805) 735-7731
(800) 528-1234
(888) 529-4667

INN OF LOMPOC
1122 North H St
(93436)
Rates: $69-$89
(805) 735-7744
(800) 548-8231

MOTEL 6
1521 North H St
(93436)
Rates: $29-$38
(805) 735-7631
(800) 466-8356

QUALITY INN & EXEC SUITES
1621 North H St
(93436)
Rates: $79-$109
(805) 735-8555
(800) 228-5151

REDWOOD INN
1200 North H St
(93436)
Rates: $40-$45
(805) 735-3737

**TALLY HO
MOTOR INN**
1020 E Ocean Ave
(93436)
Rates: $39-$65
(805) 735-6444
(800) 332-6444

LONE PINE

**ALABAMA HILLS
INN**
1920 S Main St
(93545)
Rates: $53-$78
(760) 876-8700
(800) 800-5026

**BEST WESTERN
FRONTIER MOTEL**
1008 S Main St
(93545)
Rates: $50-$94
(760) 876-5571
(800) 528-1234

**DOW VILLA
MOTEL**
310 S Main St
(93545)
Rates: $75-$105
(760) 876-5521
(800) 824-9317

**NATIONAL 9
TRAILS MOTEL**
633 S Main St
(93545)
Rates: $45-$89
(760) 876-5555

LONG BEACH

**BELMONT SHORE
INN**
3946 E Ocean Blvd
(90803)
Rates: $40+
(562) 434-6236

COMFORT INN
1133 Atlantic Ave
(90813)
Rates: $69-$129
(562) 590-8858
(800) 228-5150

DAYS INN
1500 E Pacific
Coast Hwy (90806)
Rates: $50-$75
(562) 591-0088
(800) 329-7466

**GUESTHOUSE
HOTEL**
5325 E Pacific
Coast Hwy
(90804)
Rates: $68+
(562) 597-1341
(800) 214-8378

HILTON HOTEL
Two World Trade
Center (90831)
Rates: $129-$350
(562) 983-3400
(800) 445-8667

MOTEL 6
5665 E 7th St
(90804)
Rates: $47-$62
(562) 597-1311
(800) 466-8356

LOS ALAMOS

SKYVIEW MOTEL
9150 Hwy 101
(93440)
Rates: $75-$125
(805) 344-3770

LOS ANGELES

(Find additional
L A area lodging in
the following cities:
Beverly Hills,
Hollywood, West
Hollywood and
Westwood)

**BEVERLY HILLS
PLAZA HOTEL**
10300 Wilshire
Blvd (90024)
Rates: $135-$385
(323) 275-5575
(800) 800-1234

**BEVERLY LAUREL
MOTOR HOTEL**
8018 Beverly Blvd
(90048)
Rates: $69-$83
(323) 651-2441
(800) 962-3824

**CENTURY PLAZA
HOTEL & TOWER**
2025 Avenue of
the Stars (90067)
Rates: $325-$475
(310) 277-2000

**CENTURY
WILSHIRE HOTEL**
10776 Wilshire
Blvd (90029)
Rates: $65-$85
(800) 421-7223

**CHATEAU
MARMONT HOTEL**
8221 Sunset Blvd
(90046)
Rates: $160-$550
(323) 656-1010
(800) 242-8328

**HILTON &
TOWERS/LAX**
5711 W Century
Blvd (90045)
Rates: $148-$168
(310) 410-4000
(800) 445-8667

**HOLIDAY INN
DOWNTOWN**
750 Garland Ave
(90017)
Rates: $129-$169
(213) 628-5242
(800) 465-4329

**HOLLYWOOD
CELEBRITY HOTEL**
1775 Orchid Ave
(90028)
Rates: $65-$83
(800) 222-7090

**HOTEL INTER-
CONTINENTAL**
251 S Olive St
(90012)
Rates: $260-$316
(213) 617-3300
(800) 442-5251

**HOWARD
JOHNSON PLAZA**
2619 Wilshire Blvd
(90057)
Rates: $99-$159
(213) 387-5311
(800) 446-4656

KAWADA HOTEL
200 S Hill St
(90012)
Rates: $99-$129
(213) 621-4455
(800) 752-9232

**MARRIOTT
HOTEL/LAX**
5855 W Century
Blvd (90045)
Rates: $99-$159
(310) 641-5700
(800) 228-9290

**QUALITY HOTEL/
LAX**
5249 W Century
Blvd (90045)
Rates: $80-$100
(310) 645-2200
(800) 228-5151

**RADISSON
WILSHIRE PLAZA
HOTEL**
3515 Wilshire Blvd
(90010)
Rates: $125-$145
(213) 381-7411
(800) 333-3333

**RESIDENCE INN
BY MARRIOTT**
1177 S Beverly Dr
(90035)
Rates: $149+
(310) 277-4427
(800) 331-3131

**SKYWAYS
KNIGHTS INN**
9250 Airport Blvd
(90045)
Rates: $40-$55
(800) 336-0025

**TRAVELODGE
HOTEL/LAX**
5547 W Century
Blvd (90045)
Rates: $69-$109
(310) 649-4000
(800) 578-7878

**VAGABOND
INN/USC**
3101 S Figueroa St
(90007)
Rates: $78-$88
(213) 746-1531
(800) 522-1555

**W LOS ANGELES
HOTEL**
930 Hilgard Ave
(Westwood
Village 90024)
Rates: $279-$419
(310) 208-8765
(800) 421-2317

**WESTIN
HOTEL/LAX**
5400 W Century
Blvd (90045)
Rates: $169-$179
(310) 216-5858
(800) 937-8461

**WESTWOOD
VILLAGE SUITE
HOTEL**
930 Hilgard Ave
(90024)
Rates: $279-$419
(310) 208-8765

WILSHIRE MOTEL
12023 Wilshire
Blvd (90025)
Rates: $50-$60
(323) 478-3545

LOS BANOS

**BEST WESTERN
JOHN JAY INN**
301 W Pacheco
Blvd (93635)
Rates: $45-$115
(209) 827-0954
(800) 528-1234
(888) 529-4667

REGENCY INN
349 W Pacheco
Blvd (93635)
Rates: $37-$50
(209) 826-3871

LOS GATOS

**LOS GATOS
LODGE**
50 Los Gatos-
Saratoga Rd
(95032)
Rates: $119-$169
(408) 354-3300

LOS OSOS

BACK BAY INN
1391 Second St
(93402)
Rates: $29-$110
(805) 528-1233

LOST HILLS

DAYS INN
14684 Aloma St
(93249)
Rates: $26-$60
(805) 797-2371
(800) 329-7466

AREA CODES - If the local number doesn't connect, check for a new area code.

MOTEL 6
14685 Warren St
(93249)
Rates: $27-$36
(805) 797-2346
(800) 466-8356

LOTUS

**GOLDEN LOTUS
B&B INN**
1006 Lotus Rd
(95651)
Rates: $80-$95
(916) 621-4562

LUCERNE

**BEACHCOMBER
RESORT**
6345 E Hwy 20
(95458)
Rates: $40-$85
(707) 274-6639

**LAKE SANDS
RESORT**
6335 E Hwy 20
(95458)
Rates: $50
(707) 274-7732

STARLITE MOTEL
5960 E Hwy 20
(95458)
Rates: $40-$85
(707) 274-5515

MADERA

**BEST WESTERN
MADERA VALLEY
INN**
317 North G St
(93637)
Rates: $67-$85
(559) 673-5164
(800) 528-1234

DAYS INN
25327 Ave 16 (93637)
Rates: $40-$60
(559) 674-8817
(800) 329-7466

LIBERTY INN
22683 Ave 18 1/2
(93637)
Rates: $45-$65
(559) 675-8697

SUPER 8 MOTEL
1855 W Cleveland
Ave (93637)
Rates: $46-$70
(559) 661-1131
(800) 800-8000

MALIBU

**MALIBU RIVIERA
MOTEL**
28920 Pacific
Coast Hwy
(90265)
Rates: $50-$70
(310) 457-9503

MAMMOTH LAKES

**AUSTRIA HOF
LODGE**
924 Canyon Blvd
(93546)
Rates: $80-$125
(760) 934-2764
(800) 922-2966

**CONVICT LAKE
RESORT**
Rt 1, Box 204
(93546)
Rates: $65-$350
(760) 934-3800
(800) 992-2260

**CRYSTAL CRAG
LODGE**
307 Crystal Crag
Dr (93546)
Rates: $58-$215
(760) 934-2436

**ECONOLODGE
WILDWOOD INN**
3626 Main St
(93546)
Rates: $59-$105
(760) 934-6855
(800) 553-2666
(800) 845-8764

EXECUTIVE INN
54 Sierra Blvd
(93546)
Rates: $59-$109
(760) 934-8892
(888) 500-4754

**HOLIDAY INN
EXPRESS**
3262 Main St
(93546)
Rates: $99-$149
(760) 924-1234
(800) 465-4329

**INTERNATIONAL
INN**
3554 Main St
(93546)
Rates: $45-$65
(760) 934-2542
(800) 457-1997

MOTEL 6
3372 Main St
(93546)
Rates: $42-$66
(760) 934-6660
(800) 466-8356

**NORTH VILLAGE
INN**
103 Lake Mary Rd
(93546)
Rates: $70-$115
(760) 934-2925
(800) 257-3781

QUALITY INN
3537 Main St
(93546)
Rates: $74-$159
(760) 934-5114
(800) 228-5151

**RODEWAY INN
SIERRA NEVADA**
164 Old
Mammoth Rd
(93546)
Rates: $99-$369
(760) 934-2515
(800) 228-2000

**ROYAL PINES
RESORT**
3814 Viewpoint
Rd (93546)
Rates: $65-$95
(760) 934-2306

SHILO INN
2963 Main St
(93546)
Rates: $85-$150
(760) 934-4500
(800) 222-2244

**ZWART HOUSE,
THE FAMILY
LODGE**
76 Lupine St
(93546)
Rates: $50-$80
(760) 934-2217

MANHATTAN BEACH

**BARNABEY'S
HOTEL**
3501 N Sepulveda
Blvd (90266)
Rates: $109-$169
(310) 545-8466
(800) 552-5285
(800) 874-1093

**RESIDENCE INN
BY MARRIOTT**
1700 N Sepulveda
Blvd (90266)
Rates: $145-$208
(310) 546-7627
(800) 331-3131

MARINA

MOTEL 6
100 Reservation
Rd (93933)
Rates: $39-$71
(831) 384-1000
(800) 466-8356

MARIPOSA

**BEST WESTERN
YOSEMITE
WAY STATION**
4999 S Hwy 140
(95338)
Rates: $79-$87
(209) 966-7545
(800) 528-1234
(800) 321-5261

THE CLUBB'S B&B
5060 Charles St
(95338)
Rates: $45-$75
(209) 966-5085

**E. C. YOSEMITE
MOTEL**
5180 Jones St
(95338)
Rates: $59-$64
(209) 742-6800

**GUEST HOUSE
INN**
4962 Triangle Rd
(95338)
Rates: $68-$98
(209) 742-6869

**MARIPOSA
LODGE**
5052 Hwy 140
(95338)
Rates: $60-$89
(209) 966-3607
(888) 315-2378

MINERS INN
5181 Hwy 49 N
(95338)
Rates: $59-$159
(209) 742-7777
(800) 321-5261

**MOTHERLODE
LODGE**
6051 Hwy 140
(95338)
Rates: $29-$65
(209) 966-2521
(800) 398-9770

**MOUNTAIN OAKS
GUEST HOUSE**
5070 Allred Rd
(95338)
Rates: $45-$95
(209) 966-6033

**THE PELENNOR
BED & BREAKFAT**
3871 Hwy 49 S
(95338)
Rates: $35-$45
(209) 966-2832

**TWELVE OAKS
CARRIAGE
HOUSE**
4877 Wildwood
Dr (95338)
Rates: $65+
(209) 966-3231

MARKLEEVILLE

**J. MARKLEE TOLL
STATION HOTEL**
14856 Hwy 89
(96120)
Rates: $40
(530) 694-2507

**THE MOUNTAIN &
GARDEN B&B**
250 Old Pony
Express Rd
(96120)
Rates: n/a
(530) 694-0012

MARYSVILLE

AMERIHOST INN
1111 N Beale Rd
(95901)
Rates: n/a
(530) 742-2700
(800) 434-5800

HOLIDAY LODGE
530 10th St (95901)
Rates: $29-$38
(530) 742-7147

**MARYSVILLE
MOTOR LODGE**
904 E St (95901)
Rates: $30-$50
(530) 743-1531

MCCLOUD

**STONEY BROOK
BED & BREAKFAST**
309 W Colombero
Dr (96057)
Rates: $20-$70
(530) 964-2300
(800) 369-6118

MCKINLEYVILLE

SEA VIEW MOTEL
1186 Central Ave
(95521)
Rates: $35-$125
(707) 839-1321

MENDOCINO

BLACKBERRY INN
44951 Larkin Rd
(95460)
Rates: $90-$145
(707) 937-5281
(800) 950-7806

**BLAIR HOUSE
BED & BREAKFAST**
45110 Little Lake
St (95460)
Rates: $75-$130
(707) 937-1800

**COAST
GETAWAYS
VACATION
HOMES**
45068 Ukiah St
(95460)
Rates: $100-$350
(707) 937-9200
(800) 525-0049

**THE ENCHANTED
COTTAGE**
Box 838 (95460)
Rates: $125-$175
(707) 937-4040

**L.L. MENDOCINO
COTTAGES**
10940 Lansing St
(95460)
Rates: $131-$191
(800) 944-3278

**MENDOCINO
COAST
VACATION
RENTALS**
1000 Main St
(95460)
Rates: $130-$525
(707) 937-5033
(800) 262-7801

**MENDOCINO
SEASIDE
COTTAGE B&B**
10940 Lansing St
(95460)
Rates: $100-$561
(707) 485-0239
(800) 94-HEART

**MENDOCINO
VILLAGE
COTTAGES**
45320 Little Lake
St (95460)
Rates: $50-$100
(707) 937-0866

**SALLIE & EILEEN'S
PLACE FOR
WOMEN ONLY**
P.O. Box 409
(95460)
Rates: $65-$80
(707) 937-2028

**STANFORD INN
BY THE SEA**
44850 Comptche-
Ukiah Rd (95460)
Rates: $215-$365
(707) 937-5615
(800) 331-8884

**SWEETWATER
SPA & INN**
44840 Main St
(95460)
Rates: $55-$200
(707) 937-4076
(800) 300-4140

MERCED

**BEST WESTERN
SEQUOIA INN**
1213 "V" St (95340)
Rates: $54-$110
(209) 723-3711
(800) 528-1234
(800) 735-3711

DAYS INN
1199 Motel Dr
(95340)
Rates: $68-$95
(209) 722-2726
(800) 329-7466

GATEWAY MOTEL
1407 W 16th St
(95340)
Rates: n/a
(209) 722-5734

**MOTEL 6-
CENTRAL**
1215 R St (95340)
Rates: $32-$40
(209) 722-2737
(800) 466-8356

MOTEL 6-NORTH
1410 V St (95340)
Rates: $32-$40
(209) 384-2181
(800) 466-8356

PS HAPPY INN
740 Motel Dr
(95340)
Rates: n/a
(209) 722-6291

**SAN JOAQUIN
MOTEL**
1439 W 16th St
(95340)
Rates: n/a
(209) 722-2761

**SANDPIPER
LODGE**
1001 Motel Dr
(95340)
Rates: $36-$58
(209) 723-1034

SIERRA LODGE
951 Motel Dr
(95340)
Rates: n/a
(209) 722-3926

SLUMBER MOTEL
1315 W 16th St
(95340)
Rates: n/a
(209) 722-5783

SUPER 8 MOTEL
1983 E Childs Ave
(95340)
Rates: $49-$69
(209) 384-1303
(800) 800-8000

MI-WUK VILLAGE

**MI-WUK MOTOR
LODGE**
24680 Hwy 108
(95346)
Rates: $50-$117
(209) 586-3031
(800) 341-8000

MIDPINES

**HOMESTEAD
GUEST RANCH**
P. O. Box 113 (95345)
Rates: $95-$130
(209) 966-2820

**LION'S DEN
RETREAT**
5125 Chamberlain
Rd (95345)
Rates: $75-$110
(209) 966-5254

**MUIR LODGE
HOTEL**
6833 Hwy 140
Midpines (95345)
Rates: $28-$78
(209) 966-2468

MILL CREEK

**CHILDS MEADOW
ALL SEASON
RESORT**
41500 Hwy 36 E
(96061)
Rates: $46-$100+
(530) 595-3383

MILLBRAE

**WESTIN SF
AIRPORT**
1 Old Bayshore
Hwy (94030)
Rates: $205-$245
(650) 692-3500
(800) 937-8461

MILPITAS

**BEST WESTERN
BROOKSIDE INN**
400 Valley Way
(95035)
Rates: $99-$139
(408) 263-5566
(800) 528-1234
(800) 995-8834

**CANDLEWOOD
SUITES**
40 Ranch Dr
(95035)
Rates: $159-$179
(408) 719-1212

**HAWTHORN
SUITES**
321 Cypress Dr
(95035)
Rates: n/a
(408) 383-9500
(800) 527-1133

INNS OF AMERICA
270 S Abbott Ave
(95035)
Rates: $94+
(408) 946-8889
(800) 826-0778

**RESIDENCE INN
BY MARRIOTT**
1501 California
Cir (95035)
Rates: $129-$209
(408) 941-9222
(800) 331-3131

MIRANDA

**MIRANDA
GARDENS RESORT**
6766 Avenue of
the Giants (95553)
Rates: $75-$195
(707) 943-3011

**WHISPERING
PINES**
Avenue of the
Giants (95553)
Rates: $40-$65
(707) 943-3182

MISSION HILLS

**BEST WESTERN
MISSION HILLS
INN**
10621 Sepulveda
Blvd (91345)
Rates: $68-$80
(818) 891-1771
(800) 528-1234
(800) 352-5670

MODESTO

**BEST WESTERN
TOWN HOUSE
LODGE**
909 16th St (95354)
Rates: $58-$74
(209) 524-7261
(800) 528-1234
(800) 772-7261

CHALET MOTEL
115 Downey Ave
(95354)
Rates: $38-$52
(209) 529-4370

**DOUBLETREE
HOTEL**
1150 9th St (95354)
Rates: $99-$129
(209) 526-6000
(800) 733-5466

AREA CODES - If the local number doesn't connect, check for a new area code.

MOTEL 6
1920 W
Orangeburg Ave
(95350)
Rates: $38-$52
(209) 522-7271
(800) 466-8356

TRAVELODGE
722 Kansas Ave
(95351)
Rates: $49-$85
(209) 524-3251
(800) 578-7878

TROPICS MOTOR HOTEL
936 McHenry Ave
(95350)
Rates: $32-$48
(209) 523-7701

VAGABOND INN
1525 McHenry
Ave (95350)
Rates: $64-$78
(209) 521-6340
(800) 522-1555

MOJAVE

DESERT INN
1954 Hwy 58
(93501)
Rates: $35-$49
(661) 824-2518
(800) 305-1625

ECONO LODGE
2145 Hwy 58
(93501)
Rates: $36-$49
(661) 824-2463
(800) 553-2666

MOTEL 6
16958 Hwy 58
(93501)
Rates: $31-$40
(661) 824-4571
(800) 466-8356

SCOTTISH INNS
16352 Sierra Hwy
(93501)
Rates: $40-$60
(661) 824-9317
(800) 251-1962

MONROVIA

HOLIDAY INN
924 W Huntington
Dr (91016)
Rates: $95-$275
(626) 357-1900
(800) 465-4329

HOMESTEAD VILLAGE EXTENDED STAY
930 S Fifth Ave
(91016)
Rates: $79-$99
(626) 256-6999
(888) 782-9473

MONTARA

FARALLONE INN BED & BREAKFAST
1410 Main St
(94037)
Rates: $75-$150
(415) 728-8200
(800) 350-9777

MONTE RIO

ANGELO'S RESORT
20285 River Blvd
(95462)
Rates: $50-$150
(707) 865-9080

HIGHLAND DELL INN B&B
21050 River Blvd
(95462)
Rates: $85-$250
(707) 865-1759
(800) 767-1759

MONTECITO

FOUR SEASONS BILTMORE HOTEL
1260 Channel Dr
(93108)
Rates: $225-$595
(805) 969-2261
(800) 332-3442

SAN YSIDRO RANCH
900 San Ysidro Ln
(93108)
Rates: $195-$995
(805) 969-5046
(800) 368-6788

MONTEREY

BAY PARK HOTEL
1425 Munras Ave
(93940)
Rates: $99-$170
(831) 649-1020
(800) 338-3564

BAYSIDE INN
2055 Fremont St
(93940)
Rates: $35+
(831) 372-8071

BEST WESTERN MONTEREY BEACH HOTEL
2600 Sand Dunes
Dr (93940)
Rates: $129-$249
(831) 394-3321
(800) 528-1234
(800) 242-8627

BEST WESTERN VICTORIAN INN
487 Foam St
(93940)
Rates: $199-$499
(831) 373-8000
(800) 528-1234
(800) 232-4141

CARMEL HILL LODGE
1374 Munras Ave
(93940)
Rates: $69-$189
(831) 373-3252

CYPRESS GARDENS MOTEL
1150 Munras Ave
(93940)
Rates: $105-$139
(831) 373-2761
(800) 433-4732

DRIFTWOOD MOTEL
2362 N Fremont St
(93940)
Rates: $30-$199
(831) 372-5059

EL ADOBE INN
936 Munras Ave
(93940)
Rates: $49-$179
(831) 372-5409
(800) 433-4732

HYATT REGENCY MONTEREY RESORT
1 Old Golf Course
Rd (93940)
Rates: $175-$200
(831) 372-1234
(800) 233-1234

MONTEREY BAY LODGE
55 Camino
Aquajito (93940)
Rates: $89-$179
(831) 372-8057
(800) 558-1900

MONTEREY EXPRESS INN
2041 N Fremont St
(93940)
Rates: $40+
(831) 373-2911

MONTEREY FIRESIDE LODGE
1131 10th St
(93940)
Rates: $55-$169
(831) 373-4172

MOTEL 6
2124 N Fremont
St, Old Hwy 1
(93940)
Rates: $49-$75
(831) 646-8585
(800) 466-8356

MONTEREY PARK

DAYS INN & SUITES HOTEL
434 Potrero
Grande Dr (91755)
Rates: $56-$129
(626) 728-8444
(800) 329-7466

MORENO VALLEY

MOTEL 6-NORTH
24630 Sunnymead
Blvd (92553)
Rates: $32
(909) 243-0075
(800) 466-8356

MOTEL 6-SOUTH
23581 Alessandro
Blvd (92553)
Rates: $28-$34
(909) 656-4451
(800) 466-8356

MORGAN HILL

BEST WESTERN COUNTRY INN
16525 Condit Rd
(95037)
Rates: $70-$95
(408) 779-0447
(800) 528-1234

MORRO BAY

ADVENTURE INN ON THE SEA
1148 Front St
(93442)
Rates: $49-$139
(805) 772-5607
(800) 799-5607

BEST WESTERN EL RANCHO INN
2460 Main St
(93442)
Rates: $59-$119
(805) 772-2212
(800) 528-1234
(800) 628-3500

BEST WESTERN TRADEWINDS
225 Beach St
(93442)
Rates: $79-$149
(805) 772-7376
(800) 528-1234

BEST VALUE INN
220 Beach St
(93442)
Rates: $28-$98
(805) 772-3333
(800) 549-2022

COFFEY BREAK BED & BREAKFAST
213 Dunes St
(93442)
Rates: $75-$125
(805) 772-4378

DAYS INN
1095 Main St
(93442)
Rates: $55-$145
(805) 772-2711
(800) 329-7466

GOLDEN PELICAN
3270 N Main St
(93442)
Rates: $40-$125
(805) 772-7135

MORRO CREST INN
670 Main St
(93442)
Rates: $35-$115
(805) 772-7740

MORRO HILLTOP HOUSE
1200 Morro Ave
(93442)
Rates: $40-$75
(805) 772-1890

MOTEL 6
298 Atascadero Rd
(93442)
Rates: $32-$58
(805) 772-5641
(800) 466-8356

PLEASANT INN MOTEL
235 Harbor St
(93442)
Rates: $35-$89
(805) 772-8521
(888) 772-8521

SUNDOWN MOTEL
640 Main St (93442)
Rates: $38-$95
(805) 772-7381
(800) 696-6928

TRAVELODGE
1080 Market Ave
(93442)
Rates: $49-$98
(805) 772-1259
(800) 578-7878

VILLAGER MOTEL
1098 Main St
(93442)
Rates: $35-$145
(805) 772-1235

MOUNT SHASTA

AYER PROPERTY CABIN RENTALS
P. O. Box 594
(96067)
Rates: $75-$135
(530) 926-3200

BEST WESTERN TREE HOUSE MOTOR INN
I-5 & Lake St
(96067)
Rates: $78-$100
(530) 926-3101
(800) 528-1234
(800) 545-7164

ECONO LODGE
908 S Mt. Shasta
Blvd (96067)
Rates: $45-$79
(530) 926-3145
(800) 553-2666

EVERGREEN LODGE
1312 S Mt. Shasta
Blvd (96067)
Rates: $39-$60
(530) 926-2143

MOUNT SHASTA CABINS / COTTAGES
500 S Mt. Shasta
Blvd (96067)
Rates: $35-$150
(530) 926-5396

MOUNTAIN AIR LODGE
1121 S Mt. Shasta
Blvd (96067)
Rates: $42-$125
(530) 926-3411

PINE NEEDLES MOTEL
1340 S Mt. Shasta
Blvd (96067)
Rates: $39-$59
(530) 926-4811

SHASTA LODGE MOTEL
724 N Mt. Shasta
Blvd (96067)
Rates: $29-$55
(530) 926-2815
(800) 742-7821

SHELDON HOUSE & COTTAGE RENTAL
624 S Mt. Shasta
Blvd (96067)
Rates: $75-$250
(530) 926-0619

SWISS HOLIDAY LODGE
2400 S Mt. Shasta
Blvd (96067)
Rates: $36-$90
(530) 926-3446

TRAVEL INN
504 S Mt. Shasta
Blvd (96067)
Rates: $24-$60
(530) 926-4617

VILLAS VACATION RENTAL/CABINS
P. O. Box 344
(96067)
Rates: $30-$125
(530) 926-3313

WAGON CREEK INN B&B
1239 Woodland
Park Dr (96067)
Rates: $65-$75
(530) 926-0838
(800) 995-9260

MOUNTAIN VIEW

BEST WESTERN TROPICANA LODGE
1720 El Camino
Real W (94040)
Rates: $90-$105
(650) 961-0220
(800) 528-1234
(888) 961-0502

RESIDENCE INN BY MARRIOTT
1854 El Camino
Real (94040)
Rates: $179-$209
(650) 940-1300
(800) 331-3131

MYERS FLAT

LOG CHAPEL INN
P. O. Box 195 (95554)
Rates: $35-$50
(707) 943-3315

NAPA

NAPA VALLEY BUDGET INN
3380 Solano Ave
(94558)
Rates: $70-$120
(707) 257-6111
(877) 872-6272

NATIONAL CITY

E-Z 8 MOTEL
607 Roosevelt St
(91950)
Rates: $35-$50
(619) 575-8808

E-Z 8 MOTEL
1700 E Plaza
(91950)
Rates: $35-$50
(619) 474-6491

HOLIDAY INN SOUTH BAY
700 National City
Blvd (91950)
Rates: $79
(619) 474-2800
(800) 465-4329

RADISSON SUITES
810 National City
Blvd (91950)
Rates: $89
(619) 336-1100
(800) 333-3333

NEEDLES

BEST WESTERN COLORADO RIVER INN
2271 W Broadway
(92363)
Rates: $65-$150
(760) 326-4552
(800) 528-1234

BEST WESTERN ROYAL INN
1111 Pashard St
(92363)
Rates: $60-$75
(760) 326-5660
(800) 528-1234

BEST MOTEL
1900 W Broadway
(92363)
Rates: $21-$30
(760) 326-3824

DAYS INN & SUITES
1215 Hospitality
Ln (92363)
Rates: $35-$75
(760) 326-5836
(800) 329-7466

IMPERIAL 400 MOTOR INN
644 W Broadway
(92363)
Rates: $28-$48
(760) 326-2145

MOTEL 6-NORTH
1420 J St. (92363)
Rates: $29-$38
(760) 326-3399
(800) 466-8356

OLD TRAILS INN BED & BREAKFAST
304 Broadway
(92363)
Rates: $40-$65
(760) 326-3523

OVERLAND INN
712 W Broadway
(92363)
Rates: $25-$30
(760) 326-8808

RIVER VALLEY MOTOR LODGE
1707 W Broadway
(92363)
Rates: $23-$35
(760) 326-3839
(800) 346-2331

SUPER 8 MOTEL
1102 E. Broadway
(92363)
Rates: $38-$55
(760) 326-4501
(800) 800-8000

NEVADA CITY

NEVADA STREET COTTAGES
690 Nevada St
(95959)
Rates: $60-$100
(530) 265-8071

OUTSIDE INN
575 E Broad St
(95959)
Rates: $55-$120
(530) 265-2233

NEWARK

HAWTHORN SUITES
39270 Cedar Blvd
(94560)
Rates: n/a
(800) 527-1133

MOTEL 6
5600 Cedar Ct
(94560)
Rates: $39-$56
(510) 791-5900
(800) 466-8356

PARK INN LIMITED
5977 Mowry Ave
(94560)
Rates: $70-$150
(510) 795-7995
(800) 670-7275

NEWBERRY PARK

RODEWAY INN
2850 Camino dos
Rios (91320)
Rates: $31-$40
(805) 499-2414
(800) 228-2000

NEWPORT BEACH

BALBOA INN
105 Main St
(92661)
Rates: $90-$160
(949) 675-3412

FOUR SEASONS HOTEL
690 Newport
Center Dr (92660)
Rates: $265-$375
(949) 759-0808
(800) 268-6282

HYATT NEWPORTER
1107 Jamboree Rd
(92660)
Rates: $159-$200
(949) 729-1234
(800) 233-1234
(800) 532-7496

MARRIOTT HOTEL
900 Newport
Center Dr (92660)
Rates: $149+
(949) 640-4000
(800) 228-9290

MARRIOTT SUITES
500 Bayview Cir
(92660)
Rates: $129+
(949) 854-4500
(800) 228-9290

OAKWOOD CORP HOUSING
880 Irvine Ave
(92660)
Rates: $31-$60
(949) 574-3725
(800) 456-9351

NICE

GINGERBREAD COTTAGES B&B
4057 E Hwy 20
(95464)
Rates: $99-$195
(707) 274-0200

TALLEY'S FAMILY RESORT
3827 E Hwy 20
(95464)
Rates: $45-$90
(707) 274-1177

NIPINNAWASSEE

DEER VALLEY INN BED & BREAKFAST
45013 Hwy 49
(93601)
Rates: $49-$175
(209) 683-2155

NIPOMO

KALEIDOSCOPE INN B&B
130 E Dana St
(93444)
Rates: $90
(805) 929-5444

NORCO

HOWARD JOHNSON EXP
1695 Hamner Ave
(91760)
Rates: $35-$70
(909) 278-8886
(800) 446-4656

NORTH FORK

SOUTH FORK MOTEL
57714 Mammoth
Pool Rd (93643)
Rates: $38+
(209) 877-2237

NORTH HIGHLANDS

MOTEL 6
4600 Watt Ave
(95660)
Rates: $39-$52
(916) 973-8637
(800) 466-8356

NORTH HILLS

HOWARD JOHNSON
9401 Sepulveda
Blvd (91343)
Rates: $45-$79
(818) 892-0751
(800) 446-4656

MOTEL 6
15711 Roscoe Blvd
(91343)
Rates: $39-$52
(818) 894-9341
(800) 466-8356

NORWALK

MOTEL 6
10646 E Rosecrans
Ave (90650)
Rates: $39-$50
(562) 864-2567
(800) 466-8356

NOVATO

INN MARIN
250 Entrada Dr
(94949)
Rates: $89-$109
(415) 883-5952

TRAVELODGE RUSH CREEK
7600 Redwood
Blvd (94945)
Rates: $54-$112
(415) 892-7500
(800) 578-7878

OAKHURST

BEST WESTERN YOSEMITE GATEWAY INN
40530 Hwy 41
(93644)
Rates: $79-$136
(559) 683-2378
(800) 528-1234
(800) 545-5462

PINE ROSE INN BED & BREAKFAST
41703 Road 222
(93644)
Rates: $40-$100
(559) 642-2800

OAKLAND

BROWN'S YOSEMITE CABIN
7187 Yosemite
Pkwy (94605)
Rates: $55-$75
(510) 430-8466

CLARION SUITES LAKE MERRITT HISTORIC HOTEL
1800 Madison St
(94612)
Rates: $139-$279
(510) 832-2300
(800) 933-4683
(800) 252-7466

COMFORT INN & SUITES
8452 Edes Ave
(94621)
Rates: $69-$175
(510) 522-6866
(800) 228-5150

HILTON HOTEL OAKLAND AIRPORT
1 Hegenberger Rd
(94614)
Rates: $114-$249
(510) 635-5000
(800) 445-8667

MOTEL 6 AIRPORT
8480 Edes Ave
(94612)
Rates: $45-$61
(510) 638-1180
(800) 466-8356

MOTEL 6 EMBARCADERO
1801 Embarcadero
(94606)
Rates: $59-$76
(510) 436-0103
(800) 466-8356

OCCIDENTAL

NEGRI'S OCCIDENTAL LODGE
3610 Bohemian
Hwy (95465)
Rates: $45-$98
(707) 874-3623

UNION HOTEL
3731 Main St
(95465)
Rates: $38-$55
(707) 874-3555

OCEANSIDE

DAYS INN
1501 Carmelo Dr
(92054)
Rates: $60-$95
(760) 722-7661
(800) 329-7466

ECONO LODGE
1403 Mission Ave
(92054)
Rates: $49-$99
(760) 721-6663
(800) 553-2666

MOTEL 6
3708 Plaza Dr
(92056)
Rates: $37-$52
(760) 941-1011
(800) 466-8356

RAMADA LIMITED
1440 Mission Ave
(92054)
Rates: $69-$129
(760) 967-4100
(800) 272-6232

OJAI

BEST WESTERN CASA OJAI
1302 E Ojai Ave
(93023)
Rates: $70-$139
(805) 646-8175
(800) 528-1234
(800) 255-8175

BLUE IGUANA INN
11794 N Ventura
Ave (93023)
Rates: $99-$145
(805) 646-5277

LOS PADRES INN
1208 E Ojai Ave
(93023)
Rates: $50-$115
(805) 646-4365
(800) 228-3744

OAKRIDGE INN
780 N Ventura Ave
(93023)
Rates: $45-$95
(805) 649-4018

OJAI MANOR HOTEL
210 E Matilija St
(93023)
Rates: $50-$100
(805) 646-0961

OJAI VALLEY INN & SPA
Country Club Rd
(93023)
Rates: $245-$4000
(805) 646-5511
(800) 422-6524

OLEMA

RIDGETOP INN & COTTAGES
9865 Sir Francis
Drake Bl (94950)
Rates: $95-$150
(415) 663-1500

ONTARIO

COUNTRY INN
2359 S Grove Ave
(91761)
Rates: $39-$49
(800) 770-1887

**GOOD NITE INN
ONTARIO
AIRPORT**
1801 East G St
(91764)
Rates: $55-$70
(909) 983-3604
(800) 648-3466

**HOLIDAY INN
ONTARIO
AIRPORT**
3400 Shelby St
(91764)
Rates: $105-$125
(909) 466-9600
(800) 465-4329

**LA QUINTA INN
& SUITES**
3555 Inland
Empire Blvd
(91764)
Rates: $79-$99
(909) 476-1112
(800) 687-6667

MOTEL 6
1560 E 4th St
(91764)
Rates: $35-$43
(909) 984-2424
(800) 466-8356

ONTARIO INN
5361 W Holt Ave
(91763)
Rates: $25-$35
(909) 625-3806

**QUALITY INN
AIRPORT**
1655 E 4th St
(91764)
Rates: $45-$65
(909) 986-8898
(800) 228-5151

RED ROOF INN
1818 E Holt Blvd
(91761)
Rates: $60-$105
(909) 988-8466
(800) 843-7663

**RESIDENCE INN
BY MARRIOTT**
2025 Convention
Center Way
(91764)
Rates: $125-$154
(909) 937-6788
(800) 331-3131

ORANGE

**HAWTHORN
SUITES**
720 The City Dr
(92868)
Rates: n/a
(714) 740-2700
(800) 527-1133

HILTON SUITES
400 N State
College Blvd
(92868)
Rates: $115-$205
(714) 938-1111
(800) 445-8667

**MOTEL 6-
ANAHEIM
STADIUM**
2920 W Chapman
Ave (92868)
Rates: $39-$51
(714) 634-2441
(800) 466-8356

**RESIDENCE INN
BY MARRIOTT**
201 N State
College Blvd
(92868)
Rates: $92-$199
(714) 978-7700
(800) 423-9315
(800) 331-3131

ORICK

**ROLF'S PARK
MOTEL**
Davidson Rd
(95555)
Rates: $29-$35
(707) 488-3841

ORLAND

**AMBER LIGHT
INN**
828 Newville Rd
(95963)
Rates: $36-$42
(530) 865-7655

ORLAND INN
1052 South St
(95963)
Rates: $35-$48
(530) 865-7632

**ORLANDA INN
MOTEL**
827 Newville Rd
(95963)
Rates: $27+
(530) 865-4162

OROVILLE

BEST INN & SUITES
1470 Feather River
Blvd (95965)
Rates: $69-$85
(530) 553-9673

DAYS INN
1745 Feather River
Blvd (95965)
Rates: $45-$99
(530) 533-3297
(800) 329-7466

MOTEL 6
505 Montgomery
St (95965)
Rates: $33-$42
(530) 532-9400
(800) 466-8356

TRAVELODGE
580 Oro Dam Blvd
(95965)
Rates: $55-$65
(530) 533-7070
(800) 578-7878

OXNARD

**AMBASSADOR
MOTEL**
1631 S Oxnard
Blvd (93030)
Rates: $49
(805) 486-8404

**BEST WESTERN
OXNARD INN**
1156 S Oxnard
Blvd (93030)
Rates: $69-$99
(805) 483-9581
(800) 528-1234
(800) 469-6273

**CASA SIRENA
HOTEL & MARINA**
3605 Peninsula Rd
(93035)
Rates: $79-$170
(805) 985-6311
(800) 447-3529

RADISSON HOTEL
600 Esplanade Dr
(93030)
Rates: $89+
(805) 485-9666
(800) 333-3333

**RESIDENCE IN AT
RIVER EDGE**
2101 W Vineyard
Ave (93030)
Rates: $114
(805) 278-2200
(800) 331-3131

VAGABOND INN
1245 N Oxnard
Blvd (93030)
Rates: $52-$69
(805) 983-0251
(800) 522-1555

VILLA MOTEL
1715 S Oxnard
Blvd (93030)
Rates: $49
(805) 487-1370

PACIFIC GROVE

**ANDRIL FIREPLACE
COTTAGES**
569 Asilomar Blvd
(93950)
Rates: $64-$100
(831) 375-0994

**LIGHTHOUSE
LODGE & SUITES**
1150 Lighthouse
Ave (93950)
Rates: $129-$179
(831) 655-2111
(800) 528-1234

PALM DESERT

**CASA LARREA
RESORT**
73-811 Larrea St
(92260)
Rates: $64-$104
(760) 568-0311

COMFORT SUITES
39589 Washington
St (92211)
Rates: $59-$189
(760) 360-3337
(800) 228-5150

DESERT PATCH INN
73-758 Shadow
Mtn Dr (92260)
Rates: $56-$98
(760) 346-9161
(800) 350-9758

**INN AT
DEEP CANYON**
74-470 Abronia Tr
(92260)
Rates: $99-$209
(760) 346-8061
(800) 253-0004

MOTEL 6
78100 Varner Rd
(92261)
Rates: $36-$43
(760) 345-0550
(800) 466-8356

**RESIDENCE INN
BY MARRIOTT**
38-305 Cook St
(92211)
Rates: $119-$325
(760) 776-0050
(800) 331-3131

PALM SPRINGS

**ALPINE VILLA
MOTEL**
1586 E Palm Cnyn
Dr (92262)
Rates: $75-$115
(760) 323-2231

**CASA CODY
COUNTRY INN**
175 S Cahuilla Rd
(92262)
Rates: $59-$349
(760) 320-9346
(800) 231-2639

COMFORT INN
390 S Indian Cnyn
Dr (92264)
Rates: $59-$119
(760) 778-3699
(800) 228-5150

**ESTRELLA INN
& VILLAS**
415 S Belardo Rd
(92262)
Rates: $165-$265
(760) 320-4117
(800) 237-3687

HILTON RESORT
400 E Tahquitz
Cnyn Way (92262)
Rates: $175-$235
(760) 320-6868
(800) 445-8667
(800) 522-6900

HOTEL CALIFORNIA
424 E Palm
Canyon Dr (92264)
Rates: $69-$135
(760) 322-8855

HOWARD JOHNSON
701 E Palm
Canyon Dr (92264)
Rates: $45-$99
(760) 320-2700
(800) 446-4656

IRONSIDE HOTEL
310 E Palm
Canyon Dr (92264)
Rates: $35-$75
(760) 325-1995

LA SERENA VILLAS
339 S Belardo Rd
(92262)
Rates: $55-$180
(760) 325-3216

MOTEL 6-DOWNTOWN
660 S Palm
Canyon Dr (92264)
Rates: $36-$43
(760) 327-4200
(800) 466-8356

MOTEL 6-EAST
595 E Palm
Canyon Dr (92264)
Rates: $34-$42
(760) 325-6129
(800) 466-8356

MOTEL 6-NORTH
63950 20th Ave
(North Palm
Springs 92258)
Rates: $36-$43
(760) 251-1425
(800) 466-8356

MUSICLAND HOTEL
1342 S Palm
Canyon Dr (92264)
Rates: $29-$99
(760) 325-1326
(800) 428-3939

PALM GARDEN RESORT
950 N Indian
Canyon Dr (92262)
Rates: $35-$149
(760) 323-1328

PLAZA RESORT
2601 Golf Club Dr
(92264)
Rates: $79-$169
(760) 324-1802
(800) 438-6493

QUALITY INN RESORT
1269 E Palm
Canyon Dr (92264)
Rates: $99-$139
(760) 323-2775
(800) 228-5151

RAMADA RESORT INN & CONF CTR
1800 E Palm
Canyon Dr (92264)
Rates: $109-$199
(760) 323-1711
(800) 272-6232

RIVIERA RESORT & RACQUET CLUB
1600 N Indian
Canyon Dr (92262)
Rates: $149+
(760) 327-8311
(800) 444-8311

ROYAL SUN HOTEL
1700 S Palm
Canyon Dr (92262)
Rates: $69-$99
(760) 327-1564
(800) 619-4786

SAN MARINO HOTEL
225 W Baristo Rd
(92262)
Rates: $69-$169
(760) 325-6902

SUPER 8 LODGE
1900 N Palm
Canyon Dr (92262)
Rates: $66-$86
(760) 322-3757
(800) 800-8000

VILLA ROSA INN
1577 S Indian Tr
(92264)
Rates: $75-$135
(760) 327-5915

VILLE ORLEANS RESORT HOTEL
269 Chuckwalla
Rd (92262)
Rates: $69-$225
(760) 864-6200
(800) 700-8075

PALMDALE

MOTEL 6
407 W Palmdale
Blvd (93551)
Rates: $38-$44
(661) 272-0660
(800) 466-8356

PALO ALTO

CARDINAL HOTEL
235 Hamilton Ave
(94301)
Rates: $70-$200
(650) 323-5101

CORONET MOTEL
2455 El Camino
Real (94306)
Rates: $38-$40
(650) 326-1081

CROWNE PLAZA CABANA HOTEL
4290 El Camino
Real (94306)
Rates: $195
(650) 857-0787
(800) 227-6963

MOTEL 6
4301 El Camino
Real (94306)
Rates: $57-$76
(650) 949-0833
(800) 466-8356

SHERATON PALO ALTO HOTEL
625 El Camino
Real (94301)
Rates: $209-$279
(650) 328-2800
(800) 325-3535

PARADISE

BEST INN & SUITES
5475 Clark Rd
(95969)
Rates: $59-$88
(530) 876-0191
(800) 237-8466

LIME SADDLE MARINA
3428 Pentz Road
(95969)
Rates: $225/
2-Days
(530) 877-2414
(800) 834-7571

PARADISE INN
5423 Skyway
(95969)
Rates: $42-$55
(530) 877-2127

PONDEROSA GARDENS MOTEL
7010 Skyway
(95969)
Rates: $58-$85
(530) 872-9094

PARKFIELD

PARKFIELD INN
First & Oak Sts
(93451)
Rates: $41-$65
(805) 463-2323

PASADENA

QUALITY INN
3321 E Colorado
Blvd (91107)
Rates: $65-$199
(626) 796-9291
(800) 228-5151

VAGABOND INN
1203 E Colorado
Blvd (91106)
Rates: $58-$75
(626) 449-3170
(800) 522-1555

PASO ROBLES

FARMHOUSE MOTEL
425 Spring St
(93446)
Rates: $25+
(805) 238-1720

MOTEL 6
1134 Black Oak Dr
(93446)
Rates: $35-$48
(805) 239-9090
(800) 466-8356

SHAMROCK INN BED & BREAKFST
1640 Circle B Rd
(93446)
Rates: $41-$65
(805) 239-8585

SUBURBAN LODGE
1955 Theatre Dr
(93446)
Rates: $40-$65
(805) 238-3814

TRAVELODGE
2701 Spring St
(93446)
Rates: $45-$72
(805) 238-0078
(800) 578-7878

PEBBLE BEACH

THE LODGE AT PEBBLE BEACH
1700 17-Mile
Drive (93953)
Rates: $395-$2750
(831) 624-3811
(800) 654-9300

PETALUMA

MOTEL 6-SOUTH
1368 N McDowell
Blvd (94952)
Rates: $39-$51
(707) 765-0333
(800) 466-8356

PETROLIA

MATTOLE RIVER RESORT
42354 Mattole Rd
(95558)
Rates: $45-$90
(707) 629-3445
(800) 845-4607

PICO RIVERA

TRAVELODGE
7222 Rosemead
Blvd (90660)
Rates: $45-$55
(562) 949-6648
(800) 578-7878

PINOLE

MOTEL 6
1501 Fitzgerald Dr
(94564)
Rates: $54-$63
(510) 222-8174
(800) 466-8356

PIONEERTOWN

PIONEERTOWN MOTEL
5040 Curtis (92268)
Rates: $35-$42
(760) 365-4879

RIMROCK RANCH CABINS
P.O. Box 313 (92268)
Rates: $75-$145
(760) 228-1297

AREA CODES - If the local number doesn't connect, check for a new area code.

PISMO BEACH

MOTEL 6
860 4th St (93449)
Rates: $32-$48
(805) 773-2665
(800) 466-8356

OXFORD SUITES RESORT
651 Five Cities Dr (93449)
Rates: $89-$129
(805) 773-3773
(800) 982-7848

PITTSBURG

MOTEL 6
2101 Loveridge Rd (94565)
Rates: $39-$49
(925) 427-1600
(800) 466-8356

PLACENTIA

RESIDENCE INN BY MARRIOTT
700 W Kimberly Ave (92870)
Rates: $84-$190
(714) 996-0555
(800) 331-3131

PLACERVILLE

BEST WESTERN
6850 Greenleaf Dr (95667)
Rates: $79-$99
(530) 622-9100
(800) 528-1234
(800) 854-9100

GOLD TRAIL MOTOR LODGE
1970 Broadway (95667)
Rates: $36-$51
(530) 622-2906

MOTHER LODE MOTEL
1940 Broadway (95667)
Rates: $34-$51
(530) 622-0895

PLEASANT HILL

RESIDENCE INN BY MARRIOTT
700 Ellinwood Way (94523)
Rates: $159-$199
(925) 689-1010
(800) 331-3131

PLEASANTON

CANDLEWOOD SUITES
5535 Johnson Dr (94588)
Rates: $119-$129
(925) 463-1212

CROWNE PLAZA HOTEL
11950 Dublin Cnyn Rd (94588)
Rates: $69-$165
(925) 847-6000
(800) 227-6963

HILTON HOTEL
7050 Johnson Dr (94588)
Rates: $69-$234
(925) 463-8000
(800) 445-8667

MOTEL 6
5102 Hopyard Rd (94588)
Rates: $55-$64
(925) 463-2626
(800) 466-8356

SUPER 8 LODGE
5375 Owens Ct (94588)
Rates: $70-$95
(925) 463-1300
(800) 800-8000

POINT REYES STATION

BERRY PATCH COTTAGE B&B
P. O. Box 712 (94956)
Rates: $100-$120
(415) 663-1942
(888) 663-1942

GRAY'S RETREAT AT POINT REYES
P. O. Box 547 (94956)
Rates: $135
(415) 663-2000
(800) 887-2880

JASMINE COTTAGE AT POINT REYES
P.O. Box 547 (94956)
Rates: $125
(415) 663-2000
(800) 887-2880

POINT REYES COUNTRY INN & COTTAGES ON THE BEACH
12050 Hwy One (94956)
Rates: $105-$150
(415) 663-9696

THE TREE HOUSE BED & BREAKFST
P.O. Box 1075 (94956)
Rates: $100-$150
(415) 663-8720
(800) 495-8720

THIRTY NINE CYPRESS B&B
39 Cypress Rd (94956)
Rates: $110-$130
(415) 663-1709

POLLOCK PINES

STAGECOACH MOTOR INN
5940 Pony Express Tr (95726)
Rates: $58-$78
(530) 644-2029

WESTHAVEN INN
5658 Pony Express Tr (95726)
Rates: $68-$78
(530) 644-7800
(800) 341-8000

POMONA

MOTEL 6
2470 S Garey Ave (91766)
Rates: $33-$41
(909) 591-1871
(800) 466-8356

SHERATON SUITES FAIRPLEX
601 W McKinley Ave (91768)
Rates: $139-$189
(909) 622-2220
(800) 722-4055

SHILO HOTEL
3200 Temple Ave (91768)
Rates: $79-$129
(909) 598-0073
(800) 222-2244

PORT HUENEME

SURFSIDE MOTEL
615 E Hueneme Rd (93041)
Rates: $49
(805) 488-3686

PORTERVILLE

MOTEL 6
935 W Morton Ave (93257)
Rates: $29-$40
(559) 781-7600
(800) 466-8356

PORTOLA

SLEEPY PINES MOTEL
74631 Hwy 70 (96122)
Rates: $40+
(530) 832-4291

POWAY

POWAY COUNTRY INN
13845 Poway Rd (92064)
Rates: $55-$79
(858) 748-6320
(800) 648-6320

RAMADA LIMITED
12448 Poway Rd (92064)
Rates: $65-$95
(858) 748-7311
(800) 272-6232

QUINCY

GOLD PAN MOTEL
200 Cresent (95971)
Rates: $38-$64
(530) 283-3686
(800) 804-6541

NEW ENGLAND RANCH
2571 Quincy Jct Rd (95971)
Rates: $85-$105
(530) 283-2223

RAMONA

RAMONA VALLEY INN
416 Main St (92065)
Rates: $50-$77
(760) 789-6433
(800) 648-4618

RANCHO BERNARDO

DOUBLETREE CARMEL HIGHLAND
14455 Penasquitos Dr (92129)
Rates: $139-$179
(858) 672-9100
(800) 222-8733

LA QUINTA INN
10185 Paseo Montril (92129)
Rates: $69-$89
(858) 484-8800
(800) 687-6667

RADISSON SUITE HOTEL
11520 W Bernardo Ct (92127)
Rates: $119
(858) 451-6600
(800) 333-3333

RESIDENCE INN BY MARRIOTT
11002 Rancho Carmel Dr (92128)
Rates: $209
(858) 673-1900
(800) 331-3131

TRAVELODGE
16929 W Bernardo Dr (92127)
Rates: $60-$80
(858) 487-0445
(800) 578-7878

RANCHO CORDOVA

AMERISUITES
10744 Gold Center Dr (95670)
Rates: $69-$126
(916) 635-4799
(800) 833-1516

AREA CODES - If the local number doesn't connect, check for a new area code.

BEST WESTERN HERITAGE INN
11269 Point East Dr (95742)
Rates: $89-$95
(916) 635-4040
(800) 528-1234

INNS OF AMERICA
12249 Folsom Blvd (95670)
Rates: $52-$59
(916) 351-1213
(800) 826-0778

MATHER INN MOTEL
3240 Mather Field Rd (95670)
Rates: n/a
(916) 363-3344

MOTEL 6
10694 Olson Dr (95670)
Rates: $39-$52
(916) 635-8784
(800) 466-8356

RANCHO MIRAGE

MOTEL 6
69-570 Hwy 111 (92270)
Rates: $36-$43
(760) 324-8475
(800) 466-8356

RANCHO SANTA FE

INN AT RANCHO SANTA FE
5951 Linea del Cielo (92067)
Rates: $130-$560
(858) 756-1131
(800) 654-2928
(800) 843-4661

RANCHO VALENCIA RESORT
5921 Valencia Circle (92091)
Rates: $425-$700
(858) 756-1123

RAVENDALE

RAVENDALE LODGE
Hwy 395 (96123)
Rates: $25-$30
(916) 728-0028

RED BLUFF

CINDERELLA RIVERVIEW MOTEL
600 Rio St (96080)
Rates: $32-$48
(530) 527-5490

DAYS INN & SUITES
5 John Sutter (96080)
Rates: $38-$100
(530) 527-6130
(800) 328-7466

MOTEL 6
20 Williams Ave (96080)
Rates: $33-$44
(530) 527-9200
(800) 466-8356

RED BLUFF INN-IMA
30 Gilmore Rd (96080)
Rates: $37-$52
(530) 529-2028
(800) 341-8000

RELAX INN
250 S Main St (96080)
Rates: $25-$46
(530) 527-3545

SPORTSMAN LODGE
768 Antelope Blvd (96080)
Rates: $33-$55
(530) 527-2888

SUPER 8 MOTEL
203 Antelope Blvd (96080)
Rates: $39-$59
(530) 527-8882
(800) 800-8000

TRAVELODGE
38 Antelope Blvd (96080)
Rates: $39-$79
(530) 527-6020
(800) 578-7878

RED MOUNTAIN

OLD OWL INN COTTAGES & B&B
701 Hwy 395 (93558)
Rates: $45-$105
(888) 653-6954

REDCREST

REDCREST RESORT
26459 Ave of the Giants (95569)
Rates: $47-$85
(707) 722-4208

REDDING

AMERICANA LODGE
1250 Pine St (96001)
Rates: $27-$34
(530) 241-7020
(800) 626-1900

BEST WESTERN HOSPITALITY HOUSE
532 N Market St (96003)
Rates: $59-$79
(530) 241-6464
(800) 528-1234
(800) 700-3019

BEST WESTERN PONDEROSA INN
2220 Pine St (96001)
Rates: $44-$66
(530) 241-6300
(800) 528-1234
(800) 626-1900

CAPRI MOTEL
4620 Hwy 90 S (96001)
Rates: $30-$40
(530) 241-1900
(800) 626-1900

COMFORT INN
2059 Hilltop Dr (96002)
Rates: $49-$80
(530) 221-6530
(800) 228-5150

DOUBLETREE HOTEL
1830 Hilltop Ln (96002)
Rates: $85-$100
(530) 221-8700
(800) 222-8733

ECONO LODGE
2010 Pine St (96001)
Rates: $39-$84
(530) 243-3336
(800) 553-2666

ECONOMY INNS OF AMERICA
525 N Market St (96001)
Rates: $35+
(530) 246-9803
(800) 826-0778

HOLIDAY INN EXPRESS
1080 Twin View Blvd (96003)
Rates: $89-$120
(530) 241-5500
(800) 465-4329

LA QUINTA INN
2180 Hilltop Dr (96002)
Rates: $69-$89
(530) 221-8200
(800) 687-6667

MICROTEL INN & SUITES
2600 Larkspur Lane (96002)
Rates: $41-$51
(888) 771-7171

MOTEL 6-CENTRAL
1640 Hilltop Dr (96002)
Rates: $36-$48
(530) 221-1800
(800) 466-8356

MOTEL 6-NORTH
1250 Twin View Blvd (96003)
Rates: $36-$52
(530) 246-4470
(800) 466-8356

MOTEL 6-SOUTH
2385 Bechelli Ln (96002)
Rates: $36-$52
(530) 221-0562
(800) 466-8356

MOTEL 99
533 N Market St (96001)
Rates: $35+
(530) 241-4942

NORTH GATE LODGE
1040 Market St (96001)
Rates: $30
(530) 243-4900

OXFORD SUITES
1967 Hilltop Ln (96002)
Rates: $69-$99
(530) 221-0100
(800) 762-0133

PALISADES PARADISE B&B
1200 Palisades Ave (96003)
Rates: $60-$95
(530) 223-5305

RAMADA LIMITED
1286 Twin View Blvd (96003)
Rates: $79-$149
(530) 246-2222
(800) 272-6232

REDDING LODGE
1135 Market St (96001)
Rates: $32-$36
(530) 243-5141

RIVER INN
1835 Park Marina Dr (96001)
Rates: $46-$60
(530) 241-9500
(800) 995-4341

SARATOGA MOTEL
3025 S Market St (96001)
Rates: $25+
(530) 243-8586

SHASTA LODGE
1245 Pine St (96001)
Rates: $28-$45
(530) 243-6133

STAR DUST MOTEL
1200 Pine St (96001)
Rates: $30-$35
(530) 241-6121

**THRIFTLODGE
CASA BLANCA
MOUNTAIN**
413 N Market St
(96003)
Rates: $26-$59
(530) 241-3010
(800) 578-7878

**TIFFANY HOUSE
B&B INN**
1510 Barbara Rd
(96003)
Rates: $75-$125
(530) 244-3225

VAGABOND INN
536 E Cypress Ave
(96002)
Rates: $55-$65
(530) 223-1600
(800) 522-1555

REDLANDS

**BEST WESTERN
SANDMAN MOTEL**
1120 W Colton
Ave (92374)
Rates: $46-$95
(909) 793-2001
(800) 528-1234

DYNASTY SUITES
1235 W Colton
Ave (92373)
Rates: $45-$57
(909) 793-6648
(800) 842-7899

GOOD NITE INN
1675 Industrial
Park Ave (92374)
Rates: $40-$70
(909) 793-3723
(800) 648-3466

REDONDO BEACH

VAGABOND INN
6226 Pacific Coast
Hwy (90277)
Rates: $65-$90
(310) 378-8555
(800) 522-1555

REDWAY

**BUDGET WEST
REDWAY INN**
3223 Redwood Dr
(95560)
Rates: $36
(707) 923-2660
(800) 732-5380

REDWOOD CITY

GOOD NITE INN
485 Veterans Blvd
(94063)
Rates: $40-$71
(650) 365-5500
(800) 648-3466

**HOTEL SOFITEL
SAN FR. BAY**
233 Twin Dolphin
Dr (94065)
Rates: $119-$310
(650) 598-9000

REEDLEY

EDGEWATER INN
1977 W Manning
Ave (93654)
Rates: $51-$66
(559) 637-7777
(800) 479-5855 (CA)

RIALTO

**BEST WESTERN
EMPIRE INN**
475 W Valley Blvd
(92376)
Rates: $59-$119
(909) 877-0690
(800) 528-1234
(800) 281-1771

RICHARDSON GROVE

**RICHARDSON
GROVE LDG/CBNS**
Richardson Grove
State Pk (95542)
Rates: $55-$65
(707) 247-3415

RICHMOND

**QUALITY INN
& SUITES**
915 W Cutting
Blvd (94804)
Rates: $69-$139
(510) 237-3000
(800) 228-5151

RIDGECREST

**BEST WESTERN
CHINA LAKE INN**
400 S China Lake
Inn (93555)
Rates: $60-$80
(760) 371-2300
(800) 528-1234

ECONO LODGE
201 Inyokern Rd
(93555)
Rates: $44-$54
(760) 446-2551
(800) 553-2666

**EL DORADO
MOTEL**
400 S China Lake
Blvd (93555)
Rates: $28-$95
(760) 375-1354

**HACIENDA
COURT**
150 W Miguel
(93555)
Rates: $50-$70
(760) 375-5066

**HERITAGE INN
& SUITES**
1050 N Norma Dr
(93555)
Rates: $69-$75
(760) 446-7951
(800) 843-6543

MOTEL 6
535 S China Lake
Blvd (93555)
Rates: $31-$40
(760) 375-6866
(800) 466-8356

**PANAMINT
SPRINGS RESORT**
Hwy 190 (93555)
Rates: $46-$56
(760) 764-2010

QUALITY INN
507 S China Lake
Blvd (93555)
Rates: $45-$59
(760) 375-9731
(800) 228-5151

**RIDGECREST
MOTOR INN**
329 E Ridgecrest
Blvd (93555)
Rates: $30-$50
(760) 371-1695

RIO DELL

**HUMBOLDT
GABLES MOTEL**
40 W Davis St
(95562)
Rates: $40-$65
(707) 764-5609

RIO NIDO

**RIO NIDO
LODGE RESORT**
1458 River Rd
(95471)
Rates: $50-$80
(707) 869-0821

RIVERSIDE

BEST WESTERN
10518 Magnolia
Ave (92505)
Rates: $59-$129
(909) 359-0770
(800) 528-1234

DYNASTY SUITES
3735 Iowa Ave
(92507)
Rates: $48-$54
(909) 369-8200
(800) 842-7899

ECONO LODGE
10705 Magnolia
Ave (92505)
Rates: $35-$109
(909) 351-2424
(800) 553-2666

MOTEL 6-EAST
1260 University
Ave (92507)
Rates: $34-$42
(909) 784-2131
(800) 466-8356

MOTEL 6-SOUTH
3663 La Sierra Ave
(92505)
Rates: $31-$40
(909) 351-0764
(800) 466-8356

SUPER 8 MOTEL
1350 University
Ave (92507)
Rates: $36-$43
(909) 682-1144
(800) 800-8000

ROCKLIN

**FIRST CHOICE
INN**
4420 Rocklin Rd
(95677)
Rates: $88-$100
(916) 624-4500
(800) 462-2400

**MICROTEL INN
& SUITES**
4480 Rocklin Rd
(95677)
Rates: $49-$79
(916) 632-3366
(888) 771-7171

ROHNERT PARK

BEST WESTERN
6500 Redwood Dr
(94928)
Rates: $57-$76
(707) 584-7435
(800) 528-1234

GOOD NITE INN
5040 Redwood Dr
(94928)
Rates: $39-$70
(707) 584-8180
(800) 648-3466

MOTEL 6
6145 Commerce
Blvd (94928)
Rates: $35-$49
(707) 585-8888
(800) 466-8356

RAMADA LIMITED
6288 Redwood Dr
(94928)
Rates: $39-$45
(707) 584-1600
(800) 272-6232

ROSAMOND

**DEVONSHIRE INN
MOTEL**
2076 Rosamond
Blvd (93560)
Rates: $54-$69
(661) 256-3454

ROSEMEAD

MOTEL 6
1001 S San Gabriel
Blvd (91770)
Rates: $32-$46
(323) 572-6076
(800) 466-8356

VAGABOND INN
3633 N Rosemead
Blvd (91770)
Rates: n/a
(323) 288-6661
(800) 522-1555

AREA CODES - If the local number doesn't connect, check for a new area code.

ROSEVILLE

BEST WESTERN ROSEVILLE INN
220 Harding Blvd
(95678)
Rates: $68-$95
(916) 782-4434
(800) 528-1234

OXFORD SUITES
130 N Sunrise Ave
(95661)
Rates: $79-$99
(916) 784-2222

RESIDENCE INN BY MARRIOTT
1930 Taylor Rd
(95661)
Rates: $129
(916) 772-5500
(800) 331-3131

ROWLAND HEIGHTS

MOTEL 6
18970 E Labin Ct
(91748)
Rates: $36-$44
(626) 964-5333
(800) 466-8356

RUBIDOUX

MOTEL 6
6830 Valley Way
(92509)
Rates: $33-$42
(909) 681-6666
(800) 466-8356

RUNNING SPRINGS

GIANT OAKS MOTEL & CABIN
32180 Hilltop Blvd
(92382)
Rates: $49-$159
(916) 867-2231
(800) 786-1689

SACRAMENTO

AAA RESIDENCE INN
3721 Watt Ave
(95821)
Rates: $46
(916) 485-7125
(800) 786-4926

BEST WESTERN EXPO INN
1413 Howe Ave
(95825)
Rates: $70-$120
(916) 922-9833
(800) 528-1234
(800) 643-4422

BEST WESTERN HARBOR INN & SUITES
1250 Halyard Dr
(95691)
Rates: $79-$105
(916) 371-2100
(800) 528-1234

CANDLEWOOD SUITES
555 Howe Ave
(95825)
Rates: $69-$120
(916) 646-1212

CANTERBURY INN
1900 Canterbury Rd (95815)
Rates: $69-$74
(916) 927-0927
(800) 932-3492

CLARION HOTEL
700 16th St (95814)
Rates: $114-$139
(916) 444-8000
(800) 443-0880
(800) 252-7466

DAYS INN DISCOVERY PARK
350 Bercut Dr
(95814)
Rates: $69-$79
(916) 442-6971
(800) 329-7466

DOUBLETREE HOTEL
2001 Point West Way (95815)
Rates: $149-$219
(916) 929-8855
(800) 222-8733

ECONO LODGE
711 16th St (95814)
Rates: $45-$82
(916) 443-6631
(800) 553-2666

GOLDEN TEE INN
3215 Auburn Blvd
(95821)
Rates: $25-$40
(916) 482-7440

GUEST SUITES
2806 Grassland Dr
(95833)
Rates: $45-$80
(916) 641-2617
(800) 227-4903

HERITAGE HOTEL
1780 Tribute Rd
(95815)
Rates: $74-$145
(916) 929-7900

HILTON INN
2200 Harvard St
(95815)
Rates: $79-$159
(916) 922-4700
(800) 344-4321
(800) 445-8667

HOMESTEAD GUEST STUDIOS
2810 Gateway Oaks Dr (95833)
Rates: $59-$64
(916) 564-7500
(888) 782-9473

HOST AIRPORT HOTEL
6945 Airport Blvd
(95837)
Rates: $75-$115
(916) 922-8071

HOWARD JOHNSON PLAZA
3343 Bradshaw Rd
(95827)
Rates: $65-$90
(916) 366-1266
(800) 446-4656

INNS OF AMERICA
25 Howe Ave
(95826)
Rates: $49-$58
(916) 386-8408
(800) 826-0778

LA QUINTA INN
4604 Madison Ave
(95841)
Rates: $75-$95
(916) 348-0900
(800) 687-6667

LA QUINTA INN
200 Jibboom St
(95814)
Rates: $79-$99
(916) 448-8100
(800) 687-6667

MANSION VIEW LODGE
771 16th St (95814)
Rates: $36-$42
(916) 443-6631
(800) 409-9595

MARRIOTT RESIDENCE INN
1530 Howe Ave
(95825)
Rates: $134-$139
(916) 920-9111
(800) 331-3131

MOTEL 6-CENTRAL
7850 College Town Dr (95826)
Rates: $39-$52
(916) 383-8110
(800) 466-8356

MOTEL 6-DOWNTOWN
1415 30th St
(95816)
Rates: $39-$52
(916) 457-0777
(800) 466-8356

MOTEL 6-NORTH
5110 Interstate Ave (95842)
Rates: $39-$52
(916) 331-8100
(800) 466-8356

MOTEL 6-OLD SACRAMENTO
227 Jibboom St
(95814)
Rates: $39-$52
(916) 441-0733
(800) 466-8356

MOTEL 6 SOUTH
7407 Elsie Ave
(95828)
Rates: $39-$46
(916) 689-6555
(800) 466-8356

MOTEL 6-SOUTHWEST
7780 Stockton Blvd (95823)
Rates: $39-$46
(916) 689-9141
(800) 466-8356

POINT WEST APARTMENTS
1761 Heritage Ln
(95815)
Rates: $80+
(916) 922-5882

RADISSON HOTEL
500 Leisure Ln
(95815)
Rates: $79-$139
(916) 922-2020
(800) 333-3333

RED LION'S SACRAMENTO INN
1401 Arden Way
(95815)
Rates: $115-$168
(916) 922-8041
(800) 547-8010

RED ROOF INN
3796 Northgate Blvd (95834)
Rates: n/a
(916) 927-7117
(800) 843-7663

SANDS MOTEL
2160 Auburn Blvd
(95821)
Rates: $34-$46
(916) 925-8584

SKY RIDERS MOTEL
6100 Freeport Blvd (95822)
Rates: $45-$80
(916) 421-5700

SUPER 8 MOTEL
7216 55th St
(95823)
Rates: $40-$56
(916) 427-7925
(800) 800-8000

VAGABOND INN
1319 30th St
(95816)
Rates: $39-$49
(916) 454-4400
(800) 522-1555

SALINAS

BARLOCKER'S RUSTLNG OAKS RANCH
25252 Limekiln Rd
(93908)
Rates: $75-$150
(831) 675-9121

BEST WESTERN JOHN JAY INN
175 Kern St
(93905)
Rates: $60-$175
(831) 784-0176
(800) 528-1234
(888) 529-4667

AREA CODES - If the local number doesn't connect, check for a new area code.

CABANA HOLIDAY RV PARK/CABINS
8710 Prunedale North Rd (93907)
Rates: n/a
(831) 663-2886

EL DORADO MOTEL
1351 N Main St (93906)
Rates: $36-$90
(831) 449-2442
(800) 523-6506

GOOD NITE INN
5454 Work St (93907)
Rates: n/a
(831) 758-6483
(800) 648-3466

MOTEL 6-NORTH
140 Kern St (93901)
Rates: $35-$51
(831) 753-1711
(800) 466-8356

MOTEL 6-SOUTH
1257 De La Torre Blvd (93905)
Rates: $35-$46
(831) 757-3077
(800) 466-8356

VAGABOND INN
131 Kern St (93905)
Rates: $75-$80
(831) 758-4693
(800) 522-1555

WESTERN MOTEL
1161 N Main St (93907)
Rates: n/a
(831) 422-4738

SAN ANDREAS

BLACK BART INN & MOTEL
35 Main St (95249)
Rates: $47-$60
(209) 754-3808
(800) 225-3764

COURTYARD B&B INN
334 W St. Charles (95249)
Rates: $65-$90
(209) 754-1518

SAN BERNARDINO

DAYS INN
1386 E Highland Ave (92404)
Rates: $39-$99
(909) 881-1702
(800) 329-7466

E-Z 8 MOTEL
1750 S Waterman Ave (92408)
Rates: $29-$37
(909) 888-4827

LA QUINTA INN
205 E Hospitality Ln (92408)
Rates: $69-$89
(909) 888-7571
(800) 687-6667

MOTEL 6-NORTH
1960 Ostrems Way (92407)
Rates: $33-$42
(909) 887-8191
(800) 466-8356

MOTEL 6-SOUTH
111 Redlands Blvd (92408)
Rates: $33-$42
(909) 825-6666
(800) 466-8356

SANDS MOTEL
606 North H St (92410)
Rates: $40-$49
(909) 889-8391

TRAVELODGE
225 E Hospitality Lane (92408)
Rates: $40-$55
(909) 888-6777
(800) 578-7878

SAN BRUNO

DAYS INN
1550 El Camino Real (94066)
Rates: $75-$110
(650) 616-9600
(800) 329-7466

SUMMERFIELD SUITES HOTEL
1350 Huntington Ave (94066)
Rates: $170-$300
(650) 588-0770
(800) 833-4353

SAN CARLOS

HOMESTEAD GUEST STUDIOS EXTENDED STAY
3 Circle Star Way (94070)
Rates: $518-$623 Weekly
(650) 368-2600
(888) 782-9473

INNS OF AMERICA
555 Skyway Rd (94070)
Rates: $129-$139
(650) 631-0777
(800) 826-0778

SAN CLEMENTE

HOLIDAY INN
111 S Avenida de Estrella (92672)
Rates: $129-$149
(949) 361-3000
(800) 465-4329

SAN DIEGO

BEACH HAVEN INN
4740 Mission Blvd (92109)
Rates: $90-$155
(858) 272-3812
(800) 831-6323

BUDGET MOTELS OF AMERICA
133 Encinitas Blvd (92024)
Rates: n/a
(619) 944-0260
(800) 795-6044

BUDGET MOTELS OF AMERICA
641 Camino del Rio South (92108)
Rates: n/a
(619) 295-6886
(800) 624-1257

CROWN POINT VIEW SUITE HOTEL
4088 Crown Point Dr (92109)
Rates: $115-$250
(858) 272-0676
(800) 338-3331

DIAMOND HEAD INN MOTEL
605 Diamond St (92109)
Rates: $109-$169
(858) 273-1900

DOUBLETREE HOTEL MISSION VALLEY
7450 Hazard Center Dr (92108)
Rates: $139-$159
(619) 297-5466
(800) 222-8733

E-Z 8 MOTEL OLD TOWN
4747 Pacific Hwy (92110)
Rates: $35-$50
(619) 294-2512

EBB TIDE MOTEL
5082 West Pt Loma Blvd (92107)
Rates: n/a
(619) 224-9339

GOOD NITE INN SEA WORLD
3880 Greenwood St (92110)
Rates: $47-$70
(619) 543-9944
(800) 648-3466

GROSVENOR INN DOWNTOWN
810 Ash St (92101)
Rates: $40-$59
(619) 233-8826
(800) 232-1212

HANALEI HOTEL
2270 Hotel Circle N (92108)
Rates: $94-$129
(619) 297-1101
(800) 882-0858

HILTON HOTEL SAN DIEGO MISSION VALLEY
901 Camino Del Rio S (92108)
Rates: $134-$219
(619) 543-9000
(800) 445-8667

HOLIDAY INN ON THE BAY
1355 N Harbor Dr (92101)
Rates: $149-$189
(619) 232-3861
(800) 465-4329

HORTON GRAND HISTORIC HOTEL
311 Island Ave (92101)
Rates: $119-$179
(619) 544-1886
(800) 542-1886

INN SUITES HOTEL-BALBOA PARK
2223 El Cajon Blvd (92104)
Rates: $69-$149
(619) 296-2101
(877) 343-4648

LAMPLIGHTER INN & SUITES
6474 El Cajon Blvd (92115)
Rates: $65-$100
(619) 582-3088
(800) 545-0778

LAWRENCE WELK RESORT
8860 Lawrence Welk Drive (Escondido 92026)
Rates: $139-$525
(760) 749-3000
(800) 932-9355

MARRIOTT HOTEL & MARINA
333 W Harbor Dr (92101)
Rates: $275-$300
(619) 234-1500
(800) 228-9290

AREA CODES - If the local number doesn't connect, check for a new area code.

MARRIOTT HOTEL MISSION VALLEY
8757 Rio San Diego Dr (92108)
Rates: $159-$189
(619) 692-3800
(800) 228-9290

MARRIOTT SUITES DOWNTOWN
701 "A" St (92101)
Rates: $130
(619) 696-9800
(800) 962-1367
(800) 228-9290

MIDWAY MOTEL
3325 Midway Dr (92110)
Rates: $32-$39
(619) 740-9006

MOTEL 6
2424 Hotel Circle N (92108)
Rates: $46-$66
(619) 296-1612
(800) 466-8356

MOTEL 6-DOWNTOWN
1546 2nd Ave (92101)
Rates: $45-$62
(619) 236-9292
(800) 466-8356

MOTEL 6-NORTH
5592 Clairemont Mesa Blvd (92117)
Rates: $46-$66
(619) 268-9758
(800) 466-8356

OLD TOWN INN
4444 Pacific Hwy (92110)
Rates: $55-$95
(619) 260-8024
(800) 643-3025

OUTRIGGER MOTEL
1370 Scott St (92106)
Rates: $35-$50
(619) 223-7105

PACIFIC INN HOTEL & SUITES BY THE BAY
1655 Pacific Hwy (92101)
Rates: $59-$99
(619) 232-6391

PACIFIC SANDS MOTEL & CONDOS
4449 Ocean Blvd (92109)
Rates: $40-$60
(619) 483-7555

PACIFIC SHORES INN ON THE BEACH
4802 Mission Blvd (92109)
Rates: $63-$108
(619) 483-6300
(800) 826-0715

PICKWICK HOTEL
132 W Broadway (92101)
Rates: $35-$50
(619) 234-0141

PREMIER INNS
2484 Hotel Circle Pl (92108)
Rates: $39-$89
(619) 291-8252

RAMADA LIMITED HARBORSIDE
1403 Rosecrans St (92106)
Rates: $69-$129
(619) 225-9461
(800) 272-6232

RESIDENCE INN BY MARRIOTT
5400 Kearny Mesa Rd (92111)
Rates: $147
(858) 278-2100
(800) 331-3131

RESIDENCE INN DOWNTOWN
1747 Pacific Coast Hwy (92101)
Rates: $125-$150
(619) 338-8200
(800) 331-3131

SOUTH BAY LODGE
1101 Hollister St (92154)
Rates: $27-$47
(619) 428-7600

U.S. GRANT HOTEL
326 Broadway (92101)
Rates: $175-$195
(619) 232-3121
(800) 237-5029

VAGABOND INN MISSION BAY
4540 Mission Bay Dr (92109)
Rates: $67-$87
(858) 274-7888
(800) 522-1555

VAGABOND INN MISSION VALLEY
625 Hotel Circle S (92108)
Rates: $73-$88
(619) 297-1691
(800) 522-1555

VAGABOND INN POINT LOMA
1325 Scott St (92106)
Rates: $64-$78
(619) 224-3371
(800) 522-1555

SAN DIMAS

MOTEL 6
502 W Arrow Hwy (91773)
Rates: $36-$48
(909) 592-5631
(800) 466-8356

RED ROOF INN
204 N Village Ct (91773)
Rates: $56-$82
(909) 599-2362
(800) 843-7663

SAN FRANCISCO

ALEXANDER INN
415 O'Farrell St (94102)
Rates: $48-$84
(415) 928-6800
(800) 843-8709

BERESFORD ARMS
701 Post St (94109)
Rates: $105-$185
(415) 673-2600
(800) 533-6533

BEST WESTERN TUSCAN INN AT FISHERMANS WHARF
425 Northpoint Rd (94133)
Rates: $189-$218
(415) 561-1100
(800) 528-1234
(800) 648-4626

CAMPTON PLACE HOTEL
340 Stockton St (94108)
Rates: $325-$445
(415) 781-5555
(800) 235-4300

THE CLIFT HOTEL
495 Geary St (94102)
Rates: $215-$360
(415) 775-4700
(800) 437-4824

DAYS INN
2358 Lombard St (94123)
Rates: $69-$169
(415) 922-2010
(800) 329-7466

FAIRMONT HOTEL & TOWERS
950 Mason St (94108)
Rates: $159-$299
(415) 772-5000

GOLDEN GATE HOTEL B&B
775 Bush St (94108)
Rates: $65-$99
(415) 392-3702
(800) 835-1118

GROSVENOR HOUSE
899 Pine St (94108)
Rates: $109-$275
(415) 421-1899
(800) 999-9189

HILTON-SF AIRPORT
PO Box 8355
SF Airport (94128)
Rates: $139-$175
(415) 589-0770
(800) 445-8667

HOLIDAY INN CIVIC CENTER
50 8th St (94103)
Rates: $179-$199
(415) 626-6103
(800) 465-4329

HOTEL BERESFORD
635 Sutter St (94102)
Rates: $115-$145
(415) 673-9900
(800) 533-6533

HOTEL BERESFORD MANOR
860 Sutter St (94102)
Rates: $60-$70
(415) 673-3330
(800) 533-6533

HOTEL MONACO
501 Geary St (94102)
Rates: $179-$279
(415) 292-0100
(800) 214-4220

HOTEL PALOMAR
12 Fourth St (94103)
Rates: $150-$449
(877) 294-9711
(888) 546-7866

HOTEL TRITON
342 Grant Ave (94108)
Rates: $199-$329
(415) 394-0500
(888) 546-7866

THE INN SAN FRANCISCO B&B
943 S Van Ness Ave (94110)
Rates: $85-$225
(415) 641-0188
(800) 359-0913

LAUREL MOTOR INN
444 Presidio Ave (94115)
Rates: $99-$149
(415) 567-8467
(800) 552-8735

MANDARIN ORIENTAL HOTEL
222 Sansome St (94104)
Rates: $325-$550
(415) 276-9888

MANSIONS HOTEL
2220 Sacramento St (94115)
Rates: $114-$350
(415) 929-9444
(800) 826-9398

MARRIOTT AT FISHERMANS WHARF
1250 Columbus Ave (94133)
Rates: $289
(415) 775-7555
(800) 228-9290

MARRIOTT HOTEL
55 Fourth St (94103)
Rates: $279
(415) 896-1600
(800) 228-9290

OCEAN PARK MOTEL
2690 46th Ave (94116)
Rates: $53-$65
(415) 566-7020

PACIFIC HEIGHTS INN
1555 Union St (94123)
Rates: $85-$130
(415) 776-3310
(800) 523-1801

THE PRESCOTT HOTEL
545 Post St (94102)
Rates: $190-$225
(415) 563-0303

SERRANO HOTEL
405 Taylor St (94102)
Rates: $209-$259
(415) 885-2500
(888) 546-7866

SHEEHAN HOTEL
620 Sutter St (94102)
Rates: $40-$99
(415) 775-6500
(800) 848-1529

THE STEINHART
952 Sutter St (94109)
Rates: $2100+ Monthly
(415) 928-3855

TRAVELODGE BY THE BAY
1450 Lombard St (94123)
Rates: $130-$160
(415) 673-0691
(800) 578-7878

THE WESTIN ST. FRANCIS
335 Powell St (94102)
Rates: $229-$345
(415) 397-7000
(800) 937-8461

SAN JACINTO

CROWN MOTEL
138 S Ramona Blvd (92583)
Rates: $37-$43
(909) 654-7133

SAN JOSE

DOUBLETREE HOTEL
2050 Gateway Pl (95110)
Rates: $239
(408) 453-4000
(800) 222-8733

HILTON & TOWERS
300 Almaden Blvd (95110)
Rates: $139-$240
(408) 287-2100
(800) 445-8667

HOMESTEAD GUEST STUDIOS
1560 N First St (95112)
Rates: $89-$124
(408) 573-0648
(888) 782-9473

HOMEWOOD SUITES
10 W Trimble Rd (95131)
Rates: $189-$354
(408) 428-9900
(800) 225-5466

MOTEL 6-AIRPORT
2081 N First St (95131)
Rates: $59-$74
(408) 436-8180
(800) 466-8356

MOTEL 6-SOUTH
2560 Fontaine Rd (95121)
Rates: $46-$62
(408) 270-3131
(800) 466-8356

SUMMERFIELD SUITES
1602 Crane Ct (95122)
Rates: $99-$299
(408) 436-1600
(800) 833-4353

VAGABOND INN
1488 N First St (95112)
Rates: $54-$64
(408) 453-8822
(800) 522-1555

SAN JUAN BAUTISTA

SAN JUAN INN
410 Alameda (95045)
Rates: $60-$99
(831) 623-4380

SAN JUAN CAPISTRANO

BEST WESTERN CAPISTRANO INN
27174 Ortega Hwy (92675)
Rates: $69-$119
(949) 493-5661
(800) 528-1234
(800) 441-9438

SAN LEANDRO

ISLANDER LODGE MOTEL
2398 E 14th St (94577)
Rates: $33-$45
(510) 352-5010

SAN LUIS OBISPO

AVILA HOT SPRINGS SPA
250 Avila Beach Dr (93405)
Rates: $19-$26
(805) 595-2359
(800) 332-2359

BEST WESTERN OLIVE TREE INN
1000 Olive St (93405)
Rates: $79-$159
(805) 544-2800
(800 528-1234

BEST WESTERN ROYAL OAK MOTOR HOTEL
214 Madonna Rd (93405)
Rates: $79-$195
(805) 544-4410
(800) 528-1234
(800) 545-4410

HERITAGE INN BED & BREAKFAST
978 Olive St (93405)
Rates: $65-$150
(805) 544-7440

MOTEL 6-NORTH
1433 Calle Joaquin (93401)
Rates: $36-$49
(805) 549-9595
(800) 466-8356

MOTEL 6-SOUTH
1625 Calle Joaquin (93401)
Rates: $36-$49
(805) 541-6992
(800) 466-8356

SANDS SUITES & MOTEL
1930 Monterey St (93401)
Rates: $89-$139
(805) 544-0500
(800) 441-4657

TRAVELODGE
1825 Monterey St (93401)
Rates: $79-$149
(805) 543-5110
(800) 578-7878

VAGABOND INN
210 Madonna Rd (93405)
Rates: $69-$84
(805) 544-4710
(800) 522-1555

SAN MARCOS

QUAILS INN AT LAKE SAN MARCOS
1025 La Bonita Dr (92069)
Rates: $99-$225
(760) 744-0120
(800) 447-6556

SAN MATEO

HOMESTEAD GUEST STUDIOS EXTENDED STAY
1830 Gateway Dr (94404)
Rates: $518-$658 Weekly
(650) 344-3219
(888) 782-9473

RESIDENCE INN BY MARRIOTT
2000 Winward Way (94404)
Rates: $109-$219
(650) 574-4700
(800) 331-3131

VILLA HOTEL AIRPORT SOUTH
4000 S El Camino Real (94403)
Rates: $89-$269
(650) 341-0966
(800) 341-2345

SAN PEDRO

VAGABOND INN
215 S Gaffey St (90731)
Rates: $55-$80
(310) 831-8911
(800) 522-1555

SAN RAFAEL

CASA SOLDAVINI GUESTHOUSE
531 C St (94901)
Rates: n/a
(415) 454-3140

VILLA INN
1600 Lincoln Ave (94901)
Rates: $70-$99
(415) 456-4975

AREA CODES - If the local number doesn't connect, check for a new area code.

SAN RAMON

MARRIOTT AT BISHOP RANCH
2600 Bishop Dr (94583)
Rates: $169
(925) 867-9200
(800) 228-9290

RESIDENCE INN BY MARRIOTT
1071 Market Pl (94583)
Rates: $159-$199
(925) 277-9292
(800) 331-3131

SAN SIMEON

BEST WESTERN CAVALIER INN
9415 Hearst Dr (93452)
Rates: $69-$189
(805) 927-4688
(800) 528-1234
(800) 826-8168

BEST WESTERN COURTESY INN
9450 Castillo Dr (93452)
Rates: $50-$125
(805) 927-4691
(800) 528-1234
(800) 555-5773

MOTEL 6-HEARST CASTLE
9070 Castillo Dr (93452)
Rates: $66-$95
(805) 927-8691
(800) 466-8356

SILVER SURF MOTEL
9390 Castillo Dr (93452)
Rates: $69-$119
(805) 927-4661
(800) 621-3999

SAN YSIDRO

ECONOMY INNS OF AMERICA-MEXICAN BORDER
230 Via de San Ysidro (92173)
Rates: $25-$40
(619) 428-6191
(800) 826-0778

INTERNATIONAL MOTOR INN-MEXICAN BORDER
190 E Calle Primera (92173)
Rates: $65-$75
(619) 428-4486

MOTEL 6-MEXICAN BORDER
160 E Calle Primera (92173)
Rates: $27-$40
(619) 690-6663
(800) 466-8356

SANGER

TOWN HOUSE MOTEL
1308 Church Ave (93657)
Rates: $40-$45
(559) 875-5531

SANTA ANA

GUESTHOUSE INN & SUITES
2151 E First St (92701)
Rates: $49-$79
(714) 558-2772
(800) 214-8378

HOWARD JOHNSON
939 E 17th St (92701)
Rates: $69-$85
(714) 558-3700
(800) 446-4656

MOTEL 6
1623 E First St (92701)
Rates: $37-$51
(714) 558-0500
(800) 466-8356

RED ROOF INN
2600 N Main St (92701)
Rates: $56-$82
(714) 542-0311
(800) 843-7663

SANTA BARBARA

BACARA RESORT & SPA
8301 Holister Ave (93117)
Rates: $125+
(805) 968-0100

BEACH HOUSE INN & APARTMENTS
320 W Yanonali St (93101)
Rates: $75-$175
(805) 966-1126

BLUE SANDS MOTEL
421 S Milpas (93103)
Rates: $75-$185
(805) 965-1624

CASA DEL MAR INN
18 Bath St (93101)
Rates: $69-$219
(805) 963-4418
(800) 433-3097

FESS PARKERS DOUBLETREE RESORT
633 E Cabrillo Blvd (93103)
Rates: $195-$289
(805) 564-4333
(800) 222-8733

FOUR SEASONS BILTMORE HOTEL
1260 Channel Dr (93108)
Rates: $290-$650
(805) 969-2261
(800) 332-3442

IVANHOE INN
1406 Castillo St (93101)
Rates: $125+
(805) 963-8832

LA PLAYA MOTEL
212 W Cabrillo Blvd (93102)
Rates: $45-$150
(805) 962-6436
(800) 554-9324

MIRAMAR RESORT HOTEL
1555 S Jameson Lane (93108)
Rates: $75-$125
(805) 962-2203
(800) 322-6983

MOTEL 6-BEACH
443 Corona Del Mar (93103)
Rates: $54-$81
(805) 564-1392
(800) 466-8356

OCEAN PALMS BEACH RESORT
232 W Cabrillo Blvd (93101)
Rates: $65-$355
(805) 966-9133
(800) 350-2326

PACIFIC CREST INN BY THE SEA
433 Corona Del Mar Dr (93103)
Rates: $75-$125
(805) 966-3103

PACIFICA SUITES
5490 Hollister Ave (93111)
Rates: $125-$185
(805) 683-6722
(800) 338-6722

SANDY BEACH INN
122 W Cabrillo Blvd (93102)
Rates: $55-$150
(805) 963-0405
(800) 662-1451

SANTA BARBRA VACATION RENTALS
23 S Hope Ave, A-125 (93105)
Rates: $125+
(805) 682-2731

TRAVELER'S MOTEL
3222 State St (93105)
Rates: $75-$125
(805) 687-6009

VILLA ELEGANTE VACATION RENTALS
402 Orilla del Mar (93103)
Rates: $1200/Wkly
(805) 966-4410

SANTA CATALINA ISLAND
(See Avalon)

SANTA CLARA

GUESTHOUSE INN & SUITES-SILICON VALLEY
2930 El Camino Real (95051)
Rates: $109-$220
(408) 241-3010
(800) 214-8378

MARRIOTT HOTEL
2700 Mission College Blvd (95054)
Rates: $89-$265
(408) 988-1500
(800) 228-9290

MOTEL 6
3208 El Camino Real (95051)
Rates: $55-$66
(408) 241-0200
(800) 466-8356

VAGABOND INN
3580 El Camino Real (95051)
Rates: $89-$99
(408) 241-0771
(800) 522-1555

WESTIN HOTEL
5101 Great America Pkwy (95054)
Rates: $280-$325
(408) 986-0700
(800) 937-8461

SANTA CLARITA

BEST WESTERN RANCH HOUSE INN
27413 Tourney Rd (91355)
Rates: $70-$110
(661) 255-0555
(800) 528-1234

SANTA CRUZ

CAPRI MOTEL
337 Riverside Ave (95060)
Rates: $29-$189
(831) 426-4611

CLIFF CREST B&B
407 Cliff St (95060)
Rates: $95-$150
(831) 427-2609

EDGEWATER BEACH MOTEL
525 Second St (95060)
Rates: $59-$289
(831) 423-0440
(888) 809-6767

GUESTHOUSE PACIFIC INN
330 Ocean St (95060)
Rates: $59-$199
(831) 425-3722

LAGUNA CREEK INN B&B
2727 Smith Grade (95060)
Rates: $85-$125
(831) 425-0692
(800) 730-5398

OCEAN FRONT HOUSE
1600 W Cliff Dr (95060)
Rates: $850-$1230 Weekly
(831) 266-4453
(800) 801-4453

OCEAN PACIFIC LODGE
120 Washington St (95060)
Rates: $110-$130
(831) 457-1234
(800) 995-0289

REDWOOD CROFT B&B
276 Northwest Dr (95060)
Rates: $75
(831) 458-1939

SUNNY COVE MOTEL
2-1610 E Cliff Dr (95062)
Rates: $40-$100
(831) 475-1741

TRAVELODGE RIVIERA MOTEL
619 Riverside Ave (95060)
Rates: $94-$189
(831) 423-9515
(800) 578-7878

SANTA FE SPRINGS

MOTEL 6
13412 Excelsior Dr (90670)
Rates: $35-$48
(562) 921-0596
(800) 466-8356
(800) 426-3213

SANTA MARIA

BEST WESTERN BIG AMERICA
1725 N Broadway (93454)
Rates: $69-$99
(805) 922-5200
(800) 528-1234
(800) 426-3213

COMFORT INN
210 S Nicholson Ave (93454)
Rates: $69-$89
(805) 922-5891
(800) 228-5150

HISTORIC SANTA MARIA INN
801 S Broadway (93454)
Rates: $99-$139
(805) 928-7777
(800) 462-4276

HOLIDAY INN HOTEL & SUITES
2100 N Broadway (93454)
Rates: $78-$148
(805) 928-6000
(800) 465-4329

HOLIDAY MOTEL
605 S Broadway (93454)
Rates: n/a
(805) 925-2497

HUNTER'S INN
1514 S Broadway (93454)
Rates: $49-$95
(805) 922-2123
(800) 950-2123

MOTEL 6
2040 N Preisker Lane (93454)
Rates: $35-$52
(805) 928-8111
(800) 466-8356

ROSE GARDEN INN
1007 E Main St (93454)
Rates: $35-$79
(805) 922-4505

SANTA MONICA

THE GEORGIAN
1415 Ocean Ave (90401)
Rates: $212-$325
(310) 395-6333
(800) 538-8147

HOLIDAY INN AT THE PIER
120 Colorado Blvd (90401)
Rates: $175-$275
(310) 451-0676
(800) 465-4329

LOEWS SANTA MONICA BEACH
1700 Ocean Ave (90401)
Rates: $290-$450
(310) 458-6700
(800) 235-6397

SANTA NELLA

BEST WESTERN ANDERSEN'S INN
12367 S Hwy 33 (95322)
Rates: $66-$83
(209) 826-5534
(800) 528-1234
(800) 527-5534

HOLIDAY INN EXPRESS
28976 W Plaza Dr (95322)
Rates: $59-$75
(209) 826-8282
(800) 465-4329

MOTEL 6
12733 S Hwy 33 (95322)
Rates: $34-$49
(209) 826-6644
(800) 466-8356

RAMADA INN MISSION DE ORO
13070 S Hwy 33 (95322)
Rates: $50-$89
(209) 826-4444
(800) 272-6232

SUPER 8 MOTEL
28821 W Gonzaga Rd (95322)
Rates: $39-$69
(209) 827-8700
(800) 800-8000

SANTA ROSA

BEST WESTERN GARDEN INN
1500 Santa Rosa Ave (95404)
Rates: $85-$110
(707) 546-4031
(800) 528-1234
(800) 929-2771

COOPERS GROVE RANCH B&B
5800 Sonoma Mtn Rd (95404)
Rates: $110-$185
(707) 571-1928

HILLSIDE INN MOTEL
2901 4th St (95409)
Rates: $58-$68
(707) 546-9353

LOS ROBLES LODGE
1985 Cleveland Ave (95401)
Rates: $78-$118
(707) 545-63308
(800) 255-6330

MICROTEL INN & SUITES
3000 Santa Rosa Ave (95407)
Rates: $39-$109
(707) 544-0464
(888) 771-7171
(888) 466-2687

MOTEL 6-NORTH
3145 Cleveland Ave (95403)
Rates: $45-$56
(707) 525-9010
(800) 466-8356

MOTEL 6-SOUTH
2760 Cleveland Ave (95403)
Rates: $41-$56
(707) 546-1500
(800) 466-8356

TRAVELODGE
1815 Santa Rosa Ave (95403)
Rates: $55-$90
(707) 542-3472
(800) 578-7878

SANTA YNEZ

SANTA COTA MOTEL
3099 Mission Dr (93460)
Rates: $75-$125
(805) 688-5525

SANTA YSABEL

APPLE TREE INN
4360 Hwy 78 (92070)
Rates: $55-$79
(760) 765-0222

SANTEE

CARLTON OAKS COUNTRY CLUB
9200 Inwood Dr (92071)
Rates: $50-$80
(619) 448-4242
(800) 831-6757

SEA RANCH

SEA RANCH VACATION RENTALS
P.O. Box 123 (95497)
Rates: $220-$730
(707) 785-2427
(800) 785-3455

SEAL BEACH

RADISSON INN
600 Marina Dr (90740)
Rates: $110-$124
(562) 493-7501
(800) 333-3333

SEASIDE

THRIFTLODGE BAY BREEZE INN
2049 Fremont Blvd (93955)
Rates: $50-$130
(831) 899-7111
(800) 578-7878
(800) 899-7129

AREA CODES - If the local number doesn't connect, check for a new area code.

SELMA

BEST WESTERN JOHN JAY INN
2799 Floral Ave (93662)
Rates: $55-$110
(559) 891-0300
(800) 528-1234
(877) 529-4667

SUPER 8 MOTEL
3142 S Highland Ave (93662)
Rates: $45-$75
(559) 896-2800
(800) 800-8000

SHASTA LAKE CITY

BRIDGE BAY RESORT
10300 Bridge Bay Rd (Redding 96003)
Rates: $89
(530) 275-3021
(800) 752-9669

FAWNDALE LODGE & RV
15215 Fawndale Rd (Redding 96003)
Rates: $43-$75
(530) 275-8000
(800) 338-0941

SHASTA DAM MOTEL
1529 Cascade Blvd (Project City 96079)
Rates: $39-$62
(530) 275-1065

SHELL BEACH

SHELL BEACH MOTEL
653 Shell Beach Rd (93449)
Rates: n/a
(805) 773-4373

SHELTER COVE

MARINA MOTEL
533 Machi Rd (95589)
Rates: $52-$62
(707) 986-7595

SHELTER COVE MOTOR INN
205 Wave Dr (95589)
Rates: $63-$78
(707) 986-7521
(888) 870-9676

SHERMAN OAKS

BEST WESTERN CARRIAGE INN
5525 Sepulveda Blvd (91411)
Rates: $99-$195
(818) 787-2300
(800) 528-1234
(877) 787-2300

SIERRA CITY

HERRINGTONS SIERRA PINES
SR 49 (96125)
Rates: $49-$73
(530) 862-1151
(800) 682-9848

SIMI VALLEY

CLARION HOTEL
1775 Madera Rd (93065)
Rates: $84-$400
(805) 584-6300
(800) 252-7466

MOTEL 6
2566 N Erringer Rd (93065)
Rates: $45-$58
(805) 526-3533
(800) 466-8356

RADISSON HOTEL
999 Enchanted Way (93065)
Rates: $99
(805) 583-2000
(800) 333-3333

SKY FOREST

STORYBOOK INN BED & BREAKFST
28717 Hwy 18 (92352)
Rates: $75-$145
(909) 337-0011
(877) 337-0011

SMITH RIVER

BEST WESTERN SHIP ASHORE MOTEL
12340 Hwy 101 (95567)
Rates: $58-$88
(707) 487-3141
(800) 528-1234
(800) 487-3141

CASA RUBIO BEACH HOUSE
17285 Crissey Rd (95567)
Rates: $68-$98
(707) 487-4313
(800) 357-6199

SEA ESCAPE MOTEL
15370 Hwy 101 N (95567)
Rates: $60-$65
(707) 487-7333

SOLEDAD

MOTEL 8
1013 S Front St (93960)
Rates: $39-$64
(831) 678-3814

PARAISO HOT SPRINGS LODGE
Paraiso Springs Rd (93960)
Rates: $110-$160
(831) 678-2882

SOLVANG

MEADOWLARK MOTEL
2644 Mission Dr (93463)
Rates: $40-$70
(805) 688-4631
(800) 549-4658

VIKING MOTEL
1506 Mission Dr (93463)
Rates: $38-$125
(508) 688-1337
(800) 368-5611

SOMES BAR

MARBLE MTN RANCH CABINS
92520 Hwy 96 (95568)
Rates: $27-$200
(800) 552-6284

SONOMA

BEST WESTERN SONOMA VALLEY INN
550 2nd St W (95476)
Rates: $129-$369
(707) 938-9200
(800) 528-1234
(800) 334-5784

MARTHA'S COTTAGE B&B
19377 Orange Ave (95476)
Rates: $110-$125
(707) 996-6918

SPARROW'S NEST INN B&B
424 Denmark St (95476)
Rates: $85-$125
(707) 996-3750

STONE GROVE BED & BREAKFAST
240 2nd St E (95476)
Rates: $65-$115
(707) 939-8249

TREE HOUSE B&B
431 2nd St E (95476)
Rates: $125-$150
(707) 938-1628

VILLA CASTILLO BED & BREAKFAST
1100 Castle Rd (95476)
Rates: $150
(707) 996-4616

SONORA

ALADDIN MOTOR INN
14260 Mono Way (95370)
Rates: $68-$76
(209) 533-4971

BEST WESTERN SONORA OAKS MOTOR HOTEL
19551 Hess Ave (95370)
Rates: $89-$109
(209) 553-4400
(800) 528-1234
(800) 532-1944

DAYS INN
160 S Washington St (95370)
Rates: $71-$145
(209) 532-2400
(800) 329-7466

HAMMONS HOUSE INN B&B
22963 Robertson Ranch Rd (95370)
Rates: $130-$150
(209) 532-7921
(888) 666-7923

KENNEDY MEADOWS RESORT CABINS
P. O. Box 4010 (95370)
Rates: $52-$105
(209) 965-3900

MINERS MOTEL
18740 Hwy 108 (95370)
Rates: $45-$75
(209) 532-7850
(800) 451-4176

MOUNTAIN VIEW B&B
12980 Mountain View Rd (95370)
Rates: $60-$80
(209) 533-0628
(800) 446-1333

QUALITY INN
18730 Hwy 108 (95327)
Rates: $49-$99
(209) 984-0315
(800) 228-5151

RAIL FENCE MOTEL
19950 Hwy 108 (95370)
Rates: $35-$47
(209) 532-9191

SONORA GOLD LODGE
480 Stockton St (95370)
Rates: $44-$74
(209) 532-3952

SOQUEL

BLUE SPRUCE INN B&B
2815 Main St (95073)
Rates: $85-$150
(408) 464-1137
(800) 559-1137

SOUTH LAKE TAHOE

ALDER INN
1072 Ski Run Blvd
(96150)
Rates: $58-$105
(530) 544-4485
(800) 544-0056

BEACHSIDE INN & SUITES
930 Park Ave
(96150)
Rates: $33-$125
(530) 544-2400
(800) 884-4920

BLUE JAY LODGE
4133 Cedar Ave
(96150)
Rates: $49-$169
(530) 544-5232
(800) 258-3529

BLUE LAKE MOTEL
1055 Ski Run Blvd
(96150)
Rates: $50-$80
(530) 541-2399

CARNEY'S CABINS
P. O. Box 601748
(96153)
Rates: $70-$100
(530) 542-3361

DAYS INN STATELINE
968 Park Ave
(96150)
Rates: $42-$99
(530) 541-4800
(800) 329-7466

ECHO CREEK RANCH
P. O. Box 20088
(96151)
Rates: $100+
(530) 544-5397
(800) 462-5397

HARRAH'S LAKE TAHOE HOTEL & CASINO
15 Hwy 50
(Stateline, NV 89449)
Rates: $179-$269
(775) 588-6611
(800) 427-7247
(Kennels provided)

HIGH COUNTRY LODGE
1227 Emerald Bay Rd (96150)
Rates: $30-$70
(530) 541-0508

INN AT HEAVENLY B&B
1261 Ski Run Blvd
(96150)
Rates: $75-$395
(530) 544-4244
(800) 692-2246

LA BAER INN
4133 Lake Tahoe Blvd (96150)
Rates: $49-$109
(530) 544-2139
(800) 544-5575

LAKEPARK LODGE
4081 Cedar Ave
(96150)
Rates: $40-$75
(530) 541-5004

LAMPLITER MOTEL
4143 Cedar Ave
(96150)
Rates: $45-$100
(530) 544-2936

MATTERHORN MOTEL
2187 Lake Tahoe Blvd (96150)
Rates: $40-$185
(530) 541-0367

MONTGOMERY INN
966 Modesto Ave
(96151)
Rates: $49-$69
(530) 544-3871
(800) 624-8224

MOTEL 6
2375 Lake Tahoe Blvd (96150)
Rates: $34-$70
(530) 542-1400
(800) 466-8356

PARK AVENUE/ MEADOWOOD LODGE
904 Park Ave
(96150)
Rates: $70-$100
(530) 544-3503

RAVEN WOOD HOTEL
4075 Manzanita Ave (96150)
Rates: $52-$169
(800) 659-4185

RIDGEWOOD INN MOTEL
1341 Emerald Bay Rd (96150)
Rates: $40-$75
(530) 541-8595

RODEWAY INN
4082 Lake Tahoe Blvd (96150)
Rates: $29-$99
(530) 541-7900
(800) 228-2000

SAFARI MOTEL
966 LaSalle St
(96150)
Rates: $70-$100
(530) 544-2912

SHENANDOAH MOTEL
4074 Pine Blvd
(95729)
Rates: $30-$79
(530) 544-2985

SLEEPY RACCOON MOTEL
1180 Ski Run Blvd
(96150)
Rates: $40-$70
(530) 544-5890

SOUTH LAKE TAHOE CABIN RENTAL
4 Miles South at Hwy 89 & 50 Jct (96150)
Rates: $120-$250
(619) 246-0678
(888) 818-3283

SUPER 8 MOTEL
3600 Lake Tahoe Blvd (96150)
Rates: $44-$118
(530) 544-3476
(800) 800-8000
(800) 237-8882

TAHOE COLONY INN
3794 Montreal
(96150)
Rates: $48-$110
(530) 655-6481
(800) 338-5552

TAHOE HACIENDA MOTEL
3820 Lake Tahoe Blvd (96150)
Rates: $35-$85
(530) 541-3805

TAHOE KEYS RESORT
599 Tahoe Keys Blvd (96150)
Rates: $200-$400
(530) 544-5397
(800) 438-8246

TAHOE MARINA INN
930 Bal Bijou Rd
(96150)
Rates: $79-$140
(530) 541-2180

TAHOE QUEEN MOTEL
932 Poplar St
(96157)
Rates: $40-$70
(530) 544-2291

TAHOE SUNDOWNER MOTEL
1211 Emerald Bay
(96150)
Rates: $30-$85
(530) 541-2282

TAHOE SUNSET LODGE
1171 Emerald Bay
(96150)
Rates: $26-$60
(530) 541-2940

TAHOE TROPICANA LODGE
4132 Cedar Ave
(96154)
Rates: $40-$70
(530) 541-3911

TAHOE VALLEY LODGE
2241 Lake Tahoe Blvd (96150)
Rates: $95-$195
(530) 541-0353
(800) 669-7544

TRADE WINDS RESORT
944 Friday Ave
(96150)
Rates: $35-$125
(530) 544-6459
(800) 628-1829

SOUTH SAN FRANCISCO

LA QUINTA INN
20 Airport Blvd
(94080)
Rates: $105-$125
(650) 583-2223
(800) 687-6667

QUALITY INN & SUITES
410 S Airport lvd
(94080)
Rates: $105-$180
(650) 875-7878
(800) 228-5151

VAGABOND INN
222 S Airport Blvd
(94080)
Rates: $48-$95
(650) 589-9055
(800) 522-1555

SPRING VALLEY

CROWN INN SUITES
9603 Campo Rd
(91977)
Rates: $43-$64
(619) 589-1111

STANTON

MOTEL 6
7450 Katella Ave
(90680)
Rates: $33-$46
(714) 891-0717
(800) 466-8356

ST. HELENA

EL BONITA MOTEL
195 Main St
(94574)
Rates: $120-$250
(707) 963-3216
(800) 541-3284

HARVEST INN
One Main St
(94574)
Rates: $149-$650
(707) 963-9463
(800) 950-8466

STINSON BEACH

SEADRIFT COMPANY VACATION RENTALS
2 Dipsea Rd (94970)
Rates: n/a
(415) 868-1791

STOCKTON

BEST WESTERN
550 W Charter Way (95206)
Rates: $50-$65
(209) 948-0321
(800) 528-1234

COMFORT INN
3951 E Budweiser Ct (95215)
Rates: $48-$99
(209) 931-9341
(800) 228-5150

DAYS INN CITY CENTER
33 N Center St (95202)
Rates: $42-$60
(209) 948-6151
(800) 329-7466

ECONO LODGE
2210 Manthey Rd (95206)
Rates: $44-$56
(209) 466-5741
(800) 553-2666

LA QUINTA INN
2710 W March Ln (95219)
Rates: $69-$89
(209) 952-7800
(800) 687-6667

MOTEL 6
1625 French Camp Tpk (95206)
Rates: $36-$43
(209) 467-3600
(800) 466-8356

MOTEL 6
817 Navy Dr (95206)
Rates: $38-$45
(209) 946-0923
(800) 466-8356

MOTEL 6
6717 Plymouth Rd (95207)
Rates: $38-$45
(209) 951-8120
(800) 466-8356

RESIDENCE INN BY MARRIOTT
3240 W March Ln (95219)
Rates: $119-$139
(209) 472-9800
(800) 331-3131

SUNSHINE INN
8009 N Hwy 99 (95212)
Rates: $25-$50
(209) 956-5200

STRAWBERRY

3 RIVERS RESORT
P. O. Box 81 (95375)
Rates: $85-$185
(209) 965-3278
(800) 514-6777

SUISUN CITY

ECONOMY INNS OF AMERICA
4376 Central Pl (94585)
Rates: $30-$42
(707) 864-1728
(800) 826-0778

SUN CITY

TRAVELODGE
27955 Encanto Dr (92586)
Rates: $49-$65
(909) 679-1133
(800) 578-7878

SUN VALLEY

SCOTTISH INNS
8365 Lehigh Ave (91352)
Rates: $40+
(818) 504-2671
(800) 251-1962

SUNNYVALE

CAPTAIN'S COVE MOTEL
600 N Mathilda Ave (94086)
Rates: $59-$61
(800) 322-2683

HOMESTEAD VILLAGE
1255 Orleans Dr (94086)
Rates: $99-$134
(408) 734-3431
(888) 782-9473

MOTEL 6 NORTH
775 N Mathilda Ave (94086)
Rates: $55-$62
(408) 736-4595
(800) 466-8356

MOTEL 6 SOUTH
806 Ahwanee Ave (94086)
Rates: $55-$62
(408) 720-1222
(800) 466-8356

RESIDENCE INN BY MARRIOTT
1080 Stewart Dr (94086)
Rates: $199-$239
(408) 720-8893
(800) 331-3131

RESIDENCE INN BY MARRIOTT
750 Lakeway Dr (94086)
Rates: $199-$239
(408) 720-1000
(800) 331-3131

SUMMERFIELD SUITES
900 Hamlin Ct (94089)
Rates: $160-$190
(408) 745-1515
(800) 833-4353

VAGABOND INN
816 Ahwanee Ave (94086)
Rates: $65-$75
(408) 734-4607
(800) 522-1555

SUSANVILLE

BUDGET HOST FRONTIER INN
2685 Main St (96130)
Rates: $31-$41
(530) 257-4141
(800) 283-4678

COZY MOTEL
2829 Main St (96130)
Rates: $25-$30
(530) 257-2319

DIAMOND VIEW MOTEL
1529 Main St (96130)
Rates: $27-$34
(530) 257-4585

KNIGHTS INN MOTEL
1705 Main St (96130)
Rates: $37-$49
(530) 257-2168
(800) 843-5644

MT. LASSEN HOTEL
27 S Lassen St (96130)
Rates: $37+
(530) 257-6609

RIVER INN MOTEL
1710 Main St (96130)
Rates: $46-$54
(530) 257-6051

SIERRA VISTA MOTEL
1067 Main St (96130)
Rates: $29-$34
(530) 257-6721

SUPER 8 MOTEL
2975 Johnstonville Rd (96130)
Rates: $48-$62
(530) 257-2782
(800) 800-8000

SYLMAR

GOOD NITE INN
12835 Encinitas Ave (91342)
Rates: $45-$65
(818) 362-8899
(800) 648-3466

MOTEL 6
12775 Encinitas Ave (91342)
Rates: $36-$48
(818) 362-9491
(800) 466-8356

TAHOE CITY

THREE BUCK INN
135 Alpine Meadows Rd #34 (96146)
Rates: $95-$175
(530) 550-8600

TAHOE VISTA

BEESLEY'S COTTAGES
6674 N Lake Blvd (96148)
Rates: $70-$140
(530) 546-2448

HOLIDAY HOUSE
7276 N Lake Blvd (96148)
Rates: $95-$145
(530) 546-2369
(800) 294-6378 (CA)

RUSTIC COTTAGES
7499 N Lake Blvd (96148)
Rates: $49-$139
(530) 546-3523

TAHOMA

NORFOLK WOODS INN CABINS
6941 W Lake Blvd (96142)
Rates: $100-$180
(530) 525-5000

TAHOE LAKE COTTAGES
7030 W Lake Blvd (96142)
Rates: $125-$185
(530) 525-4411
(800) 824-6348

TAHOMA LODGE
7018 W Lake Blvd (96142)
Rates: $45-$115
(530) 525-7721
(800) 824-6348

TECOPA

DELIGHT'S HOT SPA ROOMS & CABINS
368 Tecopa Hot Springs Rd (92389)
Rates: $32-$50
(760) 852-4343
(800) 854-5007

AREA CODES - If the local number doesn't connect, check for a new area code.

TEHACHAPI

**BEST WESTERN
MOUNTAIN INN**
416 W Tehachapi
Blvd (93561)
Rates: $55-$75
(661) 822-5591
(800) 528-1234

**GOLDEN HILLS
MOTEL**
22561 Woodford-
Tehachapi Rd
(93561)
Rates: $24-$49
(661) 822-4488
(800) 434-1118

**TRAVELODGE
TEHACHAPI
SUMMIT**
500 Steuber Rd
(93561)
Rates: $46-$60
(661) 823-8000
(800) 578-7878

TEMECULA

COMFORT INN
27338 Jefferson
Ave (92590)
Rates: $47-$159
(909) 699-5888
(800) 228-5150

MOTEL 6
41900 Moreno Dr
(92590)
Rates: $33-$46
(909) 676-7199
(800) 466-8356

**TEMECULA VALLEY
INN**
27660 Jefferson
Ave (92590)
Rates: $109-$119
(909) 699-2444

THOUSAND OAKS

E-Z 8 MOTEL
2434 W Hillcrest
Dr (91362)
Rates: $31+
(805) 499-0755

MOTEL 6
1516 Newbury Rd
(91320)
Rates: $36-$46
(805) 499-0711
(800) 466-8356

**THOUSAND
OAKS INN**
75 W Thousand
Oaks Blvd (91360)
Rates: $72-$95
(805) 497-3701

**THOUSAND
OAKS VILLAGE
INN**
1425 Thousand
Oaks Blvd (91360)
Rates: n/a
(805) 496-0102

THREE RIVERS

**BEST WESTERN
HOLIDAY LODGE**
40105 Sierra Dr
(93271)
Rates: $79-$93
(559) 561-4119
(800) 528-1234
(888) 523-9909

**BUCKEYE TREE
LODGE**
46000 Sierra Dr
(93271)
Rates: $73-$103
(559) 561-5900

**LAZY J RANCH
MOTEL-IMA**
39625 Sierra Dr
(93271)
Rates: $60-$95
(559) 561-4449
(800) 341-8000

THE RIVER INN
45176 Sierra Dr
(93271)
Rates: $55-$59
(559) 561-4367

SEQUOIA MOTEL
43000 Sierra Dr
(93271)
Rates: $45-$169
(559) 561-4453

**SEQUOIA
VILLAGE INN**
45971 Sierra Dr
(93271)
Rates: $50-$180
(559) 561-3652

SIERRA LODGE
43175 Sierra Dr
(93271)
Rates: $40-$95
(559) 561-3681

TORRANCE

**RESIDENCE INN
BY MARRIOTT**
3701 Torrance
Blvd (90503)
Rates: $178
(310) 543-4566
(800) 331-3131

**SUMMERFIELD
SUITES HOTEL**
19901 Prairie Ave
(90503)
Rates: $198-$228
(310) 371-8525
(800) 833-4353

TRACY

MOTEL 6
3810 Tracy Blvd
(95376)
Rates: $35-$48
(209) 836-4900
(800) 466-8356

TRINIDAD

**BISHOP PINE
LODGE**
1481 Patrick's
Point Dr (95570)
Rates: $70-$80
(707) 677-3314

**EMERALD FOREST
RESORT**
753 Patrick's Point
Dr (95570)
Rates: $55-$135
(707) 677-3554

**HARBOR HOUSE
VACATION
RENTAL**
P. O. Box 1244
(95570)
Rates: $135-$150
(707) 677-1606

SHADOW LODGE
687 Patrick's Pt Dr
(95570)
Rates: $49-$95
(707) 677-0532

TRINIDAD INN
1170 Patrick's Pt
Dr (95570)
Rates: $50-$100
(707) 677-3349

TRINITY CENTER

**BECKER'S
BOUNTY LODGE**
HCR 3, Box 4659
(96091)
Rates: $400-$650
Weekly
(530) 266-3277

**ENRIGHT GULCH
CABINS**
3500 Hwy 3, P.O.
Box 244 (96091)
Rates: $30-$35
(530) 266-3600

**RIPPLE CREEK
CABINS**
Rt 2, Box 4020
(96091)
Rates: $60-$115
(530) 266-3505

**WYNTOON
RESORT**
Hwy 3 (96091)
Rates: $16-$110
(530) 266-3337
(800) 715-3337

TRONA

**DESERT ROSE
MOTEL**
84368 Trona Rd
(93562)
Rates: $30-$42
(619) 372-4572

TRUCKEE

**ALPINE VILLAGE
MOTEL**
12660 Deerfield
Dr (96161)
Rates: $50-$79
(530) 587-3801
(800) 933-1787

**THE INN AT
TRUCKEE**
11506 Deerfield Dr
(96161)
Rates: $89-$139
(530) 587-8888
(888) 773-6888

RICHARDS MOTEL
15758 Donner
Pass Rd (96160)
Rates: $60-$110
(530) 587-3662

TULARE

**BEST WESTERN
TOWN &
COUNTRY LODGE**
1051 N Blackstone
Dr (93274)
Rates: $60-$76
(559) 688-7537
(800) 528-1234
(888) 488-5273

COMFORT SUITES
1021 N Blackstone
(93274)
Rates: $54-$89
(800) 228-5150

**GREEN GABLE
INN**
1010 E Prosperity
Ave (93274)
Rates: $53-$85
(559) 686-3432

**HOWARD
JOHNSON EXP**
1050 E Rankin Ave
(93274)
Rates: $35-$90
(559) 688-6671
(800) 446-4656

**INNS OF
AMERICA**
1183 N Blackstone
Dr (93274)
Rates: $49-$58
(559) 686-3432
(800) 826-0778

MOTEL 6
1111 N Blackstone
Dr (93274)
Rates: $31-$42
(559) 686-1611
(800) 446-8356

**TULARE INN
MOTEL**
1301 E Paige
(93274)
Rates: $29-$38
(800) 333-8571

TULELAKE

ELLIS MOTEL
2238 Hwy 139
(96134)
Rates: $30-$57
(530) 667-5242

AREA CODES - If the local number doesn't connect, check for a new area code.

TURLOCK

BEST WESTERN ORCHARD INN
5025 N Golden State Blvd (95380)
Rates: $59-$75
(209) 667-2827
(800) 528-1234
(800) 521-5025

BEST WESTERN THE GARDENS MOTOR INN
1119 Pedras Rd (95382)
Rates: $65-$78
(209) 634-9351
(800) 528-1234
(800) 847-2378

MOTEL 6
250 S Walnut Ave (95380)
Rates: $32-$40
(209) 667-4100
(800) 466-8356

THE TREE INN
200 W Glenwood Ave (95380)
Rates: $49-$75
(209) 668-3400

TWAIN HARTE

ELDORADO MOTEL
22678 Blackhawk Dr (95383)
Rates: $42-$65
(209) 586-4479

TWENTYNINE PALMS

29 PALMS INN
73950 Inn Ave (92277)
Rates: n/a
(760) 367-3505

CIRCLE "C" LODGE
6340 El Rey Ave (92277)
Rates: $70-$85
(760) 367-7615

MOTEL 6
72562 29 Palms Hwy (92277)
Rates: $35-$43
(760) 367-2833
(800) 466-8356

ROUGHLEY MANOR B&B
74744 Joe Davis Rd (92277)
Rates: $75+
(760) 367-3238

TWIN PEAKS

ARROWHEAD PINE ROSE CABINS
25994 Hwy 189 (92391)
Rates: $49-$159
(909) 337-2341
(800) 429-7463

UKIAH

DAYS INN REDWOODS-WINE COUNTRY
950 N State St (95482)
Rates: $55-$105
(707) 462-7584
(800) 329-7466
(800) 922-3388

MOTEL 6
1208 S State St (95482)
Rates: $32-$52
(707) 468-5404
(800) 466-8356

RODEWAY INN
1050 S State St (95482)
Rates: $40-$69
(707) 462-2906
(800) 228-2000

SUPER 8 MOTEL
1070 S State St (95482)
Rates: $40-$95
(707) 462-6657
(800) 800-8000

WESTERN TRAVELER MOTEL
693 S Orchard Ave (95482)
Rates: $45-$65
(707) 468-9167
(800) 794-3557

UPPER LAKE

BLUE LAKES LODGE & RESTAURANT
5135 W Hwy 20 (95485)
Rates: $32-$59
(707) 275-2181
(800) 423-2181

NARROWS LODGE RESORT
5690 Blue Lakes Rd (95485)
Rates: $50-$85
(707) 275-2718

PINE ACRES BLUE LAKE RESORT
5328 Blue Lakes Rd (95485)
Rates: $85+
(707) 275-2811

VACAVILLE

BEST WESTERN HERITAGE INN
1420 E Monte Vista Ave (95688)
Rates: $70-$115
(707) 448-8453
(800) 528-1234

MOTEL 6
107 Lawrence Dr (95687)
Rates: $37-$48
(707) 447-5550
(800) 466-8356

SUPER 8 MOTEL
101 Allison Court (95688)
Rates: $49-$69
(707) 449-8884
(800) 800-8000

VALENCIA

HILTON GARDEN INN-SIX FLAGS
27710 The Old Rd (91355)
Rates: $99-$129
(661) 254-8800
(800) 445-8667

VALLEJO

HOLIDAY INN SIX FLAGS-MARINE WORLD
1000 Fairgrounds Dr (94590)
Rates: $109-$129
(707) 644-1200
(800) 465-4329
(800) 533-5753

KNIGHTS INN
160 Lincoln Rd E (94591)
Rates: n/a
(707) 552-7220
(800) 843-5644

MOTEL 6 FAIRGROUNDS-MARINE WORLD EAST
458 Fairgrounds Dr (94589)
Rates: $39-$52
(707) 642-7781
(800) 466-8356

MOTEL 6-MARINE WORLD WEST
1455 Marine World Pkwy (94589)
Rates: $39-$52
(707) 643-7611
(800) 466-8356

MOTEL 6 MARITIME NORTH
597 Sandy Beach Rd (94590)
Rates: $34-$48
(707) 552-2912
(800) 466-8356

QUALITY INN
44 Admiral Callaghan Ln (94594)
Rates: $49-$109
(707) 643-1061
(800) 228-5151

RAMADA INN
1000 Admiral Callaghan Ln (94594)
Rates: $70-$145
(707) 643-2700
(800) 272-6232

VALLEY FORD

VALLEY FORD HOTEL
14415 Coast Hwy One (94972)
Rates: $55-$90
(707) 876-3600
(800) 696-6679

VALLEY SPRINGS

10TH GREEN INN BED & BREAKFAST
14 St. Andrews Rd (95252)
Rates: $59-$89
(209) 772-1084

VENTURA

BEST WESTERN VENTURA INN
708 E Thompson Blvd (93001)
Rates: $99-$119
(805) 648-3101
(800) 528-1234
(800) 648-1508

LA QUINTA INN
5818 Valentine Rd (93003)
Rates: $59-$79
(805) 658-6200
(800) 687-6777

MOTEL 6-BEACH
2145 E Harbor Blvd (93001)
Rates: $39-$54
(805) 643-5100
(800) 466-8356

MOTEL 6-SOUTH
3075 Johnson Dr (93003)
Rates: $39-$54
(805) 650-0080
(800) 466-8356

OCEAN VIEW MOTEL
1690 E Thompson Blvd (93001)
Rates: n/a
(805) 648-6440

REX MOTEL
2406 E Thompson Blvd (93001)
Rates: n/a
(805) 643-5681

VAGABOND INN
756 E Thompson
Blvd (93001)
Rates: $66-$85
(805) 648-5371
(800) 522-1555

VICTORIA MOTEL
2350 S Victoria
Ave (93003)
Rates: $33-$60
(805) 642-2173

WHITE CAPS MOTEL
1612 E Thompson
Blvd (93001)
Rates: n/a
(805) 648-4924

VICTORVILLE

BUDGET INN
14153 Kentwood
Blvd (92392)
Rates: $32-$44
(760) 241-8010

HI DESERT RED ROOF INN
13409 Mariposa
Rd (92392)
Rates: $51-$77
(760) 241-1577
(800) 843-7663

MOTEL 6
16901 Stoddard
Wells Rd (92392)
Rates: $31-$39
(760) 243-0666
(800) 466-8356

SUNSET INN
15765 Mojave Dr
(92392)
Rates: $25-$36
(760) 243-2342

TRAVELODGE
16868 Stoddard
Wells Rd (92394)
Rates: $39-$65
(760) 243-7700
(800) 578-7878

VISALIA

BEST WESTERN VISALIA INN
623 W Main St
(93277)
Rates: $76-$80
(559) 732-4561
(800) 528-1234
(877) 500-4771

JOHN JAY INN & SUITES
9300 W Airport Dr
(93277)
Rates: $69-$156
(559) 651-3700

OAK TREE INN
401 Woodland
Dr (93277)
Rates: $30-$36
(559) 732-8861
(800) 554-7664

VISTA

HILLTOP MOTOR LODGE
330 Mar Vista Dr
(92083)
Rates: $36-$44
(760) 726-7010

LA QUINTA INN
630 Sycamore Ave
(92083)
Rates: $65-$85
(760) 727-8180
(800) 687-6667

WALNUT CREEK

EMBASSY SUITES HOTEL
1345 Treat Blvd
(94596)
Rates: $149-$199
(925) 934-2500
(800) 362-2779

HOLIDAY INN
2730 N Main St
(94596)
Rates: $124+
(925) 932-3332
(800) 465-4329

MOTEL 6
2389 N Main St
(94596)
Rates: $49-$68
(925) 935-4010
(800) 466-8356

WALNUT CREEK MOTOR LODGE
1960 N Main St
(94596)
Rates: $65-$80
(925) 932-2811
(800) 824-0334

WATSONVILLE

BEST WESTERN INN
740 Freedom Blvd
(95076)
Rates: $67-$130
(831) 724-3367
(800) 528-1234
(888) 685-5760

COUNTRY SUNRISE B&B
3085 Freedom
Blvd (95076)
Rates: $70-$95
(831) 722-4793

EL RANCHO MOTEL
976 Salinas Rd
(95076)
Rates: $30-$69
(831) 722-2766

KOA KAMPING CABINS
1186 San Andreas
Rd (95076)
Rates: $34-$42
(831) 722-0551
(800) 562-7701

MOTEL 6
125 Silver Leaf Dr
(95076)
Rates: $39-$66
(831) 728-4144
(800) 466-8356

RED ROOF INN
1620 W Beach St
(95076)
Rates: $65-$96
(831) 740-4520
(800) 843-7663

WAWONA STATION

THE REDWOOD GUEST COTTAGES
P. O. Box 2085
(95389)
Rates: $95-$400
(209) 375-6666

WEAVERVILLE

BEST WESTERN VICTORIAN INN
1709 Main St
(96093)
Rates: $55-$159
(530) 623-4432
(800) 528-1234

49ER GOLD COUNTRY INN
718 Main St
(96093)
Rates: $34-$79
(530) 623-4937

MOTEL TRINITY
1112 Main St
(96093)
Rates: $49-$79
(530) 623-2129

RED HILL MOTEL
Red Hill Rd
(96093)
Rates: $30-$75
(530) 623-4331

WEED

BEST INN & SUITES-GRAND MANOR
1844 Shastina Dr
(96094)
Rates: $69-$96
(530) 938-1982
(800) 237-8466

MOTEL 6
466 N Weed Blvd
(96094)
Rates: $35-$46
(530) 938-4101
(800) 466-8356

SIS-Q-INN MOTEL
1825 Shastina Dr
(96094)
Rates: $46-$66
(530) 938-4194

STEWART MINERAL SPRINGS CABINS
4617 Stewart Spgs
Rd (96094)
Rates: $25-$65
(530) 938-2222
(800) 322-9223

TOWN HOUSE MOTEL
157 S Weed Blvd
(96094)
Rates: $35-$38
(530) 938-4431

Y MOTEL
90 N Weed Blvd
(96094)
Rates: $27-$40
(530) 938-4481

WEST COVINA

COMFORT INN
2804 E Garvey
Ave (91791)
Rates: $59-$150
(626) 915-6077
(800) 228-5150

HAMPTON INN
3145 E Garvey
Ave N (91791)
Rates: $69-$89
(626) 967-5800
(800) 426-7866

HOLIDAY INN
3223 E Garvey
Ave N (91791)
Rates: $79
(626) 966-8311
(800) 465-4329

WEST HOLLYWOOD

THE ARGYLE HISTORIC HOTEL
8358 Sunset Blvd
(90069)
Rates: $170-$1200
(323) 654-7100

LE MONTROSE SUITE HOTEL
900 Hammond St
(90069)
Rates: $295-$480
(323) 855-1115
(800) 776-0666

LE PARC DE GRAN LUXE HOTEL
733 N West Knoll
Dr (90069)
Rates: $195-$285
(323) 855-8888
(800) 578-4837

MONDRIAN HOTEL
8440 Sunset Blvd
(90069)
Rates: $235-$475
(323) 650-8999
(800) 525-8029

SUMMERFIELD SUITES HOTEL
1000 Westmount
Dr (90069)
Rates: $149-$179
(310) 657-7400
(800) 833-4353

AREA CODES - If the local number doesn't connect, check for a new area code.

SUNSET MARQUIS HOTEL & VILLAS
1200 N Alta Loma Rd (90069)
Rates: $315-$1200
(310) 657-1333

WEST SACRAMENTO

MOTEL 6
1254 Halyard Dr (95691)
Rates: $37-$42
(916) 372-3624
(800) 466-8356

WESTLEY

DAYS INN
7144 McCracken Rd (95387)
Rates: $46-$85
(209) 894-5500
(800) 329-7466

ECONO LODGE
7100 McCracken Rd (95387)
Rates: $38-$65
(209) 894-3900
(800) 553-2666

SUPER 8 MOTEL
7115 McCracken Rd (95387)
Rates: $45-$64
(209) 894-3888
(800) 800-8000

WESTMINSTER

MOTEL 6 NORTH
13100 Goldenwest (92683)
Rates: $33-$46
(714) 895-0042
(800) 466-8356

MOTEL 6 SOUTH
6266 Westminster Ave (92683)
Rates: $33-$46
(714) 891-5366
(800) 466-8356

WESTPORT

BLUE VICTORIAN INN
38921 N Hwy 1 (95488)
Rates: $75-$130
(707) 964-6310
(800) 466-8356

HOWARD CREEK RANCH B&B
40501 N Hwy 1 (95488)
Rates: $75-$160
(707) 964-6725

WESTPORT INN
37040 N Hwy 1 (95488)
Rates: $45+
(707) 964-5135

WHITTIER

BEST WHITTIER INN
14226 Whittier Blvd (90606)
Rates: $34-$80
(562) 698-0323

MOTEL 6
8221 S Pioneer Blvd (90606)
Rates: $33-$46
(562) 692-9101
(800) 466-8356

VAGABOND INN
14125 E Whittier Blvd (90605)
Rates: $60-$70
(562) 698-9701
(800) 522-1555

WILLIAMS

COMFORT INN
400 C St (95987)
Rates: $49-$80
(530) 473-2381
(800) 228-5150

GRANZELLA'S INN
391 6th St (95987)
Rates: $60-$95
(530) 473-3310

MOTEL 6
455 4th St (95987)
Rates: $33-$43
(530) 473-5337
(800) 466-8356

STAGE STOP MOTEL
330 7th St (95987)
Rates: $33-$50
(530) 473-2281

WILLITS

BAECHTEL CREEK INN MOTEL
101 Gregory Ln (95490)
Rates: $59-$108
(707) 459-9063
(800) 459-9911

ETTA PLACE B&B INN
909 Exley Ln (95490)
Rates: n/a
(707) 459-5953

LARK MOTEL
1411 S Main St (95490)
Rates: $30-$40
(707) 459-2421

PEPPERWOOD MOTEL
452 S Main St (95490)
Rates: $30-$50
(707) 459-2231

PINE CONE MOTEL
1350 S Main (95490)
Rates: $29-$32
(707) 459-5044

SKUNK TRAIL MOTEL
500 S Main (95490)
Rates: $38+
(707) 459-2302

WESTERN VILLAGE INN
1440 S Main St (95490)
Rates: $34+
(707) 459-4011

WILLOWS

BEST WESTERN GOLDEN PHEASANT INN
249 N Humboldt Ave (95988)
Rates: $59-$150
(530) 934-4603
(800) 528-1234
(800) 838-1387

BLUE GUM INN
Rt 2637, Road 99 W (95988)
Rates: $32-$48
(530) 934-5401

CROSS ROADS WEST INN
452 N Humboldt Ave (95988)
Rates: $39-$59
(530) 934-7026

ECONOMY INNS OF AMERICA
435 N Tehama (95988)
Rates: $33+
(530) 934-4224

GROVE MOTEL
Rt 2, Hwy 99 W (95988)
Rates: $32+
(530) 934-5067

SUPER 8 MOTEL
457 Humboldt Ave (95988)
Rates: $45-$60
(530) 934-2871
(800) 800-8000

WESTERN MOTEL
601 N Tehama (95988)
Rates: $30+
(530) 934-3856

WISHON

MILLER'S LANDING
37976 Rd 222 (93669)
Rates: $40-$125
(209) 642-3633

WOODLAND

CINDERELLA MOTEL
99 W Main St (95776)
Rates: $42-$68
(530) 662-1091
(800) 782-9403

MOTEL 6
1564 Main St (95776)
Rates: $36-$51
(530) 666-6777
(800) 466-8356

WOODLAND HILLS

HOLIDAY INN
21101 Ventura Blvd (91364)
Rates: $99-$159
(818) 883-6110
(800) 465-4329

VAGABOND INN
20157 Ventura Blvd (91364)
Rates: $65-$77
(818) 347-8080
(800) 522-1555

YORKVILLE

SHEEP DUNG ESTATES COTTAGES
P. O. Box 49 (95494)
Rates: $80
(707) 894-5322

YOSEMITE NATIONAL PARK

THE REDWOODS GUEST CTTAGES
8038 Chilnualna Falls Rd (95389)
Rates: $101-$500
(209) 375-6666

YOSEMITE'S FOUR SEASONS
7519 Henness Cir (95389)
Rates: $79-$500
(209) 372-9000
(800) 669-9300

YOUNTVILLE

VINTAGE INN
6541 Washington St (94599)
Rates: $225-$300
(707) 944-1112
(800) 351-1133

YREKA

AMERIHOST INN
148 Moonlit Oaks Ave (96097)
Rates: $62-$72
(530) 841-1300
(800) 434-5800

BEST WESTERN MINER'S INN
122 E Miner St (96097)
Rates: $59-$89
(530) 842-4355
(800) 528-1234
(800) 444-1320

DAYS INN
1804 B Fort Jones
Rd (96097)
Rates: $46-$75
(530) 842-1612
(800) 329-7466

MOTEL 6
1785 S Main St
(96097)
Rates: $33-$44
(530) 842-4111
(800) 466-8356

RODEWAY INN
526 S Main St
(96097)
Rates: $34-$70
(530) 842-4404
(800) 228-2000

SUPER 8 MOTEL
136 Montague Rd.
(96097)
Rates: $48-$54
(530) 842-5781
(800) 800-8000

WAYSIDE INN
1235 S Main St
(96097)
Rates: $45-$78
(530) 842-4412
(800) 795-7974

YUBA CITY

DAYS INN
700 N Palora Ave
(95991)
Rates: $42-$84
(530) 674-1711
(800) 329-7466

**GARDEN COURT
INN**
4228 S Hwy 99
(95991)
Rates: $26-$38
(530) 674-0210

MOTEL ORLEANS
730 N Palora Ave
(95991)
Rates: $34-$62
(530) 674-1592
(800) 626-1900

YUCCA VALLEY

**OASIS OF EDEN
INN & SUITES**
56377 Twentynine
Palms Hy (92284)
Rates: $49-$106
(760) 365-6321
(800) 606-6686

SANDS MOTEL
55446 Twentynine
Palms Hy (92284)
Rates: $25-$35
(760) 365-4615

SUPER 8 MOTEL
57096 Twentynine
Palms Hy (92284)
Rates: A44-$78
(760) 228-1773
(800) 800-8000

YUCCA INN
7500 Camino Del
Cielo (92284)
Rates: $39-$55
(760) 365-3311

COLORADO

ALAMOSA

ALAMOSA KOA KAMPING CABINS
6900 Juniper Lane (81101)
Rates: $31+
(719) 589-9757
(800) 562-9157

BEST WESTERN
1919 Main St (81101)
Rates: $65-$99
(719) 589-2567
(800) 528-1234
(800) 459-5123

COMFORT INN
6301 Rd 107 S (81101)
Rates $65-$90
(719) 587-9000
(800) 228-5150

HOLIDAY INN
333 Santa Fe Ave (81101)
Rates: $92
(719) 589-5833
(800) 465-4329

ALLENSPARK

PINE GROVE CABINS
P. O. Box 85 (80510)
Rates: $62-$145
(303) 747-2529

ALMONT

ALMONT RESORT
P O Box 306 (81210)
Rates: $50-$75
(970) 641-4009

THREE RIVERS RESORT CABINS
130 CR 742 (81210)
Rates: $35-$120
(970) 641-1303
(888) 761-3474

ANTONITO

CONEJOS CABINS
Box 519 (81120)
Rates: $55-$90
(719) 376-2547

COTTONWOOD MEADOWS CABINS
34591 Hwy 17 (81120)
Rates: $45-$100
(719) 376-5660

JOSEY'S MOGOTE MEADOW CABINS
34127 Hwy 17 (81120)
Rates: $38
(719) 376-5774
(800) 877-2133

MENKHAVEN LODGE CABINS
20900 Hwy 17 (81120)
Rates: $38-$70
(719) 376-5767

NARROW GAUGE RR INN & CABOOSE RV PARK
P. O. Box 636 (81120)
Rates: $40-$54
(719) 376-5441
(800) 323-9469

PONDEROSA CAMPGROUND & CABINS
19600 W Hwy 17 (81120)
Rates: $45
(719) 376-5857

TWIN RIVERS CABINS & RV PARK
34044 Hwy 17 (81120)
Rates: $38-$60
(719) 376-5710
(888) 689-6787

ARVADA

ON GOLDEN POND
7831 Eldridge (80005)
Rates: $70-$130
(720) 424-2296
(800) 682-0913

ASPEN

ALPINE LODGE
1240 E Cooper Ave (81611)
Rates: $50-$155
(970) 925-7351
(888) 253-4671

ASPEN CLUB LODGE
709 E Durant (81611)
Rates: $220-$495
(970) 925-6760
(800) 882-2582

BEAUMONT INN
1301 E Cooper Ave (81611)
Rates: $80-$235
(970) 925-7081
(800) 344-3853

HOTEL ASPEN
110 W Main St (81611)
Rates: $69-$299
(970) 925-3441

HISTORIC HOTEL JEROME
330 E Main St (81611)
Rates: $710-$2400
(970) 920-1000
(800) 331-7213

HOTEL LENADO
200 S Aspen St (81611)
Rates: $119-$429
(970) 925-6246
(800) 321-3457

LIMELITE LODGE
228 E Cooper St (81611)
Rates: $185-$375
(970) 925-3025
(800) 433-0832

THE LITTLE NELL RESORT HOTEL
675 E Durant Ave (81611)
Rates: $185-$550
(970) 920-4600
(800) 525-6200

THE ST. REGIS HOTEL ASPEN
315 E Dean St (81611)
Rates: $339-$709
(970) 920-3300

AURORA

AMERISUITES
16250 E 40th Ave (80012)
Rates: $119
(303) 371-0700
(800) 833-1516

DENVER MEADOWS CAMPER CABINS
2075 Potomac St (80011)
Rates: $25
(303) 364-9483
(800) 364-9847

DOUBLETREE HOTEL SE
13696 Iliff Pl (80014)
Rates: $65-$102
(303) 337-2800
(800) 222-8733

HOLIDAY INN
15500 40th Ave (80239)
Rates: $80
(303) 371-9494
(800) 465-4329

LA QUINTA INN
1011 S Abilene (80012)
Rates: $69-$89
(303) 337-0206
(800) 687-6667

MOTEL 6
14031 E Iliff Ave (80014)
Rates: $41-$58
(303) 873-3025
(800) 466-8356

SLEEP INN
15900 E 40th Ave (80011)
Rates: $72-$81
(303) 373-1616
(800) 753-3746

AVON

COMFORT INN VAIL/BEAVER CREEK
0161 W Beaver Creek Blvd (81620)
Rates: $75-$280
(970) 949-5511
(800) 228-5150

BAILEY

GLEN-ISLE RESORT LODGE & CABINS
P. O. Box 128 (80421)
Rates: $48-$75
(303) 838-5461

MOOREDALE RANCH RESORT
P. O. Box 845 (80421)
Rates: $60-$100
(303) 838-2775

BAYFIELD

BEAR PAW LODGE
18011 CR 501 (81122)
Rates: $56-$150
(970) 884-2508

CIRCLE S LODGE CABINS
18022 CR 501 (81122)
Rates: $60-$90
(970) 884-2473
(970) 884-9495

GRANITE PEAKS RANCH CABINS
25080 CR 501 (81122)
Rates: $125-$150
(970) 884-2626
(888) 825-2486

LAKE HAVEN RESORT CABINS & RENTALS
14452 CR 501 (81122)
Rates: $45-$70
(970) 884-2517

LONE WOLF LODGE
18001 CR 501 (81122)
Rates: $70-$80
(970) 884-0414

PINE RIVER LODGE
14443 CR 501 (81122)
Rates: $65-$180
(970) 884-2563

VALLECITO RESORT
13030 CR 501 (81122)
Rates: $50-$150
(800) 258-9548

BELLEVUE

GLEN ECHO RESORT
31503 Poudre Cnyn, Hwy 14 (80512)
Rates: $40-$125
(970) 881-2208
(800) 348-2208

INDIAN MEADOWS RESORT
29839 Poudre Cnyn Road (80512)
Rates: $45-$125
(970) 881-2281

MOUNTAIN GREENERY RESORT
32595 Poudre Cnyn Road (80512)
Rates: $45-$65
(970) 881-2242

SPORTSMAN'S LODGE & STORE
44174 Poudre Cnyn Road (80512)
Rates: $48-$79
(970) 881-2272
(800) 270-2272

BLACK HAWK

GOLD DUST LODGE
5312 Hwy 119 (80422)
Rates: $55-$65
(303) 582-5415

BOULDER

BEST WESTERN
770 28th St (80303)
Rates: $64-$114
(303) 449-3800
(800) 528-1234
(800) 233-8469

BOULDER MTN LODGE
91 Four Mile Canyon Rd (80302)
Rates: $44-$90
(303) 444-0882
(800) 458-0882

THE BROKER INN
555 30th St (80303)
Rates: $128-$138
(303) 444-3330
(800) 338-5407

DAYS INN
5397 S Boulder Rd (80303)
Rates: $94-$104
(303) 499-4422
(800) 329-7466

FOOT OF THE MOUNTAIN MOTEL
200 Arapahoe Ave (80302)
Rates: $60-$75
(303) 442-5688

HIGHLANDER INN MOTEL
970 28th St (80303)
Rates: $45-$83
(303) 443-7800

HOLIDAY INN UNIVERSITY AREA
800 28th St (80303)
Rates: $94-$109
(303) 443-3322
(800) 465-4329

HOMEWOOD SUITES
4950 Baseline Rd (80303)
Rates: $149-$210
(303) 499-9922
(800) 225-5466

PEARL STREET INN
1800 Pearl St (80302)
Rates: $78-$103
(303) 444-5584
(888) 810-1302

RAMADA INN
800 28th St (80303)
Rates: $71-$105
(303) 443-3322
(800) 272-6232

RESIDENCE INN BY MARRIOTT
3030 Center Green Dr (80301)
Rates: $199
(303) 449-5545
(800) 331-3131

SUPER 8 MOTEL
970 28th St (80303)
Rates: $85-$125
(303) 443-7800
(800) 800-8000

BRUSH

BEST WESTERN
1208 N Colorado Ave (80723)
Rates: $60-$78
(970) 842-5146
(800) 528-1234
(877) 224-6999

BUDGET HOST EMPIRE MOTEL
1498 Edison (80723)
Rates: $30-$48
(970) 842-2876
(800) 283-4678

MICROTEL INN
975 N Colorado Ave (80723)
Rates: $39-$56
(970) 842-4241
(888) 771-7171

BUENA VISTA

COLLEGIATE PEAKS FAMILY INN & RV PARK
516 Hwy 24 (81211)
Rates: n/a
(719) 395-2251
(888) 732-5466

COTTONWOOD INN
18999 County Rd 306 (81211)
Rates: n/a
(719) 395-6434

SAGEWOOD CABINS
38951-B N Hwy 24 (81211)
Rates: $65+
(719) 395-2582

THUNDER LODGE
Box 504 (81211)
Rates: $45-$64
(719) 395-2245
(800) 330-9194

TOPAZ LODGE MOTEL
115 N US 24 (81211)
Rates: $40-$70
(719) 395-2427

VISTA INN
733 N US 24 (81211)
Rates: $75-$95
(719) 395-8009

WOODLAND BROOK CABINS
226 S San Juan, PO Bx 418 (81211)
Rates: $50-$75
(719) 395-2922

BURLINGTON

CHAPARRAL BUDGET HOST
405 S Lincoln (80807)
Rates: $35-$55
(719) 346-5361
(800) 283-4678

COMFORT INN
282 S Lincoln (80807)
Rates: $59-$120
(719) 346-776
(800) 228-5150

SLOAN'S MOTEL
1901 Rose Ave (80807)
Rates: $34-$44
(719) 346-5333
(800) 362-0464

CAÑON CITY

BEST WESTERN ROYAL GORGE
1925 Fremont Dr (81212)
Rates: $69-$89
(719) 275-3377
(800) 231-7317
(800) 528-1234

CAÑON INN
3075 E Hwy 50 (81212)
Rates: $68-$84
(719) 275-8676
(800) 525-7727

FORT GORGE CAMPER CABINS
45044 Hwy 50 (81212)
Rates: $25
(719) 275-5111

HOLIDAY MOTEL
1502 Main St (81212)
Rates: $22-$40
(719) 275-3317

PARK LANE MOTEL
1401 Main St (81212)
Rates: $38-$55
(719) 275-7240

CARBONDALE

BRB CRYSTAL RIVER RESORT CABINS
7202 Hwy 133 (81623)
Rates: $60-$85
(970) 963-2341
(800) 963-2341

THUNDER RIVER LODGE
Hwy 133 (81623)
Rates: $40-$62
(970) 963-2543

CASTLE ROCK

BEST WESTERN INN & SUITES
595 Genoa Way (80104)
Rates: $84-$129
(303) 814-8800
(800) 528-1234

COMFORT INN
200 Wolfensberger Rd (80104)
Rates: $59-$145
(303) 660-2222
(800) 228-5150

HOLIDAY INN EXPRESS
884 Park St (80104)
Rates: $89-$109
(303) 660-9733
(800) 465-4329

SUPER 8 MOTEL
1020 Park St (80104)
Rates: $39-$50
(303) 688-0880
(800) 800-8000

CEDAREDGE

ASPEN TRAILS CAMPER CABINS
1997 Hwy 65 (81413)
Rates: $30
(970) 856-6321

GRAND MESA LODGE
P O Box 49 (81413)
Rates: $35-$90
(970) 856-3250
(800) 551-6372

SUPER 8 MOTEL
530 S Grand Mesa Dr (81413)
Rates: $62-$103
(970) 856-7824
(800) 800-8000

CIMARRON

PLEASANT VALLEY CABINS CAMPGROUND
84100 E Hwy 50 (81220)
Rates: $35-$49
(970) 249-8330

CLARK

HAHN'S PEAK GUEST RANCH
60880 CR 129 (80428)
Rates: $85
(970) 879-5878

COALDALE

HIDDEN VALLEY RANCH CAMPER CABINS
Box 220 (81222)
Rates: n/a
(719) 942-4171

LAZY J RESORT & RAFTING COMPANY
Box 109 (81222)
Rates: $30-$70
(719) 942-4274
(800) 678-4274

COLLBRAN

HILL'S SUMMER CHUCKWAGON & BED & BREAKFAST
Rt 1, Box 189 (81624)
Rates: $90
(970) 487-3433

VEGA LODGE CABINS & RV
P O Box 166 (81624)
Rates: $35
(970) 487-3733

COLORADO CITY

TRAVELODGE
Hwy 165 (81019)
Rates: $49-$69
(719) 676-3315
(800) 578-7878

COLORADO SPRINGS

THE ALIKAR GARDEN RESORT
1123 Verde Dr (80903)
Rates: $109-$169
(719) 475-2564

ANTLERS ADAM'S MARK HOTEL
4 S Cascade (80903)
Rates: $205-$220
(719) 473-5600
(800) 444-2326

APOLLO PARK EXECUTIVE SUITES
805 S Circle Dr, 2-B (80910)
Rates: $69-$99
(719) 635-1539
(800) 279-3620

BEST WESTERN LE BARON HOTEL
314 W Bijou St (80905)
Rates: $70-$179
(719) 471-8680
(800) 528-1234
(800) 477-8610

BEST WESTERN PALMER HOUSE
3010 N Chestnut (80907)
Rates: $79-$105
(719) 636-5201
(800) 528-1234
(800) 223-9127

CHIEF MOTEL
1624 S Nevada Ave (80906)
Rates: $45-$70
(719) 473-5228

COMFORT SUITES
1055 Kelly Johnson Blvd (80920)
Rates: $89-$149
(719) 536-0731
(800) 228-5150

DOUBLETREE HOTEL-WORLD ARENA
1775 E Cheyenne Mtn Blvd (80906)
Rates: $99-$149
(719) 576-8900
(800) 222-8733

DRURY INN PIKES PEAK
8155 N Academy Blvd (80920)
Rates: $74-$100
(719) 598-2500
(800) 378-7946

HAMPTON INN NORTH
7245 Commerce Center Dr (80919)
Rates: $59-$78
(719) 593-9700
(800) 426-7866

HAMPTON INN WORLD ARENA
1410 Harrison Rd (80906)
Rates: $65-$105
(719) 579-6900
(800) 426-7866

HOLIDAY INN GARDEN OF THE GODS
505 Popes Bluff Tr (80907)
Rates: $89-$99
(719) 598-7656
(800) 962-5470
(800) 465-4329

LA QUINTA INN GARDEN OF THE GODS
4385 Sinton Rd (80907)
Rates: $75-$105
(719) 528-5060
(800) 687-6667

MOTEL 6
3228 N Chestnut St (80907)
Rates: $60-$76
(719) 520-5400
(800) 466-8356

MOUNTAINDALE CAMPGROUD & CABINS
2000 Barrett Rd (80926)
Rates: $40-$55
(719) 576-0619

QUALITY INN GARDEN OF THE GODS
555 W Garden of the Gods Rd (80907)
Rates: $81-$111
(719) 593-9119
(800) 228-5151

RADISSON INN & SUITES
1645 Newport Dr (80916)
Rates: $129
(719) 597-7000
(800) 333-3333

RADISSON INN NORTH
8110 N Academy Blvd (80920)
Rates: $109-$140
(719) 598-5770
(800) 333-3333

RAINTREE INN
2625 Ore Mill Rd (80904)
Rates: $40-$75
(719) 632-4600

RAMADA INN EAST
520 N Murray Blvd (80915)
Rates: $59-$109
(719) 596-7660
(800) 272-6232

RED ROOF INN
8280 Hwy 83 (80920)
Rates: $38-$95
(719) 598-6700
(800) 843-7663

RESIDENCE INN BY MARRIOTT
3880 N Academy Blvd (80917)
Rates: $122-$166
(719) 574-0370
(800) 331-3131

RESIDENCE INN BY MARRIOTT SOUTH
2765 Geyser Dr (80906)
Rates: $169
(719) 576-0101
(800) 331-3131

RODEWAY INN
2409 E Pikes Peak Ave (80909)
Rates: $75-$85
(719) 471-0990
(800) 228-2000

AREA CODES - If the local number doesn't connect, check for a new area code.

SHERATON HOTEL
2886 S Circle Dr (80906)
Rates: $79-$116
(719) 576-5900
(800) 325-3535
(800) 981-4012

SLEEP INN
1075 Kelly Johnson Blvd (80920)
Rates: $84-$104
(719) 260-6969
(800) 753-3746

STAGECOACH MOTEL
1647 S Nevada Ave (80906)
Rates: $45-$69
(719) 633-3894

SWISS CHALET
3410-3420 W Colorado Ave (80904)
Rates: $24-$65
(719) 471-2260

TRAVELODGE
2625 Ore Mill Rd (80904)
Rates: $199-$285
(719) 632-4600
(800) 578-7878

CONEJOS

CONEJOS RIVER GUEST RANCH
P. O. Box 175 (81129)
Rates: $50-$95
(719) 376-2464

CORTEZ

ANASAZI MOTOR INN
640 S Broadway (81321)
Rates: $57-$71
(970) 565-3773
(800) 972-6232

ANETH LODGE
645 E Main St (81321)
Rates: $36-$65
(970) 565-3453
(877) 263-8454

BEST WESTERN TURQUOISE INN & SUITES
535 E Main St (81321)
Rates: $89-$119
(970) 565-3778
(800) 528-1234
(800) 547-3376

BUDGET HOST INN
2040 E Main St (81321)
Rates: $52-$78
(970) 565-3738
(800) 283-4678

COMFORT INN
2321 E Main St (81321)
Rates: $79-$99
(970) 565-3400
(800) 228-5150

DAYS INN
430 N State Hwy 145 (81321)
Rates: $64-$89
(970) 565-8577
(800) 329-7466

ECONO LODGE
2020 E Main (81321)
Rates: $55-$99
(970) 565-3474
(800) 553-2666

HOLIDAY INN EXP
2121 E Main St (81321)
Rates: $99-$137
(970) 565-6000
(800) 465-4329

NORTH BROADWAY MOTEL
510 N Broadway (81321)
Rates: $23+
(970) 565-2481

TOMAHAWK LODGE
728 S Broadway (81321)
Rates: $43-$69
(970) 565-8521

TRAVELODGE
440 S Broadway (81321)
Rates: $49-$79
(970) 585-7778
(800) 578-7878

UTE MOUNTAIN MOTEL
531 S Broadway (81321)
Rates: $26-$40
(970) 565-8507

COTOPAXI

ARKANSAS RIVER KOA & LOMA LINDA MOTEL
21435 Hwy 50 (81223)
Rates: $34-$60
(719) 275-9308
(800) 562-2686

CRAIG

BEST WESTERN
755 E Victory Way (81625)
Rates: $59-$89
(970) 824-8101
(800) 528-1234

BLACK NUGGET MOTEL
2855 W Victory Way (81625)
Rates: $32-$48
(970) 824-8161

CRAIG MOTEL
894 Yampa Ave (81625)
Rates: $30-$58
(970) 824-4491

HOLIDAY INN & SUITES
300 S Hwy 13 (81625)
Rates: $82-$102
(970) 824-4000
(800) 465-4329

RAMADA LIMITED
262 Commerce St (81625)
Rates: $65-$119
(970) 824-9282
(800) 272-6232

SUPER 8 MOTEL
200 Hwy 13 S (81625)
Rates: $32-$99
(970) 824-3471
(800) 800-8000

TRAVELODGE
2690 W Hwy 40 (81625)
Rates: $39-$110
(970) 824-7066
(800) 578-7878

CRAWFORD

BLACK CANYON RANCH B&B
P. O. Box 3 (81415)
Rates: $75
(970) 921-4252

LAST FRONTIER LODGE
Box 248 (81415)
Rates: $90
(970) 921-6363

STEWART HOMESTEAD CABIN
4156 B Rd (81415)
Rates: $85
(970) 921-6751

WESTERN RECREATION RANCH CABINS
P. O. Box 162 (81415)
Rates: $80
(970) 921-4386
(888) 921-4677

CREEDE

BROKEN ARROW RANCH CABINS
32728 Hwy 149 (81130)
Rates: $39-$49
(719) 658-2484

SOWARD RANCH CABINS
Box 130 (81130)
Rates: $40-$65
(719) 658-2295
(719) 658-2228

CRESTED BUTTE

SHERATON CRESTED BUTTE RESORT
6 Emmons Rd (81224)
Rates: $218-$240
(970) 349-8000

CRIPPLE CREEK

CRIPPLE CREEK GOLD CAMP-GROUND & CAMPER CABINS
Box 601 (80813)
Rates: $18
(719) 689-2342

THE COZY CABINS
232 & 234 Thurlow Ave (80813)
Rates: $75-$95
(719) 689-3351

DEL NORTE

DEL NORTE MOTEL
1050 Grand Ave (81132)
Rates: n/a
(719) 657-3581
(800) 372-2331

DELTA

BEST WESTERN SUNDANCE
903 Main St (81416)
Rates: $60-$75
(970) 874-9781
(800) 528-1234
(800) 626-1994

BUDGET HOST SOUTHGATE INN
2124 S Main St (81416)
Rates: $45-$60
(970) 874-9726
(800) 283-4678
(800) 621-2271

DENVER

ADAMS MARK HOTEL
1550 Court Pl (80202)
Rates: $169-$184
(303) 893-3333
(800) 444-2326

BEST BUDGET MOTOR BAR X
5001 W Colfax Ave (80204)
Rates: $32-$37
(303) 534-7191

AREA CODES - If the local number doesn't connect, check for a new area code.

BEST WESTERN EXECUTIVE INN
4411 Peoria St (80239)
Rates: $82
(303) 373-5730
(800) 528-1234
(800) 848-4060

BEST WESTERN LANDMARK INN
455 S Colorado Blvd (80246)
Rates: $99-$109
(303) 388-5561
(800) 528-1234

BURNSLEY HOTEL
1000 Grant St (80203)
Rates: $65-$135
(303) 830-1000

CAMERON MOTEL
4500 E Evan Ave (80222)
Rates: $53-$64
(303) 757-2100

DAYS INN CENTRAL
620 Federal Blvd (80204)
Rates: $45-$69
(303) 571-1715
(800) 329-7466

DOUBLETREE HOTEL
3203 Quebec St (80207)
Rates: $69-$99
(303) 321-3333
(800) 243-3112
(800) 222-8733

DRURY INN
4400 Peoria St (80239)
Rates: $67-$99
(303) 373-1983
(800) 378-7946

EMBASSY SUITES AIRPORT
4444 N Havana (80239)
Rates: $107-$124
(303) 375-0400
(800) 362-2779

EXECUTIVE TOWER HOTEL
1405 Curtis St (80202)
Rates: $85-$110
(303) 571-0300
(800) 525-6651

HAWTHORN SUITES
5001 S Ulster (80239)
Rates: $149
(303) 804-9900
(800) 527-1133

HOLIDAY CHALET B&B HOTEL
1820 E Colfax Ave (80218)
Rates: $99-$160
(303) 321-9975
(800) 626-4497

HOTEL MONACO
1717 Champa St (80239)
Rates: $170-$205
(303) 296-1717

LA QUINTA INN AIRPORT
6801 Tower Rd (80249)
Rates: $79-$99
(303) 371-0888
(800) 687-6667

LA QUINTA INN AIRPORT SOUTH
3975 Peoria Way (80239)
Rates: $53-$77
(303) 371-5640
(800) 687-6667

LA QUINTA INN DOWNTOWN
3500 Park Ave W (80216)
Rates: $75-$95
(303) 458-1222
(800) 687-6667

LA QUINTA INN SOUTH-CHERRY CREEK
1975 S Colorado Blvd (80222)
Rates: $85-$105
(303) 758-8886
(800) 687-6667

LOEWS GIORGIO HOTEL
4150 E Mississippi Ave (80222)
Rates: $79-$259
(303) 782-9300
(800) 235 6397

MARRIOTT HOTEL CITY CENTER
1701 California St (80202)
Rates: $169
(303) 297-1300
(800) 228-9290

MARRIOTT HOTEL SOUTHEAST
6363 E Hampden Ave (80222)
Rates: $139-$169
(303) 758-7000
(800) 228-9290

MARRIOTT TECH CENTER
4900 S Syracuse St (80237)
Rates: $169
(303) 779-1100
(800) 228-9290

MOTEL 6-CENTRAL
3050 W 49th Ave (80221)
Rates: $36-$54
(303) 455-8888
(800) 466-8356

MOTEL 6-EAST
12020 E 39th Ave (80239)
Rates: $40-$61
(303) 371-1980
(800) 466-8356

QUALITY INN
401 E 58th Ave (80218)
Rates: $59-$100
(303) 297-1717
(800) 228-5151

QUALITY INN & SUITES
4590 Quebec St (80216)
Rates: $74-$103
(303) 320-0260
(800) 228-5151

QUALITY INN TECH CENTER NORTH
6300 E Hampden Ave (80222)
Rates: $69-$113
(303) 758-2211
(800) 228-5151

RAMADA INN AIRPORT
3737 Quebec St (80207)
Rates: $59-$97
(303) 388-6161
(800) 272-6232

RAMADA INN DOWNTOWN WEST
1975 Bryant St (80204)
Rates: $102-$114
(303) 433-8331
(800) 272-6232

RED ROOF INN SUITES
6890 Tower Rd (80249)
Rates: $45-$72
(303) 371-5300
(800) 843-7663

RESIDENCE INN BY MARRIOTT DOWNTOWN
2777 Zuni St (80211)
Rates: $135
(303) 458-5318
(800) 331-3131

ROCKIES LODGE
4760 E Evans Ave (80222)
Rates: $26-$48
(303) 757-7601

RODEWAY INN
12033 E 38th Ave (80239)
Rates: $39-$61
(303) 371-0740
(800) 228-2000

SUPER 8 MOTEL
2601 Zuni St (80211)
Rates: $39-$54
(303) 433-6677
(800) 800-8000

SUPER 8 MOTEL
5888 N Broadway (80216)
Rates: $44-$54
(303) 296-3100
(800) 800-8000

SUPER 8 MOTEL
7201 E 36th Ave (80206)
Rates: $60-$75
(303) 393-7666
(800) 800-8000

TOWNEPLACE SUITES BY MARRIOTT
3696 S Monaco St Pkwy (80237)
Rates: $69-$119
(303) 759-9393

TRAVELODGE
6090 Smith Rd (80216)
Rates: $40-$49
(303) 388-4051
(800) 578-7878

VICTORIA OAKS INN
1575 Race St (80206)
Rates: $39-$79
(303) 355-1818

WARWICK HOTEL
1776 Grant St (80203)
Rates: $89-$170
(303) 861-2000
(800) 525-2588

WESTIN TABOR CENTER HOTEL
1672 Lawrence St (80202)
Rates: $134-$222
(303) 572-9100
(800) 228-3000

DILLON

ANNABELLE'S BED & BREAKFAST
276 Snowberry Way (80435)
Rates: $60-$100
(970) 468-8667

AREA CODES - If the local number doesn't connect, check for a new area code.

BEST WESTERN PTARMIGAN LODGE
652 Lake Dillon Dr (80435)
Rates: $65-$145
(970) 468-2341
(800) 528-1234
(800) 842-5939

PARADOX LODGE & CABINS
5040 Montezuma Rd (80435)
Rates: $55-$120
(970) 468-9445

DOLORES

CIRCLE K GUEST RANCH
27758 Hwy 145 (81323)
Rates: $35-$68
(970) 562-3826
(800) 477-6381

DOLORES MOUNTAIN INN
701 Railroad Ave (81323)
Rates: $36-$57
(970) 882-7203
(800) 842-8113

DOLORES RIVER RV PARK & CABINS
18680 Hwy 145 (81323)
Rates: $24-$69
(970) 882-7761
(800) 200-2399

GREEN SNOW OASIS CABINS
28434 Hwy 145 (81323)
Rates: $65-$75
(970) 562-3829

GROUNDHOG LAKE FISHING CAMP CABINS
P. O. Box 27 (81323)
Rates: $24-$30
(970) 882-4379

LOST CANYON LAKE LODGE
P. O. Box 1289 (81323)
Rates: $75
(970) 882-4913

OUTPOST MOTEL & CABINS
1800 Central Ave (81323)
Rates: $46-$89
(970) 882-7271
(800) 382-4892

PRIEST GULCH RANCH CAMP
2670 Hwy 145 (81323)
Rates: $54-$59
(970) 562-3810

RAG O'MUFFIN RANCH
26030 Hwy 145 (81323)
Rates: $75+
(970) 562-3803

DURANGO

ADOBE INN
2178 Main Ave (81301)
Rates: $38-$102
(970) 247-2743

ALPINE MOTEL
3515 N Main Ave (81301)
Rates: $50-$84
(970) 247-4042
(800) 818-4042

BEST WESTERN LODGE AT PURGATORY
49617 Hwy 550 N (81301)
Rates: $69-$179
(970) 247-9669
(800) 528-1234
(800) 637-7727

BUDGET INN
3077 Main Ave (81301)
Rates: $38-$74
(970) 247-5222
(800) 257-2222

CABOOSE MOTEL
3363 Main Ave (81301))
Rates: $48-$68
(970) 247-1191

COTTONWOOD CAMPER CABIN
21636 US 160 (81302)
Rates: $30
(970) 247-1977

COUNTRY VIEW LODGE
28295 US 160 E (81302)
Rates: $25-$48
(970) 247-5701

DAYS INN
1700 County Rd 203 (81301)
Rates: $79-$104
(970) 259-1430
(800) 329-7466

DOUBLETREE HOTEL
501 Camino Del Rio (81301)
Rates: $154-$171
(970) 259-6580
(800) 222-8733

DURANGO EAST KOA KAMPING KABINS & KOTTAGES
30090 US 160 (81301)
Rates: $35-$125
(970) 247-0783
(800) 562-0793

EDELWEISS INN
689 Animas View Dr (81301)
Rates: $48-$58
(970) 247-5685

HOLIDAY INN
800 Camino Del Rio (81301)
Rates: $100-$140
(970) 247-5393
(800) 465-4329

IRON HORSE INN
5800 N Main Ave (81301)
Rates: $99-$119
(970) 259-1010

LELAND HOUSE BED & BREAKFST SUITES
721 E 2nd Ave (81301)
Rates: $99-$159
(970) 385-1920
(800) 664-1920

NATIONAL 9 SUNSET
2855 N Main Ave (81301)
Rates: $29-$79
(970) 247-2653

QUALITY INN & SUITES
455 S Camino Del Rio (81301)
Rates: $55-$149
(970) 259-7900
(800) 228-5151

RESIDENCE INN BY MARRIOTT
21691 Hwy 160 W (81301)
Rates: $169-$220
(970) 259-6200
(800) 331-3131

ROCHESTER HISTORIC B&B HOTEL
726 E 2nd Ave (81301)
Rates: $139-$199
(970) 385-1920
(800) 664-1920

RODEWAY INN
2701 N Main Ave (81301)
Rates: $79-$109
(970) 259-2540
(800) 228-2000

WESTERN STAR MOTEL
3310 N Main Ave (81301)
Rates: $28-$58
(970) 247-4895

EADS

COUNTRY MANOR MOTEL
609 East 15th St (81036)
Rates: $27-$36
(719) 438-5451

EAGLE

BEST WESTERN EAGLE LODGE
200 Loren Ln (81631)
Rates: $67-$250
(970) 328-6316
(800) 528-1234
(800) 475-4824

EDWARDS

THE INN AT RIVERWALK
27 Main St (81632)
Rates: $160-$290
(970) 926-0606

LAZY RANCH B&B
0057 Lake Creek Rd (81632)
Rates: $70-$125
(970) 926-3876
(800) 655-9343

EMPIRE

CONESTOGA WAGON STOP CABINS
7364 US Hwy, P. O. Box 334 (80438)
Rates: $40-$75
(303) 569-3066

ENGLEWOOD

HAMPTON INN
9231 E Arapahoe Rd (80112)
Rates: $89-$99
(303) 792-9999
(800) 426-7886

HOLTZE EXECUTIVE VILLAGE
6380 S Boston St (80112)
Rates: $69
(303) 290-1100

LA QUINTA INN & SUITES TECH CTR
7077 S Clinton St (80112)
Rates: $59-$82
(303) 649-9969
(800) 687-6667

MAINSTAY SUITES DENVER TECH CENTER
I-25, Exit 199 (80112)
Rates: $79-$99
(303) 858-1669

QUALITY SUITES TECH CENTER SO.
7374 S Clinton St (80112)
Rates: $89-$139
(303) 858-0700
(800) 228-5151

RESIDENCE INN BY MARRIOTT
6565 S Yosemite St (80111)
Rates: $130
(303) 740-7177
(800) 331-3131

SUMMERFIELD SUITES
9280 E Costilla Ave (80112)
Rates: $169-$260
(303) 706-1945
(800) 833-4353

SUPER 8 MOTEL
5150 S Quebec St (80111)
Rates: $59-$89
(303) 771-8000
(800) 800-8000

WOODFIELD SUITES TECH CENTER
9009 E Arapahoe Rd (80112)
Rates: $129
(303) 799-4555
(800) 338-0008

ESTES PARK

A TELEMARK RESORT & COTTAGES
P. O. Box 100 (80517)
Rates: $60-$80
(970) 586-4343
(800) 669-0650

ANDERSON'S WONDER VIEW COTTAGES
Box 427CD (80517)
Rates: $44-$185
(970) 586-4158
(800) 327-0113

CASTLE MOUNTAIN LODGE
1520 Fall River Rd (80517)
Rates: $110-$185
(970) 586-3664

EDGEWATER HEIGHTS COTTAGES
P O Box 3195 (80517)
Rates: $55-$75
(970) 586-8493
800 530-3942

ELKHORN LODGE, CABINS, GUEST RANCH, CAMPING
P O Box 1560 (80517)
Rates: $40-$100
(970) 586-4416

FOUR WINDS MOTOR LODGE
1120 Big Thompson Ave (80517)
Rates: $66-$85
(970) 586-3313

MACHIN'S COTTAGES IN THE PINES
P O Box 2867 (80517)
Rates: $76-$120
(970) 586-4276

NATIONAL PARK RESORT CAMPGROUND & CABINS
3501 Fall River Rd (80517)
Rates: $50-$130
(970) 586-4563

OLYMPUS LODGE
US 34 (80517)
Rates: $45-$110
(970) 586-8141
(800) 248-8141

SKYLINE COTTAGES
2752 Hwy 66 (80517)
Rates: $88-$95
(970) 586-2886

TIMBER CREEK CHALETS
2115 Fall River Rd (80517)
Rates: $95-$185
(970) 586-8803

EVANS

MOTEL 6
3015 8th Ave (80620)
Rates: $31-$42
(970) 351-6481
(800) 466-8356

SLEEP INN
3025 8th Ave E (80620)
Rates: $75
(970) 356-2180
(800) 753-3746

TRAVELODGE
3301 W Service Rd (80620)
Rates: $49-$189
(970) 339-5900
(800) 578-7878

WINTERSET INN
800 31 St (80620)
Rates: $26-$76
(970) 339-2493

EVERGREEN

BAUER'S SPRUCE ISLAND CHALETS
5937 S Brook Forest Rd (80439)
Rates: $60-$180
(303) 674-4757

FAIRPLAY

SOUTH PARK LODGE & RV PARK
801 Main (80440)
Rates: $45-$55
(719) 836-3278

WESTERN INN MOTEL
490 Hwy 285 (80440)
Rates: $55-$70
(719) 836-2026
(800) 613-1976

FORT COLLINS

BEST WESTERN UNIVERSITY INN
914 S College Ave (80524)
Rates: $55-$75
(970) 484-1984
(800) 528-1234

DAYS INN
3625 E Mulberry St (80524)
Rates: $41-$81
(970) 221-5490
(800) 329-7466

HOLIDAY INN HOLIDOME
3836 E Mulberry St (80524)
Rates: n/a
(970) 484-4660
(800) 465-4329

HOLIDAY INN UNIVERSITY PARK
425 W Prospect Rd (80526)
Rates: $81-$119
(970) 482-2626
(800) 465-4329

MOTEL 6
3900 E Mulberry (80524)
Rates: $33-$52
(970) 482-6466
(800) 466-8356

MULBERRY INN
4333 E Mulberry St (80524)
Rates: $39-$90
(970) 493-9000

SLEEP INN
3808 E Mulberry St (80524)
Rates: $69-$89
(970) 484-5515
(800) 753-3746

SUPER 8 MOTEL
409 Centro Way (80524)
Rates: $51-$81
(970) 493-7701
(800) 800-8000

FORT GARLAND

THE LODGE MOTEL
P. O. Box 160 (81133)
Rates: $29-$33
(719) 379-3434

FORT LUPTON

MOTEL 6
65 S Grand (80621)
Rates: $37-$46
(303) 857-1800
(800) 466-8356

FORT MORGAN

BEST WESTERN PARK TERRACE
725 Main (80701)
Rates: $52-$78
(970) 867-8256
(800) 528-1234

CENTRAL MOTEL
201 W Platte Ave (80701)
Rates: $39-$56
(970) 867-2401

COUNTRY COMFORT MOTEL
16466 Hwy 34 (80701)
Rates: $25-$30
(970) 867-0260

ECONO LODGE
1409 Barlow Rd (80701)
Rates: $42-$59
(970) 867-9481
(800) 553-2666

QUALITY INN
14378 Hwy 34 (80701)
Rates: $45-$119
(970) 867-8208
(800) 228-5151

FOUNTAIN

KOA COLORADO SPRINGS SOUTH KAMPING KABINS
8100 S Bandley Dr (80817)
Rates: $40-$50
(719) 382-7575
(800) 562-8609

FRISCO

BEST WESTERN LAKE DILLON LODGE
1202 Summit Blvd (80443)
Rates: $119- $229
(970) 668-5094
(800) 528-1234
(800) 727-0607

NEW SUMMIT INN
1205 N Summit Blvd (80443)
Rates: $105-$140
(970) 668-3220

SNOWSHOE MOTEL
521 Main St
(80443)
Rates: $80-$115
(970) 668-3444

FRUITA

H-MOTEL
333 Hwy 6 & 50
(81521)
Rates: $35-$55
(970) 858-7198

SUPER 8 MOTEL
399 Jurrasic Ave
(81521)
Rates: $55-$60
(970) 858-0808
(800) 800-8000

GEORGETOWN

GEORGETOWN MOTOR INN
1100 Rose St
(80444)
Rates: $54-$60
(303) 569-3201
(800) 884-3201

GLENWOOD SPRINGS

AFFORDABLE INNS
51823 Hwys 6 & 24 (81601)
Rates: $29-$79
(970) 945-8888

BEST WESTERN CARAVAN INN
1826 Grand Ave
(81601)
Rates: $75-$99
(970) 945-7451
(800) 528-1234
(800) 945-5495

BUDGET HOST INN
51429 Hwy 6 & 24 (81601)
Rates: $32-$68
(970) 945-5682
(800) 283-4678

HISTORIC HOTEL COLORADO
526 Pine St (81601)
Rates: $80-$89
(970) 945-6511
(800) 544-3998

HOMESTEAD INN NATIONAL 9
52039 Hwys 6 & 24 (81601)
Rates: $35-$95
(970) 945-8817
(800) 456-6685

PONDEROSA LODGE
51793 Hwy 6 & 24 (81601)
Rates: $36-$118
(970) 945-5058
(800) 843-5449

RAMADA INN
124 W 6th St
(81601)
Rates: $90-$130
(970) 945-2500
(800) 272-6232

RIVERSIDE COTTAGES
1287 CR 154
(81601)
Rates: $65-$158
(970) 945-5509
(800) 945-5509

SILVER SPRUCE MOTEL
162 W 6th St
(81601)
Rates: $55-$100
(970) 945-5458
(800) 523-4742

GOLDEN

CENTRAL CITY-DORY HILL KOA KABINS
661 Hwy 46
(80403)
Rates: $34
(303) 582-9979
(800) 562-1620

DAYS INN SUITES WEST
15059 W Colfax Ave (80401)
Rates: $79-$99
(303) 277-0200
(800) 329-7466

GOLDEN MOTEL
510 24th St (80401)
Rates: n/a
(303) 279-5581

HOLIDAY INN WEST
14707 W Colfax Ave (80401)
Rates: $99-$125
(303) 279-7611
(800) 465-4329

LA QUINTA INN
3301 Youngfield Service Rd (80401)
Rates: $75-$95
(303) 279-5565
(800) 687-6667

MARRIOTT WEST
1717 Denver West Blvd (80401)
Rates: $75-$150
(303) 279-9100
(800) 228-9290

QUALITY SUITES
29300 US 40
(80401)
Rates: $99-$136
(303) 526-2000
(800) 228-5151

GRANBY

BROKEN ARROW MOTEL
Box 143 (80446)
Rates: $25-$40
(970) 887-3532

THE INN AT SILVER CREEK
62927 Hwy 40
(80446)
Rates: $89-$189
(970) 887-2131

LITTLETREE INN
P. O. Box 800
(80446)
Rates: $66-$72
(970) 887-2551

SHADOW MOUNTAIN GUEST RANCH
5043 Hwy 125
(80446)
Rates: $105-$165
(970) 887-9524
(800) 647-4236

GRAND JUNCTION

ADAM'S MARK HOTEL
743 Horizon Dr
(81506)
Rates: $79
(970) 241-8888
(800) 444-2326

BEST WESTERN CLIFTON INN
3228 I-70 (81520)
Rates: $59-$94
(970) 434-3400
(800) 528-1234

BEST WESTERN HORIZON INN
754 Horizon Dr
(81506)
Rates: $55-$74
(970) 245-1410
(800) 528-1234
(800) 544-3782

BUDGET HOST INN
721 Horizon Dr
(81506)
Rates: $44-$61
(970) 243-6050
(800) 283-4678

DAYS INN
733 Horizon Dr
(81506)
Rates: $60-$95
(970) 245-7200
(800) 329-7466

GRAND VISTA HOTEL
2790 Crossroads Blvd (81506)
Rates: $72-$99
(970) 241-8411
(800) 800-7796

HOLIDAY INN
755 Horizon Dr
(81502)
Rates: $79-$84
(970) 243-6790
(800) 465-4329

LA QUINTA INN & SUITES
2761 Crossroads Blvd (81506)
Rates: $75-$95
(970) 241-2929
(800) 687-6667

MOTEL 6
776 Horizon Dr
(81506)
Rates: $33-$52
(970) 243-2628
(800) 466-8356

PEACHTREE INN
1600 North Ave
(81501)
Rates: $32-$48
(970) 245-5770
(800) 525-0030

SUPER 8 MOTEL
728 Horizon Dr
(81506)
Rates: $50-$60
(970) 248-8080
(800) 800-8000

VALUE LODGE
104 White Ave
(81501)
Rates: $30-$42
(970) 242-0651

WEST GATE INN-IMA
2210 Hwys 6 & 50 (81505)
Rates: $49-$69
(970) 241-3020
(800) 341-8000

GRAND LAKE

ELK CREEK CAMPBER CABINS
P O Box 549
(80447)
Rates: $33
(970) 627-8502
(800) 355-2733

MOUNTAIN LAKES LODGE
P O Box 160
(80447)
Rates: $40-$140
(970) 627-8448

NONEHSHE CABINS
450 Broadway
(80447)
Rates: $60-$140
(970) 627-8012

RIVERSIDE GUESTHOUSES
P O Box 1469
(80447)
Rates: n/a
(970) 627-3619

AREA CODES - If the local number doesn't connect, check for a new area code.

WINDING RIVER RESORT VILLAGE
P O Box 269 (80447)
Rates: $80-$125
(970) 627-3215
(800) 282-5121

GREAT SAND DUNES NATIONAL MONUMENT

GREAT SAND DUNES LODGE
7900 Hwy 150 N (81146)
Rates: $70-$80
(719) 378-2900

GREELEY

BEST WESTERN RAMKOTA INN
701 8th St (80631)
Rates: $59-$105
(970) 353-8444
(800) 528-1234

HOLIDAY INN EXPRESS
2563 W 29th St (80631)
Rates: $65-$90
(970) 330-7495
(800) 465-4329

MICROTEL INN & SUITES
5630 W 10th St (80631)
Rates: $53-$85
(970) 392-1530
(888) 771-7171

RAMADA INN
609 8th Ave (80631)
Rates: $48-$86
(970) 356-3000
(800) 272-6232

GREEN MOUNTAIN FALLS

ROCKY TOP MOTEL
10090 W Hwy 24 (80819)
Rates: $30-$65
(719) 684-9044

GREENWOOD VILLAGE

DAYS INN
5150 S Quebec St (80111)
Rates: $79-$99
(303) 721-1144
(800) 329-7466

MAINSTAY SUITES
9253 E Costilla Ave (80112)
Rates: $45-$95
(303) 858-1669
(800) 660-6246

MOTEL 6-SOUTH TECH CENTER
9201 E Arapahoe Rd (80112)
Rates: $42-$58
(303) 790-8220
(800) 466-8356

SLEEP INN DENVER TECH
9257 E Costilla Ave (80112)
Rates: $59-$69
(303) 662-9950
(800) 753-3746

WELLESLEY INN & SUITES
5200 S Quebec St (80112)
Rates: $84
(303) 220-8448
(800) 444-8888

GUNNISON

ABC MOTEL
212 E Tomichi Ave (81230)
Rates: $56-$69
(970) 641-2400

FERRO'S BLUE MESA CABINS
P O Box 853 (81230)
Rates: $25-$45
(970) 641-4671

HARMEL'S GUEST RANCH
Box 955M (81230)
Rates: $110-$170
(970) 641-1740

HYLANDER INN
412 E Tomichi Ave (81230)
Rates: $58-$82
(970) 641-0700

ISLAND ACRES MOTEL LOG LODGE
38339 W Hwy 50 (81230)
Rates: $33-$58
(970) 641-1442

LAKE SOREST RESORT
P O Box 1807 (81230)
Rates: $65-$95
(970) 641-3564
(800) 368-9421

LOST CANYON RESORT CABINS
8264 Hwy 135 (81230)
Rates: $56-$89
(970) 641-0181

ROCKY RIVER RESORT CABINS
4359 CR 10 (81230)
Rates: $34-$72
(970) 641-0174

SHADY ISLAND RESORT CABINS
2776 Hwy 135 N (81230)
Rates: $35-$45
(970) 641-0416

SILENT SPRINGS RESORT CABINS
805 W Tomichi Ave (81230)
Rates: $50-$90
(970) 641-0583

GYPSUM

GOLDEN EAGLE RANCH CABINS
15877 Gypsum Creek Rd (81637)
Rates: $75
(970) 524-9311

HEENEY

GREEN MOUNTAIN CABINS
0255 CR 1782 (80498)
Rates: $40
(970) 724-9748

MELODY LODGE & CABINS
1534 Heeney Rd 30 (80498)
Rates: $60-$100
(970) 468-8497
(800) 468-8495
(888) 8MELODY

HESPERUS

CANYON MOTEL
Hwy 160 & CR 124 (81326)
Rates: n/a
(303) 259-6277

HIGHLANDS RANCH

RESIDENCE INN BY MARRIOTT
93 W Centennial Blvd (80126)
Rates: $116-$153
(303) 683-5500
(800) 331-3131

HOT SULPHUR SPRINGS

BRIDGES STAGECOACH COUNTRY INN BED & BREAKFAST
412 Nevada St (80451)
Rates: $45-$74
(970) 725-3910

CANYON MOTEL
221 Byers Ave (80451)
Rates: $42-$70
(970) 725-3395

HOTCHKISS

HOTCHKISS INN
406 Hwy 133 (81419)
Rates: $39-$59
(970) 872-2200

IDAHO SPRINGS

H & H MOTOR LODGE
2445 Colorado Blvd (80452)
Rates: $54-$84
(303) 567-2838
(800) 445-2893

PEORIANA MOTEL
2901 Colorado Blvd (80452)
Rates: $38-$65
(303) 567-2021

6 & 40 MOTEL
2920 Colorado Blvd (80452)
Rates: $45-$95
(303) 567-2691

JULESBURG

PLATTE VALLEY INN
15225 Hwy 385 & I-76 (80737)
Rates: $45-$58
(970) 474-3336
(800) 563-5166

KIT CARSON

STAGE STOP MOTEL
P. O. Box 207 (80825)
Rates: $26-$34
(719) 962-3277

LA JARA

TEXAN COURT CABINS
P O Box 692 (81140)
Rates: $25-$75
(719) 376-2321
(970) 483-6394

LA JUNTA

HOLIDAY INN EXP
27994 US Hwy 50 (81050)
Rates: $74-$84
(719) 384-2900
(800) 465-4329

QUALITY INN
1325 E 3rd St (81050)
Rates: $44-$62
(719) 384-2571
(800) 228-5151

STAGECOACH MOTEL
905 W 3rd St (81050)
Rates: $40-$50
(719) 384-5476

TRAVEL INN
110 E 1st St
(81050)
Rates: $34-$42
(719) 384-2504

LA VETA

**CUCHARA
RIVER CABINS
& CAMPGROUND**
Box 397 (81055)
Rates: $45-$75
(719) 742-5303
(800) 375-2656

**SECURITY
PROPERTIES
VACATION
RENTALS**
P O Box 25A
(81055)
Rates: $65-$250
(800) 282-4272

LAKE CITY

CINNAMON INN
426 Gunnison Ave
(81235)
Rates: $60-$85
(970) 944-2641

G & M CABINS
P O Box 503
(81235)
Rates: $45-$80
(970) 944-2282

**LAKE CITY
RESORT**
307 S Gunnison
Ave (81235)
Rates: $44-$84
(970) 944-2866
(970) 944-2437

**LAKEVIEW
RESORT, SUITES,
CABINS**
P O Box1000
(81235)
Rates: $45-$115
(970) 944-2401
(800) 456-0170

**TOWN SQUARE
CABINS & STORE**
P O Box 1025
(81235)
Rates: $30-$55
(970) 944-2236

VICKERS RANCH
Hwy 149 S (81235)
Rates: $80
(970) 944-2249

**WESTERN BELLE
LODGE**
1221 Hwy 149 N
(81235)
Rates: n/a
(970) 944-2415

**WOODLAKE PARK
CAMPGROUND &
CABINS**
2690 Hwy 149
(81235)
Rates: $25-$60
(970) 944-2283
(800) 201-2694

LAKE GEORGE

**LAKE GEORGE
CABINS & RV
PARK**
8966 CR 90
(80827)
Rates: $60-$90
(719) 748-3822

**UTE TRAIL RIVER
RANCH CABINS**
21446 CR 77,
Tarryall River Vly
(80827)
Rates: $50-$90
(719) 748-3015

LAKEWOOD

**BEST WESTERN
DENVER WEST**
11595 W 6th Ave
(80215)
Rates: $59-$89
(303) 238-7751
(800) 528-1234

**COMFORT INN
SOUTHWEST**
3440 S Vance St
(80227)
Rates: $51-$115
(303) 989-5500
(800) 228-5150

**FOOTHILLS
EXECUTIVE
LODGING**
7150 W Colfax
Ave (80215)
Rates: $40-$65
(303) 232-2932
(800) 456-0425

**FOUR POINTS
HOTEL WEST**
137 Union Blvd
(80228)
Rates: $69-$109
(303) 969-9900
(800) 325-3535

MOTEL 6
480 Wadsworth
Blvd (80226)
Rates: $36-$54
(303) 232-4924
(800) 466-8356

RAMADA INN
7150 W Colfax
Ave (80215)
Rates: $69-$79
(303) 238-1251
(800) 272-6232

**RESIDENCE INN
BY MARRIOTT**
7050 W Hampden
Ave (80215)
Rates: $99-$159
(303) 985-7676
(800) 331-3131

**TOWNEPLACE
SUITES BY
MARRIOTT**
800 Tabor St
(80215)
Rates: $49-$99
(303) 232-7790

LAMAR

**BEST WESTERN
COW PALACE INN**
1301 N Main St
(81052)
Rates: $81-$114
(719) 336-7753
(800) 528-1234
(800) 678-0344

**BLUE SPRUCE
MOTEL**
1801 S Main St
(81052)
Rates: $30-$37
(719) 336-7454

**LAMAR KOA
KAMPING CABINS**
5385 Hwy 50
(81052)
Rates: $18-$26
(719) 336-7625
(800) 562-7626

PASSPORT INN
113 N Main St
(81052)
Rates: $32-$47
(719) 336-7746

SUPER 8 MOTEL
1202 N Main St
(81052)
Rates: $34-$50
(719) 336-3427
(800) 800-8000

TRAVELODGE
1201 N Main St
(81052)
Rates: $36-$75
(719) 336-7471
(800) 578-7878

LAS ANIMAS

**BEST WESTERN
BENT'S FORT INN**
East Hwy 50
(81054)
Rates: $48-$68
(719) 456-0011
(800) 528-1234
(877) 236-8738

LEADVILLE

ALPS MOTEL
207 Elm St (80461)
Rates: $43-$64
(719) 486-1223

BEL-AIR MOTEL
Hwy 24 S at Elm
(80461)
Rates: n/a
(719) 486-0881

CLUB LEAD
500 E 7th St
(80461)
Rates: n/a
(719) 486-2202

LEADVILLE INN
25 Jacktown Pl
(80461)
Rates: $40-$50
(719) 486-3637

**MOUNTAIN
PEAKS MOTEL**
1 Harrison Ave
(80461)
Rates: n/a
(719) 486-3178

**SILVER KING
MOTOR INN**
2020 N Poplar
(80461)
Rates: $42-$59
(719) 486-2610
(800) 871-2610

**TIMBERLINE
MOTEL**
216 Harrison Ave
(80461)
Rates: n/a
(719) 486-1876
(800) 352-1876

LIMON

**BEST WESTERN
LIMON INN**
925 "T" Ave
(80828)
Rates: $65-$85
(719) 775-0277
(800) 528-1234

ECONO LODGE
985 Hwy 24
(80828)
Rates: $38-$65
(719) 775-2867
(800) 553-2666

**HOLIDAY INN
EXPRESS**
2505 6th St (80820)
Rates: $85
(719) 775-0700
(800) 465-4329

**LIMON KOA
KAMPING KABINS**
575 Colorado Ave
(80828)
Rates: $29
(719) 775-2151
(800) 562-2129

**PREFERRED
MOTOR INN**
158 E Main St
(80828)
Rates: $38-$60
(719) 775-2385

SAFARI MOTEL
637 Main St
(80828)
Rates: $44-$62
(719) 775-2363

SUPER 8 MOTEL
937 Hwy 24
(80828)
Rates: $52-$65
(719) 775-2889
(800) 800-8000

LONGMONT

FIRST INTERSTATE INN
3940 Hwy 119
(80504)
Rates: $49+
(303) 772-6000
(800) 462-4667

RAINTREE PLAZA HOTEL & CONFERENCE CENTER
1900 Ken Pratt
Blvd (80501)
Rates: $144-$184
(303) 776-2000
(800) 843-8240

SUPER 8 MOTEL
10805 Turner Ave
(80504)
Rates: $62-$86
(303) 772-0888
(800) 800-8000

SUPER 8 MOTEL-TWIN PEAKS
2446 N Main St
(80501)
Rates: $44-$72
(303) 772-8106
(800) 800-8000

TRAVELODGE
3815 Hwy 119
(80504)
Rates: $35-$85
(303) 776-8700
(800) 578-7878

LOUISVILLE

COMFORT INN
1196 Dillon Rd
(80027)
Rates: $99-$203
(303) 604-0181
(800) 228-5150

LA QUINTA INN
902 Dillon Rd
(80027)
Rates: $59-$82
(303) 664-0100
(800) 687-6667

LOVELAND

BEST WESTERN COACH HOUSE
5542 Hwy 34E
(80537)
Rates: $60-$115
(970) 667-7810
(800) 528-1234
(888) 818-6223

BUDGET HOST
2716 SE Frontage
Rd (80538)
Rates: $38-$69
(970) 667-5202
(800) 283-4676

COMFORT INN
1500 N Cheyenne
Ave (80538)
Rates: $69-$149
(970) 593-0100
(800) 228-5150

MANCOS

A&A MESA VERDE RV PARK RESORT & CABINS
34979 Hwy 160
(81328)
Rates: $26-$55
(970) 565-7141
(800) 972-6620

BLUE SPRUCE MOTEL
40700 Hwy 160
West (81328)
Rates: $27-$50
(970) 533-7073

ECHO BASIN GUEST RANCH RESORT/RV PARK
43747 Rd M
(81328)
Rates: $89-$101
(970) 533-7000
(800) 426-1890

PONDEROSA CABINS
Cty Road 37 &
Hwy 184 (81328)
Rates: $55-$60
(970) 882-7396

RYTER HOUSE BED & BREAKFAST
40580 CR H
(81328)
Rates: $65
(970) 533-7661

MANITOU SPRINGS

RED EAGLE MOUNTAIN B&B
616 Ruxton Ave
(80829)
Rates: $85-$125
(719) 685-4541
(800) 686-9861

RED WING MOTEL
56 El Paso Blvd
(80829)
Rates: $49-$64
(719) 685-5656
(800) 733-9547

MARBLE

CHAIR MOUNTAIN RANCH CABINS
0178 CR 3 (81623)
Rates: $25-$100
(970) 963-9522

UTE MEADOWS INN B&B
2880 CR 3 (81623)
Rates: $120-$150
(970) 963-7088

MEEKER

LOST CREEK LODGE
2638 CR 12
(81641)
Rates: $85-$120
(970) 878-5214
(800) 522-5187

POLLARD'S UTE LODGE
393 CR 75 (81641)
Rates: $25-$60
(970) 878-4669
(888) 414-2022

RIMROCK RV PARK & CAMPGROUND CABINS
73179 Hwy 64
(81641)
Rates: $28-$32
(970) 878-4486

SLEEPY CAT GUEST RANCH
16064 CR 8
(81641)
Rates: $60
(970) 878-4413

MESA

MESA LAKES RESORT CABINS
P O Box 230
(81643)
Rates: $20-$130
(970) 268-5467

WAGON WHEEL MOTEL
1090 Hwy 65
(81643)
Rates: $40-$45
(970) 268-5224

MESA VERDE NATIONAL PARK

FAR VIEW LODGE IN MESA VERDE
P. O. Box 277
(Mancos 81328)
Rates: $98
(970) 529-4421
(800) 449-2288

MONARCH

MONARCH MOUNTAIN LODGE
#1 Power Pl
(81227)
Rates: $54-$175
(719) 539-2581
(800) 332-3668

MONTE VISTA

BEST WESTERN MOVIE MANOR MOTOR INN
2830 W Hwy 160
(81144)
Rates: $80-$110
(719) 852-5921
(800) 528-1234
(800) 771-9468

COMFORT INN
1519 Grande Ave
(81144)
Rates: $60-$95
(719) 852-0612
(800) 228-5150

MONTROSE

BLACK CANYON MOTEL
1605 E Main
(81401)
Rates: $50-$95
(970) 249-3495
(800) 348-3495

BLUE FOX MOTEL
1150 N Townsend
Ave (81401)
Rates: n/a
(970) 249-4595

COMFORT INN
2100 E Main St
(81401)
Rates: $41-$86
(970) 240-8000
(800) 228-5150

SAN JUAN INN
1480 Hwy 550S
(81401)
Rates: $48-$70
(970) 249-6644
(888) 681-4159

SUPER 8 MOTEL
1705 E Main
(81401)
Rates: $50-$66
(970) 249-9294
(800) 800-8000

UNCOMPAHGRE BED & BREAKFST
21049
Uncompahgre Rd
(81401)
Rates: $45-$65
(970) 240-4000

WESTERN MOTEL
1200 E Main St
(81401)
Rates: $38-$46
(970) 249-3481

MOSCA

GREAT SAND DUNES LODGE
7900 Hwy 150 N
(81146)
Rates: $69-$79
(719) 378-2900

INN AT HISTORICAL ZAPATA RANCH
5303 Hwy 150
(81146)
Rates: $95-$225
(800) 284-9213

NATURITA

RAY MOTEL
123 Main St
(81422)
Rates: $26-$46
(970) 865-2235

AREA CODES - If the local number doesn't connect, check for a new area code.

NEDERLAND

ARAPAHO RANCH CABINS
1250 Eldora Rd
(80466)
Rates: $70
(303) 258-3405

BEST WESTERN LODGE
55 Lakeview Dr
(80466)
Rates: $87-$115
(303) 258-9463
(800) 279-9643
(800) 528-1234

NEDERHAUS MOTEL
686 Hwy 119
South (80466)
Rates: $38-$90
(303) 444-4705
(800) 422-4629

NEW CASTLE

NEW CASTLE/ GLENWOOD SPRINGS KOA KABINS
0581 CR 241
(81647)
Rates: $38-$42
(970) 984-2240
(800) 562-3240

NORTHGLENN

DAYS INN NORTH
36 E 120th Ave
(80233)
Rates: $47-$72
(303) 457-0688
(800) 329-7466

HOLIDAY INN
10 E 120th Ave
(80233)
Rates: $89-$99
(303) 452-4100
(800) 465-4329

RAMADA INN
110 W 104th Ave
(80234)
Rates: $72-$87
(303) 451-1234
(800) 272-6232

NORWOOD

ANNIE'S COUNTRY BED & BREAKFAST
551 CR 44ZN
(81423)
Rates: $40
(970) 327-4331

BUCKHORN / DREAM CATCHER RANCH
SR 1 (81423)
Rates: $40-$60
(253) 588-7737

LONE CONE ELK RANCH B&B
P O Box 220
(81423)
Rates: $45
(970) 327-4300

OHIO CITY

BIG HORN GUEST RANCH
9102 CR 76
(81237)
Rates: $31-$51
(970) 641-1800

OURAY

4J+1+1 RV PARK & CAMPGROUND CABIN
790 Oak St (81427)
Rates: $25
(970) 325-4418

OURAY COTTAGE MOTEL
4th & Main Sts
(81427)
Rates: $45-$115
(970) 325-4370

OURAY KOA KAMPING KABINS
P O Box J (81427)
Rates: $38
(970) 325-4736
(800) 562-8026

OURAY VICTORIAN INN
50 3rd Ave (81427)
Rates: $84-$190
(970) 325-7222
(800) 846-8729

RIVERS EDGE MOTEL
110 7th Ave
(81427)
Rates: $55-$90
(970) 325-4621

RIVERSIDE INN & CABINS
1805 Hwy 550
(81427)
Rates: $25-$125
(970) 325-4061
(800) 432-4170

TIMBER RIDGE MOTEL
1515 North Main
St (81427)
Rates: n/a
(970) 325-4523

PAGOSA SPRINGS

BE OUR GUEST BED & BREAKFAST
19 Swiss Village
Dr (81147)
Rates: $47-$65
(970) 264-6814

BEST WESTERN OAK RIDGE LODGE
158 Hot Springs
Blvd (81147)
Rates: $56-$89
(970) 264-4173
(800) 528-1234

BRUCE SPRINGS RANCH, RV, CAMPGROUND & CABINS
Box 296 (81147)
Rates: $33-$48
(970) 264-5374
(800) 622-1346

ELK MEADOWS CAMPGROUND & CAMPER CABINS
P O Box 238
(81147)
Rates: $25-$30
(970) 264-5482
(800) 273-7462

FIRESIDE INN CABINS
1600 E Hwy 160
(81147)
Rates: $94-$139
(970) 264-9204
(888) 264-9204

INDIAN HEAD LODGE
P O Box 2499
(81147)
Rates: $24-$65
(970) 731-2282
(970) 358-4853

PAGOSA HIGH COUNTRY LODGE
3821 E Hwy 160
(81147)
Rates: $66-$100
(970) 264-4181

PAGOSA RIVERSIDE CAMPER CABINS
2270 E Hwy 160
(81147)
Rates: $24-$28
(970) 264-5874

PIEDRA RIVER RESORT
P O Box 4190
(81147)
Rates: $36-$50
(970) 731-4630
(800) 898-2006

SPA MOTEL
P O Box 37 (81147)
Rates: $45-$70
(970) 264-5910
(800) 832-5523

SUPER 8 MOTEL
34 Piedra Rd
(81147)
Rates: $36-$63
(970) 731-4005
(800) 800-8000

PAONIA

COLORADO GUEST RANCH / CHIPETA RANCH
1938 Hwy 133
(81428)
Rates: $43-$60
(970) 929-6260
(800) 521-4055

PARACHUTE

SUPER 8 MOTEL
252 Green St
(81635)
Rates: $39-$60
(970) 285-7936
(800) 800-8000

PARLIN

7 - 11 RANCH CABINS
5291 CR 76
(81239)
Rates: $30
(970) 641-0666

PUEBLO

BEST WESTERN TOWN HOUSE MOTOR HOTEL
730 N Santa Fe
(81003)
Rates: $55-$85
(719) 543-6530
(800) 528-1234

HAMPTON INN
4703 N Frwy
(81108)
Rates: $79-$99
(719) 544-4700
(800) 426-7866

HOLIDAY INN
4001 N Elizabeth
St (81008)
Rates: $69-$79
(719) 543-8050
(800) 465-4329

MOTEL 6
960 Hwy 50 W
(81008)
Rates: $39-$61
(719) 543-8900
(800) 466-8356

MOTEL 6 EXTENDED STAY
4103 N Elizabeth
(81008)
Rates: $33-$52
(719) 543-6221
(800) 466-8356

PUEBLO KOA KAMPING KABINS
4131 I-25 N
(81008)
Rates: $27-$32
(719) 542-2273
(800) 562-7453

QUALITY INN & SUITES
3910 Outlook Blvd
(81008)
Rates: $50-$110
(719) 544-5500
(800) 228-5151

AREA CODES - If the local number doesn't connect, check for a new area code.

RAMADA INN
2001 N Hudson
(81001)
Rates: $59-$109
(719) 542-3750
(800) 272-6232

PURGATORY

**BEST WESTERN
LODGE AT
PURGATORY**
49617 Hwy 550 N
(81301)
Rates: $89-$179
(970) 247-9669
(800) 528-1234
(800) 637-7727

**SHERATON
TAMARRON
RESORT**
40292 Hwy 550 N
(81301)
Rates: $129-$449
(970) 259-2000

RED CLIFF

PANDO CABINS
1088 Hwy 24
(81649)
Rates: $125
(970) 949-4232
(888) 949-6682

RED FEATHER LAKES

**BEAVER
MEADOWS
RESORT RANCH**
100 Marmot
(80545)
Rates: $39-$150
(800) 462-5870

**TROUT LODGE
CABINS**
P O Box 126
(80545)
Rates: $49-$99
(970) 881-2964

REDSTONE

**AVALANCHE
RANCH CABINS**
12863 Hwy 133
(81623)
Rates: $70-$155
(970) 963-2846

RIDGWAY

SUPER 8 MOTEL
373 Palomino Tr
(81432)
Rates: $73-$93
(970) 626-5444
(800) 800-8000
(800) 368-5444

RIFLE

**RUSTY CANNON
MOTEL-IMA**
701
Taughenbaugh
Blvd (81650)
Rates: $34-$55
(970) 625-4004
(800) 341-8000

ROCKY FORD

**MELON VALLEY
INN**
1319 Elm Ave
(81067)
Rates: $30-$45
(719) 254-3306

RYE

**THE LODGE AT
SAN ISABEL**
HCR 75, Box 123
(81069)
Rates: $45-$95
(719) 489-2280

SALIDA

**ASPEN LEAF
LODGE**
7350 Hwy 50W
(81201)
Rates $39-$69
(719) 539-6733
(800) 759-0338

BUDGET LODGE
1146 E Hwy 50
(81201)
Rates: $27-$47
(719) 539-6695
(800) 933-4823
(CO)

CIRCLE R MOTEL
304 E Rainbow
Blvd (81201)
Rates: $40-$62
(719) 539-6296

**PIÑON & SAGE
B&B INN**
803 F St (81201)
Rates: $45-$75
(719) 539-3227
(800) 840-3156

RAINBOW INN
105 E Hwy 50
(81201)
Rates: $50-$75
(719) 539-4444
(800) 539-4447

**RANCH HOUSE
LODGE**
7545 W Hwy 40
(81201)
Rates: $32-$68
(719) 539-6655

**REDWOOD
LODGE**
7310 Hwy 50
(81201)
Rates: $42-$79
(719) 539-2528

**SILVER RIDGE
LODGE**
545 W Rainbow
Blvd (81201)
Rates: $55-$75
(719) 539-2553

SUPER 8 MOTEL
525 W Rainbow
(81201)
Rates: $55-$89
(719) 539-6689
(800) 800-8000

TRAVELODGE
7310 Hwy 50
(81201)
Rates: $65-$85
(719) 539-2528
(800) 578-7878

**THE TUDOR ROSE
BED & BREAKFAST**
6720 Paradise Rd
(81201)
Rates: $50-$120
(719) 539-2002
(800) 379-0889

**WOODLAND
MOTEL**
903 W 1st (81201)
Rates: $41-$82
(719) 539-4980
(800) 488-0456

SAPINERO

**LEY-Z-B AT
SAPINERO
CABINS**
16020 W Hwy 50
(81247)
Rates: $25
(970) 641-2340

SILVER CREEK

**THE INN AT
SILVER CREEK**
62927 Hwy 40
(80446)
Rates: $69-$218
(970) 887-2131
(800) 926-4386

SILVERTHORNE

DAYS INN
580 Silverthorne
Ln (80498)
Rates: $59-$189
(970) 468-8661
(800) 329-7466

I-70 INN
361 Blueriver
Pkwy (80498)
Rates: n/a
(970) 468-5170

SILVERTON

**ALMA HOUSE
BED & BREAKFAST**
220 E 10th St
(81433)
Rates: $65-$110
(970) 387-5336
(800) 267-5336

**MOLAS LAKE
PARK CAMPER
CABINS**
P O Box 776
(81433)
Rates: $25
(970) 387-5848
(800) 846-2177

**RED MOUNTAIN
MOTEL &
CAMPGROUND**
P O Box 346
(81433)
Rates: $40-$65
(970) 387-5512
(888) 970-5512

**VILLA
DALLAVALLE B&B**
1257 Blair (81433)
Rates: $60-$95
(970) 387-5555

**WYMAN HOTEL
& INN B&B**
1370 Greene St
(81433)
Rates: $85-$170
(970) 387-5372
(800) 609-7845

SNOWMASS VILLAGE

**SILVERTREE
HOTEL**
100 Elbert Ln
(81615)
Rates: $145-$525
(970) 923-3520

**SNOWMASS
MOUNTAIN
CHALET**
115 Daly Ln
(81615)
Rates: $130-$210
(970) 923-3900

**WILDWOOD
LODGE**
40 Elbert Ln
(81615)
Rates: $89-$275
(970) 923-3520
(800) 525-9402

SOMERSET

**CRYSTAL
MEADOWS
RANCH LODGING**
30682 CR 12
(81434)
Rates: $40-$135
(970) 929-5656

SOUTH FORK

**ASPENRIDGE
CABINS &
RV PARK**
0710 W Hwy 149
(81154)
Rates: $40-$45
(719) 873-5921

BLUE CREEK LODGE & CABINS
Hwy 149,
MP 11-12,
HC 33 (81154)
Rates: $32-$64
(719) 658-2479
(800) 326-6408

BUDGET HOST UTE BLUFF LODGE
27680 W Hwy 160 (81154)
Rates: $40-$95
(719) 873-5595
(800) 473-0595
(800) 283-4678

COMFORT INN
0182 E Frontage Rd (81154)
Rates: $59-$150
(719) 873-5600
(800) 228-5150

COTTONWOOD COVE LODGE & CABINS
Hwy 149, HC 33 (81154)
Rates: $39-$74
(719) 658-2242

GOODNIGHT'S LONESOME DOVE CABINS
P O Box 157 (81154)
Rates: $55-$65
(719) 873-1072
(800) 551-3683

THE INN MOTEL
30362 West Hwy 160 (81154)
Rates: $26-$75
(719) 873-5514
(800) 233-9723

RIVEREND RESORT CABINS & RV PARK
Box 129 (81154)
Rates: $42-$140
(719) 873-5344
(800) 621-6512

SOUTH FORK LODGE & RV PARK
P O Box 43 (81154)
Rates: $45-$75
(719) 873-5303
(800) 457-9156

SPRUCE LODGE B&B AND CABINS
Box 156 (81154)
Rates: $28-$55
(719) 873-5605
(800) 228-5606

WOLF CREEK SKI LODGE
31042 Hwy W 160 (81154)
Rates: $50-$68
(719) 873-5547
(800) 874-0416

SPRINGFIELD

PLUM BEAR RANCH
29461 CR 21 (81073)
Rates: $45-$50
(719) 523-4344

STEAMBOAT SPRINGS

THE ALPINER LODGE
424 Lincoln Ave (80477)
Rates: $60-$130
(970) 879-1430
(800) 538-7519

BEST WESTERN PTARMIGAN INN
2304 Apres Ski Way (80487)
Rates: $99-$229
(970) 879-1730
(800) 528-1234
(800) 538-7519

HOLIDAY INN
3190 S Lincoln Ave (80487)
Rates: $90-$170
(970) 879-2250
(800) 465-4329

RABBIT EARS MOTEL
201 Lincoln Ave (80487)
Rates: $129-$169
(970) 879-1150
(800) 828-7702

SHERATON STEAMBOAT RESORT
2200 Village Inn Court (80487)
Rates: $79-$369
(970) 879-2220

STEAMBOAT LOG CABINS AT PERRY MANSFIELD
40755 CR 36 (80487)
Rates: $105-$350
(970) 879-1060
(800) 538-7519

SUPER 8 MOTEL
3195 Hwy 40 E (80487)
Rates: $72-$90
(970) 879-5230
(800) 800-8000

STERLING

BEST WESTERN SUNDOWNER
125 Overland Trail St (80751)
Rates: $74-$105
(970) 522-6265
(800) 528-1234

COLONIAL MOTEL
915 S Division (80751)
Rates: $33-$38
(970) 522-3382

FIRST INTERSTATE INN
20930 Hwy 6 (80751)
Rates: $25-$43
(970) 522-7274

RAMADA INN
I-76 & Hwy 6 E (80751)
Rates: $85-$105
(970) 522-2625
(800) 272-6232

SUPER 8 MOTEL
12883 Hwy 61 (80751)
Rates: $42-$52
(970) 522-0300
(800) 800-8000

STRASBURG

DENVER EAST-STRASBURG KOA KAMPING CABINS
P O Box 597 (80136)
Rates: $29-$35
(303) 662-9274
(800) 562-6538

STRASBURG INN BED & BREAKFAST
1406 Main (80136)
Rates: $35-$50
(303) 622-4314

STRATTON

BEST WESTERN GOLDEN PRAIRIE
700 Colorado Ave (80836)
Rates: $45-$99
(719) 348-5311
(800) 528-1234
(800) 626-0043

SWEETWATER

SWEETWATER LAKE RESORT
3406 Sweetwater Rd (81637)
Rates: $50-$90
(970) 524-7344

TABERNASH

HURD CREEK RANCH LODGE & CABIN RENTAL
P O Box 516 (80478)
Rates: $150-$250
(970) 726-5304
(800) 471-5122

TELLURIDE

HOTEL COLUMBIA
300 W San Juan Ave (81435)
Rates: $395
(970) 728-0660
(800) 201-9505

THE PEAKS AT TELLURIDE
136 Country Club Dr (81435)
Rates: $235-$1750
(970) 728-6800
(800) 789-2220

TEXAS CREEK

WHISPERING PINES RESORT
24871 Hwy 50 W (81223)
Rates: $35-$45
(719) 275-3827
(888) 275-3827

THORNTON

MOTEL 6
6 W 83rd Pl (80221)
Rates: $36-$54
(303) 429-1550
(800) 466-8356

SLEEP INN
12101 Grant St (80229)
Rates: $54-$99
(303) 280-9819
(800) 753-3746

TRINIDAD

BEST WESTERN COUNTRY CLUB INN
900 W Adams St (81082)
Rates: $79-$99
(719) 846-2215
(800) 528-1234
(800) 955-2215

BUDGET HOST DERRICK MOTEL
10301 Santa Fe Trail Dr (81082)
Rates: $53-$70
(719) 846-3307
(800) 283-4678

BUDGET SUMMIT INN
9800 Santa Fe Trail Dr (81082)
Rates: $44-$119
(719) 846-2251

CHICOSA CANYON B&B
32391 CR 40 (81082)
Rates: $75-$95
(719) 846-6199

DAYS INN
702 W Main St (81082)
Rates: $59-$99
(719) 846-2271
(800) 329-7466

AREA CODES - If the local number doesn't connect, check for a new area code.

HOLIDAY INN
3125 Toupal Dr
(81082)
Rates: $129
(719) 846-4491
(800) 465-4329

SUPER 8 MOTEL
1924 Freedom Rd
(81082)
Rates: $52-$90
(719) 846-8280
(800) 800-8000

TWIN LAKES

**MOUNT ELBERT
LODGE & CABINS**
10764 Hwy 82
(81251)
Rates: $59-$88
(719) 486-0594
(800) 381-4433

**TWIN LAKES
NORDIC INN**
6435 Hwy 82
(81251)
Rates: $48-$65
(719) 486-1830
(800) 626-7812

**TWIN PEAKS
CABINS**
6889 Hwy 82
(81251)
Rates: $45-$80
(719) 486-2667

VAIL

ANTLERS AT VAIL
680 W Lionshead
Place (81657)
Rates: $160-$410
(970) 476-2471
(800) 843-8245

VALLECITO LAKE

**SAWMILL POINT
LODGE CABINS &
VACATION
RENTALS**
14737 CR 501
(Bayfield 81122)
Rates: $50-$125
(970) 884-2669

VICTOR

**HISTORIC VICTOR
HOTEL**
397 Victor Ave
(80860)
Rates: $85-$99
(970) 689-3553
(800) 748-0870 (CO)

WALDEN

**LAKE JOHN
RESORT**
2521 CR 7A
(80480)
Rates: $35-$45
(970) 723-3226

**NORTH PARK
MOTEL**
625 Main St
(80480)
Rates: $30-$60
(970) 723-4271

WALSENBURG

**BEST WESTERN
RAMBLER MOTEL**
457 Hwy 8587
(81089)
Rates: $65-$89
(719) 738-1121
(800) 528-1234

**BUDGET HOST
COUNTRY HOST
MOTEL**
553 US 85 & 87
(81089)
Rates: $48-$64
(719) 738-3800
(800) 283-4678

WESTCLIFFE

**CROSS D BAR
TROUT RANCH &
CAMPGROUND**
2299 CR 328
(81252)
Rates: $80
(719) 783-2007
(313) 733-5577

WESTCLIFFE INN
S Hwy 69 &
Hermit Rd (81252)
Rates: $33-$75
(719) 783-9275
(800) 284-0850

WESTMINSTER

**HAWTHORN INN
& SUITES**
10179 Church
Ranch Way
(80234)
Rates: $85-$112
(303) 438-5800
(800) 527-1133

**LA QUINTA INN
NORTH**
345 W 120th Ave
(80234)
Rates: $69-$89
(303) 252-9800
(800) 687-6667

**LA QUINTA INN
WESTMINSTER
MALL**
8701 Turnpike Dr
(80230)
Rates: $79-$99
(303) 425-9099
(800) 687-6667

SUPER 8 MOTEL
12055 Melody Dr
(80234)
Rates: $48-$72
(303) 451-7200
(800) 800-8000

WHEAT RIDGE

**HOLIDAY INN
EXPRESS**
4700 Kipling St
(80033)
Rates: $59-$79
(303) 423-4000
(800) 465-4329

MOTEL 6
9920 W 49th Ave
(80033)
Rates: $34-$52
(303) 424-0658
(800) 466-8356

MOTEL 6
10300 S I-70
Frontage Rd
(80033)
Rates: $35-$52
(303) 467-3172
(800) 466-8356

QUALITY INN
12100 W 44th Ave
(80033)
Rates: $49-$89
(303) 467-2400
(800) 228-5151

WINTER PARK

**BEST WESTERN
WINTER PARK
MOUNTAIN
LODGE**
81699 US Hwy 40
(80482)
Rates: $85-$400
(800) 528-1234
(800) 726-3340

**SITZMARK
CHALETS
& CABINS**
Hwy 40 at King's
Crossing (80482)
Rates: $40-$80
(970) 726-5453

VINTAGE HOTEL
100 Winter Park
Dr (80482)
Rates: $485
(970) 726-8801
(800) 472-7017

YAMPA

**VAN CAMP
CABINS**
P O Box 170
(80483)
Rates: $45-$55
(970) 638-4254

AREA CODES - If the local number doesn't connect, check for a new area code.

CONNECTICUT

AVON

AVON OLD FARMS HOTEL
279 Avon Mtn Rd (006001)
Rates: $180
(860) 677-1651

BERLIN

HAWTHORNE INN
2387 Wilbur Cross Hwy (06037)
Rates: $51-$75
(860) 828-4181

BRANFORD

DAYS INN
375 E Main St (06405)
Rates: $50-150
(203) 488-8314
(800) 329-7466

MOTEL 6
320 E Main St (06405)
Rates: $41-$59
(203) 483-5828
(800) 466-8356

BRIDGEPORT

HOLIDAY INN
1070 Main St (06604)
Rates: $119-$159
(203) 334-1234
(800) 465-4329

BROOKFIELD

TWIN TREE INN
1030 Federal Rd (06804)
Rates: $76-$99
(203) 775-0220

CHAPLIN

PLEASANT VIEW LODGE MOTEL
Rt 6 (06235)
Rates: $30-$50
(860) 455-9588

CHESTER

INN AT CHESTER
318 W Main St (06412)
Rates: $95-$105
(860) 526-9541
(800) 949-7829

CLINTON

CLINTON MOTEL
163 East Main St (06413)
Rates: $48-$78
(860) 669-8850

CORNWALL

THE CORNWALL INN
Route 7 (06754)
Rates: $50-$150
(800) 786-6884

COVENTRY

MILL BROOK FARM B & B
110 Wall St (06238)
Rates: $45-$60
(860) 742-5761

CROMWELL

COMFORT INN
111 Berlin Rd (06416)
Rates: $89-$104
(860) 635-4100
(800) 228-5150

RADISSON HOTEL & CONFERENCE CENTER
100 Berlin Rd (06416)
Rates: $125
(860) 635-2000
(800) 333-3333

SUPER 8 MOTEL
1 Industrial Park Rd (06416)
Rates: $56-$68
(860) 632-8888
(800) 800-8000

DANBURY

COMFORT SUITES
89 Mill Plain Rd (06811)
Rates: $59-$109
(800) 228-5150

HILTON & TOWERS
18 Old Ridgebury Rd (06810)
Rates: $95-$176
(203) 794-0600
(800) 445-8667

HOLIDAY INN
80 Newtown Rd (06810)
Rates: $121-$125
(203) 792-4000
(800) 465-4329

RAMADA INN
116 Newtown Rd (06810)
Rates: $89-$155
(203) 792-3800
(800) 272-6232

RESIDENCE INN BY MARRIOTT
22 Segar St (06810)
Rates: $129-$149
(203) 797-1256
(800) 331-3131

EAST HARTFORD

HOLIDAY INN
363 Roberts St (06108)
Rates: $119-$129
(860) 528-9611
(800) 465-4329

RAMADA INN
100 E River Dr East (06108)
Rates: $69-$139
(860) 528-9703
(800) 272-6232

WELLESLY INN & SUITES

333 Roberts St (06108)
Rates: $79-$110
(860) 289-4950
(800) 444-8888

EAST WINDSOR

BEST WESTERN COLONIAL INN
161 Bridge St (06088)
Rates: $85-$325
(860) 623-9411
(800) 528-1234

ENFIELD

MOTEL 6
11 Hazard Ave (06082)
Rates: $37-$52
(860) 741-3685
(800) 466-8356

RED ROOF INN
5 Hazard Ave (06082)
Rates: $50-$107
(860) 741-2571
(800) 843-7663

SUPER 8 MOTEL
1543 King St (06082)
Rates: $45-$115
(860) 741-3636
(800) 800-8000

ESSEX

GRISWOLD HISTORIC COUNTRY INN
36 Main St (06426)
Rates: $90-$195
(860) 767-1776

FAIRFIELD

FAIRFIELD MOTOR INN
417 Post Rd (06430)
Rates: $63-$70
(203) 255-0491
(800) 257-0496

FARMINGTON

CENTENNIAL INN SUITES
5 Spring Ln (06032)
Rates: $129-$210
(860) 677-4647
(800) 852-2052

FARMINGTON INN
827 Farmington Ave (06032)
Rates: $99-$129
(860) 677-2821
(800) 648-9804

GROTON

BENHAM MOTEL
107 Benham Rd (06340)
Rates: $76-$99
(860) 449-5700

CLARION INN
156 Kings Hwy (06340)
Rates: $59-$179
(860) 446-0660
(800) 252-7466

MORGAN INN & SUITES
135 Gold Star Hwy (06340)
Rates: $85-$150
(860) 448-3000
(800) 280-0054

TRAILS CORNER MOTOR INN
580 Poquannock Rd (06340)
Rates: n/a
(860) 445-0220

AREA CODES - If the local number doesn't connect, check for a new area code.

GUILFORD

B&B AT B
279 Boston St
(06437)
Rates: $76-$99
(203) 453-6490

HARTFORD

CROWNE PLAZA
50 Morgan St
(06120)
Rates: $79-$219
(860) 549-2400
(800) 227-6963

DAYS INN
207 Brainard Rd
(06114)
Rates: $76-$89
(860) 247-3297
(800) 329-7466

GOODWIN HOTEL
1 Haynes St
(06103)
Rates: $79-$228
(860) 246-7500

HOMEWOOD SUITES
2 Farm Glen Blvd
(06032)
Rates: n/a
(860) 321-0000
(800) 225-5466

RAMADA INN DOWNTOWN-CAPITOL HILL
440 Asylum St
(06103)
Rates: $68-$125
(860) 246-6591
(800) 272-6232

RED ROOF INN
100 Weston St
(06120)
Rates: $56-$93
(860) 724-0222
(800) 843-7663

SUPER 8 MOTEL
57 W Service Rd
(06120)
Rates: $54-$68
(860) 246-8888
(800) 800-8000

KENT

THE GIBBS HOUSE
87 N Main St
(06757)
Rates: $76-$99
(860) 927-1754

LAKEVILLE

INN AT IRON MASTERS
229 Main St
(06039)
Rates: $95-$145
(860) 435-9844

INTERLAKEN INN RESORT & CONFERENCE CENTER
74 Interlaken Rd
(06039)
Rates: $149-$189
(860) 435-9878
(800) 222-2909

LEDYARD

APPLEWOOD FARMS BED & BREAKFAST
528 Colonel
Ledyard Hwy
(06372)
Rates: $100+
(860) 536-2022

THE MARE'S INN BED & BREAKFAST
333 Colonel
Ledyard Hwy
(06372)
Rates: $100-$175
(860) 572-7556

LITCHFIELD

HISTORIC TOLLGATE HILL INN
Rt 202 & Tollgate
Rd (06759)
Rates: $100-$175
(860) 567-4545
(800) 445-3903

MANCHESTER

CLARION SUITES INN
191 Spencer St
(06040)
Rates: $106-$186
(860) 643-5811
(800) 992-4004

MERIDEN

EAST INN HOTEL & CONF CENTER
900 E Main St
(06450)
Rates: $51-$75
(203) 238-1211

RAMADA PLAZA HOTEL & CONFERNCE CENTER
275 Research
Pkwy (06450)
Rates: $79-$169
(203) 238-2380
(800) 272-6232

RESIDENCE INN BY MARRIOTT
390 Bee St (06450)
Rates: $174
(203) 634-7770
(800) 331-3131

MILFORD

RED ROOF INN
10 Rowe Ave
(06460)
Rates: $61-$73
(203) 877-6060
(800) 843-7663

MILLDALE

DAYS INN
I-84 & Rt 322
(06467)
Rates: $60-$129
(860) 621-9181
(800) 329-7466

MONTVILLE

CHESTERFIELD LODGE
1596 Rt 85
(06370)
Rates: $30-$50
(860) 442-0039

MYSTIC

AMERISUITES
224 Greenmanville
Ave (06355)
Rates: $99-$209
(860) 536-9997
(800) 833-1516

HARBOUR INNE & COTTAGE
15 Edgemont St
(06355)
Rates: $76-$99
(860) 572-9253

NEW HAVEN

MOTEL 6
270 Foxon Blvd
(06513)
Rates: $51-$62
(203) 469-0343
(800) 466-8356

RESIDENCE INN BY MARRIOTT
3 Long Wharf Dr
(06513)
Rates: $145-$180
(203) 777-5337
(800) 331-3131

NEW LONDON

RED ROOF INN
707 Colman St
(06320)
Rates: $60-$100
(860) 444-0001
(800) 843-7663

NEW MILFORD

THE HERITAGE INN OF LITCHFIELD COUNTY
34 Bridge St
(06776)
Rates: $75-$100
(860) 354-8883

NEW PRESTON

ATHA HOUSE COTTAGE
Wheaton Rd off
Rt 202 (06777)
Rates: $76-$99
(860) 355-7387

NIANTIC

MOTEL 6
269 Flanders Rd
(06357)
Rates: $45-$66
(860) 739-6991
(800) 466-8356

NORFOLK

BLACKBERRY RIVER INN BED & BREAKFAST
536 Greenwoods
Rd W (06058)
Rates: $95-$195
(860) 542-5100

NORTH HAVEN

HOLIDAY INN
201 Washington
Ave (06473)
Rates: $79-$129
(203) 239-4225
(800) 465-4329

NORTH STONINGTON

BUDGET INN
593 Providence-
New London
Tpke (06359)
Rates: $51-$75
(860) 599-0835

THE JOHN YORK HOUSE 1741 BED & BREAKFAST
One Clarks Falls
Rd (06359)
Rates: $65-$125
(860) 599-3075

NORWALK

GARDEN PARK MOTEL
351 Westport Ave
(06851)
Rates: $51-$75
(203) 847-7303

HOMESTEAD GUEST STUDIOS
400 Main Ave
(06851)
Rates: n/a
(203) 847-6888
(888) 782-9473

SILVER MINE TAVERN BED & BREAKFAST
194 Perry Ave
(06851)
Rates: $75-$125
(203) 847-4558

OLD LYME

OLD LYME INN
85 Lyme St
(06371)
Rates: $99-$175
(860) 434-2600
(800) 434-5352

OLD SAYBROOK

SANDPIPER INN
1750 Boston Post
Rd (06475)
Rates: $65-$135
(860) 399-7973

PLAINFIELD

**PLAINFIELD
MOTEL**
Box 101, RR 2
(Moosup 06354)
Rates: $37-$64
(860) 564-2791

PLAINVILLE

**HOWARD
JOHNSON
HOTEL**
400 New Britain
Ave (06062)
Rates: $60-$70
(860) 747-6876
(800) 446-4656

PUTNAM

KING'S INN
5 Heritage Rd
(06260)
Rates: $62-$78
(860) 928-7961
(800) 541-7304

RIVERSIDE

**HOWARD
JOHNSON**
1114 Boston Post
Rd (06878)
Rates: $89-$139
(203) 637-3691
(800) 446-4656

RIVERTON

**OLD RIVERTON
INN**
436 E River Rd
(06065)
Rates: $55-$130
(860) 379-8678

SHARON

**SHARON
MOTOR LODGE**
SR 41 (06069)
Rates: $62-$125
(860) 364-0036

SHELTON

AMERISUITES
695 Bridgeport
Ave (06484)
Rates: $154
(203) 925-5900
(800) 833-1516

**RAMADA PLAZA
HOTEL**
780 Bridgeport
Ave (06484)
Rates: $69-$155
(203) 929-1500
(800) 272-6232

**RESIDENCE INN
BY MARRIOTT**
1001 Bridgeport
Ave (06484)
Rates: $145-$190
(203) 926-9000
(800) 331-3131

SIMSBURY

IRONHORSE INN
969 Hopmeadow
St (06070)
Rates: $79-$89
(860) 658-2216
(800) 245-9938

**THE SIMSBURY
1820 HOUSE**
731 Hopmeadow
St (06070)
Rates: $109-$169
(860) 658-7658
(800) TRY-1820

SOUTHBURY

HILTON HOTEL
1284 Strongtown
Rd (06488)
Rates: $136-$151
(203) 598-7600
(800) 445-8667

SOUTHING-TON

MOTEL 6
625 Queen St
(06489)
Rates: $39-$56
(860) 621-7351
(800) 466-8356

STAMFORD

**BUDGET HOST
HOSPITALITY
INN**
19 Clarks Hill
Ave (06902)
Rates: $52-$75
(203) 327-4300
(800) 362-7666

**HOLIDAY INN
SELECT**
700 Main St
(06901)
Rates: $209
(203) 358-8400
(800) 465-4329

STRATFORD

RAMADA INN
225 Lordship
Blvd (06497)
Rates: $69-$135
(203) 375-8866
(800) 272-6232

UNCASVILLE

**BEST WESTERN
CRISTATA INN**
2265 Rt 32
(06382)
Rates: $89-$179
(860) 848-0660
(800) 528-1234

VERNON

**HOWARD
JOHNSON EXP**
451 Hartford Tpk
(06066)
Rates: $45-$80
(860) 875-0781
(800) 446-4656

VOLUNTOWN

**TAMARACK
LODGE**
21 Ten Rod Rd
(06384)
Rates: $51-$75
(860) 376-0640
(860) 376-0224

WATERBURY

**HOUSE ON THE
HILL B&B**
92 Woodlawn Ter
(06710)
Rates: $125-$165
(203) 757-9901

**SHERATON
HOTEL**
3580 E Main St
(06710)
Rates: $139
(203) 573-1000
(800) 325-3535

WATERFORD

**LAMPLIGHTER
MOTEL**
211 Waterford
Pkwy N (06385)
Rates: $76-$110
(860) 442-7227

WEST GOSHEN

GOSHEN MOTEL
Rt 4 W (06756)
Rates: $30-$50
(860) 491-9989

WEST HAVEN

SUPER 8 MOTEL
7 Kimberly Ave
(06516)
Rates: $48-$65
(203) 931-8888
(800) 800-8000

WESTBROOK

MAPLES MOTEL
1935 Boston Post
Rd (06498)
Rates: $55-$75
(860) 399-9345

WETHERS-FIELD

MOTEL 6
1341 Silas Deane
Hwy (06109)
Rates: $37-$50
(860) 563-5900
(800) 466-8356

RAMADA INN
1330 Silas Deane
Hwy (06109)
Rates: $62-$75
(860) 563-2311
(800) 272-6232

WILLINGTON

SLEEP INN
327 Ruby Rd
(06279)
Rates: $59-$109
(860) 684-1400
(800) 753-3746

WINDSOR

**RESIDENCE INN
BY MARRIOTT**
100 Dunfey Ln
(06095)
Rates: $128
(860) 688-7474
(800) 331-3131

WINDSOR LOCKS

**BAYMONT INN
& SUITES**
64 Ella Grasso
Tpk (06096)
Rates: $77-$87
(860) 623-3336
(800) 301-0200

**HOMEWOOD
SUITES**
65 Ella Grasso
Tpke (06096)
Rates: $159-$179
(860) 627-8463
(800) 225-5466

MOTEL 6
3 National Dr
(06096)
Rates: $37-$50
(860) 292-6200
(800) 466-8356

**SHERATON
HOTEL AT
BRADLEY INTL
AIRPORT**
1 Bradley Intl
Airport (06096)
Rates: $145-$160
(860) 627-5311
(800) 325-3535

DELAWARE

BETHANY BEACH

ATLANTIC SURF
Rt 1 & 4th St
(19930)
Rates: n/a
(302) 539-6552

WESTWARD PINES MOTEL
10 Kent Ave
(19930)
Rates: $75-$90
(302) 539-7426

BRIDGEVILLE

TEDDY BEAR B&B
303 Market St
(19933)
Rates: $45-$65
(302) 337-3134

DEWEY BEACH

ATLANTIC OCEANSIDE MOTEL
1700 Hwy 1
(19971)
Rates: $89-$229
(302) 227-8811
(800) 422-0481

BELLBUOY MOTEL
21 Van Dyke St
(19971)
Rates: $65-$165
(302) 227-6000

BEST WESTERN GOLD LEAF
1400 Hwy One
(19971)
Rates: $99-$245
(302) 226-1100
(800) 528-1234
(800) 422-8566

SEA ESTA MOTEL I
2306 Hwy 1
(19971)
Rates: $49-$139
(302) 227-7666
(800) 436-6591

SEA ESTA MOTEL 3
1409 Hwy 1 (19971)
Rates: $55-$179
(302) 227-4343
(800) 436-6591

DOVER

BUDGET INN
1426 N DuPont
Hwy (19901)
Rates: $40-$55
(302) 734-4433

FENWICK ISLAND

ATLANTIC BUDGET INN
Ocean Hwy & Rt
54 (19944)
Rates: $79-$129
(302) 539-7673

ISKANDER'S ISLAND INN
Rt 1 (19944)
Rates: $99-$169
(302) 537-1900

SANDS MOTEL & APARTMENTS
Rt 1 & James St
(19944)
Rates: $69-$114
(302) 539-7745

LEWES

COUNTRY LANE BED&BREAKFAST
7 Country Ln
(19958)
Rates: $85-$95
(302) 945-1586

FIRST PORT OF CALL
28 Cape
Henlopen (19958)
Rates: $55+
(302) 645-7266

MILLSBORO

ATLANTIC BUDGET INN
210 W DuPont
Hwy (19966)
Rates: $99-$189
(302) 934-6711

NEW CASTLE

MOTEL 6
1200 West Ave
(19720)
Rates: $40-$46
(302) 571-1200
(800) 466-8356

QUALITY INN SKYWAYS
147 N DuPont
Hwy (19720)
Rates: $84-$159
(302) 328-6666
(800) 228-5151

RODEWAY INN
111 S DuPont
Hwy (19720)
Rates: $59-$74
(302) 328-6246
(800) 228-2000

SUPER 8 MOTEL
215 S DuPont
Hwy (19720)
Rates: $47+
(302) 322-9480
(800) 800-8000

TRAVELODGE
1213 West Ave
(19720)
Rates: $48-$100
(302) 654-5544
(800) 578-7878

NEWARK

BEST WESTERN
260 Chapman Rd
(19702)
Rates: $55-$75
(302) 738-3400
(800) 528-1234
(800) 633-3203

HOMESTEAD VILLAGE GUEST STUDIOS
333 Continental
Dr (19713)
Rates: $73-$78
(302) 283-0800
(888) 782-9473

HOWARD JOHNSON HOTEL & SUITES
1119 S College
Ave (19713)
Rates: $59-$125
(302) 368-8521
(800) 446-4656

RED ROOF INN
415 Stanton
Christiana Rd
(19713)
Rates: $57-$73
(302) 292-2870
(800) 843-7663

RESIDENCE INN BY MARRIOTT
240 Chapman Rd
(19702)
Rates: $88-$179
(302) 453-9200
(800) 331-3131

TRAVELODGE
268 E Main St
(19711)
Rates: $45-$55
(302) 737-5050
(800) 578-7878

REHOBOTH BEACH

AIRPORT MOTEL
Rt 14 (19971)
Rates: $55-$96
(302) 227-6737

ATLANTIC BUDGET INN
154 Rehoboth
Ave (19971)
Rates: $89-$149
(302) 227-9446

ATLANTIC SANDS HOTEL
101 N Boardwalk
(19971)
Rates: $145-$290
(302) 227-2511

CAPE SUITES
47 Baltimore Ave
(19971)
Rates: $110-$135
(302) 226-3342

CORNER CUPBOARD INN
50 Park Ave
(19971)
Rates: $155-$240
(302) 227-8553

LORD BALTIMORE INN
16 Baltimore Ave
(19971)
Rates: $35-$65
(302) 227-2855

LOVE CREEK MOTEL
Rt 24 (19971)
Rates: $48+
(302) 945-8909

RENEGADE MOTEL
Hwy 1 (19971)
Rates: $85-$120
(302) 227-1222

SEA ESTA MOTEL 2
140 Rehoboth
Ave (19971)
Rates: $85-$119
(302) 227-1223
(800) 436-6591

SEAFORD

BEST WESTERN
225 N Dual Hwy
(19973)
Rates: $69-$89
(302) 629-8385
(800) 528-1234

WILMINGTON

BEST WESTERN
1807 Concord
Pike (19803)
Rates: $72-$132
(302) 656-9436
(800) 528-1234
(800) 537-7772

TALLY-HO MOTOR LODGE
5209 Concord
Pike (19803)
Rates: $48-$55
(302) 478-0300
(800) 445-0852

DISTRICT OF COLUMBIA

WASHINGTON
(Downtown
and vicinity)

**BEST WESTERN-
NEW HAMPSHIRE**
1121 New
Hampshire Ave
NW (20037)
Rates: $169-$239
(202) 457-0565
(800) 528-1234
(800) 762-3777

CAPITAL HILTON
16th & K Sts NW
(20036)
Rates: $225-$295
(202) 393-1000
(800) 445-8667

**THE CARLTON
HISTORIC HOTEL**
923 16th St at K
St NW (20006)
Rates: $160-$325
(202) 638-2626

CARLYLE SUITES
1731 New
Hampshire Ave
(20009)
Rates: $55-$119
(202) 234-3200

DAYS INN
2700 New York
Ave NE (20002)
Rates: $49-$119
(202) 832-5800
(800) 329-7466

**DOUBLETREE
GUEST SUITES**
801 New
Hampshire Ave
NW (20037)
Rates: $109-$179
(202) 785-2000
(800) 222-8733

**DOUBLETREE
GUEST SUITES**
2500
Pennsylvania
Ave NW (20037)
Rates: $199
(202) 333-8060
(800) 222-8733

FOUR SEASONS
2800 Pennsylvania
Ave NW (20007)
Rates: $350-$565
(202) 342-0444
(800) 332-3442

**GEORGETOWN
DUTCH INN**
1075 Thomas
Jefferson NW
(20007)
Rates: n/a
(202) 337-0900

**GEORGETOWN
INN HOTEL**
1310 Wisconsin
Ave NW (20007)
Rates: $185-$235
(202) 333-8900
(800) 424-2979

**GEORGETOWN
MEWS**
1111 20th St NW
(20007)
Rates: n/a
(202) 298-7731

**GEORGETOWN
SUITES
HARBOUR BLDG
APT HOTEL**
1000 29th St NW
(20007)
Rates: $165-$210
(202) 298-1600

**THE GRAND
HOTEL**
2350 M St NW
(20037)
Rates: $155-$300
(202) 429-0100

THE HAY-ADAMS
1 Lafayette Sq
(20006)
Rates: $300-$240
(202) 638-6600

**HILTON
& TOWERS**
1919 Connecticut
Ave NW (20009)
Rates: $209-$399
(202) 483-3000
(800) 445-8667

**HISTORIC HOTEL
WASHINGTON**
515 15th St NW
(20004)
Rates: $185-$260
(202) 638-5900

HOTEL SOFITEL
1914 Connecticut
Ave NW (20009)
Rates: $199-$239
(202) 797-2000

**HOWARD JOHN-
SON EXPRESS**
600 New York
Ave NE (20002)
Rates: $51-$74
(202) 546-9200
(800) 446-4656

**THE JEFFERSON
HOTEL**
1200 16th St NW
(20036)
Rates: $210-$950
(202) 347-2200

**LINCOLN SUITES
DOWNTOWN**
1823 L St NW
(20036)
Rates: $149-$179
(202) 223-4320
(800) 424-2970

**LOEWS L'ENFANT
PLAZA HOTEL**
480 L'Enfant
Plaza SW (20024)
Rates: $189-$259
(202) 484-1000
(800) 235-6397

**THE LUXURY
COLLECTION
HISTORIC HOTEL**
2100
Massachusetts
Ave NW (20008)
Rates: $150-$326
(202) 293-2100

**THE MADISON
HOTEL**
1177 15th St NW
(20005)
Rates: $350-$400
(202) 862-1600

**MARRIOTT
HOTEL**
1221 22nd St at M
St NW (20037)
Rates: $109-$189
(202) 872-1500
(800) 228-0290

**MARRIOTT
WARDMAN PARK
HOTEL**
2660 Woodley Rd
NW (20008)
Rates: $289
(202) 328-2000
(800) 228-9290

**MONARCH
HOTEL**
2401 M St NW
(20037)
Rates: $298
(202) 429-2400

**OMNI
SHOREHAM
HOTEL**
2500 Calvert St
NW (20008)
Rates: $189-$309
(202) 234-0700
(800) 843-6664

**ONE
WASHINGTON
CIRCLE HOTEL**
One Washington
Cir NW (20037)
Rates: $75-$290
(202) 872-1680

**PARK HYATT
WASHINGTON**
1201 124th St NW
(20037)
Rates: $300-$325
(202) 789-1234

PLAZA HOTEL
10 Thomas Circle
NW (20005)
Rates: $89-$130
(202) 842-1300
(800) 272-6232

**RADISSON PARK
TERRACE HOTEL**
1515 Rhode
Island Ave NW
(20005)
Rates: $99
(800) 333-3333

RED ROOF INN
500 H St, NW
(20001)
Rates: n/a
(202) 289-5959
(800) 843-7663

**RENAISSANCE
MAYFLOWER
HISTORIC HOTEL**
1127 Connecticut
Ave NW (20036)
Rates: $149-$365
(202) 347-3000
(800) 468-3571

**RENAISSANCE
HOTEL**
999 9th St NW
(20001)
Rates: $205-$245
(202) 898-9000
(800) 468-3571

THE RIVER INN
924 25th St NW
(20036)
Rates: $109-$160
(202) 337-7600

**SAVOY SUITES
HOTEL
GEORGETOWN**
2505 Wisconsin
Ave NW (20007)
Rates: $79-$199
(202) 337-9700
(800) 944-5377

**SHERATON
HOTEL**
923 16th St NW
(20006)
Rates: n/a
(202) 638-2626
(800) 325-3535

AREA CODES - If the local number doesn't connect, check for a new area code.

SWISS INN HOTEL-NW
1204 Massachusetts Ave (20005)
Rates: n/a
(202) 371-1816

SWISSOTEL WASHINGTON, THE WATERGATE
2650 Virginia Ave NW (20037)
Rates: $435-$495
(202) 965-2300

TRAVELODGE
1917 Bladensburg Rd (20002)
Rates: $57-$80
(202) 832-8600
(800) 578-7878

WASHINGTON COURT CAPITAL HILL
525 New Jersey Ave NW (20001)
Rates: n/a
(202) 628-2100

WESTIN HOTEL
24th & M St NW (20037)
Rates: $185-$550
(202) 429-2400
(800) 228-3000

THE WILLARD INTER-CONTINENTAL
1401 Pennsylvania Ave NW (20004)
Rates: $398-$510
(202) 628-9100

WYNDHAM BRISTOL HOTEL
2430 Pennsylvania Ave NW (20037)
Rates: $235-$255
(202) 955-6400
(800) 996-3426

WYNDHAM WASHINGTON
1400 M St NW (20001)
Rates: $219
(202) 429-1700
(800) 996-3426

WASHINGTON
(Maryland)

BEST WESTERN WASHINGTON GATEWAY HOTEL
1251 W Montgomery Ave (Rockville 20850)
Rates: $79-$149
(301) 424-4940
(800) 528-1234
(800) 366-1251

BRAGG MOTEL
7001 Crain Hwy (Upper Marlboro 20772)
Rates: n/a
(301) 627-1880

COMFORT INN
16216 Frederick (Gaithersburg 20877)
Rates: $59-$119
(301) 330-0023
(800) 228-5150

COMFORT SUITES-LAUREL LAKES
14402 Laurel Pl (Laurel 20707)
Rates: $79-$195
(301) 206-2600
(800) 228-5150

ECONO LODGE LAUREL RACETRACK
9700 Washington Blvd (Laurel 20723)
Rates: $44-$74
(301) 776-8008
(800) 553-2666

ECONO LODGE
18715 N Frederick Ave (Gaithersburg 20879)
Rates: $45-$75
(301) 963-3840
(800) 553-2666

EMBASSY SUITES CHEVY CHASE PAVILLION
4300 Military Rd NW (Chevy Chase 20015)
Rates: $119-$165
(202) 362-9300
(800) 362-2779

FOREST HILLS MOTEL
2901 Crain Hwy (Upper Marlboro 20772)
Rates: $45-$55
(301) 627-3969

HILTON HOTEL
620 Perry Pkwy (Gaithersburg 20879)
Rates: $79-$109
(301) 977-8900
(800) 445-8667

HOLIDAY INN-GAITHERSBURG
2 Montgomery Village Ave (Gaithersburg 20879)
Rates: $69-$89
(301) 948-8900
(800) 465-4329

HOMESTEAD VILLAGE GUEST STUDIOS
20141 Century Blvd (Germantown 20874)
Rates: $69-$104
(301) 515-4500
(888) 782-9473

HOWARD JOHNSON
5811 Annapolis Rd (Cheverly 20784)
Rates: $56-$105
(301) 779-7700
(800) 446-4656

MARRIOTT SUITES BETHESDA
6711 Democracy Blvd (Bethesda 20817)
Rates: $99-$160
(301) 897-5600
(800) 228-9290

MARRIOTT-GREENBELT
6400 Ivy Ln (Greenbelt 20770)
Rates: $69-$119
(301) 441-3700
(800) 228-9290

MOTEL 6
75 Hampton Park Blvd (Capital Heights 20743)
Rates: $46-$52
(301) 499-0800
(800) 466-8356

MOTEL 6
5701 Allentown Rd (20746)
Rates: $39-$51
(301) 702-1061
(800) 466-8356

PARK VIEW INN-COLLEGE PARK
9020 Baltimore Blvd (College Park 20740)
Rates: $50-$60
(301) 441-8110

QUALITY SUITES SHADY GROVE
3 Research Ct (Rockville 20850)
Rates: $69-$169
(301) 840-0200
(800) 228-5151

QUALITY INN & SUITES
7200 Baltimore Blvd (College Park 20740)
Rates: $49-$129
(301) 864-5820
(800) 228-5151

RAMADA INN
5151 Allentown Rd (Camp Springs 20746)
Rates: $50-$89
(301) 899-7700
(800) 272-6232

RED ROOF INN
497 Quince Orchard Rd (Gaithersburg 20879)
Rates: $70-$95
(301) 977-3311
(800) 843-7663

RED ROOF INN
12525 Laurel Bowie Rd (Laurel 20708)
Rates: $56-$74
(301) 498-8811
(800) 843-7663

RED ROOF INN
9050 Lanham Severn Rd (Lanham 20706)
Rates: $57-$77
(301) 731-8830
(800) 843-7663

RED ROOF INN
6170 Oxon Hill Rd (Oxon Hill 20745)
Rates: $56-$83
(301) 567-8030
(800) 843-7663

RED ROOF INN
16001 Shady Grove Rd (Rockville 20850)
Rates: $90-$120
(301) 987-0965
(800) 843-7663

RESIDENCE INN BETHESDA
7335 Wisconsin Ave (Bethesda 20814)
Rates: $209
(301) 718-0200
(800) 331-3131

RESIDENCE INN GAITHERSBURG
9721 Washingtonian Blvd (Gaithersburg 20879)
Rates: $194
(301) 590-3003
(800) 331-3131

SHERATON GREENBELT HOTEL
8500 Annapolis Rd (New Carrollton 20784)
Rates: $72-$112
(301) 459-6700
(800) 325-3535

SHERATON HOTEL
4095 Powder Mill (Beltsville 20705)
Rates: $149
(301) 937-4422
(800) 325-3535

AREA CODES - If the local number doesn't connect, check for a new area code.

SLEEP INN SHADY GROVE
2 Research Ct
(Rockville 20850)
Rates: $69-$119
(301) 948-8000
(800) 753-3746

SUMMERFIELD SUITES
200 Skidmore Blvd
(Gaithersburg 20879)
Rates: $150
(301) 527-6000
(800) 833-4353

TOWNPLACE SUITES BY MARRIOTT
212 Perry Pkwy
(Gaithersburg 20879)
Rates: $59-$109
(301) 590-2300
(800) 257-3000

WOODFIN SUITES HOTEL
1380 Piccard Dr
(Rockville 20850)
Rates: $124
(301) 590-9880
(800) 237-8811

WASHINGTON
(Virginia)

ALEXANDRIA SUITES HOTEL
420 N Van Dorn St (Alexandria, 22303)
Rates: $99-$119
(703) 370-1000

BEST WESTERN BATTLEFIELD INN
10820 Balls Ford
(Manassas 22109)
Rates: $59-$105
(703) 361-8000
(800) 528-1234

BEST WESTERN KEY BRIDGE
1850 N Fort Myer Dr (Arlington, 22209)
Rates: $129-$169
(703) 522-0400
(800) 528-1234
(800) 539-2743

BEST WESTERN TYSONS WESTPARK
8401 Wstpark Dr
(McLean 22102)
Rates: $79-$149
(703) 723-2800
(800) 528-1234
(800) 533-3301

COMFORT INN
6560 Loisdale Ct
(Springfield 22150)
Rates: $79-$99
(703) 922-9000
(800) 228-5150

COMFORT INN GUNSTON CORNER
8180 Silverbook Rd (Lorton 22079)
Rates: $59-$129
(703) 643-3100
(800) 228-5150

COMFORT INN MOUNT VERNON
7212 Richmond Hwy (Alexandria 22306)
Rates: $50-$85
(703) 765-9000
(800) 228-5150

CROWNE PLAZA AIRPORT
1489 Jefferson Davis Hwy
(Arlington 22202)
Rates: n/a
(703) 416-1600
(800) 227-6963

DAYS INN-RICHMOND HIGHWAY
6100 Richmond Hwy (Alexandria 22303)
Rates: $45-$70
(703) 329-0500
(800) 329-7466

DAYS INN
110 S Bragg St
(Alexandria 22303)
Rates: $66-$85
(703) 354-4950
(800) 329-7466

DOUBLETREE HOTEL NATIONAL AIRPORT
300 Army Navy Dr (Arlington 22202)
Rates: $65-$155
(703) 416-4100
(800) 222-8733

DOUBLETREE GUEST SUITES
100 S Reynolds St (Alexandria 22304)
Rates: $119-$159
(703) 370-9600
(800) 222-8733

ECONO LODGE-MOUNT VERNON
8849 Richmond Hwy
(Alexandria 22309)
Rates: $50-$70
(703) 780-0300
(800) 553-2666

ECONO LODGE-WOODBRIDGE
13317 Gordon Blvd (Woodbridge 22191)
Rates: $46-$85
(703) 491-5196
(800) 553-2666

EXECUTIVE CLUB SUITES
610 Bashford Ln
(Alexandria 22303)
Rates: $110-$130
(703) 739-2582

EXECUTIVE CLUB SUITES
108 S Courthouse Rd (Arlington 22209)
Rates: $110
(703) 522-2582

FRIENDSHIP INN
13964 Jefferson Davis Hwy
(Woodbridge 22191)
Rates: $44-$80
(703) 494-4144
(800) 453-4511

HAMPTON INN
6550 Loisdale Ct (Springfield 22150)
Rates: $89-$129
(703) 924-9444
(800) 426-7866

HAMPTON INN DULLES AIRPORT
45440 Holiday Dr
(Sterling 22170)
Rates: $59-$115
(703) 471-4300
(800) 426-7866

HILTON HOTEL WASH/DULLES AIRPORT
13869 Park Center Rd
(Herndon 22070)
Rates: $95-$167
(703) 478-2900
(800) 445-8667

HILTON MARK CENTER
5000 Seminary Rd
(Alexandria 22309)
Rates: $119-$239
(703) 845-1010
(800) 445-8667

HILTON TYSONS CORNER
7920 Jones Branch Rd
(McLean 22102)
Rates: n/a
(703) 847-5000
(800) 445-8667

HOLIDAY INN EISENHOWER METRO
2460 Eisenhower Ave (Alexandria 22314)
Rates: $99-$139
(703) 960-3400
(800) 465-4329

HOLIDAY INN
17133 Dumfries Rd (Dumfries 22026)
Rates: $65-$85
(703) 221-1141
(800) 465-4329

HOLIDAY INN EXPRESS WASH/DULLES
485 Elden St
(Herndon 22070)
Rates: $104
(703) 478-9777
(800) 465-4329

HOLIDAY INN-FAIR OAKS
11787 Lee Jackson Hwy
(Fairfax 22033)
Rates: $134
(703) 352-2525
(800) 465-4329

HOLIDAY INN-OLD TOWN
480 King St
(Alexandria 22314)
Rates: $161-$171
(703) 549-6080
(800) 465-4329

HOLIDAY INN ROSSLYN
1900 N Ft Myer Dr (Arlington 22209)
Rates: $120
(703) 807-2000
(800) 465-4329

HOLIDAY INN AT CARRODOC HALL
1500 E Market St
(Leesburg 22075)
Rates: $109-$159
(703) 771-9200
(800) 465-4329

HOLIDAY INN WASH/DULLES
1000 Sully Rd
(Sterling 22170)
Rates: $189
(703) 471-7411
(800) 465-4329

HOMESTEAD VILLAGE GUEST STUDIOS
200 Blue Stone Rd (Alexandria 22309)
Rates: $89-$94
(703) 329-3399
(888) 782-9473

HOMESTEAD VILLAGE GUEST STUDIOS
4504 Brookfield Corp Dr
(Arlington 22309)
Rates: $89-$134
(703) 263-3361
(888) 782-9473

HOMESTEAD VILLAGE GUEST STUDIOS
12104 Monument Dr (Fairfax 22033)
Rates: $75-$105
(703) 273-3444
(888) 782-9473

HOWARD JOHNSON
5821 Richmond Hwy (Alexandria 22303)
Rates: $59-$109
(703) 329-1400
(800) 446-4656

HOWARD JOHNSON PLAZA HOTEL
2650 Jefferson Davis Hwy
(Arlington 22202)
Rates: $69-$189
(703) 684-7200
(800) 446-4656

HYATT ARLINGTON AT KEY BRIDGE
1325 Wilson Blvd
(Arlington 22209)
Rates: $69-$181
(703) 525-1234
(800) 233-1234

HYATT FAIR LAKES
12777 Fair Lakes Cir (Fairfax 22033)
Rates: $59-$79
(703) 818-1234
(800) 233-1234

MARRIOTT CRYSTAL GATEWAY HOTEL
1700 Jefferson Davis Hwy
(Arlington 22202)
Rates: $105-$192
(703) 920-3230
(800) 228-9290

MARRIOTT HOTEL-TYSONS CORNER
8028 Leesburg Pike (Vienna 22182)
Rates: $136-$172
(703) 734-3200
(800) 228-9290

MARRIOTT DULLES AIRPORT
333 W Service Rd
(Chantilly 22021)
Rates: $59-$110
(703) 471-9500
(800) 228-9290

MARRIOTT HOTEL
3111 Fairview Park Dr (Falls Church 22042)
Rates: $79-$145
(703) 849-9400
(800) 228-9290

MARRIOTT KEY BRIDGE
1401 Lee Hwy
(Arlington 22209)
Rates: $164-$184
(703) 524-6400
(800) 228-9290
(800) 327-9789

QUALITY HOTEL
1200 N Courthouse Rd
(Arlington 22201)
Rates: $79-$179
(703) 524-4000
(800) 228-5151

QUALITY INN-IWO JIMA
1501 Arlington Blvd (Arlington 22203)
Rates: $90-$109
(703) 524-5000
(800) 228-5151

QUALITY INN
1109 Horner Rd
(Woodbridge 22191)
Rates: $49-$95
(703) 494-0300
(800) 228-5151

RADISSON HOTEL-OLD TOWN
901 Fairfax St
(Alexandria 22314)
Rates: $89
(703) 683-6000
(800) 333-3333

RED ROOF INN
10610 Automotive Dr
(Manassas 22110)
Rates: $55-$82
(703) 335-9333
(800) 843-7663

RESIDENCE INN
315 Elden St
(Herndon 22070)
Rates: $65-$155
(703) 435-0044
(800) 331-3131

RESIDENCE INN TYSONS CORNER
8616 Westwood Center Dr
(Vienna 22182)
Rates: $129-$169
(800) 331-3131

SHERATON SUITES
801 N St. Asaph St (Alexandria 22314)
Rates: $139-$155
(703) 836-4700
(800) 325-3535

STOUFFER CONCOURSE HOTEL
2399 Jefferson Davis Hwy
(Arlington 22202)
Rates: $89-$240
(703) 418-6800

SUMMERFIELD SUITES
13700 Coppermine Rd
(Herndon 22071)
Rates: $99-$178
(703) 713-6800
(800) 833-4353

TOWN PLACE SUITES BY MARRIOTT
22744 Holiday Park Dr (Sterling 22170)
Rates: $89-$99
(703) 707-2017
(800) 257-3000

WELLESLEY INN OF FAIRFAX
10327 Lee Hwy
(Fairfax 22030)
Rates: $80-$155
(703) 359-2888
(800) 444-8888

AREA CODES - If the local number doesn't connect, check for a new area code.

FLORIDA

ALACHUA

COMFORT INN
15405 MLK Blvd
(32615)
Rates: $55-$145
(904) 462-2414
(800) 228-5150

DAYS INN
16301 MLK Blvd
(32615)
Rates: $44-$130
(904) 462-3251
(800) 329-7466

RAMADA INN
16305 NW 163rd
Ln (32615)
Rates: $65-$140
(904) 462-4200
(800) 272-6232

ALTAMONTE SPRINGS

**CLUB ESPRIT
APT SUITES**
525 One Center
Blvd (32701)
Rates: $46-$90
(407) 331-3132
(800) 800-3332

EMBASSY SUITES
225 E Altamonte
Dr (32701)
Rates: $109-$134
(407) 834-2400
(800) 362-2779

HAMPTON INN
151 N Douglas
Ave (32714)
Rates: $85
(407) 869-9000
(800) 426-7866

LA QUINTA INN
150 S Westmonte
Dr (32714)
Rates: $89-$109
(407) 788-1411
(800) 687-6667

RESIDENCE INN BY MARRIOTT
270 Douglas Ave
(32714)
Rates: $128-$159
(407) 788-7991
(800) 331-3131

ALTOONA

**FIDDLERS GREEN
RANCH**
Demko Road,
(32702)
Rates: n/a
(352) 669-7111
(800) 947-2624

AMELIA ISLAND

**1857 FLORIDA
HOUSE INN B&B**
22 S 3rd St
(32034)
Rates: $70-$140
(904) 261-3300
(800) 258-3301

**RITZ CARLTON
HOTEL**
4750 Amelia Is.
Pkwy (32034)
Rates: $229-$429
(904) 277-1100
(800) 627-4688

ANNA MARIA ISLAND

**ANNA MARIA
RESORT MTL/APT**
808 Bay Blvd N
(34216)
Rates: $50-$100
(941) 778-1269
(800) 829-3150

**SUGAR SANDS
APARTMENTS**
2219 Gulf Dr N
(34216)
Rates: $50-$149
(941) 778-4178
(888) 266-2627

APALACHI-COLA

**APALACHICOLA
RIVER INN**
123 Water St
(32320)
Rates: n/a
(850) 653-8139

**BREAKAWAY
MARINA &
MOTEL**
200 Waddell Rd
(32320)
Rates: $30-$50
(850) 653-8897

**COOMBS HOUSE
INN**
80 6th St (32320)
Rates: n/a
(850) 653-2191

FIVE OAKS INN
145 Avenue E
(32320)
Rates: $55-$75
(850) 653-8980

**THE HISTORIC
GIBSON
COUNTRY INN**
Market St &
Ave C (32329)
Rates: $75-$120
(850) 653-2191

**RAINBOW INN
& MARINA**
123 Water St
(32320)
Rates: n/a
(850) 653-8139

RANCHO INN
240 Hwy 98
(32320)
Rates: $47-$73
(850) 653-9435

**THE RANEY
GUEST COTTAGE**
46 Avenue F
(32320)
Rates: $190/
Two Nights
(850) 653-2501

WITHERSPOON INN
94 5th St (32320)
Rates: $70-$75
(850) 653-9186

APOLLO BEACH

**RAMADA
BAYSIDE INN
& RESORT**
6414 Surfside
Blvd (33572)
Rates: $85-$150
(813) 641-2700
(800) 272-6232
(800) 67-BEACH

APOPKA

**CROSBY'S
MOTOR INN**
1440 W Orange
Blossom Tr
(32712)
Rates: $50-$69
(407) 886-3220
(800) 821-6685

ARCADIA

**BEST WESTERN
ARCADIA INN**
504 S Brevard
(34266)
Rates: $79-$129
(941) 494-4884
(800) 528-1234

AUBURNDALE

**FISH HAVEN
LODGE &
CABINS**
Fish Haven Rd
(33823)
Rates: n/a
(941) 984-1183

AVON PARK

**SIGNUM RESORT
LAS PALMAS**
600 E Canfield St
(33825)
Rates: $80-$165
(863) 452-2020
(800) 528-0823

BAL HARBOUR

**SHERATON
BAL HARBOUR**
9701 Collins Ave
(33154)
Rates: $165-$320
(305) 865-7511
(800) 325-3535
(800) 998-9898

BALDWIN

**BEST WESTERN
INN**
1088 US 301 &
I-10 (32234)
Rates: $45-$95
(904) 266-9759
(800) 528-1234

BARTOW

**DAVIS BROS
MOTEL**
1035 N Broadway
Ave (33830)
Rates: $50-$75
(941) 533-0711
(800) 424-0711

EL JON MOTEL
1460 E Main St
(33830)
Rates: $39-$75
(941) 533-8191
(800) 533-8191

BASEBALL CITY

DAYS INN
2425 Frontage Rd
(33837)
Rates: $39-$159
(863) 424-2596
(800) 329-7466

BAY HARBOR ISLAND

**BAY HARBOR
INN**
9660 E Bay
Harbor Dr
(33154)
Rates: $80-$115
(305) 868-4141

AREA CODES - If the local number doesn't connect, check for a new area code.

BIG PINE KEY

CAPTAIN VARRIEUR'S
P. O. Box 430744 (33043)
Rates: $650-$750 Weekly
(508) 394-4338
(888) 394-4338

OLD WOODEN BRIDGE FISHING CAMP
1791 Bogie Dr (33043)
Rates: $69-$90
(305) 872-2241

PARADISE LODGING
31316 Ave J (33043)
Rates: $75-$100
(305) 872-9009

BLUE MOUNTAIN BEACH

SANDCASTLES BY THE SEA
229 Blue Mountain Rd #101 (32541)
Rates: $115
(504) 845-8126

BOCA RATON

DOUBLETREE GUEST SUITES
701 NW 53rd St (33487)
Rates: $139-$259
(561) 997-9500
(800) 222-8733

RADISSON SUITE HOTEL
7920 Glades Rd (33434)
Rates: $199-$245
(561) 483-3600
(800) 333-3333

RAMADA INN
2901 N Federal Hwy (33431)
Rates: $105-$135
(561) 395-6850
(800) 272-6232

RESIDENCE INN BY MARRIOTT
525 NW 77th St (33487)
Rates: $159-$229
(407) 994-3222
(800) 331-3131

BRADENTON

BAHIA COURT
1905 Cortez Rd W (34207)
Rates: $50-$100
(941) 755-2188

BLUE BOY MOTEL
1839 14th St W (34205)
Rates: $50-$100
(941) 748-6909

DAYS INN
3506 1st St W (34208)
Rates: $30-$130
(941) 746-1141
(800) 329-7466

ECONO LODGE AIRPORT
6727 14th St W (34207)
Rates: $59-$95
(941) 758-7199
(800) 553-2666

HOWARD JOHNSON EXPRESS
6511 14th St W (34207)
Rates: $55-$89
(941) 756-8399
(800) 446-4656

KNIGHTS INN
668 67th St Cir E (34208)
Rates: $50-$100
(941) 745-1876
(800) 843-5644

MOTEL 6
660 67 St Cir W (34208)
Rates: $33-$48
(941) 747-6005
(800) 466-8356

PARK INN CLUB & BREAKFAST
4450 47th St W (34210)
Rates: $104-$134
(941) 795-4633
(800) 670-PARK

SUPER 8 MOTEL
6516 14th ST W (34207)
Rates: $50-$87
(941) 756-6656
(800) 800-8000

BRADENTON BEACH

THE BREAKERS
2512 Gulf Drive N (34217)
Rates: n/a
(941) 778-5588

CAPRI INN INTL APTS MOTEL
210 & 300 Gulf Drive S (34217)
Rates: $51-$100
(941) 778-5243

ISLAND BREEZE APARTMENTS
2516 Gulf Dr N (34217)
Rates: $51-$100
(941) 778-9593

PELICAN COVE RESORT CONDO
904 Gulf Dr S (34217)
Rates: n/a
(941) 778-4800
(800) 237-2252

QUEENSGATE APARTMENTS
1101 Gulf Dr N (34217)
Rates: $51-$100
(941) 778-7153

SAND PEBBLE APARTMENTS
2218 Gulf Dr N (34217)
Rates: $49-$140
(941) 778-3053
(800) 500-7263

TORTUGA INN
1325 Gulf Dr N (34217)
Rates: $100-$230
(941) 778-6611

TRADEWINDS RESORT
1603 Gulf Dr N (34217)
Rates: $116-$263
(941) 779-0010

BRANDON

BEHIND THE FENCE B&B
1400 Viola Dr (33511)
Rates: $79-$99
(813) 685-8201

BRANDON MOTOR LODGE
906 E Brandon Blvd (33511)
Rates: $32-$60
(813) 689-1261

LA QUINTA INN & SUITES
310 Grand Regency Blvd (33511)
Rates: $95-$125
(813) 643-0574
(800) 687-6667

BROOKSVILLE

HOLIDAY INN
30307 Cortez Blvd (34602)
Rates: $65-$70
(352) 796-9481
(800) 465-4329

SUNRISE MOTEL
250 N Broad St (34601)
Rates: n/a
(352) 796-8634

THE OAKS MOTEL
630 S Broad St (34601)
Rates: n/a
(352) 796-4807

BUNNELL

BEST WESTERN PLANTATION INN
2251 S Old Dixie Hwy (32110)
Rates: $60-$180
(904) 437-3737
(800) 528-1234

BUSHNELL

BEST WESTERN GUEST HOUSE INN
2224 W-CR 48 (33513)
Rates: $49-$79
(352) 793-5010
(800) 528-1234

CALLAHAN

SHIP INN
US 1 & 23, 301 N (32011)
Rates: $33-$49
(904) 879-3451

CAPE CANAVERAL

RADISSON RESORT AT THE PORT
8701 Astronaut Blvd (32920)
Rates: $100-$149
(407) 784-0000

CAPE CORAL

DEL PRADO INN
1502 Miramar St (33904)
Rates: $60-$75
(941) 542-3151
(800) 231-6818

QUALITY INN NAUTILUS
1538 Cape Coral Pkwy (33904)
Rates: $90-$125
(941) 542-2121
(800) 228-5151

CAPTIVA ISLAND

TWEEN WATERS INN
15951 Sanibel/ Captiva Rd (33924)
Rates: $150-$250+
(941) 472-5161
(800) 223-5865

CARRABELLE

MOORINGS AT CARRABELLE
1000 US 98 (32322)
Rates: $85
(850) 697-2800

CEDAR KEY

BEACHFRONT MOTEL
1st & G Sts (32625)
Rates: $44-$55
(352) 543-5113

CEDAR KEY B&B
3rd & F Sts (32625)
Rates: $65-$85
(352) 543-9000
(800) 453-5051

DOCKSIDE MOTEL
11 Dock St (32625)
Rates: $49-$69
(352) 545-5432

FARAWAY INN
3rd & F Sts (32625)
Rates: $40-$65
(352) 543-5330
(888) 543-5330

MERMAID'S LANDING
12865 Hwy 24 (32625)
Rates: $40-$65
(352) 543-5949
(800) 741-9224

PARK PLACE MOTEL/CONDOS
211 2nd St Cedar Key (32625)
Rates: $65-$80
(352) 543-5737

PIRATES COVE WATERFRONT COTTAGES
Hwy 24 (32625)
Rates: $40-$55
(352) 543-5141

CHARLOTTE HARBOR

BANANA BAY WATERFRONT MOTEL
23285 Bayshore Rd (33980)
Rates: $49-$72
(941) 743-4441

HARBOUR INN
5000 Tamiami Tr (33980)
Rates: $38-$85
(941) 625-6126
(800) 646-6037

CHATTAHOO-CHEE

MORGAN MOTEL
E US 90 (32324)
Rates: $27-$36
(850) 683-4336

CHIEFLAND

BEST WESTERN SUWANNEE VALLEY INN
1125 N Young Blvd (32626)
Rates: $56-$75
(352) 493-0663
(800) 528-1234

CHIPLEY

DAYS INN
1593 Main St (32428)
Rates: $38-$95
(850) 638-7335
(800) 329-7466

HOLIDAY INN EXPRESS
1700 A Main St (32428)
Rates: n/a
(850) 638-3996
(800) 465-4329

RESIDENCE INN BY MARRIOTT
5050 Ulmerton Rd (34620)
Rates: $139-$185
(850) 573-4444
(800) 331-3131

SUPER 8 MOTEL
1700 Main St (32428)
Rates: $40-$45
(850) 638-8530
(800) 800-8000

CHULUOTA

BIG OAKS RANCH
1900 Brumley Rd (32766)
Rates: n/a
(407) 365-8885

CITRA

ORANGE BLOSSOM MOTEL
17575 N Hwy 301 (32113)
Rates: n/a
(352) 595-8836

CLEARWATER

CLEARWATER TRAVEL RESORT
2946 Gulf to Bay Blvd (33765)
Rates: $30-$49
(727) 791-0550

HAMPTON INN
21030 US Hwy 19 N (33765)
Rates: $59-$75
(727) 797-8173
(800) 426-7866

HOLIDAY INN EXPRESS
13625 ICOT Blvd (33760)
Rates: $80-$105
(727) 536-7275
(800) 465-4329

HOMESTEAD VILLAGE GUEST STUDIOS
2311 Ulmerton Rd (33762)
Rates: $109
(727) 572-4800
(888) 782-9473

HOMEWOOD SUITES
2233 Ulmerton Rd (33762)
Rates: n/a
(727) 573-1500
(800) 225-5466

LA QUINTA INN AIRPORT
3301 Ulmerton Rd (33762)
Rates: $69-$109
(727) 572-7222
(800) 687-6667

RESIDENCE INN BY MARRIOTT
5050 Ulmerton Rd (33762)
Rates: n/a
(727) 573-4444
(800) 331-3131

CLEARWATER BEACH

AGEAN SANDS MOTEL
421 S Gulfview Blvd (34630)
Rates: $55-$130
(727) 447-3464
(800) 942-3432

BEST WESTERN SEA STONE RESORT/SUITES
445 Hamden Dr (34630)
Rates: $59-$184
(727) 441-1722
(800) 528-1234
(800) 444-1919

CLEARWATER BEACH GARDEN APT & MOTEL
14 Somerset St (34630)
Rates: n/a
(727) 442-8874

CLEARWATER BEACH HOTEL
500 Mandalay Ave (33767)
Rates: $100-$249
(727) 441-2425
(800) 292-2295

THE DOCKSIDER SUITES
116 Brightwater Dr (33767)
Rates: $50-$149
(727) 442-9881

DOUBLETREE RESORT SURFSIDE
400 Mandalay Ave (33767)
Rates: $117-$136
(727) 461-3222
(800) 222-8733

DRIFTWOOD INN
462 East Shore Dr (34630)
Rates: n/a
(727) 442-9389

THE GREY HOUSE
27 Idlewild St (33767)
Rates: $50-$140
(727) 461-9142
(888) 453-6726

SPYGLASS MOTEL
215 S Gulfview Blvd (34630)
Rates: n/a
(800) 942-3432

VIKING MOTEL
124 Brightwater Dr (34630)
Rates: $55-$75
(727) 441-3001

CLERMONT

MULBERRY INN BED & BREAKFST
915 Montrose St (34711)
Rates: $70-$95
(352) 242-0670
(800) 641-0670

VACATION VILLAGE RESORT
10301 US Hwy 27 (34711)
Rates: $46-$90
(352) 394-4091
(800) 962-9969

CLEWISTON

BEST WESTERN
1020 W Sugarland (33440)
Rates: $59-$129
(941) 983-3400
(800) 528-1234
(877) 478-1700

COCOA

BEST WESTERN COCOA INN
4225 W King St (32926)
Rates: $69-$89
(321) 632-1065
(800) 528-1234

BUDGET INN
4150 King St (32926)
Rates: n/a
(321) 632-5721

DAYS INN
5600 Hwy 524 (32926)
Rates: $39-$75
(321) 636-6500
(800) 329-7466

ECONO LODGE SPACE CENTER
3220 N Cocoa Blvd (32926)
Rates: $60-$150
(321) 632-4561
(800) 553-2666

RAMADA INN KENNEDY SPACE CENTER
900 Friday Rd (32926)
Rates: $89-$99
(321) 631-1210
(800) 272-6232

SPACE COAST MOTEL
860 W Cocoa Blvd (32922)
Rates: $30-$89
(321) 639-8700
(888) 672-4897

SUPER 8 MOTEL
900 Friday Rd (32926)
Rates: $69-$79
(321) 631-1212
(800) 800-8000

COCOA BEACH

BEST WESTERN OCEAN INN
5500 N Atlantic Ave (32931)
Rates: $89-$169
(321) 784-2550
(800) 528-1234
(888) 799-1631

DAYS INN
5600 N Atlantic Ave (32931)
Rates: $89-$219
(321) 783-7621
(800) 329-7466

ECONO LODGE RESORT
1275 N Atlantic Ave (32931)
Rates: $45-$150
(321) 783-2257
(800) 553-2666

HOLIDAY INN OCEANFRONT
1300 N Atlantic Ave (32931)
Rates: n/a
(321) 783-2271
(800) 465-4329

HOWARD JOHNSON EXPRESS
2082 N Atlantic Ave (32931)
Rates: $59-$79
(321) 783-8855
(800) 446-4656

MOTEL 6
3701 N Atlantic Ave (32931)
Rates: $41-$56
(321) 783-3103
(800) 466-8356

SATELLITE MOTEL ON OCEAN
1600 N Atlantic Ave (32931)
Rates: n/a
(321) 783-7714

SILVER SANDS MOTEL
225 N Atlantic Ave (32931)
Rates: $50-$99
(321) 783-2415
(800) 647-0761

SOUTH BEACH INN
1701 S Atlantic Ave (32931)
Rates: $80-$130
(321) 784-3333

SURF STUDIO BEACH RESORT
1801 S Atlantic Ave (32931)
Rates: $80-$145
(321) 783-7100

COCONUT GROVE

MAYFAIR HOUSE HOTEL
3000 Florida Ave (33133)
Rates: $199-$649
(305) 441-0000

CORAL GABLES

HOWARD JOHNSON
1430 S Dixie Hwy (33146)
Rates: $58-$85
(305) 665-7501
(800) 446-4656

CORAL SPRINGS

LA QUINTA INN
3701 University Dr (33065)
Rates: $105-$135
(954) 753-9000
(800) 687-6667

RADISSON RESORT
11775 Heron Bay Blvd (33076)
Rates: $169-$249
(954) 753-5598
(800) 333-3333

WELLESLEY INN & SUITES
3100 N University Dr (33065)
Rates: $84-$109
(954) 344-2200
(800) 444-8888

CRESCENT CITY

LAKE VIEW MOTEL
1004 N Summit St (32112)
Rates: $38-$50
(904) 698-1090

LEONARD'S LANDING LAKE CRESCENT RESORT
100 Grove Ave (32112)
Rates: n/a
(904) 698-2485

ST JOHNS RIVER RESORT
1269 County Rd 309 (32112)
Rates: $45-$110
(904) 467-7050

CRESTVIEW

DAYS INN
4255 S Ferdon Blvd (32536)
Rates: $39-$115
(850) 682-8842
(800) 329-7466

HOLIDAY INN
4050 S Ferdon Blvd (32536)
Rates: $64-$70
(850) 682-6111
(800) 465-4329

SUPER 8 MOTEL
3925 S Ferdon Blvd (32536)
Rates: $38-$63
(850) 682-9649
(800) 800-8000

CROSS CITY

CARRIAGE INN
280 E Main (32628)
Rates: $38-$45
(352) 498-0001
(800) 682-4816

CRYSTAL RIVER

BEST WESTERN CRYSTAL RIVER RESORT
614 NW Hwy 19 (34428)
Rates: $75-$105
(352) 795-3171
(800) 528-1234
(800) 435-4409

COMFORT INN
4486 N Suncoast Blvd (34428)
Rates: $50-$85
(352) 563-1500
(800) 228-5150

DAYS INN RESORT
2380 NW Hwy 19 (34428)
Rates: $50-$80
(352) 795-2111
(800) 329-7466

ECONO LODGE
2575 NW Hwy 19 (34428)
Rates: $45-$119
(352) 795-9447
(800) 553-2666

HAYES MOTEL
1151 NW Hwy 19 (34428)
Rates: n/a
(352) 795-2075

KING'S BAY LODGE
506 NW 1st Ave (34428)
Rates: n/a
(352) 795-2850

PLANTATION INN/GOLF RESORT
9301 W Fort Island Tr (34428)
Rates: $79-$125
(352) 795-4211
(800) 632-6262

CUTLER RIDGE

BAYMONT INN
10821 Carribean Blvd (33189)
Rates: $75-$80
(305) 278-0001
(800) 301-0200

HOWARD JOHNSON PLAZA HOTEL
10775 Caribbean Blvd (33189)
Rates: $55-$99
(305) 253-9960
(800) 446-4656

DANIA BEACH

MOTEL 6
825 E Dania Beach Blvd (33004)
Rates: $37-$56
(954) 921-5505
(800) 466-8356

SHERATON FT. LAUDERDALE AIRPORT HOTEL
1825 Griffin Rd (33004)
Rates: $139-$179
(954) 920-3500
(800) 325-3535

DAVENPORT

DAYS INN-SO MAGIC KNGDOM
2425 Frontage Rd (33837)
Rates: $49-$159
(863) 424-2596
(800) 329-7466

AREA CODES - If the local number doesn't connect, check for a new area code.

SUPER 8 MOTEL
5620 US Hwy 27
N (33837)
Rates: $39-$89
(863) 420-8888
(800) 800-8000

DAVIE

HOMESTEAD VILLAGE GUEST STUDIOS
7550 SR 84 E
(33316)
Rates: n/a
(954) 476-1211
(888) 782-9473

DAYTONA BEACH

ADAM'S MARK DAYTONA BEACH RESORT
100 N Atlantic Ave
(32118)
Rates: $50-$149
(904) 254-8200
(800) 228-9290

ARUBA INN
1254 N Atlantic
Ave (32118)
Rates: $32-$69
(904) 253-5643
(800) 214-1406

BREAKERS BEACH OCEAN-FRONT MOTEL
27 S Ocean Ave
(32118)
Rates: $45-$91
(904) 252-0863
(800) 441-8459

BUDGET HOST CANDLELIGHT
1305 S
Ridgewood Ave
(32114)
Rates: $32-$42
(904) 252-1142
(800) 283-4678

CARDINAL MOTEL
738 N Atlantic
Ave (32118)
Rates: $50-$70
(904) 252-1035

COMFORT INN
730 N Atlantic
Ave (32118)
Rates: $55-$189
(904) 255-5491
(800) 228-5150

DAYS INN OCEANFRONT
1909 S Atlantic
Ave (32118)
Rates: $95-$165
(904) 255-4492
(800) 329-7466

DAYS INN SPEEDWAY
2900 W Int'l
Speedway Blvd
(32124)
Rates: $49-$165
(904) 255-0541
(800) 329-7466

DEL AIRE MOTEL
744 N Atlantic
Ave (32118)
Rates: n/a
(904) 252-2563

FOUNTAIN BEACH RESORT
313 S Atlantic
Ave (32118)
Rates: $39-$199
(904) 255-7491
(800) 556-8855

LA QUINTA INN
2725 Int'l
Speedway Blvd
(32114)
Rates: $50-$62
(904) 255-7412
(800) 687-6667

THE PLAZA RESORT & SPA
600 N Atlantic
Ave (32118)
Rates: $149-$189
(904) 255-4471

RADISSON RESORT
640 N Atlantic Ave
(32118)
Rates: $109-$169
(904) 239-9800
(888) 568-9610

RAMADA INN SPEEDWAY
1798 W Int'l
Speedway Blvd
(32114)
Rates: $79-$259
(904) 255-2422
(800) 272-6232

SCOTTISH INNS
1515 S
Ridgewood Ave
(32114)
Rates: $95-$120
(904) 258-5742
(800) 251-1962

SUPER 8 MOTEL
2992 W Int'l
Speedway Blvd
(32124)
Rates: $39-$69
(904) 253-0643
(800) 800-8000

WHITE SANDS MOTEL
1122 N Atlantic
Ave (32118)
Rates: $30-$110
(904) 253-7461

DAYTONA BEACH SHORES

ATLANTIC OCEAN PALM INN
3247 S Atlantic
Ave (32118)
Rates: $60-$190
(904) 761-8450
(800) 634-0098

JASMIN MOTEL
3621 S Atlantic
Ave (32118)
Rates: n/a
(904) 760-9196

PALM CIRCLE VILLAS
2327 S Atlantic
Ave (32118)
Rates: $35-$130
(904) 255-4004
(800) 217-3947

PARADISE INN
335 S Atlantic
Ave (32118)
Rates: $89-$99
(904) 255-8827

QUALITY INN OCEAN PALMS
2323 S Atlantic
Ave (32118)
Rates: $120-$279
(904) 255-0476
(800) 228-5151

SAND CASTLE MOTEL
3619 S Atlantic
Ave (32127)
Rates: $28-$65
(904) 767-3182
(800) 967-4757

DE FUNIAK SPRINGS

BEST WESTERN CROSSROADS INN
2343 Freeport Rd
(32433)
Rates: $59-$89
(850) 892-5111
(800) 528-1234

DAYS INN
472 Hugh Adams
Rd (32433)
Rates: $50-$85
(850) 892-6115
(800) 329-7466

DEERFIELD BEACH

COMFORT INN OCEANSIDE
50 SE 20th Ave
(33441)
Rates: $69-$169
(954) 428-0650
(800) 228-5150

COMFORT SUITES
1040 E Newport
Center Dr (33442)
Rates: $119-$209
(954) 570-8887
(800) 228-5150

EMBASSY SUITES RESORT
950 SE 20th Ave
(33441)
Rates: $150-$300
(954) 426-0478
(800) 362-2779

HOWARD JOHNSON PLAZA HOTEL & RESORT
2096 NE 2nd St
(33441)
Rates: $95-$189
(954) 428-2850
(800) 446-4656

LA QUINTA INN
351 W Hillsboro
Blvd (33441)
Rates: $99-$115
(954) 421-1004
(800) 687-6667

QUALITY SUITES HOTEL
1050 E Newport
Center Dr (33441)
Rates: $129-$219
(954) 570-8888
(800) 228-5151

RAMADA INN
1401 S Fed Hwy
US 1 (33441)
Rates: $45-$105
(954) 421-5000
(800) 272-6232

WELLESLEY INN
100 SW 12th Ave
(33442)
Rates: n/a
(954) 428-0661
(800) 444-8888

DELAND

DELAND COUNTRY INN BED & BREAKFAST
228 W Howry
Ave (32724)
Rates: n/a
(904) 736-4244

HOLIDAY INN
350 E Int'l
Speedway Blvd
(32724)
Rates: $85-$109
(904) 738-5200
(800) 465-4329

HOWRY MANOR HOLIDAY SUITE
422 W New York
Ave (32724)
Rates: n/a
(904)736-2483

QUALITY INN
2801 E New York
Ave (32724)
Rates: $49-$275
(904) 736-3440
(800) 228-5151

RIVIERA RESORT & MARINA
2760 Botts
Landing Rd
(32724)
Rates: n/a
(904) 822-5662

TROPICAL APTS & MARINA
1485 Lakeview
Dr (32724)
Rates: n/a
(904) 734-3080

UNIVERSITY INN
644 N Woodland
Blvd (32724)
Rates: n/a
(904) 734-5711

DELRAY BEACH

THE CITATION CLUB APTS
4801 S Citation
Dr (33445)
Rates: n/a
(561) 496-7700

COLONY HOTEL & CABANA CLUB
525 E Atlantic
Ave (33483)
Rates: $100-$165
(561) 276-4123
(800) 552-2363

LAKEVIEW APARTMENTS
1915 Lavers
Circle (33444)
Rates: n/a
(561) 272-4126

SEA HORSE BATH/TENNIS CLUB
4001 N Ocean
Blvd (33483)
Rates: n/a
(561) 276-4111

DESTIN

COMFORT INN
20003 Emerald
Coast Pkwy
(32541)
Rates: $69-$195
(850) 654-8611
(800) 228-5150

DAYS INN
1029 Old Hwy
98 E (32541)
Rates: $40-$130
(850) 837-2599
(800) 329-7466

EMERALD COAST VACATION RENTALS
www.ecvr.com
Rates: n/a
(850) 837-6100
(888) 232-3224

MOTEL 6
405 Hwy 98 E, #A
(32541)
Rates: $37-$70
(850) 837-0007
(800) 466-8356

SUNRAY VACATION COTTAGE
291 Tang-O-Mar
(32541)
Rates: $1000-
$1300 Weekly
(615) 352-6405

DUNDEE

HOLIDAY INN CYPRESS GARDENS
339 Hwy 27N
(33838)
Rates: $54-$89
(941) 439-1591
(800) 465-4329

DUNEDIN

SAILWINDS WATERFRONT RESORT
1414 Bayshore
Blvd (34698)
Rates: $50-$149
(727) 734-8851
(800) 331-2548

VERMONTER MOTEL
1035 Broadway
(35698)
Rates: $35-$99
(727) 733-3228

EASTPOINT

SPORTSMAN'S LODGE MOTEL
99 N Bayshore Dr
(32328)
Rates: $36-$46
(850) 670-8423

ELKTON

COMFORT INN
2625 SR 207
(32033)
Rates: $49-$149
(904) 829-3435
(800) 228-5150

ELLENTON

BEST WESTERN ELLENTON INN
5218 17th St E
(34222)
Rates: $80-$110
(941) 729-8505
(800) 528-1234
(800) 581-3953

SHONEYS INN
4915 17th St E
(34222)
Rates: n/a
(941) 729-0600
(800) 222-2222

ENGLEWOOD

DAYS INN
2540 S McCall Rd
(34224)
Rates: $48-$135
(941) 474-5544
(800) 329-7466

VERANDA INN
2073 S McCall Rd
(34224)
Rates: $85-$100
(941) 475-6533
(800) 633-8115

WESTON'S RESORT
985 Gulf Blvd
(34224)
Rates: $100-$149
(941) 474-3431

EVERGLADES

FLAMINGO LODGE MARINA & OUTPOST RESORT
1 Flamingo
Lodge Hwy
(33030)
Rates: $59-$102
(941) 253-2241
(800) 600-3813

EVERGLADES CITY

ON THE BANKS OF THE EVERGLADES
201 W Broadway
(34139)
Rates: $50-$149
(941) 695-3151
(888) 431-1977

FERNANDINA BEACH

AMELIA ISLAND LODGING SYSTEMS
584 S Fletcher
(32034)
Rates: n/a
(904) 261-4148
(800) 872-8531

FLORIDA HOUSE INN
22 S 3rd St (32034)
Rates: $70-$160
(904) 261-3300

INN AT FERNANDINA
2707 Sadler Rd
(32034)
Rates: $69-$94
(904) 277-2300

FLAGLER BEACH

BEACH FRONT MOTEL
1544 S A1A
(32136)
Rates: $45-$110
(904) 439-0089

LUXURY ON THE OCEAN
2815 S
Oceanshore Blvd
(32136)
Rates: $150
(904) 439-1826

TOPAZ MOTEL
1224 S
Oceanshore Blvd
(32136)
Rates: $45-$90
(904) 439-3301

FLORAL CITY

MOONRISE RESORT
8501 E Moonrise
Ln (34436)
Rates: $35-$99
(352) 726-2553
(800) 665-6701

FLORIDA CITY

CORAL ROC MOTEL
1100 N Krome
Ave (33034)
Rates: $45-$78
(305) 246-2888

HAMPTON INN
124 E Palm Dr
(33034)
Rates: $99
(305) 247-8833
(800) 426-7866

FORT LAUDERDALE

ADMIRAL'S COURT MOTEL
21 Hendricks Isle
(33301)
Rates: $195-$795
Weekly
(954) 462-5072
(800) 248-6669

AMERISUITES
1851 SE 10th St
(33316)
Rates: $174
(954) 763-7670
(800) 833-1516

BAHAMA HOTEL
401 N Atlantic
Blvd (33304)
Rates: $50-$149
(954) 467-7315
(800) 622-9995

BAY PALMS VILLAS
8 Isle of Venice
(33301)
Rates: $290-$450
Weekly
(954) 552-2821

BIRCH PATIO MOTEL
617 N Birch Rd
(33304)
Rates: $35-$95
(954) 563-9540

CORTLEIGH RESORT HOTEL
2100 NE 33rd
Ave (33305)
Rates: $50-$149
(954) 564-5868

COURTYARD VILLA
4312 El Mar Dr
(Lauderdale by
the Sea 33308)
Rates: $120
(954) 776-1164

DOUBLETREE GUEST SUITES
2670 E Sunrise
Blvd (33304)
Rates: $239
(954) 565-3800
(800) 222-8733

HOTEL OCEAN
205 N Atlantic
Blvd (33304)
Rates: n/a
(954) 763-3452
(888) 456-2326

HOWARD JOHNSON PLAZA HOTEL & RESORT
700 N Atlantic
Blvd (33304)
Rates: $75-$125
(954) 563-2451
(800) 446-4656
(800) 327-8578

LA QUINTA INN
999 W Cypress
Creek Rd (33309)
Rates: $99-$119
(954) 491-7666
(800) 687-6667

MARK 2100 RESORT HOTEL
2100 N Atlantic
Blvd (33305)
Rates: $45-$199
(954) 566-8383
(800) 334-6275

MOTEL 6
1801 SR 84
(33315)
Rates: $56-$72
(954) 760-7999
(800) 466-8356

OCEAN HACIENDA INN
1924 N Atlantic
Blvd (33305)
Rates: $50-$275
(954) 564-7800
(800) 562-8467

OCEAN MILE MOTOR LODGE
4101 N Ocean
Blvd (33308)
Rates: $35-$99
(954) 565-1691

RAMADA INN
2275 SR 84
(33312)
Rates: $69-$139
(954) 584-4000
(800) 272-6232

RED ROOF INN
4800 NW 9th Ave
(33309)
Rates: $90-$101
(954) 776-6333
(800) 843-7663

SUPER 8 MOTEL
2935 N Federal
Hwy (33306)
Rates: $45-$87
(954) 565-7761
(800) 800-8000

TRAVELODGE
1500 W
Commercial Blvd
(33309)
Rates: $59-$139
(954) 776-4222
(800) 578-7878

TREVERS AT THE BEACH
552 N Birch Rd
(33304)
Rates: $36-$145
(954) 564-9601
(800) 533-4744

VENICE BEACH GUEST QUARTERS
552 N Birch Rd
(33304)
Rates: $50-$149
(954) 564-9601
(800) 533-4744

WELLESLEY INN WEST
5070 N St. Rd 7
(33319)
Rates: n/a
(954) 484-6909
(800) 444-8888

WESTIN HOTEL-CYPRESS CREEK
400 Corporate Dr
(33304)
Rates: $129-$209
(954) 772-1331
(800) 228-3000

WISH YOU WERE HERE INN
7 N Birch Rd
(33304)
Rates: $30-$90
(954) 462-0531
(800) 462-0531

FORT MYERS

BAYMONT INN
2717 Colonial
Blvd (33907)
Rates: $98
(941) 274-3500
(800) 301-0200

BEST WESTERN SPRINGS RESORT
18051 S Tamiami
Tr (33908)
Rates: $99-$120
(941) 267-7900
(800) 528-1234
(800) 344-9794

COMFORT INN
4171 Boatways
Rd (33905)
Rates: $54-$134
(941) 694-9200
(800) 228-5150

COMFORT SUITES AIRPORT
13651-A Indian
Paint Lane
(33912)
Rates: $119-$149
(941) 768-0005
(800) 228-5150

DAYS INN AIRPORT
11435 Cleveland
Ave (33907)
Rates: $39-$114
(941) 936-1311
(800) 329-7466

DAYS INN
13353 N
Cleveland Ave
(33903)
Rates: $79-$129
(941) 995-0535
(800) 329-7466

ECONO LODGE
13301 N
Cleveland Ave
(33903)
Rates: $65-$95
(941) 995-0571
(800) 553-2666

GOLF VIEW MOTEL
3523 Cleveland
Ave (33901)
Rates: $39-$75
(941) 936-1858

HOWARD JOHNSON
4811 Cleveland
Ave (33907)
Rates: $55-$150
(941) 936-3229
(800) 446-4656

LA QUINTA INN
4850 Cleveland
Ave (33907)
Rates: $75-$92
(941) 275-3300
(800) 687-6667

MOTEL 6
3350 Marinatown
Lane (33903)
Rates: $33-$56
(941) 656-5544
(800) 466-8356

RADISSON INN SAINBEL GTWY
20091 Summerlin
Rd SW (33908)
Rates: $75-$119
(941) 466-1200
(800) 333-3333

RESIDENCE INN BY MARRIOTT
2960 Colonial
Blvd (339907)
Rates: n/a
(941) 936-0110
(800) 331-3131

ROCK LAKE MOTEL
2930 Palm Beach
Blvd (33916)
Rates: n/a
(941) 334-3242

RUSTY'S RESORT
309 San Carlos
(33916)
Rates: n/a
(941) 463-4691

SLEEP INN AIRPORT
13651-B Indian
Paint Ln (33912)
Rates: $54-$99
(941) 561-1117
(800) 753-3746

STONES THROW APARTMENTS
183 Washington
Ave (33916)
Rates: n/a
(941) 463-0052

TA KI-KI MOTEL
2631 1st St
(33916)
Rates: $58-$80
(941) 334-2135

WELLESLEY INN & SUITES
440 Ford St Ext
(33916)
Rates: $95-$115
(941) 278-3949
(800) 444-8888

FORT MYERS BEACH

ABACO BEACH VACATION VILLAS
131 Estero Blvd
(33931)
Rates: n/a
(941) 463-2611

ANCHOR INN COTTAGES
285 Virginia Ave
(33931)
Rates: $330-$1085
Weekly
(941) 463-2630

BEST WESTERN BEACH RESORT
684 Estero Blvd
(33931)
Rates: $99-$269
(941) 463-6000
(800) 528-1234
(800) 336-4045

CASA PLAYA BEACH RESORT
510 Estero Blvd (33931)
Rates: $199-$305
(941) 765-0510

OLD ESTERO ISLAND SUITES
510-520 Estero Blvd (33931)
Rates: $50-$170
(941) 463-2611
(800) 569-4876

RESIDENCE INN BY MARRIOTT
2960 Colonial Blvd (33912)
Rates: $89-$179
(941) 936-0110
(800) 331-3131

SILVER SANDS VILLAS
1207 Estero Blvd (33931)
Rates: $50-$149
(941) 463-2755
(800) 603-0501

FORT PIERCE

ANGLER MOTEL
1172 Seaway Dr (34949)
Rates: $55-$60
(561) 466-0131

COMFORT INN
3236 S Hwy 1 (34982)
Rates: $45-$159
(561) 461-2323
(800) 228-5150

DAYS INN
6651 Darter Ct (34945)
Rates: $59-$94
(561) 466-4066
(800) 329-7466

HOLIDAY INN EXPRESS
7151 Okeechobee Rd (34945)
Rates: $82
(561) 464-5000
(800) 465-4329

LEEWARD APARTMENTS
1730 Seaway Dr (34949)
Rates: $200 Weekly
(561) 464-0879

MOTEL 6
2500 Peters Rd (34945)
Rates: $33-$44
(561) 461-9937
(800) 466-8356

ROYAL INN
222 Hernando St (34949)
Rates: $59-$79
(561) 464-0405

FT WALTON BEACH

BEST INN
100 SW Miracle Strip Pkwy (32548)
Rates: $62-$175
(850) 244-0121
(800) 237-8466

BEST WESTERN
349 SW Miracle Strip Pkwy (32548)
Rates: $45-$130
(850) 302-0460
(800) 528-1234

DAYS INN
135 Miracle Strip Pwy, SW (32548)
Rates: $62-$66
(850) 244-6184
(800) 329-7466

HOWARD JOHNSON
314 Miracle Strip Pkwy (32548)
Rates: $48-$85
(850) 243-6162
(800) 446-4656

HOWARD JOHNSON EXP
866 Santa Rosa Blvd (32548)
Rates: n/a
(800) 446-4656

MARINA MOTEL & EFFICIENCIES
1345 Miracle Strip Pkwy E (32548)
Rates: $70-$80
(850) 244-1129
(800) 237-7021

SANDMAN MOTEL SUITES
480 Santa Rosa Blvd (32548)
Rates: n/a
(850) 243-5954
(800) 622-1511

SHONEY'S INN
203 Miracle Strip Pkwy (32548)
Rates: n/a
(850) 244-8663
(800) 222-2222

GAINESVILLE

APARTMENT INN MOTEL
4401 SW 13th St (32608)
Rates: $165+
(352) 371-3811

BEST INN
3455 SW Williston Rd (32608)
Rates: $47-$85
(352) 378-2405
(800) 237-8466

BUDGET LODGE
6901 NW 8th Ave (32605)
Rates: n/a
(352) 331-1601

DAYS INN
7516 Newberry Rd (32608)
Rates: $46-$119
(352) 332-3033
(800) 329-7466

ECONO LODGE-U OF FL
2649 SW 13th St (32608)
Rates: $42-$90
(352) 373-7816
(800) 553-2666

FLORIDA MOTEL
2603 SW 13th St (32608)
Rates: n/a
(352) 376-3742

HOWARD JOHNSON EXP
3451 SW Williston Rd (32608)
Rates: $45-$90
(352) 335-6355
(800) 446-4656

LA QUINTA INN
920 NW 69th Terr (32601)
Rates: $69-$99
(352) 332-6466
(800) 687-6667

MOTEL 6-U OF FL
4000 SW 40th Blvd (32608)
Rates: $34-$41
(352) 373-1604
(800) 466-8356

RAMADA LTD
4021 SW 40th Blvd (32608)
Rates: $54-$140
(352) 373-0392
(800) 272-6232

RED ROOF INN
3500 SW 42nd St (32608)
Rates: $59-$75
(352) 336-3311
(800) 843-7663

RESIDENCE INN BY MARRIOTT
4001 SW 13th St (32608)
Rates: $95-$160
(352) 371-2101
(800) 331-3131

RUSH LAKE MOTEL
1410 SW 16th Ave (32608)
Rates: n/a
(352) 373-5000
(800) 523-1996

SUPER 8 MOTEL
4202 SW 40th Blvd (32608)
Rates: $43-$62
(352) 378-3888
(800) 800-8000

GREENVILLE

TARTARUGA CREEK RESORT
Rt 2 (32331)
Rates: n/a
(904) 997-0036
(800) 465-2958

GULF BREEZE

HOLIDAY INN
51 Gulf Breeze Pkwy (32561)
Rates: n/a
(850) 932-2214
(800) 465-4329

GULFPORT

MOTEL PINE GROVE COTTAGES
5139 Tangerine Ave S (33707)
Rates: n/a
(727) 321-7263

HAINES CITY

BEST WESTERN LAKE HAMILTON
605 B Moore Rd (33844)
Rates: $81
(941) 421-6929
(800) 421-6928

HOWARD JOHNSON INN
1504 US Hwy 27 S (33844)
Rates: $55-$85
(941) 422-8621
(800) 446-4656

HERNANDO

BEST WESTERN CITRUS HILL LODGE
350 E Norvell Bryant Hwy (34442)
Rates: $85-$105
(352) 527-0015
(888) 424-5634

HERNANDO BEACH

HERNANDO BEACH MOTEL & CONDOS
4291 Shoal Line Blvd (34607)
Rates: n/a
(352) 596-2527

HIALEAH

DAYS INN
1950 W 49th St
(33012)
Rates: $59-$109
(305) 823-2121
(800) 329-7466

HIGH SPRINGS

**THE RUSTIC INN
BED & BREAKFAST**
65 N Main St
(32643)
Rates: $80+
(904) 454-1223

HOBE SOUND

RED CARPET INN
8605 SE Federal
Hwy (33455)
Rates: n/a
(561) 546-3600
(800) 251-1962

HOLIDAY

**BEST WESTERN
TAHITIAN
RESORT**
2337 US 19
(34691)
Rates: $69-$99
(727) 937-4121
(800) 528-1234
(800) 931-0333

HOLLY HILL

**TRAVELERS REST
INN**
749 Ridgewood
Ave (32117)
Rates: $39-$100
(904) 255-6511

HOLLYWOOD

**COMFORT INN
HOLLYWOOD
AIRPORT**
2520 Stirling Rd
(33020)
Rates: $54-$159
(954) 922-1600
(800) 333-1492
(800) 228-5150

**DAYS INN
AIRPORT SOUTH**
2601 N 29th Ave
Hollywood
(33020)
Rates: $46-$159
(954) 923-7300
(800) 329-7466

**GREEN SEAS
MOTEL**
1419 S Federal
Hwy Hollywood
(33020)
Rates: $37-$99
(954) 923-6564

**HOWARD
JOHNSON
EXPRESS**
2900 Polk St
(33020)
Rates: $45-$99
(954) 923-1516
(800) 446-4656

**LA QUINTA INN
& SUITES**
2620 N 26th Ave
(33019)
Rates: $109-$119
(954) 922-2295
(800) 687-6667

**MIRADOR
RESORT MOTEL**
901 S Ocean Dr
(33019)
Rates: $195-$860
Weekly
(954) 922-7581

MONTREAL INN
324-336 Balboa St
(33019)
Rates: $30-$79
(954) 925-4443

RAMADA INN
1925 Harrison St
(33020)
Rates: $59-$189
(954) 927-3341
(800) 272-6232

**THREE PALM
MOTEL**
930 N 17th Ct
(33020)
Rates: n/a
(954) 923-7683

HOLMES BEACH

**AQUARIUS
BEACH RESORT**
105 39th St
(34217)
Rates: $50-$150
(941) 778-7477

**GULF DRIVE
APARTMENTS**
6505 Gulf Drive
N (34217)
Rates: $30-$50
(941) 251-2952

HALEYS MOTEL
8102 Gulf Dr
(34217)
Rates: $30-$100
(941) 778-5405
(800) 367-7824

**THE INN
BETWEEN MOTEL**
105 66th St
(34217)
Rates: $310-$525
Weekly
(941) 778-0751

**ISLAND WEST
EFFICIENCIES**
3605 Gulf Dr
(34217)
Rates: $30-$100
(941) 778-6569

**PELICAN COVE
RESORT CONDO**
901 Gulf Dr S
(34217)
Rates: n/a
(941) 778-4800
(800) 237-2252

HOMESTEAD

DAYS INN
51 S Homestead
Blvd (33030)
Rates: $52-$99
(305) 245-1260
(800) 329-7466

**EVERGLADES
MOTEL**
605 S Krome Ave
(33030)
Rates: $39-$68
(305) 247-4117

**HOWARD
JOHNSON
EXPRESS**
990 N Homestead
Blvd (33030)
Rates: n/a
(800) 446-4656

**KATY'S PLACE
BED & BREAKFAST**
31850 SW 195th
Ave (33030)
Rates: n/a
(305) 246-0783
(800) 428-3438

**RAMADA
LIMITED**
990 N
Homestead Blvd
(33030)
Rates: $69-$129
(305) 247-7020
(800) 272-6232

HOMOSASSA

**HOWARD
JOHNSON
RESORT**
5297 S Cherokee
Way (34448)
Rates: $60-$96
(352) 628-2474
(800) 446-4656

HOMOSASSA SPRINGS

RAMADA INN
4076 S Suncoast
Blvd (34446)
Rates: $59-$69
(352) 628-4311
(800) 272-6232

HUDSON

**GULFCOVE
WATERFRONT
RESORT**
6525 Clark St
(34667)
Rates: n/a
(800) 600-1955

INDIALANTIC

BUDGET INN
2900 N A1A Hwy
(32903)
Rates: $39-$140
(321) 779-9994

**CASABLANCA
INN**
1805 N A1A Hwy
(32903)
Rates: $60-$80
(321) 728-7188

**HILTON
MELBOURNE
BEACH**
3003 N Hwy A1A
(32903)
Rates: n/a
(321) 777-5000
(877) 843-8786

**OCEANFRONT
COTTAGES**
612 Wavecrest
Ave (32903)
Rates: $99-$125
(321) 725-8474

**QUALITY SUITES
OCEANFRONT**
1665 N SR A1A
(32903)
Rates: $159-$199
(321) 723-4222
(800) 228-5151

INDIAN ROCKS BEACH

ISLAND RENTALS
319 Gulf Blvd
(33785)
Rates: n/a
(813) 595-4949

**UNCLE MILT'S
COURTYARD
COTTAGES**
701 Gulf Blvd
(33785)
Rates: n/a
(813) 595-8013

INDIAN SHORES

**CASA CHICA
COTTAGES**
19000 Gulf Blvd
(34635) ·
Rates: n/a
(727) 596-1602
(800) 562-5335

**EDGEWATER
BEACH RESORT**
19130 Gulf Blvd
(34635)
Rates: $50-$100
(727) 595-4028

FLORENTINE APARTMENTS
19722 Gulf Blvd (34635)
Rates: n/a
(727) 595-8820

HOLIDAY VILLAS II CONDO
19610 Gulf Blvd (34635)
Rates: $50-$149
(727) 596-4852
(800) 428-4852

INDIAN PASS APARTMENTS
19417 Gulf Blvd (34635)
Rates: n/a
(727) 595-5444

LA REGINA MOTEL
19600 Gulf Blvd (34635)
Rates: n/a
(727) 595-8067

VICTORIA APTS & COTTAGES
19738 Gulf Blvd (34635)
Rates: n/a
(727) 595-4004

INVERNESS

THE CROWN HOTEL
109 N Seminole Ave (34450)
Rates: $50-$85
(352) 344-5555
(800) 856-4455

ISLAMORADA

B&B ISLAMORADA
81175 Old Hwy (33036)
Rates: $40-$60
(305) 664-9321

COCONUT COVE RESORT/MARINA
84801 Old Hwy (33036)
Rates: $65-$125
(305) 664-0123
(800) 801-1079

GAME FISH RESORT
Rt 1 (33036)
Rates: $55-$75
(305) 664-5568

LOOKOUT LODGE
87770 Overseas Hwy (33036)
Rates: $69-$159
(305) 852-9915
(800) 870-1772

OCEAN DAWN LODGE
82885 Old Hwy (33036)
Rates: $65-$115
(305) 664-4844

SANDS OF ISLAMORADA
80051 Overseas Hwy (33036)
Rates: $150-$240
(305) 664-2791
(888) 741-4518

WHITE GATE COURT
76010 Overseas Hwy (33036)
Rates: $98-$200
(305) 664-4136

JACKSONVILLE

ADMIRAL BENBOW INN
10550 Balmoral Cir (32218)
Rates: $39-$65
(904) 757-8338

ADMIRAL BENBOW INN-AIRPORT
14691 Duvall Rd (32218)
Rates: $39-$49
(904) 741-4254

AMERISUITES/ BAY MEADOWS
8277 Western Way Cir (32256)
Rates: $89-$149
(904) 737-4477
(800) 833-1516

BAYMONT INN & SUITES
3199 Hartley Rd (32257)
Rates: $54-$63
(904) 268-999
(800) 301-0200

BEST INNS OF AMERICA
8220 Dix Ellis Tr (32256)
Rates: $47-$64
(904) 739-3323
(800) 237-8466

COMFORT SUITES HOTEL
8333 Dix Ellis Tr (32256)
Rates: $60-$130
(904) 739-1155
(800) 228-5150

HAMPTON INN
1170 Airport Entrance Rd (32218)
Rates: $89-$99
(904) 741-4980
(800) 426-7866

HOLIDAY INN
9150 Baymeadows Rd (32256)
Rates: $59-$79
(904) 737-1700
(800) 465-4329

HOLIDAY INN AIRPORT
14670 Duvall Rd (32218)
Rates: $68-$86
(904) 741-4404
(800) 465-4329

HOMESTEAD VILLAGE GUEST STUDIOS
10020 Skinner Lake Dr (32246)
Rates: $59-$79
(904) 642-9911
(888) 782-9473

HOMESTEAD VILLAGE GUEST STUDIOS
8300 Western Way (32256)
Rates: $49-$99
(904) 739-1881
(888) 782-9473

HOMEWOOD SUITES
8737 Baymeadows Rd (32256)
Rates: $139-$175
(904) 733-9299
(800) 225-5466

HOWARD JOHNSON HOTEL
3233 Emerson St (32207)
Rates: $45-$70
(904) 398-3333
(800) 446-4656

INNS OF AMERICA
4300 Salisbury Rd N (32216)
Rates: $55
(904) 281-0198

JACKSONVILLE AIRPORT MOTEL
1153 Airport Rd (32229)
Rates: $32+
(904) 741-4600

LA QUINTA INN
4868 Lenoir Ave S (32216)
Rates: $65-$105
(904) 296-0703
(800) 687-6667

LA QUINTA INN
8555 Blanding Blvd (32244)
Rates: $59-$86
(904) 778-9539
(800) 687-6667

LA QUINTA INN NORTH
812 Dunn Ave (32218)
Rates: $59-$89
(904) 751-6960
(800) 687-6667

LA QUINTA INN-BAYMEADOWS
8255 Dix Ellis Tr (32256)
Rates: $59-$99
(904) 731-9940
(800) 687-6667

MAINSTAY SUITES
4693 Salisbury Rd (32256)
Rates: $49-$99
(904) 296-9661
(800) 660-6246

MOTEL 6 AIRPORT
10885 Harts Rd (32218)
Rates: $35-$44
(904) 757-8600
(800) 466-8356

MOTEL 6 BAYMEADOWS SOUTHEAST
8765 Baymeadows Rd (32256)
Rates: n/a
(904) 731-7317
(800) 466-8356

MOTEL 6-SOUTHEAST
8285 Dix Ellis Tr (32256)
Rates: $38-$44
(904) 731-8400
(800) 466-8356

MOTEL 6-SOUTHWEST
6107 Youngerman Cir (32244)
Rates: $36-$42
(904) 777-6100
(800) 466-8356

QUALITY HOTEL SOUTHPOINT
4660 Salisbury Rd (32256)
Rates: $59-$129
(904) 281-0900
(800) 228-5151

RAMADA INN CONFERENCE CENTER
3130 Hartley Rd (32257)
Rates: $70-$80
(904) 268-8080
(800) 272-6232

RED CARPET INN
5331 University Blvd (32216)
Rates: $28+
(904) 733-8110
(800) 251-1962

RED ROOF INN AIRPORT
14701 Airport Entrance Rd (32218)
Rates: $40-$73
(904) 741-4488
(800) 843-7663

RED ROOF INN AIRPORT
6969 Lenoir Ave E (32216)
Rates: $50-$71
(904) 296-1006
(800) 843-7663

AREA CODES - If the local number doesn't connect, check for a new area code.

RED ROOF INN
6099
Youngerman Cir
(32244)
Rates: $44-$57
(904) 777-1000
(800) 843-7663

**RESIDENCE INN
BY MARRIOTT**
8365 Dix Ellis
Trail (32256)
Rates: $119-$175
(904) 733-8088
(800) 331-3131

SUPER 8 MOTEL
10901 Harts Rd
(32218)
Rates: $40-$58
(904) 751-3888
(800) 800-8000

VALU-LODGE
351 Airport Rd
(32218)
Rates: $34+
(904) 741-0094

JACKSONVILLE BEACH

THE ATLANTIS
731 N 1st St
(32250)
Rates: $33-$53
(904) 249-5006

**DAYS INN
OCEANFRONT
RESORT**
1031 S 1st St
(32250)
Rates: $79-$129
(904) 249-7231
(800) 329-7466

EMBASSY SUITES
9300 Baymeadows
Rd (32256)
Rates: $60-$135
(904) 731-3555
(800) 362-2779

SURFSIDE MOTEL
1236 N 1st St
(32250)
Rates: $46-$75
(904) 246-1583

JASPER

DAYS INN
Rt 3 (32052)
Rates: $35-$80
(904) 792-1987
(800) 329-7466

SCOTTISH INNS
Rt 3, Box 136
(32052)
Rates: $30-$40
(904) 792-1234
(800) 251-1962

JENNINGS

**JENNINGS
HOUSE INN**
SR 143
(32053)
Rates: $20-$25
(904) 938-3305

QUALITY INN
1846 Hamilton
Ave (32053)
Rates: $34-$110
(904) 938-3501
(800) 228-5151

JENSEN BEACH

**RIVER PALM
COTTAGES &
FISH CAMP**
2325 NE Indian
River Dr (34957)
Rates: $125-$199
(561) 334-0401
(800) 305-0511

JUNO BEACH

**HOLIDAY INN
EXPRESS**
13950 US Hwy 1
(33408)
Rates: $79-$199
(561) 622-4366
(800) 465-4329

JUPITER

**JUPITER BAY
RENTALS**
351 S US Hwy 1
(33477)
Rates: n/a
(561) 743-8178

KENDALL

AMERISUITES
11520 SW 88th St
(33176)
Rates: $129-$179
(305) 279-8688
(800) 833-1516

**HOWARD
JOHNSON**
10201 S Dixie
Hwy (33156)
Rates: $66-$76
(305) 666-2531
(800) 446-4656

WELLESLEY INN
11750 Mills Dr
(33183)
Rates: $80-$100
(305) 270-0359
(800) 444-8888

KEY LARGO

**BAY HARBOR
LODGE**
97702 Overseas
Hwy (33037)
Rates: $50-$149
(305) 852-5695
(800) 385-0986

**COCONUT BAY
RESORT**
97770 Overseas
Hwy (33037)
Rates: $50-$149
(305) 852-5695
(800) 385-0986

**HOWARD
JOHNSON**
10245 Overseas
Hwy (33037)
Rates: $139-$349
(305) 451-1400
(800) 446-4656

KELLY'S MOTEL
104220 Overseas
Hwy (33037)
Rates: $44-$75+
(305) 451-1622

**SEA TRAIL
MOTEL**
Rt 5 (33037)
Rates: $35-$55
(305) 852-8001

KEY WEST

**ALEXANDER
PALMS COURT**
715 South St
(33040)
Rates: $145-$395
(305) 296-6413

**BOATHOUSE
RESORT &
MARINA**
1445 S Roosevelt
Blvd (33040)
Rates: $170-$300
(305) 292-0017
(800) 958-2128

**CARIBBEAN
HOUSE MOTEL**
226 Petronia St
(33040)
Rates: $39-$79
(305) 296-1600

**CASA ALANTE
GUEST
COTTAGES B&B**
1435 S Roosevelt
Blvd (33040)
Rates: $60-$150
(305) 293-0702
(800) 688-3942

**CASABLANCA AT
BOGART'S**
916 Center St
(33040)
Rates: $85-$155
(305) 296-0637

**CENTER COURT
HISTORIC INN &
COTTAGES B&B**
916 Center St
(33040)
Rates: $178-$338
(305) 296-9292
(800) 797-8787

**CHELSEA HOUSE
HISTORIC BED
& BREAKFAST**
707 Truman Ave
(33040)
Rates: $130-$210
(305) 296-2211

**COURTNEY'S
PLACE HISTORIC
COTTAGES**
720 Whitmarsh
Ln (33040)
Rates: $109-$189
(305) 294-3480

**THE CUBAN
CLUB SUITES
APT MOTEL**
1102-1108 Duval
St (33040)
Rates: $249-$399
(305) 296-0465
(800) 432-4849

**CURRY MANSION
INN B&B**
511 Caroline St
(33040)
Rates: $180-$325
(305) 294-5349
(800) 253-3466

DAYS INN
3852 N Roosevelt
Blvd (33040)
Rates: $94-$285
(305) 294-2742
(800) 329-7466

DEJA VU RESORT
611 Truman Ave
(33040)
Rates: $100-$249
(305) 292-9339
(800) 724-5351

**DOUGLAS
GUEST HOUSE**
419 Amelia St
(33040)
Rates: $88-$275
(305) 294-5269

**FRANCES STREET
BOTTLE INN B&B**
535 Frances St
(33040)
Rates: $135-$165
(305) 294-8530

HALFRED MOTEL
512 Truman Ave
(33040)
Rates: $65-$143
(305) 296-5565

**HIDEAWAY
COTTAGES**
6531 Maloney
Ave (33040)
Rates: $125+
(305) 296-0294
(800) 484-8777

**INCENTRA
CARRIAGE
HOUSE**
729 Whitehead St
(33040)
Rates: $59-$290
(305) 296-5565

**JABOUR'S
TRAILER
COURT/CABINS**
223 Elizabeth St
(33040)
Rates: n/a
(305) 294-5723

AREA CODES - If the local number doesn't connect, check for a new area code.

LA CASA DE LUCES
422 Amelia St (33040)
Rates: $55-$155
(305) 296-0582

MAHOGANY HOUSE
812 Simonton St (33040)
Rates: $45-$175
(305) 293-9464

NASSAU HOUSE
1016 Fleming St (33040)
Rates: $49-$199
(305) 296-8513
(800) 296-8513

OLD CUSTOMS HOUSE INN
124 Duval St (33040)
Rates: $50-$200
(305) 294-8507

OLIVIA BY DUVAL HOTEL
511 Olivia St (33040)
Rates: $40-$249
(305) 296-5169
(800) 413-1978

THE PALMS HOTEL HISTORIC B&B
820 White St (33040)
Rates: $140-$225
(305) 294-3146

PIER HOUSE RESORT & CABIBBEAN SPA
One Duval St (33040)
Rates: $150-$350
(305) 296-4600
(800) 327-8340

RAMADA INN
3420 N Roosevelt Blvd (33040)
Rates: $79-$249
(305) 294-5541
(800) 272-6232

SEA ISLE RESORT
915 Windsor Ln (33040)
Rates: $65-$140
(305) 294-5188

SEA SHELL MOTEL
718 South St (33040)
Rates: $45-$95
(305) 296-5719

SOUTHERN CROSS MOTEL
326 Duval St (33040)
Rates: $80-$115
(305) 294-3200

SPEAK EASY INN
1117 Duval St (33040)
Rates: $70-$163
(305) 296-2680

SUITE DREAMS ALL SUITES
1001 Von Phister (33040)
Rates: $100-$249
(305) 296-5169
(800) 730-2483

TRAVELERS PALM GARDEN COTTAGE
815 Catherine St (33040)
Rates: $105-$350
(305) 294-9560

WHISPERS BED & BREAKFAST INN
409 William St (33040)
Rates: $69-$150
(305) 294-5969
(800) 856-7444

WILLIAM HOUSE
1317 Duval St (33040)
Rates: $83-$170
(305) 294-8223

KISSIMMEE

BEST WESTERN EASTGATE
5565 W Irlo Bronson Hwy (34746)
Rates: $49-$159
(407) 396-0707
(800) 528-1234
(800) 223-5361

CONDOTELS OF MAGIC WORLDS
3501 W Vine St (34741)
Rates: $91-$151+
(407) 847-6007

DAYS INN
2095 E Irlo Bronson Hwy (34744)
Rates: $30-$99
(407) 846-7136
(800) 329-7466

DAYS INN SUITES MAIN GATE
5820 W Bronson Hwy (34746)
Rates: $259-$399
(407) 396-7900
(800) 329-7466

FAMILIES FIRST VACATION HOMES
7801 W Irlo Bronson Hwy (34747)
Rates: $100-$200
(407) 396-3960
(800) 393-8800

FANTASY WORLD CLUB VILLAS
3000 Hart Ave (34746)
Rates: $130-$180
(407) 396-1808
(800) 874-8047

FLAMINGO INN
801 E Vine St (34744)
Rates: $25-$60
(407) 846-1935
(800) 780-7617

HOLIDAY INN DOWNTOWN
2009 W Vine St (34741)
Rates: $145-$165
(407) 846-2713
(800) 624-5905

HOLIDAY INN-MAINGATE EAST
5678 W Irlo Bronson Hwy (34746)
Rates: $89-$126
(407) 396-4488
(800) 465-4656

HOLIDAY INN-MAINGATE WEST
7601 Black Lake Rd (34747)
Rates: $89-$189
(407) 396-1100
(800) 465-4656

HOMEWOOD SUITES WALT DISNEY WORLD RESORT
3100 Parkway Blvd (34747)
Rates: $139-$189
(407) 396-2229
(800) 225-5466
(800) 225-4543

HOWARD JOHNSON
4643 W Hwy 192 (34706)
Rates: $28-$90
(407) 396-1340
(800) 446-4656

HOWARD JOHNSON HOTEL
2323 Hwy 192 E (34744)
Rates: $29-$89
(407) 846-4900
(800) 446-4656

IFC-VACATION RENTALS
3179 W Vine St (34741)
Rates: $46-$90
(407) 870-8888
(800) 937-3567

LARSON'S LODGE & FAMILY SUITES
6075 W Irlo Bronson Hwy (34747)
Rates: $69-$99
(407) 396-6100
(800) 327-9074

MAGIC CASTLE INN & SUITES
5055 W Irlo Bronson Hwy (34747)
Rates: $49-$89
(407) 396-1212
(800) 446-5669

MASTERS INN
5367 W Irlo Bronson Hwy (34746)
Rates: $59-$79
(407) 396-4020

MASTERS INN-MAINGATE
2945 Entry Point Blvd (34747)
Rates: $59-$79
(407) 396-7743

MOTEL 6
5731 W Irlo Bronson Hwy (34746)
Rates: $30-$56
(407) 396-6333
(800) 466-8356

MOTEL 6-DISNEYWORLD MAIN GATE
7455 W Irlo Bronson Hwy (34747)
Rates: $40-$56
(407) 396-6422
(800) 466-8356

PHOENIX PROPERTIES-RENTALS
911 N Main St, Ste 98 (34741)
Rates: $91-$150
(407) 870-8011
(800) 828-7127

PREMIER VACATION HOMES
3160 Vineland Rd Suite 1 (34746)
Rates: n/a
(407) 396-9031
(800) 396-2401

RAMADA INN RESORT MAINGATE
2950 Reedy Creek Blvd (34747)
Rates: $89-$259
(407) 396-4466
(800) 272-6232

RED ROOF INN
4970 Kyng's Heath Rd (34746)
Rates: $41-$68
(407) 396-0065
(800) 843-7663

RED ROOF INN MAINGATE
7491 W Irlo Bronson Hwy (34747)
Rates: n/a
(407) 396-6000
(800) 843-7663

AREA CODES - If the local number doesn't connect, check for a new area code.

SHONEY'S INN
4156 W Vine St
(34741)
Rates: $54+
(407) 870-7374
(800) 222-2222

**SUMMERFIELD
CONDO RESORT**
2422
Summerfield
Way (34741)
Rates: $250-$299
(407) 847-7222
(800) 207-9582

SWEET WATER
91 Lasona Bay
(32747)
Rates: $50-$149
(407) 396-3230
(800) 209-4006

TRAVELODGE
201 Simpson Rd
(32744)
Rates: $39-$79
(407) 846-1530
(800) 578-7878

LABELLE

**THE RIVER'S
EDGE MOTEL**
285 N River Rd
(33935)
Rates: $45+
(941) 675-6062

LAKE BUENA VISTA

CASA ADOBE
9107 South Rt 535
(32819)
Rates: n/a
(407) 876-5432

CLARION SUITES
8451 Palm Pkwy
(32836)
Rates: $113-$225
(407) 238-1700
(800) 252-7466

COMFORT INN
8442 Palm Pkwy
(32830)
Rates: $99-$150
(407) 239-7300
(800) 228-5150

DAYS INN
12799 Apopka-
Vineland Rd
(32836)
Rates: $73-$240
(407) 239-4441
(800) 329-7466

**FANTASYWORLD
CLUB VILLAS**
3000 Hart Ave
(34746)
Rates: $100-$150
(407) 396-1808
(800) 874-8047

**HOLIDAY INN-
SUNSPREE
RESORT**
13351 SR 535
(32821)
Rates: $68-$189
(407) 239-4500
(800) 465-4329
(800) 366-6299

**ORLANDO
WORLD CENTER
MARRIOTT**
8701 World Center
Dr (32821)
Rates: $150-$225
(407) 239-4200
(800) 621-0638

**RESIDENCE INN
BY MARRIOTT**
8800 Meadow
Creek Dr (32821)
Rates: $219-$289
(407) 239-7700
(800) 331-3131

LAKE CITY

**BEST WESTERN
LAKE CITY INN**
1720 Hwy 90 W
(32055)
Rates: $49-$80
(904) 752-3801
(800) 528-1234
(800) 718-0244

COMFORT INN
Hwy 90 & I-75
(32055)
Rates: $64-$95
(904) 755-1344
(800) 228-5150

CYPRESS INN
Rt 13 (32055)
Rates: $25-$39
(904) 752-9369

**DRIFTWOOD
MOTEL**
4380 Hwy 90 W
(32055)
Rates: $29-$40
(904) 755-3545

**DYNASTY INN
& SUITES**
4670 Hwy 90 W
(32024)
Rates: $45-$50
(904) 752-6262

ECONO LODGE
4680 Hwy 90 W
(32024)
Rates: $32-$79
(904) 752-7891
(800) 553-2666

**ECONO LODGE
SOUTH**
Rt 2 (32024)
Rates: $39-$99
(904) 755-9311
(800) 553-2666

**HOWARD
JOHNSON**
Rt 13 (32055)
Rates: $42-$59
(904) 752-6262
(800) 446-4656

KNIGHTS INN
Rt 13, Box 201
(32055)
Rates: $23-$60
(904) 752-7720
(800) 843-5644

MOTEL 6
4587 W Hwy 90
(32055)
Rates: $26-$30
(904) 755-4664
(800) 466-8356

**PINEY WOODS
LODGE**
Rt 13 (32055)
Rates: $20-$45
(904) 752-8334

**QUAIL HEIGHTS
COUNTRY CLUB**
SR 247 (32025)
Rates: n/a
(904) 752-3339

RODEWAY INN
4570 Commerce
Blvd (32025)
Rates: $25-$45
(904) 755-5203
(800) 228-2000

SCOTTISH INNS
4450 W Hwy 90
(32055)
Rates: $29-$39
(904) 755-0230
(800) 251-1962

TRAVELODGE
I-75 Exit 80 US
441 & 41 (32035)
Rates: $40+
(904) 752-7582
(800) 578-7878

**TRAVELODGE
HOTEL**
4557 90 W
(32055)
Rates: $36-$70
(904) 755-9306
(800) 578-7878

**VILLAGER
LODGE**
Hwy 90 (32055)
Rates: $25-$49
(904) 752-9369

LAKE MARY

**LA QUINTA INN
& SUITES**
1060 Greenwood
Blvd (32746)
Rates: $99-$125
(407) 805-9901
(800) 687-6667

**MAINSTAY
SUITES**
1040 Greenwood
Blvd (32746)
Rates: $80-$125
(407) 829-2332
(800) 660-6246

LAKE PLACID

RAMADA INN
2165 US 27 S
(33852)
Rates: $59-$89
(941) 465-3133
(800) 272-6232

LAKE WALES

**CHALET
SUZANNE INN**
3800 Chalet
Suzanne Ln
(33853)
Rates: $135-$195
(941) 676-6011
(800) 433-6011

DELUXE INN
795 Hwy 27 S
(33853)
Rates: $25-$30
(941) 676-8667

EMERALD MOTEL
530 S Scenic Hwy
(33853)
Rates: $30-$50
(941) 676-3310

KNIGHTS INN
541 W Central
Ave (33853)
Rates: $31-$55
(941) 676-7925
(800) 843-5644

LANTERN MOTEL
3949 Hwy 27 N
(33853)
Rates: n/a
(941) 676-4821

LAKE WORTH

**LAGO MOTOR
INN**
714 S Dixie Hwy
(33460)
Rates: $58-$68
(561) 585-5246

**MARTINIQUE
MOTOR LODGE**
801 S Dixie Hwy
(33460)
Rates: $45-$75
(561) 585-2502

**SHANGRI-LA
MOTEL**
1700 S Federal
Hwy (33460)
Rates: $35-$99
(561) 582-1700
(888) 303-9966

**WHITE MANOR
MOTEL**
1618 S Federal
Hwy (33460)
Rates: $50-$62
(561) 582-7437

LAKELAND

**AMERISUITES
LAKELAND CTR**
525 W Oange St
(33815)
Rates: $109-$129
(863) 413-1122
(800) 833-1515

AREA CODES - If the local number doesn't connect, check for a new area code.

BAYMONT INN & SUITES
4315 Lakeland Park Dr (33809)
Rates: $74-$81
(863) 815-0606
(800) 301-0200

COMFORT INN
1817 E Memorial Blvd (33801)
Rates: $65-$80
(863) 688-9221
(800) 228-5150

DAYS INN
508 E Memorial Blvd (33801)
Rates: $40-$95
(863) 682-0303
(800) 329-7466

LA QUINTA INN & SUITES
1024 Crevasse St (33809)
Rates: $105-$119
(863) 859-2866
(800) 687-6667

MOTEL 6
3120 US Hwy 98 N (33809)
Rates: $35-$44
(863) 682-0643
(800) 466-8356

ROYALTY INN
3425 Hwy 98 N (33805)
Rates: $55-$95
(863) 858-4481

WELLESLEY INN
3520 N Hwy 98 (33805)
Rates: $105-$125
(863) 859-3399
(800) 444-8888

LANTANA

INNS OF AMERICA
7051 Seacrest Blvd (33462)
Rates: $49-$95
(561) 588-0456

MOTEL 6
1310 W Lantana Rd (33462)
Rates: $39-$48
(561) 585-5833
(800) 466-8356

LEESBURG

SCOTTISH INNS
1321 N 14th St (34748)
Rates: $29-$40
(352) 787-3343
(800) 251-1962

SHONEY'S INN
1308 N 14th St (34748)
Rates: $49-$60
(352) 787-1210
(800) 222-2222

SUPER 8 MOTEL
1392 N Blvd W (34748)
Rates: $43-$67
(352) 787-6363
(800) 800-8000

LITTLE TORCH KEY

OCEAN BREEZE HOUSE
Rt 747 Lafitte Rd (33042)
Rates: $1250+ Weekly
(305) 754-1299
(800) 772-4560

LIVE OAK

BEST WESTERN SUWANNEE RIVER INN
6819 US 129 (320642
Rates: $42-$95
(904) 362-6000
(800) 528-1234
(877) 211-5448

ECONO LODGE
US 129 & I-10, (32060)
Rates: $50-$80
(904) 362-7459
(800) 553-2666

SPIRIT/SUWANNE E MUSIC PARK CABINS
3076 95th Dr (32060)
Rates: n/a
(904) 364-1683

LONG KEY

FIESTA KEY KAMPGROUNDS OF AMERICA
MM 70 Hwy 1 (33001)
Rates: $50-$75
(305) 664-4922
(800) 562-7730

LONGBOAT KEY

CEDARS EAST TENNIS RESORT
545 Cedars Court (34228)
Rates: n/a
(941) 383-4621
(800) 237-9505

FLORIDA VACATION CONNECTION RENTALS
4030 Gulf of Mexico Dr (34228)
Rates: n/a
(941) 383-9505
(800) 237-9505

RIVIERA BEACH MOTEL
5451 Gulf of Mexico Dr (34228)
Rates: $800-$1100 Weekly
(941) 383-2552

ROLLING WAVES COTTAGES
6351 Gulf of Mexico Dr (34228)
Rates: $90-$202
(941) 383-1323

LONGWOOD

RAMADA INN
2025 W SR 434 (32779)
Rates: $64-$82
(407) 862-4000
(800) 272-6232

MACCLENNY

ECONO LODGE
I-10 & SR 121 (32063)
Rates: $50-$75
(904) 259-3000
(800) 553-2666

MADEIRA BEACH

LIGHTHOUSE MOTEL & APTS
13355 Second St E (33708)
Rates: n/a
(727) 391-0015

SANDY SHORES CONDOMINIUMS
12924 Gulf Blvd (33708)
Rates: $77-$101
(727) 392-1281

SCHOONER MOTEL
14500 Gulf Blvd (33708)
Rates: $40-$249
(727) 392-5167
(800) 573-5187

SEA DAWN MOTEL
13733 Gulf Blvd (33708)
Rates: $27-$60
(727) 391-7500

STARGAZER ON THE GULF
14048 Gulf Blvd (33708)
Rates: n/a
(727) 393-7200
(800) 775-3732

WAVES MOTEL
13343 Gulf Blvd (33708)
Rates: $35-$45
(727) 391-3641

MADISON

DAYS INN
Rt 1, Box 3329-F (32340)
Rates: $49-$64
(850) 973-3330
(800) 329-7466

DEERWOOD RESORT MOTEL
I-10 Exit 37 (32340)
Rates: $50-$99
(850) 973-2504

MAITLAND

WELLESLEY INN & SUITES
1951 Summer Tower Blvd (32751)
Rates: $89-$129
(407) 659-0066
(800) 444-8888

MARATHON

BONEFISH RESORT
Rt 1, Box 343 (33050)
Rates: $29-$77
(305) 743-7107

CAPT. PIPS VACATION SUITES
11410 Overseas Hwy (33050)
Rates: $760-$1100 Weekly
(305) 754-4403

CORAL LAGOON RESORT
12399 US 1 Hwy (33050)
Rates: $65-$130
(305) 289-0121

FARO BLANCO MARINE RESORT
1996 Overseas Hwy (33050)
Rates: $55-$233
(305) 743-2918

GRASSY KEY BEACH MOTEL
Rt 1, Box 357 (33050)
Rates: $45-$95
(305) 743-0533

HOLIDAY INN
13201 Overseas Hwy (33050)
Rates: n/a
(305) 289-0222
(800) 465-4329

HOWARD JOHNSON
13351 Overseas Hwy (33050)
Rates: $69-$239
(305) 743-8550
(800) 446-4656

LAGOON RESORT
7200 Aviation Blvd (33050)
Rates: $49-$129
(305) 743-5463

PEACE INN
7931 US 1 Hwy (33050)
Rates: $30-$55
(305) 743-5124

PELICAN MOTEL
Rt 1 (33050)
Rates: $34-$78
(305) 289-0011

RAINBOW BEND RESORT
Rt 1 (33050)
Rates: $120-$210
(305) 289-1505
(800) 929-1505

SEA COVE MOTEL
12685 Overseas Hwy (33050)
Rates: $24-$99
(305) 289-0800

SEASHELL BEACH
Resort Rt 1 (33050)
Rates: $39-$49
(305) 289-0265

SEAWARD RESORT MOTEL
8700 US 1 (33050)
Rates: $35-$80
(305) 754-5711

TROPICAL COTTAGES MOTEL
243 61st St.Gulf (33050)
Rates: $50-$99
(305) 743-6048

YARDARM MOTEL
6200 Overseas Hwy (33050)
Rates: $45-$50
(305) 743-2541

YELLOWTAIL INN
Rt 1 (33050)
Rates: $50-$95
(305) 743-8400

MARCO ISLAND

BOAT HOUSE MOTEL
1180 Edington Pl (34145)
Rates: $66+
(941) 642-2400
(800) 528-6345

MORAN'S BARGE MARINA & MOTEL
3200 SR 92 (34146)
Rates: n/a
(941) 642-1920
(800) 642-1921

MARIANNA

BEST WESTERN MARIANNA INN
2086 Hwy 71 (32448)
Rates: $46-$60
(850) 526-5666
(800) 528-1234

COMFORT INN
2175 Hwy 71 (32446)
Rates: $49-$65
(850) 526-5600
(800) 228-5150

DAYS INN
4132 Lafayette St (32446)
Rates: $38-$60
(850) 482-3500
(800) 329-7466

MICROTEL INN & SUITES
I-10 & SR 71 (32446)
Rates: $39-$69
(888) 771-7171

MAYO

JIM HOLLIS' RIVER RNDVOUZ CABINS
Rt 2 (32066)
Rates: n/a
(904) 294-2510
(800) 533-5276

MELBOURNE

BAYMONT INN & SUITES
7200 George T Edwards Dr (32940)
Rates: $72-$79
(321) 242-9400
(800) 301-0200

BEST WESTERN HARBORVIEW
964 S Harbor City Blvd (32901)
Rates: $49-$99
(321) 724-4422
(800) 528-1234
(888) 329-8901

CASABLANCA INN
1805 N A1A Hwy (32903)
Rates: $39-$79
(421) 728-7188
(800) 333-7273

HILTON AT RIALTO PLACE
200 Rialto Pl (32901)
Rates: $109-$119
(321) 768-0200
(800) 445-8667

QUALITY SUITES
1665 SR A1A N (32903)
Rates: $89-$199
(321) 723-4222
(800) 228-5151

RAMADA LIMITED
4500 W New Haven Rd (32904)
Rates: $49-$125
(321) 724-2050
(800) 272-6232

RIO VISTA MOTEL
1046 S Harbor City Blvd (32901)
Rates: $29-$49
(321) 727-2818

SUPER 8 MOTEL
1515 S Harbor City Blvd (32901)
Rates: $60
(321) 723-4430
(800) 800-8000

TRAVELODGE
4505 W New Haven Ave (32904)
Rates: $36-$60
(321) 724-5450
(800) 578-7878

MEXICO BEACH

OCEAN BREEZE LODGE
4103 Hwy 98 & 42nd St (34210)
Rates: n/a
(850) 648-4800

PELICAN POINT MOTEL
4001 40th St (34210)
Rates: n/a
(850) 648-4361

SANDMAN MOTEL & APTS
2303 Hwy 98 (34210)
Rates: n/a
(850) 648-8244

MIAMI

CLARION HOTEL & SUITES
100 SE 4th St (33131)
Rates: $89-$199
(305) 374-5100
(800) 252-7466

CLUB HOTEL BY DOUBLETREE
1101 NW 57th Ave (33126)
Rates: $84-$119
(305) 266-0000
(800) 222-8733

EMBASSY SUITES INTL AIRPORT
3974 NW South River Rd (33142)
Rates: $100-$165
(305) 634-5000
(800) 362-2779

GROVE ISLE RESORT
4 Grove Isle Dr (33133)
Rates: n/a
(305) 858-8300
(800) 884-7683

HAMPTON INN DOWNTOWN
2500 Brickell Ave (33129)
Rates: $110-$120
(305) 854-2070
(800) 426-7866

HAMPTON INN-AIRPORT WEST
3620 NW 79th Ave (33166)
Rates: $109-$139
(305) 573-0777
(800) 426-7866

HILTON HOTEL-MIAMI AIRPORT
5101 Blue Lagoon Dr (33126)
Rates: $145-$210
(305) 262-1000
(800) 445-8667

HOLIDAY INN AIRPORT WEST
3255 NW 87th Ave (33126)
Rates: n/a
(305) 500-9000
(800) 465-4329

HOLIDAY INN DOWNTOWN
200 SE 2nd Ave (33131)
Rates: $109-$149
(305) 374-3000
(800) 465-4329

HOMESTEAD VILLAGE GUEST STUDIOS-AIRPT
8720 NW 33rd St (33122)
Rates: n/a
(305) 436-1811
(888) 782-9472

HOWARD JOHNSON
7330 NW 36th St (33166)
Rates: $65-$100
(305) 592-5440
(800) 446-4656

HOWARD JOHNSON HOTEL
1850 NW LeJeune Rd (33126)
Rates: $55-$120
(305) 871-4350
(800) 446-4656

HOWARD JOHNSON HOTEL
16500 NW 2nd Ave (33169)
Rates: $59-$109
(305) 945-2621
(800) 446-4656
(800) 477-5429

LA QUINTA INN
7401 NW 36th St (33166)
Rates: $76-$91
(305) 599-9902
(800) 687-6667

LA QUINTA INN & SUITES AIRPORT WEST
8730 NW 27th St (33172)
Rates: $99-$129
(305) 436-0830
(800) 687-6667

QUALITY INN SOUTH
14501 S Dixie Hwy (33176)
Rates: $81-$135
(305) 251-2000
(800) 228-5151

STAYBRIDGE SUITES BY HOLIDAY INN
3265 NW 57th Ave (33172)
Rates: n/a
(305) 500-9100
(800) 238-8000

WELLESLEY INN
8436 NW 36th St (33166)
Rates: n/a
(305) 892-4799
(800) 444-8888

MIAMI BEACH

HISTORIC BREAKWATER HOTEL
940 Ocean Dr (33139)
Rates: 149-$249
(305) 532-1220
(800) 454-1220

BRIGHAM GARDENS BED & BREAKFAST
1411 Collins Ave (33139)
Rates: $60-$130
(305) 531-1331

COMFORT INN ON THE BEACH
6261 Collins Ave (33140)
Rates: $85-$225
(305) 868-1200
(800) 228-5150

DAYS INN OCEANSIDE
4299 Collins Ave (33140)
Rates: $79-$169
(305) 673-1513
(800) 329-7466

DAYS INN ART DECO BEACHFRONT
100 21st St E (33139)
Rates: $109-$159
(305) 538-6631
(800) 329-7466

FONTAINEBLEAU HILTON RESORT
4441 Collins Ave (33140)
Rates: $239-$355
(305) 538-2000
(800) 548-8886
(800) 221-2424

HOWARD JOHNSON HOTEL
4101 Collins Ave (33140)
Rates: $95-$165
(305) 673-3337
(800) 446-4656

HOWARD JOHNSON RESORT HOTEL
4000 Alton Rd (33140)
Rates: $61-$120
(305) 532-4411
(800) 446-4656
(800) 633-8573

LOEWS MIAMI BEACH HOTEL
1601 Collins Ave (33139)
Rates: $329-$419
(305) 604-1601
(800) 235-6397

NEWPORT BEACHSIDE CROWNE PLAZA
16701 Collins Ave (33160)
Rates: $109-$205
(305) 949-1300
(800) 327-5476

OCEAN FRONT HOTEL
1230-38 Ocean Dr (33139)
Rates: $125-$335
(305) 672-2579
(800) 783-1725

REGAL HOTEL-SOUTH BEACH
436 Ocean Dr (33140)
Rates: $95-$155
(305) 532-7093

SEACOAST SUITE HOTEL
5151 Collins Ave (33140)
Rates: n/a
(305) 865-5152
(800) 523-3671

MIAMI LAKES

WELLESLEY INN
7925 NW 154th St (33016)
Rates: n/a
(305) 821-8274
(800) 444-8888

MAIMI SPRINGS

BAYMONT INN & SUITES
3501 NW Le Jeune Rd (33142)
Rates: $99-$109
(305) 871-1777
(800) 301-0200

CLARION HOTEL AIRPORT
5301 NW 36th St (33166)
Rates: $120-$199
(305) 871-1000
(800) 252-74566

COMFORT INN AIRPORT EAST
5125 NW 36th St (33166)
Rates: $116-$199
(305) 887-2153
(800) 228-5150

COMFORT INN & SUITES MIAMI AIRPORT
5301 NW 36th St (33166)
Rates: $110-$199
(305) 871-6000
(800) 228-5150

MAINSTAY SUITES
101 Fairway Dr (33166)
Rates: $65-$125
(305) 871-0448
(800) 660-6246

RED ROOF INN MIAMI AIRPORT
3401 NW Le Jeune Rd (33142)
Rates: $70-$100
(305) 871-4221
(800) 843-7663

SLEEP INN MIAMI AIRPORT
105 Fairways Dr (33166)
Rates: $116-$199
(305) 871-7553
(800) 753-3746

MICANOPY

SCOTTISH INNS
Rt 2, Box 804 (32667)
Rates: $21-$25
(352) 466-3163
(800) 251-1962

SHADY OAK BED & BREAKFAST
203 Cholokka Blvd, Bx 236 (32667)
Rates: n/a
(352) 466-3476

MILTON

COMFORT INN
4962 SR 87 S (32583)
Rates: $49-$99
(850) 623-1511
(800) 228-5150

RED CARPET INN
4905 Hwy 87 S (32583)
Rates: n/a
(850) 626-7631
(800) 251-1962

MOUNT DORA

LAKE OLA BEACH MOTEL
4816 N Orange Blossom Tr (32757)
Rates: n/a
(352) 383-4713

NAPLES

BAYMONT INN & SUITES
185 Bedzel Cir (33942)
Rates: $84-$102
(941) 352-8400
(800) 301-0200

FLORIDA VACATION ACCOMMODATIONS
3757 Tamiami Tr N (34103)
Rates: $140-$300+
(941) 261-7577
(800) 828-0042

KNIGHTS INN
6600 Dudley Dr (33999)
Rates: $40-$100
(941) 434-0444
(800) 843-5644

NAPLES BATH & TENNIS CLUB
4995 Airport Rd N (33942)
Rates: $90-$235
(941) 261-5777

RED ROOF INN
1925 Davis Blvd (33942)
Rates: $100-$140
(941) 774-3117
(800) 843-7663

RESIDENCE INN BY MARRIOTT
4075 Tamiami Tr N (34103)
Rates: $100-$249
(941) 659-1300
(800) 331-3131

WATERSIDE VILLAS
2864 Gulfview Dr (33942)
Rates: $525-$740/Weekly
(941) 732-2007

WELLESLEY INN & SUITES
1555 5th Ave S (33942)
Rates: $99-$149
(941) 793-4646
(800) 444-8888

WORLD TENNIS CENTER & RESORT
4800 Airport Rd (33942)
Rates: $50-$249
(941) 263-1900
(800) 292-6662

NAVARRE

COMFORT INN & CONFERENCE CENTER
8680 Navarre Pkwy (32566)
Rates: $89-$113
(850) 939-1761
(800) 228-5150

NEW PORT RICHEY

ECONO LODGE
7631 US Hwy 19 (34652)
Rates: $60-$110
(727) 845-4990
(800) 553-2666
(800) 889-9083

NEW SMYRNA BEACH

BUENA VISTA MOTEL
500 N Causeway (32169)
Rates: $35-$60
(904) 428-5565

SMYRNA MOTEL
1050 N Dixie Frwy (32168)
Rates: $45-$75
(904) 428-2495

NICEVILLE

COMFORT INN
101 Hwy 85 N (32578)
Rates: $60-$120
(850) 678-8077
(800) 228-5150

HOLIDAY INN EXPRESS
106 Bayshore Dr (32578)
Rates: n/a
(850) 678-9131
(800) 465-4329

NOKOMIS

ROYAL COACHMAN RESORT
1070 Laurel Rd E (34275)
Rates: n/a
(941) 488-9674

OCALA

BEST WESTERN OCALA PARK CENTRE
3701 SW 38th Ave (34474)
Rates: $49-$77
(352) 237-4848
(800) 528-1234
(800) 704-0849

BUDGET HOST
4013 NW Blitchton Rd (34482)
Rates: $36-$62
(352) 732-6940
(800) 283-4678

COMFORT INN
4040 W Silver Springs Blvd (34482)
Rates: $55-$75
(352) 629-8850
(800) 228-5150

DAYS INN
3620 W Silver Springs Blvd (34475)
Rates: $40-$85
(352) 629-0091
(800) 329-7466

DAYS INN
3811 NW Blitchton Rd (34482)
Rates: $55-$125
(352) 629-7041
(800) 329-7466

HOLIDAY INN
3621 W Silver Sprgs Blvd (34475)
Rates: $109
(352) 629-0381
(800) 465-4329
(800) 942-4420

HOWARD JOHNSON
3951 NW Blitchton Rd (34482)
Rates: $40-$150
(352) 629-7021
(800) 446-4656

LA QUINTA INN & SUITES
3530 SW 36th Ave (34474)
Rates: $75-$109
(352) 861-1137
(800) 687-6667

MOTOR INNS MOTEL & RV RESORT
3601 W Silver Spgs Blvd (34475)
Rates: n/a
(352) 629-6902

QUALITY INN
3767 NW Blitchton Rd (34475)
Rates: $49-$75
(352) 732-2300
(800) 228-5151

RAMADA INN & CONFERENCE CENTER
3810 NW Blitchton Rd (34482)
Rates: $55-$85
(352) 732-3131
(800) 272-6232

SOUTHLAND MOTEL
1260 E Silver Sprgs Blvd (34470)
Rates: $19-$39
(352) 351-0113

SUPER 8 MOTEL
3924 W Silver Sprgs Blvd (34482)
Rates: $39-$62
(352) 629-8794
(800) 800-8000

OKEECHOBEE

BUDGET INN
201 S Parrott Ave (34974)
Rates: $59-$89
(863) 763-3185

ECONOMY INN
507 N Parrott Ave (34974)
Rates: $45-$79
(863) 763-1148

FORD'S WANTA LINGA MOTEL
3225 SE Hwy 441 (34974)
Rates: n/a
(863) 763-1020
(800) 754-0428

OLD TOWN

SUWANNEE GABLES MOTEL
HC 3, Box 208 (32680)
Rates: $48-$115
(352) 542-7752

ORANGE PARK

BEST WESTERN OF ORANGE PARK
300 Park Ave N (32073)
Rates: $61-$66
(904) 264-1211
(800) 528-1234
(800) 533-1211

CLUB CONTINENTAL SUITES
2143 Astor St (32073)
Rates: n/a
(904) 264-6070
(800) 877-6070

COMFORT INN
341 Park Ave (32073)
Rates: $69-$84
(904) 264-3297
(800) 228-5150

WILSON INN
4580 Collins Rd (32073)
Rates: $40-$55
(904) 264-4466

ORLANDO

AMERISUITES AIRPORT
7500 Augusta Natl Dr (32822)
Rates: $99-$109
(407) 240-3939
(800) 833-1516

AMERISUITES ORLANDO CONV CENTER
8741 Int'l Dr (32819)
Rates: $89-$149
(407) 370-4720
(800) 833-1516
(800) 787-0353

BAYMONT INN & SUITES
2051 Consulate Dr (32837)
Rates: $64
(407) 240-0500
(800) 301-0200

BEST WESTERN INN ORLANDO
2014 W Colonial Dr (32804)
Rates: $69-$129
(407) 841-8600
(800) 528-1234
(800) 645-6386

COMFORT INN NORTH
830 Lee Rd (32810)
Rates: $79-$125
(407) 629-4000
(800) 228-5150

COMFORT SUITES AIRPORT
7900 Conway Rd (32817)
Rates: $55-$109
(407) 581-7900
(800) 228-5150

DAYS INN E OF UNIVERSITY STUDIO
5827 Caravan Ct (32819)
Rates: $89-$159
(407) 351-3800
(800) 327-2111

AREA CODES - If the local number doesn't connect, check for a new area code.

DAYS INN ORLANDO
2500 W 33rd St (32839)
Rates: $39-$250
(407) 841-3731
(800) 329-7466

DAYS INN ORLANDO AIRPORT
2323 McCoy Rd (32809)
Rates: $39-$150
(407) 959-6100
(800) 329-7466

DAYS INN INT'L DRIVE
7200 Int'l Dr (32819)
Rates: $62-$130
(407) 351-1200
(800) 329-7466

DAYS INN-SEA WORLD
9990 Int'l Dr (32819)
Rates: $59-$118
(407) 352-8700
(800) 329-7466

DELTA ORLANDO RESORT
5715 Major Blvd (32819)
Rates: $118-$158
(407) 351-3340
(800) 634-4763
(800) 268-1133

ECONO LODGE CENTRAL
3300 W Colonial Dr (32808)
Rates: $46-$85
(407) 293-7221
(800) 553-2666
(800) 293-7234

FLORIDA CONDOMINIUMS
3905 Coronation Ct (32839)
Rates: $46-$90
(407) 425-2999
(800) 247-2999

HOLIDAY INN INTERNATIONAL DRIVE RESORT
6515 Int'l Dr (32819)
Rates: $89-$225
(407) 351-3500
(800) 465-4329

HOLIDAY INN SELECT
5750 T.G. Lee Blvd (32822)
Rates: n/a
(407) 851-6400
(800) 465-4329

HOLIDAY INN-UNIVERSAL STUDIOS
5905 Kirkman Rd (32819)
Rates: $89-$109
(407) 351-3333
(800) 465-4329

HOMES 4U - DISNEY AREA VACATION HOMES
1020 Elmwood St Suite 6 (32801)
Rates: $100-$149
(407) 898-9758
(888) 746-5446

HOWARD JOHNSON
929 W Colonial Dr (32804)
Rates: $35-$95
(407) 843-1360
(800) 382-6261

HOWARD JOHNSON HOTEL & SUITES
9956 Hawaiian Ct (32819)
Rates: $49-$169
(407) 351-5100
(800) 446-4656

HOWARD JOHNSON PLAZA HOTEL
3835 McCoy Rd (32812)
Rates: $59-$129
(407) 859-2711
(800) 446-4656

HOWARD JOHNSON PLAZA RESORT-UNIVERSAL GATEWAY
7050 Kirkman Rd (32819)
Rates: $64-$102
(407) 351-2000
(800) 446-4656

KNIGHTS INN
221 E Colonial Dr (32801)
Rates: $39-$69
(407) 425-9065
(800) 843-5644

LA QUINTA INN AIRPORT
7931 Daetwyler Dr (32812)
Rates: $85-$105
(407) 857-9215
(800) 687-6667

LA QUINTA INN & SUITES AIRPORT NORTH
7160 N Frontage Rd (32812)
Rates: $102-$122
(407) 240-5000
(800) 687-6667

LA QUINTA INN & SUITES-UCF
11805 Research Pkwy (32812)
Rates: $50-$99
(407) 737-6075
(800) 687-6667

LA QUINTA INN-INT'L DRIVE
8300 Jamaican Ct (32819)
Rates: $75-$105
(407) 351-1660
(800) 687-6667

MASTERS INN
8222 Jamaican St (32819)
Rates: $69-$89
(407) 345-1172

MOTEL 6 UNIVERSAL STUDIOS
5909 American Way (32819)
Rates: $38-$44
(407) 351-6500
(800) 466-8356

MOTEL 6
5300 Adanson Rd (32810)
Rates: $35-$42
(407) 647-1444
(800) 466-8356

QUALITY INN
7600 Int'l Dr (32819)
Rates: $39-$99
(407) 996-1600
(800) 228-5151

QUALITY INN PLAZA
9000 Int'l Dr (32819)
Rates: $39-$99
(407) 345-8585
(800) 999-8585
(800) 228-5151

RED ROOF INN
9922 Hawaiian Ct (32819)
Rates: $50-$100
(407) 352-1507
(800) 843-7663

RODEWAY INN
6327 Int'l Dr (32819)
Rates: $39-$95
(407) 996-4444
(800) 228-2000

SILVER LEAF SUITES
5630 Monterey Dr (32811)
Rates: $79-$119
(407) 295-0883

TRAVELODGE
409 N Magnolia Ave (32801)
Rates: $55-$80
(407) 423-1671
(800) 578-7878

VERANDA BED & BREAKFAST INN
115 N Summerlin Ave (32801)
Rates: $46-$90
(407) 849-0321
(800) 420-6822

WELLESLEY INN & SUITES
5635 Windhover Dr (32819)
Rates: $70-$100
(407) 345-0026
(800) 444-8888

WELLESLEY INN & SUITES
8687 Commodity Cir (32819)
Rates: $95-$115
(407) 248-8010
(800) 444-8888

ORMOND BEACH

BUDGET HOST INN
1633 US 1 & I-95 (32174)
Rates: $29-$79
(904) 672-7310
(800) 283-4678

COMFORT INN INTERSTATE
1567 N US 1 & I-95 (32174)
Rates: $79-$160
(904) 672-8621
(800) 228-5150

COMFORT INN ON THE BEACH
507 S Atlantic Ave (32176)
Rates: $60-$180
(904) 677-8550
(800) 228-5150

DAYS INN
1608 N US 1 & I-95 (32174)
Rates: $40-$189
(904) 672-7341
(800) 329-7466

DAYS INN OCEANFRONT-N
839 S Atlantic Ave (32176)
Rates: $45-$295
(904) 677-6600
(800) 329-7466

DRIFTWOOD BEACH MOTEL
657 S Atlantic Ave (32176)
Rates: $45-$71
(904) 677-1331
(800) 490-8935

JAMAICAN BEACH MOTEL
505 S Atlantic Ave (32176)
Rates: $30-$130
(904) 677-3353
(800) 336-3353

MAKAI BEACH LODGE
707 S Atlantic Ave (32174)
Rates: $50-$149
(904) 677-8060
(800) 799-1112

AREA CODES - If the local number doesn't connect, check for a new area code.

SCOTTISH INNS
1608 US 1 N
(32174)
Rates: n/a
(904) 677-8860
(800) 251-1962

PALATKA

THE OAKS MOTEL
Rt 3, Box 50,
Hwy 17 (32131)
Rates: $50-$89
(904) 328-1545

PALM BAY

MOTEL 6
1170 Malabar Rd
(32909)
Rates: $33-$46
(407) 951-8222
(800) 466-8356

PALM BEACH

**BRAZILIAN
COURT HOTEL**
301 Australian
Ave (33480)
Rates: $100-$170
(561) 655-7740
(800) 552-0355

**CHESTERFIELD
HOTEL DELUXE**
363 Cocoanut
Row (33480)
Rates: $229-$450
(561) 659-5800
(800) 243-7871

**FOUR SEASONS
OCEAN GRAND**
2800 S Ocean
Blvd (33480)
Rates: $385-$660
(561) 582-2800
(800) 432-2335
(800) 332-3442

**HEART OF PALM
BEACH HOTEL**
160 Royal Palm
Way (33480)
Rates: $149-$259
(561) 655-5600
(800) 523-5377

PLAZA INN
215 Brazilian Ave
(33480)
Rates: $195-$250
(561) 832-8666
(800) 233-2632

PALM BEACH GARDENS

**EDWARD'S
VACATION
RENTAL**
13107 Flamingo
Terr (33410)
Rates: $900-$1300
Weekly
(561) 622-2077

**HERON CAY BED
& BREAKFAST**
15106 Palmwood
Rd (33410)
Rates: n/a
(561) 744-6315

**INNS OF
AMERICA**
4123 Northlake
Blvd (33410)
Rates: $81
(407) 626-4918
(800) 826-0778

PALM BEACH SHORES

**BEST WESTERN
SEASPRAY INN-
SINGER ISLAND**
123 S Ocean Dr
(33404)
Rates: $100-$170
(561) 844-0233
(800) 528-1234
(800) 330-0233

PALM COAST

**MICROTEL INN
& SUITES**
16 Kingswood Dr
(32137)
Rates: $39-$69
(888) 771-7171

**PALM COAST
VILLAS**
5454 N
Oceanshore Blvd
(32137)
Rates: $40-$45
(904) 445-3525

PALM HARBOR

**FOUR POINTS
SHERATON**
34611 US 19 N
(34684)
Rates: $50-$99
(727) 942-0358

KNIGHTS INN
34106 US 19 N
(34684)
Rates: $79
(727) 789-2002
(800) 843-5644

**PALM HARBOR
RESORT/CABINS**
2119 Alt 19 N
(34683)
Rates: n/a
(727) 785-3402

RED ROOF INN
32000 US 19 N
(34684)
Rates: $60-$76
(727) 786-2529
(800) 843-7663

PALMETTO

BAYSHORE INN
3512 US 41 N
(34221)
Rates: $35-$50
(941) 722-7761

LEE'S MOTEL
3311 US Hwy 41
N (34221)
Rates: $30-$50
(941) 729-2676

**PELICAN PERCH
APARTMENTS**
4111 10th St W
(34221)
Rates: $50-$100
(941) 729-6653

SEA INN B&B
515 US Hwy 19 N
(34221)
Rates: $50-$100
(941) 721-0365

PANAMA CITY

DAYS INN
301 W 23rd St
(32405)
Rates: $40-$110
(850) 785-0001
(800) 329-7466

**DAYS INN
CENTRAL**
4111 W Hwy 98
(32401)
Rates: $40-$125
(850) 784-1777
(800) 329-7466

**HOWARD
JOHNSON**
4601 W Hwy 98
(32401)
Rates: $60-$125
(850) 785-0222
(800) 446-4656

**LA QUINTA INN
& SUITES**
1030 E 23rd St
(32405)
Rates: $72-$95
(850) 914-0022
(800) 687-6667

SCOTTISH INNS
4907 W Hwy 98
(32401)
Rates: n/a
(850) 769-2432
(800) 251-1962

SUPER 8 MOTEL
207 N Hwy 231
(32405)
Rates: $46-$57
(850) 784-1988
(800) 800-8000

PANAMA CITY BEACH

**ADMIRAL
IMPERIAL INN
MOTEL**
16819 Front
Beach Rd (32413)
Rates: n/a
(850) 234-2142

**COCONUT
GROVE MOTOR
INN**
9725 Front Beach
Rd (32407)
Rates: $35-$99
(850) 234-3366
(800) 527-6980

CONDO WORLD
8815-A Thomas
Dr (32408)
Rates: $50-$300
(850) 234-5564
(800) 232-6636

**DOLPHIN INN AT
PINEAPPLE
BEACH RESORT**
19935 Front
Beach Rd (32413)
Rates: $40-$149
(850) 234-1788
(800) 234-1788

**EDGEWATER
BEACH RESORT
& CONFERENCE
CENTER**
11212 Front
Beach Rd (32407)
Rates: n/a
(850) 235-4044
(800) 874-8686

**HOWARD
JOHNSON
RESORT HOTEL**
9400 S Thomas
Dr (32408)
Rates: $39-$195
(850) 234-3484
(800) 446-4656
(800) 224-GULF

**PANAMA PALMS
MOTEL**
5607 Thomas Dr
(32408)
Rates: n/a
(850) 234-2806
(877)310-2267

RIVIERA MOTEL
21504 W Front
Beach Rd (32413)
Rates: $50-$135
(850) 234-2150

**SURF HIGH INN
ON THE GULF**
10611 Front
Beach Rd (32407)
Rates: $35-$61
(850) 234-2129

PEMBROKE PINES

**GRAND PALMS
GOLF &
COUNTRY CLUB
RESORT**
110 Grand Palms
Dr (33027)
Rates: $135-$155
(954) 431-8800

PENSACOLA

**COMFORT INN-
NAS CORRY**
3 New
Warrington Rd
(32506)
Rates: $79-$89
(850) 455-3233
(800) 228-5150

AREA CODES - If the local number doesn't connect, check for a new area code.

CROWNE PLAZA PENSACOLA GRAND
200 E Gregory (32501)
Rates: $50-$99
(850) 433-3336
(800) 465-4329

DAYS INN NORTH
7051 Pensacola Blvd (32505)
Rates: $49-$89
(850) 476-9090
(800) 329-7466

HOSPITALITY INN
6900 Pensacola Blvd (32506)
Rates: $50-$99
(850) 477-2333
(800) 321-0052

HOWARD JOHNSON
4126 Mobile Hwy (32506)
Rates: $30-$75
(850) 456-5731
(800) 446-4656

LA QUINTA INN
7750 N Davis Hwy (32514)
Rates: $69-$95
(850) 474-0411
(800) 687-6667

MOTEL 6 EAST
7226 Plantation Rd (32504)
Rates: $35-$49
(850) 474-1060
(800) 466-8356

MOTEL 6 NORTH
7827 N Davis Hwy (32514)
Rates: $35-$49
(850) 476-5386
(800) 466-8356

MOTEL 6 WEST
5829 Pensacola Blvd (32505)
Rates: $31-$40
(850) 477-7522
(800) 466-8356

RAMADA INN
6550 Pensacola Blvd (32505)
Rates: $56-$74
(850) 477-0711
(800) 272-6232

RAMADA INN BAYVIEW
7601 Scenic Hwy (32504)
Rates: $72-$98
(850) 477-7155
(800) 282-1212
(800) 272-6232

RAMADA LIMITED
8060 Lavelle Way (32526)
Rates: $58-$100
(850) 944-0333
(800) 272-6232

RED ROOF INN
7340 Plantation Rd (32504)
Rates: $46-$60
(850) 476-7960
(800) 843-7663

RED ROOF INN
6919 Pensacola Blvd (32504)
Rates: $44-$93
(850) 478-4499
(800) 843-7663

RESIDENCE INN BY MARRIOTT
601 E Chase St (32501)
Rates: n/a
(850) 432-0202
(800) 331-3131

SEVILLE INN
223 E Garden St (32501)
Rates: $35-$69
(850) 433-8331
(800) 277-7275

SHONEY'S INN
8080 N Davis Hwy (32514)
Rates: $67-$85
(850) 484-8070
(800) 222-2222

SUPER 8 MOTEL
7220 Plantation Rd (32504)
Rates: $39-$55
(850) 476-8038
(800) 800-8000

SUPER 8 MOTEL
5 N New Warrington Rd (32506)
Rates: $58-$73
(850) 457-7277
(800) 800-8000

TRAVELODGE INN & SUITES
6950 Pensacola Blvd (32505)
Rates: $39-$89
(850) 473-0222
(800) 578-7878

PERRY

BEST BUDGET INN
2220 S Byron Butler Pkwy (32347)
Rates: $38-$43
(850) 584-6231
(800) 458-7215

DAYS INN
2277 S Byron Butler Pkwy (32347)
Rates: $40-$70
(850) 584-5311
(800) 329-7466

GANDY MOTOR LODGE
2239 S Byron Butler Pkwy (32347)
Rates: n/a
(850) 584-4947

SOUTHERN INN MOTEL
2238 S Byron Butler Pkwy (32347)
Rates: $30-$45
(850) 584-4221

PINELLAS PARK

DAYS INN
9359 US Hwy 19 N Park (34665)
Rates: $39-$69
(727) 577-3838
(800) 329-7466

LA MARK CHARLES MOTEL
6200 34th St N (34665)
Rates: $75-$120
(727) 527-7334
(800) 448-6781

LA QUINTA INN
7500 US 19 N (34665)
Rates: $75-$105
(727) 545-5611
(800) 687-6667

PLANT CITY

DAYS INN
301 S Frontage Rd (33566)
Rates: $70-$85
(813) 752-0570
(800) 329-7466

RAMADA INN
2011 N Wheeler St Plant City (33566)
Rates: $64-$130
(813) 752-3141
(800) 272-6232

PLANTATION

AMERISUITES
8530 W Broward Blvd (33324)
Rates: $116-$134
(954) 370-2220
(800) 833-1516

HOLIDAY INN
1711 N University Dr (33322)
Rates: $159
(954) 472-5600
(800) 465-4329

LA QUINTA INN & SUITES
8101 Peters Rd (33324)
Rates: $85-$129
(954) 476-6047
(800) 687-6667

RESIDENCE INN BY MARRIOTT
130 N University Dr (33324)
Rates: $89-$179
(954) 723-0300
(800) 331-3131

WELLESLEY INN
7901 SW 6th St (33324)
Rates: $110
(954) 473-8257
(800) 444-8888

PLANTATION KEY

TROPIC VISTA MOTEL
90701 Overseas Hwy (33070)
Rates: $38-$95
(305) 852-8799

POMPANO BEACH

CARIB TERRACE MOTEL
552 N Ocean Blvd (33062)
Rates: n/a
(954) 941-9130

GLENDORI APTS. OF POMP BEACH
2441 NE 10th Ct (33062)
Rates: n/a
(954) 781-0311

MOTEL 6
1201 NW 31st Ave (33069)
Rates: $37-$42
(954) 577-3838
(800) 466-8356

SEA CASTLE RESORT MOTEL
730 N Ocean Blvd (33062)
Rates: $91-$169
(954) 941-2570
(800) 331-4666

WELLESLEY INN & SUITES
1401 SW 15th Ave (33062)
Rates: $119-$129
(954) 783-1050
(800) 444-8888

PORT CHARLOTTE

ECONO LODGE
4100 Tamiami Tr (33952)
Rates: $35-$95
(941) 743-2442
(800) 553-2666

PORT CHARLOTTE MOTEL
3491 Tamiami Tr (33952)
Rates: $30+
(941) 625-4177
(800) 559-5961

QUALITY INN DOWNTOWN
3400 Tamiami Tr (33952)
Rates: $85-$130
(941) 625-4181
(800) 228-5151

PORT RICHEY

COMFORT INN
11810 US 19
(34668)
Rates: $65-$80
(727) 863-3336
(800) 228-5150

DAYS INN
11736 US Hwy 19
(34668)
Rates: $38-$8
(727) 863-1502
(800) 329-7466

PORT SALERNO

PIRATES COVE RESORT/MARINA
4307 SE Bayview
St (34992)
Rates: $80-$130
(561) 287-2500
(800) 332-1414

PUNTA GORDA

BEST WESTERN WATERFRONT
300 Retta
Esplanade
(33950)
Rates: $89-$109
(941) 639-1165
(800) 528-1234
(800) 525-1022

MOTEL 6
9300 Knights Dr
(33950)
Rates: $31-$50
(941) 639-9585
(800) 466-8356

PALMS & PINES RIVERSIDE RESORT
5400 Riverside
Dr (33950)
Rates: $150-$350
Weekly
(941) 639-5461

QUINCY

ALLISON HOUSE BED & BREAKFAST
215 N Madison St
(32351)
Rates: $80-$95
(850) 875-2511

HOLIDAY INN EXPRESS
Rt 3, Box 3950
(32351)
Rates: n/a
(850) 875-2500
(800) 465-4329

HOWARD JOHNSON EXP
500 W Orange
Ave (32351)
Rates: n/a
(800) 446-4656

QUINCY MOTOR LODGE
368 E Jefferson
(32351)
Rates: n/a
(850) 627-8929

WHIPPOORWILL SPRTSMNS LDG
Rt 3 (32351)
Rates: n/a
(850) 875-2605

REDINGTON SHORES

MONTEREY CONDO MOTEL
17880 Gulf Blvd
(33708)
Rates: n/a
(813) 391-5083

SAN REMO BEACH CLUB RESORT
18320 Gulf Blvd
(33708)
Rates: n/a
(813) 393-4810
(800) 950-7366

RIDGE MANOR

RIDGE MANOR MOTEL
5205 Treiman
Blvd (33523)
Rates: $34-$49
(352) 583-2109

RUSKIN

BAHIA BEACH ISLAND RESORT & MARINA
611 Destiny Dr
(33570)
Rates: $89-$109
(813) 645-3291

SOUTHERN COMFORT B&B
2309 Ravine Dr
(33570)
Rates: $95
(813) 645-6361

SAFETY HARBOR

SAFETY HARBOR RESORT & SPA
105 N Bayshore
Dr (34695)
Rates: $139-$249
(727) 726-1161
(899) 237-8772

ST. AUGUSTINE

ANCHORAGE MOTOR INN
1 Dolphin Dr
(32084)
Rates: $50-$99
(904) 829-9041

BALI HAI MOTEL
601 Anastasia
Blvd (32084)
Rates: $30-$45
(904) 825-4535

BAREFOOT TERRACE CONDOS
6240 A1A S
(32084)
Rates: n/a
(904) 471-9750

BUDGET INN
12 Anastasia Blvd
(32084)
Rates: $30-$100
(904) 824-1962

DAYS INN HISTORIC
2800 N Ponce de
Leon Blvd
(32084)
Rates: $41-$120
(904) 829-6581
(800) 329-7466
(800) 331-9995

DAYS INN WEST
2560 SR 16
(32092)
Rates: $44-$89
(904) 824-4341
(800) 329-7466
(800) 584-1473

ECONOMY INN
94 San Marco Ave
(32084)
Rates: n/a
(904) 824-4406

FIVE STAR REALTY & VACATION RENTALS
6233 A1A S
(32084)
Rates: n/a
(904) 471-9750

GUESTHOUSE LION INN
420 Anastasia
Blvd (32084)
Rates: $45-$150
(904) 824-2831

HOLIDAY RESORT MOTEL
530 A1A Beach
Blvd (32084)
Rates: $30-$100
(904) 471-3505

HOWARD JOHNSON RESORT HOTEL
300 A1A Beach
Blvd (32084)
Rates: $40-$150
(904) 471-2575
(800) 446-4656
(800) 752-4037

MONSON BAYFRONT INN
32 Avenida
Menendez (32084)
Rates: $46-$100
(904) 829-2277

OCEAN BLUE MOTEL
10 Vilano Rd
(32095)
Rates: $30-$100
(904) 829-5939

OCEAN CLUB CONDOS
11 Dondanville
Rd (32084)
Rates: n/a
(904) 471-6852

OCEAN CLUB CONDOS
21 Dondanville
Rd (32084)
Rates: n/a
(904) 461-3352

RAMADA INN
116 San Marco
Ave (32084)
Rates: $59-$120
(904) 824-4352
(800) 272-6232

RAMADA LIMITED
2535 St. Rd 16
(32092)
Rates: $54-$145
(904) 829-5643
(800) 272-6232

SEA SHORE MOTEL
480 A1A Beach
Blvd (32084)
Rates: $30-$100
(904) 471-3101

SUPER 8 MOTEL
3552 N Ponce de
Leon Blvd
(32084)
Rates: $35-$100
(904) 824-6399
(800) 800-8000

ST. AUGUSTINE BEACH

BEST WESTERN OCEAN INN
3955 Hwy A1A
(32084)
Rates: $69-$170
(904) 471-8010
(800) 528-1234

HOLIDAY INN BEACHSIDE
860 A1A Beach
Blvd (32084)
Rates: $110-$130
(904) 471-2555
(800) 465-4329
(800) 626-7263

ST. GEORGE ISLAND

ANCHOR VACATION PROPERTIES
119 Franklin Blvd
(32328)
Rates: n/a
(904) 927-2625
(800) 824-0416

AREA CODES - If the local number doesn't connect, check for a new area code.

PRUDENTIAL RESORT/VAC RENTALS
123 Gulf Beach Dr W (32328)
Rates: $160-$760/ Two nights
(904) 927-2666
(800) 332-5196

ST. PETERSBURG

HILTON HOTEL BEACHFRONT
333 1st St S (33711)
Rates: $145-$205
(727) 894-5000
(800) 445-8667

HOWARD JOHNSON
4601 34th St S (33711)
Rates: $44-$109
(800) 446-4656

LA QUINTA INN
4999 34th St N (33714)
Rates: $69-$95
(727) 527-8421
(800) 687-6667

VALLEY FORGE MOTEL
6825 Central Ave (33710)
Rates: $35-$99
(727) 345-0135

ST. PETERSBURG BEACH

BAY PALMS MOTEL APTS
7241 Bay St (33706)
Rates: n/a
(727) 360-1754

BAY STREET VILLAS/RESORT MARINA
7201 Bay St (33706)
Rates: $90-$140
(727) 360-5591
(800) 566-8358

HOWARD JOHNSON RESORT HOTEL
6100 Gulf Blvd (33706)
Rates: $75-$115
(727) 360-7041
(800) 446-4656
(800) 231-1419

RITZ MOTEL
4237 Gulf Blvd (33706)
Rates: $59-$99
(727) 360-7642

SANFORD

DAYS INN
4650 SR 46 W (32771)
Rates: $40-$120
(407) 323-6500
(800) 329-7466

KATIE'S WEKIVA RIVER LANDNG
190 Katie's Cove (32771)
Rates: $30-$45
(407) 628-1482

MARINA HOTEL & CONFERENCE CENTER
530 N Palmetto Ave (32771)
Rates: $55-$125
(407) 323-1910
(800) 290-1910

SUPER 8 MOTEL
4750 SR 46 W (32771)
Rates: $45-$85
(407) 323-3445
(800) 800-8000

SANIBEL ISLAND

CARIBE BEACH RESORT
2669 W Gulf Dr (33957)
Rates: $100-$249
(941) 472-1166
(800) 330-1593

WATERSIDE INN ON THE BEACH
3033 W Gulf Dr (33957)
Rates: $184-$270
(941) 472-1345

SARASOTA

ALINA MOTEL
6926 15th St E (34243)
Rates: $50-$100
(941) 755-6601

AZURE TIDES RESORT MOTEL
1330 Ben Franklin Dr (34236)
Rates: $99-$250
(941) 388-2101
(800) 326-8433

CALAIS MOTEL-APARTMENTS
1735 Stickney Point Rd (34231)
Rates: $79-$98
(941) 921-5797

COMFORT INN
4800 N Tamiami Tr (34234)
Rates: $55-$105
(941) 355-7091
(800) 228-5150

COMFORT INN
5778 Clark Rd (34233)
Rates: $79-$129
(941) 921-7750
(800) 228-5150

COQUINA ON THE BEACH RESORT
1008 Ben Franklin Dr (34236)
Rates: $169-$199
(941) 388-2141
(800) 833-2141

DAYS INN-AIRPORT
4900 N Tamiami Tr (34234)
Rates: $72-$110
(941) 355-9721
(800) 329-7466

HOWARD JOHNSON EXP
811 S Tamiami Tr (34234)
Rates: $39-$120
(941) 365-0350
(800) 446-4656

RAMADA INN
5774 Clark Rd (34233)
Rates: $100-$130
(941) 921-7812
(800) 272-6232

REGENCY INN & SUITES
4200 N Tamiami Tr (34234)
Rates: $50-$149
(941) 355-7616
(888) 773-4362

WELLESLEY INNS
1803 N Tamiami Tr (34234)
Rates: $100-$130
(941) 366-5128
(800) 444-8888

SATELLITE BEACH

DAYS INN
180 Hwy A1A (32937)
Rates: $69-$100
(521) 777-3552
(800) 329-7466

SEBASTIAN

SPORTSMAN'S MARINE & LODGE
412 S Indian River Dr (32958)
Rates: n/a
(561) 589-2020

SEBRING

INN ON THE LAKES
3100 Golfview Rd (33870)
Rates: $65-$82
(941) 471-9400
(800) 531-LAKE

SEFFNER

MASTERS INN
6010 SR 579 N (33584)
Rates: $30-$99
(813) 621-4681

SIESTA KEY

GULF TERRACE VACATION APARTMENTS
1105 Point of Rocks Rd (34242)
Rates: $620-$755/ Weekly
(941) 349-4444

MIRAMAR BEACH APTS
92 Avenida Messina (34242)
Rates: $100-$150
(941) 349-6800

SURFRIDER BEACH APTS
6400 Midnight Pass Rd (34242)
Rates: $69-$130
(941) 349-2121

TROPICAL BREEZE INN
140 Columbus Blvd (34242)
Rates: $375-$1500/Weekly
(941) 349-1125
(800) 300-2492

TURTLE BEACH RESORT
9049 Midnight Pass Rd (34242)
Rates: $1400-$2035/Weekly
(941) 349-4554

SILVER SPRINGS

DAYS INN
5001 E Silver Spgs Blvd (32688)
Rates: $45-$80
(352) 236-2891
(800) 329-7466

SUN PLAZA MOTEL
5461 E Silver Spgs Blvd (32689)
Rates: $35-$55
(352) 236-2343

AREA CODES - If the local number doesn't connect, check for a new area code.

SINGER ISLAND

DAYS INN OCEANFRONT RESORT
2700 N Ocean Dr (33404)
Rates: $59-$209
(561) 848-8661
(800) 329-7466

SOUTH BAY

OKEECHOBEE INN
265 N US Hwy 27 (33493)
Rates: $40-$45
(561) 996-7617

SOUTH DAYTONA

RED CARPET INN
1855 S Ridgewood Ave (32119)
Rates: $150
(904) 767-6681
(800) 251-1962

SOUTH PALM BEACH

PALM BEACH HAWAIIAN OCEAN INN
3550 S Ocean Blvd (33480)
Rates: $140-$310
(561) 582-5631

SPRING HILL

BEST WESTERN WEEKI WACHEE RESORT
6172 Commercial Way (34606)
Rates: $59-$89
(352) 596-2007
(800) 528-1234
(800) 490-8268

STARKE

BEST WESTERN MOTOR INN
1290 N Temple Ave (32091)
Rates: $40-$130
(904) 964-6744
(800) 528-1234

DAYS INN
1101 N Temple Ave (32091)
Rates: $50-$99
(904) 964-7600
(800) 329-7466

SLEEPY HOLLOW MOTEL
2317 N Temple Ave (32091)
Rates: $25-$28
(904) 964-5006

STEINHATCHEE

STEINHATCHEE LANDING RSRT
Hwy 51 N (32359)
Rates: $140-$367
(352) 498-3513
(800) 584-1709

STEINHATCHEE RIVER INN
1111 Riverside Dr (32359)
Rates: $60-$70
(352) 498-4049

SUNSET PLACE RESORT MOTEL
115 1st St SW (32359)
Rates: $85-$95
(352) 498-0860

STUART

HOWARD JOHNSON
950 S Federal Hwy (34994)
Rates: $65-$90
(561) 287-3171
(800) 446-4656

INDIAN RIVER PLANTATION MARRIOTT RESORT
555 NE Ocean Blvd (34996)
Rates: $179-$250
(561) 225-3700
(800) 775-5936

PIRATES COVE RESORT/MARINA
4307 SE Bayview St (34992)
Rates: $145-$249
(561) 287-2500
(800) 332 1414

SUGARLOAF KEY

SUGARLOAF LODGE RESORT
US 1 (33044)
Rates: $65-$175
(305) 745-3211
(800) 553-6097

SUN CITY CENTER

SUN CITY CENTER HOTEL
1335 Rickenbacker Dr (33573)
Rates: $79
(813) 634-3331
(800) 237-8200

SUNNY ISLES

NEWPORT BEACHSIDE-CROWNE PLAZA RESORT
16701 Collins Ave (33160)
Rates: $149-$245
(305) 949-1300

SUNRISE

BAYMONT INN
13651 NW 2nd St (33325)
Rates: $96-$106
(954) 846-1200
(800) 301-0200

WELLESLEY INN-SUNRISE AT SAWGRASS
13600 NW 2nd St (33325)
Rates: $110
(954) 845-9929
(800) 444-8888

TALLAHASSEE

BEST INNS OF AMERICA
3090 N Monroe (32303)
Rates: $42-$63
(850) 562-2378
(800) 237-8466

CLARION CAPITAL HOTEL
316 W Tennessee St (32301)
Rates: $69-$199
(850) 222-9555
(800) 252-7466

COLLEGIATE VILLAGE INN
2121 W Tennessee St (32304)
Rates: $40+
(850) 576-6121

ECONO LODGE
2681 N Monroe St (32303)
Rates: $45-$94
(850) 385-6155
(800) 553-2666

HOWARD JOHNSON EXP
2726 N Monroe St (32303)
Rates: $40-$60
(850) 386-5000
(800) 446-4656

KILLEARN COUNTRY CLUB & INN
100 Tyron Cir (32308)
Rates: $54-$80
(850) 893-2186

LA QUINTA INN NORTH
2905 N Monroe St (32303)
Rates: $59-$92
(850) 385-7172
(800) 687-6667

LA QUINTA INN SOUTH
2850 Apalachee Pkwy (32301)
Rates: $59-$89
(850) 878-5099
(800) 687-6667

MOTEL 6 DOWNTOWN
1027 Apalachee Pkwy (32301)
Rates: $37-$44
(850) 877-6171
(800) 466-8356

MOTEL 6 NORTH
1481 Timberlane Rd (32312)
Rates: $40-$56
(850) 668-2600
(800) 466-8356

MOTEL 6 WEST
2738 N Monroe St (32303)
Rates: $36-$43
(850) 386-7878
(800) 466-8356

RED ROOF INN
2930 Hospitality St (32303)
Rates: $47-$62
(850) 385-7884
(800) 843-7663

RESIDENCE INN BY MARRIOTT
1880 Raymond Diehl Rd (32308)
Rates: $89-$150
(850) 422-0093
(800) 331-3131

SHONEY'S INN
2801 N Monroe St (32303)
Rates: $65-$73
(850) 386-8286
(800) 222-2222

TAMARAC

BAYMONT INN & SUITES
3800 W Commercial Blvd (33309)
Rates: $86
(954) 485-7900
(800) 301-0200

HOMESTEAD VILLAGE GUEST STUDIOS
3873 W Commercial Blvd (33309)
Rates: $62-$110
(954) 733-6644
(888) 782-9473

WELLESLEY INN & SUITES
5070 N SR 7 (33319)
Rates: $95
(954) 484-6909
(800) 444-8888

AREA CODES - If the local number doesn't connect, check for a new area code.

TAMPA

AMERISUITES AIRPORT
4811 W Main St (33607)
Rates: $139-$199
(813) 282-1037
(800) 833-1516

AMERISUITES BUSCH GARDENS
11408 N 30th St (33610)
Rates: $89-$119
(813) 979-1922
(800) 833-1516

BAYMONT INN-BUSCH GARDNS
9202 30th St N (33612)
Rates: $79
(813) 930-6900
(800) 301-0200

BAYMONT INN FAIRGROUNDS
4811 US 301 N (33610)
Rates: $69-$76
(813) 626-0885
(800) 301-0200

BUDGETEL INN SOUTHEAST
602 S Falkenburg Rd (33619)
Rates: $85-$92
(813) 684-4007
(800) 301-0200

BEST WESTERN ALL SUITES HOTEL-USF
3001 University Center Dr (33612)
Rates: $109-$149
(813) 971-8930
(800) 528-1234
(800) SUNSHINE

DAYS INN AIRPORT/ STADIUM
2522 N Dale Mabry (33607)
Rates: $79-$145
(813) 877-6181
(800) 329-7466

DAYS INN-BUSCH GARDENS EAST
2520 N 50th St (33619)
Rates: $49-$175
(813) 247-3300
(800) 329-7466

DAYS INN-BUSCH GARDENS NORTH
701 E Fletcher Ave (33612)
Rates: $58-$90
(813) 977-1550
(800) 329-7466

EAST LAKE INN MOTEL
6529 E Hillsborough Ave (33610)
Rates: $30-$50
(813) 622-8339

ECONO LODGE BUSCH GRDNS
1701 E Busch Blvd (33612)
Rates: $44-$89
(813) 933-7681
(800) 553-2666

EMBASSY SUITES
555 N Westshore Blvd (33609)
Rates: $139-$159
(813) 875-1555
(800) 362-2779

FOUR POINT SHERATON TAMPA EAST
7401 E Hillsborough Ave (33610)
Rates: $149-$275
(813) 626-0999
(800) 325-3535

HOLIDAY INN BUSCH GRDNS
2701 E Fowler Ave (33612)
Rates: $72-$130
(813) 971-4710
(800) 465-4329

HOLIDAY INN EXPRESS HOTEL & SUITES STADIUM/AIRPORT
4732 N Dale Mabry Hwy (33614)
Rates: $95-$105
(813) 877-6061
(800) 465-4329

HOLIDAY INN EXPRESS-USF
400 E Bears (33613)
Rates: $79
(813) 961-1000
(800) 465-4329

HOWARD JOHNSON AIRPORT-STADIUM
2055 N Dale Mabry Hwy Tampa (33607)
Rates: $64-$99
(813) 875-8818
(800) 446-4656

HOWARD JOHNSON BUSCH GRDNS
4139 E Busch Blvd (33617)
Rates: $29-$98
(813) 988-9191
(800) 446-4656

LA QUINTA INN AIRPORT
4730 Spruce St (33607)
Rates: $79-$109
(813) 287-0440
(800) 687-6667

LA QUINTA INN BUSCH GARDENS
2904 Melbourne Blvd (33605)
Rates: $50-$75
(813) 623-3591
(800) 687-6667

LA QUINTA INN & SUITES-USF
3701 E Fowler Ave (33612)
Rates: $79-$129
(813) 910-7500
(800) 687-6667

MASTERS INN-FAIRGROUNDS
6606 E Dr Martin Luth Kng (33619)
Rates: $35-$99
(813) 623-6667

MOTEL 6 DOWNTOWN
333 E Fowler Ave (33612)
Rates: $40-$61
(813) 932-4948
(800) 466-8356

MOTEL 6 FAIRGROUNDS
6510 N Hwy 301 (33610)
Rates: $40-$56
(813) 628-0888
(800) 466-8356

RED ROOF INN BRANDON
10121 Horace Ave (33619)
Rates: $66-$89
(813) 681-8484
(800) 843-7663

RED ROOF INN BUSCH GRDNS
2307 E Busch Blvd (33612)
Rates: $66-$88
(813) 932-0073
(800) 843-7663

RED ROOF INN FAIRGROUNDS
5001 N US 301 (33610)
Rates: $64-$96
(813) 623-5245
(800) 843-7663

TAHITIAN INN
601 S Dale Mabry Hwy (33609)
Rates: $44-$59
(813) 877-6721
(800) 876-1397

TAMPA STATE FAIR MOTOR INN
2708 N 50th St (33619)
Rates: $60-$90
(813) 621-2081
(800) 237-1510

TRAVELODGE
820 E Busch Blvd (33612)
Rates: $59-$119
(813) 933-4011
(800) 578-7878
(800) 228-4011

WELLESLEY INN & SUITES
1805 N Westshore Blvd (33607)
Rates: $139-$169
(813) 637-8990
(800) 444-8888

YBOR SUITES
1503 E 7th Ave (33605)
Rates: $50-$99
(813) 247-9267
(800) 254-9267

TARPON SPRINGS

DAYS INN
40050 US 19 N (34689)
Rates: $67-$125
(727) 936-8000
(800) 329-7466

GULF MANOR MOTEL
548 Whitcomb Blvd (34689)
Rates: $49-$59
(727) 937-4207

SCOTTISH INNS ON SPRING BAYOU
110 W Tarpon Ave (34689)
Rates: $30-$55
(727) 937-6121
(800) 251-1962
(888) 615-6681

TAVARES

BUDGET INN
101 W Burleigh Blvd (32778)
Rates: $65-$79
(352) 343-4666

INN ON THE GREEN
700 E Burleigh Blvd (32778)
Rates: $56-$74
(352) 343-6373
(800) 935-2935

TEMPLE TERRACE

RESIDENCE INN BY MARRIOTT
13420 N Telecom Pkwy (33637)
Rates: $139-$179
(813) 972-4400
(800) 331-3131

TITUSVILLE

BEST WESTERN SPACE SHUTTLE INN
3455 Cheney Hwy (32780)
Rates: $89-$119
(321) 269-9100
(800) 528-1234
(800) 523-7654

DAYS INN KENNEDY SPACE CENTER
3755 Cheney Hwy (32780)
Rates: $59-$149
(321) 269-4480
(800) 329-7466

HOLIDAY INN KENNEDY SPACE CENTER
4951 S Washington Ave (32780)
Rates: $79-$129
(321) 269-2121
(800) 465-4329

HOWARD JOHNSON KENNEDY SPACE CENTER
1829 Riverside Dr (32780)
Rates: $45-$79
(321) 267-7900
(800) 654-2000

TREASURE ISLAND

ANCHOR INN MOTEL APTS
10133 Gulf Blvd (33706)
Rates: $40-$149
(727) 360-1871
(800) 385-9184

CAPTAIN'S QUARTERS INN
10035 Gulf Blvd (33706)
Rates: n/a
(727) 360-1659
(800) 526-9547

COMMODORE RESORT
11760 Capri Circle (33706)
Rates: n/a
(727) 367-3100

CORAL LEE MOTEL & APTS
7925 Gulf Blvd (33706)
Rates: n/a
(727) 360-1530

GREEN GABLES MOTEL & APTS
11160 1st St E (33706)
Rates: n/a
(727) 360-0206

LORELEI RESORT
10273 Gulf Blvd (33706)
Rates: $45-$95
(727) 360-4351
(800) 354-6364

RENFRO'S BEACH COTTAGE
12108 Lagoon Ln (33706)
Rates: n/a
(727) 360-6690

SEA HORSE COTTAGES & APARTMENTS
10356 Gulf Blvd (33706)
Rates: $35-$105
(727) 367-2291
(800) 741-2291

SEA OATS BY THE GULF
12626 Sunshine Ln (33706)
Rates: $52-$125
(727) 367-7568

SURFSIDE MOTEL
11270 Gulf Blvd (33706)
Rates: $50-$99
(727) 360-6551
(800) 362-1882

VENICE

DAYS INN
1710 S Tamiami Tr (34293)
Rates: $94-$228
(941) 493-4558
(800) 329-7466

INN AT THE BEACH RESORT
725 W Venice Ave (34285)
Rates: $165-$359
(941) 484-8471
(800) 255-8471

MOTEL 6
281 US Hwy 41 Bypass N (34292)
Rates: $56-$72
(941) 485-8255
(800) 466-8356

RAMBLERS REST RESORT
1300 N River Rd (34293)
Rates: $30-$49
(941) 493-4354

VERANDA INN & CAFÉ OF VENICE
625 Tamiami Tr S (34285)
Rates: $35-$99
(941) 484-9559
(800) 345-9559

VERO BEACH

BUDGET INN
2022 US 1 (32961)
Rates: n/a
(561) 567-4331

DAYS INN
8800 20th St (32966)
Rates: $64-$79
(561) 562-9991
(800) 329-7466

HAMPTON INN
9350 19th Lane (32966)
Rates: $71-$80
(561) 770-4299
(800) 426-7866

HOLIDAY INN COUNTRYSIDE
8797 20th St (32966)
Rates: n/a
(561) 567-8321
(800) 465-4329

SOUTH BEACH MOTEL & RESORT
1705 S Ocean Dr (32961)
Rates: n/a
(561) 231-5366

WAKULLA SPRINGS

WAKULLA SPRINGS STATE PARK & LODGE
1 Spring Dr (32305)
Rates: $50-$99
(904) 224-5950

WEEKI-WACHEE

BEST WESTERN WEEKI WACHEE RESORT
6172 Commercial Way (34613)
Rates: $69-$79
(352) 596-2007
(800) 528-1234

COMFORT INN
9373 Cortez Blvd (34613)
Rates: $55-$90
(352) 596-9000
(800) 228-5150

WESLEY CHAPEL

COMFORT INN
5642 Oakley Blvd (33544)
Rates: $55-$95
(813) 991-4600
(800) 228-5150

MASTERS INN
27807 SR 54W (33543)
Rates: $49-$99
(813) 973-0155

SLEEP INN
5703 Oakley Blvd (33543)
Rates: $44-$125
(813) 973-1665
(800) 753-3746

WEST MELBOURNE

HOWARD JOHNSON
4431 W New Haven Ave (32904)
Rates: $75-$89
(321) 768-8439
(800) 446-4656

WEST PALM BEACH

COMFORT INN/ PALM BEACH LAKES
1901 Palm Beach Lakes Blvd (33409)
Rates: $109-$179
(561) 689-6100
(800) 228-5150

DAYS INN TURNPIKE
6255 Okeechobee Blvd (33417)
Rates: $48-$99
(561) 686-6000
(800) 329-7466

DAYS INN AIRPORT NORTH
2300 45th St (33407)
Rates: $59-$129
(561) 689-0450
(800) 329-7466

FAIRFIELD INN
5981 Okeechobee Blvd (33417)
Rates: $40-$89
(561) 697-3399
(800) 228-2800

HIBISCUS HOUSE HISTORIC BED & BREAKFAST
501 30th St (33407)
Rates: $95-$240
(561) 863-5633
(800) 203-4927

KNIGHTS INN
2200 45th St (33407)
Rates: $35-$129
(561) 478-1554
(800) 843-5644

MOUNT VERNON MOTOR LODGE
310 Belvedere Rd (33405)
Rates: $35-$99
(561) 832-0094
(800) 545-1520

RED ROOF INN
2421 Metro Center Blvd E (33407)
Rates: $70-$102
(561) 697-7710
(800) 846-7663

WELLESLEY INN
1910 Palm Beach
Lakes Blvd
(33409)
Rates: $64-$149
(561) 689-8540
(800) 444-8888

WILDWOOD

DAYS INN
551 E SR 44
(34785)
Rates: $60-$110
(352) 748-7766
(800) 329-7466

RED CARPET INN
US 301 & FL Tpk
(34785)
Rates: $20-$34
(352) 748-4488
(800) 251-1962

SUPER 8 MOTEL
344 E SR 44
(34785)
Rates: $40-$70
(352) 748-3783
(800) 800-8000

WILLISTON

**WILLISTON
MOTOR INN**
606 W Noble Ave
(32696)
Rates: $32-$35
(352) 528-4801

WINDERMERE

**FAMILIES FIRST
VACATION
HOMES**
7801 W Irlo
Bronson Hwy
Suite A (34786)
Rates: n/a
(407) 876-1989
(800) 393-8800

WINTER
HAVEN

**BEST WESTERN
ADMIRAL'S INN**
5665 Cypress
Gardens Blvd
(33884)
Rates: $82-$112
(941) 324-5950
(800) 528-1234
(800) 247-2799

**BUDGET HOST
DRIFTWOOD**
970 Cypress
Gardens Blvd
(33880)
Rates: $38-$46
(863) 294-4229
(800) 283-4678

CYPRESS MOTEL
5651 Cypress
Gardens Blvd
(33884)
Rates: $65-$65
(863) 324-5867
(800) 729-6706

**DAYS INN
CYPRESS
GARDESN**
200 Cypress
Gardens Blvd
(33880)
Rates: $49-$109
(941) 299-1151
(800) 329-7466

**ECONOMY
MOTOR LODGE**
329 US Hwy 27 N
(33880)
Rates: n/a
(863) 439-3688

HOLIDAY INN
1150 3rd St SW
(33880)
Rates: $46-$124
(863) 294-4451
(800) 465-4329

**HOWARD
JOHNSON**
1300 US 17 SW
(33880)
Rates: $80-$109
(863) 294-7321
(800) 446-4656

**LAKE ROY
MOTOR LODGE**
1823 Cypress
Gardens Blvd
(33884)
Rates: $46-$124
(863) 324-6320
(800) 437-9431

MILLIE'S MOTEL
2850 Lake Alred
Rd (33880)
Rates: n/a
(863) 293-5211

SCOTTISH INNS
1901 Cypress
Gardens Blvd
(33884)
Rates: $32-$62
(863) 324-3954
(800) 251-1962

WINTER PARK

**LANGFORD
RESORT HOTEL**
300 E New
England Ave
(32789)
Rates: $39-$95
(407) 644-3400
(800) 203-2581

YULEE

COMFORT INN
126 Sidney Pl
(32097)
Rates: $49-$109
(904) 225-2600
(800) 228-5150

DAYS INN
3250 US 17 N
(32097)
Rates: $35-$44
(904) 225-2011
(800) 329-7466

**HOLIDAY INN
EXP**
3276 US 17 N
(32097)
Rates: $36-$53
(904) 225-5114
(800) 465-4329

**NASSAU
HOLIDAY MOTEL**
US 17 South A1A
(32097)
Rates: $30-$49
(904) 225-2397

ZEPHYRHILLS

**CRYSTAL
SPRINGS
MOTOR INN**
6736 Gall Blvd
(33541)
Rates: $35-$170
(813) 782-1214

GEORGIA

ACWORTH

BEST WESTERN FRONTIER INN
Hwy 92, I-75,
Exit 120 (30101)
Rates: $50-$65
(770) 974-0116
(800) 528-1234

QUALITY INN
4980 Cowan Rd
(30101)
Rates: $40-$85
(770) 974-1922
(800) 228-5151

RED ROOF INN
5320 Glade Rd
(30101)
Rates: $40-$46
(770) 974-5400
(800) 843-7663

SUPER 8 MOTEL
4970 Cowan Rd
(30101)
Rates: $44-$65
(770) 966-9700
(800) 800-8000

ADAIRSVILLE

COMFORT INN
107 Princeton
Blvd (30103)
Rates: $45-$95
(770) 773-2886
(800) 228-5150

RAMADA LIMITED
500 Georgia
North Cir (30103)
Rates: $40-$75
(770) 769-9726
(800) 272-6232

ADEL

DAYS INNS
1200 W 4th St
(31620)
Rates: $36-$44
(912) 896-4574
(800) 329-7466

HAMPTON INN
1500 W 4th St
(31620)
Rates: $57-$65
(912) 896-3099
(800) 426-7866

HOWARD JOHNSON
1103 W 4th St
Adel (31620)
Rates: $34-$39
(912) 896-2244
(800) 446-4656

SCOTTISH INNS
911 W 4th St
(31620)
Rates: $21-$28
(912) 896-2259
(800) 251-1962

SUPER 8 MOTEL
1102 W 4th St
(31620)
Rates: $33-$38
(912) 896-4523
(800) 800-8000

ALBANY

GRAND MOTEL
904 Radium Spgs
Rd (31705)
Rates: $39-$38
(912) 435-8919

HOWARD JOHNSON
Dowson Rd
(31701)
Rates: n/a
(912) 446-8000
(800) 446-4656

KNIGHTS INN
1201 Schley Ave
(31707)
Rates: $35-$43
(912) 888-9600
(800) 843-5644

MOTEL 6
201 S Thornton
Dr (31705)
Rates: $36-$42
(912) 439-0078
(800) 466-8356

RAMADA INN
2505 N Slappey
Blvd (31701)
Rates: $50-$75
(912) 883-3211
(800) 272-6232

SUPER 8 MOTEL
2444 N Slappey
Blvd (31701)
Rates: $39-$51
(912) 777-8388
(800) 800-8000

ALPHARETTA

AMERISUITES
5595 Windward
(30201)
Rates: $109-$149
(770) 343-9566
(800) 833-1516

HOMEWOOD SUITES
10775 Davis Dr
(30201)
Rates: $98-$162
(770) 998-1622
(800) 225-5466

LA QUINTA INN & SUITES
1350 N Point Dr
(30202)
Rates: $59-$129
(770) 754-7800
(800) 687-6667

RESIDENCE INN BY MARRIOTT
5465 Windward
Pkwy W (30201)
Rates: $149-$165
(770) 664-0664
(800) 331-3131

STAYBRIDGE SUITES BY HOLIDAY INN
3980 North Point
Pkwy (30005)
Rates: n/a
(770) 569-7200
(800) 238-8000

AMERICUS

COTTAGE INN
Hwy 49 N (31709)
Rates: $65-$195
(912) 934-0579
(912) 924-9316

1906 PATHWAY INN B&B
501 S Lee St
(31709)
Rates: $65-$125
(912) 928-2078
(800) 889-1466

RAMADA INN
1205 MLK Jr Blvd
So (31709)
Rates: $40-$70
(912) 924-4431
(800) 272-6232

REES PARK GARDEN INN
504 Rees Park
(31709)
Rates: $65-$75
(912) 931-0122

ASHBURN

COMFORT INN
820 Shoneys Dr
(31714)
Rates: $35-$68
(912) 567-0080
(800) 228-5150

DAYS INN
823 E
Washington Ave
(31714)
Rates: $32-$48
(912) 567-3346
(800) 329-7466

RAMADA LIMITED
156 Whittle Cir
(31714)
Rates: $32-$62
(912) 567-3295
(800) 272-6232

SUPER 8 MOTEL
749 E
Washington Ave
(31714)
Rates: $32-$49
(912) 567-4688
(800) 800-8000

ATHENS

BEST WESTERN COLONIAL INN
170 N Milledge
Ave (30601)
Rates: $49-$79
(706) 546-7311
(800) 528-1234
(800) 592-9401

BULLDOG INN
1120 Newton
Bridge Rd
(30607)
Rates: $38-$59
(706) 543-3611

DOWNTOWNER INNS
1198 S Millege
Ave (30605)
Rates: $59-$79
(706) 549-2626
(800) 251-1962

HI WAY HOST
525 Macon Hwy
Athens (30605)
Rates: $38-$60
(706) 549-0697

HOLIDAY INN EXPRESS
513 W Broad St
(30601)
Rates: n/a
(706) 546-8122
(800) 465-4329

MAGNOLIA TERRACE GUESTHOUSE
277 Hill St
(30601)
Rates: $95-$135
(706) 548-3860
(800) 891-1912

AREA CODES - If the local number doesn't connect, check for a new area code.

SCOTTISH INNS
410 Macon Hwy
(30606)
Rates: $23-$27
(706) 546-8161
(800) 251-1962

SUPER 8 MOTEL
3425 Atlanta
Hwy (30606)
Rates: $35-$75
(706) 549-0251
(800) 800-8000

TRAVELODGE
898 W Broad St
(30601)
Rates: $33-$70
(706) 549-5400
(800) 578-7878

ATLANTA

**AMERISUITES-
PERIMETER CTR**
1005 Crestline
Pkwy (30328)
Rates: $85-$109
(770) 730-9300
(800) 833-1516

**ANGUS &
AGATHA'S
LUXURY B&B**
670 Old Ivy Rd
NE (30342)
Rates: $100-$150
(404) 848-0022

ANSLEY INN
253 15th St NE
(30309)
Rates: $109-$169
(404) 872-9000
(800) 446-5416

**BAYMONT INN-
LENOX**
2535 Chantilly Dr
NE (30324)
Rates: $57
(404) 321-0999
(800) 301-0200

**BED&BREAKFAST
ATLANTA
RESERVATION
SERVICE**
1608 Briarcliff
Rd, Suite 5
(30306)
Rates: $60-$195
(404) 875-0525
(800) 967-3224

**BEST WESTERN
GRANADA SUITE
HOTEL**
1302 W Peachtree
St (30309)
Rates: $89-$159
(404) 876-6100
(800) 528-1234
(800) 548-5631

**BEST WESTERN
INN AT
PEACHTREES**
330 W Peachtree
St (30308)
Rates: $79-$159
(404) 577-6970
(800) 528-1234
(800) 242-4642

**BEVERLY HILLS
INN B&B**
65 Sheridan Dr
(30305)
Rates: $90-$160
(404) 233-8520
(800) 331-8520

**CROWNE PLAZA
ATLANTA-
POWERS FERRY**
6345 Powers
Ferry Rd NW
(30339)
Rates: $69-$164
(770) 955-1700
(800) 227-6963

EMORY INN
1641 Clifton Rd
(30329)
Rates: $89
(404) 712-6700

**FOUR SEASONS
HOTEL**
75 14th St (30309)
Rates: $235-$1900
(404) 881-9898
(800) 332-3442

**GEORGIAN
TERRACE**
659 Peachtree St
(30308)
Rates: $98-$375
(404) 897-1991
(800) 651-2316

HARVEY HOTEL
6345 Powers
Ferry Rd (30339)
Rates: $98-$149
(678) 955-1700
(800) 922-9222

**HAWTHORN
SUITES**
1500 Parkwood
Cir (30339)
Rates: $119-$179
(770) 952-9595
(800) 338-7812

**HILTON
ATLANTA
AIRPORT**
1031 Virginia Ave
(30354)
Rates: $79-$209
(404) 767-9000
(800) 445-8667

HILTON&TOWERS
255 Courtland St
NE (30303)
Rates: $185-$400
(404) 659-2000
(800) 445-8667

**HOLIDAY INN
AIRPORT**
1325 Virginia Ave
(30344)
Rates: n/a
(404) 768-6660
(800) 465-4329

**HOLIDAY INN
AIRPORT NORTH**
1380 Virginia Ave
(30344)
Rates: n/a
(404) 762-8411
(800) 465-4329

**HOLIDAY INN
PERIMETER**
4386 Chamblee-
Dunwoody Rd
(30341)
Rates: $59-$149
(770) 457-6363
(800) 465-4329

**HOMESTEAD
VILLAGE GUEST
STUDIOS**
1050 Hammond
Dr (30328)
Rates: n/a
(770) 522-0025
(888) 782-9473

**HOMESTEAD
VILLAGE GUEST
STUDIOS**
1339 Executive
Park Dr NE
(30329)
Rates: n/a
(404) 325-1223
(888) 782-9473

**HOMEWOOD
SUITES
CUMBERLAND**
3200 Cobb Pkwy
(30339)
Rates: $89-$169
(770) 988-9449
(800) 225-5466

**LA QUINTA INN
& SUITES**
2415 Paces Ferry
Rd SE (30326)
Rates: $59-$99
(770) 801-9002
(800) 687-6667

**LA QUINTA INN
& SUITES**
6260 Peachtree-
Dunwoody
(30328)
Rates: $59-$129
(770) 350-6177
(800) 687-6667

**MASTERS
ECONOMY INN
SIX FLAGS**
4120 Fulton
Industrial Blvd
(30336)
Rates: $59-$73
(404) 696-4690
(800) 633-3434

MOTEL 6
3585 Chamblee-
Tucker Rd
(30341)
Rates: $40-$46
(678) 455-8000
(800) 466-8356

QUALITY INN
2960 NE
Expressway
(30341)
Rates: $45-$179
(678) 451-5231
(800) 228-5151

RAMADA INN
418 Armour Dr
NE (30324)
Rates: $49-$259
(404) 873-4661
(800) 272-6232

**RED ROOF INN
AIRPORT NORTH**
1200 Virginia Ave
(30344)
Rates: n/a
(404) 209-1800
(800) 843-7663

RED ROOF INN
1960 N Druid
Hills Rd (30329)
Rates: $50-$64
(404) 321-1653
(800) 843-7663

**RED ROOF INN
SIX FLAGS**
4265 Shirley Dr
SW (30336)
Rates: $56-$83
(678) 696-4391
(800) 843-7663

**RESIDENCE INN
BY MARRIOTT
DOWNTOWN**
134 Peachtree St
NW (30303)
Rates: $185
(404) 522-0950
(800) 331-3131

**RESIDENCE INN
BY MARRIOTT
DUNWOODY**
1901 Savoy Dr
(30341)
Rates: $69-$119
(770) 455-4446
(800) 331-3131

**RESIDENCE INN
BY MARRIOTT**
1041W Peachtree
St (30309)
Rates: $114-$154
(404) 872-8885
(800) 331-3131

**RESIDENCE INN
BY MARRIOTT-
BUCKHEAD**
2960 Piedmont
Rd NE (30305)
Rates: $145-$175
(404) 239-0677
(800) 331-3131

**RESIDENCE INN
BY MARRIOTT-
BUCKHEAD/
LENOX**
2220 Lake Blvd
(30317)
Rates: $134
(404) 467-1660
(800) 331-3131

AREA CODES - If the local number doesn't connect, check for a new area code.

RESIDENCE INN BY MARRIOTT-PERIMETER W.
6096 Barfield Rd (30328)
Rates: $115-$166
(404) 252-5066
(800) 331-3131

SUMMERFIELD SUITES HOTEL
760 Mt Vernon Hwy NE (30328)
Rates: $99-$195
(404) 250-0110
(800) 833-4353

SUMMERFIELD SUITES HOTEL-BUCKHEAD
505 Pharr Rd (30305)
Rates: $109-$259
(404) 262-7880
(800) 833-4353

SUMMIT INN
3900 Fulton Ind. Blvd (30336)
Rates: $31-$49
(404) 691-2444

SUPER 8 MOTEL
111 Cone St (30303)
Rates: $79-$129
(404) 524-7000
(800) 800-8000

SUPER 8 MOTEL
3701 Jonesboro Rd (30354)
Rates: $50-$70
(404) 361-1111
(800) 800-8000

UNIVERSITY INN
1767 N Decatur Rd (30307)
Rates: $84-$134
(404) 634-7327
(800) 654-8591

W ATLANTA
111 Perimeter Center W (30346)
Rates: $119-$209
(770) 396-6800

WELLESLEY INN & SUITES
2225 Interstate N Pkwy West SE (30339)
Rates: $85-$105
(770) 226-0242
(800) 444-8888

WESTIN ATLANTA SOUTH
7 Concourse Pkwy (30328)
Rates: $99-$165
(770) 395-3900
(800) 228-3000

WESTIN PEACHTREE PLAZA
210 NW Peachtree St (30303)
Rates: $155-$295
(404) 659-1400
(800) 228-3000

WYNDHAM GARDEN HOTEL AT VININGS
2857 Paces Ferry Rd (30327)
Rates: $125
(770) 432-5555
(800) 996-3426

AUGUSTA

AMERISUITES
1062 Claussen Rd (30907)
Rates: $71
(706) 733-4656
(800) 833-1516

COMFORT INN
629 Frontage Rd NW (30907)
Rates: $63-$68
(706) 855-8000
(800) 228-5150

COMFORT INN MEDICAL CENTER
1455 Walton Way (30901)
Rates: $56-$225
(706) 722-2224
(800) 228-5150

COURTESY MOTEL
605 15th St (30901)
Rates: $25-$30
(706) 722-2525

ECONO LODGE
444 Broad St (30901)
Rates: $44-$175
(706) 724-8100
(800) 553-2666

GROVE SUITES
2901 Deans Bridge Rd (30906)
Rates: $30-$45
(706) 796-0258

HOLIDAY INN AT BOBBY JONES
2155 Gordon Hwy (30909)
Rates: $78-$96
(706) 737-2300
(800) 465-4329

HOLIDAY INN WEST
1075 Stevens Creek Rd (30907)
Rates: $59-$79
(706) 738-8811
(800) 343-4538

HORNES MOTOR LODGE
1520 Gordon Hwy (30906)
Rates: $25-$30
(706) 798-2230

HOWARD JOHNSON
1238 Gordon Hwy (30901)
Rates: $31-$65
(706) 724-9613
(800) 446-4656

KNIGHTS INN
210 Boy Scout Rd (30909)
Rates: $25-$37
(706) 737-3166
(800) 843-5644

LA QUINTA INN
3020 Washington Rd (30907)
Rates: $56-$98
(706) 733-2660
(800) 687-6667

MASTERS ECONOMY INN
3027 Washington Rd (30907)
Rates: $26-$39
(706) 863-5566

MOTEL 6
2560 Center West Pkwy (30909)
Rates: $38+
(706) 736-1934
(800) 466-8356

PARTRIDGE INN
2110 Walton Way (30904)
Rates: $89
(706) 737-8888

RADISSON RIVERWALK HOTEL
2 10th St (30901)
Rates: $104-$114
(706) 722-8900
(800) 333-3333

RADISSON SUITES INN
3038 Washington Rd (30907)
Rates: $79-$99
(706) 868-1800
(800) 333-3333

RAMADA LIMITED
4324 Belair Frontage Rd (30909)
Rates: $45-$200
(706) 860-8840
(800) 272-6232

RAMADA PLAZA
640 Broad St (30901)
Rates: $72-$229
(706) 722-5541
(800) 257-5060

RED CARPET INN
2050 Gordon Hwy (30909)
Rates: n/a
(706) 733-5566
(800) 251-1962

SHERATON HOTEL
2651 Perimeter Pkwy (30909)
Rates: $84-$120
(706) 855-8100
(800) 325-3535

SHONEY'S INN
3023 Washington Rd (30907)
Rates: $30-$46
(706) 736-2596
(800) 222-2222

SUPER 8 MOTEL-RIVERWALK
954 5th St (30901)
Rates: $33-$50
(706) 724-0757
(800) 800-8000

TELFAIR INN-VICTORIAN VILLAGE
326 Greene St (30901)
Rates: $67-$177
(706) 724-3315
(800) 241-2407

AUSTELL

KNIGHTS INN WEST SIX FLAGS
1595 Blair Bridge Rd (30001)
Rates: $32-$67
(770) 944-0824
(800) 843-5644

LA QUINTA WEST SIX FLAGS
7377 Six Flags Dr (300019
Rates: $77-$109
(770) 944-2110
(800) 687-6667

BAINBRIDGE

CHARTER HOUSE INN
1401 Tallahassee Hwy (31718)
Rates: $41-$50
(912) 246-8550
(800) 768-8550

SUPER 8 MOTEL
751 W Shotwell St (31717)
Rates: $40-$50
(912) 246-0015
(800) 800-8000

BAXLEY

HOLIDAY INN EXPRESS
103 Heritage St (31523)
Rates: n/a
(912) 367-6653
(800) 465-4329

PINE LODGE MOTEL
500 S Main St (31513)
Rates: $32-$46
(912) 367-3622
(800) 841-6052

AREA CODES - If the local number doesn't connect, check for a new area code.

SCOTTISH INNS
1179 Hatch Pkwy
S (31513)
Rates: n/a
(912) 367-3652
(800) 251-1962

BLACKSHEAR

**POND VIEW INN
BED & BREAKFAST**
4200 Grady St
(31516)
Rates: $60-$125
(912) 449-3697
(800) 585-8659

BLAIRSVILLE

**BLAIR HOUSE
CABIN RENTALS**
P. O. Box 1337
(30514)
Rates: $59+
(706) 745-3399

**EL JOE LODGE
MOTEL**
1639 Murphy
Hwy (30512)
Rates: $32-$60
(706) 745-6991

**GOOSE CREEK
CABINS**
P. O. Box 906
(30514)
Rates: $38-$129
(706) 745-5111

**HELTON CREEK
DELUXE
COTTAGES**
1989 Helton
Creek Rd (30512)
Rates: $79-$99
(706) 745-2104

**LAKE NOTTELY
LUXURY
VACATION
RENTALS**
230 Kiutuestia
Creek Rd (30512)
Rates: $125+
(706) 745-4119

**MISTY
MOUNTAIN INN
& COTTAGES**
4376 Misty Mtn
Ln (30512)
Rates: $50-$85
(706) 745-4786
(888) 647-8966

**NOTTLEY DAM
GUEST HOUSE
BED & BREAKFAST**
2266 Nottley
Dam Rd (30512)
Rates: $55-$85
(706) 745-7939

**OLD HOLLOW
CABINS**
1976 Honaker Rd
(30512)
Rates: $55-$65
(706) 745-4696

PARADISE CABINS
3163 Paradise Rd
(30514)
Rates: $89-$119
(706) 745-7483

**PROPERTY MGMT
SERVICE OF NE
GEORIGA
RENTALS**
1545 Stoney
Ridge Rd (30512)
Rates: $50-$115
(706) 745-8932

**RIVERBENDS
OLD LOG
CABINS**
1426 Riverbend
Farm Rd (30574)
Rates: $85-$180
(706) 745-7143

**7 CREEKS
CABINS**
5109 Horseshoe
Cove Rd (30512)
Rates: $55-$250
(706) 745-4753

**T-RANCH
CABINS**
509 Emmette
Walker Rd
(30512)
Rates: $85-$150
(706) 374-6159

**TOWN CREEK
CABINS**
4863 Seabolt Rd
(30512)
Rates: $79-$119
(706) 745-8891

BLAKELY

BUDGET INN
Hwy 27 N
(31723)
Rates: n/a
(912) 723-3011

BLUE RIDGE

**ABOVE THE REST
LUXURY CABINS**
My Mountain
(30513)
Rates: $95-$115
(706) 374-2057

**BLUE RIDGE
MOUNTAIN
CABINS**
10144 Blue Ridge
Dr (30513)
Rates: $85-$135
(706) 632-8999

DAYS INN
4970 Appalachian
Hwy (30513)
Rates: $50-$95
(706) 632-2100
(800) 329-7466

**FANNIN INN
MOTEL**
APD Hwy 515,
PO Box 605
(30513)
Rates: n/a
(800) 533-9834

**TICA CABIN
RENTALS**
699 E Main St
(30513)
Rates: $75-$125
(706) 374-2939
(800) 871-8422

BREMEN

DAYS INN
35 Price Creek Rd
(30110)
Rates: $45-$110
(770) 537-4646
(800) 329-7466

TRAVELODGE
1077 Alabama
Ave (30110)
Rates: $39-$125
(770) 537-3833
(800) 578-7878

BRUNSWICK

**BAYMONT INN
& SUITES**
105 Tourist Dr
(31523)
Rates: $49-$54
(912) 265-7725
(800) 301-0200

**BEST WESTERN
BRUNSWICK INN**
5323 New Jesup
Hwy (31523)
Rates: $51-$66
(912) 264-0144
(800) 528-1234

COMFORT INN
5308 New Jesup
Hwy (31523)
Rates: $59-$89
(912) 264-6540
(800) 228-5150
(800) 551-7591

DAYS INN
2307 Gloucester
St (31520)
Rates: $38-$55
(912) 265-8830
(800) 329-7466

EMBASSY SUITES
500 Mall Blvd
(31520)
Rates: $89-$119
(912) 264-6100
(800) 362-2779

HOLIDAY INN
5252 New Jesup
Hwy (31523)
Rates: $59-$89
(912) 264-4033
(800) 465-4329

KNIGHTS INN
5044 New Jesup
Hwy (31523)
Rates: $34-$40
(912) 267-6500
(800) 843-5644

MOTEL 6
403 Butler Dr
(31523)
Rates: $30-$40
(912) 264-8582
(800) 466-8356

OAK PARK INN
3104 Glynn Ave
(31520)
Rates: $30-$34
(912) 265-9301

**OLEANDER
MOTEL**
2101 Glynn Ave
(31520)
Rates: $20-$30
(912) 265-3911

PALMS MOTEL
2715 Glynn Ave
(31520)
Rates: $28-$34
(912) 265-8825

RAMADA INN
3040 Scarlet St
(31523)
Rates: $59-$79
(912) 264-3621
(800) 272-6232

RED ROOF INN
121 Tourist Dr
(31520)
Rates: n/a
(912) 264-4720
(800) 843-7663

**SEABREEZE
MOTEL**
2697 Glynn Ave
(31520)
Rates: $24-$34
(912) 265-2282

SLEEP INN
5272 New Jesup
Hwy (31523)
Rates: $39-$89
(912) 261-0670
(800) 261-0670

SUPER 8 MOTEL
5280 New Jesup
Hwy (31523)
Rates: $50-$99
(912) 264-8800
(800) 800-8000

BYRON

**BEST WESTERN
INN & SUITES**
101 Dunbar Hwy
49 Rd (31008)
Rates: $55-$99
(912) 956-3056
(800) 528-1234

ECONO LODGE
106 Old Mason
Rd (31008)
Rates: $38-$46
(912) 956-5600
(800) 553-2666

MASTERS INN
Rt 3, Box 1540
(31008)
Rates: $28-$37
(912) 956-5300

AREA CODES - If the local number doesn't connect, check for a new area code.

PASSPORT INN
111 Chapman Rd
(31008)
Rates: $23-$35
(912) 956-5200
(800) 251-1962

CAIRO

**BEST WESTERN
EXECUTIVE INN**
2800 US 84 E
(31728)
Rates: $55-$75
(912) 377-8000
(800) 528-1234

DAYS INN
35 US Hwy 84 E
(31728)
Rates: $40-$60
(912) 377-4400
(800) 329-7466

CALHOUN

**BUDGET HOST
SHEPHERD MOTL**
3900 Fairmont
Hwy (30703)
Rates: $33-$42
(706) 629-8644
(800) 283-4678

DAYS INN
742 Hwy 53 SE
(30701)
Rates: $36-$75
(706) 629-8271
(800) 329-7466

**DUFFY'S MOTEL
NORTH**
1441 US 41 N
(30701)
Rates: $23-$31
(706) 629-4436

ECONO LODGE
1438 US 41 (30701)
Rates: $30-$49
(706) 625-5421
(800) 553-2666

**HOWARD
JOHNSON**
1220 Red Bud Rd
(30701)
Rates: $40-$74
(706) 629-9191
(800) 446-4656

KNIGHTS INN
2261 Hwy 41 NE
(30701)
Rates: $37-$49
(706) 629-4521
(800) 843-5644

QUALITY INN
915 Hwy 53 E
(30701)
Rates: $45-$60
(706) 629-9501
(800) 228-5151

**RAMADA
LIMITED**
1204 Redbud Rd
NE (30701)
Rates: $44-$49
(706) 629-9207
(800) 272-6232

SCOTTISH INNS
1510 Red Bud Rd
NE (30701)
Rates: $23-$89
(706) 629-8261
(800) 251-1962

SUPER 8 MOTEL
1446 Hwy 41 N
(30701)
Rates: $35-$50
(706) 602-1400
(800) 800-8000

CAMILLA

**BEST WESTERN
COURTLAND
CLUB**
600 US Hwy 19
(31730)
Rates: $56-$66
(912) 336-0731
(800) 528-1234

CANTON

DAYS INN
291 Ball Ground
Hwy (30114)
Rates: $39-$49
(770) 479-0301
(800) 329-7466

CARROLLTON

**BEST WESTERN
CROSSROADS
HOTEL CENTER**
1202 S Park St
(30117)
Rates: $55-$89
(770) 832-2611
(800) 528-1234

CARTERSVILLE

**BUDGET HOST
INN**
851 Cass-White
Rd NW (30120)
Rates: $24-$59
(770) 386-0350
(800) 283-4678

COMFORT INN
28 Hwy 294 SE
(30120)
Rates: $34-$60
(770) 387-1800
(800) 228-5150

DAYS INN
5618 Hwy 20 SE
(30120)
Rates: $46-$88
(770) 382-1824
(800) 329-7466

ECONO LODGE
26 Hwy, 20 Spur
(30120)
Rates: $25-$69
(770) 386-3303
(800) 553-2666

**HOWARD
JOHNSON
EXPRESS**
25 Carson Loop
NW (30121)
Rates: $50-$85
(770) 386-0700
(800) 446-4656

KNIGHTS INN
420 E Church St
(30120)
Rates: $40-$85
(770) 386-7263
(800) 843-5644

MOTEL 6
5657 Hwy 20 NE
(30120)
Rates: $34-$50
(770) 386-1449
(800) 466-8356

RED CARPET INN
851 Cass-White
Rd NW (30120)
Rates: $20-$45
(770) 382-8000
(800) 251-1962

**RED TOP MTN
STATE PARK
& LODGE**
781 Red Top Mtn
Rd SE (30121)
Rates: $55-$75
(770) 975-4226
(800) 864-7275

SUPER 8 MOTEL
41 SR 20 Spur SE
(30120)
Rates: $35-$60
(770) 382-8881
(800) 800-8000

TRAVELODGE
35 Carson Loop
(30121)
Rates: $40-$45
(770) 387-2696
(800) 578-7878

CHAMBLEE

**LODGE ON
BUFORD**
4815 Buford Hwy
(30341)
Rates: $39-$148
(770) 458-8011

CHATSWORTH

KEY WEST INN
501 GI Maddox
Pkwy (30705)
Rates: $45-$60
(706) 517-1155
(800) 833-0555

SCOTTISH INNS
1279 Hwy 411 S
(30706)
Rates: n/a
(706) 695-6894
(800) 251-1962

CHERRY LOG

**COZY ACRES
CABIN RENTALS**
434 Whispering
Pine Ln (30522)
Rates: $100
(706) 273-7321
(888) 273-7321

CHULA

RED CARPET INN
I-75 & Chula-
Brookfield Rd
(31733)
Rates: n/a
(912) 382-2686
(800) 251-1962

CLARKESVILLE

**BURTON
WOODS CABINS**
220 Brookwood
Ln (30523)
Rates: $79+
(706) 947-3926

**BURTON
WOODS II**
155 Fox Valley
Rd (30523)
Rates: $79+
(706) 754-7442

**HABERSHAM
HOLLOW
CABINS**
254 Habersham
Hollow Ln
(30523)
Rates: $75+
(706) 754-5147

CLAXTON

**REST HAVEN
MOTEL**
Hwy 301 N
(30417)
Rates: $26-$31
(912) 739-1016

CLAYTON

**BACK-IN-THE-
WOODS**
1331-A
Warwoman Rd,
RR 1 (30525)
Rates: $175-$375
(706) 782-4421

**BLACK ROCK
RANCH RENTAL**
#1 Screamer Mtn
(30525)
Rates: $250-$550
(706) 782-3315

**CLIFFSIDE CABIN
ON SCREAMER
MOUNTAIN**
RR 1, Box 1241
(30525)
Rates: $150-$450
(706) 782-3318

**ENGLISH
MANOR INN**
US Hwy 76
(30525)
Rates: n/a
(706) 782-5780

AREA CODES - If the local number doesn't connect, check for a new area code.

SHONEY'S INN & SUITES
US 441 S (30525)
Rates: $89-$109
(706) 782-2214
(800) 222-2222

CLERMONT

HISTORIC CLERMONT HOTEL
101 Dean St
(30527)
Rates: $85
(770) 983-0704

CLEVELAND

GABBY'S COUNTRY CABINS
3083 Helen Hwy
(30528)
Rates: $65-$140
(706) 865-6772

HIDE AWAY CABINS
1415 Harkins Rd
(30528)
Rates: $75
(706) 865-4410

VILLAGIO DI MONTAGNA
Hwy 129 N
(30528)
Rates: $80-$120
(800) 367-3922

COLLEGE PARK

BAYMONT INN-AIRPORT
2400 Old National Hwy
(30349)
Rates: $59-$88
(404) 766-0000
(800) 301-0200

CLUB HOTEL BY DOUBLETREE
5010 Old Natl Hwy (30349)
Rates: $65-$90
(404) 761-4000
(800) 222-8733

HOLIDAY INN SELECT
4669 Airport Blvd (30337)
Rates: n/a
(404) 763-8800
(800) 465-4329

LA QUINTA INN
4874 Old National Hwy
(30337)
Rates: $59-$71
(404) 768-1241
(800) 687-6667

MARRIOTT ATLANTA AIRPORT
4711 Best Rd
(30337)
Rates: $139-$174
(404) 766-7900
(800) 228-9290

RED ROOF INN AIRPORT SOUTH
2471 Old National Pkwy
(30349)
Rates: $46-$73
(404) 761-9701
(800) 843-7663

SLEEP INN
1911 Sullivan Rd
(30337)
Rates: $70-$150
(770) 996-6100
(800) 753-3746

WESTIN-INT'L AIRPORT
4736 Best Rd
(30337)
Rates: $105-$600
(404) 762-7676
(800) 228-3000

COLUMBUS

BAYMONT INN
2919 Warm Springs Rd
(31909)
Rates: $54-$59
(706) 323-4344
(800) 301-0200

DAYS INN
3452 Macon Rd
(31907)
Rates: $49-$59
(706) 561-4400
(800) 329-7466

ECONO LODGE
4483 Victory Dr
(31903)
Rates: $39-$55
(706) 682-3803
(800) 553-2666

HOLIDAY INN
2800 Manchester Expwy (31904)
Rates: $59-$89
(706) 324-0231
(800) 465-4329

HOWARD JOHNSON EXP
1011 Veterans Pkwy (31901)
Rates: $55-$74
(706) 322-6641
(800) 446-4656

LA QUINTA INN
3201 Macon Rd
(31906)
Rates: $62-$82
(706) 568-1740
(800) 687-6667

MOTEL 6
3050 Victory Dr
(31903)
Rates: $35-$44
(706) 687-7214
(800) 466-8356

SUPER 8 MOTEL
2935 Warm Spgs Rd (31909)
Rates: $45-$70
(706) 322-6580
(800) 800-8000

COMMERCE

GUESTHOUSE INN-BANKS CROSSING
30934 US 441 S
(30529)
Rates: $39-$99
(706) 335-5147
(800) 878-0837

HOLIDAY INN
30747 US 441 S
(30529)
Rates: $52-$76
(706) 335-5183
(800) 465-4329

HOWARD JOHNSON
30591 US 441
(30529)
Rates: $44-$99
(706) 335-5581
(800) 446-4656

RAMADA LIMITED
30537 US 441 S
(30529)
Rates: $39-$89
(706) 335-5191
(800) 272-6232

CONYERS

COMFORT INN
1363 Klondike Rd
(30207)
Rates: $69-$99
(770) 760-0300
(800) 228-5150

LA QUINTA INN & SUITES
1184 Dogwood Ln (30012)
Rates: $79-$109
(770) 918-0092
(800) 687-6667

RAMADA LIMITED
1070 Dogwood Dr (30207)
Rates: $69-$125
(770) 760-0777
(800) 272-6232

CORDELE

BEST WESTERN COLONIAL INN
1706 16th Ave E
(31015)
Rates: $38-$49
(912) 273-5420
(800) 528-1234
(800) 721-3352

CORDELE CONF CENTER
1711 E 16th Ave
(31015)
Rates: $45
(912) 273-4117

DAYS INN
215 7th St S
(31015)
Rates: $45-$85
(912) 273-1123
(800) 329-7466

ECONOMY INN
1618 E 16th Ave
(31015)
Rates: $27-$50
(912) 273-2456

HOLIDAY INN EXPRESS
416 Greer St
(31015)
Rates: n/a
(800) 465-4329

PASSPORT INN
1602 16th Ave E
(31015)
Rates: $22-$30
(912) 273-4088
(800) 251-1962

RAMADA INN
2016 16th Ave E
(31015)
Rates: $48-$99
(912) 273-5000
(800) 272-6232

RODEWAY INN
1609 16th Ave E
(31015)
Rates: $30-$55
(912) 273-3390
(800) 228-2000

SUPER 8 MOTEL
566 Farmers Market Rd
(31015)
Rates: $34-$38
(912) 276-1008
(800) 800-8000

CORNELIA

COMFORT INN
2965 J. Warren Rd
(30531)
Rates: $55-$95
(706) 778-9573
(800) 228-5150

COVINGTON

BEST WESTERN WHITE COLUMNS INN
I-20 & Alcovy Rd
(30209)
Rates: $55-$85
(770) 786-5800
(800) 528-1234

HOLIDAY INN
10111 Alcovy Rd
(30209)
Rates: $70-$75
(770) 787-4900
(800) 465-4329

DAHLONEGA

WRIGHT'S R&R CHALET & CABIN RENTALS
319 Horseshoe Ln (30533)
Rates: $80-$150
(706) 219-2040

DALTON

BEST INNS OF AMERICA
1529 W Walnut Ave (30720)
Rates: $55-$69
(706) 226-1100
(800) 237-8466

BEST WESTERN DALTON INN
2106 Rd Dalton (30720)
Rates: $39-$53
(706) 226-5022
(800) 528-1234

DAYS INN
1518 W Walnut Ave (30720)
Rates: $40-$62
(706) 278-0850
(800) 329-7466

HOLIDAY INN
515 Holiday Dr (30720)
Rates: $60-$100
(706) 278-0500
(800) 465-4329

HOWARD JOHNSON
2107 Chattanooga Rd (30720)
Rates: $35-$47
(706) 278-1448
(800) 446-4656

MOTEL 6
2200 Chattanooga Rd (30720)
Rates: $31-$42
(706) 278-5522
(800) 466-8356

RAMADA LIMITED
2208 Chattanooga Rd (30720)
Rates: $28-$34
(706) 226-4545
(800) 272-6232

SUPER 8 MOTEL
236 Connector 3 SW (30720)
Rates: $40-$60
(706) 277-9323
(800) 800-8000

DARIEN

SUPER 8 MOTEL
Hwy 251 & 195 (31305)
Rates: $37-$58
(912) 437-6660
(800) 800-8000

DAWSON VILLE

COMFORT INN
127 Beartooth Pkwy (30534)
Rates: $48-$86
(706) 216-1900
(800) 228-5150

DAYS INN
750 North Ave (30534)
Rates: $59-$180
(706) 216-4410
(800) 329-7466

DECATUR

DAYS INN
4300 Snapfinger Woods Dr (30035)
Rates: $49-$129
(770) 981-5670
(800) 329-7466

MOTEL 6
2565 Wesley Chapel Rd (30035)
Rates: $40-$46
(404) 288-6911
(800) 466-8356

DILLARD

BEST INN & SUITES
US 441 (30537)
Rates: $45-$129
(706) 746-5321
(800) 237-8466

CHALET VILLAGE
Hwy 441, Old Dillard Rd (30537)
Rates: $55-$139
(706) 746-5348
(800) 742-1416

DILLARD HOUSE MOTOR INN
US 441 (30537)
Rates: $55-$169
(706) 746-5348
(800) 541-0671

HOLIDAY INN EXPRESS
64 White Oak Ln (30537)
Rates: n/a
(800) 465-4329

DONALSON-VILLE

DAYS INN
Hwy 84, 204 W 3rd St (31745)
Rates: $40-$100
(912) 524-2185
(800) 329-7466

DORAVILLE

HOWARD JOHNSON HOTEL
4422 NE Expswy (30340)
Rates: $45-$65
(770) 448-7220
(800) 446-4656

MASTERS INN
3092 Presidential Pkwy (30340)
Rates: $45-$59
(770) 454-8373

DOUGLAS

HOLIDAY INN
1750 S Peterson Ave (31533)
Rates: $49-$63
(912) 384-9100
(800) 465-4329

DUBLIN

COMFORT INN
I-16 & US 441 (31040)
Rates: $50-$75
(912) 274-8000
(800) 228-5150

HOLIDAY INN HOTEL & SUITES
2190 Hwy 441 S (31040)
Rates: $58
(912) 272-7862
(800) 465-4329

SHAMROCK INN
Hwy 441 N (31040)
Rates: n/a
(912) 275-2650

DULUTH

AMERISUITES OF GWINNETT
3390 Venture Pkwy (30136)
Rates: $99-$149
(770) 623-6800
(800) 833-1516

AMERISUITES JOHN'S CREEK
11505 Medlock Bridge Rd (30155)
Rates: $105-$145
(770) 622-5858
(800) 833-1516

COMFORT SUITES GWINNETT
3700 Shackleford Rd (30096)
Rates: $95-$115
(770) 931-9299
(800) 228-5150

HAMPTON INN
1725 Pineland Rd (30096)
Rates: $89-$119
(770) 931-9800
(800) 426-7866

HOMESTEAD VILLAGE GUEST STUDIOS
3525 Breckenridge Blvd (30136)
Rates: $79
(770) 931-3113
(888) 782-9473

EAST POINT

CROWNE PLAZA ATLANTA AIRPORT
1325 Virginia Ave (30344)
Rates: $79-$179
(404) 768-6660
(800) 227-6963

DRURY INN & SUITES
1270 Virginia Ave (30344)
Rates: $79-$99
(404) 761-4900
(800) 378-7946

ELLIJAY

BUDGET HOST INN
10 Jeff Dr (30540)
Rates: $35-$79
(706) 635-5311
(800)283-4678

ELLIJAY INN
30 S Main St (30540)
Rates: $34-$65
(706) 635-4615

OVERLAND TRAILS LOG HOMES RENTALS
Hwy 282 & 76 (30540)
Rates: $95-$150
(706) 276-2211
(706) 276-2702

STRATFORD MOTOR INN
Hwy 515 at Maddox Dr East (30539)
Rates: $38-$60
(706) 276-1080

FITZGERALD

THE INN AT FITZGERALD
235 Ocilla Hwy (31750)
Rates: $35-$65
(912) 423-6661
(800) 222-2222

FOLKSTON

DAYS INN
1201 S 2nd St (31537)
Rates: $38-$68
(912) 496-2514
(800) 329-7466

WESTERN MOTEL
US 1 & 301 S (31537)
Rates: $35-$65
(912) 496-4711

FOREST PARK

MOTEL 6
5060 Frontage Rd
(30050)
Rates: $44-$56
(404) 363-6429
(800) 466-8356

SUPER 8 MOTEL
410 Old Dixie
Way (30050)
Rates: $50-$70
(404) 363-8811
(800) 800-8000

FORSYTH

**BEST WESTERN
HILLTOP INN**
I-75 & SR 42
(31029)
Rates: $37-$55
(912) 994-9260
(800) 528-1234

DAYS INN
I-75 & Lee Rd,
Exit 62 (31029)
Rates: $39-$70
(912) 994-2900
(800) 329-7466

ECONO LODGE
320 Cabiness Rd
(31029)
Rates: $36-$48
(912) 994-5603
(800) 553-2666

HAMPTON INN
520 Holiday Cir
(31029)
Rates: $59-$64
(912) 994-9697
(800) 426-7866

HOLIDAY INN
480 Holiday Cir
(31029)
Rates: $39-$56
(912) 994-5691
(800) 465-4329

**INN
AMBASSADOR**
I-75 & Juliette Rd
(31029)
Rates: $38
(912) 994-5101

**NEW FORSYTH
INN**
130 N Frontage
Rd (31029)
Rates: $24-$32
(912) 994-5161

TRADEWINDS
I-75 & SR 83
(31029)
Rates: n/a
(912) 994-9383

FORT VALLEY

**DAYS INN
& SUITES**
300 Commercial
Hts (31030)
Rates: $40-$70
(912) 971-1249
(800) 329-7466

VALLEY INN
204 Commercial
Hts (31030)
Rates: $36-$58
(912) 822-9090

GAINESVILLE

HOLIDAY INN
726 Jesse Jewell
Pkwy (30501)
Rates: $40-$75
(770) 536-4451
(800) 465-4329

**MASTERS INN
MOTEL**
Hwy 129 &
Monroe Dr
(30507)
Rates: $38-$59
(770) 532-7531

GARDEN CITY

MASTERS INN
4200 Hwy 21 N
(31408)
Rates: $45-$59
(912) 964-4344

GLENNVILLE

CHERI-O MOTEL
US 301, P. O. Box
393 (30427)
Rates: $33-$40
(912) 654-2176

GRAY

DAYS INN
Hwy 129 (31032)
Rates: $35-$75
(912) 934-9500
(800) 329-7466

GREENSBORO

MICROTEL INN
2470 Old
Eatonton Rd
(30642)
Rates: $37-$55
(706) 453-7300
(888) 771-7171

GRIFFIN

SCOTTISH INNS
1709 N Expwy
(30223)
Rates: n/a
(770) 228-6000
(800) 251-1962

HAHIRA

HAHIRA INN
1300 Hwy 122 W
(31632)
Rates: $34-$39
(912) 794-3000

HAPEVILLE

**RESIDENCE INN
BY MARRIOTT**
3401 Intl Blvd
(30354)
Rates: $115-$155
(404) 761-0511
(800) 331-3131

HAZELHURST

DAYS INN
312 Coffee St
(31539)
Rates: $38-$46
(912) 375-4527
(800) 329-7466

HELEN

**BAVARIAN
BROOK RENTALS**
859 Edelweiss
(30545)
Rates: $38-$175
(706) 878-2840
(800) 422-6355

**HELENDORF
RIVER INN &
TOWERS**
33 Munich
Strasse (30545)
Rates: $74-$160
(706) 878-2271
(800) 445-2271

**LUND'S
HIDEAWAY**
7489 Hwy 75 Alt
(30545)
Rates: n/a
(706) 878-3111

HIAWASSEE

**HENSON COVE
PLACE**
3840 Car Miles
Rd (30546)
Rates: $70-$75
(706) 896-6195
(800) 714-5542

**HORNE'S
HIDEAWAY**
1 Hornes
Hideaway
(30546)
Rates: $65-$85
(706) 896-6292

HIAWASSEE INN
193 E Main St
(30546)
Rates: $41-$88
(706) 896-4121
(800) 711-6961

SALALE LODGE
1340 Palmer
Place US 76E
(30546)
Rates: $49-$79
(706) 896-3943

HOGANSVILLE

DAYS INN
1630 Bass Cross
Rd (30230)
Rates: $40-$100
(706) 637-5400
(800) 329-7466

**KEY WEST INN
MOTEL**
1888 E Main St
(30230)
Rates: $48-$60
(706) 637-9395
(800) 833-0555

JEKYLL ISLAND

**BEACHVIEW
CLUB**
721 N Beachview
Dr (31527)
Rates: $99-$299
(912) 635-2256
(888) 412-7770

**CLARION
BUCCANEER
RESORT**
85 S Beachview
Dr (31527)
Rates: $99-$179
(912) 635-2261
(800) 253-5955

**COMFORT INN
ISLAND SUITES**
711 N Beachview
Dr (31527)
Rates: $99-$179
(912) 635-2211
(800) 228-5150
(800) 204-0202

**HOLIDAY INN
BEACH RESORT**
200 S Beachview
Dr (31527)
Rates: $64-$129
(912) 635-3311
(800) 753-5955

JEKYLL INN
975 N Beachview
Dr (31527)
Rates: $99-$129
(912) 635-232
(800) 736-1046

**SEAFARER INN
& SUITES**
700 N Beachview
Dr (31527)
Rates: $49-$130
(912) 635-2202
(800) 281-4446

**VILLAS BY THE
SEA HOTEL
CONDO**
1175 N
Beachview Dr
(31527)
Rates: $74-$239
(912) 635-2521
(800) 841-6262

JESUP

DAYS INN
384 Hwy 301 S
(31545)
Rates: $35-$45
(912) 427-3751
(800) 329-7466

WESTERN MOTEL
194 Hwy 301 S
(31545)
Rates: $37-$57
(912) 427-7600

JONESBORO

HOLIDAY INN
6288 Old Dixie
Hwy (30236)
Rates: $69-$119
(770) 968-4300
(800) 465-4329

SHONEYS INN
6358 Old Dixie
Hwy (30236)
Rates: $49-$63
(770) 968-5018
(800) 222-2222

KENNESAW

**BEST WESTERN
KENNESAW INN**
3375 George
Busbee Pkwy
(30144)
Rates: $55-$86
(770) 424-7666
(800) 528-1234

**COUNTRY INN
& SUITES**
3192 Barrett
Lakes Blvd
(30144)
Rates: n/a
(770) 423-7105
(800) 456-4000

**RED ROOF INN-
TOWN CENTER**
520 Roberts Ct
NW (30144)
Rates: $50-$62
(770) 429-0323
(800) 843-7663

KINGSLAND

**BEST WESTERN
KINGS BAY INN**
1353 SR 40
(31548)
Rates: $55-$99
(912) 729-7666
(800) 528-1234
(800) 728-7666

COMFORT INN
I-95 & SR 40
(31548)
Rates: $49-$89
(912) 729-6979
(800) 228-5150

DAYS INN
1050 E King Ave
(31548)
Rates: $45-$60
(912) 729-5454
(800) 329-7466

ECONO LODGE
1135 E King Ave
(31548)
Rates: $48-$88
(912) 673-7336
(800) 553-2666

HOLIDAY INN
930 40 E (31548)
Rates: $69-$99
(912) 729-3000
(800) 465-4329

**MARINERS
SUITES INN**
2343 Village Dr
(31548)
Rates: $58-$79
(912) 882-3004

SUPER 8 MOTEL
120 Edenfield Dr
(31548)
Rates: $39-$59
(912) 729-6888
(800) 800-8000

LA FAYETTE

**DAYS INN
& SUITES**
2209 N Main St
(30728)
Rates: $50-$150
(706) 639-9362
(800) 329-7466

LA GRANGE

**ADMIRAL
BENBOW INN**
2575 Whitesville
Rd (30240)
Rates: $38-$58
(706) 884-1114
(800) 451-1986

AMERIHOST INN
107 Hoffman Dr
(30240)
Rates: $56-$82
(706) 885-9002

COMFORT INN
Lafayette Pkwy
at ColtonRd
(30240)
Rates: $49-$84
(800) 228-5150

**DAYS INN-
CALLAWAY
GARDENS**
2606 Whitesville
Rd (30240)
Rates: $45-$72
(706) 882-8881
(800) 329-7466

**HIGHLAND
MARINA &
RESORT**
1000 Seminole Rd
(30240)
Rates: n/a
(706) 882-3437

**TOWN &
COUNTRY
MOTEL**
712 New
Franklin Rd
(30240)
Rates: n/a
(706) 884-8965

LAKE PARK

DAYS INN
4913 Timber Dr
(31636)
Rates: $36-$48
(912) 559-0229
(800) 329-7466

**HOLIDAY INN
EXPRESS**
1198 Lakes Blvd
(31636)
Rates: $49-$70
(912) 559-5181
(800) 465-4329

SHONEY'S INN
1075 Lakes Blvd
(31636)
Rates: $36-$42
(912) 559-5660
(800) 222-2222

SUPER 8 MOTEL
4907 Timber Dr
(31636)
Rates: $42-$44
(912) 559-8111
(800) 800-8000

TRAVELODGE
4912 Timber Dr
(31636)
Rates: $38-$60
(912) 559-0110
(800) 578-7878

LAKEMONT

FOREST LODGES
Lake Rabun Rd
(30552)
Rates: $59-$79
(706) 782-6250

LAVONIA

**BEST WESTERN
REGENCY INN &
SUITES**
13705 Jones St
(30553)
Rates: $39-$99
(706) 356-4000
(800) 528-1234

**SOUTHERN
TRACE INN**
14 Baker St (30553)
Rates: $38+
(706) 356-1033

LAWRENCE-VILLE

**A TOUCH OF
HOME BED &
BREAKFAST**
489 Hearth Place
(30243)
Rates: $35-$50
(770) 277-3579

DAYS INN
731 Duluth Hwy
(30245)
Rates: $48-$100
(770) 995-7782
(800) 329-7466

LITHONIA

LA QUINTA INN
2859 Panola Rd
(30058)
Rates: $49-$79
(770) 981-6411
(800) 687-6667

LOCUST GROVE

EXECUTIVE INN
4854 Hampton
Rd (30248)
Rates: $29-$40
(770) 957-2671

RED CARPET INN
4829 Hampton
Rd (30248)
Rates: $22-$33
(770) 957-2601
(800) 251-1962

SCOTTISH INNS
4679 Hampton
Rd (30248)
Rates: $25-$131
(770) 957-9001
(800) 251-1962

SUPER 8 MOTEL
4605 Hampton
Rd (30248)
Rates: $40-$53
(770) 957-2936
(800) 800-8000

LOUISVILLE

**ALLENWOOD
MOTEL**
525 Hwy 1
Bypass (30434)
Rates: $38+
(912) 625-7205

**LOUISVILLE
MOTOR LODGE**
308 Hwy 1
Bypass (30434)
Rates: $49
(912) 625-7168

MACON

**BEST WESTERN
INN & SUITES**
4681 Chambers
Rd (31206)
Rates: $56-$99
(912) 781-5300
(800) 528-1234

COMFORT INN
2690 Riverside
Dr (31204)
Rates: $59-$79
(912) 746-8855
(800) 228-5150

ECONO LODGE
4951 Romeiser
Rd (31206)
Rates: $35-$45
(912) 474-1661
(800) 553-2666

**FAMILY INNS
OF AMERICA**
4173 Interstate
Pkwy (31204)
Rates: n/a
(912) 474-8800

HAMPTON INN
3680 Riverside
Dr (31210)
Rates: $69
(912) 471-0660
(800) 426-7866

HOLIDAY INN EXPRESS
2720 Riverside Dr (31204)
Rates: $55-$65
(912) 743-1482
(800) 465-4329

HOLIDAY INN/ CONFERENCE CENTER
3590 Riverside Dr (31210)
Rates: $74-$80
(912) 474-2610
(800) 465-4329

HOWARD JOHNSON
2566 Riverside Dr (31204)
Rates: $50-$65
(912) 746-7671
(800) 446-4656

INN AMBASSADOR
2772 Riverside Dr (31204)
Rates: $38
(912) 742-3687

INN AMBASSADOR
I-75 & Hartley Bridge Rd (31204)
Rates: $38
(912) 788-7500

KNIGHTS INN
4952 Romeiser Dr (31206)
Rates: $32-$48
(912) 471-1230
(800) 843-5644

LA QUINTA INN & SUITES
3944 River Place Dr (31204)
Rates: $59-$89
(912) 475-0206
(800) 687-6667

MACON INN
1044 Riverside Dr (31204)
Rates: n/a
(912) 746-3561

MASTERS INN
4295 Pio Nono Ave (31206)
Rates: $29-$43
(912) 788-8910

MOTEL 6
4991 Harrison Rd (31206)
Rates: $30-$38
(912) 474-2870
(800) 466-8356

QUALITY INN
4630 Chambers Rd (31206)
Rates: $45-$70
(912) 781-7000
(800) 228-5151

RAMADA INN
5009 Harrison Rd (31206)
Rates: $52-$71
(912) 474-0871
(800) 272-6232

RAMADA INN NORTH
3850 Riverside Dr (31210)
Rates: $47-$65
(912) 474-9902
(800) 272-6232

RED ROOF INN
3950 River Place Dr (31210)
Rates: $40-$64
(912) 477-7477
(800) 843-7663

RESIDENCE INN BY MARRIOTT
3900 Sheraton Dr (31204)
Rates: n/a
(912) 475-4280
(800) 331-3131

RODEWAY INN
4999 Eisenhower Pkwy (31206)
Rates: $45
(912) 781-4200
(800) 228-2000

SCOTTISH INNS
5022 Romeiser Dr (31206)
Rates: n/a
(912) 474-2665
(800) 251-1962

SUPER 8 MOTEL
3935 Arkwright Rd (31210)
Rates: $55-$74
(912) 757-8688
(800) 800-8000

MADISON

BURNETT PLACE
317 Old Post Rd (30650)
Rates: $75-$100
(706) 342-4034

COMFORT INN
1972 Eatonton Rd (30650)
Rates: $45-$65
(706) 342-0054
(800) 228-5150

DAYS INN
2001 Eatonton Hwy (30650)
Rates: $50-$85
(706) 342-1839
(800) 329-7466

RAMADA INN
US 441 & I-20, (30650)
Rates: $44-$85
(706) 342-2121
(800) 272-6232

MANCHESTER

WESTERN MOTEL
1119 Warm Sprgs Hwy (31816)
Rates: $45-$100
(706) 846-4410

MARIETTA

BEST INNS OF AMERICA
1255 Franklin Rd (30067)
Rates: $46-$65
(770) 955-0004
(800) 237-8466

DRURY INN
1170 Powers Ferry Pl (30067)
Rates: $67-$87
(770) 612-0900
(800) 325-8300

ECONO LODGE
1940 Leland Dr (30067)
Rates: $44-$88
(770) 952-0052
(800) 553-2666

HOLIDAY INN HOTEL/SUITES
2265 Kingston Ct (30067)
Rates: $92-$102
(770) 952-7581
(800) 465-4329

HOWARD JOHNSON
I-75 & Delk Rd (30067)
Rates: $48-$88
(770) 951-1144
(800) 446-4656

LA QUINTA INN
2170 Delk Rd (30067)
Rates: $49-$95
(770) 951-0026
(800) 687-6667

MASTERS INN
2682 Windy Hill Rd (30067)
Rates: $39-$53
(770) 951-2005

MOTEL 6
2360 Delk Rd (30067)
Rates: $38-$59
(770) 952-8161
(800) 466-8356

RAMADA INN
2767 Windy Hill Rd (30067)
Rates: $65-$75
(770) 952-3251
(800) 272-6232

RAMADA LIMITED
630 Franklin Rd (30067)
Rates: $55-$99
(770) 919-7878
(800) 272-6232

SUPER 8 MOTEL
610 Franklin Rd (30067)
Rates: $45-$60
(770) 919-2340
(800) 800-8000

MCDONOUGH

BRITTANY AMERICAN INN
1171 Hwy 20/81 (30253)
Rates: $35-$42
(770) 957-5291
(800) 654-6305

BUDGET INN
1136 Hampton Rd (30253)
Rates: $25-$45
(770) 957-9683

COMFORT INN
80 SR 81 W (30253)
Rates: $55-$175
(770) 954-9110
(800) 228-5150

DAYS INN
744 Hwy 155 S (30253)
Rates: $47-$60
(770) 957-5261
(800) 329-7466

ECONO LODGE
1279 Hampton Rd (30253)
Rates: $35-$145
(770) 957-2651
(800) 553-2666

HOLIDAY INN
930 Hwy 155 S (30253)
Rates: $69-$84
(770) 957-5291
(800) 465-4329

MASTERS INN
1311 Hampton Rd (30253)
Rates: $38+
(770) 957-5818

RED CARPET INN
1170 Hampton Rd (30253)
Rates: n/a
770) 957-2458
(800) 251-1962

WELCOME INN
688 Hwy 155 S (30253)
Rates: $38-$80
(770) 957-5858

METTER

COMFORT INN
I-16 & US 121 (30439)
Rates: $42-$58
(912) 685-4100
(800) 228-5150

DAYS INN
720 S Lewis St (30349)
Rates: $35-$65
(912) 685-2700
(800) 329-7466

AREA CODES - If the local number doesn't connect, check for a new area code.

MILLEDGEVILLE

DAYS INN
2551 N Columbia
St (31061)
Rates: $54-$69
(912) 453-8471
(800) 329-7466

SCOTTISH INNS
2474 N Columbia
St (31061)
Rates: $20-$29
(912) 453-9491
(800) 251-1962

MORGANTON

**A COUNTRY
HEARTH CABIN
RENTALS**
My Mountain Rd
(30560)
Rates: $90-$125
(706) 374-2057

MORROW

**BEST WESTERN
SOUTHLAKE INN**
6347 Jonesboro
Rd (30260)
Rates: $50-$129
(770) 961-6300
(800) 528-1234
(888) 277-5253

**DRURY INN-
SOUTH**
6520 S Lee St
(30260)
Rates: $68-$88
(770) 960-0500
(800) 325-8300

**QUALITY INN
SOUTHLAKE**
6597 Jonesboro
Rd (30260)
Rates: $45-$159
(770) 960-1957
(800) 228-5151

RED ROOF INN
1348 Southlake
Plaza Dr (30260)
Rates: $49-$61
(770) 968-1483
(800) 843-7663

SLEEP INN
2185 Mt. Zion
Prkwy (30260)
Rates: $49-$179
(770) 472-9800
(800) 753-3746

MT. AIRY

**MT. AIRY BED
& BREAKFAST**
1675 Dicks Hill
Pkwy (30563)
Rates: $38-$79
(706) 776-2319

NEWNAN

**ADMIRAL
BENBOW INN**
40 Parkway N
(30263)
Rates: $44-$55
(770) 251-4580
(800) 451-1986

**BEST WESTERN
SHENANDOAH
INN**
620 Hwy 34 E
(30263)
Rates: $60-$70
(770) 304-9700
(800) 528-1234
(877) 455-1245

COMFORT INN
590 Bullsboro Dr
(30265)
Rates: $65-$140
(770) 502-8688
(800) 228-5150

DAYS INN
1344 S Hwy
(30263)
Rates: $45-$89
(770) 253-8550
(800) 329-7466

**HOLIDAY INN
EXPRESS**
6 Herring Rd
(30265)
Rates: $61-$65
(770) 251-2828
(800) 465-4329

MOTEL 6
40 Parkway North
(30265)
Rates: $35-$44
(770) 251-4580
(800) 466-8356

NICHOLLS

**BURNHAM
COTTAGE**
46 John Coffee
Rd (31554)
Rates: $125
(912) 384-7082

**GENERAL
COFFEE CABINS**
46 John Coffee
Rd (31554)
Rates: $38-$79
(912) 384-7082

NORCROSS

**AMBERLEY
SUITE HOTEL**
5885 Oakbrook
Pkwy (30093)
Rates: $59-$99
(770) 263-0515
(800) 365-0659

AMERISUITES
5600 Peachtree
Pkwy (30071)
Rates: $119-$129
(770) 416-7655
(800) 833-1516

COMFORT INN
5990 Western Hills
Dr (30071)
Rates: $45-$110
(770) 368-0218
(800) 228-5150

DRURY INN
5655 Jimmy
Carter Blvd
(30071)
Rates: $67-$87
(770) 729-0060
(800) 325-8300

**HILTON HOTEL
NORTHEAST**
5993 Peachtree
Ind Blvd (30071)
Rates: n/a
(770) 447-4747
(800) 445-8667

**HOLIDAY INN
SELECT**
6050 Peachtree
Ind Blvd (30071)
Rates: n/a
(770) 446-4400
(800) 465-4329

**HOMESTEAD
VILLAGE GUEST
STUDIOS**
7049 Jimmy
Carter Blvd
(30071)
Rates: n/a
(770) 449-9966
(888) 782-9473

**HOMEWOOD
SUITES**
450 Technology
Pkwy (30092)
Rates: $195
(770) 448-4663
(800) 225-5466

LA QUINTA INN
5375 Peachtree
Ind. Blvd (30071)
Rates: $45-$82
(770) 449-5144
(800) 687-6667

LA QUINTA INN
6187 Dawson
Blvd (30093)
Rates: $45-$147
(770) 448-8686
(800) 687-6667

MICROTEL INN
Jimmy Carter &
I-85 (30092)
Rates: $39-$49
(888) 771-7171

MOTEL 6
6015 Oakbrook
Pkwy (30093)
Rates: $38-$58
(770) 446-2311
(800) 466-8356

QUALITY INN
6045 Oakbrook
Pkwy (30093)
Rates: $49-$109
(770) 449-7322
(800) 228-5151

**RAMADA
LIMITED &
SUITES**
5395 Peachtree
Industrial Blvd
(30092)
Rates: $50-$89
(770) 446-2882
(800) 272-6232

RED ROOF INN
5171 Brook
Hollow Pkwy
(30071)
Rates: $47-$53
(770) 448-8944
(800) 843-7663

OAKWOOD

**ADMIRAL
BENBOW**
4500 Oakwood
Rd (30566)
Rates: $58-$79
(770) 531-9929
(800) 451-1986

**OAKWOOD
COUNTRY INN
& SUITES**
4335 Oakwood
Rd (30566)
Rates: $60-$121
(770) 535-8080

PAVO

**FAST TURTLE INN
BED & BREAKFST**
Off County Rd
167 (31778)
Rates: $75-$95
(912) 859-2775

PEACHTREE
CITY

**BEST WESTERN
PEACHTREE CITY
INN & SUITES**
976 Crosstown
Dr (30269)
Rates: $69-$87
(770) 632-9700
(800) 528-1234
(877) 455-1234

PERRY

**BEST INN
& SUITES**
202 Valley Dr
(31069)
Rates: $36-$125
(912) 987-2585
(800) 237-8466

COMFORT INN
1602 Sam Nunn
Blvd (31069)
Rates: $45-$65
(912) 987-7710
(800) 228-5150

**CROSSROADS
MOTEL**
317 Gn Courtney
Hodges Blvd
(31069)
Rates: $28-$33
(912) 987-3030

HAMPTON INN
102 Hampton Ct
(31069)
Rates: $57-$63
(912) 987-7681
(800) 426-7866

NEW PERRY HOTEL/MOTEL
800 Main St
(31069)
Rates: $30-$51
(912) 987-1000
(800) 877-3779

PASSPORT INN
1519 Sam Nunn
Blvd (31069)
Rates: $22-$40
(912) 987-9709
(800) 251-1962

QUALITY INN
1504 Sam Nunn
Blvd (31069)
Rates: $50-$75
(912) 987-1345
(800) 228-5151

RAMADA INN
100 Market Place
Dr (31069)
Rates: $45-$90
(912) 987-8400
(800) 272-6232

RED CARPET INN
105 Gn. Courtney
Hodges Blvd
(31069)
Rates: $20-$30
(912) 987-2200
(800) 251-1962

REGENCY INN
405 Gn Courtney
Hodges Blvd
(31069)
Rates: $28-$49
(912) 987-7747

RODEWAY INN
103 Marshallville
Rd (31069)
Rates: $30-$55
(912) 987-3200
(800) 228-2000

SANDMAN MOTEL
400 Gn Courtney
Hodges Blvd
(31069)
Rates: n/a
(912) 987-2393

SCOTTISH INNS
106 Gn Courtney
Hodges Blvd
(31069)
Rates: $20-$55
(912) 987-3622
(800) 251-1962

SUPER 8 MOTEL
102 Plaza Drive
(31069)
Rates: $46-$60
(912) 987-0999
(800) 800-8000

SWAN MOTEL
744 Main St
(31069)
Rates: $20-$30
(912) 987-1811

PINE MOUNTAIN

WARM SPRINGS RESORT
2541 White
House Pkwy
(31822)
Rates: $89-$179
(706) 663-7400

WHITE COLUMNS MOTEL
19727 S US 27
(31822)
Rates: $35-$55
(706) 663-2312
(800) 722-5083

PLAINS

PLAINS BED & BREAKFAST INN
100 W ChurchSt
(31780)
Rates: $60+
(912) 824-7252

POOLER

RAMADA INN
1016 E Hwy 80
(31322)
Rates: $40-$99
(912) 748-5242
(800) 272-6232

QUITMAN

MALLOY MANOR
401 W Screven St
(31643)
Rates: $55-$85
(912) 263-5704
(800) 239-5704

REGISTER

RED CARPET INN
2875 Hwy 301 S
(30417)
Rates: $39-$50
(912) 852-5200
(800) 251-1962

RICHLAND

DAYS INN
46 Nicholson St
(31825)
Rates: $40-$100
(912) 887-9000
(800) 329-7466

RICHMOND HILL

DAYS INN
I-95 & Hwy 17
(31324)
Rates: $50-$80
(912) 756-3371
(800) 329-7466

HOLIDAY INN
I-95 & Hwy 17
(31324)
Rates: n/a
(912) 756-3351
(800) 465-4329

MOTEL 6
4071 Hwy 17
(31324)
Rates: $30-$38
(912) 756-3543
(800) 466-8356

TRAVELODGE
I-95 & US 17
(31324)
Rates: $39-$65
(912) 756-3325
(800) 578-7878

RINCON

DAYS INN
582 Columbia
Ave (31326)
Rates: $44-$79
(912) 826-6966

RINGGOLD

HOLIDAY INN
5437 Alabama
Hwy (30736)
Rates: $50-$59
(706) 965-6500
(800) 465-4329

SUPER 8 MOTEL
5400 Alabama
Hwy (30736)
Rates: $46-$55
(706) 965-7080
(800) 800-8000

ROME

COMFORT INN
2209 Shorter Ave
(30165)
Rates: $56-$150
(706) 802-1223
(800) 228-5150

HOLIDAY INN
20 US Hwy
411 E (30161)
Rates: $60-$98
(706) 295-1100
(800) 465-4329

SUPER 8 MOTEL
390 Dodd Blvd
SE (30161)
Rates: $39-$56
(706) 234-8182
(800) 800-8000

ROSWELL

BAYMONT INN
575 Old Holcomb
Bridge Rd
(30076)
Rates: $61
(770) 552-0200
(800) 301-0200

BEST WESTERN ROSWELL SUITES
907 Old Holcomb
Bridge (30076)
Rates: $50-$80
(770) 552-5599
(800) 528-1234
(800) 784-8321

HAMPTON INN
9995 Old
Dogwood Rd
(30076)
Rates: $69-$89
(770) 587-5161
(800) 426-7866

HOMESTEAD VILLAGE GUEST STUDIOS
9955 Old
Dogwood Rd
(30076)
Rates:n/a
(770) 992-9449
(888) 782-9473

SAINT MARYS

CUMBERLAND KINGS BAY LODGES
603 Sand Bar Dr,
Spur 40 (31558)
Rates: $30-$49
(912) 882-8900
(800) 831-6664

GOODBREAD HOUSE B&B
209 Osborne Rd
(31558)
Rates: n/a
(912) 882-7490

GUESTHOUSE INN & SUITES
2710 Osborne Rd
(31558)
Rates: $45-$59
(912) 882-6250
(800) 768-6250

SANDERSVILLE

VILLA SOUTH MOTEL
725 South Harris
St (31082)
Rates: $41-$51
(912) 552-1234

SAUTEE

MOUNTAIN GREENERY CABINS
3621 GA Hwy
255 N (30571)
Rates: $60-$130
(706) 878-3442

NACOOCHEE VALLEY GUEST HOUSE
P. O. Box 249
(30571)
Rates: $59-$80
(706) 878-3830

ROYAL WINDSOR COTTAGE B&B
Hwy 356 (30571)
Rates: $95-$145
(706) 878-1322

AREA CODES - If the local number doesn't connect, check for a new area code.

SAVANNAH

THE AZALEA INN
217 E
Huntingdon St
(31401)
Rates: $99-$159
(912) 236-2707
(800) 582-3823

BAYMONT INN
8484 Abercorn St
(31406)
Rates: $59-$66
(912) 927-7660
(800) 301-0200

**BED &
BREAKFAST INN**
117 W Gordon St
(31401)
Rates: $95-$130
(912) 238-0518

**CLARION INN
& SUITES**
16 Gateway Blvd
E (31419)
Rates: $69-$199
(912) 920-7770
(800) 252-7466

**EAST BAY
HISTORIC
COUNTRY INN**
225 E Bay St
(31404)
Rates: $129-$189
(912) 238-1225
(800) 500-1225

ECONO LODGE
7 Gateway Blvd
W (31419)
Rates: $75-$120
(912) 925-2280
(800) 553-2666

**GUESTHOUSE
INN I-95**
390 Canebrake
Rd (31419)
Rates: $38-$58
(912) 927-2999

**THE HASLAM /
FORT HOUSE**
417 E Charlton St
(31401)
Rates: n/a
(912) 233-6380

HOLIDAY INN
I-95 & SR 204
(31419)
Rates: $67-$75
(912) 925-2770
(800) 465-4329

**HOMEWOOD
SUITES**
5820 White Bluff
Rd (31405)
Rates: $84-$109
(912) 353-8500
(800) 225-5466

**JOAN'S ON
JONES BED &
BREAKFAST**
17 W Jones St
(31401)
Rates: $135-$180
(912) 234-3863
(800) 407-3863

LA QUINTA INN
6805 Abercorn St
(31405)
Rates: $65-$95
(912) 355-3004
(800) 687-6667

LA QUINTA INN
6 Gateway Blvd
S (31419)
Rates: $59-$85
(912) 925-9505
(800) 687-6667

LEE'S RETREAT
16 Van Horn St
(31401)
Rates: $46-$95
(912) 786-5555

MASTERS INN
4200 Hwy 21 N
(31408)
Rates: $43+
(912) 964-4344

**MICROTEL INN
& SUITES**
I-95 Exit 16, Hwy
204 (31419)
Rates: $39-$89
(888) 771-7171

**OLDE HARBOUR
INN B&B**
508 E Factors
Walk (31401)
Rates: $139-$249
(912) 234-4100
(800) 553-6533

RED CARPET INN
1 Fort Argyle Rd
(31419)
Rates: $38-$58
(912) 925-2640
(800) 251-1962

RED ROOF INN
405 Al
Henderson Blvd
(31419)
Rates: n/a
(912) 920-3535
(800) 843-7663

**RESIDENCE INN
BY MARRIOTT**
5710 White Bluff
Rd (31405)
Rates: $117-$159
(912) 356-3266
(800) 331-3131

**ST. JULIAN
STREET B&B**
501 St Julian St
(31401)
Rates: $60-$120
(912) 236-9939

SUPER 8 MOTEL
15 Fort Argyle Rd
(31419)
Rates: $49-$64
(912) 927-8550
(800) 800-8000

**SUPER 8 MOTEL
TYBEE ISLAND**
16 Tybrisia St
(31328)
Rates: $55-$85
(912) 786-8806
(800) 800-8000

SENOIA

**CULPEPPER
HOUSE BED &
BREAKFAST**
35 Broad St
(30276)
Rates: $85
(770) 599-8182

SKY VALLEY

**SKY VALLEY
LODGING**
39 Sky Valley
Resort (30537)
Rates: $100-$300
(706) 746-5301
(800) 262-8259

SMYRNA

AMERIHOST
5130 S Cobb Dr
(30080)
Rates: $68-$84
(404) 794-1600
(800) 434-5800

**HOMESTEAD
VILLAGE GUEST
STUDIOS**
3103 Sports Ave
(30080)
Rates: n/a
(770) 432-4000
(888) 782-9473

MICROTEL INN
5300 S Cobb Dr
SE (30080)
Rates: $39-$64
(770) 799-7000
(888) 771-7171

RED ROOF INN
2200 Corporate
Plaza (30080)
Rates: $46-$67
(770) 952-6966
(800) 843-7663

**RESIDENCE INN
BY MARRIOTT**
2771 Hargrove
Rd (30080)
Rates: $69-$129
(770) 433-8877
(800) 331-3131

SPARKS

RED CARPET INN
Rt 1, Box 212
(31647)
Rates: $25+
(912) 549-8243
(800) 251-1962

STATESBORO

**CROSSROADS
MOTEL**
225 N Main St
(30458)
Rates: $38+
(912) 764-5651

DAYS INN
461 S Main St
(30458)
Rates: $49-$99
(912) 764-5666
(800) 329-7466

**PARKWOOD
MOTEL &
CAMPGROUND**
936 S Main St
(30458)
Rates: $25-$38
(912) 681-3105

RAMADA INN
230 S Main St
(30458)
Rates: $35-$95
(912) 764-6121
(800) 272-6232

**STATESBORO
HISTORIC
COUNTRY INN**
106 S Main St
(30458)
Rates: $85-$125
(912) 489-8628
(800) 846-9466

SUPER 8 MOTEL
109 N Main St
(30458)
Rates: $35-$55
(912) 764-5631
(800) 800-8000

STOCKBRIDGE

**AMERIHOST
INN-EAGLES
LANDING**
100 N Park Ct
(30281)
Rates: $55-$60
(770) 507-6500
(800) 434-5800

MOTEL 6
7233 Davidson
Pkwy (30281)
Rates: $40-$56
(770) 389-1142
(800) 466-8356

SUCHES

**TOCCOA
RIVERFRONT
CABIN**
292 Brown Mt.
Dr (30572)
Rates: $225
Three Nights
(352) 237-4335

SUWANEE

HOLIDAY INN
2955 Hwy 317
(30174)
Rates: $79-$109
(770) 945-4921
(800) 465-4329

RED ROOF INN
77 Swinco Blvd
(30024)
Rates: n/a
(770) 271-5559
(800) 843-7663

SWAINSBORO

BRADFORD INN
688 S Main St
(30401)
Rates: $46-$70
(912) 237-2400

COLEMAN HOUSE INN
323 N Main St
(30401)
Rates: $55-$85
(912) 237-9100

DAYS INN
654 S Main St
(30401)
Rates: $35-$55
(912) 237-9333
(800) 329-7466

SYLVESTER

DAYS INN
909 Franklin St
(31791)
Rates: $40-$109
(912) 776-9700
(800) 329-7466

TALLAPOOSA

COMFORT INN
778 Hwy 100
& I-20 (30176)
Rates: $45-$115
(770) 5874-5575
(800) 228-5150

THOMASTON

DAYS INN
1215 Hwy 19 N
(30286)
Rates: $56-$66
(706) 648-9260
(800) 329-7466

THOMASVILLE

DAYS INN
15375 US 19 S
(31792)
Rates: $34-$59
(912) 226-6025
(800) 329-7466

GUESTHOUSE INNS & SUITES
15138 Hwy 19 S
(31792)
Rates: $59-$69
(912) 226-7111

SUSINA PLANTATION INN HISTORIC B&B
1420 Meridian
Rd (31792)
Rates: $150
(912) 377-9644

THOMSON

BEST WESTERN WHITE COLUMNS INN
1890 Washington
Rd (30824)
Rates: $53-$99
(706) 595-8000
(800) 528-1234
(800) 528-9765

DAYS INN
2658 Cobbham
Rd (30824)
Rates: $45-$55
(706) 595-2262
(800) 329-7466

HOLIDAY INN EXPRESS HOTEL & SUITES
1893 Washington
Rd NE (30824)
Rates: n/a
(706) 595-6500
(800) 465-4329

TIFTON

HAMPTON INN
720 Hwy 319 S
(31794)
Rates: $59-$71
(912) 382-8800
(800) 426-7866

HOLIDAY INN
1208 Hwy 82 W
(31793)
Rates: $60-$65
(912) 382-6687
(800) 465-4329

HOWARD JOHNSON
1103 King Rd
(31794)
Rates: $42-$55
(912) 386-2100
(800) 446-4656

MASTERS INN
I-75 & US 82 W
(31793)
Rates: $29-$43
(912) 382-8100
(800) 633-3434

MOTEL 6
I-75 & Hwy 319,
Exit 17 (30281)
Rates: $32-$39
(912) 388-8777
(800) 466-8356

RAMADA LIMITED
1211 Hwy 82 W
(31793)
Rates: $45-$85
(912) 382-8500
(800) 272-6232

RED CARPET INN
1025 W 2nd St
(31794)
Rates: $24-$37
(912) 382-0280
(800) 251-1962

SUPER 8 MOTEL
I-75 & W 2nd St
(31793)
Rates: $35-$48
(912) 382-9500
(800) 800-8000

TOCCOA

DAYS INN
Hwy 17 & Rt 5
(30577)
Rates: $34-$60
(706) 886-9641
(800) 329-7466

TOWNSEND

DAYS INN
I-95 & GA 99
(31331)
Rates: $29-$60
(912) 832-4411
(800) 329-7466

TUCKER

HOMESTEAD VILLAGE GUEST STUDIOS
1795 Crescent Ctr
Blvd (30084)
Rates: n/a
(770) 934-4040
(888) 782-9473

LA QUINTA STONE MOUNTAIN
1819 Mountain
Ind Blvd (30084)
Rates: $55-$89
(770) 496-1317
(800) 687-6667

MASTERS INNS
1435 Montreal Rd
(30084)
Rates: $39-$53
(770) 938-3552

RED ROOF INN
2810
Lawrenceville
Hwy (30084)
Rates: $46-$73
(770) 496-1311
(800) 843-7663

UNADILLA

RED CARPET INN
101 Robert St
(31091)
Rates: n/a
(912) 627-3261
(800) 251-1962

UNION CITY

RED ROOF INN
6710 Shannon
Pkwy (30291)
Rates: n/a
(770) 306-7750
(800) 843-7663

SCOTTISH INNS
Rt 2, Box 100
(31091)
Rates: $26-$32
(912) 627-3228
(800) 251-1962

VALDOSTA

BEST WESTERN KING OF THE ROAD INN
1403 N St
Augustine Rd
(31601)
Rates: $49-$59
(912) 244-7600
(800) 528-1234

BRAIRWOOD MOTEL
1943 Brairwood
Dr (31601)
Rates: n/a
(912) 242-4205

COMFORT INN
2101 W Hill Ave
(31603)
Rates: $55-$89
(912) 242-1212
(800) 228-5150

DAYS INN
4958 N Valdosta
Rd (31602)
Rates: $36-$42
(912) 244-4460
(800) 329-7466

DAYS INN
1827 W Hill Ave
(316015)
Rates: $38-$44
(912) 249-8800
(800) 329-7466

HOLIDAY INN
1309 St Augustine
Rd (31601)
Rates: $57
(912) 242-3881
(800) 465-4329

MOTEL 6-VALDOSTA STATE UNIV.
2003 West Hill
Ave (31601)
Rates: $28-$44
(912) 333-0047
(800) 466-8356

QUALITY INN
1209 St Augustine
Rd (31601)
Rates: $55-$75
(912) 244-8510
(800) 228-5151

QUALITY INN
1902 W Hill Ave
(31601)
Rates: $35-$54
(912) 244-4520
(800) 228-5151

RAMADA LTD
2008 W Hill Ave
(31601)
Rates: $49-$99
(912) 242-1225
(800) 272-6232

RODEWAY INN
2015 W Hill Ave
(31601)
Rates: $29-$75
(912) 241-1177
(800) 228-2000

SCOTTISH INNS
1114 St Augustine
Rd (31601)
Rates: n/a
(912) 244-7900
(800) 251-1962

SHONEY'S INN
1828 W Hill Ave
(31601)
Rates: $38-$48
(912) 244-7711
(800) 222-2222

SUPER 8 MOTEL
1825 W Hill Ave
(31601)
Rates: $36-$44
(912) 249-8000
(800) 800-8000

TRAVELODGE
1330 St. Augustine
Rd (31601)
Rates: $39-$69
(912) 242-3464
(800) 578-7878

**VILLAGER
LODGE**
3470 Madison
Hwy (31601)
Rates: $119-$149
Weekly
(912) 242-4664
(800) 328-7829

VIDALIA

DAYS INN
1503 Lyons Hwy,
(30474)
Rates: $40-$50
(912) 537-9251
(800) 329-7466

HOLIDAY INN
2619 E First St
(30474)
Rates: $50-$67
(912) 537-9000
(800) 465-4329

VIENNA

KNIGHTS INN
1525 E Union St
(31092)
Rates: $26-$75
(912) 268-2221
(800) 843-5644

VILLA RICA

**AHAVA
PLANTATION
BED & BREAKFAST**
2236 S Van Wert
Rd (30180)
Rates: $59-$79
(770) 459-2863
(800) 858-3473

SUPER 8 MOTEL
195 Hwy 61
Connector
(30180)
Rates: $45-$65
(770) 459-8888
(800) 800-8000

WARNER ROBINS

**ADMIRAL
BENBOW INN**
2079 Watson Blvd
(31093)
Rates: $38-$58
(912) 929-9526
(800) 451-1986

**BEST WESTERN
PEACH INN**
2739 Watson Blvd
(31099)
Rates: $45-$70
(912) 953-3800
(800) 528-1234

SUPER 8 MOTEL
105 Woodcrest
Blvd (31093)
Rates: $58-$177
(912) 923-8600
(800) 800-8000

WATKINS- VILLE

**ASHFORD
MANOR B&B**
5 Harden Hill Rd
(30677)
Rates: $85
(706) 769-2633

WAYCROSS

DAYS INN
2016 Memorial
Dr (31501)
Rates: $32-$66
(912) 285-4700
(800) 329-7466

HOLIDAY INN
1725 Memorial
Dr (31501)
Rates: $60-$67
(912) 283-4490
(800) 465-4329

JAMESON INN
950 City Blvd
(31501)
Rates: $54-$66
(912) 283-3800
(800) 526-3766

**PINE CREST
MOTEL**
1761 Memorial
Dr (31501)
Rates: $28-$32
(912) 283-3580

WEST POINT

TRAVELODGE
1870 State Rd 18
(31833)
Rates: $42-$99
(706) 643-9922
(800) 578-7878

WHITE

COURTESY INN
2335 Hwy 411 NE
(30184)
Rates: $38+
(770) 382-1122

HOLIDAY INN
2336 Hwy 411 E
(30184)
Rates: n/a
(770) 386-0830
(800) 465-4329

SCOTTISH INNS
2385 Hwy 411 NE
(30184)
Rates: $25-$100
(770) 382-7011
(800) 251-1962

YOUNG HARRIS

**CREEKSIDE
HIDEAWAY
B&B/CABIN**
8970 Sharons'
Way (30582)
Rates: $40-$85
(706) 379-1509
(888) 882-7335

HAWAII

SPECIAL NOTE: In the state of Hawaii, pets are not permitted in rooms. In addition, there is a quarantine on pets arriving from the mainland. If you intend to visit Hawaii with your pet, contact the Hawaii Visitors Bureau, (800) 464-2924 or (808) 923-1811 for additional information.

IDAHO

ALBION

MOUNTAIN MANOR B&B
P. O. Box 128
(83311)
Rates: $35-$55
(208) 673-6642

AMERICAN FALLS

FALLS MOTEL
411 Lincoln
(83211)
Rates: $30-$60
(208) 226-9658

HILLVIEW MOTEL
2799 Lakeview Rd
(83211)
Rates: $28-$42
(208) 226-5151

ARCO

ARCO INN
540 W Grand
(83213)
Rates: $32-$45
(208) 527-3100

D K MOTEL
316 S Front
(83213)
Rates: $30-$65
(208) 527-8282
(800) 231-0134

LAZY A MOTEL
318 W Grand
(83213)
Rates: $27-$50
(208) 527-8263
(800) 388-3679

LOST RIVER MOTEL
405 Hwy Dr
(83213)
Rates: $27-$56
(208) 527-3600

RIVERSIDE MOTEL
P. O. Box 22
(83213)
Rates: $20-$60
(208) 527-8954
(800) 229-8954

ASHTON

FOUR SEASONS MOTEL
P. O. Box 848
(83420)
Rates: $28-$45
(208) 652-7769

JENSEN'S RV / B&B & COTTAGES
1146 N 3400 E
Hwy 20 (83420)
Rates: $39-$49
(208) 652-3356
(800) 747-3356

LOG CABIN MOTEL
1001 Main (83420)
Rates: $37-$60
(208) 652-3956

RANKIN MOTEL
120 S Yellowstone
Hwy (83420)
Rates: $33-$50
(208) 652-3570

SUPER 8 MOTEL TETON TRAVEL PLAZA
164 White Pine Dr
(83420)
Rates: $55-$57
(208) 652-7885
(800) 800-8000

ATHOL

ATHOL MOTEL
P. O. Box 275
(83801)
Rates: $25-$49
(208) 683-3476
(800) 858-6622

KELSO LAKE RESORT CABINS
1450 Kelso Lake
Rd (83801)
Rates: $35-$45
(208) 683-2297

BANKS

THE PONDEROSA
HC 76, Box 1010
(83602)
Rates: $25-$30
(208) 793-2700

TRAILS END MOTEL
HC 76, Box 1010
(83602)
Rates: $25-$40
(208) 793-2700

BAYVIEW

BAYVIEW SCENIC MOTEL & RV PARK
6th & Main Sts
(83803)
Rates: $50-$60
(208) 683-2215

MACDONALD'S HUDSON BAY RESORT CABINS
7425 Hudson Bay
Rd (83803)
Rates: $65-$190
(208) 683-2211

SCENIC BAY MARINA & MOTEL
102 Scenic Bay Dr
(83803)
Rates: $63
(208) 683-2243

BELLEVUE

COME ON INN LOG CABINS
Beech & Main St
(83313)
Rates: $50-$65
(208) 788-0825

HIGH COUNTRY MOTEL
765 Main St S
(83313)
Rates: $40-$55
(208) 788-2050
(800) 692-2050

BLACKFOOT

ALDER INN B&B
384 Alder St
(83221)
Rates: $50
(208) 785-6968

BEST WESTERN BLACKFOOT INN
750 Jensen Grove
Dr (83221)
Rates: $50-$90
(208) 785-4144
(800) 528-1234

WESTON LAMPLIGHTER
1229 Park Way Dr
(83221)
Rates: $40-$95
(208) 785-5000

BLISS

AMBER INN
17286 US Hwy 30
(83314)
Rates: $33-$46
(208) 352-4441

BOISE

AMERISUITES
925 N Milwaukee
St (83709)
Rates: $99
(208) 375-1200
(800) 833-1516

BESTREST INN
8002 Overland Rd
(83709)
Rates: $50
(208) 322-4404
(800) 733-1418

BOULEVARD MOTEL
1121 S Capitol
Blvd (83706)
Rates: $25-$45
(208) 342-4629

BUDGET INN
2600 Fairview Ave
(83702)
Rates: $28-$55
(208) 344-8617
(800) 792-8612

AREA CODES - If the local number doesn't connect, check for a new area code.

CABANA INN
1600 Main St
(83702)
Rates: $30-$55
(208) 343-6000

CAVANAUGHS PARKCENTER SUITES
424 E Parkcenter
Blvd (83706)
Rates: n/a
(208) 342-1044

DOUBLETREE HOTEL
1800 Fairview
(83702)
Rates: $129
(208) 344-7691
(800) 222-8733

DOUBLETREE RIVERSIDE
2900 Chinden
Blvd (83714)
Rates: $99-$225
(208) 343-1871
(800) 222-8733

ECONO LODGE
4060 W Fairview
Ave (83706)
Rates: $42-$52
(208) 344-4030
(800) 553-2666

HAMPTON INN
3270 S Shoshone
(83705)
Rates: $64-$84
(208) 331-5600
(800) 426-7866

HOLIDAY INN AIRPORT
3300 Vista Ave
(83705)
Rates: $99-$109
(208) 344-8365
(800) 465-4329

HOLIDAY MOTEL
5416 Fairview Ave
(83706)
Rates: $27-$45
(208) 376-4631

MIDDLE FORK LODGE
P. O. Box 16278,
Middle Fork of
the Salmon River
(83715)
Rates: $400/Week
(208) 342-7888

MOTEL 6
2323 Airport Way
(83705)
Rates: $39-$56
(208) 344-3506
(800) 466-8356

NENDELS INN
2155 N Garden
(83704)
Rates: $35-$55
(208) 344-4030

OWYHEE PLAZA HOTEL
1109 Main St
(83702)
Rates: $74-$138
(208) 343-4611
(800) 233-4611

QUALITY INN AIRPORT
2717 Vista Ave
(83705)
Rates: $59-$74
(208) 343-7505
(800) 228-5151

RESIDENCE INN BY MARRIOTT
1401 Lusk (83706)
Rates: $59-$139
(208) 344-1200
(800) 331-3131

RESTON HOTEL
1025 S Capitol
Blvd (83706)
Rates: $49-$175
(208) 344-7971
(800) 264-7377

RODEWAY INN
1115 N Curtis Rd
(83706)
Rates: $72-$130
(208) 376-2700
(800) 228-2000

SAWTOOTH LODGE
130 N Haines
(83712)
Rates: $40-$80
(208) 344-2437

SEVEN K MOTEL
3633 Chinden
Blvd (83703)
Rates: $32-$65
(208) 343-7723

SHILO INN AIRPORT
4111 Broadway
Ave (83705)
Rates: $79-$129
(208) 343-7662
(800) 222-2244

SHILO INN RIVERSIDE
3031 Main St
(83702)
Rates: $65-$115
(208) 344-3521
(800) 222-2244

SUPER 8 MOTEL
2773 Elder St
(83705)
Rates: $53-$68
(208) 344-8871
(800) 800-8000

TRAVELODGE
1314 Grove St
(83702)
Rates: $45-$85
(208) 342-9351
(800) 578-7878

U.S. SUITES CONDOMINUMS
2147 S Centurion
Place (83709)
Rates: n/a
(208) 322-3564
(800) US SUITE

WEST RIVER INN
3525 Chinden
Blvd (83714)
Rates: $28-$38
(208) 338-1155

BONNERS FERRY

BEST WESTERN KOOTENAI RIVER INN
7160 Plaza St
(83805)
Rates: $90-$105
(208) 267-8511
(800) 345-5668

BONNERS FERRY RESORT
Rt 4, Box 4700
(83805)
Rates: $20-$60
(208) 267-2422

DEEP CREEK RESORT
Rt 4, Box 628
(83805)
Rates: $37-$47
(208) 267-2729
(800) 689-2729

KOOTENAI VALLEY MOTEL
Hwy 95 S (83805)
Rates: $35-$105
(208) 267-7567
(800) 341-8000

TOWN N' COUNTRY MOTEL & RV PARK
Hwy 95, Rt 4,
Box 4664 (83805)
Rates: $35-$75
(208) 267-7915

BUHL

SIESTA MOTEL
629 Broadway S
(83316)
Rates: n/a
(208) 543-6427

BURLEY

BEST WESTERN INN & CONV CTR
800 N Overland
Ave (83318)
Rates: $54-$86
(208) 678-3501
(800) 528-1234
(800) 599-1849

BUDGET MOTEL
900 N Overland
Ave (83318)
Rates: $44-$69
(208) 678-2200
(800) 635-4952

GREENWELL MOTEL
904 E Main St
(83318)
Rates: $32-$64
(208) 678-5576
(800) 341-8000

LAMPLITER MOTEL
304 E Main
(83318)
Rates: $25-$55
(208) 678-0031

PARISH MOTEL
721 E Main
(83318)
Rates: $20-$40
(208) 678-5505

STARLITE MOTEL
500 Overland
(83318)
Rates: $25-$45
(208) 678-7766

CALDER

ST. JOE LODGE & RESORT
Rt 3, Box 350
(83808)
Rates: $50
(208) 245-3462

CALDWELL

BEST INN & SUITES
901 Specht Ave
(83605)
Rates: $59-$121
(208) 454-2222
(800) 237-8466

BEST WESTERN CALDWELL INN & SUITES
908 Specht Ave
(83605)
Rates: $59-$144
(208) 454-7225
(800) 528-1234
(888) 454-3522

HOLIDAY MOTEL
512 Frontage Rd
(83606)
Rates: $24-$50
(208) 454-3888

SUNDOWNER MOTEL
1002 Arthur St
(83606)
Rates: $32-$42
(208) 459-1585

CAMBRIDGE

CAMBRIDGE HOUSE B&B
Hwy 95 & 71
(83610)
Rates: $40-$70
(208) 257-3325

FRONTIER MOTEL & RV PARK
P. O. Box 178
(83610)
Rates: $28-$60
(208) 257-3851

HUNTER'S INN
Hwy 95 & 71
(83610)
Rates: $35-$65
(208) 257-3325

CASCADE

ARROWHEAD CABINS & RV
Hwy 55, P. O. Box 337 (83611)
Rates: $25
(208) 382-4534

AURORA MOTEL & RV PARK
P. O. Box 799
(83611)
Rates: $35-$60
(208) 382-4948
(800) 554-6175

HIGH COUNTRY INN
112 N Main
(83611)
Rates: $30-$50
(208) 382-3315

MOUNTAIN VIEW MOTEL
P. O. Box 1053
(83611)
Rates: $36-$54
(208) 382-4238
(800) 265-7666

NORTH SHORE LODGE CABINS
175 N Shorelind Dr (Warm Lake 83611)
Rates: $50-$89
(208) 632-2000
(800) 933-3193

PINEWOOD LODGE MOTEL & RV PARK
900 S Hwy 55
(83611)
Rates: $35-$63
(208) 382-4948

SILVER PINES MOTEL
403 N Main
(83611)
Rates: $40-$60
(208) 382-4370

WHITEWATER GUEST RANCH
HC 83, Frank Church River of No Return Wilderness Area
(83611)
Rates: $50-$95
(208) 882-8082

CHALLIS

CHALLIS HOT SPRINGS
HC 63, Box 1779
(83226)
Rates: $45-$55
(208) 879-4442

CHALLIS MOTOR LODGE
Hwy 93 & Main St
(83226)
Rates: $34-$54
(208) 879-2251

NORTHGATE INN
HC 63, Box 1665
(83226)
Rates: $36-$48
(208) 879-2490

THE VILLAGE INN
P. O. Box 6, Hwy 93 (83226)
Rates: $38-$64
(208) 879-2239

CHUBBUCK

OXBOW MOTOR INN
4333 Yellowstone Ave (83202)
Rates: $34-$39
(208) 237-3100

CLARK FORK

RIVER DELTA RESORT
Box 128, Hwy 200 E (83811)
Rates: $45-$65
(208) 266-1335

COEUR D'ALENE

BATES MOTEL
2018 Sherman Ave
(83814)
Rates: $35-$45
(208) 667-1411

BENNETT BAY INN
East 5144, I-90
(83814)
Rates: $55-$150
(208) 664-6168
(800) 368-8609

BEST INN& SUITES
280 W Appleway
(83814)
Rates: $69-$109
(208) 765-5500
(800) 237-8466

BOULEVARD MOTEL & RV
2400 Seltice Way
(83814)
Rates: $35-$60
(208) 664-4978

BUDGET HOST PLEASANT INN
330 W Appleway Ave (83814)
Rates: $31-$75
(208) 765-3011
(800) 283-4678

BUDGET SAVER MOTEL
1519 Sherman Ave
(83814)
Rates: $22-$60
(208) 667-9505

CEDAR MOTEL & RV PARK
319 Coeur d'Alene Lake Dr (83814)
Rates: $29-$95
(208) 664-2278

COEUR D'ALENE BED & BREAKFAST
906 Foster Ave
(83814)
Rates: $60-$100
(208) 667-7527
(800) 597-1898

COEUR D'ALENE INN & CONF CTR
414 W Appleway Ave (83814)
Rates: $115-$139
(208) 765-3200
(800) 251-7829

COEUR D'ALENE KOA CABINS
10700 Wolf Lodge Bay Rd (83814)
Rates: n/a
(208) 664-4471
(800) KOA-2609

THE COEUR D'ALENE RESORT
115 S 2nd Ave
(83814)
Rates: $179-$509
(208) 765-4000

COUNTRY RANCH BED & BREAKFAST
1495 S Green Ferry Rd (83814)
Rates: $85-$95
(208) 664-1189

DAYS INN
2200 NW Blvd
(83814)
Rates: $55-$82
(208) 667-8668
(800) 329-7466

EL RANCHO MOTEL
1915 E Sherman Ave (83814)
Rates: $26-$65
(208) 664-8794
(800) 359-9791

GARDEN MOTEL
1808 NW Blvd
(83814)
Rates: $40-$100
(208) 664-2743

HAWTHORN INN & SUITES
2209 E Sherman Ave (83814)
Rates: $99-$129
(208) 667-6777
(800) 527-1133

MONTE VISTA MOTEL & RV PRK
320 Coeur d'Alene Lake Dr (83814)
Rates: $40-$75
(208) 664-8201

MOTEL 6
416 W Appleway
(83814)
Rates: $35-$72
(208) 664-6600
(800) 466-8356

O'NEILL'S B&B
1221 Coeur d'Alene Ave
(83814)
Rates: $60
(208) 664-5356

RESORT PROPERTY VACATION HOMES RENTALS
1801 Lincoln Way #7 (83814)
Rates: n/a
(208) 667-6035

RODEWAY INN PINES RESORT MOTEL
1422 NW Blvd
(83814)
Rates: $53-$89
(208) 664-8244
(800) 228-2000
(800) 651-2510

SCENIC BAY MARINA & MOTEL
P. O. Box 36
(83814)
Rates: $55-$65
(208) 683-2243

SHILO INN
702 W Appleway
(83814)
Rates: $69-$179
(208) 664-2300
(800) 222-2244

SQUAW BAY LAKE FRONT RESORT CABINS
5733 Hwy 97 S
(83814)
Rates: $85-$155
(208) 664-6782

STAR MOTEL
1516 Sherman Ave
(83814)
Rates: $35-$90
(208) 664-5035

SUMMER HOUSE BY THE LAKE B&B
1535 Silver Beach Rd (83814)
Rates: $125
(208) 667-9395

SUPER 8 MOTEL
505 W Appleway
(83814)
Rates: $44-$65
(208) 765-8880
(800) 800-8000

COOLIN

BISHOP'S MARINA & RESORT
Box 91 (83821)
Rates: $55-$75
(208) 443-2191

THE INN AT PRIEST LAKE
P. O. Box 189
(83821)
Rates: $50-$150
(208) 443-2121
(800) 443-6240

COUNCIL

STARLITE MOTEL
102 N Dartmouth
(83612)
Rates: $30-$49
(208) 253-4868

DIXIE

LODGEPOLE PINE INN
P. O. Box 58
(83525)
Rates: $55
(208) 842-2523
(800) 242-3958

DONNELLY

LONG VALLEY MOTEL
161 S Main St
(83615)
Rates: $34-$64
(208) 325-8545

DOWNEY

DOWNATA HOT SPRINGS
25900 S Downata
Rd (83234)
Rates: $50-$275
(208) 897-5736

FLAG'S WEST TRUCK STOP MOTEL
Exit 31, I-15
(83234)
Rates: $24-$30
(208) 897-5238

DRIGGS

BEST WESTERN TETON WEST
476 N Main St
(83422)
Rates: $70-$85
(208) 354-2363
(800) 528-1234

PINES MOTEL-GUEST HAUS
105 South Main
(83422)
Rates: $35-$70
(208) 354-2774
(800) 354-2778

DUBOIS

CROSS ROADS MOTEL
391 S Reynolds
(83423)
Rates: $26-$36
(208) 374-5258

EDEN

ANDERSONS CAMP CABINS & RV PARK
Rt 1 (83325)
Rates: $45-$55
(208) 825-9800
(888) 480-9400

ELK CITY

CANTERBURY HOUSE INN B&B
501 Elk Creek Rd
(83525)
Rates: $50-$85
(208) 842-2591

ELK CITY HOTEL
P O Box 356
(83525)
Rates: $25-$48
(208) 842-2452

JUNCTION LODGE
HC 67, Box 98
(83525)
Rates: $34-$36
(208) 842-2459

PROSPECTOR CABINS
4500 Erickson
Ridge (83525)
Rates: $55
(208) 842-2557

PROSPECTOR LODGE
129 N Main
(83525)
Rates: $30
(208) 842-2557
(888) 848-2557

RED RIVER HOT SPRINGS
Elk City (83525)
Rates: $40-$100
(208) 842-2587

SABLE TRAIL RANCH
HC1 Red River Rd
(83525)
Rates: $20-$75
(208) 842-2672

ELK RIVER

HUCKLEBERRY HEAVEN LODGE
P. O. Box 165
(83827)
Rates: $50-$109
(208) 826-3405

EMMETT

HOLIDAY MOTEL
1111 S Washington
Ave (83617)
Rates: $30-$47
(208) 365-4479

FAIRFIELD

COUNTRY INN
P. O. Box 393
(83327)
Rates: $32-$38
(208) 764-2247

MOTEL 68
P. O. Box 285
(83327)
Rates: $15
(208) 764-2211

GARDEN VALLEY

GARDEN VALLEY MOTEL
1111 Banks
Lowman Rd
(83622)
Rates: $50-$65
(208) 462-2911

IDAHO CABIN KEEPERS
761 S Middle Fork
Rd (83622)
Rates: n/a
(208) 462-3451
(877) 3 CABINS

SILVER CREEK PLUNGE MOTEL
HC 76, Box 2377
(83622)
Rates: $30-$70
(208) 890-0586

GIBBONSVILLE

BROKEN ARROW CABINS
Hwy 93 N (83463)
Rates: $24
(208) 865-2241

GLENNS FERRY

REDFORD MOTEL
601 W 1st Ave
(83623)
Rates: n/a
(208) 366-2421

GOODING

GOODING HOTEL BED & BREAKFAST
112 Main St
(83330)
Rates: $25-$59
(208) 934-4374
(888) 260-6656

SKYLER INN
1331 S Main St
(83330)
Rates: $33-$48
(208) 934-4055
(800) 979-4055

GRANGEVILLE

ELKHORN LODGE
822 SW 1st (83530)
Rates: $32-$43
(208) 983-1500

JUNCTION LODGE
HC 67, Box 98
(83530)
Rates: $40
(208) 842-2459

MONTY'S MOTEL
700 W Main St
(83530)
Rates: $35-$54
(208) 983-2500

SUPER 8 MOTEL
801 SW 1st St
(83530)
Rates: $39-$62
(208) 983-1002
(800) 800-8000

HAGERMAN

HAGERMAN VALLEY INN
661 Frog's
Landing (83332)
Rates: $48
(208) 837-6196

ROCK LODGE RESORT & CREEKSIDE RV PARK
P. O. Box 449
(83332)
Rates: $41-$75
(208) 837-4822

HAILEY

AIRPORT INN
820 4th Ave S
(83333)
Rates: $65-$90
(208) 788-2477

HITCHRACK MOTEL
619 S Main (83333)
Rates: $35-$65
(208) 788-1696
(888) 431-RACK

HAMMETT

OASIS RANCH MOTEL
HC 63, Box 6
(83627)
Rates: $20-$25
(208) 366-2025

HARRISON

LAKEVIEW LODGE
P. O. Box 54
(83833)
Rates: $60-$110
(208) 689-3318

PEG'S BED N' BREAKFAST PLACE
202 Garfield Ave
(83833)
Rates: $45-$100
(208) 689-3525

AREA CODES - If the local number doesn't connect, check for a new area code.

SQUAW BAY CAMPING RESORT & MARINA
Rt 2, Box 130 (83833)
Rates: $85-$160
(208) 664-6782

HAYDEN/ HAYDEN LAKE

COEUR D'ALENE NORTH/HAYDEN LAKE KOA KABIN
4850 E Garwood Rd (83835)
Rates: $30
(208) 772-4557
(800) 562-9503

HEYBURN

SUPER 8 MOTEL
336 S 600 W (83336)
Rates: $48-$64
(208) 678-7000
(800) 800-8000

TOPS MOTEL
310 S Hwy 24 (83336)
Rates: $28-$44
(208) 436-4724

HOMEDALE

SUNNYDALE MOTEL
Hwy 95 & E Colorado (83628)
Rates: $24-$40
(208) 337-3302

HOPE

IDAHO COUNTRY RESORT CABINS
140 Idaho Country Rd (83836)
Rates: $75-$150
(208) 264-5505
(800) 307-3050

RED FIR RESORT CABINS
450 Red Fir Rd (83836)
Rates: $85-$155
(208) 264-5287

HORSESHOE BEND

TRAILS END RESTAURANT & MOTEL
P. O. Box 259 (83629)
Rates: n/a
(208) 793-2700

IDAHO CITY

IDAHO CITY HOTEL
215 Montgomery St (83631)
Rates: $34-$47
(208) 392-4290

KNOTTY PINE CABINS
P. O. Box 624 (83631)
Rates: $60-$105
(208) 392-9976
(800) 440-PINE

PROSPECTOR MOTEL
507 Main St (83631)
Rates: $34-$49
(208) 392-4290

WARM SPRINGS RESORT CABINS
P. O. Box 28 (83631)
Rates: $30-$50
(208) 392-4437

IDAHO FALLS

BEST WESTERN COTTONTREE INN
900 Lindsay Blvd (83402)
Rates: $86-$190
(208) 523-6000
(800) 528-1234
(800) 662-6886

BEST WESTERN DRIFTWOOD INN
575 River Pkwy (83405)
Rates: $75-$110
(208) 523-2242
(800) 528-1234
(800) 939-2242

BONNEVILLE MOTEL
2000 South Yellowstone (83402)
Rates: $30-$50
(208) 522-7847

CAVANAUGHS ON THE FALLS
475 River Pkwy (83405)
Rates: $68-$88
(208) 523-8000

COMFORT INN
195 E Colorado Ave (83402)
Rates: $55-$132
(208) 528-2804
(800) 228-5150

DAYS INN STARDUST
700 Lindsay Blvd (83402)
Rates: $46-$74
(208) 522-2910
(800) 329-7466
(800) 527-0274

LITTLETREE INN
888 N Holmes (83401)
Rates: $39-$79
(208) 523-5993
(800) 521-5993

MOTEL 6
1448 W Broadway (83402)
Rates: $35-$54
(208) 522-0112
(800) 466-8356

MOTEL WEST
1540 W Broadway (83402)
Rates: $34-$50
(208) 522-1112
(800) 582-1063

QUALITY INN
850 Lindsay Blvd (83402)
Rates: $49-$99
(208) 523-6260
(800) 228-5151

SHILO INN
780 Lindsay Blvd (83402)
Rates: $79-$149
(208) 523-0088
(800) 222-2244

ISLAND PARK

A-BAR MOTEL
HC 66, Box 452, Last Chance Is. Park (83429)
Rates: $38-$90
(208) 558-7358
(800) 286-7358

ASPEN LODGE CABINS
HC 66, Box 269 (83429)
Rates: $39-$85
(208) 558-7407
(800) 755-7407

ELK CREEK GUEST RANCH
P. O. Box 2 (83429)
Rates: $75
(208) 558-7404

MACK'S INN RESORT/CABINS
Hwy 20 & 191 (83433)
Rates: $50-$120
(208) 558-7272

POND'S LODGE CABINS
P. O. Box 258 (83429)
Rates: $40-$160
(208) 558-7221

SAWTELLE MOUNTAIN RESORT
HC 66, Box 15X (83429)
Rates: $54-$74
(208) 558-9366
(800) 574-0404

STALEY SPRINGS LODGE CABINS
HC 66, Box 102 (83429)
Rates: $65-$165
(208) 558-7471

WILD ROSE RANCH
340 W 7th S (83429)
Rates: $55-$185
(208) 558-7201

JEROME

BEST WESTERN SAWTOOTH INN
3057 S Lincoln (83338)
Rates: $59-$89
(208) 324-9200
(800) 528-1234

CREST MOTEL
2983 S Lincoln (83338)
Rates: $32-$50
(208) 324-2670

HOLIDAY MOTEL
401 W Main (83338)
Rates: $20-$60
(208) 324-2361

SLEEP INN
1200 Centennial Spur (83338)
Rates: $45-$106
(208) 324-6400
(800) 753-3746

KAMIAH

CLEARWATER 12 MOTEL
Hwy 12 & Cedar St (83536)
Rates: $40-$50
(208) 935-2671
(800) 935-2671

LEWIS CLARK RESORT/MOTEL
Rt 1, Box 17 (83536)
Rates: $40-$59
(208) 935-2556

SUNDOWN MOTEL
Rt 2, Box 100 (83536)
Rates: $24-$39
(208) 935-2568

WHITEWATER OUTFITTERS GUEST RANCH
P. O. Box 642 (83536)
Rates: $65
(208) 935-0631

KELLOGG

INN AT SILVER MOUNTAIN
305 S Division (83837)
Rates: $20+
(208) 786-2311
(800) SNOW-FUN

MOTEL-51
206 E Cameron Ave (83837)
Rates: $25-$40
(208) 786-9441

SILVERHORN MOTOR INN
699 W Cameron Ave (83837)
Rates: $51-$69
(208) 783-1151
(800) 437-6437

SUNSHINE INN
301 W Cameron Ave (83837)
Rates: $24-$40
(208) 784-1186

SUPER 8 MOTEL
601 Bunker Ave (83837)
Rates: $53-$72
(208) 783-1234
(800) 800-8000

TRAIL MOTEL
206 W Cameron Ave (83837)
Rates: $25-$35
(208) 784-1161

KETCHUM

BEST WESTERN TYROLEAN LODGE
260 Cottonwood St (83340)
Rates: $70-$175
(208) 726-5336
(800) 528-1234
(800) 333-7912

CHRISTIANIA MOTOR LODGE
651 Sun Valley Rd (83340)
Rates: $89-$105
(208) 726-3351
(800) 535-3241

HEIDLEBERG INN
1908 Warm Springs Rd (83340)
Rates: $85-$130
(208) 726-5361
(800) 284-4863

KETCHUM KORRAL MOTOR LODGE
310 S Main St (83340)
Rates: $58-$125
(208) 726-3510
(800) 657-2657

RIVER STREET INN
100 W River St (83340)
Rates: $140-$195
(208) 726-3611
(888) 746-3611

SKI VIEW LODGE
409 S Hwy 75 (83340)
Rates: $40-$70
(208) 726-3441

KINGSTON

KINGSTON 5 RANCH B & B
297 Silver Valley Rd (83839)
Rates: $55-$125
(208) 682-4862
(800) 254-1852

KOOSKIA

BEAR HOLLOW BED & BREAKFAST
HC 75, Box 16 (83539)
Rates: $55-$85
(208) 926-7146
(800) 831-3713

IDA-LEE MOTEL
P. O. Box 592 (83539)
Rates: $25-$36
(208) 926-0166

MOUNT STUART INN MOTEL
Clearwater River, P. O. Box 592 (83539)
Rates: $25-$48
(208) 926-0166

RYAN'S WILDERNESS INN
Lowell Hwy, MP 97.5 (83539)
Rates: $35-$45
(208) 926-4706

THREE RIVERS RESORT
HC 75, Box 61 (83539)
Rates: $39-$97
(208) 926-4430

LAKEFORK

MARY'S CABINS
Box 684 (83635)
Rates: $25+
(208) 634-5527

LAVA HOT SPRINGS

DEMPSEY CREEK LODGE
162 E Main (83246)
Rates: $29-$49
(208) 776-5000

LAVA HOT SPRINGS INN
95 E Portneuf Ave (83246)
Rates: $59-$185
(208) 776-5830
(800) 527-5830

LAVA RANCH INN MOTEL & RV
9611 Hwy 30 (83246)
Rates: $35-$75
(208) 776-9917

OREGON TRAIL LODGE
119 E Main (83246)
Rates: n/a
(208) 776-5000

RIVERSIDE INN & HOT SPRINGS
255 Portneuf (83246)
Rates: $60-$110
(208) 776-5504
(800) 733-5504

TUMBLING WATERS MOTEL
359 E Main (83246)
Rates: $45-$55
(208) 776-5589

WHITE WOLF B&B
9926 Hwy 30 E (83246)
Rates: $55-$70
(208) 776-5353
(888) 776-5344

LEMHI

MOTEL DELUXE
112 S Church (83465)
Rates: $32-$48
(208) 756-2231

LEWISTON

BEL AIR MOTEL
2018 N & S Hwy (83501)
Rates: $22-$27
(208) 743-5946

COMFORT INN
2128 8th Ave (83501)
Rates: $63-$122
(208) 798-8090
(800) 228-5150

EL RANCHO MOTEL
2240 3rd Ave N (83501)
Rates: $26-$32
(208) 743-8517

HILLARY MOTEL
2030 N & S Hwy (83501)
Rates: $21-$45
(208) 743-8514
(800) 856-8514

HO HUM MOTEL
2015 N & S Hwy (83501)
Rates: $25-$45
(208) 743-2978

HOLLYWOOD INN
3001 N & S Hwy (83501)
Rates: $40-$60
(208) 743-9424
(800) 210-6925

HOWARD JOHNSON EXPRESS INN
1716 Main St (83501)
Rates: $52-$102
(208) 743-9526
(800) 446-4656

RED LION HOTEL
621 21st St (83501)
Rates: $69-$79
(208) 799-1000
(800) 232-6730

RIVERVIEW INN
1325 Main St (83501)
Rates: $38-$60
(208) 746-3311
(800) 806-7666

SACAJAWEA SELECT INN
1824 Main St (83501)
Rates: $48-$79
(208) 746-1393
(800) 333-1393

SHEEP CREEK GUEST RANCH
227 Snake River Ave (83501)
Rates: $85-$280
(208) 746-6276
(800) 262-8874

SNAKE RIVER ADVENTURES
227 Snake River Ave (83501)
Rates: $85+
(208) 746-6276
(800) 262-8874

SUPER 8 MOTEL
3120 N & S Hwy (83501)
Rates: $37-$72
(208) 743-8808
(800) 800-8000

TRAVEL MOTOR INN
1021 Main St (83501)
Rates: $30-$49
(208) 743-4501

LOWMAN

NEW HAVEN LODGE
HC 77, Box 3608 (83637)
Rates: $38-$110
(208) 259-3344

SOURDOUGH LODGE & RV RESORT
8406 Hwy 21 (83637)
Rates: $40-$65
(208) 259-3326

MACKAY

BEAR BOTTOM INN
412 W Spruce St
(83213)
Rates: $40-$60
(208) 588-2483

WAGON WHEEL MOTEL & RV
809 W Custer
(83251)
Rates: $35-$70
(208) 588-3331

WHITE KNOB MOTEL & RV
Box 180 (83251)
Rates: $22-$42
(208) 588-2622
(800) 534-2622

MACK'S INN

MACK'S INN RESORT
P. O. Box 10
(83433)
Rates: $20-$110
(208) 558-7272

SAWTELL MOUNTAIN RESORT
P. O. Box 250
(83433)
Rates: $54-$74
(208) 558-9366
(800) 574-0404

MALAD

VILLAGE INN MOTEL
50 South 300 E
(83252)
Rates: $32-$48
(208) 766-4761

MCCALL

BEST WESTERN MCCALL
415 N 3rd St
(83638)
Rates: $70-$120
(208) 634-6300
(800) 528-1234

BRUNDAGE BUNGALOWS
308 W Lake St
(83638)
Rates: $55-$160
(208) 634-8573

BRUNDAGE INN
1005 W Lake St
(83638)
Rates: $45-$90
(208) 634-2344
(800) 643-2009

FIRCREST CONDOS
300 Washington
OFC #107 (83638)
Rates: $59-$120
(208) 634-4528

LAKEFORK LODGE GUEST RANCH
McCall Lick Creek
Rd (83638)
Rates: $150-$175
(208) 634-3713

SCANDIA INN MOTEL
401 N 3rd St
(83638)
Rates: $50-$54
(208) 634-7394

SUPER 8 MOTEL
303 S 3rd (83638)
Rates: $60-$72
(208) 634-4637
(800) 800-8000

VILLAGE INN MOTEL
P. O. Box 734
(83638)
Rates: $40-$85
(208) 634-2344
(800) 643-2009

WOODSMAN MOTEL
402 N 3rd St
(83638)
Rates: $32-$56
(208) 634-7671

MELBA

GIVEN'S HOT SPRINGS CABINS
Hwy 78 (83641)
Rates: n/a
(208) 495-2000

MONTPELIER

BEST WESTERN CLOVER CREEK INN
243 N 4th St
(83254)
Rates: $56-$72
(208) 847-1782
(800) 528-1234

BUDGET MOTEL
240 N 4th St
(83254)
Rates: $20-$35
(208) 847-1273

THE FISHER INN
601 N 4th St
(83254)
Rates: $35-$45
(208) 847-1772

MICHELLE MOTEL
401 Boise St
(83254)
Rates: $20-$33
(208) 847-1772
(800) 590-1772

PARK MOTEL
745 Washington
(83254)
Rates: $25-$50
(208) 847-1911

MOSCOW

BEST WESTERN UNIVERSITY INN
1516 Pullman Rd
(83843)
Rates: $65-$100
(208) 882-0550
(800) 528-1234

HILLCREST MOTEL
706 N Main
(83843)
Rates: $28-$60
(208) 882-7579
(800) 368-6564

MARK IV MOTOR INN
414 N Main St
(83843)
Rates: $49-$129
(208) 882-7557
(800) 833-4240

MOTEL 6
101 Baker St
(83843)
Rates: $26-$38
(208) 882-5511
(800) 466-8356

ROYAL MOTOR INN
120 West 6th St
(83843)
Rates: $25-$65
(208) 882-2581

MOUNTAIN HOME

BEST WESTERN FOOTHILLS MOTOR INN
1080 Hwy 20
(83647)
Rates: $59-$89
(208) 587-8477
(800) 528-1234

MOTEL THUNDERBIRD
910 Sunset Strip
(83647)
Rates: $34-$65
(208) 587-7927

ROSESTONE INN
495 N 3rd E
(83647)
Rates: $45-$85
(208) 587-8866
(800) 717-ROSE

SLEEP INN
1180 Hwy 20
(83647)
Rates: $59-$79
(208) 587-9743
(800) 753-3746

TOWNE CENTER MOTEL
410 N 2nd E
(83647)
Rates: $24-$40
(208) 587-3373

MUD LAKE

HAVEN MOTEL & TRAILER PARK
1079 E 1500 N
(83450)
Rates: $30-$35
(208) 663-4821

MULLAN

LOOKOUT MOTEL
201 River St
(83846)
Rates: $29-$45
(208) 744-1601

MURPHY

SILVER CITY LODGINGS-GROUP HOSTEL
P. O. Box 56
(83650)
Rates: $40
(208) 583-4111

NAMPA

BUDGET INN
908 3rd St South
(83651)
Rates: $35-$45
(208) 466-3594

DESERT INN MOTEL
115 9th Ave S
(83651)
Rates: $34-$48
(208) 467-1161

SHILO INN
617 Nampa Blvd
(83687)
Rates: $45-$85
(208) 466-8993
(800) 222-2244

SHILO INN NAMPA SUITES
1401 Shilo Dr
(83687)
Rates: $75-$109
(208) 465-3250
(800) 222-2244

SLEEP INN
1315 Industrial Rd
(83687)
Rates: $49-$105
(208) 463-6300
(800) 753-3746

STARLITE MOTEL
320 11th Ave N
(83651)
Rates: $30-$43
(208) 466-9244

SUPER 8 MOTEL
624 Nampa Blvd
(83687)
Rates: $44-$72
(208) 467-2888
(800) 800-8000

NEW MEADOWS

HARTLAND INN & MOTEL
211 Norrist St
(83654)
Rates: $44-$115
(208) 347-2114
(888) 509-7400

MEADOWS MOTEL
Hwy 95 (83654)
Rates: $35-$49
(208) 347-2175

AREA CODES - If the local number doesn't connect, check for a new area code.

NORDMAN

**ELKINS CABINS
ON PRIEST LAKE**
404 Elkins Rd
(83848)
Rates: $85-$235
(208) 443-2432

**KANIKSU RESORT
CABINS**
HCO 1, Box 152
(83848)
Rates: $60+
(208) 443-2609

NORTH FORK

**CUMMINGS LAKE
LODGE**
Box 8 (83466)
Rates: $45
(208) 865-2424

**100 ACRE WOOD
BED & BREAKFAST**
Rt 1, Hwy 93 N
(83466)
Rates: $55-$95
(208) 865-2165

**NORTH FORK
MOTEL**
P. O. Box 100
(83466)
Rates: $36-$46
(208) 865-2412

**RIVER'S FORK INN
& RV PARK**
Hwy 93 N (83466)
Rates: $48-$53
(208) 865-2301

OROFINO

**HELGESON PLACE
HOTEL**
P. O. Box 463
(83544)
Rates: $37-$50
(208) 476-5729
(800) 404-5729

**KONKOLVILLE
MOTEL**
2000 Konkolville
Rd (83544)
Rates: $40-$47
(208) 476-5584

RIVERSIDE MOTEL
10560 Hwy 12
(83544)
Rates: $24+
(208) 476-5711

**WHITE PINE
MOTEL**
222 Brown St
(83544)
Rates: $33-$55
(208) 476-7093
(800) 874-2083

PALISADES

**PALISADES RV
PARK & CABINS**
3802 Swan Valley
Hwy (83428)
Rates: $39-$45
(208) 483-4485

PARMA

**THE COURT
MOTEL**
712 Grove St
(83660)
Rates: $36-$45
(208) 722-5579

PIERCE

CEDAR INN
412 S Main (83546)
Rates: $15-$22
(208) 464-2704

**KEY BAR
HOTEL & CAFE**
Box 494 (83546)
Rates: $10-$15
(208) 464-2704

PIERCE MOTEL
509 Main St
(83546)
Rates: $25-$40
(208) 464-2324

PINE

**DEER CREEK
LODGE**
Anderson Ranch
Reservoir (83647)
Rates: $29-$50
(208) 653-2454

**FALL CREEK
RESORT
& MARINA**
HC 87, Box 85
(83647)
Rates: $45-$55
(208) 653-2242

**NESTER'S
MOUNTAIN
MOTEL**
HC 87, Box 210
(83647)
Rates: $45-$55
(208) 653-2222

PINEHURST

**KELLOGG/
SILVER VALLEY
KOA CABINS**
P. O. Box 949
(83850)
Rates: $20-$27
(208) 682-3612
(800) KOA-0799

**KELLOGG
VACATION HOME
RENTALS**
P. O. Box 944
(83850)
Rates: $50-$200
(208) 786-4261
(208) 435-2588

PLUMMER

BONNIE'S B&B
P. O. Box 258
(83851)
Rates: $50-$60
(208) 686-1165

HIWAY MOTEL
301 10th St (83851)
Rates: $25-$45
(208) 686-1310

POCATELLO

**BACK O'BEYOND
BED & BREAKFAST**
404 S Garfield
(83201)
Rates: $60-$65
(208) 232-3825
(888) 232-3820

**BEST WESTERN
COTTON TREE
INN**
1415 Bench Rd
(83201)
Rates: $75-$99
(208) 237-7650
(800) 528-1234
(800) 662-6886

**CAVANAUGH'S
POCATELLO
HOTEL**
1555 Pocatello
Creek Rd (83201)
Rates: $62-$89
(208) 233-2200
(800) 527-5202

COMFORT INN
1333 Bench Rd
(83201)
Rates: $69-$150
(208) 237-8155
(800) 228-5150

**ECONO LODGE
UNIVERSITY**
835 S 5th Ave
(83201)
Rates: $45-$59
(208) 233-0451
(800) 553-2666

HOLIDAY INN
1399 Bench Rd
(83201)
Rates: $69-$79
(208) 237-1400
(800) 465-4329

**IMPERIAL 400
MOTEL**
1055 S 5th (83201)
Rates: $23-$60
(208) 233-5120

MOTEL 6
291 W Burnside
Ave (83202)
Rates: $33-$44
(208) 237-7880
(800) 466-8356

PINE RIDGE INN
4333 Yellowstone
Ave (83202)
Rates: $35-$60
(208) 237-3100

RAINBOW MOTEL
3020 S 5th (83201)
Rates: $25-$45
(208) 232-1451

SUPER 8 MOTEL
1330 Bench Rd
(83201)
Rates: $48-$72
(208) 234-0888
(800) 800-8000

**THUNDERBIRD
MOTEL**
1415 S 5th Ave
(83201)
Rates: $36-$50
(208) 232-6330

POLLACK

**R & R
WHITEWATER
ADVENTURE
LODGE**
HC 2, Box 500
(83547)
Rates: $38-$60
(208) 628-3033
(800) 574-1224

POST FALLS

**BEST WESTERN
CAVANAUGH
TEMPLIN'S
RESORT HOTEL**
414 E First Ave
(83854)
Rates: $90-$115
(208) 773-1611
(800) 528-1234
(800) 283-6754

**HOWARD
JOHNSON
EXPRESS**
3705 W 5th Ave
(83854)
Rates: $49-$89
(208) 773-4541
(800) 446-4656

SLEEP INN
100 Pleasant View
Rd (83854)
Rates: $60-$119
(208) 777--9394
(800) 753-3746

POTLATCH

**ROLLING HILLS
BED & BREAKFAST**
Rt 1, Box 157
(83855)
Rates: $50-$55
(208) 668-1126

PRESTON

**DEER CLIFF RV
& CABINS**
1942 N Deer Cliff
(83263)
Rates: $28-$32
(208) 852-1736

AREA CODES - If the local number doesn't connect, check for a new area code.

PRIEST LAKE

HILL'S RESORT
4777 W Lakeshore
Rd (83856)
Rates: $120-$325
(208) 443-2551

PRIEST RIVER

EAGLE'S NEST MOTEL
1007 Albeni Hwy
(83865)
Rates: $43-$75
(208) 448-2000
(800) 881-6378

SELKIRK MOTEL
Hwy 2 (83856)
Rates: $35-$61
(208) 448-1112

REXBURG

BEST WESTERN COTTONTREE INN
450 W 4th St S
(83440)
Rates: $72-$92
(208) 356-4646
(800) 528-1234
(800) 662-6886

COMFORT INN
1565 W Main
(83440)
Rates: $45-$100
(208) 359-1311
(800) 228-5150

DAYS INN
271 S 2nd W
(83440)
Rates: $52-$62
(208) 356-9222
(800) 329-7466

REX MOTEL
357 W 400 S
(83440)
Rates: $25-$36
(208) 356-5477
(800) 449-5477

RIGGINS

BRUCE MOTEL
P. O. Box 208
(83549)
Rates: $29-$70
(208) 628-3005
(888) 517-3005

THE LODGE B&B
On Little Salmon
River, Hwy 95
(83549)
Rates: $30-$60
(208) 628-3863

PINEHURST RESORT CTTGES
MM 182 on Hwy
95 (83549)
Rates: $35-$60
(208) 628-3323

RAPID RIVER GUEST RANCH
HC 69, Box 100
(83549)
Rates: $40-$50
(208) 628-3264

RIGGINS MOTEL
615 S Main (83549)
Rates: $34-$95
(208) 628-3001
(800) 669-6739

SALMON RIVER MOTEL
1203 S Hwy 95
(93549)
Rates: $33-$65
(208) 628-3231
(888) 628-3025

TAYLOR MOTEL
206 S Main St
(83549)
Rates: $27
(208) 628-3914

ROGERSON

DESERT HOT SPRINGS MOTEL
General Delivery
(83302)
Rates: $25-$35
(208) 857-2233

RUPERT

FLAMINGO LODGE MOTEL
406 E 8th St
(83350)
Rates: $30-$50
(208) 436-4321

SAGLE

BOTTLE BAY RESORT & MARINA
115 Resort Rd
(83860)
Rates: $85-$135
(208) 263-5916

COUNTRY INN
7360 Hwy 95 S
(83860)
Rates: $24-$49
(208) 263-3333
(800) 736-0454

GARFIELD BAY RESORT CABINS
60 W Garfield Bay
Rd (83860)
Rates: $55
(208) 263-1078

ST. ANTHONY

SQUIRREL CREEK ELK RANCH CABINS
109 N 2nd W
(83445)
Rates: $50-$70
(208) 652-3972
(800) 734-7002

ST. MARIES

BENEWAH RESORT
Rt 1, Box 50-C
(83861)
Rates: $25-$29
(208) 245-3288

THE PINES MOTEL
1117 Main St
(83861)
Rates: $35-$65
(208) 245-2545

SALMON

BROKEN ARROW RESORT
Hwy 93 N (83467)
Rates: $28+
(208) 865-2241

MOTEL DELUXE
112 S Church St
(83467)
Rates: $30-$55
(208) 756-2231

SUNCREST MOTEL
705 S Challis St
(83467)
Rates: $33-$65
(208) 756-2294

SYRINGA LODGE
2000 Syringa Dr
(83467)
Rates: $40-$95
(208) 756-4424

SANDPOINT

BEST SPA & JACUZZI SUITES RESORT
521 N 3rd Ave
(83864)
Rates: $30-$130
(208) 263-3532
(888) 520-0555

CHALET MOTEL
3270 Hwy 95 N
(83864)
Rates: $39-$60
(208) 263-3202

COUNTRY INN
7360 Hwy 95 S
(83864)
Rates: $24-$49
(208) 263-3333
(800) 736-0454

EDGEWATER RESORT MOTOR INN
56 Bridge St
(83864)
Rates: $60-$160
(208) 263-3194
(800) 635-2534

HAWTHORN INN & SUITES
415 Cedar St
(83864)
Rates: $89-$109
(208) 263-9581
(800) 282-0660

IDAHO COUNTRY RESORT
141 Idaho
Country Rd
(83864)
Rates: $75-$150
(208) 264-5505
(800) 307-3050

K2 INN
501 N 4th Ave
(83864)
Rates: $35-$110
(208) 263-3441

LAKESIDE INN
106 Bridge St
(83864)
Rates: $64-$125
(208) 263-3717
(800) 543-8126

MICROTEL INN
477255 Hwy 95
(83864)
Rates: $50-$200
(208) 263-5383
(888) 771-7171
(888) 297-0666

MONARCH INN
Hwy 95N (83864)
Rates: $39-$95
(208) 263-1222
(800) 543-8193

MOTEL 16
317 Marion (83864)
Rates: $30-$110
(208) 263-5323

QUALITY INN
807 N 5th Ave
(83864)
Rates: $54-$129
(208) 263-2111
(800) 228-5151

SUPER 8 MOTEL
476841 Hwy 95N
(83864)
Rates: $45-$75
(208) 263-2210
(800) 800-8000

TKE VACATION RENTALS
303 Pine St (83864)
Rates: $35-$300
(208) 263-5539
(800) 765-5539

SHOSHONE

GOVERNOR'S MANSION
315 S Greenwood
(83352)
Rates: $30-$65
(208) 886-2858

SHOUP

SHOUP STORE, CAFE & CABINS
RR 2, Box 1
(83469)
Rates: $30-$100
(208) 394-2125

SMITH HOUSE B&B
49 Salmon River
Rd (83469)
Rates: $35-$55
(208) 394-2121
(800) 238-5915

AREA CODES - If the local number doesn't connect, check for a new area code.

SILVERTON

MOLLY B'DAMM MOTEL
P. O. Box 481
(83867)
Rates: $25-$45
(208) 556-4391

SILVER LEAF MOTEL
West Wallace
(83867)
Rates: $25-$30
(208) 752-0222

SODA SPRINGS

CARIBOU LODGE
110 W 2nd S
(83276)
Rates: $25-$50
(208) 547-3377
(800) 270-9178

LAKEVIEW MOTEL
341 W 2nd S
(83276)
Rates: $25-$50
(208) 547-4351

SPENCER

SPENCER STAGE STOP CABINS
HC 62, Box 54
(83446)
Rates: $30
(208) 374-5242

SPIRIT LAKE

SILVER BEACH RESORT CABINS
8350 W Spirit
Lake Rd (83869)
Rates: $20+
(208) 623-4842

STANLEY

DANNER'S LOG CABIN MOTEL
P. O. Box 196
(83278)
Rates: $50-$100
(208) 774-3539

ELK MOUNTAIN RV RESORT CABIN
P. O. Box 115,
Hwy 21 (83278)
Rates: $75
(208) 774-2202

JERRY'S COUNTRY STORE & MOTEL
HC 67, Box 300
(83278)
Rates: $55-$65
(208) 774-3566
(800) 972-4627

SAWTOOTH HOTEL
West end of Main
Street (83278)
Rates: $27-$60
(208) 774-9947
(208) 622-7922

STANLEY OUTPOST
P. O. Box 131,
Hwy 21 (83278)
Rates: $50-$90
(208) 774-3646
(888) 774-3640

TORREY'S BURNT CREEK INN
HC 67, Box 725
(83278)
Rates: $40-$60
(208) 838-2313
(888) 838-2313

TRIANGLE C RANCH CABINS
#1 Benner St &
Hwy 21 (83278)
Rates: $75-$95
(208) 774-2266
(800) 303-6258

SUN VALLEY

BALD MOUNTAIN LODGE
151 S Main (83353)
Rates: $50-$90
(208) 726-9963
(800) 892-7407

CLARION INN
600 Main St
(83353)
Rates: $55-$250
(208) 726-5900
(800) 252-7466

HIGH COUNTRY PROPERTIES/ RENTALS
180 East Ave
(83353)
Rates: $80-$3500
(208) 726-1256
(800) 726-7076

SUN VALLEY'S ELKHORN RESORT
100 Elkhorn Road
(83353)
Rates: $129-$290
(208) 622-4511
(800) 355-4676

SWAN VALLEY

SOUTH FORK LODGE
40 Conant Valley
Loop (83449)
Rates: $45-$105
(208) 483-2112
(800) 483-2110

TERRETON

B-K'S MOTEL
1073 E 1500 N
(83450)
Rates: $30-$35
(208) 663-4578

TETONIA

TETON MTN VIEW LODGE
510 Egbert Ave
(83452)
Rates: $59-$99
(208) 456-2741
(800) 625-2232

TETON SUNRISE INN
313 N 200 W
(83452)
Rates: $65-$80
(208) 456-2777
(888) 456-2777

TWIN FALLS

BEST WESTERN APOLLO MOTOR INN
296 Addison Ave
W (83301)
Rates: $50-$68
(208) 733-2010
(800) 528-1234

BEST WESTERN CAVANAUGHS CANYON SPRGS
1357 Blue Lakes
Blvd N (83301)
Rates: $83-$100
(208) 734-5000
(800) 528-1234
(800) 727-5003

COMFORT INN
1893 Canyon
Sprgs Rd (83301)
Rates: $59-$119
(208) 734-7494
(800) 228-5150

MOTEL 6
1472 Blue Lake
Blvd N (83301)
Rates: $33-$49
(208) 734-3993
(800) 466-8356

QUINN'S RAINBOW LODGE
1972 Maple Ave
(83301)
Rates: $20
(208) 487-2020

SHILO INN
1586 Blue Lakes
Blvd N (83301)
Rates: $89-$159
(208) 733-7545
(800) 222-2244

SUPER 7 MOTEL
320 Main Ave S
(83301)
Rates: $30-$50
(208) 733-8770
(888) 530-0138

SUPER 8 MOTEL
1260 Blue Lakes
Blvd N (83301)
Rates: $49-$69
(208) 734-5801
(800) 800-8000

TWIN FALLS MOTEL
2152 Kimberly Rd
(83301)
Rates: $28-$48
(208) 733-8620

WESTON INN
906 Blue Lake
Blvd (83301)
Rates: $40-$56
(208) 733-6095
(800) 551-3505

VICTOR

TETON VALLEY CAMPGROUND CABINS
128 Hwy 31
(83455)
Rates: $55
(208) 787-2647

WALLACE

BEST WESTERN WALLACE INN
100 Front St
(83873)
Rates: $70-$86
(208) 752-1252
(800) 528-1234
(888) 326-4611

STARDUST MOTEL
410 Pine St (83873)
Rates: $40-$55
(208) 752-1213
(800) 643-2386

WARM LAKE

NORTH SHORE LODGE CABINS
172 N Shoreline
Dr (83611)
Rates: $50-$85
(208) 632-2000
(800) 933-3193

WEISER

COLONIAL MOTEL
251 E Main
(83672)
Rates: $28-$66
(208) 549-0150

INDIANHEAD MOTEL & RV
747 US Hwy 95
(83672)
Rates: $30-$70
(208) 549-0331

WHITE BIRD

WHITE BIRD MOTEL & RV PARK
Hwy 95 (83554)
Rates: $32-$45
(208) 839-2308

WINCHESTER

WINCHESTER COUNTRY INN
605 Nez Perce St
(83555)
Rates: $40
(208) 924-7405

YELLOW PINE

YELLOW PINE LODGE
P. O. Box 77
(83677)
Rates: $25-$45
(208) 633-3377

AREA CODES - If the local number doesn't connect, check for a new area code.

ILLINOIS

ALORTON

LAKESIDE MOTEL
4300 Missouri Ave
(62207)
Rates: n/a
(618) 874-4700

ALSIP

BAYMONT INN
12801 S Cicero
Ave (60658)
Rates: $140
(708) 597-3900
(800) 301-0200
(800) 301-0200

**BUDGETER
MOTOR INN**
5150 W 127th St
(60658)
Rates: n/a
(708) 371-5600

RADISSON HOTEL
5000 W 127th St
(60658)
Rates: $139-$149
(708) 371-7300
(800) 333-3333

ALTAMONT

**BEST WESTERN
CARRIAGE INN**
1304 S Main St
(62411)
Rates: $42-$69
(847) 483-6101
(800) 528-1234

SUPER 8 MOTEL
3091 E Mill Dr
(62411)
Rates: $40-$90
(847) 483-6300
(800) 800-8000

ALTON

**COLLEGE CREST
MOTEL**
Rt 140 & Burling
Dr (62002)
Rates: n/a
(618) 465-3212

COMFORT INN
11 Crossroads Ct
(62002)
Rates: $59-$120
(618) 465-9999
(800) 228-5150

HOLIDAY INN
3800 Homer M
Adams Pkwy
(62002)
Rates: $92
(618) 462-1220
(800) 465-4329

DAYS INN
1900 Homer M
Adams Pkwy
(62002)
Rates: $48-$72
(618) 463-0800
(800) 329-7466

**HOTEL
STRATFORD**
229 Market St
(62002)
Rates: n/a
(618) 465-2700

SUPER 8 MOTEL
1800 Homer M
Adams Pkwy
(62002)
Rates: $45-$79
(618) 465-8885
(800) 800-8000

AMBOY

AMBOY MOTEL
1556 Rt 30 (61310)
Rates: n/a
(815) 857-3916

ANNA

**ANNA PLAZA
MOTEL**
150 E Vienna S E
(62906)
Rates: n/a
(618) 883-5215

ANTIOCH

**BEST WESTERN
REGENCY INN**
350 Hwy 173
(60002)
Rates: $90-$145
(847) 395-3606
(800)528-1234

ARCOLA

**BUDGET HOST
AMISH COUNTRY
INN**
640 E Springfield
Rd (61910)
Rates: $34-$55
(217) 268-3031
(800) 283-4678

COMFORT INN
610 E Springfield
(61910)
Rates: $35-$99
(217) 268-4000
(800) 228-5150

ARLINGTON HEIGHTS

AMERISUITES
2111 S Arlington
Hgts Rd (60005)
Rates: $109-$139
(847) 956-1400
(800) 434-5800

**BEST WESTERN
ARLINGTON INN**
948 E Northwest
Hwy (60004)
Rates: $60-$86
(847) 255-2900
(800) 528-1234
(800) 209-0009

LA QUINTA INN
1415 W Dundee
Rd (60004)
Rates: $89-$109
(847) 253-8777
(800) 687-6667

MOTEL 6
441 W Algonquin
Rd (60005)
Rates: $47-$62
(847) 806-1230
(800) 466-8356

RADISSON HOTEL
75 W Algonquin
Rd (60005)
Rates: $159-$169
(847) 364-7600
(800) 333-3333

RED ROOF INN
22 W Algonquin
Rd (60005)
Rates: $66-$95
(847) 228-6650
(800) 843-7663

SHERATON HOTEL
3400 W Euclid
Ave (60005)
Rates: $229
(847) 394-2000
(800) 325-3535

ARTHUR

**ARTHUR'S
COUNTRY INN**
785 E Columbia,
Hwy 133 (61911)
Rates: n/a
(217) 543-3321

ATLANTA

I-55 MOTEL
103 Empire St
(61723)
Rates: $30-$37
(217) 648-2322

AURORA

COMFORT SUITES
111 N Broadway
(60505)
Rates: $69-$209
(630) 896-2800
(800) 228-5150

MOTEL 6
2380 N
Farnsworth Ave
(60504)
Rates: $36-$42
(630) 851-3600
(800) 466-8356

RIVERWALK INN
77 S Stolp Ave
(60505)
Rates: n/a
(630) 892-0001

BANNOCK-BURN

**WOODFIELD
SUITES**
2000 Lakeside Dr
(60015)
Rates: $89-$139
(847) 317-7300

BARRINGTON

**BARRINGTON
MOTOR LODGE**
405 W Northwest
Hwy (60010)
Rates: $54+
(847) 381-2640
(800) 354-6605

BEARDSTOWN

SUPER 8 MOTEL
1903 Grand Ave
(62618)
Rates: $40-$60
(217) 323-5858
(800) 800-8000

BELLEVILLE

**CINDERELLA
MOTEL**
1438 Centreville
Ave (62223)
Rates: n/a
(618) 233-7410

DAYS INN
2120 West Main St
(62226)
Rates: $56-$150
(618) 234-9400
(800) 329-7466

**EXECUTIVE INN
MOTEL**
1234 Centreville
Ave (62223)
Rates: n/a
(618) 233-1234

SCOTT LODGE
1651 Old Hwy 158
(62223)
Rates: n/a
(618) 744-1244

SUPER 8 MOTEL
600 E Main St
(62220)
Rates: $39-$56
(618) 234-9670
(800) 800-8000

BENTON

**BENTON GRAY
PLAZA MOTEL**
706 W Main St
(62812)
Rates: n/a
(618) 439-3113

DAYS INN
711 W Main St
(62812)
Rates: $46-$60
(618) 439-3183
(800) 329-7466

SUPER 8 MOTEL
711 1/2 W Main St
(62812)
Rates: $39-$59
(618) 438-8205
(800) 800-8000

BLOOMINGTON

**BEST INNS OF
AMERICA**
1905 W Market St
(61701)
Rates: $42-$64
(309) 827-5333
(800) 237-8466

**COUNTRY INN
& SUITES**
923 Maple Hill Rd
(61701)
Rates: $74-$86
(309) 828-7177
(800) 456-4000

DAYS INN-WEST
1707 W Market St
(61701)
Rates: $43-$80
(309) 829-6292
(800) 329-7466

**EASTLAND SUITES
& CONF CENTER**
1801 Eastland Dr
(61701)
Rates: n/a
(309) 662-0000
(800) 53-SUITE

ECONO LODGE
401 Brock Dr (61701)
Rates: $49-$130
(309) 829-3100
(800) 553-2666

**GUESTHOUSE
INN**
1803 E Empire St
(61701)
Rates: $61-$81
(309) 663-1361
(800) 21-GUEST

**JUMER'S
CHATEAU**
1601 Jumer Dr
(61704)
Rates: $103-$173
(309) 662-2020
(800) 285-8637

**MICROTEL INN
& SUITES**
919 Maple Hill Rd
(61704)
Rates: $52-$88
(888) 771-7171

**RADISSON HOTEL
& CONF CENTER**
10 Brickyard Dr
(61704)
Rates $89-$119
(309) 664-6446
(800) 333-3333

SUPER 8 MOTEL
818 I.A.A. Dr
(61701)
Rates: $45-$79
(309) 663-2388
(800) 800-8000

BOLINGBROOK

**HOLIDAY INN
HOTEL & SUITES**
205 Remington
Blvd (60440)
Rates: $116
(630) 679-1600
(800) 465-4329

BOURBONNAIS

MOTEL 6
1311 Illinois Rt 50
N (60914)
Rates: $32-$38
(815) 933-2300
(800) 466-8356

BRADFORD

**SHALLOWBROOK
FARM EXECUTIVE
RETREAT**
Rt 2, PO Box 277
(61421)
Rates: n/a
(309) 897-8437

BRADLEY

LEES INN
1500 N Rt 50 (60914)
Rates: n/a
(815) 932-8080
(800) 733-5337

**NORTHGATE
MOTEL**
Rt 50 N (60914)
Rates: n/a
(815) 933-8261

BRAIDWOOD

SANDS MOTEL
1179 W Kennedy
Rd (60408)
Rates: n/a
(815) 458-3401

BREESE

**KNOTTY PINE
HOTEL**
Old Rt 50 W
(62230)
Rates: n/a
(618) 526-4556

BRIDGEVIEW

EXEL INN
9625 S 76th Ave
(60455)
Rates: $56-$87
(708) 430-1818
(800) 367-3935

BROADVIEW

ECONO LODGE
1150 Roosevelt Rd
(60153)
Rates: $49-$69
(708) 681-2550
(800) 553-2666

BUNCOMBE

**VALLEY VIEW
CABINS**
7025 Lick Creek
Rd (62912)
Rates: n/a
(618) 833-6356

BUREAU

**RANCH HOUSE
LODGE**
Rts 26 & 29
(61315)
Rates: n/a
(815) 659-3361

BUSHNELL

BUSHNELL INN
Rt 41 (61422)
Rates: n/a
(309) 772-3172

CACHE

**MELTON'S
FISHING CAMP**
Rural Route
(62913)
Rates: n/a
(618) 776-5504

CAHOKIA

**TRAILS END
MOTEL**
600 Water St
(62206)
Rates: n/a
(618) 337-2010

CAIRO

DAYS INN
RR 1 Box 10
(62914)
Rates: $32-$70
(618) 734-0215
(800) 329-7466

PLAZA MOTEL
3705 Sycamore St
(62914)
Rates: n/a
(618) 734-2102

CALUMET PARK

SUPER 8 MOTEL
12808 S Ashland
Ave (60827)
Rates: $62-$88
(708) 385-9100
(800) 800-8000

CANTON

SIESTA MOTEL
Rt 9 W (61520)
Rates: n/a
(309) 647-1915

CARBONDALE

**BEST INNS
OF AMERICA**
1345 E Main St
(62901)
Rates: $57
(618) 529-4801
(800) 237-8466

HOLIDAY INN
800 E Main St
(62901)
Rates: $69-$83
(618) 529-1100
(800) 465-4329

KNIGHTS INN
3000 W Main St
(62901)
Rates: $39-$89
(618) 529-2424
(800) 843-5644

RELAX INN
700 E Main St
(62901)
Rates: n/a
(618) 549-0889

SUPER 8 MOTEL
1180 E Main St
(62901)
Rates: $42-$79
(618) 457-8822
(800) 800-8000

CARLINVILLE

BEL-AIRE MOTEL
915 E 1st South St
(62626)
Rates: n/a
(217) 854-3287

**CARLIN VILLA
MOTEL-IMA**
SR 4 South (62626)
Rates: $37-$68
(217) 854-3201
(800) 341-8000

HOLIDAY INN
19067 W Frontage
Rd (62626)
Rates: $62-$82
(217) 324-2100
(800) 465-4329

CARROLLTON

**GOETTENS
SIERRA MOTEL**
Rt 3 (62016)
Rates: n/a
(217) 942-5012

AREA CODES - If the local number doesn't connect, check for a new area code.

CARTHAGE

PRAIRIE WINDS MOTEL
Hwy 136 West (62321)
Rates: n/a
(217) 357-3101

CASEYVILLE

BEST INNS OF AMERICA
2423 Old Country Inn Rd (62232)
Rates: $59-$72
(618) 397-3300
(800) 237-8466

MOTEL 6
2431 Old Country Inn Rd (62232)
Rates: $36-$42
(618) 397-8867
(800) 466-8356

CENTRALIA

BELL TOWER INN
200 E Noleman St (62801)
Rates: $46-$63
(618) 533-1300

CHAMPAIGN

BAYMONT INN & SUITES
302 W Anthony Dr (61821)
Rates: $65
(217) 356-8900
(800) 301-0200

CAMPUS INN
1701 S State St (61820)
Rates: $35-$42
(217) 359-8888

CLARION HOTEL
1501 S Neil St (61820)
Rates: $69-$91
(217) 352-7891
(800) 252-7466

COMFORT INN
305 Market View Dr (61821)
Rates: $49-$104
(217) 352-4055
(800) 228-5150

DRURY INN
905 W Anthony Dr (61821)
Rates: $65-$87
(217) 398-0030
(800) 378-7946

LA QUINTA INN
1900 Center Dr (61820)
Rates: $65-$85
(217) 356-4000
(800) 687-6667

MICROTEL INN
1615 Rion Dr (61822)
Rates: $39-$89
(217) 398-4136
(888) 771-7171

RED ROOF INN
212 W Anthony Dr (61820)
Rates: $40-$76
(217) 352-0101
(800) 843-7663

SUPER 8 MOTEL
202 Marketview Dr (61820)
Rates: $42-$65
(217) 359-2388
(800) 800-8000

CHARLESTON

BEST WESTERN WORTHINGTON INN
920 W Lincoln Ave (61920)
Rates: $56-$126
(217) 348-8161
(800) 528-1234
(800) 528-8161

CHENOA

SUPER 8 MOTEL
I-55 Exit 187 (61726)
Rates: $45-$60
(815) 945-5900
(800) 800-8000

CHESTER

BEST WESTERN REIDS' INN
2150 State St (62233)
Rates: $48-$64
(618) 826-3034
(800) 528-1234
(877) 826-4701

HI 3 MOTEL
Rt 3 N (62233)
Rates: n/a
(618) 826-4415

CHICAGO
(and Vicinity)

AMBASSADOR WEST-WYNDHAM GRAND HERTGE
1300 N State Pkwy (60610)
Rates: $215
(312) 787-3700
(800) 996-3426

BEST WESTERN HAWTHORNE TERRACE
3434 N Broadway Ave (60657)
Rates: $99-$169
(773) 244-3434
(800) 528-1234
(888) 675-2378

BLACKSTONE HOTEL
636 S Michigan Ave (60605)
Rates: $99-$109
(312) 427-4300
(800) 622-6330

CHICAGO HILTON & TOWERS
720 S Michigan Ave (60605)
Rates: $159-$345
(319) 922-4400
(800) 445-8667

CITY SUITES HISTORIC HOTEL
933 W Belmont Ave (60657)
Rates: $86-$108
(773) 404-3400
(888) 248-4667

CLARIDGE HOTEL
1244 N Dearborn Pkwy (60610)
Rates: $139-$225
(312) 787-4980
(800) 245-1258

CLARION HOTEL EXECUTIVE PLAZA
71 E Wacker Dr (60601)
Rates: $119-$209
(312) 346-7100
(800) 252-7466

ESSEX INN
800 S Michigan Ave (60605)
Rates: $89-$115
(312) 939-2800
(800) 621-6909

FAIRMONT HOTEL
200 N Columbus Dr (60601)
Rates: $199-$339
(312) 565-8000
(800) 527-4727

FOUR SEASONS HOTEL
120 E Delaware Place (60611)
Rates: $360-$3500
(312) 280-8800
(800) 332-3442

HILTON-O'HARE
O'Hare Airport (60666)
Rates: $146-$210
(773) 686-8000
(800) 445-8667

HOUSE OF BLUES A LOEWS HOTEL
333 N Dearborn St (60610)
Rates: $179-$289
(312) 245-0333
(800) 235-6397

MARRIOTT O'HARE
8535 W Higgins Rd (60631)
Rates: $119-$204
(773) 693-4444
(800) 228-9290

MOTEL 6
162 E Ontario St (60611)
Rates: $82-$90
(312) 787-3580
(800) 466-8356

THE PALMER HOUSE HILTON
17 E Monroe St (60603)
Rates: $189-$374
(312) 726-7500
(800) 445-8667

QUALITY INN DOWNTOWN
1 S Halsted (60661)
Rates: $99-$199
(312) 829-5000
(800) 228-5151

RADISSON HOTEL & SUITES
160 E Huron St (60611)
Rates: $129+
(312) 787-2900
(800) 333-3333

REGAL KNICKERBOCKER HOTEL
163 E Walton Ave (60611)
Rates: $125-$189
(312) 751-8100

RENAISSANCE CHICAGO HOTEL
1 W Wacker Dr (60601)
Rates: $219-$350
(312) 372-7200
(800) 468-3571

RESIDENCE INN BY MARRIOTT
201 E Walton Pl (60611)
Rates: $195-$310
(312) 943-9800
(800) 331-3131

RITZ-CARLTON A FOUR SEASONS HOTEL
160 E Pearson St (60611)
Rates: $365-$545
(312) 266-1000
(800) 332-3442
(800) 241-3333

SPA MOTEL
5414 N Lincoln Ave (60625)
Rates: n/a
(773) 561-0313

SUTTON PLACE HOTEL
21 E Bellevue Place (60611)
Rates: $275-$795
(312) 266-2100
(800) 543-4300

TRAVELODGE
65 E Harrison St (60605)
Rates: $59-$89
(312) 427-8000
(800) 578-7878

TREMONT HOTEL
100 E Chestnut St
(60611)
Rates: $220-$299
(312) 751-1900
(800) 621-8133

WESTIN HOTEL
909 N Michigan
Ave (60611)
Rates: $129-$324
(312) 943-7200
(800) 228-3000

CHILLICOTHE

SUPER 8 MOTEL
615 S Fourth St
(61523)
Rates: $46-$64
(309) 274-2568
(800) 800-8000

CLARENDON HILLS

MAYFLOWER MOTEL
407 Ogden Ave
(60514)
Rates: n/a
(630) 325-2500

CLINTON

DAYS INN
US 51 Bypass
(61727)
Rates: $40-$130
(217) 935-4140
(800) 329-7466

TOWN & COUNTRY MOTEL
1151 Rt 54W
(61727)
Rates: $25-$32
(217) 935-2121

WYE MOTEL
Rt 54 & 10 E
(61727)
Rates: $30-$40
(217) 935-3373

COBDEN

SHAWNEE HILL B&B
290 Water Valley
Rd (62902)
Rates: n/a
(618) 893-2211

BLACK DIAMOND RANCH
Rt 3 (62920)
Rates: n/a
(618) 833-7629

COLLINSVILLE

DRURY INN
602 N Bluff Rd
(62234)
Rates: $66-$88
(618) 345-7700
(800) 325-8300

MAGGIE'S B&B
2102 N Keebler
Ave (62234)
Rates: n/a
(618) 344-8283

MOTEL 6
295A N Bluff Rd
(62234)
Rates: $42-$58
(618) 345-2100
(800) 466-8356

PEAR TREE INN BY DRURY
552 Ramada Blvd
(62234)
Rates: $58-$78
(618) 345-9500
(800) 282-8733

SUPER 8 MOTEL
2 Gateway Dr
(62234)
Rates: $42-$79
(618) 345-8008
(800) 800-8000

CRYSTAL LAKE

SUPER 8 MOTEL
577 Crystal Point
Dr (60014)
Rates: $52-$75
(815) 455-2388
(800) 800-8000

DANVILLE

BEST WESTERN REGENCY INN
360 Eastgate Dr
(61834)
Rates: $54-$72
(217) 446-2111
(800) 528-1234

BEST WESTERN RIVERSIDE
57 S Gilbert St
(61832)
Rates: $60-$75
(217) 431-0020
(800) 528-1234

COMFORT INN
383 Lynch Dr
(61832)
Rates: $49-$99
(217) 443-8004
(800) 228-5150

GLO MOTEL
3617 N Vermillion
(61832)
Rates: $31-$45
(217) 442-2086

KNIGHTS INN
411 Lynch Dr
(61834)
Rates: $34-$49
(217) 443-3690
(800) 843-5644

RAMADA INN
338 Eastgate
(61832)
Rates: $69-$129
(217) 446-2400
(800) 272-6232

SUPER 8 MOTEL
377 Lynch Dr
(61832)
Rates: $59
(217) 443-4499
(800) 800-8000

DECATUR

BAYMONT INN
5100 Hickory Pt
Frontage Rd
(62526)
Rates: $60-$65
(217) 875-5800
(800) 301-0200

COUNTRY INN & SUITES
5150 Hickory Pt
Frontage Rd
(62526)
Rates: $73-$79
(217) 872-2402
(800) 456-4000

DAYS INN
333 N Wyckles Rd
(62522)
Rates: $40-$57
(217) 422-5900
(800) 329-7466

GREEN VALLEY MOTEL
145 W Pershing
Rd (62526)
Rates: n/a
(217) 877-3123

HOLIDAY INN SELECT CONF HOTEL
4191 W US 36
(62522)
Rates: $95-$110
(217) 422-8800
(800) 465-4329

INTOWN MOTEL
1013 E Eldorado
St (62526)
Rates: n/a
(217) 422-9080

RED CARPET INN
3035 N Water St
(62526)
Rates: $35-$55
(217) 877-3380
(800) 251-1962

SUPER 8 MOTEL
3141 N Water St
(62526)
Rates: $41-$62
(217) 877-8888
(800) 800-8000

DEERFIELD

MARRIOTT SUITES
2 Parkway Blvd N
(60015)
Rates: $149-$179
(847) 405-9666
(800) 228-9290

RESIDENCE INN BY MARRIOTT
530 Lake Cook Rd
(60015)
Rates: $119-$169
(847) 940-4644
(800) 331-3131

DEKALB

BEST WESTERN DEKALB INN & SUITES
1212 W Lincoln
Hwy (60115)
Rates: $69-$125
(815) 758-8661
(800) 528-1234

HOWARD JOHNSON EXPRESS
1321 W Lincoln
Hwy (60115)
Rates: $40-$56
(815) 756-1451
(800) 446-4656

TRAVELODGE
1116 W Lincoln
Hwy (60115)
Rates: $36-$69
(815) 756-3398
(800) 578-7878

DES PLAINES

CLUB HOTEL BY DOUBLETREE O'HARE
1450 E Touhy Ave
(60018)
Rates: n/a
(847) 296-8866

COMFORT INN O'HARE
2175 E Touhy Ave
(60018)
Rates: $104-$140
(847) 635-1300
(800) 228-5150

TRAVELODGE
3003 Mannheim
Rd (60018)
Rates: $84-$169
(847) 296-5541
(800) 578-7878

DIX

SCOTTISH INNS
I-57 Exit 103
(62830)
Rates: $23-$34
(618) 266-7254
(800) 251-1962

DIXON

BEST WESTERN BRANDYWINE LODGE
443 State Rt 2
(61021)
Rates: $59-$175
(815) 284-1890
(800) 528-1234

AREA CODES - If the local number doesn't connect, check for a new area code.

DOWNERS GROVE

MARRIOTT SUITES
1500 Opus Place
(60515)
Rates: $179
(630) 852-1500
(800) 228-9290

RED ROOF INN
1113 Butterfield
Rd (60515)
Rates: $51-$76
(630) 963-4205
(800) 843-7663

DU QUOIN

BUDGET INN
Rt 51 S (62832)
Rates: n/a
(618) 52-5014

DWIGHT

SUPER 8 MOTEL
14 E Northbrook
Dr (60420)
Rates: $39-$64
(815) 584-1888
(800) 800-8000

EAST DUBUQUE

L & L MOTEL
20170 Rt 20 W
(61025)
Rates: n/a
(815) 747-3931

EAST MOLINE
(see Quad Cities)

EAST PEORIA

BUDGET HOST COUNTRY INN
300 N Main St
(61611)
Rates: $35-$45
(309) 694-4261
(800) 283-4678

MOTEL 6
104 W Camp St
(61611)
Rates: $35-$41
(309) 699-7281
(800) 466-8356

SUPER 8 MOTEL
725 Taylor St
(61611)
Rates: $42-$79
(309) 698-8889
(800) 800-8000

EFFINGHAM

ABE LINCOLN MOTEL
1108 W Edgar St
(62401)
Rates: n/a
(217) 342-4717

ANTHONY ACRES RESORT
RR 2 (62401)
Rates: n/a
(217) 868-2950

BAYMONT INN
1103 Ave of Mid-America (62401)
Rates: $54-$69
(217) 342-2525
(800) 301-0200

BEST INNS OF AMERICA
1209 N Keller Dr
(62401)
Rates: $38-$55
(217) 347-5141
(800) 237-8466

BEST WESTERN RAINTREE INN
1811 W Fayette
Ave (62401)
Rates: $40-$57
(217) 342-4121
(800) 528-1234

COMFORT SUITES
1310 W Fayette
Ave (62401)
Rates: $55-$140
(217) 342-3151
(800) 228-5150

DAYS INN
1412 W Fayette
Ave (62401)
Rates: $34-$50
(217) 342-9271
(800) 329-7466

EFFINGHAM MOTEL
702 E Fayette Ave
(62401)
Rates: n/a
(217) 342-3991

HAMPTON INN
1509 Hampton Dr
(62401)
Rates: $62-$88
(217) 342-4499
(800) 426-7866

HOWARD JOHNSON EXPRESS
1606 W Fayette
Ave (62401)
Rates: $39-$59
(217) 342-4667
(800) 446-4656

PARADISE INN
1000 W Fayette
Ave (62401)
Rates: $23-$39
(217) 342-2165
(800) 535-0546

QUALITY INN
1600 W Fayette
Ave (62401)
Rates: $40-$84
(217) 342-4161
(800) 228-5151

RAMADA INN & CONV CENTER
1201 N Keller Dr
(62401)
Rates: $62-$90
(217) 342-2131
(800) 272-6232

SUPER 8 MOTEL
1400 Thelma
Keller Ave (62401)
Rates: $44-$79
(217) 342-6888
(800) 800-8000

EL PASO

DAYS INN
630 W Main
(61738)
Rates: $55-$120
(309) 527-7070
(800) 329-7466

SUPER 8 MOTEL
880 W Main
(61738)
Rates: $45-$63
(309) 527-4949
(800) 800-8000

ELGIN

BAYMONT INN
500 Toll Gate Rd
(60123)
Rates: $76-$96
(847) 931-4800
(800) 301-0200

DAYS INN
1585 Dundee Ave
(60120)
Rates: $60-$149
(847) 695-2100
(800) 329-7466

ELIZABETH

RIDGEVIEW B&B
8833 S Massbach
Rd (61028)
Rates: n/a
(815) 598-3150

ELK GROVE VILLAGE

DAYS INN
1920 E Higgins Rd
(60007)
Rates: $45-$189
(847) 437-1650
(800) 329-7466

EXEL INN
1000 W Devon
Ave (60007)
Rates: $61-$84
(847) 895-2085
(800) 367-3935

EXEL INN-O'HARE
2881 Touhy Ave
(6007)
Rates: $69-$88
(847) 803-9400
(800) 367-3935

HOLIDAY INN
1000 Busse Rd
(60007)
Rates: $64-$109
(847) 437-6010
(800) 465-4329

LA QUINTA INN-O'HARE AIRPORT
1900 Oakton St
(60007)
Rates: $89-$99
(847) 439-6767
(800) 687-6667

MOTEL 6
1601 Oakton St
(60007)
Rates: $38-$44
(847) 981-9766
(800) 466-8356

SHERATON SUITES O'HARE
121 Northwest
Point Blvd (60007)
Rates: $89-$219
(847) 290-1600
(800) 325-3535

ELMHURST

HOLIDAY INN
624 N York Rd
(60126)
Rates: $114-$134
(630) 279-1100
(800) 465-4329

EVANSTON

A SOMMER PLACE BED & BREAKFAST
1213 Maple Ave
(60201)
Rates: n/a
(847) 869-0543

HOMESTEAD HOTEL
1625 Hinman Ave
(60201)
Rates: n/a
(847) 475-3300

FAIRFIELD

BRIARWOOD INN
116 N Market Ave
(62837)
Rates: n/a
(618) 842-3667

FAIRVIEW HEIGHTS

BEST WESTERN CAMELOT INN
311 Salem Pl
(62208)
Rates: $45-$69
(618) 624-3636
(800) 528-1234

DRURY INN
12 Ludwig Dr
(62208)
Rates: $65-$85
(618) 398-8530
(800) 325-8300

RAMADA INN
6900 N Illinois
(62208)
Rates: $69-$85
(618) 632-4747
(800) 272-6232

SUPER 8 MOTEL
45 Ludwig Dr
(62208)
Rates: $42-$79
(618) 398-8338
(800) 800-8000

TRAILWAY MOTEL
10039 Lincoln Tr
(62208)
Rates: n/a
(618) 397-5757

FARMER CITY

BUDGET MOTEL
Rt 54 E (61842)
Rates: n/a
(309) 928-2157

DAYS INN
54 Hwy at High St
(61842)
Rates: $35-$95
(309) 928-9434
(800) 329-7466

FLORA

RANCH MOTEL
Olive St, Hwy 60
(62839)
Rates: n/a
(618) 662-2181

FORSYTH

COMFORT INN
134 Barnett Ave
(62535)
Rates: $52-$90
(217) 875-1166
(800) 228-5150

FRANKLIN PARK

COMFORT INN
2001 N Mannheim
Rd (60131)
Rates: $75-$99
(800) 228-5150

THRIFTLODGE
3010 N Mannheim
Rd (60131)
Rates: $55-$65
(847) 288-0600
(800) 525-9055

FREEBURG

GABRIEL MOTEL
600 N State St
(62243)
Rates: n/a
(618) 539-5588

FREEPORT

COUNTRYSIDE MOTEL
1535 W Galena
Ave (61032)
Rates: $27-$53
(815) 232-6148

RAMADA INN
1300 E South St
(61032)
Rates: $53-$65
(815) 297-9700
(800) 272-6232

WEST MOTEL
2084 W Galena
Ave (61032)
Rates: n/a
(815) 232-4188

GALENA

BEST WESTERN QUIET HOUSE SUITES
9915 Rt 20 E
(61036)
Rates: $91-$190
(815) 777-2577
(800) 528-1234

CLORAN MANSION B&B
1237 Franklin St
(61036)
Rates: n/a
(815) 777-0583

COUNTRY GARDENS B&B
1000 Third St
(61036)
Rates: n/a
(815) 777-3062

COUNTRY VALLEY HOMESTEAD
2690 S Blackjack
Rd (61036)
Rates: $65-$90
(815) 777-1915

FARSTER'S EXECUTIVE INN
305 N Main St
(61036)
Rates: n/a
(815) 777-9125
(800) 545-8551

PALACE MOTEL
11383 US Rt 20 W
(61036)
Rates: $55-$69
(815) 777-2043

TRIANGLE MOTEL
Rt 20 West (61036)
Rates: n/a
(815) 777-2897

GALESBURG

AARON'S THRIFTY MOTEL
1777 Grand Ave
(61401)
Rates: n/a
(309) 343-2812

COMFORT INN
907 W Carl
Sandburg Dr
(61401)
Rates: $54-$119
(309) 344-5445
(800) 228-5150

HOLIDAY INN EXPRESS
2285 Washington
St (61401)
Rates: $60-$127
(309) 343-7100
(800) 465-4329

JUMER'S CONTINENTAL INN
260 S Soangetaha
Rd (61401)
Rates: $63-$80
(309) 343-7151
(800) 285-8637

RAMADA INN
29 Public Sq On
Main St (61401)
Rates: $50-$65
(309) 343-9161
(800) 272-6232

REGENCY HOTEL
3282 N Henderson
St (61401)
Rates: n/a
(309) 344-1111
(800) 648-4707

SUPER 8 MOTEL
737 Knox Hwy 10
(61401)
Rates: $40-$61
(309) 289-2100
(800) 800-8000

GENESEO

DECK PLAZA MOTEL
2181 S Oakwood
Ave (61254)
Rates: $26-$41
(309) 944-4651

THE OAKWOOD MOTEL
225 US Hwy 6 E
(61254)
Rates: $19-$25
(309) 944-3696

GENEVA

OSCAR SWAN COUNTRY INN
1800 W State St
(60134)
Rates: n/a
(630) 232-0173

GILMAN

BUDGET HOST INN
723 S Crescent St
(60938)
Rates: $35-$99
(815) 265-7261
(800) 283-4678

DAYS INN
834 Hwy 24 W
(60938)
Rates: $45-$77
(815) 265-7283
(800) 329-7466

SUPER 8 MOTEL
1301 S Crescent St
(60938)
Rates: $49-$69
(815) 265-7000
(800) 800-8000

GLEN ELLYN

BEST WESTERN FOUR SEASONS
656 Taft Ave
(60137)
Rates: $58-$150
(630) 469-8500
(800) 528-1234

SUPER 8 MOTEL
737 Knox Hwy 10

HOLIDAY INN
1250 Roosevelt Rd
(60137)
Rates: $89-$129
(630) 629-6000
(800) 465-4329

GLENVIEW

BAYMONT INN
1625 Milwaukee
Ave (60025)
Rates: $71-$76
(847) 635-8300
(800) 301-0200

MOTEL 6
1535 Milwaukee
Ave (60025)
Rates: $45-$61
(847) 390-7200
(800) 466-8356

GODFREY

HIWAY HOUSE MOTOR INN
3023 Godfrey Rd
(62035)
Rates: n/a
(618) 466-6676

GOLCONDA

BRIDGEMICKS COTTAGE WEST
Washington Dt
(62938)
Rates: n/a
(618) 683-3601

MICHAELS MOTEL
RR 3 Adams St
(62938)
Rates: n/a
(618) 683-2424

SAN DAMIANO RETREAT
Rt 1, P. O. Box 106
(62938)
Rates: n/a
(618) 285-3507

SMITHLAND POOL LODGING
Main St, Box 435
(62938)
Rates: n/a
(618) 683-2333

AREA CODES - If the local number doesn't connect, check for a new area code.

GRANITE CITY

CHAIN OF ROCKS MOTEL
3228 W Chain of Rocks Rd (62040)
Rates: n/a
(618) 931-6600

DAYS INN
1100 Niedringhaus Ave (62040)
Rates: $39-$52
(618) 877-7100
(800) 329-7466

GRANITE CITY LODGE
1200 19th St (62040)
Rates: n/a
(618) 876-2600

GREENUP

BUDGET HOST INN
716 E Elizabeth St (62428)
Rates: $29-$43
(217) 923-3176
(800) 283-4678

FIVE STAR MOTEL
US Rt 40 & Rt 130 (62428)
Rates: n/a
(217) 923-5512

GREENVILLE

BEST WESTERN COUNTRY VIEW INN
I-70 & Rt 127 (62246)
Rates: $34-$56
(618) 664-3030
(800) 528-1234

BUDGET HOST
1525 State, Rt 127 (62246)
Rates: $28-$47
(618) 664-1950
(800) 283-4678

PRAIRIE HOUSE COUNTRY INN
RR 4, Box 47-AA (62246)
Rates: n/a
(618) 664-3003

2 ACRES MOTEL
I-70 & Rt 127 (62246)
Rates: n/a
(618) 664-3131

UPTOWN MOTEL
323 S Third St (62246)
Rates: n/a
(618) 664-3121

GURNEE

ADVENTURE INNS
3732 Grand Ave (60031)
Rates: n/a
(847) 623-7777
(800) 373-5245

BAYMONT INN & SUITES
5688 North Ridge Rd (60031)
Rates: $100-$125
(847) 662-7600
(800) 301-0200

COMFORT INN
6080 Gurnee Mills Blvd (60030)
Rates: $112-$135
(847) 855-8866
(800) 228-5150

HAMEL

INNKEEPER MOTEL
I-55 & Rt 140 (62234)
Rates: n/a
(618) 633-2111

HARRISBURG

BUDGET HOST INN
411 E Poplar St (62946)
Rates: $29-$35
(618) 253-7651
(800) 283-4678

SUPER 8 MOTEL
100 E Seright St (62946)
Rates: $44-$62
(818) 253-8081
(800) 800-8000

HARVARD

AMERIHOST INN
1701 S Division St (60033)
Rates: $63-$73
(815) 943-0700
(800) 434-5800

EL RANCHO MOTEL
5508 Rt 14 (60033)
Rates: $33-$45
(815) 943-5404

HAVANA

RED LION MOTOR LODGE
136 US E (62644)
Rates: n/a
(309) 543-4407

HENRY

HENRY HARBOR INN
208 Cromwell Dr (61537)
Rates: n/a
(309) 364-2365

HERRIN

PARK AVENUE MOTEL
900 N Park Ave (62948)
Rates: n/a
(618) 942-3159

HIGHLAND

CARDINAL INN
101 Walnut St (62249)
Rates: n/a
(618) 654-4433

HOLIDAY INN EXPRESS
20 Central Blvd (62249)
Rates: n/a
(618) 651-1100
(800) 465-4329

HILLSBORO

MANOR MOTEL
1447 Vandalia Rd (62049)
Rates: n/a
(217) 532-6144

HILLSIDE

HOLIDAY INN
4400 Frontge Rd (62162)
Rates: $98-$103
(708) 544-9300
(800) 465-4329

HOFFMAN ESTATES

AMERISUITES
2750 Greenspoint Pkwy (60195)
Rates: $129-$139
(847) 839-1800
(800) 833-1516

BAYMONT INN & SUITES
2075 Barrington Rd (60195)
Rates: $73-$80
(847) 882-8848
(800) 301-0200

LA QUINTA INN
2280 Barrington Rd (60195)
Rates: $95-$109
(847) 882-3312
(800) 687-6667

RED ROOF INN
2500 Hassell Rd (60195)
Rates: $56-$69
(847) 885-7877
(800) 843-7663

HOOPESTON

DOWNTOWN MOTEL
200 E Main St (60942)
Rates: n/a
(217) 283-6605

ITASCA

HOLIDAY INN
860 W Irving Park Rd (60143)
Rates: n/a
(630) 773-2340
(800) 465-4329

JACKSONVILLE

AMERIHOST INN
1709 W Morton Ave (62650)
Rates: n/a
(217) 245-4500
(800) 434-5800

HOLIDAY INN
1717 W Morton Ave (62650)
Rates: $48-$107
(217) 245-9571
(800) 445-1659

MOTEL 6
1716 W Morton Dr (62650)
Rates: $26-$32
(217) 243-7157
(800) 466-8356

STAR LITE MOTEL
1910 W Morton Ave (62650)
Rates: $38-$48
(217) 245-7184

JERSEYVILLE

LORTONS COLONIAL INN
114 W Arch St (62052)
Rates: n/a
(618) 498-6833

JOHNSTON CITY

FARRIS MOTEL
Rt 37 South, Box 6 (62951)
Rates: n/a
(618) 983-8086

JOLIET

COMFORT INN
135 S Larkin Ave (60436)
Rates: $42-$119
(815) 744-1770
(800) 228-5150

COMFORT INN NORTH
3235 Norman Ave (60435)
Rates: $59-$104
(815) 436-5141
(800) 228-5150

HOLIDAY INN EXPRESS
411 S LarkinAve (60436)
Rates: $69-$119
(815) 729-2000
(800) 465-4329

AREA CODES - If the local number doesn't connect, check for a new area code.

MANOR MOTEL
32926 E Eames
(60436)
Rates: n/a
(815) 467-5385

MICROTEL INN
1806 McDonough
St (60435)
Rates: $32-$99
(815) 730-8800
(888) 771-7171

MOTEL 6
1850 McDonough
Rd (60436)
Rates: $40-$56
(815) 729-2800
(800) 466-8356

MOTEL 6
3551 Mall Loop Dr
(60436)
Rates: $40-$61
(815) 439-1332
(800) 466-8356

RED ROOF INN
1750 McDonough
St (60436)
Rates: $47-$64
(815) 741-2304
(800) 843-7663

JONESBORO

**TRAIL OF TEARS
LODGE & SPORTS
RESORT**
1575 Fair City Rd
(62952)
Rates: n/a
(618) 833-8697

KANKAKEE

AVIS MOTEL
1225 E Court
(60901)
Rates: n/a
(815) 933-1717

**FAIRFIEW COURTS
MOTEL**
2745 S Rt 45-52
(60901)
Rates: n/a
(815) 933-7708

MODEL MOTEL
1245 S
Washington Ave
(60901)
Rates: n/a
(815) 932-5013

NORMA'S B&B
429 S Fourth
(60901)
Rates: n/a
(815) 937-1533

KEITHSBURG

**THE KEITHSBURG
MOTEL**
2nd & Main Sts
(61442)
Rates: n/a
(309) 374-2659

KEWANEE

**KEWANEE HOTEL
& MOTEL**
125 N Chestnut St
(61443)
Rates: n/a
(309) 852-2141

**KEWANEE
MOTOR LODGE**
400 S Main St
(61443)
Rates: $45-$50
(309) 853-4000

LA GRANGE

**J C COUNTRYSIDE
MOTEL**
6401 Joliet Rd
(60525)
Rates: n/a
(847) 352-3113

LANSING

**BEST WESTERN
SOUTH**
2505 Bernice Rd
(60438)
Rates: $49-$60
(708) 895-7810
(800) 528-1234

RED ROOF INN
2450 E 173rd St
(60438)
Rates: $56-$80
(708) 895-9570
(800) 843-7663

LE ROY

SUPER 8 MOTEL
1 Demma Dr
(61752)
Rates: $43-$70
(309) 962-4700
(800) 800-8000

LIBERTYVILLE

**BEST INNS
OF AMERICA**
1809 W
Milwaukee Ave
(60048)
Rates: $62-$89
(847) 816-8006
(800) 237-8466

**CANDLEWOOD
SUITES**
1100 N Hwy 45
(60048)
Rates: $119-$139
(847) 247-9900

LINCOLN

COMFORT INN
2811 Woodlawn
Rd (62656)
Rates: $55-$100
(217) 735-3960
(800) 228-5150

**CROSSROADS
MOTEL**
1305 Woodlawn
Rd (62656)
Rates: n/a
(217) 735-5571

HOLIDAY INN EXP
130 Olson Rd
(62656)
Rates: $68
(217) 735-5800
(800) 465-4329

SUPER 8 MOTEL
2809 Woodlawn
Rd (62656)
Rates: $42-$65
(217) 732-8886
(800) 800-8000

LINCOLNSHIRE

**MARRIOTTS
RESORT**
10 Marriott Dr
(60069)
Rates: $99-$240
(847) 634-0100
(800) 228-9290

LISLE

RADISSON HOTEL
3000 Warrenville
Rd (60532)
Rates: $169-$199
(630) 505-1000
(800) 333-3333

LITCHFIELD

**BEST WESTERN
GARDENS**
413 Columbian
Blvd N (62056)
Rates: $42-$53
(217) 324-2181
(800) 528-1234

COMFORT INN
1010 E Columbia
N Blvd (62056)
Rates: $49-$110
(217) 324-2288
(800) 228-5150

66 MOTEL
621 N Sherman St
(62056)
Rates: n/a
(217) 324-2179

SUPER 8 MOTEL
2110 Ohren Dr
(62056)
Rates: $42-$59
(217) 324-7788
(800) 800-8000

LIVINGSTON

**COUNTRY INN
MOTEL**
536 Veterans
Memorial Dr
(62058)
Rates: n/a
(618) 637-2600

LOMBARD

**HOMESTEAD
VILLAGE GUEST
STUDIOS**
2701 Technology
Dr (60148)
Rates: n/a
(630) 928-0202
(888) 782-9473

**RESIDENCE INN
BY MARRIOTT**
2001 S Highland
Ave (60148)
Rates: $113-$175
(630) 629-7800
(800) 331-3131

MACOMB

**HOLIDAY INN
EXPRESS**
1655 Jackson St
(61455)
Rates: n/a
(309) 836-6700
(800) 465-4329

MAHOMET

**HERITAGE INN
MOTEL**
I-74 & Rt 47
(61853)
Rates: n/a
(217) 586-4975

MARION

**BEST INNS
OF AMERICA**
2700 W De Young
(62959)
Rates: $37-$54
(618) 997-9421
(800) 237-8466

**BEST WESTERN
AIRPORT INN**
130 Express Dr
(62959)
Rates: $42-$65
(618) 993-3222
(800) 528-1234

**BRENTWOOD INN
& SUITES**
1806 Bittle Place
(62959)
Rates: n/a
(618) 997-7900
(800) 455-7900

COURTS INN
110 S Court
(62959)
Rates: n/a
(618) 993-8131

DAYS INN
1802 Bittle Place
(62959)
Rates: $55-$65
(618) 997-1351
(800) 329-7466

DRURY INN
2706 W De Young
(62959)
Rates: $545$78
(618) 997-9600
(800) 378-7946

GRAY PLAZA MOTEL
New Rt 13 W
(62959)
Rates: n/a
(618) 993-2174

MOTEL MARION
2100 W Main St
(62959)
Rates: n/a
(618) 993-2101

MOTEL 6
1008 Halfway Rd
(62959)
Rates: $30-$36
(618) 993-2631
(800) 466-8356

OLD SQUAT INN
RR 7, Box 246
(62959)
Rates: n/a
(618) 982-2916

SUPER 8 MOTEL
2601 W De Young
St (62959)
Rates: $42-$79
(618) 993-5577
(800) 800-8000

TOUPAL'S COUNTRY INN
RR 5 (62959)
Rates: n/a
(618) 995-2074

MARSHALL

LINCOLN MOTEL
US Rt 40 (62441)
Rates: n/a
(217) 826-2941

PEAKS MOTOR INN
I-70, Exit 147
(62441)
Rates: n/a
(217) 826-3031

MARYVILLE

ECONO LODGE
2701 Maryville Rd
(62-62)
Rates: $37-$75
(618) 345-5720
(800) 533-2666

MASON CITY

MASON CITY MOTEL
701 W Chestnut St
(62664)
Rates: n/a
(217) 482-3003

MATTESON

BAYMONT INN & SUITES
5210 Southwick
Dr (60443)
Rates: $67-$87
(708) 503-0999
(800) 301-0200
(877) 229-6668

MATTOON

BUDGET INN
I-57 & SR 45, Exit
184 (61938)
Rates: n/a
(217) 235-4011

KNIGHTS INN
4922 Paradise Rd
(61938)
Rates: $34-$75
(217) 235-4161
(800) 843-5644

SUPER 8 MOTEL
Rte 16 E & I-57
(61938)
Rates: $45-$58
(217) 235-8888
(800) 800-8000

US GRANT MOTEL
SR 45 (61938)
Rates: n/a
(217) 235-5695

MCLEAN

SUPER 8 MOTEL
South St & Elm St
(61754)
Rates: $44-$95
(309) 874-2366
(800) 800-8000

MENDOTA

COMFORT INN
1307 Kailash Dr
(61342)
Rates: $60-$95
(815) 538-3355
(800) 228-5150

SUPER 8 MOTEL
508 Hwy 34 E
(61342)
Rates: $45-$60
(815) 539-7429
(800) 800-8000

METROPOLIS

BEST INNS OF AMERICA
2055 E 5th St
(62960)
Rates: $41-$79
(618) 524-8200
(800) 237-8466

BEST WESTERN
2119 E 5th St
(62960)
Rates: $39-$59
(618) 524-3723
(800) 528-1234
(800) 577-0707

COMFORT INN
2118 E 5th St
(62960)
Rates: $48-$110
(618) 524-7227
(800) 228-5150

ISLE OF VIEW B&B
205 Metropolis St
(62960)
Rates: $43-$125
(618) 524-5838

PLAYERS AMERIHOST INN
203 E Front St
(62960)
Rates: $72-$88
(618) 524-5678
(800) 434-5800

MINONK

VICTORIAN OAKS BED & BREAKFAST
435 Locust (61760)
Rates: $59-$104
(309) 432-2771
(800) 621-9970

MOLINE
(see Quad Cities)

MONEE

COUNTRY HOST MOTEL
25512 E Sunrise
Dr (60449)
Rates: n/a
(708) 534-2150

MONMOUTH

MELING'S MOTEL
1129 N Main St
(61462)
Rates: $27-$46
(309) 734-2196

MONTROSE

MOTEL MONTAROSA
I-70, Exit 105
(62445)
Rates: n/a
(217) 924-4117

MORRIS

BEST WESTERN
Rt 47 & Hampton
St (60450)
Rates: $59-$119
(815) 942-9000
(800) 528-1234

COMFORT INN
70 W Gore Rd
(60450)
Rates: $59-$109
(815) 942-1433
(800) 228-5150

HOLIDAY INN
200 Gore Rd
(60450)
Rates: $56+
(815) 942-6600
(800) 465-4329

SUPER 8 MOTEL
70 Green Acres
(60450)
Rates: $52-$67
(815) 942-3200
(800) 800-8000

MORRISON

PARKVIEW MOTEL
15424 E Lincoln
Rd (61270)
Rates: n/a
(815) 772-2163

MORTON

COMFORT INN
210 E Ashland
Ave (61550)
Rates: $55-$95
(309) 266-8888
(800) 228-5150

HOLIDAY INN EXPRESS
115 E Ashland
(61550)
Rates: n/a
(309) 266-8310
(800) 465-4329

MORTON GROVE

BEST WESTERN INN
9424 Waukegan
Rd (60053)
Rates: $49-$85
(847) 965-6400
(800) 528-1234

MOUNT CARMEL

SHAMROCK MOTEL
1303 N Cherry St
(62863)
Rates: n/a
(618) 262-4169

MOUNT CARROLL

THE CAPTAINS QUARTERS B&B
207 S Main St
(61053)
Rates: n/a
(815) 244-2692

MOUNT MORRIS

MOUNT MORRIS MOTEL
1691 W Rt 64
(61054)
Rates: n/a
(815) 734-4114

MOUNT PROSPECT

RAMADA INN AIRPORT
200 E Rand Rd
(60058)
Rates: $72-$140
(847) 255-8800
(800) 272-6232

AREA CODES - If the local number doesn't connect, check for a new area code.

MOUNT STERLING

IRISH HOUSE MOTEL
RR 4, Box 195-B (62353)
Rates: n/a
(217) 773-4100

LAND OF LINCOLN MOTEL
403 E Main St (62353)
Rates: n/a
(217) 773-3311

MOUNT VERNON

BEST INNS OF AMERICA
222 S 44th (62864)
Rates: $34-$51
(618) 244-4343
(800) 237-8466

DRURY INN
145 N 44th St (62864)
Rates: $55-$75
(618) 244-4550
(800) 325-8300

ECONO LODGE
120 N 44th St (62864)
Rates: $43-$69
(618) 242-6370
(800) 553-2666

HOLIDAY INN
222 Potomac Blvd (62864)
Rates: $75
(618) 244-7100
(800) 465-4329

MOTEL 6
333 S 44th St (62864)
Rates: $32-$36
(618) 244-2383
(800) 466-8356

PINE TREE INN
I-57 & 64 (62864)
Rates: n/a
(618) 242-6370

SUPER 8 MOTEL
401 S 44th St (62864)
Rates: $45-$79
(618) 242-8800
(800) 800-8000

THRIFTY INN
100 N 44th St (62864)
Rates: $44-$62
(618) 244-7750

MUDDY

DAYS INN
Rt 45, Box 3 (62965)
Rates: $33-$75
(618) 252-6354
(800) 329-7466

MUNDELEIN

SUPER 8 MOTEL
1950 S Lake St (60060)
Rates: $49-$75
(847) 949-8842
(800) 800-8000

MURPHYS- BORO

APPLE TREE INN
100 North 2nd St (62966)
Rates: $30-$40
(618) 687-2345
(800) 626-4356

NAPERVILLE

COUNTRY INN & SUITES
1847 W Diehl Rd (60563)
Rates: $89-$109
(630) 548-0966
(800) 456-4000

EXEL INN
1585 N Naperville/ Wheaton Rd (60563)
Rates: $57-$85
(630) 357-0022
(800) 367-3935

HAWTHORN SUITES
1843 W Diehl Rd (60563)
Rates: $99-$179
(630) 548-0881
(800) 527-1133

HOMESTEAD VILLAGE GUEST STUDIOS
1827 Centre Point Circle (60563)
Rates: $69-$95
(630) 577-0200
(888) 782-9473

RED ROOF INN
1698 W Diehl Rd (60563)
Rates: $71-$81
(630) 369-2500
(800) 843-7663

TRAVELODGE
1617 Naperville Rd (60563)
Rates: $52-$100
(630) 505-0200
(800) 578-7878

NASHVILLE

BEST WESTERN U.S. INN
11640 SR 27 (62263)
Rates: $38-$59
(618) 478-5341
(800) 528-1234

MILL CREEK INN
560 N Mill (62263)
Rates: n/a
(618) 327-8424

NAUVOO

NAUVOO FAMILY MOTEL
1875 Mulholland (62354)
Rates: $42-$59
(217) 453-6527

NAUVOO VILLAGE INN
1350 Farley St (62354)
Rates: $20-$30
(217) 453-6634

NEBO

HEARTHLAND LODGE
RR 1, Box 8A (62355)
Rates: n/a
(217) 222-0899

NEWTON

RIVER PARK MOTEL
RR 5 (62448)
Rates: n/a
(618) 783-2327

NILES

DAYS INN
6450 W Touhy Ave (60714)
Rates: $65-$195
(847) 647-7700
(800) 329-7466

THRIFTLODGE
7247 N Waukegan Rd (60714)
Rates: $45-$70
(847) 647-9444
(800) 525-9055

NORMAL

BEST WESTERN UNIVERSITY INN
6 Traders Cir (61761)
Rates: $59-$89
(309) 454-4070
(800) 528-1234

COMFORT SUITES
310-B Greenbriar Dr (61761)
Rates: $59-$99
(309) 452-8588
(800) 228-5150

HOLIDAY INN NORTH
8 Traders Cir (61761)
Rates: $100
(309) 452-8300
(800) 465-4329

MOTEL 6
1600 N Main St (61761)
Rates: $32-$38
(309) 452-0422
(800) 466-8356

SUPER 8 MOTEL
2 Traders Cir (61761)
Rates: $35-$59
(309) 454-5858
(800) 800-8000

NORTH AURORA

HOWARD JOHNSON
306 S Lincolnway (60542)
Rates: $52-$68
(630) 892-6481
(800) 446-4656

NORTHBROOK

RADISSON HOTEL & CONF CENTER
2875 N Milwaukee Ave (60062)
Rates: $69-$89
(847) 298-2525
(800) 333-3333

RED ROOF INN
340 Waukegan Rd (60062)
Rates: $70-$100
(847) 205-1755
(800) 843-7663

OAK BROOK

MARRIOTT HOTEL
1401 W 22nd St (60523)
Rates: $84-$149
(630) 573-8555
(800) 228-9290

OAK FOREST

THE TERRACE MOTEL
15353 S Cicero Ave (60452)
Rates: n/a
(708) 687-7500

OAK PARK

THE WRITE INN
211 N Oak Park Ae (60302)
Rates: n/a
(708) 383-4800

OAKBROOK TERRACE

COMFORT SUITES O'HARE
17 W 445 Roosevelt Rd (60181)
Rates: $99-$149
(630) 916-1000
(800) 228-5150

AREA CODES - If the local number doesn't connect, check for a new area code.

HILTON SUITES
10 Drury Ln
(60181)
Rates: $139
(630) 941-0100
(800) 445-8667

LA QUINTA INN
1 South 666
Midwest Rd
(60181)
Rates: $55-$105
(630) 495-4600
(800) 687-6667

O'FALLON

COMFORT INN
1100 Eastgate Dr
(62269)
Rates: $60-$89
(618) 624-6060
(800) 228-5150

OGLESBY

HOLIDAY INN EXP
900 Holiday St
(61348)
Rates: $59-$65
(815) 883-3535
(800) 465-4329

OKAWVILLE

SUPER 8 MOTEL
812 N Henhouse
Rd (62271)
Rates: $41-$66
(618) 243-6525
(800) 800-8000

OLNEY

SUPER 8 MOTEL
Rt 130 & North
Ave (62450)
Rates: $39-$54
(618) 392-7888
(800) 800-8000

OREGON

VIP MOTEL
1326 IL 2 N (61061)
Rates: $27-$32
(815) 732-6195

ORLAND PARK

COMFORT INN
8800 W 159th St
(60462)
Rates: $89-$225
(708) 403-1100
(800) 228-5150

OTTAWA

HOLIDAY INN EXPRESS
120 W Stevenson
Rd (61350)
Rates: $63-$72
(815) 433-0029
(800) 465-4329

PALATINE

MOTEL 6
1450 E Dundee Rd
(60067)
Rates: $44-$66
(847) 359-0046
(800) 466-8356

RED GABLES MOTEL
875 W Northwest
Hwy (60067)
Rates: n/a
(847) 358-3443

PANA

ROSE BUD MOTEL
RR 2, Jct 16 & 51
(62557)
Rates: n/a
(217) 562-3929

PARIS

PINNELL MOTOR INN
11639 Hwy 1
(61944)
Rates: $45-$70
(217) 465-6441

SUPER 8 MOTEL
Hwy 150 (61944)
Rates: $39-$75
(217) 463-8888
(800) 800-8000

PEKIN

BEST WESTERN PEKIN INN
2801 E Court St
(61554)
Rates: $53-$68
(309) 347-5533
(800) 528-1234

COMFORT INN
3240 N Vandever
Ave (61554)
Rates: $59-$139
(309) 353-4047
(800) 228-5150

MINERAL SPRINGS MOTEL
1901 Court St
(61554)
Rates: $31-$41
(309) 346-2147

PEORIA

COMFORT SUITES
4021 War
Memorial Dr
(61614)
Rates: $57-$130
(309) 688-3800
(800) 228-5150

DAYS INN
2726 W Lake Ave
(61615)
Rates: $50-$140
(309) 688-7000
(800) 329-7466

HOLIDAY INN
4400 N
Brandywine Dr
(61614)
Rates: $90-$95
(309) 686-8000
(800) 465-4329

HOLIDAY INN CITY CENTRE
500 Hamilton
Blvd (61602)
Rates: $98-$138
(309) 674-2500
(800) 465-4329

JUMER'S CASTLE LODGE
117 N Western
Ave (61604)
Rates: $81-$106
(309) 673-8040
(800) 285-8637

MARK TWAIN HOTEL
225 NE Adams
(61602)
Rates: $85-$104
(309) 676-3600
(800) 325-6351

PERE MARQUETTE HISTORIC HOTEL
501 Main St
(61602)
Rates: $82-$500
(309) 637-6500
(800) 447-1676

RED ROOF INN
4031 N War
Memorial Dr
(61614)
Rates: $46-$56
(309) 684-3911
(800) 843-7663

RESIDENCE INN BY MARRIOTT
4201 N war
Memorial Dr
(61614)
Rates: $130-$140
(309) 681-9000
(800) 331-3131

SLEEP INN
4244 Brandywine
Dr (61614)
Rates: $57-$127
(309) 682-3322
(800) 753-3746

SUPER 8 MOTEL
4025 W War
Memorial Dr
(61614)
Rates: $47-$79
(309) 688-8074
(800) 800-8000

PERU

BEST INN
1841 May Rd
(61354)
Rates: $34-$49
(815) 224-1060
(800) 237-8466

MOTEL 6
1900 May Rd
(61354)
Rates: $25-$31
(815) 224-2785
(800) 466-8356

QUALITY INN
1840 May Rd
(61354)
Rates: $50-$75
(815) 224-2500
(800) 228-5151

RAMADA LIMITED
4389 Venture Dr
(61354)
Rates: $63-$84
(815) 224-9000
(800) 272-6232

SUPER 8 MOTEL
1851 May Rd
(61354)
Rates: $44-$60
(815) 223-1848
(800) 800-8000

PINCKNEYVILLE

FOUNTAIN MOTEL
112 S Main St
(62274)
Rates: $32-$34
(618) 357-2128

POCAHONTAS

POWHATAN MOTEL
I-70 & Exit 36
(62275)
Rates: n/a
(618) 669-2271

TAHOE MOTEL
Rt 40 & I-70, Exit
36 (62275)
Rates: n/a
(618) 669-2404

WIKIUP MOTEL
Plant & Johnson
Sts (62275)
Rates: n/a
(618) 669-2293

POLO

VILLAGE INN MOTEL
1007 S Division St
(61064)
Rates: n/a
(815) 946-2229

PONTIAC

COMFORT INN
1821 W Reynolds
St (61764)
Rates: $55-$125
(815) 842-2777
(800) 228-5150

FIESTA MOTEL
Rts 66 & 116
(61764)
Rates: n/a
(815) 844-7103

PALAMAR MOTEL
213 S Ladd St
(61764)
Rates: n/a
(815) 844-5191

SUPER 8 MOTEL
601 S Deerfield Rd
(61764)
Rates: $41-$58
(815) 844-6888
(800) 800-8000

PONTOON BEACH

BEST WESTERN CAMELOT INN
1240 E Old Chain
of Rocks Rd (62040)
Rates: $49-$69
(618) 931-2262
(800) 528-1234

SUPER 8 MOTEL
4141 Timberlake
Dr (62040)
Rates: $45-$64
(618) 931-8808
(800) 800-800

PRINCETON

DAYS INN
2238 N Main St
(61356)
Rates: $30-$55
(815) 875-3371
(800) 329-7466

LINCOLN INN
I-80 & Rt 26
(61356)
Rates: $32-$44
(815) 875-3371

PRAIRIE HILL BARN B&B
Rt 4, Box 74
(61356)
Rates: n/a
(815) 447-2487

PRINCETON MOTOR LODGE
1844 N Main
(61356)
Rates: $36-$44
(815) 875-1121

PROPHETSTOWN

PROPHET MOTEL
201 Washington St
(61277)
Rates: n/a
(815) 537-5333

PROSPECT HEIGHTS

EXEL INN
540 Milwaukee
Ave (60070)
Rates: $42-$66
(847) 459-0545
(800) 367-3935

FOREST LODGE
1246 S River Rd
(60070)
Rates: $29-$150
(847) 537-2000

QUAD CITIES

BEST WESTERN STEEPLEGATE INN
100 W 76th St
(Davenport 52806)
Rates: $75-$105
(319) 386-6900
(800) 528-1234
(800) 373-6900

COMFORT INN
7222 Northwest
Blvd
(Davenport 52806)
Rates: $45-$65
(319) 391-8222
(800) 228-5150

DAYS INN
3202 E Kimberly
Rd
(Davenport 52807)
Rates: $45-$75
(319) 355-1190
(800) 329-7466

ECONO LODGE
2205 Kimberly Rd
(Bettendorf 52722)
Rates: $40-$75
(319) 355-6471
(800) 553-2666

EXEL INN
6310 N Brady St
(Davenport 52806)
Rates: $33-$52
(319) 386-6350
(800) 367-3935

EXEL INN
2501 52nd Ave
(Moline 61265)
Rates: $42-$59
(309) 797-5580
(800) 367-3935

HAMPTON INN AIRPORT
6920 27th St
(Moline 61265)
Rates: $71-$85
(309) 762-1711
(800) 426-7866

HAMPTON INN
3330 E Kimberly
Rd
(Davenport 52807)
Rates: $67-$68
(319) 359-3921
(800) 426-7866

HEARTLAND INN
815 Golden
Valley Dr
(Bettendorf 52722)
Rates: $56-$76
(319) 355-6336
(800) 334-3277

HEARTLAND INN
6605 Brady St
(Davenport 52806)
Rates: $54-$71
(319) 386-8336
(800) 334-3277

HOLIDAY INN
909 Middle Rd
(Bettendorf 52722)
Rates: $69-$91
(319) 395-7141
(800) 465-4329

HOLIDAY INN
6902 27th St
(Moline 61265)
Rates: $70
(309) 762-8811
(800) 465-4329

HOLIDAY INN EXP
6910 27th St
(Moline 61265)
Rates: $59-$75
(309) 762-8300
(800) 465-4329

JUMER'S CASTLE LODGE
900 Spruce Hills
Dr
(Bettendorf 52722)
Rates: $76-$97
(319) 359-7141
(800) 528-8637

LA QUINTA INN
5450 27th St
(Moline 61265)
Rates: $65-$85
(309) 762-9008
(800) 687-6667

MOTEL 6
Airport Road
(Moline 61265)
Rates: $39-$45
(309) 764-8711
(800) 466-8356

MOTEL 6
6111 N Brady St
(Davenport 52806)
Rates: $34-$39
(319) 391-8997
(800) 466-4356

SUPER 8 MOTEL
2201 John Deere
Expy (East
Moline 61244)
Rates: $45-$64
(309) 796-1999
(800) 800-8000

TWIN BRIDGES MOTOR INN
221 15th St
(Bettendorf 52722)
Rates: $30-$65
(319) 355-6451

QUINCY

BEL-AIRE MOTEL
2314 North 12th St
(62301)
Rates: n/a
(217) 223-1356

COMFORT INN
4100 Broadway
(62301)
Rates: $49-$96
(217) 228-2700
(800) 228-5150

DAYS INN-RIVERSIDE
200 Maine St
(62301)
Rates: $29-$99
(217) 223-6610
(800) 329-7466

DIAMOND MOTEL
4703 N 12th St
(62301)
Rates: n/a
(217) 223-1436

HOLIDAY INN
201 S 3rd St
(62301)
Rates: $69-$79
(217) 222-2666
(800) 465-4329

SUPER 8 MOTEL
224 N 36th St
(62301)
Rates: $42-$62
(217) 228-8808
(800) 800-8000

TRAVELODGE
200 S 3rd St
(62301)
Rates: $45-$75
(217) 222-5620
(800) 578-7878

RANTOUL

BEST WESTERN HERITAGE INN
420 S Murray Rd
(61866)
Rates: $50-$74
(217) 892-9292
(800) 528-1234

DAYS INN
801 W Champaign
(61866)
Rates: $48-$70
(217) 893-0700
(800) 329-7466

SUPER 8 MOTEL
207 S Murray Rd
(61866)
Rates: $45-$67
(217) 893-8888
(800) 800-8000

RED BUD

RED BUD COUNTRY INN
1617 S Main
(62278)
Rates: n/a
(618) 282-4444

RED BUD MOTEL
1103 S Main St
(62278)
Rates: n/a
(618) 282-2123

RICHMOND

DRAKE MOTEL
8613 S Rt 12
(60071)
Rates: n/a
(815) 678-3501

ROBINSON

**BEST WESTERN
ROBINSON INN**
1500 W Main St
(62454)
Rates: $48-$103
(618) 544-8448
(800) 528-1234

ROCK FALLS

HOLIDAY INN
2105 S 1st Ave
(61071)
Rates: $54-$61
(815) 626-5500
(800) 465-4329

SUPER 8 MOTEL
2100 1st Ave
(61071)
Rates: $46-$69
(815) 626-8800
(800) 800-8000

ROCK ISLAND

**PLAZA ONE
HOTEL**
17th St at 3rd Ave
(61201)
Rates: $80-$248
(309) 794-1212

ROCKFORD

AIRPORT INN
4419 S 11th St
(61108)
Rates: n/a
(815) 397-4000

ALPINE INN
4404 E State St
(61108)
Rates: $36-$58
(815) 399-1890
(800) 399-3580

**BEST SUITES OF
AMERICA**
7401 Walton Ave
(61108)
Rates: $65-$93
(815) 227-1300
(800) 237-8466

**BEST WESTERN
COLONIAL INN
MOTOR LODGE**
4850 E State St
(61108)
Rates: $78-$98
(815) 398-5050
(800) 613-1234

COMFORT INN
7392 Argus Dr
(61107)
Rates: $59-$110
(815) 398-7061
(800) 228-5150

EXEL INN
220 S Lyford Rd
(61108)
Rates: $44-$64
(815) 332-4915
(800) 367-3935

**HOWARD
JOHNSON HOTEL**
3909 11th St
(61109)
Rates: $49-$89
(815) 397-9000
(800) 446-4656

KNIGHTS INN
3851 11th St
(61109)
Rates: n/a
(815) 398-6080
(800) 843-5644

RED ROOF INN
7434 E State St
(61108)
Rates: $63-$76
(815) 398-9750
(800) 843-7663

**RESIDENCE INN
BY MARRIOTT**
7542 Colosseum
Dr (61107)
Rates: $89-$129
(815) 227-0013
(800) 331-3131

SIXPENCE INN
4205 S 11th St
(61109)
Rates: $25-$29
(815) 398-0066

SUPER 8 MOTEL
7646 Colosseum
Dr (61107)
Rates: $39-$79
(815) 229-5522
(800) 800-8000

**SWEDEN HOUSE
LODGE**
4605 E State St
(61108)
Rates: $40-$70
(815) 398-4130
(800) 896-4138

ROLLING MEADOWS

MOTEL 6
1800 Winnetka Cir
(60008)
Rates: $37-$43
(847) 818-8088
(800) 466-8356

ROSEMONT

**HOLIDAY INN-
O'HARE**
5540 N River Rd
(60018)
Rates: $169-$189
(847) 671-6350
(800) 465-4329

**HOTEL SOFITEL
O'HARE**
5550 N River Rd
(60018)
Rates: $235-$275
(847) 678-4488
(800) 233-5959

**MARRIOTT SUITES
O'HARE**
6155 N River Rd
(60018)
Rates: $139-$224
(847) 696-4400
(800) 228-9290

RUSHVILLE

**THE BOTTENBERG
BED & BREAKFAST**
505 N Liberty
(62681)
Rates: n/a
(217) 322-6100

**CROSSROADS
MOTEL**
Hwy 24 (62681)
Rates: n/a
(217) 322-6702

**GREEN GABLES
MOTEL**
Rt 67 (62681)
Rates: n/a
(217) 322-4371

SAINT ANNE

**GEORGIAN
MOTEL**
Rts 1 & 17 (61964)
Rates: n/a
(815) 937-9740

SAINT ELMO

WALDORF MOTEL
1000 W
Cumberland Rd
(62458)
Rates: n/a
(618) 829-5665

SALEM

**CONTINENTAL
MOTEL**
1600 E Main St
(62881)
Rates: $26-$36
(618) 548-3090

HOLIDAY INN
1812 W Main St
(62881)
Rates: $56-$61
(618) 548-4212
(800) 465-4329

**MOTEL
LAKEWOOD**
1500 E Main St
(62881)
Rates: $23-$27
(618) 548-2785

RESTWELL MOTEL
700 W Main St
(62881)
Rates: n/a
(618) 548-2040

SUPER 8 MOTEL
118 Paragon Rd
(62881)
Rates: $43-$79
(618) 548-5882
(800) 800-8000

SAVANNA

**BLACKHAWK
MOTEL**
7418 Rt 84 N
(61074)
Rates: n/a
(815) 273-2041

**INDIAN HEAD
MOTEL**
3523 Rt 84 N
(61074)
Rates: n/a
(815) 273-2154

LAW'S MOTEL II
2000 Oakton Rd
(61074)
Rates: n/a
(815) 273-7728

**PINE LODGE
MOTEL**
2017 Chicago Ave
(61074)
Rates: n/a
(815) 273-2291

RADKE HOTEL
422 Main St
(61074)
Rates: n/a
(815) 273-3713

SAVOY

**BEST WESTERN
PARADISE INN**
1001 N Dunlap
(61874)
Rates: $50-$70
(217) 356-1824
(800) 528-1234

SCHAUMBURG

AMERISUITES
1851 McConnor
Pkwy (60173)
Rates: $89-$154
(847) 330-1060
(800) 833-1516

**CORPORATE
SUITES & APTS**
1813 Hemlock Pl
(60173)
Rates: n/a
(847) 397-8021

DRURY INN
600 N Martingale
Rd (60173)
Rates: $81-$99
(847) 517-7737
(800) 325-8300

HOLIDAY INN
1550 N Roselle Rd
(60195)
Rates: n/a
(847) 310-0500
(800) 465-4329

**HOMESTEAD
VILLAGE GUEST
STUDIOS**
51 E State Pkwy
(60173)
Rates: $89-$94
(847) 882-6900
(888) 782-9473

HOMEWOOD SUITES
815 E American Ln (60173)
Rates: $79-$169
(847) 605-0400
(800) 225-5466

LA QUINTA INN
1730 E Higgins Rd (60173)
Rates: $85-$105
(847) 517-8484
(800) 687-6667

MARRIOTT HOTEL
50 N Martingale Rd (60173)
Rates: $82-$199
(847) 240-0100
(800) 228-9290

SUMMERFIELD SUITES HOTEL
901 E Woodfield Office Ct (60173)
Rates: $79-$230
(847) 619-6677
(800) 833-4353

SCHILLER PARK

HOWARD JOHNSON EXPRESS
4101 N Mannheim Rd (60176)
Rates: $89-$124
(847) 678-4470
(800) 446-4656

MOTEL 6
9408 W Lawrence Ave (60176)
Rates: $42-$48
(847) 671-4282
(800) 466-8356

SHEFFIELD

DAYS INN
16733 Hwy 40 (61361)
Rates: $40-$85
(815) 454-2361
(800) 329-7466

HIDDEN LAKE COUNTRY CLUB GUEST HOUSES
Buda on Rt 40 (61361)
Rates: n/a
(815) 454-2603

SHELBYVILLE

LITHIA RESORT
RR 4, Box 105 (62565)
Rates: $52-$109
(217) 774-2882

SPILLWAY MOTEL
Hwy 16 E (62565)
Rates: n/a
(217) 774-9591

SHOREWOOD

DAYS INN
19747 Frontage Rd (60435)
Rates: $49-$145
(815) 725-2180
(800) 329-7466

SKOKIE

DOUBLETREE NORTH SHORE
9599 Skokie Blvd (60077)
Rates: $109-$165
(847) 679-7000
(800) 222-8733

HOLIDAY INN NORTH SHORE
5300 W Touhy Ave (60077)
Rates: $130-$150
(847) 679-8900
(800) 465-4329

HOWARD JOHNSON
9333 Skokie Blvd (60077)
Rates: $107-$149
(847) 679-4200
(800) 654-2000

SOUTH HOLLAND

BAYMONT INN
17225 S Holland St (60473)
Rates: n/a
(708) 596-3900
(877) 229-6668
(800) 301-0200

RED ROOF INN
17301 S Halsted St (60473)
Rates: $48-$66
(708) 331-1621
(800) 843-7663

SPARTA

MAC'S SPARTA MOTEL
700 S St. Louis St (62286)
Rates: n/a
(618) 443-3614

POOLSIDE MOTEL
402 E Broadway (62286)
Rates: n/a
(618) 443-3187

SPRING VALLEY

RIVIERA MOTEL
I-80 & Rt 89 (61362)
Rates: n/a
(815) 894-2225

SPRINGFIELD

BAYMONT INN
5871 S Sixth St (62703)
Rates: $65-$72
(217) 529-6655
(800) 301-0200

BEST INNS OF AMERICA
500 N 1st St (62702)
Rates: $55-$85
(217) 522-1100
(800) 237-8466

BEST WESTERN CLEARLAKE PLAZA
3440 Clearlake Ave (62702)
Rates: $60-$95
(217) 525-7420
(800) 528-1234

CAPITOL PLAZA HOTEL
418 E Jefferson St (62701)
Rates: n/a
(217) 525-1700

COMFORT INN
3442 Freedom Dr (62704)
Rates: $58-$100
(217) 787-2250
(800) 228-5150

DAYS INN
3000 Stevenson Dr (62703)
Rates: $54-$84
(217) 529-0171
(800) 329-7466

DRURY INN
3180 S Dirksen Pkwy (62703)
Rates: $65-$85
(217) 529-3900
(800) 378-7946

HILTON HOTEL
700 E Adams St (62701)
Rates: $79-$149
(217) 789-1530
(800) 445-8667

HOLIDAY INN EAST-HOTEL & CONF CENTER
3100 S Dirksen Pkwy (62703)
Rates: $78-$90
(217) 529-7171
(800) 465-4329

PEAR TREE INN BY DRURY
3190 S Dirksen Pkwy (62703)
Rates: $46-$65
(217) 529-9100
(800) 282-8733

RAMADA INN
625 E St Joseph St (62703)
Rates: $60-$150
(217) 529-7131
(800) 272-6232

RAMADA LIMITED
5970 S 6th St (62703)
Rates: $49-$90
(217) 529-1410
(800) 272-6232

RED ROOF INN
3200 Singer Ave (62703)
Rates: $50-$68
(217) 753-4302
(800) 843-7663

SKY HARBOR INN & CONF CENTER
1701 J David Jones Pkwy (62703)
Rates: n/a
(217) 541-8762
(800) 349-4081

SLEEP INN
3470 Freedom Dr (62704)
Rates: $49-$89
(217) 787-6200
(800) 753-3746

STEVENSON INN
2860 Stevenson Dr (62703)
Rates: n/a
(217) 585-4002
(888) 993-REST

SUPER 8 MOTEL
1330 S Dirksen Pkwy (62703)
Rates: $39-$55
(217) 528-8889
(800) 800-8000

SUPER 8 MOTEL
3675 S 6th St (62703)
Rates: $42-$57
(217) 529-8898
(800) 800-8000

STAUNTON

SUPER 8 MOTEL
1527 Herman Rd (62088)
Rates: $39-$55
(618) 635-5353
(800) 800-8000

SULLIVAN

GATEWAY INN
S Hamilton (61951)
Rates: n/a
(217) 728-4314

SYCAMORE

AMERIHOST INN
1475 S Peace Rd (60178)
Rates: $60-$85
(815) 895-4979
(800) 434-5800

TAYLORVILLE

RYAN'S INN
Rt 29 S & 48 Bypass (62568)
Rates: n/a
(217) 287-7211
(800) 252-4748

AREA CODES - If the local number doesn't connect, check for a new area code.

29 WEST MOTEL
709 Springfield Rd
(62568)
Rates: $30-$38
(217) 824-2216

TINLEY PARK

**BAYMONT INN
& SUITES**
7255 W 183rd St
(60477)
Rates: $68-$92
(708) 633-1200
(800) 301-0200
(877) 229-6668

TONICA

**KISHAUWAU ON
THE VERMILION**
901 N 2129 Rd
(61370)
Rates: n/a
(815) 442-8453

TROY

SCOTTISH INNS
909 Edwardsville
Rd (62294)
Rates: $30-$40
(618) 667-9969
(800) 251-1962

TUSCOLA

**HOLIDAY INN
EXPRESS**
1201 Tuscola Blvd
(61953)
Rates: $70-$88
(217) 253-6363
(800) 465-4329

SUPER 8 MOTEL
1007 E Hwy
36(61953)
Rates: $47-$65
(217) 253-5488
(800) 800-8000

ULLIN

**BEST WESTERN
CHEEKWOOD**
128 Cheekwood
Lane (62992)
Rates: $48-$68
(618) 845-3773
(800) 528-1234

URBANA

**JUMER'S CASTLE
LODGE**
209 S Broadway
(61801)
Rates: $75-$94
(217) 384-8800
(800) 285-8637

MOTEL 6
1906 N
Cunningham Ave
(61801)
Rates: $30-$36
(217) 344-1082
(800) 466-8356

**PARK INN &
CONFERENCE
CENTER**
2408 N
Cunningham Ave
(61801)
Rates: $55-$60
(217) 344-8000
(800) 437-7275

**RAMADA
LIMITED**
902 W Killaraney
(61801)
Rates: $58-$150
(217) 328-4400
(800) 272-6232

SLEEP INN
1908 N Lincoln
Ave (61801)
Rates: $48-$85
(217) 367-6000
(800) 753-3746

VANDALIA

DAYS INN
1920 Kennedy
Blvd (62471)
Rates: $52-$90
(618) 283-4400
(800) 329-7466

JAY'S INN
720 Gochenour St
(62471)
Rates: $34-$52
(618) 283-1200

RAMADA LIMITED
Rt 40 W (62471)
Rates: $50-$78
(618) 283-1400
(800) 272-6232

TRAVELODGE
1500 N 6th St
(62471)
Rates: $37-$70
(618) 283-2363
(800) 578-7878

VERNON HILLS

AMERISUITES
450 N Milwaukee
Ave (60061)
Rates: $87-$114
(847) 918-1400
(800) 833-1516

**HOMESTEAD
VILLAGE GUEST
STUDIOS**
675 Woodlands
Pkwy (60061)
Rates: $50-$74
(847) 955-1111
(888) 782-9473

VILLA PARK

MOTEL 6
10 W Roosevelt
Rd (60181)
Rates: $43-$49
(630) 941-9100
(800) 466-8356

WARRENILLE

AMERISUITES
4305 Weaver
Pkwy (62379)
Rates: $79-$169
(630) 393-0400
(800) 833-1516

WASHINGTON

**CRESTVIEW
MOTEL**
1216 Peoria St
(61571)
Rates: n/a
(309) 444-4421

SUPER 8 MOTEL
1884 Washington
Rd (61571)
Rates: $46-$56
(309) 444-8881
(800) 800-8000

WATSEKA

**CAROUSEL INN
MOTEL**
1120 E Walnut St
(60970)
Rates: $33-$40
(815) 432-4966

SUPER 8 MOTEL
710 W Walnut St
(60970)
Rates: $52-$71
(815) 432-6000
(800) 800-8000

WATSEKA MOTEL
814 E Walnut St
(60970)
Rates: n/a
(815) 432-2426

WAUKEGAN

AIRPORT INN
3651 Lewis Ave
(60087)
Rates: n/a
(847) 249-7777

**BEST INNS
OF AMERICA**
31 N Green Bay
Rd (60085)
Rates: $52-$102
(847) 336-9000
(800) 237-8466

**BEST WESTERN
OF WAUKEGAN**
411 S Greenbay
Rd (60085)
Rates: $45-$110
(847) 244-6100
(800) 528-1234

**LUMBERLAND
MOTEL**
3030 Belvedere Rd
(60085)
Rates: n/a
(847) 623-6830

WENONA

SUPER 8 MOTEL
5 Cavalry Dr
(61377)
Rates: $40-$58
(815) 853-4371
(800) 800-8000

WEST
FRANKFORT

**GRAY PLAZA
MOTEL**
1010 W Main St
(62896)
Rates: n/a
(618) 932-3116

WESTMONT

**BEST WESTERN
AMBASSADOR
INN**
669 Pasquinelli Dr
(60559)
Rates: $60-$85
(630) 323-1515
(800) 528-1234

**HOMESTEAD
VILLAGE GUEST
STUDIOS**
855 Pasquinelli Dr
(60559)
Rates: n/a
(630) 323-9292
(888) 782-9473

WILLOW-
BROOK

BAYMONT INN
855 W 79th St
(60521)
Rates: $48-$71
(630) 654-0077
(800) 301-0200

HOLIDAY INN
7800 S Kingery
Hwy (60521)
Rates: $89-$95
(630) 325-6400
(800) 465-4329

RED ROOF INN
7535 Robt Kingery
Hwy (60521)
Rates: $67-$79
(630) 323-8811
(800) 843-7663

WINDSOR

**THE DEERFIELD
BED & BREAKFAST**
RR 1, Box 99-A
(61957)
Rates: n/a
(217) 459-2750

WINTHROP
HARBOR

SANDPIPER INN
301 N Sheridan Rd
(60096)
Rates: $69-$109
(847) 746-7380

AREA CODES - If the local number doesn't connect, check for a new area code.

WOOD RIVER

BEL AIR MOTEL
542 West Ferguson
Ave (62095)
Rates: n/a
(618) 254-0683

WOODSTOCK

**BUNDLING
BOARD INN**
220 E South St
(60098)
Rates: n/a
(815) 338-7054

**CONCORD
COUNTRY INN**
1122 Cass St
(60098)
Rates: n/a
(815) 338-1100

SUPER 8 MOTEL
1220 Davis Rd
(66098)
Rates: $49-$72
(815) 337-8808
(800) 800-8000

INDIANA

ALEXANDRIA

COUNTRY GAZEBO INN
RR 1 Box 323 (46001)
Rates: n/a
(765) 754-8783

ANDERSON

BEST INNS
5706 Scatterfield Rd (46013)
Rates: $47-$65
(765) 644-2000
(800) 237-8466

COMFORT INN
2205 E 59th St (46013)
Rates: $54-$150
(765) 644-4422
(800) 228-5150

LEES INN
2114 E 59th St (46013)
Rates: $64-$159
(765) 649-2500
(800) 733-5337

MARK MOTOR INN
2400 S Scatterfield Rd (46013)
Rates: $29-$45
(765) 642-9966

MOTEL 6
5810 Scatterfield Rd (46013)
Rates: $32-$65
(765) 642-9023
(800) 466-8356

RAMADA INN
5901 Scatterfield Rd (46013)
Rates: $68-$95
(765) 649-0451
(800) 272-6232

SUPER 8 MOTEL
2215 E 59th St (46013)
Rates: $49-$59
(765) 642-2222
(800) 800-8000

AUBURN

HOLIDAY INN EXP
404 Touring Dr (46706)
Rates: $78-$105
(219) 925-1900
(800) 465-4329

RAMADA LIMITED
400 Touring Dr (46706)
Rates: $78-$99
(219) 920-1900
(800) 272-6232

BEDFORD

MARK III MOTEL
1711 M St (47421)
Rates: $29-$45
(812) 275-5935

PLAZA MOTEL
US 50 E (47421)
Rates: $30-$50
(812) 834-5522

ROSEMOUNT MOTEL
1923 M St (47421)
Rates: $32-$45
(812) 275-5953

BLOOMINGDALE

CHEROKEE VILLAGE CAMPING CABINS
RR Box 140 (47832)
Rates: $15-$17
(765) 597-2029

COUNTRY HAVEN COTTAGE
RR 1, Box 188 (47832)
Rates: n/a
(765) 498-2532

BLOOMINGTON

BEST WESTERN FIRESIDE INN
4501 E Third St (47401)
Rates: $46-$129
(812) 332-2141
(800) 528-1234

COMFORT INN
1722 N Walnut St (47408)
Rates: $39-$94
(812) 339-1919
(800) 228-5150

DAYS INN
200 Matlock Rd (47401)
Rates: $49-$150
(812) 336-0905
(800) 329-7466

HAMPTON INN
2100 N Walnut St (47408)
Rates: $69-$87
(812) 334-2100
(800) 426-7866

MOTEL 6
126 S Franklin Rd (47401)
Rates: $29-$45
(812) 332-0337
(800) 466-8356

MOTEL 6
1800 N Walnut (47402)
Rates: $35-$44
(812) 332-0820
(800) 466-8356

SUPER 8 MOTEL
1000 W State Rd (47401)
Rates: $52-$69
(812) 323-8000
(800) 800-8000

TRAVELODGE
2615 E 3rd St (47401)
Rates: $525$99
(812) 339-6191
(800) 578-7878

BLUFFTON

BUDGET INN
1420 N Main St (46714)
Rates: $35-$45
(219) 824-0820

HOLIDAY INN EXPRESS

1782 N SR 1 (46714)
Rates: n/a
(219) 824-4455
(800) 465-4329

BOSWELL

BOSWELL MOTEL
307 S Old US 41 (47921)
Rates: $29-$45
(765) 869-5060

BRAZIL

HOWARD JOHNSON EXPRESS
935 W State Rd 42 (47834)
Rates: $55-$100
(812) 446-2345
(800) 446-4656

BROWNSBURG

COMFORT SUITES
500 W Northfield Dr (46112)
Rates: $74-$275
(317) 852-2000
(800) 228-5150

CARLISLE

SUPER 8 MOTEL
8435 S Old Hwy (47838)
Rates: $39-$54
(812) 398-2500
(800) 800-8000

CARMEL

COMFORT SUITES
151st St & US 31 (46074)
Rates: $75-$115
(800) 228-5150

CENTERVILLE

SUPER 8 MOTEL
2407 N Centerville Rd (47330)
Rates: $31-$54
(765) 855-5461
(800) 800-8000

CLARKSVILLE

BEST WESTERN GREEN TREE INN
1425 Broadway (47129)
Rates: $59-$74
(812) 288-9281
(800) 528-1234
(800) 950-9281

HAMPTON INN
1501 Broadway (47129)
Rates: $59-$69
(812) 280-1500
(800) 426-7866

KNIGHTS INN
I-65 & Eastern Blvd (47129)
Rates: $39-$65
(800) 858-8937

CLOVERDALE

HOLIDAY INN EXPRESS
1017 N Main St (46120)
Rates: $69-$99
(765) 795-5050
(800) 465-4329

RAMADA INN
1035 N Main St (46120)
Rates: $39-$64
(765) 795-3500
(800) 272-6232

COLUMBIA CITY

COLUMBIA CITY MOTEL
500 Old US 30W (46725)
Rates: $21-$38
(219) 244-5103

LEES INN
235 Frontage Rd
(46725)
Rates: $59-$149
(219) 244-5300
(800) 733-5337

SUPER 8 MOTEL
351 W Plaza Dr
(46725)
Rates: $48-$72
(219) 244-2655
(800) 800-8000

COLUMBUS

DAYS INN
3445 Jonathan
Moore Pike
(47201)
Rates: $44-$64
(812) 376-9951
(800) 329-7466

HOLIDAY INN
2480 Jonathan
Moore Pike
(47201)
Rates: $79-$99
(812) 372-1541
(800) 465-4329

KNIGHTS INN
101 Carrie Lane
(47201)
Rates: $39-$75
(812) 378-3100
(800) 843-5644

SUPER 8 MOTEL
110 Brexpark Dr
(47201)
Rates: $47-$67
(812) 372-8828
(800) 800-8000

CRAWFORDS-VILLE

COMFORT INN
2991 N Gandhi St
(47933)
Rates: $65-$250
(765) 361-0665
(800) 228-5150

**DAVIS HOUSE
BED & BREAKFAST**
1010 W Wabash
Ave (47933)
Rates: $50-$60
(765) 364-0461

**GENERAL LEW
WALLACE INN**
309 W Pike St
(47933)
Rates: $37-$43
(765) 362-8400

HOLIDAY INN
2500 N Lafayette
Rd (47933)
Rates: $59-$85
(765) 362-8700
(800) 465-4329

SUPER 8 MOTEL
1025 Corey Blvd
(47933)
Rates: $46-$59
(765) 364-9999
(800) 800-8000

DALE

**BAYMONT INN
& SUITES**
20857 N US 231
(47523)
Rates: $69-$179
(812) 937-7000
(800) 301-0200

MOTEL 6
20840 N Hwy 231
(47523)
Rates: $43-$56
(812) 937-2294
(800) 466-8356

SCOTTISH INNS
231 A,best Plaza
(47523)
Rates: $33-$42
(812) 937-2816
(800) 251-1962

**YELLOW BANKS
RECREATION
CENTER CABINS**
RR 2, Box 160
(47523)
Rates: $55-$65
(812) 567-4703

DALEVILLE

SUPER 8 MOTEL
15701 W
Commerce St
(47334)
Rates: $43-$52
(765) 378-0888
(800) 800-8000

DECATUR

DAYS INN
1033 N 13th St
(46733)
Rates: $49-$85
(219) 728-2196
(800) 329-7466

MATADOR INN
922 N 13th St
(46733)
Rates: $34-$40
(219) 728-2101

DERBY

**OHIO RIVER
CABINS**
13445 SR 66
(47525)
Rates: $70-$99
(812) 836-2289

DUNREITH

**FLAMINGO
MOTEL**
108 First St (47337)
Rates: $33-$55
(765) 987-7111

EDINBURGH

**BEST WESTERN
HORIZON INN**
11780 N US 31
(46124)
Rates: $39-$139
(812) 526-9883
(800) 528-1234

ELKHART

DIPLOMAT MOTEL
3300 Cassopolis
Rd (46514)
Rates: $34-$45
(219) 264-4118

ECONO LODGE
4550 Cassopolis
Rd (46514)
Rates: $37-$135
(219) 262-0540
(800) 553-2666

THE FAIRWAY INN
115 North Pointe
Blvd (46514)
Rates: $44-$90
(219) 266-1940
(877) 843-4667

**QUALITY INN
& SUITES**
3321 Plaza Ct
(46514)
Rates: $55-$135
(219) 264-0404
(800) 228-5151

RAMADA INN
3011 Belvedere Rd
(46514)
Rates: n/a
(219) 262-1581
(800) 272-6232

RED ROOF INN
2902 Cassopolis St
(46514)
Rates: $51-$100
(219) 262-3691
(800) 843-7663

SUPER 8 MOTEL
345 Windsor Ave
(46514)
Rates: $54-$68
(219) 264-4457
(800) 800-8000

TURNPIKE MOTEL
3500 Cassopolis St
(46514)
Rates: $34-$46
(219) 264-1108

EVANSVILLE

COMFORT INN
5006 E Morgan
Ave (47715)
Rates: $65-$91
(812) 477-2211
(800) 228-5150

DAYS INN
4819 Tecumseh Ln
(47715)
Rates: $45-$110
(812) 473-7944
(800) 329-7466

**DRURY INN &
SUITES-EAST**
100 Cross Pointe
Blvd (47710)
Rates: $59-$81
(812) 471-3400
(800) 378-7946

**DRURY INN &
SUITES-NORTH**
3901 US 41 N
(47711)
Rates: $59-$81
(812) 423-5818
(800) 378-7946

LEES INN
5538 E Indiana St
(47715)
Rates: $69-$169
(812) 477-6663
(800) 733-5337

MOTEL 6
4321 US 41 N
(47711)
Rates: $35-$48
(812) 424-6431
(800) 466-8356

RED ROOF INN
8331 E Walnut St
(47715)
Rates: $50-$91
(812) 476-3600
(800) 843-7663

**RESIDENCE INN
BY MARRIOTT**
8283 E Walnut St
(47715)
Rates: $96
(812) 471-7191
(800) 331-3131

SUPER 8 MOTEL
4600 Morgan Ave
(47715)
Rates: $49-$64
(812) 476-4008
(800) 800-8000

FISHERS

**FREDERICK-
TALBOTT INN
B&B**
13805 Allisonville
Rd (46038)
Rates: $99-$199
(317) 578-3600

HOLIDAY INN
9780 North by
Northeast Blvd
(46038)
Rates: $84-$96
(317) 578-9000
(800) 465-4329

**HOLIDAY INN
EXPRESS**
9790 North by
Northeast Blvd
(46038)
Rates: $69-$85
(317) 578-2000
(800) 465-4329

AREA CODES - If the local number doesn't connect, check for a new area code.

SLEEP INN
9791 North by
Northeast Blvd
(46038)
Rates: $69-$175
(317) 558-4100
(800) 753-3746

FORT WAYNE

BAYMONT INN
1005 W
Washington Ctr
Rd (46825)
Rates: $54-$109
(219) 489-2220
(800) 301-0200

**BEST INNS
OF AMERICA**
3017 W Coliseum
Blvd (46808)
Rates: $41-$66
(219) 483-0091
(800) 237-8466

COMFORT SUITES
5775 Coventry Ln
(46804)
Rates: $79-$200
(219) 436-4300
(800) 228-5150

COMFORT SUITES
3302 E Dupont Rd
(46802)
Rates: $64-$136
(213) 480-7030
(800) 228-5150

**DAYS INN EAST
DOWNTOWN**
3730 E
Washington Blvd
(46803)
Rates: $40-$90
(219) 424-1980
(800) 329-7466

DAYS INN NORTH
5250 Distribution
Dr (46825)
Rates: $33-$48
(219) 484-9681
(800) 329-7466

**HAMPTON INN
& SUITES**
5702 Challenger
Pkwy (46818)
Rates: $99
(219) 489-0908
(800) 426-7866

HOMETOWN INN
6910 US 30E
(46803)
Rates: $32-$40
(219) 749-5058

**KNIGHT'S INN-
NORTH**
2901 Goshen Rd
(46808)
Rates: $40-$51
(219) 464-2669
(800) 843-5644

LEES INN
5707 Challenger
Pkwy (46818)
Rates: $69-$160
(219) 489-8888
(800) 733-5337

MARRIOTT HOTEL
305 E Washington
Center Rd (46825)
Rates: $130-$140
(219) 484-0411
(800) 228-9290

MOTEL 6
3003 Coliseum
Blvd W (46808)
Rates: $29-$45
(219) 482-3972
(800) 466-8356

RED ROOF INN
2920 Goshen Rd
(46808)
Rates: $29-$38
(219) 484-8641
(800) 843-7663

**RESIDENCE INN
BY MARRIOTT**
4919 Lima Rd
(46808)
Rates: $69-$135
(219) 484-4700
(800) 331-3131

SLEEP INN
I-69 Exit 116
(46825)
Rates: $45-$200
(800) 753-3746

FRANKFORT

**HOLIDAY INN
EXPRESS**
592 S CR 200
(46041)
Rates: $61-$110
(765) 659-4400
(800) 465-4329

FRANKLIN

DAYS INN
2180 E King St
(46131)
Rates: $42-$70
(317) 736-8000
(800) 329-7466

FREMONT

E & L MOTEL
35 W SR 120
(46737)
Rates: $25-$42
(219) 495-3300

FRENCH LICK

**THE PINES AT
PATOKA LAKE
VILLAGE**
7900 W CR 1025S
(47432)
Rates: $79-$89
(812) 936-9854

GOSHEN

**BEST WESTERN
INN**
900 Lincolnway E
(46526)
Rates: $64-$69
(219) 533-0408
(800) 528-1234

COUNTRY B&B
27727 CR 36
(46526)
Rates: n/a
(219) 862-2748

GREENCASTLE

COLLEGE INN
315 Bloomington
St (46135)
Rates: $28-$48
(765) 653-4167

GREENFIELD

BUDGET MOTEL
1310 W Main St
(46140)
Rates: $34-$52
(317) 462-4493

COMFORT INN
178 Martindale Dr
(46140)
Rates: $52-$100
(317) 467-9999
(800) 228-5150

LEES INN
2270 N State St
(46140)
Rates: $64-$160
(317) 462-7112
(800) 733-5337

GREENSBURG

**BEST WESTERN
PINES INN**
2317 N State Rd 3
(47240)
Rates: $64-$95
(812) 663-6055
(800) 528-1234

LEES INN
2211 N State Rd 3
(47240)
Rates: $59-$160
(812) 663-9998
(800) 733-5337

GREENWOOD

COMFORT INN
110 Sheek Rd
(46143)
Rates: $54-$225
(317) 887-1515
(800) 228-5150

HAMMOND

HOLIDAY INN
3830 179th St
(46323)
Rates: $85-$100
(219) 844-2140
(800) 465-4329

MOTEL 6
3840 179th St
(46324)
Rates: $39-$50
(219) 845-0330
(800) 466-8356

**RESIDENCE INN
BY MARRIOTT**
7740 Corinne Dr
(46324)
Rates: $109-$169
(219) 844-8440
(800) 331-3131

HOBART

COMFORT INN
1915 Mississippi
St (46342)
Rates: $80-$94
(219) 947-7677
(800) 228-5150

HOWE

SUPER 8 MOTEL
7333 N SR 9
(46746)
Rates: $60-$74
(219) 562-2828
(800) 800-8000

**TRAVEL INN
MOTEL**
50 W 815 N
(46746)
Rates: $29-$59
(219) 562-3481

HUNTINGTON

DAYS INN
2996 W Park Dr
(46750)
Rates: $44-$100
(219) 359-8989
(800) 329-7466

**SHERYL MANOR
MOTEL**
1800 Etna Ave
(46750)
Rates: $39-$45
(219) 356-0626

INDIANAPOLIS

AMERISUITES
9104 Keystone
Crossing (46240)
Rates: $99-$119
(317) 843-0064
(800) 833-1516

**BAYMONT INN &
SUITES-AIRPORT**
2650 Executive Dr
(46241)
Rates: $70-$75
(317) 244-8100
(800) 301-0200

**BAYMONT INN &
SUITES-INDY EAST**
2349 Post Dr
(46219)
Rates: $60-$65
(317) 897-2300
(800) 301-0200

**COMFORT INN
CITY CENTER**
530 S Capitol Ave
(46225)
Rates: $98-$108
(317) 631-9000
(800) 228-5150

COMFORT INN NORTH
3880 W 92nd St (46268)
Rates: $54-$74
(317) 872-3100
(800) 228-5150

DAYS INN EAST
7314 E 21st St (46219)
Rates: $39-$59
(317) 359-5500
(800) 329-7466

DAYS INN NORTHEAST
4326 Sellers St (46226)
Rates: $34-$119
(317) 542-1031
(800) 329-7466

DAYS INN - NW
3740 N High School Rd (46224)
Rates: $41-$66
(317) 293-6550
(800) 329-7466

DAYS INN & SUITES
8275 Craig St (46250)
Rates: $59-$119
(317) 841-9700
(800) 329-7466

DRURY INN
9320 N Michigan Rd (46268)
Rates: $60-$80
(317) 876-9777
(800) 378-7946

ECONO LODGE
4505 S Harding St (46217)
Rates: $36-$150
(317) 788-9361
(800) 553-2666

FOUR POINTS BY SHERATON
7701 E 42nd St (46256)
Rates: $79-$109
(317) 897-4000
(800) 325-3535

HAMPTON INN NORTHWEST
7220 Woodland Dr (46278)
Rates: $77-$92
(317) 290-1212
(800) 426-7866

HAWTHORN SUITES LTD
3871 W 92nd St (46268)
Rates: n/a
(317) 879-1700
(800) 527-1133

HOLIDAY INN EAST
6990 E 21st St (46219)
Rates: $74-$89
(317) 359-5341
(800) 465-4329

HOLIDAY INN EXPRESS
5151 S East St (46227)
Rates: n/a
(317) 783-5151
(800) 465-4329

HOLIDAY INN-SE
5120 Victory Dr (46203)
Rates: $109
(317) 783-7751
(800) 465-4329

HOMEWOOD SUITES AT THE CROSSING
2501 E 86th St (46240)
Rates: $99-$109
(317) 253-1919
(800) 225-5466

HOWARD JOHNSON EXPRESS
7050 E 21st St (46219)
Rates: $36-$48
(317) 352-0481
(800) 446-4656

HOWARD JOHNSON EXPRESS
2602 N High School Rd (46224)
Rates: $30-$60
(317) 291-8800
(800) 446-4656

HOWARD JOHNSON EXPRESS INN & SUITES
7202 E 82nd St (46256)
Rates: $69-$150
(317) 841-8585
(800) 446-4656

HOWARD JOHNSON HOTEL
8401 W Washington St (46231)
Rates: n/a
(800) 446-4656

INDIANAPOLIS MOTOR SPEED-WAY BRICKYARD CROSSING GOLF RESORT & INN
4400 W 16th St (46202)
Rates: $65-$130
(317) 241-2500

LA QUINTA INN-AIRPORT
5316 W Southern Ave (46241)
Rates: $60-$85
(317) 247-4281
(800) 687-6777

LA QUINTA INN-EAST
7304 E 21st St (46219)
Rates: $75-$95
(317) 359-1021
(800) 687-6777

LEES INN
5011 N Lafayette Rd (46241)
Rates: $69-$225
(317) 297-8880
(800) 733-5337

MAINSTAY SUITES
8520 Northwest Blvd (46278)
Rates: $79-$179
(317) 334-7829
(800) 660-6246

MARRIOTT HOTEL
7202 E 21st St (46219)
Rates: $89-$139
(317) 352-1231
(800) 228-9290

MOTEL 6
5241 W Bradbury Ave (46241)
Rates: $33-$52
(317) 248-1231
(800) 466-8356

MOTEL 6 EAST
2851 Shadeland Ave (46219)
Rates: $33-$46
(317) 546-5864
(800) 466-8356

MOTEL 6 SOUTH
5151 Elmwood Dr (46203)
Rates: $33-$50
(317) 783-5555
(800) 466-8356

NEW ENGLAND SUITES HOTEL
3871 W 92nd St (46268)
Rates: $39-$65
(317) 879-1700

OMNI NORTH HOTEL
8181 N Shadeland Ave (46250)
Rates: $175-$195
(317) 849-6668
(800) 843-6664

OMNI SEVERIN HOTEL
40 W Jackson Place (46225)
Rates: $119-$249
(317) 634-6664
(800) 843-6664

PICKWICK FARMS AIRPORT APARTMENT MOTEL
25 Beachway Dr (46260)
Rates: $78-$85
(317) 240-3567
(800) 736-8390

PICKWICK FARMS SHORT-TERM FURNISHED APARTMENTS
9300 N Ditch Rd (46260)
Rates: $35-$95
(317) 872-6506
(800) 869-7368

QUALITY INN & SUITES
9090 Wesleyan Rd (46268)
Rates: $59-$250
(317) 875-7676
(800) 228-5151

QUALITY INN I-70 EAST
2141 N Post Rd (46219)
Rates: $49-$250
(317) 897-2000
(800) 228-5151

QUALITY INN SOUTH
520 E Thompson Rd (46227)
Rates: $69-$150
(317) 787-8341
(800) 228-5151

RADISSON HOTEL CITY CENTRE
31 W Ohio St (46204)
Rates: $119-$194
(317) 635-2000
(800) 333-3333

RAMADA INN
4514 S Emerson Ave (46203)
Rates: $45-$68
(317) 787-3344
(800) 272-6232

RAMADA LIMITED
108 Pennsylvania (46204)
Rates: $97-$150
(317) 614-1400
(800) 272-6232

RAMADA LIMITED
4950 S East St (46227)
Rates: $60-$87
(317) 784-0047
(800) 272-6232

RED ROOF INN AIRPORT
2653 Lynhurst Dr (46241)
Rates: n/a
(800) 843-7663

RED ROOF INN
450 Bixler Rd (46227)
Rates: $39-$64
(317) 788-0811
(800) 843-7663

RED ROOF INN NORTH
9520 Vaparaiso Ct (46268)
Rates: $38-$70
(317) 872-3030
(800) 843-7663

RED ROOF INN SOUTH
5221 Victory Dr (46203)
Rates: $40-$63
(317) 788-9551
(800) 843-7663

AREA CODES - If the local number doesn't connect, check for a new area code.

**RED ROOF INN
SPEEDWAY**
6415 Debonair Ln
(46224)
Rates: $45-$84
(317) 293-6881
(800) 843-7663

**RESIDENCE INN
BY MARRIOTT**
350 W New York
St (46204)
Rates: $139-$279
(317) 822-0840
(800) 331-3131

**RESIDENCE INN
BY MARRIOTT**
5224 W Southern
Ave (46241)
Rates: $109-$179
(317) 244-1500
(800) 331-3131

**RESIDENCE INN
BY MARRIOTT**
3553 Founders Rd
(46268)
Rates: $109-$169
(317) 872-0462
(800) 331-3131

**RESIDENCE INN
BY MARRIOTT**
9765 Cross Point
Blvd (46256)
Rates: $119-$159
(317) 842-1111
(800) 331-3131

SHERATON NORTH
8787 Keystone
Crossing (46240)
Rates: $89-$139
(317) 846-2700
(800) 325-3535

SUPER 8 MOTEL
4502 S Harding
(46217)
Rates: $41-$60
(317) 788-4774
(800) 800-8000

SUPER 8 MOTEL
8850 E 21st St
(46219)
Rates: $41-$52
(317) 895-5402
(800) 800-8000

SUPER 8 MOTEL
McFarland Blvd
(46237)
Rates: $45-$64
(317) 859-8888
(800) 800-8000

**WELLESLEY INN
& SUITES**
5350 W Southern
Ave (46241)
Rates: $89-$159
(317) 241-0700
(800) 444-8888

**WELLSLEY INN &
SUITES**
9370 Waldemar Dr
Rates: $89-$139
(317) 471-0700
(800) 444-8888

**THE WESTIN
SUITES NORTH**
8787 Keystone
Crossing (46240)
Rates: $99-$159
(317) 574-6770
(800) 228-3000

JASPER

DAYS INN
272 Brucke Strasse
(47547)
Rates: $65-$109
(812) 482-6000
(800) 329-7466

JEFFERSON-VILLE

DAYS INN
350 Eastern Blvd
(47130)
Rates: $35-$38
(812) 288-9331
(800) 329-7466

MOTEL 6
2016 Old Hwy 31
E (47130)
Rates: $31-$45
(812) 283-2703
(800) 466-8356

KENTLAND

**TRI-WAY INN
MOTEL**
611 E Dunlap St
(47951)
Rates: $35-$51
(219) 474-5141

KNOX

RODEWAY INN
2001 S Hwy 35
(46534)
Rates: $49-$129
(219) 772-2227
(800) 228-2000

KOKOMO

COMFORT INN
522 Essex Dr
(46901)
Rates: $62-$125
(765) 452-5050
(800) 228-5150

MOTEL 6
2808 S Reed Rd
(46902)
Rates: $37-$50
(765) 457-8211
(800) 466-8356

SUPER 8 MOTEL
5110 Clinton St
(46902)
Rates: $48-$72
(765) 455-3288
(800) 800-8000

LA PORTE

RAMADA INN
444 Pine Lake Ave
(46350)
Rates: $69-$129
(219) 362-4595
(800) 272-6232

LAFAYETTE

BUDGET INN
139 N Frontage Rd
(47905)
Rates: $38-$75
(765) 447-7566

COMFORT SUITES
31 Frontage Rd
(47905)
Rates: $74-$150
(765) 447-0016
(800) 228-5150

**HAWTHORN
SUITES**
163 Frontage Rd
(47905)
Rates: n/a
(765) 446-8668
(800) 527-1133

**HOLIDAY INN
EXPRESS**
201 Frontage Rd
(47905)
Rates: $75-$150
(765) 449-4808
(800) 465-4329

**HOMEWOOD
SUITES**
3939 SR 26E
(47905)
Rates: $92-$225
(765) 448-9700
(800) 225-5466

KNIGHTS INN
4110 SR 26E
(47905)
Rates: $149
(765) 447-5611
(800) 843-5644

LEES INN
4701 Meijer Ct
(47905)
Rates: $69-$199
(765) 447-3434
(800) SEE-LEES

**LOEB HOUSE
HISTORIC INN**
708 Cincinnati St
(47905)
Rates: $79
(765) 420-7737

**MICROTEL INN
& SUITES**
151 Frontage Rd
(47905)
Rates: $49-$99
(765) 446-8558
(888) 771-7171

RADISSON INN
4343 SR 26 E
(47905)
Rates: $99-$199
(765) 447-0575
(800) 333-3333

RAMADA INN
4221 SR 26E
(47905)
Rates: $70-$150
(765) 447-9460
(800) 272-6232

RED ROOF INN
4201 SR 26
(47905)
Rates: $51-$62
(765) 448-4671
(800) 843-7663

LAGRANGE

APPLEWOOD INN
11135 E 100 S
(46761)
Rates: $50-$80
(219) 351-3267
(888) 404-3267

LEBANON

COMFORT INN
210 Sam Ralston
Rd (46052)
Rates: $57-$225
(765) 482-4800
(800) 228-5150

LEES INN
1245 W SR 32
(46052)
Rates: $59-$149
(765) 482-9611
(800) 733-5337

SUPER 8 MOTEL
405 N Mount Zion
Rd (46052)
Rates: n/a
(765) 482-9999
(800) 800-8000

LINGONIER

MINUETTE B&B
210 S Main St
(46767)
Rates: n/a
(219) 894-4494

LOGANSPORT

HOLIDAY INN
3550 E Market St
(46947)
Rates: $150
(219) 753-6351
(800) 465-4329

SUPER 8 MOTEL
3601 E Market St
(46947)
Rates: $55-$67
(219) 722-1273
(800) 800-8000

MADISON

**BEST WESTERN
OF MADISON**
700 Clifty Dr,
Hwy 62 (47250)
Rates: $52-$125
(812) 273-5151
(800) 528-1234
(800) 497-8863

**PRESIDENT
MADISON MOTEL**
Center Center
(47250)
Rates: $35-$60
(812) 265-2361
(800) 456-6835

AREA CODES - If the local number doesn't connect, check for a new area code.

ROTH'S GET-AWAY COTTAGES
203 S Walnut (47250)
Rates: $59-$85
(812) 265-6636

MANSFIELD

CHARTWELL FARMS GUEST HOUSE
RR 1, Box 155 (47837)
Rates: n/a
(765) 344-1510

MARION

BROADMOOR MOTEL
1323 N Baldwin Ave (46952)
Rates: $32-$40
(765) 664-0501

COMFORT SUITES
1345 N Baldwin Ave (46952)
Rates: $89-$125
(765) 651-1006
(800) 228-5150

SUPER 8 MOTEL
5172 S Kaybee Dr (Gas City 46953)
Rates: $50-$75
(765) 998-6800
(800) 800 8000

MARKLE

SLEEP INN
730 W Logan St (46770)
Rates: $59-$69
(219) 758-8111
(800) 753-3746

SUPER 8 MOTEL
610 Annette Dr (46770)
Rates: $46-$62
(219) 758-8888
(800) 800-8000

MARSHALL

CHEROKEE VILLAGE CAMPING CABINS
RR 1, Box 140 (47859)
Rates: $16-$18
(765) 597-2029

MARTINSVILLE

LEES INN
50 Bills Blvd (46151)
Rates: $59-$159
(765) 342-1842
(800) 733-5337

MERRILLVILLE

KNIGHTS INN
8250 Louisiana St (46410)
Rates: $40-$65
(219) 736-5100
(800) 843-5644

LA QUINTA INN
8210 Louisiana St (46410)
Rates: $65-$85
(219) 738-2870
(800) 687-6667

LEES INN
6201 Opportunity Lane (46410)
Rates: $64-$149
(219) 942-8555
(800) 733-5337

MOTEL 6
8290 Louisianna St (46410)
Rates: $36-$52
(219) 738-2701
(800) 466-8356

RADISSON HOTEL AT STAR PLAZA
800 E 81st Ave (46410)
Rates: $99-$159
(219) 769-6311
(800) 333-3333

RED ROOF INN
8290 Georgia St (46410)
Rates: $51-$71
(219) 738-2430
(800) 843-7663

RESIDENCE INN BY MARRIOTT
8018 Delaware Place (46410)
Rates: $119-$169
(219) 791-9000
(800) 331-3131

SUPER 8 MOTEL
8300 Louisianna St (46410)
Rates: $43-$61
(219) 736-8383
(800) 800-8000

METAMORA

THORPE HOUSE COUNTRY INN
10941 Clayborne St (47030)
Rates: $70-$125
(765) 647-5425
(888) 427-7932

MICHIGAN CITY

KNIGHTS INN
201 W Kieffer Rd (46360)
Rates: $55-$109
(219) 874-9500
(800) 843-5644

RED ROOF INN
110 W Kieffer Rd (46360)
Rates: $57-$78
(219) 874-5251
(800) 843-7663

MIDDLEBURY

THE THAYER HOUSE
14604 CR 22 (46540)
Rates: n/a
(219) 825-7926

MISHAWAKA

DAYS INN
2754 Lincolnway E (46544)
Rates: $42-$63
(219) 256-2300
(800) 329-7466

SUPER 8 MOTEL
535 W University Dr (46545)
Rates: $45-$90
(219) 247-0888
(800) 800-8000

MITCHELL

SHARP'S FAMILY INN
Hwy 37 S & 60 E (47446)
Rates: $29-$45
(812) 849-9048

MONTGOMERY

RED ROOF INN
Box 60, CR 650 E (47558)
Rates: $45-$53
(812) 486-2600
(800) 843-7663

MONTICELLO

1887 BLACK DOG INN
2830 Untaluti (47960)
Rates: n/a
(219) 583-8297

QUIET WATER B&B
4794 E Harbor Ct (47960)
Rates: $59-$85
(219) 583-6023

MOUNT VERNON

FOUR SEASONS MOTEL
2400 W 4th St (47620)
Rates: $50-$91
(812) 838-4821
(800) 264-1405

SUPER 8 MOTEL
6225 Hwy 69 S (47620)
Rates: $50-$91
(812) 838-8888
(800) 800-8000

MUNCIE

COMFORT INN
4011 W Bethel Ave (47305)
Rates: $54-$150
(765) 282-6666
(800) 228-5150

DAYS INN
3509 N Everbrook Ln (47304)
Rates: $53-$63
(765) 288-2311
(800) 329-7466

LEES INN
3302 N Everbrook Ln (47304)
Rates: $69-$199
(765) 282-7557
(800) 733-5337

RADISSON HOTEL ROBERTS
420 S High St (47304)
Rates: $65-$225
(765) 741-7777
(800) 333-3333

SUPER 8 MOTEL
3601 W Fox Ridge Ln (47304)
Rates: $46-$57
(765) 286-4333
(800) 800-8000

NAPPANEE

VICTORIAN GUEST HOUSE
302 E Market (46550)
Rates: n/a
(219) 773-4383

NASHVILLE

SALT CREEK INN
Box 397 (47448)
Rates: $40-$110
(812) 988-1149

STORY INN
6404 S SR 135 (47448)
Rates: n/a
(812) 988-2273

WESTWARD HO CAMPGROUND & CABINS
4557 E SR 46 (47448)
Rates: n/a
(812) 988-0008

NEW ALBANY

HOLIDAY INN EXPRESS
411 W Spring St (47150)
Rates: $99
(812) 945-2771
(800) 465-4329

NEW CASTLE

BEST WESTERN RAINTREE INN
2836 S SR 3 (47362)
Rates: $56-$120
(765) 521-0100
(800) 528-1234
(800) 521-0015

AREA CODES - If the local number doesn't connect, check for a new area code.

DAYS INN
5343 S State Rd 3
(47362)
Rates: $37-$54
(765) 987-8205
(800) 329-7466

MULBERRY LANE INN
5256 N CR 75 W
(47362)
Rates: $59-$85
(765) 836-4500

NEW CASTLE INN
2005 S Memorial
Dr (47362)
Rates: $30-$44
(765) 529-1670

WALNUT RIDGE RESORT CABINS
408 N CR 300 W
(47362)
Rates: $40-$55
(765) 533-6611

NEW HARMONY

WRIGHT PLACE BED & BREAKFST
515 S Arthur St
(47631)
Rates: $80-$130
(812) 682-3453

NEW HAVEN

HOMETOWN INN
6910 US 30 E
(46774)
Rates: $37-$62
(219) 749-5058

NORTH VERNON

NORTH VERNON'S RAILROAD INN
302 Summit St
(47265)
Rates: $39-$65
(812) 346-7345

PATOKA LAKE

THE PINES AT PATOKA LAKE CABINS
7000 W CR 1025
S (French Lick
47432)
Rates: n/a
(812) 936-9854
(888) 324-5350

PLAINFIELD

LEES INN & SUITES
6010 Gateway Dr
(46168)
Rates: $79-$249
(317) 837-9000
(800) 733-5337

PLYMOUTH

DAYS INN
2229 N Michigan
St (46563)
Rates: $35-$55
(219) 935-4276
(800) 329-7466

MOTEL 6
2535 N Michigan
Ave (46563)
Rates: $31-$38
(219) 935-5911
(800) 466-8356

RAMADA INN
2550 N Michigan
St (46563)
Rates: $73-$90
(219) 936-4013
(800) 272-6232

SUPER 8 MOTEL
2160 N Oak Rd
(46563)
Rates: $50-$130
(219) 936-8856
(800) 800-8000

POLAND

WASATCH LAKE CABIN RENTALS
General Delivery
(47868)
Rates: $100-$400
(317) 488-7373

PORTAGE

COMFORT INN
2300 Willow
Creek (46368)
Rates: $99
(219) 763-7177
(800) 228-5150

DAYS INN
6161 Melton Rd
(46368)
Rates: $55-$135
(219) 762-2136
(800) 329-7466

HAMPTON INN
6353 Melton Rd
(46368)
Rates: $64-$99
(219) 764-1919
(800) 426-7866

RAMADA INN
6200 Melton Rd
(46368)
Rates: $54-$68
(219) 762-5546
(800) 272-6232

PORTLAND

HOOSIER INN
1620 Maridian St
(47371)
Rates: $38-$50
(219) 726-7113

PRINCETON

DAYS INN
2110 W Broadway
(47670)
Rates: $49-$100
(812) 386-1200
(800) 329-7466

RENSSELAER

INTERSTATE MOTEL
8530 W St Rd
Hwy (47978)
Rates: $30-$40
(219) 866-4164

REYNOLDS

PARK VIEW MOTEL
RR 1, Box 4
(47980)
Rates: $25-$55
(219) 984-5380

RICHMOND

BEST WESTERN IMPERIAL MOTOR LODGE
3020 E Main St
(47374)
Rates: $36-$66
(765) 966-1505
(800) 528-1234

DAYS INN
540 W Eaton Pike
(47374)
Rates: $45-$90
(765) 966-7591
(800) 329-7466

HOLIDAY INN
5501 E National
Rd (47374)
Rates: $86-$325
(765) 966-7511
(800) 465-4329

LEES INN
6030 National Rd
E (47374)
Rates: $59-$149
(765) 966-6449
(800) 733-5337

RAMADA INN
4700 E National
Rd (47374)
Rates: $39-$62
(765) 962-5551
(800) 272-6232

SUPER 8 MOTEL
2525 Chester Blvd
(47374)
Rates: $48-$75
(765) 962-7576
(800) 800-8000

VILLA MOTEL
533 W Eaton Pike
(47374)
Rates: $23-$42
(765) 962-5202

RISING SUN

ANDERSON'S RIVIERA SUITES
119 Industrial
Access Rd (47040)
Rates: $99
(812) 438-2121
(888) 243-6446

THE JELLY HOUSE COUNTRY INN B&B
222 S Walnut St
(47040)
Rates: $110-$170
(812) 438-2319
(877) 429-0695

RIVERVIEW COTTAGE
222 S Front St
(47040)
Rates: n/a
(812) 438-4057

ROCKVILLE

BILLIE CREEK VILLAGE & INN
US 36 E, Billie
Creek Dr (47872)
Rates: $69-$99
(765) 569-3430

RACOON LAKESIDE LODGE
RR 1, Box 870
(47873)
Rates: $63-$200
(765) 344-1162

RENT A VICTORIAN HOUSE
Main St., Box 1883
(47872)
Rates: $80+
(765) 344-1510

SALEM

DELANEY PARK CABINS
Delaney Park Rd
(47167)
Rates: $29-$45
(812) 883-5101

SANTA CLAUS

LAKE RANDOLPH CMPGRND/RV/ CABIN RENTALS
Hwy 245 (47579)
Rates: n/a
(812) 937-4458
(877) 478-3657

SCOTTSBURG

BEST WESTERN SCOTTSBURG INN
1525 W McClain
St (47170)
Rates: $60-$139
(812) 752-2212
(800) 528-1234

HAMPTON INN
1535 W McClain
Ave (47170)
Rates: $64-$81
(812) 752-1999
(800) 426-7866

MARIANN TRAVEL INN
SR 56 & I-65
(47170)
Rates: $39-$58
(812) 752-3396
(800) 648-0662

YOGI BEAR JELLYSTONE PARK CABIN RENTALS
4577 W SR 56
(47170)
Rates: n/a
(812) 752-4062
(812) 752-7046
(800) 437-0566

SEYMOUR

DAYS INN
302 S Commerce
Dr (47274)
Rates: $35-$100
(812) 522-3678
(800) 329-7466

ECONO LODGE
220 Commerce Dr
(47274)
Rates: $28-$70
(812) 522-8000
(800) 553-2666

HOLIDAY INN
2025 E Tipton St
(47274)
Rates: n/a
(812) 522-6767
(800) 465-4329

KNIGHTS INN
207 N Frontage Rd
(47274)
Rates: $44-$55
(812) 522-3523
(800) 843-5644

LEES INN
2075 E Tipton St
(47274)
Rates: $69-$149
(812) 523-1850
(800) 733-5337

SHELBYVILLE

LEES INN
111 Lee Blvd (46176)
Rates: $59-$139
(765) 392-2299
(800) 733-5337

RAMADA INN
1810 N Riley Hwy
(46176)
Rates: $48-$135
(765) 392-3221
(800) 272-6232

SUPER 8 MOTEL
20 Rampart Dr
(46176)
Rates: $43-$52
(765) 392-6239
(800) 800-8000

SHIPSHEWANA

**COUNTRY INN
& SUITES**
3440 N SR 5
(46565)
Rates: $55-$85
(219) 768-7780

SUPER 8 MOTEL
470 S Van Buren
(46565)
Rates: $60-$79
(219) 768-4004
(800) 800-8000

SOUTH BEND

**BEST INNS OF
AMERICA**
425 Dixie Hwy N
(46637)
Rates: $54-$70
(219) 277-7700
(800) 237-8466

COMFORT SUITES
52939 US 33 N
(46637)
Rates: $69-$185
(219) 272-1500
(800) 228-5150

**DAYS INN-
NOTRE DAME**
52757 US 31 N
(46637)
Rates: $59-$79
(219) 277-0510
(800) 329-7466

**ECONO LODGE
AIRPORT**
3233 Lincoln Way
W (46628)
Rates: $39-$145
(219) 232-9019
(800) 553-2666

**HOLIDAY INN
UNIVERSITY AREA**
515 Dixie Way N
(46637)
Rates: $69-$110
(219) 272-6600
(800) 465-4329

MOTEL 6
52624 Hwy 31 N
(46637)
Rates: $36-$46
(219) 272-7072
(800) 466-8356

**RESIDENCE INN
BY MARRIOTT**
716 N Niles (46637)
Rates: $99-$129
(219) 289-5555
(800) 331-3131

SPEEDWAY

MOTEL 6
6330 Debonair Ln
(46224)
Rates: $33-$46
(317) 293-3220
(800) 466-8356

SULLIVAN

DAYS INN
Jct 41 & 154
(47882)
Rates: $50-$55
(812) 268-6391
(800) 329-7466

TAYLORSVILLE

COMFORT INN
10330 N US 31
(47280)
Rates: $58-$175
(812) 526-9747
(800) 228-5150

TELL CITY

DAYSTOP
Hwy 66 & 14th St
(47586)
Rates: $34-$60
(812) 547-3474
(800) 329-7466

RAMADA LIMITED
235 Orchard Hill
Dr (47586)
Rates: $59-$73
(812) 547-3234
(800) 272-6232

TERRE HAUTE

COMFORT SUITES
501 E Margaret
Ave (47802)
Rates: $58-$150
(812) 235-1770
(800) 228-5150

DRURY INN
3040 US Hwy 41 S
(47802)
Rates: $62-$78
(812) 238-1206
(800) 378-7946

HOLIDAY INN
3300 Hwy 41 S
(47802)
Rates: $89
(812) 232-6081
(800) 465-4329

KNIGHTS INN
401 Margaret Ave
(47802)
Rates: $53-$79
(812) 234-9931
(800) 843-5644

**MID TOWN
MOTEL**
400 S 3rd St
(47807)
Rates: $30-$40
(812) 232-0383

MOTEL 6
1 W Honey Creek
Dr (47802)
Rates: $29-$46
(812) 238-1586
(800) 466-8356

PEAR TREE INN
3050 S Hwy 41
(47802)
Rates: $55-$71
(812) 234-4268
(800) 282-8733

SUPER 8 LODGE
3089 S 1st St
(47802)
Rates: $75-$90
(812) 232-4890
(800) 800-8000

TRAVELODGE
530 S 3rd St
(47807)
Rates: $38-$75
(812) 232-7075
(800) 578-7878

VINCENNES

HOLIDAY INN
600 Wheatland Rd
(47591)
Rates: $49-$74
(812) 886-9900
(800) 465-4329

**VINCENNES
LODGE**
1411 Willow St
(47591)
Rates: $28-$38
(812) 882-1282

WALKERTON

**HESTERS CABIN
BED & BREAKFST**
71880 SR 23
(46574)
Rates: n/a
(219) 586-2105

WARREN

**HUGGY BEAR
MOTEL**
7588 S Warren Rd
(46792)
Rates: $59-$85
(219) 375-2504
(800) 523-5972

RAMADA LIMITED
7275 S Co. Rd 75 E
(46792)
Rates: $59-$85
(219) 375-4800
(800) 272-6232

WARSAW

DAYS INN
3521 Lake City
Hwy (46580)
Rates: $52-$200
(219) 269-3031
(800) 329-7466

**RAMADA PLAZA
HOTEL**
2519 E Center St
(46580)
Rates: $82-$88
(219) 269-2323
(800) 272-6232

SUPER 8 MOTEL
3014 Frontage Rd
(46580)
Rates: $44-$64
(219) 268-2888
(800) 800-8000

WASHINGTON

**BAYMONT INN
& SUITES**
7 Cumberland Dr
(47501)
Rates: $54-$91
(812) 254-7000
(800) 301-0200

WEST
LAFAYETTE

HOLIDAY INN
5600 SR 4 3N
(47906)
Rates: $59-$99
(765) 567-2131
(800) 465-4329

SUPER 8 MOTEL
2030 Northgate Dr
(47906)
Rates: $56-$79
(765) 567-7100
(800) 800-8000

AREA CODES - If the local number doesn't connect, check for a new area code.

TRAVELODGE
200 Brown St
(47906)
Rates: $45-$120
(765) 743-9661
(800) 578-7878

WHITELAND

**WISHING WELL
MOTEL**
RR 1, Box 93
(46184)
Rates: $21-$25
(317) 535-7548

IOWA

ADAIR

BUDGET INN
100 S 5th St
(50002)
Rates: $33-$50
(515) 742-5553

SUPER 8 MOTEL
111 S 5th St
(50002)
Rates: $40-$60
(515) 742-5251
(800) 800-8000

ALBIA

INDIAN HILLS INN
100 Hwy 34 E
(52531)
Rates: $44-$66
(515) 932-7181

ALGONA

BURR OAK MOTEL
Hwy 169 S (50511)
Rates: $39-$47
(515) 295-7213
(877) 745-6315

ALTOONA

HEARTLAND INN
5000 NE 56th St
(50009)
Rates: $52-$79
(515) 967-2400
(800) 334-3277

MOTEL 6
3225 Adventureland
Drive (50009)
Rates: $37-$56
(515) 967-5252
(800) 466-8356

AMANA COLONIES

COMFORT INN
I-80, Exit 225
(52203)
Rates: $62-$100
(319) 668-2700
(800) 228-5150

HOLIDAY INN
I-80 Exit 225
(52203)
Rates: $84-$100
(319) 668-1175
(800) 465-4329
(800) 633-9244

AMES

BAYMONT INN
2500 Elwood Dr
(50010)
Rates: $55-$65
(515) 296-2500
(800) 301-0200

BEST WESTERN STARLITE VILLAGE
2601 E 13th St
(50010)
Rates: $56-$76
(515) 232-9260
(800) 528-1234
(800) 903-0009

COMFORT INN
1605 S Dayton Ave
(50010)
Rates: $55-$89
(515) 232-0689
(800) 228-5150

HEARTLAND INN
Hwy 30 & I-35
(50010)
Rates: $42-$56
(515) 233-6060
(800) 334-3277

HOLIDAY INN-GATEWAY CENTER
US 30 & Elwood
Dr (50010)
Rates: $95-$125
(515) 292-8600
(800) 465-4329

HOWARD JOHNSON EXPRESS
1709 S Duff Ave
(50010)
Rates: $55-$69
(515) 232-8363
(800) 446-4656

RAMADA INN
1206 S Duff
(50010)
Rates: $66-$200
(515) 232-3410
(800) 272-6232

UNIVERSITY INN
229 S Duff Ave
(50010)
Rates: $55-$85
(515) 232-0280

ANKENY

BEST WESTERN STARLITE VILLAGE
133 SE Delaware
(50021)
Rates: $55-$75
(515) 964-1717
(800) 528-1234
(800) 903-0009

DAYS INN
103 NE Delaware
(50021)
Rates: $40-$61
(515) 965-1995
(800) 329-7466

SUPER 8 MOTEL
206 SE Delaware
St (50021)
Rates: $48-$63
(515) 964-4503
(800) 800-8000

ARNOLDS PARK

FILLENWARTH BEACH COTTAGES
87 Lake Shore Dr
(51331)
Rates: $240-$960/
Weekly
(712) 332-5646

ATLANTIC

ECONO LODGE
I-80 & US 71
(50022)
Rates: $50-$60
(712) 243-4067
(800) 553-2666

AVOCA

CAPRI MOTEL
Hwy 59 (51521)
Rates: $33-$60
(712) 343-6301
(800) 222-6301

BETTENDORF
(also see Quad
Cities)

HEARTLAND INN
815 Golden Valley
Dr (52722)
Rates: n/a
(319) 355-6336
800-334-3277

BLOOMFIELD

SOUTHFORK INN
Hwys 2 & 63
(52537)
Rates: $30-$39
(515) 664-1063
(800) 926-2860

BOONE

SUPER 8 MOTEL
1715 S Story St
(50036)
Rates: $43-$58
(515) 432-8890
(800) 800-8000

BROOKLYN

SLEEP INN
4130 SR 21 (52211)
Rates: $55-$69
(319) 685-4500
(800) 753-3746

BURLINGTON

ARROWHEAD MOTEL-IMA
2520 Mt. Pleasant
St (52601)
Rates: $36-$82
(319) 752-6353
(800) 341-8000

CARROLL (header continues)

BEST WESTERN PZAZZ MOTOR INN
3001 Winegard Dr
(52601)
Rates: $60-$78
(319) 753-2223
(800) 528-1234
(800) 373-1223

COMFORT INN
3051 Kirkwood
Ave (52601)
Rates: $45-$70
(319) 753-0000
(800) 228-5150

RAMADA INN
2759 Mt. Pleasant
St (52601)
Rates: $50-$78
(319) 754-5781
(800) 272-6232

CARROLL

NICE STAY INN
1507 Radiant Rd
(51401)
Rates: $30-$43
(712) 792-9214

71-30 MOTEL
Jct US 30 & 71
(51401)
Rates: $30-$44
(712) 792-1100

CARTER LAKE

SUPER 8 MOTEL
3000 Airport Dr
(51510)
Rates: $59-$75
(712) 347-5588
(800) 800-8000

CEDAR FALLS

BLACKHAWK MOTOR INN
122 Washington
(50613)
Rates: $36-$39
(319) 271-1161
(888) 577-1161

AREA CODES - If the local number doesn't connect, check for a new area code.

HOLIDAY INN
5826 University
Ave (50613)
Rates: $59-$79
(319) 277-2230
(800) 465-4329

MIDWEST LODGE
4410 University
Ave (50613)
Rates: n/a
(319) 277-1550

UNIVERSITY INN
4711 University
Ave (50613)
Rates: $35-$109
(319) 277-1412
(800) 962-7784

CEDAR RAPIDS

BEST INN
3233 Southridge
Dr SW (52404)
Rates: $56-$100
(319) 363-9999
(800) 237-8466

**BEST WESTERN
LONGBRANCH
HOTEL & CONV
CENTER**
90 Twixt Town Rd
(52402)
Rates: $59-$250
(319) 377-6386
(800) 528-1234

**COLLINS PLAZA
HOTEL & CONV.
CENTER**
1200 Collins Rd
NE (52402)
Rates: $109-$119
(319) 393-6600
(800) 541-1067

**COMFORT INN-
NORTH**
5055 Rockwell Dr
(52402)
Rates: $59-$84
(319) 393-8247
(800) 228-5150

**COMFORT INN-
SOUTH**
390 33rd Ave SW
(52404)
Rates: $60-$120
(319) 363-7934
(800) 228-5150

DAYS INN
3245 Southgate
Place SW (52404)
Rates: $43-79
(319) 365-4339
(800) 329-7466

EXEL INN
616 33rd Ave SW
(52404)
Rates: $36-$90
(319) 366-8888
(800) 367-3935

**HOWARD
JOHNSON
EXPRESS INN
& SUITES**
700 Wright
Brothers Blvd
(52404)
Rates: $59-$130
(319) 363-3789
(800) 446-4656

RED ROOF INN
3325 Southgate Ct
SW (52404)
Rates: $36-$68
(319) 366-7523
(800) 843-7663

**RESIDENCE INN
BY MARRIOTT**
1900 Dodge Rd
NE (52402)
Rates: $84-$159
(319) 395-0111
(800) 331-3131

**SHERATON FOUR
POINTS HOTEL**
525 33rd Ave SW
(52404)
Rates: $90-$100
(319) 366-8671
(800) 325-3535

**VILLAGE INN
HOTEL & CONV
CENTER**
100 F Ave NW
(52405)
Rates: $45-$70
(319) 366-5323
(800) 858-5511

CHARITON

**ROYAL REST
MOTEL**
Hwy 14 & 34 E
(50049)
Rates: $38-$60
(515) 774-5961

CHARLES CITY

HARTWOOD INN
1312 Gilbert St
(50616)
Rates: $34-$50
(515) 228-4352
(800) 972-2335

CHEROKEE

**BEST WESTERN
LA GRANDE
HACIENDA**
1401 N 2nd St,
Hwy 59N (51012)
Rates: $55-$73
(712) 225-5701
(800) 528-1234
(800) 924-3765

SUPER 8 MOTEL
1400 N Second St
(51012)
Rates: $41-$58
(712) 225-4278
(800) 800-8000

CLARINDA

SUPER 8 MOTEL
US 71 & 12th St
(51632)
Rates: $45-$59
(712) 542-6333
(800) 800-8000

CLEAR LAKE

**BEST WESTERN
HOLIDAY LODGE**
2023 Hwy 18
(50248)
Rates: $56-$80
(515) 357-5253
(800) 528-1234
(800) 606-3552

BUDGET INN
1306 N 25th St
(50428)
Rates: $43-$57
(515) 357-8700
(888) 357-8700

HEARTLAND INN
1603 S Shore Dr
(50428)
Rates: $89-$139
(515) 357-5123
(800) 334-3277

**LAKE COUNTRY
INN MOTEL**
518 Hwy 18 W
(50428)
Rates: $30-$45
(515) 357-2184

MICROTEL INN
1305 N 25th St
(50428)
Rates: $37-$63
(515) 357-0966
(888) 771-7171

**PHEASANT
COUNTRY INN
BED & BREAKFST**
4497 190th St
(50428)
Rates: $85
(515) 357-3528
(Dog kennel
provided)

SUPER 8 MOTEL
P. O. Box 340
(50428)
Rates: $37-$56
(515) 357-7521
(800) 800-8000

CLINTON

**BEST WESTERN
FRONTIER
MOTOR INN**
2300 Lincolnway
(52732)
Rates: $54-$99
(319) 242-7112
(800) 528-1234
(800) 728-7112

**COUNTRY INN
& SUITES
BY CARLSON**
2224 Lincolnway
(52732)
Rates: $69-$109
(319) 244-9922
(800) 456-4000

RAMADA INN
1522 Lincolnway
(52732)
Rates: $48-$95
(319) 243-8841
(800) 272-6232

TIMBER MOTEL
2225 Lincolnway
(52732)
Rates: $27-$39
(319) 243-6901

TRAVELODGE
302 6th Ave S
(52732)
Rates: $38-$48
(319) 243-4730
(800) 578-7878

CLIVE

**BAYMONT INN
& SUITES**
1390 NW 118th St
(50325)
Rates: $67-$74
(515) 221-9200
(800) 301-0200

**FOUR POINTS
HOTEL
BY SHERATON**
11040 Hickman
Rd (50325)
Rates: $69
(515) 278-5575
(800) 325-3535

**THE INN
AT UNIVERSITY**
11001 University
Ave (50325)
Rates: $55-$75
(515) 225-2222
(800) 369-7476

**RESIDENCE INN
BY MARRIOTT**
11428 Forest Ave
(50325)
Rates: $109-$145
(515) 223-7700
(800) 331-3131

*COLUMBUS
JUNCTION*

**COLUMBUS
MOTEL**
Hwy 92 E (52738)
Rates: $39-$53
(319) 728-8080

COOK

**VERMILLION DAM
LODGE**
P. O. Box 1105-AA
(55723)
Rates: $700-
$1040/Weekly
(800) 325-5780

AREA CODES - If the local number doesn't connect, check for a new area code.

CORALVILLE

**BEST WESTERN
CANTERBURY
INN & SUITES**
704 1st Ave
(52241)
Rates: $70-$140
(319) 351-0400
(800) 528-1234
(800) 798-0400

COMFORT INN
209 W 9th St
(52241)
Rates: $60-$119
(319) 351-8144
(800) 228-5150

HEARTLAND INN
87 2nd St (52241)
Rates: $65-$80
(319) 351-8132
(800) 334-3277

MOTEL 6
810 1st Ave (52241)
Rates: $35-$50
(319) 354-0030
(800) 466-8356

**RAMADA
WESTFIELD INN**
2530 Holiday Rd
(52241)
Rates: $60-$90
(319) 354-7770
(800) 272-6232

COUNCIL BLUFFS

**BEST WESTERN
CROSSROADS OF
THE BLUFFS INN**
2216 27th Ave
(51501)
Rates: $59-$74
(712) 322-3150
(800) 528-1234

**BEST WESTERN
METRO INN &
SUITES**
3537 W Broadway
(51501)
Rates: $55-$89
(712) 328-3171
(800) 528-1234
(800) 556-6242

DAYS INN
3619 9th Ave
(51501)
Rates: $54-$75
(712) 323-2200
(800) 329-7466

HEARTLAND INN
1000 Woodbury
Ave (51503)
Rates: $50-$57
(712) 322-8400
(800) 334-3277

MOTEL 6-SOUTH
3032 S Expwy
(51501)
Rates: $37-$50
(712) 366-2405
(800) 466-8356

SUPER 8 MOTEL
2712 S 24th St
(51501)
Rates: $50-$60
(712) 322-2888
(800) 800-8000

TRAVELODGE
2325 Ave N
(51501)
Rates: $64-$70
(712) 328-3881
(800) 578-7878

CRESCO

CRESCO MOTEL
620 2nd Ave SE
(42136)
Rates: $35-$65
(319) 547-240

CRESTON

CAROL'S B&B
1873 High & Dry
Rd (50801)
Rates: n/a
(515) 782-7347
(800) 253-4354
(Dog kennel
provided)

DAVENPORT
(also see Quad
Cities)

**BAYMONT INN
& SUITES**
400 Jason Way Ct
(52807)
Rates: $59
(319) 386-1600
(800) 302-0200

**BEST WESTERN
STEEPLEGATE INN**
100 W 76th St
(Davenport 52806)
Rates: $75-$105
(319) 386-6900
(800) 528-1234
(800) 373-6900

COMFORT INN
7222 Northwest
Blvd (52806)
Rates: $45-$145
(319) 391-8222
(800) 228-5150

**COUNTRY INN
& SUITES
BY CARLSON**
140 E 55th St
(52805)
Rates: $78
(319) 388-6444
(800) 456-4000

DAYS INN
3202 E Kimberly
Rd (52807)
Rates: $45-$75
(319) 355-1190
(800) 329-7466

**EXEL INNS
OF AMERICA**
6310 N Brady Ave
(52806)
Rates: $39-$62
(319) 386-6350
(800) 367-3935

HAMPTON INN
3330 E. Kimberly
Rd (52807)
Rates: $79
(319) 359-3921
(800) 426-7866

HOLIDAY INN
5202 Brady
(52806)
Rates: n/a
(319) 391-1230
(800) 465-4329

MOTEL 6
6111 N Brady St
(52806)
Rates: $34-$46
(319) 391-8997
(800) 466-8356

**RESIDENCE INN
BY MARRIOTT**
120 E 55th St
(52807)
Rates: $99-$109
(319) 391-8877
(800) 331-3131

SUPER 8 MOTEL
410 E 65th St
(52807)
Rates: $42-$58
(319) 388-9810
(800) 800-8000

DE SOTO

**EDGETOWNER
MOTEL**
I-80, Exit 110
(50069)
Rates: $36-$40
(515) 834-2641

DECORAH

HEARTLAND INN
705 Commerce Dr
(52101)
Rates: $55-$76
(319) 382-2269
(800) 334-3277

SUPER 8 MOTEL
810 Hwy 9 E
(52101)
Rates: $40-$70
(319) 382-8771
(800) 800-8000

DENISON

**BEST WESTERN
INN**
502 Boyer Valley
Rd (51442)
Rates: $36-$57
(712) 263-5081
(800) 528-1234
(800) 428-0684

DAYS INN
315 Chamberlin
Dr (51442)
Rates: $35-$58
(712) 263-2500
(800) 329-7466

DES MOINES

ARCHER MOTEL
4965 Hubbell Ave
(50317)
Rates: $30-$60
(515) 265-0368

**BEST INNS OF
AMERICA**
5050 Merle Hay
Rd (50322)
Rates: $64-$94
(515) 270-1111
(800) 237-8466

**BEST WESTERN
BAVARIAN INN**
5220 NE 14th St
(50313)
Rates: $64-$89
(515) 265-5611
(800) 528-1234
(800) 383-7378

**BEST WESTERN
COLONIAL**
5020 NE 14th St
(50313)
Rates: $43-$61
(515) 265-7511
(800) 528-1234
(877) 823-0701

**BEST WESTERN
STARLITE
VILLAGE**
929 3rd St (50309)
Rates: $70-$95
(515) 282-5251
(800) 528-1234
(800) 903-0009

**BROADWAY
MOTEL**
5100 Hubbell Ave
(50317)
Rates: $30-$75
(515) 262-5659

COMFORT INN
5231 Fleur Dr
(50321)
Rates: $59-$109
(515) 287-3434
(800) 228-5150

EMBASSY SUITES
101 E Locust St
(50309)
Rates: $109-$149
(515) 244-1700
(800) 362-2779

**FORT DES
MOINES HOTEL**
1000 Walnut St
(50309)
Rates: $61-$160
(800) 532-1466

HEARTLAND INN
11414 Forest Ave
(50325)
Rates: $51-$150
(515) 226-0414
(800) 334-3277

**HEARTLAND INN
AIRPORT**
1901 Hackley Ave
(50315)
Rates: $59-$79
(515) 256-0603
(800) 334-3277

**HICKMAN
MOTOR LODGE**
6500 Hickman Rd
(50322)
Rates: $40-$55
(515) 276-8591

HOLIDAY INN
5000 Merle Hay
Rd (50322)
Rates: $79-$109
(515) 278-0271
(800) 465-4329

KIRKWOOD CIVIC CENTER HOTEL
400 Walnut St
(50309)
Rates: $54-$200
(515) 244-9191
(800) 798-9191

MARRIOTT HOTEL DOWNTOWN
700 Grand Ave
(50309)
Rates: $74-$174
(515) 245-5500
(800) 228-9290

MOTEL 6-AIRPORT
4817 Fleur Dr
(50321)
Rates: $40-$56
(515) 287-6364
(800) 466-8356

MOTEL 6-NORTH
4940 NE 14th St
(50313)
Rates: $37-$52
(515) 266-5456
(800) 466-8356

QUALITY INN & SUITES
4995 NW Merle
Hay Rd (50322)
Rates: $69-$170
(515) 278-2381
(800) 228-5151

SAVERY HOTEL & SPA
401 Locust St
(50309)
Rates: $139-$169
(515) 244-2151
(800) 798-2151

SUPER 8 LODGE
4755 Merle Hay
Rd (50322)
Rates: $47-$75
(515) 278-8858
(800) 800-8000

DUBUQUE

BEST WESTERN INN
3434 Dodge St
(52003)
Rates: $71-$169
(319) 556-7760
(800) 528-1234
(800) 747-7760

BEST WESTERN MIDWAY HOTEL
3100 Dodge St
(52003)
Rates: $79-$109
(319) 557-800
(800) 528-1234
(800) 336-4392

COMFORT INN
4055 McDonald
Dr (52003)
Rates: $59-$109
(319) 556-3006
(800) 228-5150

DAYS INN
1111 Dodge St
(52001)
Rates: $49-$79
(319) 583-3297
(800) 329-7466
(800) 772-3297

HEARTLAND INN SOUTH
2090 Southpark Ct
(52003)
Rates: $55-$75
(319) 556-6555
(800) 334-3377

HEARTLAND INN WEST
4025 McDonald
Dr (52003)
Rates: $55-$75
(319) 582-3752
(800) 334-3277

HOLIDAY INN FIVE FLAGS
450 Main St
(52001)
Rates: $54-$84
(319) 556-2000
(800) 465-4329

MOTEL 6
2670 Dodge St
(52003)
Rates: $33-$40
(319) 556-0880
(800) 466-8356

DYERSVILLE

COLONIAL INN MOTEL
1110 9th St SE
(52040)
Rates: $36-$52
(319) 875-7194

EARLY

EARLY MOTEL
403 Hwys 71 & 20
(50535)
Rates: $20-$25
(712) 273-5599

ELDORA

VILLAGE MOTEL
2005 E Edgington
Ave (50627)
Rates: $30-$45
(515) 858-3441

FAIRFIELD

BEST WESTERN INN
2200 W Burlington
(52556)
Rates: $57-$74
(515) 472-2200
(800) 528-1234

ECONOMY INN
Hwy 34 W (52556)
Rates: $30-$55
(515) 472-4161

FORT DODGE

BEST WESTERN STARLITE VILLAGE
1518 3rd Ave NW
(50501)
Rates: $48-$69
(515) 573-7177
(800) 528-1234
(800) 903-0009

COMFORT INN
2938 5th Ave S
(50501)
Rates: $49-$127
(515) 573-3731
(800) 228-5150

HOLIDAY INN
2001 Hwy 169 S
(50501)
Rates: $45-$65
(515) 955-3621
(800) 465-4329

FORT MADISON

BEST WESTERN IOWAN MOTOR LODGE
Hwy 61 S (52627)
Rates: $55-$80
(319) 372-7510
(800) 528-1234
(800) 423-2693

MADISON INN MOTEL
3440 Ave L (52627)
Rates: $42-$55
(319) 372-7740

MERICANA MOTEL
Hwy 61 West
(52627)
Rates: $30-$65
(319) 372-5123
(800) 982-5640

GLENWOOD

BULL VIEW MOTEL
57902 190 S
(51534)
Rates: $38-$42
(712) 622-8191

WESTERN INN
707 S Locust
(51534)
Rates: $31-$50
(712) 527-3175

GRINNELL

CLAYTON FARMS BED & BREAKFST
621 Newburg Rd
(50112)
Rates: $57-$120
(641) 236-3011
(888) 634-0503
(Horses allowed
only)

DAYS INN
I-80 & Hwy 146
(50112)
Rates: $48-$75
(641) 236-6710
(800) 329-7466

ECONO LODGE
2210 West St
(50112)
Rates: $47-$79
(641) 236-6116
(800) 553-2666

SUPER 8 MOTEL
I-80 & Hwy 146,
Exit 182 (50112)
Rates: $43-$61
(641) 236-7888
(800) 800-8000

HAMPTON

AMERICINN MOTEL & SUITES
702 Central Ave W
(50441)
Rates: $75-$130
(515) 456-5559
(800) 634-3444

GOLD KEY MOTEL
1570 B Hwy 65
(50441)
Rates: $32-$55
(515) 456-2566

HUMBOLT

CORNER INN MOTEL-IMA
1004 13th St N
(50548)
Rates: $36-$53
(515) 332-1672
(800) 341-8000

SUPER 8 MOTEL
Hwy 3 W (50548)
Rates: $42-$58
(515) 332-1131
(800) 800-8000

IDA GROVE

DELUX MOTEL
5981 US 175
(51445)
Rates: $35-$50
(712) 364-3317

INDEPENDENCE

SUPER 8 MOTEL
2000 1st St W
(50644)
Rates: $45-$61
(319) 334-7041
(800) 800-8000

SUPER 8 MOTEL
2730 Dodge St
(52003)
Rates: $44-$62
(319) 582-8898
(800) 800-8000

INDIANOLA

WOODS MOTEL
906 South
Jefferson (50125)
Rates: $24-$40
(515) 961-5311

IOWA CITY

**SHERATON
IOWA CITY
PLAZA HOTEL**
210 S Dubuque St
(52240)
Rates: $69-$149
(319) 337-4058
(800) 325-3535

JEFFERSON

REDWOOD MOTEL
209 E US 30
(50129)
Rates: $33-$45
(515) 386-3116

SUPER 8 MOTEL
Jct Hwy 30 & 4
(50129)
Rates: $41-$58
(515) 386-2464
(800) 800-8000

JOHNSTON

**BEST INNS
OF AMERICA**
5050 Merle Hay
Rd (50131)
Rates: $49-$87
(515) 270-1111
(800) 237-8466

**THE INN &
CONFERENCE
CENTER**
5055 Merle Hay
Rd (50131)
Rates: $69-$79
(515) 276-5411

KEOKUK

CHIEF MOTEL
2701 Main St
(52632)
Rates: $30-$50
(319) 524-2565
(800) 728-0599

ECONO LODGE
3764 Main St
(52632)
Rates: $39-$67
(319) 524-3252
(800) 553-2666

LE CLAIRE
(see Quad Cities)

LE MARS

**AMBER INN
MOTEL**
635 Eighth Ave
SW (51031)
Rates: $40-$60
(712) 546-7066
(800) 338-0298

MANCHESTER

SUPER 8 MOTEL
1020 W Main
(52057)
Rates: $50-$96
(319) 927-2533
(800) 800-8000

MAPLETON

MAPLE MOTEL
Hwy 141 & 175
(51034)
Rates: $30-$40
(712) 882-1271

MAQUOKETA

KEY MOTEL
Hwy 61 & 64
(52060)
Rates: $25-$40
(319) 652-5131

MARQUETTE

**THE FRONTIER
MOTEL**
101 S 1st St
(52158)
Rates: $40-$85
(319) 873-3497

MARSHALL-TOWN

**BEST WESTERN
REGENCY INN**
3303 S Center St
(50158)
Rates: $69-$106
(641) 752-6321
(800) 528-1234
(800) 241-2974

COMFORT INN
2613 S Center St
(50158)
Rates: $50-$87
(641) 752-6000
(800) 228-5150

ECONO LODGE
3315 S Center St
(50158)
Rates: $39-$72
(641) 753-3333
(800) 553-2666

MASON CITY

DAYS INN
2301 4th St SW
(50401)
Rates: $40-$76
(641) 424-0210
(800) 329-7466

HOLIDAY INN
2101 4th St SW
(50401)
Rates: $69-$89
(641) 423-1640
(800) 465-4329
(800) 859-2737

THRIFTLODGE
24 5th St SW
(50401)
Rates: $44-$62
(641) 424-2910
(800) 578-7878
(800) 525-9055

MISSOURI VALLEY

DAYS INN
1967 Hwy 30 (51555)
Rates: $45-$90
(712) 642-4003
(800) 329-7466

MOUNT PLEASANT

HEARTLAND INN
Hwy 218 N
(52641)
Rates: $48-$56
(319) 385-2102
(800) 334-3277

RAMADA LIMITED
1200 E Baker
(52641)
Rates: $50-$125
(319) 385-0571
(800) 272-6232

MUSCATINE

HOLIDAY INN
2915 N Hwy 61
(52761)
Rates: $69-$109
(319) 264-5550
(800) 465-4329

NEWTON

**BEST WESTERN
INN**
I-80 & Hwy 14,
Exit 164 (50208)
Rates: $49-$89
(641) 792-4200
(800) 528-1234
(800) 373-6350

DAYS INN
1605 W 19th St S
(50208)
Rates: $45-$70
(641) 792-2330
(800) 329-7466

**HOLIDAY INN
EXPRESS**
1700 W 19th St S
(50208)
Rates: $40-$65
(641) 792-7722
(800) 465-4329
(888) 249-1468

RADISSON INN
208 W 4th St N
(50208)
Rates: $74-$82
(641) 792-3333
(800) 333-3333

RAMADA LIMITED
1405 W 19th St S
(50208)
Rates: $50-$105
(641) 792-8100
(800) 272-2632

SUPER 8 MOTEL
1635 S 12th Ave W
(50208)
Rates: $49-$62
(641) 792-8868
(800) 800-8000

**TERRACE LODGE
MOTEL**
Hwy 14 & I-80
(50208)
Rates: $46-$100
(800) 383-7722

OKOBOJI

**COUNTRY CLUB
MOTEL**
1107 Sanborn Ave
(51355)
Rates: $65-$120
(712) 332-5617
(800) 831-5615

**VILLAGE EAST
RESORT**
1405 US 71 (51355)
Rates: $149-$165
(712) 332-2161

ONAWA

SUPER 8 MOTEL
I-29, exit 112
(51040)
Rates: $43-$55
(712) 423-2101
(800) 800-8000

OSCEOLA

**AMERICINN
MOTEL & SUITES**
111 Ariel Cir
(50213)
Rates: $137
(515) 342-9400
(800) 634-3444

**BEST WESTERN
REGAL INN**
1520 Jeffries Dr
(50213)
Rates: $42-$54
(515) 342-2123
(800) 528-1234
(800) 252-2289

**BLUE HAVEN
MOTEL**
325 S Main St
(50213)
Rates: $34-$55
(515) 342-2115
(800) 333-3180

OSKALOOSA

COMFORT INN
2401 A Ave W
(52577)
Rates: $40-$200
(515) 672-0375
(800) 228-5150

RED CARPET INN
2278 Hwy 63
North (52577)
Rates: $30-$60
(515) 673-8641
(800) 251-1962
(800) 255-2110

**TRAVELER
BUDGET INN**
1210 A Ave East
(52577)
Rates: $32-$75
(515) 673-8333
(800) 391-0123

AREA CODES - If the local number doesn't connect, check for a new area code.

OTTUMWA

**COLONIAL
MOTOR INN**
1534 Albia Rd
(52501)
Rates: $33-$60
(515) 683-1661

DAYS INN
206 Church St
(52501)
Rates: $50-$60
(515) 682-8131
(800) 329-7466

HEARTLAND INN
125 W Joseph Ave
(52501)
Rates: $45-$57
(515) 682-8526
(800) 334-3277

PACIFIC JUNCTION

BLUFF VIEW MOTEL
I-29 & Hwy 34
(51561)
Rates: $30-$40
(712) 622-8191
(800) 582-9366

QUAD CITIES

**BAYMONT INN
& SUITES**
400 Jason Way Ct
(Davenport 52807)
Rates: $59
(319) 386-1600
(800) 302-0200

**BEST WESTERN
STEEPLEGATE INN**
100 W 76th St
(Davenport 52806)
Rates: $75-$105
(319) 386-6900
(800) 528-1234
(800) 373-6900

COMFORT INN
7222 Northwest
Blvd
(Davenport 52806)
Rates: $45-$145
(319) 391-8222
(800) 228-5150

COMFORT INN
902 Mississippi
View Ct
(Le Claire 52753)
Rates: $70-$139
(319) 289-4747
(800) 228-5150

**COUNTRY INN
& SUITES
BY CARLSON**
140 E 55th St
(Davenport 52805)
Rates: $78
(319) 388-6444
(800) 456-4000

DAYS INN
3202 E Kimberly
Rd (Davenport
52807)
Rates: $45-$75
(319) 355-1190
(800) 329-7466

ECONO LODGE
2205 Kimberly Rd
(Bettendorf 52722)
Rates: $50-$75
(319) 355-6471
(800) 553-2666

**EXEL INNS
OF AMERICA**
6310 N Brady Ave
(52806)
Rates: $39-$62
(319) 386-6350
(800) 367-3935

EXEL INN
2501 52nd Ave
(Moline 61265)
Rates: $36-$52
(309) 797-5580
(800) 367-3935

**HAMPTON INN
AIRPORT**
6920 27th St
(Moline 61265)
Rates: $65-$79
(309) 762-1711
(800) 426-7866

HAMPTON INN
3330 E Kimberly
Rd (Davenport
52807)
Rates: $79
(319) 354-3921
(800) 426-7866

HEARTLAND INN
815 Golden Valley
Dr (Bettendorf
52722)
Rates: $56-$76
(319) 355-6336
(800) 334-3277

HEARTLAND INN
6605 Brady St
(Davenport 52806)
Rates: $54-$71
(319) 386-8336
(800) 334-3277

HOLIDAY INN
5202 Brady
(Davenport 52806)
Rates: $54-$157
(319) 391-1230
(800) 465-4329

HOLIDAY INN
6902 27th St
(Moline 61265)
Rates: $50-$145
(309) 762-8811
(800) 465-4329

HOLIDAY INN EXP
6910 27th St
(Moline 61265)
Rates: $55-$140
(309) 762-8300
(800) 465-4329

HOLIDAY INN
909 Middle Rd
(Bettendorf 52722)
Rates: $59-$91
(319) 395-7141
(800) 465-4329

**JUMER'S CASTLE
LODGE**
900 Spruce Hills
Drive
(Bettendorf 52722)
Rates: $78-$146
(319) 359-7141
(800) 285-8637

LA QUINTA INN
5450 27th St
(Moline 61265)
Rates: $50-$58
(309) 762-9008
(800) 687-6667

MOTEL 6
Airport Road
(Moline 61265)
Rates: $39-$45
(309) 764-8711
(800) 466-8536

MOTEL 6
6111 N Brady St
(Davenport 52806)
Rates: $34-$39
(319) 391-8997
(800) 466-8356

**RESIDENCE INN
BY MARRIOTT**
120 E 55th St
(Davenport 52807)
Rates: $99-$109
(319) 391-8877
(800) 331-3131

SUPER 8 MOTEL
2201 John Deere
Expy (East Moline
(61244)
Rates: $45-$64
(309) 796-1999
(800) 800-8000

SUPER 8 MOTEL
1522 Welcome
Center Rd (Le
Claire 52753)
Rates: $54-$85
(319) 289-5888
(800) 800-8000

**TWIN BRIDGES
MOTOR INN**
221 15th St
(Bettendorf 52722)
Rates: $39-$48
(319) 355-6451

SHELDON

SHELDON MOTEL
3 Blks W on US 18
(51201)
Rates: $24-$34
(712) 324-2568

SHENANDOAH

**COUNTRY INN
MOTEL**
1503 W Sheridan
Ave (51601)
Rates: $35-$75
(712) 246-1550

SIBLEY

SUPER 8 MOTEL
1108 2nd Ave
(51249)
Rates: $42-$60
(712) 754-3603
(800) 800-8000

SIOUX CENTER

**COLONIAL
MOTEL**
1367 South Main
(51250)
Rates: $27-$50
(712) 722-2614
(800) 762-9149

MOTEL 6
6166 Harbor Dr
(51111)
Rates: $31-$42
(712) 277-3131
(800) 466-8356

SIOUX CITY

BAYMONT INN
3101 Singing Hills
Blvd (51106)
Rates: $56-$100
(712) 233-2302
(800) 301-0200

**BEST WESTERN
CITY CENTRE**
130 Nebraska St
(51101)
Rates: $55-$77
(712) 277-1550
(800) 528-1234

COMFORT INN
4202 E Lakeport St
(51106)
Rates: $69-$109
(712) 274-1300
(800) 228-5150

ELMDALE MOTEL
US 75 N at 22nd St
(51105)
Rates: $28-$59
(712) 277-1012

HAMILTON INN
1401 Zenith Dr
(51101)
Rates: n/a
(712) 277-3211

HILTON HOTEL
707 4th St (51101)
Rates: $99-$115
(712) 277-4101
(800) 445-8667
(800) 593-0555

MARINA INN
4th & B Sts (51101)
Rates: $64-$74
(800) 798-7980

MOTEL 6
6166 Harbor Dr
(51101)
Rates: $37-$53
(712) 277-3131
(800) 466-8356

AREA CODES - If the local number doesn't connect, check for a new area code.

RIVERBOAT INN
701 Gordon Dr
(51101)
Rates: $55-$75
(712) 277-9400
(800) 236-6146

SUPER 8 MOTEL
4307 Stone Ave
(51106)
Rates: $50-$70
(712) 274-1520
(800) 800-8000

SIOUX RAPIDS

**HANSEN HOUSE
B&B INN**
402 Third St
(50585)
Rates: $50-$65
(712) 283-2179
(Pet kennel
provided)

SLOAN

**WINNA
VEGAS INN**
1862 Hwy 141
(51055)
Rates: $48-$58
(712) 428-4280

SPIRIT LAKE

OAKS MOTEL
1701 Chicago
(51360)
Rates: $79
(712) 336-2940

SHAMROCK INN
2231 18th St
(51360)
Rates: $40-$85
(812) 336-2668

STORM LAKE

**CROSS ROADS
MOTEL**
Hwys 3 & 71
(50588)
Rates: $23-$38
(712) 732-1456
(800) 383-1456

PALACE MOTEL
E Lake Shore Dr
(50588)
Rates: $30-$50
(712) 732-5753

**VISTA ECONOMY
INN**
1316 N Lake Ave
(50588)
Rates: $28-$44
(712) 732-2342
(800) 826-0778
(800) 451-6261

STORY CITY

SUPER 8 MOTEL
515 Factory Outlet
Dr (50248)
Rates: $44-$60
(515) 733-5281
(800) 800-8000

**VIKING
MOTOR INN**
West of I-35, Exit
124 (50248)
Rates: $45-$60
(515) 733-4306
(800) 233-4306

STUART

SUPER 8 MOTEL
203 SE 7th St
(50250)
Rates: $39-$59
(515) 523-2888
(800) 800-8000

TOLEDO

SUPER 8 MOTEL
207 Hwy 30 W
(52342)
Rates: $42-$64
(515) 484-5888
(800) 800-8000

URBANDALE

COMFORT INN
5900 Sutton Dr
(50322)
Rates: $70-$94
(515) 270-1037
(800) 228-5150

DAYS INN
10841 Douglas
Ave (50322)
Rates: $55-$115
(515) 278-2811
(800) 329-7466

SLEEP INN
11211 Hickman Rd
(50322)
Rates: $59-$129
(515) 270-2424
(800) 753-3746

WALCOTT

DAYS INN
2889 N Plainview
Dr (52773)
Rates: $40-$65
(319) 284-6600
(800) 329-7466

SUPER 8 MOTEL
241 Interstate St
(52773)
Rates: $43-$59
(319) 284-5083
(800) 800-8000

WALNUT

RED CARPET INN
33246 Antique
City Dr (51577)
Rates: $49-$79
(712) 784-2233
(800) 251-1962
(800) 711-5409

SUPER 8 MOTEL
Exit 46, I-80
(51577)
Rates: $49-$59
(712) 784-2221
(800) 800-8000

WAPELLO

ROY EL MOTEL
405 Hwy 61 S
(52653)
Rates: $28-$38
(319) 523-2991
(877) 523-2111

WASHINGTON

SUPER 8 MOTEL
119 Westview Dr
(52353)
Rates: $43-$63
(319) 653-6621
(800) 800-8000

WATERLOO

**BEST WESTERN
STARLITE
VILLAGE**
214 Washington St
(50701)
Rates: $58-$76
(319) 235-0321
(800) 528-1234
(800) 903-0009

COMFORT INN
1945 La Porte Rd
(50702)
Rates: $65-$104
(319) 234-7411
(800) 228-5150

EXEL INN
3350 University
Ave (50701)
Rates: $37-$57
(319) 235-2165
(800) 367-3935

HEARTLAND INN
1809 La Porte Rd
(50702)
Rates: $52-$135
(319) 235-4461
(800) 334-3277

HEARTLAND INN
3052 Marnie Ave
(50701)
Rates: $48-$135
(319) 232-7467
(800) 334-3277

**HOLIDAY INN
CONVENTION
CENTER**
205 W 4th St
(50701)
Rates: $79
(319) 233-7560
(800) 465-4329

MOTEL 6
2343 Logan Ave
(50703)
Rates: $40-$48
(319) 236-3238
(800) 466-8356

**QUALITY INN
& SUITES**
226 W 5th St
(50701)
Rates: $54-$259
(319) 235-0301
(800) 228-5151

SUPER 8 MOTEL
1825 La Porte Rd
(50702)
Rates: $53-$68
(319) 233-1800
(800) 800-8000

WAVERLY

AMERIHOST INN
404 29th Ave SW
(50677)
Rates: $58-$68
(319) 352-0399
(800) 434-5800

**BEST WESTERN
RED FOX INN**
1900 Heritage
Way (50677)
Rates: $58-$149
(319) 352-5330
(800) 528-1234
(800) 397-5330

WEBSTER CITY

EXECUTIVE INN
1700 Superior St
(50595)
Rates: $53-$70
(515) 832-3631
(800) 322-3631

SUPER 8 MOTEL
305 Closz Dr
(50595)
Rates: $45-$60
(515) 832-2000
(800) 800-8000

WEST BEND

**WEST BEND
MOTEL**
West of Hwy 15
(50597)
Rates: $22-$42
(515) 887-3611

WEST BRANCH

**PRESIDENTIAL
MOTOR INN**
711 S Downey
(52358)
Rates: $35-$49
(319) 643-2526

**WEST
BURLINGTON**

**AMERICINN
MOTEL & SUITES**
628 S Gear Ave
(52655)
Rates: $66-$106
(319) 758-9000
(800) 634-3444

**WEST DES
MOINES**

**CANDLEWOOD
SUITES**
7625 Office Plaza
Dr North (50266)
Rates: $85
(515) 221-0001

AREA CODES - If the local number doesn't connect, check for a new area code.

MOTEL 6
7655 Office Plaza
Dr North (50266)
Rates: $40-$56
(515) 267-8885
(800) 466-8356

WEST LIBERTY

ECONO LODGE
1943 Garfield Ave
(52776)
Rates: $45-$69
(319) 627-2171
(800) 553-2666

WEST UNION

ELMS MOTEL
705 Hwy 150
South (52175)
Rates: $30-$60
(319) 422-3841
(800) 422-3843

SUPER 8 MOTEL
108 Hwy 18 & 150
(52175)
Rates: $45-$65
(319) 422-3464
(800) 800-8000

WILLIAMS

**BEST WESTERN
NORSEMAN INN**
3086 220th St
(50271)
Rates: $40-$64
(515) 854-2281
(800) 528-1234
(800) 292-1450

WILLIAMSBURG

**BEST WESTERN
QUIET HOUSE
SUITES**
1708 N Highland
St (52361)
Rates: $76-$155
(319) 668-9777
(800) 528-1234

DAYS INN
2214 U Ave
(52361)
Rates: $42-$68
(319) 668-2097
(800) 329-7466

RAMADA LIMITED
120 Hawkeye Dr
(52361)
Rates: $47-$135
(319) 668-1000
(800) 272-6232

SUPER 8 MOTEL
1708 N Highland
St (52361)
Rates: $59-$88
(319) 668-9718
(800) 800-8000

SUPER 8 MOTEL
2228 U Ave
(52361)
Rates: $36-$53
(319) 668-2800
(800) 800-8000

WINTERSET

SUPER 8 MOTEL
1312 N 10th St
(50273)
Rates: $41-$58
(515) 462-4888
(800) 800-8000

**VILLAGE VIEW
MOTEL**
711 Hwy 92 E
(50273)
Rates: $35-$48
(515) 462-1218

WYOMING

SUNSET MOTEL
7032 Hwy 64
(52362)
Rates: $25-$48
(319) 488-2240

AREA CODES - If the local number doesn't connect, check for a new area code.

KANSAS

ABILENE

BALFOUR'S HOUSE BED & BREAKFAST
940 1900 Ave
(67410)
Rates: $40-$65+
(785) 263-4262

BEST WESTERN ABILENE'S PRIDE
1709 N Buckeye
(67410)
Rates: $40-$65
(785) 263-2800
(800) 528-1234

BEST WESTERN PRESIDENTS INN
2210 N Buckeye
(67410)
Rates: $36-$69
(785) 263-2050
(800) 528-1234

DIAMOND MOTEL
1407 NW 3rd St
(67410)
Rates: $22-$45
(785) 263-2360

SPRUCE HOUSE
604 N Spruce
(67410)
Rates: $50-$65
(785) 263-3900

SUPER 8 MOTEL
2207 N Buckeye
(67410)
Rates: $41-$55
(785) 263-4545
(800) 800-8000

WHITE HOUSE MOTEL
101 NW 14th
(67410)
Rates: $22-$42
(785) 263-3600

ARKANSAS CITY

BEST WESTERN HALLMARK MOTOR INN
1617 N Summit St
(67005)
Rates: $54-$64
(316) 442-1400
(800) 528-1234

ASHLAND

ROLLIING HILLS BED & BREAKFAST
204 E 4th Ave
(67831)
Rates: $45-$50
(316) 635-2859

ATCHISON

ATCHISON MOTOR INN
401 S 10th (66002)
Rates: $30-$45
(913) 367-7000

AUBURN

LIPPINCOTT'S FYSHE HOUSE
8720 W 85th St
(66402)
Rates: $60-$75
(913) 256-2436

BAXTER SPRINGS

BAXTER INN-4-LESS
2451 Military Ave
(66713)
Rates: $26-$42
(316) 856-2106

BELLEVILLE

BEST WESTERN BEL VILLA MOTEL
215 US Hwy 36
(66935)
Rates: $38-$54
(785) 527-2231
(800) 528-1234

BELOIT

MAINLINER INN
RFD 1, Box 47 A
(67420)
Rates: $28-$60
(785) 738-3531

SUPER 8 MOTEL
205 W Hwy 24
(67420)
Rates: $42-$57
(785) 738-4300
(800) 800-8000

BERN

LEAR ACRES B & B
Rt 1, Box 31
(66408)
Rates: $32-$38
(913) 336-3903

BURLINGTON

COUNTRY HAVEN INN
207 Cross St
(66839)
Rates: $49-$69
(316) 364-8260
(800) 9HAVEN9

CAWKER CITY

OAK CREEK LODGE
1787 Rain Road
(67431)
Rates: $55-$85
(913) 263-8755

CHANUTE

GUEST HOUSE INN
1814 S Santa Fe
(66720)
Rates: $25-$32
(316) 431-0600
(800) 523-6128

HOLIDAY PARK MOTEL 65
3030 S Santa Fe
(66720)
Rates: $37-$45
(316) 431-0850

SAFARI INN-IMA
3428 S Santa Fe
(66720)
Rates: $40-$60
(316) 431-9460
(800) 341-8000

SKYLINE MOTEL
1216 W Main St
(66720)
Rates: $26-$45
(316) 431-1500

CLAY CENTER

CEDAR COURT MOTEL
905 Crawford
(67432)
Rates: $25-$44
(785) 632-2148

COFFEYVILLE

APPLETREE INN
820 E 11th (67337)
Rates: $40-$48
(316) 251-0002

SUPER 8 MOTEL
104 W 11th St
(67337)
Rates: $41-$61
(316) 251-2250
(800) 800-8000

COLBY

BEST WESTERN CROWN MOTEL
2320 S Range
(67701)
Rates: $45-$79
(785) 462-3943
(800) 528-1234

BUDGET HOST INN
1745 W 4th St
(67701)
Rates: $40-$70
(785) 462-3338
(800) 283-4678

COMFORT INN
2225 S Range
(67701)
Rates: $55-$79
(785) 462-3833
(800) 228-5150

DAYS INN
1925 S Range
(67701)
Rates: $45-$65
(785) 462-8691
(800) 329-7466

RAMADA INN
1950 S Range
(67701)
Rates: $39-$70
(785) 462-3933
(800) 272-6232

SUPER 8 MOTEL
1040 Zelfer Ave
(67701)
Rates: $40-$60
(785) 462-8248
(800) 800-8000

CONCORDIA

BEST WESTERN THUNDERBIRD INN
89 Lincoln (66901)
Rates: $40-$60
(785) 243-4545
(800) 528-1234

COTTON-WOOD FALLS

1874 STONE-HOUSE ON MULBERRY HILL
Rt 1, Box 67A
(66845)
Rates: $75
(316) 273-8481

GRAND CENTRAL HOTEL
215 Broadway
(66845)
Rates: $109-$179
(316) 273-6763

COUNCIL GROVE

THE COTTAGE HOUSE HOTEL
25 N Neosho
(66846)
Rates: $60-$130
(316) 767-6828
(800) 727-7903

AREA CODES - If the local number doesn't connect, check for a new area code.

DODGE CITY

ASTRO MOTEL
2200 Wyatt Earp
Blvd (67801)
Rates: $42-$60
(316) 227-8146

**BEST WESTERN
SILVER SPUR
LODGE**
1510 W Wyatt
Earp Blvd (67801)
Rates: $47-$65
(316) 227-2125
(800) 528-1234

**DAYS INN
DODGE HOUSE**
2408 W Wyatt
Earp Blvd (67801)
Rates: $28-$120
(316) 225-9900
(800) 553-9901

ECONO LODGE
1610 W Wyatt
Earp Blvd (67801)
Rates: $47-$80
(315) 225-0231
(800) 553-2666

**HOLIDAY INN
EXPRESS**
2320 W Wyatt
Earp Blvd (67801)
Rates: $65-$70
(316) 227-5000
(800) 465-4329

HOLIDAY MOTEL
2100 W Wyatt
Earp Blvd (67801)
Rates: $23-$33
(316) 227-2169

**NENDELS INN &
SUITES**
2523 E Wyatt Earp
Blvd (67801)
Rates: $40-$58
(316) 225-3000

SUPER 8 MOTEL
1708 W Wyatt
Earp Blvd (67801)
Rates: $43-$56
(316) 225-3924
(800) 800-8000

**THUNDERBIRD
MOTEL**
2300 W Wyatt
Earp Blvd (67801)
Rates: $23-$33
(316) 225-4143

EL DORADO

**BEST WESTERN
RED COACH INN**
2525 W Central
(67042)
Rates: $44-$89
(316) 321-6900
(800) 528-1234

HERITAGE INN
2515 W Central
Ave (67042)
Rates: $38-$44
(316) 321-6800

ELLSWORTH

**BEST WESTERN
GARDEN INN**
Jct Hwy 156 & 140
(67439)
Rates: $42-$58
(785) 472-3116
(800) 528-1234

ELWOOD

CAPRI MOTEL
P. O. Box 97-C
(Wathena 66090)
Rates: $17-$24
(913) 365-0209

EMPORIA

**BEST WESTERN
HOSPITALITY
HOUSE**
3021 W Hwy 50
(66801)
Rates: $49-$69
(316) 342-7587
(800) 528-1234
(800) 362-2036

**BUDGET HOST-
SUNRISE MOTEL**
1830 E Hwy 50
(66801)
Rates: $26-$42
(316) 343-6922
(800) 283-4678

COMFORT INN
2511 W 18th
(66801)
Rates: $38-$56
(316) 343-7750
(800) 228-5150

DAYS INN
3032 W Hwy 50
(66801)
Rates: $42-$54
(316) 342-1787
(800) 329-7466

MOTEL 6
2630 W 18th Ave
(66801)
Rates: $30-$37
(316) 343-1240
(800) 466-8356

**RAMADA INN
& CONFERENCE
CENTER**
2700 W 18th Ave
(66801)
Rates: $49-$69
(316) 343-2200
(800) 272-6232

**RANCH HOUSE
MOTEL**
4215 W Hwy 50
(66801)
Rates: $25-$40
(316) 343-7920

SUPER 8 MOTEL
2913 W Hwy 50
(66801)
Rates: $40-$60
(316) 342-7567
(800) 800-8000

ERIE

**LAND OF AH'S
MOTOR INN**
700 W Canville &
Hwy 59
(66733)
Rates: $29-$34
(316) 244-5231

ENTERPRISE

**EHRSAM PLACE
BED &
BREAKFAST**
103 S Grant
(67441)
Rates: $55-$65
(913) 263-8747
(800) 470-7774

EUREKA

**BLUE STEM
LODGE**
1314 E River St
(67045)
Rates: $28-$38
(316) 583-5531

FLORENCE

HOLIDAY MOTEL
630 W 5th (66851)
Rates: $22-$31
(316) 878-4246

FORT SCOTT

**BEST WESTERN
FORT SCOTT INN**
101 State St
(66701)
Rates: $48-$55
(316) 223-0100
(800) 528-1234
(888) 800-3175

**FRONTIER INN
4 LESS**
2222 S Main
(66701)
Rates: $29-$39
(316) 223-5330

**THE LYONS
HOUSE BED &
BREAKFAST**
742 S National
(66701)
Rates: $85
(316) 223-3644

**RANCH HOUSE
MOTEL**
Hwy 54 West
(66701)
Rates: n/a
(316) 223-9734

RED RAM MOTEL
Hwy 54 West
(66704)
Rates: n/a
(316) 223-2400

GARDEN CITY

**BEST WESTERN
RED BARON
MOTOR INN**
US 50 & Hwy 83
(67846)
Rates: $40-$66
(316) 275-4164
(800) 528-1234

**BEST WESTERN
WHEAT LANDS
INN**
1311 E Fulton
(67846)
Rates: $45-$72
(316) 276-2387
(800) 528-1234

**CONTINENTAL
INN**
1408 Jones Ave
(67846)
Rates: $33-$53
(316) 276-7691
(800) 621-0318

GARDEN CITY INN
1202 W Kansas
Ave
(67846)
Rates: $45-$53
(316) 276-7608

**HOLIDAY INN
EXPRESS**
2502 E Kansas Ave
(67846)
Rates: $67-$75
(316) 275-5900
(800) 465-4329

**HOLIDAY INN
EXPRESS**
1818 Commanche
(67846)
Rates: $43-$77
(316) 275-5095
(800) 465-4329

NATIONAL 9 INN
1502 E Fulton
(67846)
Rates: $36-$54
(316) 276-0677
(800) 333-4164

PLAZA INN
1911 E Kansas Ave
(67846)
Rates $50-$120
(316) 275-7471
(800) 875-5201

GARDNER

SUPER 8 MOTEL
2001 E Santa Fe
(66030)
Rates: $53-$67
(913) 856-8887
(800) 800-8000

GLASCO

**RUSTIC
REMEMBRANCES
BED & BRKFAST**
Rt 1, Box 68
(67445)
Rates: $45-$75
(785) 546-2552

GOODLAND

**BEST WESTERN
BUFFALO INN**
830 W Hwy 24
(67735)
Rates: $40-$75
(785) 899-3621
(800) 528-1234
(800) 433-3621

COMFORT INN
2519 Enterprise
Rd (67735)
Rates: $49-$79
(785) 899-7181
(800) 228-5150

HOWARD JOHNSON
2218 Commerce
Rd (67735)
Rates: $39-$69
(785) 899-3644
(800) 446-4656

MOTEL 6
2420 Commerce
Rd (67735)
Rates: $32-$40
(785) 899-5672
(800) 466-8356

SUPER 8 MOTEL
2520 S Hwy 27
(67735)
Rates: $38-$55
(785) 899-7566
(800) 800-8000

WELCOME INN MOTEL
2721 Enterprise
Rd (67735)
Rates: $30-$45
(785) 899-7566

GREAT BEND

BEST WESTERN ANGUS INN
2920 10th St
(67530)
Rates: $49-$79
(316) 792-3541
(800) 528-1234
(800) 862-6487

DAYS INN
4701 10th St
(67601)
Rates: $32-$60
(316) 792-8235
(800) 329-7466

HOLIDAY INN
3017 W 10th St
(67530)
Rates: $50-$65
(316) 792-2431
(800) 465-4329

PEACEFUL ACRES BED & BREAKFAST
Rt 5, Box 153
(67530)
Rates: $25-30
(316) 793-7527

SUPER 8 MOTEL
3500 10th St
(67530)
Rates: $39-$61
(316) 793-8486
(800) 800-8000

GREENSBURG

BEST WESTERN J-HAWK MOTEL
515 W Kansas Ave
(67054)
Rates: $49-$69
(316) 723-2121
(800) 528-1234

ECONO LODGE
800 E Kansas Ave
(67054)
Rates: $26-$41
(316) 723-2141
(800) 553-2666

HALLOWELL

CLAYTHORNE LODGE
Rt 1, Box 13
(66725)
Rates: n/a
(316) 597-2568

HAYS

BEST WESTERN VAGABOND MOTEL
2524 Vine St
(67601)
Rates: $44-$65
(785) 625-2511
(800) 528-1234
(800) 432-2776

BUDGET HOST VILLA
810 E 8th (67601)
Rates: $30-$55
(785) 625-2563
(800) 950-5015

DAYS INN
3205 N Vine St
(67601)
Rates: $40-$96
(785) 628-8261
(800) 329-7466

ECONO LODGE
3503 Vine St
(67601)
Rates: $35-$55
(785) 625-4839
(800) 553-2666

HAMPTON INN
3801 Vine St
(67601)
Rates: $53-$60
(785) 625-8103
(800) 426-7866

HOLIDAY INN
3603 Vine St
(67601)
Rates: $58-$63
(785) 625-7371
(800) 465-4329

MOTEL 6
3404 Vine St
(67601)
Rates: $34-$44
(785) 625-4282
(800) 466-8356

HIAWATHA

HEARTLAND INN
1100 S 1st (66434)
Rates: $35-$43
(785) 742-7401

HILL CITY

PHEASANT RUN BED & BREAKFAST
609 N 4th Ave
(67642)
Rates: $35-$45
(913) 674-2955

HUTCHINSON

ASTRO MOTEL
15 E 4th (67501)
Rates: $28-$46
(316) 663-1151

BEST WESTERN SUN DOME
11 Des Moines
(67505)
Rates: $60-$85
(316) 663-4444
(800) 528-1234

DAYS INN
100 E Second Ave
(67501)
Rates: $39-$250
(316) 663-7100
(800) 329-7466

HOLIDAY INN
1601 Super Plaza
(67501)
Rates: $65-$90
(316) 669-5200
(800) 465-4329

MICROTEL INN & SUITES
17th Ave &
Lorraine St
(67501)
Rates: $42-$65
(888) 771-7171

QUALITY INN CITY CENTER
15 W 4th St
(67501)
Rates: $35-$130
(316) 663-1211
(800) 228-5151

RAMADA INN
1400 N Lorraine
(67501)
Rates: $77-$90
(316) 669-9311
(800) 272-6232

SUPER 8 MOTEL
1315 E 11th Ave
(67501)
Rates: $40-$60
(316) 662-6394
(800) 800-8000

INDEPEN-DENCE

APPLETREE INN
201 N 8th St
(67301)
Rates: $44-$55
(316) 331-5500

BEST WESTERN PRAIRIE INN
US 75 & 160 West
(67301)
Rates: $41-$59
(316) 331-7300
(800) 528-1234

IOLA

BEST WESTERN INN
1315 N State
(66749)
Rates: $40-$50
(316) 365-5161
(800) 528-1234
(800) 769-0007

JUNCTION CITY

BEST WESTERN JAYHAWK INN
110 E Flint Hills
Blvd (66441)
Rates: $35-$65
(785) 238-5188
(800) 528-1234

DAYS INN
1024 S
Washington St
(66441)
Rates: $38-$55
(785) 762-2727
(800) 329-7466

DREAMLAND MOTEL
520 E Flint Hills
Blvd (66441)
Rates: $24-$36
(785) 238-1108

ECONO LODGE
211 E Flint Hills
Blvd (66441)
Rates: $30-$59
(785) 238-8181
(800) 424-4777

HOLIDAY INN EXPRESS
120 N East St
(66441)
Rates: n/a
(785) 762-4200
(800) 465-4329

RAMADA LTD
1133 S Washington
St (66441)
Rates: $39-$79
(785) 238-1141
(800) 272-6232

SUPER 8 MOTEL
1001 E 6th (66441)
Rates: $41-$68
(785) 238-8101
(800) 800-8000

KANSAS CITY

BEST WESTERN INN & CONFERENCE CENTER
501 Southwest
Blvd (66103)
Rates: $69-$149
(913) 677-3060
(800) 528-1234

KINGMAN

BUDGET HOST COPA MOTEL
1113 Hwy 54 E
(67068)
Rates: $33-$43
(316) 532-3118
(800) 283-4678

LAKIN

WINDY HEIGHTS BED & BREAKFAST
607 Country Hts Rd (67860)
Rates: $40-$60
(316) 355-7699

LANSING

ECONO LODGE
504 N Main St (66043)
Rates: $32-$55
(913) 727-2777
(800) 553-2666

LARNED

BEST WESTERN TOWNSMAN INN
123 E 14th St (67550)
Rates: $41-$60
(316) 285-3114
(800) 528-1234
(800) 399-3114

COUNTRY INN MOTEL
135 E 14th St (67550)
Rates: $22-$40
(316) 285-3216

LAWRENCE

BEST WESTERN HALLMARK INN
730 Iowa St (66044)
Rates: $50-$69
(785) 841-6500
(800) 528-1234
(800) 923-2888

DAYS INN
2309 Iowa St (66046)
Rates: $43-$95
(785) 843-9100
(800) 329-7466

GROVE HOUSE BED & BREAKFAST
807 Grove St, Box 212 (66046)
Rates: $50-$95
(785) 594-2947

HOLIDAY INN
200 McDonald Dr (66044)
Rates: $59-$86
(785) 749-8923
(800) 465-4329

RAMADA INN
2222 W 6th St (66049)
Rates: $58-$80
(785) 842-7030
(800) 272-6232

SUPER 8 MOTEL
515 McDonald Dr (66049)
Rates: $43-$63
(785) 842-5721
(800) 800-8000

TRAVELODGE
801 Iowa St (66049)
Rates: $44-$85
(785) 842-5100
(800) 578-7878

WESTMINSTER INN
2525 W 6th St (66049)
Rates: $44-$60
(785) 841-8410

LEAVENWORTH

BEST WESTERN HALLMARK INN
3211 S Fourth St (66048)
Rates: $49-$70
(913) 651-6000
(800) 528-1234

RAMADA INN
101 S 3rd St (66048)
Rates: $50-$76
(913) 651-5500
(800) 272-6232

SUPER 8 MOTEL
303 Montana Ct (66048)
Rates: $37-$59
(913) 682-0744
(800) 800-8000

LENEXA

LA QUINTA INN
9461 Lenexa Dr (66215)
Rates: $51-$79
(913) 492-5500
(800) 687-6667

MOTEL 6
9725 Lenexa Dr (66215)
Rates: $38-$44
(913) 541-8558
(800) 466-8356

LIBERAL

BEST WESTERN LAFONDA MOTEL
229 W Pancake Blvd (67901)
Rates: $35-$91
(316) 624-5601
(800) 528-1234

CIMARRON INN
564 E Pancake Blvd (67901)
Rates: $33-$47
(316) 624-6203

KANSAN MOTEL
310 E Pancake Blvd (67901)
Rates: n/a
(316) 624-7215

LIBERAL INN
603 E Pancake Blvd (67901)
Rates: $43-$64
(316) 624-7254
(800) 458-4667

THUNDERBIRD INN
2100 N Hwy 83 (67901)
Rates: $29-$35
(316) 624-7271

WESTERN HO MOTEL-IMA
754 E Pancake (67901)
Rates: $23-$40
(316) 624-1921
(800) 341-8000

LINDSBORG

CORONADO MOTEL
305 N Harrison (67456)
Rates: $30-$46
(913) 227-3943
(800) 747-2793

LOUISBURG

RED MAPLE INN
201 S 11th St (66053)
Rates: $55-$75
(913) 837-2840

LYONS

LYONS INN
817 W Main (67554)
Rates: $36-$45
(316) 257-5185
(800) 220-9393

MANHATTAN

BEST WESTERN CONTINENTAL INN
100 Bluemont Ave (66502)
Rates: $44-$66
(785) 776-4771
(800) 528-1234

DAYS INN
1501 Tuttle Creek Blvd (66502)
Rates: $46-$78
(785) 539-5391
(800) 329-7466

HAMPTON INN
501 E Poyntz Ave (66502)
Rates: $65-$70
(785) 539-5000
(800) 426-7866

HOLIDAY INN-HOLIDOME
530 Richards Dr (66502)
Rates: $109
(785) 539-5311
(800) 465-4329

MOTEL 6
510 Tuttle Creek Blvd (66502)
Rates: $30-$36
(785) 537-1022
(800) 466-8356

RAMADA INN
17th & Anderson KSU (66502)
Rates: $78-$119
(785) 539-7531
(800) 272-6232

MANKATO

CREST-VUE MOTEL
1/2 Mi East on US 36 (66956)
Rates: $25-$31
(913) 378-3515

DREAMLINER MOTEL
RR 2, Box 8 (66956)
Rates: $30-$45
(913) 378-3107

MARION

COUNTRY DREAMS
Rt 3, Box 82 (66861)
Rates: $50-$60
(316) 382-2250
(800) 570-0540

MARYSVILLE

BEST WESTERN SURF MOTEL
2005 Center Rd (66508)
Rates: $38-$58
(785) 562-2354
(800) 528-1234

SUPER 8 MOTEL
1155 Pony Express Rd (66508)
Rates: $38-$52
(785) 562-5588
(800) 800-8000

THUNDERBIRD MOTEL
Hwy 36W (66508)
Rates: $28-$40
(785) 562-2373

MCPHERSON

BEST WESTERN HOLIDAY MANOR
2211 E Kansas Ave (67460)
Rates: $40-$60
(316) 241-5343
(800) 528-1234

RED COACH INN
2111 E Kansas Ave (67460)
Rates: $43-$59
(316) 241-6960

SUPER 8 MOTEL
2110 E Kansas
(67460)
Rates: $40-$60
(316) 241-8881
(800) 800-8000

WHEAT STATE MOTEL
1137 W Kansas
Ave (67460)
Rates: $27-$50
(316) 241-6981

MEADE

DALTON'S BEDPOST MOTEL
519 Carthage
(67864)
Rates: $28-$36
(316) 873-2131

MOON MIST MOTEL
804 W Carthage
(67864)
Rates: $27-$35
(316) 873-2121

MEDICINE LODGE

COPA MOTEL
401 W Fowler
(67104)
Rates: $32-$40
(316) 886-5673

MERRIAM

COMFORT INN
6401 E Frontage
Rd (66202)
Rates: $59-$84
(913) 262-2622
(800) 228-5150

DRURY INN
9009 Shawnee
Mission Pkwy
(66202)
Rates: $58-$69
(913) 236-9200
(800) 325-8300

HOMESTEAD VILLAGE
6451 E Frontage
Rd (66202)
Rates: $239-$309
(913) 236-6006

NESS CITY

DERRICK INN
Hwy 96 E (67560)
Rates: $36-$85
(913) 798-3617
(800) 561-3409

NEWTON

BEST WESTERN RED COACH INN
1301 E 1st St
(67114)
Rates: $44-$89
(316) 283-9120
(800) 528-1234
(800) 777-9120

DAYS INN
105 Manchester
(67114)
Rates: $48-$75
(316) 283-3300
(800) 329-7466

1ST INTERSTATE INN
P. O. Box 772
(67114)
Rates: $32-$46
(316) 283-8850
(800) 462-4667

SUPER 8 MOTEL
1620 E 2nd St
(67114)
Rates: $39-$60
(316) 283-7611
(800) 800-8000

NORTON

HILLCREST MOTEL
Hwy 36 W (67654)
Rates: $33-$50
(785) 877-3343

OAKLEY

ANNIE OAKLEY MOTEL
428 Center St
(67748)
Rates: $27-$37
(785) 672-3223

BEST WESTERN GOLDEN PLAINS MOTEL
3506 US 40 (67748)
Rates: $43-$62
(785) 672-3254
(800) 528-1234

FIRST TRAVEL INN
708 Center Ave
(67748)
Rates: $29-$49
(785) 672-3226

KANSAS KOUNTRY INN
3538 US 40 (67748)
Rates: $34-$48
(785) 672-3131

OBERLIN

FRONTIER MOTEL
207 E Frontier
Pkwy (67749)
Rates: $26-$50
(913) 475-2203

OLATHE

BEST WESTERN HALLMARK INN
211 N Rawhide Dr
(66061)
Rates: $57-$72
(913) 782-4343
(800) 528-1234
(800) 336-9393

OSAWATOMIE

LANDMARK INN
304 Eastgate Dr
(66064)
Rates: $38-$49
(913) 755-3051

OSBORNE

CAMELOT INN
933 N 1st (67473)
Rates: $30-$36
(913) 436-5413

OTTAWA

BEST WESTERN HALLMARK INN
2209 S Princeton
(66067)
Rates: $47-$64
(785) 242-7000
(800) 528-1234
(888) 540-4024

DAYS INN
1641 S Main
(66067)
Rates: $36-50
(785) 242-4842
(800) 329-7466

ECONO LODGE
2331 S Cedar Rd
(66067)
Rates: $42-$60
(785) 242-3400
800) 424-4777

VILLAGE INN MOTEL
2520 S Main
(66067)
Rates: $22-$31
(785) 242-5512

OVERBROOK

PINEMOORE INN
RR 1, Box 44
(66524)
Rates: $60
(913) 453-2304

OVERLAND PARK

DOUBLETREE HOTEL
10100 College
Blvd (66210)
Rates: $79-$109
(913) 451-6100
(800) 222-8733

DRURY INN
10951 Metcalf
(66210)
Rates: $63-$89
(913) 345-1500
(800) 325-8300

EMBASSY SUITES HOTEL
10601 Metcalf
(66212)
Rates: $139-$159
(913) 649-7060
(800) 362-2779

HOLIDAY INN
7240 Shawnee
Mission Pky
(66202)
Rates: $79-$89
(913) 262-3010
(800) 465-4329

RED ROOF INN
6800 W 108th St
(66211)
Rates: $34-$53
(913) 341-0100
(800) 843-7663

RESIDENCE INN BY MARRIOTT
6300 W 110th St
(66211)
Rates: $109-$159
(913) 491-3333
(800) 331-3131

WHITE HAVEN MOTEL
8039 Metcalf Ave
(66204)
Rates: $41-$50
(913) 649-8200
(800) 752-2892

PARSONS

TOWNSMAN MOTEL
P. O. Box 813
(67357)
Rates: $28-$41
(800) 552-4008

PHILLIPSBURG

THE NEW COTTONWOOD INN
Rt 1, Box 108
(67661)
Rates: $35-$45
(785) 543-2125
(800) 466-7332

PITTSBURG

SUNSET MOTEL
RR 3, Box 737
(66762)
Rates: $21-$32
(316) 231-3950

PRATT

BEST WESTERN HILLCREST MOTEL
1336 E 1st St
(67124)
Rates: $32-$41
(316) 672-6407
(800) 528-1234
(800) 336-2279

DAYS INN
1901 E First St
(67124)
Rates: $38-$70
(316) 672-9465
(800) 329-7466

ECONOMY INN
1401E FirstSt
(67124)
Rates: $24-$34
(316) 672-5588

EVERGREEN INN
20001 W Hwy 54
(67124)
Rates: $27-$36
(800) 456-6424

HOLIDAY INN EXPRESS
1401 W Hwy 54
(67124)
Rates: $52-$70
(316) 672-9433
(800) 465-4329

SUPER 8 MOTEL
1906 E 1st St
(67124)
Rates: $36-$51
(316) 672-5945
(800) 800-8000

QUINTER

BUDGET HOST "Q" MOTEL
P. O. Box 398
(67752)
Rates: $35-$46
(785) 754-3337
(800) 283-4678

ROSE HILL

QUEEN ANNE'S LACE B & B
15335 SW Queen Anne's Lace
(67133)
Rates: $40-70
(316) 733-4075

RUSSELL

BUDGET HOST WINCHESTER INN
Frontage Rd, Hwy 281 S (67665)
Rates: $30-$52
(785) 483-6660
(800) 283-4678

DAYS INN
1225 S Fossil St
(67665)
Rates: $40-$60
(785) 483-6660
(800) 329-7466

SABETHA

SABETHA COUNTRY INN
1423 S 75 Hwy
(66534)
Rates: $39-$45
Tela: (913) 284-2300

ST. JOHN

COUNTRY INN MOTEL
RR 2, Box 135
(67576)
Rates: $24-$37
(316) 549-6604

SALINA

AIRLINER MOTEL
781 N Broadway
(67401)
Rates: $20-$32
(785) 827-5586

BEST WESTERN HEART OF AMERICA
632 Westport Blvd
(67401)
Rates: $45-$65
(785) 827-9315
(800) 528-234

BEST WESTERN MID-AMERICA INN
1846 N 9th St
(67401)
Rates: $45-$64
(785) 827-0356
(800) 528-1234

BUDGET INN VAGABOND MOTEL
217 S Broadway
(67401)
Rates: $32-$60
(785) 825-7265
(800) 283-4678

COMFORT INN
1820 W Crawford St (67401)
Rates: $59-$89
(785) 826-1711
(800) 228-5150

HOLIDAY INN
1616 W Crawford St (67401)
Rates: $58-$62
(785) 823-1739
(800) 465-4329

HOWARD JOHNSON
2403 S 9th St
(67401)
Rates: $36-$44
(785) 827-5511
(800) 446-4656

HUNTERS LEIGH BED & BREAKFAST
4109 E North St
(67401)
Rates: $60-$70
(785) 823-6750

MOTEL 6
635 W Diamond Dr (67401)
Rates: $33-$43
(785) 827-8397
(800) 466-8356

RAMADA INN
1949 N 9th St
(67401)
Rates: $52-$68
(785) 825-8211
(800) 272-6232

RED COACH INN
2020 W Crawford
(67401)
Rates: $47-$65
(785) 825-2111

SALINA INN MOTEL
222 E Diamond Dr
(67401)
Rates: $40-$60
(785) 827-0292

SUPER 8 MOTEL
1640 W Crawford St (67401)
Rates: $38-$75
(785) 823-9215
(800) 800-8000

SENECA

STARLITE MOTEL
410 North St
(66538)
Rates: $21-$32
(913) 336-2191

SHARON SPRINGS

HEYL'S TRAVELER MOTEL
Jct US 40 & KS27
(67758)
Rates: n/a
(913) 852-4293

SMITH CENTER

MODERN AIRE MOTEL
117 W US 36
(66967)
Rates: $23-$40
(800) 727-7332

SOUTH HUTCHINSON

BEST WESTERN SUN DOME HOTEL
11 Des Moines
(67505)
Rates: $60-$75
(316) 663-4444
(800) 528-1234

STAFFORD

KOUNTRY KORNER MOTEL
506 E Martin
(67578)
Rates: $20-$30
(316) 234-5232

STERLING

STERLING INN
430 S Broadway
(67579)
Rates: $23-$35
(315) 278-3291

TECUMSAH

OLD STONE HOUSE
6033 SE Hwy 40
(66542)
Rates: $45-$55
(913) 379-5568

TOPEKA

BEST WESTERN MEADOW ACRES MOTEL
2950 S Topeka Blvd (66611)
Rates: $49-$84
(785) 267-1681
(800) 528-1234
(800) 432-3949

COMFORT INN
1518 SW Wanamaker Rd
(66604)
Rates: $50-$99
(785) 273-5365
(800) 228-5150

COUNTRY VIEW ESTATE
5420 SW Fairlawn Rd (66610)
Rates: $55-$125
(785) 862-0335
(785) 862-1975

DAYS INN
1510 SW Wanamaker Rd
(66604)
Rates: $39-$79
(785) 272-8538
(800) 329-7466

ECONO LODGE
1240 SW Wanamaker Rd
(66604)
Rates: $43-$63
(785) 273-6969
(800) 553-2666

HOLIDAY INN CAPITAL CITY CTR
914 SE Madison St
(66607)
Rates: $49-$80
(785) 232-7721
(800) 465-4329

HOLIDAY INN WEST
605 SW Fairlawn
(66606)
Rates: $64-$79
(785) 272-8050
(800) 465-4329

LIBERTY INN
3839 S Topeka Blvd (66609)
Rates: $37-$55
(785) 266-4700

LIPPINCOTT'S FYSHE HOUSE BED & BREAKFAST
8720 W 85th St
(66609)
Rates: $60-$80
(785) 256-2772

MOTEL 6
709 Fairlawn Rd
(66608)
Rates: $43-$40
(785) 272-8283
(800) 466-8356

MOTEL 6
1224 Wanamaker Rd SW (66604)
Rates: $37-$46
(785) 273-9888
(800) 466-8356

RAMADA INN
420 E 6th St
(66607)
Rates: $62-$88
(785) 234-5400
(800) 272-6232

**RAVENWOOD
MISSION CREEK
LODGE B&B**
10147 SW 61st St
(66606)
Rates: $150
(800) 656-2454

**RESIDENCE INN
BY MARRIOTT**
1620 SW Westport
Dr (66604)
Rates: $89-$136
(913) 271-8903
(800) 331-3131

SUPER 8 MOTEL
5968 SW 10th Ave
(66604)
Rates: $43-$71
(785) 273-5100
(800) 800-8000

TRAVELODGE
3846 SW Topeka
Blvd (66609)
Rates: $40-$60
(785) 267-1222
(800) 578-7878

UDALL

**IMPRINT HORSE
FARM B&B**
RR 2, Box 350
(67146)
Rates: $65-$85
(316) 782-3893

ULYSSES

SINGLE TREE INN
2033 W Oklahoma
St (67880)
Rates: $52-$57
(316) 356-1500

WAKEENEY

**BEST WESTERN
WHEEL MOTEL**
I-70 & US 283
(67672)
Rates: $36-$62
(785) 743-2118
(800) 528-1234

**BUDGET HOST
TRAVEL INN**
I-70 & US 283
(67672)
Rates: $28-$60
(785) 743-2121
(800) 283-4678

**KANSAS
KOUNTRY INN**
223 S 1st St
(67672)
Rates: $28-$42
(785) 743-2129

WAMEGO

SUMMER MOTEL
1215 Hwy 24 W
(66547)
Rates: $33-$42
(913) 456-2304

WASHINGTON

K-MOTEL
112 W 7th (66968)
Rates: $25-$35
(785) 325-2100

**WASHINGTON
MOTEL**
310 W 7th (66968)
Rates: $30-$40
(785) 325-2281

WELLINGTON

OAK TREE INN
1177 E 16th St
(67152)
Rates: $49
(316) 326-8191

WICHITA

**BEST WESTERN
AIRPORT RED
COACH INN**
6815 W Kellogg
(67209)
Rates: $69-$89
(316) 942-5600
(800) 528-1234
(888) 942-5666

**BEST WESTERN
RED COACH INN**
915 E 53rd St N
(67219)
Rates: $59-$76
(316) 832-9387
(800) 528-1234
(800) 362-0095

COMFORT INN
9525 E Corporate
Hills (67207)
Rates: $50-$69
(316) 686-2844
(800) 228-5150

COMFORT INN
4849 S Laura
(67216)
Rates: $54-$59
(316) 522-1800
(800) 228-5150

**COMFORT SUITES
AIRPORT**
658 Westdale
(67209)
Rates: $79-$94
(316) 945-2600
(800) 228-5150

DELUXE INN
8401 Hwy 54W
(67209)
Rates: $26-$42
(316) 722-4221

**GRAND PALACE
INN**
607 E 47th St S
(67216)
Rates: $32-$38
(316) 529-4100

HAMPTON INN
9449 E. Corporate
Hills (67207)
Rates: $69-$89
(316) 686-3576
(800) 426-7866

HARVEY HOTEL
549 S Rock Rd
(67207)
Rates: $69-$129
(316) 686-7131
(800) 922-9222

**HOLIDAY INN
WICHITA /
AIRPORT**
5500 W Kellogg
(67209)
Rates: $69-$85
(316) 943-2181
(800) 465-4329

KANSAS INN
1011 N Topeka
Ave (67214)
Rates: $42-$55
(316) 269-9999

LA QUINTA INN
7700 E Kellogg
(67207)
Rates: $44-$73
(316) 681-2881
(800) 687-6667

MARRIOTT HOTEL
9100 Corporate
Hills Dr (67207)
Rates: $99-$275
(316) 651-0333
(800) 229-9290

MOTEL 6
5736 W Kellogg
(67209)
Rates: $34-$42
(316) 945-8440
(800) 466-8356

**QUALITY INN
AIRPORT**
600 S Holland
(67209)
Rates: $41-$55
(316) 722-8730
(800) 228-5151

RAMADA INN
7335 E Kellogg
(67207)
Rates: $79-$99
(316) 685-1281
(800) 272-6232

RED CARPET INN
607 E 47th St
(67216)
Rates: $38-$46
(316) 529-4100
(800) 251-1962

RED CARPET INN
925 N Broadway
(67214)
Rates: $42-$48
(316) 264-2323
(800) 251-1962

**RESIDENCE INN
BY MARRIOTT**
411 S Webb
(67207)
Rates: n/a
(316) 686-7331
(800) 331-3131

WINFIELD

COMFORT INN
US 77 at Quail
Ridge (67156)
Rates: $65-$170
(316) 221-7529
(800) 228-5150

**TOWNHOUSE
MOTEL**
601 W 9th Ave
(67156)
Rates: $28-$40
(316) 221-2110

YATES CENTER

STAR MOTEL
206 S Fry (66783)
Rates: $25-$33
(316) 625-2175

**TOWNSMAN
MOTEL**
609 W Mary
(66783)
Rates: $27-$38
(316) 625-2131

AREA CODES - If the local number doesn't connect, check for a new area code.

KENTUCKY

ALBANY

WISDOM DOCK COTTAGES
553 W (42602)
Rates: n/a
(800) 840-8523

ASHLAND

ASHLAND INN
3320 Winchester Ave (41101)
Rates: n/a
(606) 325-0776

DAYS INN
12700 SR 180 (41101)
Rates: $45-$65
(606) 928-3600
(800) 329-7466

DEAN'S INN
539 Summit Rd (41101)
Rates: n/a
(606) 929-9005
(888) 929-9005

KNIGHTS INN
7216 US 60 (41102)
Rates: $38-$48
(606) 928-9501
(800) 843-5644

AUBURN

AUBURN GUEST HOUSE
421 W Main St (42206)
Rates: n/a
(502) 542-6019

AURORA

CEDAR LANE RESORT COTTAGES
16984 Hwy 68 (42048)
Rates: n/a
(270) 474-8042

EARLY AMERICAN MOTEL
16749 Hwy 68 E (42048)
Rates: $38-$42
(270) 474-2000

FIN 'N' FEATHER
16695 Hwy 68 E (42048)
Rates: n/a
(270) 474-2351
(800) 486-3961

KEN OAK COTTAGES
16918 Hwy 68 E (42048)
Rates: n/a
(800) 995-5844

LAKELAND RESORT
16410 Hwy 68 E (42048)
Rates: n/a
(270) 474-2292
(888) 684-3526

BARBOURVILLE

BEST WESTERN WILDERNESS TRAIL INN
Box 1896 (40906)
Rates: $48-$68
(606) 546-8500
(800) 528-1234

BARDSTOWN

COMFORT INN
984 Frost Ave (40004)
Rates: $39-$55
(502) 349-9400
(800) 228-5150

HAMPTON INN
985 Chambers Blvd (40004)
Rates: $65-$80
(502) 349-0100
(800) 426-7866

HOLIDAY INN CONVENTION CENTER
1875 New Haven Rd (40004)
Rates: $62-$74
(502) 348-9253
(800) 465-4329

RAMADA INN
523 N 3rd St (40004)
Rates: $55-$180
(502) 349-0363
(800) 272-6232

RED CARPET INN
1714 New Haven Rd (40004)
Rates: $35-$51
(502) 348-1112
(800) 251-1962

BARREN RIVER LAKE

VALLEY ON THE BARREN RETREAT
US 31 E (42156)
Rates: n/a
(502) 646-4672

BEATTYVILLE

LOGO LINDA COTTAGES
850 Black Ridge Rd (41311)
Rates: n/a
(606) 464-2876

THE OLD SCHOOL HOUSE BED & BREAKFST
124 Mt. Paran Rd (41311)
Rates: n/a
(606) 464-9991

TINCHER'S MOTEL
1182 Hwy 11 (41311)
Rates: n/a
(606) 464-9231

BENTON

COZY COVE WATERFRONT RESORT
1917 Reed Rd (42025)
Rates: $59-$1529/ Weekly
(270) 354-8168
(800) 467-8168

HESTER'S SPOT IN THE SUN COTTAGES
350 Hester Rd (42025)
Rates: n/a
(270) 354-8280
(800) 455-7481

HOLIDAY INN EXPRESS HOTEL & SUITES
173 Carroll Rd (42025)
Rates: n/a
(270) 527-5300
(800) 465-4329

KING CREEK RESORT & MARINA
972 King Creek Rd (42025)
Rates: $475
$850/Weekly
(270) 354-8268
(800) 733-6710

SHAMROCK MOTEL
806 Main (42025)
Rates: n/a
(270) 527-1341

SOUTHERN KOMFORT
460 S Komfort Rd (42025)
Rates: n/a
(270) 354-6422
(800) 526-4946

SPORTSMAN'S LODGE
12710 US 68 E (42025)
Rates: n/a
(270) 354-8333
(800) 733-6716

WHISPERING OAKS RESORT COTTAGES
267 Millers Rd (42025)
Rates: n/a
(270) 354-6628
(800) 788-1061

BEREA

BUDGET INN
215 Mt Vernon Rd (40403)
Rates: n/a
(606) 986-3771

CABIN FEVER B&B
112 Adams St (40403)
Rates: n/a
(606) 986-9075

DAYS INN
1202 Walnut Meadow Rd (40403)
Rates: $45-$59
(606) 986-7373
(800) 366-9358

ECONO LODGE
1010 Paint Lick Rd (40403)
Rates: $45-$75
(606) 986-9324
(800) 553-2666

HOLIDAY MOTEL
100 Jane St (40403)
Rates: $45-$55
(606) 986-9311

KNIGHTS INN
715 Chestnut St (40403)
Rates: $38-$60
(606) 986-2384
(800) 843-5644

SUPER 8 MOTEL
196 Prince Royal Dr (40403)
Rates: $39-$60
(606) 986-8426
(800) 800-8000

AREA CODES - If the local number doesn't connect, check for a new area code.

BOWLING GREEN

ALPINE LODGE B&B
5310 Morgantown
Rd (42104)
Rates: n/a
(270) 843-4846

COUNTRY HEARTH INN
396 Corvette Dr
(42103)
Rates: n/a
(888) 294-6491

DRURY INN
3250 Scottsville
Rd (42103)
Rates: $62-$82
(270) 842-7100
(800) 378-7946

GREENWOOD EXECUTIVE INN
1000 Executive
Way (42104)
Rates: n/a
(800) 354-4394

HOLIDAY INN
3240 Scottsville
Rd (42104)
Rates: $45-$99
(270) 781-1500
(800) 465-4329

MICROTEL INN
1980 Mel
Browning Rd
(42101)
Rates: $35-$65
(270) 745-9922
(888) 771-7171

MOTEL 6
3139 Scottsville
Rd (42104)
Rates: $39-$50
(270) 843-0140
(800) 466-8356

NEWS INN OF BOWLING GREEN
3160 Scottsville
Rd (42104)
Rates: $42-$65
(270) 781-3460
(800) 443-3701

QUALITY INN
1919 Mel
Browning St
(42104)
Rates: $39-$75
(270) 846-4588
(800) 228-5151

RAMADA INN
4767 Scottsville
Rd (42104)
Rates: $55-$100
(270) 781-3000
(800) 272-6232

SCOTTISH INNS
3140 Scottsville
Rd (42104)
Rates: $30-$45
(270) 781-6550
(800) 251-1962

SUPER 8 MOTEL
250 Cumberland
Trace Rd (42104)
Rates: $39-$54
(270) 781-9594
(800) 800-8000

TRAVEL INN
409 Hwy 31 W
BP (42104)
Rates: n/a
(270) 843-3264

UNIVERSITY PLAZA HOTEL
1021 Wilkenson
Trace (42104)
Rates: n/a
(800) 801-1777

VALUE LODGE
I-65 Exit 28
(42104)
Rates: n/a
(270) 781-6181

WESTERN HILLS MOTEL
Hwy 231 & 68
(42101)
Rates: n/a
(270) 842-5633

BRANDEN-BURG

OTTER CREEK PARK MOTEL
850 Otter Creek
Park Rd (40108)
Rates: n/a
(502) 583-3361

BROOKS

BUDGETEL INN
191 Brenton Way
(40165)
Rates: $50-$65
(502) 955-9550
(800) 428-3438

BURKESVILLE

HENDRICKS CREEK RESORT COTTAGES
General Delivery
(42717)
Rates: n/a
(800) 321-4000

RIVERFRONT LODGE MOTEL
305 King St
(42717)
Rates: $40-$48
(270) 864-3300

BURNSIDE

SOUTH FORK CABIN RENTALS
56 Narrows Ln
(42519)
Rates: n/a
(606) 561-4704

VILLAGER RESORT COTTAGES
US 27 S, Hwy 90
W (42519)
Rates: n/a
(606) 561-4707

CADIZ

GATEWAY VACATION APARTMENTS
97 Canton Lane
(42211)
Rates: n/a
(270) 924-9216

HOLIDAY INN EXPRESS
153 Broadbent
Blvd (42211)
Rates: $64-$85
(270) 522-3700
(800) 465-4329

KNIGHTS INN
5698 Hopkinsville
Rd (42211)
Rates: $35-$60
(270) 522-9395
(800) 843-5644

PARKVIEW COTTAGES
3535 Blue Springs
Road (42211)
Rates: n/a
(270) 924-5351

PRIZER POINT MARINA & RESORT
1777 Prizer Point
(42211)
Rates: n/a
(270) 522-3762
(800) 548-2048

SUPER 8 MOTEL
154 Hospitality Ln
(42211)
Rates: $43-$63
(270) 522-7007
(800) 800-8000

CALVERT CITY

FOXFIRE MOTOR INN
3457 US 62 (42029)
Rates: n/a
(270) 395-7162

KENTUCKY DAM MOTEL
4020 US 62 (42029)
Rates: n/a
(270) 395-5633

CAMPBELLS-VILLE

A LUCKY VISTA MOTEL
1409 S Columbia
(42718)
Rates: n/a
(800) 649-4692

BEST WESTERN LODGE
1400 E Broadway
(42718)
Rayes: $54-$67
(270) 465-7001
(800) 528-1234
(800) 770-0430

CARROLLTON

BLUE GABLES COURT
1501 Highland
Ave (41008)
Rates: $26-$30
(502) 732-4248
(800) 382-0364

DAYS INN
61 Inn Rd (41008)
Rates: $55-$59
(502) 732-9301
(800) 329-7466

HOLIDAY INN EXPRESS
141 Inn Rd (41008)
Rates: $59-$69
(502) 732-6661
(800) 465-4329

SUNSET MOTEL
I-71 Exit 44
(41008)
Rates: n/a
(502) 732-5985

SUPER 8 MOTEL
130 Slumber Lane
(41008)
Rates: $49-$55
(502) 732-0252
(800) 800-8000

CAVE CITY

CAVE LAND MOTEL
451 Dixie Hwy
(42127)
Rates: $18-$36
(270) 773-2321

COMFORT INN
801 Mammoth
Cave St (42127)
Rates: $40-$100
(270) 773-2030
(800) 228-5150

DAYS INN
822 Mammoth
Cave St (42127)
Rates: $56-$76
(270) 773-2151
(800) 329-7466

HOLIDAY INN EXPRESS
102 Happy Valley
St (42127)
Rates: $64-$85
(270) 773-3101
(800) 465-4329

PARKVIEW MOTEL
3906 Mammoth
Cave Rd (42127)
Rates: n/a
(270) 773-3467
(877) 482-2262

QUALITY INN
1006 A Doyle Rd
(42127)
Rates: $49-$105
(270) 773-2181
(800) 228-5151

AREA CODES - If the local number doesn't connect, check for a new area code.

SCOTTISH INNS
414 N Dixie Hwy
(42127)
Rates: n/a
(270) 773-3118
(800) 251-1962

SUPER 8 MOTEL
799 Mammoth
Cave St (42127)
Rates: $49-$85
(270) 773-3200
(800) 800-8000

CENTRAL CITY

CORONODO MOTEL
US 431& US 67
(42330)
Rates: n/a
(270) 754-1320

CLARKSON

PONDEROSA BOAT DOCK MOTEL
865 Ponderosa Rd
(42726)
Rates: n/a
(270) 242-7215

COLUMBIA

DREAMLAND MOTEL
510 Burkesville St
(42728)
Rates: n/a
(270) 384-2131

HOLMES BEND RESORT COTTAGES
5380 Holmes Bend
Rd (42728)
Rates: n/a
(800) 801-8154

CORBIN

BAYMONT INN & SUITES
174 Adams Rd
(40701)
Rates: $40-$65
(606) 523-9040
(888) 301-0200

DAYS INN
I-75 & US 25W
(40701)
Rates: $30-$60
(606) 528-8150
(800) 329-7466

KNIGHTS INN
37 Hwy 770
(40701)
Rates: $29-$75
(606) 523-1500
(800) 843-5644

MOM & DAD'S PLACE B&B
Corinth Rd
(40701)
Rates: n/a
(513) 625-8270

QUALITY INN
264 W
Cumberland Gap
Pky (40701)
Rates: $41-$125
(606) 528-4802
(800) 228-5151

RAMADA LIMITED
2615 Cumberland
Falls Hwy (40701)
Rates: $29-$59
(606) 528-6301
(800) 272-6232

SUBURBAN MOTEL
1320 Cumberland
Falls Hwy (40701)
Rates: n/a
(606) 528-1370

SUPER 8 MOTEL
171 W
Cumberland Gap
Pkwy (40701)
Rates: $39-$61
(606) 528-8888
(800) 800-8000

SWEETHOLLOW RESORT COTTAGES
I-75 Exit 29 E
(40701)
Rates: n/a
(606) 523-1094

CORINTH

K & T MOTEL
Hwy 330 & I-75
Exit 144 (41010)
Rates: n/a
(506) 824-4371

MULLINS LOG CABIN
Scaffold Lick Rd
(41010)
Rates: n/a
(888) 392-5077

COVINGTON

CARNEAL HOUSE INN B&B
405 E 2nd (41011)
Rates: n/a
(606) 431-6130

CLARION HOTEL RIVERVIEW
668 W 5th St
(41011)
Rates: $104-$114
(606) 491-1200
(800) 252-7466

EMBASSY SUITES AT RIVERCENTER
10 E Rivercenter
Blvd (410118)
Rates: $139-$179
(606) 261-8400
(800) 362-2779

SANDFORD HOUSE B&B
1026 Russell St
(41011)
Rates: $50-$105
(606) 291-9133
(888) 291-9133

CUMBERLAND

CUMBERLAND MOTEL
US 119 S (40823)
Rates: n/a
(606) 589-2181

CYNTHIANA

EVERGREEN MOTEL
US 27 N (41031)
Rates: n/a
(606) 234-5460

DANVILLE

BRYANTS CAMP MOTEL
Hwy 34 & 3373
(40422)
Rates: n/a
(606) 236-5601

COMFORT SUITES
864 Ben-Ali Dr
(40422)
Rates: $65-$74
(606) 936-9300
(800) 228-5150

DAYS INN
US 127/150
Bypass (40422)
Rates: $60+
(606) 236-8601
(800) 329-7466

GWINN ISLAND RESORT
1200 Gwinn
Island Rd (40422)
Rates: n/a
(606)236-4286

HOLIDAY INN EXPRESS
96 Daniel Dr
(40422)
Rates: $59-$65
(606) 236-8600
(800) 465-4329

OFF-BROADWAY TERRACE
US 127 & 150
(40422)
Rates: n/a
(606) 236-7474

ROYALTY'S FISH CAMP COTTAGES
US 68 & Hwy
342N (40422)
Rates: n/a
(606) 748-5459

SUPER 8 MOTEL
3663 Hwy
150/127 Bypass
(40422)
Rates: $42-$65
(606) 236-8881
(800) 800-8000

DAWSON SPRINGS

SPRINGS INN
208 E Arcadia
(42408)
Rates: n/a
(502) 797-2029

DRY RIDGE

DRY RIDGE INN
69 Broadway
(41035)
Rates: n/a
(606) 824-7005
(800) 837-5150

MICROTEL INN & SUITES
79 Blackburn Lane
(41035)
Rates: $46-$59
(606) 824-2000
(888) 771-7171

SUPER 8 MOTEL
88 Blackburn Ln
(41035)
Rates: $42-$50
(606) 824-3700
(800) 800-8000

EDDYVILLE

EDDY BAY LODGING RESORT MOTEL
75 Forest Glen Dr
(42038)
Rates: $64-$125
(270) 388-9960
(800) 324-8807

HOLIDAY HILLS TOWNHOUSES
5631 KY 93 S
(42038)
Rates: $140
(270) 388-7236
(800) 337-8550

PALISADES RESORT COTTAGES
1564 Palisades Dr
(42038)
Rates: n/a
(800) 890-1374

ELIZABETH-TOWN

BEST WESTERN CARDINAL INN
642 E Dixie Ave
(42701)
Rates: $59-$129
(270) 765-6139
(800) 528-1234

COMFORT INN ATRIUM GARDENS
1043 Executive Dr
(42701)
Rates: $64-$149
(270) 769-3030
(800) 228-5150

AREA CODES - If the local number doesn't connect, check for a new area code.

DAYS INN
2010 N Mulberry
(42701)
Rates: $48-$54
(270) 769-5522
(800) 329-7466

HOLIDAY INN
1058 N Mulberry
(42701)
Rates: n/a
(270) 769-2344
(800) 465-4329

MOTEL 6
Hwy 62 & I-65
(42701)
Rates: $33-$46
(270) 769-3102
(800) 466-8356

**THE OLDE
BETHLEHEM
ACADEMY INN**
7051 St John Rd
(42701)
Rates: $65-$150
(270) 862-9003

RED ROOF INN
2009 N Mulberry
St (42701)
Rates: $41-$68
(270) 765-4166
(800) 843-7663

SUPER 8 MOTEL
2028 N Mulberry
St (42701)
Rates: $45-$99
(270) 737-1088
(800) 800-8000

ERLANGER

**BAYMONT INN
& SUITES**
1805 Airport
Exchange (41018)
Rates: $60-$105
(606) 746-0300
(800) 301-0200

**COMFORT INN
CINCINNATI
AIRPORT**
630 Donaldson Rd
(41018)
Rates: $62-$115
(606) 727-3400
(800) 228-5150

ECONO LODGE
633 Donaldson Rd
(41018)
Rates: $30-$55
(606) 342-5500
(800) 553-2666

**RESIDENCE INN
BY MARRIOTT
AIRPORT**
2811 Circleport Dr
(41018)
Rates: $159
(606) 282-7400
(800) 331-3131

FLORENCE

AMERISUITES
300 Meijer Dr
(41042)
Rates: $89-$139
(606) 647-1170
(800) 833-1516

**ASHLEY
QUARTERS
EXTENDED STAY**
4880 Houston Rd
(41042)
Rates: n/a
(888) 525-9997

**BEST WESTERN
FLORENCE INN**
7821 Commerce
Dr (41042)
Rates: $70-$90
(606) 525-0909
(800) 528-1234

KNIGHTS INN
8049 Dream St
(41042)
Rates: $47-$60
(606) 371-9711
(800) 843-5644

MOTEL 6
7937 Dream St
(41042)
Rates: $27-$36
(606) 283-0909
(800) 466-8356

SUPER 8 MOTEL
7928 Dream St
(41042)
Rates: $52-$64
(606) 283-1221
(800) 800-8000

TRAVELODGE
8075 Steilen Dr
(41042)
Rates: $40-$55
(606) 371-0277
(800) 578-7878

FORT CAMPBELL

BUDGETEL INNS
12759 Fort
Campbell Blvd
(42262)
Rates: n/a
(502) 439-0022
(800) 428-3438

FORT MITCHELL

**HOLIDAY INN
SOUTH**
2100 Dixie Hwy
(41017)
Rates: $79-$119
(606) 331-1500
(800) 465-4329

FORT WRIGHT

**DAYS INN
CINCINNATI-
FT. WRIGHT**
1945 Dixie Hwy
(41011)
Rates: $35-$46
(606) 341-8801
(800) 329-7466

FRANKFORT

ANCHOR INN
790 E Main
(40601)
Rates: n/a
(502) 227-7404

BLUEGRASS INN
635 Versailles Rd
(40601)
Rates: $40-$58
(502) 695-1800
(800) 322-1802

DAYS INN
I-64 Exit 53B
(40601)
Rates: $36-$56
(502) 875-2200
(800) 329-7466

SUPER 8 MOTEL
1225 US Hwy 127
S (40601)
Rates: $46-$66
(502) 875-3220
(800) 800-8000

FRANKLIN

BEST WESTERN
162 Anand Dr
(42134)
Rates: $35-$65
(800) 528-1234

COMFORT INN
3794 Nashville Rd
(42134)
Rates: $40-$70
(270) 586-6100
(800) 228-5150

DAYS INN
103 Trotter's Ln
(42134)
Rates: $40-$80
(270) 598-0163
(800) 329-7466

**FRANKLIN KOA
COTTAGES**
I-65 Exit 6 (42134)
Rates: n/a
(270) 586-5622

**HOLIDAY INN
EXPRESS**
3811 Nashville Rd
(42134)
Rates: $60-$70
(270) 586-5090
(800) 465-4329

QUALITY INN
3894 Nashville Rd
(42134)
Rates: $36-$69
(270) 586-3291
(800) 228-5151

SUPER 8 MOTEL
2805 Scottsville
Rd (42134)
Rates: $33-$45
(270) 586-8885
(800) 800-8000

FULTON

GUEST INN
Purchase Pkwy &
US 52 (42041)
Rates: n/a
(270) 472-2342

GEORGETOWN

DAYS INN
385 Cherry
Blossom Way
(40324)
Rates: $35-$110
(502) 863-5000
(800) 329-7466

ECONO LODGE
3075 Paris Pike
(40324)
Rates: $28-$85
(502) 863-2240
(800) 553-2666

**GAYLA
EQUESTRIAN
CARRIAGE
GUEST HOUSE**
3329 Cynthiana
(40324)
Rates: n/a
(502) 863-5113
(800) 360-5774

HAMPTON INN
128 Darby Dr
(40324)
Rates: $59-$75
(502) 867-4888
(800) 426-7866

HOMEWOOD B&B
5301 Bethel
(40324)
Rates: n/a
(502) 355-2814

LOG CABIN B&B
350 N
Georgetown Rd
(40324)
Rates: n/a
(502) 863-3514

MICROTEL INN
111 Darby Dr
(40324)
Rates: $35-$60
(502) 868-8000
(888) 771-7171

MOTEL 6
401 Cherry
Blossom Way
(40324)
Rates: $32-$42
(502) 863-1166
(800) 466-8356

**RACER'S REST
FARM
VACATION
HOUSE**
519 Anderson Rd
(40324)
Rates: n/a
(502) 863-6342

SHONEY'S INN
200 Shoney Dr
(40324)
Rates: $54-$65
(502) 868-9800
(800) 222-2222

SUPER 8 MOTEL
250 Shoney Dr
(40324)
Rates: $40-$63
(502) 863-4888
(800) 800-8000

GILBERTSVILLE

CLOVERLEAF INN MOTEL
2237 US 62 (42044)
Rates: n/a
(888) 462-5926

LAKE HOLIDAY MOTEL
6918 US 62 (42044)
Rates: n/a
(270) 362-8143

MOORS RESORT & MARINA
570 Moors Rd
(42044)
Rates: n/a
(800) 626-5472

RAMADA INN RESORT AT KY DAM-CALVERT CITY
2184 US 62 (42044)
Rates: $50-$89
(502) 362-4278
(800) 272-6232
(800) 628-6538

GLASGOW

COMFORT INN
210 Calvary Dr
(42141)
Rates: $49-$75
(270) 651-9009
(800) 228-5150

HAPPY VALLEY INN
500 Happy Valley Rd (42141)
Rates: n/a
(270) 651-5177

TOWNE MOTEL
604 Happy Valley Rd (42141)
Rates: n/a
(270) 651-2169

GOODY

SUPER 8 MOTEL
65 State Hwy 292 E (41514)
Rates: $45-$63
(606) 237-5898
(800) 800-8000

GRAND RIVERS

BARKLEY DAM MOTEL
1054 Stringtown (42045)
Rates: n/a
(270) 362-4263
(800) 863-9009

BEST WESTERN KENTUCKY-BARKLEY LAKES INN
720 Complex Dr (42045)
Rates: $52-$87
(270) 928-2700
(800) 528-1234
(800) 928-2711

MICROTEL INN & SUITES
1017 Dover Rd (42045)
Rates: $35-$79
(270) 928-2740
(888) 771-7171
(877) 890-0111

GRAVEL SWITCH

LOGAN HILL LODGE
Hwy 243 (40328)
Rates: n/a
(502) 692-1741

GRAYSON

COUNTRY SQUIRE INN
I-64 Exit 172 (41143)
Rates: n/a
(606) 474-6605

ECONO LODGE
205 State Hwy 1947 (41143)
Rates: $36-$55
(606) 474-7854
(800) 553-2666

GREENUP

WRIGHTS MOTEL
505 Hwy 23 (41144)
Rates: n/a
(606) 473-7782

GUTHRIE

HOLIDAY MOTEL
10085 Russelville Rd (42234)
Rates: n/a
(270) 483-2509

HARLAN

BEST WESTERN HARLAN INN
2608 S Hwy 421 (40831)
Rates: $69-$85
(606) 573-3385
(800) 528-1234

MOUNT AIRE MOTEL
355 Skidmore Dr (40831)
Rates: n/a
(800) 988-4660

HARNED

MOUNTAIN LAUREL LAKE COTTAGES
US 60 & Hwy 86 (40144)
Rates: n/a
(502) 756-2737

HARRODS-BURG

BEST WESTERN INN
1680 Danville Rd (40330)
Rates: $53-$68
(606) 734-9431
(800) 528-1234

ROYALTY'S FISH CAMP COTTAGES
US 68 & Hwy 342 (40330)
Rates: n/a
(606) 748-5459

STONE MANOR MOTEL
774 S College St (40330)
Rates: n/a
(606) 734-4371

HEBRON

RADISSON INN-CINCINNATI AIRPORT
Cincinnati N KY Airport (41048)
Rates: $115-$129
(606) 371-6166
(800) 333-3333

HENDERSON

DAYS INN
2044 US 41 N (42420)
Rates: $48-$105
(270) 826-6600
(800) 329-7466

SCOTTISH INNS
2820 US 41 N (42420)
Rates: $38-$55
(270) 827-1806
(800) 251-1962

SUPER 8 MOTEL
2030 Hwy 41 N (42420)
Rates: $46-$70
(270) 827-5611
(800) 800-8000

HOPKINSVILLE

BEST WESTERN INN
4101 Fort Campbell Blvd (42240)
Rates: $54-$65
(270) 886-9000
(800) 528-1234

ECONO LODGE
2916 Fort Campbell Blvd (42240)
Rates: $42-$48
(270) 886-5242
(800) 553-2666

RODEWAY INN
2923 Fort Campbell Blvd (42240)
Rates: $38-$55
(270) 885-1126
(800) 228-2000

HORSE CAVE

BUDGET HOST INN
I-65 & SR 218 (42749)
Rates: $37-$47
(270 786-2165
(800) 283-4678

IRVINE

OAK TREE INN MOTEL
1075 Richmond Rd (40336)
Rates: n/a
(606) 723-2600

IVEL

ALPIKE MOTEL
US 23 (41642)
Rates: n/a
(606) 874-2560

JACKSON

JACKSON INN
19 Brewers Dr (41339)
Rates: n/a
(606) 666-7551
(800) 521-5271

JAMESTOWN

SASSAFRAS HILLS CABIN RENTALS
US 127 S (42629)
Rates: n/a
(270) 343-4667

KENLAKE STATE RESORT PARK

EARLY AMERICAN MOTEL
Rt 1 (Hardin 42048)
Rates: $30-$58
(502) 474-2241

KEVIL

WALDON HUNTING LODGE
779 Colvin Lake (42053)
Rates: n/a
(270) 224-2020

AREA CODES - If the local number doesn't connect, check for a new area code.

KUTTAWA

DAYS INN
Factory Outlet
Ave (42055)
Rates: $59-$80
(270) 388-5420
(800) 329-7466

RELAX INN
224 New Circle
(42055)
Rates: n/a
(270) 388-2285

LAGRANGE

DAYS INN
I-71 & SR 53
(40031)
Rates: $30-$51
(502) 222-7192
(800) 329-7466

LAWRENCE-BURG

**DOWLING HALL
BED & BREAKFST**
321 S Main St
(40342)
Rates: n/a
(502) 839-8798

LEBANON

**COUNTRY
HEARTH INN**
720 W Main St
(40033)
Rates: $46-$56
(270) 692-4445
(888) 294-6493

LEITCHFIELD

**COUNTRYSIDE
INN**
315 Commerce Dr
(42754)
Rates: $29-$41
(270) 259-4021

**MOUNTARDIER
RESORT
COTTAGES**
1990 Mountardier
Rd (42754)
Rates: n/a
(270) 286-4069

LEXINGTON

**BEST WESTERN
REGENCY INN**
2241 Elkhorn Dr
(40505)
Rates: $69-$104
(606) 293-2202
(800) 528-1234

**BRYAN STATION
INN**
273 E New Circle
(40505)
Rates: n/a
(606) 299-4162

**CONTINENTAL
INN**
801 New Circle
NE (40505)
Rates: n/a
(800) 432-9388

DAYS INN
1987 N Broadway
(40505)
Rates: $39-$59
(606) 299-1202
(800) 329-7466

DAYS INN-SOUTH
5575 Athens-
Boonesboro Rd
(40509)
Rates: $39-$65
(606) 263-3100
(800) 329-7466

ECONO LODGE
5527 Athens-
Boonesboro Rd
(40509)
Rates: $28-$55
(606) 263-5101
(800) 553-2666

**HALIFAX LANE
FARM B&B**
1201 N Yarrollton
Rd (40509)
Rates: n/a
(606) 225-5485

**HILTON
GARDEN INN**
1973 Plaudit Pl
(40509)
Rates: $99-$149
(606) 543-8300
(800) 445-8667

**HOLIDAY INN-
NORTH**
1950 Newtown
Pike (40511)
Rates: $100-$115
(606) 233-0512
(800) 465-4329

**HOLIDAY INN
SOUTH**
5532 Athens-
Boonesboro Rd
(40509)
Rates: $65-$99
(606) 263-5241
(800) 465-4329

KNIGHTS INN
1935 Stanton Way
(40511)
Rates: $36-$99
(606) 231-0232
(800) 843-5644

LA QUINTA INN
1919 Stanton Way
(40511)
Rates: $99
(606) 231-7551
(800) 687-6667

**MARRIOTT'S
GRIFFIN GATE
RESORT**
1800 Newtown
Pike (40511)
Rates: $139-$169
(606) 231-5100
(800) 228-9290

MICROTEL INN
2240 Buena Vista
(40505)
Rates: $39-$69
(606) 299-9600
(888) 771-7171

MOTEL 6
2260 Elkhorn Rd
(40505)
Rates: $35-$52
(606) 293-1431
(800) 466-8356

**QUALITY INN
NORTHWEST**
1050 Newtown
Pike (40511)
Rates: $49-$84
(606) 233-0561
(800) 228-5151

**RADISSON PLAZA
HOTEL**
369 W Vine St
(40507)
Rates: $159-$179
(606) 231-9000
(800) 333-3333

**RED ROOF INN-
NORTH**
1980 Haggard Ln
(40505)
Rates: $46-$74
(606) 293-2626
(800) 843-7663

**RED ROOF INN-
SOUTH**
2651 Wilhite Dr
(40503)
Rates: $44-$82
(606) 277-9400
(800) 843-7663

**RED ROOF INN
SOUTHEAST**
100 Canebrake Dr
(40509)
Rates: n/a
(606) 543-1877
(800) 843-7663

**RESIDENCE INN
BY MARRIOTT**
1080 Newtown
Pike (40511)
Rates: $134-$159
(606) 231-6191
(800) 331-3131

SHONEYS INN
2753 Richmond
Rd (40509)
Rates: $53-$71
(606) 269-4999
(800) 222-2222

SLEEP INN
1920 Plaudet Pl
(40509)
Rates: $47-$108
(606) 543-8400
(800) 753-3746

SUPER 8 MOTEL
2351 Buena Vista
Rd (40505)
Rates: $48-$72
(606) 299-6241
(800) 800-8000

LIBERTY

**THE BROWN
MOTEL**
176 Wolford Ave
(42539)
Rates: $49-$58
(606) 787-6224

LONDON

**BEST WESTERN
HARVEST INN**
207 W 80 (40741)
Rates: $41-$70
(606) 864-2222
(800) 528-1234

**BUDGET HOST
WESTGATE INN**
254 W Daniel
Boone Pkwy
(40741)
Rates: $36-$49
(606) 878-7330
(800) 283-4678

DAYS INN
2035 Hwy 192 W
(40741)
Rates: $45-$75
(606) 864-7331
(800) 329-7466

**HOLIDAY INN
EXPRESS**
400 GOP (40741)
Rates: n/a
(606) 878-7678
(800) 465-4329

RED ROOF INN
110 Melcon Ln
(40741)
Rates: $41-$68
(606) 862-8844
(800) 843-7663

SUPER 8 MOTEL
I-75 Exit 41
(40741)
Rates: $39-$59
(606) 878-9800
(800) 800-8000

**TOWN CENTER
MOTEL**
500 Main (40741)
Rates: n/a
(606) 864-4101

LOUISA

BEST WESTERN VILLAGE INN
117 E Madison St (41230)
Rates: $40-$47
(606) 638-9417
(800) 528-1234

SUPER 8 MOTEL
US 23 & KY 3 (41230)
Rates: $47-$67
(606) 638-7888
(800) 800-8000

LOUISVILLE
(And vicinity)

ALEKSANDER HOUSE B&B
1213 S 1st St (40220)
Rates: $80-$150
(502) 637-4985

AMERISUITES
701 S Hurstbourne Pkwy (Jeffersontown 40220)
Rates: $79-$129
(502) 426-0119
(800) 833-1516

BEST WESTERN SOUTH
211 S Lakeview Dr (Shepherdsville 40165)
Rates: $55-$66
(502) 543-7097
(800) 528-1234

BRECKINRIDGE INN HOTEL
2800 Breckinridge Ln (40220)
Rates: $59-$75
(502) 456-5050

DAYS INN
I-65 & KY 44 (Shepherdsville 40165)
Rates: $30-$51
(502) 543-3011
(800) 329-7466

DAYS INN EAST
4621 Shelbyville Rd (40207)
Rates: $58-$88
(502) 896-8871
(800) 329-7466

DAYS INN SOUTHEAST
1850 Embassy Sq Blvd (40299)
Rates: $30-$75
(502) 491-1040
(800) 329-7466

DOUBLETREE CLUB HOTEL EAST
9700 Bluegrass Pkwy (Jeffersontown 40299)
Rates: $89
(502) 491-4830
(800) 289-1009

EXECUTIVE INN HOTEL
978 Phillips Ln (40209)
Rates: $86-$96
(502) 367-6161
(800) 626-2706

EXECUTIVE WEST
830 Phillips Ln (40209)
Rates: $68-$104
(502) 367-2251
(800) 626-2708

HOLIDAY INN AIRPORT EAST
1465 Gardiner Ln (40213)
Rates: $103-$134
(502) 452-6361
(800) 465-4329

HOLIDAY INN DOWNTOWN
120 W Broadway (40202)
Rates: $96-$116
(502) 426-2600
(800) 465-4329

HOLIDAY INN SOUTHEAST
3255 Bardstown Rd (40205)
Rates: $85-$99
(502) 454-0451
(800) 465-4329

HOLIDAY INN SOUTH-AIRPORT
3317 Fern Valley Rd (40213)
Rates: $85+
(502) 964-3311
(800) 465-4329

THE INN AT JEWISH HOSPITAL
100 E Jefferson (40202)
Rates: n/a
(502) 582-2481

LOUISVILLE SOUTH KOA COTTAGES
I-65 Exit 117 (Shepherdsville 40165)
Rates: n/a
(502) 543-2041

MAINSTAY SUITES
1650 Alliante Ave (40299)
Rates: $95-$250
(502) 267-4454
(800) 660-6246

MOTEL 6
144 Paroquet Springs Dr (Shepherdsville 40165)
Rates: $35-$50
(502) 543-4400
(800) 466-8356

RED ROOF INN-AIRPORT
4704 Preston Hwy (40213)
Rates: $45-$157
(502) 968-0151
(800) 843-7663

RED ROOF INN-EAST
9330 Blairwood Rd (Hurstbourne 40222)
Rates: $46-$73
(502) 426-7621
(800) 843-7663

RED ROOF INN-SOUTHEAST
3322 Red Roof Inn Pl (40218)
Rates: $50-$83
(502) 456-2993
(800) 843-7663

RESIDENCE INN BY MARRIOTT
120 Hurstbourne Pkwy (Jeffersontown 40222)
Rates: $92-$120
(502) 425-1821
(800) 331-3131

SEELBACH HILTON HOTEL
500 Fourth Ave (40202)
Rates: $179-$274
(502) 585-3200
(800) 445-8667

SLEEP INN
1850 Priority Way (Jeffersontown 40299)
Rates: $49-$240
(502) 266-6776
(800) 753-3746

SLEEP INN SIX FLAGS
3330 Preston Hwy, Gate #6 (40213)
Rates: $69-$200
(502) 368-9597
(800) 753-3746

SUPER 8 MOTEL
4800 Preston Hwy (40213)
Rates: $43-$68
(502) 968-0088
(800) 800-8000

SUPER 8 MOTEL
927 S 2nd St (40213)
Rates: $43-$63
(502) 584-8888
(800) 800-8000

THRIFTY DUTCHMAN MOTEL
3357 Fern Valley Rd (40213)
Rates: $35-$43
(502) 968-8124

TRAVELODGE
9340 Blairwood Rd (Hurstbourne 40222)
Rates: $43-$79
(502) 425-8010
(800) 578-7878

TRAVELODGE AIRPORT
3315 Bardstown Rd (40218)
Rates: $47-$79
(502) 452-1501
(800) 578-7878

WOODHAVEN BED & BREAKFAST
401 S Hubbards (40207)
Rates: n/a
(502) 895-1011

MADISONVILLE

BIG SPRING INN
1750 E Center (42431)
Rates: n/a
(270) 821-8700

DAYS INN
1900 Lantaff Blvd (42431)
Rates: $59-$125
(270) 821-8620
(800) 329-7466

ECONO LODGE
1117 E Center St (42431)
Rates: $37-$59
(270) 821-0364
(800) 553-2666

MAMMOTH CAVE NATIONAL PARK
(Kennels provided)

MAMMOTH CAVE HOTEL & COTTAGES
11 Mi W of Jct I-65 & SR 70 (42259)
Rates: $62-$73
(270) 758-2225

MANCHESTER

BOONE PARKWAY MOTEL
Hwy 80 (40962)
Rates: n/a
(606) 598-5122

MARION

TOBIN TOURTEL
225 Sturgis Rd (42064)
Rates: n/a
(270) 965-5241

MAYFIELD

DAYS INN
1101 W Housman St (42066)
Rates: $49-$55
(502) 247-3700
(800) 329-7466

SUPER 8 MOTEL
1100 Links Ln
(42066)
Rates: $43-$58
(270) 247-8899
(800) 800-8000

MCKEE

**TOWN &
COUNTRY MOTEL**
390 US 421 S
(40447)
Rates: n/a
(606) 287-8235

MONTICELLO

ANCHOR MOTEL
1077 N Main
(42633)
Rates: n/a
(606) 348-8441

**HIDDEN VALLEY
LODGE**
Hwy 92 W (42633)
Rates: n/a
(606) 348-4567

MORTONS
GAP

**BEST WESTERN
INN**
Pennyrile Pkwy,
Exit 37 (42440)
Rates: $44-$65
(502) 258-5201
(800) 528-1234
(888) 298-2115

MOUNT
STERLING

BUDGET INN
I-64 Exit 110
(40353)
Rates: n/a
(606) 498-9600

DAYS INN
705 Maysville Rd
(40353)
Rates: $25-$55
(606) 498-4680
(800) 329-7466

RAMADA LIMITED
115 Stone Trace Dr
(40353)
Rates: $62-$72
(606) 497-9400
(800) 272-6232

SCOTTISH INNS
517 Maysville Rd
(40353)
Rates: $22-$28
(606) 498-3424
(800) 251-1962

MOUNT
VERNON

ECONO LODGE
1630 Richmond St
(40456)
Rates: $40-$70
(606) 256-4621
(800) 553-2666

**KASTLE INN
MOTEL**
I-75 & US 25, Exit
59 (40456)
Rates: $46-$60
(606) 256-5156
(800) 956-4366

MUNFORD-
VILLE

SUPER 8 MOTEL
88 Stockpen Rd
(42765)
Rates: $42-$54
(502) 524-4888
(800) 800-8000

MURRAY

DAYS INN
517 S 12th St
(42071)
Rates: $40-$125
(270) 753-6706
(800) 329-7466

**LYNHURST
RESORT
& MARINA**
270 Lynhurst Dr
(42071)
Rates: n/a
(888) 244-2277

**PARADISE
RESORT
COTTAGES**
1024 Paradise Dr
(42071)
Rates: n/a
(270) 436-2767
(800) 340-2767

NANCY

NANCY'S PLACE
131 Everett Lane
Spur (42544)
Rates: n/a
(606) 341-7789

NEW
CONCORD

**CYPRESS SPRINGS
RESORT**
2740 Cypress Trail
(42076)
Rates: n/a
(270) 436-5496

**LAKEVIEW
COTTAGES
& MARINA**
165 Lakeview
Cabin Dr (42076)
Rates: n/a
(270) 436-5876

**MISSING HILLS
RESORT
COTTAGES**
HC Box 215-A
(42076)
Rates: n/a
(270) 436-5519

NICHOLAS-
VILLE

**CEDAR HAVEN
FARM COUNTRY
HOME**
2380 Bethel Rd
(40356)
Rates: n/a
(606) 858-3849

PRINCESS MOTEL
US 27 N (40356)
Rates: n/a
(606) 885-6808

OAK GROVE

BAYMONT INN
12759 Ft Campbell
(42262)
Rates: n/a
(270) 439-0022
(800) 301-0200

DAYS INN
212 Auburn St
(42262)
Rates: $49-$99
(270) 640-3888
(800) 329-7466

OLIVE HILL

CARROLL'S INN
I-64 Exit 161
(41164)
Rates: n/a
(606) 286-4141

OWENSBORO

DAYS INN
3720 New
Hartford Rd
(42301)
Rates: $44-$52
(270) 684-9621
(800) 329-7466

HOLIDAY INN
3136 W 2nd St
(42301)
Rates: $79
(270) 685-3941
(800) 465-4329

MOTEL 6
4585 Frederica St
(42301)
Rates: $33-$46
(270) 686-8606
(800) 466-8356

SUPER 8 MOTEL
1027 Goetz Dr
(42301)
Rates: $46-$59
(270) 685-3388
(800) 800-8000

PADUCAH

**BAYMONT INN
& SUITES**
5300 Old Cairo Rd
(42002)
Rates: $46-$57
(270) 443-4343
(800) 301-0200

**BEST INNS
OF AMERICA**
5001 Hinckleville
Rd (42002)
Rates: $45-$69
(270) 442-3334
(800) 237-8466

BUDGET INN
3300 Park Ave
(42002)
Rates: n/a
(270) 442-8236

DRURY INN
3975 Hinkleville
Rd (42001)
Rates: $59-$86
(270) 443-3313
(800) 378-7946

**DRURY SUITES
HOTEL**
120 McBride Ln
(42001)
Rates: $76-$96
(270) 441-0024
(800) 378-7946

**FARLEY PLACE
BED & BREAKFAST**
166 Farley Pl
(42003)
Rates: n/a
(270) 442-2488

HAMPTON INN
4930 Hinkleville
Rd (42001)
Rates: $61-$79
(270) 442-4500
(800) 426-7866

**HOLIDAY INN
EXPRESS**
3994 Hinkleville
Rd (42001)
Rates: n/a
(270) 442-8874
(800) 465-4329

MOTEL 6
5120 Hinkleville
Rd (42001)
Rates: $35-$46
(270) 443-3672
(800) 466-8356

PEAR TREE INN
4910 Hinkleville
Rd (42001)
Rates: $47-$65
(270) 444-7200
(800) 282-8733
(800) 378-7946

QUALITY INN
1380 S Irvin Cobb
Dr (42003)
Rates: $44-$64
(270) 443-8751
(800) 228-5150

RED CARPET INN
2701 HC Mathis
Dr (42001)
Rates: n/a
(270) 443-5500
(800) 251-1962

RIVER INN PLACE
4050 Clarks River
Rd (42003)
Rates: n/a
(270) 442-3595

**TRINITY HILLS
FARM B&B**
10455 Old
Lovelaceville
(42003)
Rates: n/a
(800) 488-3998

WESTOWNE INN
I-24 Exit 4 (42003)
Rates: n/a
(270) 442-5666

PAINTSVILLE

DAYS INN
512 S Mayo Trail
(41240)
Rates: $50-$90
(606) 789-3551
(800) 329-7466

STARFIRE MOTEL
US 23 & Hwy 321
S (41240)
Rates: n/a
(606) 789-5341

PARIS

**COLONIAL
MOTEL**
1493 S Main
(40361)
Rates: n/a
(606) 987-3250

PARK CITY

**PARKLAND
MOTEL**
2400 Louisville Rd
(42160)
Rates: n/a
(800) 647-2880

PARKERS LAKE

**HOLIDAY
MOTOR LODGE**
Hwy 90, Box 300
(42634)
Rates: n/a
(606) 376-2732

PHELPS

**COUNTRY INN
MOTEL**
US 23 & Hwy 194
E (41553)
Rates: n/a
(606) 456-3349

PIKEVILLE

COLLEY MOTEL
US 23 S (41501)
Rates: n/a
(606) 432-0834

**DANIEL BOONE
MOTOR INN**
US 23 N (41501)
Rates: n/a
(606) 432-0365

LANDMARK INN
146 S Mayo Trail
(41501)
Rates: $55-$65
(606) 432-2545

**MODERNE VILLA
MOTEL**
510 S Mayo Trail
(41501)
Rates: n/a
(606) 432-2188

PINSON MOTEL
2nd & Pike Ave
(41501)
Rates: n/a
(606) 437-7346

PRESTONS-BURG

SUPER 8 MOTEL
80 Shoppers Path
(41653)
Rates: $46-$55
(606) 886-3355
(800) 800-8000

PRINCETON

PARKWAY INN
112 US 62 W
(42445)
Rates: n/a
(502) 365-2001

PROSPECT

**MELROSE INN
& MOTEL**
13306 US 42
(40059)
Rates: $36-$60
(502) 228-1136

RADCLIFF

FORT KNOX INN
1400 N Dixie Hwy
(40160)
Rates: n/a
(502) 351-3199
(800) 852-6164

**GATEWAY VILLA
MOTEL**
US 31 W (40160)
Rates: n/a
(502) 351-3449

**OTTER CREEK
PARK MOTEL &
CABINS**
US 31 W (40160)
Rates: n/a
(502) 583-3577

SUPER 8 MOTEL
395 Redmar Blvd
(40160)
Rates: $49-$60
(502) 352-1888
(800) 800-8000

RICHMOND

**BEST WESTERN
ROAD STAR INN**
1751 Lexington Rd
(40475)
Rates: $69-$99
(606) 623-9121
(800) 528-1234
(800) 575-5339

DAYS INN
2109 Belmont Dr
(40475)
Rates: $53-$70
(606) 624-5769
(800) 329-7466

ECONO LODGE
230 Eastern
Bypass (40475)
Rates: $34-$59
(606) 623-8813
(800) 553-2666

RED ROOF INN
Lexington Rd
(40475)
Rates: n/a
(606) 625-0084
(800) 843-7663

SUPER 8 MOTEL
107 N Keeneland
(40475)
Rates: $45-$65
(606) 624-1550
(800) 800-8000

TRAVELODGE
1698 Northgate Dr
(40475)
Rates: $35-$50
(606) 623-0881
(800) 578-7878

WISE MOTEL
105 N Killarney
Ln (40475)
Rates: $31-$32
(606) 623-8126

RICHWOOD

**HOLIDAY INN
EXPRESS**
164 Winning
Colors Dr (41094)
Rates: n/a
(606) 485-2330
(800) 465-4329

**RICHWOOD
MOTEL**
10805 Dixie Hwy
(41094)
Rates: n/a
(606) 525-9525

RUSSELL
SPRINGS

**CUMBERLAND
LODGE**
S Hwy 127 (42642)
Rates: n/a
(270) 866-4208

**POPPLEWELL'S
ALLIGATOR
DOCK #1
COTTAGES**
6956 S Hwy 76
(42642)
Rates: n/a
(270) 866-3634

**SHILOH MOTOR
INN**
60 Steve Wariner
(42642)
Rates: n/a
(270) 866-5920

**WHITE PILLARS
BED & BREAKFAST**
100 Thrasher Ct
(42642)
Rates: n/a
(502) 866-7231

RUSSELLVILLE

SCOTTISH INNS
815 W 9th St
(42276)
Rates: n/a
(270) 726-8351
(800) 251-1962

TOWN MOTEL
Hwy 80 & 68
(42276)
Rates: n/a
(270) 726-7665

SCOTTSVILLE

DAYS INN
57 Burnley Rd
(42164)
Rates: $42-$55
(502) 622-7770
(800) 329-7466

SHELBYVILLE

**BEST WESTERN
SHELBYVILLE
LODGE**
115 Isaac Shelby
Dr (40065)
Rates: $49-$89
(502) 633-4400
(800) 528-1234

**GREENVIEW
MOTEL**
2366 US 60 (40065)
Rates: n/a
(502) 633-2080

SMITHS GROVE

BRYCE INN
592 S Main St
(42171)
Rates: $39-$53
(270) 563-5141

SOMERSET

**BUCK CREEK
BOAT DOCK
COTTAGES**
9700 Rush Branch
(42501)
Rates: n/a
(606) 382-5542

COMFORT INN
82 Jolin Dr (42503)
Rates: $64-$130
(606) 677-1500
(800) 228-5150

CUMBERLAND MOTEL
6050 S Hwy 27
(42501)
Rates: n/a
(606) 561-5131

LANDMARK INN
1201 US 27 S
(42501)
Rates: n/a
(606) 678-8115

TRIPLE J & I RENTAL COTTAGES
Hwy 27 S (42501)
Rates: n/a
(606) 679-7864

SPRINGFIELD

GLENMAR PLANTATION BED & BREAKFST
Rt 1, Box 682
(40069)
Rates: $75
(606) 284-7791

SULPHUR

SULPHUR TRACE FARM B&B
8793 Sulphur Rd
(40070)
Rates: n/a
(502) 743-5956

VERSAILLES

1823 HISTORIC ROSE HILL INN B&B
233 Rose Hill
(40383)
Rates: $69-$140
(606) 873-5957

TYRONE PIKE BED & BREAKFST
3820 Tyrone Pike
(40383)
Rates: $89-$125
(606) 873-2408

WESTERN FIELDS GUEST HOUSE
5018 Fords Mill
Rd (40383)
Rates: n/a
(800) 600-4935

WALTON

DAYS INN
11177 Frontage Rd
(41094)
Rates: $30-$51
(606) 485-4151
(800) 329-7466

WEST SOMERSET

BECKETT MOTEL
2001 Lees Ford
Dock (42564)
Rates: n/a
(606) 636-6411

WILLIAMSBURG

ADKINS MOTOR INN
1746 US 25 W
(40769)
Rates: n/a
(606) 549-4450

CUMBERLAND INN BY MARRIOTT
649 S 10th St
(40769)
Rates: n/a
(800) 315-0286

HOLIDAY INN EXPRESS
30 W Hwy 92
(40769)
Rates: $51-$85
(606) 549-3450
(800) 465-4329

WILLIAMSBURG MOTEL
I-75 Exit 11 (40769)
Rates: n/a
(606) 549-2300

WILLIAMS-TOWN

DAYS INN
211 SR 36 W
(41097)
Rates: $42-$85
(606) 824-5025
(800) 329-7466

HOWARD JOHNSON EXPRESS
10 Skyway Dr
(41097)
Rates: $34-$55
(606) 824-7177
(800) 446-4656

WINCHESTER

BEST WESTERN COUNTRY SQUIRE MOTEL
1307 W Lexington
Ave (40391)
Rates: $49-$89
(606) 744-7210
(800) 528-1234

COMFORT SUITES
960 Interstate Dr
(40391)
Rates: $75-$80
(606) 737-3990
(800) 228-5150

SUPER 8 MOTEL
5100 Revilo Rd
(40391)
Rates: $40-$65
(606) 745-0751
(800) 800-8000

THOROUGHBRED MOTEL
I-64 Exit 96
(40391)
Rates: n/a
(606) 744-1262

LOUISIANA

ALEXANDRIA

BEST WESTERN
2720 W
MacArthur Dr
(71303)
Rates: $60-$97
(318) 445-5530
(800) 528-1234
(888) 338-2008

DAYS INN
2300 N
MacArthur Dr
(71303)
Rates: $40-$62
(318) 443-7331
(800) 329-7466

**HOWARD
JOHNSON
EXPRESS**
6014 Old Boyce
Rd (71301)
Rates: $57-$70
(318) 442-5190
(800) 446-4656

**LA QUINTA INN
& SUITES**
6116 W Calhoun
Dr (71303)
Rates: $59-$99
(318) 442-3700
(800) 687-6667

RODEWAY INN
742 MacArthur Dr
(71303)
Rates: $45-$70
(318) 448-1611
(800) 228-2000

SUPER 8 MOTEL
700 MacArthur Dr
(71301)
Rates: $45-$65
(318) 445-6541
(800) 800-8000

AMITE

**BLYTHEWOOD
PLANTATION
BED & BREAKFAST**
400 Daniel St
(70422)
Rates: $75-$150
(504) 345-6419

ARCADIA

DAYS INN
1061 Hwy 151
(71001)
Rates: $45-$80
(318) 263-3555
(800) 329-7466

BASTROP

COUNTRY INN
1815 E Madison
(71220)
Rates: $39-$43
(318) 281-8100

BATON ROUGE

AMERISUITTES
6080 Bluebonnet
Blvd (70809)
Rates: $79-$149
(225) 769-4400
(800) 833-1516

**BAYMONT INN
& SUITES**
10555 Rieger Rd
(70809)
Rates: $49-$54
(225) 291-6600
(800) 301-0200

COMFORT INN
2445 S Acadian
Thruway (70808)
Rates: $69-$95
(225) 927-5790
(800) 228-5150

DAYS INN
10245 Airline
Hwy (70816)
Rates: $50-$95
(225) 291-8152
(800) 329-7466

**HOMEWOOD
SUITES**
5860 Corporate
Blvd (70808)
Rates: n/a
(225) 927-1700
(800) 225-5466

LA QUINTA INN
2333 S Acadian
Thruway (70808)
Rates: $69-$95
(225) 924-9600
(800) 687-6667

MOTEL 6
9901 Gwen Adele
Ave (70816)
Rates: $34-$42
(225) 924-2130
(800) 466-8356

QUALITY INN
10920 Mead
Frontage Rd (70816)
Rates: $49-$76
(225) 293-9370
(800) 228-5151

RED ROOF INN
11314 Boardwalk
Dr (70816)
Rates: $44-$53
(225) 275-6600
(800) 843-7663

**RESIDENCE INN
BY MARRIOTT**
5522 Corporate
Blvd (70816)
Rates: $105-$135
(225) 927-5630
(800) 331-3131

**SHONEY'S INN
& SUITES**
9919 Gwen Adele
Dr (70816)
Rates: $55-$63
(225) 925-8399
(800) 222-2222

SLEEP INN
10332 Plaza
Americana Dr
(70816)
Rates: $59-$72
(225) 926-8488
(800) 753-3746

BOSCO

**BOSCOBEL
COTTAGE B&B**
185 Cordell Ln
(71202)
Rates: $75-$95
(318) 325-1550

BOSSIER CITY

**BEST WESTERN
AIRLINE MOTOR
INN**
1984 Airline Dr
(71112)
Rates: $65-$125
(318) 742-6000
(800) 528-1234
(800) 635-7639

DAYS INN
200 John Wesley
Blvd (71112)
Rates: $29-$70
(318) 742-9200
(800) 329-7466

LA QUINTA INN
309 Preston Blvd
(71112)
Rates: $69-$95
(318) 747-4400
(800) 687-6667

MOTEL 6
210 John Wesley
Blvd (71112)
Rates: $32-$46
(318) 742-3472
(800) 466-8356

QUALITY INN
4300 Industrial Dr
(71112)
Rates: $49-$89
(318) 746-5050
(800) 228-5151

RAMADA INN
750 Isle of Capri
Blvd (71111)
Rates: $57-$81
(318) 746-8410
(800) 272-6232

**RESIDENCE INN
BY MARRIOTT**
1001 Gould Dr
(71111)
Rates: $94-$135
(318) 747-6220
(800) 331-3131

BOYCE

LA QUINTA INN
6116 W Calhoun
Dr (71303)
Rates: $49-$59
(318) 442-3700
(800) 687-6667

BREAUX BRIDGE

BEST WESTERN
2088-B Rees St
(70517)
Rates: $65-$150
(337) 332-1114
(800) 528-1234
(888) 783-0007

**HOLIDAY INN
EXPRESS**
2924 Grand Point
Hwy (70517)
Rates: n/a
(337) 332-3017
(800) 465-4329

CHALMETTE

**QUALITY INN
MARINA**
5353 Paris Rd
(70043)
Rates: $49-$135
(504)277-5353
(800) 228-5151

CHENEYVILLE

**LOYD HALL
PLANTATION
B & B**
292 Loyd Bridge
Rd (71325)
Rates: $95-$145
(318) 776-5641
(800) 240-8135

CROWLEY

BEST WESTERN
9571 Egan Hwy
(70526)
Rates: $65-$110
(337) 783-2378
(800) 528-1234
(800) 940-0003

AREA CODES - If the local number doesn't connect, check for a new area code.

CROWLEY INN
2111 N Cherokee
Dr (70526)
Rates: n/a
(337) 788-0970
(800) 256-4565

DARROW

**TEZCUCO
PLANTATION B&B**
3138 Hwy 44
(70725)
Rates: $65-$165
(225) 562-3929

DE RIDDER

RED CARPET INN
806 N Pine St
(70634)
Rates: $27-$39
(318) 463-8605
(800) 251-1962

DELHI

**BEST WESTERN
DELHI INN**
35 Snider Rd
(71232)
Rates: $42-$68
(318) 878-5126
(800) 528-1234

DAYS INN
13 Snider Rd
(71232)
Rates: $40-$58
(318) 878-9000
(800) 329-7466

DENHAM SPRINGS

QUALITY INN
2605 S Range Ave
(70726)
Rates: $55-$150
(225) 667-7177
(800) 228-5151

EUNICE

**SEALE GUEST-
HOUSE B & B**
P. O. Box 568
(70535)
Rates: $65-$75
(318) 457-3753

GRETNA

LA QUINTA INN
50 Terry Pkwy
(70053)
Rates: $79-$99
(504) 368-5600
(800) 687-6667

QUALITY INN
100 Westbank
Expwy (70053)
Rates: $55-$150
(504) 366-8531
(800) 228-5151

HAMMOND

QUALITY INN
14175 Hwy 190
(70401)
Rates: $59-$99
(504) 542-8555
(800) 228-5151

RAMADA INN
42309 S Morrison
Blvd (70403)
Rates: $45-$80
(504) 542-1000
(800) 272-6232

HOUMA

**CROCHET HOUSE
B&B**
301 Midland Dr
(71073)
Rates: $45-$65
(504) 879-3033

HAMPTON INN
1728 Martin
Luther King Blvd
(71073)
Rates: $67-$77
(504) 873-3140
(800) 426-7866

JACKSON

ASPHODEL INN
4626 Hwy 68
(70748)
Rates: $55-$130
(504) 654-6868

JENNINGS

**CREOLE ROSE
MANOR B & B**
214 W Plaquemine
(70546)
Rates: $50-$75
(318) 824-3145

DAYS INN
2502 Port Dr
(70546)
Rates: $55-$85
(318) 824-6550
(800) 329-7466

HOLIDAY INN
603 Holiday Dr
(70546)
Rates: n/a
(318) 824-5280
(800) 465-4329

KENNER

**DAYS INN
AIRPORT**
1300 Veterans
Memorial Blvd
(70062)
Rates: $42-$140
(504) 469-2531
(800) 329-7466

**HILTON HOTEL-
NEW ORLEANS
AIRPORT**
901 Airline Hwy
(70063)
Rates: $110-$212
(504) 469-5000
(800) 445-8667

LA QUINTA INN
2610 Williams
Blvd (70063)
Rates: $85-$119
(504) 466-1401
(800) 687-6667

KINDER

COMFORT INN
13894 US 165
(70648)
Rates: $59-$260
(318) 738-3240
(800) 228-5150

**HOLIDAY INN
EXPRESS HOTEL
& SUITES**
11750 US Hwy 165
(70648)
Rates: $99
(318) 738-3381
(800) 465-4329

KROTZ SPRINGS

**COUNTRY STORE
B & B INN**
P. O. Drawer 457
(70750)
Rates: $45-$75
(318) 566-2331

LA PLACE

BEST WESTERN
4289 Main St
(70068)
Rates: $69-$179
(504) 651-4000
(800) 528-1234

LAFAYETTE

**BEST WESTERN
HOTEL
ACADIANA**
1801 Pinhook Rd
(70508)
Rates: $79-$122
(337) 233-8120
(800) 528-1234
(800) 826-8386

**BOIS DES CHENES
INN B&B**
338 N Sterling
(70501)
Rates: $75-$105
(337) 233-7816

COMFORT INN
1421 SE
Evangeline Thrwy
(70501)
Rates: $74-$120
(337) 232-9000
(800) 228-5150

COMFORT SUITES
2300 NE
Evangeline Thrwy
(70501)
Rates: 74-$164
(337) 291-6008
(800) 228-5150

DAYS INN
1620 N
University&
I-10 (70506)
Rates: $52+
(337) 237-8880
(800) 329-7466

**HOLIDAY INN
EXPRESS**
2503 SE
Evangeline Thrwy
(70508)
Rates: n/a
(337) 234-2000
(800) 465-4329

LA QUINTA INN
2100 NE
Evangeline Thrwy
(70501)
Rates: $69-$99
(337) 233-5610
(800) 687-6777

QUALITY INN
1605 N University
(70506)
Rates: $54-$72
(337) 232-6131
(800) 228-5151

RAMADA INN
2716 NE
Evangeline Thrwy
(70507)
Rates: $49-$85
(337) 233-0003
(800) 272-6232

RED ROOF INN
1718 N University
Ave (70507)
Rates: $51-$67
(337) 233-3339
(800) 843-7663

SHONEYS INN
2216 NE
Evangeline Thrwy
(70501)
Rates: n/a
(337) 234-0383
(800) 222-2222

SUPER 8 MOTEL
2224 NE
Evangeline Thrwy
(70501)
Rates: $34-$54
(337) 232-8826
(800) 800-8000

LAKE CHARLES

**BEST SUITES
OF AMERICA**
401 Lakeshore Dr
(70601)
Rates: $69-$150
(337) 439-2444

DAYS INN
1010 Hwy 171 N
(70601)
Rates: $45+
(337) 433-1711
(800) 329-7466

HOWARD JOHNSON EXPRESS
825 Broad St
(70601)
Rates: $44-$65
(337) 436-4311
(800) 446-4656

MOTEL 6
335 Hwy 171
(70601)
Rates: $36-$50
(337) 433-1773
(800) 466-8356

LIVONIA

OAK TREE INN
7875 Airline Hwy
(70755)
Rates: $59-$69
(225) 637-2590

MANSFIELD

MANSFIELD INN
1055 Washington Ave (71052)
Rates: $39-$48
(318) 872-5034

METARIE

DOUBLETREE HOTEL LAKESIDE
3838 N Causeway Blvd (70002)
Rates: $80-$99
(504) 836-5253
(800) 222-8733

LA QUINTA INN CAUSEWAY
3100 I-10 Service Rd (70001)
Rates: $79-$105
(504) 835-8511
(800) 687-6777

LA QUINTA INN
5900 Veterans Memorial Blvd
(70002)
Rates: $79-$99
(504) 456-0003
(800) 687-6667

QUALITY HOTEL
2261 N Causeway Blvd (70001)
Rates: $89-$159
(504) 833-8211
(800) 228-5151

MINDEN

BEST WESTERN MINDEN
1411 Sibley Rd
(71055)
Rates: $55-$70
(318) 377-1001
(800) 528-1234

MONROE

BEST WESTERN AIRPPORT INN
1475 Garrett Rd
(71202)
Rates: $54-$70
(318) 345-4000
(800) 528-1234

BOSCOBEL COTTAGE B&B
185 Cordell Lane
(71202)
Rates: $65-$95
(318) 325-1550
(800) 254-3529

LA QUINTA INN
1035 US 165S
Bypass (71203)
Rates: $59-$79
(318) 322-3900
(800) 687-6667

MOTEL 6
1501 US Hwy 165
Bypass (71202)
Rates: $29-$35
(318) 322-5430
(800) 466-8356

MORGAN CITY

RAMADA INN
7408 Hwy 90 E
(70380)
Rates: $65-$85
(504) 384-5750
(800) 272-6232

NATCHITOCHES

CLOUTIER TOWN-HOUSE B&B
Front St/Ducoumau Square (71457)
Rates: $50-$150
(318) 352-5242
(800) 351-7666

COMFORT INN
5362 SR 6 W
(71457)
Rates: $67-$140
(318) 352-7500
(800) 228-5150

DAYS INN
1000 College Ave
(71457)
Rates: $45-$75
(318) 352-4426
(800) 329-7466

SUPER 8 MOTEL
801 Hwy 1 Bypass
(71457)
Rates: $45-$105
(318) 352-1700
(800) 800-8000

NEW IBERIA

BEST WESTERN INN & SUITES
2714 Hwy 14
(70560)
Rates: $60-$109
(318) 364-3030
(800) 528-1234

COMFORT SUITES
SR 14 (70560)
Rates: $57-$129
(800) 228-5150

HOLIDAY INN AVERY ISLAND
2915 Hwy 14
(70560)
Rates: $51-$61
(318) 367-1201
(800) 465-4329

LA MAISON B&B
8317 Weeks Island Rd (70560)
Rates: $75-$140
(318) 364-2970
(800) 225-8671

MAISON MARCELINE B&B
442 E Main
(70560)
Rates: $50-$175
(318) 364-5922

NEW ORLEANS

AMBASSADOR HOTEL
535 Tchoupitoulas
(70130)
Rates: $89-$260
(504) 527-5271
(888) 527-5271

THE FAIRMONT HOTEL
123 Baronne St
(70130)
Rates: n/a
(504) 529-7111

FRENCH QUARTER COURTYARD HOTEL
1101 Rampart St
(70140)
Rates: $59-$189
(504) 522-7333

HILTON HOTEL NEW ORLEANS RIVERSIDE
2 Poydras St
(70140)
Rates: $119-$234
(504) 561-0500
(800) 445-8667

LA QUINTA INN
12001 I-10 Service Rd (70127)
Rates: $69-$89
(504) 246-3003
(800) 687-6667

LA QUINTA INN CROWDER BLVD
8400 I-10 Service Rd (70127)
Rates: $69-$89
(504) 246-5800
(800) 687-6667

LA MERIDIEN HOTEL
614 Canal St
(70127)
Rates: $270-$285
(504) 525-6500

MAISON ESPLANADE GUEST HOUSE BED & BREAKFAST
1244 Esplanade Ave (70116)
Rates: $39-$149
(504) 523-8080
(800) 892-5529

THE OLIVER ESTATE-A B&B
1425 N Prieur St
(70116)
Rates: $79-$295
(504) 949-9600

RATHBONE INN BED & BREAKFST
1227 Esplanade
(70116)
Rates: $90-$145
(504) 947-2100
(800) 947-2101

ROBERT GORDY HOUSE B&B
2630 Bell St
(70119)
Rates: $75-$95+
(504) 486-9424
(800) 889-7359

ROYAL SONESTA HOTEL
300 Bourbon St
(70130)
Rates: $185-$360
(504) 586-0300

RUE ROYAL INN
1006 Royal St
(70116)
Rates: $75-$145
(504) 524-3900
(800) 776-3901

SULLY MANSION
2631 Prtania St
(70130)
Rates: $50-$150
(504) 891-0457

WINDSOR COURT HOTEL
300 Gravier St
(70140)
Rates: $275-$675
(504) 523-6000

NEW ROADS

RIVER BLOSSOM INN B&B
300 N Carolina St
(70760)
Rates: $55-$75
(504) 638-8650

OPELOUSAS

BEST WESTERN OF OPELOUSAS
5791 I-49 Service Rd S (70570)
Rates: $65-$150
(337) 942-5540
(800) 528-1234
(888) 942-5540

DAYS INN
1649 I-49 Service
Rd S (70570)
Rates: $60-$80
(800) 329-7466

PORT ALLEN

SUPER 8 MOTEL
I-10 & Hwy 415
(70767)
Rates: $42-$52
(225) 381-9134
(800) 800-8000

RAYVILLE

COTTONLAND INN
116 Cottonland
(71269)
Rates: $45
(318) 728-5985
(800) 528-7732

RUSTON

ECONO LODGE
1301 Goodwin Rd
(71270)
Rates: $39-$79
(318) 255-0354
(800) 553-2666

RAMADA LIMITED
1951 N Service Rd
E (71270)
Rates: $65-$85
(318) 242-0070
(800) 272-6232

ST. FRANCISVILLE

BUTLER GREEN-WOOD B&B
8345 US Hwy 61
(70775)
Rates: $80-$100
(225) 635-6312

GREEN SPRINGS B&B
7463 Tunica Trace
(70775)
Rates: $95-$195
(225) 635-4232

LAKE ROSEMOUND INN B&B
10473 Lindsey Ln
(70775)
Rates: $70-$105
(225) 635-3176

ST. MARTINVILLE

MAISON BLEUE BED & BREAKFAST
417 N Main St
(70582)
Rates: $65-$75
(318) 394-1215

SCOTT

SLEEP INN
2140 W Willow St
(70583)
Rates: $59-$167
(318) 264-0408
(800) 753-3746

SHREVEPORT

DAYS INN
4935 W
Monkhouse Rd
(71109)
Rates: $29-$70
(318) 636-0800
(800) 329-7466

ECONO LODGE AIRPORT
4911 Monkhouse
Dr (71109)
Rates: $32-$59
(318) 636-0771
(800) 553-2666

HOWARD JOHNSON INN
1906 N Market St
(71107)
Rates: $44-$74
(318) 424-6621
(800) 446-4656

LA QUINTA INN
6700 Financial Cir
(71129)
Rates: $89-$109
(318) 671-1100
(800) 687 6667

MOTEL 6
4915 Monkhouse
Dr (71109)
Rates: $28-$32
(318) 631-9691
(800) 466-8356

RED ROOF INN
7296 Greenwood
Rd (71119)
Rates: $46-$68
(318) 938-5342
(800) 843-7663

SUPER 8 MOTEL
5204 Monkhouse
Dr (71109)
Rates: $41-$66
(318) 635-8888
(800) 800-8000

2439 FAIRFIELD-A B&B
2439 Fairfield Ave
(71104)
Rates: $95-$165
(318) 424-2424

SLIDELL

ECONO LODGE
58512 Tyler Dr
(70459)
Rates: $45-$100
(504) 641-2153
(800) 553-2666

LA QUINTA INN
794 E I-10 Service
Rd (70461)
Rates $49-$62
(504) 643-9770
(800) 687-6777

MOTEL 6
136 Taos St (70458)
Rates: $36-$40
(504) 649-7925
(800) 466-8356

SULPHUR

LA QUINTA INN
2600 S Ruth St
(70663)
Rates: $69-$89
(337) 527-8303
(800) 687-6667

TALLULAH

SUPER 8 MOTEL
1604 New Hwy 65
S (71282)
Rates: $39-$62
(318) 574-2000
(800) 800-8000

THIBODAUX

HOWARD JOHNSON
201 N Canal Blvd
(70301)
Rates: $67-$90
(504) 447-9071
(800) 952-2968

OAKES BED & BREAKFAST
1418 Himalaya
Ave (70301)
Rates: $75-$150
(504) 447-3764

WEST MONROE

HOLIDAY INN EXPRESS
401 Constitution
Dr (71292)
Rates: n/a
(318) 388-3810
(800) 465-4329

RED ROOF INN
102 Constitution
Dr (71292)
Rates: $45-$52
(318) 388-2420
(800) 843-7663

WINNSBORO

BEST WESTERN WINNSBORO
4198 Front St
(71295)
Rates: $45-$75
(318) 435-2000
(800) 528-1234

AREA CODES - If the local number doesn't connect, check for a new area code.

MAINE

AUBURN

AUBURN INN
Washington St at
Exit 12 (04210)
Rates: $49-$89
(207) 777-1777

AUGUSTA

**BEST WESTERN
SENATOR INN**
284 Western Ave
(04330)
Rates: $89-$149
(207) 622-5804
(800) 528-1234
(877) 772-2224

**ECHO LAKE
LODGE &
COTTAGES**
Rt 17 in Fayette
(04330)
Rates: n/a
(207) 685-9550

MOTEL 6
18 Edison Dr
(04330)
Rates: $42-$58
(207) 622-0000
(800) 466-8356

**TRAVELODGE
HOTEL**
390 Western Ave
(04330)
Rates: $70
(207) 622-6371
(800) 578-7878

BAILEY ISLAND

**LOG CABIN
LODGING**
Rt 24 (04003)
Rates: $120-$210
(207) 833-5546

BANGOR

BEST INN
570 Main St
(04401)
Rates: $75-$120
(207) 947-0566
(800) 237-8466

**BEST WESTERN
WHITE HOUSE**
155 Littlefield Ave
(04401)
Rates: $85-$100
(207) 862-3737
(800) 528-1234

COMFORT INN
750 Hogan Rd
(04401)
Rates: $39-$99
(207) 942-7899
(800) 228-5150

**COUNTRY INN
AT THE MALL**
936 Stillwater Ave
(04401)
Rates: $60-$80
(207) 941-0200

DAYS INN
250 Odlin Rd
(04401)
Rates: $44-$84
(207) 942-8272
(800) 329-7466

ECONO LODGE
327 Odlin Rd
(04401)
Rates: $45-$89
(207) 945-0111
(800) 553-2666

**HOLIDAY INN
MAIN STREET**
500 Main St
(04401)
Rates: $75-$90
(207) 947-8651
(800) 465-4329

**HOLIDAY INN
ODLIN ROAD**
404 Odlin Rd
(04401)
Rates: $73-$89
(207) 947-0101
(800) 465-4329

MAIN STREET INN
480 Main St
(04401)
Rates: $52-$62
(207) 942-5282
(800) 928-9877

MOTEL 6
1100 Hammond St
(04401)
Rates: $30-$43
(207) 947-6921
(800) 466-8356

**THE PHENIX INN
B&B**
20 Broad St (04401)
Rates: $90-$159
(207) 947-0411

RAMADA INN
357 Odlin Rd
(04401)
Rates: $49-$99
(207) 947-6961
(800) 272-6232

RIVERSIDE INN
495 State St
(04401)
Rates: $50-$88
(207) 947-3800
(800) 252-4044

RODEWAY INN
482 Odlin Rd
(04401)
Rates: $40-$80
(207) 942-6301
(800) 228-2000

BAR HARBOR

**BALANCE ROCK
INN HISTORIC
BED & BREAKFST**
21 Albert Meadow
(04609)
Rates: $225-$525
(207) 288-2610
(800) 753-0494

BEST WESTERN
Rt 3, RR 2, Box
1127 (04609
Rates: $98-$105
(207) 288-5823
(800) 528-1234

**CARRIAGE
HOUSE LOFT
APARTMENT**
Eagle Lake Rd
(04609)
Rates: $400-$800
Weekly
(207) 288-5154

**DAYS INN
FRENCHMANS
BAY**
120 Eden St
(04609)
Rates: $145
(207) 288-3321
(800) 329-7466

**GUEST
APARTMENT**
Eagle Lake Rd
(04609)
Rates: $400-$800
Weekly
(207) 288-5154

**HUTCHIN'S
MOUNTAIN VIEW
COTTAGES**
RFD 2, Box 1190
(04609)
Rates: $58-$84
(207) 288-4833
(800) 775-4833

**LEDGELAWN INN
HISTORIC B&B**
66 Mt. Desert St
(04609)
Rates: $95-$275
(207) 288-4596
(800) 274-5334

SUMMER HOUSE
Eagle Lake Rd
(04609)
Rates: $500-$1000
Weekly
(207) 288-5154

**WONDER VIEW
INN**
Box 25 (04609)
Rates: $55-$129
(207) 288-3358

BASS HARBOR

**BASS HARBOR
GABLES**
P.O. Box 396
(04653)
Rates: $125
(207) 244-3699

**QUIETSIDE
CAMPGROUND
& CABINS**
P O Box 10 (04653)
Rates: n/a
(207) 244-5992

BATH

**ADMIRAL'S
OCEAN INN**
RR 1, Box 5373
(04915)
Rates: $29-$75
(207) 338-4260

**BELFAST BAY
MEADOWS INN**
192 Northport Ave
(04915)
Rates: $75-$165
(207) 338-5715
(800) 335-2370

FAIRHAVEN INN
North Bath Rd
(04530)
Rates: $60-$90
(207) 443-4391

HOLIDAY INN
139 Richardson
Ave (04530)
Rates: $89-$134
(207) 443-9741
(800) 465-4329

**NEW MEADOWS
INN**
Bath Rd (West
Bath 04530)
Rates: $30-$58
(207) 443-3921

BELFAST

**ADMIRAL'S
OCEAN INN**
RR 1, Box 99A
(04915)
Rates: $48-$75
(207) 338-4260

**BELFAST BAY
MEADOWS INN**
192 Northport Ave
(04915)
Rates: $85-$165
(207) 338-5715
(800) 335-2370

BELFAST HARBOR INN
RR 5, Box 5230
(04915)
Rates: $59-$119
(207) 338-2740
(800) 545-8576

COMFORT INN
US 1, Box 35,
RR 5 (04915)
Rates:$129-$165
(207) 338-2090
(800) 228-5150

GULL MOTEL
RR 5, Box 5377
(04915)
Rates: $65-$79
(207) 338-4030

SEASCAPE MOTEL & COTTAGES
Rt 1 (04915)
Rates: $75-$99
(207) 338-2130

BETHEL

BETHEL INN & COUNTRY CLUB
1 Bethel Inn Dr
(04217)
Rates: $75-$400
(207) 824-2175
(800) 654-0125

THE BRIAR LEA BED & BREAKFAST
150 Mayville Rd
(04217)
Rates: $42-$129
(207) 824-4717

THE CAMERON HOUSE
Maston St Box 468
(04217)
Rates: n/a
(207) 824-3219

THE INN AT THE ROSTAY
186 Mayville Rd
(04217)
Rates: $45-$108
(207) 824-3111

L'AUBERGE HISTORIC COUNTRY INN
Mill Hill Rd
(04217)
Rates: $79-$129
(207) 824-2774

BINGHAM

BINGHAM MOTOR INN
Route 201 (04920)
Rates: $30-$68
(207) 672-4135

BLUE HILL

DEWING VACATION RENTAL
P. O. Box 988
(04614)
Rates: $600
Weekly
(207) 374-2888

BOOTHBAY

HILLSIDE ACRES MOTOR COURT
Adams Pond Rd
(04537)
Rates: $55-$75
(207) 633-3411

WHITE ANCHOR MOTEL
SR 27 (04537)
Rates: $39-$75
(207) 633-3788

BOOTHBAY HARBOR

CATWALK ON THE MILL POND
P.O. Box 447
(East Boothbay,
04554)
Rates: $750
Weekly
(207) 633-3270

HARBORSIDE RESORT
P. O. Box 516B
(04575)
Rates: $59-$109
(207) 633-5381
(800) 235-5402

THE LAWNMEER INN
SR 27, Box 505
(West Boothbay
Harbor 04538)
Rates: $95-$175
(207) 633-2544
(800) 633-7645

LEEWARD VILLAGE
Rt 96 Ocean Point
Rd (East Boothbay
04544)
Rates: $50-$150
(207) 633-3681

OCEAN POINT CABIN
HC Box 936 (East
Boothbay 04544)
Rates: n/a
(207) 633-2981

THE PINES MOTEL
Sunset Rd (04538)
Rates: $70-$90
(207) 633-4555

WELCH HOUSE INN B&B
56 McKown St
(04538)
Rates: $80-$155
(207) 633-3431
(800) 279-7313

BREWER

BREWER MOTOR INN
359 Wilson St
(04412)
Rates: $49-$59
(207) 989-4476

BROWNFIELD

FOOTHILLS FARM BED & BREAKFST
RR 1, Box 598
(04010)
Rates: n/a
(207) 935-3799

BRUNSWICK

THE ATRIUM MOTEL
Cooks Corner exit
(04011)
Rates: $45-$97
(207) 729-5555

MAINELINE MOTEL
133 Pleasant St
(04011)
Rates: $70-$100
(207) 725-8761

VIKING MOTOR INN
287 Bath Rd
(04011)
Rates: $64-$89
(207) 729-6661
(800) 429-6661

BUCKSPORT

BEST WESTERN JED PROUTY INN
52 Main St (04416)
Rates: $79-$119
(207) 469-3113
(800) 528-1234

BUCKSPORT MOTOR INN
151 Main St
(04416)
Rates: $33-$55
(207) 469-3111

SPRING FOUNTAIN MOTEL
RFD 2, Box 710
(04416)
Rates: $34-$75
(207) 469-3139

CALAIS

CALAIS MOTOR INN
293 Main St
(04619)
Rates: $69-$74
(207) 454-7111

INTERNATIONAL MOTEL
276 Main St
(04619)
Rates: $45-$120
(207) 454-7515

CAMDEN

BELOIN'S MOTEL & COTTAGES
U S Rt 1 (04843)
Rates: n/a
(207) 236-3262

BLUE HARBOR HOUSE COUNTRY INN
67 Elm St (04843)
Rates: $95-$175
(207) 236-3196
(800) 248-3196

CAMDEN HARBOUR INN
83 Bayview St
(04843)
Rates: $195-$255
(207) 236-4200

CAPE ELIZABETH

INN BY THE SEA
40 Bowery Beach
Rd (04107)
Rates: $269-$549
(207) 799-3134

CAPE NEDDICK

COUNTRY VIEW MOTEL & GUESTHOUSE
1521M Rt One
(03902)
Rates: n/a
(207) 363-7160
(800) 258-6598

CARIBOU

CARIBOU INN & CONV CENTER
Rt 3 (04736)
Rates: $60-$118
(207) 498-3733

CASTINE

THE HOLIDAY HOUSE
Box 215, Perkins
St (04421)
Rates: n/a
(207) 326-4335

THE MANOR
P. O. Box 276
(04421)
Rates: $65-$150
(207) 326-4861

PENTAGOT INN HISTORIC B&B
Main St (04421)
Rates: $99-$150
(207) 326-8616

CENTER LOVELL

HEWNOAKS HOUSEKEEPING COTTAGES
RR 1, Box 65
(04016)
Rates: n/a
(207) 925-6051

**WESTWAYS
ON KEZAR LAKE**
Rt 5 (04016)
Rates: $90+
(207) 928-2663

CORNISH

MIDWAY MOTEL
S Hiram Rd
(04020)
Rates: $49-$89
(207) 625-8835

DAMARISCOTTA

**COUNTY FAIR
MOTEL**
RFD 1, Box 36
(04543)
Rates: $64-$71
(207) 563-3769

EAGLE LAKE

**OVERLOOK
MOTEL**
N Main St (04739)
Rates: $94
(207) 444-4535

EAST BOOTHBAY

**SMUGGLER'S
COVE MOTOR
INN**
SR 96 (East
Boothbay 04544)
Rates: $89-$159
(207) 633-2800
(800) 633-3008

EAST HOLDEN

THE LUCERNE INN
Bar Harbor Rd
(04429)
Rates: $59-$89
(207) 843-5123

EAST WINTHROP

**LAKESIDE MOTEL
CABINS
& MARINA**
P. O. Box 236
(04343)
Rates: $35+
(800) 532-6892

EASTPORT

TODD HOUSE
Todd's Head
(04631)
Rates: $45-$80
(207) 853-2328

EDGECOMB

BAYVIEW INN
Rt 1 & Rt 27 S
(04556)
Rates: $60-$90
(207) 882-6911
(800) 530-2445

**SHEEPSCOT RIVER
INN**
306 Eddy Rd
(04556)
Rates: $80-$120
(207) 882-6343
(800) 437-5503

ELLSWORTH

**BROOKSIDE
MOTEL**
High St (04605)
Rates: $38-$88
(207) 667-2543

COMFORT INN
130 High St
(04605)
Rates: $129-$139
(207) 667-1345
(800) 228-5150

HOLIDAY INN
215 High St
(04605)
Rates: $130-$170
(207) 667-9341
(800) 465-4329
(800) 401-9341

JASPER'S MOTEL
200 High St
(04605)
Rates: $66-$87
(207) 667-5318

SUNRISE MOTEL
Bar Harbor Rd
(04605)
Rates: $25-$96
(207) 667-8452
(800) 419-2473

TRAVELODGE
321 High St
(04605)
Rates: $84-$108
(207) 667-5548
(800) 578-7878

TWILITE MOTEL

147 Bucksport Rd
(04605)
Rates: $66-$86
(207) 667-8165
(800) 395-5097

**THE WHITE
BIRCHES**
Hwy 1 (04605)
Rates: $90-$100
(207) 667-3621
(800) 435-1287
(800) 660-3621

FALMOUTH

**FALMOUTH INN
MOTEL**
209 US 1 (04105)
Rates: $38-$82
(207) 781-2120

FARMINGTON

MOUNT BLUE MOTEL
Wilton Rd (04938)
Rates: $40-$60
(207) 778-6004

FREEPORT

EAGLE MOTEL
215 US 1 S (04032)
Rates: $84-$94
(207) 865-4088
(800) 334-4088

FREEPORT INN
335 US 1 S (04032)
Rates: $100-$120
(207) 865-3106
(800) 998-2583

**ISAAC RANDALL
HOUSE HISTORIC
B&B**
5 Independence
Dr (04032)
Rates: $105-$145
(207) 865-9295
(800) 865-9295

**MAINE IDYLL
MOTOR COURT**
325 US Rt 1 N
(04032)
Rates: n/a
(207) 865-4201

GLEN COVE

**CLADDAGH
MOTEL**
US 1 (04846)
Rates: $36-$75
(207) 594-8479

GRAND LAKE STREAM

**LEEN'S LODGE
COTTAGES**
P O Box 40 (04637)
Rates: $90-$180
(207) 796-5575

GREENVILLE

**GREENWOOD
MOTEL**
SR 6 & 15 (04441)
Rates: $54-$75
(207) 695-3321

**KINEO VIEW
MOTOR LODGE**
SR 15 (04441)
Rates: $69-$79
(207) 695-4470
(800) 659-8439

**SPENCER POND
CAMPS CABINS**
Star Rt 76, Box 580
(04441)
Rates: $36-$48
(207) 695-2821

GREENVILLE JUNCTION

**CHALET
MOOSEHEAD
MOTEL**
Box 327 (04442)
Rates: $55-$65
(207) 695-2950
(800) 290-3645

**GREENWOOD
MOTEL**
SR 6 & 15 (04442)
Rates: $39-$75
(207) 695-3321
(800) 477-4386

HOULTON

SCOTTISH INNS
US 2A Bangor Rd
(04730)
Rates: $40-$60
(207) 532-2236
(800) 251-1962

JACKMAN

**BRIARWOOD
MOUNTAIN
RESORT**
P. O. Box 490
(04945)
Rates: $46-$54
(207) 668-7756

**SKY LODGE
MOTEL/CABINS**
U S 201 (04945)
Rates: $50-$165
(207) 668-2171

**TUCKAWAY
SHORES**
Forest St (04945)
Rates: $25
(207) 668-3351

JONESBORO

WINDRISE FARM
Box 47, Evergreen
Pt Rd (04648)
Rates: $250-$500
Weekly
(207) 434-2701

KENNEBUNK

**LODGE AT
KENNEBUNK**
95 Alewive Rd
(04043)
Rates: $69-$99
(207) 985-9010

KENNEBUNK-PORT

**THE COLONY
RESORT HOTEL**
140 Ocean Ave
(04046)
Rates: $175-$427
(207) 967-3331

**CABOT COVE
COTTAGES**
South Maine St,
Box 1082 (04046)
Rates: $85-$145
(207) 967-5424
(800) 962-5424

**FOUR ACRES
COTTAGES**
44 Mills Rd
(04046)
Rates: n/a
(207) 967-2735

**LODGE AT
TURBAT'S CREEK**
Turbat's Creek Rd
(04046)
Rates: $95-$139
(207) 967-8700

**SEASIDE HOUSE
MOTOR INN &
COTTAGES**
Beach St, Gooch's
Beach (04046)
Rates: $85-$160
(207) 967-4461

KINGFIELD

**THE HERBERT
HOTEL**
Box 67 (04947)
Rates: $38-$125
(800) 843-4372

KITTERY

**ENCHANTED
NIGHTS B&B**
29 Wentworth St
(03904)
Rates: $58-$132
(207) 439-1489

SUPER 8 MOTEL
85 US Rt 1 Bypass
S (03904)
Rates: $35-$94
(207) 439-2000
(800) 800-8000

LEEDS

**ANGELL COVE
COTTAGES**
Box 29, Bishop
Hill Rd (04263)
Rates: $575
Weekly
(207) 524-5041

LEWISTON

HOLIDAY MOTEL
1905 Lisbon Rd
(04240)
Rates: $19-$41
(207) 783-2277

MOTEL 6
516 Pleasant St
(04240)
Rates: $43-$59
(207) 782-6558
(800) 466-8356

LIMERICK

**JEREMIAH
MASON HOUSE
BED & BREAKFAST**
5 Main St (04048)
Rates: $50-$60
(207) 793-4858

LINCOLN

**BRIARWOOD
MOTOR INN**
P. O. Box 628 (04457)
Rates: $40-$55
(207) 794-6731

**LINCOLN HOUSE
MOTEL**
85 Main St (04457)
Rates: $32-$42
(207) 794-3096

LINCOLNVILLE

**PINE GROVE
COTTAGES**
RR 3 (04849)
Rates: $65-$125
(207) 236-2929
(800) 530-5265

LUBEC

EASTLAND MOTEL
US 1 & SR 189
(04652)
Rates: $38-$60
(207) 733-5501

MACHIAS

BLUEBIRD MOTEL
US 1, Box 45 (04654)
Rates: $54-$60
(207) 255-3332

**MACHIAS
MOTOR INN**
26 E Main St (04654)
Rates: $60-$65
(207) 255-4861

**MAINELAND
MOTEL**
RR 1 (East
Machias 04630)
Rates: $35-$53
(207) 255-3334

MANSET

SEAWALL MOTEL
Rt 102A (04656)
Rates: $40-$85
(207) 244-9250
(800) 248-9250

MATINICUS

**TUCKANUCK
LODGE**
Shag Hollow Rd
(04851)
Rates: $40-$80
(207) 366-3830

MEDWAY

GATEWAY INN
Rt 157 (04460)
Rates: $45-$100
(207) 746-3193

**KATAHDIN
SHADOWS
MOTEL**
I-95, Exit 56
(04460)
Rates: $29-$39
(207) 746-5162
(800) 794-5267

MILFORD

MILFORD MOTEL
Rt 2 E (04461)
Rates: $54-$84
(207) 827-3200
(800) 282-3330

MILLINOCKET

**THE ATRIUM INN
& HEALTH CLUB**
740 Central St
(04462)
Rates: $65-$90
(207) 723-4555

**BEST WESTERN
HERITAGE
MOTOR INN**
935 Central St
(04462)
Rates: $79-$99
(207) 723-9777
(800) 528-1234

**PAMOLA
MOTOR LODGE**
973 Central St
(04462)
Rates: $29-$54
(207) 723-9746

MOODY

**NE'R BEACH
MOTEL**
SR 98 (US 1,
Box 389, 04054)
Rates: $44-$109
(207) 646-2636

MOOSE RIVER

**SKY LODGE
CABINS & MOTEL**
Sky Lodge, Rt 201
(05945)
Rates: n/a
(207) 668-2171
(800) 307-0098

NAPLES

**AUGUSTUS BOVE
HOUSE B&B**
Rts 302 & 114
(04055)
Rates: $79-$175
(207) 693-6365

NEWPORT

LOVLEY'S MOTEL
P. O. Box 147
(04953)
Rates: $30-$90
(207) 368-4311

NOBLEBORO

**HOUSEKEEPING
COTTAGE**
RR1, Box 820
(Jefferson, 04348)
Rates: $150-$300
Weekly
(207) 832-7055

**NOBLEBORO
CABIN**
631 W Neck Rd
(04555)
Rates: $500
Weekly
(207) 563-8152
(207) 563-8677

NORTH ANSON

**EMBDEN LAKE
RESORT**
RR 1, Box 3395
(04958)
Rates: $110-$130
(207) 566-7501

NORWAY

**LEDGEWOOD
MOTEL**
RFD 2, Box 30
(04268)
Rates: $38-$60
(207) 743-6347

OGUNQUIT

**THE CAPTAIN
THOMAS RESORT
MOTEL**
305 US 1 (03907)
Rates: $129-$219
(207) 646-4600

NORSEMAN MOTOR INN

P. O. Box 896
(03907)
Rates: $50-$185
(207) 646-7024

**STUDIO EAST
MOTOR INN**
43 Main St (03907)
Rates: $109-$129
(207) 646-7297

WHITE ROSE INN
89 Rt 1 (03907)
Rates: $95-$150
(207) 646-3432

OLD ORCHARD BEACH

**BEAU RIVAGE
MOTEL**
54 E Grand Ave
(04064)
Rates: $99-$160
(207) 934-4668
(800) 939-4668

CREST MOTEL
35 E Grand Ave
(04064)
Rates: $128-$162
(207) 934-4060
(800) 909-4060

FLAGSHIP MOTEL
54 W Grand Ave
(04064)
Rates: $69-$109
(207) 934-4866
(800) 486-1681

**GRAND BEACH
INN**
198 E Grand Ave
(04064)
Rates: $59-$179
(207) 934-4621
(800) 926-3242

**OLD COLONIAL
MOTEL**
61 W Grand Ave
(04064)
Rates: $105-$175
(207) 934-9862
(888) 225-5989

SEA VIEW MOTEL
65 W Grand Ave
(04064)
Rates: $70-$190
(207) 934-4180

WAVES OCEAN-FRONT RESORT
87 W Grand Ave
(04064)
Rates: $100-$159
(207) 934-4949

ORONO

BEST WESTERN BLACK BEAR INN
4 Godfrey Dr
(04473)
Rates: $70-$110
(207) 866-7120
(800) 528-1234

UNIVERSITY MOTOR INN
5 College Ave
(04473)
Rates: $45-$68
(207) 866-4921

PATTEN

MT CHASE LODGE & COUNTRY INN
Shin Pond Rd,
Box 281 (04765)
Rates: n/a
(207) 528-2183

SHIN POND VILLAGE
RR 1, Box 280-M
(04765)
Rates: $30-$62
(207) 528-2900

PORTLAND

ANDREWS LODGING B&B
417 Auburn St
(04103)
Rates: $78-$150
(207) 797-9157

BLACK COVE INN BED & BREAKFST
575 Forest Ae
(04103)
Rates: $100
(207) 772-2557

DOUBLETREE HOTEL
1230 Congress St
(04103)
Rates: $153
(207) 774-5611
(800) 222-8733

HOLIDAY INN WEST
81 Riverside St
(04103)
Rates: $114-$143
(207) 774-5601
(800) 465-4329

HOWARD JOHNSON
155 Riverside
(04103)
Rates: $99-$135
(207) 774-5861
(800) 446-4656

INN AT ST. JOHN
939 Congress St
(04102)
Rates: $35-$115
(207) 773-6481
(800) 636-9127

MOTEL 6
One Riverside St
(04103)
Rates: $36-$66
(207) 775-0111
(800) 466-8356

RADISSON EASTLAND
157 High St
(04101)
Rates: $85-$135
(207) 775-5411
(800) 333-3333

RAMADA LIMITED
1150 Brighton Ave
(04102)
Rates: $49-$149
(207) 775-3711
(800) 272-6232

PRESQUE ISLE

COUNTRY VIEW HOTEL & CONV CENTER
US 1 (04769)
Rates: $60-$120
(207) 764-3321

NORTHERN LIGHTS MOTEL
692 Main St
(04769)
Rates: $24-$39
(207) 764-4441

RANGELEY

GRANTS KENNEBAGO CAMP CABINS
P O Box 786
(04970)
Rates: n/a
(207) 282-5264
(207) 864-3608

RANGELEY INN & MOTOR LODGE
Box 160 (04970)
Rates: $52-$120
(207) 864-3341
(800) 666-3687

TOWN & LAKE MOTEL
Main St (04970)
Rates: $40-$50
(207) 864-3755

ROCKLAND

NAVIGATOR MOTOR INN
520 Main St
(04841)
Rates: $75-$110
(207) 594-2131
(800) 545-8026

OAKLAND SEASHORE COTTAGES & MOTEL
112 Dearborn Ln
(04841)
Rates: $35-$100
(207) 594-8104

TRADE WINDS MOTOR INN
2 Park Drive
Center (04841)
Rates: $69-$139
(207) 596-6661
(800) 834-3130

ROCKWOOD

ABNAKI COTTAGES
Abnaki Rd,
P. O. Box 6 (04478)
Rates: n/a
(207) 534-7318

THE BIRCHES RESORT
Box 81 (04478)
Rates: $35-$950
(207) 534-7305

MAYNARDS IN MAINE
P. O. Box 228
(04478)
Rates: n/a
(207) 534-7702

RUMFORD

LINNELL MOTEL & RESTINN CONF CENTER
US 2 (04276)
Rates: $50-$75
(207) 364-4511

MADISON MOTOR INN
Rt 2 (04276)
Rates: $55-$125
(207) 364-7973

SACO

SACO MOTEL
473 Main St
(04072)
Rates: $45-$70
(207) 284-6952

TOURIST HAVEN MOTEL
757 Portland Rd
(04072)
Rates: $35-$60
(207) 284-7251

SANFORD

BAR-H MOTEL
581 Main St
(04073)
Rates: $45-$89
(207) 324-4662

SCARBOROUGH

PRIDE MOTEL & COTTAGES
677 US 1 (04070)
Rates: $60-$105
(207) 883-4816
(800) 424-3350

RESIDENCE INN BY MARRIOTT
800 Roundwood
Dr (04074)
Rates: n/a
(207) 883-0400
(800) 331-3131

SEAL COVE

THE DOCKSIDE
P O Box 124
(04674)
Rates: $60+
(207) 244-5221

SEARSPORT

LIGHT'S MOTEL
RFD Box 349
(04974)
Rates: $33-$46
(207) 548-2405

SEBASCO ESTATES

SMALL POINT BED & BREAKFAST
HCR 32, Box 250
(04565)
Rates: $40-$120
(207) 389-1716

SKOWHEGAN

BELMONT MOTEL
P. O. Box 160
(04976)
Rates: $45-$55
(207) 474-8315
(800) 235-6669

BREEZY ACRES MOTEL
US 201 (04976)
Rates: $40-$68
(207) 474-2703

SOUTH PORTLAND

AMERISUITES
303 Sable Oaks Dr
(04106)
Rates: $99-$159
(207) 775-3900
(800) 833-1516

BEST WESTERN MERRY MANOR INN
700 Main St
(04106)
Rates: $119-$149
(207) 774-6151
(800) 528-1234

HOWARD JOHNSON
675 Main St
(04106)
Rates: $94-$159
(207) 775-5343
(800) 446-4656

AREA CODES - If the local number doesn't connect, check for a new area code.

MARRIOTT HOTEL
200 Sable Oaks Dr
(04106)
Rates: $189
(207) 871-8000
(800) 228-9290

SOUTH PRINCETON

HIDEAWAY ON POCOMOOSHINE LAKE
Mary Wallace, The Hideaway (04668)
Rates: n/a
(207) 427-6183

SPRUCE HEAD

CRAIGNAIR INN AT CLARK IS.
533 Clark Island Rd (04859)
Rates: $48-$120
(207) 594-7644

STRATTON

SPILLOVER MOTEL
P. O. Box 427
(04982)
Rates: $42-$68
(207) 246-6571

TRENTON

DAYS INN
Rt 1 (04605)
Rates: $49-$89
(207) 667-9506
(800) 329-7466

WATERFORD

WATERFORD INNE
Box 149 (04088)
Rates: $74-$99
(207) 583-4037

WATERVILLE

THE ATRIUM MOTEL
332 Main St
(04901)
Rates: $45-$80
(207) 873-2777

BEST WESTERN INN
356 Main St
(04901)
Rates: $95-$140
(207) 873-3335
(800) 528-1234

BUDGET HOST AIRPORT INN
400 Kennedy Memorial Dr
(04901)
Rates: $60-$100
(207) 873-3366
(800) 876-2463

ECONO LODGE
455 Kennedy Memorial Dr
(04901)
Rates: $65-$80
(207) 872-5577
(800) 553-2666

HOLIDAY INN
375 Main St
(04901)
Rates: $75-$105
(207) 873-0111
(800) 465-4329
(800) 785-0111

WATERVILLE MOTOR LODGE
320 Kennedy Memorial Dr
(04901)
Rates: $28-$54
(207) 873-0141

WELLS

GARRISON SUITES MOTEL & COTTAGES
1099 Post Rd
(04090)
Rates: $35-$110
(207) 646-3497
(800) 646-3497

WEST KENNEBUNK

ALEWIFE COUNTRY MOTOR INN
P. O. Box 575
(04094)
Rates: $40-$70
(207) 985-6525

WEST TREMONT

QUIETSIDE CAMPGROUND & CABINS
P O Box 8 (04692)
Rates: n/a
(207) 244-5992

WESTBROOK

SUPER 8 MOTEL
208 Larrabee Rd
(04092)
Rates: $41-$84
(207) 854-1881
(800) 800-8000

WILTON

WHISPERING PINES MOTEL
183 Lake Rd
(04294)
Rates: $51-$91
(207) 645-3721

WINTERPORT

THE COLONIAL WINTERPORT INN
P. O. Box 525
(04496)
Rates: $50-$65
(207) 223-5307

YARMOUTH

DOWN-EAST VILLAGE MOTEL
705 US Rt 1
(04096)
Rates: $89-$99
(207) 846-5161
(800) 782-9338

YORK

YORK COMMONS INN
362 U S 1 (03909)
Rates: $100-$110
(207) 363-8903

MARYLAND

ABERDEEN

BUDGET INN
1112 S
Philadelphia Blvd
(21001)
Rates: n/a
(410) 272-2401

CAVALIER MOTEL
1109 S
Philadelphia Blvd
(21001)
Rates: n/a
(410) 272-4100

DAYS INN
783 W Bel Air Ave
(21001)
Rates: $45-$55
(410) 272-8500
(800) 329-7466

**FOUR POINTS
SHERATON
HOTEL**
980 Hospitality
Way (21001)
Rates: $79-$109
(410) 273-6300
(800) 325-3535

**HOLIDAY INN
CHESAPEAKE
HOUSE**
1007 Beards Hill
Rd (21001)
Rates: $95-$125
(410) 272-8100
(800) 465-4329

KNIGHTS INN
744 S Philadelphia
Blvd (21001)
Rates: $35-$49
(410) 272-3600
(800) 843-5644

MURLYN INN
424 S Philadelphia
Blvd (21001)
Rates: n/a
(410) 272-3666

RED ROOF INN
988 Hospitality
Way (21001)
Rates: $60-$74
(410) 273-7800
(800) 842-7663

SUPER 8 MOTEL
1008 Beards Hill
Rd (21001)
Rates: $43-$63
(410) 272-5420
(800) 800-8000

ANNAPOLIS

**AMERICAN
HERITAGE B&B**
108 Charles St
(21401)
Rates: n/a
(410) 280-1620

DAYS INN
1542 Whitehall Rd
(21401)
Rates: $49-$129
(410) 974-4440
(800) 329-7466

ECONO LODGE
2451 Riva Rd
(21401)
Rates: $59-$295
(410) 224-4317
(800) 553-2666

**LOEWS
ANNAPOLIS
HOTEL**
126 West St (21401)
Rates: $135-$185
(410) 263-7777
(800) 526-2593

MAINSTAY SUITES
120 Admiral
Cochrane Dr
(21401)
Rates: $59-$125
(410) 571-6600
(800) 660-6246

RADISSON HOTEL
210 Holiday Ct
(21401)
Rates: $69-$119
(410) 224-3150
(800) 333-3333

**RESIDENCE INN
BY MARRIOTT**
170 Admiral
Cochrane Dr
(21401)
Rates: $160-$184
(410) 573-0300
(800) 331-313

BALTIMORE

**ADMIRAL FELL
INN**
888 S Broadway
(21201)
Rates: $139-$219
(410) 522-7377

**BEST INN &
SUITES**
5701 Baltimore
Natl Pike (21228)
Rates: $55-$150
(410) 747-8900
(800) 237-8466

**BILTMORE SUITES
HOTEL**
205 W Madison St
(21201)
Rates: n/a
(410) 728-6550

**COMFORT INN
BWI AIRPORT**
6921 Baltimore-
Annapolis Blvd
(21225)
Rates: $89-$129
(410) 789-9100
(800) 228-5150

**DOUBLETREE INN
AT THE
COLONNADE**
4 W University
Pkwy (21218)
Rates: $119-$275
(410) 235-5400
(800) 222-8733

**HOLIDAY INN
BWI AIRPORT**
1800 Belmont Ave
(21244)
Rates: $77
(410) 265-1400
(800) 465-4329

**HOWARD
JOHNSON
EXPRESS**
5701 Baltimore
Natl Pike (21228)
Rates: $45-$90
(410) 744-8900
(800) 446-4656

MOTEL 6
1654 Whitehead
Ct (21207)
Rates: $40-$46
(410) 265-7660
(800) 466-8356

**SHERATON INTL
HOTEL**
7032 Elm Rd
(21240)
Rates: $65-$150
(410) 859-3300
(800) 638-5858

**SLEEP INN &
SUITES AIRPORT**
6055 Belle Grove
Rd (21225)
Rates: $69-$129
(410) 789-9100
(800) 753-3746

SUPER 8 MOTEL
98 Stemmers Run
Rd (21221)
Rates: $43-$71
(410) 780-0030
(800) 800-8000

**THE TREMONT
HOTEL**
8 E Pleasant St
(21202)
Rates: $115
(410) 576-1200
(800) 873-6668

**TREMONT PLAZA
HOTEL**
222 St. Paul Pl
(21202)
Rates: $115-$155
(410) 727-2222
(800) 873-6668

BELTSVILLE

**SHERATON
HOTEL**
4095 Powder Mill
(20705)
Rates: $149
(301) 937-4422
(800) 325-3535

BETHESDA

MARRIOTT SUITES
6711 Democracy
Blvd (20817)
Ratews: $99-$160
(301) 897-5600
(800) 228-9290

**RESIDENCE INN
BY MARRIOTT**
7335 Wisconsin
Ave (20814)
Rates: $209
(301) 718-0200
(800) 331-3131

BOWIE

**RIP'S COUNTRY
INN**
3809 N Crain Hwy
(20717)
Rates: n/a
(301) 262-0900

BRANDYWINE

CADILLAC MOTEL
16101 Crain Hwy
SW (20613)
Rates: n/a
(301) 372-6600

BUCKEYSTOWN

**CATOCTIN INN &
CONFERENCE
CENTER B&B**
3619 Buckeystown
Pike (21717)
Rates: n/a
(301) 874-5555
(800) 730-5550

AREA CODES - If the local number doesn't connect, check for a new area code.

CALIFORNIA

SUPER 8 MOTEL
290 Three Notch
Rd (20619)
Rates: $48-$68
(301) 862-9822
(800) 800-8000

CAMBRIDGE

**COMMODORES
COTTAGE**
215 Glenburn Ave
(21613)
Rates: n/a
(410) 228-6938
(800) 228-6938

**SARKE
PLANTATION B&B**
6033 Todd Point
Rd (21613)
Rates: n/a
(410) 228-7020
(800) 814-7020

SHOALS INN
Rt 50 E (21612)
Rates: n/a
(410) 228-6900

CAMP SPRINGS

MOTEL 6
5701 Allentown
Rd (20746)
Rates: $39-$51
(301) 702-1061
(800) 466-8356

**RAMADA INN
ANDREWS AFB**
5151 Allentown
Rd (20746)
Rates: $50-$89
(301) 899-7700
(800) 272-6232

CAPITAL
HEIGHTS

MOTEL 6
75 Hampton Park
Blvd (20743)
Rates: $46-$52
(301) 499-0800
(800) 466-8356

CENTREVILLE

HILLSIDE MOTEL
2630 Centreville
Rd (21617)
Rates: n/a
(410) 758-2270
(800) 705-2270

ROSE TREE B&B
116 S Commerce
St (21617)
Rates: n/a
(410) 758-3991

CHESTERTOWN

COURTYARD INN
Rt 213 S (21620)
Rates: n/a
(410) 778-2755

**FOXLEY MANOR
MOTEL**
609 Washington
Ave (21620)
Rates: n/a
(410) 778-3200

**IMPERIAL HOTEL
& RESTAURANT**
208 High St (21620)
Rates: n/a
(410) 778-2100

**THE PARKER
HOUSE B&B**
108 Spring Ave
(21620)
Rates: n/a
(410) 778-9041

**THE RIVER INN AT
ROLPH'S WHARF**
1008 Rolph's
Wharf Rd (21620)
Rates: n/a
(410) 778-6347
(800) 894-6347

CHEVERLY

**HOWARD
JOHNSON INN**
5811 Anapolis Rd
(20784)
Rates: $56-$105
(301) 779-7700
(800) 274-4938

CHEVY CHASE

**EMBASSY SUITES
CHEVY CHASE
PAVILLION**
4300 Military Rd
NW (20015)
Ratews: $119-$165
(301) 362-9300
(800) 362-2779

CHURCH CREEK

**LOBLOLLY
LANDINGS /
LODGE**
2142 Liners Rd
(21622)
Rates: n/a
(410) 397-3033
(800) 862-7452

CLEAR
SPRINGS

**CEDAR CREST
COTTAGE B&B**
12527 Rockdale
Rd (21722)
Rates: n/a
(202) 363-0976
(800) 484-1453

COCKEYSVILLE

**RESIDENCE INN
BY MARRIOTT**
10710 Beaver Dam
Rd (21030)
Rates: n/a
(410) 584-7370
(800) 331-3131

COLLEGE PARK

**COLLEGE MOTOR
INN**
5043 Branchville
Rd (20740)
Rates: n/a
(301) 441-3707

PARK VIEW INN
9020 Baltimore
Blvd (20740)
Rates: $50-$60
(301) 441-8110

**QUALITY INN
& SUITES**
7200 Baltimore
Blvd (20740)
Rates: $49-$129
(301) 864-5820
(800) 228-5151

COLUMBIA

**COLUMBIA INN
HOTEL & CONF
CENTER**
10207 Wincopin
Circle (21044)
Rates: $139-$149
(410) 730-3900
(800) 638-2817

**RESIDENCE INN
BY MARRIOTT**
4910 Executive
Park Dr (21045)
Rates: n/a
(410) 997-7200
(800) 331-3131

**STAYBRIDGE
SUITES BY
HOLIDAY INN**
8844 Columbia
200 Pkwy (21045)
Rates: n/a
(410) 964-9494
(800) 238-8000

**WELLESLEY INN &
SUITES**
8890 Stanford
Blvd (21045)
Rates: $79-$125
(410) 872-2994
(800) 444-8888

CUMBERLAND

**CUMBERLAND
MOTEL**
10900 Mason Rd
(21502)
Rates: n/a
(301) 724-7790

DIPLOMAT MOTEL
17012 McMullen
Hwy (21502)
Rates: n/a
(301) 729-2311

HOLIDAY INN
100 S George St
(21502)
Rates: $89-$109
(301) 724-8800
(800) 465-4329

EASTON

**ATLANTIC
BUDGET INN**
8058 Ocean
Gateway (21601)
Rates: n/a
(410) 822-2200

COMFORT INN
8523 Ocean
Gateway (21601)
Rates: $59-$149
(410) 820-8333
(800) 228-5150

DAYS INN
7018 Ocean
Gateway (21601)
Rates: $86-$115
(410) 822-4600
(800) 329-7466

ECONO LODGE
8175 Ocean
Gateway (21601)
Rates: $49-$99
(410) 820-5555
(800) 553-2666

**THE TIDEWATER
INN**
101 E Dover St
(21601)
Rates: $95-$295
(410) 822-1300

EDGEWOOD

**BEST WESTERN
INVITATION INN**
1709 Edgewood
Rd (21040)
Rates: $59-$99
(410) 679-9700
(800) 528-1234
(800) 408-4748

**COMFORT INN
CONFERENCE CTR**
1700 Van Bibber
Rd (21040)
Rates: $55-$195
(410) 679-0770
(800) 228-5150

**MOTEL
EDGEWOOD**
2209 Pulaski Hwy
(21040)
Rates: $36-$42
(410) 676-4466

ELKRIDGE

**COPPER
STALLION INN**
7615 Washington
Blvd (21075)
Rates: n/a
(410) 799-1900

EXEC MOTEL
6265 Washington
Blvd (21075)
Rates: n/a
(410) 796-4466

MARYLAND

ELKTON

ECONO LODGE
311 Belle Hill Rd
(21921)
Rates: $35-$70
(410) 392-5010
(800) 553-2666

ELKTON LODGE
200 Belle Hill Rd
(21921)
Rates: n/a
(410) 398-9400

GARDEN COTTAGE AT SINKING SPRINGS FARM
234 Blair Shore Rd
(21921)
Rates: n/a
(410) 398-5566

KNIGHTS INN
626 Belle Hill Rd
(21921)
Rates: $35-$75
(410) 392-6680
(800) 843-5644

MOTEL 6
223 Belle Hill Rd
(21921)
Rates: $34-$40
(410) 392-5020
(800) 466-8356

SUTTON MOTEL
405 E Pulaski
Hwy (21921)
Rates: $31-$37
(410) 398-3830

ELLICOTT CITY

FOREST MOTEL
10021 Baltimore
Natl Pike (21042)
Rates: n/a
(410) 465-2090

FAULKNER

TOWN & COUNTRY MOTEL
10870 Crain Hwy
(20632)
Rates: n/a
(301) 934-8252

FREDERICK

COMFORT INN
420 Prospect Blvd
(21701)
Rates: $69-$89
(301) 695-6200
(800) 228-5150

ECONO LODGE
6005 Urbana Pike
(21704)
Rates: $45-$69
(301) 698-0555
(800) 553-2666

HAMPTON INN
5311 Buckeystown
Pike (21701)
Rates: $89
(301) 698-2500
(800) 426-7866

HOLIDAY INN
999 W Patrick St
(21702)
Rates: $70-$85
(301) 662-5141
(800) 465-4329

HOLIDAY INN EXPRESS FSK MALL
5579 Spectrum Dr
(21701)
Rates: $72
(301) 695-2881
(800) 465-4329

HOLIDAY INN FSK MALL
5400 Holiday Dr
(21701)
Rates: $79-$99
(301) 694-7500
(800) 465-4329

MAINSTAY SUITES
7310 Executive
Way (21703)
Rates: $59-$119
(800) 660-6246

MASSER'S MOTEL
1505 W Patrick St
(21701)
Rates: n/a
(301) 663-3698

RED HORSE MOTOR INN
998 W Patrick St
(21702)
Rates: $44-$67
(301) 662-0281
(800) 245-6701

SLEEP INN
5361 Spectrum Dr
(21703)
Rates: $59-$99
(800) 753-3746

TRAVELODGE
200 E Walser Dr
(21704)
Rates: $38-$85
(301) 663-0500
(800) 578-7878

FROSTBURG

CHARLIE'S MOTEL
220 W Main St
(21532)
Rates: n/a
(301) 689-6557

COMFORT INN
11100 New George
Creek Rd (21532)
Rates: $56-$87
(301) 689-2050
(800) 228-5150

FAILINGER'S HOTEL GUNTER
11 W Main St
(21532)
Rates: n/a
(301) 689-6511

GAITHERS-BURG

COMFORT INN
16216 Frederick
(20877)
Rates: $59-$119
(301) 330-0023
(800) 228-5150

ECONO LODGE
18715 Frederick Ave
(20879)
Rates: $45-$75
(301) 963-3840
(800) 553-2666

HILTON HOTEL
620 Perry Pkwy
(20877)
Rates: $79-$109
(301) 977-8900
(800) 445-8667

RED ROOF INN
497 Quince
Orchard Rd
(20878)
Rates: $70-$95
(301) 977-3311
(800) 843-7663

RESIDENCE INN BY MARRIOTT
9721
Washingtonian
Blvd (20879)
Rates: $194
(301) 590-3003
(800) 331-3131

SUMMERFIELD SUITES
200 Skidmore
Blvd (20879)
Rates: $150
(301) 527-6000
(800) 833-4353

TOWNPLACE SUITES BY MARRIOTT
212 Perry Pkwy
(20879)
Rates: $59-$109
(301) 590-2300
(800) 257-3000

GERMANTOWN

HOMESTEAD VILLAGE GUEST STUDIOS
20141 Century
Blvd (20874)
Rates: $69-$104
(301) 515-4500
(888) 782-9473

GLEN BURNIE

DAYS INN
6600 Ritchie Hwy
(21061)
Rates: $89-$119
(410) 761-8300
(800) 329-7466

HOLIDAY INN NORTH
6323 Ritchie Hwy
(21061)
Rates: $99
(410) 636-4300
(800) 465-4329

GRANTSVILLE

HOLIDAY INN
2541 Chestnut
Ridge Rd (21536)
Rates: $49-$79
(301) 895-5993
(800) 465-4329

LITTLE MEADOWS MOTEL
12676 National
Hwy (21536)
Rates: n/a
(301) 895-5142

WALNUT RIDGE BED & BREAKFST
92 Main St (21536)
Rates: $65-$75
(301) 895-4248

GRASONVILLE

CHESAPEAKE MOTEL
107 Hissey Rd
(21638)
Rates: n/a
(410) 827-7272
(800) 822-7272

LANDS END MANOR ON THE BAY B&B
232 Prospect Bay
Dr (21638)
Rates: n/a
(410) 827-6284

GREENBELT

MARRIOTT SUITES
6400 Ivy Lane
(20770)
Rates: $69-$119
(301) 441-3700
(800) 228-9290

HAGERSTOWN

ECONO LODGE
18221 Mason-
Dixon Rd (21740)
Rates: $56-$65
(301) 791-3560
(800) 553-2666

FOUR POINTS SHERATON INN
1910 Dual Hwy
(21740)
Rates: $56-$69
(301) 790-3010
(800) 325-3535

MOTEL 6
11321 Massey
Blvd (21740)
Rates: $44-$60
(301) 582-4445
(800) 466-8356

SLEEP INN
I-70 Exit 29 & Rt
65 (21740)
Rates: $39-$89
(800) 753-3746

STATE LINE MOTEL
18221 Mason
Dixon Rd (21740)
Rates: $32-$42
(301) 733-8262

SUNDAY'S B&B
39 Broadway
(21740)
Rates: n/a
(301) 797-4331
(800) 221-4828

SUPER 8 MOTEL
1220 Dual Hwy
(21740)
Rates: $42-$55
(301) 739-5800
(800) 800-8000

VENICE INN
431 Dual Hwy
(21740)
Rates: $65-$74
(301) 733-0830

HANOVER

HOLIDAY INN BWI AIRPORT
7481 Ridge Rd
(21076)
Rates: $89-$150
(410) 684-3388
(800) 465-4329

RED ROOF INN BWI PARKWAY
7306 Parkway Dr
(21076)
Rates: $55-$81
(410) 712-4070
(800) 843-7663

HUNT VALLEY

EMBASSY SUITES HOTEL
213 International
Cir (21030)
Rates: $99-$189
(410) 584-1400
(800) 362-2779

MARRIOTT'S INN
245 Shawan Rd
(21031)
Rates: $95+
(410) 785-7000
(800) 228-9290

RESIDENCE INN BY MARRIOTT
10710 Beaver Dam
Rd (21030)
Rates: $125-$169
(410) 584-7370
(800) 331-3131

JESSUP

GREENWAY MOTEL
7731 Washington
Blvd (20794)
Rates: n/a
(410) 799-2975

RED ROOF INN
8000 Washington
Blvd (20794)
Rates: $58-$71
(410) 796-0380
(800) 843-7663

JOPPA

SUPER 8 MOTEL
1015 Pulaski Hwy
(21085)
Rates: $60-$76
(410) 676-2700
(800) 800-8000

KNOXVILLE

HILLSIDE MOTEL
19105 Keep Tryst
Rd (21758)
Rates: n/a
(301) 834-8144

LA PLATA

BEST WESTERN INN
400 South Hwy
(20646)
Rates: $73-$103
(301) 934-4900
(800) 528-1234
(877) 356-4900

LANHAM

BEST WESTERN HOTEL CAPITAL BELTWAY
5910 Princess
Garden Pkwy
(20706)
Rates: $59-$99
(301) 459-1000
(800) 528-1234
(800) 866-4458

RED ROOF INN
9050 Lanham
Severn Rd (20706)
Rates: $41-$58
(301) 731-8830
(800) 843-7663

LARGO

CLUB HOTEL BY DOUBLETREE
9100 Basil Ct
(20774)
Rates: $93-$103
(301) 773-0700
(888) 444-2582

LAUREL

COMFORT SUITES LAUREL LAKE
13302 Laurel Pl
(20707)
Rates: $79-$195
(301) 206-2600
(800) 228-5150

ECONO LODGE LAUREL RACETRACK
9700 Washington
Blvd (20723)
Rates: $44-$74
(301) 776-8008
(800) 553-2666

MOTEL 6
3510 Old
Annapolis Rd
(20724)
Rates: $37-$52
(301) 497-1544
(800) 466-8356

RED ROOF INN
12525 Laurel
Bowie Rd (20708)
Rates: $56-$74
(301) 498-8811
(800) 848-7878

LINTHICUM HEIGHTS

AMERISUITES BWI AIRPORT
940 Int'l Dr
(21090)
Rates: $99-$209
(410) 859-3366
(800) 833-1516

COMFORT INN AIRPORT
6921 Baltimore
Annapolis Blvd
(21090)
Rates: $89-$129
(410) 789-9100
(800) 228-5150

COMFORT INN BWI AIRPORT
815 Elkridge
Landing Rd
(21090)
Rates: $79-$139
(410) 691-1000
(800) 228-5150

DOUBLETREE GUEST SUITES HOTEL BWI
1300 Concourse
Dr (21090)
Rates: $89-$189
(410) 850-0747
(800) 222-8733

HAMPTON INN WASHINGTON INTL AIRPORT
829 Elkridge
Landing Rd
(21090)
Rates: $99-$119
(410) 850-0600
(800) 426-7866

HOLIDAY INN BWI AIRPORT
890 Elkridge
Landing Rd
(21090)
Rates: $99-$119
(410) 859-8400
(800) 465-4329

HOMESTEAD VILLAGE GUEST STUDIOS
939 Int'l Dr
(21090)
Rates: $72-$84
(410) 691-2500
(888) 782-9473

HOMEWOOD SUITES HOTEL BWI AIRPORT
1181 Winterson
Rd (21090)
Rates: $139-$174
(410) 684-6100
(800) 225-5466

MOTEL 6
5179 Raynor Ave
(21090)
Rates: $39-$51
(410) 636-9070
(800) 466-8356

RED ROOF INN BWI AIRPORT
827 Elkridge
Landing Rd
(21090)
Rates: $66-$93
(410) 850-7600
(800) 843-7663

SHERATON INTL HOTEL BWI AIRPORT
7032 Elm Rd (21090)
Rates: $79-$225
(410) 859-3300
(800) 325-3535

LOTHIAN

DUNCAN'S FAMILY CAMPGROUND CABINS
5381 Sands Rd
(20711)
Rates: n/a
(410) 741-9558
(800) 222-2086

MCHENRY

A&A REALTY VACATION RENTALS
Rt 219 & Deep
Creek Lake
(21541)
Rates: n/a
(301) 387-4700
(800) 336-7303

COMFORT INN
2704 Deep Creek
Dr (21541)
Rates: $60-$109
(301) 387-4200
(800) 228-5150

DEEP CREEK LAKE VACATION RENTALS
24439 Garrett Hwy,
Suite 101 (21541)
Rates: n/a
(301) 387-6187
(800) 769-5300

INNLET MOTOR LODGE
Deep Creek Dr (21541)
Rates: n/a
(301) 387-5596
(800) 540-0763

THE LODGE
Lakeshore Dr (21541)
Rates: n/a
(301) 469-6617

MOUNTAIN LAKE VACATION RENTALS
P. O. Box 929 (21541)
Rates: n/a
(800) 846-RENT

WISP MOUNTAIN RESORT/HOTEL & CONF CENTER
290 Marsh Hill Rd (21541)
Rates: $79-$169
(301) 387-5581

MECHANICS-VILLE

CHARLOTTE HALL MOTEL
Rt 5 (20659)
Rates: n/a
(301) 884-3172

WIDE BAY COTTAGE AT DAMERON B&B
997 Old Rt 5 (20659)
Rates: n/a
(301) 884-3254

NEW CARROLLTON

SHERATON GREENBELT HOTEL
8500 Annapolis Rd (20784)
Rates: $72-$112
(301) 459-6700
(800) 325-3535

NORTH EAST

CRYSTAL INN
1 Center Dr (21901)
Rates: $89
(410) 287-7100
(800) 631-3803

OAKLAND

THE BOARD ROOM MOTEL
12678 Garrett Hwy (21550)
Rates: n/a
(301) 334-2126

TIMBERLAKE RENTALS
19139 Garrett Hwy (21550)
Rates: n/a
(301) 387-0336

OCEAN CITY

BAREFOOT MAILMAN MOTEL
35th S, Oceanfront (21842)
Rates: n/a
(410) 289-5343
(800) 395-3668

BAY SAILS INN
102 60th St (21842)
Rates: n/a
(410) 524-5634
(800) 776-5634

BEST WESTERN SEA BAY INN
6007 Coastal Hwy (21842)
Rates: $29-$299
(410) 524-6100
(800) 528-1234
(800) 888-2229

BUDGET BEACH MOTEL
32nd St, Coastal Hwy (21842)
Rates: n/a
(410) 289-1808

CAROUSEL HOTEL & RESORT
118th St, Oceanfront (21842)
Rates: n/a
(410) 524-1000
(800) 641-0011

CAYMAN SUITES HOTEL
125 St & Oceanside (21842)
Rates: n/a
(410) 250-7600
(800) 546-0042

EMPRESS MOTEL
1910 Baltimore Ave (21842)
Rates: n/a
(410) 289-6745

GEORGIA BELLE HOTEL
12004 Coastal Hwy (21842)
Rates: $29-$175
(410) 250-4000
(800) 542-4444

HARRISON HALL HOTEL
15th St, Boardwalk (21842)
Rates: n/a
(410) 289-6222
(800) 638-2106

KING CHARLES HOTEL
1209 Baltimore Ave (21842)
Rates: n/a
(410) 289-6141
(800) 498-0356

KING'S ARMS MOTEL
2403 Baltimore Ave (21842)
Rates: n/a
(410) 289-6257

MISTY HARBOR MOTEL & APTS
25th St & Philadelphia Ave (21842)
Rates: n/a
(410) 289-7284
(800) 638-3344

OCEAN MANOR ROOMS, APTS & COTTAGES
107 Wicomico St (21842)
Rates: n/a
(410) 289-9050
(877) 222-3133

PLAYLAND APARTMENTS
Worcester St, Boardwalk (21842)
Rates: n/a
(410) 289-7271

PLIM PLAZA HOTEL
2nd St, Boardwalk (21842)
Rates: n/a
(410) 289-6181
(800) 837-3587

SAFARI MOTEL
13th St, Boardwalk (21842)
Rates: n/a
(410) 289-6411
(800) 787-2183

SHERATON FONTAINBLEAU HOTEL
10100 Ocean Hwy (21842)
Rates: $239-$299
(410) 524-3535
(800) 638-2100

SURF VILLA HOTEL
705 N Baltimore Ave (21842)
Rates: n/a
(410) 289-9434
(800) 303-SURF

TAKE-A-MITSIA
401 11th St, Bayside (1842)
Rates: n/a
(410) 289-3200

WINDJAMMER APARTMENT MOTEL
4503 Atlantic Ave (21842)
Rates: n/a
(410) 289-9409

OXON HILL

RED ROOF INN
6170 Oxon Hill Rd (20745)
Rates: $56-$83
(301) 567-8030
(800) 843-7663

PERRYVILLE

COMFORT INN
61 Heather Ln (21903)
Rates: $55-$86
(410) 642-2866
(800) 228-5150

EL CAPITAN MOTEL
5271 Pulaski Hwy (21903)
Rates: n/a
(410) 642-2282

PERRYVILLE MOTEL
5288 Pulaski Hwy (21903)
Rates: n/a
(410) 642-2044

PIKESVILLE

COMFORT INN NW
10 Wooded Way (21208)
Rates: $55-$149
(410) 484-7700
(800) 228-5150

PINEY POINT

SWANNS HOTEL
Rt 235 (20674)
Rates: n/a
(301) 994-0774

POCOMOKE CITY

DAYS INN
1540 Ocean Hwy (21851)
Rates: $53-$58
(410) 957-3000
(800) 329-7466

QUALITY INN
825 Ocean Hwy (21851)
Rates: $56-$90
(410) 957-1300
(800) 228-5151

PRINCESS ANNE

ECONO LODGE
10936 Market Ln (21853)
Rates: $54-$89
(410) 651-9400
(800) 553-2666
(800) 615-GOLF

WATERLOO COUNTRY INN
28822 Mt Vernon Rd (21853)
Rates: $100-$225
(410) 651-0883

RAWLINGS

DIPLOMAT MOTEL
17012 McMullen
Hwy (21502)
Rates: $35-$48
(301) 729-2311

ROCK HALL

**BAY BREEZE INN
BED & BREAKFAST**
5758 Main St
(21661)
Rates: $65-$98
(410) 639-2061

**HUNTINGFIELD
MANOR B&B**
4928 Eastern Neck
Rd (21661)
Rates: $90-$140
(410) 639-7779

MARINERS MOTEL
5681 S Hawthorne
Ave (21661)
Rates: $60-$70
(410) 639-2291

**NORTH POINT
MARINA**
5639 Walnut St
(21661)
Rates: n/a
(410) 639-2907

ROCKVILLE

**BEST WESTERN
WASHINGTON
GATEWAY HOTEL**
1251 W
Montgomery Ave
(20850)
Rates: $79-$149
(301) 424-4940
(800) 528-1234
(800) 366-1251

**QUALITY SUITES
SHADY GROVE**
3 Research Ct
(20850)
Rates: $69-$169
(301) 840-0200
(800) 228-5151

RED ROOF INN
16001 Shady
Grove Rd (20850)
Rates: $56-$83
(301) 948-0965
(800) 843-7663

**SLEEP INN
SHADY GROVE**
2 Research Ct
(20850)
Rates: $69-$119
(301) 948-8000
(800) 753-3746

**WOODFIN
SUITES HOTEL**
1380 Piccard Dr
(20850)
Rates: $124-$179
(301) 590-9880
(800) 237-8811

ROYAL OAK

**THE OAKS,
A COUNTRY INN**
25876 Royal Oak
Rd (21662)
Rates: n/a
(410) 745-5053

ST. MICHAELS

**BEST WESTERN
ST. MICHAELS
MOTOR INN**
1228 S Talbot St
(21663)
Rates: $68-$115
(410) 745-3333
(800) 528-1234

**CYGNET HOUSE
BED & BREAKFAST**
201 Carpenter St
(21663)
Rates: n/a
(410) 745-2929

**FOX RUN FARM
BED & BREAKFAST**
24060 St. Michaels
Rd (21663)
Rates: n/a
(410) 745-2381

KEMP HOUSE INN
412 S Talbot St
(21663)
Rates: n/a
(410) 745-2243

SALISBURY

**BEST WESTERN
SALISBURY PLAZA**
1735 N Salisbury
Blvd (21801)
Rates: $98-$135
(410) 546-1300
(800) 528-1234
(800) 636-7554

BUDGET HOST
1510 Salisbury
Blvd (21801)
Rates: $40-$90
(410) 742-3284
(800) 272-7829

COMFORT INN
2701 N Salisbury
Blvd (21801)
Rates: $53-$139
(410) 543-4666
(800) 228-5150

**ECONO LODGE
STATESMAN**
712 N Salisbury
Rd (21801)
Rates: $34-$99
(410) 749-7155
(800) 553-2666

**HOWARD
JOHNSON**
2625 N Salisbury
Blvd (21801)
Rates: $66-$120
(410) 742-7194
(800) 446-4656

**LORD SALISBURY
MOTEL**
2637 N Salisbury
Blvd (21801)
Rates: $39-$75
(410) 742-3251
(800) 299-3232

SUPER 8 MOTEL
2615 N Salisbury
Blvd (21801)
Rates: $39-$54
(410) 749-5131
(800) 800-8000

**THRIFT TRAVEL
INN**
603 N Salisbury
Blvd (21801)
Rates: n/a
(410) 742-5135
(800) 457-3341

SHARPSBURG

**CLIPP'S MILL &
LOG CABIN B&B**
110 E Chaplain St
(21782)
Rates: n/a
(202) 363-0976
(800) 484-1453

SILVER SPRING

**LITTLE HOUSE AT
WIND SWEPT B&B**
17000 Carwell Rd
(20905)
Rates: n/a
(301) 384-3336
(800) 861-2434

**THE PARK CREST
HOME B&B**
8101 Park Crest
Dr (20910)
Rates: n/a
(301) 588-2845

SNOW HILL

**RIVER HOUSE INN
BED & BREAKFST**
201 E Market St
(21863)
Rates: $99-$195
(410) 632-2722

SOLOMONS

BOWEN'S INN
14630 Solomons
Island Rd S
(20688)
Rates: n/a
(410) 326-9880

HOLIDAY INN
155 Holiday Dr
(20688)
Rates: $94-$130
(410) 326-6311
(800) 465-4329

**LOCUST INN
ROOMS B&B**
14478 Solomons
Island Rd S (20688)
Rates: n/a
(410) 326-9817

TAYLORS
ISLAND

**BECKY PHIPP'S
INN B&B**
Taylor's Island
Marina Rd, Rt 16
(21669)
Rates: n/a
(410) 221-2911

**TAYLORS ISLAND
CAMPGROUND
APT RENTALS**
Bayshore Rd
(21669)
Rates: n/a
(410) 397-3275

THURMONT

**COZY COUNTRY
INN**
103 Frederick Rd
(21788)
Rates: n/a
(301) 271-4301

RAMBLER INN
426 W Church St
(21788)
Rates: $42-$62
(301) 271-2424

SUPER 8 MOTEL
300 Tippin Dr
(21788)
Rates: $48-$68
(301) 271-7888
(800) 800-8000

TILGHMAN
ISLAND

**HARRISON'S
COUNTRY INN**
21551 Chesapeake
House Dr (21671)
Rates: n/a
(410) 886-2121

**TILGHMAN
ISLAND INN**
21384 Cooper Rd
(21671)
Rates: n/a
(410) 886-2141
(800) 866-2141

TIMONIUM

RED ROOF INN
111 W Timonium
Rd (21093)
Rates: $60-$78
(410) 666-0380
(800) 843-7663

TOWSON

DAYS INN-EAST
8801 Loch Raven
Blvd (21204)
Rates: $64-$139
(410) 882-0900
(800) 329-7466

RAMADA INN
8712 Loch Raven
Blvd (21286)
Rates: $49-$125
(410) 823-8750
(800) 272-6232

AREA CODES - If the local number doesn't connect, check for a new area code.

SHERATON BALTIMORE
903 Dulaney
Valley Rd (21204)
Rates: n/a
(410) 321-7400
(800) 433-7619

UPPER MARLBORO

BRAGG MOTEL
7001 Crain Hwy
(20772)
Rates: n/a
(301) 627-1880

FOREST HILLS MOTEL
2901 Crain Hwy
(20772)
Rates: $45-$55
(301) 627-3969

WALDORF

ECONO LODGE
11770 Business
Park Dr (20601)
Rates: $55-$89
(301) 645-0022
(800) 553-2666

HOWARD JOHNSON EXPRESS
3125 Crain Hwy
(20602)
Rates: $44-$70
(301) 932-5090
(800) 446-4656
(800) 826-4504

MASTER SUITES HOTEL
2228 Old
Washington Rd
(20601)
Rates: n/a
(301) 870-5500

SUPER 8 MOTEL
3550 Crain Hwy
(20602)
Rates: $45-$59
(301) 932-8957
(800) 800-8000

WESTMINSTER

THE BOSTON INN
533 Baltimore
Blvd (21157)
Rates: $36-$70
(410) 848-9095
(800) 634-0846

COMFORT INN
451 WMC Dr
(21158)
Rates: $49-$99
(410) 857-1900
(800) 228-5150

DAYS INN
25 S Cranberry Rd
(21157)
Rates: $58-$84
(410) 857-0500
(800) 329-7466

WHITEHAVEN

WHITEHAVEN BED & BREAKFAST
23844-48 River St
(21856)
Rates: n/a
(410) 873-3294

WILLIAMSPORT

RED ROOF INN
310 E Potomac St
(21795)
Rates: $42-$49
(301) 582-3500
(800) 843-7663

AREA CODES - If the local number doesn't connect, check for a new area code.

MASSACHUSETTS

AMHERST

**LORD JEFFERY
INN**
30 Boltwood Ave
(01002)
Rates: $70-$109
(413) 253-2576
(800) 742-0358

**UNIVERSITY
MOTOR LODGE**
345 N Pleasant St
(01002)
Rates: $65-$105
(413) 256-8111

ANDOVER

**ANDOVER
COUNTRY NN**
Chapel Ave
(01810)
Rates: $99-$115
(978) 475-5903
(800) 242-5903

WYNDHAM HOTEL
123 Old River Rd
(01810)
Rates: $155
(978) 975-3600
(800) 996-3426

AUBURN

BAYMONT INN
444 Southbridge
St (01501)
Rates: $52-$72
(508) 832-7000
(800) 301-0200

BARNSTABLE

LAMB & LION INN
2504 Main St
(02630)
Rates: $110-$150
(508) 362-6823

BARRE

**JENKINS
HISTORIC
COUNTRY INN**
7 West St (01005)
Rates: $110-$150
(978) 355-6444
(800) 378-7373

BASS RIVER

**WAYFARERS ALL
COTTAGES**
186 Seaview Ave
(02664)
Rates: $600
Weekly
(508) 771-4532

BEDFORD

**RENNAISSANCE
BEDFORD HOTEL**
44 Middlesex Tpk
(01730)
Rates: $194-$204
(781) 275-5500
(800) 468-3571

BLANDFORD

**PLEASURE HORSE
PASO FINO FARM
BED & BREAKFAST**
43 Russell Rd
(01008)
Rates: $70-$110
(413) 848-2214

BOSTON

**BOSTON
HARBOR HOTEL**
70 Rowes Wharf
(02110)
Rates: $235-$510
(617) 439-7000
(800) 752-7077

**COLONNADE
HOTEL**
120 Huntington
Ave (02116)
Rates: $150+
(617) 424-7000
(800) 962-3030

**FAIRMONT
COPLEY PLAZA
HOTEL**
138 St James Ave
(02116)
Rates: $219-$379
(617) 267-5300
(800) 527-4727

FOUR SEASONS
HOTEL BOSTON
200 Boylston St
(02116)
Rates: $465-$610
(617) 338-4400
(800) 332-3442
(800) 268-6282

**HILTON-BOSTON
BACK BAY**
40 Dalton St
(02115)
Rates: $155-$250
(617) 236-1100
(800) 445-8667
(800) 874-0663

**HOWARD
JOHNSON**
575 Commonwealth
Ave (02215)
Rates: $135-$235
(617) 267-3100
(800) 446-4656

**HOWARD
JOHNSON**
1271 Boylston St
(02215)
Rates: $115-$199
(617) 267-8300
(800) 446-4656

**LE MERIDIEN
HOTEL**
250 Franklin St
(02110)
Rates: $333-$370
(617) 451-1900
(800) 543-4300

SEAPORT HOTEL
1 Seaport Lane
(02110)
Rates: $250-$349
(617) 385-4000

**SHERATON
HOTEL**
39 Dalton St
(02199)
Rates: $259
(617) 236-2000
(800) 325-3535

SWISSOTEL
BOSTON
One Ave de
Lafayette (02111)
Rates: $379-$449
(617) 451-2600

**THE WESTIN
COPLEY PLACE**
10 Huntington
Ave (02116)
Rates: $260-$355
(617) 262-9600
(800) 937-8461

BOURNE

**YANKEE THRIFT
MOTEL**
114 Trowbridge Rd
(02532)
Rates: n/a
(508) 759-3883

BRAINTREE

**CANDLEWOOD
SUITES**
235 Wood Rd
(02184)
Rates: $50-$109
(781) 849-7450
(800) 946-6200

DAYS INN
190 Wood Rd
(02184)
Rates: $99-$200
(781) 848-1260
(800) 329-7466

MOTEL 6
125 Union St
(02184)
Rates: $60-$76
(781) 848-7890
(800) 466-8356

BREWSTER

GREYLIN HOUSE
2311 Main St
(02631)
Rates: $70-$175
(508) 896-0004
(800) 233-6662

HIGH BREWSTER
INN
964 Satucket Rd
(02631)
Rates: $90-$120
(508) 896-3636
(800) 203-2634

**JOLLY WHALER
VILLAGE**
Rt 6A (02631)
Rates: $35-$70
(508) 896-3474

**PINE HILLS
COTTAGES**
800 Main St
(02631)
Rates: $100-$750
Weekly
(508) 896-1999

BROOKLINE

BEECH TREE INN
83 Longwood Ave
(02146)
Rates: $40-$109
(617) 277-1620
(800) 544-9660

BERTRAM INN
92 Sewall Ave
(021462)
Rates: $70-$164
(617) 566-2334
(800) 295-3822

BURLINGTON

**HOMESTEAD
VILLAGE GUEST
STUDIOS**
40 South St
(01803)
Rates: n/a
(781) 359-9099
(888) 782-9473

**SUMMERFIELD
SUITES HOTEL**
2 Van de Graaf Dr
(01803)
Rates: $109-$199
(781) 270-0800
(800) 833-4353

AREA CODES - If the local number doesn't connect, check for a new area code.

BUZZARDS BAY

BAY MOTOR INN
223 Main St
(02532)
Rates: $79-$100
(508) 759-3989

THE POND HOUSE
44 Monument
Neck Rd (02532)
Rates: $45-$95
(508) 759-1994

SHIPSWAY MOTEL & COTTAGES
51 Canal Rd
(02532)
Rates: $70-$109
(508) 888-0206

CAMBRIDGE

ALL-NEW WINDSOR HOUSE
283 Windsor St
(02139)
Rates: $70-$109
(617) 354-3116

CHARLES HOTEL IN HARVARD SQUARE
1 Bennett St
(02138)
Rates: $240-$430
(617) 864-1200
(800) 882-1818

HOWARD JOHNSON HOTEL
777 Memorial Dr
(02139)
Rates: $135-$234
(617) 492-7777
(800) 446-4656

RESIDENCE INN BY MARRIOTT
6 Cambridge
Center (02142)
Rates: n/a
(800) 331-3131

CAPE COD TOWNS

See listings under
the following cities;
Barnstable
Bass River
Bourne
Brewster
Buzzards Bay
Centerville
Chatham
Dennis Port
East Falmouth
East Sandwich
Eastham
Falmouth
Harwich Port
Hyannis
Hyannis Port
North Eastham
North Truro
Orleans
Provincetown
Sandwich
South Orleans
South Wellfleet
South Yarmouth
Wellfleet
West Barnstable
West Dennis
West Harwich
West Yarmouth
Yarmouth Port

CENTERVILLE

CENTERVILLE CORNERS MOTOR LODGE
369 S Main St
(02632)
Rates: $115-$130
(508) 775-7223
(800) 242-1137

CHATHAM

MORGAN WATER-FRONT HOUSES
444 Old Harbor
Rd (02633)
Rates: $400-$1800
Weekly
(508) 945-1870

OCEANFRONT APARTMENTS & COTTAGES
Seagull Ln (02633)
Rates: n/a
(508) 945-5907

CHELMSFORD

BEST WESTERN INN
187 Chelmsford St
(01824)
Rates: $79-$109
(978) 256-7511
(800) 528-1234
(888) 770-9992

CHICOPEE

MOTEL 6
Rt 291, Burnett Rd
(01020)
Rates: $40-$49
(413) 592-5141
(800) 466-8356

SUPER 8 MOTEL
463 Memorial Dr
(01020)
Rates: $57-$75
(413) 592-6171
(800) 800-8000

CLINTON

CLINTON MOTOR INN
146 Main St
(01510)
Rates: $35-$50
(978) 368-8133
(800) 368-8134

CONCORD

BEST WESTERN AT HISTORIC CONCORD
740 Elm St (01742)
Rates: $94-$129
(978) 369-6100
(800) 528-1234

CUMMINGTON

SWIFT RIVER INN
151 South St
(01026)
Rates: $49-$99
(413) 634-5751

DANVERS

COMFORT INN NORTH SHORE
50 Dayton St
(01923)
Rates: $69-$159
(978) 777-1700
(800) 228-5150

MOTEL 6
65 Newbury St
(01923)
Rates: $48-$72
(978) 774-8045
(800) 466-8356

RESIDENCE INN BY MARRIOTT
51 Newbury St
(01923)
Rates: $148-$227
(978) 777-7171
(800) 331-3131

DEDHAM

HILTON HOTEL AT DEDHAM PLACE
25 Allied Dr
(02026)
Rates: $224-$239
(781) 329-7900
(800) 445-8667

RESIDENCE INN BY MARRIOTT
259 Elm St (02026)
Rates: n/a
(781) 407-0999
(800) 331-3131

DENNIS PORT

ACORN COTTAGES
927 Main St
(02639)
Rates: $495-$895
Weekly
(508) 760-2101

BAY LIGHT COTTAGES
235 Division St
(02639)
Rates: $100-$750
(508) 398-5989

THE BEACH ROSE COTTAGE
46 Chase Ave
(02639)
Rates: $400-$750
Weekly
(508) 760-1140

BETH'S BEACH HOUSE
General Delivery
(02639)
Rates: $650
Weekly
(508) 385-4588

HURRICANE PINES VACATION RENTAL
94 Old Wharf Rd
(02639)
Rates: $200-$400
Weekly
(508) 398-2616

LAMPLIGHTER MOTOR LODGE
329 Main St
(02639)
Rates: $28-$55
(508) 398-8469

MARINE LODGE COTTAGES
15 North St
(02639)
Rates: $300-$750
Weekly
(508) 398-2963
(888) 398-2963

SEA LORD RESORT MOTEL
Chase Ave (02639)
Rates: $35-$110
(508) 398-6900

TOWN COTTAGES
319 Main St
(02639)
Rates: $429
Weekly
(508) 398-8469
(800) 328-8812

UNION WHARF VILLAGE
68 Union Wharf
Dr (02639)
Rates: $300-$750
Weekly
(508) 881-1381

EAST BOSTON

HILTON-LOGAN AIRPORT
75 Service Rd,
Logan Intl Airport
(02128)
Rates: $105-$200
(617) 569-9300
(800) 445-8667

EAST FALMOUTH

GREEN HARBOR WATERFRONT MOTOR LODGE
134 Acapesket Rd
(02536)
Rates: $80-$109
(508) 548-4747
(800) 548-5556

EAST SANDWICH

AZARIAH SNOW HOUSE
529 Rt 6A (02537)
Rates: $40-$70
(508) 888-6677

CEDAR COTTAGES
59 Ploughed Neck
(02537)
Rates: n/a
(508) 888-0464

THE EARL OF SANDWICH MOTOR MANOR
378 Rt 6A (02537)
Rates: $45-$89
(508) 888-1415
(800) 442-EARL

PINE GROVE COTTAGES
358 Rt 6A (02537)
Rates: $70-$100
(508) 888-8179

WINGSCORTON FARM INN
11 Wing Blvd
(02537)
Rates: $90-$175
(508) 888-0534

EASTHAM

CRANBERRY COTTAGES
785 State Hwy
(02642)
Rates: $45-$85
(508) 255-0602
(800) 292-6631

GIBSON COTTAGES
80 Depot Rd
(02642)
Rates: $70-$109
(508) 255-0882

SMITH HEIGHTS COTTAGES
1420 Rt 6 (02642)
Rates: $420-$680
Weekly
(508) 255-5895

TOWN CRIER MOTEL
3260 Rt 6 (02642)
Rates: $70-$105
(508) 255-4000
(800) 932-1434

EASTON

EASTON 138 MOTEL
25 Washington St
(02356)
Rates: $35-$69
(508) 238-4321

FAIRHAVEN

THE HUTTLESTON MOTEL
128 Huttleston
Ave (02719)
Rates: $40-$69
(508) 997-7655

FALMOUTH

BAYBERRY INN BED & BREAKFST
226 Trotting Park
(02536)
Rates: $50-$109
(508) 540-2962

FALMOUTH INN
824 Main St
(02540)
Rates: $70-$100
(508) 540-2500
(800) 255-4157

MARINER MOTEL
555 Main St
(02540)
Rates: $70-$110
(508) 548-1331
(800) 233-2939
(800) 949-2939

OCEAN VIEW MOTEL
263 Grand Ave
(02540)
Rates: $50-$140
(508) 540-4120
(800) 294-8888

FITCHBURG

BEST WESTERN ROYAL PLAZA HOTEL & TRADE CENTER
150 Royal Plaza
Dr (01420)
Rates: $75-$135
(978) 342-7100
(800) 528-1234
(888) 976-0254

FLORIDA

WHITCOMB SUMMIT MOTEL
229 Mohawk Tr
(01247)
Rates: $45-$109
(413) 662-2625
(800) 547-0944

FOXBORO

RESIDENCE INN BY MARRIOTT
250 Foxborough
Blvd (02035)
Rates: $110-$149
(508) 698-2800
(800) 331-3131

FRAMINGHAM

MOTEL 6
1668 Worcester Rd
(01702)
Rates: $48-$62
(508) 620-0500
(800) 466-8356

RED ROOF INN
650 Cochituate Rd
(01701)
Rates: $65-$105
(508) 872-4499
(800) 843-7663

GLOUCESTER

CAPE ANN MOTOR INN
33 Rockport Rd
(01930)
Rates: $115-$130
(978) 281-2900
(800) 464-8439

THE MANOR INN
141 Essex Ave
(01930)
Rates: $89-$139
(978) 283-0614

GREAT BARRINGTON

CHEZ GABRIELLE BED & BREAKFAST
320 State Rd
(01230)
Rates: $110-$149
(413) 528-2799

CHICADEE COTTAGE
27 Division St
(01230)
Rates: $65-$75
(413) 528-0002

MOUNTAIN VIEW MOTEL
304 State Rd
(01230)
Rates: $45-$125
(413) 528-0250

SEEKONK PINES INN
142 Seekonk Cross
Rd (01230)
Rates: $70-$160
(413) 528-4192
(800) 292-4192

WAINWRIGHT INN
518 S Main St
(01230)
Rates: $65-$175
(413) 528-2062

GREENFIELD

THE BRANDT HOUSE HISTORIC BED & BREAKFST
29 Highland Ave
(01301)
Rates: $125-$195
(413) 774-3329
(800) 235-3329

CANDLELIGHT MOTOR INN
208 Mohawk Tr
(01301)
Rates: $38-$84
(413) 772-0101
(888) 262-0520

OLD TAVERN FARM B&B
817 Colrain Rd
(01301)
Rates: $70-$109
(413) 772-0474

HADLEY

HOWARD JOHNSON
401 Russell St
(01036)
Rates: $75-$145
(413) 586-0114
(800) 446-4656

HANCOCK

JERICHO VALLEY INN
2541 Hancock Rd
(01237)
Rates: $68-$138
(413) 458-9511

HARWICH PORT

HARBOR WALK GUEST HOUSE
6 Freeman St
(02646)
Rates: n/a
(508) 432-1675

HOUSATONIC

BROOK COVE
30 Linda Ln
(01236)
Rates: $65-$85
(413) 274-6653

CHRISTINE'S BED & BREAKFAST CARRIAGE HOUSE
325 N Plain Rd
(01236)
Rates: $70-$200+
(413) 274-6149

HYANNIS

ANGEL MOTEL
Rt 132 (02601)
Rates: $41-$54
(508) 775-2440

CASCADE MOTOR LODGE
201 Main St
(02601)
Rates: $39-$70
(508) 775-9717

COMFORT INN
1470 SR 132
(02601)
Rates: $54-$175
(508) 771-4804
(800) 228-5150

ECONO LODGE
59 E Main St
(02601)
Rates: $34-$84
(508) 771-0691
(800) 553-2666

GLO-MIN COTTAGES & MOTEL
182 Sea St (02601)
Rates: $59-$149
(508) 775-1423
(800) 696-1423

HYANNIS SANDS MOTOR LODGE
921 Rt 132 (02601)
Rates: $35-$69
(508) 790-1700

RAINBOW RESORT MOTEL
Rt 132 (02601)
Rates: $48-$56
(508) 362-3217

SNUG HARBOUR MOTOR LODGE
48 E Main St
(02601)
Rates: $35-$70
(508) 771-0699
(800) 345-0130

HYANNIS PORT

HARBOR VILLAGE
160 Marstons Ave
(02647)
Rates: $90-$150
(508) 775-7581

SEA BREEZE COTTAGES BY THE BEACH
337 Sea St (02647)
Rates: $450-$850
Weekly
(508) 775-4269

SEASIDE COLONIAL VACATION RENTAL
60 Crocker St
(02647)
Rates: $400-$1125
Weekly
(508) 778-1439

THE SIMMONS HOMESTEAD INN BED & BREAKFAST
288 Scudder Ave
(02647)
Rates: $101-$175
(508) 778-4999
(800) 637-1649

KINGSTON

BAY VIEW MOTEL
20 Main St (02364)
Rates: $35-$65
(781) 585-2268

THE INN AT PLYMOUTH BAY
149 Main St
(02364)
Rates: $99-$130
(781) 585-3831
(800) 941-0075

LANESBORO

ARSENAULT'S LAKE HOUSE
Ocean St (01237)
Rates: n/a
(413) 442-6304

BERKSHIRE NORTH COTTAGES
121 S Main St
(01237)
Rates: $35-$70
(413) 44207469

LAMPOST MOTEL
P.O. Box 335
(01237)
Rates: n/a
(413) 443-2979

LANESBORO MOUNTAIN MOTEL
P.O. Box 355
(01237)
Rates: n/a
(413) 442-6717

MT. VIEW MOTEL
499 S Main St
(01237)
Rates: $48-$125
(413) 442-1009

WEATHERVANE MOTEL
475 S Main St
(01237)
Rates: $35-$125
(413) 443-3230

LAWRENCE

HAMPTON INN NORTH
224 Winthrop Ave
(01843)
Rates: $79-$99
(978) 975-4050
(800) 426-7866

LEE

DEVONFIELD B&B
85 Stockbridge Rd
(01238)
Rates: $70-$175
(413) 243-3298
(800) 664-0880

LENOX

QUALITY INN
130 Pittsfield Rd
(01240)
Rates: $44-$179
(413) 637-4244
(800) 228-5150

SEVEN HILLS COUNTRY INN
40 Plunkett St
(01240)
Rates: $85-$325
(413) 637-0060
(800) 869-6518

WALKER HOUSE INN B&B
64 Walker St
(01240)
Rates: $70-$165
(413) 637-1271
(800) 235-3098

LEOMINSTER

THE INN ON THE HILL
450 N Main St
(01453)
Rates: $46
(978) 537-1661

MOTEL 6
Commercial St
(01453)
Rates: $36-$45
(978) 537-8161
(800) 466-8356

LEXINGTON

BATTLE GREEN MOTOR INN
1720 Massachusetts Ave (02173)
Rates: $99-$109
(781) 862-6100
(800) 343-0235

HOLIDAY INN EXPRESS
440 Bedford St
(02173)
Rates: n/a
(781) 861-0850
(800) 465-4329

MARY VAN & JIMS "THIS OLD HOUSE" B&B
12 Plainfield St
(02173)
Rates: $50-$109
(781) 861-7057

LYNN

DIAMOND DISTRICT B & B INN
142 Ocean St
(01902)
Rates: $85-$225
(781) 599-5122
(800) 666-3076

MALDEN

NEW ENGLANDER MOTOR COURT
551 Broadway
(02148)
Rates: $69-$89
(781) 321-0505
(800) 334-1043

MANSFIELD

MOTEL 6
60 Forbes Blvd
(02048)
Rates: $54-$70
(508) 339-2323
(800) 466-8356

MARBLEHEAD

THE NESTING PLACE B&B
16 Village St
(01945)
Rates: $50-$110
(781) 631-6655

SEAGULL INN BED & BREAKFAST
106 Harbor Ave
(01945)
Rates: $70-$175
(781) 631-1893

MARION

VILLAGE LANDING B&B
13 South St
(02738)
Rates: $70-$109
(508) 748-0350

MARLBOROUGH

EMBASSY SUITES
123 Boston Post
Rd W (01752)
Rates: $95-$175
(508) 485-5900
(800) 362-2779

SUPER 8 MOTEL
880 Donald J
Lynch Blvd
(01752)
Rates: $55-$69
(508) 460-1000
(800) 800-8000

MARTHA'S VINEYARD

THE BED & BISCUIT VACATION HOME
20 Jennie Lane
(Edgartown 02539)
Rates: $2000-$2500
Weekly
(508) 627-3666

BUNNY RUN COTTAGE AT HIDDEN HILL
Dunham Ave
(Vineyard Haven 02658)
Rates: $750
(508) 693-2809

ISLAND INN RESORT
Beach Rd,
Box 1585
(Oak Bluffs 02557)
Rates: $70-$285
(508) 693-2002
(800) 462-0269

MARTHA'S VINEYARD SURFSIDE MOTEL
Oak Bluffs Ave
(Oak Bluffs 02557)
Rates: $60-$285
(508) 693-2500
(800) 537-3007

MILL HILL B&B
22 Mill Hill Rd
(Edgartown 02539)
Rates: $110-$149
(508) 627-8807

NEST EGG COTTAGE AT HIDDEN HILL
P O Box 1644
(Vineyard Haven 02568)
Rates: $800-$900
(508) 693-2809

POINT WAY INN B&B
Main St & Pease's Point Way
(Edgartown 02539)
Rates: $110-$250
(508) 627-8633

TIVOLI INN B&B
125 Circuit Ave
(Oak Bluffs 02557)
Rates: $50-$149
(508) 693-7928

THE VICTORIAN INN
24 S Water St
(Edgartown 02539)
Rates: $125-$265
(508) 627-4784

WIND SONG APARTMENT AT HIDDEN HILL
P O Box 1644
(Vineyard Haven 02568)
Rates: $800-$950
(508) 693-2809

MIDDLE-BOROUGH

DAYS INN
30 E Clark St
(02346)
Rates: $77-$95
(508) 946-4400
(800) 329-7466

MIDDLEFIELD

BLUE HEAVEN BLUEBERRY FARM
246 Skyline Trail
(01243)
Rates: $100
(413) 623-5519

STRAWBERRY BANKE FARM B&B
Skyline Trail
(01243)
Rates: $70-$109
(413) 623-6481

NANTUCKET ISLAND

BACK-A-BIT COTTAGE
4 Walsh St (02554)
Rates: n/a
(508) 228-2623

BARTLETT'S BEACH COTTAGES
Hummock Pond Rd (02554)
Rates: $110-$200
(508) 228-3906

BOAT HOUSE
15 Old N Wharf
(02554)
Rates: $250-$500
(508) 228-9552
(800) 245-9552

CORKISH COTTAGES
320 Polpis Rd
(02554)
Rates: $150+
(508) 228-5686

FAR ISLAND COTTAGES
41 Madaket Rd
(02554)
Rates: n/a
(508) 228-4227

THE GREY LADY
34 Centre St (02554)
Rates: $95-$175
(508) 228-9552
(800) 245-9552

HALLIDAY'S NANTUCKET HOUSE
2 E York St (02554)
Rates: $400-$500/weekly
(508) 228-9450

JARED COFFIN HOUSE
29 Broad St
(02554)
Rates: $150-$400
(508) 228-2400
(800) 248-2405

NANTUCKET INN & CONF CENTER
27 Macy's Lane
(02554)
Rates: $100-$195
(508) 228-6900
(800) 321-8484

SAFE HARBOR GUEST HOUSE
2 Harbor View Way (02554)
Rates: $140-$170
(508) 228-3222

TEN HUSSEY STREET
10 Hussey St
(02554)
Rates: $95-$175
(508) 228-9552
(800) 245-9552

WEST WIND COTTAGE MADAKET HARBOR
41 Linnaean St
(01238)
Rates: n/a
(617) 868-6866

NEPONSET

SUSSE CHALET BOSTON HOTEL
900 Morrissey Blvd (02122)
Rates: $120-$165
(617) 287-9200
(800) 524-2538
(800) 258-1980

NEW ASHFORD

CARRIAGE HOUSE MOTEL
Route 7 (01237)
Rates: $35-$69
(413) 458-5359

NEWBURYPORT

MORRILL PLACE INN
209 High St
(01950)
Rates: $70-$110
(978) 462-2808
(888) 594-4667

THE WINDSO-HOUSE B&B
38 Federal St
(01950)
Rates: $110-$149
(978) 462-3778
(888) 873-5296

NEWTON

SHERATON HOTEL
320 Washington St
(02158)
Rates: n/a
(617) 969-3010
(800) 325-3535

NORTH ATTLEBORO

ARNS PARK MOTEL
515 S Washington St (02760)
Rates: $55-$70
(508) 695-5102
(800) 828-5097

PINEAPPLE INN
633 S Washington St (02760)
Rates: $35-$70
(508) 695-9324

NORTH CHELMSFORD

HAWTHORN SUITES
25 Research Pl
(01863)
Rates: 139
(978) 256-5151
(800) 527-1133

NORTH EASTHAM

THE BLUE DOLPHIN INN
5950 Rt 6 (02651)
Rates: $79-$149
(508) 255-1159
(800) 654-0504

NORTH TRURO

EBB TIDE ON THE BAY
538 Shore Rd
(02652)
Rates: 200-$750
(508) 487-2122

OUTER REACH RESORT
535 Rt 6 (02652)
Rates: $35-$109
(508) 487-9500
(800) 942-538

SEASCAPE MOTOR INN
Rt 6A (02652)
Rates: $40-$100
(508) 487-1225

NORTH HAMPTON

BEST WESTERN
117 Conz St
(01060)
Rates: $57-$115
(413) 586-1500
(800) 528-1234
(800) 941-3066

ORANGE

EXECUTIVE INN
110 Daniel Shay Hwy (01364)
Rates: $45-$65
(978) 544-8864

ORLEANS

LAKECREST COTTAGES
Arey's Ln (02653)
Rates: $400-$750
(508) 255-3334

ORLEANS B&B ASSOCIATION
P.O. Box 1312
(02653)
Rates: n/a
(508) 255-3824
(800) 541-6226

SKAKET BEACH MOTEL
203 Cranberry Hwy (02653)
Rates: $91-$164
(508) 255-1020
(800) 835-0298

OTIS

GROUSE HOUSE
P.O. Box 70
(01253)
Rates: n/a
(413) 269-4446

PEABODY

COUNTRY SIDE MOTEL
130 Newbury St
(01960)
Rates: $35-$69
(978) 535-1150
(800) 839-8757

MAINSTAY SUITES
200 Jubilee Dr
(01960)
Rates: $109-$139
(978) 531-6632
(800) 660-6246

PITTSFIELD

BONNIE BRAE CABINS
108 Broadway St
(01201)
Rates: $45-$75
(413) 442-3754

HEART OF THE BERKSHIRE MOTEL
970 W Housatonic St (01201)
Rates: $45-$100
(413) 443-1255

HUNSTMAN MOTEL
1350 W Housatonic St
(01201)
Rates: n/a
(413) 442-8714

LAKEVIEW COTTAGE
43 Thomas Rd
(01201)
Rates: $80-$120
(413) 445-7620
(413) 445-7179

PROVINCE-TOWN

BAYSHORE APTS
493 Commercial St
(02657)
Rates: $950-$1995
(508) 487-9133

BEST INN
698 Commercial St
(02657)
Rates: $154-$169
(508) 487-1711
(800) 422-4224

BREAKWATER MOTEL
Rt 6A (02657)
Rates: $79-$149
(508) 487-1134
(800) 487-1134

HOLIDAY INN
698 Commercial St
(02657)
Rates: $70-$140
(508) 487-1711
(800) 465-4329
(800) 422-4224

SURFSIDE INN
543 Commercial St
(02657)
Rates: $129-$189
(508) 487-1726

WHITE SANDS MOTEL
Rt 6A, Box 611
(02657)
Rates: $59-$250
(508) 487-0244

WHITE WIND INN
174 Commercial St
(02657)
Rates: $160-$1225
(508) 487-1526
(800) 449-9463

QUINCY

PRESIDENTS' CITY INN
845 Hancock St
(02170)
Rates: $95-$110
(617) 479-6500

RANDOLPH

HOLIDAY INN
1374 N Main St
(02368)
Rates: $82-$98
(781) 961-1000
(800) 465-4329

RAYNHAM

DAYS INN
Rt 44 (02767)
Rates: $69-$99
(508) 824-8647
(800) 329-7466

REHOBOTH

FIVE BRIDGE FARM INN B&B
154 Pine St (02769)
Rates: $78-$125
(508) 252-3190

REVERE

COMFORT INN & SUITES
101 American Legion Hwy
(02151)
Rates: $79-$199
(800) 228-5150

HOWARD JOHNSON
407 Squire Rd
(02151)
Rates: $69-$129
(781) 284-7200
(800) 446-4656

RICHMOND

A B&B IN THE BERKSHIRES
1666 Dublin Rd
(01254)
Rates: $75-$150
(413) 698-2817
(800) 795-7122

MIDDLERISE B&B
Route 41 (01254)
Rates: $90-$100
(413) 698-2687

ROCKLAND

HOLIDAY INN EXP
909 Hingham St
(02370)
Rates: $114-$129
(781) 871-5660
(800) 465-4329

RAMADA INN
929 Hingham St
(02370)
Rates: $149-$189
(781) 871-0545
(800) 272-6232

ROCKPORT

BEACH KNOLL BED & BREAKFAST
30 Beach St
(01966)
Rates: $70-$109
(978) 546-6939

THE BLUEBERRY BED & BREAKFAST
50 Stockholm Ave
(01966)
Rates: $40-$70
(978) 546-2838

CARLSON'S BED & BREAKFST
43 Broadway
(01966)
Rates: $40-$70
(978) 546-2770

SANDY BAY MOTOR INN
173 Main St
(01966)
Rates: $102-$150
(978) 546-7155
(800) 437-7155

SALEM

HAWTHORNE HOTEL
18 Washington Sq
(01970)
Rates: $140-$189
(978) 744-4080
(800) 729-7829

THE SALEM INN HISTORIC B&B
7 Summer St
(01970)
Rates: $160-$290
(978) 741-0680
(800) 446-2995

SALISBURY

CASINO OCEANFRONT MOTEL RESORT
40 North End Blvd (01952)
Rates: $110-$149
(978) 462-2228

DRIFTWOOD MOTEL
229 Beach Rd
(01952)
Rates: $50-$149
(978) 462-9424
(800) 373-8963

MICHAEL'S OCEANFRONT MOTEL
40 Central Ave
(01952)
Rates: $70-$149
(978) 499-0260

SANDISFIELD

NEW BOSTON INN
101 N Main
(01255)
Rates: $85-$95
(413) 258-4477

SANDWICH

THE EARL OF SANWICH MOTEL
378 Rt 6A (02563)
Rates: $85-$109
(508) 888-1415

SANDWICH LODGE & RESORT
54 Rt 6A (02563)
Rates: $110-$170
(508) 888-2275
(800) 282-5353

SAUGUS

COLONIAL TRAVELER MOTOR COURT
1753 Bdwy (01906)
Rates: $45-$80
(781) 233-6700
(800) 323-2731

SCITUATE

CLIPPER SHIP LODGE
7 Beaver Dam Rd
(02066)
Rates: $72-$149
(781) 545-5550
(800) 368-3818

SEEKONK

MOTEL 6
821 Fall River Ave
(02771)
Rates: $56-$71
(508) 336-7800
(800) 466-8356

RAMADA INN
940 Fall River Ave
(02771)
Rates: $65-$110
(508) 336-7300
(800) 272-6232

SHEFFIELD

**BOW WOW
ROAD INN**
570 Bow Wow Rd
(01257)
Rates: $110-$149
(413) 229-3339

**DEPOT GUEST
HOUSE**
P.O. Box 575
(01257)
Rates: $45-$95
(413) 229-2908

**IVANHOE
COUNTRY HOUSE
BED & BREAKFAST**
254 S
Undermountain
Rd (01257)
Rates: $65-$175
(413) 229-2143

**RACE BROOK
LODGE B&B**
864
Undermountain
Rd S (01257)
Rates: $70-$149
(413) 229-2916
(888) 725-6343

**STAGECOACH
HILL INN**
854
Undermountain
Rd S (01257)
Rates: $50-$125
(413) 229-8585

SOMERSET

QUALITY INN
1878 Wilbur Ave
(02725)
Rates: $75-$129
(508) 678-4545
(800) 228-5151

SOUTH DEERFIELD

MOTEL 6
Rt 5-10 (01373)
Rates: $42-$56
(413) 665-7161
(800) 466-8356

SOUTH ORLEANS

**OCEAN BAY VIEW
COTTAGES**
116 Portanimicut
Rd (02662)
Rates: n/a
(508) 255-3344

**SEA BREEZE
MOTEL**
13-17 Beach Rd
(02662)
Rates: $70-$100
(508) 240-5500

SOUTH WELLFLEET

**GREEN HAVEN
COTTAGES**
633 Rt 6 (02663)
Rates: $100-$750
Weekly
(508) 349-1715

**SURF SIDE
COTTAGES**
Ocean View Dr
(02663)
Rates: n/a
(508) 349-3959

**SWEET PEA &
VILLAGE EDGE**
249 Main St
(02663)
Rates: $100-$700
(508) 349-6396

SOUTH YARMOUTH

**BRENTWOOD
COTTAGES**
961 Main St
(02664)
Rates: n/a
(508) 398-8812
(800) 328-8812

**BRENTWOOD
MOTOR INN**
Rt 28 (02664)
Rates: $35-$65+
(508) 398-8812
(800) 328-8812

**CAPTAIN
JONATHAN
MOTEL**
1237 Rt 28 (02664)
Rates: $35-$70
(508) 398-3480
(800) 342-348

MOTEL 6
1314 Rt 28 (02664)
Rates: $75-$85
(508) 394-4000
(800) 466-8356

**WAYFARER'S ALL
COTTAGES**
186 Seaview Ave
(02664)
Rates: $200-$1125
Weekly
(508) 394-9981

**WINDJAMMER
MOTOR INN**
192 South Shore
Dr (02664)
Rates: $49-$100
(508) 398-2370
(800) 448-9744

SOUTH-BOROUGH

RED ROOF INN
367 Turnpike Rd
(01772)
Rates: $64-$104
(508) 481-3904
(800) 843-7663

STOCKBRIDGE

HIGH MEADOWS
P.O. Box 976
(01262)
Rates: n/a
(413) 298-4652
(800) 817-5665

STURBRIDGE

**BEST WESTERN
AMERICAN
MOTOR LODGE**
350 Main St
(01566)
Rates: $75-$110
(508) 347-9121
(800) 528-1234

DAYS INN
66-68 Old Rt 15,
Haynes St (01566)
Rates: $75-$120
(508) 347-3391
(800) 329-7466

**GREEN ACRES
MOTEL**
2 Shepard Rd
(01566)
Rates: $55-$95
(508) 347-3496

**PUBLICK HOUSE
HISTORIC
RESORT**
SR 131 (01566)
Rates: $100-$170
(508) 347-3313
(800) 782-5425

RODEWAY INN
172 Main St
(01566)
Rates: $60-$130
(508) 347-9673
(800) 228-2000

**STURBRIDGE
HERITAGE MOTEL**
499-501 Main St
(01566)
Rates: $35-$70
(508) 347-3943

**STURBRIDGE
HOST HOTEL
& CONFERENCE
CENTER**
366 Main St
(01566)
Rates: $119-$179
(508) 347-7393
(800) 582-3232

TEWKSBURY

HOLIDAY INN
4 Highwood Dr
(01876)
Rates: $49-$89
(978) 640-9000
(800) 465-4329

MOTEL 6
95 Main St (01876)
Rates: $47-$56
(978) 851-8677
(800) 466-8356

**RESIDENCE INN
BY MARRIOTT**
1775 Andover St
(01876)
Rates: $129-$169
(978) 640-1003
(800) 331-3131

TYRINGHAM

**SUNSET FARM
BED & BREAKFAST**
74 Tyringham Rd
(01264)
Rates: $65-$110
(413) 243-3229
(413) 243-0730

UXBRIDGE

**QUAKER MOTOR
LODGE**
442 Quaker Hwy
(01569)
Rates: $45-$55
(508) 278-2445

WALTHAM

**HOMESTEAD
VILLAGE GUEST
STUDIOS**
52 Fourth Ave
(02154)
Rates: $99-$114
(781) 890-1333
(888) 782-9473

**SUMMERFIELD
SUITES**
54 Fourth Ave
(02154)
Rates: $139-$249
(781) 290-0026
(800) 833-4353

**THE WESTIN
HOTEL**
70 Third Ave
(02154)
Rates: $119-$255
(781) 290-5600
(800) 228-3000

WELLFLEET

**FRIENDSHIP
COTTAGES**
530 Chequessett
Neck Rd (02667)
Rates: $100-$750
Weekly
(202) 722-0185

**PINE MOORINGS
COTTAGES & B&B**
Indianeck Rd
(02667)
Rates: $75-$750
(508) 349-6923

WEST BARNSTABLE

COZY NEST B&B
161 Maple St
(02630)
Rates: n/a
(508) 362-4218

WEST BROOKFIELD

COPPER LANTERN MOTOR LODGE
184 W Main St
(01585)
Rates: $35-$70
(508) 867-6441

WEST DENNIS

CAPTAIN VARRIEUR'S COTTAGES
P.O. Box 1332
(02670)
Rates: $600-$1125+
Weekly
(508) 394-4338
(888) 394-4338

ELMWOOD INN
57 Old Main St
(02670)
Rates: $38-$70
(508) 394-2798

PINE COVE INN & COTTAGES
5 Main St (02670)
Rates: $30-$70
(508) 398-8511

WOODBINE VILLAGE ON THE COVE
Rt 28 (02670)
Rates: $300
Weekly
(508) 881-1381

WEST HARWICH

BARNABY INN
36 Main St (02671)
Rates: $30-$100
(508) 432-6789
(800) 439-4764

CAPE COD CLADDAGH INN
77 Main St (02671)
Rates: $95-$135
(508) 432-9628

WEST SPRINGFIELD

BLACK HORSE MOTEL
500 Riverdale St
(01089)
Rates: $39-$69
(413) 733-2161

RAMADA LIMITED
21 Baldwin St
(01089)
Rates: $69-$74
(413) 781-2300
(800) 272-6232

RED ROOF INN
1254 Riverdale St
(01089)
Rates: $56-$93
(413) 731-1010
(800) 843-7663

WEST STOCKBRIDGE

PLEASANT VALLEY MOTEL
Rt 102 (01266)
Rates: $55-$165
(413) 232-8511

SHAKER MILL INN
Rt 102 (01266)
Rates: $70-$175
(413) 232-8596
(800) 322-8565

WEST YARMOUTH

MAYFLOWER MOTEL
504 Main St
(02673)
Rates: $35-$70
(508) 775-2758
(800) 227-1851

RED ROSE INN
6 New Hampshire
Ave (02673)
Rates: $70-$109
(508) 775-2944

RYAN'S COTTAGE
19 Sandy Ln
(02673)
Rates: $300-$750
Weekly
(508) 771-6387

THUNDERBIRD MOTOR LODGE
216 Main St
(02673)
Rates: $30-$70
(508) 775-2692
(800) 247-3006

TOWN 'N COUNTRY MOTOR LODGE
452 Main St
(02673)
Rates: $35-$70
(508) 771-0212
(800) 992-2340

YARMOUTH SHORES COTTAGES
29 Lewis Bay Rd
(02673)
Rates: $190-$750
Weekly
(508) 775-1944

WESTBOROUGH

COMFORT INN
399 Turnpike Rd
(01581)
Rates: $89-$139
(508) 366-0202
(800) 228-5150

RESIDENCE INN BY MARRIOTT
25 Connector Rd
(01581)
Rates: $89-$199
(508) 366-7700
(800) 331-3131

WYNDHAM HOTEL
5400 Computer Dr
(01581)
Rates: $84-$160
(508) 366-5511
(800) 996-3426

WESTFIELD

COUNTRY COURT MOTEL
480 Southampton
Rd (01085)
Rates: $35-$69
(413) 562-9790

WESTMINSTER

TOWN CRIER MOTEL
Rt 2A & 140
(04173)
Rates: $29-$45
(508) 874-5951

WEYMOUTH

SUPER 8 MOTEL
655 Washington St
(02188)
Rates: $47-$79
(781) 337-5200
(800) 800-8000

WILLIAMSTOWN

COZY CORNER MOTEL
284 Sand Spring
Rd (01267)
Rates: $70-$105
(413) 458-8006

GREEN VALLEY MOTEL
1214 Simonds Rd
(01267)
Rates: $35-$109
(413) 458-3864

JERICHO VALLEY INN
2541 Hancock Rd
(01267)
Rates: $48-$100
(413) 458-9511
(800) 537-4246

THE VILLAGER MOTEL
953 Simonds Rd
(01267)
Rates: $65-$95
(413) 458-4046

WILLIAMS INN
On the Green,
Rts 2 & 7 (01267)
Rates: $80-$140
(413) 458-9371
(800) 828-0133

WOBURN

HAMPTON INN
315 Mishawum
Rd (01801)
Rates: $139-$169
(781) 935-7666
(800) 426-7866

WORCESTER

REGENCY SUITES
70 Southridge St
(01608)
Rates: $95-$125
(508) 753-3512

YARMOUTH PORT

COLONIAL HOUSE INN
277 Main St
(02675)
Rates: $45-$100
(508) 362-4348
(800) 999-3416

VILLAGE INN B&B
92 Main St (02675)
Rates: $70-$109
(508) 362-3182

AREA CODES - If the local number doesn't connect, check for a new area code.

MICHIGAN

ACME

KNOLLWOOD MOTEL
5777 US 31 N, Box 37 (49610)
Rates: $38-$88
(231) 938-2040

SUN 'N SAND MOTEL
P. O. Box 307 (49610)
Rates: n/a
(231) 938-2190

ALBION

DAYS INN
27644 C Dr North (49224)
Rates: $45-$54
(517) 629-9411
(800) 329-7466

ALGONAC

LINDA'S LIGHTHOUSE INN BED & BREAKFST
5965 Pte. Tremble Rd (48001)
Rates: $70-$135
(810) 794-2992

ALLEGAN

BUDGET HOST SUNSET MOTEL
1580 Lincoln Rd (49010)
Rates: $35-$105
(616) 673-6622
(800) 283-4678

ALLEN PARK

BEST WESTERN GREENFIELD INN
3000 Enterprise Dr (48101)
Rates $89-$114
(313) 271-1600
(800) 528-1234
(800) 342-5802

HOLIDAY INN EXPRESS HOTEL & SUITES
3600 Enterprise Dr (48101)
Rates: n/a
(800) 465-4329

ALMA

PETTICOAT INN
2454 W Monroe Rd (48801)
Rates: $27-$40
(517) 681-5728

ALPENA

AMBER MOTEL
2052 State St (49707)
Rates: $35-$65
(517) 354-8573

BAY MOTEL
2107 US 23 S (49707)
Rates: $30-$150
(517) 356-6137

FIRESIDE INN
18730 Fireside Hwy (49707)
Rates: n/a
(517) 595-6369

HOLIDAY INN
1000 Hwy 23N (49707)
Rates: $84-$114
(517) 356-2151
(800) 465-4329

PARKER HOUSE MOTEL
11505 Hwy 23N (49707)
Rates: $40-$55
(517) 595-6484

WATERS EDGE MOTEL
1000 State St (49707)
Rates: $28-$49
(517) 354-5495

ANN ARBOR

COMFORT INN
2455 Carpenter Rd (48108)
Rates: $68-$140
(734) 973-6100
(800) 228-5150

HAWTHORN SUITES
3535 Green Court (48105)
Rates: n/a
(734) 327-0011
(800) 527-1133

MOTEL 6
3764 S State St (48108)
Rates: $50-$66
(734) 665-9900
(800) 466-8356

RED ROOF INN
3621 Plymouth Rd (48105)
Rates: $59-$79
(734) 996-5800
(800) 843-7663

RED ROOF INN
3505 S State St (48108)
Rates: n/a
(734) 665-3500
(800) 843-7663

RESIDENCE INN BY MARRIOTT
800 Victors Way (48108)
Rates: $99-$169
(734) 996-5666
(800) 331-3131

AU GRES

BEST WESTERN PINEWOOD LODGE
510 W US 23 (48703)
Rates: $79-$109
(517) 876-4060
(800) 528-1234
(800) 943-7769

POINT AU GRES HOTEL
3279 South Point Ln (48703)
Rates: $33-$40
(517) 876-7217

AUBURN HILLS

AMERISUITES
1545 Opdyke Rd (48326)
Rates: $69-$129
(248) 475-9393
(800) 833-1516

COMFORT SUITES
N Opdyke Rd (48326)
Rates: $59-$150
(800) 228-5150

HILTON SUITES
2300 Featherstone Rd (48326)
Rates: $129-$164
(248) 334-2222
(800) 445-8667

HOMESTEAD VILLAGE GUEST STUDIOS
3315 University Dr (48326)
Rates: n/a
(248) 340-8888
(888) 782-9473

MOTEL 6
1471 Opdyke Rd (48326)
Rates: $50-$66
(248) 373-8440
(800) 466-8356

WELLESLEY INN & SUITES
2100 Featherstone Rd (48326)
Rates: $69-$139
(248) 335-5200
(800) 444-8888

BARAGA

CARLA'S LAKE SHORE MOTEL
Rt 1, Box 233 (49908)
Rates: $45-$62
(906) 353-6256

SUPER 8 MOTEL
790 Michigan Ave (49908)
Rates: $46-$58
(906) 353-6680
(800) 800-8000

BATTLE CREEK

BATTLE CREEK INN
5050 Beckley Rd (49015)
Rates: $62-$82
(616) 979-1100
(800) 232-3405

BAYMONT INN & SUITES
4725 Beckley Rd (49017)
Rates: $63-$87
(616) 979-5400
(800) 301-0200

DAYS INN
4786 Beckley Rd (49017)
Rates: $50-$100
(616) 979-3561
(800) 329-7466

ECONO LODGE
165 Capital Ave SW (49015)
Rates: $36-$75
(616) 965-3976
(800) 553-2666

HAMPTON INN
1150 Riverside Dr (49017)
Rates: $68-$83
(616) 979-5577
(800) 426-7866

KNIGHTS INN
2595 Capital Ave SW (49015)
Rates: $39-$82
(616) 964-2600
(800) 843-5644

MCCALMY PLAZA HOTEL
50 Capital Ave SW (49017)
Rates: $129-$139
(616) 963-7050

MICHIGAN MOTEL
20475 Capital Ave NE (49017)
Rates: $35-$45
(616) 963-1565

MOTEL 6
4775 Beckley Rd (49015)
Rates: $32-$58
(616) 979-1141
(800) 466-8356

SUPER 8 MOTEL
5395 Beckley Rd (49015)
Rates: $47-$61
(616) 979-1828
(800) 800-8000

BAY CITY

AMERICINN
3915 Three Mile Rd (48706)
Rates: $59-$134
(517) 671-0071
(800) 634-3444

BAY VALLEY HOTEL & RESORT
2470 Old Bridge Rd (48706)
Rates: $70-$120
(517) 686-3500

DELTA MOTEL
1000 S Euclid Ave (48706)
Rates: $30-$60
(517) 684-4490

HOLIDAY INN
501 Saginaw St (48708)
Rates: $80-$160
(517) 892-3501
(800) 465-4329

BAY VIEW

COMFORT INN
1314 US 31 N (49770)
Rates: $48-$225
(231) 347-3220
(800) 228-5150

BEAR LAKE

BELLA VISTA MOTOR LODGE
US #31 in Village (49614)
Rates: n/a
(616) 864-3000

BELLAIRE

WINDWARD SHORE MOTEL
5812 E Torch Lake Dr (49615)
Rates: n/a
(616) 377-6321

BELLEVILLE

COMFORT INN
45945 S Service Dr (48111)
Rates: $45-$99
(734) 697-8556
(800) 228-5150

RED ROOF INN METRO AIRPORT
4550 N Expwy (48111)
Rates: $67-$84
(734) 697-2244
(800) 843-7663

SUPER 8 MOTEL
45707 I-94 Service Dr (48111)
Rates: $50-$69
(734) 699-1888
(800) 800-8000

BENTON HARBOR

MOTEL 6
2063 Pipestone Rd (49022)
Rates: $40-$56
(616) 925-5100
(800) 466-8356

RAMADA INN
798 Ferguson Dr (49022)
Rates: $69-$129
(616) 927-1172
(800) 272-6232

RED ROOF INN
1630 Mall Dr (49022)
Rates: $53-$81
(616) 927-2484
(800) 843-7663

SUPER 8 MOTEL
1950 E Napier Ave (49022)
Rates: $42-$62
(616) 926-1371
(800) 800-8000

BERGLAND

NORTHWINDS MOTEL & RESORT
1497 W M-28 (49910)
Rates: $22-$69
(906) 575-3557

BEULAH

PINE KNOT MOTEL
171 N Center St (49617)
Rates: $80-$110
(231) 882-7751

SUNNYWOODS RESORT MOTEL
14065 Honor Hwy (49617)
Rates: $30-$80
(616) 325-3952
(800) 347-9728

BIG BAY

BIG BAY DEPOT MOTEL
P. O. Box 61 (49808)
Rates: $50-$55
(906) 345-9350

BIRCH RUN

SUPER 8 MOTEL
9235 Birch Run Rd (48415)
Rates: $37-$67
(517) 624-4440
(800) 800-8000

BLOOMFIELD HILLS

QUALITY INN
1801 S Telegraph Rd (48302)
Rates: $69-$99
(248) 334-2444
(800) 228-5151

ST. CHRISTOPHER MOTEL
3915 Telegraph Rd (48302)
Rates: $35-$45
(248) 647-1800

BOYNE FALLS

BOYNE VUE MOTEL
2711 Railroad, Box 12 (49713)
Rates: $28-$125
(616) 549-2822
(800) 549-2822

BRANCH

LAZY DAYS MOTEL
P. O. Box 104 (49402)
Rates: $32
(616) 898-2252

BREVORT

CHAPEL HILL MOTEL
4422 W US 2 (49760)
Rates: $44-$54
(906) 292-5521

BRIDGEPORT

BAYMONT INN
6460 Dixie Hwy (48722)
Rates: $40-$66
(517) 777-3000
(800) 301-0200

MOTEL 6
6361 Dixie Hwy (48722)
Rates: $33-$49
(517) 777-2582
(800) 466-8356

BRIDGMAN

BRIDGMAN INN
9999 Red Arrow Hwy (49106)
Rates: $30-$70
(616) 465-3187

CADILLAC

CADILLAC SANDS RESORT
6319 E M115 (49601)
Rates: $75-$130
(231) 775-2407
(800) 647-2637

ECONO LODGE
2501 Sunnyside Dr (49601)
Rates: $65-$120
(231) 775-6700
(800) 553-2666

KNIGHTS INN
301 S Lake Mitchell Dr (49601)
Rates: $39-$125
(231) 775-9961
(800) 843-5644

MCGUIRES RESORT & CONFERENCE CENTER
7880 Mackinaw Tr (49601)
Rates: $89-$129
(231) 775-9947
(800) 662-7302

PILGRIM'S VILLAGE
181 S Lake Mitchell (49601)
Rates: $49
(231) 775-5412

PINE CHATA RESORT
5936 E M 55 (49601)
Rates: $50-$60
(231) 775-4677

PINE KNOLL MOTEL
8072 Mackinaw Tr (49601)
Rates: $35-$65
(231) 775-9471

SOUTH SHORE RESORT
1246 Sunnyside Dr (49601)
Rates: $30-$60
(231) 775-7641

CANTON

BAYMONT INN & SUITES
41211 Ford Rd (48187)
Rates: $70-$77
(734) 981-1808
(800) 301-0200

DAYS INN
40500 Michigan Ave (48187)
Rates: $48-$75
(734) 721-5200
(800) 329-7466

MOTEL 6
41216 Ford Rd
(48187)
Rates: $45-$61
(734) 981-5000
(800) 466-8356

SUPER 8 MOTEL
3933 Lotz Rd
(48187)
Rates: $55-$67
(734) 722-8880
(800) 800-8000

CARO

KINGS WAY INN
1057 E Caro Rd
(48723)
Rates: $27-$65
(517) 673-7511

CASCADE

BAYMONT INN
2873 Kraft Ave
(49512))
Rates: $42-$52
(616) 956-3300
(800) 301-0200

**COUNTRY INN
& SUITES
BY CARLSON**
5399 28th St
(49512)
Rates: $74-$98
(616) 977-0909
(800) 456-4000

EXEL INN
4855 28th St SE
(49512)
Rates: $45-$70
(616) 957-3000
(800) 367-3935

HAMPTON INN
4981 28th St SE
(49512)
Rates: $65-$94
(616) 956-9304
(800) 426-7866

RED ROOF INN
5131 E 28th St
(49512)
Rates: $59-$78
(616) 942-0800
(800) 843-7663

CASEVILLE

SURF N SAND MTL
6006 Pt Austin Rd
(48725)
Rates: $36-$84
(517) 856-4400

CASS CITY

**WILDWOOD
MOTEL**
5986 E Cass City
Rd (48726)
Rates: $34
(517) 872-3366

CEDARVILLE

COMFORT INN
106 W SR 134
(49719)
Rates: $80-$609
(906) 484-2266
(800) 228-5150
(800) 222-2949

CHARLEVOIX

CAPRI MOTEL
1455 S Bridge St
(49720)
Rates: $60-$120
(231) 547-2545

**THE LODGE
MOTEL**
US 31 N (49720)
Rates: $30-$160
(231) 547-6565

SLEEP INN
800 Petoskey Ave
(49720)
Rates: $49-$133
(231) 547-0300
(800) 753-3746

CHARLOTTE

SUPER 8 MOTEL
828 E Shepherd St
(48813)
Rates: $54-$74
(517) 543-8288
(800) 800-8000

CHEBOYGAN

**BIRCH HAUS
MOTEL**
1301 Mackinaw
Ave (49721)
Rates: $30-$55
(231) 627-5862

**CHEBOYGAN
MOTOR LODGE**
1355 Mackinaw
Ave (49721)
Rates: $30-$75
(231) 627-3129

**MONARCH
MOTEL**
1257 Mackinaw
Ave (49721)
Rates: $30-$55
(231) 627-2143

**PINE RIVER
MOTEL**
102 Lafayette
(49721)
Rates: $40-$50
(231) 627-5119

CHELSEA

COMFORT INN
Commerce Park
Dr & Brown Dr
(48118)
Rates: $75-$250
(800) 228-5150

CLARE

**DOHERTY
MOTOR HOTEL**
604 McEwan St
(48617)
Rates: $40-$75
(517) 386-3441
(800) 525-4115

KNIGHTS INN
1110 N McEwan
(48617)
Rates: $29-$100
(517) 386-7201
(800) 843-5644

**LONE PINE
MOTEL**
1508 McEwan St
(48617)
Rates: $45-$50
(517) 386-7787

CLIO

**CINNAMON STICK
BED & BREAKFAST**
12364 N Genesee
Rd (48420)
Rates: $60-$125
(810) 686-8391

COLDWATER

ECONO LODGE
884 W Chicago Rd
(49036)
Rates: $38-$69
(517) 278-4501
(800) 553-2666

**QUALITY INN
& SUITES**
1000 Orleans Blvd
(49036)
Rates: $572$175
(517) 278-2017
(800) 228-5151

SUPER 8 MOTEL
600 Orleans Blvd
(49036)
Rates: $55-$74
(517) 278-8833
(800) 800-8000

COMSTOCK
PARK

SWAN INN MOTEL
5182 Alpine Ave
NW (49321)
Rates: $45-$80
(616) 784-1224
(800) 875-7926

COOPERSVILLE

AMERIHOST INN
1040 O'Malley Dr
(49404)
Rates: $68-$78
(616) 837-8100
(800) 434-5800

COPPER
HARBOR

**ASTOR HOUSE-
MINNETONKA
RESORT**
P. O. Box 13 (49918)
Rates: $43-$85
(906) 289-4449
(800) 433-2770

**BELLA VISTA
MOTEL**
P. O. Box 26
(49918)
Rates: $38-$50
(906) 289-4213

**KING COPPER
MOTELS**
PO Box 68 (49918)
Rates: $40-$60
(906) 289-4214
(800) 833-2470

**LAKE FANNY
HOOE RESORT**
505 2nd St (49918)
Rates: $58-$68
(906) 289-4451
(800) 426-4451

NORLAND MOTEL
US 41, F #172
(49918)
Rates: $36-$64
(906) 289-4815

CURTIS

SEASONS MOTEL
Main St (49820)
Rates: $30-$43
(906) 586-3078

DEARBORN

ECONO LODGE
23730 Michigan
Ave (48124)
Rates: $45-$79
(313) 565-7250
(800) 553-2666

RED ROOF INN
24130 Michigan
Ave (48124)
Rates: $66-$82
(313) 278-9732
(800) 843-7663

RITZ CARLTON
Fairlane Plaza,
300 Town Ctr Dr
(48126)
Rates: $225-$1500
(313) 441-2000
(800) 241-3333

DETROIT

HOTEL ST. REGIS
3071 W Grand
Blvd (48202)
Rates: $79-$115
(313) 873-3000

**MARRIOTT HOTEL
DETROIT
AIRPORT**
Detroit Metro
Airport (48242)
Rates: $139-$160
(313) 941-9400
(800) 228-9290

MARRIOTT RENAISSANCE CENTER
Renaissance Center (48242)
Rates: $159-$209
(313) 568-8000
(800) 228-9290

RAMADA INN
400 Bagley Ave (48226)
Rates: $64-$139
(313) 962-2300
(800) 272-6232

RESIDENCE INN BY MARRIOTT
5777 Southfield Service Dr (48228)
Rates: $159-$175
(313) 441-1700
(800) 331-3131

RIVER PLACE HOTEL
1000 River Pl (48207)
Rates: $99-$159
(313) 259-9500

THE SHORECREST MOTOR INN
1316 E Jefferson (48207)
Rates: $52-$150
(313) 568-3000
(800) 992-9616

SUBURBAN HOUSE
16920 Telegraph (48219)
Rates: $28-$40
(313) 535-9646

WESTIN HOTEL RENAISSANCE CENTER
Renaissance Center (48243)
Rates: $175-$210
(313) 568-8000
(800) 228-3000

DOUGLAS

PINES MOTEL
56 S Blue Star Hwy (49406)
Rates: $29-$98
(616) 857-5211

DRUMMOND ISLAND

VECHELL'S CEDAR VIEW RESORT
P. O. Box 175 (49726)
Rates: $225-$255
(906) 493-5381

WOODMOOR RESORT COMPLEX
26 Maxton Rd (49726)
Rates: $69-$109
(906) 493-1000

DUNDEE

COMFORT INN
621 Tecumseh (48131)
Rates: $59-$150
(734) 529-5505
(800) 228-5150

EAGLE HARBOR

SHORELINE RESORT
201 Front St, F #2015 (49950)
Rates: $52-$72
(906) 289-4441

EAST JORDAN

WESTBROOK MOTEL
218 Elizabeth St (49727)
Rates: $45-$55
(616) 536-2674

EAST LANSING

RESIDENCE INN BY MARRIOTT
1600 E Grand River Ave (48823)
Rates: $124-$145
(517) 332-7711
(800) 331-3131

EAST TAWAS

AARON'S WOODED ACRES RESORT
On Lake Huron (48730)
Rates: n/a
(517) 362-5788

CARRIAGE INN
1500 N US 23 (48730)
Rates: $30-$55
(517) 362-2831
(800) 666-8493

HOLIDAY INN
300 E Bay St (48730)
Rates: n/a
(517) 362-8601
(800) 465-4329

NORTHLAND BEACH COTTAGES
808 East Bay St (48730)
Rates: n/a
(517) 362-2601

EASTPOINTE

EASTLAND MOTEL
21055 Gratiot Ave (48021)
Rates: $26-$32
(810) 772-1300

ELK RAPIDS

CAMELOT INN
10962 Hwy 31S (49629)
Rates: $53-$88
(231) 264-8473

EPOUFETTE

WONDERLAND MOTEL
80 West US 2 (49762)
Rates: n/a
(906) 292-5574

ESCANABA

BAY VIEW MOTEL
Hwy 2, 41 & SR 35 (49837)
Rates: $45-$60
(906) 786-2843

DAYS INN
2603 N Lincoln Rd (49829)
Rates: $50-$78
(906) 789-1200
(800) 329-7466

ECONO LODGE
921 N Lincoln Rd (49829)
Rates: $39-$79
(906) 789-1066
(800) 553-2666

HIAWATHA MOTEL
2400 Ludington St (49829)
Rates: $32-$53
(906) 786-1341

SUNSET MOTEL
P. O. Box 343 (49829)
Rates: $25-$45
(906) 786-1213

FARMINGTON HILLS

HOLIDAY INN
38123 W Ten Mile Rd (48335)
Rates: $115-$130
(248) 477-4000
(800) 465-4329

MOTEL 6
38300 Grand River Ave (48335)
Rates: $40-$46
(248) 471-0590
(800) 466-8356

RED ROOF INN
24300 Sinacola Ct (48335)
Rates: $57-$79
(248) 478-8640
(800) 843-7663

FENNVILLE

J. PAULES FENN IN BED & BREAKFAST
2254 S 58th St (49408)
Rates: $70-$200
(616) 561-2836

SPRUCE CUTTERS COTTAGE B&B
6670 126th Ave (49408)
Rates: $95-$155
(616) 543-4285
(800) 493-5888

FLINT

BAYMONT INN
4160 Pier North Blvd (48504)
Rates: $40-$64
(810) 732-2300
(800) 301-0200

HOWARD JOHNSON EXPRESS
G-3277 Miller Rd (48507)
Rates: $40-$65
(810) 733-5910
(800) 446-4656

MOTEL 6
2324 Austin Pkwy (48507)
Rates: $32-$38
(810) 767-7100
(800) 466-8356

RAMADA INN
G-4300 W Pierson Rd (48504)
Rates: $59-$80
(810) 732-0400
(800) 272-6232

RED ROOF INN
G-3219 Miller Rd (48507)
Rates: $46-$68
(810) 733-1660
(800) 843-7663

SUPER 8 MOTEL
3033 Claude Ave (48507)
Rates: $49-$60
(810) 230-7888
(800) 800-8000

FOUNTAIN

CHRISTIE'S LOG CABINS ON ROUND LAKE
6503 E Sugar Grove (49410)
Rates: $45-$80
(616) 462-3218
(800) 209-7385

FRANKEN-MUTH

DRURY INN
260 S Main St (48734)
Rates: $60-$110
(517) 652-2800
(800) 378-7946

FRANKFORT

**CHIMNEY COR-
NERS RESORT**
1602 Crystal Dr
(49635)
Rates: $37-$110
(616) 352-7522

**HOTEL
FRANKFORT B&B**
231 Main St
(49635)
Rates: $39-$230
(616) 352-4303

FREELAND

**FREELAND INN
MOTEL**
6840 Midland Rd
(48623)
Rates: n/a
(517) 695-9646

GAYLORD

**BEST WESTERN
ROYAL CREST
MOTEL**
803 S Otsego Ave
(49735)
Rates: $59-$99
(517) 732-6451
(800) 528-134

CEDARS MOTEL
701 North Center
(49735)
Rates: $25-$30
(517) 732-4525

**DOWNTOWN
MOTEL**
208 S Otsego Ave
(49735)
Rates: $42-$68
(517) 732-5010

ECONO LODGE
2880 Old 27 S
(49735)
Rates: $38-$69
(517) 732-5133
(800) 553-2666

HOLIDAY INN
833 W Main St
(49735)
Rates: $70-$97
(517) 732-2431
(800) 465-4329

**MICHAYWE
RESORT**
1535 Opal Lake
Rd (49735)
Rates: $65-$300
(517) 939-8914
(800) 322-6636

SUPER 8 MOTEL
1042 W Main St
(49735)
Rates: $45-$135
(517) 732-5193
(800) 800-8000

TIMBERLY MOTEL
881 S Otsego Ave
(49735)
Rates: $40-$76
(517) 732-5166
(888) 321-2606

GLADSTONE

**SLEEPY HOLLOW
MOTEL**
7156 US 2 & 41
(49837)
Rates: n/a
(906) 786-7092

GLADWIN

**GLADWIN
MOTOR INN**
1003 W Cedar Ave
(48624)
Rates: $25-$50
(517) 426-9661

GRAND BLANC

SCENIC INN
G8308 S Saginaw
Rd (48439)
Rates: $35-$61
(313) 694-6611

GRAND
MARAIS

HILLTOP CABINS
P. O. Box 377
(49839)
Rates: $45-$65
(906) 494-2331

**VOYAGEUR'S
MOTEL**
E Wilson St
(49839)
Rates: $50-$71
(906) 494-2389

GRAND RAPIDS

CASCADE INN
2865 Broadmoore
(49512)
Rates: $27-$43
(616) 949-0850

**DAYS INN
DOWNTOWN**
310 Pearl St NW
(49504)
Rates: $65-$98
(616) 235-7611
(800) 329-7466

ECONO LODGE
5175 28th St SE
(49512)
Rates: $36-$110
(616) 956-6601
(800) 553-2666

ECONO LODGE
250 28th St SW
(49548)
Rates: $54-$64
(616) 452-2131
(800) 553-2666

**HAWTHORN
SUITES LTD**
2985 Kraft Ave SE
(49512)
Rates: n/a
(616) 940-1777
(800) 527-1133

HOLIDAY INN
270 Ann St NW
(49504)
Rates: $76-$86
(616) 363-9001
(800) 465-4329

**HOMEWOOD
SUITES**
3920 Stahl Dr SE
(49546)
Rates: $94-$150
(616) 285-7100
(800) 225-5466

MOTEL 6
3524 28th St SE
(49508)
Rates: $32-$44
(616) 957-3511
(800) 466-8356

**NEW ENGLAND
SUITES HOTEL**
2985 Kraft Ave SE
(49512)
Rates: $55-$75
(616) 940-1777
(800) 784-8371

RIVIERA MOTEL
4350
Rememberance
Rd (49504)
Rates: $35-$50
(616) 453-2404

SLEEP INN
4284 29th St SE
(49512)
Rates: $69-$109
(616) 975-9000
(800) 753-3746

GRAYLING

CEDAR MOTEL
606 N James
(49738)
Rates: $26-$40
(517) 348-5884

ECONO LODGE
1232 I-75 Bus
Loop (49738)
Rates: $39-$89
(517) 348-8900
(800) 553-2666

HOLIDAY INN
2650 S I-75 Bus
Loop (49738)
Rates: $109-$129
(517) 348-7611
(800) 465-4329
(800) 292-9055

**NORTH COUNTRY
LODGE**
617 N I-75 Bus
Loop (49738)
Rates: $50-$160
(517) 348-8471
(800) 475-6300

**POINTE NORTH
OF GRAYLING**
N I-75 Bus Loop
(49738)
Rates: $35-$75
(517) 348-5950

**RIVER COUNTRY
MOTOR LODGE**
N I-75 Bus Loop
(49738)
Rates: $30-$65
(517) 348-8619
(800) 733-7396

SUPER 8 MOTEL
5828 NA Miles
Pkwy (49738)
Rates: $60-$75
(517) 348-8888
(800) 800-8000

**WOODLAND
MOTEL**
267 I-75 Business
Loop (49738)
Rates: $30-$80
(517) 348-9094

HAGAR SHORE

**SWEET CHERRY
RESORT**
3313 Chestnut
(49038)
Rates: n/a
(616) 849-1233

HANCOCK

**BEST WESTERN
COPPER CROWN
MOTEL**
235 Hancock Ave
(49930)
Rates: $50-$63
(906) 482-6111
(800) 528-1234

HARBOR
BEACH

**THE TRAIN
STATION MOTEL**
2044 N Lakeshore
Dr (48441)
Rates: $51-$62
(517) 479-3215

HARBOR
SPRINGS

**HARBOR
SPRINGS
COTTAGE INN**
145 Zoll St (49740)
Rates: $90-$100
(231) 526-5431

HARPER
WOODS

PARKCREST INN
20000 Harper Ave
(48225)
Rates: $59-$80
(313) 884-8800

HARRISON

**LAKESIDE MOTEL
& COTTAGES**
South Business
#27 (48625)
Rates: $32-$42
(517) 539-3796

WAGON WHEEL MOTEL
4294 North Clare Ave (48625)
Rates: $30-$40
(517) 539-7065

HARRISVILLE

WIDOW'S WATCH BED & BREAKFAST
401 Lake St (48740)
Rates: $45-$65
(517) 724-5465
(800) 868-1904

HART

BUDGET HOST HART MOTEL
715 State St (49420)
Rates: $52-$89
(231) 873-2151
(800) 283-4678

COMFORT INN
2248 Comfort Dr (49420)
Rates: $79-$119
(231) 873-3456
(800) 228-5150

HAZEL PARK

QUALITY INN
1 W 9 Mile Rd (48030)
Rates: $90
(248) 399-5800
(800) 228-5151

HESSEL

LAKEVIEW MOTEL
P. O. Box 277 (49745)
Rates: $39-$42
(906) 484-2474

HILLSDALE

BAVARIAN INN
1728 Hudson Rd (49242)
Rates: $27-$34
(517) 437-3367
(800) 779-8033

HOLLAND

BLUE MILL INN
409 US 31S (49423)
Rates: $39-$51
(616) 392-7073

HONOR

SUNNY WOODS RESORT
14065 Honor Hwy (49640)
Rates: $67-$89
(231) 325-3952

HOUGHTON

BEST WESTERN FRANKLIN SQUARE INN
820 Shelden Ave (49931)
Rates: $89-$149
(906) 487-1700
(800) 528-1234
(888) 487-1700

BEST WESTERN KING'S INN
215 Shelden Ave (49931)
Rates: $63-$108
(906) 482-5000
(800) 528-1234
(888) 482-5005

HOUGHTON LAKE

HILLSIDE MOTEL
3419 W Houghton Lake Dr (48629)
Rates: $48-$56
(517) 366-5711

HOLIDAY ON THE LAKE MOTOR INN
100 Clearview Rd (48629)
Rates: $60-$85
(517) 422-5195

LAGOON RESORT & MOTEL
6578 W Houghton Lake Dr (48629)
Rates: $30-$70
(517) 422-5761

POPULARS RESORT
10360 West Shore Dr (48629)
Rates: $38-$72
(517) 422-5132

QUALITY INN
9285 W Houghton Lake Dr (48629)
Rates: $60-$179
(517) 422-5175
(800) 228-5151

VAL HALLA MOTEL
9869 West Shore Dr (48629)
Rates: $34-$48
(517) 422-5137

WAY NORTH MOTEL
9052 N Old US 27 (48629)
Rates: $34-$58
(517) 422-5523

HOWELL

BEST WESTERN INN
1500 Pickney Rd (48843)
Rates: $69-$100
(517) 548-2900
(800) 528-1234

HUDSON

SUNSET ACRES MOTEL
400 S Meridian US 127 (49247)
Rates: $31-$51
(517) 448-8968

HULBERT

THE LEEJA MOTEL
2000 M28 (49748)
Rates: n/a
(906) 876-2323

IMLAY CITY

DAYS INN
6692 Newark Rd (48444)
Rates: $60-$102
(810) 724-8005
(800) 329-7466

SUPER 8 MOTEL
6951 Newark Rd (48444)
Rates: $49-$80
(810) 724-8700
(800) 800-8000

INDIAN RIVER

CARAVAN MOTEL COTTAGES
4904 S Straits Hwy (49749)
Rates: $45-$65
(231) 238-7537

NORTHWOODS LODGE
2390 S Straits Hwy (49749)
Rates: $44-$98
(231) 238-7729

REIDS MOTOR COURT
3977 S Straits Hwy (49749)
Rates: $29-$48
(231) 238-9353

STAR GATE MOTEL
4646 S Straits Hwy (49749)
Rates: $32-$48
(231) 238-7371

WOODLANDS LODGE
5115 S Straits Hwy (49749)
Rates: $39-$54
(231) 238-4137

IONIA

EVERGREEN MOTEL
2030 N State Rd (48846)
Rates: $29
(616) 527-0930

MIDWAY MOTEL
7076 S State Rd (48846)
Rates: $26-$51
(616) 527-2080

SUPER 8 MOTEL
7245 S State Rd (48846)
Rates: $51-$109
(616) 527-2828
(800) 800-8000

IRON MOUNTAIN

BEST WESTERN EXECUTIVE INN
1518 S Stephenson Ave (49801)
Rates: $54-$87
(906) 774-2040
(800) 528-1234

BUDGET HOST LAKE ANTOINE
1663 N Stephenson Ave (49801)
Rates: $35-$52
(906) 774-6797
(800) 283-4678

DAYS INN
W 8176 S US 2 (49801)
Rates: $50-$85
(906) 774-2181
(800) 329-7466

EDGEWATER'S COUNTRY CABINS
N4128 N US 2 (49801)
Rates: $44-$70
(906) 774-6244
(800) 236-6244

TIMBERS MOTOR LODGE
200 S Stephenson Ave (49801)
Rates: $34-$74
(906) 774-7600
(800) 443-8533

WOODLANDS MOTEL
N 3957 North US 2 (49801)
Rates: $30-$40
(906) 774-6106

IRON RIVER

IRON RIVER MOTEL
3073 East US 2 (49935)
Rates: $32
(906) 265-4212

IRONWOOD

ARMATA MOTEL
124 W Cloverland Dr (49938)
Rates: $28-$42
(906) 932-4421

BLUE CLOUD MOTEL
105 W Cloverland Dr (49938)
Rates: $30-$50
(906) 932-0920

AREA CODES - If the local number doesn't connect, check for a new area code.

CRESTVIEW COZY INN MOTEL
424 Cloverland Dr (49938)
Rates: $32-$60
(906) 932-4845

ROYAL MOTEL
715 W Cloverland Dr (49938)
Rates: $31-$41
(906) 932-4230

SUPER 8 MOTEL
160 E Cloverland Dr (49938)
Rates: $66-$84
(906) 932-3395
(800) 800-8000

TWILIGHT TIME MOTEL
930 E Cloverland Dr. (49938)
Rates: $25-$50
(906) 932-3010

ISHPEMING

BEST WESTERN COUNTRY INN
850 US 41W (49849)
Rates: $71-$81
(906) 485-6345
(800) 528-1234

BEST WESTERN JASPER RIDGE INN
1000 River Pkwy (49849)
Rates: $54-$99
(906) 485-2378
(800) 528-1234

JACKSON

BAYMONT INN
2035 N Service Dr (49202)
Rates: $62-$90
(517) 789-6000
(800) 301-0200

HOLIDAY INN
2000 Holiday Inn Dr (49202)
Rates: $94-$99
(517) 783-2681
(800) 465-4329

MOTEL 6
830 Royal Dr (49202)
Rates: $42-$86
(517) 789-7186
(800) 466-8356

SUPER 8 MOTEL
2001 Shirley Dr (49202)
Rates: $49-$65
(517) 788-8780
(800) 800-8000

JONESVILLE

PINECREST MOTEL
516 W Chicago St (49250)
Rates: $25+
(517) 849-2137

KALAMAZOO

BAYMONT INN & SUITES
2203 S 11th St (49009)
Rates: $50-$75
(616) 372-7999
(800) 301-0200

HOLIDAY INN AIRPORT
3522 Sprinkle Rd (49002)
Rates: $79
(616) 381-7070
(800) 465-4329

HOLIDAY INN WEST
2747 S 11th St (49009)
Rates: $79-$99
(616) 375-6000
(800) 465-4329

KNIGHTS INN
1211 S Westernedge Ave (49008)
Rates: $45-$90
(616) 381-5000
(800) 843-5644

MOTEL 6
3704 Van Rick Rd (49002)
Rates: $34-$42
(616) 344-9255
(800) 466-8356

QUALITY INN & SUITES
3750 Easy St (49002)
Rates: $55-$120
(616) 388-3551
(800) 228-5151

RED ROOF INN-E
3701 E Cork St (49001)
Rates: $50-$83
(616) 382-6350
(800) 843-7663

RED ROOF INN-W
5425 W Michigan Ave (49009)
Rates: $50-$80
(616) 375-7400
(800) 843-7663

RESIDENCE INN BY MARRIOTT
1500 E Kilgore Rd (49001)
Rates: $105-$134
(616) 349-0855
(800) 331-3131

SUPER 8 MOTEL
618 Maple Hill Dr (49009)
Rates: $43-$63
(616) 345-0146
(800) 800-8000

KENTWOOD

RESIDENCE INN BY MARRIOTT
2701 E Beltline SE (49546)
Rates: $99-$140
(616) 957-8111
(800) 331-3131

LAKE CITY

LAKE CITY MOTEL
704 N Morey Rd (49651)
Rates: $35
(231) 839-4857

NORTHCREST MOTEL
1341 S Lakeshore (49651)
Rates: $49-$62
(231) 839-2075

LAKESIDE

WHITE RABBIT INN BED & BREAKFAST
14634 Red Arrow Hwy (49116)
Rates: $95-$200
(616) 469-4620
(800) 967-2224

LANSING

BEST WESTERN GOVERNOR'S INN
6133 S Pennsylvania Ave (48911)
Rates: $69-$110
(517) 393-5500
(800) 528-1234

BEST WESTERN MIDWAY HOTEL
7711 W Saginaw Hwy (48917)
Rates: $79-$109
(517) 627-8471
(800) 528-1234

DAYS INN SOUTH
6501 S Pennsylvania Ave (48911)
Rates: $50-$180
(517) 393-1650
(800) 329-7466

ECONO LODGE
1100 Ramada Dr (48911)
Rates: $37-$58
(517) 394-7200
(800) 553-2666

HAWTHORN SUITES LTD
901 Delta Commerce Dr (48911)
Rates: $99
(517) 886-0600
(800) 527-1133

MOTEL 6
7326 W Saginaw Hwy (48917)
Rates: $37-$43
(517) 321-1444
(800) 466-8356

MOTEL 6
112 E Main St (48933)
Rates: $30-$36
(517) 484-8722
(800) 466-8356

RAMADA LIMITED
6741 S Cedar (48911)
Rates: $44-$59
(517) 694-0454
(800) 272-6232

RED ROOF INN EAST
3615 Dunckel Rd (48910)
Rates: $50-$82
(517) 332-2575
(800) 843-7663

RED ROOF INN WEST
7412 W Saginaw Hwy (48917)
Rates: $52-$73
(517) 321-7246
(800) 843-7663

RESIDENCE INN BY MARRIOTT
922 Delta Commerce Dr (48917)
Rates: $84-$145
(517) 886-5030
(800) 331-3131

LAPEER

TOWN AND COUNTRY MOTEL
1275 Imlay City Rd (48446)
Rates: $35-$60
(810) 664-9132

LELAND

FALLING WATERS LODGE
200 W Cedar Box 345 (49654)
Rates: $75-$175
(616) 256-9832

LEWISTON

FAIRWAY INN
County Rd 489 (49756)
Rates: $40-$50
(517) 786-2217

LIVONIA

AMERISUITES
19300 Haggerty Rd (48152)
Rates: $95-$113
(734) 953-9224
(800) 833-1516

RESIDENCE INN BY MARRIOTT
17250 Fox Dr (48152)
Rates: $139
(734) 462-4201
(800) 331-3131

AREA CODES - If the local number doesn't connect, check for a new area code.

LUDINGTON

HOLIDAY INN EXPRESS
5323 W US 10
(49431)
Rates: $89-$149
(616) 845-7004
(800) 465-4329

LUDINGTON HOUSE B&B
General Delivery
(49431)
Rates: n/a
(800) 827-7869

NADER'S LAKE SHORE MOTOR LODGE
612 N Lakeshore Dr (49431)
Rates: $50-$85
(616) 843-8757
(800) 968-0109

MARINA BAY MOTOR LODGE
604 W Ludington Ave (49431)
Rates: $30-$140
(616) 845-5124
(800) 968-1440

NOVA MOTEL
472 S Old 31 Hwy
(49431)
Rates: $28-$69
(616) 843-3454

SUPER 8 MOTEL
5005 W US 10
(49431)
Rates: $50-$68
(616) 843-2140
(800) 800-8000

TIMBERLANE LONG LAKE RENOVA MOTEL
472 S Old 31 Hwy
(49431)
Rates: $28-$69
(616) 843-3454

TIMBERLANE LONG LAKE RESORT
7410 E US 10
(49458)
Rates: n/a
(616) 757-2142
(800) 227-2142

MACKINAW CITY

AMERICAN MOTEL
14351 S US 31
(49701)
Rates: $20-$55
(231) 436-5231

BAYMONT INN & SUITES
109 S Nicolet
(49701)
Rates: $99-$129
(231) 436-7737
(800) 301-0200

BEACHCOMBER MOTEL ON THE WATER
1011 S Huron
(49701)
Rates: $59-$125
(231) 436-8451
(800) 968-1383

THE BEACH HOUSE
1035 S Huron St
(49701)
Rates: $57-$150
(231) 436-5353
(800) 262-5353

BELL'S MELODY MOTEL
P. O. Box 896
(49701)
Rates: $28-$73
(231) 436-5463

BUDGET HOST INN
517 N Huron
(49701)
Rates: $62-$138
(231) 436-5543
(800) 283-4678

CAPRI MOTEL
801 S Nicolet St
(49701)
Rates: $45-$75
(231) 436-5498

DOWNING'S DOWNTOWN MOTOR INN
202 E Central Ave
(49701)
Rates: $58-$75
(231) 436-5528
(800) 695-5528

THE GRAND MACKINAW MOTEL
907 S Huron
(49701)
Rates: $68-$135
(231) 436-8831

HOLIDAY INN EXPRESS
364 Louvigney
(49701)
Rates: $42-$159
(231) 436-7100
(800) 465-4329

KINGS INN
1020 S Nicolet St
(49701)
Rates: $40-$98
(231) 436-5322

LA MIRAGE MOTEL
699 N Huron St
(49701)
Rates: $48-$122
(231) 436-5304
(800) 729-0998

LAMPLIGHTER MOTEL
303 Jamet St
(49701)
Rates: $43-$60
(231) 436-5350

MOTEL 6
206 Nicolet St
(49701)
Rates: $49-$149
(231) 436-8961
(800) 466-8356

NICOLET INN
General Delivery
(49701)
Rates: n/a
(800) 437-7817

OTTAWA MOTEL
P. O. Box 908
(49701)
Rates: $24-$65
(231) 436-8041

PARKSIDE INN-BRIDGESIDE
102 Nicolet St
(49701)
Rates: $38-$110
(231) 436-8301

QUALITY INN BEACHFRONT
917 S Huron
(49701)
Rates: $69-$219
(231) 436-5051
(800) 228-5151

RAMADA INN
450 S Nicolet
(49701)
Rates: $59-$159
(231) 436-5535
(800) 272-6232

STARLITE BUDGET INNS
116 Old US 31
(49701)
Rates: $42-$79
(231) 436-5959
(800) 288-8190

SUPER 8 MOTEL
601 N Huron Ave
(49701)
Rates: $55-$155
(231) 436-5252
(800) 800-8000

VAL-RU MOTEL
14394 Old US 31
(49701)
Rates: $39-$59
(231) 436-7691

VINDEL MOTEL
223 W Central Ave
(49701)
Rates: $59-$89
(231) 436-5273
(800) 968-5273

WA WA TAM MOTEL
219 W Jamet St
(49701)
Rates: $26-$54
(231) 436-8871

MADISON HEIGHTS

KNIGHTS INN
32703 Stephenson Hwy (48071)
Rates: $35-$52
(248) 583-7700
(800) 843-5644

MOTEL 6
32700 Barrington Rd (48071)
Rates: $40-$46
(248) 583-0500
(800) 466-8356

RED ROOF INN
32511 Concord Dr
(48071)
Rates: $56-$78
(248) 583-4700
(800) 843-7663

RESIDENCE INN BY MARRIOTT
32650 Stephenson Hwy (48071)
Rates: $139-$189
(248) 583-4322
(800) 331-3131

MANCELONA

MANCELONA MOTEL
8306 US 131
(49659)
Rates: $35-$76
(616) 587-8621
(800) 320-1240

RAPID RIVER MOTEL
7530 US 131
(49659)
Rates: $30-$50
(616) 258-2604

MANISTEE

BEST WESTERN MANISTEE INN
200 US 31N
(49660)
Rates: $42-$150
(231) 723-9949
(800) 528-1234
(888) 296-6835

HILLSIDE MOTEL
1675 US 31S
(49660)
Rates: $50-$110
(231) 723-2584
(800) 234-1250

MANISTIQUE

COMFORT INN
726 E Lakeshore Dr (49854)
Rates: $89-$119
(906) 341-6981
(800) 228-5150

ECONO LODGE
E Lakeshore Dr
(49854)
Rates: $44-$66
(906) 341-6014
(800) 553-2666

HOLIDAY MOTEL
US 2 E (49854)
Rates: $32-$49
(906) 341-2710

MANKATO

BAYMONT INN
111 West Lind Ct
(56001)
Rates: n/a
(507) 345-8800
(800) 301-0200

MANTON

GREEN MILL MOTEL
709 N US 131
(49663)
Rates: $30-$70
(616) 824-3504

IRISH INN MOTEL
415 N Michigan
Ave (49663)
Rates: $31-$41
(616) 824-6988

MARINE CITY

MARINE BAY LODGE MOTEL
6000 River Rd
(E China 48054)
Rates: $30-$62
(810) 765-8877
(810) 765-8878

PORT SEAWAY INN
7623 River Rd
(48039)
Rates: $32-$90
(810) 765-4033

MARQUETTE

BAVARIAN INN
2782 US 41 W
(49855)
Rates: $28-$44
(906) 226-2314

BIRCHMONT MOTEL
2090 US 41S
(49855)
Rates: $38-$52
(906) 228-7538

EDGEWATER MOTEL
2050 US 41S
(49855)
Rates: $31-$47
(906) 225-1305

HOLIDAY INN
1951 US 41W
(49855)
Rates: $79
(906) 225-1351
(800) 465-4329

LAMPLIGHTER MOTEL
3600 US 41W
(49855)
Rates: $22-$44
(906) 228-4004

PARKWAY MOTEL
Upper Peninsula
(49855)
Rates: n/a
(906) 249-1404

RAMADA INN
412 W Washington
(49855)
Rates: $94-$99
(906) 228-6000
(800) 272-6232

TIROLER HOF INN
150 Carp River
Hill (49855)
Rates: $44-$60
(906) 226-7516
(800) 892-9376

TRAVELODGE
1010 M-28 E
(49855)
Rates: $52-$76
(906) 249-1712
(800) 578-7878

MARSHALL

ARBOR INN-HISTORIC MARSHALL
15435 W Michigan
Ave (49068)
Rates: $52-$64
(616) 781-7772
(800) 424-0807

MARSHALL HEIGHTS MOTEL
16147 Old US 27
N (49068)
Rates: $24-$40
(616) 781-5659

MCMILLAN

INTERLAKEN LODGE
Rt 3, Box 2542
(49853)
Rates: $65-$125
(906) 586-3545

MENOMINEE

HOWARD JOHN-SON EXPRESS
2516 10th St (49858)
Rates: $55-$75
(906) 863-4431
(800) 446-4656

MIDLAND

BEST WESTERN VALLEY PLAZA RESORT
5221 Bay City Rd
(48642)
Rates: $62-$82
(517) 496-2700
(800) 528-1234
(800) 825-2700

FAIRVIEW INN
2200 W Wackerly
St (48640)
Rates: $62-$89
(517) 631-0070
(800) 422-2744

HOLIDAY INN
1500 W Wackerly
St (48640)
Rates: $79-$140
(517) 631-4220
(800) 465-4329
(800) 622-4220

PLAZA SUITES HOTEL
5217 Bay City Rd
(48640)
Rates: $82-$165
(517) 496-0100

SLEEP INN
2100 W Wackerly
St (48640)
Rates: $55-$84
(517) 837-1010
(800) 753-3746
(888) 837-1010

MILAN

STAR MOTEL
335 E Lewis Ave
(48160)
Rates: $32-$48
(734) 439-2448

MILFORD

MILFORD'S HURON VALLEY MOTEL
640 N Milford Rd
(48381)
Rates: $35-$45
(810) 685-1020

MIO

MIO MOTEL
415 N Morenci St
(48647)
Rates: $40-$60
(517) 826-3248

MONROE

COMFORT INN
6500 E Albain Rd
(48161)
Rates: $64-$124
(734) 384-1500
(800) 228-5150

DAYS INN
1440 N Dixie Hwy
(48162)
Rates: $54-$95
(734) 289-4000
(800) 329-7466

HOLIDAY INN
1225 N Dixie Hwy
(48161)
Rates: $69+
(734) 242-6000
(800) 465-4329

HOMETOWN INN
1885 Welcome
Way (48161)
Rates: $42-$90
(734) 289-1080

MOUNT PLEASANT

COMFORT INN
2424 S Mission St
(48858)
Rates: $69-$195
(517) 772-4000
(800) 228-5150

HOLIDAY INN
5665 E Pickard St
(48858)
Rates: $79-$169
(517) 772-2905
(800) 465-4329

SOARING EAGLE HOTEL & RESORT
6800 Soaring
Eagle Dr (48858)
Rates: $60-$175
(517) 775-7777

SUPER 8 MOTEL
2323 S Mission
(48858)
Rates: $59
(517) 773-8888
(800) 800-8000

MUNISING

ALGER FALLS MOTEL
M-28 E (49862)
Rates: $48-$65
(906) 387-3536

COMFORT INN
SR 28 (M-28) E
(49862)
Rates: $565$105
(906) 387-5292
(800) 228-5150

SCOTTY'S MOTEL
415 Cedar St
(49862)
Rates: $26-$34
(906) 387-2449

STAR-LITE MOTEL
500 M-28E (49862)
Rates: $34-$40
(906) 387-2291

SUNSET MOTEL
1315 Bay St
(49862)
Rates: $48-$52
(906) 387-4574

TERRACE MOTEL
420 Prospect
(49862)
Rates: $48-$64
(906) 387-2735

YULE LOG RESORT
122 W Chocobay
(49862)
Rates: $36-$78
(906) 387-3184

MUSKEGON

BEL AIRE MOTEL
4240 Airline Rd
(49444)
Rates: $38-$68
(616) 733-2196

SEAWAY MOTEL
631 W Norton Ave
(49441)
Rates: $30-$67
(616) 733-1220

SUPER 8 MOTEL
3380 Hoyt St
(49444)
Rates: $41-$55
(616) 733-0088
(800) 800-8000

NEGAUNEE

AREA CODES - If the local number doesn't connect, check for a new area code.

QUARTZ MTN INN
791 US 41 E
(49866)
Rates: $29-$40
(906) 475-7165

NEW BALTIMORE

COUNTRY HEARTH INN
29101 23-Mile Rd
(48047)
Rates: $40-$70
(810) 949-4520
(800) 282-5711

NEW BUFFALO

COMFORT INN
11539 O'Brien Ct
(49117)
Rates: $59-$153
(616) 469-4440
(800) 228-5150

EDGEWOOD MOTEL
18716 LaPorte Rd
(49117)
Rates: $33-$43
(616) 469-3345

GRAND BEACH MOTEL
19189 US 12
(49117)
Rates: $25-$70
(616) 469-1555

SANS SOUCI B&B
19265 S Lakeside Rd (49117)
Rates: $98-$196
(616) 756-3141

NEWBERRY

GATEWAY MOTEL
Rt 4, Box 980,
M123 (49868)
Rates: n/a
(906) 293-5651

GREEN ACRES MOTEL
Rt 1, Box 736 (49868)
Rates: $38-$48
(800) 800-5398

PARK-A-WAY MOTEL
RR 4, Box 966
(49868)
Rates: $30-$60
(906) 293-5771

RAINBOW LODGE
County Rd 423,
P. O. Box 386
(49868)
Rates: $31-$75
(906) 658-3357

NORTON SHORES

BEL AIRE MOTEL
4240 Airline Rd
(49444)
Rates: $56-$72
(231) 733-2196

SEAWAY MOTEL
631 W Norton Ave
(49444)
Rates: $60-$90
(231) 733-1220

NOVI

FAIRLANE MOTEL
45700 Grand River
(48374)
Rates: $28-$35
(248) 349-6410

OAKS

GUESTHOUSE/ DOGHAVEN
P. O. Box 283
Three (49128)
Rates: $157-$295
(616) 756-3856

ONAWAY

LAKESIDE MOTEL
County Rd 489,
Rt 1 (49765)
Rates: n/a
(517) 733-4298

ONEKAMA

TRAVELERS MOTEL
5606 Eight Mile,
Box 97 (49675)
Rates: $30-$70
(231) 889-4342
(800) 769-0184

ONTONAGON

RAINBOW MOTEL & CHALETS
P. O. Box 2900
(49953)
Rates: $36-$70
(906) 885-5348

SCOTT'S SUPERIOR INN & CABINS
277 Lakeshore Rd
(49953)
Rates: $39-$58
(906) 884-4866

SUNSHINE MOTEL & CABINS
1442 M-64 (49953)
Rates: $25-$75
(906) 884-2187

SUPERIOR SHORES RESORT
1823 M-64 (49953)
Rates: $35-$115
(906) 884-2653
(800) 344-5355

OSCODA

ANCHORAGE COTTAGES RESORT
3164 N US 23
(48750)
Rates: $45-$95
(517) 739-7843

ASPEN MOTOR INN
115 N Lake St
(48750)
Rates: $29-$50
(517) 739-9152
(800) 892-7736

BLUE HORIZON COURT
4208 N US 23,
Box 151 (48750)
Rates: $30-$55
(517) 739-8487
(800) 524-5201

CEDAR LANE RESORT MOTEL
7404 N US 23
(48750)
Rates: $26-$68
(517) 739-9988

NORTHERN TRAVELER
5493 N US 23
(48750)
Rates: $34-$58
(517) 739-9261

RAINBOW RESORT
5764 N US 23
(48750)
Rates: $60-$400/Weekly
(517) 739-5695

SURFSIDE I & II CONDO & MOTEL
6504 N US 23
(48750)
Rates: $52-$150
(517) 739-5363

OWATONNA

RAMADA INN
1212 I-35 (55060)
Rates: $52-$72
(507) 455-0606
(800) 272-6232

OWOSSO

OWOSSO MOTOR LODGE
2247 E Main St
(48867)
Rates: $30-$50
(517) 725-7148
(800) 444-7148

PARADISE

TRAVELODGE
M-123 &
Whitefish Rd
(49768)
Rates: $50-$175
(906) 492-3445
(800) 578-7878

PAW PAW

GREEN ACRES MOTEL
38245 W Red Arrow (49079)
Rates: n/a
(616) 657-4037

MROCZEK INN
139 Ampey Rd
(49079)
Rates: $31-$40
(616) 657-2578

QUALITY INN & SUITES
153 Ampey Rd
(49079)
Rates: $567$110
(616) 655-0303
(800) 228-5151

PERRY

HEB'S INN MOTEL
2811 Lansing Rd
(48872)
Rates: $43-$55
(517) 625-7500

PETOSKEY

COACH HOUSE MOTEL
2445 Charlevoix Ave (49770)
Rates: $50-$65
(231) 347-2593

COMFORT INN
1314 US 31 N
(49770)
Rates: $47-$190
(231) 347-3220
(800) 228-5150

PINCONNING

PINCONNING TRAIL HOUSE
201 S M-13 (48650)
Rates: $32-$75
(517) 879-4219

PLAINWELL

COMFORT INN
622 Allegan St
(49080)
Rates: $67-$180
(616) 685-9891
(800) 228-5150

PLYMOUTH

RED ROOF INN
39700 Ann Arbor Rd (48170)
Rates: $60-$77
(734) 459-3300
(800) 843-7663

PONTIAC

RESIDENCE INN BY MARRIOTT
3333 Centerpoint Pkwy (48341)
Rates: $89-$199
(248) 858-8664
(800) 331-3131

PORT AUSTIN

LAKESIDE MOTOR LODGE
P.O. Box 358 (48467)
Rates: $35-$60
(517) 738-5201

PORT HURON

DAYS INN
2908 Pine Grove
(48060)
Rates: $40-$130
(810) 984-1522
(800) 329-7466

MAINSTREET LODGE
514 Huron Ave (48060)
Rates: $58-$81
(810) 984-3166
(888) 256-5656

PORTLAND

BEST WESTERN AMERICAN HERITAGE INN
1681 Grand River Ave (48875)
Rates: $59-$77
(517) 647-2200
(800) 528-1234

POWERS

CANDLE LITE MOTEL
P.O. Box 195 (49874)
Rates: $22-$30
(906) 497-5413

PRUDENVILLE

SHEA'S LAKE FRONT LODGE
125 Pine St (48651)
Rates: $48-$52
(517) 366-5910

RAPID RIVER

RIGHT BOWER MOTEL
9912 US 2 (49878)
Rates: $23-$36
(906) 474-6078

REDFORD

COACH & LANTERN MOTEL
25255 Grand River Ave (48240)
Rates: $29-$42
(313) 533-4020

DORCHESTER MOTEL
26825 Grand River Ave (48240)
Rates: $33-$75
(313) 533-8400

ROCHESTER HILLS

RED ROOF INN
2580 Crooks Rd (48309)
Rates: $57-$83
(248) 853-6400
(800) 843-7663

ROCHESTER MOTOR LODGE
2070 S Rochester Rd (48307)
Rates: $38-$48
(248) 651-8591

ROMULUS

BAYMONT INN & SUITES-AIRPORT
9000 Wickham Rd (48174)
Rates: $75-$80
(734) 722-6000
(800) 301-0200

COMFORT INN METRO AIRPORT
31800 Wick Rd (48174)
Rates: $79-$229
(734) 326-2100
(800) 228-5150

CROWNE PLAZA HOTEL-AIRPORT
8000 Merriman Rd (48174)
Rates: $130
(734) 729-2600
(800) 227-6963

DAYS INN AIRPORT
9501 Middlebelt Rd (48174)
Rates: $60-$80
(734) 946-4300
(800) 329-7466

HOWARD JOHNSON
9555 Middlebelt Rd (48174)
Rates: $60-$99
(734) 946-1400
(800) 446-4656

DETROIT AIRPORT MARRIOTT HOTEL
Detroit Metro Airport (48174)
Rates: $94-$350
(734) 941-9400
(800) 228-9290

RED ROOF INN
Merriman Rd (48174)
Rates: n/a
(734) 641-9006
(800) 843-7663

ROMULUS MARRIOTT AT DETROIT AIRPORT
30559 Flynn Dr (48174)
Rates: n/a
(734) 729-7555
(800) 228-9290

ROSEVILLE

BAYMONT INN & SUITES
20675 13 Mile Road (48066)
Rates: $67-$84
(810) 296-6910
(800) 301-0200

GEORGIAN INN
31327 Gratiot Ave (48066)
Rates: $69-$90
(810) 294-0400
(800) 477-1466

RED ROOF INN
31800 Little Mack Rd (48066)
Rates: $52-$70
(810) 296-0310
(800) 843-7663

SAGINAW

ECONO LODGE
2225 Tittabawassee Rd (48604)
Rates: $32-$49
(517) 791-1411
(800) 553-2666

FOUR POINTS BY SHERATON
4960 Towne Center Rd (48604)
Rates: $128-$138
(517) 790-5050
(800) 325-3535

HOLIDAY INN
1408 S Outer Dr (48601)
Rates: $81-$92
(517) 755-0461
(800) 465-4329
(888) 296-7010

KNIGHTS INN SOUTH
1415 S Outer Dr (48601)
Rates: $43-$82
(517) 754-9200
(800) 843-5644

RED ROOF INN
966 S Outer Dr (48601)
Rates: $44-$61
(517) 754-8414
(800) 843-7663

RODEWAY INN
3425 Holland Rd (48601)
Rates: $50-$89
(517) 753-2461
(800) 228-2000

SUPER 8 MOTEL
4848 Town Centre Rd (48603)
Rates: $40-$50
(517) 791-3003
(800) 800-8000

ST. CLOUD

RAMADA LIMITED SUITES
121 Park Ave S (56301)
Rates: $50-$76
(320) 253-3200
(800) 272-6232

ST. IGNACE

BAY VIEW MOTEL
1133 N State St (49781)
Rates: $52-$72
(906) 643-9444

BLUE BAY MOTEL
1071 N State St (49781)
Rates: $29-$79
(906) 643-7414

BUDGET HOST INN
700 N State St (49781)
Rates: $58-$98
(906) 643-9666
(800) 283-4678

CEDAR'S MOTEL
2040 N Business Loop I-75 (49781)
Rates: $32-$39
(906) 643-9578

THE DRIFTWOOD MOTEL
590 N State St (49781)
Rates: $30-$52
(906) 643-7744

HOWARD JOHNSON EXPRESS
913 Boulevard Dr (49781)
Rates: $79-$118
(906) 643-9700
(800) 446-4656

ROCKVIEW MOTEL
2055 N Business Loop I-75 (49781)
Rates: $32-$38
(906) 643-8839

SILVER SANDS RESORT
1519 US 2 W (49781)
Rates: $50-$125
(906) 643-8635

WAYSIDE MOTEL
751 N State St (49781)
Rates: $45-$70
(906) 643-8944

ST. JOSEPH

BEST WESTERN GOLDEN LINK
2723 Niles Ave (49085)
Rates: $39-$89
(616) 983-6321
(800) 528-1234

TRAVELODGE
3822 Red Arrow Hwy (49085)
Rates: $32-$85
(616) 429-3261
(800) 578-7878

SANDUSKY

THUMB HERITAGE INN
405 W Sanilac (48471)
Rates: $34-$70
(810) 648-4811

SAUGATUCK

KIRBY HOUSE B&B
294 W Center St (49453)
Rates: $75-$125
(616) 857-2904

SAULT STE MARIE

ADMIRALS INN
2701 I-75 Business Spur (49783)
Rates: $33-$40
(906) 632-1130

AREA CODES - If the local number doesn't connect, check for a new area code.

BAMBI MOTEL
1801 Ashmun
(49783)
Rates: $34-$65
(906) 632-7881
(800) 289-0864

BAVARIAN ECONOMY INN
2006 Ashmun St
(49783)
Rates $52-$69
(906) 632-6864

BILTMORE MOTEL
331 E Portage
(49783)
Rates: $34-$54
(906) 632-2119
(800) 528-0612

BUDGET HOST CRESVIEW INN
1200 Ashmun St
(49783)
Rates: $49-$79
(906) 635-5213
(800) 283-4678

GRAND MOTEL
1100 E Portage
Ave (49783)
Rates: $36-$110
(906) 632-2141

IMPERIAL MOTOR INN
2216 Ashmun St
(49783)
Rates: n/a
(906) 632-7334
(800) 859-9898

KING'S INN MOTEL
3755 I-75 Business
Spur (49783)
Rates: $28-$60
(906) 635-5061

LAKER INN
1712 Ashmun
(49783)
Rates: $42-$46
(906) 632-3581

MID-CITY MOTEL
304 E Portage Ave
(49783)
Rates: $44-$54
(906) 632-6832

ROYAL MOTEL
1707 Ashmun
(49783)
Rates: $38-$64
(906) 632-6323
(800) 978-4454

SUPER 8 MOTEL
3826 I-75 Business
Spur (49783)
Rates: $65-$74
(906) 632-8882
(800) 800-8000

SILVER CITY

BEST WESTERN PORCUPINE MTN LODGE
120 Lincoln at
Beaser (49953)
Rates: $79-$119
(906) 885-5311
(800) 528-1234
(800) 454-5983

TOMLINSON'S RAINBOW LODGING
2900 M 64 (49953)
Rates: $60-$68
(906) 885-5348

SMYRNA

DOUBLE R RANCH RESORT
4424 Whites
Bridge Rd (48887)
Rates: $34-$50
(616) 794-0520

SOUTH HAVEN

COLONIAL HOTEL
532 Dyckman
(49090)
Rates: $50-$125
(616) 637-2887
(800) 608-8951

ECONO LODGE
09817 M-140
(49090)
Rates: $50-$135
(616) 637-5141
(800) 553-2666

SOUTHFIELD

HILTON GARDEN INN
26000 American
Dr (48034)
Rates: $99
(248) 357-1100
(800) 445-8667

HOLIDAY INN
26555 Telegraph
Rd (48034)
Rates: $116
(248) 353-7700
(800) 465-4329

HOMESTEAD GUEST STUDIOS
28500
Northwestern
Hwy (48034)
Rates: n/a
(248) 213-4500
(888) 782-9473

RADISSON PLAZA HOTEL
1500 Town Center
(48075)
Rates: $129-$149
(248) 827-4000
(800) 333-3333

RED ROOF INN
27660 Northwestern
Hwy (48034)
Rates: $60-$73
(248) 353-7200
(800) 843-7663

RESIDENCE INN BY MARRIOTT
26700 Central
Park Blvd (48076)
Rates: $139-$169
(248) 352-8900
(800) 331-3131

SOUTHGATE

BAYMONT INN & SUITES
12888 Reeck Rd
(48195)
Rates: $67-$74
(734) 374-3000
(800) 301-0200

STANDISH

STANDISH MOTEL
US 23 & M-76
(48658)
Rates: $30-$50
(517) 846-9571

STEPHENSON

STEPHENSON MOTEL
Rt 2, Box 20, Hwy
41 (49887)
Rates: $30-$35
(906) 753-2552

STERLING HEIGHTS

KNIGHTS INN
7887 17 Mile Rd
(48313)
Rates: $50-$70
(810) 268-0600
(800) 843-5644

SUPER 8 MOTEL
34550 Van Dyke
Ave (48313)
Rates: $44-$63
(810) 795-8800
(800) 800-8000

STEVENSVILLE

BAYMONT INN & SUITES
2601 W Marquette
Woods Rd (49127)
Rates: $62-$76
(616) 428-9111
(800) 301-0200

HAMPTON INN
5050 Red Arrow
Hwy (49127)
Rates: $69-$99
(616) 429-2700
(800) 426-7866

PARK INN INTERNATIONAL
4290 Red Arrow
Hwy (49127)
Rates: $65-$90
(616) 429-3218
(800) 670-727

STURGIS

COMFORT INN
1300 E Centerville
Rd (49091)
Rates: $50-$150
(616) 651-7881
(800) 228-5150

GREEN BAY MOTOR INN
71381 S
Centerville Rd
(49091)
Rates: $38-$55
(616) 651-2361

SUTTONS BAY

RED LION MOTOR LODGE
4290 S West Bay
Shore Rd (49682)
Rates: $45-$115
(231) 271-6694
(800) 547-8010

TAWAS CITY

NORTH STAR MOTEL
1119 S US 23
(48763)
Rates: $35-$65
(517) 362-2255

TAWAS MOTEL & RESORT
1124 US 23S
(48764)
Rates: $50-$80
(517) 362-3822

TAYLOR

HOFFMAN'S COLONIAL HOUSE OF TAYLOR
10780 S Telegraph
(48180)
Rates: $27-$42
(734) 291-3000

RED ROOF INN
21230 Eureka Rd
(48180)
Rates: $60-$75
(734) 374-1150
(800) 843-7663

SUPER 8 MOTEL
15101 Huron St
(48180)
Rates: $50-$69
(734) 283-8830
(800) 800-8000

TECUMSEH

TECUMSEH INN MOTEL
1445 W Chicago
Blvd (49286)
Rates: $45-$65
(517) 423-7401

THREE RIVERS

GREYSTONE MOTEL
59271 US 131, Box
62 (49093)
Rates: $28-$42
(616) 278-1695

THREE RIVERS INN
1200 W Broadway
(49093)
Rates: $43-$80
(616) 273-9521

AREA CODES - If the local number doesn't connect, check for a new area code.

TRAVERSE CITY

BEST WESTERN FOUR SEASONS MOTEL
305 Munson Ave (49686)
Rates: $59-$149
(231) 946-8424
(800) 528-1234
(800) 823-7844

ECONOMY INN
1582 US 31 N (49686)
Rates: $30-$110
(231) 938-2080

FOX HAUS MOTOR LODGE
704 Munsion Ave (49684)
Rates: $30-$175
(231) 947-4450

HOLIDAY INN
615 E Front St (49684)
Rates: $80-$146
(231) 947-3700
(800) 465-4329
(800) 888-8020

MAIN STREET INNS
618 E Front St (49684)
Rates: $60-$150
(231) 929-0410
(800) 255-7180

MOTEL 6
1582 US 31 N (49684)
Rates: n/a
(231) 938-3002
(800) 466-8356

OLD MISSION INN
18599 Old Mission Rd (49684)
Rates: $250-$500 Weekly
(231) 223-7770

TROUT LAKE

MCGOWAN'S FAMILY MOTEL
M-123 (49793)
Rates: $45-$51
(906) 569-3366

TROY

DRURY INN
575 W Big Beaver Rd (48084)
Rates: $86-$106
(248) 528-3330
(800) 378-7946

HILTON HOTEL
5500 Crooks Rd (48083)
Rates: $189-$204
(248) 879-2100
(800) 445-8667

HOLIDAY INN
2537 Rochester Ct (48083)
Rates: $135
(248) 689-7500
(800) 465-4329

RED ROOF INN
2350 Rochester Rd (48083)
Rates: $57-$87
(248) 689-4391
(800) 843-7663

RESIDENCE INN BY MARRIOTT
2600 Livernois Rd (48083)
Rates: $129-$179
(248) 689-6856
(800) 331-3131

UTICA

BAYMONT INN & SUITES
45311 Park Dr (48315)
Rates: $89-$96
(810) 731-4700
(800) 301-0200

WAKEFIELD

INDIANHEAD MOUNTAIN RESORT
500 Indianhead Rd (49968)
Rates: $58-$160
(906) 229-5181
(800) 346-3426

WALKER

MOTEL 6
777 Three Mile Rd (49504)
Rates: $33-$44
(616) 784-9375
(800) 466-8356

RIVIERA MOTEL
4350 Remembrance Rd (49544)
Rates: $39-$45
(616) 453-2404

WARREN

BAYMONT INN & SUITES
30900 Van Dyke (48093)
Rates: $67-$74
(810) 574-0550
(800) 301-0200

HOMEWOOD SUITES
30180 N Civic Center Blvd (48093)
Rates: $89-$145
(810) 558-7870
(800) 225-5466

MOTEL 6
8300 Chicago Rd (48093)
Rates: $34-$40
(810) 826-9300
(800) 466-8356

QUALITY INN
32035 Van Dyke (48093)
Rates: $69-$79
(810) 264-0100
(800) 228-5151

RED ROOF INN
26300 DeQuindre Rd (48091)
Rates: $51-$73
(810) 573-4300
(800) 843-7663

RESIDENCE INN BY MARRIOTT
30120 Civic Center Blvd (48093)
Rates: $110-$139
(810) 558-8050
(800) 331-3131

VAN DYKE PARK HOTEL
31800 Van Dyke (48093)
Rates: $59-$500
(800) 321-1008

WATERFORD

MCGUIRE'S MOTOR INN
120 S Telegraph Rd (48328)
Rates: $46-$52
(248) 682-5100
(800) 545-0454

WATERS

NORTHLAND INN & MOTEL
9311 Old US 27 (49797)
Rates: $40-$70
(517) 732-4470

WATERSMEET

VACATIONLAND RESORT
E 19636 Hebert Rd (49969)
Rates: $60-$160
(906) 358-4380

WEST BRANCH

LA HACIENDA MOTEL
969 W Houghton Ave (48661)
Rates: $44-$63
(517) 345-2345

RED ROSE MOTEL
836 S M-33 (48661)
Rates: $39
(517) 345-2136

SUPER 8 MOTEL
2596 Austin Way (48661)
Rates: $58-$72
(517) 345-8488
(800) 800-8000

TRI-TERRACE MOTEL
2259 Business Loop I-75 (49661)
Rates: $45-$60
(517) 345-3121

WELCOME MOTEL
3308 W M-76 (48661)
Rates: $28+
(517) 345-2896

WETMORE

BEST WESTERN OF MUNISING
M-28 E (49895)
Rates: $59-$115
(906) 387-4864
(800) 528-1234

WHITE PIGEON

PLAZA MOTEL
71410 US 131 S (49099)
Rates: $25-$49
(616) 382-7285

WHITEHALL

LAKE LAND MOTEL
1002 E Colby St (49461)
Rates: $60-$65
(231) 894-5644

WHITMORE LAKE

LAKES MOTEL
8365 Main St (48189)
Rates: $35-$60
(734) 449-5991

WORTHINGTON

RAMADA INN
2015 Humiston Ave (56187)
Rates: $62-$69
(507) 372-2991
(800) 272-6232

WYOMING

JIM WILLIAMS MOTEL
3821 S Division (49548)
Rates: $28-$46
(616) 241-5461

SUPER 8 MOTEL
727 44th St SW (49509)
Rates: $53-$65
(616) 530-8588
(800) 800-8000

YPSILANTI

MAYFLOWER MOTEL
5610 Carpenter (48197)
Rates: $35-$90
(734) 434-2200

AREA CODES - If the local number doesn't connect, check for a new area code.

MINNESOTA

ADA

NORMAN MOTEL
503 W Thorpe Ave
(56510)
Rates: $25-$40
(218) 784-3781

AITKIN

**ANGLER'S INN
RESORT CABINS**
Rt 1, Box 398
(56431)
Rates: $65-$75
(218) 678-2421
(800) 289-0680

BILL'S RESORT
Rt 2, Box 521
(56431)
Rates: n/a
(218) 927-3841

**EDGEWATER
RESORT CABINS
& RV PARK**
Rt 3, Box 890
(56431)
Rates: $500-$1200
Weekly
(218) 927-2895
(800) 639-4337

40 CLUB INN
950 2nd St NW
(56431)
Rates: $76
(218) 927-2903
(800) 682-8152

**RIPPLE RIVER
MOTEL**
701 Minnesota
Ave (56431)
Rates: $36-$75
(218) 927-3734
(800) 258-3734

ALBERT LEA

**ALBERT LEA
COUNTRYSIDE
MOTEL**
2102 E Main St
(56007)
Rates: $34-$65
(507) 373-2446

BEL AIRE MOTOR INN

700 US Hwy 69 S
(56007)
Rates: $35-$100
(507) 373-3983
(800) 373-4073

COMFORT INN
I-35 & SR 46
(56007)
Rates: $45-$110
(800) 228-5150

DAYS INN
2306 E Main St
(56007)
Rates: $49-$85
(507) 373-6471
(800) 329-7466

MOTEL 65
Hwy 65, Ext 8 on
35W (56007)
Rates: $30-$37
(507) 373-9792
(800) 373-9792

SUPER 8 MOTEL
2019 E Main St
(56007)
Rates: $40-$61
(507) 377-0591
(800) 800-8000

ALEXANDRIA

**AMERICINN
MOTEL**
4520 Hwy 29S
(56308)
Rates: $50-$100
(320) 763-6808
(800) 634-3444

**ARROWWOOD-
A RADISSON
RESORT**
2100 Arrowwood
Lane (56308)
Rates: $129
(320) 762-1124
(800) 333-3333

**CARRINGTON
HOUSE B & B**
4974 Interlachen
Dr NE (56308)
Rates: $90-$140
(320) 846-7400

COUNTRY INN & SUITES

I-94 & Hwy 29S
(56308)
Rates: $69-$129
(320) 763-9900
(800) 456-4000

HOLIDAY INN
5637 Hwy 29 S
(56308)
Rates: n/a
(320) 763-6577
(800) 465-4329

"L" MOTEL
910 Hwy 27 W
(56308)
Rates: $34-$49
(320) 763-5121
(800) 733-1793

RED CARPET INN
1903 Aga Dr
(56308)
Rates: n/a
(320) 762-0512
(800) 251-1962

SKYLINE MOTEL
605 30th Ave
(56308)
Rates: $30-$50
(320) 763-3175
(800) 467-4096

SUPER 8 MOTEL
4620 Hwy 29 S
(56308)
Rates: $44-$60
(320) 763-6552
(800) 800-8000

ANNANDALE

**THAYER'S
HISTORIC B&B**
60 W Elm (55302)
Rates: $38-$265
(612) 274-8222
(800) 944-6595

ANOKA

PIERCE MOTEL
1520 S Ferry
(55303)
Rates: $33-$41
(612) 421-7000

SUPER 8 MOTEL

1129 W Hwy 10
(55303)
Rates: $49-$71
(612) 422-8000
(800) 800-8000

APPLE VALLEY

**AMERICINN
MOTEL & SUITES**
15000 Glazler Ave
(55124)
Rates: $70-$86
(612) 431-3800
(800) 634-3444

APPLETON

SUPER 8 MOTEL
900 N
Munsterman
(56208)
Rates: $36-$52
(320) 289-2500
(800) 800-8000

ARLINGTON

**ARLINGTON E-Z
REST MOTEL**
509 2nd Ave NW
(55307)
Rates: $23-$35
(507) 964-5606

AUSTIN

AUSTIN MOTEL
805 21st St NE
(55912)
Rates: $20-$39
(507) 433-9254
(800) 433-9254

**COUNTRY SIDE
INN MOTEL**
3303 W Oakland
Ave (55912)
Rates: $39-$99
(507) 437-7774

DAYS INN
700 16th Ave NW
(55912)
Rates: $64
(507) 433-8600
(800) 329-7466

HOLIDAY INN HOLIDOME

1701 4th St NW
(55912)
Rates: $62-$159
(55912)
507) 433-1000
(800) 465-4329

SUPER 8 MOTEL
1401 14th St NW
(55912)
Rates: $40-$60
(507) 433-1801
(800) 800-8000

AVON

**AMERICINN
MOTEL**
304 Blattner Dr
(56310)
Rates: $40-$53
(320) 356-2211
(800) 634-3444

BABBITT

**TIMBER BAY
LODGE &
HOUSEBOATS**
8347 Timber Bay
Rd (55706)
Rates: $745-$1245
Weekly
(218) 827-3682
(800) 846-6821

BACKUS

**PINE MOUNTAIN
INN B&B**
P.O. Box 144
(56435)
Rates: $40-$45
(218) 947-3050
(218) 682-2884

BADGER

BADGER MOTEL
Hwy 11 (56714)
Rates: $25-$35
(218) 528-3745

BAGLEY

DUTCH MILL MOTEL & VIDEO
Hwy 2 W (56621)
Rates: $29-$35
(218) 694-2050

BARNUM

NORTHWOODS MOTEL & COTTAGES
3716 Main St
(55707)
Rates: $33-$75
(218) 389-6951
(800) 228-6951

BAUDETTE

AMERICINN MOTEL & SUITES
SR 11 (56623)
Rates: $60-$72
(218) 634-3200
(800) 634-3444

BAUDETTE MOTEL
309 W Main (56623)
Rates: $27-$69
(218) 634-2600
(800) 200-2601

KEN-MAR-KE RESORT CABINS
Box 215, Rt 1
(56623)
Rates: $58+
(218) 634-2072
(800) 535-8155

ROYAL DUTCHMAN RESORT MOTEL
Hwy 11 E (56623)
Rates: $28-$55
(218) 634-1024
(800) 908-1024

BAXTER

COUNTRY INN BY CARLSON
1220 Delwood Dr
N (56401)
Rates: $79-$107
(218) 828-2161
(800) 456-4000

TWIN BIRCH MOTEL
2300 Fairview Rd
N (56401)
Rates: $34-$59
(218) 829-2833
(888) 829-2833

BEAVER BAY

THE INN AT BEAVER
1017 Main St
(55601)
Rates: $49-$150
(218) 226-4351
(800) 226-4351

BECKER

SUPER 8 MOTEL
13804 First St
(55308)
Rates: $41-$59
(612) 261-4440
(800) 800-8000

BELLE PLAINE

BELLE PLAINE MOTEL
315 S Walnut St
(56011)
Rates: $20-$69
(612) 873-2242
(888) 873-6424

BEMIDJI

BEL AIR MOTEL
1350 Paul Bunyan
Dr NW (56601)
Rates: $28-$70
(218) 751-3222
(800) 798-3222

BEST WESTERN BEMIDJI INN
2420 Paul Bunyan
Dr NW (56601)
Rates: $45-$105
(218) 751-0390
(800) 528-1234

COMFORT INN
3500 Comfort Dr
NW (56601)
Rates: $55-$110
(218) 751-7700
(800) 228-5150

HOLIDAY INN EXPRESS
2422 Ridgeway
Ave NW (56601)
Rates: $62-$75
(218) 751-2487
(800) 465-4329

LAKESIDE MOTEL
809 Paul Bunyan
Dr NE (56601)
Rates: $24-$64
(218) 751-3266
(800) 817-4930

MIDWAY MOTEL
1000 Paul Bunyan
Dr NE (56601)
Rates: $25-$38
(218) 751-1180

PAUL BUNYAN MOTEL
915 Paul Bunyan
Dr NE (56601)
Rates: $24-$64
(218) 751-1314
(800) 848-3788

PIMUSHE RESORT CABINS
Rt 4, Box 312
(56601)
Rates: $50-$130
(218) 586-2094
(800) 450-2094

RUTTGER'S BIRCHMONT LODGE
530 Birchmont
Beach Rd NE
(56601)
Rates: $48-$309
(218) 751-1630
(888) RUTTGER

BENEDICT

PINEHURST LODGE RESORT
Box 40 (56436)
Rates: $85-$155
(218) 224-2577
(800) 359-2567

BENSON

MOTEL 1
620 Atlantic Ave
(56215)
Rates: $28-$38
(320) 843-4434

SUPER 8 MOTEL
600 22nd St S
(56215)
Rates: $35-$56
(320) 843-3451
(800) 800-8000

BIG FALLS

BIG FALLS MOTEL
Hwy 71 (56627)
Rates: $25-$38
(218) 276-2261

BIG LAKE

LAKE AIRE MOTEL
340 Jefferson Blvd
(55309)
Rates: n/a
(612) 263-2405

BIWABIK

BIWABIK MOTEL
Hwy 135 (55708)
Rates: $25-$30
(218) 865-9980

BLACKDUCK

AMERICINN MOTEL
81 Brandl Dr NW
(56630)
Rates: $45-$95
(218) 835-4500
(800) 634-3444

DRAKE MOTEL
305 N Pine (56630)
Rates: $30-$35
(218) 835-4567
(888) 253-8501

BLOOMINGTON

AMERISUITES
7800 International
Dr (55425)
Rates: $79-$149
(612) 854-0700
(800) 833-1516

BAYMONT INN AIRPORT
7815 Nicollet Ave
S (55420)
Rates: $74-$90
(612) 881-7311
(800) 301-0200

BEST WESTERN THUNDERBIRD HOTEL
2201 E 78th St
(55425)
Rates: $97-$180
(612) 854-3411
(800) 528-1234
(800) 328-1931

CLARION HOTEL
8151 Bridge Rd
(55437)
Rates: $99
(612) 830-1300
(800) 252-7466

COMFORT INN
1321 E 78th St
(55425)
Rates: $59-$109
(612) 854-3400
(800) 228-5150

EXEL INN
2701 E 78th St
(55425)
Rates: $61-$85
(612) 854-7200
(800) 367-3935

HILTON HOTEL MINNEAPOLIS-ST PAUL AIRPORT
3800 E 80th St
(55425)
Rates: $105-$139
(612) 854-2100
(800) 445-8667

HOTEL SOFITEL
5601 W 78th St
(55439)
Rates: $95-$125
(612) 835-1900
(800) 876-6303

MARRIOTT HOTEL AIRPORT
2020 E 79th St
(55425)
Rates: $149-$175
(612) 854-7441
(800) 228-9290

RADISSON HOTEL SOUTH & PLAZA TOWER
7800 Normandale
Blvd (55425_
Rates: $159-$179
(612) 835-7800
(800) 333-3333

RESIDENCE INN BY MARRIOTT
7850 Bloomington Ave S (55425)
Rates: n/a
(612) 876-0900
(800) 331-3131

SELECT INN
7851 Normandale Blvd (55435)
Rates: $34-$44
(612) 835-7400
(800) 641-1000

SUPER 8 MOTEL
7800 2nd Ave S (55420)
Rates: $59-$74
(612) 888-8800
(800) 800-8000

THUNDERBIRD HOTEL
2201 E 78th St (55425)
Rates: $82-$360
(612) 854-3411
(800) 328-1931

WYNDHAM GARDEN HOTEL
4460 W 78th St (55435)
Rates: $59-$111
(800) 822-4200

BLUE EARTH

AMERICINN MOTEL
1495 Domes Dr (56013)
Rates: $57-$71
(507) 526-4215
(800) 634-3444

BUDGET INN
Hwy 169 N & 5th St (56013)
Rates: $29-$55
(507) 526-2706

SUPER 8 MOTEL
1120 N Grove St (56013)
Rates: $44-$65
(507) 526-7376
(800) 800-8000

BRAINERD

DAYS INN
1630 Fairview Dr N (56401)
Rates: $59-$79
(218) 829-0391
(800) 329-7466

DELLWOOD MOTEL
1302 S 6th St (56401)
Rates: $23-$35
(218) 828-8756

DOWNTOWN MOTEL
507 S 6th St (56401)
Rates: $23-$45
(218) 829-7489

ECONO LODGE
2655 SR 371 S (56401)
Rates: $39-$150
(218) 828-0027
(800) 553-2666

HOLIDAY INN
2115 S 6th St (56401)
Rates: $53-$72
(218) 829-1441
(800) 465-4329

RIVERVIEW INN
324 NW Washington St (56401)
Rates: $30-$70
(218) 829-8771
(800) 850-8771

BRANDON

BERNDT'S KAMP KAPPY RESORT CABINS
13110 Devils Lake Rd NW (56315)
Rates: $75-$110
(320) 524-2225
(800) 845-2566

BRECKENRIDGE

BEST INN
821 Hwy 75 N (56520)
Rates: $36-$99
(218) 643-9201
(800) 237-8466

SOUTH HAVEN INN MOTEL
1120 Buffalo Ave (56520)
Rates: $30-$55
(218) 643-3125

BROOKLYN CENTER

BAYMONT INN & SUITES
6415 James Cir N (55430)
Rates: $74-$89
(612) 561-8400
(800) 301-0200

COMFORT INN
1600 James Cir N (55430)
Rates: $59-$119
(612) 560-7464
(800) 228-5150

HILTON MINNEAPOLIS NORTH
2200 Freeway Blvd (55430)
Rates: $79+
(612) 566-8000
(800) 445-8667

SUPER 8 MOTEL
6445 James Circle (55430)
Rates: $53-$63
(612) 566-9810
(800) 800-8000

BROOKLYN PARK

NORTHWEST INN & CONFERENCE CENTER
6900 Lakeland Ave N (55428)
Rates: $79-$89
(612) 566-8855

SLEEP INN
7011 Northland Circle (55428)
Rates: $69-$109
(612) 971-8000
(800) 753-3746

BUFFALO

SUPER 8 MOTEL
303 10th Ave S (55313)
Rates: $51-$68
(612) 682-5930
(800) 800-8000

BURNSVILLE

COUNTRY INN BY CARLSON
14331 Nicollet Ct (55337)
Rates: $64-$74
(612) 892-1900
(800) 456-4000

RED ROOF INN
12920 Aldrich Ave S (55337)
Rates: $58-$72
(612) 890-1420
(800) 843-7663

SUPER 8 MOTEL
1101 Burnsville Pkwy (55337)
Rates: $50-$70
(612) 894-3400
(800) 800-8000

CALEDONIA

CREST MOTEL
Hwy 44 & 76 (55921)
Rates: $30-$46
(507) 724-3311
(800) 845-0904

CAMBRIDGE

BUDGET HOST IMPERIAL MOTOR LODGE
643 N Main (55008)
Rates: $32-$70
(612) 689-2200
(800) 283-4678

CANNON FALLS

BEST WESTERN SARATOGA INN
31591 64th Ave (55009)
Rates: $50-$95
(507) 263-7272
(800) 528-1234

CARAVAN MOTEL
Hwy 52 S (55009)
Rates: $38-$60
(507) 263-4777

COUNTRY QUIET INN
37295 112th Ave Way (55009)
Rates: $55-$130
(507) 258-4406
(800) 258-1843

EDGEWOOD MOTEL
7860 365th Streetway (55009)
Rates: $39
(507) 263-5700

CARLTON

AMERICINN MOTEL
Hwy 210 & I-35 (55718)
Rates: $40-$78
(218) 384-3535
(800) 634-3444

ROYAL PINES MOTEL
Hwy 210 & I-35 (55009)
Rates: $29-$119
(218) 384-4242
(800) 788-9622

CASS LAKE

VIEW POINT RESORT COTTAGES
RR 3, Box 642 (56633)
Rates: $500+ Weekly
(218) 335-6746

WHISPERING PINES MOTEL
6318 Hwy 2 NW (56633)
Rates: $31-$42
(218) 335-8852
(800) 371-8852

CHANHASSEN

CHANHASSEN INN MOTEL
531 W 79th St (55317)
Rates: $37-$44
(612) 934-7373

CHATFIELD

LUND'S GUEST HOUSES
218 Winona St SE (55923)
Rates: $45-$65
(507) 867-4003

AREA CODES - If the local number doesn't connect, check for a new area code.

CHISAGO CITY

SUPER 8 MOTEL
11650 Lake Blvd
(55013)
Rates: $37-$54
(612) 257-8088
(800) 800-8000

CLARA CITY

**GREEN MEADOW
INN**
300 Hwy 7 (56222)
Rates: $30-$40
(320) 847-3790
(800) 685-4266

CLEARBROOK

**PIPER'S INN
MOTEL**
223 Hwy 92 SW
(56634)
Rates: $37-$79
(218) 776-2323
(877) 776-2323

CLEARWATER

BUDGET INN
945 SR 24 (55320)
Rates: $31-$58
(320) 558-2221

CLOQUET

**AMERICINN
MOTEL**
111 Big Lake Rd
(55720)
Rates: $67-$94
(218) 879-1231
(800) 634-3444

**ROYAL PINES
MOTEL**
Hwy 210 & I-35
(55718)
Rates: $29-$119
(218) 384-4242
(800) 788-9622

**SUNNY SIDE
MOTEL**
North Hwy 33
(55720)
Rates: $28-$50
(218) 879-4655

SUPER 8 MOTEL
121 Big Lake Rd
(55720)
Rates: $53-$75
(218) 879-1250
(800) 800-8000

COLD SPRING

**AMERICINN
MOTEL**
118 3rd St S
(56320)
Rates: $46-$79
(320) 685-4539
(800) 634-3444

COOK

**MOOSEBIRDS ON
LAKE VERMILION**
3068 Vermilion Dr
(55723)
Rates: $35-$125
(218) 666-2627

COON RAPIDS

COMFORT INN
9052 NW
University (55448)
Rates: $59-$109
(612) 785-4746
(800) 228-5150

**COUNTRY SUITES
BY CARLSON**
155 Coon Rapids
Blvd (55433)
Rates: $90-$111
(612) 780-3797
(800) 456-4000

**HOLIDAY INN
EXPRESS HOTEL
& SUITES**
9333 Springbrook
Dr (55433)
Rates: $85-$125
(612) 792-9292
(800) 465-4329

CRANE LAKE

**OLSON'S
BORDERLAND**
7488 Crane Lake
Rd (55725)
Rates: n/a
(218) 993-2233

**PINE POINT
LODGE & RESORT**
HC 3, Box 91C
(55725)
Rates: $90+
(218) 993-2311
(800) 623-4446

CROOKSTON

**MOTEL COUNTRY
CLUB**
Hwy 2 & 75 NW
(56716)
Rates: $30-$40
(218) 281-1607

NORTHLAND INN
2200 University
Ave (56716)
Rates: $48-$60
(218) 281-5210

DASSEL

DASSEL MOTEL
505 Mn Hwy 15
(55325)
Rates: n/a
(320) 275-3118
(800) 732-9230

DAWSON

**THE PICKET
FENCE MOTEL**
118 1st St (56232)
Rates: $23-$48
(320) 769-4787

DEER RIVER

BAHR'S MOTEL
P. O. Box 614
(56636)
Rates: $25-$39
(218) 246-8271

MILLER'S RESORT
RR 1, Box 266
(56636)
Rates: $275-
$350/Weekly
(218) 246-8951

**WILLIAMS
NARROWS
RESORT**
53465 Williams
Narrows Rd
(56636)
Rates: $98-$225
(218) 246-8703
(800) 325-2475

DEERWOOD

**CAMP HOLIDAY
RESORT**
17467 Round Lake
Rd (56444)
Rates: $60-$90
(218) 678-2495
(800) 450-2495

COUNTRY INN
BY CARLSON

115 Front St E
(56444)
Rates: $52-$75
(218) 534-3101
(800) 456-4000

**DEERWOOD
MOTEL**
9 W Forest Rd
(56444)
Rates: $32-$65
(218) 534-3163

DETROIT
LAKES

**BEST WESTERN
HOLLAND HOUSE
& SUITES**
615 Hwy 10 E
(56501)
Rates: $89-$149
(218) 847-4483
(800) 528-1234
(800) 33-TULIP

**BUDGET HOST
INN**
895 Hwy 10 E
(56501)
Rates: $40-$80
(218) 847-4454
(800) 283-4678

**CASTAWAY INN
& RESORT**
1226 E Shore Dr
(56501)
Rates: $59-$99
(218) 847-4449
(800) 640-3395

**COUNTRY INN
& SUITES**
1330 Hwy 10 E
(56501)
Rates: $65-$99
(218) 847-2000
(800) 456-4000

**INN ON THE
LAKE-
HOLIDAY INN**
Hwy 10 E (56501)
Rates: $80-$120
(218) 847-2121
(800) 465-4329

SUPER 8 MOTEL
400 Morrow Ave
(56501)
Rates: $36-$67
(218) 847-1651
(800) 800-8000

DEXTER

MILL INN MOTEL
I-90 & SR 16 (55926)
Rates: $35-$46
(507) 584-6440

DILWORTH

**HOWARD
JOHNSON INN**
701 E Center Ave
(56529)
Rates: $35-$99
(218) 287-1212
(800) 446-4656

DULUTH

**ALLYNDALE
MOTEL**
510 N 66th Ave W
(55807)
Rates: $33-$80
(218) 628-1061
(800) 806-1061

**AMERICINN
MOTEL & SUITES**
185 Hwy 2 (55810)
Rates: $70-$155
(218) 624-1026
(800) 634-3444

**BEST WESTERN
DOWNTOWN
MOTEL**
131 W 2nd St
(55802)
Rates: $55-$90
(218) 727-6851
(800) 528-1234

**BEST WESTERN
EDGEWATER EAST
MOTEL**
2400 London Rd
(55812)
Rates: $69-$139
(218) 728-3601
(800) 528-1234
(800) 777-7925

CHALET MOTEL
1801 Lincoln Rd
(55812)
Rates: $39-$60
(218) 728-4238
(800) 235-2957

**COUNTRY INN
& SUITES**
9330 Skyline
Pkwy (55810)
Rates: $55-$106
(218) 628-0668
(800) 456-4000

DAYS INN
909 Cottonwood
Ave (55811)
Rates: $59-$109
(218) 727-3110
(800) 329-7466

FITGER'S INN HOTEL
600 E Superior St
(55802)
Rates: $75-$245
(218) 722-8826
(888) 726-2982

GRAND MOTEL
4312 Grand Ave
(55807)
Rates: n/a
(218) 624-4821
(800) 472-0841

HAWTHORN SUITES AT WATERFRONT PLAZA
325 Lake Ave S
(55802)
Rates: $119-$239
(218) 727-4663
(800) 527-1133

LAKEVIEW CASTLE
5135 N Shore Dr
(55804)
Rates: n/a
(218) 525-1014

MANOR ON THE CREEK COUNTRY INN B&B
2215 E 2nd St
(55812)
Rates: $129-$199
(218) 728-3189
(800) 428-3189

MOTEL 6
200 S 27th Ave W
(55806)
Rates: $30-$36
(218) 723-1123
(800) 466-8356

NORTH SHORE COTTAGES
7717 Congdon
Blvd (55804)
Rates: $39-$159
(218) 525-2812
(800) 787 2812

RADISSON HOTEL
505 W Superior St
(55802)
Rates: $79-$119
(218) 727-8981
(800) 333-3333

SKYLINE COURT MOTEL
4880 Miller Truck
Hwy (55811)
Rates: $35-$65
(218) 727-1563
(800) 554-0621

TRAVELODGE
9315 Westgate
Blvd (55810)
Rates: $54-$84
(218) 628-3691
(800) 578-7878

VOYAGEUR LAKEWALK INN
333 E Superior St
(55802)
Rates: $45-$175
(218) 722-3911
(800) 258-3911

WILLARD MUNGER INN
7408 Grand Ave
(55807)
Rates: $36-$122
(218) 624-4814
(800) 982-2453

EAGAN

HOLIDAY INN EXPRESS HOTEL & SUITES-MALL OF AMERICA
1950 Rahncliff Ct
(55122)
Rates: $110
(651) 681-9266
(800) 465-4329

HOMESTEAD VILLAGE GUEST STUDIOS
3015 Denmark
Ave (55122)
Rates: n/a
(651) 905-1778
(888) 782-9473

RESIDENCE INN BY MARRIOTT
3040 Eagandale Pl
(55121)
Rates: $94-$152
(651) 688-0363
(800) 331-3131

EDEN PRAIRIE

HAMPTON INN
7740 Flying Cloud
Dr (55344)
Rates: $69-$84
(612) 942-9000
(800) 426-7866

HOMESTEAD VILLAGE GUEST STUDIOS
11905 Technology
Dr (55344)
Rates: $72-$87
(612) 942-6818
(888) 782-9473

RESIDENCE INN BY MARRIOTT
7780 Flying Cloud
Dr (55344)
Rates: $135-$195
(612) 829-0033
(800) 331-3131

TOWNE PLACE SUITES
11588 Leona Rd
(55344)
Rates: $54-$114
(612) 942-6001
(800) 257-3000

EDINA

HAWTHORNE SUITES HOTEL
3400 Edinborough
Way (55435)
Rates: $125-$145
(612) 893-9300
(800) 527-1133

ELBOW LAKE

COUNTRY INN MOTEL
Hwy 79 E (56531)
Rates: $29-$45
(218) 685-4511

ELK RIVER

AMERICINN MOTEL
17432 Hwy 10
(55330)
Rates: $49-$119
(612) 441-8554
(800) 634-3444

RED CARPET INN
17291 Hwy 10
(55330)
Rates: $26-$42
(612) 441-2424
(800) 251-1962

ELY

BIG LAKE WILDERNESS LODGE
3012 Echo Trail
(55731)
Rates: $655-$1100
Weekly
(218) 365-2125
(800) 446-9080

BLUE HERON BED & BREAKFST
827 Kawishiwi
Trail (55731)
Rates: $75-$100
(218) 365-4720

BUDGET HOST-MOTEL ELY
1047 E Sheridan St
(55731)
Rates: $49-$75
(218) 365-3237
(800) 283-4678

CEDAR SHORES RESORT
2024 Grant
McMahan Blvd
(55731)
Rates: $470-$610
Weekly
(218) 365-5775
(847) 678-5398

LA TOURELL'S RESORT & OUTFITTERS
P O Box 239
(55731)
Rates: $75+
(218) 365-4531
(800) 365-4531

LODGE OF WHISPERING PINES
2700 Echo Trail
(55731)
Rates: $105+
(218) 365-2129
(800) 510-2947

NORTH COUNTRY LODGE
5865 Moose Lake
Rd (55731)
Rates: $445-$1395
Weekly
(218) 365-4976
(800) 777-4431

OJIBWAY RESORT
Farm Lake, HCR-1
(55731)
Rates: $595
Weekly
(218) 365-4106
(800) 777-7091

OLSON BAY RESORT COTTAGES
2279 Grant
McMahan Blvd
(55731)
Rates: $350-$600
Weekly
(800) 777-4419

PADDLE INN
1314 E Sheridan St
(55731)
Rates: n/a
(218) 365-6036

SHAGAWA INN RESORT ON THE LAKE
P O Box 148
(55731)
Rates: $48-$63
(218) 365-5154

SILVER RAPIDS LODGE RESORT
HC 1, Box 2992
(55731)
Rates: $50-$180
(218) 365-4877
(800) 950-9425

THREE DEER HAVEN
1850 Deer Haven
Dr (55731)
Rates: $75-$90
(218) 365-6464

TIMBER TRAIL LODGE
HC 1, Box 3111
(55731)
Rates: $49-$135
(218) 365-4879
(800) 777-7348

TIMBER WOLF LODGE
P O Box 147
(55731)
Rates: $580-$1550
Weekly
(218) 827-3512
(800) 777-8457

AREA CODES - If the local number doesn't connect, check for a new area code.

WEST GATE MOTEL
110 N 2nd Ave W (55731)
Rates: $38-$60
(218) 365-4513
(800) 806-4979

WHITE IRON BEACH RESORT
13471 White Iron Beach (55731)
Rates: $60-$120
(218) 365-4885

EMILY

WIGWAM MOTEL
Hwy 6 (56447)
Rates: $42-$52
(218) 763-2995
(800) 763-2995

ERSKINE

WIN-E-MAC MOTEL
Box 144 (56535)
Rates: $27-$50
(218) 687-2415
(800) 358-8663

EVELETH

KOKE'S DOWNTOWN MOTEL
714 Fayal Rd (55734)
Rates: $20-$38
(218) 744-4500
(800) 892-5107

EXCELSIOR

CHRISTOPHER INN
201 Mill St (55331)
Rates: $80-$155
(612) 474-0605

FAIRFAX

FAIRFAX MOTEL
403 E Lincoln Ave (55332)
Rates: n/a
(507) 426-7266

FAIRMONT

BUDGET INN
1122 N State St (56031)
Rates: $29-$39+
(507) 235-3373

COMFORT INN
2225 N State St (56031)
Rates: $64-$99
(507) 238-5444
(800) 228-5150

HIGHLAND COURT MOTEL
1245 Lake Ave (56031)
Rates: $23-$49
(507) 235-6686

HOLIDAY INN
1201 Torgerson Dr (56031)
Rates: $89-$159
(507) 238-4771
(800) 465-4329

SEBASTIANI & EDGEWATER INN
200 S Main (56031)
Rates: $28-$42
(507) 235-5541

SUPER 8 MOTEL
1200 Torgerson Dr (56031)
Rates: $54-$79
(507) 238-9464
(800) 800-8000

FARIBAULT

AMERICINN MOTEL
1801 Lavender Dr (55021)
Rates: $69-$85
(507) 334-9464
(800) 634-3444

GREAT WESTERN MOTEL
1401 Hwy 60 W (55021)
Rates: n/a
(507) 334-5508

KNIGHTS INN
841 Faribault Rd (55021)
Rates: $31-$55
(507) 334-1841
(800) 843-5644

SELECT INN
4040 Hwy 60 W (55021)
Rates: $37-$58
(507) 334-2051
(800) 641-1000

WINJUM'S SHADY ACRES RESORT
17759 W 177th St (55021)
Rates: $290-$550 Weekly
(507) 334-6661
(800) 626-2952

FEDERAL DAM

SUGAR POINT RESORT
10125 Sugar Point Dr NW (56641)
Rates: $80-$120
(218) 654-3150
(800) 733-3150

FERGUS FALLS

AMERICINN MOTEL
526 Western Ave N (56537)
Rates: $57-$114
(218) 739-3900
(800) 634-3444

BEST WESTERN
902 Frontier Dr (56537)
Rates: $59-$89
(218) 739-2211
(800) 528-1234
(800) 293-2216

DAYS INN
610 Western Ave N (56537)
Rates: $38-$69
(218) 739-3311
(800) 329-7466

JEWEL MOTEL
1602 Pebble Lake Rd (56537)
Rates: n/a
(218) 739-5430

MOTEL 7
616 Frontier Dr (56537)
Rates: $32-$45
(218) 736-2554

SUPER 8 MOTEL
2454 College Way (56537)
Rates: $38-$53
(218) 739-3261
(800) 800-8000

FINLAYSON

SUPER 8 MOTEL
2811 Hwy 23 (55735)
Rates: $44-$56
(320) 245-5284
(800) 800-8000

FOREST LAKE

FOREST LAKE MOTEL
7 NE 6th Ave (55025)
Rates: $50-$60
(612) 464-4077
(800) 470-4077

FOSSTON

SUPER 8 MOTEL
108 S Amber (56542)
Rates: $41-$57
(218) 435-1088
(800) 800-8000

FRANKLIN

MAPLE HILL COTTAGE
RR 1, Box 12 (55333)
Rates: $45-$55
(507) 557-2403

FRAZEE

MORNINGSIDE MOTEL
31348 County Hwy 10 (56544)
Rates: $30-$57
(218) 334-5021

FRIDLEY

BEST WESTERN KELLY INN
5201 Central Ave NE (55421)
Rates: $79-$209
(612) 571-9440
(800) 528-1234

GARRISON

COUNTRY INN & SUITES BY CARLSON
SR 169N (56450)
Rates: $105-$129
(320) 692-4050
(800) 456-4000

GREGORY'S RESORT
HC1, Box 42B (56540)
Rates: $20+
(320) 692-4415

ROLLING HILLS RESORT
HC1, Box 205A (56450)
Rates: $56-$82
(320) 692-4348

TWIN PINES RESORT & MOTEL
HCR 1, Box 35 (56540)
Rates: $35-$59
(320) 692-4413
(800) 450-8246

GAYLORD

GOLD LEAF INN & SUITES
330 E Main St (55334)
Rates: $45-$149
(507) 237-5860

GLENCOE

GLENCOE CASTLE BED & BREAKFST
831 13th St E (55336)
Rates: $65-$175
(320) 864-3043
(800) 517-3334

GLENWOOD

HI-VIEW MOTEL
255 N Hwy 55 (56334)
Rates: $26-$43
(612) 634-4541

SCOTWOOD MOTEL
Hwy 28 & 55 (56334)
Rates: $48-$70
(320) 634-5105

GRAND MARAIS

ASPEN LODGE
310 E Hwy 61 (55604)
Rates: $65-$110
(218) 387-2500

AREA CODES - If the local number doesn't connect, check for a new area code.

BEST WESTERN SUPERIOR INN
104 1st Ave E
(55604)
Rates: $99-$199
(218) 387-2240
(800) 842-8439

CLEARWATER LODGE
355 Gunflint Trail
(55604)
Rates: $595-$625
Weekly
(800) 527-0554

EAST BAY HOTEL
P O Box 220
(55604)
Rates: $26-$155
(218) 387-2800
(800) 414-2807

GOLDEN EAGLE LODGE
325 Gunflint Trail
(55604)
Rates: $89-$120
(218) 388-2203
(800) 346-2203

GUNFLINT LODGE
143 S Gunflint
Trail (55604)
Rates: $165-$362
(218) 388-2294
(800) 328-3325

GUNFLINT MOTEL
Gunflint Trail
(55604)
Rates: $40-$52
(218) 387-1454

GUNFLINT PINES RESORT
755 Gunflint Trail
(55604)
Rates: n/a
(800) 533-5814

HARBOR INN
207 Wisconsin St
(55604)
Rates: n/a
(218) 387-1191
(800) 595-4566

LITTLE OLLIE LAKE CABIN
590 Gunflint Trail
(55604)
Rates: $110-$125
(218) 388-9972
(800) 322-8327

LUND'S ON THE SCANDINAVIAN RIVIERA
P O Box 126
(55604)
Rates: $48-$84
(218) 387-2155

MOTEL WEDGEWOOD
HC 1, Box 100
(55604)
Rates: $30-$35
(218) 387-2944

NOR' WESTER LODGE & OUTFITTER
7778 Gunflint
Trail (55604)
Rates: $498-$1249/Weekly
(218) 388-2252

OUTPOST RESORT MOTEL
2935 E Hwy 61
(55604)
Rates: $37-$79
(218) 387-1833
(888) 380-1833

SANDGREN MOTEL
P. O. Box 1056
(55604)
Rates: $30-$45
(218) 387-2975

SEAWALL MOTEL & CABINS
Hwy 61 & 3rd Ave
(55604)
Rates: $42-$72
(218) 387-2095
(800) 245-5806

SUPER 8 MOTEL
1711 Hwy 61 W
(55604)
Rates: $69-$114
(218) 387-2448
(800) 800-8000

TOMTEBODA MOTEL
1800 Hwy 61 W
(55604)
Rates: $59-$79
(218) 387-1585

TRAILSIDE CABINS & MOTEL
P O Box 155
(55604)
Rates: $40-$70
(218) 387-1550
(800) 585-2792

WEDGEWOOD MOTEL
1663 Hwy 61 E
(55604)
Rates: $30-$42
(218) 387-2944

GRAND RAPIDS

AMERICANA MOTEL
1915 Hwy 2 W
(55744)
Rates: $28-$38
(218) 326-0369
(888) 326-0369

BEST WESTERN RAINBOW INN
1300 US 169 E
(55744)
Rates: $56-$77
(218) 326-9655
(800) 528-1234

COUNTRY INN BY CARLSON
2601 Hwy 169 S
(55744)
Rates: $68-$106
(218) 327-4960
(800) 456-4000

DAYS INN
311 Hwy 2 E
(55744)
Rates: $45-$100
(218) 326-3457
(800) 329-7466

ITASCAN MOTEL
610 S Pokegama
Ave (55744)
Rates: $38-$48
(218) 326-3489
(800) 842-7733

SAWMILL INN
2301 S Pokegama
Ave (55744)
Rates: $57-$99
(218) 326-8501

GRANITE FALLS

SUPER 8 MOTEL
845 W Hwy 212
(56241)
Rates: $45-$57
(320) 564-4075
(800) 800-8000

GREENBUSH

EMERALD INN MOTEL
Hwy 32 S (56751)
Rates: $29-$34
(218) 782-2990

HACKENSACK

GREEN ROOF LODGE ON WOMAN LAKE
945 County 5 NW
(56452)
Rates: $420-$785
Weekly
(218) 682-2399
(800) 366-2399

OWL'S NEST MOTEL & RV
Hwy 371 (56452)
Rates: $28-$49
(218) 675-6141

QUIETWOODS RESORT
4765 Alder Lane
NW (56452)
Rates: $45-$95
(218) 675-6240

HALLOCK

GATEWAY MOTEL
702 S Atlantic
(56728)
Rates: $21-$35
(218) 843-2032

HAMPTON

SILVER BELL MOTEL
Hwy 52 (55031)
Rates: $37-$40
(651) 437-9242

HARMONY

COUNTRY LODGE MOTEL
525 Main Ave N
(55939)
Rates: $45-$80
(507) 886-2515
(800) 870-1710

HASTINGS

A COUNTRY ROSE
13452 90th St S
(55033)
Rates: $65-$85
(612) 436-2237

HENDRICKS

TRIPLE L FARM BED & BREAKFAST
Rt 1, Box 141
(56136)
Rates: $40-$55
(507) 275-3740

HERMAN

LAWNDALE FARM WILDLIFE GALLERY B&B
Rt 2, Box 50
(56248)
Rates: $65
(320) 677-2687

HIBBING

ADAMS HOUSE BED & BREAKFAST
201 E 23rd St
(55746)
Rates: $48-$53
(218) 263-9742
(888) 891-9742

DAYS INN
1520 Hwy 37 E
(55746)
Rates: $41-$75
(218) 263-8306
(800) 329-7466

HIBBING PARK HOTEL
1402 E Howard St
(55746)
Rates: $70-$75
(218) 262-3481

SUPER 8 MOTEL
1411 E 40th St
(55746)
Rates: $43-$68
(218) 263-8982
(800) 800-8000

HILL CITY

BLUE MOON RESORT & MOTEL
17090 Hwy 169
(55748)
Rates: $38-$75
(218) 697-8155
(888) 94-MN-FUN

WHITETAIL INN MOTEL
Hwy 169 N
(55748)
Rates: $26-$38
(218) 697-2470

AREA CODES - If the local number doesn't connect, check for a new area code.

HINCKLEY

DAYS INN
104 Grindstone Ct
(55037)
Rates: $39-$135
(320) 384-7751
(800) 329-7466

HINCKLEY GOLD PINE INN
325 Fire Monument
(55037)
Rates: $49-$75
(320) 384-6112

HOLIDAY INN EXPRESS
604 Weber Ave
(55037)
Rates: $59-$89
(320) 384-7171
(800) 465-4329

HOWARD LAKE

HOWARD LAKE MOTEL
210 10th Ave
(55349)
Rates: $29-$34
(320) 543-2186

HUTCHINSON

BEST WESTERN VICTORIAN INN
1000 Hwy 7 W
(55350)
Rates: $58-$135
(320) 587-6030
(800) 528-1234
(800) 369-0145

ECONOMY INN
200 Hwy 7 E
(55350)
Rates: $25-$65
(320) 587-2129

KING MOTEL
Hwy 7 & 22 W
(55350)
Rates: $32-$44
(320) 587-4737

INTERNATIONAL FALLS

BUDGET HOST INN-VOYAGEUR NATL PARK AREA
10 Riverview Blvd
(56649)
Rates: $36-$60
(218) 283-2577
(800) 283-4678

DAYS INN
2331 Hwy 53 S
(56649)
Rates: $39-$49
(218) 283-9441
(800) 329-7466

HILLTOP MOTEL
2002 2nd Ave W
(56649)
Rates: $35-$59
(218) 283-2505
(800) 322-6671

HOLIDAY INN
1500 Hwy 71 W
(56649)
Rates: $84-$150
(218) 283-8000
(800) 465-4329

ISLAND VIEW LODGE & MOTEL
1817 Hwy 11E
(56649)
Rates: $47-$195
(218) 266-3511
(800) 777-7856

NORTHERNAIRE FLOATING LODGES
P. O.Box 510
(56649)
Rates: $695-$1895
Weekly
(218) 286-5221

RAMBLER MOTEL
1901 2nd Ave W
(56649)
Rates: n/a
(218) 283-8454

THUNDERBIRD LODGE
2170 CR 139
(56649)
Rates: $65-$89
(218) 286-3151

INVER GROVE HEIGHTS

AMERICINN HOTEL & SUITES
5861 Blaine Ave E
(55076)
Rates: n/a
(651) 450-7511
(800) 634-3444

ISLE

MCQUOID'S INN
1325 Hwy 47 N
(56342)
Rates: $60-$120
(320) 676-3535
(800) 862--3535

SCENIC BAY RESORT & MOTEL
610 W Main St
(56342)
Rates: $36-$50
(320) 676-3274

JACKSON

BUDGET HOST-PRAIRIE WINDS MOTEL
950 N US 71
(56143)
Rates: $29-$62
(507) 847-2020
(800) 283-4678

PARK-VU MOTEL
Hwy 71, South of
I-90 (56143)
Rates: $25-$35
(507) 847-3440

SUPER 8 MOTEL
2025 Hwy 71 N
(56143)
Rates: $54-$67
(507) 847-3498
(800) 800-8000

KASSON

AMERICINN MOTEL & SUITES
301 8th St SE
(55944)
Rates: $55-$70
(507) 634-3444
(800) 634-3444

KELLIHER

ROYAL SHOOKS MOTEL
1 & 72 (56661)
Rates: $25-$30
(218) 647-8379

LA CRESCENT

RANCH MOTEL
Hwy 14-16-61
(55947)
Rates: $30-$75
(507) 895-4422

LAKE BENTON

STEVE'S RESORT & MOTEL
N Hwys 75 & 14
(56149)
Rates: $30-$37
(507) 368-4399

LAKE BRONSON

LAKE BRONSON MOTEL
P O Box 8 (56734)
Rates: $30-$36
(218) 754-4355

LAKE CITY

EDGE O TOWN MOTEL
1756 Hwy 61 S
(55041)
Rates: $25-$53
(651) 345-2309

LAKE AIRE MOTEL
917 N Lakeshore
Dr (55041)
Rates: $26-$60
(651) 345-4586

LAKE PEPIN LODGE-MOTEL
620 Central Point
Rd (55041)
Rates: $59-$139
(651) 345-5392
(800) 644-2780

SUNSET MOTEL & RESORT
1515 N Lakeshore
Dr (55041)
Rates: $38-$87
(651) 345-5331
(800) 945-0192

LAKE GEORGE

LAKE GEORGE PINES MOTEL
HC 70, Box 309
(56458)
Rates: $27-$50
(218) 266-3914

LAKE KABETOGAMA

BIRCHAM'S LAKE-VIEW RESORT
12475 Burma Rd
(56669)
Rates: $65-$80
(218) 875-2471

CALM BAY'S WHITE EAGLE RESORT
10476 Gamma Rd
(56669)
Rates: $65-$95
(218) 875-2341

SNYDER'S IDLEWILD RESORT
10060 Gappa Rd
(56669)
Rates: $430-$840
Weekly
(218) 875-3831

WATSON'S HARMONY BEACH RESORT & LODGE
10002 Gappa Rd
(56669)
Rates: $35-$145
(218) 875-2811

LAKE OF THE WOODS

ZIPPEL BAY RESORT
HC 2, Box 51
(56686)
Rates: $35-$65
(800) 222-2537

LAKE SHORE

GULL LAKE MOTEL
7779 Interlachen
Rd (56468)
Rates: $50-$85
(218) 963-2208
(800) 599-2208

LAKE VERMILION

BAY VIEW LODGE
2001 Bay View Dr
(55790)
Rates: $70
(218) 753-4825
(800) 628-1607

WHITE EAGLE RESORT
3026 Vermilion Dr
(55723)
Rates: $550-$1300
Weekly
(218) 666-5500
(800) 542-0365

LAKESHORE

GULL LAKE MOTEL
7779 Interlachen
Rd (56468)
Rates: $40-$75
(218) 963-2208
(800) 599-2208

LAKEVILLE

COMFORT INN
10935 176th St W
(55044)
Rates: $80-$144
(612) 898-3700
(800) 228-5150

**FRIENDLY HOST
LAKEVILLE MOTEL**
17296 Kenrick Ave
(55044)
Rates: $59-$79
(612) 435-7191
(800) 341-8000

MOTEL 6
11274 210th St
(55044)
Rates: $30-$36
(612) 469-1900
(800) 466-8356

SUPER 8 MOTEL
20800 Kenrick Ave
(55044)
Rates: $58-$76
(612) 469-1134
(800) 800-8000

LAMBERTON

**LAMBERTON
MOTEL**
601 1st Ave W
(56152)
Rates: $26-$38
(507) 752-7242
(888) 785-9762

LITCHFIELD

**LAKE RIPLEY
RESORT MOTEL**
1205 S Sibley Ave
(55355)
Rates: $29-$40
(320) 693-3227
(800) 544-4792

**SCOTWOOD
MOTEL**
1017 E Frontage
Rd (55355)
Rates: $58-$89
(320) 693-2496
(800) 225-5489

LITTLE FALLS

**AMERICINN
MOTEL**
306 Lemieur St
(56345)
Rates: $49-$109
(320) 632-1964
(800) 634-3444

**CLIFFWOOD
MOTEL**
1201 N Haven Rd
(56345)
Rates: $30-$48
(320) 632-5488

**COUNTRY INN
& SUITES BY
CARLSON**
209 16th St NE
(56345)
Rates: $59-$119
(320) 632-1000
(800) 456-4000

GOODNIGHT INN
RR 6, Box 280
(56345)
Rates: $29-$70
(320) 632-2989
(800) 575-0594

PINE EDGE INN
308 1st St SE
(56345)
Rates: $35-$95
(320) 632-6681
(800) 344-6681

LONG LAKE

**LONG LAKE
MOTEL**
521 Willow Dr
(55356)
Rates: $31-$39
(612) 473-5411

LONG PRAIRIE

BUDGET HOST
417 Lake St (56347)
Rates: $40-$49
(320) 732-6118
(800) 544-0737
(800) 283-4678

LONGVILLE

**HOLIDAY HAVEN
RESORTS**
3529 State 84 N
(56655)
Rates: $60-$96
(218) 363-2473
(800) 279-5372

JOURNEY'S END
RESORT
648 Journey's End
Lane (56655)
Rates: $495-$1050
Weekly
(218) 363-2601
(800) 429-2523

LONGVILLE INN
Hwy 84 N & S
(56655)
Rates: $36-$59
(218) 363-2400
(800) 670-0810

PINES MOTEL
P O Box 115
(56655)
Rates: $36-$59
(218) 363-2035
(800) 670-0810

LUTSEN

**BEST WESTERN
CLIFF DWELLER**
Hwy 61 (55612)
Rates: $39-109
(218) 773-7273
(800) 528-1234
(800) 223 2048

**THE MOUNTAIN
INN AT LUTSEN**
Ski Hill Rd (55612)
Rates: $69-$129
(218) 663-7244

**SOLBAKKEN
RESORT**
4874 W Hwy 61
(55612)
Rates: $39-$230
(218) 663-7566
(800) 435-3950

**THOMSONITE
BEACH MOTEL**
2920 W Hwy 61
(55612)
Rates: $56-$145
(218) 387-1532
(888) 387-1532

LUVERNE

**COZY REST
MOTEL**
116 S Kniss
(56156)
Rates: $26-$48
(507) 283-4461
(800) 839-1375

SUNRISE MOTEL
I-90, Exit 12
(56156)
Rates: $26-$48
(507) 283-2347
(800) 868-4748

SUPER 8 MOTEL
I-90 & Hwy 75
(56156)
Rates: $42-$49
(507) 283-9541
(800) 800-8000

MAHNOMEN

**TRAVELERS
MOTEL**
Hwy 59 & 200
(56557)
Rates: $27-$38
(218) 935-5654
(800) 551-8587

MANKATO

**BEST WESTERN
HOTEL**
1111 Range St
(56603)
Rates: $59-$94
(507) 625-9333
(800) 528-1234

COMFORT INN
131 Apache Pl
(56601)
Rates: $59-$99
(507) 388-5107
(800) 228-5150

DAYS INN
1285 Range St
(56001)
Rates: $50-$130
(507) 387-3332
(800) 329-7466

ECONO LODGE
111 W Lind Ct
(56003)
Rates: $40-$90
(507) 345-8800
(800) 553-2666

ECONOMY INN
1255 Range St
(56001)
Rates: $35-$105
(507) 388-1644
(800) 822-2521

**HOLIDAY INN
DOWNTOWN**
101 E Main St
(56001)
Rates: $105
(507) 345-1234
(800) 465-4329

MANTORVILLE

**GRAND OLD
MANSION**
501 Clay St
(55955)
Rates: $30-$64
(507) 635-3231

MAPLE PLAIN

**MAPLE PLAIN
MOTEL**
5329 Hwy 12
(55359)
Rates: $28-$40
(612) 479-1434

MAPLEWOOD

**BEST WESTERN
INN**
1780 E CR D
(55109)
Rates: $99-$129
(651) 770-2811
(800) 528-1234
(888) 770-2811

SUPER 8 MOTEL
285 Century Ave
(55119)
Rates: $50-$71
(651) 738-1600
(800) 800-8000

MARSHALL

**BEST WESTERN
MARSHALL INN**
1500 E College Dr
(56258)
Rates: $64-$106
(507) 532-3221
(800) 528-1234
(800) 422-0897

COMFORT INN
1511 E College Dr
(56258)
Rates: $59-$100
(507) 532-3070
(800) 228-5150

AREA CODES - If the local number doesn't connect, check for a new area code.

SUPER 8 MOTEL
1106 E Main St
(56258)
Rates: $50-$62
(507) 537-1461
(800) 800-8000

TRAVELER'S LODGE
1425 E College Dr
(56258)
Rates: $36-$52
(507) 532-5721
(800) 532-5721

MCGREGOR

COUNTRY MEADOWS INN
SR 65 & 210
(55760)
Rates: $60-$99
(218) 768-7378
(888) 331-7378

TOWN & COUNTRY MOTEL
Hwy 65 & 210
(55760)
Rates: $29-$46
(218) 768-3271

MELROSE

SUPER 8 MOTEL
231 E County Rd
173 (56352)
Rates: $40-$54
(320) 256-4261
(800) 800-8000

MENAHGA

SPIRIT LAKE MOTEL
Hwy 71 (56464)
Rates: $25-$39
(218) 564-4151

MERRIFIELD

MISSION BEACH RESORT
HC 86 Box 1010
(56465)
Rates: $250-$500
Weekly
(218) 765-3447
(800) 279-5370

SHING WAKO RESORT
HC 87 Box 9580
(56465)
Rates: $75-$105
(218) 765-3226

MILACA

SUPER 8 MOTEL
215 10th Ave SE
(56353)
Rates: $52-$70
(320) 983-2660
(800) 800-8000

MILLE LACS

ST. ALBANS BAY LODGE
HCr 1 Box 40
(56450)
Rates: $46-$69
(320) 692-4552
(800) 377-2443

MINNEAPOLIS

AQUA CITY MOTEL
5739 Lyndale Ave
S (55419)
Rates: $25-$50
(612) 861-6061
(800) 861-6061

BEST WESTERN NORMANDY INN
405 S 8th St
(55404)
Rates: $69-$109
(612) 370-1400
(800) 528-1234
(800) 372-3131

CROWN PLAZA NORTHSTAR HOTEL
618 S 2nd Ave
(55402)
Rates: $89-$139
(612) 338-2288
(800) 227-6963

DOUBLETREE PARK PLACE HOTEL
1500 Park Place
Blvd (55416)
Rates: n/a
(612) 542-8600
(800) 542-5566

HILTON HOTEL
1001 Marquette
Ave (55403)
Rates: $125-$305
(612) 376-1000
(800) 445-8667

HOLIDAY INN METRODOME
1500 Washington
Ave S (55454)
Rates: $118-$159
(612) 333-4646
(800) 465-4329
(800) 448-3663

HOMEWOOD SUITES
2261 Killebrew Dr
(55425)
Rates: n/a
(612) 854-0900
(800) 225-5466

HYATT WHITNEY HOTEL
150 Portland Ave
(55401)
Rates: $165-$190
(612) 375-1223
(612) 339-1333
(800) 233-1234

THE MARQUETTE HOTEL
710 Marquette
Ave (55402)
Rates: $79-$259
(612) 333-4545

MARRIOTT CITY CENTER
30 S 7th St (55402)
Rates: $139-$209
(612) 349-4000
(800) 228-9290

METRO INN
5637 Lyndale Ave
S (55419)
Rates: $39-$64
(612) 861-6011

RADISSON HOTEL METRODOME
615 Washington
Ave SE (55414)
Rates: $129-$159
(612) 379-8888
(800) 333-3333

RADISSON PLAZA HOTEL
35 S 7th St (55402)
Rates: $89-$239
(612) 339-4900
(800) 333-3333

REGAL MINNEAPOLIS HOTEL
1313 Nicollet Mall
(55403)
Rates: $99-$199
(612) 332-6000
(800) 522-8856

RODEWAY INN
2335 3rd Ave S
(55404)
Rates: $60-$80
(612) 871-2000
(800) 228-2000

RODEWAY INN
925 4th St SE
(55414)
Rates: $60-$79
(612) 623-9490
(800) 228-2000

SHERATON MINNEAPOLIS METRODOME
1330 Industrial
Blvd (55413)
Rates: $85-$110
(612) 331-1900
(800) 325-3535

MINNESOTA CITY

SUNDOWN MOTEL
RR 2, Box 3A
(55959)
Rates: $25-$48
(507) 452-7376
(800) 469-5920

MINNETONKA

MARRIOTT SOUTHWEST
5801 Opus Pkwy
(55343)
Rates: $74-$189
(612) 935-5500
(800) 228-9290

MONTEVIDEO

COUNTRY INN & SUITES BY CARLSON
1805 E SR 7
(56265)
Rates: $63-$81
(320) 269-8000
(800) 456-4000

FIESTA CITY MOTEL
Jct 59, 212 & 7W
(56265)
Rates: $24-$55
(320) 269-8896
(800) 472-6478

THE HOTEL HUNT ON MAIN
207 N 1st St
(56265)
Rates: $43-$61
(320) 269-5554
(888) 430-4400

VIKING MOTEL
Rt 2, Box 60 E,
Hwy 7 (56265)
Rates: $23-$38
(320) 269-6545
(800) 670-0777

MONTICELLO

BEST WESTERN SILVER FOX INN
1114 Cedar St
(55362)
Rates: $59-$120
(612) 295-4000
(800) 528-1234

COMFORT INN
89 Chelsea Rd
(55362)
Rates: $59-$144
(612) 271-8880
(800) 228-5150

DAYS INN
200 E Oakwood
Dr (55362)
Rates: $55-$100
(612) 295-1111
(800) 329-7466

MOORHEAD

BEST WESTERN RED RIVER INN
600 30th Ave S
(56560)
Rates: $54-$75
(218) 233-6171
(800) 528-1234
(800) 328-6173

DAYS INN
1010 Holiday Dr
(56560)
Rates: $40-$148
(218) 233-7531
(800) 329-7466

GUEST HOUSE MOTEL
2107 SE Main
(56560)
Rates: $28-$38
(218) 233-2471

THE MADISON HOTEL
600 30 Ave S
(56560)
Rates: $39-$78
(218) 233-6171

MOTEL 75
810 Belsly Blvd
(56560)
Rates: $35-$48
(218) 233-7501
(800) 828-4171

TRAVELODGE
3027 Frontage Rd
S (56560)
Rates: $43-$74
(218) 233-5333
(800) 578-7878

MORA

AMERICINN MOTEL & SUITES
1877 Frontage Rd
(55051)
Rates: $62-$112
(320) 679-5700
(800) 634-3444

ANN RIVER SWEDISH MOTEL
1819 S Hwy 65
(55051)
1-$95
(320) 679-2972
(800) 679-2973

MOTEL MORA
301 S Hwy 65
(55051)
2-$52
(320) 679-3262
(800) 657-0167

MORRIS

BEST WESTERN PRAIRIE INN
200 Hwy 28 E
(56267)
Rates: $36-$95
(320) 589-3030
(800) 528-1234
(800) 535-3035

MORTON

THE MORTON INN
Hwy 19 & 71
(56270)
Rates: $32-$36
(507) 697-6205
(800) 245-9800

MOTLEY

EASTWOOD INN
900 Hwy 10 S
(56466)
Rates: $44-$60
(218) 352-6386
(888) 886-6719

MOUNDS VIEW

SKYLINE MOTEL
4889 Old Hwy 8
(55112)
Rates: $35-$48
(612) 784-1436

NEVIS

FREMONT'S POINT RESORT
Rt 1, Box 119
(56467)
Rates: $675-$725
Weekly
(218) 652-3299
(800) 221-0713

ISLAND VIEW RESORT
RR 2 Box 75
(56467)
Rates: $380-$465
Weekly
(218) 652-3692
(800) 429-1388

PARADISE COVE RESORT
RR 2, Box 123K
(56467)
Rates: $450-$685
Weekly
(218) 732-3779
(800) 765-2682

PARK STREET INN HISTORICAL B&B
106 Park St (56467)
Rates: $60-$125
(218) 652-4500
(800) 797-1778

NEW PRAGUE

HERITAGE INN
410 W Main St
(56071)
Rates: $27-$38
(612) 758-4100

NEW ULM

BUDGET HOLIDAY MOTEL
1316 S Broadway
(56073)
Rates: $32-$36
(507) 354-4145

HOLIDAY INN
2101 S Broadway
(56073)
Rates: $94-$144
(507) 359-2941
(800) 465-4329

NEW ULM MOTEL
1427 S Broadway
(56073)
Rates: $26-$45
(507) 359-1414

SUPER 8 MOTEL
1901 S Broadway
(56073)
Rates: $48-$72
(507) 359-2400
(800) 800-8000

NEW YORK MILLS

SUNSHINE RESORT
RR 3, Box 256
(56567)
Rates: $315+
Weekly
(218) 346-5487
(888) 346-5487

NISSWA

JOLLY ROGER'S RESORT
9937 Cty Rd 4 N
(56468)
Rates: $250-$750
Weekly
(507) 829-6752
(800) 278-6752

NISSWA MOTEL
1426 Merrill Ave
(56468)
Rates: $61-$75
(218) 963-7611

WILDERNESS POINT RESORT
Wilderness Rd
(56468)
Rates: $47-$138
(218) 568-5642
(800) 231-4050

NORTHFIELD

ARCHER HOUSE OF NORTHFIELD HISTORIC COUNTRY INN
212 Division St
(55057)
Rates: $45-$140
(507) 645-5661
(800) 247-2235

COLLEGE CITY MOTEL
875 Hwy 3 N
(55057)
Rates: $25-$65
(507) 645-4426
(800) 775-0455

SUPER 8 MOTEL
1420 Riverview Dr
(55057)
Rates: $58-$77
(507) 663-0371
(800) 800-8000

OLIVIA

THE SHEEP SHEDDE INN
2425 W Lincoln
Ave (56277)
Rates: $50-$65
(320) 523-5000

ONAMIA

ECONO LODGE OF MILLE LACS LAKE
40993 US 169
(56359)
Rates: $27-$99
(320) 532-3838
(800) 553-2666
(800) 839-7006

EDDY'S LAKE MILLE LACS RESORT
41334 Shakopee
Lake Rd (56359)
Rates: $69-$129
(320) 532-3657
(800) 657-4704

ORR

NORTH COUNTRY INN MOTEL
4483 Hwy 53 (55771)
Rates: $46-$55
(218) 757-3778

PINE ACRES RESORT
4498 Pine Acres
Rd (55771)
Rates: $375-$850
Weekly
(218) 757-3144
(800) 777-7231

SUNSET RESORT
10294 Ash River
Trail (55771)
Rates: $75+
(218) 374-3161
(800) 232-3161

ORTONVILLE

VALI-VU MOTEL
Jct 12 & 75 (56278)
Rates: $22-$34
(320) 839-2558
(800) 841-6236

OUTING

ROOSEVELT LOG CABIN RESORT & MOTEL
758 State 6 NE
(56662)
Rates: $55-$95
(218) 792-5177
(800) 691-1869

OWATONNA

BEST BUDGET INN
1100 I-35 & Hwy
14 (55060)
Rates: $30-$80
(507) 451-0776
(800) 454-2628

BUDGET HOST INN
745 State Ave
(55060)
Rates: $40-$65
(507) 451-8712
(800) 283-4678

COUNTRY INN & SUITES
130 Allen Ave SW
(55060)
Rates: $69-$99
(507) 455-9295
(800) 456-4000

OAKDALE MOTEL
1416 S Oak St
(55060)
Rates: $30-$69
(507) 451-5480

SUPER 8 MOTEL
1818 Hwy 14 W
(55060)
Rates: $45-$62
(507) 451-0380
(800) 800-8000

PARK RAPIDS

BAYSIDE RESORT
HC 06, Box 338NK
(56470)
Rates: $385-$1000
Weekly
(218) 732-3666
(888) 750-3666

**CROW WING
CREST LODGE**
Rt 2. Box 33
(56433)
Rates: $480-$785
Weekly
(218) 652-3111
(800) 279-2754

**LEE'S RIVERSIDE
RESORT-MOTEL**
700 N Park
(56470)
Rates: $44-$74
(218) 732-9711
(800) 733-9711

**LITTLE NORWAY
RESORT**
HCO 5, Box 145
(56470)
Rates: $475-$760
Weekly
(218) 732-5480

LOON SONG B&B
Lake Itasca, #27
(56470)
Rates: $80-$105
(218) 266-3333

**SPIRIT LAKE
MOTEL**
Hwy 71 (56464)
Rates: $25-$39
(218) 564-4151

**TERRACE VIEW
MOTOR LODGE**
716 N Park
(56470)
Rates: $26-$42
(218) 732-1213
(800) 731-1213

PAYNESVILLE

**BLACK SAUCER
MOTEL**
703 W Main St
(56362)
Rates: $30-$65
(320) 243-3774

PELICAN RAPIDS

**CROSS POINT
RESORT**
Rt 3, Box 453
(56572)
Rates: $50-$55
(218) 863-8593

PEQUOT LAKES

BRADMOR MOTEL
Rt 2, Box 440
(56472)
Rates: $27-$52
(218) 568-4366

PERHAM

**BUDGET HOST
OASIS INN**
Hwy 78 & 10
(56573)
Rates: $32-$40
(218) 346-7810
(800) 283-4678

PETERSON

**LILLIAN'S HOUSE
OF SEVEN
GABLES B&B**
135 N Church St
(55962)
Rates: $59-$110
(507) 875-1000
(800) 442-7969

PINE CITY

CHALET MOTEL
I-35 & Hwy 70
(55063)
Rates: $30-$52
(320) 629-7684

**SCHWARTZWALD
MOTEL**
920 S 6th St
(55063)
Rates: $33-$48
(320) 629-2511
(800) 524-2512

PINE ISLAND

PINE MOTEL
106 1st St NE
(55963)
Rates: $32-$44
(507) 356-4421

PINE RIVER

**CEDARWOOD
MOTEL**
1st & Maple
(56474)
Rates: $38-$48
(888) 390-2208

**NORWAY BROOK
MOTEL**
HCR 77 Box 24
(56474)
Rates: $39-$44
(218) 587-2118
(800) 950-7330

TRAVELODGE
2684 SR 371 W
(56474)
Rates: $74-$95
(218) 587-4499
(800) 578-7878
(800) 450-4499

PIPESTONE

ARROW MOTEL
N Hwy 75 (56164)
Rates: $25-$35
(507) 825-3331

KINGS KOURT
821 SE 7th St
(56164)
Rates: n/a
(507) 825-3314

PLYMOUTH

**BEST WESTERN
KELLY INN**
2705 N Annapolis
Lane (55441)
Rates: $79-$105
(612) 553-1600
(800) 528-1234

RADISSON HOTEL
3131 Campus Dr
(55441)
Rates: $79-$154
(612) 559-6600
(800) 333-3333

RED ROOF INN
2600 Annapolis Ln
N (55441)
Rates: $50-$66
(612) 553-1751
(800) 843-7663

PRESTON

**INN TOWN
LODGE**
205 Franklin St
(55965)
Rates: $40-$65
(507) 765-4412

**THE JAILHOUSE
HISTORIC INN**
109 Houston St
NW (55965)
Rates: $42-$149
(507) 765-2181

PRINCETON

PINE-AIRE MOTEL
3079 90th Ave
(55371)
Rates: $38
(612) 389-2812

RUM RIVER MOTEL
510 19th Ave N
(55371)
Rates: $36-$45
(612) 389-3120

PRIOR LAKE

**NATURE'S INN
BED & BREAKFST
SUITES**
2920 220th St E
(55372)
Rates: $129-$179
(612) 447-2272

PROCTOR

AMERICINN
185 US Hwy 2
(55810)
Rates: $55-$130
(218) 624-1026
(800) 634-3444

RANIER

**SANDBAY B&B AT
TARA'S WHARF**
2065 Spruce St
Landing (56668)
Rates: $85-$145
(218) 286-5699
(877) 724-6955

RED LAKE FALLS

CHATEAU MOTEL
Hwy 32 N (56750)
Rates: $35-$42
(218) 253-4144

RED WING

**AMERICINN
OF RED WING**
1819 Old Main W
(55066)
Rates: $64-$95
(651) 385-9060
(800) 634-3444

**BEST WESTERN
QUIET HOUSE
SUITES**
752 Withers
Harbor Dr (55066)
Rates: $96-$179
(651) 388-1577
(800) 528-1234

DAYS INN
955 E 7th St (55066)
Rates: $40-$85
(651) 388-3568
(800) 329-7466

PARKWAY MOTEL
3425 Hwy 61 W
(55066)
Rates: $33-$43
(651) 388-8231
(800) 762-0934

RODEWAY INN
235 Withers
Harbor Dr (55066)
Rates: $39-$95
(651) 388-1502
(800) 228-2000

SUPER 8 MOTEL
232 Withers
Harbor Dr (55066)
Rates: $46-$92
(651) 388-0491
(800) 800-8000

REDWOOD FALLS

COMFORT INN
1382 E Bridge St
(56283)
Rates: $39-$130
(507) 644-5700
(800) 228-5150

AREA CODES - If the local number doesn't connect, check for a new area code.

SUPER 8 MOTEL
1305 E Bridge St
(56283)
Rates: $34-$54
(507) 637-3456
(800) 800-8000

REMER

ANDERSEN'S FOUR SEASONS RESORT
4293 State 6 NE
(56672)
Rates: $80+
(218) 566-2555
(800) 458-6707

CEDAR BEACH RESORT
4502 Cedar Trail NE (56672)
Rates: $105-$130
(218) 566-3669
(800) 566-3669

REMER MOTEL
200 Main St
(56672)
Rates: $40-$52
(218) 566-2555

RICHFIELD

CANDLEWOOD SUITES
351 W 77th St
(55423)
Rates: $59-$120
(612) 869-7704

MOTEL 6
7640 Cedar Ave S
(55423)
Rates $40-$46
(612) 861-4491
(800) 466-8356

ROCHESTER

BEST WESTERN FIFTH AVE
20 5th Ave NW
(55901)
Rates: $59-$79
(507) 289-3987
(800) 528-1234

BLONDELL'S CROWN SQUARE MOTEL & MALL
1406 2nd St SW
(55902)
Rates: $42-$130
(507) 282-9444
(800) 441-5209

COLONIAL HOTEL
114 2nd St SW
(55902)
Rates: $25-$54
(507) 289-3363
(800) 533-2226

COMFORT INN
1625 S Broadway
(55904)
Rates: $69-$129
(507) 281-2211
(800) 228-5150

COUNTRY INN & SUITES
4323 Hwy 52 N
(55901)
Rates: $79-$109
(507) 285-3335
(800) 456-4000

COURTESY INN
510 17th Ave NW
(55901)
Rates: $30-$60
(507) 289-1801

DAYS INN
6 First Ave NW
(55901)
Rates: $45-$69
(507) 282-3801
(800) 329-7466

DAYS INN SOUTH
111 28th St SE
(55904)
Rates: $44-$59
(507) 286-1001
(800) 329-7466

DAYSTOP
11 17th Ave SW
(55902)
Rates: $39-$79
(507) 282-2733
(800) 329-7466

ECONO LODGE
519 3rd Ave SW
(55902)
Rates: $44-$59
(507) 288-1855
(800) 553-2666

ECONO LODGE SOUTH
1850 S Broadway
(55904)
Rates: $44-$59
(507) 282-9905
(800) 553-2666

EXECUTIVE SUITES HOTEL & ECONOMY INN
9 3rd Ave NW
(55901)
Rates: $80
(507) 289-8646

FIKSDAL MOTEL
1215 2nd St SW
(55902)
Rates: $35-$49
(507) 288-2671

HOLIDAY INN MAYO CLINIC
220 S Broadway
(55904)
Rates: $69-$92
(507) 288-3231
(800) 465-4329

HOLIDAY INN SOUTH
1630 S Broadway
(55904)
Rates: $69-$109
(507) 288-1844
(800) 465-4329

HOWARD JOHNSON EXPRESS INN
111 17th Ave SW
(55902)
Rates: $41-$59
(507) 289-1617
(800) 446-4656

THE KAHLER GRAND HOTEL
20 2nd Ave SW
(55903)
Rates: $99-$138
(507) 282-2581
(800) 533-1655

MARRIOTT HOTEL
101 1st Ave SW
(55902)
Rates: $189-$199
(507) 280-6000
(800) 228-9290

MICROTEL INN & SUITES
4210 Hwy 52 N
(55901)
Rates: $46-$78
(507) 286-8780
(888) 771-7171
(800) 245-9535

MOTEL 6
2107 W Frontage Rd (55901)
Rates: $30-$36
(507) 282-6625
(800) 466-8356

QUALITY INN & SUITES
1620 1st Ave SE
(55904)
Rates: $89-$189
(507) 282-8091
(800) 228-5151

RADISSON HOTEL CENTERPLACE
150 S Broadway
(55904)
Rates: $109
(507) 281-8000
(800) 333-3333

RAMADA LIMITED
435 16th Ave NW
(55901)
Rates: $69-$99
(507) 288-9090
(800) 282-6232

SUPER 8 MOTEL
106 SE 21st St
(55901)
Rates: $48-$63
(507) 282-1756
(800) 800-8000

SUPER 8 MOTEL SOUTH
1230 S Broadway
(55904)
Rates: $49-$69
(507) 288-8288
(800) 800-8000

SUPER 8 MOTEL WEST
1608 2nd St SW
(55902)
Rates: $44-$69
(507) 281-5100
(800) 800-8000

THRIFTLODGE
1837 S Broadway
(55904)
Rates: $32-$45
(507) 288-2031
(800) 578-7878

TRAVELODGE DOWNTOWN
426 2nd St SW
(55902)
Rates: $44-$69
(507) 289-4095
(800) 578-7878

ROGERS

AMERICINN MOTEL
21800 Industrial Blvd (55374)
Rates: $56-$115
(612) 428-4346
(800) 634-3444

ROSEAU

AMERICINN
1090 3rd St NW
(56751)
Rates: $49-$86
(218) 463-1045
(800) 634-3444

EVERGREEN MOTEL
304 5th Ave NW
(56751)
Rates: $29-$34
(218) 463-1642
(800) 434-7685

NORTH COUNTRY INN
902 3rd St NW
(56751)
Rates: $48-$68
(218) 463-9444

SUPER 8 MOTEL
318 West Side
(56751)
Rates: $34-$43
(218) 463-2196
(800) 800-8000

ROSEVILLE

MOTEL 6
2300 Cleveland Ave N (55113)
Rates: $37-$43
(651) 639-3988
(800) 466-8356

ROUND LAKE

THE PRAIRIE HOUSE ON ROUND LAKE B&B
RR 1, Box 105
(56167)
Rates: $55
(507) 945-8934

RUSHFORD

MEADOWS INN B&B
900 Pine Meadow Ln (55971)
Rates: $50-$120
(507) 864-2378

AREA CODES - If the local number doesn't connect, check for a new area code.

WINDSWEPT INN MOTEL
207 N Mill St
(55971)
Rates: $30-$36
(507) 864-2545

ST. CHARLES

DOWNTOWN MOTEL
843 Whitewater
Ave (55972)
Rates: $22-$40
(507) 932-4050

ST. CLOUD

AMERICINN MOTEL & SUITES
4385 Clearwater
Rd (56301)
Rates: $79-$89
(320) 253-6337
(800) 634-3444

BEST WESTERN AMERICANNA INN
520 S US Hwy 10
(56304)
Rates: $50-$121
(320) 252-8700
(800) 528-1234
(800) 950-8701

BEST WESTERN KELLY INN
1 Sunwood Dr
(56301)
Rates: $64-$179
(320) 253-0606
(800) 528-1234

BUDGET INN
I-94 & Hwy 24
(56301)
Rates: $31-$85
(320) 558-2221
(800) 950-7751

DAYS INN
420 SE Hwy 10
(56304)
Rates: $49-$125
(320) 253-0500
(800) 329-7466

GATEWAY MOTEL
310 Lincoln Ave
SE (56304)
Rates: $24-$42
(320) 252-4050

HOLIDAY INN
75 37th Ave S
(56302)
Rates: $70-$200
(320) 253-9000
(800) 465-4329

HOLIDAY INN EXPRESS
4322 Clearwater
Rd (56301)
Rates: $54-$72
(320) 240-8000
(800) 465-4329

KLEIS MOTEL
30 25th Ave S
(56301)
Rates: $28-$57
(320) 251-7450

MOTEL 6
815 1st St S
(56387)
Rates: $28-$36
(320) 253-7070
(800) 466-8356

QUALITY INN
70 S 37th Ave
(56301)
Rates: $50-$150
(320) 253-4444
(800) 228-5151

SUPER 8 MOTEL
50 Park Ave S
(56301)
Rates: $38-$49
(320) 253-5530
(800) 800-8000

THRIFTY MOTEL
130 14th Ave NE
(56304)
Rates: $32-$38
(320) 253-6320

TRAVELODGE
3820 Roosevelt Rd
(56301)
Rates: $50-$135
(320) 283-3338
(800) 578-7878

ST. JAMES

SUPER 8 MOTEL
Hwy 60 (56081)
Rates: $46-$60
(507) 375-4708
(800) 800-8000

ST. JOSEPH

SUPER 8 MOTEL
P. O. Box 721
(56374)
Rates: $44-$64
(320) 363-7711
(800) 800-8000

ST. LOUIS PARK

LAKELAND MOTEL
4025 Hwy 7
(55416)
Rates: $50-$65
(612) 926-6575

ST. PAUL

BEST WESTERN KELLY INN
161 St Anthony
Ave (55103)
Rates: $94-$114
(651) 227-8711
(800) 528-1234

EXEL INN
1739 Old Hudson
Rd (55106)
Rates: $52-$84
(651) 771-5566
(800) 367-3935

HOLIDAY INN RIVER CENTRE
175 W 7th St
(55102)
Rates: $97
(651) 292-8929
(800) 465-4329

HOLIDAY INN-3M AREA
2201 Burns Ave
(55119)
Rates: $85-$125
(651) 731-2220
(800) 465-4329

RADISSON HOTEL
11 E Kellogg Blvd
(55101)
Rates: $95-$145
(651) 292-1900
(800) 333-3333

RADISSON INN
411 Minnesota St
(55101)
Rates: $102-$150
(651) 291-8800
(800) 333-3333

SHERATON MIDWAY
400 Hamline Ave
N (55104)
Rates: $90-$120
(651) 642-1234
(800) 535-2339

TRAVELODGE
1870 Old Hudson
Rd (55119)
Rates: $71
(651) 735-2337
(800) 578-7878

ST. PETER

AMERICINN MOTEL
700 N Minnesota
Ave (56082)
Rates: $54-$109
(507) 931-6554
(800) 634-3444

VIKING JR MOTEL
169 & 90 West
(56082)
Rates: $30-$50
(507) 931-3081
(800) 221-6406

SANBORN

SOD HOUSE ON THE PRAIRIE
Rt 2, Box 75
(56083)
Rates: $75-$135
(507) 723-5138

SANDSTONE

SANDSTONE 61 MOTEL
Hwy 23 & 61
(55072)
Rates: $29-$49
(320) 245-5419

SAUK CENTRE

AMERICINN MOTEL & SUITES
1230 Timberlane
Dr (56378)
Rates: $50-$103
(320) 352-2800
(800) 634-3444

GOPHER PRAIRIE MOTEL-IMA
1222 S Getty
(56378)
Rates: $30-$53
(320) 352-2275
(800) 341-8000

SAVAGE

COMFORT INN
4601 Hwy 13 W
(55378)
Rates: $54-$88
(612) 894-6124
(800) 228-5150

SAVAGE MOTOR INN
7361 Hwy 13 W
(55378)
Rates: $35-$65
(612) 894-4181

SCHROEDER

LAMB'S RESORT
North Shore Dr
Hwy 61 (55613)
Rates: n/a
(218) 663-7292

SUPERIOR RIDGE RESORT-MOTEL
P O Box 29 (55613)
Rates: $49-$109
(218) 663-7189
(800) 782-1776

SEBEKA

SEBEKA MOTEL
Hwy 71 (56477)
Rates: $24-$40
(218) 837-5162

SHAKOPEE

HILL VIEW MOTEL
12826 Johnson
Memorial Dr
(55379)
Rates: $39-$99
(612) 445-7111

PARK INN & SUITES
1244 Canterbury
Rd (55379)
Rates: $64-$150
(612) 445-3644

SILVER BAY

LITTLE MARAIS LAKESIDE CABINS
6476 Hwy 61
(55614)
Rates: $68+
(218) 226-3456

MARINER MOTEL
46 Outer Dr (55614)
Rates: $40-$80
(218) 226-4488
(800) 777-8452

WHISPERING PINES MOTEL
5763 Hwy 61 E (55614)
Rates: $45-$57
(218) 226-4712
(800) 332-0531

SLAYTON

RIDOTTO "WACH" INN MOTEL
2436 Hwy 59 (56172)
Rates: $36-$48
(507) 836-8511

SLEEPY EYE

BEST WESTERN INN OF SEVEN GABLES
1100 E Main St (56085)
Rates: $59-$89
(507) 794-5390
(800) 528-1234
(800) 852-9451

ORCHID INN & MOTOR LODGE
Hwy 14 & 4 (56085)
Rates: $28-$36
(507) 794-3211
(800) 245-4931

SPICER

NORTHERN INN ON GREEN LAKE
154 Lake St (56288)
Rates: $45-$80
(612) 796-2091
(800) 941-0423

SPRING COVE

STRATFORD-LEE INN
RR 1, Box 108 (55974)
Rates: $75-$100
(507) 498-5707

VILLAGE HOUSE MOTEL
265 W Main (55974)
Rates: $27-$39
(507) 498-3271

SPRING VALLEY

66 MOTEL
612 North Huron Ave (55975)
Rates: $22-$25
(507) 346-9993

SUPER 8 MOTEL
North Broadway (55975)
Rates: $50-$98
(507) 346-7788
(800) 800-8000

STAPLES

SUNSET MOTEL
Rt 2, Box 330 (56479)
Rates: $29-$39
(218) 894-1965

SUPER 8 MOTEL
109 2nd Ave W (56479)
Rates: $38-$57
(218) 894-3585
(800) 800-8000

STARBUCK

CEDAR INN OF STARBUCK
604 Main St (56381)
Rates: $40-$68
(320) 239-4300

STEVENSVILLE

HAMPTON INN
5050 Red Arrow Hwy (49127)
Rates: $69-$99
(616) 429-2700
(800) 426-7866

STEWARTVILLE

AMERICINN MOTEL
1700 NW 2nd Ave (55976)
Rates: $50-$65
(507) 533-4747
(800) 634-3444

STILLWATER

BEST WESTERN INN
1750 Frontage Rd W (55082)
Rates: $58-$79
(651) 430-1300
(800) 528-1234
(800) 647-4039

STURGEON LAKE

STURGEON LAKE MOTEL
I-35 & County Rd 46 (55783)
Rates: $32-$47
(218) 372-3194

TAYLORS FALLS

PINES MOTEL
543 River St (55084)
Rates: $34-$60
(651) 465-3422
(800) 843-0329

THE SPRINGS HISTORIC COUNTRY INN
90 Government Rd (55084)
Rates: $45-$95
(651) 465-6565
(800) 851-4243

THIEF RIVER FALLS

BEST WESTERN INN
1060 Hwy 32 S (56701)
Rates: $54-$87
(218) 681-7555
(800) 528-1234
(800) 569-8123

C'MON INN
1586 Hwy 59 SE (56701)
Rates: $49-$94
(218) 681-3000
(800) 950-8111

HARTWOOD MOTEL
1010 N Main St (56701)
Rates: $29-$43
(218) 681-2640

SUPER 8 MOTEL
1915 Hwy 59 SE (56701)
Rates: $39-$56
(218) 681-6205
(800) 800-8000

T-59 MOTEL
Hwy 59 SE (56701)
Rates: $29-$49
(218) 681-2720

TOFTE

AMERICINN MOTEL & SUITES
7261 W Hwy 61 (55615)
Rates: $79-$165
(218) 663-7899
(800) 634-3444

ASPENWOOD RESORT MOTEL
130 Aspenwood (55615)
Rates: n/a
(218) 663-7978

BLUEFIN BAY RESORT ON LAKE SUPERIOR
SR 61 (55615)
Rates: $95-$495
(218) 663-7296
(800) 258-3346

CHATEAU LE VEAUX ON LAKE SUPERIOR
P. O. Box 115 (55615)
Rates: $55-$159
(218) 663-7223
(800) 445-5773

SATELLITE COUNTRY INN
9436 W Hwy 61 (55613)
Rates: $39-$75
(218) 663-7574
(800) 700-7574

SUPERIOR RIDGE RESORT & MOTEL
5041 W Hwy 61 (55615)
Rates: $49-$109
(218) 663-7189
(800) 782-1776

TOWER

THE LURE OF THE LOON RESORT
2162 Birch Point (55790)
Rates: $75-$195
(218) 753-4732
(800) 832-5988

TWO HARBORS

AMERICINN LODGE & SUITES
1088 Hwy 61 (55616)
Rates: $77-$136
(218) 834-3000
(800) 634-3444

COUNTRY INN BY CARLSON
1204 7th Ave (55616)
Rates: $54-$129
(218) 834-5557
(800) 456-4000

GRAND SUPERIOR LODGE ON LAKE SUPERIOR
2826 Hwy 61 (55616)
Rates: n/a
(218) 834-3796
(800) 627-9565

SUPERIOR SHORES RESORT & HOMES
1521 Superior Shores Dr (55616)
Rates: $119-$399
(218) 834-5671
(800) 242-1988

VOYAGEUR MOTEL
1227 7th Ave (55616)
Rates: $30-$44
(218) 834-3644

TYLER

BABETTE'S INN
308 S Tyler St (56178)
Rates: $55-$65
(507) 537-1632

VIRGINIA

LAKESHOR MOTOR INN DOWNTOWN
404 N 6th Ave (55792)
Rates: $39-$89
(218) 741-3360
(800) 569-8131

AREA CODES - If the local number doesn't connect, check for a new area code.

MIDWAY MOTEL
Hwy 53 &
Midway Rd
(55792)
Rates: $31-$46
(218) 741-6145
(800) 777-7956

SKI-VIEW MOTEL
903 N 17th St
(55792)
Rates: $30-$60
(218) 741-8918

VOYAGEUR NORTH MOTEL
8317 13th St S
(55792)
Rates: n/a
(218) 741-9235

WABASHA

THE ANDERSON HOUSE
333 W Main St
(55981)
Rates: $30-$125
(800) 535-5467

WABASHA MOTEL
1110 E Hiawatha
Dr (55981)
Rates: $32-$50
(651) 565-9932

WACONIA

SUPER 8 MOTEL
301 E Frontage Rd
(55387)
Rates: $46-$71
(612) 442-5147
(800) 800-8000

WADENA

BROOKSIDE MOTEL
1410 Jefferson St
N (56482)
Rates: $35-$46
(218) 631-9108
(800) 929-4603

JENSEN'S TERRY MOTEL
12338 Hwy 10 E
(56482)
Rates: $21-$27
(218) 631-1956

WAHKON

CJ'S ON THE BAY RESORT
550 N Main St
(56386)
Rates: $40-$70
(320) 495-3325

WALKER

ADVENTURE NORTH
HCR 84, Box 1207
(56484)
Rates: $625-$1995
Weekly
(218) 547-1532
(800) 294-1532

ANCHOR'S A-WAY FAMILY RESORT
HCR 73, Box 86
(56484)
Rates: $325-$1095
Weekly
(218) 547-1229
(800) 982-2624

ANDERSON'S CHIPPAWA LODGE
HC 84 Box 376
(56484)
Rates: $300-$2600
Weekly
(218) 836-2437
(800) 416-2216

ANDERSON'S SPIRIT OF THE NORTH
HC 84 Box 392
(56484)
Rates: $75-$105
(218) 836-2357
(800) 516-0077

BAYSIDE RESORT
8039 Onigum Rd
NW (56484)
Rates: $115-$172
(218) 547-1350
(800) 484-8056

BIRCHWOOD RESORT
8055 Onigum Rd
NW (56484)
Rates: $80-$111
(218) 547-1454
(800) 279-2683

CHASE MOTOR INN & COTTAGES
500 Cleveland Ave
W (56484)
Rates: $36-$89
(218) 547-2882
(800) 772-6769

COUNTRY INN & SUITES BY CARLSON
442 Walker Bay
Blvd (56484)
Rates: $69-$107
(218) 547-1400
(800) 456-4000

DOC'S LODGE
3425 Stony Point
Camp Rd NW
(56485)
Rates: $450-$600
Weekly
(218) 547-1772
(800) 753-1529

FOREST INN MOTEL
6615 Hwy 371
NW (56484)
Rates: $28-$48
(218) 547-2400
(800) 738-3639

GRAND VU LODGE
HCR 84 Box 1235
(56484)
Rates: $475-$2400
Weekly
(218) 547-1632
(800) 842-0783

LAKEVIEW INN
Hwy 371 (56484)
Rates: $25-$65
(218) 547-1212
(800) 252-5073

STEAMBOAT BAY RESORT ON LEECH LAKE
HCR 73 Box 585
(56484)
Rates: $75-$90
(218) 547-1575
(800) 705-9925

STONY POINT RESORT
HC 84 Box 942
(56484)
Rates: $92-$224
(218) 547-1665
(800) 338-9303

TIANNA FARMS BED & BREAKFAST
Tianna Farms Rd,
Box 968 (56484)
Rates: $45-$125
(218) 547-1306
(800) 842-6620

TRADER'S BAY LODGE
HC 84 Box 1017
(56484)
Rates: $75-$100
(218) 547-1031
(888) 667-7481

WARREN

ELM CREST MOTEL
Hwy 75 N (56762)
Rates: $26-$50
(218) 745-4721

WARROAD

CAN-AM MOTEL
406 Main Ave NE
(56763)
Rates: $38-$69
(218) 386-3807
(800) 280-2626

HOSPITAL BAY BED & BREAKFST
620 Lake St NE
(56763)
Rates: $40-$60
(218) 386-2627
(800) 568-6028

THE PATCH MOTEL
Hwy 11 W (56763)
Rates: $38-$69
(218) 386-2723
(800) 288-2753

WATERTOWN

WANDER INN BED & BREAKFAST
2590 Vega Ave
(55360)
Rates: $70-$90
(612) 955-2230

WATERVILLE

SAKATAH BAY RESORT MOTEL
815 Paquin St E
(56096)
Rates: $28+
(507) 362-8980

WHEATON

WHEATON INN
403 5th St N
(56296)
Rates: $27-$45
(320) 563-8236

WHITE BEAR LAKE

COUNTRY INN BY CARLSON
4940 Hwy 61
(55110)
Rates: $69-$120
(612) 429-5393
(800) 456-4000

WILLMAR

COMFORT INN
2200 E US 12
(56201)
Rates: $72-$129
(320) 231-2801
(800) 228-5150

DAYS INN
225 28th St SE
(56201)
Rates: $51-$81
(320) 231-1275
(800) 528-1234

HI-WAY 12 MOTEL
609 E Hwy 12
(56201)
Rates: $26-$31
(320) 235-4500
(800) 352-3218

HOLIDAY INN
2100 US 12 E
(56201)
Rates: $92-$109
(320) 235-6060
(800) 465-4329

LAKEVIEW INN MOTEL
N Business Hwy
71 & 23 (56201)
Rates: $33-$50
(320) 235-3424
(800) 718-3424

SUPER 8 MOTEL
2655 S 1st St
(56201)
Rates: $37-$55
(320) 235-7260
(800) 800-8000

AREA CODES - If the local number doesn't connect, check for a new area code.

WILLMAR-SPICER

LAKEVIEW MOTEL
15150 Hwy 23 NE
(56288)
Rates: $29-$38
(320) 796-2224

WINDOM

SUPER 8 MOTEL
222 S 3rd Ave
(56101)
Rates: $40-$59
(507) 831-1120
(800) 800-8000

WINONA

BEST WESTERN RIVERPORT INN & SUITES
900 Bruski Dr
(55987)
Rates: $59-$99
(507) 452-0606
(800) 595-0606

EL RANCHO MOTEL
1429 Gilmore Ave
(55987)
Rates: n/a
(507) 454-5920
(800) 469-5920

HOLIDAY INN HOTEL & SUITES
1025 Hwy 61 E
(55987)
Rates: n/a
(507) 453-0303
(800) 465-4329

QUALITY INN
956 Mankato Ave
(55987)
Rates: $69-$169
(507) 454-4390
(800) 228-5151

STERLING MOTEL
1450 Gilmore Ave
(55987)
Rates: $31-$60
(507) 454-1120
(800) 452-1235

SUGAR LOAF MOTEL
1066 Homer Rd
(55987)
Rates: $33-$62
(507) 452-1491

SUPER 8 MOTEL
1025 Sugar Loaf
Rd ((55987)
Rates: $45-$70
(507) 454-6066
(800) 800-8000

WOODBURY

HAMPTON INN
1450 Weir Dr
(55125)
Rates: $69-$99
(651) 578-2822
(800) 426-7866

HOLIDAY INN EXPRESS HOTEL & SUITES
9840 Norma Lane
(55125)
Rates: n/a
(651) 702-0200
(800) 465-4329

RED ROOF INN
1806 Wooddale Dr
(55125)
Rates: $60-$76
(651) 738-7160
(800) 843-7663

WORTHINGTON

AMERICINN MOTEL
1475 Darling Dr
(56187)
Rates: $54-$66
(507) 376-4500
(800) 634-3444

BEST WESTERN
1923 Dover St
(56187)
Rates: $55-$65
(507) 376-4146
(800) 528-1234

BUDGET INN
1231 Oxford St
(56187)
Rates: $28-$34
(507) 376-6136

DAYS INN
207 Oxford St
(56187)
Rates: $54-$95
(507) 376-6155
(800) 329-7466

RAMADA INN
2015 Humiston
Ave (56187)
Rates: $62-$69
(507) 372-2991
(800) 272-6232

SUPER 8 MOTEL
I-90 & 266, Exit 42
(56187)
Rates: $44-$62
(507) 372-7755
(800) 800-8000

ZUMBROTA

SUPER 8 MOTEL
Hwy 52 (55992)
Rates: $37-$59
(507) 732-7852
(800) 800-8000

MISSISSIPPI

ABERDEEN

**BEST WESTERN
ABERDEEN INN**
801 E Commerce
St (39730)
Rates: $46-$65
(662) 369-4343
(800) 528-1234
(888) 222-4345

BATESVILLE

COMFORT INN
290 Power Dr
(38606)
Rates: $55-$82
(662) 563-1188
(800) 228-5150

SKYLINE MOTEL
311 Hwy 51S
(38606)
Rates: $26-$35
(662) 563-7671

BAY ST. LOUIS

KEY WEST INN
1000 Hwy 90
(39521)
Rates: $62-$110
(228) 466-0444
(800) 833-0555

BILOXI

**THE BREAKERS
INN**
2506 W Beach
Blvd (39531)
Rates: $70-$155
(228) 388-6320
(800) 624-5031

**BROADWATER
BEACH RESORT**
2110 Beach Blvd
(39531)
Rates: $90-145
(228) 388-2211
(800) 404-9567

**HOLIDAY INN
BEACHFRONT**
2400 Beach Blvd
(39531)
Rates: $68-$135
(228) 388-3551
(800) 465-4329

**HOLIDAY INN
EXPRESS**
2416 Beach Blvd
(39531)
Rates: $75-$108
(228) 388-1000
(800) 465-4329

**LOFTY OAKS INN
BED & BREAKFAST**
17288 Hwy 67
(39532)
Rates: $98-$150
(228) 392-6722

MOTEL 6
2476 Beach Blvd
(39531)
Rates: $50-$66
(228) 388-5130
(800) 466-8356

RAMADA LIMITED
8071 Tucker Rd
(39532)
Rates: $54-$149
(228) 872-2323
(800) 272-6232

SEAVIEW RESORT
1870 Beach Blvd
(39531)
Rates: $35-$75
(228) 388-5512

BROOKHAVEN

**BEST INN &
SUITES**
1210 Broockway
Blvd (39601)
Rates: $40-$120
(601) 833-1341
(800) 237-8466

SUPER 8 MOTEL
344 Dunn Ratliff
Rd NW (39601)
Rates: $45-$65
(601) 833-8580
(800) 800-8000

CLARKSDALE

DAYS INN
1910 State St
(38614)
Rates: $39-$89
(662) 624-4391
(800) 329-7466

COLUMBUS

HOLIDAY INN
506 Hwy 45 N
(39701)
Rates: n/a
(662) 328-5202
(800) 465-4329

FOREST

**BEST WESTERN
INN**
I-20 at Hwy 35
(39074)
Rates: $54-$63
(601) 469-2640
(800) 528-1234

COMFORT INN
1250 Hwy 35 S
(39074)
Rates: $55-$85
(601) 469-2100
(800) 228-5150

GREENVILLE

DAYS INN
2500 Hwy 82 E
(38701)
Rates: $35-$50
(662) 335-1999
(800) 329-7466

GREENWOOD

BEST INN & SUITES
335 Hwy 82 W
(38930)
Rates: $40-$120
(601) 453-4364
(800) 237-8466

GRENADA

BEST WESTERN
1750 Sunset Dr
(38901)
Rates: $44-$69
(662) 226-7816
(800) 528-1234
(800) 880-8866

HOLIDAY INN
1796 Sunset Dr
(38901)
Rates: $55-$58
(662) 226-2851
(800) 465-4329

GULFPORT

**BEST WESTERN
SEAWAY INN**
9475 US Hwy 49
& I-10 (39503)
Rates: $56-$120
(228) 864-0050
(800) 528-1234
(800) 822-4141

CRYSTAL INN
9379 Canal Rd
(39503)
Rates: $49-$99
(228) 822-9600
(888) 822 9600

**HOLIDAY INN
AIRPORT**
9415 Hwy 49 N
(39503)
Rates: $72-$95
(228) 868-8200
(800) 465-4329

MOTEL 6
9355 US Hwy 49
(39503)
Rates: $36-$48
(228) 863-1890
(800) 466-8356

HATTIESBURG

**BAYMONT INN
& SUITES**
123 Plaza Dr
(39401)
Rates: $65-$80
(601) 264-8380
(800) 301-0200

COMFORT INN
6595 Hwy 49 N
(39401)
Rates: $59-$120
(601) 268-2170
(800) 228-5150

DAYS INN
6518 Hwy 49 N
(39401)
Rates: $35-$62
(601) 544-6300
(800) 329-7466

HAMPTON INN
4301 Hardy St
(39401)
Rates: $59-$84
(601) 264-8080
(800) 426-7866

HOLIDAY INN
6563 Hwy 49 N
(39401)
Rates: $57-$80
(601) 268-2850
(800) 465-4329

**HOWARD
JOHNSON**
6553 US Hwy 49
N (39401)
Rates: $40-$89
(601) 268-2251
(800) 446-4656

MOTEL 6
6508 US Hwy 49
(39401)
Rates: $32-$36
(601) 544-6096
(800) 466-8356

RAMADA LIMITED
6528 Hwy 49 N
(39401)
Rates: $54-$69
(601) 544-4530
(800) 272-6232

INDIANOLA

**HOLIDAY INN
EXPRESS**
601 Hwy 82 W
(38751)
Rates: n/a
(662) 887-7477
(800) 465-4329

IUKA

**VICTORIAN INN
MOTEL**
199 CR 180 (38852)
Rates: $38-$58
(601) 423-9221
(800) 839-1662

AREA CODES - If the local number doesn't connect, check for a new area code.

JACKSON

BEST SUITES OF AMERICA
5411 I-55 N
(39206)
Rates: $74-$139
(601) 899-8580
(800) 237-8466

BEST WESTERN METRO INN
1520 Ellis Ave
(39204)
Rates: $39-$84
(601) 355-7483
(800) 528-1234
(888) 788-9788

CLARION HOTEL
400 Greymont Ave
(39202)
Rates: $69-$99
(601) 969-2141
(800) 252-7466

CROWNE PLAZA
200 E Amite St
(39201)
Rates: $110-$145
(601) 969-5100
(800) 227-6963

DAYS INN
2616 Hwy 80 W
(39204)
Rates: $44-$86
(601) 969-5511
(800) 329-7466

THE EDISON WALTHALL HOTEL
225 E Capitol St
(39201)
Rates: $67-$185
(601) 948-6161
(800) 932-6161

HOLIDAY INN HOTEL & SUITES
5075 I-55 N
(39206)
Rates: $85-$115
(601) 366-9411
(800) 465-4329

HOLIDAY INN-SOUTHWEST
2649 Hwy 80W
(39204)
Rates: $78
(601) 355-3472
(800) 465-4329

HOJO INN
1065 S Frontage Rd (39204)
Rates: $32-$41
(601) 354-4455
(800) 446-4656

LA QUINTA INN NORTH
616 Briarwood Rd
(39211)
Rates: $55-$85
(601) 957-1741
(800) 687-6667

LA QUINTA INN SOUTH
150 Angle St
(39204)
Rates: $52-$69
(601) 373-6110
(800) 687-6667

MOTEL 6
6145 I-55 N
(39213)
Rates: $36-$42
(601) 956-8848
(800) 466-8356

QUALITY INN
400 Greymont Ave
(39202)
Rates: $49-$79
(601) 969-2230
(800) 228-5151

RED ROOF INN COLISEUM
700 Larson St
(39202)
Rates: $49-$58
(601) 969-5006
(800) 843-7663

RESIDENCE INN BY MARRIOTT
881 E River Pl
(39202)
Rates: $99-$149
(601) 355-3599
(800) 331-3131

RODEWAY INN
3880 I-55 S (39212)
Rates: $29-$60
(601) 373-1244
(800) 228-2000

SCOTTISH INNS
2263 US Hwy 80
W (39204)
Rates: $24-$36
(601) 969-1144
(800) 251-1962

SHONEY'S INN
I-55 N Exit 103
(39204)
Rates: $58-$72
(601) 956-6203
(800) 222-2222

SUPER 8 MOTEL
2655 I-55 S (39204)
Rates: $42-$55
(601) 372-1006
(800) 800-8000

TRAVELODGE
716 Hwy 80 E
(39208)
Rates: $40-$45
(601) 939-8200
(800) 578-7878

KOSCIUSKO

BEST WESTERN PARKWAY INN
1052 Veterans
Memorial Dr
(39090)
Rates: $44-$62
(662) 289-6252
(800) 528-1234

LAUREL

HOLIDAY INN EXPRESS
1608 Jefferson St
(39440)
Rates: n/a
(601) 422-0500
(800) 465-4329

RAMADA INN
1105 Sawmill Rd
(39440)
Rates: $46-$60
(601) 649-9100
(800) 272-6232

LONG BEACH

RED CREEK COLONIAL INN
7416 Red Creek Rd
(39560)
Rates: $39-$69
(228) 452-3080
(800) 729-9670

LOUISVILLE

BEST WESTERN RED HILLS INN
201 Hwy 15 N
(39339)
Rates: $54-$82
(662) 773-9090
(800) 528-1234

MAGEE

COMFORT INN
5441 Simpson
Hwy 28 W (39111)
Rates: $57-$73
(601) 849-2300
(800) 228-5150

PASSPORT INN
Hwy 49 N (39111)
Rates: n/a
(601) 849-3250
(800) 251-1962

MCCOMB

DAYS INN
2298 Delaware
Ave (39648)
Rates: $69-$99
(601) 684-5566
(800) 329-7466

RAMADA INN
1900 Delaware
Ave (39648)
Rates: $45-$64
(601) 684-6211
(800) 272-6232

SUPER 8 MOTEL
100 Commerce St
(39648)
Rates: $39-$51
(601) 684-7654
(800) 800-8000

MERIDIAN

BAYMONT INN & SUITES
1400 Roebuck Dr
(39301)
Rates: $39
(601) 693-2300
(800) 301-0200

DAYS INN
530 US Hwy 80 &
11 E (39301)
Rates: $38-$59
(601) 483-3812
(800) 329-7466

ECONO LODGE
2405 S Frontage
Rd (39301)
Rates: $40-$84
(601) 693-9393
(800) 553-2666

ECONO LODGE
109 Hwy 11/80 E
(39302)
Rates: $49-$65
(601) 485-3254
(800) 553-2666

HOLIDAY INN EXPRESS
1401 Roebuck Dr
(39301)
Rates: $65-$90
(601) 693-4521
(800) 465-4329

MOTEL 6
2309 S Frontage
Rd (39301)
Rates: $27-$31
(601) 482-1182
(800) 466-8356

SCOTTISH INNS
1903 S Frontage
Rd (39301)
Rates: $22-$32
(601) 482-2487
(800) 251-1962

MOSS POINT

BEST INN & SUITES
7105 Hwy 63 N
(39563)
Rates: $55-$79
(228) 474-9300
(800) 237-8466

BEST WESTERN FLAGSHIP INN
4830 Amoco Dr
(39563)
Rates: $39-$80
(228) 475-5000
(800) 528-1234
(800) 522-5082

ECONO LODGE
7207 Tanner Ln
(39563)
Rates: $39-$249
(228) 475-7666
(800) 553-2666

HOLIDAY INN EXPRESS
4800 Amoco Dr
(39563)
Rates: $49-$89
(228) 474-2100
(800) 465-4329

SHULAR INN
6623 Hwy 63
(39563)
Rates: $45-$54
(228) 475-8444
(800) 962-1820

SUPER 8 MOTEL
6824 Hwy 613
(39563)
Rates: $39-$59
(228) 474-1855
(800) 800-8000

NATCHEZ

**CEDAR GROVE
PLANTATION
HISTORIC B&B**
617 Kingston Rd
(39120)
Rates: $100-$145
(601) 445-0585

**THE GUEST HOUSE
HISTORIC HOTEL
BED & BREAKFAST**
201 N Pearl St
(39120)
Rates: $94-$127
(601) 442-1054

**NATCHEZ EOLA
HOTEL**
110 N Pearl St
(39120)
Rates: $60-$150
(601) 445-6000
(800) 888-9140

SCOTTISH INNS
40 Sgt Prentiss Dr
(39120)
Rates: $29-$43
(601) 442-9141
(800) 251-1962

SUPER 8 MOTEL
271 D'Evereaux
Dr (39120)
Rates: $35-$60
(601) 442-3686
(800) 800-8000

NEW ALBANY

**HOLIDAY INN
HOTEL & SUITES**
300 Hwy 30 W
(38652)
Rates: n/a
(601) 534-8870
(800) 465-4329

NEWTON

DAYS INN
I-20 & Hwy 15
(39345)
Rates: $46-$53
(601) 683-3361
(800) 329-7466

OCEAN SPRINGS

DAYS INN
7305 Washington
Ave (39564)
Rates: $43-$179
(228) 872-8255
(800) 329-7466

OXFORD

DAYS INN
1101 Frontage Rd
(38655)
Rates: $49-$99
(662) 234-9500
(800) 329-7466

DOWNTOWN INN
400 N Lamar Ave
(38655)
Rates: $70-$95
(662) 234-3031

PASCAGOULA

LA FONT INN
2703 Denny Ave
(39568)
Rates: $61-$78
(228) 762-7111
(800) 647-6077

PASS CHRISTIAN

**INN AT THE PASS
BED & BREAKFAST**
125 E Scenic Dr
(39571)
Rates: $65-$95
(228) 452-0333
(800) 217-2588

PHILADELPHIA

DAYS INN
1009 Holland Ave
(39350)
Rates: $53-$95
(601) 650-3590
(800) 329-7466

**HOLIDAY INN
EXPRESS**
1530 Hwy 16 W
(39350)
Rates: n/a
(601) 656-3553
(800) 465-4329

KEY WEST INN
1004 Central Dr
(39350)
Rates: $59-$90
(601) 656-0052
(800) 833-0555

PICAYUNE

**BUDGET HOST
MAJESTIC INN**
999 Cooper Rd
(39466)
Rates: $32-$45
(601) 798-3859
(800) 283-4678

RICHLAND

DAYS INN
1035 Hwy 49 S
(39218)
Rates: $55-$85
(601) 932-5553
(800) 329-7466

RIDGELAND

**HOMEWOOD
SUITES HOTEL**
853 Centre St
(39157)
Rates: n/a
(601) 899-8611
(800) 225-5466

RED ROOF INN
810 Adcock St
(39157)
Rates: $39-$49
(601) 956-7707
(800) 843-7663

ROBINSON-VILLE

COTTAGE INN
4235 Casino
Centre Dr (38664)
Rates: $65-$95
(601) 363-2900

DAYS INN
2440 Casino Strip
Blvd (38664)
Rates: $55-$175
(601) 363-9996
(800) 329-7466

KEY WEST INN
US 61 (38664)
Rates: $50
(601) 363-0021
(800) 833-0555

SARDIS

**BEST WESTERN
SARDIS INN**
410 E Lee St
(38666)
Rates: $45-$69
(601) 487-2424
(800) 528-1234
(800) 328-2112

SOUTHAVEN

**BEST WESTERN
INN**
8945 Hamilton Rd
(38671)
Rates: $55-$139
(662) 393-4174
(800) 528-1234

STARKVILLE

BEST WESTERN
119 Hwy 12 W
(39759)
Rates: $49-$95
(662) 324-5555
(800) 528-1234

HAMPTON IN
700 Hwy 12
(39759)
Rates: $69-$79
(662) 324-1333
(800) 426-7866

**RAMADA INN
UNIVERSITY CTR**
403 Hwy 12 &
Montgomery St
(39759)
Rates: $65-$75
(662) 323-6161
(800) 272-6232

TUNICA

**HISTORIC
HOTEL MARIE**
1195 Main St
(38676)
Rates: $49-$99
(601) 363-0100

TUPELO

AMERIHOST INN
625 Spicer Dr
(38801)
Rates: $54-$64
(662) 844-7660
(800) 434-5800

DAYS INN
1015 N Gloster
(38804)
Rates: $43-$58
(662) 842-0088
(800) 329-7466

EXECUTIVE INN
1011 N Gloster St
(38801)
Rates: $64-$77
(662) 841-2222
(800) 533-3220

**HOLIDAY INN
EXPRESS HOTEL
& SUITES**
923 N Gloster
(38802)
Rates: n/a
(601) 842-8811
(800) 465-4329

**MOCKINGBIRD
INN B&B**
305 N Gloster
(38801)
Rates: $95-$125
(662) 841-0286

RED ROOF INN
1500 MCullough
Blvd (38801)
Rates: $46-$73
(662) 844-1904
(800) 843-7663

SUPER 8 MOTEL
3898 McCullough
Blvd (38801)
Rates: $42-$54
(662) 842-0448
(800) 800-8000

VICKSBURG

BATTLEFIELD INN
4137 I-20 N
Frontage Rd
(39180)
Rates: $59-$75
(601) 638-5811

**BELLE OF THE
BENDS B&B**
508 Klein St
(39180)
Rates: $95-$150
(601) 634-0737
(800) 844-2308

**THE CORNERS
BED & BREAKFAST**
601 Klein St (39180)
Rates: $75-$125
(601) 636-7421
(800) 444-7421

**DUFF GREEN
MANSION INN
BED & BREAKFAST**
1114 First East St
(39180)
Rates: $55-$160
(601) 636-6968
(800) 992-0037

HAMPTON INN
3330 Clay St
(39180)
Rates: $56-$75
(601) 636-6100
(800) 426-7866

PARK INN INT'L
4137 I-20 Frontage
Rd (39180)
Rates: $50-$70
(601) 638-5811
(800) 359-9363

QUALITY INN
2390 S Frontage
Rd (39180)
Rates: $47-$65
(601) 634-8607
(800) 228-5151

SCOTTISH INNS
3955 E Clay St
(39180)
Rates: n/a
(601) 638-5511
(800) 251-1962

SUPER 8 MOTEL
4127 I-20 Frontage
Rd (39180)
Rates: $41-$61
(601) 638-5077
(800) 800-8000

WAVELAND

**MICROTEL INN
& SUITES**
Hyw 90 & 603
(39576)
Rates: $49-$89
(888) 225-5151

AREA CODES - If the local number doesn't connect, check for a new area code.

MISSOURI

AFFTON

OAK GROVE INN
6602 S Lindbergh
Blvd (63123)
Rates: $34-$42
(314) 894-9449

ALBANY

EASTWOOD MOTEL
US 136E (64402)
Rates: $22-$33
(816) 726-5208

ARNOLD

DRURY INN
1201 Drury Ln
(63010)
Rates: $63-$86
(636) 296-9600
(800) 378-7946

WHITE WING RESORT
P. O. Box 840
(65616)
Rates: $42-$53
(636) 338-2318

AURORA

AURORA INN MOTEL
Rt 3, Box 200
(65605)
Rates: $36-$42
(417) 678-5035

BELTON

ECONO LODGE
222 Peculiar Dr
(64012)
Rates: $40-$65
(816) 322-1222
(800) 553-2666

BETHANY

FAMILY BUDGET INN
4014 Millen
(64424)
Rates: $39-$49
(660) 425-7915

BIRCH TREE

HICKORY HOUSE MOTOR INN
P. O. Box 306
(65438)
Rates: $20-$32
(573) 292-3232

BLUE SPRINGS

MICROTEL INN & SUITES
3120 NW Jefferson
St (64015)
Rates: $39-$69
(816) 224-1122
(888) 771-7171

MOTEL 6
901 W Jefferson St
(64015)
Rates: $30-$36
(816) 228-9133
(800) 466-8356

RAMADA LIMITED
1110 N 7 Hwy
(64014)
Rates: $40-$85
(816) 229-6363
(800) 272-6232

SLEEP INN
451 NW Jefferson
St (64014)
Rates: $59-$125
(816) 224-1199
(800) 753-3746

SUPER 8 MOTEL
1501 NW
Northridge Dr
(64015)
Rates: $55-$70
(816) 224-2899
(800) 800-8000

BOLIVAR

SUPER 8 MOTEL
1919 S
Killingsworth Ave
(65613)
Rates: $44-$62
(417) 777-8888
(800) 800-8000

WELCOME INN
4710 S 128th Rd
(65613)
Rates: $25-$40
(417) 326-5268

BOURBON

BUDGET INN MOTEL
55 Hwy C (65441)
Rates: $35-$40
(573) 732-4080

BRANSON

BARRINGTON HOTEL
263 Shepherd of
the Hills Expy
(65616)
Rates: $42-$62
(417) 334-8866

BAYMONT INN & SUITES
2375 Green Mtn
Dr (65616)
Rates: $73-$145
(417) 336-6161
(800) 301-0200

BEST WESTERN BRANSON RUSTIC OAK INN
403 W Hwy 76
(65616)
Rates: $50-$99
(417) 334-6464
(800) 528-1234
(800) 828-0404

BIG VALLEY MOTEL
2005 W Hwy 76
(65616)
Rates: $45-$76
(417) 334-7676
(800) 332-7274

BRANSON INN
448 SR 248 (65616)
Rates: $55-$61
(417) 334-5121

BRANSON LODGE MOTEL
2456 SR 165
(65616)
Rates: $49-$79
(417) 334-3105

CHATEAU ON THE LAKE RESORT HOTEL & CONV CTR
415 N State Hwy
265 (65616)
Rates: $169-$269
(417) 334-1161

DAYS INN
3524 Keeter St
(65616)
Rates: $59-$100
(417) 334-5544
(800) 329-7466

FIDDLERS INN
3522 W 76th
(65616)
Rates: $29-$50
(417) 334-2212
(800) 544-6483

1ST INN GOLD
2719 W Hwy 76
(65616)
Rates: n/a
(417) 334-7000

GOOD SHEPHERD INN
1023 W Hwy 76
(65616)
Rates: $29-$60
(417) 334-1695

HALL OF FAME MOTEL
3005 W Hwy 76
(65616)
Rates: $50-$65
(417) 334-5161

HARMONY PLACE MOTEL
3514 W Hwy 76
(65616)
Rates: n/a
(417) 334-5510

HOTEL GRAND VICTORIAN
2325 W Hwy 76
(65616)
Rates: $99-$145
(417) 336-2935
(800) 324-8751

HOWARD JOHNSON
3027-A W Hwy 76
(65616)
Rates: $59-$150
(417) 336-5151
(800) 446-4656

LAKESHORE RESORT
1773 Lakeshore Dr
(65616)
Rates: $80-$150
(417) 334-6262

LIGHTHOUSE INN
2375 Green Mtn
Dr (65616)
Rates: $48-$88
(417) 336-6161

MIDTOWN INN
2330 W Hwy 76
(65616)
Rates: $49-$54
(417) 334-7474

MOTEL 6
2651 Shepherd of
the Hills Expwy
(65616)
Rates: $49-$54
(417) 336-6088
(800) 466-8356

PEACH TREE INN
2450 Green Mtn
Dr (65616)
Rates: $79
(417) 335-5900

RAMADA LIMITED
2316 Shepherd of
the Hills Expwy
(65616)
Rates: $70-$90
(417) 337-5207
(800) 272-6232

RED ROOF INN
220 S Wildwood
Dr (65616)
Rates: $59-$102
(417) 335-4500
(800) 843-7663

RESIDENCE INN BY MARRIOT
280 Wildwood Dr S (65616)
Rates: $89-$139
(417) 336-4077
(800) 331-3131

ROCK VIEW RESORT MOTEL
1049 Parkview Dr (65672)
Rates: $54-$79
(417) 334-4678

SETTLE INN RESORT & CONF CENTER
3050 Green Mtn Dr (65616)
Rates: $49-$95
(417) 335-4700
(800) 677-6906

SHADY ACRE MOTEL
US 76 (65616)
Rates: $32-$41
(417) 338-2316

SUPER 8 MOTEL CENTRAL
3060 Green Mtn Dr (65616)
Rates: $43-$78
(417) 336-3300
(800) 800-8000

SUPER 8 MOTEL NORTH
150 Church Rd (65616)
Rates: $38-$58
(417) 335-2543
(800) 800-8000

SUPER 8 MOTEL SOUTH
Hwy 65 S (65616)
Rates: $32-$52
(417) 334-2770
(800) 800-8000

TANEY MOTEL
311 Hwy 65N Business (65616)
Rates: $30-$59
(417) 334-3143
(800) 334-3193

WELK RESORT CENTER
1984 SR 165 (65616)
Rates: $94-$99
(417) 336-3575
(800) 505-WELK

BRANSON WEST

COLONIAL MOUNTAIN INN
US 65 SR 13 (65737)
Rates: $40-$48
(417) 272-8414

ECONO LODGE SILVER DOLLAR CITY AREA
SR 13 (65737)
Rates: $39-$80
(417) 272-3326
(800) 553-2666

BRIDGETON

BRIDGEPORT INN
4199 N Lindbergh Blvd (63044)
Rates: $24-$34
(314) 739-4600

ECONO LODGE
4575 N Lindbergh Blvd (63044)
Rates: $39-$65
(314) 731-3000
(800) 553-2666

KNIGHTS INN
12433 St Charles Rock Rd (63044)
Rates: $33-$50
(314) 291-8545
(800) 843-5644

MOTEL 6
3655 Pennridge Dr (63044)
Rates: $32-$39
(314) 291-6100
(800) 466-8356

RED ROOF INN
3470 Hollenberg Dr (63044)
Rates: $57-$75
(314) 291-3350
(800) 843-7663

SCOTTISH INNS-AIRPORT
4645 N Lindbergh Blvd (63044)
Rates: $32-$42
(314) 731-1010
(800) 251-1962

SUPER 8 MOTEL
12705 St Charles Rock Rd (63044)
Rates: $38-$59
(314) 291-8845
(800) 800-8000

BROOKFIELD

COUNTRY INN
800 S Main St (64628)
Rates: $31-$36
(816) 258-7262

BUFFALO

GOODNITE INN
642 S Ash (65622)
Rates: $25-$43
(417) 345-3245

BUTLER

DAYS INN
100 S Fran Ave (64730)
Rates: $40-$60
(660) 679-4544
(800) 329-7466

SUPER 8 MOTEL
1114 W Ft. Scott St (64730)
Rates: $41-$60
(660) 679-6183
(800) 800-8000

CAMDENTON

LAN-O-LAK MOTEL
P. O. Box 619 (65020)
Rates: $38-$55
(314) 346-2256

CAMERON

BEST WESTERN ACORN INN
I-35 & US 36 (644251
Rates: $47-$75
(816) 632-2187
(800) 528-1234
(800) 607-2288

DAYS INN
501 Northland Dr (64429)
Rates: $35-$60
(816) 632-6623
(800) 329-7466

ECONO LODGE
220 E Grand (64429)
Rates: $32-$55
(816) 632-6571
(800) 553-2666

CAPE GIRARDEAU

DRURY LODGE
104 S Vantage (63701)
Rates: $60-$77
(573) 334-7151
(800) 378-7946

DRURY SUITES
3303 Campster (63701)
Rates: $79-$95
(573) 339-9500
(800) 378-7946

HAMPTON INN
103 Cape West Pkwy (63701)
Rates: $68-$83
(573) 651-3000
(800) 426-7866

PEAR TREE INN
3248 William St (63701)
Rates: $48-$65
(573) 334-3000
(800) 282-8733

SANDS MOTEL
1448 N Kings Hwy (63701)
Rates: $27-$37
(573) 334-2828

VICTORIAN INN
3265 William St (63701)
Rates: $62-$82
(573) 651-4486

CARTHAGE

DAYS INN
2244 Grand Ave (64836)
Rates: $42-$53
(417) 358-2499
(800) 329-7466

ECONO LODGE
1441 W Central (64836)
Rates: $48-$100
(417) 358-3900
(800) 553-2666

CASSVILLE

BUDGET INN
SR 76, 86 & 112 (65625)
Rates: $34-$58
(417) 847-4196

HOLIDAY MOTEL & RV PARK-IMA
85 S Main St (65625)
Rates: $37-$46
(417) 847-3163
(800) 341-8000

SUPER 8 MOTEL
101 S Hwy 37 (656254
Rates: $43-$59
(417) 847-4888
(800) 800-8000

TOWNHOUSE MOTEL
HCR 81, Box 9570 (65625)
Rates: $28-$38
(417) 847-4196

CHARLESTON

CHARLESTON INN
310 S Story (63834)
Rates: $31-$50
(573) 683-2125

CHESTERFIELD

RESIDENCE INN BY MARRIOTT
15431 Conway Rd (63017)
Rates: $69-$109
(636) 537-1444
(800) 331-3131

CHILLICOTHE

BEST WESTERN
1020 S Washington (64601)
Rates: $50-$88
(660) 646-0572
(800) 528-1234
(800) 990-9150

GRAND RIVER INN
606 W Bus. 36 (64601)
Rates: $54-$70
(660) 646-6590

SUPER 8 MOTEL
580 Old Hwy 36 E (64601)
Rates: $46-$59
(660) 646-7888
(800) 800-8000

TRAVEL INN
901 Hwy 36W
(64601)
Rates: $32-$42
(660) 646-0784

CLARKSVILLE

CLARKSVILLE INN
2nd & Lewis Sts
(63336)
Rates: $29-$41
(314) 242-3324

CLAYTON

THE DANIELE HOTEL
216 N Meramec
(63105)
Rates: $139
(314) 721-0101

SEVEN GABLES INN
26 N Meramec
(63105)
Rates: $85-$130
(314) 863-8400

CLINTON

DAYS INN
Hwy 7 & Rives Rd
(64735)
Rates: $60-$70
(660) 885-6901
(800) 329-7466

SAFARI MOTEL
1505 N 2nd St
(64735)
Rates: $28-$50
(660) 885-3395

COLUMBIA

BAYMONT INN
2500 I-70 Dr SW
(65203)
Rates: $59-$67
(573) 445-1899
(800) 301-0200

DAYS INN CONFERENCE CENTER
1900 I-70 Dr SW
(65203)
Rates: $59-$175
(573) 445-8511
(800) 329-7466

DRURY INN
1000 Knipp St
(65203)
Rates: $64-$84
(573) 445-1800
(800) 378-7946

ECONO LODGE
900 I-70 Dr SW
(65203)
Rates: $45-$89
(573) 442-1191
(800) 553-2666

HAWTHORN SUITES LTD
Keene St (65201)
Rates: n/a
(800) 527-1133

HOLIDAY INN EAST- HOLIDOME
1612 N Providence Rd (65202)
Rates: $59-$69
(573) 449-2491
(800) 465-4329

HOLIDAY INN SELECT- EXECUTIVE CTR
2200 I-70 Dr SW
(65203)
Rates: $85
(573) 445-8531
(800) 465-4329

HOLIDAY INN EXPRESS
801 Keene St
(65201)
Rates: $75-$100
(573) 449-4422
(800) 465-4329

MOTEL 6-EAST
1718 N Providence Rd
(65202)
Rates: $24-$30
(573) 442-9390
(800) 466-8356

MOTEL 6-WEST
1800 I-70 Dr SW
(65203)
Rates: $26-$32
(573) 445-8433
(800) 466-8356

RAMADA INN & CONF CENTER
1100 Vandiver Dr
(65202)
Rates: $69-$139
(573) 449-0051
(800) 272-6232

RED ROOF INN
201 E Texas Ave
(65202)
Rates: $47-$62
(573) 442-0145
(800) 843-7663

TRAVELODGE
900 Vandiver Dr
(65202)
Rates: $50-$77
(573) 449-1065
(800) 578-7878

CONCORDIA

BEST WESTERN HEIDELBERG INN
406 NW 2nd St
(64020)
Rates: $45-$70
(660) 463-2114
(800) 528-1234

DAYS INN
301 NW 3rd St
(64020)
Rates: $40-$69
(660) 463-7987
(800) 329-7466

CREVE COEUR

DRURY INN & SUITES
11980 Olive Blvd
(63141)
Rates: $85-$105
(314) 989-1100
(800) 378-7946

CUBA

BEST WESTERN CUBA INN
246 Hwy P (65453)
Rates: $38-$59
(573) 885-7707
(800) 528-1234

DEXTER

SUPER 8 MOTEL
1807 Business 60 W (63841)
Rates: $41-$56
(573) 624-7465
(800) 800-8000

DONIPHAN

DAYS INN
100 Oaktree Village (63935)
Rates: $50-$99
(573) 996-2400
(800) 329-7466

TIN LIZZIE MOTEL
Hwy 160 (63935)
Rates: n/a
(573) 996-2101

EAGLE ROCK

EAGLE ROCK RESORT
HCR 01, Box 1593
(65641)
Rates: n/a
(417) 271-3222

FLETCHER'S DEVIL'S DIVE RESORT
HCR 01, Box 8
(65641)
Rates: n/a
(417) 271-3396

LAZY EAGLE RESORT
P. O. Box 141
(65641)
Rates: n/a
(417) 271-3390
(800) 232-4783

EDMUNDSON

DRURY INN-AIRPT
10490 Natural Bridge (63134)
Rates: $76-$101
(314) 423-7700
(800) 378-7946

MARRIOTT- AIRPORT
10700 Pear Tree
(63134)
Rates: $65-$119
(314) 423-9700
(800) 228-9290

EL DORADO SPRINGS

EL DORADO MOTEL
102 Hwy 54 East
(64744)
Rates: n/a
(417) 876-6888

ELLINGTON

SCENIC RIVERS MOTEL
231 N 2nd St
(63638)
Rates: $38-$43
(573) 663-7722

EUREKA

RAMADA INN SIX FLAGS
4901 Allenton Rd
(63025)
Rates: $129-$219
(636) 938-6661
(800) 272-6232

RED CARPET INN SIX FLAGS
1725 W 5th St
(63025)
Rates: $60-$76
(636) 938-5348
(800) 251-1962

SUPER 8 MOTEL
1733 W 5th St
(63025)
Rates: $32-$55
(636) 938-4368
(800) 800-8000

FARMINGTON

BEST WESTERN TRADITION INN
1627 W Columbia
(63640)
Rates: $55-$60
(573) 756-8031
(800) 528-1234

FENTON

DRURY INN & SUITES
1088 S Hwy Dr
(63026)
Rates: $68-$89
(636) 343-7822
(800) 378-7946

HOWARD JOHNSON EXPRESS INN
650 S Hwy Dr
(63026)
Rates: $39-$79
(636) 343-5710
(800) 446-4656

MOTEL 6
1860 Bowles Ave
(63026)
Rates: $37-$43
(636) 349-1800
(800) 466-8356

PEAR TREE INN
1100 S Hwy Dr
(63026)
Rates: $50-$75
(636) 343-8820
(800) 282-8733

AREA CODES - If the local number doesn't connect, check for a new area code.

FESTUS

BAYMONT INN
1303 Veterans
Blvd (63028)
Rates: $60-$65
(636) 937-2888
(800) 301-0200

DRURY INN
1001 Veterans
Blvd (63028)
Rates: $60-$85
(636) 933-2400
(800) 378-7946

FLAT RIVER

ROSENER'S INN
Hwy 67 N (63601)
Rates: $29-$45
(314) 431-4241

FLORISSANT

RED ROOF INN
307 Dunn Rd
(63031)
Rates: $53-$73
(314) 831-7900
(800) 843-7663

FORISTELL

**BEST WESTERN
WEST 70 INN**
12 Hwy West
(63348)
Rates: $50-$65
(636) 673-2900
(800) 528-1234
(888) 869-6990

FREDERICK-TOWN

ECONO LODGE
740 Madison
Plaza Dr (63645)
Rates: $44-$55
(573) 783-2500
(800) 553-2666

**LONGHORN
MOTEL**
P. O. Box 721
(63645)
Rates: $31-$50
(573) 783-7200

FULTON

**BUDGET HOST
WESTWOODS
MOTEL**
422 Gaylord Dr
(65251)
Rates: $36-$65
(573) 642-5991
(800) 283-4678

**LOGANBERRY
INN B&B**
310 W Seventh St
(65251)
Rates: $65-$85
(573) 642-9229
(888) 866-6661

GRAIN VALLEY

TRAVELODGE
105 Sunny Lane
Dr (64029)
Rates: $50-$80
(816) 224-3420
(800) 578-7878

GRAVOIS MILLS

**MILLSTONE
LODGE RESORT**
Rt 1, Box 515
(65037)
Rates: $60-$299
(314) 372-5111

HANNIBAL

DAYS INN
4070 Market St
(63401)
Rates: $46-$75
(573) 248-1700
(800) 329-7466

ECONO LODGE
3604 McMasters
Ave (63401)
Rates: $39-$99
(573) 221-0422
(800) 553-2666

HANNIBAL INN
4141 Market St
(63401)
Rates: $70-$75
(573) 221-6610

**HOWARD
JOHNSON
EXPRESS INN**
3603 McMasters
Ave (63401)
Rates: $35-$75
(573) 221-7950
(800) 446-4656

TRAVELODGE
502 Mark Twain
Ave (63401)
Rates: $56-$70
(573) 221-4100
(800) 578-7878

HARRISON-VILLE

BEST WESTERN
2201 N Rockhaven
Rd (64701)
Rates: $45-$76
(816) 884-3200
(800) 528-1234

**BUDGET HOST
CARAVAN MOTEL**
1705 Hwy 291 N
(64701)
Rates: $31-$49
(816) 884-4100
(800) 283-4678

**SLUMBER INN
MOTEL**
21400 E 275th St
(64701)
Rates: $32-$44
(816) 884-3100

HAYTI

PEAR TREE INN
1317 Hwy 84
(63851)
Rates: $50-$70
(573) 359-2702
(800) 282-8733

HAZELWOOD

BAYMONT INN
318 Taylor D
(63042)
Rates: $37-$63
(314) 731-4200
(800) 301-0200

LA QUINTA-AIRPORT
5781 Campus St
(63042)
Rates: $62-$82
(314) 731-3881
(800) 687-6667

HERMAN

**HARBOR HOUSE
INN**
113 Market St
(65041)
Rates: $45-$125
(573) 486-2222
(888) 942-7529

HIGGINSVILLE

**BEST WESTERN
CAMELOT INN**
6683 S Hwy 13
(64037)
Rates: $50-$70
(660) 584-3646
(800) 528-1234
(877) 794-5774

SUPER 8 MOTEL
I-70 & Exit 49
(64037)
Rates: $47-$63
(660) 584-7781
(800) 800-8000

HOLLISTER

**ROCK VIEW
RESORT**
HCR 2, Box 870
(65672)
Rates: $46-$63
(417) 334-4678

HOLTS SUMMIT

**SUMMIT PLAZA
HOTEL**
150 City Plaza
(65043)
Rates: $49-$65
(573) 896-8787

HOUSTON

**SOUTHERN INN
MOTEL**
1493 Hwy 63 S
(65483)
Rates: $37-$46
(417) 967-4591

INDEPEN-DENCE

**HOWARD
JOHNSON**
4200 S Noland Rd
(64055)
Rates: $79-$129
(816) 373-8856
(800) 446-4656

RED ROOF INN
13712 E 42nd Ter
(64055)
Rates: $48-$60
(816) 373-2800
(800) 843-7663

SUPER 8 MOTEL

4032 S Lynn Court
Dr (64055)
Rates: $38-$67
(816) 833-1888
(800) 800-8000

ISABELLA

**LAKEPOINT
RESORT**
HCR 1, Box 1152
(65676)
Rates: $42-$47
(417) 273-4343

JACKSON

DAYS INN
517 Jackson Blvd
(63755)
Rates: $45-$85
(573) 243-3577
(800) 329-7466

**DRURY INN &
SUITES**
225 Drury Ln
(63755)
Rates: $56-$82
(573) 243-9200
(800) 378-7946

JEFFERSON CITY

**CAPITOL PLAZA
HOTEL**
415 W McCarty St
(65101)
Rates: $95-$130
(573) 635-1234

HOTEL DEVILLE
319 W Miller St
(65101)
Rates: $69-$79
(573) 636-5231

MOTEL 6-SOUTH
1624 Jefferson St
(65109)
Rates: $30-$36
(573) 634-4220
(800) 466-8356

RAMADA INN
1510 Jefferson
(65109)
Rates: $59-$69
(573) 635-7171
(800) 272-6232

JOPLIN

**BEST WESTER
HALLMARK INN**
3600 Range Line
Rd (64804)
Rates: $47-$83
(417) 624-8400
(800) 528-1234
(800) 825-2378

**BEST WESTERN
SANDS INN**
1611 Range Line
Rd (64801)
Rates: $40-$59
(417) 624-8300
(800) 528-1234
(800) 624-8306

CAPRI MOTEL
3401 South Main
(64804)
Rates: n/a
(417) 623-0391

DRURY INN
3601 Range Line
Rd (64804)
Rates: $64-$84
(417) 781-8000
(800) 378-7946

HAMPTON INN
3107 E 36th St
(64804)
Rates: $64-$79
(417) 659-9900
(800) 426-7866

HOLIDAY INN
3615 Range Line
Rd (64804)
Rates: $79-$94
(417) 782-1000
(800) 465-4329

**HOWARD
JOHNSON**
3510 Range Line
Rd (64804)
Rates: $34-$54
(417) 623-0000
(800) 446-4656

MOTEL 6
3031 S Range Line
Rd (64804)
Rates: $36-$52
(417) 781-6400
(800) 466-8356

SLEEP INN
I-44 & St Hwy 43
S (64803)
Rates: $54-$60
(417) 782-1212
(800) 221-2222

SUPER 8 MOTEL
2830 E 36th St
(64804)
Rates: $38-$71
(417) 782-8765
(800) 800-8000

**TROPICANA
MOTEL**
2417 Range Line
Rd (64804)
Rates: $26-$32
(417) 624-8200

**WESTWOOD
MOTEL**
1700 W 30th St
(64804)
Rates: $33-$39
(417) 782-7212

KANSAS CITY

BAYMONT INN-N
2214 Taney St
(64116)
Rates: $61-$68
(816) 221-1200
(800) 301-0200

BAYMONT INN-S
8601 Hillcrest Rd
(64136)
Rates: $61-$68
(816) 822-7000
(800) 301-0200

**BENJAMIN HOTEL
& SUITES**
6101 E 87th St
(64138)
Rates: $74-$150
(816) 765-4331
(800) 532-6338

COMFORT SUITES
8200 N Church Rd
(64157)
Rates: $55-$120
(816) 781-7273
(800) 228-5150

DAYS INN & SUITES
11120 NW
Ambassador Dr
(64190)
Rates: $55-$100
(816) 746-1666
(800) 329-7466

**DRURY INN-
STADIUM**
3830 Blue Ridge
Cutoff (64133)
Rates: $69-$95
(816) 923-3000
(800) 378-7946

**DRURY INN
& SUITES**
7900 NW Tiffany
Spgs Pky (64153)
Rates: $64-$84
(816) 880-9700
(800) 378-7946

**EMBASSY SUITES
HOTEL-AIRPORT**
7640 NW Tiffany
Spgs Pky (64153)
Rates: $109-$144
(816) 891-7788
(800) 362-2779

**HISTORIC SUITES
OF AMERICA
MOTEL**
612 Central Ave
(64105)
Rates: $170-$245
(816) 842-6544

HOLIDAY INN
5701 Longview Rd
(64137)
Rates: $89-$100
(816) 765-4100
(800) 465-4329

**HOMESTEAD
VILLAGE GUEST
STUDIOS**
4535 Main St
(64153)
Rates: $80-$99
(816) 531-2212
(888) 782-9473

**HOMEWOOD
SUITES**
7312 N Polo Dr
(64153)
Rates: n/a
(816) 880-9880
(800) 225-5466

**INN TOWNE
LODGE**
2620 NE 43rd St
(64117)
Rates: $40-$55
(816) 453-6550

MAINSTAY SUITES
9701 N Shannon
Dr (64153)
Rates: $69-$99
(816) 891-8500
(800) 660-6246

**MARRIOTT
HOTEL-AIRPORT**
775 Brasilia Ave
(64153)
Rates: $79-$139
(816) 464-2200
(800) 228-9290

**MARRIOTT
DOWNTOWN**
200 W 12th St
(64105)
Rates: $92-$195
(816) 421-6800
(800) 228-9290

MAINSTAY SUITES
9701 N Shannon
Dr (64105)
Rates: $65-$100
(816) 891-8500
(800) 660-6246

MOTEL 6
6400 E 87th St
(64138)
Rates: $45-$61
(816) 333-4468
(800) 466-8356

MOTEL 6-NORTH
8230 NW Prairie
View Rd (64152)
Rates: $35-$41
(816) 741-6400
(800) 466-8356

**RADISSON SUITE
HISTORIC HOTEL**
106 W 12th St
(64105)
Rates: $89-$109
(816) 221-7000
(800) 333-3333

RED ROOF INN-N
3636 NE
Randolph Rd
(64161)
Rates: $59-$77
(816) 452-8585
(800) 843-7663

**RESIDENCE INN
BY MARRIOTT**
9900 NW Prairie
View Rd (64153)
Rates: $129
(816) 891-9009
(800) 331-3131

**RESIDENCE INN
BY MARRIOTT-
UNION HILL**
2975 Main St
(64108)
Rates: $144
(816) 561-3000
(800) 331-3131

RITZ-CARLTON
401 Ward Pkwy
(64112)
Rates: $126-$275
(816) 756-1500
(800) 241-3333

SLEEP INN
7611 NW 97th
Terrace (64153)
Rates: $60-$69
(816) 891-0111
(800) 753-3746

**SUPER 8 MOTEL-
NW**
6900 NW 83rd
Terr (64152)
Rates: $48-$67
(816) 587-0808
(800) 800-8000

**THE WESTIN
CROWN CENTER**
1 Pershing Rd
(64108)
Rates: $185-$230
(816) 474-4400
(800) 228-3000

KEARNEY

DAYS INN
400 Platte-Clay
Way (64060)
Rates: $45-$75
(816) 628-2288
(800) 329-7466

ECONO LODGE
505 Shanks Ave
(64060)
Rates: $40-$69
(816) 628-1111
(800) 553-2666

SUPER 8 MOTEL
210 Platte-Clay
Way (64060)
Rates: $50-$64
(816) 628-6800
(800) 800-8000

KENNETT

DAYS INN
110 Independence
Ave (63857)
Rates: $45-$90
(573) 888-9860
(800) 329-7466

KIMBERLING CITY

KIMBERLING ARMS RESORT
1 S Hwy 13
(65686)
Rates: $64-$79
(417) 739-2461

KIMBERLING HEIGHTS RESORT MOTEL
HCR 4, Box 980
(65686)
Rates: $44-$59
(417) 779-4158

KIMBERLING INN RESORT
Hwy 13 (65686)
Rates: $70-$160
(417) 739-4311

KIRKSVILLE

BEST WESTERN SHAMROCK INN
2501 S Business 63
(63501)
Rates: $48-$56
(660) 665-8352
(800) 528-1234

BUDGET HOST VILLAGE INN
1304 S Baltimore
(63501)
Rates: $40-$49
(660) 665-3722
(800) 283-4678

COMFORT INN
2209 N Baltimore
(63501)
Rates: $60-$75
(660) 665-2205
(800) 228-5150

KIRKWOOD

BEST WESTERN INN
1200 S Kirkwood
Rd (63122)
Rates: $73-$99
(314) 821-3950
(800) 528-1234
(800) 435-4656

KNOB NOSTER

WHITEMAN INN
2340 W Irish Ln
(65336)
Rates: $44-$75
(660) 563-3000

LAKE OZARK

HOLIDAY INN ON THE LAKE
3703 E Hwy 54
(65049)
Rates: $120-$130
(573) 365-2334
(800) 465-4329

LAKE ST. LOUIS

DAYS INN
2560 S Outer Rd
(63367)
Rates: $49-$140
(314) 625-1711
(800) 329-7466

LAKEVIEW

COLONIAL MOUNTAIN INN
P. O. Box 2068
(65737)
Rates: $36-$55
(417) 272-8414

RUSTIC GATE MOTOR INN
P. O. Box 1088
(65737)
Rates: $32-$50
(417) 272-3326

LAMAR

BEST WESTERN BLUE TOP INN
65 SE 1st Ln
(64759)
Rates: $36-$47
(417) 682-3333
(800) 528-1234
(800) 407-3030

LEBANON

BEST WESTERN WYOTA INN
1225 Mill Creek
Rd (65536)
Rates: $38-$56
(417) 532-6171
(800) 528-1234

BRENTWOOD MOTEL
1320 S Jefferson
(65536)
Rates: $29-$41
(417) 532-6131

ECONO LODGE
2125 W Elm
(65536)
Rates: $39-$54
(417) 588-3226
(800) 553-2666

QUALITY INN
2073 W Elm
(65536)
Rates: $49-$66
(417) 532-7111
(800) 228-5151

LEES SUMMIT

COMFORT INN
607 SE Oldham
Pkwy (64063)
Rates: $69-$109
(816) 524-8181
(800) 228-5150

LEXINGTON

LEXINGTON INN
Jct US 24 & SR 13
(64067)
Rates: $32-$37
(816) 259-4641

LIBERTY

BEST WESTERN HALLMARK INN
209 N 291 Hwy
(64068)
Rates: $61-$75
(816) 781-8770
(800) 528-1234
(888) 246-0026

SUPER 8 MOTEL
115 N Stewart Rd
(64068)
Rates: $39-$55
(816) 781-9400
(800) 800-8000

LICKING

SUPER 8 MOTEL
209 S Hwy 63
(65542)
Rates: $40-$54
(573) 674-4809
(800) 800-8000

LOUISIANA

RIVER'S EDGE MOTEL
201 Mansion St
(63353)
Rates: $33-$48
(573) 754-4522

MACON

BEST WESTERN INN
28933 Sunset Dr
(63552)
Rates: $43-$55
(660) 385-2125
(800) 528-1234
(800) 901-2125

SUPER 8 MOTEL
203 E Briggs Dr
(63552)
Rates: $45-$54
(660) 385-5788
(800) 800-8000

MARSTON

SUPER 8 MOTEL
501 SE Outer Rd
(63866)
Rates: $45-$60
(573) 643-9888
(800) 800-8000

MARYLAND HEIGHTS

BAYMONT INN
12330 Dorsett Rd
(63043)
Rates: $66-$73
(314) 878-1212
(800) 301-0200

DRURY INN
12220 Dorsett Rd
(63043)
Rates: $69-$89
(314) 576-9966
(800) 378-7946

HARRAH'S HOTEL AT RIVERPORT CASINO CENTER
777 Casino Center
Dr (63043)
Rates: n/a
(314) 770-8100

HOMESTEAD VILLAGE GUEST STUDIOS
12161 Lackland
Rd (63043)
Rates: $59
(314) 878-8777
(888) 782-9473

LA QUINTA INN & SUITES
11805 Lackland
Rd (63043)
Rates: $65-$85
(314) 991-3262
(800) 687-6667

RESIDENCE INN BY MARRIOTT WEST PORT PLAZA
1881 Craigshire
Rd (63043)
Rates: $75-$139
(314) 469-0060
(800) 331-3131

SUMMERFIELD SUITES
1855 Craigshire
Rd (63043)
Rates: $109-$149
(314) 878-1555
(800) 833-4353

MARYVILLE

COMFORT INN
2817 S Main St
(64468)
Rates: $39-$69
(660) 562-2002
(800) 228-5150

SUPER 8 MOTEL
Hwy 71 S (64468)
Rates: $42-$51
(660) 582-8088
(800) 800-8000

MEHLVILLE

BEST WESTERN 55 - SOUTH INN
6224 Heimos
Industrial Pk
(63129)
Rates: $75-$159
(314) 416-7639
(800) 528-1234
(800) 592-5432

AREA CODES - If the local number doesn't connect, check for a new area code.

HOLIDAY INN SOUTH I-55
4234 Butler Hill Rd (63129)
Rates: $85-$105
(314) 894-0700
(800) 465-4329

MOTEL 6-SOUTH
6500 S Lindbergh Blvd (63123)
Rates: $46-$62
(314) 892-3664
(800) 466-8356

OAK GROVE INN
6602 S Lindbergh Blvd (63123)
Rates: $42-$65
(314) 894-9449

MEXICO

BEST WESTERN INN
1010 E Liberty St (65265)
Rates: $38-$75
(573) 581-1440
(800) 528-1234

VILLA INN
4224 S Clark (65265)
Rates: $29-$40
(573) 581-8350

MOBERLY

KNOLL MOTEL
P. O. Box 146 (65270)
Rates: $28-$32
(660) 263-5000

RAMADA INN
US 24 & 63 (65270)
Rates: $56-$100
(660) 263-6540
(800) 272-6232

MONETT

HARTLAND LODGE
929 Hwy 60E (65708)
Rates: $37-$43
(417) 235-4000

OXFORD INN
868 Hwy 60 (65708)
Rates: $45-$53
(417) 235-8039

MONROE CITY

MONROE CITY INN
3 Gateway Square (63456)
Rates: $37-$50
(573) 735-4200

MOUND CITY

AUDREY'S MOTEL
1211 State St (64470)
Rates: $30-$51
(816) 442-3191

MOUNT VERNON

BEL-AIRE MOTOR INN
900 E Mt Vernon Blvd (65712)
Rates: $38-$50
(417) 466-2111

BUDGET HOST RANCH MOTEL
1015 E Mt Vernon Blvd (65712)
Rates: $40-$52
(417) 466-2125
(800) 283-4678

SUPER 8 MOTEL
I-44 & Hwy 39, Exit 46 (65712)
Rates: $39-$71
(800) 800-8000

MOUNTAIN GROVE

BEST WESTERN RANCH HOUSE INN
111 E 17th St (65711)
Rates: $38-$58
(417) 926-3152
(800) 528-1234

DAYS INN
300 E 19th St (65711)
Rates: $36-$66
(417) 926-5555
(800) 329-7466

NEOSHO

HARTLAND LODGE
1400 71 S (64850)
Rates: $47-$50
(417) 451-3784

NEOSHO INN
2500 S 71 Hwy (64850)
Rates: $42-$48
(417) 451-6500

NEVADA

COMFORT INN
2345 Marvel Dr (64772)
Rates: $50-$72
(417) 667-6777
(800) 228-5250

RAMSEY'S NEVADA MOTEL
1514 E Austin (64772)
Rates: $30-$38
(417) 667-5273

SUPER 8 MOTEL
2301 E Austin (64772)
Rates: $40-$56
(417) 667-8888
(800) 800-8000

NIXA

SUPER 8 MOTEL
418 Massey Blvd (65714)
Rates: $39-$61
(417) 725-0880
(800) 800-8000

NORTH KANSAS CITY

HARRAH'S NORTH KANSAS CITY CASINO & HOTEL
One Riverboat Dr (64116)
Rates: $119-$149
(816) 472-7777

OAK GROVE

DAYS INN
101 N Locust (64075)
Rates: $39-$90
(816) 690-8700
(800) 329-7466

OSAGE BEACH

BEST WESTERN DOGWOOD HILLS RESORT
SR KK (65065)
Rates: $45-$97
(573) 348-1735
(800) 528-1234
(800) 220-6571

LAKE CHATEAU RESORT
5066 Hwy 54 (65065)
Rates: $74-$89
(573) 348-2791

SCOTTISH INNS
5404 Hwy 54 (65065)
Rates: $43-$59
(573) 348-3123
(800) 251-1962

OVERLAND PARK

EMBASSY SUITES
10601 Metcalf Ave (66212)
Rates: $109-$154
(913) 649-7060
(800) 362-2779

OZARK

COMFORT INN
1900 W Evangel St (65721)
Rates: $63-$69
(417) 485-6688
(800) 228-5150

PALMYRA

HILLCREST INN
423 E Lafayette (63461)
Rates: $29-$38
(314) 769-2007

PERRYVILLE

BEST WESTERN COLONIAL INN
1500 Liberty St (63755)
Rates: $57-$68
(573) 547-1091
(800) 528-1234

BUDGET HOST INN
221 S Kings Hwy (63775)
Rates: $26-$42
(573) 547-4516
(800) 283-4678

COMFORT INN
1517 S Perryville Blvd (63775)
Rates: $79-$130
(573) 547-1727
(800) 228-5150

PLATTE CITY

BEST WESTERN AIRPORT INN
I-29 & Exit 19 (64079)
Rates: $54-$89
(816) 858-4588
(800) 528-1234
(877) 524-7275

COMFORT INN
1200 Hwy 92 (64079)
Rates: $59-$109
(816) 858-5430
(800) 228-5150

SUPER 8 MOTEL
Hwy I-29 & 92 (64079)
Rates: $51-$61
(816) 858-2888
(800) 800-8000

POPLAR BLUFF

COMFORT INN
2582 N Westwood blvd (63901)
Rates: $67-$94
(573) 686-5200
(800) 228-5150

DRURY INN
2220 N Westwood Blvd (63901)
Rates: $62-$82
(573) 686-2451
(800) 378-7946

PEAR TREE INN
2218 N Westwood Blvd (63901)
Rates: $50-$69
(314) 785-7100
(800) 282-8733

AREA CODES - If the local number doesn't connect, check for a new area code.

RAMADA INN
2115 N Westwood
Blvd (63901)
Rates: $55-$65
(573) 785-7711
(800) 272-6232

STUGA COTTAGE
900 Nooney St
(63901)
Rates: $40
(573) 785-4085

PORTAGEVILLE

TEROY MOTEL
903 Hwy 61 N
(63873)
Rates: $32-$38
(573) 379-5461

REEDS SPRING

**KING'S KOVE
RESORT**
Rt 5, Box 498A
(65737)
Rates: $60
(417) 739-4513

RICH HILL

APACHE MOTEL
Rt 3, Box 309A
(64779)
Rates: $32-$38
(417) 395-2161

RICHMOND

SUPER 8 MOTEL
888 Slumber Lane
(64085)
Rates: $44-$55
(816) 776-8008
(800) 800-8000

RICHMOND HEIGHTS

**RESIDENCE INN
BY MARRIOTT-
GALLERIA**
1100 McMorrow
Ave (63117)
Rates: $70-$179
(314) 862-1900
(800) 331-3131

ROCK PORT

ROCK PORT INN
Rt 4, Box 218
(64482)
Rates: $35-$44
(660) 744-6282

SUPER 8 MOTEL
I-29 & 136 Hwy
(64482)
Rates: $35-$50
(660) 744-5357
(800) 800-8000

ROCKAWAY BEACH

**EDEN ROC
RESORT**
607 Beach Blvd
(65740)
Rates: $31-$50
(417) 561-4163
(800) 955-3459

KENNY'S COURT
P. O. Box 87
(65740)
Rates: $31-$75
(417) 561-4131
(800) 942-5557

ROLLA

BESTWAY INN
1631 Martin
Springs Dr (65401)
Rates: $26-$46
(573) 341-2158

**BEST WESTERN
COACHLIGHT**
1403 Martin
Springs Dr (65401)
Rates: $65-$71
(573) 341-2511
(800) 528-1234
(800) 274-9464

DAYS INN
1207 Kings Hwy
(65401)
Rates: $46-$75
(573) 341-3700
(800) 329-7466

DRURY INN
2006 N Bishop
(65401)
Rates: $60-$76
(573) 364-4000
(800) 378-7946

ECONO LODGE
1417 Martin
Springs Dr (65401)
Rates: $37-$58
(573) 341-3130
(800) 553-2666

**HOLIDAY INN
EXPRESS**
1507 Martin
Springs Dr (65401)
Rates: $60-$90
(573) 364-8200
(800) 465-4329

**HOWARD
JOHNSON**
127 H J Dr (65401)
Rates: $49-$75
(573) 364-7111
(800) 446-4656

WESTERN INN
1605 Martin
Springs Dr (65401)
Rates: $33-$56
(573) 341-3050

ST. ANN

**HAMPTON INN
AIRPORT**
10800 Pear Tree Ln
(63074)
Rates: $75-$100
(314) 427-3400
(800) 426-7866

ST. CHARLES

BAYMONT INN
1425 S 5th St
(63301)
Rates: $59-$70
(636) 946-6936
(800) 301-0200

**MONARCH
BUDGET
MOTEL**
3717 I-70 (63303)
Rates: $22-$32
(636) 724-3717

RED ROOF INN
2010 Zumbehl Rd
(63303)
Rates: $57-$71
(636) 947-7770
(800) 843-7663

SLEEP INN
Fountain Lakes Dr
/I-370 (63301)
Rates: $49-$90
(636) 947-0330
(800) 753-3746

ST. CLAIR

**BUDGET
LODGING**
866 S Outer Rd
(63077)
Rates: $45-$69
(636) 629-1000

ST. JAMES

COMFORT INN
110 N Outer Rd
(65559)
Rates: $45-$89
(573) 265-5005
(800) 228-5150

ST. JOSEPH

**BEST WESTERN
CLASSIC INN**
4502 S I-69 (64507)
Rates: $49-$72
(816) 232-2345
(800) 528-1234
(800) 569-8378

DRURY INN
4213 Frederick
Blvd (64506)
Rates: $59-$79
(816) 364-4700
(800) 378-7946

**HOLIDAY INN-
DOWNTOWN**
102 S Third St
(64501)
Rates: $82
(816) 279-8000
(800) 465-4329

MOTEL 6
4021 Frederick
Blvd (64506)
Rates: $34-$40
(816) 232-2311
(800) 466-8356

SUPER 8 MOTEL
4024 Frederick
Blvd (64506)
Rates: $43-$64
(816) 364-3031
(800) 800-8000

ST. LOUIS
(and Vicinity)

COMFORT INN
12031 Lackland
Rd (63146)
Rates: $59-$109
(314) 878-1400
(800) 228-5150

**DRURY INN
GATEWAY ARCH**
711 N Broadway
(63102)
Rates: $75-$100
(314) 231-8100
(800) 378-7946

**DRURY INN
UNION STATION
HISTORIC MOTOR
INN**
201 S 20th St
(63103)
Rates: $106-$131
(314) 231-3900
(800) 378-7946

EMBASSY SUITES
901 N 1st St
(63102)
Rates: $130-$150
(314) 241-4200
(800) 362-2779

**HAMPTON INN
UNION STATION**
2211 Market St
(63103)
Rates: $95-$120
(314) 241-3200
(800) 426-7866

**HOLIDAY INN-
FOREST PARK**
5915 Wilson Ave
(63110)
Rates: $79-$125
(314) 645-0700
(800) 465-4329

**MARRIOTT
HOTEL-AIRPORT**
I-70 at Lambert
(63134)
Rates: $125-$375
(314) 423-9700
(800) 228-9290

**MOTEL 6
AIRPORT**
4576 Woodson Rd
(63134)
Rates: $36-$42
(314) 427-1313
(800) 466-8356

MOTEL 6-NE
1405 Dunn Rd
(63138)
Rates: $35-$41
(314) 869-9400
(800) 466-8356

AREA CODES - If the local number doesn't connect, check for a new area code.

OMNI MAJESTIC HOTEL
1019 Pine St (63110)
Rates: $99-$169
(314) 436-2355
(800) 843-6664

RED ROOF INN-HAMPTON
5823 Wilson Ave (63110)
Rates: $76-$100
(314) 645-0101
(800) 843-7663

RED ROOF INN
11837 Lackland Rd (63146)
Rates: n/a
(314) 991-4900
(800) 843-7663

REGAL RIVER-FRONT HOTEL
200 S Fourth St (63102)
Rates: $109-$119
(314) 241-9500
(800) 325-7353

SHERATON-WEST PORT INN
191 West Port Plaza (63146)
Rates: $70-$129
(314) 878-1500
(800) 822-3535

ST. PETERS

DRURY INN
80 Mid Rivers Mall Dr (63376)
Rates: $65-$86
(636) 397-9700
(800) 378-7946

HOLIDAY INN SELECT
4221 S Outer Rd (63376)
Rates: $70-$90
(636) 928-1500
(800) 465-4329

ST. ROBERT

HOLIDAY INN EXPRESS
114 Vickie Lynn Lane (65583)
Rates: n/a
(573) 336-2299
(800) 465-4329

STE. GENEVIEVE

FAMILY BUDGET INNS
17030 New Bremen (63670)
Rates: $40-$60
(573) 543-2272

SALEM

SCOTTISH INNS
1005 S Main St (65560)
Rates: $38-$47
(573) 729-4191
(800) 251-1962

SEDALIA

BEST WESTERN STATE FAIR MOTOR INN
3210 S 65 Hwy (65301)
Rates: $52-$66
(660) 826-6100
(800) 528-1234

SHELL KNOB

BASS HAVEN FAMILY RESORT
HCR 1, Box 4480E (65747)
Rates: $35-$48
(417) 858-6401

SIKESTON

BEST WESTERN COACH HOUSE INN & SUITES
220 S Interstate Dr (63801)
Rates: $59-$145
(573) 471-9700
(877) 471-9700

DAYS INN
1330 S Main St (63801)
Rates: $45-$75
(573) 471-3930
(800) 328-7466

DRURY INN
2602 East Malone (63801)
Rates: $65-$89
(573) 471-4100
(800) 378-7946

PEAR TREE INN BY DRURY
2602 Rear East Malone (63801)
Rates: $45-$65
(573) 471-8660
(800) 282-8733

SUPER 8 MOTEL
2609 E Malone (63801)
Rates: $46-$65
(573) 471-7944
(800) 800-8000

SMITHVILLE

SUPER 8 MOTEL
112 Cuttings Dr (64089)
Rates: $46-$62
(816) 532-3088
(800) 800-8000

SPRINGFIELD

BAYMONT INN & SUITES
3776 S Glenstone Ave (65803)
Rates: $54-$69
(417) 889-8188
(800) 301-0200

BEST WESTERN COACH HOUSE INN
2535 N Glenstone Ave (65803)
Rates: $44-$125
(417) 862-0701
(800) 528-1234
(800) 287-1476

BEST WESTERN ROUTE 66 RAIL HAVEN
203 S Glenstone Ave (65802)
Rates: $39-$119
(417) 866-1963
(800) 528-1234
(800) 304-0021

CLARION HOTEL
3333 S Glenstone Ave (65804)
Rates: $69-$89
(417) 883-6550
(800) 252-7466

COMFORT SUITES
1260 E Independence St (65804)
Rates: $79-$95
(417) 886-5090
(800) 228-5150

COURTYARD BY MARRIOTT
3370 E Battlefield Rd (65804)
Rates: $69-$74
(417) 883-6200
(800) 443-6000

DAYS INN
621 W Sunshine (65807)
Rates: $69-$180
(417) 862-0153
(800) 329-7466

DAYS INN
2700 N Glenstone (65803)
Rates: $45-$50
(417) 865-5511
(800) 329-7466

DRURY INN & SUITES
2715 N Glenstone Ave (65803)
Rates: $66-$87
(417) 863-8400
(800) 378-7946

GUESTHOUSE SUITES PLUS
1550 E Raynell Place (65803)
Rates: $89
(417) 520-7300
(800) 214-8378

HOLIDAY INN UNIVERSITY PLAZA
333 John Q Hammons Pkwy (65806)
Rates: $93-$126
(417) 864-7333
(800) 465-4329

HOWARD JOHNSON EXPRESS INN
2550 N Glenstone (65803)
Rates: n/a
(800) 465-4656

HOWARD JOHNSON EXPRESS INN & SUITES
2535 S Campbell Ave (65807)
Rates: $48-$80
(417) 890-6060
(800) 465-4656

KNIGHTS INN
2601 N Glenstone Ave (65803)
Rates: $24-$79
(417) 865-6565
(800) 843-5644

MARKHAM INN OF THE OZARKS
2820 N Glenstone Ave (65803)
Rates: $45-$49
(417) 866-3581

MOTEL 6-NORTH
3114 N Kentwood (65803)
Rates: $34-$50
(417) 833-0880
(800) 466-8356

MOTEL 6-SOUTH
2455 N Glenstone Ave (65803)
Rates: $26-$32
(417) 869-4343
(800) 466-8356

MOUNT VERNON MOTOR LODGE
2006 S Glenstone Ave (65804)
Rates: n/a
(417) 881-2833

PEAR TREE INN
2745 N Glenstone Ave (65803)
Rates: $44-$64
(417) 869-0001
(800) 282-8733

QUALITY INN & CONF CENTER
3050 N Kentwood (65803)
Rates: $49-$69
(417) 833-3108
(800) 228-5151

RED ROOF INN
2655 N Glenstone Ave (65803)
Rates: $36-$61
(417) 831-2100
(800) 843-7663

RESIDENCE INN BY MARRIOTT
1550 E Raynell Pl (65804)
Rates: $99-$129
(417) 883-7300
(800) 331-3131

SATELLITE MOTEL
2305 N Glenstone Ave (65803)
Rates: $25-$42
(417) 869-2527

SCOTTISH INNS
2933 N Glenstone Ave (65803)
Rates: $34-$48
(417) 862-4301
(800) 251-1962

SHERATON HAWTHORN PARK
2431 N Glenstone Ave (65803)
Rates: $69-$99
(417) 831-3131
(800) 325-3535

SKYLINE MOTEL
2120 N Glenstone Ave (65803)
Rates: $28-$44
(417) 866-4356

SLEEP INN
233 E Camino Alto (65810)
Rates: $64-$94
(417) 886-2464
(800) 753-3746

SOLAR INN
2355 N Glenstone Ve (65803)
Rates: $36-$55
(417) 866-6776

SUPER 8 MOTEL
3022 N Kentwood Ave (65803)
Rates: $41-$61
(417) 833-9218
(800) 800-8000

TRAVELODGE
3260 E Montclair St (65804)
Rates: $48-$59
(417) 882-9484
(800) 578-7878

STOCKTON

HOLIDAY MOTEL
400 Hwy 32 E (65785)
Rates: $37-$45
(417) 276-4443

STRAFFORD

SUPER 8 MOTEL
315 E Chestnut St (65757)
Rates: $36-$57
(417) 736-3883
(800) 800-8000

SULLIVAN

ECONO LODGE
307 N Service Rd (63080)
Rates: $39-$59
(573) 468-3136
(800) 553-2666
(800) 361-4185

FAMILY MOTOR INN
209 N Service Rd (63080)
Rates: $45-$65
(573) 468-4119

SUPER 8 MOTEL
601 N Service Rd (63080)
Rates: $42-$60
(573) 468-8076
(800) 800-8000

SWEET SPRINGS

PEOPLE'S CHOICE MOTEL
1001 N Locust St (65351)
Rates: $29-$45
(660) 335-6315

THEODOSIA

THEODOSIA MARINA-RESORT
HR 5, Box 5020 (65761)
Rates: $32-$50
(417) 273-4444

TIPTON

TWIN PINE MOTEL
Hwy 50 W (65081)
Rates: $29-$42
(660) 433-5525

TROY

SUPER 8 MOTEL
14 Frenchman Bluff Rd (63379)
Rates: $40-$60
(2314 528-8128
(800) 800--8000

VAN BUREN

HAWTHORNE MOTEL
P. O. Box 615 (63965)
Rates: $24-$40
(314) 323-4275

VILLAGE RIDGE

BEST WESTERN DIAMOND INN
2875 Hwy 100 E (63089)
Rates: $99-$109
(636) 742-3501
(800) 528-1234
(800) 782-8487

WAPPAPELLO

MILLERS MOTOR LODGE
Rt 2, Box 2900 (63966)
Rates: $48-$89
(573) 222-8579

WARRENS-BURG

UNIVERISTY INN CONF CENTER
Jct Hwy 13 & 50 (64093)
Rates: $49-$64
(660) 747-5125

WARRENTON

COLLIER HOSPITALITY INN
2532 W Old Hwy 40 (63383)
Rates: $33-$34
(314) 456-7272

WAYNESVILLE

BEST WESTERN MONTIS INN
14086 Hwy Z (65583)
Rates: $45-$65
(573) 336-4299
(800) 528-1234

DAYS INN
14125 Hwy Z (65583)
Rates: $47-$67
(573) 336-5556
(800) 329-7466

ECONO LODGE
309 Hwy Z (65583)
Rates: $50-$70
(573) 336-7272
(800) 553-2666

THE HOME PLACE BED & BREAKFST
302 S Benton (65583)
Rates: $45-$55
(573) 774-6637
(800) 438-3778

RAMADA INN-FORT WOOD
I-44, Ft. Wood Exit (65583)
Rates: $51-$59
(573) 336-3121
(800) 272-6232

SCOTTISH INNS
25755 Hwy 17 (65583)
Rates: n/a
(573) 774-3600
(800) 251-1962
(888) 855-6668

SUPER 8 MOTEL
I-44 & Hwy 28 (65583)
Rates: $42-$68
(573) 336-3036
(800) 800-8000

WENTZVILLE

HERITAGE MOTEL
404 N Hwy 61, Bus. Rt (63385)
Rates: $22-$26
(636) 327-6263

HOLIDAY INN
900 Corporate Pkwy (63385)
Rates: $79-$94
(636) 327-7001
(800) 465-4329

HOWARD JOHNSON
1500 Continental Dr (63385)
Rates: $35-$52
(636) 327-5212
(800) 446-4656

RAMADA LIMITED
1400 Continental Dr (63385)
Rates: $39-$79
(636) 327-5515
(800) 272-6232

SCOTTISH INNS
404 N Hwy 61, Bus. Rt (63385)
Rates: n/a
(800) 251-1962

SUPER 8 MOTEL
4 Pantera Dr (63385)
Rates: $40-$53
(636) 327-5300
(800) 800-8000

VILLAGER LODGE
404 N Business Rt 61 (63385)
Rates: $35-$55
(636) 327-6263

WEST PLAINS

DAYS INN
2105 Porter Wagoner Blvd (65775)
Rates: $34-$100
(417) 256-4135
(800) 329-7466

RAMADA INN
1301 Preacher Roe Blvd (65775)
Rates: $50-$59
(417) 256-8191
(800) 272-6232

AREA CODES - If the local number doesn't connect, check for a new area code.

MONTANA

ABSAROKEE

STILLWATER LODGE
28 Woodard Ave
(59001)
Rates: $40-$60
(406) 328-4899

ALBERTON

RIVER EDGE MOTEL
I-90 Exit 75
(59820)
Rates: $40-$60
(406) 722-4418

ANACONDA

LODGE AT SKYHAVEN
1711 Hwy 48
(59711)
Rates: $30-$40
(406) 563-8342
(800) 563-8089

PINTLAR INN
13902 Hwy 1
(59711)
Rates: $30-$40
(406) 563-5072

7 GABLES RESORT
20 Southern Cross Rd (59711)
Rates: $40-$60
(406) 563-5052

AUGUSTA

BUNKHOUSE INN
122 Main St
(59410)
Rates: $30-$40
(406) 562-3387
(800) 553-4016

BABB

(Also see Glacier National Park)

THRONSON'S MOTEL
US 89, Box 169
(59411)
Rates: $40-$60
(406) 732-5530

BAKER

ROY'S MOTEL & CAMPGROUND
327 W Montana Ave (59313)
Rates: $30-$40
(406) 778-3321
(800) 552-3321

SAGEBRUSH INN
518 US 12 W
(59313)
Rates: $40-$60
(406) 778-3341
(800) 638-3708

BASIN

MERRY WIDOW MOTEL
308 E 8th Ave
(59631)
Rates: $30-$40
(406) 225-3220
(877) 225-3220

BELGRADE

SUPER 8 MOTEL
6450 Jackrabbit Ln
(59714)
Rates: $40-$56
(406) 388-1493
(800) 800-8000

3 CHEERS MOTEL-EXTENDED STAY SUITES
19601 Frontage Rd
(59714)
Rates: $40-$60
(406) 388-4051

BIG FORK

BAYVIEW RESORT & MARINA
543 Yenne Point Rd (59911)
Rates: $60-$80
(406) 837-4843
(800) 775-3536

HOLIDAY RESORT
17001 E Shore Rd
(59911)
Rates: $60-$80
(406) 982-3710
(800) 421-9141

TIMBERS MOTEL
8540 Hwy 35
(59911)
Rates: $30-$68
(406) 837-6200
(800) 821-4546

WOODS BAY RESORT
26481 E Shore Rt
(59911)
Rates: $40-$60
(406) 837-3333

BIG SANDY

Q'S MOTEL
US 87 & Hwy 236,
Box 421 (59520)
Rates: $30-$40
(406) 378-2389

BIG SKY

BEST WESTERN BUCK'S T-4 LODGE
46625 Gallatin Rd
(59716)
Rates: $119-$169
(406) 995-4111
(800) 528-1234
(800) 822-4484

COMFORT INN
47214 Gallatin Rd
(59716)
Rates: $99-$149
(406) 995-2333
(800) 228-5150

THE HUD CABIN VACATION RENTAL
13730 Portnell Rd
(Bozeman 59718)
Rates: $225/Night
Rates: $1575/Wk
(406) 763-5215

320 GUEST RANCH
205 Buffalo Horn
(59730)
Rates: $125-$319
(406) 995-4283

BIG TIMBER

BIG TIMBER INN B&B
Yellowstone River
Ln, Box 328 (59011)
Rates: $40-$60
(406) 932-4080

LAZY J MOTEL
Hwy 10 (59011)
Rates: $40-$60
(406) 932-5533

RIPPLING WATERS GUEST HOUSE
P O. Box 1042,
Hwy 298 (59011)
Rates: n/a
(406) 932-4718

SUPER 8 MOTEL
I-90 & Hwy 10 W
(59011)
Rates: $57-$74
(406) 932-8888
(800) 800-8000

BIGFORK

TIMBERS MOTEL
8540 Hwy 35
(59911)
Rates: $32-$78
(406) 837-6200

BILLINGS

AIRPORT METRA INN
403 Main St
(59105)
Rates: $31-$40
(406) 245-6611
(800) 234-6611

BEST WESTERN BILLINGS
5610 S Frontage
Rd (59101)
Rates: $68-$99
(406) 248-9800
(800) 528-1234

BEST WESTERN PONDEROSA INN
2511 1st Ave N
(59101)
Rates: $55-$80
(406) 259-5511
(800) 528-1234
(800) 628-9081

BIG 5 MOTEL
2601 4th Ave N
(59101)
Rates: $30-$40
(406) 245-6646
(888) 544-9358

BILLINGS HOTEL & CONV CENTER
1223 Mullowney
Ln (59101)
Rates: $60-$80
(406) 248-7151
(800) 537-7286

BILLINGS INN
880 N 29th St
(59101)
Rates: $49-$65
(406) 252-6800
(800) 231-7782

CHERRY TREE INN
823 N Broadway
(59101)
Rates: $35-$50
(406) 252-5603
(800) 237-5882

COMFORT INN
2030 Overland
Ave (59102)
Rates: $70-$89
(406) 652-5200
(800) 228-5150

COUNTRY HEARTH INN
1223 Mullowney
(59101)
Rates: $40-$60
(406) 248-1954

DAYS INN
843 Parkway Ln
(59101)
Rates: $47-$75
(406) 252-4007
(800) 329-7466

AREA CODES - If the local number doesn't connect, check for a new area code.

DUDE RANCHER LODGE
415 N 29th St
(59101)
Rates: $39-$66
(406) 259-5561
(800) 221-3302

HEIGHTS INN MOTEL
1206 Main St
(59101)
Rates: $30-$40
(406) 252-8451
(800) 275-8451

HILLTOP INN
1116 N 28th St
(59101)
Rates: $51-$65
(406) 245-5000
(800) 878-9282

HOLIDAY INN
5500 Midland Rd
(59101)
Rates: $79-$99
(406) 248-7701
(800) 465-4329

HOWARD JOHNSON EXPRESS INN
101 S 27th St
(59101)
Rates: $69-$79
(406) 248-4656
(800) 446-4656

JUNIPER MOTEL
1315 N 27th St
(59101)
Rates: $41-$43
(406) 245-4128
(800) 826-7530

KELLY INN
5425 Midland Rd
(59101)
Rates: $46-$76
(406) 252-2700
(800) 635-3559

LAZY KT MOTEL
1403 1st Ave N
(59101)
Rates: $40
(406) 252-6606
(800) 290-2681

MOTEL 6 NORTH
5353 Midland Rd
(59102)
Rates: $30-$36
(406) 248-7551
(800) 466-8356

MOTEL 6 SOUTH
5400 Midland Rd,
RR 9 (59101)
Rates: $30-$36
(406) 252-0093
(800) 466-8356

OVERPASS MOTEL
615 Central Ave
(59101)
Rates: $25-$36
(406) 252-5157
(800) 579-5157

PICTURE COURT MOTEL
5146 Laurel Rd
(59101)
Rates: $40
(406) 252-8478
(800) 523-7379

QUALITY INN HOMESTEAD
2036 Overland
Ave (59102)
Rates: $56-$96
(406) 652-1320
(800) 228-5151

RADISSON NORTHERN HOTEL
19 N 28th St
(59101)
Rates: $89-$109
(406) 245-5121
(800) 333-3333

RAMADA LIMITED
1345 Mullowney
Ln (59101)
Rates: $60-$80
(406) 252-2584
(800) 272-6232

RIMROCK INN
1203 North 27th St
(59101)
Rates: $40-$60
(406) 252-7107
(800) 624-9770

RIMVIEW INN
1025 N 27th St
(59101)
Rates: $47-$58
(406) 248-2622
(800) 551-1418

SHERATON BILLINGS HOTEL
27 N 27th St
(59101)
Rates: $85-$99
(406) 252-7400
(800) 588-7666

SUPER 8 LODGE
5400 Southgate Dr
(59102)
Rates: $425$67
(406) 248-8842
(800) 800-8000

TOWNHOUSE MOTEL
3420 1st Ave N
(59101)
Rates: $26-$38
(406) 245-4191

TWIN CUBS MOTEL
1818 Main St
(59101)
Rates: $40-$60
(406) 252-9851

WAR BONNET INN
2612 Belknap Ave
(59101)
Rates: $40-$60
(406) 248-7761
(888) 242-6023

BOULDER

CASTORIA MOTEL
211 S Monroe
(59632)
Rates: $30-$40
(406) 225-3549

O-Z MOTEL
114 N Main St
(59632)
Rates: $30-$40
(406) 225-3364

BOZEMAN

ALPINE LODGE
1017 E Main
(59715)
Rates: $30-$40
(406) 586-0356
(888) 922-5746

BLUE SKY MOTEL
1010 E Main
(59715)
Rates: $30-$40
(406) 587-2311
(800) 845-9032

BOBCAT LODGE
2307 W Main
(59715)
Rates: $40-$60
(406) 587-5241
(888) 587-5241

BOZEMAN INN
1235 N 7th Ave
(59715)
Rates: $57-$79
(406) 587-3176
(800) 648-7515

BRIDGER MTNS HIGHLAND HOUSE B&B
1540 Nelson Rd
(59715)
Rates: $82-$90
(406) 587-0904

COMFORT INN
1370 N 7th Ave
(59715)
Rates: $50-$99
(406) 587-2322
(800) 228-5150

DAYS INN
1321 N 7th Ave
(59715)
Rates: $58-$99
(406) 587-5251
(800) 329-7466

HOLIDAY INN
5 Baxter Ln
(59715)
Rates: $99
(406) 587-4561
(800) 465-4329

IMPERIAL INN
122 W Main St
(59715)
Rates: $40-$60
(406) 587-4481
(800) 541-7423

RAINBOW MOTEL
510 N 7th Ave
(59715)
Rates: $50-$70
(406) 587-4201

RAMADA LIMITED
2020 Wheat Dr
(59715)
Rates: $59-$119
(406) 585-2626
(800) 272-6232

ROYAL "7" BUDGET INN
310 N 7th Ave
(59715)
Rates: $48-$58
(406) 587-3103
(800) 587-3103

SLEEP INN
817 Wheat Dr
(59715)
Rates: $79-$99
(406) 585-7888
(800) 753-3746
(800) 377-8240

SUPER 8 MOTEL
800 Wheat Dr
(59715)
Rates: $55-$75
(406) 586-1521
(800) 800-8000

TLC INN
805 Wheat Dr
(59715)
Rates: $60-$69
(406) 587-2100

WESTERN HERITAGE INN
1200 E Main St
(59715)
Rates: $58-$88
(406) 586-8534
(800) 877-1094

BROADUS

BROADUS MOTEL
101 N Park
(59317)
Rates: $40-$60
(406) 436-2671

BROWNING

WESTERN MOTEL
121 Central Ave E
(59417)
Rates: $40-$60
(406) 338-7572

BUTTE

BEST WESTERN BUTTE PLAZA INN
2900 Harrison Ave
(59701)
Rates: $89-$109
(406) 494-3500
(800) 543-5814

CAPRI MOTEL
220 N Wyoming
(59701)
Rates: $30-$50
(406) 723-4391
(800) 342-2774

COMFORT INN
2777 Harrison Ave
(59701)
Rates: $62-$99
(406) 494-8850
(800) 228-5150

EDDY'S MOTEL
1205 S Montana
(59701)
Rates: $40-$60
(406) 723-4364

MILE HI MOTEL
3499 Harrison Ave
(59701)
Rates: $40-$60
(406) 494-2250

**RAMADA INN
COPPER KING**
4655 Harrison Ave
(59701)
Rates: $89-$109
(406) 494-6666
(800) 332-8600

ROCKER INN
122001 W Brown's
Gulch Rd (59701)
Rates: $38-$48
(406) 723-5464
(800) 828-5399
(MT)

SKOOKUM MOTEL
3541 Harrison Ave
(59701)
Rates: $30-$40
(406) 494-2153

SUPER 8 MOTEL
2929 Harrison Ave
(59701)
Rates: $60-$80
(406) 494-6000
(800) 800-8000

**WAR BONNET
INN**
2100 Cornell Ave
(59701)
Rates: $69-$99
(406) 494-7800
(800) 443-1806

CAMERON

**MADISON RIVER
CABINS & RV**
1403 Hwy 287 N
(59720)
Rates: $40-$60
(406) 682-4890

**WEST FORK
CABIN CAMP**
1475 US 287 N
(59720)
Rates: $40-$60
(406) 682-4802

CASCADE

BADGER MOTEL
132 1st St N
(59421)
Rates: $40-$60
(406) 468-9330

RUSSELL'S INN
2468 Old US 91
(59421)
Rates: $40-$60
(406) 468-2855

CHESTER

**WHEATSHEAF
MOTEL**
10 Washington
Ave (59522)
Rates: $30-$40
(406) 759-5300

CHINOOK

CHINOOK HOTEL
62 3rd St (59523)
Rates: $30-$40
(406) 357-2231

**CHINOOK
MOTOR INN**
100 Indiana Ave
(59523)
Rates: $44-$58
(406) 357-2248
(800) 603-2864

CHOTEAU

BIG SKY MOTEL
209 S Main Ave
(59422)
Rates: $38-$60
(406) 466-5318

**WESTERN STAR
MOTEL**
426 Main Ave S
(59422)
Rates: $30-$40
(406) 466-5737

CIRCLE

TRAVELERS INN
Hwy 200, Box 78
(59215)
Rates: $30-$40
(406) 485-3323

CLINTON

**ROCK CREEK
LODGE**
7 Rock Creek Rd
(59825)
Rates: $30-$40
(406) 825-4868

COLSTRIP

FORT UNION INN
73 Dogwood
(59323)
Rates: $26-$37
(406) 748-2553
(800) 738-6440

SUPER 8 MOTEL
6227 Main St
(59323)
Rates: $49-$58
(406) 748-3400
(800) 800-8000

COLUMBIA FALLS

**MEADOW LAKE
RESORT**
100 St. Andrews
Dr (59912)
Rates: $89-$459
(406) 892-7601
(800) 321 4653

**SUPER 8 MOTEL-
GLACIER PARK**
7336 Hwy 2 E
(59912)
Rates: $63-$78
(406) 892-0888
(800) 800-8000

**WESTERN INNS
GLACIER
MOUNTAIN
SHADOWS
RESORT**
7285 Hwy 2 E
(59912)
Rates: $60-$80
(406) 892-7686
(800) 766-1137

COLUMBUS

**GLACIER INN
MOTEL**
1401 2nd Ave E
(59912)
Rates: $40-$60
(406) 892-4341

**GLACIER MT
SHADOWS
RESORT**
US 2 E & Hwy 206
(59912)
Rates: $40-$60
(406) 892-7686
(800) 766-1137

SUPER 8 MOTEL
602 8th Ave N
(59019)
Rates: $49-$74
(406) 322-4101
(800) 800-8000

CONDON

SUPER 8 MOTEL
Hwy 83, Box
1278 (59826)
Rates: $52-$62
(406) 754-2688
(800) 800-8000

CONRAD

CONRAD MOTEL
210 N Main
(59425)
Rates: $30-$40
(406) 278-7544

**NORTHGATE
MOTEL**
5 N Main (59425)
Rates: $30-$40
(406) 278-3516

SUPER 8 MOTEL
215 N Main St
(59425)
Rates: $49-$74
(406) 278-7676
(800) 800-8000

COOKE CITY

ELKHORN LODGE
108 Main St
(59020)
Rates: $40-$60
(406) 838-2332

**HIGH COUNTRY
MOTEL**
US 212, P. O. Box
1146 (59020)
Rates: $32-$58
(406) 838-2272

**SODA BUTTE
LODGE**
209 US 212 (59020)
Rates: $65-$75
(406) 838-2251
(800) 527-6462

CORAM

**EVERGREEN
MOTEL**
US Hwy 2 (59913)
Rates: $60-$80
(406) 387-5365

CULBERTSON

**DIAMOND
WILLOW INN**
US 2 & Hwy 16,
Box 753 (59218)
Rates: $30-$40
(406) 787-6218

CUSTER

**D & L
MOTEL/CAFE**
3rd St, Box 105
(59024)
Rates: $30-$40
(406) 856-4128

CUT BANK

CORNER MOTEL
201 E Main St
(59427)
Rates: $30-$40
(406) 873-5588
(800) 851-5541

**GLACIER
GATEWAY INN**
1121 E Railroad St
(59427)
Rates: $46-$57
(406) 873-5544
(800) 851-5541

**NORTHERN
MOTOR INN**
609 W Main St
(59427)
Rates: $40-$60
(406) 873-5662

POINT MOTEL
1109 E Main St
(59427)
Rates: $30-$40
(406) 873-5433
(800) 851-5541

TERRACE MOTEL
11 9th Ave SE
(59427)
Rates: $30-$40
(406) 873-5031

DARBY

ALTA RANCH
9203 West Fork Rd
(59829)
Rates: $85-$210
(406) 349-2142
(888) 349-2142

BUD & SHIRLEY'S MOTEL
Main St (59829)
Rates: $40-$60
(406) 821-3401

EL CAPITAN VILLAS
3300 Old Darby Rd (59829)
Rates: $40-$60
(406) 821-3111

HONEY'S MOTEL
3237 US 93 (59829)
Rates: $40-$60
(406) 821-3111

WILDERNESS MOTEL & BUNKHOUSE
308 S Main St (59829)
Rates: $30-$40
(406) 821-3405
(800) 820-2554

DE BORGIA

HOTEL ALBERT BED & BREAKFAST
#2 Yellowstone Tr (59830)
Rates: $54-$70
(406) 678-4303

DEER LODGE

COLEMAN FEE MANSION B&B
500 Missouri Ave (59722)
Rates: $65-$150
(406) 846-2922

DOWNTOWNER MOTEL
500 4th St (59722)
Rates: $40-$60
(406) 846-1021
(800) 253-4093

SCHARF'S MOTOR INN
819 Main St (59722)
Rates: $30-$50
(406) 846-2810

SUPER 8 MOTEL
1150 N Main St (59722)
Rates: $54-$79
(406) 846-2370
(800) 800-8000

DENTON

HOLM MOTEL
106 3rd N (59430)
Rates: $30-$40
(406) 567-2286

DILLON

BEST WESTERN PARADISE INN
650 N Montana St (59725)
Rates: $51-$78
(406) 683-4214
(800) 528-1234

COMFORT INN
450 N Interchange (59725)
Rates: $65-$81
(406) 683-6831
(800) 228-5150

CRESTON MOTEL
335 S Atlantic (59725)
Rates: $26-$42
(406) 683-2341

GUESTHOUSE INNS & SUITES
580 Sinclair (59725)
Rates: $65-$75
(406) 683-3636
(800) 214-8378

SACAJAWEA MOTEL
775 N Montana St (59725)
Rates: $30-$40
(406) 683-2381

SUNDOWNER MOTEL
500 N Montana St (59725)
Rates: $43-$50
(406) 683-2375
(800) 524-9746

SUPER 8 MOTEL
550 N Montana St (59725)
Rates: $42-$69
(406) 683-4288
(800) 800-8000

DRUMMOND

DRUMMOND MOTEL
170 W Front St (59832)
Rates: $30-$40
(406) 288-3272

SKY MOTEL
Front & Broadway (59832)
Rates: $30-$40
(406) 288-3206
(800) 559-3206

WAGON WHEEL CAFE & MOTEL
Front & C Sts (59832)
Rates: $30-$40
(406) 288-3201

EAST GLACIER

(Also see Glacier National Park)

BISON CREEK RANCH
20722 Hwy 2 W (59434)
Rates: $40-$60
(406) 226-4482
(888) 226-4482

DANCING BEARS MOTEL
147 Montana St (59434)
Rates: $55-$75
(406) 226-4402

GLACIER PARK CIRCLE R
402 Hwy 2 E (59343)
Rates: $40-$60
(406) 226-9331

WHISTLING SWAN MOTEL
512 Hwy 2 W (59343)
Rates: $40-$60
(406) 226-4412

EKALAKA

GUEST HOUSE
4 Main St (59324)
Rates: $25-$37
(406) 775-6337

ELLISTON

LAST CHANCE MOTEL
26 Hwy 12 S (59728)
Rates: $30-$40
(406) 492-7250

EMIGRANT

QUERENICA B&B
P. O. Box 184 (59027)
Rates: $90-$125
(406) 333-4500
(888) 603-4500

ENNIS

EL WESTERN RESORT COTTAGES
Hwy 287 S (59729)
Rates: $65-$185
(406) 682-4127
(800) 831-2773

FAN MOUNTAIN INN
207 N Main (59729)
Rates: $40-$65
(406) 682-5200

RIVERSIDE MOTEL & OUTFITTERS
346 Main St (59729)
Rates: $40-$60
(406) 682-4240
(800) 535-4139

SILVERTIP LODGE
301 Main St (59729)
Rates: $30-$40
(406) 682-4384

SPORTSMAN'S LODGE
310 US 287 N (59729)
Rates: $45-$65
(406) 682-4242
(800) 220-1690

ESSEX

(Also see Glacier National Park)

DENNY'S MOTEL
14297 US 2 (59916)
Rates: $30-$40
(406) 888-5720

EUREKA

CREEK SIDE MOTEL & RV
1333 Hwy 93 N (59917)
Rates: $29-$40
(406) 296-2361

KSANKA MOTOR INN
US 93 & Hwy 37 (59917)
Rates: $40-$60
(406) 296-3127

FAIRVIEW

KORNER MOTEL
217 W 9th (59221)
Rates: $30-$40
(406) 747-5259
(800) 656-7637

FORSYTH

BEST WESTERN SUNDOWNER INN
1018 Front St (59327)
Rates: $55-$75
(406) 356-2115
(800) 528-1234
(877) 356-2115

RAILS INN MOTEL
3rd & Front Sts (59327)
Rates: $45-$60
(406) 356-2242
(800) 621-3754

RESTWEL MOTEL
810 Front St (59327)
Rates: $34-$40
(406) 356-2771
(800) 548-3442

WESTWIND MOTOR INN
226 Westwind Lane (59327)
Rates: $39-$46
(406) 356-2038
(888) 356-2038

FORT BENTON

FORT MOTEL
1809 St Charles (59442)
Rates: $40-$60
(406) 622-3312

AREA CODES - If the local number doesn't connect, check for a new area code.

FORT PECK

FORT PECK HOTEL
Missouri &
Kansas Ave
(59223)
Rates: $40-$60
(406) 526-3266
(800) 560-4931

**LAKERIDGE
MOTEL & TACKLE**
HCR 1660 (59223)
Rates: $40-$60
(406) 526-3597

FORT SMITH

**QUILL GORDON
FLY FISHERS
MOTEL**
Box 7597 (59035)
Rates: $40-$60
(406) 666-2253

GALATA

**GALATA MOTEL
& RV OVERNITE**
Box 31 (59444)
Rates: $30-$40
(406) 432-2352

GALLATIN
GATEWAY

**CASTLE ROCK
INN**
65840 Gallatin
Gateway (59730)
Rates: n/a
(406) 763-4243

**MILLERS OF
MONTANA B&B**
US 191 (59730)
Rates: $50-$75
(406) 763-4102

GARDINER

**ABSAROKA
LODGE**
Box 10, US 89
(59030)
Rates: $60-$80
(406) 848-7414
(800) 755-7414

**BEST WESTERN BY
MAMMOTH HOT
SPRINGS**
Hwy 89 S (59030)
Rates: $85-$160
(406) 848-7311
(800) 528-1234
(800) 828-9080

**BLUE HAVEN
MOTEL**
521 Scott St W
(59030)
Rates: $47-$104
(406) 848-7719

**JIM BRIDGER
COURT**
US 89, Box 325
(59030)
Rates: $40-$60
(406) 848-7371
(888) 858-7508

MOTEL 6
109 Hell Roaring
Rd (59030)
Rates: $34-$85
(406) 848-7520
(800) 466-8356

SUPER 8 MOTEL
Hwy 89 S (59030)
Rates: $94
(406) 848-7401
(800) 800-8000

**WESTERNAIRE
MOTEL**
Hwy 89 S (59030)
Rates: $60-$80
(406) 848-7397
(888) 273-0358

**YELLOWSTONE
RIVER MOTEL**
14 E Park St
(59030)
Rates: $55-$77
(406) 848-7303
(888) 797-4837

GLACIER
NATIONAL
PARK

Also see the fol-
lowing cities for
lodging adjacent
to the park:

Babb
East Glacier
Essex
St. Mary

GLASGOW

CAMPBELL LODGE
534 3rd Ave S
(59230)
Rates: $29-$38
(406) 228-9328

**COTTONWOOD
INN**
US 2 E (59230)
Rates: $48-$66
(406) 228-8213
(800) 321-8213

KOSKI'S MOTEL
320 US 2 E (59230)
Rates: $30-$40
(406) 228-8282
(888) 238-8282

LACASA MOTEL
238 1st Ave N
(59230)
Rates: $30-$40
(406) 228-9311
(877) 228-9311

RUSTIC LODGE
700 1st Ave N
(59230)
Rates: $27-$40
(406) 228-2451
(888) 228-0772

**STAR LODGE
MOTEL**
903 6th Ave N
(59230)
Rates: $30-$40
(406) 228-2494

GLENDIVE

**BEST WESTERN
JORDAN INN**
222 N Merrill Ave
(59330)
Rates: $55-$81
(223) 365-5655
(800) 528-1234
(888) 453-6348

BUDGET MOTEL
1610 N Merrill
Ave (59330)
Rates: $26-$35
(406) 365-8334

DAYS INN
2000 N Merrill
Ave (59330)
Rates: $29-$60
(406) 365-6011
(800) 329-7466

**EL CENTRO
MOTEL**
112 S Kendrick
Ave (59330)
Rates: $25-$35
(406) 365-5211

KINGS INN
1903 N Merrill
Ave (59330)
Rates: $30-$40
(406) 365-5636

**PACKWOOD
MOTEL**
1002 W Bell
(59330)
Rates: $27-$35
(406) 365-8221

SUPER 8 MOTEL
1904 N Merrill
Ave (59330)
Rates: $36-$54
(406) 365-5671
(800) 800-8000

GRASS RANGE

**GRASS RANGE
MOTEL**
570 US 87 S
(59032)
Rates: $30-$40
(406) 428-2242

GREAT FALLS

AIRWAY MOTEL
1800 14th St SW
(59401)
Rates: $30-$40
(406) 761-8915

**BEST WESTERN
HERITAGE INN**
1700 Fox Farm Rd
(59404)
Rates: $79-$99
(406) 761-1900
(800) 528-1234
(800) 548-8256

**BEST WESTERN
PONDEROSA INN**
220 Central Ave
(59401)
Rates: $54-$77
(406) 761-3410
(800) 528-1234
(800) 266-3410

**BUDGET INN
MOTEL**
2 Treasure State
Dr (59404)
Rates: $41-$47
(406) 453-1602
(800) 362-4842

CENTRAL MOTEL
715 Central Ave W
(59404)
Rates: $40-$70
(406) 453-0161
(800) 794-7433

COMFORT INN
1120 9th St S
(59401)
Rates: $70-$89
(406) 454-2727
(800) 228-5150

CRESTVIEW INN
500 13th Ave S
(59401)
Rates: $40-$60
(406) 727-8380
(800) 727-8380

DAYS INN
101 14th Ave NW
(59404)
Rates: $63-$76
(406) 727-6565
(800) 466-8356

**EDELWEISS
MOTOR INN**
626 Central Ave W
(59404)
Rates: $28-$40
(406) 452-9503
(800) 294-9503

GREAT FALLS INN
1400 28th St S
(59405)
Rates: $49-$63
(406) 453-6000
(800) 454-6010

**HIGHWOOD
VILLAGE MOTEL**
4009 10th Ave S
(59405)
Rates: $40-$60
(406) 452-8505
(800) 253-8505

HOLIDAY INN
400 10th Ave S
(59405)
Rates: $65-$85
(406) 727-7200
(800) 465-4329

IMPERIAL INN
601 2nd Ave N
(59401)
Rates: $30-$40
(406) 452-9581
(800) 735-7173 (US)
(800) 676-6267 (Can)

AREA CODES - If the local number doesn't connect, check for a new area code.

MID-TOWN MOTEL
526 2nd Ave N
(59401)
Rates: $40-$60
(406) 453-2411
(800) 457-2411

PLAZA INN
1224 10th Ave S
(59405)
Rates: $36-$65
(406) 452-9594
(800) 354-0868

ROYAL MOTEL
1300 Central Ave
(59401)
Rates: $30-$40
(406) 452-9548

SAHARA 9 MOTEL
3460 10th Ave S
(59405)
Rates: $40-$60
(406) 761-6150
(800) 772-1330

SKI'S WESTERN MOTEL
2420 10th Ave S
(59405)
Rates: $35-$70
(406) 453-3281
(800) 354-0868

SKYLARK SUPER SEVEN MOTEL
415 10th Ave S
(59401)
Rates: $40-$60
(406) 727-7977

STARLIT MOTEL
1521 1st Ave NW
(59401)
Rates: $30-$40
(406) 452-9597
(800) 818-9597

SUPER 8 MOTEL
1214 13th St S
(59405)
Rates: $46-$70
(406) 727-7600
(800) 800-8000

TOWN & COUNTRY MOTEL
2418 10th Ave S
(59405)
Rates: $30-$40
(406) 452-5643

TOWNHOUSE INNS
1411 10th St S
(59405)
Rates: $80
(406) 761-4600
(800) 442-4667

TRIPLE CROWN MOTOR INN
621 Central Ave
(59401)
Rates: $39-$49
(406) 727-8300
(800) 722-8300

VILLAGE MTR INN
726 10th Ave S
(59405)
Rates: $30-$40
(406) 727-7666
(800) 354-0868

WAGON WHEEL MOTEL
2620 10th Ave S
(59401)
Rates: $40-$60
(406) 761-1300
(800) 800-6483

WRIGHT NITE INN RENDEZVOUS MOTEL
560 Country Club
Blvd (59401)
Rates: $40-$60
(406) 452-9525
(800) 800-6483
(MT)

GREENOUGH

LORAN'S CLEARWATER INN
Hwy 200 & 83,
Box 20 (59836)
Rates: $30-$40
(406) 244-9535

HAMILTON

BITTERROOT MOTEL
408 S 1st St
(59840)
Rates: $30-$40
(406) 363-1142

CITY CENTER MOTEL
W 415 Main
(59840)
Rates: $40-$60
(406) 363-1652

COMFORT INN
1113 N 1st St
(59840)
Rates: $59-$84
(406) 363-6600
(800) 228-5150

DEER CROSSING BED & BREAKFAST
396 Hayes Creek
Rd (59840)
Rates: $45-$95
(406) 363-2232
(800) 763-2232

RANCH B&B
1615 US 93 S
(59840)
Rates: $40-$60
(406) 363-4739

SPORTSMAN MOTEL
410 N 1st St
(59840)
Rates: $30-$40
(406) 363-2411

HARDIN

AMERICAN INN
1324 N Crawford
Ave (59034)
Rates: $45-$79
(406) 665-1870
(800) 582-8094

CAMP CUSTER MOTEL
303 E 4th St
(59034)
Rates: $30-$40
(406) 665-2504
(800) 234-2504

LARIAT MOTEL
709 North Center
Ave (59034)
Rates: $30-$54
(406) 665-2683

SUPER 8 MOTEL
I-90 & Hwy 47 N
(59034)
Rates: $47-$58
(406) 665-1700
(800) 800-8000

WESTERN MOTEL
830 W 3rd St
(59034)
Rates: $45-$70
(406) 665-2296

HARLOWTON

CORRAL MOTEL
US 12 & 191
(59036)
Rates: $35-$45
(406) 632-4331
(800) 392-4723

COUNTRYSIDE INN
309 3rd St NE
(59036)
Rates: $38-$57
(406) 632-4119
(800) 632-4120

TROY MOTEL
US 12 & 191
(59036)
Rates: $30-$40
(406) 632-4428

HAUGAN

SILVER $ INN
I-90 Exit 16, Box
W (59842)
Rates: $40-$60
(406) 678-4242
(800) 531-1968

HAVRE

BUDGET INN MOTEL
115 9th Ave
(59501)
Rates: $30-$40
(406) 265-8625
(888) 868-8625

CIRCLE INN MOTEL
3565 US 2 E
(59501)
Rates: $30-$40
(406) 265-9655

EL TORO INN
521 1st St (59501)
Rates: $36-$46
(406) 265-5414
(800) 422-5414

GREAT NORTHERN INN
1345 1st St (59401)
Rates: $60-$80
(406) 265-4200
(888) 530-4100

HI-LINE MOTEL
20 2nd St (59501)
Rates: $30-$40
(406) 265-5512

RAILS INN
537 2nd St (59501)
Rates: $30-$40
(406) 265-1438
(800) 724-5746

SHASTA MOTEL
600 1st St (59501)
Rates: $40-$60
(406) 265-5863

TOWNHOUSE INNS
601 W 1st St
(59501)
Rates: $59-$84
(406) 265-6711
(800) 442-4667

HELENA

ALADDIN MOTER INN
2101 11th Ave
(59601)
Rates: $40-$60
(406) 443-2300
(800) 541-2743

APPLETON INN BED & BRKFAST
1999 Euclid Ave
(59601)
Rates: $85-$150
(406) 449-7492
(800) 986-1999

BARRISTER B&B
416 N Ewing
(59601)
Rates: $90-$105
(406) 443-7330
(800) 823-1148

BIRDSEYE B&B
6890 Raven Rd
(59602)
Rates: $65-$85
(406) 449-4380

COMFORT INN
750 Fee St (59601)
Rates: $60-$79
(406) 443-1000
(800) 228-5150

DAYS INN
2001 Prospect Ave
(59601)
Rates: $49-$90
(406) 442-3280
(800) 329-7466

ELKHORN MOUNTAIN INN
1 Jackson Creek (59601)
Rates: $60-$67
(406) 442-6625

HOLIDAY INN
22 N Last Chance Gulch (59601)
Rates: n/a
(800) 465-4329

HOLIDAY INN EXPRESS
22 N Last Chance Gulch (59601)
Rates: n/a
(800) 465-4329

KINGS CARRIAGE INN
910 N Last Chance Gulch (59601)
Rates: $40-$60
(406) 442-6080
(888) 334-5464 (MT)

KNIGHTS REST MOTEL
1831 Euclid (59601)
Rates: $32-$46
(406) 442-6384
(888) 442-6384

LAMPLIGHTER MOTEL
1006 Madison (59601)
Rates: $42-$53
(406) 442-9200

MOTEL 6
800 N Oregon (59601)
Rates: $30-$40
(406) 442-9990
(800) 466-8356

SHILO INN
2020 Prospect Ave (59601)
Rates: $69-$99
(406) 442-0320
(800) 222-2244

SUPER 8 MOTEL
2200 11th Ave (59601)
Rates: $56-$78
(406) 443-2450
(800) 800-8000

HOT SPRINGS

HOT SPRINGS SPA
308 N Springs St (59845)
Rates: $30-$40
(406) 741-2283

HUNGRY HORSE

HUNGRY HORSE MOTEL
8808 US 2 E (59919)
Rates: $40-$60
(406) 387-5443

MINI GOLDEN INNS MOTEL
8955 US 2 E (59919)
Rates: $80-$86
(406) 387-4313
(800) 891-6464

SWEET DREAMS MOTEL
131 Alpha Rd (59919)
Rates: $40-$60
(406) 387-5705

JORDAN

FELLMAN'S MOTEL
Hwy 200 (59337)
Rates: $26-$39
(406) 557-2209
(800) 337-1863

KALISPELL

AERO INN
1830 US 93 S (59901)
Rates: $34-$87
(406) 755-3798
(800) 843-6114

BEST WESTERN OUTLAW INN
1701 Hwy 93 S (59901)
Rates: $95-$135
(406) 755-6100
(800) 528-1234
(800) 237-7445

BIG CHIEF MOTEL
1484 Hwy 35 (59901)
Rates: $40-$60
(406) 756-3434

BLUE & WHITE MOTEL
640 E Idaho (59901)
Rates: $40-$60
(406) 755-4311
(800) 382-3577

CAVANAUGH'S KALISPELL CENTER
20 N Main (59901)
Rates: $95-$150
(406) 752-6660
(800) 325-4000

DIAMOND LIL'S INN MOTEL
1680 US 93 S (59901)
Rates: $64-$66
(406) 752-3467
(800) 843-7301

FOUR SEASONS MOTOR INN
350 N Main St (59901)
Rates: $58-$79
(406) 755-6123
(800) 545-6399

FRIENDSHIP INN
1009 US 2 E (59901)
Rates: $50-$116
(406) 257-7155
(800) 453-4511

GLACIER GATEWAY MOTEL
264 N Main St (59901)
Rates: $45-$75
(406) 755-3330

KALISPELL HISTORIC GRAND HOTEL
100 Main St (59901)
Rates: $71-$91
(406) 755-8100
(800) 858-7422

MOTEL 6
1540 Hwy 93 S (59901)
Rates: $66-$82
(406) 752-6355
(800) 466-8356

RED LION INN
1330 Hwy 2W (59901)
Rates: $59-$95
(406) 755-6700
(800) 733-5466

SUPER 8 MOTEL
1341 1st Ave E (59901)
Rates: $62-$76
(406) 755-1888
(800) 800-8000

TEEPEE LODGE MOTEL
255 Montclair Dr (59901)
Rates: $40-$60
(406) 752-6533

VACATIONER MOTEL
285 7th Ave NE (59901)
Rates: $60-$80
(406) 755-7144
(888) 755-7144

WHITE BIRCH MOTEL
17 Shady Lane (59901)
Rates: $42-$47
(406) 752-4008

LAKESIDE

SUNRISE VISTA INN
7005 US 93 (59922)
Rates: $68-$88
(406) 844-3864

LAUREL

LAUREL RIDGE MOTEL
1403 E Main (59044)
Rates: $26-$38
(406) 628-2000

RUSSELL MOTEL
711 E Main (59044)
Rates: $30-$40
(406) 628-6513
(888) 275-2616

WELCOME TRAVELERS MOTEL
620 W Main (59044)
Rates: $40-$60
(406) 628-6821

LEWISTOWN

B & B MOTEL-IMA
520 E Main St (59457)
Rates: $39-$48
(406) 538-5496
(800) 341-8000

MOUNTAIN VIEW MOTEL
1422 Main St (59457)
Rates: $30-$40
(406) 538-3457
(800) 862-5786

SUNSET MOTEL
115 NE Main (59457)
Rates: $30-$40
(406) 538-8741

TRAIL'S END MOTEL
216 NE Main (59457)
Rates: $30-$40
(406) 538-5468

YOGO INN
211 E Main St (59457)
Rates: $47-$57
(406) 538-8721
(800) 860-9646

LIBBY

CABOOSE MOTEL
714 W 9th (59923)
Rates: $32-$45
(406) 293-6201
(800) 627-0206

MOUNTAIN MAGIC MOTEL
919 Mineral Ave (59923)
Rates: $40-$50
(406) 293-7795

SANDMAN MOTEL
688 Hwy 2 W (59923)
Rates: $40-$60
(406) 293-8831

SUPER 8 MOTEL
448 US 2W (59923)
Rates: $49-$77
(406) 293-2771
(800) 800-8000

AREA CODES - If the local number doesn't connect, check for a new area code.

LIMA

SPORTSMAN INN
111 Baily St
(59739)
Rates: $30-$40
(406) 276-3535

LINCOLN

BLACKFOOT RIVER INN
At 7UP Ranch,
Box 185 (59639)
Rates: $40-$60
(406) 362-4955

LEEPER'S MOTEL
SR 200 & 1st Ave
(59639)
Rates: $39-$50
(406) 362-4333

SNOWY PINES INN
Hwy 200 (59639)
Rates: $40-$60
(406) 362-4481
(800) 809-2463

THREE BEARS MOTEL
Hwy 200, Box
1191 (59639)
Rates: $30-$40
(406) 362-4355
(800) 838-9771

LIVINGSTON

BEST WESTERN YELLOWSTONE MOTOR INN
1515 West Park
(59047)
Rates: $54-$93
(406) 222-6110
(800) 826-1214

BUDGET HOST PARKWAY MOTEL
1124 W Park
(59047)
Rates: $52-$72
(406) 222-3840
(800) 727-7217
(800) 283-4678

COMFORT INN
114 Loves Ln
(59047)
Rates: $44-$100
(406) 222-4400
(800) 228-5150

COUNTRY MOTOR INN
814 E Park (59047)
Rates: $40-$60
(406) 222-1923
(800) 286-1923

ECONO LODGE
111 Rogers Ln
(59047)
Rates: $46-$89
(406) 222-0555
(800) 553-2666

GUEST HOUSE MOTEL
105 W Park
(59047)
Rates: $40-$60
(406) 222-1460
(888) 222-1460

MURRAY HOTEL
201 W Park
(59047)
Rates: $40-$60
(406) 222-1350

PARADISE INN
Park Rd & Rogers
Lane (59047)
Rates: $79-$89
(406) 222-6320
(800) 437-6291

PINE CREEK STORE & LODGE
2496 E River Rd
(59047)
Rates: n/a
(406) 222-3628
(800) 746-3990

RAINBOW MOTEL
5574 E Park St
(59047)
Rates: $40-$60
(406) 222-3780
(800) 788-2301

LOLO

DAYS INN
11225 US 93 S
(59847)
Rates: $45-$75
(406) 273-2121
(800) 329-7466

FORT FIZZLE INN
US 12 W (59847)
Rates: $40-$60
(406) 273-6993

FORT LOLO HOT SPRINGS
58300 Hwy 12 W
(59870)
Rates: $60-$80
(406) 273-2201

MALTA

GREAT NORTHERN MOTEL
2 S 1st Ave E
(59538)
Rates: $40-$60
(406) 654-2100
(888) 234-0935

RIVERSIDE MOTEL
8 N Central
(59538)
Rates: $30-$40
(406) 654-2310
(800) 854-2310

ROYALS INN
117 N 1st St
(59538)
Rates: $28-$38
(406) 654-1150

MARTIN CITY

MIDDLE FORK MOTEL
US 2, P. O. Box
260237 (59926)
Rates: $40-$60
(406) 387-5900

MARTINSDALE

CRAZY MOUNTAIN INN
100 Main St
(59053)
Rates: $30-$40
(406) 572-3307

MCALLISTER

CROSSROADS MARKET & CABINS
5564 US 287 N,
Box 155 (59740)
Rates: $30-$40
(406) 682-7652

MEDICINE LAKE

CLUB HOTEL
202 W Main St
(59247)
Rates: $30-$40
(406) 789-2208

MELROSE

SPORTSMAN MOTEL
Frontage Rd, Box
86 (59743)
Rates: $40-$60
(406) 835-2141

MELSTONE

TERRI'S MOTEL
205 Main St
(59054)
Rates: $30-$40
(406) 358-2470

MILES CITY

BEST WESTERN WAR BONNET INN
1015 S Haynes
(59301)
Rates: $60-$92
(406) 232-4560
(800) 528-1234

BUDGET HOST CUSTER'S INN
1209 S Haynes
Ave (59301)
Rates: $39-$55
(406) 232-5170
(800) 456-5026
(800) 283-4678

DAYS INN
1006 S Haynes
Ave (59301)
Rates: $35-$60
(406) 232-3550
(800) 329-7466

MOTEL 6
1314 S Haynes
Ave (59301)
Rates: $28-$34
(406) 232-7040
(800) 466-8356

SAGEBRUSH MOTEL
308 N Custer
(59301)
Rates: $26-$37
(406) 232-1875

SUPER 8 MOTEL
RR 2, Hwy 59 S
(59301)
Rates: $35-$58
(406) 232-5261
(800) 800-8000

MISSOULA

ASPEN MOTEL
3720 Hwy 200 E
(59802)
Rates: $30-$40
(406) 721-9758

BEL AIRE MOTEL
300 E Broadway
(59802)
Rates: $30-$55
(406) 543-3183
(800) 543-3184

BEST INN NORTH
4953 N Reserve St
(59802)
Rates: $63-$71
(406) 542-7550
(800) 237-8466

BEST INN SOUTH
3803 Brooks St
(59801)
Rates: $63-$71
(406) 251-2665
(800) 237-8466

BEST WESTERN EXECUTIVE INN
201 E Main St
(59802)
Rates: $50-$70
(406) 543-7221
(800) 528-1234

BEST WESTERN GRANT CREEK INN
5280 Grant Creek
Rd (59801)
Rates: $89-$149
(406) 543-0700
(800) 528-1234
(888) 543-0700

BROOKS STREET MOTOR INN
3333 Brooks St
(59802)
Rates: $34-$65
(406) 549-5115
(800) 538-3260

BROWNIE'S PLUS MOTEL
1540 W Broadway
(59802)
Rates: $30-$40
(406) 543-6614
(800) 543-6614

CAMPUS INN
744 E Broadway
(59802)
Rates: $39-$59
(406) 549-5134
(800) 232-8013

COMFORT INN
4545 N Reserve St
(59802)
Rates: $74-$199
(406) 542-0888
(800) 228-5150

CREEKSIDE INN
630 E Broadway
(59802)
Rates: $45-$80
(406) 549-2387
(800) 551-2387

**DAYS INN/
WESTGATE**
8000 Truck Stop
Rd (59802)
Rates: $66-$79
(406) 721-9776
(800) 329-7466

**DOUBLETREE
HOTEL
EDGEWATER**
100 Madison
(59802)
Rates: $105-$135
(406) 728-3100
(800) 222-8733

**DOWNTOWN
MOTEL**
502 E Broadway
(59802)
Rates: $37-$45
(406) 549-5191
(800) 303-5191

HAMPTON INN
4805 N Reserve St
(59802)
Rates: $75-$89
(406) 549-1800
(800) 426-7866

**HOLIDAY INN-
MISSOULA
PARKSIDE**
200 S Pattee St
(59802)
Rates: $89
(406) 721-8550
(800) 465-4329

**HUBBARD'S
PONDEROSA
LODGE**
800 E Broadway
(59802)
Rates: $47-$60
(406) 543-3102

**THE INN ON
BROADWAY**
1609 W Broadway
(59802)
Rates: $31-$58
(406) 543-7231
(800) 286-2316

MOTEL 6
3035 Expo Pkwy
Commerce Ctr
(59802)
Rates: $37-$48
(406) 549-6665
(800) 466-8356

**ORANGE STREET
BUDGET MOTOR
INN**
801 N Orange St
(59802)
Rates: $43-$49
(406) 721-3610
(800) 328-0801

RED LION INN
700 W Broadway
(59802)
Rates: $125
(406) 728-3300
(800) 547-8010

**REDWOOD
LODGE**
8060 Hwy 93 N
(59802)
Rates: $54-$64
(406) 721-2110
(800) 874-9412

ROYAL MOTEL
338 Washington St
(59802)
Rates: $40-$48
(406) 542-2184
(888) 541-2006

**RUBY'S INN &
CONVENTION
CENTER**
4825 N Reserve St
(59802)
Rates: $69-$89
(406) 721-0990
(800) 221-2057

SLEEP INN
3425 Dore Ln
(59801)
Rates: $58-$90
(406) 543-5883
(800) 753-3746

SUPER 7 MOTEL
1135 W Broadway
(59802)
Rates: $29-$40
(406) 549-2358

SUPER 8 MOTEL
3901 Brooks St
(59801)
Rates: $51-$61
(406) 251-2255
(800) 800-8000

**THUNDER BIRD
MOTEL**
1000 E Broadway
(59802)
Rates: $60-$80
(406) 543-7251
(800) 952-2400
(MT)

**TRAVELERS INN
MOTEL**
4850 N Reserve St
(59802)
Rates: $55-$65
(406) 728-8330
(800) 862-3363

UPTOWN MOTEL
329 Woody
(59802)
Rates: $40-$60
(406) 549-5141
(800) 315-5141

MONARCH

CUB'S DEN MOTEL
5012 US 89 S
(59463)
Rates: $40-$60
(406) 236-5922

MONTANA CITY

**ELKHORN
MOUNTAIN INN**
1 Jackson Creek
Rd (59634)
Rates: $40-$60
(406) 442-6625

NEVADA CITY

**NEVADA CITY
HOTEL & CABINS**
US 287 W, Box 338
(59755)
Rates: $40-$60
(406) 843-5377
(800) 648-7588

NOXON

NOXON MOTEL
2 Klakken Rd
(59853)
Rates: $30-$40
(406) 847-2600

OVANDO

**LAKE UPSATA
GUEST RANCH**
135 Lake Upsala
Rd (59854)
Rates: $220-$440
(406) 793-5890
(800) 594-7687

PHILIPSBURG

**THE INN
AT PHILIPSBURG**
915 W Broadway
(59858)
Rates: $30-$40
(406) 859-3959

PLAINS

TOPS MOTEL
340 E Railroad
(59859)
Rates: $40-$60
(406) 826-3412

PLENTYWOOD

**GRANDVIEW
HOTEL**
120 S Main (59254)
Rates: $30-$40
(406) 765-2730

PLAINS MOTEL
626 W 1st Ave
(59254)
Rates: $27-$39
(406) 765-1240

SHERWOOD INN
515 W 1st Ave
(59254)
Rates: $40-$60
(406) 765-2810

POLARIS

**GRASSHOPPER
INN**
Box 460511
(59746)
Rates: $40-$60
(406) 834-3456

POLSON

DAYS INN
914 Hwy 93
(59860)
Rates: $70-$75
(406) 883-3120
(800) 329-7466

SUPER 8 MOTEL
P. O. Box 308
(59860)
Rates: $39-$67
(406) 883-6266
(800) 800-8000

SWAN HILL B&B
460 Kings Point
Rd (59860)
Rates: $75-$150
(406) 883-5292
(800) 537-9489

PRAY

**CHICO HOT
SPRINGS LODGE**
Drawer D, Old
Chico Road
(59645)
Rates: $36-$275
(406) 333-4933
(800) 468-9232

RED LODGE

**BECK'S ALPINE
MOTEL**
1005 N Broadway
(59068)
Rates: $40-$60
(406) 446-2213

**BEST WESTERN
LUPINE INN**
702 S Hauser
(59068)
Rates: $49-$99
(406) 446-1321
(800) 528-1234
(888) 567-1321

CHATEAU ROUGE
1505 S Broadway
(59068)
Rates: $60-$80
(406) 446-1601
(800) 926-1601

COMFORT INN
612 N Broadway
(59068)
Rates: $80-$150
(406) 446-4469
(800) 228-5150

EAGLE'S NEST MOTEL
702 S Broadway
(59068)
Rates: $30-$40
(406) 446-2312
(800) 746-2312

RED LODGE INN
811 S Broadway
(59068)
Rates: $60-$80
(406) 446-2030

SUPER 8 MOTEL
1223 S Broadway
(59068)
Rates: $65-$120
(406) 446-2288
(800) 800-8000
(80) 813-8335

YODELER MOTEL
601 S Broadway
(59068)
Rates: $48-$68
(406) 446-1435

RONAN

STARLITE MOTEL
18 Main St SW
(59864)
Rates: $52-$67
(406) 676-7000
(800) 823-4403

ROUNDUP

BIG SKY MOTEL
740 Main (59072)
Rates: $30-$40
(406) 323-2303

IDEAL MOTEL & RV PARK
926 Main (59072)
Rates: $25-$38
(406) 323-3371
(888) 323-3371

ST. IGNATIUS

STONEHEART INN B&B
26 N Main (59865)
Rates: $40-$60
(406) 745-4999

SUNSET MOTEL
32670 Hwy 93
(59865)
Rates: $54-$63
(406) 745-3900

ST. MARY
(Also see Glacier National Park)

RED EAGLE MOTEL
Star Rt, Box 896
(59417)
Rates: $40-$60
(406) 732-4453

ST. MARY LODGE
US 89 & Going-to-the-Sun Rd
(59417)
Rates: $60-$80
(406) 732-4431
(800) 368-3689

ST. REGIS

LITTLE RIVER MOTEL
50 Old Hwy 10
(59866)
Rates: $30-$40
(406) 649-2713

ST. REGIS CAMP MOTEL
Old Hwy 10
(59866)
Rates: $29-$40
(406) 649-2428

SUPER 8 MOTEL
9 Old Hwy 10 E
(59866)
Rates: $41-$56
(406) 649-2422
(800) 800-8000

SCOBEY

CATTLE KING MOTOR INN
Hwy 13 S (59263)
Rates: $40-$60
(406) 487-5332
(800) 562-2775

SEELEY LAKE

DUCK INN MOTEL
Hwy 83 at MM 15,
Box 458 (59868)
Rates: $40-$60
(406) 677-2335
(800) 237-9978

THE EMILY A B&B
SR 83 N, MM 20
(59868)
Rates: $115
(406) 677-3474

WILDERNESS GATEWAY INN
SR 835 (59868)
Rates: $53-$59
(406) 677-2095
(800) 355-5588

SHELBY

BEACON MOTEL
722 1st St N
(59474)
Rates: $40-$60
(406) 434-2721

COMFORT INN
50 Frontage Rd
(59474)
Rates: $69-$95
(406) 434-2212
(800) 220-5150

CROSSROADS INN
1200 Hwy 2
(59474)
Rates: $46-$63
(406) 434-5134
(800) 779-7666

GLACIER MOTEL
744 US 2 (59474)
Rates: $30-$40
(406) 434-5181
(800) 764-5181

O'HAIRE MANOR MOTEL
204 2nd St (59474)
Rates: $29-$44
(406) 434-5555
(800) 541-5809

TOTEM MOTEL
730 Oilfield Ave
(59474)
Rates: $30-$40
(406) 434-2930

SHERIDAN

MILL CREEK INN
102 Mill St (59749)
Rates: $40-$60
(406) 842-5422

MORIAH MOTEL
220 S Main (59749)
Rates: $40-$60
(406) 842-5491

SIDNEY

LONE TREE MOTOR INN
900 S Central
(59270)
Rates: $40-$60
(406) 482-4520

PARK PLAZA MOTEL
601 S Central
(59270)
Rates: $30-$39
(406) 482-1520

RICHLAND MOTOR INN
1200 S Central
(59270)
Rates: $49-$54
(406) 482-6400

SILVER GATE

GRIZZLY LODGE
Hwy 212 (59081)
Rates: $40-$60
(406) 838-2219

PINE EDGE CABINS
Box 45 (59081)
Rates: n/a
(406) 838-2222

STANFORD

SUNDOWN MOTEL
Hwy 200 W, Box 126 (59479)
Rates: $30-$40
(406) 566-2316
(800) 346-2316

STEVENSVILLE

ST. MARY'S MOTEL & RV PARK
3889 US 93 N
(59870)
Rates: $40-$60
(406) 777-2838
(800) 624-7015

SUPERIOR

BELLEVUE HOTEL/MOTEL
110 Mullan Rd E
(59872)
Rates: $30-$40
(406) 822-4692

BUDGET HOST BIG SKY MOTEL
103 4th Ave E
(59872)
Rates: $44-$58
(406) 822-4831
(800) 283-4678

LAKE TOWNSEND MOTEL
413 N Pine (59644)
Rates: $35-$45
(406) 266-3461
(800) 856-3461

SWAN LAKE

ALPINE CHALET RESTAURANT & MOTEL
71284 Hwy 83
(59911)
Rates: $40-$60
(406) 886-2226

TERRY

DIAMOND MOTEL
118 E Spring
(59349)
Rates: $27-$38
(406) 635-5407
(800) 548-6407

KEMPTON HOTEL
204 Spring (59349)
Rates: $28-$35
(406) 635-5543

THOMPSON FALLS

FALLS MOTEL
112 S Gallatin
(59873)
Rates: $40-$60
(406) 827-3559
(800) 521-2184

RIMROCK LODGE
4946 Hwy 200
(59873)
Rates: $40-$60
(406) 827-3536
(888) 418-2701

THE RIVERFRONT MOTEL
4907 Scenic SR 200 W (59873)
Rates: $49-$89
(406) 827-3460

AREA CODES - If the local number doesn't connect, check for a new area code.

THREE FORKS

BROKEN SPUR MOTEL
124 W Elm (59752)
Rates: $44-$60
(406) 285-3237
(888) 354-3048

FORT THREE FORKS MOTEL
10776 Hwy 287 (59752)
Rates: $36-$72
(406) 285-3233
(800) 477-5690

PERREN PARK HOTEL
114 Main St (59752)
Rates: $26-$38
(406) 285-3457

SACAJAWEA HISTORIC COUNTRY INN
5 N Main St (59752)
Rates: $49-$99
(406) 285-6515
(800) 821-7326

TOWNSEND

BEDFORD INN BED & BREAKFAST
7408 US 287 (59644)
Rates: $40-$60
(406) 266-3629

LAKE TOWNSEND MOTEL
413 N Pine (59644)
Rates: $30-$40
(406) 266-3461
(800) 856-3461

MUSTANG MOTEL
412 North Front St (59644)
Rates: $39-$40
(406) 266-3491
(800) 349-3499

TROUT CREEK

TROUT CREEK MOTEL
2972 Hwy 200 (59874)
Rates: $40-$60
(406) 827-3268

TWIN BRIDGES

KING'S MOTEL
307 S Main (59754)
Rates: $30-$40
(406) 684-5639
(800) 222-5510

VALIER

LAKE FRANCES INN
412 Teton (59486)
Rates: $35-$45
(406) 279-3476
(800) 551-8332

VIRGINIA CITY

DAYLIGHT CREEK MOTEL
Box 62 (59755)
Rates: $40-$60
(406) 843-5377
(800) 648-7588

WEST YELLOWSTONE

BEST WESTERN CROSSWINDS INN
201 Firehole Ave (59758)
Rates: $75-$120
(406) 646-9557
(800) 528-1234

BEST WESTERN DESERT INN
133 Canyon Ave (59758)
Rates: $75-$139
(406) 646-7376
(800) 528-1234

BEST WESTERN EXECUTIVE INN
236 Dunraven (59758)
Rates: $50-$150
(406) 646-7681
(800) 528-1234

BEST WESTERN WESTON INN
103 Gibbon St (59758)
Rates: $35-$110
(406) 646-7373
(800) 528-1234

CIRCLE R MOTEL
321 Madison (59758)
Rates: $26-$85
(406) 646-7641

CROW'S NEST MOTEL
608 Hwy 20 (59758)
Rates: $40-$60
(406) 646-7873

EVERGREEN MOTEL
229 Firehole Ave (59758)
Rates: $29-$89
(406) 646-7655
(800) 488-2750

GRAY WOLF INN & SUITES
250 S Canyon St (59748)
Rates: $44-$129
(406) 646-0000
(800) 852-8602

HADLEY'S MOTEL
29 Gibbon Ave (59748)
Rates: $40-$60
(406) 646-9534

HIBERNATION STATION
212 Gray Wolf Ave (59748)
Rates: $80+
(406) 646-4200
(800) 580-3557

HO HUM MOTEL
126 Canyon Ave (59748)
Rates: $30-$40
(406) 646-7746

KELLY INN
104 S Canyon Ave (59748)
Rates: $79-$139
(406) 646-4544
(800) 259-4672

KIRKWOOD RANCH MOTEL
11505 Hebgen Lake Rd (59748)
Rates: $60-$80
(406) 646-7200

LAKE VIEW CABINS
15570 Hebgen Lake Rd (59748)
Rates: $40-$60
(406) 646-7257

PINE SHADOWS MOTEL
Hayden & US 20 (59748)
Rates: $40-$60
(406) 646-7541
(800) 624-5291

PIONEER MOTEL
515 Madison (59748)
Rates: $60-$80
(406) 646-9705

PONY EXPRESS MOTEL
4 Firehole Ave (59748)
Rates: $40-$60
(406) 646-7644
(800) 323-9708

RAMADA LIMITED
235 Canyon St (59758)
Rates: $53-$105
(800) 272-6232

SLEEPY HOLLOW LODGE
124 Electric (59748)
Rates: $60-$80
(406) 646-7707

THREE BEAR MOTOR LODGE
217 Yellowstone Ave (59758)
Rates: $70-$88
(406) 646-7353
(800) 646-7353

TRAVELERS LODGE
225 Yellowstone Ave (59758)
Rates: $70-$90
(406) 646-9561
(800) 831-5741

WEARY REST MOTEL
601 US 20 (59748)
Rates: $60-$80
(406) 646-7633
(800) 858-9224

WHISPERING PINES
321 Canyon Ave (59748)
Rates: $30-$40
(406) 646-9317

YELLOWSTONE INN
601 Hwy 20 (59748)
Rates: $80+
(406) 646-7633
(800) 858-9224

YELLOWSTONE LODGE
251 Electric St (59748)
Rates: $99-$149
(406) 646-0020

WHITE SULPHUR SPRINGS

GORDON'S HIGHLAND MOTEL
410 E Main (59645)
Rates: $30-$40
(406) 547-3880

SUPER 8 MOTEL
808 3rd Ave SW (59645)
Rates: $48-$68
(406) 547-8888
(800) 800-8000
(877) 314-0241

TENDERFOOT/ HILAND MOTEL
301 W Main (59645)
Rates: $30-$40
(406) 547-3303
(800) 898-3303

WHITEFISH

ALLEN'S MOTEL
6540 US 93 S (59937)
Rates: $40-$60
(406) 862-3995

ALPINGLOW INN
3900 Big Mountain Rd (59937)
Rates: $75-$122
(406) 862-6966

BEST WESTERN ROCKY MOUNTAIN
6510 US 93 S (59937)
Rates: $119-$179
(406) 862-2569
(800) 528-1234
(800) 862-2569

AREA CODES - If the local number doesn't connect, check for a new area code.

CHALET MOTEL
6430 US 93 S
(59937)
Rates: $37-$84
(406) 862-5581
(800) 462-3266

**CRENSHAW
HOUSE B&B**
5465 Hwy 93 S
(59937)
Rates: $65-$145
(406) 862-3496
(800) 453-2863

**DOWNTOWNER
MOTEL &
ATHLETIC CLUB**
224 Spokane Ave
(59937)
Rates: $40-$60
(406) 862-2535

**EAGLE'S ROOST
BED & BREAKFAST**
400 Wisconsin Ave
(59937)
Rates: $65-$100
(406) 862-5198
(888) 750-6378

**LAZY BEAR
LODGE**
6390 US 93S
(59937)
Rates: $80+
(406) 862-4020
(800) 888-4479

**MOUNTAIN
HOLIDAY MOTEL**
6595 US 93 S
(59937)
Rates: $40-$55
(406) 862-2548
(800) 543-8064

**NORSKMAN
MOTEL**
6400 US 93 S
(59937)
Rates: $40-$60
(406) 862-5515
(800) 862-3711

**QUALITY INN
PINE LODGE**
920 Spokane Ave
(59937)
Rates: $60-$220
(406) 862-7600
(800) 228-5151
(800) 305-7463

SUPER 8 MOTEL
800 Spokane Ave
(59937)
Rates: $78-$83
(406) 862-8255
(800) 800-8000

**WHITEFISH
MOTEL**
620 8th St (59937)
Rates: $40-$60
(406) 862-3507

WHITEHALL

CHIEF MOTEL
303 E Legion
(59759)
Rates: $40-$60
(406) 287-3921

RICE MOTEL
7 N "A" St (59759)
Rates: $30-$40
(406) 287-3895

SUPER 8 MOTEL
515 N Whitehall
St (59759)
Rates: $36-$52
(406) 287-5588
(800) 800-8000

WIBAUX

SUPER 8 MOTEL
400 W 2nd Ave N
(59353)
Rates: $36-$52
(406) 796-2666
(800) 800-8000

WISDOM

**NEZ PIERCE
MOTEL**
Hwy 43, Box 123
(59761)
Rates: $30-$40
(406) 689-3254

SANDMAN MOTEL
Old Hwy 278
(59761)
Rates: $30-$40
(406) 689-3218

WOLF CREEK

**MONTANA RIVER
OUTFITTERS
MOTEL/CABINS**
515 Recreation Rd
(59648)
Rates: $40-$60
(406) 235-4350
(800) 800-4350

WOLF POINT

BIG SKY MOTEL
Hwy 2 E (59201)
Rates: $30-$40
(406) 653-2300

**HOMESTEAD INN
MOTEL**
101 US 2 E (59201)
Rates: $25-$37
(406) 653-1300
(800) 231-0986

**SHERMAN
MOTOR INN**
200 E Main St
(59201)
Rates: $26-$35
(406) 653-1100
(800) 952-1100

YELLOWSTONE
NATIONAL
PARK, WY

The following
accommodations
are located near
the park
entrances:

**CANYON VILLAGE
LODGE & CABINS**
Box 165 (82190)
Rates: $60-$80
(307) 344-7311

**LAKE LODGE &
CABINS**
Box 165 (82190)
Rates: $60-$80
(307) 344-7311

**LAKE YELLOW-
STONE HOTEL &
CABINS**
Box 165 (82190)
Rates: $80+
(307) 344-7311

**MAMMOTH HOT
SPRINGS & HOTEL**
Box 165 (82190)
Rates: $60-$80
(307) 344-7311

**OLD FAITHFUL
LODGE & CABINS**
Box 165 (82190)
Rates: $40-$80
(307) 344-7311

**OLD FAITHFUL
SNOW LODGE**
Box 165 (82190)
Rates: $51-$100
(307) 344-7311

**ROOSEVELT
LODGE**
Box 165 (82190)
Rates: $26-$35
(307) 344-7311

ZORTMAN

**BUCKHORN
STORE, CABINS &
RV PARK**
1st & Main Sts,
Box 501 (59546)
Rates: $30-$40
(406) 673-3162

ZORTMAN MOTEL
302 Main St
(59546)
Rates: $30-$40
(406) 673-3160
(800) 517-0372

AREA CODES - If the local number doesn't connect, check for a new area code.

NEBRASKA

AINSWORTH

**AINSWORTH INN
BED & BRKFAST**
400 N Main (69210)
Rates: $35-$55
(402) 387-0540
(888) 237-0954

LAZY A MOTEL
1120 East 4th St
(69210)
Rates: $35+
(402) 387-2600

**REMINGTON
ARMS MOTEL**
1000 E 4th (69210)
Rates: $35-$55
(402) 387-2220
(800) 248-3971

**SKINNER'S
MOTOR COURT**
HC 65 (69210)
Rates: $30-$55
(402) 387-2021

**THE UPPER ROOM
BED & BRKFAST**
409 N Wilson
(69210)
Rates: $35-$75
(402) 387-0107

ALLIANCE

HOLIDAY INN EXP
1420 W 3rd St
(69301)
Rates: $39-$59
(308) 762-7600
(800) 465-4329

**MCCARROLL'S
MOTEL-IMA**
1028 E 3rd St
(69301)
Rates: $35-$55
(308) 762-3680
(800) 341-8000

SUNSET MOTEL
1210 E Hwy 2
(69301)
Rates: $45-$60
(308) 762-8660
(800) 767-8660

SUPER 8 MOTEL
1419 W 3rd St
(69301)
Rates: $41-$58
(308) 762-8300
(800) 800-8000

WEST WAY MOTEL
1207 W Hwy 2 &
385 (69301)
Rates: $38-$67
(308) 762-4040
(800) 722-4041

ALMA

**SUPER OUTPOST
MOTEL**
N Hwy 183 & 136
(68920)
Rates: $35+
(308) 928-2116

**WESTERN
HOLIDAY MOTEL**
Rt 1, Box 25-A1
(68920)
Rates: $25-$55
(308) 928-2155
(800) 258-8124

ARAPAHOE

**ARAPAHOE
MOTEL**
W Hwys 6 & 34
(68922)
Rates: $35+
(308) 962-7948

**SHADY REST
CAMP MOTEL**
309 Chestnut
(68922)
Rates: $35-$55
(308) 962-5461

AUBURN

AUBURN INN
517 J St (68305)
Rates: $30-$49
(402) 274-3143
(800) 272-3143

PALMER HOUSE
MOTEL
1918 J St (68305)
Rates: $35-$55
(402) 274-3193
(800) 272-3193

AURORA

**BUDGET HOST
KEN'S MOTEL**
1515 11th St
(68818)
Rates: $26-$34
(402) 694-3141
(800) 283-4678

**HAMILTON
MOTOR INN**
907 S Hwy 14
(68818)
Rates: $35-$65
(402) 694-6961

BASSETT

**RANCHLAND
MOTEL**
HC 75, Box 74
(68714)
Rates: $25-$55
(402) 684-3340

BEATRICE

BEATRICE INN
3500 N 6th St
(68310)
Rates: $35-$48
(402) 223-4074
(800) 232-8742

**HOLIDAY VILLA
MOTEL**
1820 N 6th St
(68310)
Rates: $35-$55
(402) 223-4036

BEAVER CITY

**FURNAS COUNTY
INN**
Rt 1, Box 86E
(68926)
Rates: $25-$55
(308) 268-7705

BELLEVUE

**AMERICAN
FAMILY INN**
1110 Fort Crook
Rd S (68005)
Rates: $40-$58
(402) 291-0804
(800) 253-2865

**OFFUTT
MOTOR COURT**
3618 Fort Crook
Rd (68005)
Rates: $35+
(402) 291-4333

BIG SPRINGS

**BUDGET 8
PANHANDLE INN**
P. O. Box 157
(69122)
Rates: $26-$50
(308) 889-3671

BLAIR

**BLAIR HOUSE
MOTEL**
W Hwy 30 (68008)
Rates: $35-$55
(402) 426-4801
(800) 793-9240

RATH INN
RR 1, Box 268E
(68008)
Rates: $27-$49
(402) 426-8703

BLOOMFIELD

**FOUR SEASONS
MOTEL**
Rt 3, Box 239
(68718)
Rates: $30-$55
(402) 373-2441
(800) 763-1261

BREWSTER

**UNCLE BUCK'S
LODGE**
P. O. Box 100
(68821)
Rates: $35-$55
(308) 547-2210
(800) 239-9190

BRIDGEPORT

BELL MOTOR INN
P. O. Box 854
(69336)
Rates: $29-$38
(308) 262-0557

BRIDGEPORT INN
P. O. Box 1106
(69336)
Rates: $35-$55
(308) 262-0290

**GOLDEN ACRES
MOTEL & RV
PARK**
Rt 1, Box 196
(69336)
Rates: $25-$55
(308) 262-0410

BROKEN BOW

**WAGON WHEEL
MOTEL &
CAMPGROUND**
1545 South E St
(68822)
Rates: $26-$35
(308) 872-2433
(800) 770-2433

WM PENN LODGE
853 South E St
(68822)
Rates: $24-$40
(308) 872-2412

BURWELL

**CALAMUS
COUNTRY MOTEL**
HC 79, Box 18A
(68823)
Rates: $35
(308) 346-4729

**CALAMUS RIVER
LODGE**
P.O. Box 305
(68879)
Rates: $25-$35
(308) 346-4331

RODEO INN
Hwys 91 & 11
(68823)
Rates: $35-$55
(308) 346-4408
(800) 926-9427

CALLAWAY

CHESLEY'S LODGE
Rt 1, Box 76
(68825)
Rates: $30-$55
(308) 836-2658

**TRAVELERS INN
CALLAWAY
HOUSE**
P. O. Box 189
(68825)
Rates: $35-$70
(308) 836-4414

CAMBRIDGE

**BUNKHOUSE
MOTEL**
E Hwy 6 & 34
(69022)
Rates: $35-$55
(308) 697-4540

**MEDICINE CREEK
LODGE**
Rt 2, Box 93
(69022)
Rates: $35
(308) 697-3774

CENTRAL CITY

**CRAWFORD
MOTEL**
RR 1, Box 270
(68826)
Rates: $18-$25
(308) 946-3051

CREST MOTEL
E Hwy 30 (68826)
Rates: $35
(308) 946-3077
(888) 879-9201

CHADRON

**BEST WESTERN
WEST HILLS INN**
1100 W 10th St
(69337)
Rates: $44-$125
(308) 432-3305
(800) 528-1234

BLAINE MOTEL
159 Bordeaux St
(69337)
Rates: $35-$55
(308) 432-5568

**ECONOMY 9
MOTEL**
1201 W Hwy 20
(69337)
Rates: 35-$65
(308) 432-3119

**THE OLDE MAIN
STREET INN B&B**
115 Main St
(69337)
Rates: $35-$60
(308) 432-3380

**ROUND UP
MOTEL**
901 E 3rd St
(69337)
Rates: $26-$34
(308) 432-5591

**WESTERNER
MOTEL**
300 Oak St (69337)
Rates: $23-$42
(308) 432-5577
(800) 341-8000

CHAPPELL

**EL RANCHO
MOTEL &
CAMPGROUND**
P. O. Box 592
(69129)
Rates: $25-$35
(308) 874-3264

CHESTER

**CHESTER
COUNTRY INN
MOTEL**
Box 3-C (68327)
Rates: $25-$33
(402) 324-8494

CODY

**CODY'S COUNTRY
COTTAGE**
Box 217 (69211)
Rates: $28-$52
(402) 823-4182

COLUMBUS

DAYS INN
371 33rd Ave
(68601)
Rates: $35-$55
(402) 564-2527
(800) 329-7466

GEMBOL'S MOTEL
3220 8th St (68601)
Rates: $35-$55
(402) 564-2729
(800) 288-3658

NEW WORLD INN
265 33rd Ave
(68601)
Rates: $43-$61
(402) 564-1492
(800) 433-1492

ROSEBUD MOTEL
154 Lakeshore Dr
(68601)
Rates: $26-$34
(402) 564-3256

**SEVEN KNIGHTS
MOTEL**
2222 23rd St
(68601)
Rates: $26-$41
(402) 563-3533
(800) 533-8365

COZAD

**BUDGET HOST
CIRCLE S MOTEL**
440 S Meridian
(69130)
Rates: $26-$34
(308) 784-2290
(800) 283-4678

MOTEL 6
809 S Meridian
(69130)
Rates: $34-$40
(308) 784-4900
(800) 466-8356

CRAWFORD

BUTTE RANCH
803 W Ashcreek
Rd (69339)
Rates: $55
(308) 665-2364

HILLTOP MOTEL
304 McPherson St
(69339)
Rates: $55
(308) 665-1144
(800) 504-1444

**TOWN LINE
MOTEL**
Hwys 2 & 20
(69339)
Rates: $35-$55
(308) 665-1450
(800) 903-1450

CREIGHTON

**THE BLACK
HORSE INN**
408 Rice St (68729)
Rates: $36-$54
(402) 358-3587

CROFTON

BOGNER'S MOTEL
Hwys 12 & 121
(68730)
Rates: $35
(402) 388-4626

DAVID CITY

FIESTA MOTEL
N Hwy 15 (68632)
Rates: $35
(402) 367-3129

DIXON

**THE GEORGES
BED & BREAKFAST**
57759 874 Rd
(68732)
Rates: $30-$55
(402) 584-2625

DONIPHAN

USA INNS
Rt 2, Box 190 E
(68832)
Rates: $33-$60
(308) 381-0111

ELM CREEK

**1ST INTERSTATE
INN**
I-80 & Hwy 183
(68836)
Rates: $30-$40
(308) 856-4652

ELWOOD

J. J.'S MARINA
4 Lakeview Acres
Dr 14 (68937)
Rates: $55+
(308) 785-2836

**THOMPSON'S
RESORT**
20 Bullhead
Expwy, Dr 28
(68937)
Rates: $35-$55
(308) 785-2298

ERICSON

WATSON CABINS
P. O. Box 82
(68637)
Rates: $25-$35
(308) 653-3106

FALLS CITY

CHECK IN MOTEL
1901 Fulton St
(68355)
Rates: $35
(402) 245-2433

**STEPHENSON
MOTEL**
2621 Harlan St
(68355)
Rates: $35-$55
(402) 245-2459

FREMONT

COMFORT INN
1649 E 23rd St
(68025)
Rates: $49-$80
(402) 721-1109
(800) 228-5150

HOLIDAY LODGE
1220 E 23rd St
(68025)
Rates: $42-$63
(402) 727-1110
(800) 743-7666

SUPER 8 MOTEL
1250 E 23rd St
(68025)
Rates: $39-$63
(402) 727-4445
(800) 800-8000

FUNK

**UNCLE SAM'S
HILLTOP LODGE**
Rt 1, Box 110
(68940)
Rates: $35-$55
(308) 995-2204

GENOA

REDWOOD MOTEL
336 N Elm St
(68640)
Rates: $25-$55
(402) 993-2817

GERING

CAVALIER MOTEL
3655 N 10th St
(69341)
Rates: $25-$55
(308) 635-3176

CIRCLE S LODGE
400 M St (69341)
Rates: $35-$55
(308) 436-2157

MICROTEL INN & SUITES
1130 M St (69341)
Rates: $42-$65
(308) 436-1950
(888) 771-7171

GIBBON

COUNTRY INN & ANTIQUES
2432 Lowell Rd
(68840)
Rates: $26-$54
(308) 468-5256
(800) 887-6324

GORDON

HACIENDA MOTEL
Rt 1, Box 85
(69343)
Rates: $26-$34
(308) 282-1400

HILLS MOTEL
107 West Hwy 20
(69343)
Rates: $35+
(308) 282-1795

MEADOW VIEW RANCH B&B
HC 91 (69343)
Rates: $40-$55
(308) 282-0679
(800) 484-5753

GOTHENBURG

TRAVEL INN
501 S Lake (69138)
Rates: $35-$55
(308) 537-3638

WESTERN MOTOR INN
1102 21st St
(69138)
Rates: $35-$55
(308) 537-3622

GRAND ISLAND

BEST WESTERN RIVERSIDE INN
3333 Ramada Rd
(68801)
Rates: $50-$65
(308) 384-5150
(800) 528-1234

BUDGET HOST ISLAND INN
2311 S Locust St
(68801)
Rates: $28-$40
(308) 382-1815
(800) 283-4678

CONOCO MOTEL
2107 W 2nd St
(68803)
Rates: $32-$36
(308) 384-2700

HOLIDAY INN I-80
7838 S US Hwy 281 (68802)
Rates: $49-$67
(308) 384-7770
(800) 465-4329

LAZY V MOTEL-IMA
2703 E Hwy 30
(68801)
Rates: $24-$30
(308) 384-0700
(800) 341-8000

MOTEL 6
3021 S Locust St
(68801)
Rates: $27-$31
(308) 384-4100
(800) 466-8356

OAK GROVE INN
3205 S Locust St
(68801)
Rates: $28-$37
(308) 384-1333
(800) 435-7144

RELAX INN
507 W 2nd St
(68801)
Rates: $27-$50
(308) 483-1000

SUPER 8 MOTEL
2603 S Locust St
(68801)
Rates: $43-$55
(308) 384-4380
(800) 800-8000

TRAVELODGE
1311 S Locust
(68801)
Rates: $38-$43
(308) 382-5003
(800) 578-7878

VALENTINE MOTEL
3518 S Locust St
(68801)
Rates: $29-$35
(308) 384-1740

GRANT

GRANT MOTEL & RV PARK
P. O. Box 400
(69140)
Rates: $25-$34
(308) 352-4844

GREENWOOD

DAYS INN
13006 238th St
(68366)
Rates: $35-$68
(402) 944-3313
(800) 329-7466

HARTINGTON

HILLCREST MOTEL
403 Robinson Ave
(68739)
Rates: $27-$54
(402) 254-6850

HASTINGS

HOLIDAY INN
2205 Osborne Dr E (68901)
Rates: $59-$76
(402) 463-6721
(800) 465-4329

MIDLANDS LODGE
910 West J St
(68901)
Rates: $29-$47
(402) 463-2428
(800) 237-1872

RAINBOW MOTEL
1000 West J St
(68901)
Rates: $29-$40
(402) 463-2989
(800) 825-7424

SUPER 8 MOTEL
2200 N Kansas Ave (68901)
Rates: $41-$52
(402) 463-8888
(800) 800-8000

WAYFAIR MOTEL
101 East J St
(68901)
Rates: $35-$55
(402) 463-2434

HAYES CENTER

MIDWAY MOTEL
Hwy 25 (69032)
Rates: $35
(308) 286-3227

HEBRON

ROSEWOOD VILLA MOTEL
140 S 13th St
(68370)
Rates: $24-$33
(402) 768-6524

WAYFARER MOTEL
104 N 13th St
(68370)
Rates: $35
(402) 768-7226

HENDERSON

WAYFARER II MOTOR INN
Jct I-80 & S-93A
(68371)
Rates: $28-$32
(402) 723-5856
(800) 543-0577

HOLDREGE

THE CROW'S NEST B&B INN
503 Grant (68949)
Rates: $44-$55
(308) 995-5440

PLAINS MOTEL-IMA

619 W Hwy 6
(68949)
Rates: $32-$46
(308) 995-8646
(800) 341-8000

SUPER 8 MOTEL
5th & Broadway
(68949)
Rates: $42-$60
(800) 800-8000

HOWELLS

BERAN B&B
1604 Road 16
(68641)
Rates: $39-$55
(402) 986-1358

KEARNEY

BEST WESTERN TEL-STAR INN
1010 3rd Ave
(68848)
Rates: $51-$79
(308) 237-5185
(800) 528-1234

BUDGET MOTEL SOUTH
411 S 2nd Ave
(68847)
Rates: $35-$65
(308) 237-5991

BUDGET MOTEL WEST & CAMP-GROUND
1910 W 24th St
(68847)
Rates: $26-$48
(308) 237-5131

PIONEER MOTEL
917 E 25thSt
(68847)
Rates: $28-$52
(308) 237-3168
(800) 359-6301

QUALITY INN
80 S 2nd Ave
(68847)
Rates: $39-$64
(308) 234-2541
(800) 228-5151

REGENCY INN
301 2nd Ave
(68848)
Rates: $61-$69
(308) 237-3141

AREA CODES - If the local number doesn't connect, check for a new area code.

SUPER 8 MOTEL
15 W 8th St
(68847)
Rates: $44-$64
(308) 234-5513
(800) 800-8000

WESTERN INN SOUTH
510 3rd Ave
(68847)
Rates: $37-$46
(308) 234-1876
(800) 437-8457

KIMBALL

ARABIAN MOTEL
607 E 3rd St
(69145)
Rates: $28-$65
(308) 235-3995

BEST WESTERN HOLIDAY MOTOR LODGE
611 E 3rd St
(69145)
Rates: $34-$64
(308) 235-4671
(800) 528-1234

FINER MOTEL
Rt 1, Box 126
(69145)
Rates: $35-$55
(308) 235-4878

MOTEL KIMBALL
Rt 1, Box 131
(69145)
Rates: $35-$55
(308) 235-4606

SLUMBER J MOTEL
Rt 1, Box 126
(69145)
Rates: $27-$34
(308) 235-4878

SUPER 8 MOTEL
I-80 & 71 (69145)
Rates: $40-$52
(308) 235-4888
(800) 800-8000

WESTERN MOTEL
914 W Hwy 30
(69145)
Rates: $55+
(308) 235-4622

LAUREL

BIG RED MOTEL
202 S Hwy 20
(68745)
Rates: $35-$55
(402) 256-9952

LEMOYNE

ADMIRAL'S COVE RESORT
999 Lemoyne Rd
(69146)
Rates: $40-$55
(308) 355-2102
(800) 928-3386

NORTH SHORE LODGE
P. O. Box 237
(69146)
Rates: $42-$70
(308) 335-2222

LEWELLEN

GANDER INN MOTEL
S Main St (69147)
Rates: $35
(308) 778-5616

J'S OTTER CREEK RESORT
1290 Hwy 92 W
(69147)
Rates: $35-$50
(308) 355-5000

LEXINGTON

BUDGET HOST MINUTE MAN MOTEL
801 S Bridge St
(68850)
Rates: $32-$42
(308) 324-5540
(800) 283-4678

DAYS INN
Hwy 285 &
Commerce Rd
(68850)
Rates: $40-$85
(308) 324-6440
(800) 329-7466

ECONO LODGE
I-80 at US 283
(68850)
Rates: $32-$49
(308) 324-5601
(800) 553-2666

GABLE VIEW INN-IMA
2701 Plum Creek
Pkwy (68850)
Rates: $26-$49
(308) 324-5595
(800) 341-8000

TODDLE INN MOTEL
2701 Plum Creek
Pkwy (68850)
Rates: $29-$49
(308) 324-5595
(800) 341-8000

LINCOLN

BEST WESTERN AIRPORT INN
3200 NW 12th St
(68521)
Rates: $47-$67
(402) 475-9541
(800) 528-1234

COMFORT INN AIRPORT
2940 NW 12th St
(68521)
Rates: $44-$99
(402) 464-2200
(800) 228-5150

COMFORT SUITES
4231 Industrial
Ave (68504)
Rates: $60-$100
(402) 476-8080
(800) 228-5150

CONGRESS INN
2001 West O St
(68528)
Rates: $32-$59
(402) 477-4488
(800) 447-2393

ECONO LODGE
2410 NW 12th St
(68521)
Rates: $34-$59
(402) 474-1311
(800) 553-2666

GUESTHOUSE INN
3245 Cornhusker
Hwy (68504)
Rates: $35-$55
(402) 466-2341

HOLIDAY INN AIRPORT
1010 W Bond St
(68521)
Rates: $54-$90
(402) 474-1417
(800) 465-4329

INN 4 LESS
1140 W
Cornhusker Hwy
(68521)
Rates: $35
(402) 475-4511

MICROTEL INN & SUITES
2505 Fairfield
(68521)
Rates: $40-$56
(402) 476-2591
(888) 569-5070

MOTEL 6
3001 NW 12th St
(68521)
Rates: $33-$41
(402) 475-3211
(800) 466-8356

OAK PARK MOTEL
926 Oak St (68521)
Rates: $26-$45
(402) 435-3258

QUALITY INN
5250 Cornhusker
Hwy (68507)
Rates: $49-$79
(402) 464-3171
(800) 228-5151

QUALITY INN AIRPORT
1101 W Bond
Circle (68521)
Rates: $44-$99
(402) 475-4971
(800) 228-5151

RESIDENCE INN BY MARRIOTT
200 S 68th Pl
(68510)
Rates: $93-$143
(402) 483-4900
(800) 331-3131

SLEEP INN
3400 NW 12th St
(68521)
Rates: $44-$80
(402) 475-1550
(800) 753-3746

STOP 'N' SLEEP
1140 Calvert St
(68502)
Rates: $42-$56
(402) 423-7111

TOWN HOUSE MINI-SUITES
1744 M St (68508)
Rates: $44-$60
(402) 475-3000
(800) 279-1744

VILLAGER MOTOR INN
5200 O St (68510)
Rates: $69-$84
(402) 464-9111
(800) 356-4321

LODGEPOLE

LODGEPOLE MOTEL
P. O. Box 114
(69149)
Rates: $25-$35
(308) 483-5890

LONG PINE

THE PINES
P. O. Box 343
(69217)
Rates: $26-$49
(402) 273-4483

LOUP CITY

COLONY INN
Rt 1, Box 184
(68853)
Rates: $35
(308) 745-0164

MCCOOK

BW CHIEF MOTEL
612 West B St
(69001)
Rates: $47-$59
(308) 345-3700
(800) 528-1234

CEDAR INN 4 LESS
1300 East C St
(69001)
Rates: $35-$55
(308) 345-7091
(800) 352-4489

HOLIDAY INN EXP
1 Holiday Bison
Dr (69001)
Rates: $40-$67
(308) 345-4505
(800) 465-4329

SUPER 8 MOTEL
1103 East B St
(69001)
Rates: $37-$53
(308) 345-1141
(800) 800-8000

MILFORD

MILFORD INN
962 238th St
(68405)
Rates: $26-$34
(402) 761-2151

MINATARE

HARRY'S MOTEL
Box 729 (69356)
Rates: $29-$45
(308) 783-1222

MINDEN

**PIONEER VILLAGE
MOTEL**
224 E Hwy 6
(68959)
Rates: $30-$55
(308) 832-1181
(800) 445-4447

MULLEN

**GLIDDEN
SANDHILLS
MOTEL**
P. O. Box 368
(69152)
Rates: $28-$35
(308) 546-2206

MURDOCK

FARM HOUSE B&B
32617 Church Rd
(68407)
Rates: $30-$55
(402) 867-2062

**NEBRASKA
CITY**

APPLE INN
502 S 11th (68410)
Rates: $38-$48
(402) 873-5959
(800) 659-4446

NELIGH

DELUXE MOTEL
101 J St (68756)
Rates: $35-$55
(402) 887-4628

**WEST HILLVIEW
MOTEL**
RR 2, Box 43
(68756)
Rates: $35-$50
(402) 887-4186

**NEWMAN
GROVE**

**CRYSTAL KEY INN
BED & BRKFAST**
P. O. Box 369
(68758)
Rates: $35-$75
(402) 447-2772

NIOBRARA

**TWO RIVERS
SALOON &
HOTEL**
254 - 12 Park Ave
(68760)
Rates: $35-$55
(402) 857-3340

NORFOLK

**BLUE RIDGE
MOTEL**
916 S 13th St (68701)
Rates: $35
(402) 371-0530

RAMADA INN
1227 Omaha Ave
(68701)
Rates: $51-$68
(402) 371-7000
(800) 272-6232

NORTH PLATTE

**BEST WESTERN
CHALET LODGE**
920 N Jeffers St
(69101)
Rates: $38-$60
(308) 532-2313
(800) 528-1234

**BEST WESTERN
CIRCLE C SOUTH
INN**
1211 S Dewey St
(69101)
Rates: $45-$73
(308) 532-0130
(800) 528-1234

**BLUE SPRUCE
MOTEL**
821 S Dewey
(69101)
Rates: $35-$55
(308) 534-2600

**CAMINO INN &
SUITES**
2102 S Jeffers
(69101)
Rates: $50-$66
(308) 532-9090
(800) 760-3333

**CEDAR LODGE
MOTEL**
421 Rodeo Rd
(69101)
Rates: $26-$45
(308) 532-9710

COUNTRY INN
321 S Dewey
(69101)
Rates: $27-$32
(308) 532-8130
(800) 532-8130

HOLIDAY INN EXP
300 Holiday
Frontage Dr
(69103)
Rates: $57-$79
(308) 532-9500
(800) 465-4329

HUSKER INN
721 E 4th St
(69101)
Rates: $25-$35
(308) 534-6960

MOTEL 6
1520 S Jeffers
(69101)
Rates: $32-$46
(308) 534-6200
(800) 466-8356

PARK MOTEL
1302 N
Jeffers(69101)
Rates: $26-$37
(308) 532-6834

PIONEER MOTEL
902 S Dewey
(69101)
Rates: $35-$55
(308) 532-8730

**QUALITY INN
& SUITES**
2102 S Jeffers
(69101)
Rates: $49-$84
(308) 532-9090
(800) 228-5151

RAMADA LIMITED
3201 S Jeffers
(69101)
Rates: $47-$76
(308) 534-3120
(800) 272-6232

RAMBLER MOTEL
1420 Rodeo Rd
(69101)
Rates: $25-$35
(308) 532-9290

**SANDS MOTOR
INN**
501 Halligan Dr
(69101)
Rates: $35-$56
(308) 532-0151

**STANFORD
MOTEL**
1400 E 4th St (69101)
Rates: $30-$49
(308) 532-9380
(800) 743-4934

STOCKMAN INN
1402 S Jeffers
(69103)
Rates: $41-$65
(308) 534-3630
(800) 624-4643

SUPER 8 MOTEL
220 Eugene Ave
(69101)
Rates: $36-$62
(308) 532-4224
(800) 800-8000

**TRAVELERS
INN-IMA**
602 E 4th St
(69101)
Rates: $30-$45
(308) 534-4020
(800) 341-8000

OGALLALA

**BEST WESTERN
STAGECOACH
INN**
201 Stagecoach Tr
(69153)
Rates: $39-$85
(308) 284-3656
(800) 662-2993

DAYS INN
601 Stagecoach Tr
(69153)
Rates: $40-$70
(308) 284-6365
(800) 329-7466

ECONO LODGE
108 Prospector Dr
(69153)
Rates: $39-$69
(308) 284-2056
(800) 553-2666

ELMS MOTEL
717 W 1st St
(69153)
Rates: $26-$34
(308) 284-3404

HOLIDAY INN EXP
501 Stagecoach Tr
(69153)
Rates: $65-$75
(308) 284-2266
(800) 465-4329

KINGSLEY LODGE
1510 N Hwy 61
(69153)
Rates: $35-$55
(308) 284-2775
(800) 883-2775

LAKEWAY LODGE
918 N Spruce St
(69153)
Rates: $35-$55
(308) 284-4431
(888) 284-4431

LAZY K MOTEL
1501 E 1st St
(69153)
Rates: $28-$40
(308) 284-4085

PLAZA INN
311 E 1st (69153)
Rates: $55-$65
(308) 284-8416

RAMADA LIMITED
201 Chuckwagon
Rd (69153)
Rates: $42-$67
(308) 284-3623
(800) 272-6232

SUNSET MOTEL
1021 W 1st (69153)
Rates: $35
(308) 284-4264

SUPER 8 MOTEL
500 East A South
(69153)
Rates: $36-$61
(308) 284-2076
(800) 800-8000

WESTERN PARADISE MOTEL
221 E 1st (69153)
Rates: $35-$55
(308) 284-3684
(800) 733-0899

OMAHA

BEN FRANKLIN MOTEL-IMA
10308 Frontage Rd (68138)
Rates: $44-$55
(402) 895-2200
(800) 341-8000

BEST WESTERN CENTRAL-EXEC CENTER
3650 S 72nd St (68124)
Rates: $59-$89
(402) 397-3700
(800) 528-1234

BUDGETEL INN
10760 M St (68127)
Rates: $38-$67
(402) 592-5200
(800) 428-3438

CLARION HOTEL CARLISLE
10909 M St (68137)
Rates: $69-$104
(402) 331-8220
(800) 252-7466

COMFORT INN
10919 J St (68137)
Rates: $44-$89
(402) 592-2882
(800) 228-5150

COMFORT INN
9595 S 145th St (68138)
Rates: $49-$84
(402) 896-6300
(800) 228-5150

ECONO LODGE
7833 W Dodge Rd(68124)
Rates: $45-$95
(402) 391-7100
(800) 553-2666

EMBASSY SUITES
555 S 10th (68102)
Rates: $139-$179
(402) 346-9000
(800) 362-2779

FOUR POINTS BY SHERATON ITT
4888 S 118th St (68137)
Rates: $79-$109
(402) 895-1000
(800) 325-3535

HAMPTON INN
10728 L St (68127)
Rates: $57-$72
(402) 593-2380
(800) 426-7866

HAWTHORN SUITES
11025 M Street (68137)
Rates: $55-$65
(402) 331-0101
(800) 527-1133

LA QUINTA INN
3330 N 104th Ave (68134)
Rates: $49-$74
(402) 493-1900
(800) 531-5900

MARRIOTT HOTEL
10220 Regency Cir (68114)
Rates: $89-$150
(402) 399-9000
(800) 228-9290

MOTEL 6
10708 M St (68127)
Rates: $33-$41
(402) 331-3161
(800) 466-8356

PARK INN INTERNATIONAL
9305 S 145th St (68138)
Rates: $43-$65
(402) 895-2555
(800) 437-7275

RAMADA LIMITED
9505 S 142nd St (68138)
Rates: $55-$85
(402) 896-9500
(800) 272-6232

RESIDENCE INN BY MARRIOTT
6990 Dodge St (68132)
Rates: $99-$130
(402) 553-8898
(800) 331-3131

RODEWAY INN
7101 Grover St (68106)
Rates: $58-$64
(402) 391-5757
(800) 228-2000

SATELLITE MOTEL
6006 L St (68117)
Rates: $32-$42
(402) 733-7373

SUBURBAN INN
11023 Sapp Brothers Dr (68138)
Rates: $26-$49
(402) 332-3911
(800) 599-3911

O'NEILL

BUDGET HOST CARRIAGE HOUSE MOTEL
929 E Douglas St (68763)
Rates: $28-$45
(402) 336-3403
(800) 283-4678

CAPRI MOTEL-IMA
1020 E Douglas St (68763)
Rates: $28-$45
(402) 336-2762
(800) 341-8000

ELMS MOTEL
Hwy 20 E (68763)
Rates: $30-$45
(402) 336-3800
(800) 526-9052

GOLDEN HOTEL
406 E Douglas St (68763)
Rates: $23-$39
(402) 336-4436
(800) 658-3148

INNKEEPER
725 E Douglas St (68763)
Rates: $35-$60
(402) 336-1640

ORCHARD

DIAMOND E TROUT RESORT GUEST RANCH
P. O. Box B (68764)
Rates: $59-$80
(402) 893-4745
(800) 974-3002

ORCHARD MOTEL
E Hwy 20 (68764)
Rates: $35
(402) 893-2165

OSHKOSH

S & S MOTEL
Hwy 26 & 27 (69154)
Rates: $35
(308) 772-3350

SHADY REST MOTEL
108 Main St (69154)
Rates: $30-$36
(308) 772-4115

PAWNEE CITY

PAWNEE INN
1021 F St (68420)
Rates: $35-$55
(402) 852-2238

PAXTON

DAYS INN
I-80 Ex 145 (69155)
Rates: $39-$90
(308) 239-4510
(800) 329-7466

PLAINVIEW

HILLCREST MOTEL
P. O. Box 848 (68769)
Rates: $26-$34
(402) 582-3299

PLATTSMOUTH

BROWN'S FAMILY MOTEL
1913 Hwy 34 E (68048)
Rates: $55-$65
(402) 296-9266

RANDOLPH

CEDAR MOTEL
107 East Hwy 20 (68771)
Rates: $25-$35
(402) 337-0500

RED CLOUD

MCFARLAND HOTEL
137 West 4th Ave (68970)
Rates: $25-$35
(402) 746-2329

REPUBLICAN CITY

DAVE'S CABINS
RR 1, Box 125 (68971)
Rates: $26-$46
(308) 799-3635

GATEWAY MOTEL
17 Hwy 136 (68971)
Rates: $35
(308) 799-2815

RUSHVILLE

ANTLERS MOTEL
607 East 2nd St (69360)
Rates: $30-$60
(308) 327-2444

NEBRASKALAND MOTEL
508 East 2nd, Box 377 (69360)
Rates: $35-$55
(308) 327-2277

ST. PAUL

KELLER'S KORNER MOTEL
1517 2nd St (68873)
Rates: $35
(308) 754-4451

SUPER 8 MOTEL
116 Howard Ave (68873)
Rates: $37-$59
(308) 754-4554
(800) 800-8000

SCHUYLER

JOHNNIE'S MOTEL
222 W 16th
(68661)
Rates: $28-$37
(402) 352-5454

VALLEY COURT MOTEL
320 W 16th St
(68661)
Rates: $35
(402) 352-3326

SCOTTSBLUFF

CAPRI MOTEL
2424 Ave I (69361)
Rates: $31-$44
(308) 635-2057
(800) 642-2774

LAMPLIGHTER MOTEL-IMA
606 E 27th St
(69361)
Rates: $32-$43
(308) 632-7108
(800) 341-8000

SCOTTSBLUFF INN
1901 21st Ave
(69361)
Rates: $50-$85
(308) 635-3111
(800) 597-3111

SEWARD

EAST HILL MOTEL
131 Hwy 34 E
(68434)
Rates: $35
(402) 643-3679

SUPER 8 MOTEL
1329 Progressive Rd (68434)
Rates: $41-$5
(402) 643-3388
(800) 800-8000

SIDNEY

CONESTOGA MOTEL
Rt 1, Box 410
(69162)
Rates: $28-$42
(308) 254-6000

DELUXE MOTEL
2201 Illinois St
(69162)
Rates: $25-$34
(308) 254-4666

EL PALOMINO MOTEL
2220 Illinois St
(69162)
Rates: $27-$46
(308) 254-5566

FORT SIDNEY INN
935 9th Ave
(69162)
Rates: $33-$85
(308) 254-5863
(888) 743-6394

GENERIC MOTEL
11552 Hwy 30
(69162)
Rates: $35-$55
(308) 254-4527
(800) 893-5309

HOLIDAY INN
664 Chase Blvd
(69162)
Rates: $75-$80
(308) 254-2000
(800) 465-4329

SUPER 8 MOTEL
2115 W Illinois St
(69162)
Rates: $40-$52
(308) 254-2081
(800) 800-8000

SOUTH SIOUX CITY

THE MARINA INN
4th & B Sts (68776)
Rates: $69-$89
(402) 494-4000
(800) 798-7980

RAMADA LIMITED
2829 Dakota Ave
(68776)
Rates: $39-$59
(402) 494-8874
(800) 962-2545

TRAVELODGE
400 Dakota Ave
(68776)
Rates: $40-$60
(402) 494-3046
(800) 578-7878

SPENCER

SKYLINE MOTEL
Hwys 281 & 12
(68777)
Rates: $35
(402) 589-1300
(800) 917-1300

STEINAUER

CONVENT HOUSE BED & BRKFAST
P. O. Box 68
(68441)
Rates: $40-$55
(402) 869-2276

STUART

STUART VILLAGE INN
P. O. Box 238
(68780)
Rates: $26-$35
(402) 924-3133

SUPERIOR

VICTORIAN INN
P. O. Box 407
(68978)
Rates: $27-$34
(402) 879-3245

SUTHERLAND

PARK MOTEL
1110 1st St (69165)
Rates: $35
(308) 386-4384
(800) 437-2565

SUTTON

SUTTON MOTEL
208 N French
(68979)
Rates: $25-$35
(402) 773-4803

SYRACUSE

MUSTANG MOTEL
940 Park St
(68446)
Rates: $25-$35
(402) 269-2185

THEDFORD

RODEWAY INN
SR 2E (69166)
Rates: $37-$80
(308) 645-2284
(800) 228-2000

TRYON

LONGHORN MOTEL
P. O. Box 94
(69167)
Rates: $26-$34
(308) 587-2345

VALENTINE

BALLARD MOTEL
227 S Hall St
(69201)
Rates: $35
(402) 376-2922

FOUNTAIN INN
237 S Cherry St
(69201)
Rates: $55
(402) 376-2300

MERRITT RESORT
HC 32, Box 23
(69201)
Rates: $60
(402) 376-3437

MOTEL RAINE
Hwy 20 W (69201)
Rates: $32-$44
(402) 376-2030
(800) 999-3066

NIOBRARA INN
525 N Main
(69201)
Rates: $60-$80
(402) 376-1779

NIOBRARA RIVER RESORT
HC 60, Box 5
(69216)
Rates: $37-$55
(402) 966-3321

TRADE WINDS LODGE-IMA
E Hwy 20 & 83
(69201)
Rates: $33-$59
(402) 376-1600
(800) 341-8000

VALENTINE MOTEL
Hwy 20 & 83
(69201)
Rates: $35-$55
(402) 376-2450
(800) 376-2450

VERDIGRE

THE VERDIGRE INN
P. O. Box 28
(68783)
Rates: $28-$50
(402) 668-2277

WAHOO

BILL'S WAHOO MOTEL
Hwys 77, 92 & 109
(68066)
Rates: $35
(402) 443-9933

WAUNETA

WAUNETA MOTEL
P. O. Box 221
(69034)
Rates: $25-$33
(308) 394-5434

WAUSA

COMMERCIAL HOTEL
Main St (68786)
Rates: $35-$55
(402) 586-2377

WAYNE

K-D INN MOTEL
311 East 7th St
(68787)
Rates: $30-$55
(402) 375-1770

SPORTS CLUB MOTEL
Rt 2, Box 195
(68787)
Rates: $29-$48
(402) 375-4222

WEST POINT

POINTERS INN MOTEL
534 S Lincoln Hwy (68788)
Rates: $30-$52
(402) 372-2491

SUPER 8 MOTEL
1211 N Lincoln
(68788)
Rates: $41-$55
(402) 372-3998
(800) 800-8000

AREA CODES - If the local number doesn't connect, check for a new area code.

WILBER

**HOTEL WILBER
BED & BREAKFAST**
P. O. Box 633
(68465)
Rates: $28-$53
(402) 821-2020
(888) 494-5237

WISNER

MIDWEST MOTEL
1612 Ave E (68791)
Rates: $35-$55
(402) 529-6910

WOOD RIVER

**WOOD RIVER
MOTEL**
11774 S Hwy 11
(68883)
Rates: $35
(308) 583-2256
(800) 587-2256

WYMORE

D & M MOTEL
601 S 14th St
(68466)
Rates: $35
(402) 645-3801

YORK

**BEST WESTERN
PALMER INN**
2426 S Lincoln
Ave (68467)
Rates: $37-$59
(402) 362-5585
(800) 528-1234

DAYS INN
3710 S Lincoln
(68467)
Rates: $38-$56
(402) 362-6355
(800) 329-7466

STAEHR MOTEL
RR 4, Box 49
(68467)
Rates: $35-$55
(402) 362-4804

SUPER 8 MOTEL
P. O. Box 532
(68467)
Rates: $40-$56
(402) 362-3388
(800) 800-8000

AREA CODES - If the local number doesn't connect, check for a new area code.

NEVADA

ALAMO

**MEADOW LANE
MOTEL**
US Hwy 93
(89001)
Rates: $30-$49
(775) 725-3371
(888) 740-8009

AMARGOSA VALLEY

**DESERT VILLAGE
MOTEL**
Rt 373 & Mecca
Rd (89020)
Rates: $39-$49
(775) 372-1405

**LONGSTREET
INN/CASINO &
RV PARK**
373 Stateline
(89020)
Rates: $69-$89
(775) 372-1777
(800) 508-9493

AUSTIN

LINCOLN MOTEL
728 Main (89310)
Rates: $29-$43
(775) 964-2698

**PONY CANYON
MOTEL**
Hwy 50 (89310)
Rates: $34-$52
(775) 964-2605

**PONY EXPRESS
HOUSE B&B**
115 NW Main St
(89310)
Rates: $35+
(775) 964-2306

BAKER

BORDER INN
Hwys 50 & 6
(89311)
Rates: $29-$39
(775) 234-7300

**HIDDEN CANYON
GUEST RANCH**
P O Box 180
(89311)
Rates: $44-$124
(775) 234-7267
(888) 711-7552

**SILVERJACK
MOTEL**
Main St (89311)
Rates: $36-$70
(775) 234-7323

BATTLE MOUNTAIN

**BEL COURT
MOTEL**
292 E Front St
(89820)
Rates: $20-$30
(775) 635-2569

BEST INN
650 W Front St
(89820)
Rates: $44-$79
(775) 635-5200
(800) 237-8466

**BEST WESTERN
BIG CHIEF MOTEL**
434 W Front St
(89820)
Rates: $54-$87
(775) 635-2416
(800) 528-1234

COMFORT INN
521 E Front St
(89820)
Rates: $49-$59
(775) 635-5880
(800) 228-5150

HO MOTEL
150 W Front St
(89820)
Rates: $20
(775) 635-5101

**OWL HOTEL
& CASINO**
8 E Front St
(89820)
Rates: $30+
(775) 635-5155

BEATTY

BURRO INN
Third St & Hwy
95 (89003)
Rates: $37-$65
(775) 553-2225
(800) 843-2078

**EL PORTAL
MOTEL**
420 Main St
(89003)
Rates: $30-$60
(775) 553-2912
(800) 352-3068

PHOENIX INN
Hwy 95 & First St
(89003)
Rates: $30-$50
(775) 553-2250
(800) 845-7401

**STAGECOACH
HOTEL & CASINO**
Hwy 95 (89003)
Rates: $35-$100
(775) 553-2419
(800) 424-4946

BOULDER CITY

**BEST WESTERN
LIGHTHOUSE INN
& RESORT**
110 Vile Dr (89005)
Rates: $60-$80
(702) 293-6444
(800) 528-1234
(800) 934-8282

**DESERT INN OF
BOULDER CITY**
800 Nevada Hwy
(89005)
Rates: $40-$120
(702) 293-2827

**FLAMINGO INN
MOTEL**
804 Nevada Hwy
(89005)
Rates: $27-$60
(702) 293-3565

LAKE MEAD RESORT & MARINA

322 Lakeshore Rd
(89005)
Rates: $50-$125
(702) 293-2074
(800) 752-9669

**NEVADA INN
MOTEL**
1009 Nevada Hwy
(89005)
Rates: $30-$75
(702) 293-2044
(800) 638-8890

STARVIEW MOTEL
1017 Nevada Hwy
(89005)
Rates: $27-$90
(702) 293-1658

SUPER 8 MOTEL
704 Nevada Hwy
(89005)
Rates: $50-$300
(702) 294-8888
(800) 800-8000

CALIENTE

**CALIENTE
HOT SPRINGS
MOTEL**
Hwy 93 N (89008)
Rates: $34-$75
(775) 726-3777
(888) 726-3777

**LONGHORN
CATTLE COMPANY
GUEST RANCH**
Rainbow Canyon
Rd (89008)
Rates: $100+
(775) 388-9955

**RAINBOW
CANYON MOTEL**
884 A St (89008)
Rates: $35-$45
(775) 726-3291

SHADY MOTEL
450 Front St
(89008)
Rates: $38-$47
(775) 726-3106

CARLIN

**BEST INN
& SUITES**
1018 Fir St (89822)
Rates: $49-$84
(775) 754-6110
(800) 237-8466

CAVALIER MOTEL
10th & State Rt 40
(89822)
Rates: $32-$50
(775) 754-6311

CARSON CITY

**BEST VALUE
MOTEL**
2731 S Carson St
(89701)
Rates: $33-$99
(775) 882-2007
(800) 231-6326

**BEST WESTERN
TRAILSIDE INN**
1300 N Carson St
(89701)
Rates: $39-$69
(775) 883-7300
(800) 528-1234
(800) 626-1900

CARSON CITY INN
1930 N Carson St
(89701)
Rates: $30-$37
(775) 882-1785

DAYS INN
3103 N Carson St
(89701)
Rates: $37-$130
(775) 883-3343
(800) 329-7466

**DOWNTOWNER
MOTOR INN**
801 N Carson St
(89701)
Rates: $32-$99
(775) 882-1333
(800) 364-4908

FRONTIER MOTEL
1718 N Carson St
(89701)
Rates: $25-$179
(775) 882-1377

AREA CODES - If the local number doesn't connect, check for a new area code.

MOTEL 6
2749 S Carson St
(89701)
Rates: $31-$40
(775) 885-7710
(800) 466-8356

NUGGET MOTEL
651 N Stewart St
(89701)
Rates: $40-$75
(775) 882-7711
(800) 948-9111

PIONEER MOTEL
907 S Carson St
(89701)
Rates: $36-$75
(775) 882-3046
(800) 882-3046

RAND AVENUE MOTEL
1464 Rand Ave
(89706)
Rates: $30-$35
(775) 841-7200

ROUND HOUSE INN
1400 N Carson St
(89701)
Rates: $29-$99
(775) 882-3446

SIERRA SAGE MOTEL
801 S Carson St
(89701)
Rates: $25-$60
(775) 882-1419

SIERRA VISTA MOTEL
711 S Plaza St
(89701)
Rates: $30-$75
(775) 883-9500
(800) NEVADA-1

SUPER 8 MOTEL
2829 S Carson St
(89701)
Rates: $46-$82
(775) 883-7800
(800) 800-8000

DENIO

DENIO JUNCTION MOTEL
P. O. Box 10
(89404)
Rates: $40+
(775) 941-0371

ECHO BAY

ECHO BAY RESORT
On Lake Mead
(Overton 89040)
Rates: $90-$100
(702) 394-4000
(800) 752-9669

ELKO

BEST WESTERN ELKO INN EXPRESS
837 Idaho St
(89801)
Rates: $54-$99
(775) 738-7261
(800) 528-1234

BEST WESTERN GOLD COUNTRY MOTOR INN
2050 Idaho St
(89801)
Rates: $69-$109
(775) 738-8421
(800) 528-1234
(800) 621-1332

COMFORT INN
2970 Idaho St
(89801)
Rates: $49-$89
(775) 777-8762
(800) 228-5150

ELKO MOTEL
1243 Idaho St
(89801)
Rates: $32-$95
(775) 738-4433

ESQUIRE INN
505 Idaho St
(89801)
Rates: $32-$70
(775) 738-3157
(800) 822-7473

HIGH DESERT INN
3015 Idaho St
(89801)
Rates: $59-$109
(775) 738-8425
(888) 394-8303

HOLIDAY MOTEL
1276 Idaho St
(89801)
Rates: $32-$36
(775) 738-7187

KEY MOTEL
650 W Idaho St
(89801)
Rates: $34-$58
(775) 738-8081

LOUIS MOTEL
2100 Idaho St
(89801)
Rates: $26-$108
(775) 738-3536

MANOR MOTOR LODGE
185 Idaho St
(89801)
Rates: $30-$60
(775) 738-3311

MID-TOWN MOTEL
294 Idaho St
(89801)
Rates: $30-$65
(775) 738-3515

MOTEL 6
3021 Idaho St
(89801)
Rates: $33-$39
(775) 738-4337
(800) 466-8356

O.K. 7 MOTEL
291 W Idaho St
(89801)
Rates: $27-$31
(775) 738-4644

OAK TREE INN
95 Spruce Rd
(89801)
Rates: $52-$79
(775) 777-2222
(888) 897-9647

ONCE UPON A TIME B&B
537 14th St (89801)
Rates: $65-$95
(775) 738-1200

RED LION INN & CASINO
2065 Idaho St
(89801)
Rates: $79-$109
(775) 738-2111
(800) 733-5466
(800) 545-0044

RUBY CREST GUEST RANCH
HC 30, Box 197
(89801)
Rates: 150+
(775) 744-2277

RUBY MARSHES GUEST RANCH
HC 30, Box 197
(89801)
Rates: $150+
(775) 744-2277

SHILO INN
2401 Mountain
City Hwy (89801)
Rates: $69-$125
(775) 738-5522
(800) 222-2244

STAMPEDE 7 MOTEL
129 W Idaho St
(89801)
Rates: $30-$50
(775) 738-8471

THUNDERBIRD MOTEL
345 Idaho St
(89801)
Rates: $49-$79
(775) 738-7115

TOWNE HOUSE MOTEL
500 W Oak St
(89801)
Rates: $32-$42
(775) 738-7269

TRAVELERS MOTEL
1181 Idaho St
(89801)
Rates: $26-$38
(775) 738-4048

ELY

BEST WESTERN MAIN MOTEL
1101 Aultman St
(89301)
Rates: $41-$69
(775) 289-4529
(800) 528-1234

BEST WESTERN PARK VUE
930 Aultman St
(89301)
Rates: $43-$65
(775) 289-4497
(800) 528-1234

DESER-EST MOTOR LODGE
1425 Aultman St
(89301)
Rates: $28-$49
(775) 289-8885

EL RANCHO MOTEL
1400 Aultman St
(89301)
Rates: $25-$40
(775) 289-3644

FIRESIDE INN
McGill Hwy
(89301)
Rates: $38-$44
(775) 289-3765
(800) 732-8288

GRAND CENTRAL MOTEL
1498 Lyons Ave
(89301)
Rates: $32-$36
(775) 289-6868

GREAT BASIN INN
701 Ave F (89301)
Rates: $39-$45
(775) 289-4468

HOTEL NEVADA & GAMBLING HALL
501 Aultman St
(89301)
Rates: $20-$85
(775) 289-6665
(888) 406-3055

IDLE INN MOTEL
150 Fourth St
(89301)
Rates: $22-$35
(775) 289-4411

JAILHOUSE MOTEL
Fourth & High Sts
(89301)
Rates: $40-$65
(775) 289-3033
(800) 841-5430

LANE'S RANCH MOTEL
State Rt 318 at
Preston (89301)
Rates: $29-$43
(775) 238-5246

MOTEL 6
770 Ave O (89301)
Rates: $32-$42
(775) 289-6671
(800) 466-8356

AREA CODES - If the local number doesn't connect, check for a new area code.

RAMADA INN COPPER QUEEN HOTEL & CASINO
805 Great Basin Blvd (89301)
Rates: $60-$125
(775) 289-4884
(800) 851-9526
(800) 272-6232

SHAKESPEARE INN
1550 High St (89301)
Rates: $25-$45
(775) 289-2512
(888) 866-8253

WHITE PINE MOTEL
1301 Aultman St (89301)
Rates: $24-$43
(775) 289-3800

EUREKA

COLONNADE HOTEL
Clark & Monroe Sts (89316)
Rates: $25-$44
(775) 237-9988

RUBY HILL MOTEL
Hwy 50 (89316)
Rates: $28-$38
(775) 237-5339

SUNDOWN LODGE
Main St (89316)
Rates: $31-$44
(775) 237-5334

FALLON

BONANZA INN & CASINO
855 W Williams Ave (89406)
Rates: $36-$70
(775) 423-6031

BUDGET INN
1705 S Taylor (89406)
Rates: $40-$65
(775) 423-2277

FALLON MOTEL
390 W Williams Ave (89406)
Rates: $40-$90
(775) 423-4648

MICROTEL INN & SUITES
1051 W Williams Ave (89406)
Rates: $50-$80
(775) 428-0300
(888) 771-7171

OXBOW MOTOR INN
60 S Allen Rd (89406)
Rates: $46-$65
(775) 423-7021

VALUE INN
180 W Williams Ave (89406)
Rates: $32-$65
(775) 423-5151

WESTERN MOTEL
125 S Carson St (89406)
Rates: $37-$57
(775) 423-5118

FERNLEY

BEST WESTERN FERNLEY INN
1405 E Newlands Dr (89408)
Rates: $49-$110
(775) 575-6776
(800) 528-1234

LAZY INN
325 Main (89408)
Rates: $30-$60
(775) 575-4452
(800) 682-6445

GABBS

GABBS MOTEL
100 S Main St (89409)
Rates: $28-$45
(775) 285-4019

GARDNERVILLE

BEST WESTERN INN AT TOPAZ LAKE
1929 Hwy 395 S (89410)
Rates: $50-$150
(775) 266-4000
(800) 528-1234

THE NENZEL MANSION B&B
1431 Ezell St (89410)
Rates: $90-$110
(775) 782-7644

TOPAZ LODGE & CASINO
1979 Hwy 395 S (89410)
Rates: $39-$53
(775) 266-3338
(800) 962-0732

GENOA

GENOA HOUSE INN B&B
180 Nixon St (89411)
Rates: $105-$150
(775) 782-7075

GERLACH

SOLDIER MEADOWS GUEST RANCH & LODGE
Soldier Meadows Rd (89412)
Rates: $50-$120
(530) 233-4881

HAWTHORNE

ANCHOR MOTEL
965 Sierra Way (89415)
Rates: $25-$29
(775) 945-2573

BEST INN & SUITES
1402 E 5th St (89415)
Rates: $55-$60
(775) 945-2660
(800) 237-8466

CLIFF HOUSE LAKESIDE RESORT
1 Cliff House Rd (89415)
Rates: $30-$40
(775) 945-2444
(888) 320-5253

EL CAPITAN RESORT/CASINO
540 F St (89415)
Rates: $26-$42
(775) 945-3321
(800) 922-2311

HAWTHORNE MOTEL
720 Sierra Hwy 95 (89415)
Rates: $25-$30
(775) 945-2544

HOLIDAY LODGE
Fifth & J Sts (89415)
Rates: $26-$32
(775) 945-3316

MONARCH MOTEL
1291 E Fifth St (89415)
Rates: $28-$50
(775) 945-3117

ROCKET MOTEL
694 Sierra Way (89415)
Rates: $22-$25
(775) 945-2143

SAND N SAGE MOTEL
1301 E 5th St (89415)
Rates: $30-$45
(775) 945-3352

WRIGHT MOTEL
W Fifth & I Sts (89415)
Rates: $26-$33
(775) 945-2213

HENDERSON

BOBY MOTEL
2100 S Boulder Hwy (89015)
Rates: $30-$75
(702) 565-9711

OUTPOST MOTEL
1104 N Boulder Hwy (89015)
Rates: $38-$75
(702) 564-2664

RESIDENCE INN BY MARRIOTT
2190 Olympic Rd (89014)
Rates: $99-$139
(702) 434-2700
(800) 331-3131

SKY MOTEL
1713 N Boulder Hwy (89015)
Rates: $35-$45
(702) 564-1534

TOWNHOUSE MOTOR LODGE
43 Water St (89015)
Rates: $25-$65
(702) 564-3111

INDIAN SPRINGS

INDIAN SPRINGS MOTOR HOTEL
300 Tonapah Hwy (89018)
Rates: $33-$49
(702) 879-3700

JACKPOT

BARTON'S CLUB 93
Hwy 93 (89825)
Rates: $35-$65
(775) 755-2341
(800) 258-2937

COVERED WAGON MOTEL
1601 Hwy 93 (89825)
Rates: $20-$40
(775) 755-2241
(800) 838-1241

HORSESHU HOTEL & CASINO
1385 Hwy 93, Dice Rd (89825)
Rates: $42-$67
(775) 755-7777
(800) 821-2321

JARBIDGE

OUTDOOR INN
Main St (89826)
Rates: $30-$75
(775) 488-2311

LAKE TAHOE

(SEE ADDITIONAL LISTINGS IN CALIFORNIA)

HARRAH'S LAKE TAHOE HOTEL & CASINO
15 Hwy 50 (Stateline 89449)
Rates: $179-$269
(775) 588-6611
(800) 427-7247
(Kennels provided)

HORIZON CASINO RESORT
P. O. Box C (89449)
Rates: $69-$200
(775) 588-6211
(800) 322-7723

AREA CODES - If the local number doesn't connect, check for a new area code.

LAMOILLE

BREITENSTEIN HOUSE B&B
P. O. Box 281381 (89828)
Rates: $55-$125
(775) 753-6356

LAS VEGAS

A FISHERS INN
3565 Boulder Hwy (89121)
Rates: $25-$65
(702) 457-3900

AMERISUITES HOTEL
4520 Paradise Rd (89109)
Rates: $69-$179
(702) 369-3366
(800) 833-1516

BEST INN & SUITES
4288 N Nellis Blvd (89115)
Rates: $59-$175
(702) 632-0229
(800) 237-8466

BEST WESTERN MAIN STREET INN
1000 N Main St (89101)
Rates: $39-$139
(702) 382-3455
(800) 528-1234
(800) 851-1414

BEST WESTERN NELLIS MOTOR INN
5330 E Craig Rd (89115)
Rates: $49-$500
(702) 643-6111
(800) 528-1234
(800) 546-1119

BEST WESTERN PARKVIEW INN
905 Las Vegas Blvd N (89101)
Rates: $49-$125
(702) 385-1213
(800) 528-1234
(800) 548-6122

BLAIR HOUSE SUITES
344 E Desert Inn Rd (89109)
Rates: $45-$125
(702) 792-2222
(800) 553-9111

BLUE ANGEL MOTEL
2110 E Fremont St (89101)
Rates: $30-$100
(702) 386-9500

BUDGET SUITES OF AMERICA
4625 Boulder Hwy (89121)
Rates: $49-$69
(702) 454-4625
(800) 752-1501

BUDGET SUITES OF AMERICA
4855 Boulder Hwy (89121)
Rates: $49-$69
(702) 433-3644

CITY CENTER MOTEL
700 E Fremont St (89101)
Rates: $35-$130
(702) 382-4766

CROWNE PLAZA
4255 S Paradise Rd (89109)
Rates: $125-$185
(702) 369-4400
(800) 227-6963

DAISY MOTEL & APARTMENTS
415 S Main St (89101)
Rates: $29-$35
(702) 382-0707

FERGUSONS MOTEL
1028 E Fremont St (89101)
Rates: $35-$150
(702) 382-3500
(800) 933-7829

FOUR SEASONS HOTEL
3960 Las Vegas Blvd S (89193)
Rates: $200-$400
(702) 632-5000
(877) 632-5000

GATEWAY MOTEL
928 Las Vegas Blvd S (89101)
Rates: $26-$100
(702) 382-2146

GATEWOOD MOTEL
3075 E Fremont St (89104)
Rates: $25-$125
(702) 457-3600

GLASS POOL INN
4613 Las Vegas Blvd S (89119)
Rates: $39-$109
(702) 739-6636
(800) 527-7118

GOLDEN INN MOTEL
120 Las Vegas Blvd N (89101)
Rates: $27-$80
(702) 384-8204

HAWTHORN SUITES
4975 S Valley View Blvd (89118)
Rates: $79-$170
(702) 798-7736
(800) 527-1133

HAWTHORN SUITES
5051 Duke Ellington Way (89119)
Rates: $115-$199
(702) 739-7000
(800) 527-1133

HOLIDAY INN EMERALD SPRINGS
325 E Flamingo Rd (89109)
Rates: $79-$150
(702) 732-9100
(800) 465-4329
(800) 732-7889

HOLIDAY INN EXPRESS
8669 W Sahara Ave (89117)
Rates: $89-$175
(702) 256-3766
(800) 465-4329

HOWARD JOHNSON INN
1401 Las Vegas Blvd (89104)
Rates: $49-$129
(702) 388-0301
(800) 446-4656

HOWARD JOHNSON PLAZA HOTEL
3111 W Tropicana Ave (89103)
Rates: $49-$149
(702) 798-1111
(800) 446-4656

KING ALBERT MOTEL
185 Albert Lane (89109)
Rates: $39+
(702) 732-1555
(800) 553-7753

LA PALM MOTEL
2512 E Fremont St (89104)
Rates: $30-$65
(702) 384-5874

LA QUINTA INN
3782 Las Vegas Blvd S (89109)
Rates: $69-$99
(702) 739-7457
(800) 687-6667

LAMPLIGHTER MOTEL
2805 E Fremont St (89104)
Rates: $30-$50
(702) 382-8791

MEADOWS INN
525 E Bonanza Rd (89101)
Rates: $35-$55
(702) 366-0456
(800) 932-1499

MOTEL 8/MR. DELI
3961 Las Vegas Blvd S (89119)
Rates: $29-$105
(702) 798-7223

MOTEL REGENCY
700 N Main St (89101)
Rates: $32-$49
(702) 382-2332

MOTEL 6
4125 Boulder Hwy (89121)
Rates: $32-$56
(702) 457-8051
(800) 466-8356

MOTEL 6
5085 S Industrial Rd (89118)
Rates: $32-$56
(702) 739-6747
(800) 466-8356

PARADISE RESORT INN
3450 Paradise Rd (89109)
Rates: $38-$55
(702) 733-3900

RESIDENCE INN BY MARRIOTT
3225 S Paradise Rd (891095
Rates: $95-$399
(702) 796-9300
(800) 331-3131
(800) 244-3364

RESIDENCE INN BY MARRIOTT
370 Hughes Ctr Dr (89109)
Rates: $119-$149
(702) 837-0592
(800) 331-3131
(800) 244-3364

RODEWAY INN
167 E Tropicana Ave (89109)
Rates: $35-$345
(702) 795-3311
(800) 228-2000

SILVER QUEEN MOTEL
1401 E Carson St (89101)
Rates: $28-$130
(702) 384-8157

SUPER 8 MOTEL
4250 Koval Lane (89109)
Rates: $50-$72
(702) 794-0888
(800) 800-8000

TAM O'SHANTER MOTEL
3317 Las Vegas Blvd S (89109)
Rates: $38-$64
(702) 735-7331
(800) 727-3423

THRIFTLODGE
4244 Las Vegas Blvd (89115)
Rates: $45-$89
(702) 644-9595
(800) 525-9055

TRAVEL INN MOTEL
217 Las Vegas Blvd N (89101)
Rates: $30-$50
(702) 384-3040

TRAVELODGE
2028 E Fremont St (89101)
Rates: $39-$99
(702) 384-7540
(800) 578-7878

VAGABOND INN CENTER STRIP
3265 Las Vegas Blvd S (89109)
Rates: $45-$1150
(702) 735-5102
(800) 522-1555
(800) 828-8032

VALLEY MOTEL
1313 E Fremont St (89101)
Rates: $30-$40
(702) 384-6890

VEGAS CHALET MOTEL
2401 Las Vegas Blvd N (89030)
Rates: $35-$125
(702) 642-2115

WALDEN MOTEL
3085 E Fremont (89104)
Rates: $25-$125
(702) 457-9090

WELLESLEY INN & SUITES
1550 E Flamingo Rd (89109)
Rates: $50-$80
(702) 731-3111
(800) 444-8888

WHITE SANDS MOTEL
3889 Las Vegas Blvd S (89109)
Rates: $30-$85
(702) 736-2515

LAUGHLIN

(Also see Bullhead City, AZ)

BAY SHORE INN
1955 Casino Dr (89029)
Rates: $25-$125
(702) 299-9010

DON LAUGHLIN'S RIVERSIDE RESORT HOTEL & CASINO
1650 Casino Dr (89029)
Rates: $25-$109
(702) 298-2535
(800) 227-3849

LOVELOCK

CADILLAC INN
1395 Cornell Ave (89419)
Rates: $20-$42
(775) 273-2798

COVERED WAGON MOTEL
945 Dartmouth Ave (89419)
Rates: $38-$45
(775) 273-2961

DESERT PLAZA INN
1435 Cornell Ave (89419)
Rates: $35-$55
(775) 273-2500

LOVELOCK INN
55 Cornell Ave (89419)
Rates: $39-$65
(775) 273-2937

RAMADA INN & CASINO
1420 Cornell Ave (89419)
Rates: $49-$75
(775) 273-2971
(800) 272-6232
(800) 234-6835

SAGE MOTEL
1335 Cornell Ave (89419)
Rates: $17-$32
(775) 273-0444

SIERRA MOTEL
14th & Dartmouth Sts (89419)
Rates: $20-$42
(775) 273-2798

MCDERMITT

MCDERMITT MOTEL
55 Hwy 95 N (89421)
Rates: $40-$60
(775) 532-8588
(800) 841-3058

MESQUITE

BUDGET INN & SUITES
390 N Sandhill (89024)
Rates: $35-$110
(702) 346-7444
(800) 463-6302

DESERT PALMS MOTEL
Mesquite Blvd (89024)
Rates: $15-$45
(702) 346-5756

SI REDD'S OASIS RESORT HOTEL & CASINO
897 W Mesquite Blvd (89024)
Rates: $29-$109
(702) 346-5232
(800) 216-2747

VALLEY INN MOTEL
791 W Mesquite Blvd (89024)
Rates: $30-$69
(702) 346-5281

VIRGIN RIVER HOTEL & CASINO
915 Mesquite Blvd N (89024)
Rates: $22-$69
(702) 346-7777
(800) 346-7721

MILL CITY

SUPER 8 MOTEL
6000 E Frontage Rd (89418)
Rates: $39-$53
(775) 538-7311
(800) 800-8000

MINDEN

BEST WESTERN MINDEN INN
1795 Ironwood Dr (89423)
Rates: $65-$150
(775) 782-7766
(800) 528-1234

HOLIDAY LODGE
1591 US 395N (89423)
Rates: $32-$48
(775) 782-2288
(800) 266-2289

MOUNT CHARLESTON

MT. CHARLESTON HOTEL
2 Kyle Canyon Rd (89124)
Rates: $49-$155
(702) 872-5500
(800) 794-3456

MT. CHARLESTON LODGE
Kyle Canyon Rd (89124)
Rates: $125-$220
(702) 872-5408
(800) 955-1314

MOUNTAIN CITY

CHAMBERS' MOTEL
P. O. Box 188 (89831)
Rates: $30-$45
(775) 763-6626

MOUNTAIN CITY MOTEL
Hwy 225 (89831)
Rates: $28-$60
(775) 763-6622

NORTH LAS VEGAS

BARKER MOTEL
26001 Las Vegas Blvd N (89030)
Rates: n/a
(702) 642-1138

COMFORT INN
910 E Cheyenne Rd (89030)
Rates: $59-$250
(702) 399-1500
(800) 228-5150

OASIS

OASIS MOTEL
I-80, Exit 378 (89835)
Rates: $23-$45
(702) 478-5113

OLD NEVADA

BONNIE SPRINGS MOTEL
1 Gunfighter Lane (89004)
Rates: $55-$125
(702) 875-4400

OROVADA

ROCKY VIEW INN
Hwy 95 N (89425)
Rates: $30-$40
(775) 272-3337

OVERTON

BEST WESTERN THE NORTH SHORE INN AT LAKE MEAD
520 N Moapa Vly Blvd (89040)
Rates: $55-$115
(702) 397-6000
(800) 528-1234

PAHRUMP

DAYS INN
Hwy 160 N (89041)
Rates: $42-$99
(775) 727-5100
(800) 329-7466

SADDLE WEST HOTEL & CASINO
1220 S Hwy 160 (89041)
Rates: $37-$52
(775) 727-1111

PIOCHE

HUTCHINGS MOTEL
Hwy 93 (89043)
Rates: $35+
(775) 962-5404

MOTEL PIOCHE
100 LaCour St (89043)
Rates: $35+
(775) 962-5551

OVERLAND HOTEL
85 Main St (89043)
Rates: $37-$52
(775) 962-5895

RACHEL

LITTLE A'LE'INN
Hwy 375 (89001)
Rates: $30+
(775) 729-2515

AREA CODES - If the local number doesn't connect, check for a new area code.

RENO

BONANZA MOTOR INN
215 W Fourth St
(89501)
Rates: $38-$125
(775) 322-8632
(800) 808-3303

CITY CENTER MOTEL
365 West St
(89501)
Rates: $30-$90
(775) 323-8880

DAYS INN
701 E 7th St
(89512)
Rates: $29-$125
(775) 786-4070
(800) 329-7466
(800) 448-4555

DOWNTOWNER MOTOR LODGE
150 Stevenson St
(89503)
Rates: $32+
(775) 322-1188

EASY 8 MOTEL
255 W Fifth St
(89503)
Rates: $22+
(775) 322-4588

EL RAY MOTEL
330 N Arlington
(89501)
Rates: $30-$125
(775) 329-6669

EL TAVERN MOTEL
1801 W Fourth St
(89503)
Rates: $30-$40
(775) 322-4504

FLAMINGO MOTEL
520 N Center St
(89501)
Rates: $30-$80
(775) 323-3202

GOLD COIN MOTEL
2555 E Fourth St
(89512)
Rates: $28-$50
(775) 323-0237

HARRAH'S RENO CASINO/HOTEL
219 Center St
(89504)
Rates: $39-$139
(775) 786-3232
(800) HARRAHS
(Kennels provided)

HIGHWAY 40 MOTEL
1750 E Fourth St
(89512)
Rates: $25+
(775) 329-1911

HOLIDAY HOTEL & CASINO
111 Mill St (89504)
Rates: $20-$50
(775) 329-0411
(800) 648-5431

HOLIDAY INN DOWNTOWN
1000 E 6th St
(89512)
Rates: $79-$109
(775) 786-5151
(800) 465-4329
(800) 648-4877

KAY MARTIN LODGE
6950 S Virginia St
(89511)
Rates: $35-$75
(775) 853-6504

KENO MOTEL NO. 1
322 N Arlington Ave (89501)
Rates: $25-$80
(775) 322-6281

LA QUINTA INN
4001 Market St
(89501)
Rates: $65-$85
(775) 348-6100
(800) 687-6667

MINER'S INN
1651 N Virginia St
(89506)
Rates: $39-$95
(775) 329-3464
(800) 626-1900

MONTE CARLO MOTEL
500 N Virginia St
(89501)
Rates: $35-$110
(775) 329-2010

MOTEL 500
500 S Center St
(89501)
Rates: $30-$95
(775) 786-2777

MOTEL 6
1400 Stardust St
(89503)
Rates: $35-$58
(775) 747-7390
(800) 466-8356

MOTEL 6
866 N Wells Ave
(89512)
Rates: $35-$48
(775) 786-9852
(800) 466-8356

MOTEL 6
1901 S Virginia
(89502)
Rates: $35-$42
(775) 827-0255
(800) 466-8356

OLYMPIC APARTMENT HOTEL
195 W Second St
(89501)
Rates: $30-$60
(775) 323-0726

OX-BOW MOTOR LODGE
941 S Virginia St
(89509)
Rates: $30-$95
(775) 786-3777

PONDEROSA HOTEL
515 S Virginia St
(89501)
Rates: $29-$70
(775) 786-6820
(800) 228-6820

RESIDENCE INN BY MARRIOTT
9845 Gateway Dr
(89511)
Rates: $112-$149
(775) 853-8800
(800) 331-3131

SAVOY MOTOR LODGE
705 N Virginia St
(89501)
Rates: $28-$55
(775) 322-4477
(877) 200-4099

SEASONS INN
495 West St
(89503)
Rates: $40-$115
(775) 322-6000
(800) 322-8588

SHOWBOAT INN
660 N Virginia St
(89501)
Rates: $35-$125
(775) 786-4032
(800) 648-3960

SILVER DOLLAR MOTOR LODGE
817 N Virginia St
(89501)
Rates: $30-$50
(775) 323-6875

SUNDANCE MOTEL
850 N Virginia St
(89501)
Rates: $30-$60
(775) 329-9248

SUPER 8 MOTEL
1651 N Virginia St
(89503)
Rates: $39-$59
(775) 329-3464
(800) 800-8000

SUPER 8 AT MEADOWOOD COURTYARD
5851 S Virginia St
(89502)
Rates: $45-$75
(775) 825-2940
(800) 800-8000

TOWN HOUSE MOTOR LODGE
303 W Second St
(89503)
Rates: $29-$78
(775) 323-1821
(800) 438-5660

TRAVELODGE CENTRAL
2050 Market St
(89502)
Rates: $53-$90
(775) 786-2500
(800) 578-7878

TRAVELODGE DOWNTOWN
655 W 4th St
(89503)
Rates: $49-$75
(775) 329-3451
(800) 578-7878

TRUCKEE RIVER LODGE
501 W 1st St
(89503)
Rates: $31-$220
(775) 786-8888
(800) 635-8950

UPTOWN MOTEL
570 N Virginia St
(89501)
Rates: $35+
(775) 323-8906

VAGABOND INN
3131 S Virginia St
(89501)
Rates: $65-$70
(775) 825-7134
(800) 522-1555

WHITE POST INN
567 W Fourth St
(89503)
Rates: $38-$55
(775) 322-8181

SEARCHLIGHT

EL REY MOTEL
430 S Hobson
(89046)
Rates: $32-$60
(702) 297-1144

SILVER CITY

HARDWICKE HOUSE B&B
99 Main St (89428)
Rates: $35-$60
(775) 847-0215

SILVER SPRINGS

A SECRET GARDEN B&B
P O Box 1150
(89429)
Rates: $55-$65
(775) 577-0837

PIPERS MOTEL
1190 Hwy 50 W
(89429)
Rates: $35+
(775) 577-2295

SMITH

WALKER RIVER RESORT
Hudson Way, P O Box 90 (89430)
Rates: $64+
(775) 465-2573
(800) 446-2573

SPARKS

BLUE FOUNTAIN INN
1590 B St (89431)
Rates: n/a
(775) 359-0359

MOTEL 6
2405 Victorian Ave (89431)
Rates: $35-$75
(775) 358-1080
(800) 466-8356

PONY EXPRESS LODGE
2406 Prater Way (89431)
Rates: $28-$46
(775) 358-7110

SUPER 8 MOTEL
1900 E Greg St (89431)
Rates: $47-$62
(775) 358-8884
(800) 800-8000

WESTERN VILLAGE INN & CASINO
815 E Nichols Blvd (89432)
Rates: $20-$100
(775) 331-1069
(800) 648-1170

STATELINE

HARRAH'S LAKE TAHOE HOTEL CASINO
15 Hwy 50, Casino Area (89449)
Rates: $119-$259
(775) 588-6611
(800) 427-7247
(Kennels provided)

SUMMERLIN

HAMPTON INN
7100 Cascade Valley Ct (89128)
Rates: $59-$74
(702) 360-5700
(800) 426-7866

TONOPAH

BEST WESTERN HI-DESERT INN
320 Main St (89049)
Rates: $49-$79
(775) 482-3511
(800) 528-1234
(877) 286-2208

CLOWN MOTEL
521 N Main St (89049)
Rates: $35+
(775) 482-5920

GOLDEN HILLS MOTEL
826 E Main St (89049)
Rates: $24-$65
(775) 482-6238

JIM BUTLER MOTEL
100 S Main St (89049)
Rates: $34-$55
(775) 482-3577
(800) 635-9455

OK CORRAL MOTEL
Hwy 95 N (89049)
Rates: $24-$47
(775) 482-8202

SILVER QUEEN MOTEL
255 Erie Main (89049)
Rates: $31-$45
(775) 482-6291
(800) 210-9218

SUNDOWNER MOTEL
700 Hwy 95 (89049)
Rates: $27-$34
(775) 482-6224

TONOPAH MOTEL
325 Main St (89049)
Rates: $27-$33
(775) 482-3987

TOPAZ LAKE

TOPAZ LODGE
1979 US 395 S (89410)
Rates: $39-$53
(775) 266-3338

UNIONVILLE

OLD PIONEER GARDEN B&B
2805 Unionville Rd (89418)
Rates: $65-$85
(775) 538-7585

VALMY

VALMY STATION MOTEL
I-80 E, Exit 216 (89438)
Rates: $22-$35
(775) 635-5511

VIRGINIA CITY

SILVER QUEEN HOTEL
28 North C St (89440)
Rates: $45-$125
(775) 847-0440

SPARGO HOUSE BED & BREAKFST
395 B St (89440)
Rates: $75-$150
(775) 847-7455

WELLS

BEST WESTERN SAGE INN
576 6th St (89835)
Rates: $46-$80
(775) 752-3353
(800) 528-1234

LONE STAR MOTEL
676 6th St (89835)
Rates: $24-$39
(775) 752-3632

MOTEL 6
I-80/US 40 & 93 (89835)
Rates: $34-$50
(775) 752-2116
(800) 466-8356

OVERLAND HOTEL
P. O. Box 79 (89835)
Rates: $19-$27
(775) 752-3373

REST INN SUITES MOTEL
1509 E 6th St (98935)
Rates: $37-$49
(775) 752-2277
(800) 935-5768

SHARON MOTEL
633 6th St (89835)
Rates: $24-$39
(775) 752-3232

SHELL CREST MOTEL
573 6th St (89835)
Rates: $24-$39
(775) 752-3755

SUPER 8 MOTEL
930 6th St (89835)
Rates: $60-$85
(775) 752-3384
(800) 800-8000

WAGON WHEEL MOTEL
340 Sixth St (89835)
Rates: $19-$37
(775) 752-2151

WENDOVER

SUPER 8 MOTEL
1325 Wendover Blvd (89883)
Rates: $30-$84
(702) 664-2888
(800) 800-8000

WENDOVER, UTAH

MOTEL 6
561 E Wendover Blvd (84083)
Rates: $30-$36
(435) 665-2267

WESTERN RIDGE MOTEL
895 E Wendover Blvd (84083)
Rates: $26-$80
(435) 665-2211

WINNEMUCCA

BEST WESTERN GOLD COUNTRY INN
921 W Winnemucca Blvd (89445)
Rates: $79-$119
(775) 623-6999
(800) 528-1234
(800) 346-5306

BEST WESTERN HOLIDAY MOTEL
670 W Winnemucca Blvd (89445)
Rates: $59-$89
(775) 623-3684
(800) 528-1234
(800) 262-8901

BUDGET INN
251 E Winnemucca Blvd (89445)
Rates: $25-$55
(775) 623-2394

BULL HEAD MOTEL
500 E Winnemucca Blvd (89445)
Rates: $33-$50
(775) 623-3636

COZY MOTEL
344 E Winnemucca Blvd (89445)
Rates: $30-$40
(775) 623-2615

DAYS INN
511 E Winnemucca Blvd (89445)
Rates: $64-$84
(775) 623-3661
(800) 329-7466

ECONOMY MOTEL
635 W Winnemucca Blvd (89445)
Rates: $38-$75
(775) 623-5281

FRONTIER MOTEL
410 E Winnemucca Blvd (89445)
Rates: $38-$65
(775) 623-2915

HOLIDAY INN EXPRESS
1987 W Winnemucca Blvd (89445)
Rates: $55-$180
(775) 625-3100
(800) 465-4329

MOTEL 6
1600 Winnemucca
Blvd (89445)
Rates: $33-$52
(775) 623-1180
(800) 466-8356

PARK MOTEL
740 W Winnemucca
Blvd (89445)
Rates: $30-$40
(775) 623-2810

**PONDEROSA
MOTEL**
705 W Winnemucca
Blvd (89445)
Rates: $28-$59
(775) 623-4898

PYRENEES MOTEL
714 W Winnemucca
Blvd (89445)
Rates: $43-$63
(775) 623-1116

RAMADA LIMITED
1620 W Winnemucca
Blvd (89445)
Rates: $59-$99
(775) 623-1119
(800) 272-6232

**RED LION INN
& CASINO**
741 W Winnemucca
Blvd (89445)
Rates: $79-$164
(775) 623-2565
(800) 633-6435

**SCOTT
SHADY COURT**
400 First St (89445)
Rates: $35-$75
(775) 623-3646

SCOTTISH INNS
333 N Winnemucca
Blvd (89445)
Rates: $32-$75
(775) 623-3703
(800) 251-1962

SUPER 8 MOTEL
1157 W Winnemucca
Blvd (89445)
Rates: $46-$61
(775) 625-1818
(800) 800-8000

VAL-U INN MOTEL
125 E Winnemucca
Blvd (89445)
Rates: $62
(775) 623-5248
(800) 443-7777

**WINNERS
HOTEL & CASINO**
185 W Winnemucca
Blvd (89445)
Rates: $42-$80
(775) 623-2511
(800) 648-4770

YERINGTON

CASINO WEST
11 N Main St
(89447)
Rates: $34-$60
(775) 463-2481
(800) 227-4661

**COPPER INN
MOTEL**
307 N Main St
(89447)
Rates: $35-$45
(775) 463-2135

IN TOWN MOTEL
111 S Main St
(89447)
Rates: $35-$45
(775) 463-2164

**RANCH HOUSE
MOTEL**
311 W Bridge St
(89447)
Rates: $32-$44
(775) 463-2200

ZEPHYR COVE

**ZEPHYR COVE
RESORT**
760 Hwy 50
(89448)
Rates: $60-$260
(775) 588-6644

AREA CODES - If the local number doesn't connect, check for a new area code.

NEW HAMPSHIRE

ALTON

EYE JOY COTTAGES
Roberts Cove Rd (03809)
Rates: n/a
(603) 569-4973

ALTON BAY

HORSE & BUGGY COTTAGES
Bay Hill Rd (03810)
Rates: $50-$390
(603) 875-5600

LEMAY'S BY THE BAY
Rt 28A, Box 127 (03810)
Rates: n/a
(603) 875-3629

ANTRIM

MAPLEHURST INN
155 Main St (03440)
Rates: $60-$85
(603) 588-8000

ASHLAND

BLACK HORSE MOTOR COURT
RR 1, Box 46, Rt 3 (03217)
Rates: n/a
(603) 968-7116

BARTLETT

THE VILLAGER MOTEL
Main St, Rt 302 (03812)
Rates: $69-$119
(603) 374-2742
(800) 334-6988

BENNINGTON

ECONO LODGE
634 Francistown Rd (03442)
Rates: $69-$199
(603) 588-2777
(800) 553-2666

BERLIN

TRAVELER MOTEL
25 Pleasant St (03570)
Rates: $39-$99
(603) 752-2500
(800) 365-9391

BRADFORD

BRADFORD INN
RFD 1, Box 40 (03221)
Rates: n/a
(603) 938-5309

CAMPTON

GILCREST COTTAGES & MOTEL
RFD 1, Box 927 (03223)
Rates: n/a
(603) 726-3330
(888) 741-0129

PLYMOUTH WHITE MTN HOTEL
Rt 3 (03223)
Rates: $76-$125
(603) 536-3520

CENTER HARBOR

LAKE SHORE MOTEL & COTTAGES
RR 2, Box 16H (03226)
Rates: n/a
(603) 253-6244
(941) 439-6625

THE MEADOWS LAKESIDE LODGING
SR 25 (03226)
Rates: $65-$110
(603) 253-4347

SACO RIVER MOTOR LODGE
Rt 302, P. O. Box 9A (03813)
Rates: $39-$139
(603) 447-3720

WATCH HILL BED & BREAKFAST
P. O. Box 1605 (03226)
Rates: $65+
(603) 253-4334

CHESTERFIELD

CHESTERFIELD COUNTRY INN
399 Cross Rd (03466)
Rates: $105-$225
(603) 256-3211
(800) 365-5515

CLAREMONT

BEST BUDGET INN
24 Sullivan St (03743)
Rates: $38-$65
(603) 542-9567

CLAREMONT MOTOR LODGE
Beauregard St (03743)
Rates: $45-$60
(603) 542-2540

COLEBROOK

COLEBROOK HOUSE & MOTEL
132 Main St (03576)
Rates: n/a
(603) 237-5521
(800) 626-7331

NORTHERN COMFORT MOTEL
RR 1, Box 520 (03576)
Rates: $48-$72
(603) 237-4440

CONCORD

BRICK TOWER MOTOR INN
414 S Main St (03301)
Rates: $39-$64
(603) 224-9565

COMFORT INN
71 Hall St (03301)
Rates: $59-$165
(603) 226-4100
(800) 228-5150

HOLIDAY INN
172 N Main St (03301)
Rates: $79-$149
(603) 224-9534
(800) 465-4329

CONWAY

SUNNY BROOK COTTAGES
Rt 16, P. O. Box 1429 (03818)
Rates: $49-$59
(603) 447-3922

TANGLEWOOD MOTEL & COTTAGES
Rt 16, Box 108 (03818)
Rates: n/a
(603) 447-5932

WHITE DEER MOTEL
379 White Mtn Hwy (03818)
Rates: $49-$119
(603) 447-5366

DIXVILLE NOTCH

THE BALSAMS GRAND HOTEL
Off SR 26 (03576)
Rates: $195-$400
(603) 255-3400
(800) 255-0600

DOVER

DAYS INN
481 Central Ave (03820)
Rates: $80-$140
(603) 742-0400
(800) 329-7466

DURHAM

HICKORY POND INN HISTORIC BED & BREAKFST
1 Stagecoach Rd (03824)
Rates: $59-$99
(603) 659-2227

EAST SULLIVAN

POST & BEAM BED & BREAKFST
18 Centre St (03445)
Rates: n/a
(603) 847-3330
(888) 376-6262

EAST SWANZEY

COACH AND FOUR MOTOR INN
755 Monadnock Hwy (03446)
Rates: n/a
(603) 357-3705

EAST WAKEFIELD

LAKE IVANHOE CAMPING & BED & BREAKFAST INN
631 Acton Ridge Rd (03830)
Rates: n/a
(603) 522-8824

EXETER

BEST WESTERN HEARTHSIDE MOTOR INN
137 Portsmouth Ave (03833)
Rates: $60-$110
(603) 772-3794
(800) 528-1234

EXETER INN
90 Front St (03833)
Rates: $73-$135
(603) 772-5901

FITZWILLIAM

THE UNIQUE YANKEE B&B
354 Upper Troy
Rd (03447)
Rates: $60-$130
(603) 242-6706

FRANCESTOWN

THE INN AT CROTCHED MTN
Mountain Rd
(03043)
Rates: $45-$120
(603) 588-6840

FRANCONIA

"FRANCONIA NOTCH VACATIONS" HOME RENTALS
P O Box 906,
Mittersill (03580)
Rates: na
(800) 247-5536

GALE RIVER MOTEL
1 Main St (03580)
Rates: $82-$110
(603) 823-5655
(800) 255-7989

THE HORSE & HOUND INN
205 Wells Rd
(03580)
Rates: $65-$120
(603) 823-5501

LOVETT'S INN BY LAFAYETTE BROOK
Route 18 (03580)
Rates: $75-$180
(603) 823-7761
(800) 356-3802

FRANKLIN

D K MOTEL
Rt 3A & 11 (03235)
Rates: n/a
(603) 934-3311

GILMANTON

TEMPERANCE TAVERN HISTORIC BED & BRKFAST
Old Province Rd
(03237)
Rates: $75-$125
(603) 267-7349

GORHAM

COLONIAL COMFORT INN
370 Main St
(03581)
Rates: $42-$125
(603) 466-2732
(800) 470-4224

GORHAM MOTOR INN
324 Main St
(03581)
Rates: $39-$86
(603) 466-3381
(800) 445-0913

MOOSE BROOK MOTEL
65 Lancaster Rd
(03581)
Rates: $39-$69
(603) 466-5400

NORTHERN PEAKS MOTEL
289 Main St
(03581)
Rates: $32-$62
(603) 466-3374

ROYALTY INN
130 Main St
(03581)
Rates: $57-$88
(603) 466-3312
(800) 437-3529

TOWN & COUNTRY MOTOR INN
US Rt 2 (03581)
Rates: $48-$94
(603) 466-3315
(800) 325-4386

HAMPTON

LAMIE'S COUNTRY INN & TAVERN
490 Lafayette Rd
(03842)
Rates: $85-$125
(603) 926-0330

STONE GABLE INN
869 Lafayette Rd
(03842)
Rates: $44-$55
(603) 926-6883
(800) 737-6606

HAMPTON FALLS

HAMPTON FALLS INN
11 Lafayette Rd
(03844)
Rates: $99-$169
(603) 926-9545
(800) 356-1729

HANOVER

HANOVER INN-DARTMOUTH COLLEGE ON THE GREEN
Main & Wheelocke
St (03755)
Rates: $217-$287
(603) 643-4300
(800) 443-7024

HENNIKER

HENNIKER MOTEL
Craney Pond Rd
(03242)
Rates: $49-$74
(603) 428-3536

HILLSBORO

1830 HOUSE MOTEL
626 W Main St
(03244)
Rates: $45+
(603) 478-3135

HOLDERNESS

MANOR ON GOLDEN POND COUNTRY INN
Shepard Hill
Rd (03245)
Rates: $175-$375
(603) 968-3348

YANKEE TRAIL MOTEL
Rt 3 (03245)
Rates: $45-$65
(603) 968-3535
(800) 972-1492

INTERVALE

RIVERSIDE INN
Rt 16A (03845)
Rates: $45-$95
(603) 356-9060

SWISS CHALETS VILLAGE INN
Rt 16A (03845)
Rates: $49-$139
(603) 356-2232
(800) 831-2727

JACKSON

DANA PLACE INN
Jct SR 16A & 16B
(03846)
Rates: $99-$155
(603) 383-6822
(800) 537-9276

MOUNTAINSIDE FARM B&B
Carter Notch Rd
(03846)
Rates: $26-$60
(603) 383-6531
(800) 782-4270

THE VILLAGE HOUSE INN
Rt 16 A (03846)
Rates: $26-$50
(603) 383-6666
(800) 972-8343

WHITNEY'S INN
Rt 16-B (03846)
Rates: $135-$155
(603) 383-8916
(800) 677-5737

JAFFREY

WOODBOUND INN
Woodbound Rd
(03452)
Rates: $65-$190
(800) 688-7770

JEFFERSON

APPLEBROOK BED & BREAKFAST
Rt 115-A (03583)
Rates; $55-$90
(603) 586-7713
(800) 545-6504

EVERGREEN MOTEL
Rt 2 (03583)
Rates: $30-$60
(603) 586-4449

JEFFERSON NOTCH MOTEL & CABINS
Rt 2, Randolph
(03583)
Rates: $50+
(603) 466-3833
(800) 345-3833

JOSSELYN'S GETAWAY LOG CABINS
RFD 1, Box 51A,
North Rd (03583)
Rates: $56+
(800) 586-4507

KEARSARGE

ISAAC E. MERRILL HOUSE INN B&B
720 Kearsarge Rd
(03847)
Rates: $55-$155
(603) 356-9041
(800) 328-9041

KEENE

BEST WESTERN SOVEREIGN HOTEL
401 Winchester St
(03431)
Rates: $103-$150
(603) 357-3038
(800) 528-1234
(800) 533-6364

DAYS INN
175 Key Rd
(03431)
Rates: $125-$155
(603) 352-7616
(800) 329-7466

THE MOTOR INN MOTEL
921 Main St, Rt 12
S (03431)
Rates: n/a
(603) 352-4138

VALLEY GREEN MOTEL
379 West St
(03431)
Rates: $30-$69
(603) 352-7350

WINDING BROOK LODGE
Box 372 (03431)
Rates: $34-$50
(603) 352-3111

LACONIA

SUN VALLEY COTTAGES & CONDOS
686 Endicott St N (03246)
Rates: $45-$60
(603) 366-4945

TIN WHISTLE INN
1047 Union Ave (03246)
Rates: n/a
(603) 528-4185

LANCASTER

LANCASTER MOTOR INN
112 Main St (03584)
Rates: $39-$55
(603) 788-4921

THE OLD MORSE LODGE B&B
39 Portland St (03584)
Rates: $45-$100
(603) 788-4600

PINETREE MOTEL
RFD 2, Box 281 (03584)
Rates: $28-$40
(603) 636-2479

LEBANON

HOLIDAY INN EXPRESS
135 SR 120 (03766)
Rates: $129-$155
(603) 448-5070
(800) 465-4329

LINCOLN

COMFORT INN & SUITES
10 Railroad St (03251)
Rates: $50-$125
(800) 228-5150

PARKER'S MOTEL
Rt 3, Box 100 (03251)
Rates: $54-$89
(603) 745-8341
(800) 766-6835

PEMI MOTOR COURT CABINS
RFD 1, Box 97 (03251)
Rates: $50+
(603) 745-8323

LISBON

AMMONOOSUC COUNTRY INN
641 Bishop Rd (03585)
Rates: $60-$130
(603) 838-6118

LITTLETON

CONTINENTAL 93 MOTOR INN
516 Meadow St (03561)
Rates: $49-$89
(603) 444-5366

EASTGATE MOTOR INN
335 Cottage St (03561)
Rates: $64-$70
(603) 444-3971

MAPLE LEAF MOTEL
150 W Main St (03561)
Rates: $42-$58
(603) 444-5105

LOUDON

LOVEJOY FARM BED & BREAKFST
268 Lovejoy Rd (03301)
Rates: $69-$87
(603) 783-4007

LYME

LOCH LYME LODGE
NH 10, RFD 278 (03768)
Rates: $26-$65
(603) 795-2141
(800) 423-2141

MANCHESTER

COMFORT INN
298 Queen City Ave (03102)
Rates: $64-$134
(603) 668-2600
(800) 221-5150

ECONO LODGE
75 W Hancock St (03102)
Rates: $55-$150
(603) 624-0111
(800) 553-2666

HOLIDAY INN
700 Elm St (03101)
Rates: $99-$119
(603) 625-1000
(800) 465-4329

SHERATON FOUR POINTS HOTEL
55 John E Devine Dr (03103)
Rates: $80-$102
(603) 668-6110

MERRIMACK

DAYS INN
242 Daniel Webster Hwy (03054)
Rates: $44-$77
(603) 429-4600
(800) 329-7466

MERRIMACK HOTEL & CONF CENTER
4 Executive Park Dr (03054)
Rates: $89-$149
(603) 424-8000

RESIDENCE INN BY MARRIOTT
246 Daniel Webster Hwy (03054)
Rates: $110-$170
(603) 424-8100
(800) 331-3131

MOULTON-BOROUGH

MATTERHORN MOTOR LODGE
340 Rt 25 (03254)
Rates: $95-$125
(603) 253-4314

ROB ROY MOTOR LODGE
P. O. Box 420 (03254)
Rates: $49-$75
(603) 476-5571

MOUNT SUNAPEE

BEST WESTERN SUNAPEE LAKE LODGE
1403 Rt 103 (03255)
Rates: $89-229
(603) 763-2010
(800) 528-1234
(800) 606-5253

NASHUA

HOLIDAY INN
9 Northeastern Blvd (03062)
Rates: $69-$109
(603) 888-1551
(800) 465-4329

MOTEL 6
2 Progress Ave (03062)
Rates: $48-$64
(603) 889-4151
(800) 466-8356

MARRIOTT HOTEL
2200 Southwood Dr (03063)
Rates: $85-$125
(603) 880-9100
(800) 228-9290

RED ROOF INN
77 Spitbrook Rd (03063)
Rates: $59-$89
(603) 888-1893
(800) 843-7663

NEWPORT

HISTORIC EAGLE INN AT COIT MOUNTAIN
523 N Main St (03773)
Rates: $49-$127
(603) 863-3583
(800) 367-2364

NEWPORT MOTEL
467 Sunapee St (03773)
Rates: $53-$75
(603) 863-1440

NORTH CONWAY

ISAAC E MERRILL HOUSE INN B&B
720 Kearsarge Rd (03860)
Rates: $59-$179
(603) 356-9041

MAPLE LEAF MOTEL
Rt 16 (03860)
Rates: n/a
(603) 356-5388

MT. WASH VALLEY MOTOR LODGE
1567 White Mtn Hwy (03860)
Rates: $69-$149
(603) 356-5486
(800) 634-2383

NORTH CONWAY MOUNTAIN INN
White Mtn Hwy (03860)
Rates: $69-$169
(603) 356-2803

OXEN YOKE B&B, MOTEL & COTTAGES
Kearsarge St (03860)
Rates: $40+
(603) 356-6321
(800) 862-1600

STONEHURST MANOR HISTORIC COUNTRY INN
SR 16 & US 302 (03860)
Rates: $96-$186
(603) 356-3113
(800) 525-9100

NORTH WOODSTOCK

PITRE'S CABINS
Rt 112 West (03262)
Rates: n/a
(603) 745-8646

NORTHWOOD

LAKE SHORE FARM RESORT
275 Jenness Pond Rd (03261)
Rates: $285-$305
(603) 942-5921

AREA CODES - If the local number doesn't connect, check for a new area code.

OSSIPEE

PINE COVE MOTEL
Rts 16 & 28
(03864)
Rates: $45-$70
(603) 539-4491

PITTSBURG

THE GLEN LODGE
77 The Glen Rd
(03592)
Rates: $77-$192
(603) 538-6500
(800) 445-4536

LOPSTICK LODGE & CABINS
First Connecticut
Lake (03592)
Rates: n/a
(800) 538-6659

SNOWFIELD CABINS
RR 1, Box 94-B,
Covill Rd (03592)
Rates: n/a
(603) 538-7008

SPRUCE CONE CABINS
Rt 3, Box 13
(03592)
Rates: $20-$28
(603) 538-6572
(800) 538-6361

TALL TIMBER LODGE
Back Lake (03592)
Rates: n/a
(603) 538-6651
(800) 835-6343

TIMBERLAND LODGE & CABINS
First Connecticut
Lake (03592)
Rates: $35-$62
(603) 538-6613
(800) 545-6613

PITTSFIELD

APPLE MOUNTAIN LODGE
1301 Upper City
Rd (03263)
Rates: n/a
(603) 435-7641

PLYMOUTH

BEST WESTERN WHITE MOUNTAINS
I-93, Exit 27
(03264)
Rates: $39-$150
(603) 536-3520
(800) 370-8666

PILGRIM INN & COTTAGES
307 Main St
(03264)
Rates: n/a
(603) 536-1319
(800) 216-1900

PORTSMOUTH

ANCHORAGE INN
417 Woodbury
Ave (03801)
Rates: $52-$99
(603) 431-8111
(800) 370-8111

HOWARD JOHNSON HOTEL
Interstate Traffic
Circle (03801)
Rates: $59-$195
(603) 436-7600
(800) 446-4656

RESIDENCE INN BY MARRIOTT
1 Int'l Dr (03801)
Rates: $169-$199
(603) 436-8880
(800) 331-3131

WREN'S NEST VILLAGE INN
3548 Lafayette Rd
(03801)
Rates: $69-$169
(603) 436-2481

RINDGE

WOODBOUND COUNTRY INN
62 Woodbound
Rd (03641)
Rates: $69-$190
(603) 532-8341
(800) 688-7770

ROCHESTER

ANCHORAGE INNS
80 Main St (03839)
Rates: $59-$89
(603) 332-3350

HI-VU MOTOR INN
Rochester Hill Rd,
Rt 108 (03839)
Rates: n/a
(603) 332-1230

SALEM

RED ROOF INN
15 Red Roof Ln
(03079)
Rates: $76-$86
(603) 898-6422
(800) 843-7663

SEABROOK

BEST WESTERN SEABROOK INN
9 Stard Rd & Rt
107 (03874)
Rates: $49-$99
(603) 474-3078
(800) 528-1234

SHELBURNE

PHILBROOK FARM INN
881 North Rd
(03581)
Rates: $122-$475
(603) 466-3831

SUGAR HILL

THE HILLTOP INN BED & BREAKFST
1348 Main St
(03585)
Rates: $129-$155
(603) 823-5695
(800) 770-5695

HOMESTEAD HISTORIC COUNTRY INN
Rt 117 (03585)
Rates: $30-$70
(603) 823-9599
(800) 823-5564

SUNAPEE

BURKEHAVEN RESORT
179 Burkehaven
Hill Rd (03782)
Rates: $69-$84
(603) 763-2788
(800) 567-2788

DEXTER'S INN
258 Stagecoach Rd
(03782)
Rates: $95-$180
(603) 763-5571
(800) 232-5571

SEVEN HEARTHS INN HISTORIC BED & BREAKFST
26 Seven Hearths
Ln (03782)
Rates: $100-$140
(603) 763-5657

SWANZEY

LOAFER INN AT THE 1792 WHITECOMB HOUSE B&B
27 Main St (03431)
Rates: n/a
(603) 357-6624

TAMWORTH

THE TAMWORTH HISTORIC COUNTRY INN
15 Cleveland Hill
Rd (03886)
Rates: $140-$220
(603) 323-7721
(800) 642-7352

THORNTON

GILCREST COTTAGES & MOTEL
Rt 3, Exit 29 I-93
(03223)
Rates: n/a
(603) 726-3330
(888) 741-0129

TILTON

TILTON MANOR
40 Chestnut St
(03276)
Rates: $60-$70
(603) 286-3457

TROY

THE INN AT EAST HILL FARM
Monadnock St
(03465)
Rates: $68-$88
(603) 242-6495
(800) 242-6495

TUFTONBORO

19 MILE BAY LODGES
HC 69, Box 110
(03853)
Rates: n/a
(603) 569-3507

TWIN MOUNTAIN

CHARLMONT MOTOR INN
Rt 3, Box G
(03595)
Rates: $35-$60
(603) 846-5549

WEIRS BEACH

CEDAR LODGE AT BRICKYARD MOUNTAIN
Rt 3 (03247)
Rates: n/a
(603) 366-4316
(800) 366-4883

CHANNEL INN & COTTAGES
P O Box 5106
(03247)
Rates: n/a
(603) 366-4673

LANGLEY COVE MOTEL & COTTAGES
563 Weirs Blvd,
Rt 3 (03247)
Rates: n/a
(603) 366-5540

WENTWORTH

HILLTOP ACRES BED & BREAKFAST
Eastside & Buffalo
Rds (03282)
Rates: $100-$125
(603) 764-5896

WEST LEBANON

ECONOMY INN AIRPORT
45 Airport Rd
(03784)
Rates: $50-$95
(603) 298-8888
(800) 845-3557

AREA CODES - If the local number doesn't connect, check for a new area code.

RADISSON INN NORTH COUNTRY
25 Airport Rd
(03784)
Rates: $99-$110
(603) 298-5996
(800) 962-3198

WHITEFIELD

SPALDING INN
Mountain View
Rd (03598)
Rates: n/a
(603) 837-2572
(800) 368-VIEW

WILTON CENTER

AUK'S NEST BED & BREAKFAST
East Road, RFD 1
(03086)
Rates: $45-$60
(603) 878-3443

STEPPING STONES B&B
Bennington Battle
Trail (03086)
Rates: $50-$55
(603) 654-9048

WINNISQUAM

LYNNMERE MOTEL & COTTAGES
850 Laconia Rd
(03289)
Rates: $35-$85
(603) 524-0912

WOLFEBORO

ALLEN 'A' MOTOR INN
Rt 28 (03894)
Rates: n/a
(603) 569-1700
(800) 732-8507

THE LAKE MOTEL
280 S Main St
(03894)
Rates: $100-$110
(603) 569-1100
(888) 569-1110

MUSEUM LODGES
HC 69, P. O. Box
680 (03894)
Rates: $80-$130
(603) 569-1551

WOODSTOCK

WHEELOCK MOTOR COURT
Rt 3 (03293)
Rates: n/a
(603) 745-8771

WOODSVILLE

ALL SEASONS MOTEL
36 Smith St
(03785)
Rates: $50-$75
(603) 747-2157

NOOTKA LODGE
36 Smith St
(03785)
Rates: $50-$110
(603) 747-2418

NEW JERSEY

ABSECON

DAYS INN
224 E White Horse Pike (08201)
Rates: $60-$175
(609) 652-2200
(800) 329-7466
(800) 755-9987

ANDOVER

PANTHER LAKE CAMPGROUND CABINS
6 Panther Lake Rd (07821)
Rates: $23+
(973) 347-4440
(800) 543-2056

ATLANTIC CITY

SUNSET INN ON THE BAY
1600 Albany Ave (06401)
Rates: $40-$110
(609) 344-2515
(800) 223-6370

(The following pet care facility is provided as a service for pet owners visiting the casinos)

ATLANTIC CITY BEACH PET CARE KENNEL
547 N Trenton Ave (08401)
Rates: n/a
(609) 348-8660
(800) 965-5555

BARNEGAT

SCRUBBLE PINES FAMILY CAMPGROUND CABINS
30 Rt 72 (08005)
Rates: $18-$45
(609) 698-5684
(800) 590-2879

BAYVILLE

CEDAR CREEK CAMPGROUND CABINS
1052 Rt 9 (08721)
Rates: n/a
(732) 269-1413

BEACH HAVEN

ENGLESIDE INN
30 Engleside Ave (08008)
Rates: $170-$255
(609) 492-1251
(800) 762-2214

BELMAR

DOWN THE SHORE BED & BREAKFAST
201 7th Ave (07719)
Rates: $55-$90
(732) 681-9023

BERLIN

RED CARPET INN
1036 Rt 73 S (08009)
Rates: n/a
(609) 768-5353
(800) 251-1962

BLACKWOOD

HOWARD JOHNSON EXPRESS
832 N Black Horse Pk (08012)
Rates: $45-$95
(856) 228-4040
(800) 446-4656
(800) 796-4040

BORDENTOWN

DAYS INN
1073 US 206 N (08505)
Rates: $80-$94
(609) 298-6100
(800) 329-7466

ECONO LODGE
187 US 130 N (08505)
Rates: $49-$109
(609) 298-5000
(800) 553-2666

BRANCHVILLE

HARMONY RIDGE FARM & CAMPGROUND CABINS
23 Risdon Dr (07826)
Rates: $15+
(973) 948-4941
(800) 462-2670

KYMER CAMPGROUND CABINS
69 Kymer Rd (07826)
Rates: $20+
(973) 875-3167
(800) 526-2267

BUENA

BUENA VISTA CAMPING PARK CABINS
1775 Harding Hwy Rt (08301)
Rates: $21+
(856) 697-2004

CAPE MAY

BEACHCOMBER CAMPING RESORT CABINS
462 Seashore Rd (08204)
Rates: $29-$35
(800) 233-0150

MARQUIS DE LAFAYETTE HOTEL
501 Beach Dr (08204)
Rates: $219-$359
(609) 884-3500
(800) 257-0432

THE MOFFETT HOUSE B&B
715 Broadway (08204)
Rates: $75-$100
(609) 898-0915
(800) 498-0915

CAPE MAY COURT HOUSE

BIG TIMBER LAKE CAMPGROUND CABINS
116 Goshen-Swanton Rd (08210)
Rates: $31+
(609) 465-4456
(800) 542-CAMP

KING NUMMY TRAIL CAMPGROUND CABINS
205 Rt 47S (08210)
Rates: $19-$23
(609) 465-4242

NORTH WILDWOOD CAMPGROUND CABINS
240 W Shellbay Ave (08210)
Rates: $25+
(609) 465-4440
(800) 752-4882

SHELLBAY CAMPGROUND CABINS
277 W Shellbay Ave (08210)
Rates: $25+
(609) 465-4770

CARTERET

HOLIDAY INN
1000 Roosevelt Ave (07008)
Rates: $90-$138
(732) 541-9500
(800) 465-4329

CHATSWORTH

WADING PINES CAMPGROUND CABINS
85 Godfrey Bridge Rd (08019)
Rates: $25+
(609) 726-1313

CHERRY HILL

HOLIDAY INN
Rt 70 & Sayer Ave (08002)
Rates: $94
(856) 663-5300
(800) 465-4329

HOWARD JOHNSON EXPRESS INN & CONF CENTER
2389 W Marlton Pike (08002)
Rates: $45-$75
(856) 317-1900
(800) 446-4656

RESIDENCE INN BY MARRIOTT
1821 Old Cuthbert Rd (08034)
Rates: $150
(856) 429-6111
(800) 331-3131

CLARKESBORO

TIMBERLANE CAMPGROUND CABINS
117 Timber Lane (08020)
Rates: $19+
(856) 423-6677

CLERMONT

AVALON CAMPGROUND CABINS
1917 Rt 9 N (08210)
Rates: $24+
(609) 624-0075
(800) 814-2267

DRIFTWOOD CAMPING RESORT CABINS
1955 Rt 9 & Rt 83 (08210)
Rates: $24+
(609) 624-1899
(800) 624-3743

HIDDEN ACRES CAMPGROUND CABINS
1142 Rt 83 (08210)
Rates: $28+
(609) 624-9015
(800) 874-7576

COLESVILLE

HIGH POINT COUNTRY INN MOTEL
1328 SR 23 N (07461)
Rates: $64-$85
(973) 702-1860

DELAWARE

DELAWARE RIVER CABINS
Rt 46, Box 100 (07833)
Rates: $20+
(908) 475-4517
(800) 543-0271

DOROTHY

COUNTRY MOUSE CAMPGROUND CABINS
13 S Jersey Ave (08317)
Rates: $22+
(609) 476-2143
(800) 694-0315

EAST BRUNSWICK

HILTON & TOWERS
3 Tower Center (08816)
Rates: $89-$225
(732) 828-2000
(800) 445-8667

MOTEL 6
244 Rt 18 (08816)
Rates: $53-$60
(732) 390-4545
(800) 466-8356

EAST HANOVER

RAMADA HOTEL & CONFERENCE CENTER
130 Rt 10 W (07936)
Rates: $60-$159
(973) 386-5622
(800) 272-6232

EAST RUTHERFORD

HOMESTEAD GUEST STUDIOS
300 SR 3 E (07073)
Rates: n/a
(201) 939-8866

SHERATON MEADOWLANDS
2 Meadowlands Plaza (07073)
Rates: $109-$160
(201) 896-0500
(800) 325-3535

EAST WINDSOR

DAYS INN
460 Rt 33 (08520)
Rates: $89-$124
(856) 448-3200
(800) 329-7466

EATONTOWN

CRYSTAL MOTOR LODGE
170 Main St (07724)
Rates: $38-$66
(732) 542-4900
(800) 562-5290

EDISON

RAMADA PLAZA HOTEL
3050 Woodbridge Ave (08817)
Rates: $89-$99
(732) 661-1000
(800) 272-6232

RED ROOF INN
860 New Durham Rd (08817)
Rates: $69-$88
(732) 248-9300
(800) 843-7663

SHERATON HOTEL
125 Raritan Center Pkwy (08817)
Rates: $199
(732) 225-8300
(800) 325-3535

WELLESLEY INN & SUITES
831 Rt 1S (08817)
Rates: $99-$149
(732) 287-0171
(800) 444-8888

ELIZABETH

HILTON NEWARK AIRPORT
1170 Spring St (07201)
Rates: $99-$279
(908) 351-3900
(800) 445-8667

ELMER

YOGI BEAR AT TALL PINES RESORT CABINS
49 Beal Rd (08318)
Rates: $31
(856) 451-7479
(800) 252-2890

ENGLEWOOD

RADISSON HOTEL
401 S Van Brunt St (07631)
Rates: $209-$239
(201) 871-2020
(800) 333-3333

ESTELLE MANOR

PLEASANT VALLEY CAMPGROUND CABINS
60 S River Rd (08319)
Rates: $25+
(609) 625-1238

FAIR LAWN

AMERISUITES
41-01 Broadway (07410)
Rates: $134-$170
(201) 475-3888
(800) 833-1516

FAIRFIELD

RADISSON HOTEL & SUITES
690 US 46 E (07004)
Rates: $179-$199
(973) 227-9200
(800) 333-3333

FLEMINGTON

RAMADA INN
250 Rts 202 & 31 (08822)
Rates: $89-$102
(908) 782-7472
(800) 272-6232

FRANKLINVILLE

THE ROCK AT VILLAGE DOCK CAMPGROUND CABINS
1664 Delsea Dr [(08322
Rates: $20+
(856) 694-4935

HAMMONTON

PARADISE LAKES CAMPGROUND CABINS
500 Paradise Dr (08037)
Rates: $21+
(609) 561-7095

HASBROUCK HEIGHTS

HILTON HOTEL
650 Terrace Ave (07604)
Rates: $99-$189
(201) 288-6100
(800) 445-8667

HAZLET

WELLESLEY INN & SUITES
3215 Hwy 35 N (07730)
Rates: $99-$159
(732) 888-2800
(800) 444-8888

HOPE

THE INN AT MILL-RACE POND B&B
313 Johnsonburg Rd (07844)
Rates: $85-$165
(908) 459-4884
(800 746-6467

JACKSON

BUTTERFLY CAMPGROUND CABINS
360 Butterfly Rd (08527)
Rates: $24+
(732) 928-2107

TIP TAM CAMPING RESORT CABINS
Brewers Bridge Rd (08527)
Rates: $27+
(732) 363-4036

JERSEY CITY

HOLLAND MOTOR LODGE
Holland Tunnel Plaza E (07302)
Rates: $52-$70
(201) 963-6200

LAKEWOOD

BEST WESTERN LEISURE INN
1600 Rt 70 (08701)
Rates: $59-$105
(732) 367-0900
(800) 528-1234

LAWRENCEVILLE

HOWARD JOHNSON INN
2995 Brunswick Pike (08648)
Rates: $51-$150
(609) 896-1100
(800) 446-4656

RED ROOF INN
3203 Brunswick Pike (08648)
Rates: $66-$98
(609) 896-3388
(800) 843-7663

LYNDHURST

NOVOTEL MEADOWLANDS
1 Polito Ave (07071)
Rates: $88-$120
(201) 896-6666
(800) 668-6835

AREA CODES - If the local number doesn't connect, check for a new area code.

MAHWAH

COMFORT INN
160 SR 17 S
(07430)
Rates: $60-$150
(201) 512-0800
(800) 228-5150

**SHERATON
CROSSROADS
HOTEL**
1 Int'l Blvd (07495)
Rates: $199-$219
(201) 529-1660
(800) 325-3535

MAPLE SHADE

MOTEL 6
Rt 73 N (08052)
Rates: $39-$47
(609) 235-3550
(800) 466-8356

MARMORA

**WHIPPOORWIL
CAMPGROUND
CABINS**
810 S Shore Rd
(08223)
Rates: $34+
(609) 390-3458
(800) 424-8275

MAYS LANDING

**WINDING RIVER
CAMPGROUND
CABINS**
6752 Weymouth
Rd (08330)
Rates: $20+
(609) 625-3191

**YOGI BEAR'S
JELLYSTONE PARK
CABINS**
1079 12th Ave
(08330)
Rates: $20+
(609) 476-2811
(800) 355-0264

MIDDLETOWN

**HOWARD
JOHNSON
MOTOR LODGE**
750 Hwy 35 S
(07748)
Rates: $86-$150
(732) 671-3400
(800) 446-4656

MILLVILLE

**MILLVILLE
MOTOR INN**
1701 N 2nd St
(08332)
Rates: $54-$100
(856) 327-3300
(800) 428-4373

MONMOUTH JUNCTION

RED ROOF INN
208 New Rd
(08852)
Rates: $56-$88
(732) 821-8800
(800) 843-7663

**RESIDENCE INN
BY MARRIOTT**
4225 Rt 1 (08852)
Rates: n/a
(732) 329-9600
(800) 331-3131

MONROEVILLE

**OLD CEDAR CAMP-
GROUND CABINS**
274 Richwood Rd
(08343)
Rates: $17+
(609) 358-2406
(609) 358-4881

**OLDMAN'S CREEK
CAMPGROUND
CABINS**
174 Laux Rd (08343)
Rates: $17+
(609) 478-4502

MONTAGUE

**SHIPPEKONK
FAMILY
CAMPGROUND
CABINS**
59 River Rd
(07827)
Rates: $19+
(973) 293-3383

MOUNT ARLINGTON

**FOUR POINTS
HOTEL BY
SHERATON**
15 Howard Blvd
(07856)
Rates: $85-$119
(973) 770-2000
(800) 325-3535

MOUNT HOLLY

**BEST WESTERN
INN**
2020 Rt 541
(08060)
Rates: $86-$122
(609) 261-3800
(800) 528-1234

**HOWARD
JOHNSON INN**
Mt. Holly Rd
(08060)
Rates: $59-$105
(609) 267-6550
(800) 446-4656

MOUNT LAUREL

MAINSTAY SUITES
SR 38 & Bishops
Gate (08054)
Rates: $59+
(800) 660-6246

RED ROOF INN
603 Fellowship Rd
(08054)
Rates: $51-$83
(856) 234-5589
(800) 843-7663

**SUMMERFIELD
SUITES**
3000 Crawford Pl
(08054)
Rates: $179
(856) 222-1313
(800) 833-4353

**TRAVELODGE
HOTEL**
1111 Rt 73 (08054)
Rates: $119-$149
(856) 234-7000
(800) 578-7878

NEW BRUNSWICK

**HOWARD
JOHNSON
EXPRESS INN**
26, Rt 1 N (08901)
Rates: $70-$115
(800) 446-4656

NEWARK

**MARRIOTT HOTEL
AIRPORT**
Newark Intl
Airport (07114)
Rates: $89-$195
(973) 623-0006
(800) 228-9290

**SHERATON
HOTEL NEWARK
AIRPORT**
128 Frontage Rd
(07114)
Rates: $206
(973) 690-5500
(800) 325-3535

NORTH BERGEN

DAYS INN
2750 Tonnelle Ave
(07047)
Rates: $79-$500
(201) 348-3600
(800) 329-7466

NORTH PLAINFIELD

**HOWARD
JOHNSON
EXPRESS INN**
1011 Rt 22 W
(07060)
Rates: $65-$129
(908) 753-6500
(800) 446-4656

OCEAN CITY

**CROSSINGS
MOTOR INN**
3420 Haven Ave
(08226)
Rates: $95-$170
(609) 398-4433

OCEAN VIEW

**OCEAN VIEW
CAMPGROUND
CABINS**
255 Rt 9, Shore Rd
(08230)
Rates: $29+
(609) 624-1675

**PINE HAVEN
CAMPGROUND
CABINS**
Rt 9 (08230)
Rates: $27+
(609) 624-3437

SEA GROVE CAMPING

RESORT CABINS
2665 Rt 9 (08230)
Rates: $23+
(609) 624-3529
(800) 432-6629

**TAMERLANE
CAMPGROUND
CABINS**
2241 Rt 9 (08230)
Rates: $21+
(609) 624-0767

PARAMUS

**HOWARD
JOHNSON INN**
393 Rt 17S (07652)
Rates: $80-$115
(201) 265-4200
(800) 446-4656

RADISSON INN
601 From Rd
(07652)
Rates: $160
(201) 262-6900
(800) 333-3333

PARKERTOWN

**BAKER'S ACRES
CAMPGROUND
CABINS**
230 Willets Ave
(08087)
Rates: $20+
(609) 296-2664
(800) 648-2227

PARSIPPANY

HILTON HOTEL
1 Hilton Court
(07054)
Rates: $79-$199
(973) 267-7373
(800) 445-8667

**HOWARD
JOHNSON
EXPRESS**
625 Rt 46 E (07054)
Rates: $55-$75
(973) 882-8600
(800) 446-4656

RAMADA LIMITED
949 Rt 46 (07054)
Rates: $95-$120
(973) 263-0404
(800) 272-6232

AREA CODES - If the local number doesn't connect, check for a new area code.

RED ROOF INN
855 Rt 46 E (07054)
Rates: $80-$90
(973) 334-3737
(800) 843-7663

RESIDENCE INN BY MARRIOTT
3 Gatehall Dr
(07054)
Rates: n/a
(800) 331-3131

PENNS GROVE

WELLESLEY INN & SUITES
517 S Pennsville
Auburn Rd
(08069)
Rates: $50-$150
(856) 299-3800
(800) 444-8888

PILESGROVE

FOUR SEASONS CABIN RENTALS
158 Woodstown-
Daretown Rd
(08098)
Rates: $18-$20
(856) 769-3635
(888) 372-2267

PISCATAWAY

EMBASSY SUITES HOTEL
121 Centennial
Ave (08854)
Rates: $99-$225
(732) 980-0500
(800) 362-2779

MOTEL 6
1012 Stelton Rd
(08854)
Rates: $53-$60
(732) 981-9200
(800) 466-8356

POMONA

EVERGREEN WOODS CAMPING RESORT CABINS
Rt 575 & Moss
Mill Rd (08240)
Rates: $24-$26
(609) 652-1577

PRINCETON

AMERISUITES
3565 US 1 S (08543)
Rates: $175-$200
(609) 720-0200
(800) 833-1516

NOVOTEL HOTEL
100 Independence
Way (08540)
Rates: $89-$169
(609) 520-1200
(800) 668-6835

RESIDENCE INN BY MARRIOTT
4225 Rt 1 (08543)
Rates: $69-$149
(609) 683-0001
(800) 331-3131

SUMMERFIELD SUITES HOTEL
4375 US 1 S
(08543)
Rates: $139-$199
(609) 951-0009
(800) 833-4353

RAMSEY

THE INN AT RAMSEY
1315 Rt 17S
(07446)
Rates: $60-$150
(201) 327-6700
(800) 678-5683

WELLESLEY INN & SUITES
946 Rt 17N (07446)
Rates: $59-$124
(201) 934-9250
(800) 444-8888

RUNNEMEDE

HOLIDAY INN
109 9th Ave
(08078)
Rates: $99-$120
(856) 939-4200
(800) 465-4329

SADDLE BROOK

HOLIDAY INN & CONFERENCE CTR
50 Kenney Pl
(07662)
Rates: $89-$109
(201) 843-0600
(800) 465-4329

SECAUCUS

AMERISUITES
575 Park Plaza Dr
(07094)
Rates: $159-$269
(201) 422-9480
(800) 833-1516

MAINSTAY SUITES
50 Plaza Dr
(07094)
Rates: $79
(800) 660-6246

MEADOWLANDS CROWNE PLAZA
2 Harmon Plaza
(07094)
Rates: $129-$299
(201) 348-6900
(800) 227-6963

RADISSON SUITE HOTEL
350 Rt 3W, Mill
Creek Dr (07094)
Rates: $119-$209
(201) 863-8700
(800) 333-3333

RED ROOF INN
15 Meadowlands
Pkwy (07094)
Rates: $70-$142
(201) 319-1000
(800) 843-7663

SOMERS POINT

RESIDENCE INN BY MARRIOTT AT GREATE BAY GOLF CLUB
900 Mays Landing
Rd (08244)
Rates: $149-$199
(609) 927-6400
(800) 331-3131

SOMERSET

HOLIDAY INN
195 Davidson Ave
(08873)
Rates: $149
(732) 356-1700
(800) 465-4329

QUALITY INN
1850 Easton Ave
(08873)
Rates: $64-$125
(732) 469-5050
(800) 228-5151

SUMMERFIELD SUITES HOTEL
260 Davidson Ave
(08873)
Rates: $129-$159
(732) 356-8000
(800) 833-4353

SOUTH PLAINFIELD

HOLIDAY INN
4701 Stelton Rd
(07080)
Rates: $69-$129
(908) 753-5500
(800) 465-4329

SPRINGFIELD

HOLIDAY INN
304 Rt 22 W
(07081)
Rates: $125
(973) 376-9400
(800) 465-4329

TINTON FALLS

RED ROOF INN
11 Centre Plaza-
Hope Rd (07724)
Rates: $56-$83
(732) 389-4646
(800) 843-7663

RESIDENCE INN BY MARRIOTT
90 Park Rd (07724)
Rates: $109-$149
(732) 389-8100
(800) 331-3131

SUNRISE SUITES HOTEL
3 Centre Plaza
(07724)
Rates: $209
(732) 389-4800
(800) 833-4353

TOMS RIVER

HOLIDAY INN
290 Hwy 37 E
(08753)
Rates: $84-$114
(732) 244-4000
(800) 465-4329

HOWARD JOHNSON HOTEL
955 Hooper Ave
(08753)
Rates: $110-$189
(732) 244-1000
(800) 446-4656

TUCKERTON

ATLANTIC CITY NORTH BASS RIVER KOA KABINS
Stage Rd (08087)
Rates: $22+
(609) 296-9163
(888) 229-9776

VINELAND

RAMADA INN
2216 W Landis
Ave & Rt 55
(08360)
Rates: $60-$75
(856) 696-3800
(800) 272-6232

VOORHEES

HAMPTON INN
121 Laurel Oak Rd
(08043)
Rates: $93-$99
(856) 346-4500
(800) 426-7866

WALL

ECONO LODGE
5309 SR 33 & 34
(07727)
Rates: $54-$125
(732) 938-3110
(800) 553-2666

WARREN

SOMERSET HILLS HOTEL
200 Liberty
Corner Rd (07059)
Rates: $115-$235
(908) 647-6700

WAYNE

HOWARD JOHNSON INN
1850 Rt 23 (07470)
Rates: $70-$115
(973) 696-8050
(800) 446-4656

WEEHAWKEN

SHERATON SUITES OF LINCOLN HARBOR
500 Harbor Blvd (07087)
Rates: $289-$319
(201) 617-5600
(800) 325-3535

WEST CREEK

SEA PIRATE CAMPGROUND CABINS
154 Rt 9 N (08092)
Rates: $21+
(609) 296-7400
(800) 822-CAMP

WHIPPANY

HOMESTEAD VILLAGE GUEST STUIODS
125 Rt 10 E (07981)
Rates: $99
(973) 463-1999
(888) 782-9473

HOWARD JOHNSON INN
1255 Rt 10 (07981)
Rates: $59-$125
(973) 539-8350
(800) 446-4656

MARRIOTT HOTEL
1401 Rt 10E
(07981)
Rates: $99-$205
(973) 538-8811
(800) 228-9290

SUMMERFIELD SUITES
1 Ridgedale Ave
(07981)
Rates: $120-$280
(973) 605-1001
(800) 833-4353

WINSLOW

KNIGHTS INN
530 Rt 73 (08095)
Rates: $40-$99
(609) 561-6200
(800) 843-5644

WOODBRIDGE

HOMESTEAD VILLAGE GUEST STUDIOS
1 Hoover Way
(07095)
Rates: $99
(732) 442-8333
(888) 782-9473

WOODCLIFF LAKE

HILTON HOTEL
200 Tice Blvd
(07675)
Rates: $186-$206
(201) 391-3600
(800) 445-8667

WRIGHTS-TOWN

DAYS INN
507 E Main St
(08562)
Rates: $41-$84
(609) 723-6900
(800) 329-7466

NEW MEXICO

ALAMOGORDO

ALL AMERICAN INN
508 S White Sands Blvd (88310)
Rates: $30-$38
(505) 437-1850

BEST WESTERN DESERT AIRE MOTOR HOTEL
1021 S White Sands Blvd (88310)
Rates: $57-$68
(505) 437-2110
(800) 528-1234

HOLIDAY INN EXPRESS
1401 S White Sands Blvd (88310)
Rates: $65
(505) 437-7100
(800) 465-4329

MOTEL 6
251 Panorama Blvd (88310)
Rates: $34-$60
(505) 434-5970
(800) 466-8356

SATELLITE INN
2224 N White Sands Blvd (88310)
Rates: $32-$40
(505) 437-8454

SUPER 8 MOTEL
3204 N White Sands (88310)
Rates: $35-$53
(505) 434-4205
(800) 800-8000

ALBUQUERQUE

111 BNB JAZZ INN
111 Walter NE (87103)
Rates: $65-$95
(505) 242-1530
(888) JAZZ-INN

AMBERLEY SUITE HOTEL
7620 Pan American Frwy NE (87109)
Rates: $89-$155
(505) 823-1300
(800) 333-9806

AMERISUITES
6901 Arvada Ave NE (87110)
Rates: $69-$107
(505) 872-9000
(800) 833-1516

AMERISUITES
1400 Sunport Pl SE (87106)
Rates: $85-$107
(505) 242-9300
(800) 833-1516

BAYMONT INN AIRPORT
1511 Gibson Blvd SE (87106)
Rates: $65-$75
(505) 242-1555
(800) 789-4103
(800) 301-0200

BAYMONT INN & SUITES
7439 Pan American Frwy NE (87109)
Rates: $55-$66
(505) 345-7500
(800) 789-4103
(800) 301-0200

BEST WESTERN AIRPORT INN
2400 Yale Blvd SE (87106)
Rates: $49-$109
(505) 242-7022
(800) 528-1234

BEST WESTERN AMERICAN MOTOR INN
12999 Central Ave NE (87123)
Rates: $49-$99
(505) 298-7426
(800) 528-1234
(800) 366-3252

BRITTANIA & W. E. MAUGER ESTATE BED & BREAKFAST
701 Roma Ave NE (87102)
Rates: $89-$199
(505) 242-8755
(800) 719-9189

CASITA CHAMISA BED & BREAKFAST
850 Chamisal Rd NW (87107)
Rates: n/a
(505) 897-4644

CLUBHOUSE INN & SUITES
1315 Menaul Blvd NE (87107)
Rates $89-$133
(505) 345-0010
(800) 258-2466

COMFORT INN
13031 Central Ave NE (87123)
Rates: $50-$100
(505) 294-1800
(800) 228-5150

COMFORT INN AIRPORT
2300 Yale Blvd SE (87106)
Rates: $39-$119
(505) 243-2244
(800) 228-5150

COMFORT INN MIDTOWN
2015 Menaul Blvd NE (87107)
Rates: $49-$110
(505) 881-3210
(800) 228-5150

COMFORT INN & SUITES
5811 Signal Ave NE (87113)
Rates: $59-$149
(505) 822-1090
(800) 228-5150

DAYS INN
6031 Iliff Rd NW (87105)
Rates: $50-$100
(505) 836-3297
(800) 329-7466

DAYS INN
13317 Central Ave NE (87123)
Rates: $45-$95
(505) 294-3297
(800) 329-7466

DAYS INN
10321 Hotel Ave NE (87123)
Rates: $45-$105
(505) 275-3297
(800) 329-7466

DE ANZA MOTOR LODGE
4302 Central Ave NE (87108)
Rates: $20-$37
(505) 255-1654

ECONO LODGE
13211 Central Ave NE (87123)
Rates: $30-$80
(505) 292-7600
(800) 553-2666

ECONO LODGE OLD TOWN
2321 Central Ave NW (87104)
Rates: $44-$89
(505) 243-8475
(800) 553-2666

HAMPTON INN NORTH
5101 Ellison NE (87109)
Rates: $60-$110
(505) 344-1555
(800) 426-7866

HAMPTON INN UNIVERSITY NM
2300 Carlisle NE (87110)
Rates: $59-$69
(505) 837-9300
(800) 426-7866

HOLIDAY INN EXPRESS
10330 Hotel Ave NE (87123)
Rates: $68-$115
(505) 275-8900
(800) 465-4329

HOLIDAY INN EXPRESS-COORS
6100 Iliff Rd (87121)
Rates: $70-$87
(505) 836-8600
(800) 465-4329

HOLIDAY INN MOUNTAIN VIEW
2020 Menaul Blvd NE (87107)
Rates: $90-$119
(505) 884-2511
(800) 465-4329

HOMESTEAD VILLAGE GUEST STUDIOS
2401 Wellesley Dr NE (87107)
Rates: $39-$99
(505) 883-8888
(888) 782-9473

HOMESTEAD VILLAGE GUEST STUDIOS
4441 Osuna Rd NE (87109)
Rates: $39-$44
(505) 344-7744
(888) 782-9473

HOWARD JOHNSON EXPRESS
7630 Pan American Frwy NE (87109)
Rates: $55-$69
(505) 828-1600
(800) 446-4656

LA QUINTA INN-AIRPORT
2116 Yale Blvd SE (87106)
Rates: $75-$95
(505) 243-5500
(800) 687-6667

AREA CODES - If the local number doesn't connect, check for a new area code.

LA QUINTA INN-NORTH
5241 San Antonio
Dr NE (87109)
Rates: $69-$89
(505) 821-9000
(800) 687-6667

LA QUINTA INN
2424 San Mateo
Blvd NE (87110)
Rates: $65-$85
(505) 884-3591
(800) 687-6667

LA QUINTA INN WEST
6101 Iliff Rd NW
(87212)
Rates: $65-$85
(505) 839-1744
(800) 687-6667

MAGGIE'S RASPBERRY RANCH B&B
9817 Eldridge Rd
NW (87114)
Rates: n/a
(505) 897-1523
(800) 897-1523

MOTEL 6
3400 Prospect Ave
NE (87107)
Rates: $31-$52
(505) 883-8813
(800) 466-8356

MOTEL 6
5701 Iliff Rd NW
(87105)
Rates: $31-$52
(505) 831-8888
(800) 466-8356

MOTEL 6-EAST
13141 Central Ave
NE (87123)
Rates: $30-$52
(505) 294-4600
(800) 466-8356

MOTEL 6-MIDTOWN
1701 University
Blvd NE (87102)
Rates: $30-$52
(505) 843-9228
(800) 466-8356

MOTEL 6-NORTH
8510 Pan
American Frwy
NE (87109)
Rates: $37-$62
(505) 821-1472
(800) 466-8356

MOTEL 6-PREMIER
6015 Iliff Rd NW
(87121)
Rates: $35-$52
(505) 831-3400
(800) 466-8356

MOTEL 6-STADIUM
1000 Avenida
Cesar Chavez SE
(87102)
Rates: $35-$54
(505) 243-8017
(800) 466-8356

PLAZA INN
900 Medical Arts
NE (87120)
Rates: $80-$95
(505) 243-5693
(800) 237-1307

QUALITY SUITES
5251 San Antonio
Blvd (87109)
Rates: $59-$150
(505) 797-0850
(800) 228-5151

RADISSON HOTEL & CONF CENTER
2500 Carlisle Blvd
NE (87110)
Rates: $82-$99
(505) 888-3311
(800) 333-3333

RAMADA LIMITED
5601 Alameda NE
(87113)
Rates: $52-$77
(505) 858-3297
(800) 272-6232

RED ROOF IN
1635 Candelaria
Blvd NE (87104)
Rates: n/a
(505) 344-5311
(800) 843-7663

RESIDENCE INN BY MARRIOTT
3300 Prospect NE
(87107)
Rates: $126
(505) 881-2661
(800) 331-3131

RODEWAY INN
2108 Menaul Blvd
NE (87107)
Rates: $34-$70
(505) 884-2480
(800) 228-2000

ROYAL HOTEL
4119 Central Ave
NE (87108)
Rates: $24-$49
(505) 265-3585
(800) 843-8572

SLEEP INN AIRPORT
2300 International
Ave SE (87106)
Rates: $59-$99
(505) 244-3325
(800) 753-3746

SUPER 8 MOTEL
2500 University
Blvd NE (87107)
Rates: $49-$75
(505) 888-4884
(800) 800-8000

SUPER 8 MOTEL
450 Paisano St NE
(87123)
Rates: $43-$75
(505) 271-4807
(800) 800-8000

TRAVELODGE
13139 Central Ave
NE (87123)
Rates: $36-$110
(505) 292-4878
(800) 578-7878

WYNDHAM HOTEL
2910 Yale Blvd SE
(87106)
Rates: $59-$99
(505) 843-7000
(800) 996-3426
(800) 227-1117

ALTO

HIGH COUNTRY LODGE
N Hwy 48 (88312)
Rates: $79-$139
(505) 336-4321
(800) 845-7265

LA JUNTA GUEST RANCH
P. O. Box 139
(88312)
Rates: $70-$200
(800) 443-8423

ANGEL FIRE

ANGEL FIRE RESORT
1 N Angel Fire Rd
(87710)
Rates: $195-$315
(505) 377-6401

ARROYO SECO

ADOBE & STARS BED & BREAKFAST
584 SR 150 (87514)
Rates: $105-$180
(505) 776-2776

ARTESIA

ARTESIA INN
1820 S 1st St
(88210)
Rates: $38-$55
(505) 746-9801

BELEN

BEST WESTERN INN
2101 Sosimo
Padilla Blvd
(87002)
Rates: $59-$74
(505) 861-3181
(800) 528-1234

BUDGET HOST RIO COMMUNITIES RESORT MOTEL
502 Rio
Communities
Blvd (87002)
Rates: $30-$40
(505) 864-4451
(800) 283-4678

SUPER 8 MOTEL
428 S Main St
(87002)
Rates: $45-$62
(505) 864-8188
(800) 800-8000

BERNALILLO

SUPER 8 MOTEL
265 Hwy 44 E
(87004)
Rates: $39-$65
(505) 867-0766
(800) 800-8000

BLOOMFIELD

SUPER 8 MOTEL
525 W Broadway
(87413)
Rates: $41-$55
(505) 632-8886
(800) 800-8000

CARLSBAD

BEST WESTERN STEVENS INN
1829 S Canal St
(88220)
Rates: $54-$79
(505) 887-2851
(800) 528-1234
(800) 730-2851

CARLSBAD INN
2019 S Canal St
(88220)
Rates: $32-$45
(505) 887-1171

COMFORT INN
2429 W Pierce St
(88220)
Rates: $48-$83
(505) 887-1994
(800) 228-5150

CONTINENTAL INN
3820 National
Parks Hwy
(88220)
Rates: $38-$55
(505) 887-0341

DAYS INN
3910 National
Parks Hwy
(88220)
Rates: $50-$95
(505) 887-7800
(800) 329-7466

HOLIDAY INN
601 S Canal
(88220)
Rates: $80-$104
(505) 885-8500
(800) 465-4329

MOTEL 6
3824 National
Parks Hwy
(88220)
Rates: $26-$36
(505) 885-0011
(800) 466-8356

AREA CODES - If the local number doesn't connect, check for a new area code.

PARKVIEW MOTEL
401 E Greene St
(88220)
Rates: $28-$39
(505) 885-3117

QUALITY INN
3706 National
Parks Hwy
(88220)
Rates: $49-$80
(505) 887-2861
(800) 228-5151

STAGECOACH INN
1819 S Canal
(88220)
Rates: $36-$46
(505) 887-1148

SUPER 8 MOTEL
3817 National
Parks Hwy
(88220)
Rates: $41-$55
(505) 887-8888
(800) 800-8000

CHAMA

ELK HORN LODGE MOTEL
Rte 1, Box 45
(87520)
Rates: $46-$104
(505) 756-2105
(800) 532-8874

RIVER BEND LODGE
2625 Hwy 64/84
(87520)
Rates: $63-$78
(505) 756-2264

CLAYTON

BEST WESTERN KOKOPELLI LODGE
702 S First St
(88415)
Rates: $59-$109
(505) 374-2589
(800) 528-1234
(800) 392-6691

SUPER 8 MOTEL
1425 Hwy 87
(88415)
Rates: $50-$66
(505) 374-8127
(800) 800-8000

CLOUDCROFT

SUMMIT INN MOTEL
P. O. Box 627
(88317)
Rates: $38-$93
(505) 682-2814

CLOVIS

COMFORT INN
1616 Mabry Dr
(88101)
Rates: $41-$65
(505) 762-4591
(800) 228-5150

DAYS INN
1720 Mabry Dr
(88101)
Rates: $40-$58
(505) 762-2971
(800) 329-7466

HOLIDAY INN
2700 Mabry Dr
(88101)
Rates: $55-$105
(505) 762-4491
(800) 465-4329

MOTEL 6
2620 Mabry Dr
(88101)
Rates: $29-$35
(505) 762-2995
(800) 466-8356

DEMING

ANSELMENT'S BUTTERFIELD STAGE MOTEL
309 W Pine
(88030)
Rates: $29-$38
(505) 544-0011

BEST WESTERN MIMBRES VALLEY INN
1500 W Pine St
(88030)
Rates: $42-$59
(505) 546-4544
(800) 528-1234

DAYS INN
1601 E Pine St
(88030)
Rates: $36-$51
(505) 546-8813
(800) 329-7466

DEMING MOTEL
500 W Pine St
(88030)
Rates: $28-$38
(505) 546-2737

GRAND MOTOR INN
1721 E Spruce St
(88030)
Rates: $38-$48
(505) 546-2632

HOLIDAY INN
I-10 Exit 85
(88031)
Rates: $50-$60
(505) 546-2661
(800) 465-4329

MOTEL 6
I-10 & Motel Dr
(88031)
Rates: $34-$50
(505) 546-2623
(800) 466-8356

WAGON WHEEL MOTEL
1109 W Pine St
(88030)
Rates: $24-$34
(505) 546-2681

DULCE

BEST WESTERN JICARILLA INN
233 Jicarilla Blvd
(87528)
Rates: $55-$110
(505) 759-3663
(800) 742-1938

ELEPHANT BUTTE

QUALITY INN
Hwy 195 (87935)
Rates: $75-$89
(505) 744-5431
(800) 228-5151

ESPAÑOLA

CHAMESA INN
920 N Riverside
Dr (87532)
Rates: $53-$63
(505) 753-7291

COMFORT INN
604-B S Riverside
Dr (87532)
Rates: $58-$88
(505) 753-2419
(800) 228-5150

SUPER 8 MOTEL
811 S Riverside Dr
(87532)
Rates: $38-$56
(505) 753-5374
(800) 800-8000

FARMINGTON

BEST WESTERN INN & SUITES
700 Scott Ave
(87401)
Rates: $79-$109
(505) 327-5221
(800) 528-1234
(800) 600-5221

COMFORT INN
555 Scott Ave
(87401)
Rates: $50-$72
(505) 325-2626
(800) 228-5150

HOLIDAY INN
600 E Broadway
(87401)
Rates: $75-$81
(505) 327-9811
(800) 465-4329

HOLIDAY INN EXP
2110 Bloomfield
Hwy (87401)
Rates: $69-$75
(505) 325-2545
(800) 465-4329

LA QUINTA INN
675 Scott Ave
(87401)
Rates: $69-$89
(505) 327-4706
(800) 687-6667

MOTEL 6
1600 Bloomfield
Hwy (87401)
Rates: $33-$46
(505) 326-4501
(800) 466-8356

SUPER 8 MOTEL
1601 Bloomfield
Hwy (87401)
Rates: $48-$64
(505) 325-1813
(800) 800-8000

GALLUP

AMBASSADOR MOTEL
1601 US 66 W
(87301)
Rates: $27-$31
(505) 722-3843

BEST WESTERN INN & SUITES
3009 W US 66
(87301)
Rates: $69-$99
(505) 722-2221
(800) 528-1234
(800) 722-6399

BEST WESTERN ROYAL HOLIDAY MOTEL
1903 W Hwy 66
(87301)
Rates: $45-$149
(505) 722-4900
(800) 528-1234

BLUE SPRUCE LODGE
1119 US 66E
(87301)
Rates: $24-$36
(505) 863-5211

BUDGET INN
3150 US 66 W
(87301)
Rates $26-$49
(505) 722-6631

COLONIAL MOTEL
1007 W Coal Ave
(87301)
Rates: $18-$30
(505) 863-6821

COMFORT INN
3208 US 66 W
(87305)
Rates: $46-$62
(505) 722-0982
(800) 228-5150
(888) 722-0982

DAYS INN CENTRAL
1603 US 66 W
(87301)
Rates: $50-$60
(505) 863-3891
(800) 329-7466

AREA CODES - If the local number doesn't connect, check for a new area code.

DAYS INN WEST
3201 US 66 W
(87301)
Rates: $45-$65
(505) 863-6889
(800) 329-7466

ECONO LODGE
3101 US 66 W
(87301)
Rates: $34-$109
(505) 722-3800
(800) 553-2666

ECONOMY INN
1709 US 66 W
(87301)
Rates: $25-$45
(505) 863-9301

EL CAPITAN MOTEL
1300 US 66 E
(87301)
Rates: $22-$40
(505) 863-6828

EL RANCHO HOTEL & MOTEL
1000 US 66E
(87301)
Rates: $36-$54
(505) 863-9311

HOLIDAY INN HOLIDOME
2915 US 66 W
(87301)
Rates: $65-$105
(505) 722-2201
(800) 465-4329

MOTEL 6
3306 US 66 W
(87301)
Rates: $33-$46
(505) 863-4492
(800) 466-8356

RAMADA LIMITED
1440 W Maloney
Ave (87301)
Rates: $39-$59
(800) 272-6232

ROAD RUNNER MOTEL
3012 US 66 E
(87301)
Rates: $26-$36
(505) 863-3804

ROSEWAY INN
2003 Hwy 66 W
(87301)
Rates: $34-$45
(505) 863-9385
(800) 454-5444

SLEEP INN
3820 US 66 E
(87301)
Rates: $53-$75
(505) 863-3535
(800) 753-3746

SUPER 8 MOTEL
1715 W Hwy 66
(87301)
Rates: $40-$61
(505) 722-5300
(800) 800-8000

TRAVELODGE
3275 W Hwy 66
(87301)
Rates: $40-$60
(505) 722-2100
(800) 578-7878

GLENWOOD

LOS OLMOS GUEST RANCH HISTORIC COTTAGE
1 Los Olmos Rd
(880393)
Rates: $60-$103
(505) 539-2311

GRANTS

BEST WESTERN INN & SUITES
1501 E Santa Fe
Ave (87020)
Rates: $59-$89
(505) 287-7901
(800) 528-1234

COMFORT INN
1551 E Santa Fe
Ave (87020)
Rates: $50-$65
(505) 797-9347
(800) 228-5150

DAYS INN
1504 E Santa Fe
Ave (87020)
Rates: $50-$90
(505) 287-8883
(800) 329-7466

ECONO LODGE
1509 E Santa Fe
Ave (87020)
Rates: $34-$89
(505) 287-7700
(800) 553-2666

HOLIDAY INN EXPRESS
1496 E Santa Fe
Ave (87020)
Rates: $59-$89
(505) 285-4676
(800) 465-4329

LEISURE LODGE
1204 E Santa Fe
Ave (87020)
Rates: $29-$38
(505) 287-2991

MOTEL 6
1505 E Santa Fe
Ave (87020)
Rates: $31-$43
(505) 285-4607
(800) 466-8356

SANDS MOTEL
112 McArthur St
(87020)
Rates: $35-$50
(505) 287-2996

TRAVELODGE
1608 E Santa Fe
Ave (87020)
Rates: $35-$60
(505) 287-7800
(800) 578-7878

HERNANDEZ

CASA DEL RIO BED & BREAKFAST
Hwy 84,
MM 199.46
(87532)
Rates: $95-$125
(505) 753-2035

HOBBS

BEST INN
501 N Marland
Blvd (88240)
Rates: $42-$47
(505) 397-3251
(800) 237-8466

DAYS INN
211 N Marland
Blvd (88240)
Rates: $35-$60
(505) 397-6541
(800) 329-7466

ECONO LODGE
619 N Marland
Blvd (88240)
Rates: $32-$43
(505) 397-3591
(800) 553-2666

INNKEEPERS
309 N Marland
Blvd (88240)
Rates: $40-$50
(505) 397-7171

TRAVELODGE
1301 E Broadway
(88240)
Rates: $40-$70
(505) 393-4101
(800) 578-7878

LAS CRUCES

BAYMONT INN & SUITES
1500 Hickory Dr
(88005)
Rates: $38-$43
(505) 523-0100
(800) 789-4103
(800) 301-0200

BEST WESTERN MESILLA VALLEY INN
901 Avenida de
Mesilla (88005)
Rates: $59-$79
(505) 524-8603
(800) 528-1234
(800) 327-3314

BEST WESTERN MISSION INN
1765 S Main St
(88005)
Rates: $45-$78
(505) 524-8591
(800) 528-1234
(800) 390-1440

COMFORT SUITES
2101 S Triviz
(88001)
Rates: $64-$99
(505) 522-1300
(800) 228-5150

DAYS INN
2600 S Valley Dr
(88001)
Rates: $55-$70
(505) 526-4441
(800) 329-7466

DESERT LODGE MOTEL
1900 W Picacho St
(88005)
Rates: $24-$32
(505) 524-1925

HAMPTON INN
755 Avenida de
Mesilla (88005)
Rates: $52-$69
(505) 526-8311
(800) 426-7866

HILLTOP HACIENDA B&B
2600
Westmoreland
NM (88012)
Rates: $75-$85
(606) 382-3556

HILTON INN
705 S Telshor
(88001)
Rates: $77+
(505) 522-4300
(800) 445-8667

HOLIDAY INN
201 E University
Ave (88004)
Rates: $49-$69
(505) 526-4411
(800) 465-4329

HOLIDAY INN EXPRESS
2200 S Valley Dr
(88005)
Rates: $45-$99
(505) 527-9947
(800) 465-4329

LA QUINTA INN
790 Avenida de
Mesilla (88005)
Rates: $59-$79
(505) 524-0331
(800) 531-5900

LUNDEEN INN OF THE ARTS B&B
618 S Alameda
Blvd (88005)
Rates: $53-$150
(505) 526-3327

MOTEL 6
235 La Posada Ln
(88001)
Rates: $36-$52
(505) 525-1010
(800) 466-8356

ROYAL HOST MOTEL
2146 W Picacho St
(88005)
Rates: $30-$38
(505) 524-8536

AREA CODES - If the local number doesn't connect, check for a new area code.

SLEEP INN
2121 S Triviz
(88001)
Rates: $49-$89
(505) 522-1700
(800) 753-3746

THE SMITH B&B
909 N Alameda
Blvd (88005)
Rates: $56-$132
(505) 525-2525

SUPER 8 MOTEL
245 La Posada Ln
(88001)
Rates: $37-$47
(505) 523-8695
(800) 800-8000

WESTERN INN
2155 W Picacho
Ave (88005)
Rates: $27-$42
(505) 523-5399

LAS VEGAS

EL CAMINIO MOTEL
1152 N Grand Ave
(87701)
Rates: $40-$60
(505) 425-5994

**HISTORIC PLAZA
HOTEL**
230 Old Town
Plaza (87701)
Rates: $63-$97
(505) 425-3591
(800) 328-1882

**INN ON THE
SANTA FE TRAIL**
1133 N Grand Ave
(87701)
Rates: $64-$79
(505) 425-6791
(800) 425-6791

**TOWN HOUSE
MOTEL**
1215 N Grand Ave
(87701)
Rates: $26-$37
(505) 425-6717

LORDSBURG

**BEST WESTERN
AMERICAN
MOTOR INN**
994 E Motel Dr
(88045)
Rates: $39-$70
(505) 542-3591
(800) 528-1234

**BEST WESTERN
WESTERN SKIES**
1303 S Main
(88045)
Rates: $53-$58
(505) 542-8807
(800) 528-1234

DAYS INN
1100 W Motel
Blvd (88045)
Rates: $55-$78
(505) 542-3600
(800) 329-7466

**HOLIDAY INN
EXPRESS**
1408 S Main
(88045)
Rates: $59
(505) 542-3666
(800) 465-4329

**ORANGE STREET
INN**
3496 Orange St
(87544)
Rates: $52-$75
(505) 662-2651
(800) 662-3180

LOS LUNAS

DAYS INN
1919 Main St SW
(87031)
Rates: $44-$60
(505) 865-5995
(800) 329-7466

**MICROTEL INN
& SUITES**
2258 Sun Ranch
Village Loop
(87031)
Rates: $45-$65
(505) 865-0001
(888) 771-7171

MESILLA

**HAPPY TRAILS
BED & BREAKFAST**
1857 Paisaho Rd
(88005)
Rates: $75-$100
(505) 527-8471

MILAN

**CROSSROADS
MOTEL**
1600 W Hwy 66
(87021)
Rates: $24-$27
(505) 287-9264

MORIARTY

DAYS INN
US 66 W & I-40
(87035)
Rates: $43-$72
(505) 832-4451
(800) 329-7466

MOTEL 6
109 Rt 66 E (87035)
Rates: $40-$56
(505) 832-6666
(800) 466-8356

SUNSET MOTEL
501 Old Rt 66
(87035)
Rates: $39-$47
(505) 832-4234

SUPER 8 MOTEL
1611 W Old Rt 66
(87035)
Rates: $50-$70
(505) 832-6730
(800) 800-8000

PLACITAS

**HACIENDA DE
PLACITAS INN OF
THE ARTS B&B**
491 Hwy 165
(87043)
Rates: $99-$199
(505) 867-0082

PORTALES

DUNES MOTEL
1613 West 2nd St
(88130)
Rates: $26-$40
(505) 356-6668

PORTALES INN
218 West 3rd St
(88130)
Rates: $29-$42
(505) 359-1208

*RANCHO
DE TAOS*

BUDGET MOTEL
1798 Paseo Del
Pueblo Sur Ave
(87557)
Rates: $39-$55
(505) 758-2524

RATON

**BUDGET HOST
MELODY LANE
MOTEL**
136 Canyon Dr
(87740)
Rates: $44-$49
(505) 445-3655
(800) 283-4678

CAPRI MOTEL
304 Canyon Dr
(87740)
Rates: $29-$55
(505) 445-3641

**HARMONY
MOTOR MOTEL**
351 Clayton Rd
(87740)
Rates: $36-$58
(505) 445-2763

**HOLIDAY CLASSIC
MOTEL**
P. O. Box 640
(87740)
Rates: $60-$73
(505) 445-5555
(800) 255-8879

MOTEL 6
1600 Cedar St
(87740)
Rates: $33-$49
(505) 445-2777
(800) 466-8356

SUPER 8 MOTEL
1610 Cedar St
(87740)
Rates: $48-$68
(505) 445-2355
(800) 800-8000

RED RIVER

**TALL PINE
RESORT**
P. O. Box 567
(87558)
Rates: $60-$95
(505) 754-2241

**TERRACE
TOWERS LODGE**
P. O. Box 149
(87558)
Rates: $34-$95
(505) 754-2962
(800) 695-6343

RIO RANCHO

**BEST WESTERN
INN**
1465 Rio Rancho
Dr (87124)
Rates: $79-$139
(505) 892-1700
(800) 528-1234
(800) 658-9558

DAYS INN
4200 Crestview Dr
(87124)
Rates: $75-$100
(505) 892-8800
(800) 329-7466

RAMADA LIMITED
4081 High Resort
Blvd (87124)
Rates: $47-$150
(505) 892-5998
(800) 272-6232

SUPER 8 MOTEL
4100 Barbara Loop
SE (87124)
Rates: $80+
(505) 896-8888
(800) 800-8000

**WELLESLEY INN
& SUITES**
2221 Rio Rancho
Blvd (87124)
Rates: $49-$99
(505) 892-7900
(800) 444-8888

ROAD FORKS

**DESERT WEST
MOTEL**
I-10, Exit 5 (88045)
Rates: $40-$45
(505) 542-8801

ROSWELL

**BEST WESTERN
EL RANCHO
PALACIO
MOTOR LODGE**
2205 N Main St
(88201)
Rates: $42-$65
(505) 622-2721
(800) 528-1234

**BEST WESTERN
SALLY PORT INN**
2000 N Main St
(88201)
Rates: $69-$99
(505) 622-6430
(800) 528-1234

AREA CODES - If the local number doesn't connect, check for a new area code.

BUDGET INN NORTH
2101 N Main St (88201)
Rates: $30-$55
(505) 623-6050
(800) 752-4667

BUDGET INN WEST
2200 W 2nd St (88201)
Rates: $27-$48
(505) 623-3811

DAYS INN
1310 N Main St (88201)
Rates: $44-$65
(505) 623-4021
(800) 329-7466

FRONTIER MOTEL
3010 N Main St (88201)
Rates: $28-$48
(505) 622-1400
(800) 678-1401

LEISURE INN
2700 W 2nd St (88201)
Rates: $32-$46
(505) 622-2575

MOTEL 6
3307 N Main St (88201)
Rates: $36-$46
(505) 625-6666
(800) 466-8356

NATIONAL 9 INN
2001 N Main St (88201)
Rates: $29-$40
(505) 622-0110
(800) 524-9999

RAMADA INN
2803 W 2nd (88201)
Rates: $64-$78
(505) 623-9440
(800) 272-6232

TRAVELODGE
2700 W 2nd St (88201)
Rates: $36-$46
(505) 622-2575
(800) 578-7878

RUIDOSO

BEST WESTERN SWISS CHALET INN
1451 Mechem (88345)
Rates: $59-$129
(505) 258-3333
(800) 528-1234
(800) 477-9477

INN AT PINE SPRINGS RESORT
Hwy 70 E (88346)
Rates: $40-$82
(505) 378-8100
(800) 237-3607

TRAVELODGE
159 W Hwy 70 (88345)
Rates: $57-$59
(505) 378-4471
(800) 578-7878

VILLAGE LODGE SUITE MOTEL
1000 Mecham Dr (88345)
Rates: $79-$129
(505) 258-5442

RUIDOSO DOWNS

BESTWAY INN
2052 Hwy 70 W (88346)
Rates: $110-$185
(505) 378-8000

RAMADA LIMITED
1420 E Hwy 70 (88346)
Rates: $49-$89
(505) 378-8100
(800) 272-6232

SANTA FE

ALEXANDER'S INN HISTORIC B&B
529 E Palace Ave (87501)
Rates: $90-$170
(505) 986-1431
(888) 321-5123

BEST WESTERN OF SANTA FE
3650 Cerrillos Rd (87505)
Rates: $65-$125
(505) 438-3822
(800) 528-1234

CACTUS LODGE MOTEL
2864 Cerrillos Rd (87505)
Rates: $48-$88
(505) 471-7699

CASAPUEBLO INN BED & BREAKFST
138 Park Ave (87501)
Rates: $159-$269
(505) 988-4455

CITIES OF GOLD CASINO HOTEL
Rt 11, Box 21-B (87501)
Rates: $75-$85
(505) 455-0515

COMFORT INN
4312 Cerrillos Rd (87505)
Rates: $75-$139
(505) 474-7330
(800) 228-5150

DAYS INN
2900 Cerrillos Rd (87505)
Rates: $69-$85
(505) 424-3297
(800) 329-7466

EL DORADO HOTEL
309 W San Francisco St (87501)
Rates: $239-$279
(505) 988-4455
(800) 955-4455
(800) 385-6073

EL PARADERO HISTORIC B&B
220 W Manhattan (87501)
Rates: $65-$150
(505) 988-1177

HACIENDA NICHOLAS B&B
320 E Marcy St (87501)
Rates: $95-$160
(505) 986-1431
(888) 321-5123

HOLIDAY INN
4048 Cerrillos Rd (87501)
Rates: $129-$159
(505) 473-4646
(800) 465-4329

HOTEL SANTA FE
1501 Paseo De Peralta (87501)
Rates: $169-$259
(505) 982-1200
(800) 210-6442

INN OF THE ANASAZI
113 Washington Ave (87501)
Rates: $265-$415
(505) 988-3030
(800) 688-8100

INN ON THE ALAMEDA
303 E Alameda St (87501)
Rates: $147-$342
(505) 984-2121
(800) 506-9205

LA QUINTA INN
4298 Cerrillos Rd (87505)
Rates: $95-$115
(505) 471-1142
(800) 687-6667

LAS PALOMAS HISTORIC MOTEL
119 Park Ave (87501)
Rates: n/a
(505) 988-4455

THE MADELEINE HISTORIC B&B
106 Faithway (87501)
Rates: $80-$165
(505) 982-1431
(888) 321-5123

MOTEL 6-NORTH
3007 Cerrillos Rd (87505)
Rates: $52-$68
(505) 473-1380
(800) 466-8356

MOTEL 6-SOUTH
3695 Cerrillos Rd (87505)
Rates: $39-$66
(505) 471-4140
(800) 466-8356

OPEN SKY BED & BREAKFAST
134 Turquoise Trail (87505)
Rates: $70-$120
(505) 471-3475
(800) 244-3475

PECOS TRAIL INN
2239 Old Pecos Tr (87505)
Rates: $59-$90
(505) 984-2146

QUALITY INN
3011 Cerillos Rd (87501)
Rates: $95-$105
(505) 471-1211
(800) 228-5151

RESIDENCE INN BY MARRIOTT
1698 Galisteo St (87505)
Rates: $95-$199
(505) 988-7300
(800) 331-3131

RIO VISTA SUITES CONDO MOTEL
320 Artist Rd (87501)
Rates: $135-$165
(505) 982-6636
(800) 745-9910

TRAVELODGE
3450 Cerrillos Rd (87505)
Rates: $79-$125
(505) 471-4000
(800) 578-7878

SANTA ROSA

BEST WESTERN ADOBE INN
1501 E Will Rogers Dr (88435)
Rates: $45-$65
(505) 472-3446
(800) 528-1234

BEST WESTERN SANTA ROSA INN
3022 E Will Rogers Dr (88435)
Rates: $50-$65
(505) 472-5877
(800) 528-1234

COMFORT INN
3343 E Will Rogers Blvd (88435)
Rates: $56-$99
(505) 472-5570
(800) 228-5150

DAYS INN
1830 Will Rogers Dr (88435)
Rates: $45-$65
(505) 472-5985
(800) 329-7466

AREA CODES - If the local number doesn't connect, check for a new area code.

HOLIDAY INN EXPRESS
3202 Will Rogers Dr (88435)
Rates: $45-$70
(505) 472-5411
(800) 465-4329

MOTEL 6
3400 Will Rogers Dr (88435)
Rates: $42-$58
(505) 472-3045
(800) 466-8356

RAMADA LIMITED
1701 Will Rogers Dr (88435)
Rates: $50-$85
(505) 472-4800
(800) 272-6232

TRAVELODGE
1819 Will Rogers Dr (88435)
Rates: $34-$54
(505) 472-3494
(800) 578-7878

SILVER CITY

BEAR MOUNTAIN GUEST RANCH
2251 Bear Mtn Rd (88061)
Rates: $90-$105
(505) 538-2538
(800) 880-2538

COPPER MANOR MOTEL
710 Silver Heights Blvd (88062)
Rates: $43-$58
(505) 538-5392

DRIFTER MOTEL
711 Silver Heights Blvd (88062)
Rates: $41-$50
(505) 538-2916

ECONO LODGE
1120 Hwy 180 E (88061)
Rates: $40-$70
(505) 534-1111
(800) 553-2666

HOLIDAY INN EXPRESS
1103 Superior St (88061)
Rates: n/a
(505) 538-2525
(800) 465-4329

HOLIDAY MOTOR HOTEL
3420 Hwy 180 E (88061)
Rates: $47-$59
(505) 538-3711
(800) 828-8291

SUPER 8 MOTEL
1040 Hwy 180 E (88061)
Rates: $39-$60
(505) 388-1983
(800) 800-8000

SOCORRO

BEST INN
507 N California Ave (87801)
Rates: $39-$69
(505) 835-0230
(800) 237-8466

ECONO LODGE
713 NW California St (87801)
Rates: $32-$58
(505) 835-1500
(800) 553-2666

HOLIDAY INN EXPRESS
1100 NE California St (87801)
Rates: $79-$104
(505) 838-0556
(800) 465-4329

MOTEL 6
807 US Hwy 85 (87801)
Rates: $36-$52
(505) 835-4300
(800) 466-8356

TAOS

AUSTING HAUS INN
P. O. Box 8 (Ski Valley 87525)
Rates: $88-$110
(505) 776-2649
(800) 748-2932

EL MONTE LODGE
317 E Kit Carson Rd (87571)
Rates: $55-$125
(505) 758-3171
(800) 828-8267

EL PUEBLO LODGE
412 Paseo del Pueblo Norte (87571)
Rates: $50-$125
(505) 758-8700
(800) 433-9612

EL RINCON BED & BREAKFAST
114 E Kit Carson Rd (87571)
Rates: $59-$125
(505) 758-4874

FECHIN INN
227 Paseo del Pueblo Norte (87571)
Rates: $109-$319
(505) 751-1000
(800) 746-2764

HOLIDAY INN DON FERNANDO DE TAOS
1005 Paseo del Pueblo Sur (87571)
Rates: $100-$165
(505) 758-4444
(800) 759-2736

INN ON THE RIO
910 E Kit Carson Rd (87571)
Rates: $69-$129
(505) 758-7199
(800) 859-6752

LAUGHING HORSE INN
729 Paseo del Pueblo Norte (87571)
Rates: n/a
(505) 758-8350
(800) 776-0161

QUALITY INN
1043 Camino del Pueblo Sur (87571)
Rates: $59-$99
(505) 758-2200
(800) 228-5151
(888) 908-8267

RAMADA INN
615 Paseo del Pueblo Sur (87571)
Rates: $79-$120
(505) 758-2900
(800) 659-8267

SAGEBRUSH HISTORIC INN
1508 Paseo del Pueblo Sur (87571)
Rates: $85-$115
(505) 758-2254
(888) 782-8267

SUN GOD LODGE
919 Paseo del Pueblo Sur (87571)
Rates: $75-$105
(505) 758-3162
(800) 821-2437

TAOS MOTEL & RV PARK
Hwy 68 (87571)
Rates: $30-$38
(505) 758-2524
(800) 323-6009

TOUCHSTONE HISTORIC BED & BREAKFAST
110 Mabel Dodge Ln (87571)
Rates: $90-$250
(505) 758-0192

THOREAU

ZUNI MOUNTAIN LODGE COUNTRY INN
40 W Perch Dr (87323)
Rates: $55-$85
(505) 862-7769

TRUTH OR CONSEQUENCES

ACE LODGE MOTEL
1302 Date St (87901)
Rates: $29-$60
(505) 894-2151

BEST WESTERN HOT SPRINGS MOTOR INN
2270 N Date St (87901)
Rates: $55-$70
(505) 894-6665
(800) 528-1234

HOLIDAY IN
2000 N Date St (87901)
Rates: n/a
(800) 465-4329

SUPER 8 MOTEL
2151 N Date St (87901)
Rates: $50-$61
(505) 894-7888
(800) 800-8000

TUCUMCARI

AMERICANA MOTEL
406 E Tucumcari Blvd (88401)
Rates: $24-$42
(505) 461-0431

APACHE MOTEL
1106 E Tucumcari Blvd (88401)
Rates: $20-$34
(505) 461-3367

BEST WESTERN DISCOVERY INN
200 E Estrella (88401)
Rates: $69-$74
(505) 461-4884
(800) 528-1234

BEST WESTERN POW WOW INN
801 W Tucumcari Blvd (88401)
Rates: $49-$150
(505) 461-0500
(800) 528-1234
(800) 527-6996

BUCKAROO MOTEL
1315 W Tucumcari Blvd (88401)
Rates: $18-$22
(505) 461-1650

COMFORT INN
2800 E Tucumcari Blvd (88401)
Rates: $59-$89
(505) 461-4094
(800) 228-5150

DAYS INN
2623 S First St (88401)
Rates: $43-$79
(505) 461-3158
(800) 329-7466

ECONO LODGE
3400 E Tucumcari Blvd (88401)
Rates: $41-$66
(505) 461-4194
(800) 553-2666

HOLIDAY INN
3716 E Tucumcari
Blvd (88401)
Rates: $65-$95
(505) 461-3780
(800) 465-4329

MICROTEL INN
2420 S 1st St
(88401)
Rates: $40-$65
(505) 461-0600
(888) 771-7171

MOTEL 6
2900 E Tucumcari
Blvd (88401)
Rates: $32-$46
(505) 461-4791
(800) 466-8356

RELAX INN
1010 E Tucumcari
Blvd (88401)
Rates: $20-$30
(505) 461-3862

**RODEWAY INN
EAST**
1023 E Tucumcari
Blvd (88401)
Rates: $24-$68
(505) 461-0360
(800) 228-2000

**ROYAL PALACIO
MOTEL**
1620 E Tucumcari
Blvd (88401)
Rates: $27-$35
(505) 461-1212

SAFARI MOTEL
722 E Tucumcari
Blvd (88401)
Rates: $26-$40
(505) 461-3642

SUPER 8 MOTEL
4001 E Tucumcari
Blvd (88401)
Rates: $40-$69
(505) 461-4444
(800) 800-8000

TRAVELODGE
1214 E Tucumcari
Blvd (88401)
Rates: $32-$75
(505) 461-1401
(800) 578-7878

VAUGHN

BEL-AIR MOTEL
US 54, 60 & 285
(88353)
Rates: $30-$40
(505) 584-2241

WHITE ROCK

**BANDELIER INN
MOTEL**
132 SR 4 (87544)
Rates: $62-$69
(505) 672-3838

WHITES CITY

**BEST WESTERN
CAVERN INN**
17 Carlsbad
Caverns Hwy
(88268)
Rates: $65-$85
(505) 785-2291
(800) 528-1234
(800) 228-3767

NEW YORK

ACRA

SLEEPY DUTCHMAN
Rt 23, Box 59B
(12405)
Rates: n/a
(518) 622-2050

ALBANY

HOWARD JOHNSON HOTEL
416 Southern Blvd
(12209)
Rates: $65-$150
(518) 462-6555
(800) 446-4656
(800) 562-7253

HOWARD JOHNSON HOTEL
1614 Central Ave
(12205)
Rates: $69-$100
(518) 869-0281
(800) 446-4656
(800) 293-3794

MANSION HILL INN B&B
115 Phillip St at
Park Ave (12205)
Rates: $125-$165
(518) 465-2038

MARRIOTT HOTEL
189 Wolf Rd
(12205)
Rates: $76-$150
(518) 458-8444
(800) 228-9290
(800) 541-1881

MOTEL 6
100 Watervliet Ave
(12206)
Rates: $39-$49
(518) 438-7447
(800) 466-8356

RAMADA INN
1228 Western Ave
(12205)
Rates: $92-$125
(518) 489-2981
(800) 272-6232

RAMADA LIMITED
1630 Central Ave
(12205)
Rates: $64-$119
(518) 456-0222
(800) 272-6232

RAMADA INN-DOWNTOWN
300 Broadway
(12207)
Rates: $69-$119
(518) 434-4111
(800) 272-6232

RED ROOF INN
188 Wolf Rd
(12205)
Rates: n/a
(518) 459-1971
(800) 843-7663

ALEXANDRIA BAY

RIVEREDGE RESORT & HOTEL
17 Holland St
(13607)
Rates: $218-$298
(315) 482-9917
(800) 977-9101
(800) 365-6987

ALTMAR

BRENDA'S MOTEL & CAMPGROUND
644 CR 48 (13302)
Rates: n/a
(315) 298-2268

CANNON'S PLACE
P. O. Box 209, CR
48 (13302)
Rates: n/a
(315) 298-5054

FOX HOLLOW
2740 SR 13 (13302)
Rates: n/a
(315) 298-2876

JAYHAWKERS BUNKHOUSE
CC Rd, Box 132
(13302)
Rates: n/a
(315) 964-2557

AMENIA

DEER RUN
P O Box 302
(12501)
Rates: $50-$99
(914) 373-9558

AMHERST

LORD AMHERST MOTOR HOTEL
5000 Main St
(14226)
Rates: $59-$85
(716) 839-2200
(800) 544-2200

MARRIOTT HOTEL
1340 Millersport
Hwy (14221)
Rates: $99-$159
(716) 689-6900
(800) 228-9290

MOTEL 6
4400 Maple Rd
(14226)
Rates: $36-$56
(716) 834-2231
(800) 466-8356

RED ROOF INN
42 Flint Rd (14226)
Rates: $70-$90
(716) 689-7474
(800) 843-7663

AMSTERDAM

BEST WESTERN AMSTERDAM INN
10 Market St
(12010)
Rates: $60-$85
(518) 843-5760
(800) 528-1234

VALLEY VIEW MOTOR INN
Rts 5 S & 30
(12010)
Rates: $31-$58
(518) 842-5637

ANGELICA

ANGELICA INN BED & BREAKFAST
64 W Main St
(14709)
Rates: $60-$100
(716) 466-3295

AUBURN

DAYS INN
37 William St
(13021)
Rates: $42-$89
(315) 252-7567
(800) 329-7466

HOLIDAY INN
75 North St
(13021)
Rates: $89-$139
(315) 253-4531
(800) 465-4329

THE IRISH ROSE BED & BREAKFAST
102 South St
(13021)
Rates: $55-$95
(315) 255-0196

MICROTEL INN & SUITES
12 Seminary Ave
(13021)
Rates: $39-$89
(315) 253-5000
(888) 771-7171

AVOCA

CABOOSE MOTEL
8620 State Rt 415
(14809)
Rates: $50-$75
(607) 566-2216

BAINBRIDGE

ALGONKIN MOTEL
262 State Hwy 7
(13733)
Rates: $50-$75
(607) 967-5911

BALLSTON LAKE

WESTWOOD MOTEL
1012 Saratoga Rd
(12019)
Rates: $45-$80
(518) 339-3612

BATAVIA

BEST WESTERN BATAVIA INN
8204 Park Rd
(14020)
Rates: $74-$109
(716) 343-1000
(800) 528-1234
(800) BATAVIA

CROWN INN
8212 Park Rd
(14020)
Rates: $56-$89
(716) 343-2311
(800) 228-2000

DAYS INN
200 Oak St (14020)
Rates: $42-$69
(716) 343-1440
(800) 329-7466

BATH

DAYS INN
330 W Morris St
(14810)
Rates: $60-$95
(607) 776-7644
(800) 329-7466

OLD NATIONAL HOTEL
13 E Steuben St
(14810)
Rates: $44-$50
(607) 776-4104

BELLPORT

THE GREAT SOUTH BAY INN B&B
160 S Country Rd
(11713)
Rates: $105-$125
(631) 286-8588

AREA CODES - If the local number doesn't connect, check for a new area code.

BERLIN

THE SEDGWICK INN
17971 Rt 22 (12022)
Rates: $65-$95
(518) 658-2334

BERNHARDS BAY

SNUG HARBOR
Rt 9, Box 44 (13028)
Rates: n/a
(315) 675-3527

BINGHAMTON

COMFORT INN
1156 Front St (13905)
Rates: $55-$160
(607) 722-5353
(800) 228-5150

HOLIDAY INN ARENA
2-8 Hawley St (13901)
Rates: $90
(607) 722-1212
(800) 465-4329

HOWARD JOHNSON EXPRESS
690 Front St (13905)
Rates: $34-$70
(607) 724-1341
(800) 446-4656

MOTEL 6
1012 Front St (13905)
Rates: $39-$55
(607) 771-0400
(800) 466-8356

SUPER 8 MOTEL
650 Old Front St (13905)
Rates: $35-$105
(607) 773-8111
(800) 800-8000

SUPER 8 MOTEL
771 Upper Court St (13904)
Rates: $42-$60
(607) 775-3443
(800) 800-8000

BOONVILLE

HEADWATERS MOTOR LODGE
Rt 12 (13309)
Rates: $45-$65
(315) 952-4493

BOWMANSVILLE

RED ROOF INN
146 Maple Dr (14026)
Rates: $63-$87
(716) 633-1100
(800) 843-7663

BRIGHTON

HAMPTON INN
717 E Henrietta Rd (14623)
Rates: $99
(716) 272-7800
(800) 426-7866

WELLESLEY INN & SUITES
797 E Henrietta Rd (14623)
Rates: $60-$105
(716) 427-0130
(800) 444-8888

BRISTOL CENTER

THE ACORN INN BED & BRKFAST
4508 SR 64 S (14424)
Rates: $76-$140
(716) 229-2834

BROCKPORT

ECONO LODGE
6575 4th Section Rd (14420)
Rates: $49-$90
(716) 637-3157
(800) 553-2666

BROOKLYN

COMFORT INN
8315 4th Ave (11209)
Rates: $159-$199
(718) 238-3737
(800) 228-5150

BUFFALO

ADAM'S MARK HOTEL
120 Church St (14202)
Rates: $106-$160
(716) 845-5100
(800) 444-2326

BEST WESTERN INN-ON THE AVENUE
510 Delaware Ave (14202)
Rates: $99-$125
(716) 886-8333
(800) 528-1234
(888) 868-3033

BUFFALO EXIT 53 MOTOR LODGE
475 Dingens St (14206)
Rates: $50-$70
(716) 896-2800
(800) 437-3744

COMFORT SUITES
901 Dick Rd (14225)
Rates: $79-$199
(716) 633-6000
(800) 228-5150

HOLIDAY INN EXPRESS HOTEL & SUITES
601 Dingens St (14206)
Rates: n/a
(716) 896-2900
(800) 465-4329

CALCIUM

MICROTEL INN
8000 Virginia Smith Dr (13616)
Rates: $36-$49
(315) 629-5000
(888) 771-7171
(800) 447-9660

CAMBRIDGE

BLUE WILLOW MOTEL
51 S Park St (12816)
Rates: $35-$65
(518) 677-3552

CAMBRIDGE INN BED & BRKFAST

16 W Main St (12816)
Rates: $48-$75
(518) 677-5741

TOWN HOUSE MOTOR INN
16 W Main (12816)
Rates: $45-$50
(518) 677-5524

CANANDAIGUA

CAMPUS LODGE
4341 Lakeshore Dr (14424)
Rates: $50-$95
(716) 394-1250
(800) 836-3299

CANANDAIGUA INN ON THE LAKE
770 S Main St (14424)
Rates: $104-$144
(716) 394-7800

ECONO LODGE MUAR LAKE
170 Eastern Blvd (14424)
Rates: $61-$75
(716) 394-9000
(800) 553-2666

FINGER LAKES INN
4343 Rts 5 & 20 E (14424)
Rates: $50-$75
(800) 727-2775

CANASTOTA

DAYS INN
NYS Rte 13 (13032)
Rates: $59-$89
(315) 697-3309
(800) 329-7466

CANTON

BEST WESTERN UNIVERSITY INN
90 E Main St (13617)
Rates: $78-$88
(315) 386-8522
(800) 528-1234
(888) 386-8522

COMFORT SUITES

6000 US Hwy 11 (13617)
Rates: $85-$159
(315) 386-1161
(800) 228-5150

CASTLETON

BEL-AIR MOTEL
1036 Rt 9 (12033)
Rates: $40-$55
(518) 732-7744

CATSKILL

DAYS INN
I-87/Exit 21 (12414)
Rates: $60-$125
(518) 943-5800
(800) 329-7466

CAZENOVIA

LINCKLAEN HOUSE
79 Albany St (13035)
Rates: $65-$130
(315) 655-3461

CENTRAL SQUARE

TOWN & COUNTRY MOTEL
1436 Brewerton Rd (13036)
Rates: n/a
(315) 668-6751

CHAFFEE

JOSIE'S BROOKSIDE MOTEL
SR 16 & 39 (14030)
Rates: $29-$45
(716) 496-5057

CHEEKTOWAGA

HOMEWOOD SUITES HOTEL
760 Dick Rd (14225)
Rates: $109-$149
(716) 685-0700
(800) 225-5466

WELLESLEY INN & SUITES
4630 Genesee St (14225)
Rates: $85-$115
(716) 631-8966
(800) 444-8888

AREA CODES - If the local number doesn't connect, check for a new area code.

CLARENCE

**HERITAGE HOUSE
COUNTRY INN**
8261 Main St
(14221)
Rates: $53-$100
(716) 633-4900
(800) 283-3899

CLAYTON

**WEST WINDS
MOTEL &
COTTAGES**
Box 56 RD 2
(Thousand Islands
13624)
Rates: $38-$67
(315) 686-3352

CLIFTON

**HOWARD
JOHNSON INN**
680 Rt 3 W (07014)
Rates: $89-$139
(973) 471-3800
(800) 446-4656

CLINTON

THE HEDGES B&B
180 Sanford Ave
(13323)
Rates: $65-$125
(315) 853-3031

COBLESKILL

**BEST WESTERN
INN**
12 Campus Dr
Extenstion (12043)
Rates: $126-$149
(518) 234-4321
(800) 528-1234

COHOES

HAMPTON INN
981 New Loudon
Rd (12047)
Rates: $99-$109
(518) 785-0000
(800) 426-7866

**INN AT THE
CENTURY**
997 New Loudon
Rd (12047)
Rates: $72-$110
(518) 785-0931

COLONIE

**AMBASSADOR
MOTOR INN**
1600 Central Ave
(12205)
Rates: $55-$88
(518) 456-8982

MARRIOTT HOTEL
189 Wolf Rd
(12205)
Rates: $109-$185
(518) 458-8444
(800) 228-9290

COMMACK

**HOWARD
JOHNSON INN**
450 Moreland Rd
(11725)
Rates: $75-$119
(516) 864-8820
(800) 446-4656

COOPERS
PLAIN

STILES MOTEL
9239 Victory Hwy
(14827)
Rates: $42-$52
(607) 962-5221

COOPERSTOWN

**AALSMEER
MOTEL**
Box 790, RD 2
(13326)
Rates: $75+
(607) 547-8819

**BEST WESTERN
INN AT
COMMONS**
50 Commons Dr
(13326)
Rates: $140-$210
(607) 547-9439
(800) 528-1234

CORFU

**ECONO LODGE-
DARIEN LAKES**
8493 Rt 77 (14036)
Rates: $39-$80
(716) 599-4681
(800) 553-2666

CORNING

RADISSON HOTEL
125 Denison Pkwy
E (14870)
Rates: $109-$165
(607) 962-5000
(800) 333-3333

CORTLAND

COMFORT INN
2 1/2 Locust Ave
(13045)
Rates: $79-$159
(607) 753-7721
(800) 228-5150

SUPER 8 MOTEL
188 Clinton Ave
(13045)
Rates: $58-$98
(607) 756-5622
(800) 800-8000

**WATERFALLS
MOTEL**
Rt 9A & Furnace
Dock Rd (10520)
Rates: $60-$70
(914) 271-4322

CUBA

**CUBA COACH-
LIGHT MOTEL**
1 N Branch Rd
(14727)
Rates: $39-$55
(716) 968-1992

DANSVILLE

DAYSTOP
I-390, Exit 5 (14437)
Rates: $44-$55
(716) 335-6023
(800) 329-7466

DELHI

**BUENA VISTA
MOTEL**
Andes Rd, Rt 28
(13753)
Rates: $42-$82
(607) 746-2135

DEPOSIT

**ALEXANDER'S INN
ON OQUAGA
LAKE B&B**
770 Oquaga Lake
Rd (13754)
Rates: $59-$99
(607) 467-6023

DEWITT

ECONO LODGE
3400 Erie Blvd E
(13214)
Rates: $42-$90
(315) 446-3300
(800) 553-2666

DIAMOND
POINT

**DIAMOND COVE
COTTAGES**
3648 Lake Shore
Dr (12845)
Rates: $595-$1650
Weekly
(518) 668-5787

DOVER PLAINS

**OLD DROVERS
HISTORIC
COUNTRY INN**
Old Rt 22 (12522)
Rates: $105-$395
(914) 832-9311

DUNKIRK

**BEST WESTERN
DUNKIRK INN**
3929 Vineyard Dr
(14048)
Rates: $69-$139
(716) 366-4400
(716) 366-7100
(800) 528-1234

COMFORT INN
3925 Vineyard Dr
(14048)
Rates: $70-$139
(716) 672-4450
(800) 228-5150

**DRAKES
MOTOR INN**
5361 West Lake
Rd (14048)
Rates: n/a
(716) 672-4867

**FOUR POINTS
SHERATON
HARBORFRONT
HOTEL**
30 Lake Shore Dr
(14048)
Rates: $69-$199
(716) 366-8350
(800) 325-3535

RODEWAY INN
310 Lake Shore Dr
(14048)
Rates: $39-$79
(716) 366-2200
(800) 228-2000

**SOUTHSHORE
MOTOR LODGE**
5040 W Lake Rd
(14048)
Rates: $49-$98
(716) 366-2822

DURHAM

**GOLDEN
HARVEST B&B**
37 Golden Hill Rd
(E Durham 12423)
Rates: n/a
(518) 634-2305

ROSE MOTEL
Rt 145 (12422)
Rates: n/a
(518) 239-8496

EAST
ELMHURST
(See Queens)

EAST
GREENBUSH

**MOUNT VERNON
MOTEL**
576 Columbia
Tpke (12061)
Rates: $29-$69
(518) 477-9352
(800) 321-4681

EAST
HAMPTON

DUTCH MOTEL
488 Montauk Hwy
(11937)
Rates: $115-$150
(631) 324-4550

EAST
HERKIMER

**GLEN RIDGE
MOTEL**
Rt 5 (13350)
Rates: n/a
(315) 866-4149

AREA CODES - If the local number doesn't connect, check for a new area code.

EAST SYRACUSE

EMBASSY SUITES
6646 Old Collamer
Rd (13057)
Rates: $108-$139
(315) 446-3200
(800) 362-2779

**HOLIDAY INN
EAST-CARRIER
CIRCLE**
6555 Old Collamer
Rd (13057)
Rates: $94-$109
(315) 437-2761
(800) 465-4329

MICROTEL INN
6608 Old Collamer
Rd (13057)
Rates: $44-$59
(315) 437-3500
(888) 771-7171
(800) 435-1665

MOTEL 6
6577 Court St Rd
(13057)
Rates: $33-$48
(315) 433-1300
(800) 466-8356

**RESIDENCE INN
BY MARRIOTT**
6420 Yorktown Cir
(13057)
Rates: $115-$131
(315) 432-4488
(800) 331-3131

SUPER 8 MOTEL
6620 Old Collamer
Rd (13057)
Rates: $45-$66
(315) 432-5612
(800) 800-8000

EAST WINDHAM

**POINT LOOKOUT
MOUNTAIN INN**
The Mohican Trail
Rte 23 (12439)
Rates: $55-$125
(518) 734-3381

ELBRIDGE

COZY COTTAGE
4987 Kingston Rd
(13060)
Rates: n/a
(315) 689-2082

ELKA PARK

**DIAMOND
HORSESHOE
RANCH & SKI
RESORT**
Dale Lane (12427)
Rates: $90-$135
(518) 589-5197
(800) 926-2771

ELLICOTTVILLE

**JEFFERSON INN
B&B**
3 Jefferson St
(14731)
Rates: $110-$145
(716) 699-5869

ELMHURST

**MARRIOTT HOTEL
LA GUARDIA**
102-05 Ditmars
Blvd (11369)
Rates: $143-$175
(718) 565-8900
(800) 228-9290

ELMIRA

**COACHMAN
MOTOR LODGE**
908 Pennsylvania
Ave (14904)
Rates: $53-$63
(607) 733-5526

**HOLIDAY INN-
DOWNTOWN**
760 E Water St
(14901)
Rates: $129
(607) 734-4211
(800) 465-4329

**NEW PLANTA-
TION MOTEL**
2046 Rt 17 (14901)
Rates: n/a
(607) 737-9008
(800) 836-0310

RED JACKET INN
489 Rt 17 (14902)
Rates: $35-$65
(607) 734-1616
(800) 562-5808

ELMSFORD

HAMPTON INN
200 Tarrytown Rd
(10523)
Rates: $117-$129
(914) 592-5680
(800) 426-7866

ENDICOTT

ECONO LODGE
749 W Main St
(13760)
Rates: $39-$149
(607) 754-1533
(800) 553-2666

FAIRPORT

**TRAIL BREAK
MOTOR INN**
7340 Pittsford-
Palmyra Rd
(14450)
Rates: $35-$69
(716) 223-1710

FALCONER

MOTEL 6
1980 E Main St
(14733)
Rates: $48-$64
(716) 665-3670
(800) 466-8356

FARMINGTON

BUDGET INN
6001 Rt 96 (14425)
Rates: $36-$70
(716) 924-5020

**SUNRISE HILL
COUNTRY INN**
6108 Loomis Rd
(14424)
Rates: $25-$95
(716) 924-2131
(800) 333-0536

FISHKILL

MAINSTAY SUITES
25 Merritt Blvd
(12524)
Rates: $125-$135
(914) 897-2800
(800) 660-6246

**RESIDENCE INN
BY MARRIOTT**
2481 Rt 9 (12524)
Rates: $139-$225
(914) 896-5210
(800) 331-3131

**WELLESLEY INN
& SUITES**
2477 Rt 9 (12524)
Rates: $75-$150
(914) 896-4995
(800) 444-8888

FLEISCHMANNS

**RIVER RUN
BED & BRKFAST**
Main St (12430)
Rates: $50-$100
(914) 254-4884

FREDONIA

DAYS INN
10455 Bennett Rd
(14063)
Rates: $36-$71
(716) 673-1351
(800) 329-7466

FREEPORT

**FREEPORT
MOTOR INN
& BOATEL**
445 S Main St
(11520)
Rates: $76-$99
(516) 623-9100

FULTON

KNIGHTS INN
163 S First St
(13069)
Rates: $49-$89
(315) 598-6100
(800) 843-5644

MINI MOTEL
RR 8, Box 160
(13069)
Rates: n/a
(315) 592-7238

**192 EXECUTIVE
SUITES**
192 S 1st St
(13069)
Rates: n/a
(315) 593-6631
(315) 593-7304

FULTONVILLE

TRAVELODGE
123 Riverside Dr
(12072)
Rates: $55-$85
(518) 853-4511
(800) 578-7878

GALES

MOTEL 6
155 Buell Rd
(14624)
Rates: $39-$54
(716) 436-2170
(800) 466-8356

GANSEVOORT

**MCGREGOR INN
MOTEL**
Rt 9 (12831)
Rates: n/a
(518) 587-1394

GARDEN CITY

**THE GARDEN
CITY HOTEL**
45 Seventh St
(11530)
Rates: $160-$340
(516) 747-3000
(800) 547-0400

GASPORT

**HARTLAND
MOTEL**
8464 Ridge Rd
(14067)
Rates: n/a
(716) 772-2266

GATES

MOTEL 6
155 Buell Rd
(14624)
Rates: $42-$48
(716) 436-2170
(800) 466-8356

GENEVA

MOTEL 6
485 Hamilton St
(14456)
Rates: $50-$66
(315) 789-4050
(800) 466-8356

**99 WILLIAM
STREET B&B**
99 William St
(14456)
Rates: $65
(315) 789-1273

RAMADA INN LAKEFRONT
41 Lakefront Dr (14456)
Rates: $99-$149
(315) 789-0400
(800) 272-6232
(800) 990-0907

GILBERTSVILLE

SIGNATURE QUILT B&B
6 Commercial St (13776)
Rates: $85+
(607) 783-2722

GRAND GORGE

GOLDEN ACRES FARM RANCH
Windy Ridge Rd (12076)
Rates: $80-$330
(607) 588-7329

GRAND ISLAND

CHATEAU MOTOR LODGE
1810 Grand Island Blvd (14072)
Rates: $31-$69
(716) 773-2868

CINDERELLA MOTEL
2797 Grand Island Blvd (14072)
Rates: $35-$69
(716) 773-2872

GREAT NECK

INN AT GREAT NECK
30 Cutter Mill Rd (10021)
Rates: $195-$325
(516) 773-2000

GREECE

COMFORT INN-WEST
1501 W Ridge Rd (14615)
Rates: $59-$150
(716) 621-5700
(800) 228-5150
(800) 892-9348

HAMPTON INN
500 Center Place Dr (14615)
Rates: $78-$96
(716) 663-6070
(800) 426-7866

RESIDENCE INN BY MARRIOTT
500 Paddy Creek Cir (14615)
Rates: $84-$169
(716) 865-2090
(800) 331-3131

WELLESLEY INN & SUITES
1635 W Ridge Rd (14615)
Rates: $60-$105
(716) 621-2060
(800) 444-8888

GREENPORT

SILVER SANDS MOTEL
P. O. Box 285 (11944)
Rates: $70-$100
(516) 477-0011

HAGUE

TROUT HOUSE VILLAGE
Lake Shore Dr, Rt 9N (12836)
Rates: n/a
(518) 543-6088
(800) 368-6088

HAMBURG

PENNY WISE INN
5245 Camp Rd (14075)
Rates: $32-$95
(716) 648-2000

RED ROOF INN
5370 Camp Rd (14075)
Rates: $44-$71
(716) 648-7222
(800) 843-7663

HAMLIN

SANDY CREEK MANOR HOUSE BED & BRKFAST
1960 Redman Rd (14464)
Rates: $60-$95
(716) 964-7528
(800) 594-0400

HAMMONDS-PORT

VINEHURST MOTEL
Box 203, Rt 54 (14840)
Rates: n/a
(607) 569-2300

HANCOCK

SMITHS COLONIAL MOTEL
RR 1, Box 172-D (13783)
Rates: $45-$75
(607) 637-2989

HAUPPAUGE

WYNDHAM WIND WATCH HOTEL & HAMLET GOLF CLUB
1717 Vanderbilt Motor Pky (11788)
Rates: $185
(631) 232-9800
(800) 996-3426

HENRIETTA

DAYS INN
4853 W Henrietta Blvd (14467)
Rates: $49-$95
(716) 334-9300
(800) 329-7466

ECONO LODGE-SOUTH
940 Jefferson Rd (14623)
Rates: $64-$130
(716) 427-2700
(800) 553-2666
(800) 837-9906

MICROTEL INN
905 Lehigh Station Rd (14467)
Rates: $36-$69
(716) 334-3400
(888) 771-7171
(800) 999-2005

RED CARPET INN
4600 W Henrietta Rd (14467)
Rates: n/a
(716) 334-4280
(800) 251-1962

RED ROOF INN
4820 W Henrietta Rd (14467)
Rates: $48-$83
(716) 359-1100
(800) 843-7663

RESIDENCE INN BY MARRIOTT
1300 Jefferson Rd (14467)
Rates: $97-$130
(716) 272-8850
(800) 331-3131

HERKIMER

HERKIMER MOTEL
100 Marginal Rd (13350)
Rates: $46-$68
(315) 866-0490

INN TOWNE MOTEL
227 N Washington St (13350)
Rates: $36-$58
(315) 866-1101

HIGHLAND FALLS

BEST WESTERN PALISADE MOTEL
17 Main St (10928)
Rates: $80-$120
(914) 446-9400
(800) 528-1234

HILLSDALE

LINDEN VALLEY INN
E on NY 23 (12529)
Rates: $115-$145
(518) 325-7100

SWISS HUTTE MOTEL
Rt 23 (12529)
Rates: $75-$179
(518) 325-3333

HOLBROOK

RED CARPET INN
4444 Veterans Memorial Hwy (11741)
Rates: $47-$65
(516) 588-7700
(800) 251-1962

HORNELL

ECONO LODGE
7464 Old SR 36 (14843)
Rates: $45-$75
(607) 324-0800
(800) 553-2666

HORSEHEADS

BEST WESTERN MARSHALL MANOR
3527 Watkins Glen Rd (14845)
Rates: $38-$76
(607) 739-3891
(800) 528-1234

HOWARD JOHNSON
2671 Corning Rd (14845)
Rates: $39-$99
(607) 739-5636
(800) 446-4656

MOTEL 6
4133 Rt 17 (14845)
Rates: $42-$58
(607) 739-2525
(800) 466-8356

HUDSON

ST. CHARLES HISTORIC HOTEL
16-18 Park Place (12534)
Rates: $79-$109
(518) 822-9900

HUNTER

EVERGREEN COTTAGES
P.O. Box 161 (12442)
Rates: n/a
(518) 263-4932

HUNTER INN
Rt 23A (12442)
Rates: $80-$915
(518) 263-3777

ILION

WHIFFLETREE MOTEL
345 E Main St (13357)
Rates: $40-$75
(315) 895-7777

AREA CODES - If the local number doesn't connect, check for a new area code.

ITHACA

BEST WESTERN UNIVERSITY INN
1020 Ellis Hollow Rd (14850)
Rates: $69-$199
(607) 272-6100
(800) 528-1234

CLARION HOTEL
1 Sheraton Dr (14850)
Rates: $95-$299
(607) 257-2000
(800) 252-7466
(800) 257-6992

COLLEGETOWN MOTOR LODGE
312 College Ave (14850)
Rates: $48-$100
(607) 273-3542
(800) 745-3542

ECONOMY INN
658 Elmira Rd (14850)
Rates: $28-$85
(607) 277-0370
(800) 826-0778

HOLIDAY INN-EXECUTIVE TOWER
222 S Cayuga St (14850)
Rates: $99-$159
(607) 272-1000
(800) 465-4329

LA TOURELLE COUNTRY INN
1150 Danby Rd (14850)
Rates: $79-$299
(607) 273-2734
(800) 765-1492

MEADOW COURT INN
529 S Meadow St (14850)
Rates: $75-$150
(607) 273-3885
(800) 852-4014

SPRING WATER MOTEL
1083 Dryden (14850)
Rates: $42-$70
(607) 272-3721
(800) 548-1890

JAMAICA
(See Queens)

JAMESTOWN

COMFORT INN
2800 N Main St (14701)
Rates: $99-$149
(716) 664-5920
(800) 228-5150

JOHNSON CITY

BEST WESTERN INN
569 Harry L Dr (13790)
Rates: $54-$67
(607) 729-9194
(800) 528-1234

RED ROOF INN
590 Fairview St (13790)
Rates: $56-$73
(607) 729-8940
(800) 843-7663

JOHNSTOWN

HOLIDAY INN
308 N Comrie Ave (12095)
Rates: $60-$91
(518) 762-4686
(800) 465-4329

KENMORE

SUPER 8 MOTEL
1288 Sheridan Dr (14217)
Rates: $37-$55
(716) 876-4020
(800) 800-8000

KINGSTON

HOLIDAY INN
503 Washington Ave (12401)
Rates: $119-$159
(914) 338-0400
(800) 465-4329

SUPER 8 MOTEL
487 Washington Ave (12401)
Rates: $54-$77
(914) 338-3078
(800) 800-8000

LAKE GEORGE

BALMORAL MOTEL
444 Canada St (12845)
Rates: $59-$99
(518) 668-2673
(800) 457-2673

GREEN HAVEN RESORT MOTEL
3136 Lake Shore Dr (12845)
Rates: $64-$114
(518) 668-2489
(800) 269-9978

LAKE GEORGE ESCAPE-EVERGREEN CAMPING RESORT CABINS
E Schroon River Rd (12845)
Rates: n/a
(518) 623-3207
(800) 327-3188

LYN AIRE MOTEL
1872 SR 9 (12845)
Rates: $99-$149
(518) 668-4612

TRAVELODGE
2011 Rt 9N (12845)
Rates: $39-$99
(518) 668-2346
(800) 578-7878
(888) 389-4554

LAKE LUZERNE

LUZERNE COURT
508 Lake Ave (12846)
Rates: $50-$90
(518) 696-2734

LAKE PLACID

ART DEVLIN'S OLYMPIC MOTOR INN
350 Main St (12946)
Rates: $58-$118
(518) 523-3700

BEST WESTERN GOLDEN ARROW
150 Main St (12946)
Rates: $79-$169
(518) 523-3353
(800) 528-1234
(800) 582-5540

EDGE OF THE LAKE MOTEL
56 Saranac Ave (12946)
Rates: $61-$109
(518) 523-9430
(800) 523-9430

HILTON RESORT
1 Mirror Lake Dr (12946)
Rates: $119-$199
(518) 523-4411
(800) 445-8667
(800) 755-5598

HOWARD JOHNSON
90 Saranac Ave (12946)
Rates: $70-$130
(518) 523-9555
(800) 446-4656
(800) 858-4656

LAKE PLACID RESORT HOTEL & GOLF CLUB
1 Olympic Dr (12946)
Rates: $69-$229
(518) 523-2556
(800) 874-1980

RAMADA INN
8-12 Saranac Ave (12946)
Rates: $59-$140
(518) 523-2587
(800) 272-6232
(800) 741-7841

SWISS ACRES INN
189 Saranac Ave (12946)
Rates: $50-$85
(518) 523-3040

LAKEWOOD

STAR MOTEL
270 E Fairmount Ave (14750)
Rates: $38-$50
(716) 763-8578

LANSING

ECONO LODGE
2303 N Triphammer Rd (14882)
Rates: $46-$150
(607) 257-1400
(800) 553-2666

RAMADA INN AIRPORT
2310 N Triphammer Rd (14882)
Rates: $95-$179
(607) 257-3100
(800) 272-6232

LATHAM

THE CENTURY HOUSE HOTEL
997 New Loudon Rd (12110)
Rates: $109-$225
(518) 785-0931
(888) 674-6873

HOLIDAY INN EXPRESS
946 New Loudon Rd (12110)
Rates: $67-$105
(518) 783-6161
(800) 465-4329

MICROTEL INN
7 Rensselaer Ave (12110)
Rates: $47-$80
(518) 782-9161
(888) 771-7171

RESIDENCE INN BY MARRIOTT
1 Residence Inn Dr (12110)
Rates: $155-$205
(518) 783-0600
(800) 331-3131

LIBERTY

RAMADA LIMITED
7 E Route 52 (12754)
Rates: $99-$120
(914) 292-7171
(800) 272-6232

LITTLE FALLS

BEST WESTERN INN
20 Albany St (13365)
Rates: $60-$77
(315) 823-4954
(800) 528-1234

AREA CODES - If the local number doesn't connect, check for a new area code.

LIVERPOOL

ECONO LODGE NORTH
401 7th North St (13088)
Rates: $44-$99
(315) 451-6000
(800) 553-2666

HOLIDAY INN
441 Electronics Pkwy (13088)
Rates: $120-$150
(315) 457-1122
(800) 465-4329

HOMEWOOD SUITES
275 Elwood Davis Rd (13088)
Rates: $199
(315) 451-3800
(800) 225-5466

KNIGHTS INN
430 Electronics Pkwy (13088)
Rates: $35-$99
(315) 453-6330
(800) 843-5644

LIVINGSTON MANOR

LANZA'S INN
Rd 2, Box 446 (12758)
Rates: $54-$84
(914) 439-5070

THE MAGICAL LAND OF OZ B&B
455 Shandlee Rd (12758)
Rates: $75-$85
(914) 438-3418

LOCKPORT

TWIN OAKS MOTEL
4660 Ridge Rd (14094)
Rates: n/a
(716) 433-2447

LONG LAKE

JOURNEY'S END COTTAGES
Deerland Rd, Rt 30 (12847)
Rates: $625-$700 Weekly
(518) 624-5381

LONG VIEW LODGE
Rt 28 N & 30 (12847)
Rates: $65-$85
(518 624-2862

LOWMAN

FOUNTAIN MOTEL
Rt 17, Box 11 (14861)
Rates: n/a
(607) 732-8617

RED JACKET MOTOR INN
Rt 17 (14861)
Rates: $39-$75
(607) 734-1616

LYONS

KREISS FARM BED & BREAKFST
2097 Highland Fruit Farm Rd (14489)
Rates: n/a
(315) 946-9448

MALONE

ECONO LODGE
227 W Main St (12953)
Rates: $42-$65
(518) 483-0500
(800) 553-2666

FLANAGAN HOTEL
One Elm St (12953)
Rates: $30-$60
(518) 483-1400

SUPER 8 MOTEL AT JONS
Finny Blvd, Rt 30 S (12953)
Rates: $60-$66
(518) 483-8123
(800) 800-8000

MALTA

POST ROAD LODGE
2865 Rt 9 (12020)
Rates: n/a
(518) 584-4169
(800) 836-2687

RIVIERA MOTEL
2539 Rt 9 (12020)
Rates: n/a
(518) 899-2600

MASONVILLE

BUDGET MOTOR LODGE/MASON INN
Rt 206, Box 8 (13804)
Rates: $38-$45
(607) 265-3287
(800) 828-3691

MASSENA

BOB'S MOTEL
Rt 2, Box 301 (13662)
Rates: n/a
(315) 769-9497

FLANDERS INN
Main & W Orvis Sts (13662)
Rates: $50-$75
(315) 769-2441
(800) 654-0162

HILLSIDE MOTEL
15 Smith Rd (13662)
Rates: n/a
(315) 769-5403

PARK INN MOTEL
528 CR 42 (13662)
Rates: n/a
(315) 769-7799

MELVILLE

HILTON HOTEL
598 Broad Hollow Rd (11747)
Rates: $149+
(516) 845-1000
(800) 445-8667

MEXICO

STRIKE KING LODGE
286 SR 104B (13114)
Rates: n/a
(315) 963-7826

WALTON'S MOTEL
3210 US Rt 11, Box 92 (13114)
Rates: n/a
(315) 963-7120

MIDDLE GROVE

DAYBREAK MOTEL
2909 Rt 9 (12850)
Rates: $35-$125
(518) 882-6838

MIDDLEPORT

CANAL COUNTRY INN
4021 Peet St (14105)
Rates: n/a
(716) 735-7572

MIDDLETOWN

HOWARD JOHNSON HOTEL
551 Rt 211 E (10940)
Rates: $55-$115
(914) 342-5822
(800) 446-4656

MIDDLETOWN MOTEL
501 Rt 211 E (10940)
Rates: $50-$90
(914) 342-2535
(800) 343-2535

SUPER 8 LODGE
563 Rt 211 E (10940)
Rates: $65-$95
(914) 692-5828
(800) 800-8000

MILLBROOK

COTTONWOOD MOTEL
RR2, Box 25 (12545)
Rates: $50-$99
(914) 677-3283

MONTAUK

SEPP'S SURF-SOUND COTTAGES
Ditch Plains Rd (11954)
Rates: $80+
(516) 668-2215

MONTGOMERY

SUPER 8 MOTEL
207 Montgomery Rd (12549)
Rates: $45-$70
(914) 457-3143
(800) 800-8000

MONTOUR FALLS

FALLS MOTEL
239 N Genesee St (14865)
Rates: $65-$125
(607) 535-7262

RELAX INN
100 Clawson Blvd (14865)
Rates: $44-$89
(607) 535-7183

MOUNT KISCO

HOLIDAY INN
1 Holiday Inn Dr (10549)
Rates: $160
(914) 241-2600
(800) 465-4329

MOUNT TREMPER

LA DUCHESSE ANNE HISTORICAL B&B
1564 Wittenberg Rd (12457)
Rates: $60-$150
(914) 688-5260

NAPLES

LANDMARK RETREAT B&B
6006 Rt 21 (14512)
Rates: $40-$60
(716) 396-2383

NEW BALTIMORE

BEST WESTERN NEW BALTIMORE INN
Rt 9 W (12192)
Rates: $55-$144
(518) 731 8100
(800) 528-1234
(877) 731-8100

NEW HAMPTON

DAYS INN
Rt 17 M & 6 (10958)
Rates: $49-$119
(914) 374-2411
(800) 329-7466

NEW HARTFORD

HOLIDAY INN UTICA
1777 Burrstone Rd (13413)
Rates: $89-$159
(315) 797-2131
(800) 465-4329

NEW YORK CITY
(Manhattan)

THE BRYANT PARK HOTEL
40 W 40th St (10018)
Rates: $575+
(212) 869-0100
(877) 640-9300

THE CARLYLE
35 E 76th St (10021)
Rates: $325-$455
(212) 744-1600
(800) 227-5737

COMFORT INN CENTRAL PARK WEST
31 W 71st St (10023)
Rates: $99-$169
(212) 721-4770
(800) 228-5150

CROWNE PLAZA MANHATTAN
1605 Broadway (10019)
Rates: $185-$235
(212) 977-4000
(800) 227-6963
(800) 243-6969

CROWNE PLAZA UNITED NATIONS
304 E 42nd St (10017)
Rates: $150+
(212) 986-8800
(800) 227-6963
(800) 879-8836

DUMONT PLAZA SUITE HOTEL
150 E 34th (10016)
Rates: $321-$351
(212) 481-7600
(800) 627-8483

FOUR SEASONS HOTEL
57 E 57th St (10022)
Rates: $535-$665
(212) 758-5700
(800) 487-3769
(800) 332-3442

HILTON & TOWERS
1335 Ave of the Americas (10019)
Rates: $169-$305
(800) 445-8667
(800) 586-7000

HOLIDAY INN WALL STREET DISTRICT
15 Gold St (10038)
Rates: $219
(212) 232-7700
(800) 465-4329

HOTEL PIERRE-A FOUR SEASONS HOTEL
2 E 61st St (10021)
Rates: $395-$575
(212) 838-8000
(800) 332-3442

HOTEL PLAZA ATHENEE
37 E 64th St (10021)
Rates: $430-$620
(212) 734-9100
(800) 447-8800

LA GUARDIA MARRIOTT HOTEL
102-05 Ditmars Blvd (10019)
Rates: $239
(718) 565-8900
(800) 228-9290

LE PARKER MERIDIEN
118 W 57th St (10019)
Rates: $365-$435
(212) 245-5000
(800) 543-4300

LOEWS NEW YORK
569 Lexington Ave (10022)
Rates: $319
(212) 752-7000
(800) 235-6397

THE LOWELL
28 E 63rd St (10021)
Rates: $315-$1015
(212) 838-1400
(800) 221-4444

MARRIOTT MARQUIS
1535 Broadway (10036)
Rates: $335-$520
(212) 398-1900
(800) 228-9290

MAYFLOWER HOTEL ON THE PARK
15 Central Park W (10023)
Rates: $190-$250
(212) 265-0060
(800) 223-4164

MILLENIUM BROADWAY HOTEL
145 W 44th St (10036)
Rates: $290-$410
(212) 768-4400
(800) 622-5569

MORGANS HOTEL
237 Madison Ave (10016)
Rates: $195-$275
(212) 686-0300
(800) 334-3408

THE MUSE HOTEL
130 W 46th St (10036)
Rates: $355+
(212) 485-2400

NEW YORK PALACE HISTORIC HOTEL
455 Madison Ave (10022)
Rates: $540-$690
(212) 888-7000
(800) 697-2522

NOVOTEL NEW YORK
226 W 52nd St (10019)
Rates: $119-$249
(212) 315-0100
(800) 221-3185

THE PENINSULA
700 5th Ave (10019)
Rates: $550-$1750
(212) 956-2888
(800) 262-9467

THE PLAZA HOTEL
19 W 58th St (10019)
Rates: $220-$500
(212) 759-3000
(800) 228-3000

THE REGENCY HOTEL
540 Park Ave (10021)
Rates: $260-$320
(212) 759-4100
(800) 233-2356

RENAISSANCE HOTEL
714 7th Ave (10036)
Rates: $299-$415
(212) 765-7676
(800) 228-9892

SHERATON MANHATTAN HOTEL
790 7th Ave (10019)
Rates: $179-$305
(212) 581-3300
(800) 325-3535

SHERATON NEW YORK HOTEL & TOWERS
811 7th Ave (10019)
Rates: $179-$305
(212) 581-1000
(800) 325-3535

SOHO GRAND HOTEL
310 W Broadway (10013)
Rates: $454+
(212) 965-3000
(800) 965-3000

NEWARK

QUALITY INN
125 N Main St (14513)
Rates: $79-$160
(315) 331-9500
(800) 228-5151

SOUTHGATE TOWER SUITE HOTEL
371 7th Ave (10001)
Rates: $278-$308
(212) 563-1800
(800) ME-SUITE

THE STANHOPE
995 Fifth Ave (10028)
Rates: $300-$2500
(212) 288-5800
(800) 828-1123

SURREY HOTEL
20 E 76th St (10022)
Rates: $450-$480
(212) 288-3700
(800) 637-8483

SWISSOTEL-THE DRAKE
440 Park Ave (10022)
Rates: $185-$355
(212) 421-0900
(800) 372-5369

TRIBECA GRAND HOTEL
2 Ave of the Americas (10013)
Rates: $399+
(212) 519-6600
(877) 519-6000

WALDORF TOWERS
100 E 50th St (10022)
Rates: $375-$1150
(212) 355-3100
(800) 445-8667

WARWICK HOTEL
65 W 54th St (10019)
Rates: $245-$260
(212) 247-2700
(800) 223-4099

NEWBURGH

HOWARD JOHNSON
95 RT 17K (12550)
Rates: $69-$199
(914) 564-4000
(800) 446-4656

KELSAY'S HOUSE OF NATIONS
1 Scenic Dr
(12550)
Rates: n/a
(914) 562-1477

NEWFANE

LAKE ONTARIO MOTEL
3330 Lockport-Olcott Blvd
(14108)
Rates: $37-$84
(716) 778-5004
(800) 446-5767

NIAGARA FALLS
(New York, USA)

BEST WESTERN INN ON THE RIVER
7001 Buffalo Ave
(14304)
Rates: $89-$169
(716) 283-7612
(800) 245-7612

BEST WESTERN SUMMIT INN
9500 Niagara Falls
Blvd (14304)
Rates: $89-$139
(716) 297-5050
(800) 528-1234
(800) 404-8217

BIT O' PARIS MOTEL
9890 Niagara Falls
Blvd (14304)
Rates: n/a
(716) 297-1710

BOYLE'S HOUSE BED & BREAKFAST
2478 River Rd
(14304)
Rates: n/a
(716) 693-3070

CARAVAN MOTEL
6730 Niagara Falls
Blvd (14304)
Rates: n/a
(716) 236-0752

THE COACHMAN MOTEL
523 Third St (14301)
Rates: $36-$109
(716) 285-2295
(800) 335-2295

DAYS INN
401 Buffalo Ave
(14303)
Rates: $40-$120
(716) 285-2541
(800) 329-7466

DUNES MOTEL
5655 Niagara Falls
Blvd (14304)
Rates: n/a
(716) 283-6114

FALLS MOTEL
5820 Buffalo Ave
(14304)
Rates: n/a
(716) 283-3239

HOWARD JOHNSON LODGE AT THE FALLS
454 Main St (14301)
Rates: $45-$140
(716) 285-5261
(800) 446-4656
(800) 282-5621

JUNIOR'S MOTOR INN
5647 Niagara Falls
Blvd (14304)
Rates: n/a
(716) 283-4914

KNIGHTS INN
9900 Niagara Falls
Blvd (14304)
Rates: $68-$89
(716) 297-3647
(800) 843-5644

NIAGARA RAINBOW MOTEL
7900 Niagara Falls
Blvd (14304)
Rates: $25-$89
(716) 283-1760

PELICAN MOTEL
6817 Niagara Falls
Blvd (14304)
Rates: $29-$99
(716) 283-2278
(716) 283-3169

PLAZA COURT MOTEL
7680 Niagara Falls
Blvd (14304)
Rates: n/a
(716) 283-2638
(716) 283-3151

SANDS MOTEL
9393 Niagara Falls
Blvd (14304)
Rates: $24-$108
(716) 297-3797

SUNRISE INN
6225 Niagara Falls
Blvd (14304)
Rates: n/a
(716) 283-9952

TRAVELERS BUDGET INN
9001 Niagara Falls
Blvd (14304)
Rates: $29-$109
(716) 297-3228

TRAVELODGE HOTEL
201 Rainbow Blvd
(14303)
Rates: $39-$129
(716) 285-9321
(800) 578-7878

NIAGARA FALLS
(Ontario, Canada)

BEST WESTERN FALLVIEWS MOTOR HOTEL
5551 Murray St
(L2G 2J4)
Rates: $79-$229
(905) 356-0551
(800) 528-1234
(800) 263-2580

CAMELOT INN
5640 Stanley Ave
(L2G 3X5)
Rates: $34-$80
(905) 354-3754

FLAMINGO MOTOR INN
7701 Lundy's Ln
(L2H 1H3)
Rates: $39-$129
(905) 356-4646
(800) 738-7701

GLENGATE MOTEL
5534 Stanley Ave
(L2G 3X2)
Rates: $39-$99
(905) 357-1333

HOLIDAY INN BY THE FALLS
5339 Murray Hill
(L2G 2J3)
Rates: $59-$199
(905) 356-1333
(800) 263-9393

HOWARD JOHNSON PLAZA HOTEL
5905 Victoria Ave
(L2G 3L8)
Rates: n/a
(905) 357-4040
(800) 446-4656

INN ON THE NIAGARA PARKWAY
7857 Niagara
River Pkwy
Rates: n/a
(905) 295-4371

NIAGARA PARKWAY COURT MOTEL
3708 Main St
(L2G 6B1)
Rates: $50-$100
(905) 295-3331

PENINSULA INN & RESORT
7373 Niagara
Square Dr
Rates: n/a
(905) 354-8812

SHERATON INN
6045 Stanley Ave
(L2G 3Y3)
Rates: $88-$249
(905) 374-4142
(800) 267-5439

STANLEY MOTOR INN
6220 Stanley Ave
Rates: n/a
(905) 358-9238

SUNSET INN
5803 Stanley Ave
(L2G 3X8)
Rates: $34-$75
(905) 354-7513

THRIFTLODGE
6000 Stanley Ave
(L2G 3Y1)
Rates: $99-$199
(905) 358-6243
(800) 578-7878

NORTH CREEK

BLACK MOUNTAIN SKI LODGE & MOTEL
2999 SR 8 (12853)
Rates: $55-$65
(518) 251-2800
(888) 846-4858

THE INN ON GORE MOUNTAIN
Peaceful Valley Rd
(12853)
Rates: $59-$75
(518) 251-2111

NORTH SYRACUSE

CLUB HOTEL BY DOUBLETREE AIRPORT
6701 Buckley Rd
(13212)
Rates: $99
(315) 457-4000
(800) 222-8733
(800) 572-1602

NORTH TONAWANDA

ROYAL MOTEL
3333 Niagara Falls
Blvd (14120)
Rates: n/a
(716) 692-2724
(716) 692-4546

STARFIRE MOTEL
3466 Niagara Falls
Blvd (14120)
Rates: n/a
(716) 694-3600

NORWICH

HOWARD JOHNSON
75 N Broad St (13815)
Rates: $99-$159
(607) 334-2200
(800) 446-4656

OGDENSBURG

ALTA COURTS MOTEL
Riverside Dr (13669)
Rates: $35-$75
(315) 393-6860

DAYS INN
1200 Paterson St (13669)
Rates: $47-$75
(315) 393-3200
(800) 329-7466

QUALITY INN GRAN-VIEW
6765 SR 37 (13669)
Rates: $53-$99
(315) 393-4550
(800) 228-5151
(800) 392-4550

STONE FENCE LODGING
7191 SR 37 (13669)
Rates: $63-$119
(315) 393-1545
(800) 253-1545

OLCOTT

BAYSIDE GUEST HOUSE
1572 Lockport-Olcott Rd (14126)
Rates: n/a
(716) 778-7767
(800) 438-2192

OLD FORGE

BEST WESTERN SUNSET INN
Rt 28, Box 261 (13420)
Rates: $99-$189
(315) 369-6836
(800) 528-1234

ONEONTA

CELTIC MOTEL
112 Oneida St (13820)
Rates: n/a
(607) 432-0860

HOLIDAY INN
Rt 23 Southside (13820)
Rates: $199
(607) 433-2250
(800) 465-4329

SUPER 8 MOTEL
4973 Southside (13820)
Rates: $58-$79
(607) 432-9505
(800) 800-8000

OSWEGO

BEST WESTERN THE CAPTAIN'S QUARTERS
26 E First St (13126)
Rates: $68-$200
(315) 342-4040
(800) 528-1234

CHESTNUT GROVE INN
7096 SR 104 W (13126)
Rates: n/a
(315) 342-2547

DAYS INN
101 SR 104 (13126)
Rates: $49-$105
(315) 343-3136
(800) 329-7466

K & G LODGE
94 Creamery Rd (13126)
Rates: n/a
(315) 343-8171

SUNSET CABINS
RR 10 (13126)
Rates: n/a
(315) 343-2166

THE THOMAS INN
309 W Seneca St (13126)
Rates: n/a
(315) 343-4900

TWIN PINES CABINS
1881 CR 1 (13126)
Rates: n/a
(315) 343-2475

OWEGO

SUNRISE MOTEL
3778 Waverly Rd (13827)
Rates: $58-$73
(607) 687-5667
(800) 806-9074

PAINTED POST

BEST WESTERN LODGE ON THE GREEN
3171 Canada Rd (14870)
Rates: $80
(607) 962-2456
(800) 528-1234

LAMPLITER MOTEL
9316 Victory Hwy (14870)
Rates: $30-$43
(607) 962-1184

STILES MOTEL
9239 Victory Hwy (14870)
Rates: $25-$47
(607) 962-5221
(800) 331-3920

PALENVILLE

HICKORY NOTCH CABINS
P.O. Box 279 (12463)
Rates: n/a
(518) 678-3259

PARISH

MONTCLAIR MOTEL
Rt 69 (13131)
Rates: $39-$44
(315) 625-7100

PARKSVILLE

BEST WESTERN PARAMOUNT
Tanzman Rd (12768)
Rates: $45-$220
(914) 292-6700
(800) 528-1234
(800) 922-3498

PEEKSKILL

PEEKSKILL INN
634 Main St (10566)
Rates: $95-$120
(914) 739-1500
(800) 526-9466

PEMBROKE

ECONO LODGE-DARIEN LAKES
8493 SR 77 (14036)
Rates: $60-$80
(716) 599-4681
(800) 553-2666

PENN YAN

VIKING MOTEL
680 E Lake Rd (14527)
Rates: $42-$135
(315) 536-7061

PINE CITY

RUFUS TANNER HOUSE
60 Sagetown Rd (14871)
Rates: n/a
(607) 732-0213

PITTSFORD

THE DELMONTE LODGE
41 N Main St (14534)
Rates: $68-$75
(716) 381-9900
(800) 836-3376

PLAINVIEW

RESIDENCE INN BY MARRIOTT
9 Gerhard Rd (11803)
Rates: $189-$199
(516) 433-6200
(800) 331-3131

PLATTSBURGH

BAYMONT INN & SUITES
16 Plaza Blvd (12901)
Rates: $67-$77
(518) 562-4000
(800) 301-0200

BEST WESTERN-THE INN AT SMITHFIELD
446 Rt 3 (12901)
Rates: $79-$99
(518) 561-7750
(800) 528-1234
(800) 243-4656

ECONO LODGE
528 Rt 3 (12901)
Rates: $35-$75
(518) 561-1500
(800) 553-2666

HOLIDAY INN
412 Rt 3 (12901)
Rates: $50-$75
(518) 561-5000
(800) 465-4329

SUPER 8 MOTEL
7129 Rt 9 N (12901)
Rates: $40-$57
(518) 562-8888
(800) 800-8000

PORT JEFFERSON

DANFORDS INN ON THE SOUND
25 E Broadway (11777)
Rates: $100-$400
(516) 928-5200
(800) 332-6367

PORT JERVIS

COMFORT INN
Rt 23 & Greenville Tpk (12771)
Rates: $69-$119
(914) 856-6611
(800) 228-5150

PORT ONTARIO

MANNING'S PORT ONTARIO
RS 1, Rt 3 (13142)
Rates: n/a
(315) 298-2509

POUGHKEEPSIE

HOLIDAY INN EXP
341 South Rd (12601)
Rates: $109-$169
(914) 473-1151
(800) 465-4329

TRAVELODGE
313 Manchester Rd (12601)
Rates: $60-$87
(914) 454-3080
(800) 578-7878

PULASKI

BIG A SPORT SHOP & LODGE
7542 Salina St (13142)
Rates: n/a
(315) 298-5509

CLARK'S COTTAGES
RD 2, Lake Rd (13142)
Rates: n/a
(315) 298-4778

DOUBLE EAGLE LODGE
3268 SR 13 (13142)
Rates: n/a
(315) 298-3326

DRIFTWOOD MOTEL
5240 US Rt 11 (13142)
Rates: n/a
(315) 298-5000

1880 HOUSE BED & BREAKFAST
7536 S Jefferson St (13142)
Rates: n/a
(315) 298-6088

FISH HAWK LODGE
1091 Albion Cross Rd (13142)
Rates: n/a
(315) 298-5841

GOLDEN FISH CABINS
RD 1, Rt 3 (13142)
Rates: n/a
(315) 298-6556

LAURDON HEIGHTS
7489-90 Lewis St (13142)
Rates: n/a
(315) 298-6091

MAPLE GROVE SPORT & ANGLER RESORT
2870 SR 13 (13142)
Rates: n/a
(315) 298-7256

PORT LODGE MOTEL
7469 Scenic Hwy (13142)
Rates: n/a
(315) 298-6876

PORTLY ANGLER LODGE
CR 2A at Rt 13 (13142)
Rates: $50-$75
(315) 298-4773

RAINBOW SHORES HOTEL
RD 2 (13142)
Rates: n/a
(315) 298-9982
(315) 298-5110

RAINBOW SHORES MOTEL
348 Rainbow Shores Rd (13142)
Rates: n/a
(315) 298-4407

REDWOOD MOTEL
I-81 & NY 13 (13142)
Rates: $50-$75
(315) 298-4717

RUPERT'S TRADING POST
7539 Rome St (13142)
Rates: n/a
(315) 298-4042

SEQUOIA INN
7686 N Jefferson St (13142)
Rates: n/a
(315) 298-4407
(315) 298-2460

WHITAKERS MOTEL
7700 Rome Rd (13142)
Rates: n/a
(315) 298-6162

WILD BILL'S LODGE
7453 Lewis St (13142)
Rates: $18+
(315) 298-2461

PURLING

BAVARIAN MANOR COUNTRY INN
CR 24 (12470)
Rates: n/a
(518) 622-3261

QUEENS

CLARION HOTEL LA GUARDIA AIRPORT
9400 Ditmars Blvd (East Elmhurst 11369)
Rates: $165-$265
(718) 335-1200
(800) 252-7466

COMFORT INN-JFK AIRPORT
14436 153rd Lane (Jamaica 11434)
Rates: $115-$175
(718) 977-0001
(800) 228-5150

HILTON HOTEL-JFK AIRPORT
138-10 135th Ave (Jamaica 11436)
Rates: $109-$169
(718) 322-8700
(800) 445-8667

PLAZA HOTEL-JFK AIRPORT
135-30 140th St (Jamaica 11436)
Rates: n/a
(718) 659-6003

QUEENSBURY

SUSSE CHALET
24 Big Boom Rd (12804)
Rates: $48-$88
(518) 793-8891
(800) 524-2538

RHINEBECK

BEEKMAN ARMS MOTEL
4 Mill St (12572)
Rates: $80-$140
(914) 876-7077

RHINEBECK MOTEL
117 Rt 9 (12572)
Rates: $40-$99
(914) 876-5900

WHISTLE WOOD FARM
11 Pells Rd (12572)
Rates: $99-$150
(914) 876-6838

RIPLEY

BUDGET HOST COLONIAL SQUIRE
Shortman Rd (14775)
Rates: $49-$55
(716) 736-8000
(800) 283-4678

ROCHESTER

COMFORT INN
395 Buell Rd (14624)
Rates: $54-$99
(716) 436-4400
(800) 228-5150

CROWNE PLAZA
70 State St (14614)
Rates: $89-$129
(716) 546-3450
(800) 227-6963
(800) 243-7760

HAMPTON INN
717 E Henrietta Rd (14623)
Rates: $95-$105
(716) 272-7800
(800) 426-7866

HOLIDAY INN AIRPORT
911 Brooks Ave (14624)
Rates: n/a
(716) 328-6000
(800) 465-4329

QUALITY INN
1273 Chili Ave (14624)
Rates: $49-$89
(716) 464-8800
(800) 228-5151

TOWPATH MOTEL
2323 Monroe Ave (14618)
Rates: $40-$46
(716) 271-2147

ROCKVILLE CENTRE

HOLIDAY INN
173 Sunrise Hwy (11570)
Rates: $155-$165
(516) 678-1300
(800) 465-4329
(877) 241-7544

ROME

ADIRONDACK THIRTEEN PINES MOTEL
7353 River Rd (13440)
Rates: $40-$55
(315) 337-4930

AMERICAN HERITAGE MOTOR INN
799 Lower Lawrence St (13440)
Rates: $35-$60
(315) 339-3610
(800) 836-1203

BEECHES-PAUL REVERE MOTOR LODGE
7900 Turin Rd (13440)
Rates: $59-$85
(315) 336-1776

FAMILY INNS OF AMERICA
145 E Whitesboro St (13440)
Rates: $45+
(315) 337-9400
(800) 348-3377

ROSCOE

ROSCOE MOTEL
Box 608 (12776)
Rates: $45-$65
(607) 498-5220

SACKETS HARBOR

ONTARIO PLACE HOTEL
103 General Smith Dr (13685)
Rates: $49-$69
(315) 646-8000
(800) 564-1812

SALAMANCA

DUDLEY HOTEL
132 Main St
(14779)
Rates: $40-$50
(716) 945-3200

SANDY CREEK

HARRIS LODGING
P.O. Box 547
(13145)
Rates: n/a
(315) 387-5907
(315) 387-5504

TUG HILL LODGE
216 Salisbury St
(13145)
Rates: n/a
(315) 387-5326

SARANAC LAKE

ADIRONDACK MOTEL
23 Lake Flower Ave (12983)
Rates: $50-$135
(518) 891-2116

COMFORT INN
148 Lake Flower Ave (12983)
Rates: $75-$120
(518) 891-1970
(800) 228-5150

HOTEL SARANAC OF PAUL SMITH'S COLLEGE
101 Main St
(12983)
Rates: $75-$105
(518) 891-2200
(800) 937-0211

LAKE FLOWER INN
15 Lake Flower Ave (12983)
Rates: $68-$92
(518) 891-2310

LAKE SIDE MOTEL
27 Lake Flower Ave (12983)
Rates: $50-$99
(518) 891-4333

THE POINT
HCR 1, Box 65
(12983)
Rates: $825-$1350
(518) 891-5674
(800) 255-3530

SARATOGA SPRINGS

ADIRONDACK MOTEL
230 West Ave
(12866)
Rates: $49-$169
(518) 584-3510

BEST WESTERN PLAYMORE FARMS
3291 S Broadway
(12866)
Rates: $49-$189
(518) 584-2350
(800) 528-1234

COMMUNITY COURT MOTEL
248 Broadway
(12866)
Rates: $40-$60+
(518) 584-6666

COUNTRY CLUB MOTEL
306 Church St
(12866)
Rates: $55-$175
(518) 882-6838

GRAND UNION MOTEL
120 S Broadway
(12866)
Rates: $50-$75
(518) 584-9001

HOLIDAY INN
232 Broadway
(12866)
Rates: $219-$279
(518) 584-4550
(800) 465-4329

ROBIN HOOD MOTEL
2205 Rt 50 (12866)
Rates: n/a
(518) 885-8899

ST. CHARLES/ST. FRANCIS MOTEL
160 Broadway
(12866)
Rates: $45-$135
(518) 584-2050

THOROBRED MOTEL
P.O. Box 195
(12866)
Rates: n/a
(518) 583-4903

UNION GABLES BED & BRKFAST

55 Union Ave
(12866)
Rates: $240-$300
(518) 584-1558
(800) 398-1558

SAUGERTIES

HOWARD JOHNSON INN
2764 Rt 32 (12477)
Rates: $55-$80
(914) 246-9511
(800) 446-4656

SCHENECTADY

DAYS INN
167 Nott Ter (12308)
Rates: $79-$119
(518) 370-3297
(800) 329-7466

HOLIDAY INN
100 Nott Ter (12308)
Rates: $89-$129
(518) 393-4141
(800) 465-4329

SUPER 8 MOTEL
3083 Carman Rd
(12303)
Rates: $45-$65
(518) 355-2190
(800) 800-8000

SCHROON LAKE

BLUE RIDGE MOTEL
RR 1, Box 321
(12870)
Rates: $55-$75
(518) 532-7521

DUN ROAMIN CABINS
Rt 9, P. O. Box 535
(12870)
Rates: $40-$75
(518) 532-7277

RAWLINS MOTEL AND CABINS
P.O. Box 9 (12870)
Rates: n/a
(518) 532-7907
(800) 901-5253

SENECA FALLS

MICROTEL INN & SUITES
1966 Rt 5 & 20
(13148)
Rates: $39-$76
(315) 539-8438
(888) 771-7171

SHARON SPRINGS

BUDGET HOST INN-SHARON SPRINGS MOTEL
Rt 20 (13459)
Rates: $45-$159
(518) 284-2114
(800) 283-4678

SHELTER ISLAND HEIGHTS

BEACH HOUSE INN
P. O. Box 648 (11965)
Rates: $90-$125
(516) 749-0264

SIDNEY

COUNTRY MOTEL
Rt 7 & E of Rt 8
(13838)
Rates: n/a
(607) 563-1035

SOUTH WORCESTER

CHARLOTTE VALLEY INN B&B
480 CR 40 (12197)
Rates: $115-$125
(607) 397-8164

SOUTHAMP-TON

OAK TREE INN BED & BREAKFST
606 Major's Path
(11968)
Rates: $85-$210
(516) 287-2057

SPRING GLEN

GOLD MOUNTAIN CHALET RESORT
36 Tice Rd (12483)
Rates: $100-$150
(914) 647-4332
(800) 395-5200

STAMFORD

REXMERE LODGE
5 Lake St (12167)
Rates: $48-$85
(607) 652-7394
(800) 932-1090

SUFFERN

WELLESLEY INN
17 N Airmont Rd
(10901)
Rates: $71-$103
(914) 368-1900
(800) 444-8888

SYRACUSE

COMFORT INN
6491 Thompson Rd (13206)
Rates: $54-$129
(315) 437-0222
(800) 228-5150

COMFORT INN FAIRGROUNDS
7010 Interstate Island Rd (13209)
Rates: $66-$159
(315) 453-0045
(800) 228-5150

DAYS INN-EAST
6609 Thompson Rd (13206)
Rates: $55-$99
(315) 437-5998
(800) 329-7466

ECONO LODGE UNIVERSITY
454 James St
(13203)
Rates: $35-$110
(315) 425-0015
(800) 553-2666

HOLIDAY INN FAIRGROUNDS
100 Farrell Rd
(13209)
Rates: $89-$119
(315) 457-8700
(800) 465-4329

JOHN MILTON INN
6578 Thompson Rd (13206)
Rates: $35-$60
(315) 463-8555
(800) 352-1061

AREA CODES - If the local number doesn't connect, check for a new area code.

RAMADA LIMITED UNIVERSITY
6590 Thompson Rd N (13206)
Rates: $59-$99
(315) 463-0202
(800) 272-6232

RED ROOF INN
6614 Thompson Rd (13206)
Rates: $56-$85
(315) 437-3309
(800) 843-7663

TARRYTOWN

HILTON HOTEL
455 S Broadway (10591)
Rates: $109-$279
(914) 631-5700
(800) 445-8667

TICONDEROGA

CIRCLE COURT MOTEL
440 Montcalm St (12883)
Rates: $54-$64
(518) 585-7660

RANCH HOUSE AT BALDWIN
RR 1, 79 Baldwin Rd (12883)
Rates: $69
(518) 585-6596

TONAWANDA

MICROTEL INN
1 Hospitality Centre Way (14150)
Rates: $45-$71
(716) 693-8100
(888) 771-7171

TUPPER LAKE

PINE TERRACE MOTEL & TENNIS CLUB
94 Moody Rd (12986)
Rates: $50-$450
(518) 359-9258

RED TOP INN
90 Moody Rd (12986)
Rates: $50-$55
(518) 359-9209

SUNSET PARK MOTEL
De Mars Blvd (12986)
Rates: $44-$56
(518) 359-3995

UNIONDALE

LONG ISLAND MARRIOTT HOTEL & CONF CENTER
101 James Doolittle Blvd (11553)
Rates: $179-$215
(516) 794-3800
(800) 228-9290
(800) 832-6255

UPPER SARANAC LAKE

THE WAWBEEK RESORT CABINS & RESTAURANT
553 Panther Mtn Rd (12986)
Rates: $95-$150
(518) 359-2656
(800) 953-2656

UTICA

A-1 MOTEL
238 N Genesee St (13502)
Rates: $50-$60
(315) 735-6698
(800) 809-6885

BEST WESTERN GATEWAY ADIRONDACK INN
175 N Genesee St (13502)
Rates: $75-$199
(315) 732-4121
(800) 528-1234

HAPPY JOURNEY MOTEL
300 N Genesee St (13502)
Rates: $28-$45
(315) 738-1959

MOTEL 6
150 N Genesee St (13502)
Rates: $37-$56
(315) 797-8743
(800) 466-8356

RADISSON HOTEL
200 N Genesee St (13502)
Rates: $119-$159
(315) 797-8010
(800) 333-3333

RED ROOF INN
20 Weaver St (13502)
Rates: $65-$105
(315) 724-7128
(800) 843-7663

SUPER 8 MOTEL
309 N Genesse St (13502)
Rates: $37-$62
(315) 797-0964
(800) 800-8000

VALATIE

BLUE SPRUCE INN & SUITES
3093 US 9 (12184)
Rates: $55-$80
(518) 758-9711
(888) 261-9823

VESTAL

HAMPTON INN
3708 Vestal Pkwy E (13850)
Rates: $85-$109
(607) 797-5000
(800) 426-7866

HOLIDAY INN
4105 Vestal Pkwy E (13850)
Rates: n/a
(607) 729-6371
(800) 465-4329

HOWARD JOHNSON EXPRESS INN
3601 Vestal Pkwy E (13850)
Rates: $45-$149
(607) 729-6181
(800) 446-4656

PARKWAY MOTEL
900 Vestal Pkwy E 434 (13851)
Rates: $30-$68
(607) 785-3311

RESIDENCE INN BY MARRIOTT
4610 Vestal Pkwy E (13850)
Rates: $99-$150
(607) 770-8500
(800) 331-3131

VICTOR

MICROTEL INN
7498 Main St Fishers (14564)
Rates: $54-$80
(716) 924-9240
(888) 771-7171
(800) 278-8884

WADDINGTON

RIVERVIEW MOTEL & COTTAGES
RR 1, Box 14 (13694)
Rates: $38-$48
(315) 388-5912

WALLKILL

AUDREY'S FARM HOUSE B&B
2188 Brunswyck Rd (12589)
Rates: $90-$110
(914) 895-3440

WATERLOO

HOLIDAY INN
2468 SR 414 (13165)
Rates: $119-$139
(315) 539-5011
(800) 465-4329

WATERTOWN

BEST WESTERN CARRIAGE HOUSE INN
300 Washington St (13601)
Rates: $62-$81
(315) 782-8000
(800) 528-1234

CITY LINE MOTEL
19226 US Rt 11 (13601)
Rates: $24-$66
(315) 782-9619

ECONO LODGE
1030 Arsenal St (13601)
Rates: $40-$75
(315) 762-5500
(800) 553-2666

NEW PARROT MOTEL
19325 Washington St (13601)
Rates: $30-$68
(315) 788-5080
(800) 479-9889

RAINBOW MOTEL
RD 6, Box 20 (13601)
Rates: n/a
(315) 788-2830
(800) 421-8989

ROYAL INN MOTEL
25791 State Rt 37 (13601)
Rates: $25-$50
(315) 788-2910

THE INN
1190 Arsenal St (13601)
Rates: $50-$70
(315) 788-6800

WATKINS GLEN

CHALET LEON AT HECTOR FALLS
Box 388 (14891)
Rates: $40-$69
(607) 546-7171

CHIEFTAN MOTEL
3815 SR 14 (14891)
Rates: $49-$83
(607) 535-4759

FARM SANCTUARY BED & BREAKFAST
P. O. Box 150 (14891)
Rates: $55-$95
(607) 583-2225

GLEN MOTOR INN
3380 Rt 14 (14891)
Rates: $73-$90
(607) 535-2706

AREA CODES - If the local number doesn't connect, check for a new area code.

WAVERLY

O'BRIENS INN
6312 CR 60
(14892)
Rates: $38-$58
(607) 565-2817

WEEDSPORT

BEST WESTERN INN
2709 Erie Dr
(13166)
Rates: $59-$120
(315) 834-6623
(800) 528-1234

WEST NYACK

NYACK MOTOR LODGE
Rt 303 (10994)
Rates: $44-$68
(914) 358-4100

WESTBURY

ISLAND INN
Old Country Rd
(11590)
Rates: $99-$350
(516) 228-9500

WESTMORE-LAND

CARRIAGE MOTOR INN
SR 223 (13490)
Rates: $38-$55
(315) 853-3561

WHITE PLAINS

THE ESPLANADE HOTEL
95 S Broadway
(10601)
Rates: $69-$79
(914) 761-8100
(800) 247-5322

WESTCHESTER RESIDENCE INN BY MARRIOTT
5 Barker Ave
(10601)
Rates: $90-$200
(914) 761-7700
(800 331-3131

WHITEHALL

APPLE ORCHARD INN
Old Fairhaven Rd
(12887)
Rates: $65
(518) 499-0180

WILLIAMSVILLE

MICROTEL INN
50 Freeman Rd
(14221)
Rates: $45-$50
(716) 633-6200
(888) 771-7171

RESIDENCE INN BY MARRIOTT
100 Maple Rd
(14221)
Rates: $120-$200
(716) 632-6622
(800) 331-3131

WILMINGTON

GRAND VIEW MOTEL
SR 86 (12987)
Rates: $62-$89
(518) 946-2209

HIGH VALLEY MOTEL
HCR 2, Box 13
(12997)
Rates: $40-$61
(518) 946-2355

HOLIDAY LODGE
P. O. Box 38
(12997)
Rates: $30-$90
(518) 946-2251

HUNGRY TROUT MOTOR INN
SR 86 (12997)
Rates: $69-$139
(518) 946-2217
(800) 766-9137

LEDGE ROCK AT WHITEFACE MTN MOTEL
Placid Rd, SR 86
(12997)
Rates: $79-$160
(518) 946-2379
(800) 336-4754

NORTH POLE MOTOR INN
SR 86 (12997)
Rates: $59-$79
(518) 946-7733
(800) 245-0228

WINKELMAN MOTEL
E of Jct NY 86
(12997)
Rates: $48-$56
(518) 946-7761

WILSON

FISHERMAN'S CHOICE B&B
4793 E Lake Rd
(14172)
Rates: n/a
(716) 751-9481

YOUNGSTOWN

RIVER LOFT
425 Main St
(14174)
Rates: n/a
(716) 745-3217

TRAVEL NOTES

AREA CODES - If the local number doesn't connect, check for a new area code.

NORTH CAROLINA

ABERDEEN

**INN AT THE
BRYANT HOUSE
BED & BREAKFAST**
214 N Poplar St
(28315)
Rates: $40-$75
(919) 944-3300
(800) 453-4019

MOTEL 6
1408 Sandhills
Blvd (28315)
Rates: $39-$55
(910) 944-5633
(800) 466-8356

APEX

**PEARSON PLACE
BED & BREAKFST**
1009 N Salem St
(27502)
Rates: n/a
(919) 362-4290

ASHEBORO

SUPER 8 MOTEL
1020 Albermarle
Rd (27203)
Rates: $44-$78
(336) 625-1880
(800) 800-8000

ASHEVILLE

**ASHEVILLE
ACCOMMODA-
TIONS**
109 Circadian Way
(Chapel Hill
27516)
Rates: n/a
(919) 929-5553
(800) 770-9055

**BEST INNS OF
AMERICA**
1435 Tunnel Rd
(28805)
Rates: $43-$79
(828) 298-4000
(800) 237-4667

**COMFORT INN
RIVER EDGE**
800 Fairview Rd
(28803)
Rates: $79-$149
(828) 298-9141
(800) 228-5150
(800) 836-6732

DAYS INN
1500 Tunnel Rd
(28805)
Rates: $50-$145
(828) 298-5140
(800) 329-7466

DAYS INN
199 Tunnel Rd
(28805)
Rates: $55-$90
(828) 254-4311
(800) 329-7466

**DOGWOOD
COTTAGE INN**
40 Canterbury Rd
N (28801)
Rates: n/a
(828) 258-9725

ECONO LODGE
190 Tunnel Rd
(28805)
Rates: $65-$90
(828) 254-9521
(800) 553-2666

HILL HOUSE B&B
120 Hillside St
(28801)
Rates: $95-$250
(800) 379-0002

**HOLIDAY INN-
ASHEVILLE MALL**
201 Tunnel Rd
(28805)
Rates: $66-$99
(828) 252-4000
(800) 465-4329

**HOLIDAY INN-
EAST**
1450 Tunnel Rd
(28805)
Rates: $59-$109
(828) 298-5611
(800) 465-4329

MOTEL 6
1415 Tunnel Rd
(28805)
Rates: $37-$53
(828) 299-3040
(800) 466-8356

**RED ROOF INN-
WEST**
16 Crowell Rd
(28806)
Rates: $47-$91
(828) 667-9803
(800) 843-7663

**RESIDENCE INN
BY MARRIOTT**
701 Biltmore Ave
(28803)
Rates: n/a
(828) 281-3361
(800) 331-3131

SUPER 8 MOTEL
1329 Tunnel Rd
(28805)
Rates: $49-$89
(828) 298-7952
(800) 800-8000

ATLANTIC
BEACH

**ATLANTIS LODGE
OCEANFRONT**
MP 5, Salter Path
Rd (28512)
Rates: n/a
(252) 726-5168
(800) 682-7057

SEA GULL MOTEL
102 Henderson
Blvd (28512)
Rates: n/a
(252) 726-3613
(800) 257-2196

TRIPLE S MOTEL
502 Henderson
Blvd (28512)
Rates: n/a
(252) 726-8156

AVON

**AVON
COTTAGES**
40279 Younce Rd
(27915)
Rates: n/a
(252) 995-4123

**COLONY REALTY
VACATION
RENTALS**
40197 Bonito Rd
(27915)
Rates: n/a
(252) 995-5891
(800) 962-5256

**HATTERAS
REALTY
VACATION
RENTALS**
Hwy 12 (27915)
Rates: n/a
(252) 995-5466
(800) 428-8372

**OUTER BEACHES
REALTY
VACATION
RENTALS**
Hwy 12 & Tigrone
Blvd (27915)
Rates: n/a
(252) 995-4477
(800) 627-3150

**SURF OR SOUND
REALTY
VACATION
RENTALS**
Hwy 12 (27915)
Rates: n/a
(252) 995-5801
(800) 237-1138

BANNER ELK

**BANNER ELK INN
BED & BREAKFAST**
407 Main St E
(28604)
Rates: $85-$130
(828) 898-6223

**EAGLE RIDGE
LOG CABIN
RENTALS**
190 McGuire Mtn
Rd (28604)
Rates: n/a
(828) 963-5299

**HIGH COUNTRY
RENTALS**
Hwy 105 S (28604)
Rates: n/a
(828) 963-6521
(800) 221-6521

BAT CAVE

**BURCH REAL
ESTATE
VACATION
RENTALS**
US 64/74A
(28710)
Rates: n/a
(828) 625-8000
(800) 200-2309

**ROCKY BROAD
COTTAGES**
Scenic Hwy 9
(28710)
Rates: n/a
(828) 625-2177
(888) 577-7721

BATTLEBORO

**COMFORT INN
NORTH**
7084 Hwy 4
(27809)
Rates: $50-$90
(252) 972-9426
(800) 228-5150

**DAYS INN
GOLDROCK**
6970 Hwy 4
(27809)
Rates: $40-$75
(252) 446-0621
(800) 329-7466

DELUXE INN
Rt 1, Box 161B
(27809)
Rates: n/a
(252) 446-2411

HOWARD JOHNSON INN
7568 Hwy 48 (27809)
Rates: $24-$95
(252) 977-9595
(800) 446-4656

MASTERS ECONOMY INN
Rt 1, Box 162 (27809)
Rates: $26-$33
(252) 442-8075

RED CARPET INN
Rt 1, Box 162C (27809)
Rates: $20-$35
(252) 446-0771
(800) 251-1962

SCOTTISH INNS
Rt 1, Box 158 (27809)
Rates: $20-$32
(252) 446-1831
(800) 251-1962

TRAVELODGE
7531 Hwy 48 (27809)
Rates: $30-$50
(252) 977-3505
(800) 578-7878

BEAUFORT

CARTERET COUNTY HOME B&B
299 Hwy 101 (28516)
Rates: n/a
(252) 728-4611

BEECH MOUNTAIN

BEECH MT CHALET RENTALS
405 Beech Mtn Pkwy (28604)
Rates: n/a
(828) 387-4231
(800) 368-7404

BEECH MOUNTAIN SLOPESIDE CHALET RENTALS
503 Beech Mtn Pkwy (28604)
Rates: n/a
(828) 387-4251
(800) 692-2061

BISCOE

DAYS INN
531 E Main St (27209)
Rates: $50-$135
(910) 428-2525
(800) 329-7466

BLACK MOUNTAIN

BLACK MT INN
718 W Old Hwy 70 (28711)
Rates: n/a
(828) 669-6528
(800) 735-6128

IN THE OAKS EPISCOPAL CENTER RESORT
P O Box 1117 (28711)
Rates: n/a
(828) 669-2117

SUPER 8 MOTEL
101 Flat Creek Rd (28711)
Rates: $32-$71
(828) 669-8076
(800) 800-8000

TYLER'S COVE COTTAGE
Rock Creek Rd (28711)
Rates: n/a
(828) 669-6989
(800) 849-2730

WILDFLOWER COTTAGES
451 N Fork Rd (28711)
Rates: n/a
(828) 669-0433

BLOWING ROCK

APPLE RIDGE CABINS
120 Apple Ridge Ln (28605)
Rates: n/a
(828) 295-6622
(800) 268-4748

BLOWING ROCK PROPERTIES RENTALS
232 Ransom St (28605)
Rates: n/a
(828) 295-9899

PEACOCK RIDGE CABINS
292 Peacock Dr (28605)
Rates: n/a
(828) 295-3873

PILOT RIDGE INN
8353 Hemlock Ridge Rd (28605)
Rates: n/a
(828) 295-6509
(828) 964-5420

BOONE

CARDINAL MOTEL
2135 Blowing Rock Rd (28607)
Rates: n/a
(828) 264-3630
(800) 222-5638

FLETCHER'S VACATION RENTALS
607 Norman Rd (28607)
Rates: n/a
(828) 963-7588

JANICE ANDERSON VACATION RENTALS
184 N Water St, Suite 13 (28607)
Rates: n/a
(828) 262-1004

THE LION'S DEN B&B & CHALET
109 Red Rhododendron (28607)
Rates: n/a
(828) 863-5785
(800) 963-5785

RED CARPET INN
862 Blowing Rock Rd (28607)
Rates: n/a
(828) 264-2457
(800) 251-1962
(800) 443-7179

SCOTTISH INNS
782 Blowing Rock Rd (28607)
Rates: $29-$64
(828) 264-2483
(800) 251-1962
(800) 524-5214

BRASSTOWN

TROUT COVE CABINS
1629 Trout Cove Rd (28902)
Rates: n/a
(828) 389-3584
(888) 389-3584

BREVARD

HAMPTON INN
800 Forest Gate Center (28712)
Rates: $90-$119
(828) 883-4800
(800) 426-7866

LAS PRADERAS STABLES & COTTAGES
Rt 1, Box 12A (28712)
Rates: n/a
(828) 883-3375

SUNSET MOTEL
415 S Broad St (28712)
Rates: $44-$70
(828) 884-9106

BRYSON CITY

FALLING WATERS ADVENTURE RESORT
US 74 W (28713)
Rates: n/a
(864) 647-9587
(800) 451-9972

FONTANA LAKE CABIN RENTALS
1570 Greasy Branch Rd (28713)
Rates: n/a
(828) 488-1935
(877) 366-5253

LAUREL CREEK CABINS
78 Almond Boat Park Rd (28713)
Rates: n/a
(850) 386-7229

MOUNTAIN LAUREL MOTEL
250 Main St (28713)
Rates: n/a
(828) 488-6641

SHEPHERD'S RETREAT CABINS
P O Box 2198 (28713)
Rates: n/a
(828) 488-9836

WEST OAK B&B & COTTAGES
101 Fryemont St (28713)
Rates: n/a
(828) 488-2438

BURLINGTON

COMFORT INN
978 Plantation Dr (27215)
Rates: $62-$99
(336) 227-3681
(800) 228-5150

MOTEL 6
2155 Hanford Rd (27215)
Rates: $37-$48
(336) 226-1325
(800) 446-8356

RED ROOF INN
2133 W Hanford Rd (27215)
Rates: n/a
(336) 227-1270
(800) 843-7663

BURNSVILLE

A NORTH CAROLINA GETAWAY
Cold Springs Rd (28714)
Rates: n/a
(828) 682-3528
(877) 275-5144

ALBERT'S INN & BAVARIAN VILLAGE
20 S Toe River Rd (28714)
Rates: n/a
(828) 675-5011

BOXWOOD LODGE CABINS
Rt 6, Box 615 (28714)
Rates: n/a
(828) 682-9643

CAROLINA COUNTRY MOTEL
600 W Main (28714)
Rates: n/a
(828) 682-6033

MOUNTAIN VIEW MOTEL
Hwy 19 E (28714)
Rates: n/a
(828) 682-2115
(800) 967-8885

7TH HEAVEN
6370 Seven Mile Ridge Rd (28714)
Rates: n/a
(828) 675-4011
(800) 562-9625

WEST RIDGE VACATION RENTAL
19 E (28714)
Rates: n/a
(828) 682-1310
(734) 676-2946

CANTON

RIVERMONT CABINS
162 Rivermont Dr (28716)
Rates: n/a
(828) 648-3066
(888) 648-6373

CAROLINA BEACH

BENSON'S LANDING MOTEL
801 Carolina Beach Ave N (28428)
Rates: n/a
(910) 458-5886
(800) 932-0498

COLE'S MOTEL
213 Raleigh Ave (28428)
Rates: n/a
(910) 458-5176

SANDSTEP MOTEL
716-701 Carolina Beach Ave (28428)
Rates: n/a
(910) 458-8387
(800) 934-4076

CARY

CANDLEWOOD SUITES
1020 Buck Jones Rd (27511)
Rates: $119
(919) 468-4222

COMFORT SUITES
350 Asheville Ave (27511)
Rates: $69-$129
(919) 852-4318
(800) 228-5150

GUEST SUITES
6211 St. Regis Cir, Ste 101 (27511)
Rates: n/a
(919) 851-1511
(800) 533-2370

LA QUINTA INN & SUITES
191 Crescent Commons (27511)
Rates: $79-$119
(919) 851-2850
(800) 687-6667

RED ROOF INN
1800 Walnut St (27511)
Rates: $45-$65
(919) 469-3400
(800) 843-7663

RESIDENCE INN BY MARRIOTT
2900 Regency Pkwy (27511)
Rates: n/a
(800) 331-3131

CASHIERS

DOHERTY & WILLSON RENTALS
280 Hwy 64 E (28717)
Rates: n/a
(828) 743-3242

HIGH HAMPTON INN RESORT COMPLEX
Hwy 107 S (28717)
Rates: $88-$188
(828) 743-2411
(800) 344-2551

LAKESHORE MOUNTAIN HIDE-AWAY
286 Scenic Lake Ln (28717)
Rates: n/a
(828) 743-4252

LAKEVIEW MOUNTAIN CABINS
P O Box 471 (28717)
Rates: n/a
(828) 743-5421

MOUNTAIN VILLAGE VACATION COTTAGES
Hwy 107 S (28717)
Rates: n/a
(828) 743-2377

TUMBLIN' CREEK CHALET RENTAL
Springvalley Rd (28717)
Rates: n/a
(828) 743-2504
(407) 268-8349

VALLEY AIRE MOTEL
Hwy 107 N & Slab Town Rd (28717)
Rates: n/a
(828) 743-3998

CEDAR ISLAND

DRIFTWOOD MOTEL & CAMPGROUND
Hwy 12 (28520)
Rates: n/a
(252) 225-4861

CHAPEL HILL

THE SIENA HOTEL
1505 E Franklin St (27514)
Rates: $165
(919) 929-4000
(800) 223-7379

CHARLOTTE

AMERISUITES
7900 Forest Point Blvd (28273)
Rates: $99-$109
(704) 522-8400
(800) 833-1516

BEST WESTERN MERCHANDISE MART HOTEL
3024 E Independence Blvd (28205)
Rates: $59-$89
(704) 358-3755
(800) 528-1234

BRADLEY MOTEL
4200 I-85S (28214)
Rates: $27-$36
(704) 392-3206

CLARION HOTEL
321 W Woodlawn Rd (28217)
Rates: $59-$209
(704) 523-1400
(800) 252-7466

COMFORT INN EXECUTIVE PARK
5822 Westpark Dr (28217)
Rates: $59-$179
(704) 525-2626
(800) 228-5150

DAYS INN
118 E Woodlawn Rd (28217)
Rates: $49-$125
(704) 525-5500
(800) 329-7466

DAYS INN
601 N Tryon (28202)
Rates: $45-$135
(704) 333-4733
(800) 329-7466

DAYS INN
1408 W Sugar Creek Rd (28212)
Rates: $29-$54
(704) 597-8110
(800) 329-7466

DRURY INN & SUITES
415 W W T Harris Blvd (28262)
Rates: $79-$99
(704) 593-0700
(800) 378-7946

EXECUSTAY CONDOS
3301D Woodpark Blvd (28206)
Rates: n/a
(704) 599-1575
(800) 789-8929

HILTON HOTEL EXECUTIVE PARK
5624 Westpark Dr (28217)
Rates: $99-$164
(704) 527-8000
(800) 445-8667

HOLIDAY INN AIRPORT HOTEL & CONF CENTER
2707 Little Rock Rd (28214)
Rates: n/a
(704) 394-4301
(800) 465-4329

HOLIDAY INN UNIVERSITY EXECUTIVE PARK
8520 University Exec Park Dr (28262)
Rates: $94-$129
(704) 547-0999
(800) 465-4329

HOMEWOOD SUITES/AIRPORT COLISEUM
2770 Yorkmont Rd (28208)
Rates: n/a
(704) 357-0500
(800) 225-5466

LA QUINTA INN AIRPORT
3100 S I-85 Service Rd (28208)
Rates: $55-$79
(704) 393-5306
(800) 687-6667

LA QUINTA INN COLISEUM
4900 S Tryon St (28202)
Rates: $69-$99
(704) 523-5599
(800) 687-6667

LA QUINTA INN-SOUTH
7900 Nations Ford Rd (28217)
Rates: $55-$70
(704) 522-7110
(800) 687-6667

MICROTEL INN
3412 S I-85 Service Rd (28208)
Rates: $44-$96
(704) 398-9601
(800) 840-2972
(888) 771-7171

AREA CODES - If the local number doesn't connect, check for a new area code.

MOTEL 6-SOUTH
3430 St. Vardell Ln
(28210)
Rates: $36-$40
(704) 527-0144
(800) 466-8356

QUALITY INN CROWN POINT
2501 Sardis Rd N
(28227)
Rates: $86-$110
(704) 845-2810
(800) 228-5151

QUALITY INN & SUITES
4330 N I-85
(28206)
Rates: $58-$339
(704) 596-0182
(800) 228-5151

QUALITY SUITES
1700 S I-85 Service Rd (28208)
Rates: $74-$87
(704) 399-1600
(800) 228-5151

RED ROOF INN AIRPORT
3300 S I-85 (28208)
Rates: $46-$73
(704) 392-2316
(800) 843-7663

RED ROOF INN AT UNIVERSITY
5116 I-85 N
(28206)
Rates: $38-$70
(704) 596-8222
(800) 843-7663

RED ROOF INN COLISEUM
131 Red Roof Dr
(28217)
Rates: $54-$68
(704) 529-1020
(800) 843-7663

RESIDENCE INN BY MARRIOTT
8503 N Tryon St
(28262)
Rates: $119-$139
(704) 547-1122
(800) 331-3131

RESIDENCE INN BY MARRIOTT
5816 Westpark Dr
(28216)
Rates: $129-$139
(704) 527-8110
(800) 331-3131

SHERATON AIRPORT PLAZA
3315 I-85 S
at Billy Graham Pkwy (28208)
Rates: $85-$145
(704) 392-1200
(800) 325-3535

SLEEP INN
8525 N Tryon St
(28262)
Rates: $68-$199
(704) 549-4544
(800) 753-3746

STAYBRIDGE SUITES BY HOLIDAY INN
7924
Forest Pine Rd
(28273)
Rates: n/a
(704) 527-6767
(800) 238-8000

CHEROKEE

BAYMONT INN
Acquoni Rd
(28719)
Rates: n/a
(828) 497-2102
(800) 301-0200

CHEROKEE PLAZA MOTEL
Hwy 19 & 441 Bus
(28719)
Rates: n/a
(828) 497-2301
(800) 535-4798

HAMPTON INN
Hwy 19 S (28719)
Rates: $59-$99
(828) 497-3115
(800) 426-7866

PIONEER MOTEL & COTTAGES
Hwy 19 S (28719)
Rates: $58-$78
(828) 497-2435

SLEEP INN
US 441 S (28719)
Rates: $45-$135
(828) 497-4730
(800) 753-3746

CHIMNEY ROCK

CHIMNEY ROCK INN
126 Main St
(28720)
Rates: n/a
(828) 625-1429
(800) 625-2003

FALLS COUNTRY MOTEL
US 64 & 74 A
(28720)
Rates: n/a
(828) 625-2771

CLAREMONT

SUPER 8 MOTEL
3054 N Oxford St
(28610)
Rates: $45-$52
(704) 459-7777
(800) 800-8000

CLAYTON

SLEEP INN
105 Commerce Pkwy (27520)
Rates: $55-$75
(919) 772 7771
(800) 753-3746

CLEMMONS

TANGLEWOOD PARK MOTEL
Hwy 158 W (27012)
Rates: n/a
(336) 778-6300

CLINTON

A & J GUESTHOUSES AND APARMENTS
216 Simpson St
(28328)
Rates: n/a
(910) 592-2634
(800) 462-9817

CLYDE

MIDWAY MOTEL
3708 Crabtree Rd
(28786)
Rates: n/a
(828) 627-8401

COLUMBUS

LY NAVD HILLS GUEST HOUSE B&B
Rt 2, Box 1723
(28722)
Rates: n/a
(828) 863-2603

CONCORD

HOLIDAY INN EXPRESS
1601 Hwy 29 N
(28025)
Rates: n/a
(704) 786-5181
(800) 465-4329

CORNELIUS

HAMPTON INN
19501 Statesville Rd (28031)
Rates: $69-$79
(704) 892-9900
(800) 426-7866

HOLIDAY INN LAKE NORMAN
19901 Holiday Ln
(28031)
Rates: $79-$104
(704) 892-9120
(800) 465-4329

COROLLA

B&B ON THE BEACH
1023 Ocean Trail
(27927)
Rates: n/a
(252) 453-3033
(800) 962-0201

KARICHELE REALTY VACATION RENTALS
66 Sunset Blvd, TimBuck II
(27927)
Rates: n/a
(252) 453-4400
(800) 453-2377

R&R RESORT RENTAL PROPERTIES
821 Ocean Tr, Suite 1 (27927)
Rates: n/a
(252) 453-8854
(800) 849-6189

VILLAGE REALTY VACATION RENTALS
655 Sound & Sea Ct (27927)
Rates: n/a
(252) 453-0409
(800) 548-9688

CREEDMOOR

ECONO LODGE
2574 Lyons Station Rd (27522)
Rates: $38-$60
(919) 575-6451
(800) 553-2666

CRUSO

HERITAGE COVE CABINS
101 Heritage Cove Dr (28716)
Rates: n/a
(828) 648-4020
(800) 646-4020

CULLOWHEE

FOX DEN COTTAGES
P. O. Box 129
(28723)
Rates: n/a
(828) 293-9847
(800) 721-9847

DILLSBORO

APPLE REALTY CABIN RENTALS
Hwy 441 S & Macktown Rd
(28725)
Rates: n/a
(828) 584-3450
(800) 766-2776

THE DILLSBORO INN
146 N River Rd
(28725)
Rates: n/a
(828) 586-3898

DORTCHES

HOLIDAY INN
5350 Dortches Blvd (27804)
Rates: $55-$73
(252) 937-6300
(800) 465-4329

DUCK

CAROLINA DESIGNS REALTY VACATION RENTALS
1197 Duck Rd (27949)
Rates: n/a
(252) 261-3934
(800) 368-3825

R&R RESORT RENTAL PROPERTIES
1184 Duck Rd (27949)
Rates: n/a
(252) 261-1136
(800) 433-8805

DUNN

BEST WESTERN MIDWAY INN
603 Spring Branch Rd (28334)
Rates: $39-$49
(910) 892-2162
(800) 528-1234

BUDGET INN
513 Spring Branch Rd (28334)
Rates: n/a
(910) 892-6181

ECONO LODGE
1125 E Broad St (28334)
Rates: $29-$69
(910) 892-1293
(800) 553-2666

RAMADA INN
1011 E Cumberland St (28334)
Rates: $34-$59
(910) 892-8101
(800) 272-6232

SUPER 8 MOTEL
510 Spring Branch Rd (28334)
Rates: $32-$39
(910) 892-8711
(800) 800-8000

DURHAM

BEST WESTERN SKYLAND INN
5400 US 70 (27705)
Rates: $58-$72
(919) 383-2508
(800) 528-1234

CANDLEWOOD SUITES
Hwys 54 & 55 (27705)
Rates: n/a
(888) 226-3539

CAROLINA DUKE MOTOR INN
2517 Guess Rd (27705)
Rates: $45-$57
(919) 286-0771
(800) 438-1158

COMFORT INN UNIVERSITY
3508 Mt. Moriah Dr (27707)
Rates: $69-$129
(919) 490-4949
(800) 228-5150

DAYS INN
I-85 & Redwood Rd,Ext 183 (27704)
Rates: $35-$79
(919) 688-4338
(800) 329-7466

DUKE TOWER RESIDENTIAL SUITES
807 Trinity Ave (27701)
Rates: n/a
(919) 687-4444

HOMEGATE STUDIOS & SUITES
4419 S Miami Blvd (27703)
Rates: n/a
(919) 998-0400

HOMESTEAD VILLAGE
4515 Hwy 55 (27713)
Rates: n/a
(919) 544-9991
(888) 782-9473

HOMESTEAD VILLAGE GUEST STUDIOS
1920 Ivy Creek Blvd (27707)
Rates: n/a
(919) 402-1700
(888) 782-9473

LA QUINTA INN & SUITES
1919 W Park Dr (27713)
Rates: n/a
(919) 484-1422
(800) 687-6667

LA QUINTA INN & SUITES
4414 Durham-Chapel Hill Blvd (27707)
Rates: $79-$109
(919) 401-9660
(800) 687-6667

RED ROOF INN
5623 Chapel Hill Blvd (27707)
Rates: $51-$78
(919) 489-9421
(800) 843-7663

RED ROOF INN
1915 N Pointe Dr (27705)
Rates: $48-$74
(919) 471-9882
(800) 843-7663

RED ROOF INN
4405 Hwy 55 E (27713)
Rates: $36-$45
(919) 361-1950
(800) 843-7663

RESIDENCE INN BY MARRIOT
1919 Hwy 54 E (27713)
Rates: $109-$142
(919) 361-1266
(800) 331-3131

WELLESLEY INN & SUITES
4919 S Miami Blvd (27703)
Rates: $89-$129
(919) 998-0400
(800) 444-8888

WINGATE INN
5228 Page Rd (27717)
Rates: n/a
(919) 941-2854
(800) 228-1000

EDENTON

COACH HOUSE INN
823 N Broad St (27932)
Rates: n/a
(252) 482-2107

ELIZABETH CITY

DAYS INN
308 S Hughes Blvd (27909)
Rates: $50-$125
(252) 335-4316
(800) 329-7466

HOLIDAY INN
522 S Hughes Blvd (27909)
Rates: n/a
(252) 338-3951
(800) 465-4329

QUEEN ELIZABETH MOTEL
1160 Hwy 17 S (27909)
Rates: n/a
(252) 338-3961

TRAVELLERS INN
1211 N Road St (27909)
Rates: n/a
(252) 338-5451

EMERALD ISLE

BLUEWATER ASSOCIATES VACATION RENTALS
200 Mangrove Dr (28594)
Rates: n/a
(252) 354-2323
(888) 258-9287

CENTURY 21 VACATION RENTALS
7603 Emerald Dr (28594)
Rates: n/a
(252) 354-2131
(800) 822-2121

EMERALD ISLE REALTY VACATION RENTALS
7501 Emerald Dr (28594)
Rates: n/a
(252) 354-3315
(800) 849-3315

ENGELHARD

JENNETT'S LODGE & GUIDE SERVICE
572 Lazy Lane (27824)
Rates: n/a
(252) 925-1461

FAIRFIELD

HYDE-AWAY MOTEL
6491 Hwy 94 (27826)
Rates: n/a
(252) 926-8101

MATTAMUSKEET INN
6217 Hwy 94 (27826)
Rates: n/a
(252) 926-3021
(800) 910-3021

FAISON

MAGNOLIA HALL BED & BREAKFAST
701 W Main (28341)
Rates: n/a
(910) 267-9241
(888) 267-2941

FAYETTEVILLE

BEST WESTERN FAYETTEVILLE-FT. BRAGG
2910 Sigman St (28303)
Rates: $53-$125
(910) 485-0520
(800) 528-1234
(877) 485-0520

BUDGET INN
1830 Dunn Rd (28301)
Rates: n/a
(910) 483-9038

BUDGET INN II
442 Eastern Blvd
(28301)
Rates: n/a
(910) 323-4008

COLISEUM INN
2507 Gillespie St
(23806)
Rates: n/a
(910) 485-5161

COMFORT INN
1957 Cedar Creek
Rd (28301)
Rates: $60-$79
(910) 323-8333
(800) 228-5150

**COTTONADE
SQUARE GUEST
INN**
6264 Yadkin Rd
(28303)
Rates: n/a
(910) 864-6655

ECONOMY INN
525 Eastern Blvd
(28301)
Rates: n/a
(910) 323-3938

**HOLIDAY INN
BORDEAUX**
1707 Owen Dr
(28304)
Rates: $71-$80
(910) 323-0111
(800) 465-4329

MOTEL 6
2076 Cedar Creek
Rd (28301)
Rates: $32-$38
(910) 485-8122
(800) 466-8356

SUNSET INN
333 Person St
(28301)
Rates: n/a
(910) 483-0431

**FONTANA
VILLAGE**

THE HIKE INN
Hwy 28, Box 5,
Fontana Dam
(28733)
Rates: $35-$80
(828) 479-3677

**JOHNNY REB
MOTOR LODGE**
Hwy 28 S (28733)
Rates: n/a
(828) 479-8519

FOREST CITY

COMFORT INN
205 Commercial
Dr (28043)
Rates: $52-$69
(828) 248-3400
(800) 228-5150

RAMADA LIMITED
2600 Hwy 74-A
(28043)
Rates: $48-$68
(828) 248-1711
(800) 272-6232

FRANKLIN

**ALPINE
COTTAGES**
64 Pennington Dr
(28734)
Rates: n/a
(828) 524-2644

BARBER'S MOTEL
3108 S Georgia Rd
(28734)
Rates: n/a
(828) 524-2444

**BEARABLE
LODGE,
CORNERSTONE
CABIN, FOXLAIR**
Woodland Hgts
(28734)
Rates: n/a
(828) 524-9128

**CAROLINA
MOUNTAIN TOP
HOMES**
144 Deer Crossing
Rd (28734)
Rates: n/a
(828) 369-3469
(800) 820-1210

COLONIAL INN
3157 Georgia Rd
(28734)
Rates: $45-$70
(828) 524-6600

DAYS INN
1320 E Main St
(28734)
Rates: $84-$95
(828) 524-6491
(800) 329-7466

**DOGWOOD
COUNTRY
COTTAGES**
1115 Lowery Ln
(28734)
Rates: n/a
(828) 524-2558

**EAGLE'S NEST
COTTAGE**
128 Sugar Fork Rd
(28734)
Rates: n/a
(828) 524-3649

**GEMSTONE
COTTAGES**
196 Gemstone Dr
(28734)
Rates: n/a
(828) 524-9854
(800) 428-9118

**HIGH COUNTRY
HAVEN INN**
29 Bates Branch
Rd (28734)
Rates: n/a
(828) 524-4783
(888) 815-4783

MICROTEL
81 Allman Dr
(28734)
Rates: $50-$60
(828) 349-9000
(888) 771-7171

**MINI NIAGARA
FALLS RENTAL**
4912 Wayah Rd
(28734)
Rates: n/a
(828) 524-6513

**MOUNTAIN VIEW
COTTAGES**
74 Stonehouse Dr
(28734)
Rates: n/a
(828) 524-4605

**MOUNTAINSIDE
VACATION
LODGING**
8356 Sylva Rd
(28734)
Rates: $55-$70
(828) 524-6209

**PINE HILL
COTTAGES**
28 Hill St (28734)
Rates: n/a
(828) 524-8328

**PREFERRED
PROPERTY
RENTALS**
33 Pine Ln (28734)
Rates: n/a
(828) 349-4663
(800) 442-6400

**PRUDENTIAL
MARKHAM
BANKSTON
CABIN RENTALS**
144 Porter St
(28734)
Rates: n/a
(828) 524-8088
(800) 499-9310

**SLEEPY HOLLOW
COTTAGES**
130 Sleepy Hollow
Ln (28734)
Rates: n/a
(828) 524-4311
(877) 682-8850

**SMOKY
MOUNTAIN
VACATION
VILLAS**
45 Wells Grove
Rd, #1 (28734)
Rates: n/a
(828) 524-7524
(800) 818-7524

**FUQUAY-
VARINA**

COMFORT INN
7616 Purfoy Rd
(27526)
Rates: $63-$84
(919) 557-9000
(800) 228-5150

GARNER

HAMPTON INN
110 Drexmere St
(27529)
Rates: $69-$101
(919) 772-6500
(800) 426-7866

GASTONIA

DAYS INN
1700 N Chester St
(28052)
Rates: $45-$150
(704) 864-9981
(800) 329-7466

MOTEL 6
1721 Broadcast St
(28052)
Rates: $36-$52
(704) 868-4900
(800) 466-8356

**GLADE
VALLEY**

**WYMARA FARM
COTTAGE**
715 Scenic Valley
Rd (28627)
Rates: n/a
(336) 657-8514

**GLENDALE
SPRINGS**

**MOUNTAIN VIEW
LODGE & CABINS**
Blue Ridge Pkwy,
MP 256 (28629)
Rates: $50-$95
(336) 982-2233
(800) 903-6811

GOLDSBORO

**BEST WESTERN
INN**
801 US 70 E
Bypass (27534)
Rates: $57-$65
(919) 735-7911
(800) 528-1234

DAYS INN
2000 Wayne
Memorial Dr
(27534)
Rates: $46-$59
(919) 734-9471
(800) 329-7466

MOTEL 6
701 US 70 E
Bypass (27534)
Rates: $29-$42
(919) 734-4542
(800) 466-8356

QUALITY INN
708 US Hwy 70
Bypass (27533)
Rates: $49-$152
(919) 735-7901
(800) 228-5151

RAMADA INN
808 W Graham St
(27530)
Rates: $39-$79
(919) 736-4590
(800) 272-6232

AREA CODES - If the local number doesn't connect, check for a new area code.

GRAHAM

ECONO LODGE
640 E Harden St
(27253)
Rates: $37-$69
(336) 228-0231
(800) 553-2666

GRASSY CREEK

**RIVER HOUSE INN
& RESTAURANT**
1896 Old Field
Creek Rd (28631)
Rates: n/a
(336) 982-2109

GREENSBORO

**BEST INNS OF
AMERICA**
6452 Burnt Poplar
Rd (27409)
Rates: $42-$59
(336) 668-9400
(800) 237-8466

**BILTMORE
GREENSBORO
HOTEL**
111 W Washington
St (27409)
Rates: $85-$120
(336) 272-3474

**COMFORT SUITES
AIRPORT**
7619 Thorndike
Rd (27409)
Rates: $85-$260
(336) 882-6666
(800) 228-5150

DRURY INN
3220 High Point
Rd (27407)
Rates: $75-$95
(336) 856-9696
(800) 378-7946

**LA QUINTA INN
& SUITES**
I-40 at Wendover
& Stanley (27407)
Rates: n/a
(336) 316-0100
(800) 687-6667

**MOTEL 6-
AIRPORT**
605 Regional Rd S
(27409)
Rates: $36-$46
(336) 668-2085
(800) 466-8356

MOTEL 6-SOUTH
831 Greenhaven
Dr (27406)
Rates: $34-$46
(336) 854-0993
(800) 466-8356

RED ROOF INN
2101 W
Meadowview Rd
(27403)
Rates: $43-$62
(336) 852-6560
(800) 843-7663

RED ROOF INN
615 Regional Rd S
(27409)
Rates: $41-$82
(336) 271-2636
(800) 843-7663

**RESIDENCE INN
BY MARRIOTT**
2000 Veasley St
(27407)
Rates: n/a
(336) 294-8600
(800) 331-3131

GREENVILLE

ECONOMY INN
1901 Stantonsburg
Rd (27834)
Rates: n/a
(252) 754-8047

RED ROOF INN
301 SE Greenville
Blvd (27858)
Rates: $36-$70
(252) 756-2792
(800) 843-7663

HAMPTON-VILLE

**WELBORN'S
MOTEL**
3012 US 421
(27020)
Rates: n/a
(336) 468-2622

HATTERAS

**HATTERAS
CABANAS &
CONDOMINIUMS**
Hwy 12 S (27943)
Rates: n/a
(252) 986-2241
(800) 338-4775

**MIDGETT REALTY
VACATION
RENTALS**
Hwy 12 (27943)
Rates: n/a
(252) 986-2841
(800) 527-2903

**OUTER BEACHES
REALTY
VACATION
RENTALS**
Hwy 12 & Eagle
Pass Rd (27943)
Rates: n/a
(252) 986-2900
(800) 627-3150

**SEASIDE INN AT
HATTERAS B&B**
Hwy 57303
(27943)
Rates: n/a
(252) 986-2700

HAVELOCK

DAYS INN
1220 E Main
(28532)
Rates: $50-$65
(252) 447-1122
(800) 329-7466

HAYESVILLE

**BRISTOL ROAD
CABINS**
520 Bristol Rd
(28904)
Rates: n/a
(828) 389-0440

**CHATUGE
MOUNTAIN INN**
P O Box 565
(28904)
Rates: n/a
(828) 389-9340
(800) 948-2755

ELF SCHOOL INN
982 Elf School Rd
(28904)
Rates: n/a
(828) 389-6987
(888) 515-0554

HENDERSON

SLEEP INN
18 Market St
(27536)
Rates: $55-$75
(800) 753-3746

HENDERSON-VILLE

COMFORT INN
206 Mitchelle Dr
(28792)
Rates: $59-$199
(828) 693-8800
(800) 228-5150
(800) 882-3843

**MOUNTAIN AIRE
SUITES**
1351 Asheville
Hwy (28792)
Rates: n/a
(828) 692-9173

**SOUTHERNAIRE
MOTEL**
Rt 9 Hwy 64 E
(28792)
Rates: n/a
(828) 685-1131

**VILLA CAPRI
COTTAGES**
920 Greenville
Hwy (28792)
Rates: n/a
(828) 692-7660

**WALDROP'S
CAROLINA
MOTEL**
1004 Greenville
Hwy (28792)
Rates: n/a
(828) 692-7460

HERTFORD

**BEECHTREE INN
COTTAGES**
Pender Rd (27944)
Rates: n/a
(252) 426-7815

HICKORY

**HICKORY MOTOR
LODGE**
484 Hwy 70 SW
(28602)
Rates: n/a
(828) 322-1740

**HOLIDAY INN
EXPRESS**
2250 Hwy 70 SE
(28602)
Rates: n/a
(828) 328-2081
(800) 465-4329

**HOWARD
JOHNSON INN**
483 Hwy 70 & 321
SW (28603)
Rates: $48-$75
(828) 322-1600
(800) 446-4656

RED ROOF INN
1184 Lenoir Rhyne
Blvd (28602)
Rates: $47-$61
(828) 323-1500
(800) 843-7663

HIGH POINT

**RAMADA INN &
CONF CENTER**
236 S Main St
(27260)
Rates: $75-$265
(336) 886-7011
(800) 272-6232

TRAVELODGE
200 Ardale Dr
(27260)
Rates: $45-$120
(336) 841-7717
(800) 578-7878

HIGHLANDS

**FIRE MOUNTAIN
INN & CABINS**
P. O. Box 2772
(28741)
Rates: n/a
(828) 526-4446
(800) 775-4466

**MOUNTAIN HIGH
MOTEL**
200 Main St
(28741)
Rates: $79-$175
(828) 526-2790
(800) 445-7293

SKYLINE LODGE
Flat Mtn Rd
(28741)
Rates: n/a
(828) 526-2121
(800) 575-9546

HOT SPRINGS

**THE BRICK
HOUSE**
257 Henderson Dr
(28743)
Rates: n/a
(828) 622-3425
(800) 999-0831

MOUNTAIN SIDE CABINS
441 Rebel Dr (28743)
Rates: n/a
(828) 622-7647

JACKSONVILLE

ONSLOW INN
201 Marine Blvd (28540)
Rates: $37-$41
(910) 347-3151
(800) 763-3151

SUPER 8 MOTEL
2149 N Marine Blvd (28546)
Rates: $45-$66
(910) 455-6888
(800) 800-8000

JONESVILLE

HOLIDAY INN
1713 Hwy 67 (28642)
Rates: n/a
(336) 835-6000
(800) 465-4329

ROSE'S VILLAGE MOTEL
407 N Bridge St (28642)
Rates: n/a
(336) 835-3609

KENLY

BEST WESTERN INN
843 Johnston Pkwy (27542)
Rates: $45-$100
(919) 284-3800
(800) 528-1234

ECONO LODGE
US 301 & I-95 (27542)
Rates: $38-$59
(919) 284-1000
(800) 553-2666

KILL DEVIL HILLS

ANCHORAGE MOTEL
903 S Virginia Dare Tr (27948)
Rates: n/a
(252) 441-7226

BUDGET HOST INN
1003 S Croatan Rd (27948)
Rates: $35-$125
(252) 441-2503
(800) 283-4678

KITTY HAWK VACATION RENTALS
2901 N Croatan Hwy (27948)
Rates: n/a
(252) 441-7166
(800) 635-1559

NAGS HEAD BEACH HOTEL
804 N Virginia Dare Tr (27948)
Rates: $49-$95
(252) 441-0411
(800) 338-7761

OCEAN VACATIONS
2501 N Croatan Hwy (27948)
Rates: n/a
(252) 441-3127
(800) 548-2033

RAMADA INN-NAGS HEAD BEACH
1701 Virginia Dare Tr (27948)
Rates: $57-$209
(252) 441-2151
(800) 272-6232

SUN REALTY OF NAGS HEAD VACATION RENTALS
1500 S Croatan Rd (27948)
Rates: n/a
(252) 441-7033
(800) 334-4745

KITTY HAWK

WRIGHT PROPERTY VACATION RENTALS
3630 N Croatan Hwy (27949)
Rates: n/a
(252) 261-2186

KURE BEACH

EAST WIND COTTAGES
217 Ft Fisher Blvd N (28449)
Rates: n/a
(910) 458-5234

LAKE LURE

GENEVA RIVERSIDE LODGING & GATHERING PLACE
3147 Memorial Hwy (28746)
Rates: n/a
(828) 625-4121

PINE GABLES
328 Boys Camp Rd (28746)
Rates: n/a
(828) 625-8846

LAUREL SPRINGS

DOUGHTON HALL B&B INN
12668 Hwy 18 S (28644)
Rates: $75
(336) 359-2341

LAURINBURG

HAMPTON INN
115 Hampton Cir (28352)
Rates: $58-$70
(910) 277-1516
(800) 426-7866

RAMADA INN
1609 Hwy 15-401 By-Pass (28352)
Rates: $60-$109
(910) 276-6555
(800) 272-6232

LENOIR

RAMADA LIMITED
142 Wilkesboro Blvd SE (28645)
Rates: $40-$89
(828) 758-4403
(800) 272-6232

LINCOLNTON

DAYS INN
614 Clark Dr (28092)
Rates: $39-$59
(704) 735-8271
(800) 329-7466

LINVILLE FALLS

BLUE RIDGE COUNTRY CLUB & INN
US 221 N (28647)
Rates: n/a
(828) 756-4013
(800) 845-8430

HUMPBACK HOLLOW CABINS
16 Luther Franklin Ln (28647)
Rates: n/a
(828) 766-6555
(888) 263-3632

PARKVIEW LODGE
US 221 & Blue Ridge Pkwy (28647)
Rates: n/a
(828) 765-4787
(800) 849-4452

LITTLE SWITZERLAND

LOG CABIN LODGING
888 Little Switzerland Rd (Marion 28752)
Rates: n/a
(828) 756-4339

LUMBERTON

BEST WESTERN INN
201 Jackson Ct (28358)
Rates: $55-$90
(910) 618-9799
(800) 528-1234

COMFORT SUITES
215 Wintergreen Dr (28358)
Rates: $80-$115
(910) 739-8800
(800) 228-5150

ECONO LODGE
I-95 & SR 211 (28359)
Rates: $36-$89
(910) 738-7121
(800) 553-2666

MOTEL 6
2361 Lackey Rd (28358)
Rates: $29-$38
(910) 738-2410
(800) 466-8356

QUALITY INN & SUITES
3608 Kahn Dr (28358)
Rates: $49-$86
(910) 738-8261
(800) 228-5151

SUPER 8 MOTEL
150 Jackson Ct (28358)
Rates: $45-$85
(910) 671-4444
(800) 671-4444

MAGGIE VALLEY

ABBEY INN MOTEL
6375 Soco Rd (28751)
Rates: n/a
(828) 926-1188
(800) 545-5853

ALAMO MOTEL & COTTAGES
1485 Soco Rd (28751)
Rates: n/a
(828) 926-8750
(800) 467-7485

APPLECOVER INN MOTEL & RV PRK
4077 Soco Rd (28751)
Rates: $35-$80
(828) 926-9100
(800) 787-4788

BEAR RUN LOG CABIN RENTALS
1604 Moody Farm Rd (28751)
Rates: n/a
(828) 926-7566
(888) 926-7566

CAROLINA MOUNTAIN VACATION HOMES
Soco Rd (28751)
Rates: n/a
(828) 926-9681

COUNTRY CABINS
171 Bradley St (28751)
Rates: n/a
(828) 926-0612
(888) 222-4611

CREEK WOOD VILLAGE CABINS
3340 Soco Rd (28751)
Rates: n/a
(828) 926-3321

ED'S MOTEL
6262 Soco Rd (28751)
Rates: n/a
(828) 926-1879

GEISHA GARDENS COTTAGE
985 Fie Top Rd (28751)
Rates: n/a
(828) 926-1182

HEARTH & HOME INN
Hwy 19 (28751)
Rates: n/a
(828) 926-1845
(888) 926-1845

LAUREL PARK INN
257 Soco Rd (28751)
Rates: n/a
(828) 926-1700
(800) 451-4424

MAGGIE CREST MOTEL
P O Box 96 (28751)
Rates: n/a
(828) 926-1369

MAGGIE MOUNTAIN VILLAS & CHALET
60 Twin Hickory Ln (28751)
Rates: n/a
(828) 452-4285
(800) 308-1808

MAGGIE VALLEY VILLAS
130 Country Club Dr (28751)
Rates: n/a
(828) 926-0951

MOUNTAIN JOY COTTAGES
121 Setzer Cove Rd (28751)
Rates: n/a
(828) 926-1257
(888) 926-1257

MOUNTAINSIDE COTTAGES
27 Mountainside Cir (28751)
Rates: n/a
(828) 926-0689

THE NELSON CABIN
Hwy 19 (28751)
Rates: n/a
(828) 926-0033
(800) 327-5271

O'BRIEN CHALET
100 NE 48th Ct (Ft Lauderdale, FL 33334)
Rates: n/a
(954) 491-8138

PIONEER REALTY VACATION RENTALS
3197 Soco Rd (28751)
Rates: n/a
(828) 926-6025
(800) 923-6025

PIONEER VILLAGE
219 Campbell Creek Rd (28751)
Rates: n/a
(828) 926-1881

REALTY WORLD VACATION RENTALS
1986 Soco Rd (28751)
Rates: n/a
(828) 926-0871
(800) 968-5817

SNUGGLE INN
279 Soco Rd (28751)
Rates: n/a
(828) 926-3782

TOWN & MTN REALTY CABIN RENTALS
461 Moody Farm Rd (28751)
Rates: n/a
(828) 926-3164
(800) 338-8228

THE VALLEY INN
236 Soco Rd (28751)
Rates: n/a
(828) 926-1240
(800) 948-6880

MANNS HARBOR

MANNS HARBOR MARINA & MOTEL
Manns Harbor (27953)
Rates: n/a
(252) 473-5150

MANTEO

PIRATE'S COVE VACATION RENTALS
Rt 64/264, Nags Head /Manteo Causeway (27954)
Rates: n/a
(252) 473-6800
(800) 537-7245

MARION

BROOKS & BROADWELL CABIN RENTAL
1020 Sugar Hill Rd (28752)
Rates: n/a
(828) 652-7757
(800) 842-7253

MARSHALL

MARSHALL HOUSE B&B INN
100 Hill St (28753)
Rates: $30-$75
(828) 649-9205

MILL SPRING

MORNING GLORY FARM COTTAGE
Hwy 9 S (28756)
Rates: n/a
(828) 894-5595

SWISS CHALET COTTAGES
730 Hwy 108 E (28756)
Rates: n/a
(828) 894-8096

MOCKSVILLE

OLD MOCKS FIELDS B&B
1189 Jericho Church Rd (27028)
Rates: n/a
(336) 751-2738

MONTREAT

GREYBEARD REALTY VACATION RENTALS
113 John Knox Rd (28757)
Rates: n/a
(828) 669-1072

MOORESVILLE

SLEEP INN & SUITES
I-77 & US 150 SW Quad (28115)
Rates: $60-$100
(800) 753-3746

MORGANTON

CABINS IN THE LAUREL
Hwy 181 N (28655)
Rates: n/a
(828) 438-8185

RED CARPET INN
125 Bush Dr (28655)
Rates: $37-$48
(828) 437-6980
(800) 251-1962
(800) 849-7770

MORRISVILLE

BAYMONT INN & SUITES
1001 Aerial Center Pkwy (27560)
Rates: $59-$66
(919) 481-3600
(800) 301-0200

LA QUINTA INN & SUITES-AIRPORT
1001 Hospitality Ct (27560)
Rates: $59-$119
(919) 461-1771
(800) 687-6667

MOUNT AIRY

BLUE-VUE WELCOME LODGE
1421 Fancy Gap Rd (27030)
Rates: n/a
(336) 786-6101

CITY VIEW MOTEL
1002 Hwy 52 N Bypass (27030)
Rates: n/a
(336) 786-2136

MURPHY

APPALACHIAN CABINS
1550 Hwy 60 (28906)
Rates: n/a
(828) 837-2393

BEST WESTERN INN
1522 Andrews Rd (28906)
Rates: $69-$99
(828) 837-3060
(800) 528-1234

BOYD'S RIDGE CABINS
430 Boyd Ridge Dr (28906)
Rates: n/a
(941) 739-2575

COBB CREEK CABINS
106 Cobb Cir (28906)
Rates: n/a
(828) 837-0270

COMFORT INN
754 US 64 W (28906)
Rates: $59-$115
(828) 837-8030
(800) 228-5150

HAMLET O' CABINS
451 Hilltop Lane (28906)
Rates: $50-$75
(828) 644-5957
(800) 644-5957

PARK PLACE B&B
54 Hill St (28906)
Rates: n/a
(828) 837-8842

PINE CREEK CABINS
596 Taylor Hensen Rd (28906)
Rates: n/a
(828) 837-4228

RIVER'S EDGE CABIN
531 Granite Ln (28906)
Rates: n/a
(813) 787-6623

SOMMERS RENTAL CABIN
Rt 2, Box 506C (28906)
Rates: n/a
(828) 837-9805

WEST MOTEL
105 Andrews Rd (28906)
Rates: n/a
(828) 837-2012

NAGS HEAD

CAROLINIAN HOTEL
2313 Virginia Dare Trail (27959)
Rates: n/a
(252) 441-7171
(800) 852-0756

CAREFREE COTTAGES
6721 S Virginia Dare Trail (27959)
Rates: n/a
(252) 441-5340
(252) 441-2343

COLA VAUGHAN VACATION RENTALS
P O Box 1375 (27959)
Rates: n/a
(877) 247-2652

COLEMAN'S COTTAGES
500 Sterling Rd (Virginia Beach, VA 23464)
Rates: n/a
(800) 989-4571

COVE REALTY VACATION RENTALS
105 E Dunn (27959)
Rates: n/a
(252) 441-6391
(800) 635-7007

DEWEY COTTAGE
MP 11 (27959)
Rates: n/a
(252) 441-5128

GULL RENTALS ON THE OCEAN
Beach Rd, MP 17 (27959)
Rates: $89-$99
(252) 441-5005

NAGS HEAD REALTY VACATION RENTALS
2300 S Croatan Hwy (27959)
Rates: n/a
(252) 441-4311
(800) 222-1531

PELICAN COTTAGES
MP 12.5 (27959)
Rates: n/a
(252) 441-6729

VILLAGE REALTY VACATION RENTALS
103 E Mall Dr (27959)
Rates: n/a
(252) 480-2224
(800) 548-9688

VIVIANNA MOTEL
6905 Virginia Dr (27959)
Rates: n/a
(252) 441-7409

WHALEBONE MOTEL
Beach Rd, MP 17 (27959)
Rates: n/a
(252) 441-7423

NEW BERN

SHERATON GRAND HOTEL
100 Middle St (28562)
Rates: $95-$120
(252) 638-3585
(800) 326-3745

NORTH TOPSAIL BEACH

EGRETS NEST CONDOS
895 New River Inlet Rd (28460)
Rates: n/a
(910) 328-3772

OAK CITY

SOUTHERN COMFORT B&B
15909 Hwy 125 N (27857)
Rates: n/a
(252) 798-7081

OAK ISLAND

OAK ISLAND ACCOMMODA-TIONS
300 Country Club Dr (28465)
Rates: n/a
(910) 278-6011
(800) 243-8132

OCRACOKE

ANCHORAGE INN
Silver Lake Rd (27960)
Rates: $114-$125
(252) 928-1101

BLACKBEARD'S LODGE
111 Back Rd (27960)
Rates: n/a
(252) 928-2503
(800) 892-5314

OCRACOKE ISLAND VACATION RENTALS
1055 Irvin Garrish Hwy (27960)
Rates: n/a
(252) 928-6261
(800) 699-9082

SHARON MILLER REALTY VACATION RENTALS
Hwy 12 S (27960)
Rates: n/a
(252) 928-5711
(800) 955-0630

OXFORD

RAMADA IN
913 Linden Ave (27565)
Rates: $45-$75
(919) 693-9151
(800) 272-6232

PINEBLUFF

PINE CONE MANOR BED & BREAKFAST
450 E Philadelphia Ave (28373)
Rates: n/a
(910) 281-5307

PINEHURST

CONDOTELS OF PINEHURST
305 N Page Rd (28374)
Rates: n/a
(910) 295-8864
(800) 272-8588

PLEASANT GARDEN

WALNUT LANE BED & BREAKFAST INN
7119 Racine Rd (27313)
Rates: n/a
(336) 674-7093

RAEFORD

DAYS INN
Hwy 401 Bypass & Teal Dr (28376)
Rates: $49-$150
(910) 904-1050
(800) 329-7466

RALEIGH

AMERISUITES
3301 Wake Forest Rd (27609)
Rates: $79-$99
(919) 877-9997
(800) 833-1516

BEST WESTERN CRABTREE INN
6619 Glenwood Ave (27612)
Rates: $72-$180
(919) 782-8650
(800) 528-1234

CANDLEWOOD SUITES
1020 Buck Jones Rd (27606)
Rates: n/a
(800) 946-6200

COMFORT INN NORTH
2910 Capital Blvd (27604)
Rates: $59-$69
(919) 878-9550
(800) 228-5150

DAYS INN
6329 Glenwood Ave (27612)
Rates: $45-$79
(919) 781-7904
(800) 329-7466

FARIFIELD INN-CRABTREE
2201 Summit Park Lane (27612)
Rates: $49-$94
(919) 881-9800
(800) 228-2800

HOLIDAY INN-CRABTREE
4100 Glenwood Ave (27612)
Rates: $89
(919) 782-8600
(800) 465-4329

HOMESTEAD VILLAGE GUEST STUDIOS
3531 Wake Forest Rd (27612)
Rates: n/a
(919) 981-7353
(888) 782-9473

HOWARD JOHNSON EXPRESS INN
3120 New Bern Ave (27610)
Rates: $38-$58
(919) 231-3000
(800) 446-4656

AREA CODES - If the local number doesn't connect, check for a new area code.

LA QUINTA INN & SUITES-AIRPORT
1001 Hospitality Ct (27560)
Rates: n/a
(919) 461-1771
(800) 687-6667

LA QUINTA INN & SUITES-CRABTREE MALL
2211 Summit Park Ln (27622)
Rates: $79-$129
(919) 785-0071
(800) 687-6667

MAINSTAY SUITES
2601 Appliance Ct (27604)
Rates: $85-$99
(919) 807-9970
(800) 660-6246

MOTEL 6-NORTHWEST
3921 Arrow Dr (27612)
Rates: $37-$44
(919) 782-7071
(800) 466-8356

MOTEL 6-SOUTHWEST
1401 Buck Jones Rd (27606)
Rates: $37-$44
(919) 467-6171
(800) 466-8356

PLANTATION INN RESORT
6401 Capital Blvd (27604)
Rates: $50-$70
(919) 876-1411
(800) 992-9662
(800) 521-1932 (NC)

QUALITY SUITES
4400 Capital Blvd (27604)
Rates: $79-$169
(919) 876-2211
(800) 228-5151

RED ROOF INN
3520 Mailtland Dr (27610)
Rates: $53-$78
(919) 231-0200
(800) 843-7663

RED ROOF INN-N
3201 Old Wake Forest Rd (27609)
Rates: $39-$89
(919) 878-9310
(800) 843-7663

RED ROOF INN-S
1813 S Saunders St (27603)
Rates: $64-$89
(919) 833-6005
(800) 843-7663

RESIDENCE INN BY MARRIOTT
1000 Navaho Dr (27609)
Rates: $69-$144
(919) 878-6100
(800) 331-3131

SLEEP INN
2617 Appliance Ct (27604)
Rates: $50-$79
(919) 755-6005
(800) 753-3746

SUNDOWN INN
3801 Capital Blvd (27612)
Rates: $39-$61
(919) 790-8480
(800) 533-7749

SUPER 8 MOTEL
3804 New Bern Ave (27610)
Rates: $58-$68
(919) 231-8818
(800) 800-8000

TRAVELODGE
2813 Capital Blvd (27604)
Rates: $54-$69
(919) 850-9986
(800) 578-7878

VELVET CLOAK INN
1505 Hillsborough St (27605)
Rates: $65-$85
(919) 828-0333
(800) 334-4372
(800) 662-8829 (NC)

WYNNE RESIDENTIAL SUITES
6008 Triangle Dr, Ste 121 (27612)
Rates: n/a
(919) 781-6922
(800) 477-6922

RESEARCH TRIANGLE PARK

RADISSON GOVERNORS INN
Davis Dr (27709)
Rates: $134-$139
(919) 549-8631
(800) 333-3333

ROANOKE RAPIDS

INN AT ROANOKE RAPIDS
100 Holiday Dr (27870)
Rates: n/a
(252) 537-1031

INTERSTATE INN
1606 Roanoke Rapids Rd (27870)
Rates: $30-$40
(252) 536-4111

MOTEL 6
1911 Julian R Allsbrook Hwy (27870)
Rates: $38-$54
(252) 537-5252
(800) 466-8356

RAMADA INN
100 Holiday Dr (27870)
Rates: $49-$89
(252) 537-1031
(800) 272-6232

ROBBINSVILLE

MASON COTTAGE
1 U Gap 743 (28771)
Rates: n/a
(828) 479-3892

ROCKY MOUNT

COMFORT INN
200 Gateway Blvd (27804)
Rates: $45-$90
(252) 937-7765
(800) 228-5150
(888) 449-0050

RED ROOF INN
1370 N Wesleyan Blvd (27803)
Rates: $36-$63
(252) 984-0907
(800) 843-7663

SUNSET INN B&B
1210 Sunset Ave (27804)
Rates: $65-$125
(252) 446-9524

RODANTHE

MIDGETT REALTY VACATION RENTALS
Hwy 12 (27968)
Rates: n/a
(252) 987-2350
(800) 527-2903

PARADISE-HATTERAS STYLE COTTAGE
Oceanfront (27968)
Rates: n/a
(800) 989-4571

SEA SOUND MOTEL
24224 Sea Sound Rd (27968)
Rates: n/a
(252) 987-2224

SURF OR SOUND VACATION RENTALS
Hwy 12 (27968)
Rates: n/a
(252) 987-1444
(888) 919-7686

ROWLAND

DAYS INN
14723 US Hwy 301 (28383)
Rates: $33-$70
(910) 422-3366
(800) 329-7466

ROXBORO

DAYS INN
1006 N Madison Blvd (27573)
Rates: $45-$80
(336) 599-9276
(800) 329-7466

TIMBERLAND MOTEL
720 N Mdison Blvd (27573)
Rates: n/a
(336) 599-2144

RUTHERFORD-TON

CARRIER HOUSES BED & BREAKFST
225 N Main St (28139)
Rates: $40-$60
(828) 287-4222

SALIDA

SANDY CUT CABINS
Pearson Falls Rd (28773)
Rates: n/a
(828) 749-9555

SALISBURY

DAYS INN
1810 Lutheran Synod Dr (28144)
Rates: $41-$140
(704) 633-4211
(800) 329-7466

HAMPTON INN
1001 Klumac Rd (28144)
Rates: $59-$75
(704) 637-8000
(800) 426-7866

HOLIDAY INN
530 Jake Alexander Blvd (28144)
Rates: $61-$71
(704) 637-3100
(800) 465-4329

RODEWAY INN
321-R Bendix Dr (28146)
Rates: $60-$110
(704) 636-7065
(800) 228-2000

SALTER PATH

WILLIAM & GARLAND MOTEL
Hwy 58 (28575)
Rates: n/a
(252) 247-3733

SALVO

CAPE ESCAPE REALTY VACATION RENTALS
Hwy 12 (27972)
Rates: n/a
(252) 987-2336
(800) 996-2336

**SALVO
REAL ESTATE
COTTAGE
RENTALS**
26204 Monitor Ln
(27972)
Rates: n/a
(252) 987-2343

SANFORD

**PALOMINO
MOTEL**
15 & 501 Bypass
(27330)
Rates: $40-$44
(919) 776-7531

SAPPHIRE

**HUMMINGBIRD
REALTY
VACATION
RENTALS**
425 Hwy 64 W
(28774)
Rates: n/a
(828) 966-4737

**WOODLANDS
INN OF
SAPPHIRE**
1305 Hwy 64 W
(28774)
Rates: n/a
(828) 966-4709

SCALY

**FIRE MOUNTAIN
INNS, CABINS &
TOWNHOUSES**
700 Happy Hill
Rd (28775)
Rates: n/a
(828) 526-4446
(800) 775-4446

SELMA

DAYS INN
419 US 70 E
(27576)
Rates: $23-$100
(919) 965-3762
(800) 329-7466

MASTERS INN
318 US 70 E
(27576)
Rates: n/a
(919) 965-3771
(800) 633-3434

SHELBY

**TOWN HOUSE
MOTEL**
1530 E Dixon Blvd
(28152)
Rates: n/a
(704) 484-8539

SKYLAND

**GLENN & EDNA'S
VACATION
COTTAGE**
P. O. Box 98
(28176)
Rates: n/a
(704) 684-9938

SMITHFIELD

**HOWARD
JOHNSON**
I-96 Exit 95
(27577)
Rates $35-$85
(919) 934-7176
(800) 446-4656

**LOG CABIN
MOTEL**
Rt 2, Box 447
(27577)
Rates: $47-$54
(919) 934-1534

**MASTERS
ECONOMY INN**
318 US 70 E
(27577)
Rates: n/a
(919) 965-3771
(800) 633-3434

SUPER 8 MOTEL
735 Industrial
Park Dr (27577)
Rates: $51-$63
(919) 989-8988
(800) 800-8000

TRAVELERS INN
I-95 Exit 90, 96 S
(27577)
Rates: n/a
(919) 934-4194

**VILLAGE MOTOR
LODGE &
RESTAURANT**
198 Mallard Rd
(27577)
Rates: n/a
(919) 934-7126
(800) 531-0063

WAVERLY'S B&B
1321 E Market St
(27577)
Rates: n/a
(919) 989-2161

**SOUTHERN
PINES**

**BEST WESTERN
PINEHURST
MOTOR INN**
1500 Sandhills
Blvd (28315)
Rates: $65-$85
(910) 944-2367
(800) 528-1234

FAIRWAY MOTEL
1410 US 1 S
(28387)
Rates: n/a
(910) 692-2711

JEFFERSON INN
150 W New
Hampshire Ave
(28388)
Rates: n/a
(910) 692-5300

**SOUTHERN
SHORES**

**SOUTHERN
SHORES
VACATION
RENTALS**
5 Ocean Blvd
(27949)
Rates: n/a
(252) 261-2000
(800) 334-1000

SOUTHPORT

CAPE FEAR INN
308 W Bay St
(28461)
Rates: n/a
(910) 457-5989

PORT MOTEL
4821 Long Beach
Rd SE (28461)
Rates: $40
(910) 457-4800

STATESVILLE

**BEST WESTERN
INN**
1121 Morland Dr
(28677)
Rates: $70-$181
(704) 881-0111
(800) 528-1234

MOTEL 6
1137 Moreland Dr
(28677)
Rates: $38-$50
(704) 871-1116
(800) 466-8356

RED ROOF INN
1508 E Broad St
(28677)
Rates: $42-$63
(704) 878-2051
(800) 843-7663

SUPER 8 MOTEL
1125 Greenland Dr
(28677)
Rates: $46-$120
(704) 878-9888
(800) 800-8000

SURF CITY
(On Topsail
Island)

**CENTURY 21
VACATION
RENTALS**
518 Roland Ave
(28445)
Rates: n/a
(910) 328-2511
(800) 255-2233

SEA STAR MOTEL
2108 N New River
Dr (28445)
Rates: n/a
(910) 328-5191
(800) 343-0087

SURF SIDE MOTEL
121 N Shore Dr
(28445)
Rates: n/a
(910) 328-4099
(877) 404-9162

TIFFANY'S MOTEL
1502 New River
Dr (28445)
Rates: n/a
(910) 328-1397
(800) 758-3818

**WARD REALTY
VACATION
RENTALS**
116 S Topsail Dr
(28445)
Rates: n/a
(910) 328-3221
(800) 782-6216

SWANSBORO

SUNRISE LANE B&B
603 Sunrise Lane
(28584)
Rates: n/a
(910) 326-6208

SYLVA

AZALEA MOTEL
97 Skyland Dr
(28779)
Rates: n/a
(828) 586-2051

LINE SHAK KABIN
2105 Blanton
Branch Rd (28779)
Rates: n/a
(828) 586-2346

**THE WOODLAND
MOTEL**
2444 Hwy 441 S
(28779)
Rates: n/a
(828) 586-4331
(800) 366-4331

TARBORO

**LADY ANN OF
HISTORIC
TARBORO B&B**
1205 Main St N
(27886)
Rates: $50-$70
(919) 641-1438

THOMASVILLE

DAYS INN
895 Lake Rd
(27360)
Rates: $52-$145
(336) 472-6600
(800) 329-7466

RAMADA LIMITED
5 Laura Lane (27360)
Rates: $70-$125
(336) 472-0700
(800) 272-6232

**TOPSAIL
BEACH**
(On Topsail Island)

**BEACH
COTTAGE
REALTY RENTALS**
804 Carolina Ave
(28445)
Rates: n/a
(910) 328-5000
(800) 720-5184

AREA CODES - If the local number doesn't connect, check for a new area code.

SEA VISTA MOTEL
1521 Ocean Blvd
(28445)
Rates: n/a
(910) 328-2171
(800) 732-8478

TOPSAIL REALTY VACATION RENTALS
712 S Anderson
Blvd (28445)
Rates: n/a
(910) 328-5241
(800) 526-6432

TRYON

FENCE BED & BARN B&B
500 Hunting
Country Rd
(28782)
Rates: n/a
(828) 859-9021

HISTORIC BLOCK HOUSE FARM INN
1 Block House
(28782)
Rates: n/a
(828) 859-6306

THE MELROSE COUNTRY INN
211 Melrose Ave
(28782)
Rates: n/a
(828) 859-7014

VALLE CRUCIS

VALLE CRUCIS LOG CABIN RENTALS
Valle Landing,
Hwy 194 (28691)
Rates: n/a
(828) 963-7774

VALLE CRUCIS RUSTIC RENTALS
3657-3 Hwy 194 S
(28691)
Rates: n/a
(828) 963-2784

VILAS

BEULAH LAND FARM & GUEST HOUSE
170 Beulah Land
Ln (28692)
Rates: n/a
(828) 297-1329
(888) 550-8006

COTTAGES OF GLOWING HEARTH
171 Glowing
Hearth Ln (28692)
Rates: n/a
(828) 963-8800

ROBIN'S NEST & THE SUGAR GROVE INN
867 Georges Gap
Rd (28692)
Rates: n/a
(828) 297-3336

WADE

DAYS INN
Rt 1, Box 216-BB
(28395)
Rates: $42-$72
(910) 323-1255
(800) 329-7466

WADESBORO

DAYS INN
209 E Caswell St
(28170)
Rates: $40-$150
(704) 694-7070
(800) 329-7466

WASHINGTON

ECONO LODGE NORTH
1220 W 15th St
(27889)
Rates: $36-$65
(252) 946-7781
(800) 553-2666

WAVES

OUTER BEACHES VACATION RENTALS
Hwy 12 & Sea
Vista Dr (27982)
Rates: n/a
(252) 987-2771
(800) 627-3150

WAYNESVILLE

MOUNTAIN CREEK BED & BREAKFAST
146 Chestnut
Walk Dr (28786)
Rates: n/a
(828) 456-5509
(800) 557-9766

SON COUNTRY CABINS
577 Woodmore Dr
(28786)
Rates: n/a
(828) 926-8767
(800) 790-8767

WEAVERVILLE

ANTIQUE CABINS/ DUNROMIN VACATION RENTALS
64 Green Ridge
Rd (28787)
Rates: n/a
(828) 658-3345
(800) 457-2740

OX GLEN VACATION RENTALS
376 Ox Creek Rd
(28787)
Rates: n/a
(828) 645-2974
(800) 326-2373

WELDON

DAYS INN
1611 Roanoke
Rapids Rd (27890)
Rates: $45-$100
(252) 536-4867
(800) 329-7466

INTERSTATE INN
1606 Julian
Allsbrook Hwy
(27890)
Rates: n/a
(252) 536-4111

WEST JEFFERSON

CAROLINA MOUNTAIN PROPERTY RENTALS
5 N Jefferson Ave
(28694)
Rates: n/a
(336) 246-2803
(800) 628-2663

GREENFIELD RESORT COTTAGES
1795 Mt Jefferson
Rd (28694)
Rates: n/a
(336) 246-9106

WHITTIER

ARROWHEAD MOTEL
5801 Ela Rd
(28789)
Rates: n/a
(828) 488-3305

MOUNTAIN CREEK COTTAGES
2672 Dicks Creek
Rd (28789)
Rates: n/a
(828) 586-6042

SAWBUCK FARM & VINTAGE SPRINGS COTTAGES
546 Jericho Rd
(28789)
Rates: n/a
(828) 516-2687

WILLIAMSTON

COMFORT INN
100 E Blvd (27892)
Rates: $55-$65
(252) 792-8400
(800) 228-5150

HOLIDAY INN
101 E Blvd (27892)
Rates: $59-$69
(252) 792-3184
(800) 465-4329

WILMINGTON

ANDERSON GUEST HOUSE BED & BREAKFAST
520 Orange St
(28401)
Rates: n/a
(910) 343-8128
(888) 265-1216

BLUE HEAVEN BED & BREAKFST
517 Orange St
(28401)
Rates: n/a
(910) 772-9929
(800) 338-1748

CAMELLIA COTTAGE BED & BREAKFAST
118 S 4th St
(28401)
Rates: n/a
(910) 763-9171
(800) 763-9171

COMFORT INN EXECUTIVE CENTER
151 S College Rd
(28403)
Rates: $75-$125
(910) 791-4841
(800) 228-5150

HAMPTON INN
1989 Eastwood Rd
(28403)
Rates: $89-$139
(910) 256-9600
(800) 426-7866

HILTON HOTEL RIVERSIDE
301 N Water St
(28401)
Rates: n/a
(910) 763-5900
(800) 445-8667

LIVE OAKS BED & BREAKFAST
318 S 3rd St
(28401)
Rates: n/a
(910) 762-6733
(888) 762-6732

MOTEL 6
2828 Market
(28403)
Rates: $37-$52
(910) 762-0120
(800) 466-8356

219 S. 5TH BED & BREAKFAST
219 S 5th Ave
(28401)
Rates: n/a
(910) 763-5539
(800) 219-7634

WATERWAY LODGE
7246 Wrightsville
Ave (28403)
Rates: n/a
(910) 256-3771
(800) 677-3771

WILSON

DAYS INN
1815 Hwy 301
(27893)
Rates: $52-$57
(252) 243-5111
(800) 329-7466

AREA CODES - If the local number doesn't connect, check for a new area code.

**HEART OF
WILSON MOTEL**
501 W Nash St
(27893)
Rates: n/a
(252) 237-3124

**MATTHEWS
MOTEL**
2421 Hwy 301 S
(27893)
Rates: n/a
(252) 243-4133
(800) 884-7703

QUALITY INN
2901 Hwy 301 S
(27893)
Rates: $59-$89
(252) 243-5165
(800) 228-5151

WINDSOR

WINDSOR MOTEL
1523 S King St
(27983)
Rates: n/a
(252) 794-3444

WINSTON-SALEM

**AUGUSTUS
ZEVELY INN
HISTORIC B&B**
803 S Main St (Old
Salem 27101)
Rates: $80-$205
(336) 748-9299
(800) 928-9299

**HAWTHORNE INN
& CONF CENTER**
420 High St
(27101)
Rates: $62-$98
(336) 777-3000
(800) 972-3774

**LA QUINTA INN
& SUITES**
2020 Griffith Rd
(27103)
Rates: n/a
(336) 765-8777
(800) 687-6667

MOTEL 6
3810 Patterson
Ave (27105)
Rates: $35-$48
(336) 661-1588
(800) 466-8356

**RESIDENCE INN
BY MARRIOTT**
7835 N Point Blvd
(27106)
Rates: $114
(336) 759-0777
(800) 331-3131

SALEM INN
127 S Cherry St
(27101)
Rates: $54-$96
(336) 725-8561
(800) 533-8760

**TRAVEL HOST OF
AMERICA**
4191 Patterson
Ave (27105)
Rates: n/a
(336) 767-1930

WRIGHTSVILLE BEACH

**WATERWAY
LODGE**
7246 Wrightsville
Ave (28480)
Rates: $110-$170
(910) 256-3771

YANCEYVILLE

DAYS INN
1858 Hwy 86 N
(27379)
Rates: $45-$125
(336) 694-9494
(800) 329-7466

YAUPON BEACH

**OAK ISLAND
REALTY
VACATION
RENTALS**
300 Country Club
Dr (28465)
Rates: n/a
(910) 278-6011
(800) 243-8132

NORTH DAKOTA

BEACH

BUCKBOARD INN
1191 1st Ave NW
(58621)
Rates: $31-$37
(701) 872-4794
(888) 449-3599

BISMARCK

**BEST WESTERN
DOUBLEWOOD
INN**
1400 E
Interchange Ave
(58501)
Rates: $61-$76
(701) 258-7000
(800) 528-1234
(800) 554-7077

**BISMARCK
MOTOR HOTEL**
2301 E Main
(58502)
Rates: $20-$32
(701) 223-2474

COMFORT INN
1030 Interstate
Ave (58502)
Rates: $44-$70
(701) 223-1911
(800) 228-5150

DAYS INN
1300 Capitol Ave
(58501)
Rates: $34-$74
(701) 223-9151
(800) 329-7466

EXPRESSWAY INN
200 Bismarck
Expwy (58504)
Rates: $42-$54
(701) 222-2900
(800) 456-6388

**EXPRESSWAY
SUITES**
180 E Bismarck
Expwy (58504)
Rates: $50-$60
(701) 222-3311

**HOLIDAY INN
HOTEL BISMARCK**
605 E Broadway
(58502)
Rates: $59-$83
(701) 255-6000
(800) 465-4329

KELLY INN
1800 N 12th St
(58501)
Rates: $51-$56
(701) 233-8001
(800) 635-3559

MOTEL 6
2433 State St
(58501)
Rates: $29-$38
(701) 255-6878
(800) 466-8356

RADISSON INN
800 S 3rd St
(58504)
Rates: $64-$100
(701) 258-7700
(800) 333-3333

**RAMADA LIMITED
SUITES**
3808 E Divide Ave
(58501)
Rates: $60-$100
(701) 221-3030
(800) 272-6232

SELECT INN
1505 Interchange
Ave (58501)
Rates: $34-$50
(701) 223-8060
(800) 641-1000

SUPER 8 MOTEL
1124 E Capitol Ave
(58501)
Rates: $40-$59
(701) 255-1314
(800) 800-8000

BOWMAN

**BUDGET HOST
4U MOTEL**
704 Hwy 12 W
(58623)
Rates: $28-$44
(701) 523-3243
(800) 283-4678

EL VU MOTEL
Hwy 12 & 85
(58623)
Rates: n/a
(701) 523-5224
(800) 521-0379

**NORTH WINDS
LODGE**
503 Hwy 85 S
(58623)
Rates: $37-$47
(701) 523-5641
(888) 684-9463

SUPER 8 MOTEL
614 3rd Ave SW
(58623)
Rates: $35-$56
(701) 523-5613
(800) 800-8000

CARRINGTON

**CHIEFTAIN
CONFERENCE
CENTER**
60 4th Ave S
(58421)
Rates: $40-$85
(701) 652-3131

SUPER 8 MOTEL
101 4th Ave S
(58421)
Rates: $40-$81
(701) 652-3982
(800) 800-8000

DEVILS LAKE

COMFORT INN
215 Hwy 2 E
(58301)
Rates: $50-$70
(701) 662-6760
(800) 228-5150

DAVIS MOTEL
Hwy 2 W (58301)
Rates n/a
(701) 662-4927

DAYS INN
Hwy 2 & 20
(58301)
Rates: $49-$58
(701) 662-5381
(800) 329-7466

ECONO LODGE
Hwy 2 E (58301)
Rates: $39-$59
(701) 662-4001
(800) 553-2666

SUPER 8 MOTEL
1001 Hwy 2 E
(58301)
Rates: $39-$59
(701) 662-8656
(800) 800-8000

**TRAILS WEST
MOTEL**
Hwy 2 W (58301)
Rates: $34-$40
(701) 662-5011
(800) 453-5011

DICKINSON

**AMERICINN
MOTEL & SUITES**
229 15th St W
(58601)
Rates: $66-$78
(701) 225-1400
(800) 634-3444

**BEST WESTERN
BADLANDS INN**
71 Museum Dr
(58601)
Rates: $45-$82
(701) 227-4310
(800) 528-1234
(800) 285-1122

BUDGET INN
529 12th St W
(58601)
Rates: $31-$44
(701) 225-9123

COMFORT INN
493 Elk Dr (58601)
Rates: $40-$69
(701) 264-7300
(800) 228-5150

**HARTFIEL INN
HISTORIC B&B**
509 3rd Ave W
(58601)
Rates: $60-$90
(701) 225-1184

NODAK MOTEL
600 E Villard St
(58601)
Rates: $23-$38
(701) 225-5119
(888) 663-2598

OASIS MOTEL
1000 W Villard St
(58601)
Rates: $40-$65
(701) 225-6703

SELECT INN
642 12 St W (58601)
Rates: $21-$34
(701) 227-1891
(800) 641-1000

SUPER 8 MOTEL
637 12th St W
(58601)
Rates: $32-$50
(701) 227-1215
(800) 800-8000

**TRAVELODGE
HOTEL**
532 15th St W
(58601)
Rates: $57-$149
(701) 227-1853
(800) 578-7878

DRAYTON

MOTEL 66
I-29 & Hwy 66
(58225)
Rates: $27-$35
(701) 454-6464

FARGO

AMERICINN MOTEL
1423 35th St SW
(58103)
Rates: $54-$69
(701) 234-9946
(800) 634-3444

**BEST WESTERN
DOUBLEWOOD
INN**
3333 13th Ave S
(58103)
Rates: $79-$173
(701) 235-3333
(800) 528-1234
(800) 433-3235

AREA CODES - If the local number doesn't connect, check for a new area code.

BEST WESTERN KELLY INN
3800 Main Ave (58103)
Rates: $59-$89
(701) 282-2143
(800) 528-1234
(800) 635-3559

COMFORT INN EAST
1407 35th St S (58103)
Rates: $59-$99
(701) 280-9666
(800) 228-5150

COMFORT SUITES
1415 35th St S (58103)
Rates: $64-$99
(701) 237-5911
(800) 228-5150

COUNTRY SUITES BY CARLSON
3316 13th Ave S (58103)
Rates: $67-$149
(701) 234-0565
(800) 456-4000

DAYS INN & SUITES-AIRPORT/DOME
1507 19th Ave N (58102)
Rates: $54-$135
(701) 232-0000
(800) 329-7466

ECONO LODGE
1401 35th St S (58103)
Rates: $42-$68
(701) 232-3412
(800) 553-2666

EXPRESSWAY INN
1340 21st Ave S (58103)
Rates: $48-$63
(701) 235-3141
(800) 437-0044

FLYING J MOTEL
3150 39th St SW (58106)
Rates: $38-$58
(701) 282-8473
(800) 845-1311

HOLIDAY INN
3803 13th Ave (58106)
Rates: $125
(701) 282-2700
(800) 465-4329

HOLIDAY INN EXPRESS
1040 40th St S (58103)
Rates: $60+
(701) 282-2000
(800) 465-4329

KELLY INN
4207 13th Ave SW (58106)
Rates: $54-$89
(701) 277-8821
(800) 635-3559

MOTEL 6-WEST
1202 36th St S (58103)
Rates: $29-$38
(701) 232-9251
(800) 466-8356

MOTEL 75
3402 14th Ave S (58103)
Rates: $35-$48
(701) 232-1321
(800) 828-5962

QUALITY INN & SUITES
301 3rd Ave N (58102)
Rates: $59-$139
(701) 232-8850
(800) 228-5151

RADISSON HOTEL
201 5th St N (58102)
Rates: $79-$109
(701) 232-7363
(800) 333-3333

RED ROOF INN
901 38th St SW (58103)
Rates: $40-$55
(701) 282-9100
(800) 843-7663

RODEWAY INN
2202 S University Dr (58103)
Rates: $29-$65
(701) 239-8022
(800) 228-2000

SELECT INN
1025 38th St SW (58103)
Rates: $32-$61
(701) 282-6300
(800) 641-1000

SLEEP INN
1921 44th St SW (58103)
Rates: $59-$69
(701) 281-8240
(800) 753-3746

SUPER 8 MOTEL
3518 Interstate Blvd (58103)
Rates: $36-$92
(701) 232-9202
(800) 800-8000

GARRISON

GARRISON MOTEL
Frontage Rd & Hwy 37 (58540)
Rates: $25-$35
(701) 463-2858

GRAFTON

IRLENE SHIRLEY'S GINGERBREAD HOUSE B&B
603 Eastern Ave (58237)
Rates: n/a
(701) 352-0856

LEONARD MOTEL
Hwy 17 West (58237)
Rates: n/a
(701) 352-1730

SUPER 8 MOTEL
948 W 12th St (58237)
Rates: $36-$53
(701) 352-0888
(800) 800-8000

GRAND FORKS

BEST WESTERN TOWN HOUSE
710 1st Ave N (58203)
Rates: $55-$89
(701) 746-5411
(800) 528-1234
(800) 867-9797

COMFORT INN
3251 30th Ave S (58201)
Rates: $54-$89
(701) 775-7503
(800) 228-5150

COUNTRY INN & SUITES BY CARLSON
3350 32nd Ave S (58201)
Rates: $49-$82
(701) 775-5000
(800) 456-4000

DAYS INN
3101 34th St S (58201)
Rates: $49-$89
(701) 775-0600
(800) 329-7466

ECONO LODGE
900 N 43rd St (58201)
Rates: $44-$65
(701) 746-6666
(800) 553-2666

PLAINSMAN MOTEL
2201 Gateway Dr (58203)
Rates: $29-$41
(701) 775-8134
(888) 775-8134

RODEWAY INN
4001 Gateway Dr (58203)
Rates: $45-$60
(701) 795-9960
(800) 228-2000
(800) 795-4001

SELECT INN
1000 N 42nd St (58203)
Rates: $30-$45
(701) 775-0555
(800) 641-1000

SUPER 8 MOTEL
1122 N 43rd St (58203)
Rates: $39-$54
(701) 775-8138
(800) 800-8000

TRAVELODGE
2100 S Washington (58201)
Rates: $39-$89
(701) 772-8151
(800) 578-7878

WESTWARD HO MOTEL
US 2 W (58201)
Rates: $40-$61
(701) 775-5341

JAMESTOWN

COMFORT INN
811 20 St SW (58401)
Rates: $59-$99
(701) 252-7125
(800) 228-5150

DAYS INN
824 SW 20th St (58401)
Rates: $38-$53
(701) 251-9085
(800) 329-7466

GLADSTONE SELECT INN
111 2nd St NE (58402)
Rates: $42-$57
(701) 252-0700
(800) 641-1000

RANCH HOUSE MOTEL-IMA
408 Business Loop W (58401)
Rates: $35-$45
(701) 252-0222
(800) 341-8000

LAKOTA

SUNLAC INN
310 4th Ave SE (58344)
Rates: $29-$38
(701) 701-2487

LANGDON

LANGDON MOTOR INN
210 Ninth Ave (58249)
Rates: $26-$34
(701) 256-3600

LINTON

WILLOWS MOTEL
Hwy 83 S (58552)
Rates: $24-$38
(701) 254-4555
(800) 584-9278

MANDAN

BEST WESTERN SEVEN SEAS INN
2611 Old Red Tr (58554)
Rates: $57-$67
(701) 663-7401
(800) 528-1234
(800) 597-7327

AREA CODES - If the local number doesn't connect, check for a new area code.

MCCLUSKY

R & H MOTEL
404 Ave (58463)
Rates: n/a
(701) 363-2275

MINOT

**BEST WESTERN
INTERNATIONAL
INN**
1505 N Broadway
(58701)
Rates: $56-$76
(701) 852-3161
(800) 528-1234
(800) 735-4493

**BEST WESTERN
KELLY INN**
1510 26th Ave SW
(58701)
Rates: $54-$100
(701) 852-4300
(800) 528-1234
(800) 735-5868

CASA MOTEL
1900 US 2 & 52
Bypass (58701)
Rates: $22-$32
(701) 852-2352

COMFORT INN
1515 22nd Ave SW
(58701)
Rates: $48-$80
(701) 852-2201
(800) 228-5150

DAKOTA INN
US 2 & 52 Bypass
(58701)
Rates: $35-$55
(701) 838-2700

DAYS INN
2100 4th St SW
(58701)
Rates: $40-$60
(701) 852-3646
(800) 329-7466

**HOLIDAY INN
RIVERSIDE**
2200 Burdick Expy
(58702)
Rates: $55-$89
(701) 852-2504
(800) 465-4329

SELECT INN
225 22nd Ave NW
(58702)
Rates: $30-$46
(701) 852-3411
(800) 641-1000

SUPER 8 MOTEL
1315 N Broadway
(58703)
Rates: $36-$49
(701) 852-1817
(800) 800-8000

NEW TOWN

**4 BEARS CASINO
& LODGE**
SR 23 W (58763)
Rates: $55+
(701) 627-4018
(800) 294-5454

PARSHALL

**PARSHALL
MOTOR INN**
North Main St,
Box 38 (58770)
Rates: n/a
(701) 862-3127

ROLLA

**NORTHERN
LIGHTS**
Hwy 5 East
(58367)
Rates: n/a
(701) 477-6164
(800) 535-6145

RUGBY

DAYS INN
Hwy 2 E (58368)
Rates: $44-$70
(701) 776-5776
(800) 329-7466

STEELE

**LONE STEER
MOTEL**
I-94 Hwy #3
(58482)
Rates: n/a
(701) 475-2221
(888) 4L-STEER

O K MOTEL
301 3rd Ave
Northeast (58482)
Rates: n/a
(701) 475-2440

VALLEY CITY

**WAGON WHEEL
INN & SUITES**
930 4th Ave SW
(58072)
Rates: $38-$52
(701) 845-5333

WAHPETON

COMFORT INN
209 13th St S
(58075)
Rates: $49-$109
(701) 642-1115
(800) 228-5150

**HOLIDAY INN
EXPRESS**
1800 Two Ten Dr
(58075)
Rates: $54-$61
(701) 642-5000
(800) 465-4329

SUPER 8 MOTEL
995 21st Ave N
(58075)
Rates: $41-$49
(701) 642-8731
(800) 800-8000

WASHBURN

**SCOTWOOD
MOTEL**
1323 Frontage Rd
(58577)
Rates: $35-$46
(701) 462-8191

WATFORD CITY

MCKENZIE INN
120 SW 3rd St
(58854)
Rates: $29-$37
(701) 842-3980

WEST FARGO

DAYS INN
525 E Main Ave
(58078)
Rates: $52-$100
(701) 281-0000
(800) 329-7466

SUPER 8 MOTEL
825 E Main Ave
(58078)
Rates: $30-$44
(701) 282-7121
(800) 800-8000

WILLISTON

**AIRPORT
INTERNATIONAL
INN**
Hwy 2 & 85 N
(58802)
Rates: $38-$70
(701) 774-0241

**EL RANCHO
MOTOR HOTEL**
1623 2nd Ave W
(58802)
Rates: $42-$52
(701) 572-6321
(888) 452-3706

SELECT INN
213 35th St W
(58801)
Rates: $29-$37
(701) 572-4242
(800) 641-1000

SUPER 8 MOTEL
2324 2nd Ave W
(58801)
Rates: $43-$53
(701) 572-8371
(800) 800-8000

OHIO

AKRON

DAYS INN
3237 Arlington Rd
(44333)
Rates: $55-$99
(330) 644-1204
(800) 329-7466

HOLIDAY INN EXP
2940 Chenoweth
Rd (44312)
Rates: $89-$139
(330) 644-7126
(800) 465-4329

**RED ROOF INN
SOUTH**
2939 S Arlington
Rd (44312)
Rates: $47-$60
(330) 644-7748
(800) 843-7663

ALLIANCE

COMFORT INN
2500 W State St
(44601)
Rates: $59-$94
(330) 821-5555
(800) 228-5150

AMHERST

MOTEL 6
704 N Leavitt Rd
(44001)
Rates: $35-$56
(440) 988-3266
(800) 466-8356

ASHLAND

DAYS INN
1423 CR 1575
(44805)
Rates: $45-$80
(419) 289-0101
(800) 329-7466

**HOLIDAY INN
EXPRESS HOTEL
& SUITES**
1392 TR 743
(44805)
Rates: n/a
(419) 281-2900
(800) 465-4329

SUPER 8 MOTEL
736 US 250 E
(44805)
Rates: $44-$66
(419) 281-0567
(800) 800-8000

ASHTABULA

CEDARS MOTEL
2015 W Prospect
Rd (44004)
Rates: $45-$70
(440) 992-5406

HO HUM MOTEL
3801 N Ridge
West (44004)
Rates: $40-$65
(440) 969-1136

ATHENS

SUPER 8 MOTEL
2091 E State St
(45701)
Rates: $49-$65
(740) 594-4900
(800) 800-8000

AURORA

THE AURORA INN
30 E Garfield Rd
(44202)
Rates: $165-$195
(330) 562-6121
(800) 444-6121

AUSTINTOWN

**HOWARD
JOHNSON
EXPRESS INN**
5425 Clarkins Dr
(44515)
Rates: $50-$84
(330) 792-9740
(800) 446-4656

MOTEL 6
5431 76th Dr (44516)
Rates: $50-$60
(330) 793-9305
(800) 466-8356

BATAVIA

HOLIDAY INN
4501 Eastgate
Blvd (45245)
Rates: $109-$119
(513) 752-4400
(800) 465-4329

BEACHWOOD

MARRIOTT HOTEL
3663 E Park Dr
(44122)
Rates: $109-$189
(216) 464-5950
(800) 228-9290

**RESIDENCE INN
BY MARRIOTT**
3628 E Park Dr
(44122)
Rates: $169-$299
(216) 831-3030
(800) 331-3131

TRAVELODGE
3795 Orange Pl
(44122)
Rates: $57-$78
(216) 831-7200
(800) 578-7878

BELLE-FONTAINE

COMFORT INN
260 Northview
(43311)
Rates: $62-$99
(937) 599-6666
(800) 228-5150

BLUE ASH

AMERISUITES
11435 Reed-
Hartman Hwy
(45241)
Rates: $89-$129
(513) 489-3666
(800) 833-1516

MAINSTAY SUITES
4630 Creek Rd
(45242)
Rates: $59-$95
(513) 985-9992
(800) 660-6246

RED ROOF INN-NORTHEAST
5900 Pfeiffer Rd
(45242)
Rates: $63-$96
(513) 793-8811
(800) 843-7663

**RESIDENCE INN
BY MARRIOTT**
11401 Reed-
Hartman Hwy
(45241)
Rates: $169
(513) 530-5060
(800) 331-3131

**STUDIO PLUS
APARTMENT
HOTEL**
4260 Hunt Rd
(45242)
Rates: $74-$84
(513) 793-6750

BLUE ROCK

MCNUTT FARM
6120 Cutler Lake
Rd (43720)
Rates: $40-$45
(614) 674-4555

BLUFFTON

COMFORT INN
117 Commerce
Lane (45817)
Rates: $49-$89
(419) 358-6000
(800) 228-5150

BOARDMAN

DAYS INN
8392 Market St
(44512)
Rates: $49-$165
(330) 758-2371
(800) 329-7466

ECONOMY INN
10145 Market St
(44512)
Rates: $45-$85
(330) 549-3224

MICROTEL INN
7393 South Ave
(44512)
Rates: $32-$47
(330) 758-1816
(888) 771-7171
(800) 804-8385

**WAGON WHEEL
MOTEL**
7015 Market St
(44512)
Rates: $30-$65
(330) 758-4551

BOWLING GREEN

**BUCKEYE BUDGET
INN**
1740 E Wooster St
(43402)
Rates: $38-$49
(419) 352-1520

BROOK PARK

**HOWARD
JOHNSON HOTEL**
16161 Brook Park
Rd (44135)
Rates: $39-$86
(216) 267-5100
(800) 446-4656

QUALITY INN
15541 Brook Park
Rd (44142)
Rates: $59-$139
(216) 267-9800
(800) 228-5151

BROOKVILLE

DAYS INN
100 Parkview Dr
(45309)
Rates: $60-$70
(937) 833-4003
(800) 328-7466

BUCKEYE LAKE

SUPER 8 MOTEL
I-70 & SR 79
(43008)
Rates: $43-$53
(740) 929-1015
(800) 800-8000

BUCYRUS

DAYS INN
1515 N Sandusky
St (44820)
Rates: $50-$175
(419) 562-3737
(800) 329-7466

BURBANK

MOTEL PLAZA
Rt 1, Box 8 (44214)
Rates: $27-$32
(216) 624-3012

CAMBRIDGE

**BEST WESTERN
INN**
1945 Southgate
Pkwy (43725)
Rates: $49-$89
(740) 439-3581
(800) 528-1234

**BUDGET HOST
DEER CREEK MOTEL**
2321 Southgate
Pkwy (43725)
Rates: $33-$65
(740) 432-6391
(800) 283-4678

BUDGET INN
6405 Glenn Hwy
(43725)
Rates: $30-$50
(740) 432-2304

**COLONEL
TAYLOR INN B&B**
633 Upland Rd
(43725)
Rates: $90-$95
(740) 432-1123

COMFORT INN
2327 Southgate
Pkwy (43725)
Rates: $84-$109
(740) 435-3200
(800) 228-5150

HOLIDAY INN
2248 Southgate
Pkwy (43725)
Rates: $99
(740) 432-7313
(800) 465-4329

TRAVELODGE
I-70 & SR 209,
Exit 178 (43725)
Rates: $45-$75
(740) 432-7375
(800) 578-7878

CANTON

**BEST SUITES
OF AMERICA**
4914 Everhard Rd
(44718)
Rates: $70-$88
(330) 499-1011
(800) 237-8466

MOTEL 6
6880 Sunset Strip
Ave NW (44720)
Rates: $37-$49
(330) 494-7611
(800) 466-8356

PARKE SUITES
4285 Everhart Rd
(44718)
Rates: $80-$100
(330) 494-2233

RED ROOF INN
5353 Inn Circle Ct
NW (44720)
Rates: $46-$73
(330) 499-1970
(800) 843-7663

**RESIDENCE INN
BY MARRIOTT**
5280 Broadmoor
Cir NW (44709)
Rates: $129-$179
(330) 493-0004
(800) 331-3131

CELINA

**COMFORT INN
GRAND LAKE**
1421 SR 703 E
(45822)
Rates: $49-$159
(419) 586-4656
(800) 228-5150

CHERRY GROVE

MOTEL 6
3960 Nine Mile Rd
(45255)
Rates: $40-$71
(513) 752-2262
(800) 466-8356

**RED ROOF INN
EAST**
4035 Mt Carmel
Tobasco Rd
(45255)
Rates: $66-$80
(513) 528-2741
(800) 843-7663

CHILLICOTHE

**CHRISTOPHER
INN**
30 N Plaza Blvd
(45601)
Rates: $59-$129
(740) 774-6835

COMFORT INN
20 N Plaza Blvd
(45601)
Rates: $60-$135
(740) 775-3500
(800) 228-5150

**COUNTRY
HEARTH INN**
1135 E Main St
(45601)
Rates: $48-$85
(740) 775-2500

DAYS INN
1250 N Bridge St
(45601)
Rates: $52-$90
(740) 775-7000
(800) 329-7466

HOLIDAY INN
1003 E Main
(45601)
Rates: n/a
(740) 779-2424
(800) 465-4329

CINCINNATI

COMFORT INN
11440 Chester Rd
(45246)
Rates: $39-$175
(513) 771-3400
(800) 228-5150

DAYS INN-EAST
4056 Mt. Carmel-
Tobasco Rd
(45255)
Rates: $43-$110
(513) 528-3800
(800) 329-7466

**GARFIELD SUITES
HOTEL**
2 Garfield Pl
(45202)
Rates: $199-$1200
(513) 421-3355

HAMPTON INN
858 Eastgate N Dr
(45245)
Rates: $69-$99
(513) 752-8584
(800) 426-7866

HOLIDAY INN
3855 Hauck Rd
(45241)
Rates: n/a
(513) 563-8330
(800) 465-4329

HOLIDAY INN
800 W 8th St
(45203)
Rates: $71
(513) 241-8660
(800) 465-4329

**HOWARD
JOHNSON INN**
5410 Ridge Ave
(45213)
Rates: $57-$85
(513) 631-8500
(800) 446-4656

**HOWARD
JOHNSON INN**
400 Glensprings
Dr (45246)
Rates: $49-$77
(513) 825-3129
(800) 446-4656

IMPERIAL HOUSE
5510 Rybolt Rd
(45248)
Rates: $48-$58
(513) 574-6000

**QUALITY HOTEL
& SUITES**
4747 Montgomery
Rd (45212)
Rates: $75-$150
(513) 351-6000
(800) 228-5151

TRAVELODGE
3244 Central
Pkwy (45225)
Rates: $41-$72
(513) 559-1800
(800) 578-7878

VILLAGER LODGE
7313 Kingsgate
Way (45225)
Rates: $30-$70
(513) 777-5170

CIRCLEVILLE

KNIGHTS INN
23897 US 23S
(43113)
Rates: $40-$55
(740) 474-6006
(800) 843-5644

**MONTECELLO
MOTEL**
21530 US 23S
(43113)
Rates: $30-$35
(740) 474-8884

**TRAVELODGE
HOTEL**
24701 US 23 S
(43113)
Rates: $42-$50
(740) 474-7511
(800) 578-7878

CLEVELAND

**BAYMONT INN
AIRPORT**
4222 W 150th St
(44135)
Rates: $68-$80
(216) 251-8500
(800) 301-0200

**MARRIOTT HOTEL
AIRPORT**
4277 W 150th St
(44135)
Rates: $89-$164
(216) 252-5333
(800) 228-9290

RADISSON HOTEL
651 Huron Rd
(44145)
Rates: $129-$139
(216) 377-9000
(800) 333-3333

**RESIDENCE INN
BY MARRIOTT**
30100 Clemens Rd
(44145)
Rates: n/a
(216) 892-2254
(800) 331-3131

**RITZ CARLTON
HOTEL**
1515 W 3rd St
(44113)
Rates: $199-$279
(216) 623-1300
(800) 241-3333

CLYDE

PLAZA MOTEL
500 E McPherson
Hwy (43410)
Rates: $25-$52
(419) 547-6514

COLUMBUS

ADAMS MARK HOTEL
50 N 3rd St
(43215)
Rates: $89-$200
(614) 228-5050
(800) 444-2326

AMERISUITES
7490 Vantage Dr
(43235)
Rates: $98-$118
(614) 846-4355
(800) 833-1516

BEST WESTERN UNIVERSITY INN
3232 Olentangy
River Rd (43202)
Rates: $55-$75
(614) 261-7141
(800) 528-1234
(800) 628-0508

COMFORT SUITES
4270 Sawyer Rd
(43219)
Rates: $84-$184
(614) 237-5847
(800) 228-5150

DAYS INN FAIRGROUNDS
1700 Clara St
(43211)
Rates: $50-$75
(614) 299-4300
(800) 329-8466

DAYS INN UNIVERSITY
3160 Olentangy
River Rd (43202)
Rates: $36-$65
(614) 261-0523
(800) 329-7466

DAYS INN-WEST
1559 W Broad St
(43222)
Rates: $35-$70
(614) 275-0388
(800) 329-7466

DOUBLETREE GUEST SUITES
50 S Front St
(43222)
Rates: $89-$144
(614) 228-4600
(800) 222-8733

ECONO LODGE
5950 Scarborough
Blvd (43232)
Rates: $45-$85
(614) 864-4670
(800) 553-2666

ECONO LODGE
6125 Zumstein Dr
(43229)
Rates: $39-$90
(614) 436-0800
(800) 553-2666

HAWTHORN SUITES LTD
5505 Keim Cir
(43026)
Rates: $139
(614) 853-6199
(800) 527-1133

HOLIDAY INN
175 Hutchinson
Ave (43235)
Rates: $109
(614) 885-3334
(800) 465-4329

HOLIDAY INN ON THE LANE
328 W Lane Ave
(43201)
Rates: $119
(614) 294-4848
(800) 465-4329

HOMEWOOD SUITES
115 Hutchinson
Ave (43235)
Rates: $109-$150
(614) 785-0001
(800) 225-5466

HOWARD JOHNSON EXPRESS
1070 Dublin-
Grandview Ave
(43215)
Rates: $32-$75
(614) 486-4554
(800) 446-4656

KNIGHTS INN-EAST
4320 Groves Rd
(43232)
Rates: $50-$89
(614) 864-0600
(800) 843-5644

LANSING ST B&B
180 Lansing St
(43206)
Rates: $70
(614) 444-8488
(800) 383-7839

MARRIOTT NORTH
6500 Doubletree
Ave (43229)
Rates: $79-$119
(614) 885-1885
(800) 228-0290

MICROTEL INN
7500 Vantage Dr
(43235)
Rates: $64
(614) 436-0556
(888) 771-7171
(800) 433-3690

MOTEL 6
5500 Renner Rd
(43228)
Rates: $36-$44
(614) 870-0993
(800) 466-8356

MOTEL 6-EAST
5910 Scarborough
Blvd (43232)
Rates: $37-$50
(614) 755-2250
(800) 466-8356

MOTEL 6-EXTENDED STAY
7480 N High St
(43235)
Rates: $35-$46
(614) 431-2525
(800) 466-8356

MOTEL 6-NORTH
1289 Dublin-
Granville Rd
(43229)
Rates: $37-$51
(614) 846-9860
(800) 466-8356

PARKE UNIVERSITY HOTEL
3025 Olentangy
River Rd (43202)
Rates: $65-$130
(614) 267-1111
(800) 277-6158

QUALITY INN
4801 E Broad St
(43213)
Rates: $45-$89
(614) 861-0321
(800) 228-5151

QUALITY INN & SUITES
1001 Schrock Rd
(43229)
Rates: $59-$119
(614) 431-0208
(800) 228-5151

RADISSON NORTH
4900 Sinclair Rd
(43229)
Rates: $70
(614) 846-0300
(800) 333-3333

RAMADA INN WEST
4601 W Broad St
(43228)
Rates: $69+
(614) 878-5301
(800) 272-6232

RED ROOF INN DOWNTOWN
111 Nationwide
Blvd (43215)
Rates: n/a
(614) 224-6539
(800) 843-7663

RED ROOF INN NORTH
750 Morse Rd
(43229)
Rates: $54-$86
(614) 846-8520
(800) 843-7663

RED ROOF INN-OSU
441 Ackerman Rd
(43202)
Rates: $60-$88
(614) 267-9941
(800) 843-7663

RED ROOF INN-WEST
5001 Renner Rd
(43228)
Rates: $48-$74
(614) 878-9245
(800) 843-7663

RESIDENCE INN BY MARRIOTT
2084 S Hamilton
Rd (43232)
Rates: $109-$153
(614) 864-8844
(800) 331-3131

RESIDENCE INN BY MARRIOTT
6191 Zumstein Dr
(43229)
Rates: $119-$159
(614) 431-1819
(800) 331-3131

SHERATON SUITES
201 Hutchinson
Ave (43235)
Rates: $170-$190
(614) 436-0004
(800) 325-3535

SUPER 8 MOTEL
1078 E Dublin-
Granville Rd
(43229)
Rates: $39-$54
(614) 885-1601
(800) 800-8000

TRAVELODGE EAST
5930 Scarborough
Blvd (43232)
Rates: $30-$66
(614) 868-9200
(800) 578-7878

TRAVELODGE NORTH
999 E Dublin-
Granville Rd
(43229)
Rates: $44-$50
(614) 885-4484
(800) 578-7878

UNIVERSITY PLAZA HOTEL
3110 Olentangy
River Rd (43202)
Rates: $80-$90
(614) 267-7461

VICTORIAN B&B
78 Smith Pl
(43201)
Rates: n/a
(614) 299-1656

THE WESTIN
GREAT SO.
COLUMBUS
310 S High St
(43215)
Rates: $99-$175
(614) 228-3800
(800) 937-8461

COSHOCTON

TRAVELODGE
275 S
Whitewoman St
(43812)
Rates: $42-$59
(740) 622-9823
(800) 578-7878

CURTICE

ECONO LODGE
10530 Corduroy
Rd (42413)
Rates: $35-$90
(419) 836-2822
(800) 553-2666

CUYAHOGA FALLS

SHERATON
SUITES
1989 Front St
(44221)
Rates: $149-$164
(330) 929-3000
(800) 325-3535

DAYTON

BEST WESTERN
EXECUTIVE HOTEL
2401 Needmore
Rd (45414)
Rates: $49-$69
(800) 528-1234

ECONO LODGE
2140 Edwin C.
Moses Blvd
(45408)
Rates: $35-$69
(937) 223-0166
(800) 553-2666

ECONO LODGE
2221 Wagoner
Ford Rd (45414)
Rates: $36-$85
(937) 278-1500
(800) 553-2666

HOWARD
JOHNSON
EXPRESS
7575 Poe Ave
(45414)
Rates: $60-$100
(937) 454-0550
(800) 446-4656

MARRIOTT HOTEL
1414 S Patterson
Blvd (45409)
Rates: $79-$140
(937) 223-1000
(800) 228-9290

MOTEL 6-NORTH
7130 Miller Lane
(45414)
Rates: $36-$56
(937) 898-3606
(800) 466-8356

RAMADA INN
AIRPORT
4079 Little York
Rd (45414)
Rates: $60-$80
(937) 890-9500
(800) 272-6232

RED ROOF INN-N
7370 Miller Ln
(45414)
Rates: $46-$72
(937) 898-1054
(800) 843-7663

RESIDENCE INN
BY MARRIOTT
7070 Poe Ave
(45414)
Rates: $140
(937) 898-7764
(800) 331-3131

TRAVELODGE
7911 Brandt Pike
(45424)
Rates: $35-$57
(937) 236-9361
(800) 578-7878

DELAWARE

TRAVELODGE
1001 US 23 N
(43015)
Rates: $43-$52
(740) 369-4421
(800) 578-7878

DOVER

KNIGHTS INN
889 Commercial
Pkwy (44622)
Rates: $40-$85
(330) 364-7724
(800) 843-5644

DUBLIN

BAYMONT INN
6145 Park Center
Circle (43017)
Rates: $70-$75
(614) 792-8300
(800) 301-0200

MARRIOTT
NORTHWEST
5605 Paul Blazer
Mem Pkwy
(43017)
Rates: $99-$159
(614) 791-1000
(800) 228-9290

RED ROOF INN
5125 Post Rd
(43017)
Rates: $57-$82
(614) 764-3993
(800) 843-7663

RESIDENCE INN
BY MARRIOTT
435 Metro Place S
(43017)
Rates: $99-$154
(614) 791-0403
(800) 331-3131

WOODFIN SUITES
HOTEL
4130 Tuller Rd
(43017)
Rates: $99-$189
(614) 766-7762
(800) 237-8811

WYNDHAM
DUBLIN HOTEL
600 Metro Place N
(43017)
Rates: $129-$160
(614) 764-2200
(800) 996-3426

EATON

ECONO LODGE
Rt 127 N (45320)
Rates: $36-$69
(937) 456-5959
(800) 553-2666

ELYRIA

COMFORT INN
739 Leona St
(44035)
Rates: $80-$108
(440) 324-7676
(800) 228-5150

HOWARD
JOHNSON
EXPRESS INN
1724 Lorain Blvd
(44035)
Rates: $35-$80
(440) 323-1515
(800) 446-4656

SUPER 8 MOTEL
910 Lorain Blvd
(44035)
Rates: $54-$104
(440) 323-7488
(800) 800-8000

ENGLEWOOD

MOTEL 6
1212 S Main St
(45322)
Rates: $31-$44
(937) 832-3770
(800) 466-8356

FAIRBORN

HOLIDAY INN
2800 Presidential
Dr (45324)
Rates: $85-$115
(937) 426-7800
(800) 465-4329

HOMEWOOD
SUITES
2750 Presidential
Dr (45324)
Rates: $119-$139
(937) 429-0600
(800) 225-5466

RED ROOF INN
2580 Col. Glenn
Hwy (45324)
Rates: $59-$86
(937) 426-6116
(800) 843-7663

FAIRFIELD

STUDIO PLUS
APARTMENT
MOTEL
9651 Seward Rd
(45014)
Rates: $65-$75
(513) 860-5733

FAIRLAWN

BEST WESTERN
INN & SUITES
160 Montrose
West Ave (44321)
Rates: $89-$999
(330) 670-0888
(800) 528-1234

HILTON INN
3180 W Market St
(44313)
Rates: $89-$159
(330) 867-5000
(800) 445-8667

RED ROOF INN
NORTH
99 Rothrock Rd
(44321)
Rates: $61-$81
(330) 666-0566
(800) 843-7663

RESIDENCE INN
BY MARRIOTT
120 W Montrose
Ave (44321)
Rates: $143
(330) 666-4811
(800) 331-3131

SUPER 8 MOTEL
79 Rochrock Rd
(44321)
Rates: $35-$110
(330) 666-8887
(800) 800-8000

FINDLAY

ECONO LODGE
316 Emma St
(45840)
Rates: $35-$70
(419) 422-0154
(800) 553-2666

HAWTHORN
SUITES LTD
2355 Tiffin Ave
(45840)
Rates: $89
(419) 425-9696
(800) 527-1133

RAMADA INN
820 Trenton Ave
(45840)
Rates: $39-$65
(419) 423-8212
(800) 272-6232

SUPER 8 MOTEL
1600 Fox St
(45840)
Rates: $38-$52
(419) 422-8863
(800) 800-8000

FOREST PARK

AMERISUITES-NW
12001 Chase Plaza
Dr (45240)
Rates: $79-$129
(513) 825-9035
(800) 833-1516

FOSTORIA

DAYS INN
601 Findlay St
(44830)
Rates: $50-$80
(419) 435-6511
(800) 329-7466

FRANKLIN

SUPER 8 MOTEL
3553 Commerce
Dr (45005)
Rates: $44-$59
(513) 422-4888
(800) 800-8000

FREDERICK-TOWN

**HEARTLAND
COUNTRY
RESORT B&B**
2994 Township
Rd 190 (43019)
Rates: $80-$175
(419) 768-9300

FREMONT

**FREMONT
TURNPIKE MOTEL**
520 CR 84E
(43420)
Rates: $46-$80
(419) 332-6489

HOLIDAY INN
3422 Port Clinton
Rd (43420)
Rates: $79-$149
(419) 334-2682
(800) 465-4329

TRAVELODGE
1750 Cedar St
(43420)
Rates: $39-$57
(419) 334-9517
(800) 578-7878

GALION

HOMETOWN INN
172 N Portland
Way (44833)
Rates: $50-$140
(419) 468-9909

GALLIPOLIS

**WILLIAM ANN
MOTEL**
918 2nd Ave
(45631)
Rates: $40-$45
(740) 446-3373

GIRARD

DAYS INN
1610 Motor Inn Dr
(44420)
Rates: $100-$150
(330) 759-3410
(800) 329-7466

GREENVILLE

GREENVILLE INN
851 E Martin
(45331)
Rates: $55-$100
(937) 548-3613

GROVE CITY

**BEST WESTERN
EXECUTIVE INN**
4026 Jackpot Rd
(43123)
Rates: $55-$75
(614) 875-7770
(800) 528-1234

COMFORT INN
4197 Marlane Dr
(43123)
Rates: $59-$75
(614) 539-3500
(800) 228-5150

RED ROOF INN
1900 Stringtown
Rd (43123)
Rates: $57-$84
(614) 875-8543
(800) 843-7663

HAMILTON

**HAMILTONIAN
HOTEL**
1 Riverfront Plaza
(45011)
Rates: $91-$115
(513) 896-6200
(800) 522-5570

HARRISON

COMFORT INN
New Haven Rd
(45030)
Rates: $52-$100
(800) 228-5150

HEATH

HOLIDAY INN
733 Hebron Rd
(43056)
Rates: $56-$64
(740) 522-1165
(800) 465-4329

HOMETOWN INN
1266 Hebron Rd
(43056)
Rates: $38-$42
(740) 522-6112

SUPER 8 MOTEL
1177 S Hebron Rd
(43056)
Rates: $50-$70
(740) 788-9144
(800) 800-8000

HILLIARD

COMFORT SUITES
3831 Park Mill
Run Dr (43026)
Rates: $70-$120
(614) 529-8118
(800) 228-5150

**HOMEWOOD
SUITES**
3841 Park Mill Rd
(43026)
Rates: $129-$159
(614) 529-4100
(800) 225-5466

MOTEL 6
3950 Parkway Ln
(43026)
Rates: $37-$49
(614) 771-1500
(800) 466-8356

HOLLAND

**CROSS COUNTRY
INN**
1201 E Mall Dr
(43528)
Rates: $41-$55
(419) 866-6565

RED ROOF INN
1214 Corporate Dr
(43528)
Rates: $47-$58
(419) 866-5512
(800) 843-7663

**RESIDENCE INN
BY MARRIOTT**
6101 Trust Dr
(43528)
Rates: $159
(419) 867-9555
(800) 331-3131

HUBER HEIGHTS

**HOLIDAY INN
EXPRESS HOTEL
& SUITES**
5612 Merily Way
(45424)
Rates: n/a
(937) 235-2000
(800) 465-4329

TRAVELODGE
7911 Brandt Pike
(45424)
Rates: $55-$70
(937) 236-9361
(800) 578-7878

HURON

**PLANTATION
MOTEL**
2815 E Cleveland
Rd (44839)
Rates: $59-$88
(419) 433-4790

INDEPENDENCE

AMERISUITES
6025 Jefferson Dr
(44131)
Rates: $114-$134
(216) 328-1060
(800) 833-1516

BAYMONT INN
6161 Quarry Ln
(44131)
Rates: $75-$87
(216) 447-1133
(800) 301-0200

**HILTON INN
SOUTH**
6200 Quarry Ln
(44131)
Rates: $109
(216) 447-1300
(800) 445-8667

RED ROOF INN
6020 Quarry Ln
(44131)
Rates: $72-$100
(216) 447-0030
(800) 843-7663

**RESIDENCE INN
BY MARRIOTT**
5101 W Creek Rd
(44131)
Rates: $129-$179
(216) 520-1450
(800) 331-3131

IRONTON

GRANDVIEW INN
154 County Rd
(45680)
Rates: $40-$75
(614) 377-4388
(800) 424-9849

JACKSON

KNIGHTS INN
404 Chillicothe St
(45640)
Rates: $40-$54
(740) 286-2135
(800) 843-5644

JEFFERSONVILLE

AMERIHOST INN
11431 Allen Rd
NW (43128)
Rates: $65-$125
(740) 948-2104
(800) 434-5800

KENT

HOLIDAY INN
4363 SR 43 (44240)
Rates: $98
(330) 678-0101
(800) 465-4329

KINGS ISLAND

HOLIDAY INN EXP
5589 Kings Mills
Rd (45034)
Rates: n/a
(514) 398-8075
(800) 465-4329

LAKEWOOD

DAYS INN
12019 Lake Ave
(44107)
Rates: $49-$79
(216) 226-4800
(800) 329-7466

AREA CODES - If the local number doesn't connect, check for a new area code.

TRAVELODGE
11837 Edgewater
Dr (44107)
Rates: $45-$75
(216) 221-9000
(800) 578-7878

LANCASTER

BEST WESTERN INN
1858 N Memorial
Dr (43130)
Rates: $58-$94
(740) 653-3040
(800) 528-1234

KNIGHTS INN
1327 River Valley
Blvd (43130)
Rates: $44-$69
(740) 687-4823
(800) 843-5644

LEBANON

ECONO LODGE
674 N Broadway
(45036)
Rates: $30-$75
(513) 932-4111
(800) 553-2666

LIMA

COMFORT INN
1210 Neubrecht
Rd (45801)
Rates: $45-$100
(419) 228-4251
(800) 228-5150

DAYS INN
1250 Neubrecht
Rd (45801)
Rates: $40-$75
(419) 227-6515
(800) 329-7466

ECONO LODGE
1201 Neubrecht
Rd (45801)
Rates: $44-$52
(419) 222-0596
(800) 553-2666

KNIGHTS INN
2285 N Eastown
Rd (45807)
Rates: $40-$60
(419) 331-9215
(800) 843-5644

MOTEL 6
1800 Harding
Hwy (45804)
Rates: $40-$56
(419) 228-0456
(800) 466-8356

LANCASTER

SUPER 8 MOTEL
1430 Bellefontaine
Ave (45804)
Rates: $38-$56
(419) 227-2221
(800) 800-8000

LOGAN

HOCKING HILLS HOMESTEAD
General Delivery
(43138)
Rates: n/a
(740) 385-0449

SHAWNEE INN
30916 Lake Logan
Rd (43138)
Rates: $45-$59
(740) 385-5674

LORAIN

CLARION CARRIAGE HOUSE INN-SPITZER PLAZA HOTEL & MARINA
301 Broadway
(44052)
Rates: $80-$105
(440) 246-5767
(800) 252-7466

MACEDONIA

BAYMONT INN
268 E Highland
Rd (44056)
Rates: $101-$111
(330) 468-5400
(800) 301-0200

KNIGHTS INN
240 E Highland
Rd (44056)
Rates: $52-$72
(330) 467-1981
(800) 843-5644

MOTEL 6
311 E Highland
Rd (44056)
Rates: $37-$52
(330) 468-1670
(800) 466-8356

MANSFIELD

BAYMONT INN
120 Stander Ave
(44903)
Rates: $43-$61
(419) 774-0005
(800) 301-0200

BEST WESTERN INN
880 Laver Rd
(44905)
Rates: $69
(419) 589-2200
(800) 528-1234

COMFORT INN
500 N Trimble Rd
(44906)
Rates: $66-$85
(419) 529-1000
(800) 228-5150

ECONO LODGE
1017 Roogle Rd
(44903)
Rates: $46-$85
(419) 589-3333
(800) 553-2666

42 MOTEL
2444 Lexington
Ave (44907)
Rates: $33-$65
(419) 884-1315

HAMPTON INN
1051 N Lexington
Springmil (44906)
Rates: $63-$71
(419) 747-5353
(800) 426-7866

KNIGHTS INN
555 N Trimble Rd
(44906)
Rates: $50-$100
(419) 529-2100
(800) 843-5644

SUPER 8 MOTEL
2425 Interstate Cir
(44903)
Rates: $47-$65
(419) 756-8875
(800) 800-8000

TRAVELODGE
90 Hanley W Rd
(44903)
Rates: $38-$85
(419) 756-7600
(800) 578-7878

VILLAGER LODGE
191 W Park Ave
(44902)
Rates: $38-$53
(419) 522-7275

MARBLEHEAD

SURF MOTEL
230 E Main St
(43440)
Rates: $45-$60
(419) 798-4823

MARIETTA

BEST WESTERN MARIETTA INN
279 Muskingum
Dr (45750)
Rates: $49-$79
(740) 374-7211
(800) 528-1234

ECONO LODGE
702 Pike St (45750)
Rates: $48-$65
(740) 374-8481
(800) 553-2666

KNIGHTS INN
506 Pike St (45750)
Rates: $40-$75
(740) 373-7373
(800) 843-5644

LAFAYETTE HOTEL
101 Front St
(45750)
Rates: $75-$200
(614) 373-5522
(800) 331-9336

SUPER 8 MOTEL
46 Acme St
(45750)
Rates: $44-$63
(740) 374-8888
(800) 800-8000

MARION

COMFORT INN
256 Jamesway
(43302)
Rates: $66-$96
(740) 398-5552
(800) 228-5150

DAYS INN
1838 Marion Mt-
Gilead Rd (43302)
Rates: $45-$100
(740) 389-4651
(800) 329-7466

HARDING MOTOR LODGE
1065 Delaware
Ave (43302)
Rates: $37-$46
(740) 383-6771

TRAVELODGE
1952 Marion-Mt
Gilead Rd (43302)
Rates: $45-$62
(740) 389-4671
(800) 578-7878

MARYSVILLE

DAYS INN
16510 Square Dr
(43040)
Rates: $69-$99
(937) 644-8821
(800) 329-7466

HAMPTON INN
16610 Square Dr
(43040)
Rates: $69-$89
(937) 642-3777
(800) 426-7866

SUPER 8 MOTEL
10220 US 42 (43040)
Rates: $45-$78
(937) 873-4100
(800) 800-8000

MASON

BAYMONT INN
9918 Escort Dr
(45040)
Rates: $97-$102
(513) 459-1111
(800) 301-0200

DAYS INN KINGS ISLAND
9735 Mason/Mont-
gomery Rd (45040)
Rates: $39-$149
(513) 398-3297
(800) 329-7466

HOLIDAY INN EXP KINGS ISLAND
5589 Kings Mill
Rd (45040)
Rates: $109-$169
(513) 398-8075
(800) 465-4329

QUALITY INN
9845 Escort Dr
(45040)
Rates: $59-$189
(513) 398-8015
(800) 228-5151

RED ROOF INN KINGS ISLAND
9847 Escort Dr (45040)
Rates: $35-$150
(513) 398-3633
(800) 843-7663

MASSILLON

SUPER 8 MOTEL
242 Lincoln Way W (44646)
Rates: $56-$62
(330) 837-8880
(800) 800-8000

MAUMEE

COUNTRY INN & SUITES
541 W Dussel Dr (43537)
Rates: $71-$110
(419) 893-8576
(800) 456-4000

DAYS INN
150 W Dussel Dr (43537)
Rates: $60-$85
(419) 893-9960
(800) 329-7466

HOMEWOOD SUITES HOTEL
1410 Arrowhead Rd (43537)
Rates: n/a
(419) 897-0980
(800) 225-5466

KNIGHTS INN
1520 S Holland-Sylvania Rd (43537)
Rates: $44-$90
(419) 865-1380
(800) 843-5644

RED ROOF INN
1570 Reynolds Rd (43537)
Rates: $46-$64
(419) 893-0292
(800) 843-7663

MAYFIELD HEIGHTS

BAYMONT INN
1421 Golden Gate Blvd (44124)
Rates: $70-$82
(440) 442-8400
(800) 301-0200

MIAMISBURG

HOMEWOOD SUITES HOTEL
3100 Contemporary Ln (45342)
Rates: $135
(937) 432-0000
(800) 225-5466

MOTEL 6-STUDIO 6
8101 Springboro Pike (45342)
Rates: n/a
(937) 434-8750
(800) 466-8356

RED ROOF INN
222 Byers Rd (45342)
Rates: $57-$80
(937) 866-0705
(800) 843-7663

RESIDENCE INN BY MARRIOTT
155 Prestige Pl (45342)
Rates: $125-$140
(937) 434-7881
(800) 331-3131

MIDDLEBURG HEIGHTS

CLARION HOTEL AIRPORT WEST
17000 Bagley Rd (44130)
Rates: $69-$109
(440) 243-4200
(800) 252-7466

COMFORT INN
17550 Rosbough Dr (44130)
Rates: $79-$129
(440) 234-3131
(800) 228-5150

MOTEL 6
7210 Engle Rd (44130)
Rates: $52-$64
(440) 234-0990
(800) 466-8356

RED ROOF INN
17555 Bagley Rd (44130)
Rates: $68-$83
(440) 243-2441
(800) 843-7663

RESIDENCE INN BY MARRIOTT
17525 Rosbough Dr (44130)
Rates: $98-$179
(440) 234-6688
(800) 331-3131

MIDDLETOWN

HOLIDAY INN EXPRESS
6575 Terhune Dr (450424
Rates: n/a
(513) 727-8440
(800) 465-4329

MANCHESTER INN & CONF CENTER HISTORIC HOTEL
1027 Manchester Ave (45042)
Rates: $68-$140
(513) 422-5481
(800) 523-9126

RAMADA INN
6147 W SR 122 (45042)
Rates: $69
(513) 424-1201
(800) 272-6232

MILAN

MOTEL 6
11406 Rt 250 N (44846)
Rates: $75-$155
(419) 499-8001
(800) 466-8356

MONROE

ECONO LODGE
150 Garver Rd (45050)
Rates: $40-$75
(513) 539-9221
(800) 553-2666

MONTPELIER

ECONO LODGE
13485 SR 15 (43543)
Rates: $40-$105
(419) 485-3139
(800) 553-2666

HOLIDAY INN
13508 SR 15 (43543)
Rates: $99-$169
(419) 485-5555
(800) 465-4329

MORAINE

SUPER 8 MOTEL
2450 Dryden Rd (45439)
Rates: $47-$86
(937) 298-0380
(800) 800-8000

MOUNT GILEAD

KNIGHTS INN
5898 SR 95 (43338)
Rates: $42-$80
(419) 946-6010
(800) 843-5644

MOUNT VERNON

CURTIS MOTOR HOTEL
6 Public Sq (43050)
Rates: $52-$60
(740) 397-4334
(800) 934-6835

THE DAN EMMETT HOUSE HOTEL
150 Howard St (43050)
Rates: $54-$85
(740) 392-6886

HOLIDAY INN EXP
11555 Upper Gillcrest Rd (43050)
Rates: $68-$74
(740) 392-1900
(800) 465-4329

MOUNT VERNON INN
601 W High St (43058)
Rates: $48-$78
(740) 392-9881

NAPOLEON

QUALITY INN
2395 N Scott St (43545)
Rates: $55-$65
(419) 592-5010
(800) 228-5151

NEW PARIS

GOLDEN INN MOTEL
8868 Rt 40 W (45347)
Rates: $35-$50
(937) 437-0722

NEW PHILADELPHIA

HOLIDAY INN
131 Bluebell Dr SW (44663)
Rates: $89-$125
(330) 339-7731
(800) 465-4329

MOTEL 6
181 Bluebell Dr (44663)
Rates: $40-$56
(330) 339-6446
(800) 466-8356

SCHOENBRUNN INN BY CHRISTOPHER
118 McDonald Dr SW (44663)
Rates: $79-$130
(330) 339-4334

SUPER 8 MOTEL
131 1/2 Bluebell Dr SW (44663)
Rates: $49-$84
(330) 339-6500
(800) 800-8000

TRAVELODGE
1256 W High Ave (44663)
Rates: $44-$55
(330) 339-6671
(800) 578-7878

NEWARK

CHERRY VALLEY LODGE
2299 Cherry Valley Rd (43055)
Rates: $159-$169
(740) 788-1200

NEWCOMERS-TOWN

SUPER 8 MOTEL
299 Adena Dr (43832)
Rates: $43-$53
(740) 498-4116
(800) 800-8000

NEWTON FALLS

RODEWAY INN
4248 SR 5 (44444)
Rates: $35-$110
(330) 872-0988
(800) 228-2000

NORTH BALTIMORE

CROWN INN
P. O. Box 82
(45872)
Rates: $35-$40
(419) 257-3821

NORTH CANTON

DAYS INN
3970 Convenience
Circle (44718)
Rates: $43-$68
(330) 493-8883
(800) 329-7466

HOLIDAY INN
4520 Everhart Rd
(44718)
Rates: $89-$169
(330) 494-2770
(800) 465-4329

SUPER 8 MOTEL
3950 Convenience
Cir NW (44718)
Rates: $44-$68
(330) 492-5030
(800) 800-8000

NORTH LIMA

RODEWAY INN
10650 Market St
(44452)
Rates: $49-$69
(330) 549-3988
(800) 228-2000

SUPER 8 MOTEL
10076 Market St
(44452)
Rates: $49-$65
(330) 549-2187
(800) 800-8000

NORTH OLMSTED

HOMESTED VILLAGE GUEST STUDIOS
24851 Country
Club Dr (44070)
Rates: $59-$74
(440) 777-8585
(888) 782-9473

NORTH-RIDGEVILLE

TRAVELERS INN
32751 Lorain Rd
(44039)
Rates: $32-$62
(216) 327-6311

NORWALK

L K MOTEL
283 Benedict Ave
(44857)
Rates: $33-$68
(419) 668-8255
(800) 282-5711

NORWOOD

RED ROOF INN CENTRAL
5300 Kennedy Ave
(45213)
Rates: $50-$65
(513) 531-6589
(800) 843-7663

OBERLIN

OBERLIN INN
7 N Main St
(44074)
Rates: $81-$141
(440) 775-1111

OREGON

COMFORT INN EAST
2930 Navarre Ave
(43616)
Rates: $59-$112
(419) 691-8911
(800) 228-5150

SLEEP INN & SUITES
1761 Meijer Circle
(43616)
Rates: $62-$150
(419) 693-6199
(800) 753-3746

ORRVILLE

ORRVILLE INN
10355 E Lincoln
Way (44667)
Rates: $32-$47
(330) 682-4080

ROYAL STAR INN
11980 E Lincoln
Way (44667)
Rates: $58-$70
(330) 683-7827

OXFORD

COLLEGE VIEW MOTEL
4000 Oxford-
Millville Rd
(45056)
Rates: $32-$48
(513) 523-6311

SCOTTISH INNS
5235 College
Corner Rd (45056)
Rates: $42-$52
(513) 523-6306
(800) 251-1962

PAINESVILLE

RIDER'S INN
792 Mentor Ave
(44077)
Rates: $75-$95
(216) 354-8200

PENINSULA

VIRGINIA MOTEL
5374 Akron-
Cleveland Rd
(44264)
Rates: $29-$50
(216) 650-0449

PERRYSBURG

BAYMONT INN
1154 Professional
Dr (43551)
Rates: $65-$72
(419) 872-0000
(800) 301-0200

DAYS INN
10667 Fremont
Pike (43551)
Rates: $62-$77
(419) 874-8771
(800) 329-7466

HOWARD JOHNSON
I-280 & Hanley Rd
(43551)
Rates: $37-$58
(419) 837-5245
(800) 446-4656

RED CARPET INN
26054 N Dixie
Hwy (43551)
Rates: $35-$60
(419) 872-2902
(800) 251-1962

PIQUA

COMFORT INN
987 E Ash St
(45356)
Rates: $56-$129
(937) 778-8100
(800) 228-5150

HOWARD JOHNSON EXPRESS
902 Scot Dr
(45356)
Rates: $40-$55
(937) 773-2314
(800) 446-4656

RAMADA LIMITED
950 E Ash St
(45356)
Rates: $66-$87
(937) 615-0140
(800) 262-6232

RED CARPET INN
9060 Country
Club Rd (45356)
Rates: n/a
(937) 773-6275
(800) 251-1962

POLAND

RED ROOF INN
1051 Tiffany South
(44514)
Rates: $49-$70
(330) 758-1999
(800) 843-7663

RESIDENCE INN BY MARRIOTT
7396 Tiffany South
(44514)
Rates: $169
(330) 726-1747
(800) 331-3131

PORT CLINTON

COUNTRY HEARTH INN
1815 E Perry St
(43452)
Rates: $60-$160
(419) 732-2111

PORTSMOUTH

BEST WESTERN OF PORTSMOUTH
3762 Hwy 32 N
(45662)
Rates: $54-$66
(740) 354-2851
(800) 528-1234

PUT-IN-BAY

PERRY HOLIDAY HOTEL
99 Concord Ave
(43456)
Rates: $65-$139
(419) 285-2107

REYNOLDS-BURG

BEST WESTERN COLUMBUS EAST
2100 Brice Rd
(43068)
Rates: $59-$73
(614) 864-1280
(800) 528-1234

LA QUINTA INN
2447 Brice Rd
(43068)
Rates: $65-$85
(614) 866-6456
(800) 687-6667

LENOX INN
13700
Reynoldsburg-
Baltimore Rd
(43068)
Rates: $59-$66
(614) 861-7800

RED ROOF INN
2449 Brice Rd
(43068)
Rates: $56-$83
(614) 864-3683
(800) 843-7663

SUPER 8 MOTEL
6201 Oaktree Ln
(43068)
Rates: $45-$70
(614) 866-8000
(800) 800-8000

RICHFIELD

HOLIDAY INN
4742 Brecksville
Rd (44286)
Rates: $89-$119
(330) 659-6151
(800) 465-4329

HOWARD JOHNSON
5171 Brecksville
Rd (44286)
Rates: $39-$90
(330) 659-6116
(800) 446-4656

SCOTTISH INNS
5175 Brecksville
Rd (44286)
Rates: n/a
(330) 659-6661
(800) 251-1962

RIO GRANDE

**COLLEGE HILL
MOTEL**
10987 SR 588
(45674)
Rates: $34-$43
(740) 245-5326

ST.
CLAIRSVILLE

FISCHER MOTEL
P. O. Box 63
(43950)
Rates: $28-$35
(740) 782-1715

KNIGHTS INN
51260 National Rd
(43950)
Rates: $46-$69
(740) 695-5038
(800) 843-5644

RED ROOF INN
68301 Red Roof
Ln (43950)
Rates: $51-$73
(740) 695-4057
(800) 843-7663

SUPER 8 MOTEL
68400 Matthews
Dr (43950)
Rates: $38-$59
(740) 695-1994
(800) 800-8000

**TWIN PINES
MOTEL**
46079 National Rd
(43950)
Rates: n/a
(740) 695-3720

ST. MARYS

**S & W MOTEL
& SUITES**
1321 Celina Rd
(45885)
Rates: $49-$66
(419) 394-2341

SANDUSKY

CLARION INN
1119 Sandusky
Mall Blvd (44870)
Rates: $100-$150
(419) 625-6280
(800) 252-7466

**CORNADO
MOTEL**
4319 Venice Rd
(44870)
Rates: $30-$105
(419) 625-2954

**QUALITY INN
& SUITES**
3304 Milan Rd
(44870)
Rates: $48-$305
(419) 626-6766
(800) 228-5151

RED ROOF INN
6100 US Rt 250
(44870)
Rates: n/a
(419) 609-9000
(800) 843-7663

SEVILLE

COMFORT INN
4949 Park Ave W
(44273)
Rates: $43-$115
(330) 769-4949
(800) 228-5150

**HOWARD
JOHNSON
EXPRESS**
I-71 & I-76 (44273)
Rates: $34-$43
(330) 769-2053
(800) 446-4656

SUPER 8 MOTEL
6116 Speedway Dr
(44273)
Rates: $49-$77
(330) 769-8880
(800) 800-8000

SHARONVILLE

DAYS INN
111075 Lebanon
Rd (45241)
Rates: $41-$140
(513) 554-1400
(800) 329-7466

**HOMEWOOD
SUITES-NORTH**
2670 E Kemper Rd
(45241)
Rates: $103-$200
(513) 772-8888
(800) 225-5466

MARRIOTT HOTEL
11320 Chester Rd
(45246)
Rates: $109-$149
(513) 772-1720
(800) 228-9290

MOTEL 6-EAST
3850 Hauck Rd
(45241)
Rates: $33-$48
(513) 563-1123
(800) 466-8356

MOTEL 6-WEST
2000 E Kemper Rd
(45241)
Rates: $33-$46
(513) 772-5944
(800) 466-8356

PRESTON HOTEL
2235 Sharon Rd
(45241)
Rates: $79-$109
(513) 771-0700

RADISSON HOTEL
11320 Chester Rd
(45241)
Rates: $99-$159
(513) 772-1720
(800) 333-3333

RED ROOF INN
2301 E Sharon Rd
(45241)
Rates: $60-$75
(513) 771-5552
(800) 843-7663

RED ROOF INN
11345 Chester Rd
(45246)
Rates: $50-$76
(513) 771-5141
(800) 843-7663

**RESIDENCE INN
BY MARRIOTT**
11689 Chester Rd
(45246)
Rates: $119
(513) 771-2525
(800) 331-3131

**WOODFIELD
SUITES**
11029 Dowlin Dr
(45241)
Rates: $99-$189
(513) 771-0300
(800) 338-0008

SHELBY

L K MOTEL
178 Mansfield Ave
(44875)
Rates: $30-$46
(419) 347-2141
(800) 282-5711

SIDNEY

DAYS INN
420 Folkerth Ave
(45365)
Rates: $45-$55
(937) 492-1104
(800) 329-7466

**GREATSTONE
CASTLE B&B**
429 N Ohio Ave
(45365)
Rates: $75-$115
(937) 498-4728

HOLIDAY INN
400 Folkerth Ave
(45365)
Rates: $69-$79
(937) 492-1131
(800) 465-4329

SOUTH POINT

**BEST WESTERN
SOUTHERN HILLS
INN**
803 Solida Rd
(45680)
Rates: $40-$50
(740) 894-3391
(800) 528-1234

**COMFORT INN
& SUITES**
70 Private Rd
(45680)
Rates: $40-$100
(740) 377-2766
(800) 228-5150

SPRINGDALE

BAYMONT INN
12150 Springfield
Pike (45246)
Rates: $65
(513) 671-2300
(800) 301-0200

**BEST WESTERN
HOTEL &
CONF CENTER**
11911 Sheraton Ln
(45246)
Rates: $69-$129
(513) 671-6600
(800) 528-1234

SPRINGFIELD

KNIGHTS INN
2207 W Main St
(45504)
Rates: $50-$60
(937) 325-8721
(800) 843-5644

RAMADA LIMITED
319 E Leffel Lane
(45504)
Rates: $59-$74
(937) 328-0123
(800) 272-6232

RODEWAY INN
1715 W North St
(45504)
Rates: $37-$89
(937) 324-5561
(800) 228-2000

STEUBENVILLE

HOLIDAY INN
1401 University
Blvd (43952)
Rates: $71
(740) 282-0901
(800) 465-4329

STOW

STOW INN
4601 Darrow Rd
(44224)
Rates: $60-$85
(330) 688-3508

STRONGSVILLE

DAYS INN
9029 Pearl Rd
(44136)
Rates: $40-$65
(440) 234-3575
(800) 329-7466

**HOLIDAY INN
SELECT**
15471 Royalton
Rd (44136)
Rates: n/a
(440) 238-8800
(800) 465-4329

AREA CODES - If the local number doesn't connect, check for a new area code.

RED ROOF INN
15385 Royalton
Rd (44136)
Rates: $52-$68
(440) 238-0170
(800) 843-7663

TIFFIN

TIFFIN MOTEL
315 West Market
St (44883)
Rates: n/a
(419) 447-7411

TOLEDO

BUDGET INN
2450 S Reynolds
Rd (43614)
Rates: $31-$41
(419) 865-0201

**CLARION INN
WESTGATE**
3536 Secor Rd
(43606)
Rates: $79-$89
(419) 535-7070
(800) 252-7466

COMFORT INN
3560 Secor Rd
(43606)
Rates: $62
(419) 531-2666
(800) 228-5150

**COMFORT INN
NORTH**
445 E Alexis Rd
(43612)
Rates: $59-$80
(419) 476-0170
(800) 228-5150

CROWN INN
1727 W Alexis Rd
(43613)
Rates: $47-$130
(419) 473-1485

DAYS INN
1800 Miami St
(43605)
Rates: $52-$139
(419) 666-5120
(800) 329-7466

ECONO LODGE
2429-B South
Reynolds Rd
(43614)
Rates: $79+
(419) 381-8765
(800) 553-2666

HOLIDAY INN
2340 S Reynolds
Rd (43614)
Rates: n/a
(419) 865-1361
(800) 465-4329

MOTEL 6
5335
Heatherdowns
Blvd (43614)
Rates: $33-$46
(419) 865-2308
(800) 466-8356

QUALITY HOTEL
2429-A South
Reynolds Rd
(43614)
Rates: $59-$99
(419) 381-8765
(800) 228-5151

**RED ROOF INN
SECOR**
3530 Executive
Pkwy (43606)
Rates: $49-$78
(419) 536-0118
(800) 843-7663

TROY

ECONO LODGE
1210 Brukner Dr
(45373)
Rates: $35-$75
(937) 335-0013
(800) 553-2666

**HOLIDAY INN
EXPRESS HOTEL
& SUITES**
60 Troy Town Dr
(45373)
Rates: $94
(937) 332-1700
(800) 465-4329

KNIGHTS INN
30 Troy Town Dr
(45373)
Rates: $40-$58
(937) 339-1515
(800) 843-5644

**QUALITY INN
& SUITES**
1375 W SR 55
(45373)
Rates: $69-$109
(937) 335-0021
(800) 228-5151

**RESIDENCE INN
BY MARRIOTT**
83 Troy Town Dr
(45373)
Rates: $71-$104
(937) 440-9303
(800) 331-3131

TWINSBURG

SUPER 8 MOTEL
8848 Twins Hills
Dr (44087)
Rates: $63-$69
(330) 425-2889
(800) 800-8000

UPPER SANDUSKY

AMERIHOST INN
1726 E Wyandot
Ave (43351)
Rates: $59-$85
(419) 294-3919
(800) 434-5800

URBANA

**LOGAN LODGE
MOTEL**
2551 SR 68 (43078)
Rates: $58-$63
(937) 652-2188

UHRICHSVILLE

**BEST WESTERN
COUNTRY INN**
111 McCauley Dr
(44683)
Rates: $45-$80
(740) 922-0774
(800) 528-1234

VAN WERT

DAYS INN
820 N Washington
St (45891)
Rates: $43-$58
(419) 238-5222
(800) 329-7466

TRAVELODGE
875 N Washington
St (45891)
Rates: $40-$50
(419) 238-3700
(800) 578-7878

VANDALIA

**PARK INN INTL
AIRPORT**
75 Corporate
Center Dr (45377)
Rates: $50-$90
(937) 898-8321
(800) 670-7275

VERMILION

**HOLIDAY INN
EXPRESS**
2417 State Rd 60
(44089)
Rates: $99-$129
(440) 967-8770
(800) 465-4329

WAPAKONETA

BEST WESTERN
1510 Saturn Dr
(45895)
Rates: $65-$85
(419) 738-8181
(800) 528-1234

DAYS INN
1659 Bellefontaine
St (45895)
Rates: $50-$90
(419) 738-2184
(800) 329-7466

SUPER 8 MOTEL
1011 Lunar Dr
(45895)
Rates: $43-$54
(419) 738-8810
(800) 800-8000

WARREN

**BEST WESTERN
INN**
777 Mahoning Ave
NW (44483)
Rates: $55-$69
(330) 392-2515
(800) 528-1234

**HISTORIC PARK
HOTEL**
136 N Park Ave
(44481)
Rates: $60-$70
(330) 393-1200

WASHINGTON COURT HOUSE

KNIGHTS INN
1820 Columbus
Ave (43160)
Rates: $46-$62
(740) 335-9133
(800) 843-5644

WAUSEON

**ARROWHEAD
MOTEL**
8225 SR 108
(43567)
Rates: $36-$58
(419) 335-5811

WAYNESVILLE

**THE APPLE
BARN B&B**
88 Plott Valley Rd
(28786)
Rates: $100
(704) 452-1860

THE CABIN
1500 Eagles Nest
Rd (28786)
Rates: $165
(704) 452-7514

WESTERVILLE

**CORNELIA'S
CORNER B&B**
93 W College Ave
(43081)
Rates: $60-$85
(614) 882-2678
(800) 745-2678

KNIGHTS INN
32 Heatherdown
Dr (43081)
Rates: $49-$99
(614) 890-0426
(800) 843-5644

WESTLAKE

HOLIDAY INN
1100 Crocker Rd
(44145)
Rates: n/a
(440) 871-6000
(800) 465-4329

RED ROOF INN
29595 Clemens Rd
(44145)
Rates: $70-$93
(440) 892-7920
(800) 843-7663

RESIDENCE INN BY MARRIOTT
30100 Clemens Rd (44145)
Rates: $119-$169
(440) 892-2254
(800) 331-3131

WHEELERS-BURG

COMFORT INN
8226 Ohio River Rd (45694)
Rates: $98
(740) 574-1046
(800) 228-5150

WILLARD

LODGE KEEPER INN
117 E Walton (44890)
Rates: n/a
(419) 935-6321
(800) 282-5711

WILLOUGHBY

RED ROOF INN
4166 SR 306 (44094)
Rates: $40-$64
(440) 946-9872
(800) 843-7663

TRAVELODGE
34600 Maplegrove Rd (44094)
Rates: $59-$91
(440) 585-1900
(800) 578-7878

WILMINGTON

HOLIDAY INN EXPRESS
155 Holiday Dr (45177)
Rates: $74-$125
(937) 382-5858
(800) 465-4329

L K INN
264 W Curry Rd (45177)
Rates: $39-$59
(937) 382-6605
(800) 282-5711

WOOSTER

ECONO LODGE
2137 E Lincoln Way (44691)
Rates: $39-$69
(330) 264-8883
(800) 553-2666

SUPER 8 MOTEL
969 Timken Rd (44691)
Rates: $40-$65
(330) 264-6211
(800) 800-8000

WOOSTER INN
801 E Wayne Ave (44691)
Rates: $60-$120
(330) 264-2341

WORTHINGTON

ECONO LODGE
50 E Wilson Bridge Rd (43235)
Rates: $35-$80
(614) 888-3666
(800) 553-2666

RED ROOF INN
7474 N High St (43235)
Rates: $65-$81
(614) 846-3001
(800) 843-7663

RESIDENCE INN BY MARRIOTT
Northwoods (43235)
Rates: n/a
(800) 331-3131

XENIA

ALLENDALE GARDEN INN
38 S Allison Ave (45385)
Rates: $38-$44
(937) 376-8124

BEST WESTERN REGENCY INN
600 Little Main St (45385)
Rates: $45-$60
(937) 372-9954
(800) 528-1234

YOUNGSTOWN

BEST WESTERN MEANDER INN
870 N Canfield-Niles Rd (44515)
Rates: $65-$90
(330) 544-2378
(800) 528-1234

RED ROOF INN
1051 N Canfield-Niles Rd (44515)
Rates: n/a
(330) 793-9851
(800) 843-7663

SUPER 8 MOTEL
4250 Belmont Ave (44505)
Rates: $36-$50
(330) 759-0040
(800) 800-8000

ZANESVILLE

BEST WESTERN TOWN HOUSE
135 N 7th St (43701)
Rates: $65-$104
(740) 452-4511
(800) 528-1234

COMFORT INN
500 Monroe St (43701)
Rates: $75-$149
(740) 454-4144
(800) 228-5150

HOLIDAY INN
4645 E Pike (43701)
Rates: $74-$109
(740) 453-0771
(800) 465-4329

RED ROOF INN
4929 E Pike (43701)
Rates: $60-$100
(740) 453-6300
(800) 843-7663

SUPER 8 MOTEL
2440 National Rd (43701)
Rates: $59-$80
(740) 455-3124
(800) 800-8000

AREA CODES - If the local number doesn't connect, check for a new area code.

OKLAHOMA

ADA

HOLIDAY INN
400 NE
Richardson Loop
(74820)
Rates: n/a
(580) 332-9000
(800) 465-4329

AFTON

**GRAND LAKE
COUNTRY INN**
I-44, Exit 302
(74331)
Rates: $29-$49
(918) 257-8313

ALTUS

**BEST WESTERN
ALTUS INN**
2804 N Main St
(73521)
Rates: $58-$69
(580) 482-9300
(800) 528-1234

DAYS INN
3202 N Main St
(73521)
Rates: $36-$55
(580) 477-2300
(800) 329-7466

RAMADA INN
2515 E Broadway
(73521)
Rates: $50-$68
(580) 477-3000
(800) 272-6232

ALVA

**BEST WESTERN
REDBUD INN**
800 E Oklahoma
Blvd (73717)
Rates: n/a
(580) 327-1111
(800) 528-1234

**RANGER INN
MOTEL**
420 E Oklahoma
Blvd (73717)
Rates: $26-$32
(580) 327-1981

**WHARTON'S
VISTA MOTEL**
1330 W Oklahoma
Blvd (73717)
Rates: $20-$29
(580) 327-3232

ARDMORE

BEST WESTERN INN
6 Holiday Dr
(73401)
Rates: $50-$64
(580) 223-7525
(800) 528-1234

COMFORT INN
2700 W Broadway
(73401)
Rates: $55-$125
(580) 226-1250
(800) 228-5150

DAYS INN
2432 Veterans
Blvd (73401)
Rates: $39-$61
(580) 223-7976
(800) 329-7466

HOLIDAY INN
2705 Holiday Dr
(73401)
Rates: $69
(580) 223-7130
(800) 465-4329

MOTEL 6
120 Holiday Dr
(73401)
Rates: $27-$33
(580) 226-7666
(800) 466-8356

SUPER 8 MOTEL
2120 Veterans
Blvd (73401)
Rates: $34-$48
(580) 223-2201
(800) 800-8000

ATOKA

**BEST WESTERN
ATOKA INN**
2101 S Mississippi
(74525)
Rates: n/a
(580) 889-7381
(800) 528-1234

BARTLESVILLE

**BEST WESTERN
WESTON INN**
222 SE
Washington Blvd
(74006)
Rates: $49-$69
(918) 335-7755
(800) 528-1234
(800) 336-2415

HOLIDAY INN
1410 SE
Washington Blvd
(74006)
Rates: $55-$76
(918) 333-8320
(800) 465-4329

SUPER 8 MOTEL
211 SE
Washington Blvd
(74006)
Rates: $43-$51
(918) 335-1122
(800) 800-8000

BLACKWELL

COMFORT INN
1201 N 44th St
(74631)
Rates: $60-$68
(580) 363-7000
(800) 228-5150

DAYS INN
4302 W Doolin
(74631)
Rates: $37-$54
(580) 363-2911
(800) 329-7466

SUPER 8 MOTEL
1014 W Doolin
(74631)
Rates: $35-$48
(580) 363-5945
(800) 800-8000

BOISE CITY

**TOWNSMAN
MOTEL**
1205 E Main
(73933)
Rates: $27-$35
(580) 544-2506

BROKEN ARROW

CANTERBURY INN
1301 N Elm Pl
(74012)
Rates: $29-$34
(918) 258-7556

HOLIDAY INN
2600 N Aspen
(74012)
Rates: $66-$84
(918) 258-7085
(800) 465-4329

BROKEN BOW

**BROKEN BOW
LAKE CABIN &
BOAT RENTALS**
P O Box 234
(74728)
Rates: $85
(580) 494-6349

**CHARLES WESLEY
MOTOR LODGE**
302 N Park Dr
(74728)
Rates: $30-$37
(580) 584-3303

**END OF TRAIL
MOTEL**
11 N Park Dr
(74728)
Rates: n/a
(580) 584-3350

CATOOSA

SUPER 8 MOTEL
19250 Timbercrest
Dr (74015)
Rates: $33-$60
(918) 266-7000
(800) 800-8000

CHANDLER

ECONO LODGE
600 N Price
(74834)
Rates: $45-$65
(405) 258-2131
(800) 553-2666

CHECOTAH

BUDGET INN
Old 69 & I-40
(74426)
Rates: n/a
(918) 473-2331

DAYS INN
Hwy 69 & 150
(74426)
Rates: $55-$70
(918) 689-3999
(800) 329-7466

**LAKE EUFAULA
INN**
I-40 & S Hwy 150
(74426)
Rates: $42-$62
(918) 473-2376

**SHARPE HOUSE
BED & BREAKFAST**
301 NW 2nd
(74426)
Rates: $35-$50
(918) 473-2832

CHEROKEE

CHEROKEE INN
1720 S Grand
(73728)
Rates: $57-$60
(580) 596-2828

CHICKASHA

**BEST WESTERN
INN**
2101 S 4th (73018)
Rates: $50-$65
(405) 224-4890
(800) 528-1234
(877) 489-0647

DAYS INN
2701 S 4th St
(73018)
Rates: $39-$49
(405) 222-5800
(800) 329-7466

CLAREMORE

BEST WESTERN WILL ROGERS INN
940 S Lynn Riggs Blvd (74017)
Rates: $49-$67
(918) 341-4410
(800) 528-1234
(800) 644-WILL

CLAREMORE MOTOR INN
1709 N Lynn Riggs (74017)
Rates: $33-$42
(918) 342-4545

DAYS INN
1720 S Lynn Riggs (74017)
Rates: $50-$75
(918) 343-3297
(800) 329-7466

MOTEL CLAREMORE
812 E Will Rogers Blvd (74017)
Rates: $39-$47
(918) 341-3254

CLINTON

BEST WESTERN TRADE WINDS COURTYARD INN
2128 Gary Blvd (73601)
Rates: $44-$95
(580) 323-2610
(800) 528-1234
(800) 321-2209

BUDGET INN
1413 Neptune Dr (73601)
Rates: $16-$26
(580) 323-9333
(800) 283-4678

RED ROOF INN
2140 Gary Blvd (73601)
Rates: n/a
(580) 323-2010
(800) 843-7663

RELAX INN
1116 S 10th St (73601)
Rates: $20-$24
(580) 323-1888

DEL CITY

LA QUINTA INN
5501 Tinker Diagonal (73115)
Rates: $62-$79
(405) 672-0067
(800) 687-6667

DUNCAN

DUNCAN INN
3402 N Hwy 81 (73533)
Rates: $25-$36
(580) 252-5210

HERITAGE INN
1515 S Hwy 81 (73533)
Rates: $30-$43
(580) 252-5612

HILLCREST MOTEL
1417 S 81 Bypass (73533)
Rates: $18-$20
(580) 255-1640
(800) 710-7788

HOLIDAY INN
1015 N Hwy 81 (73533)
Rates: $43-$53
(580) 252-1500
(800) 465-4329

DURANT

BEST WESTERN MARKITA INN
2401 W Main St (74701)
Rates: $40-$65
(580) 924-7676
(800) 528-1234

COMFORT INN & SUITES
2112 W Main St (74701)
Rates: $649$129
(580) 924-8881
(800) 228-5150

EDMOND

BROADWAY SUITES
1305 Broadway Ave (73034)
Rates: $75
(405) 341-6068

RAMADA PLAZA HOTEL

930 E 2nd St (73034)
Rates: $69-$79
(405) 341-3577
(800) 272-6232

EL RENO

BEST WESTERN INN
2701 S Country Club Rd (73036)
Rates: $44-$57
(405) 262-6490
(800) 528-1234
(800) 263-3844

COMFORT INN
1707 SW 27th St (73036)
Rates: $47-$64
(405) 262-3050
(800) 228-5150

DAYS INN
2700 S Country Club Rd (73036)
Rates: $40-$55
(405) 262-8720
(800) 329-7466

RAMADA LIMITED
2851 Hwy 81 S (73036)
Rates: $32-$58
(405) 262-1022
(800) 272-6232

RED CARPET INN
2706 S Country Club Rd (73036)
Rates: $26-$32
(405) 262-1526
(800) 251-1962

SUPER 8 MOTEL
2820 Hwy 81 S (73036)
Rates: $41-$70
(405) 262-8240
(800) 800-8000

ELK CITY

BEST WESTERN ELK CITY INN
2015 W 3rd St (73644)
Rates: $45-$65
(580) 225-2331
(800) 528-1234

BUDGET HOST INN

2000 W 3rd St (73644)
Rates: $30-$65
(580) 225-1811
(800) 283-4678

DAYS INN
1100 Hwy 34 (73644)
Rates: $40-$50
(580) 225-9210
(800) 329-7466

ECONO LODGE
108 Meadow Ridge (73644)
Rates: $34-$50
(580) 225-5120
(800) 553-2666

HOLIDAY INN
101 Meadow Ridge (73648)
Rates: $55-$67
(580) 225-6637
(800) 465-4329

MOTEL 6
2500 E Hwy 66 (73644)
Rates: $24-$31
(580) 225-6661
(800) 466-8356

QUALITY INN
102 B. J. Hughes Access Rd (73644)
Rates: $45-$65
(580) 225-8140
(800) 228-5151

RAMADA INN
2500 S Main St (73644)
Rates: $54-$75
(580) 225-0305
(800) 272-6232

SUPER 8 MOTEL
2801 E Hwy 66 (73644)
Rates: $35-$49
(580) 225-9430
(800) 800-8000

TRAVELODGE
301 Sleepy Hollow Ct (73644)
Rates: $30-$45
(580) 243-0150
(800) 578-7878

ENID

BEST WESTERN ENID INN
2818 S Van Buren (73703)
Rates: $50-$59
(580) 242-7110
(800) 528-1234
(800) 378-6308

COMFORT INN
210 N Van Buren (73703)
Rates: $62-$80
(580) 234-1200
(800) 228-5150

DAYS INN
200 N Van Buren (73703)
Rates: $46-$51
(580) 234-0080
(800) 329-7466

HOLIDAY INN
2901 S Van Buren (73703)
Rates: $34-$41
(580) 237-6000
(800) 465-4329

RAMADA INN
3005 W Garriot Rd (73703)
Rates: $42-$62
(580) 234-0440
(800) 272-6232

ERICK

DAYS INN
I-40 & Hwy 30 (73645)
Rates: $41-$59
(580) 526-3315
(800) 329-7466

FREDERICK

SCOTTISH INNS
1015 S Main St (73542)
Rates: $25-$32
(580) 335-2129
(800) 251-1962

GLENPOOL

BEST WESTERN INN
14831 S Casper St (74033)
Rates: $52-$99
(918) 322-5201
(800) 528-1234
(800) 678-5201

AREA CODES - If the local number doesn't connect, check for a new area code.

GUTHRIE

**BEST WESTERN
TERRITORIAL INN**
2323 Territorial Tr
(73044)
Rates: $55-$75
(405) 282-8831
(800) 528-1234

**HARRISON
HOUSE INN B&B**
124 West Harrison
(73044)
Rates: $52-$87
(405) 282-1000
(800) 375-1001

**TOWN HOUSE
MOTEL**
223 E Oklahoma
Ave (73044)
Rates: $27-$39
(405) 282-2400

GUYMON

**AMBASSADOR
INN**
1909 NW US 54
(73942)
Rates: $60
(580) 338-5555

**BEST WESTERN
TOWNSMAN INN**
212 NE Hwy 54
(73942)
Rates: $51-$75
(580) 338-6556
(800) 528-1234
(800) 245-0335

ECONO LODGE
923 Hwy 54 E
(73942)
Rates: $37-$60
(580) 338-5431
(800) 553-2666

SUPER 8 MOTEL
1201 Hwy 54 NE
(73942)
Rates: $47-$59
(580) 338-0507
(800) 800-8000

HENRYETTA

GATEWAY INN
Hwy 75 &
Trudgeon St
(74430)
Rates: $32-$38
(918) 652-4448

LEBARON MOTEL
1001 E Main
(74437)
Rates: $28-$35
(918) 652-2531

SUPER 8 MOTEL
Rt 1, Box 98
(74437)
Rates: $32-$49
(918) 652-2533
(800) 800-8000

HOOKER

SUNSET MOTEL
710 Hwy 54
(73945)
Rates: $23-$30
(405) 652-3250

KETCHUM

**SUMMERSIDE
INN B&B**
7 Summerside
(74349)
Rates: $150
(918) 782-3301

KINGSTON

**LAKE TEXOMA
RESORT**
US 70 E (73439)
Rates: $62-$96
(580) 564-2311
(800) 654-8240

LAWTON

DAYS INN
3110 Cache Rd
(73505)
Rates: $42-$48
(580) 353-3104
(800) 329-7466

**HOWARD
JOHNSON**
1125 E Gore Blvd
(73501)
Rates: $63-$78
(580) 353-0200
(800) 446-4656

MOTEL 6
202 SE Lee Blvd
(73501)
Rates: $35-$42
(580) 355-9765
(800) 466-8356

RAMADA INN
601 NW 2nd St
(73507)
Rates: $48-$56
(580) 355-7115
(800) 272-6232

**SUPER 8-
SANDPIPER INN**
2202 NW Hwy
277 (73507)
Rates: $42-$64
(580) 353-0310
(800) 800-8000

LOCUST GROVE

**HOLIDAY INN
EXPRESS HOTEL
& SUITES**
106 Holiday Lane
(74352)
Rates: $75-$105
(918) 479-8082
(800) 465-4329

LONE WOLF

**QUARTZ
MOUNTAIN
RESORT**
Rt 1 (73655)
Rates: $50-$88
(800) 654-8240

McALESTER

**BEST WESTERN
INN**
1215 George Nigh
Expwy (74501)
Rates: $49-$64
(918) 426-0115
(800) 528-1234

DAYS INN
1217 George Nigh
Expwy (74501)
Rates: $49-$69
(918) 426-5050
(800) 329-7466

RAMADA INN
1500 S George
Nigh Expy (74501)
Rates: $49-$54
(580) 423-7766
(800) 272-6232

SUPER 8 MOTEL
2400 S Main Bus
69 (74501)
Rates: $45-$65
(580) 426-5400
(800) 800-8000

MIAMI

**BEST WESTERN
INN**
2225 E Steve
Owens Blvd
(74354)
Rates: $49-$69
(918) 542-6681
(800) 528-1234

MIDWEST CITY

MOTEL 6
6166 Tinker
Diagonal (73110)
Rates: $32-$38
(405) 737-6676
(800) 466-8356

MOTEL STUDIO 6
5801 Tinker
Diagonal (73110)
Rates: n/a
(405) 737-8851
(800) 466-8356

SUPER 8 MOTEL
6821 SE 29th St
(73110)
Rates: $38-$50
(405) 737-8880
(800) 800-8000

MOORE

DAYS INN
1701 N Moore Ave
(73160)
Rates: $30-$50
(405) 794-5070
(800) 329-7466

MOTEL 6
1417 N Moore Ave
(73160)
Rates: $29-$36
(405) 799-6616
(800) 466-8356

SUPER 8 MOTEL
1520 N Service Rd
(73160)
Rates: $44-$71
(405) 794-4030
(800) 800-8000

MUSKOGEE

DAYS INN
900 S 32nd St
(74401)
Rates: $50-$55
(918) 683-3911
(800) 329-7466

MOTEL 6
903 S 32nd St
(74401)
Rates: $27-$33
(918) 683-8369
(800) 466-8356

MUSKOGEE INN
2360 E Shawnee
(74401)
Rates: $46-$51
(918) 683-6551

RAMADA INN
800 S 32nd St
(74401)
Rates: $50-$95
(918) 682-4341
(800) 272-6232

SUPER 8 MOTEL
2240 S 32nd
(74401)
Rates: $40-$53
(918) 683-8888
(800) 800-8000

TRAVELODGE
534 S 32nd St
(74401)
Rates: $49-$70
(918) 683-2951
(800) 578-7878

NORMAN

ECONO LODGE
100 26th Dr NW
(73069)
Rates: $48-$66
(405) 364-5554
(800) 553-2666

LA QUINTA INN
930 Ed Noble Dr
(73069)
Rates: $69-$85
(405) 579-4000
(800) 687-6667

**RESIDENCE INN
BY MARRIOTT**
2681 Jefferson St
(73072)
Rates: $89-$115
(405) 366-0900
(800) 331-3131

SUPER 8 MOTEL
2600 West Main
(73069)
Rates: $46-$56
(405) 329-1624
(800) 800-8000

AREA CODES - If the local number doesn't connect, check for a new area code.

TRAVELODGE
225 N Interstate
Dr (73069)
Rates: $39-$89
(405) 329-7194
(800) 578-7878

OKLAHOMA CITY

**AMERISUITES
AIRPORT**
1818 S Meridian
Ave (73108)
Rates: $115-$125
(405) 682-3900
(800) 833-1516

**AMERISUITES
QUAIL SPRINGS**
3201 W Memorial
Dr (73134)
Rates: $80-$107
(405) 749-1595
(800) 833-1516

**BEST WESTERN
SADDLEBACK INN**
4300 SW 3rd St
(73108)
Rates: $65-$93
(405) 947-7000
(800) 528-1234
(800) 228-3903

**BEST WESTERN
TRADE WINDS
CENTRAL INN**
1800 E Reno
(73117)
Rates: $50-$75
(405) 235-4531
(800) 528-1234
(800) 615-2647

**CLARION
MERIDIAN HOTEL**
737 S Meridian
Ave (73108)
Rates: $79-$94
(405) 942-8511
(800) 252-7466

CLARION INN
4345 N Lincoln
Blvd (73105)
Rates: $59-$79
(405) 528-2741
(800) 252-7466

**COMFORT INN
EAST**
5653 Tinker
Diagonal (73110)
Rates: $55-$74
(405) 73301339
(800) 228-5150

**COMFORT INN
HISTORIC RT 66**
4017 NW 39th
Expwy (73131)
Rates: $49-$55
(405) 947-0038
(800) 228-5150

**COMFORT INN
NORTH**
4625 NE 120th St
(73131)
Rates: $65-$110
(405) 478-7282
(800) 228-5150

**COMFORT INN
& SUITES**
5405 N Lincoln
Blvd (73105)
Rates: $65-$175
(405) 528-7563
(800) 228-5150

**DAYS INN
AIRPORT**
4712 W I-40
(73128)
Rates: $41-$59
(405) 947-8721
(800) 329-7466

DAYS INN NORTH
12013 I-35 N
Service Rd (73131)
Rates: $55-$135
(405) 478-2554
(800) 329-7466

DAYS INN NW
2801 NW 39th St
(73112)
Rates: $40-$175
(405) 946-0741
(800) 329-7466

DAYS INN SOUTH
2616 I-35 S (73129)
Rates: $41-$175
(405) 677-0521
(800) 329-7466

ECONO LODGE
4601 SW Third St
(73128)
Rates: $41-$79
(800) 553-2666

ECONO LODGE
8200 W I-40
Service Rd (73128)
Rates: $30-$55
(405) 787-7051
(800) 553-2666

EMBASSY SUITES
1815 S Meridian
Ave (73108)
Rates: $99-$139
(405) 682-6000
(800) 362-2779

**GOVERNORS
SUITES HOTEL**
2308 S Meridian
Ave (73108)
Rates: $54-$65
(405) 682-5299

**HAWTHORN
SUITES**
1600 Richmond
Square (73118)
Rates: $75
(405) 840-1440
(800) 527-1133

**HILTON HOTEL
NORTHWEST**
2945 NW Expwy
(73112)
Rates: $69-$154
(405) 848-4811
(800) 445-8667

**HOLIDAY INN
AIRPORT**
2101 S Meridian
(73108)
Rates: $82
(405) 685-4000
(800) 465-4329

HOLIDAY INN EXP
5405 N Lincoln
Blvd (73105)
Rates: $65-$79
(405) 528-7563
(800) 465-4329

**HOWARD
JOHNSON EXP**
1629 S Prospect
(73129)
Rates: $39-$56
(405) 677-0551
(800) 446-4656

**HOWARD
JOHNSON EXP**
400 S Meridian
Ave (73108)
Rates: $47-$68
(405) 943-9841
(800) 446-4656

**LA QUINTA INN
AIRPORT**
800 S Meridian
Ave (73108)
Rates: $69-$89
(405) 942-0040
(800) 687-6667

**LA QUINTA INN-
SOUTH**
8315 I-35 S (73149)
Rates: $59-$79
(405) 631-8661
(800) 687-6667

**LA QUINTA INN
& SUITES**
4829 NW Expwy
(73131)
Rates: $109
(4050 773-5575
(800) 687-6667

MARRIOTT HOTEL
3233 NW Expwy
(73112)
Rates: $119-$145
(405) 842-6633
(800) 228-9290

**MICROTEL INN
& SUITES**
624 S MacArthur
Blvd (73128)
Rates: $45-$95
(405) 942-0011
(888) 771-7171

MOTEL 6
12121 NE Expwy
(73131)
Rates: $32-$51
(405) 478-4030
(800) 466-8256

**MOTEL 6-
AIRPORT**
820 S Meridian
Ave (73108)
Rates: $38-$54
(405) 946-6662
(800) 466-8356

MOTEL 6-NORTH
11900 NE Expwy
(73131)
Rates: $26-$32
(405) 478-8666
(800) 466-8356

MOTEL 6-WEST
4200 I-40 W
(73108)
Rates: $42-$58
(405) 947-6550
(800) 466-8356

QUALITY INN
3850 S Prospect
Ave (73129)
Rates: $49-$59
(405) 670-5800
(800) 228-5151

**QUALITY INN
AT FOUNDERS
TOWER**
5704 Mosteller Dr
(73112)
Rates: $54-$107
(405) 810-1100
(800) 228-5151

**QUALITY INN
NORTH**
12001 NE Expwy
(73131)
Rates: $45-$70
(405) 478-0400
(800) 228-5151

**QUALITY INN
SOUTHWEST**
7800 C A
Henderson Blvd
(73139)
Rates: $58-$79
(405) 632-6666
(800) 228-5151

**QUALITY INN
WEST**
720 S MacArthur
Blvd (73128)
Rates: $50-$70
(405) 943-2393
(800) 228-5151

RADISSON INN
401 S Meridian
Ave (73108)
Rates: $59-$190
(800) 333-3333

RAMADA INN
2001 E Reno Ave
(73117)
Rates: $48-$73
(405) 235-2761
(800) 272-6232

RAMADA LIMITED
1400 63rd St (73111)
Rates: $49-$79
(405) 478-5221
(800) 272-6232

**RAMADA LIMITED
AIRPORT**
7400 S May Ave
(73119)
Rates: $49-$55
(405) 682-2211
(800) 272-6232

AREA CODES - If the local number doesn't connect, check for a new area code.

RED ROOF INN
309 S Meridian
Ave (73108)
Rates: n/a
(405) 947-8777
(800) 843-7663

RESIDENCE INN BY MARRIOTT
4361 W Reno
(73107)
Rates: $122
(405) 942-4500
(800) 331-3131

SOUTHGATE INN
5245 S I-35 (73129)
Rates: n/a
(405) 672-5561

SUPER 8 MOTEL
2821 NW 39th St
(73112)
Rates: $37-$49
(405) 946-9170
(800) 800-8000

TRAVELODGE
820 S MacArthur
Blvd (73128)
Rates: $35-$55
(405) 947-8651
(800) 578-7878

TRAVELODGE HOTEL
3535 NW 39th
Expwy (73112)
Rates: $45-$55
(405) 947-2351
(800) 578-7878

TRAVELODGE HOTEL
6200 N Robinson
(73118)
Rates: $66-$95
(405) 843-5558
(800) 578-7878

THE WATERFORD MARRIOTT
6300 Waterford
Blvd (73118)
Rates: $139-$195
(405) 848-4782

OKMULGEE

BEST WESTERN INN
3499 N Wood Dr
(74447)
Rates: $47-$66
(918) 756-9200
(800) 528-1234
(800) 552-9201

DAYS INN
1221 S Wood Dr
(74447)
Rates: $40-$55
(918) 758-0660
(800) 329-7466

PAULS VALLEY

AMISH INN MOTEL
3101 W Grant Ave
(73075)
Rates: $26-$36
(405) 238-7545

DAYS INN
Rt 3, Box 295-C
(73075)
Rates: $41-$62
(405) 238-7548
(800) 329-7466

GARDEN INN MOTEL
S Hwy 19 & I-35
(73075)
Rates: $22-$31
(405) 238-7313

PERRY

BEST WESTERN CHEROKEE STRIP MOTEL
I-35 & US 77 (73077)
Rates: $129-$159
(580) 336-2218
(800) 528-1234

DAN-D-MOTEL
515 Fir St (73077)
Rates: $18-$24
(580) 336-4463

PONCA CITY

DAYS INN
1415 E Bradley
(74604)
Rates: $31-$46
(580) 767-1406
(800) 329-7466

HOLIDAY INN
2215 N 14th St
(74601)
Rates: $62-$108
(580) 762-8311
(800) 465-4329

PRYOR

DAYS INN
Hwy 69 S & 69A
(74362)
Rates: $42-$68
(918) 825-7600
(800) 329-7466

HOLIDAY MOTEL
701 S Mill (74361)
Rates: $25-$39
(918) 825-1204

PRYOR HOUSE MOTOR INN
123 S Mill (74361)
Rates: $32-$42
(918) 825-6677

PURCELL

ECONO LODGE
2500 Hwy 74 S
(73080)
Rates: $40-$55
(405) 527-5603
(800) 553-2666

ROLAND

BEST WESTERN ROLAND INN
900 S Paw Paw St
(74954)
Rates: $40-$59
(918) 427-6600
(800) 528-1234

DAYS INN
201 Cherokee
Blvd (74954)
Rates: $35-$45
(918) 427-1000
(800) 329-7466

SALLISAW

BEST WESTERN BLUE RIBBON INN
706 S Kerr (74955)
Rates: $40-$59
(918) 775-6294
(800) 528-1234
(800) 554-9532

DAYS INN
1700 W Cherokee
(74955)
Rates: $34-$58
(918) 775-4406
(800) 329-7466

ECONO LODGE
2403 E Cherokee
(74955)
Rates: $28-$45
(918) 775-7981
(800) 553-2666

GOLDEN SPUR INN
601 S Kerr Blvd
(74955)
Rates: $26-$34
(918) 775-4443

MOTEL 6
1300 E Cherokee
(74955)
Rates: $30-$36
(918) 775-7791
(800) 466-8356

SUPER 8 MOTEL
924 S Kerr Blvd
(74955)
Rates: $37-$48
(918) 775-8900
(800) 800-8000

SAND SPRINGS

BEST WESTERN INN & SUITES
211 S Lake Dr
(74063)
Rates: $65-$75
(918) 245-4999
(800) 528-1234
(888) 297-7466

DAYS INN
1110 Charles Page
Blvd (74063)
Rates: $30-$55
(918) 245-0283
(800) 329-7466

SAPULPA

SUPER 8 MOTEL
1505 New Sapulpa
Rd (74066)
Rates: $38-$52
(918) 227-3300
(800) 800-8000

SAVANNA

BUDGET HOST COLONIAL INN
P. O. Box 323 (74565)
Rates: $22-$27
(800) 283-4678

TRAVELODGE
Hwy 69 & Panola
St (74565)
Rates: $32-$68
(918) 548-3506
(800) 578-7878

SHAWNEE

BEST WESTERN CINDERELLA MOTOR INN
623 Kickapoo
Spur (74801)
Rates: $49-$72
(405) 273-7010
(800) 528-1234
(800) 480-5111

MOTEL 6
4981 N Harrison
St (74801)
Rates: $34-$41
(405) 275-5310
(800) 466-8356

RAMADA INN
4900 N Harrison
St (74801)
Rates: $58-$75
(405) 275-4404
(800) 272-6232

SUPER 8 MOTEL
4900 N Harrison
St (74801)
Rates: $37-$57
(405) 275-0089
(800) 800-8000

STILLWATER

BEST WESTERN INN
600 E McElroy
(74075)
Rates: $65-$109
(405) 377-7010
(800) 528-1234
(800) 353-6894

DAYS INN
5010 W 6th
(74074)
Rates: $35-$60
(405) 743-2570
(800) 329-7466

HOLIDAY INN
2515 W 6th
(74074)
Rates: $45-$62
(405) 372-0800
(800) 465-4329

MOTEL 6
5122 W 6th
(74074)
Rates: $29-$36
(405) 624-0433
(800) 466-8356

STROUD

BEST WESTERN INN
1200 N 8th Ave
(74079)
Rates: $47-$60
(918) 968-9515
(800) 528-1234

SULPHUR

SUPER 8 MOTEL
2110 W Broadway
(73086)
Rates: $39-$49
(405) 622-6500
(800) 800-8000

TAHLEQUAH

**BUDGET HOST
TAHLEQUAH
MOTOR LODGE**
2501 S Muskogee
(74464)
Rates: $49-$60
(918) 456-2350
(800) 487-8705

**OAK HILL
MOTEL SUITES**
2600 S Muskogee
(74464)
Rates: $51-$70
(918) 458-1200

TONKAWA

WESTERN INN
I-35 & US 60
(74653)
Rates: $34-$44
(580) 628-2577

TULSA

AMERISUITES
7037 S Zurich Ave
(74136)
Rates: $109-$139
(918) 491-4010
(800) 833-1516

**BAYMONT INN
& SUITES**
4530 E Skelly Dr
(74135)
Rates: $55-$61
(918) 488-8777
(800) 301-0200

**BEST WESTERN
TRADEWINDS
CENTRAL INN**
3141 E Skelly Dr
(74105)
Rates: $66-$71
(918) 749-5561
(800) 528-1234
(800) 685-4564

**BEST WESTERN
TRADEWINDS
EAST INN**
3337 E Skelly Dr
(74135)
Rates: $55-$65
(918) 743-7931
(800) 528-1234
(800) 254-7449

**COMFORT SUITES
AIRPORT**
1737 S 101st Ave
(74127)
Rates: $59-$94
(918) 628-0900
(800) 228-5150

DAYS INN
5525 W Skelly Dr
(74107)
Rates: $39-$60
(918) 446-1561
(800) 329-7466

**DAYS INN
AIRPORT**
1016 N Garnett Rd
(74116)
Rates: $40-$48
(918) 438-5050
(800) 329-7466

**DOUBLETREE
HOTEL**
6110 S Yale Ave
(74136)
Rates: $164
(918) 495-1000
(800) 222-8733

**DOUBLETREE
HOTEL**
616 W 7th St
(74127)
Rates: $100
(918) 587-8000
(800) 222-8733

**GUESTHOUSE
SUITES PLUS**
8181 E 41st St
(74145)
Rates: $99-$125
(918) 664-7241

**HOLIDAY INN
AIRPORT**
1010 N Garnett Rd
(74116)
Rates: $96-$116
(918) 437-7660
(800) 465-4329

**HOLIDAY INN
WOODLAND
HILLS**
9010 E 71st St
(74133)
Rates: n/a
(918) 459-5321
(800) 465-4329

LA QUINTA INN
10829 E 41st St
(74146)
Rates: $62-$79
(918) 665-0220
(800) 687-6667

**LA QUINTA INN-
AIRPORT**
35 N Sheridan Rd
(74115)
Rates: $62-$82
(918) 836-3931
(800) 687-6667

**LA QUINTA INN-
SOUTH**
12525 E 52nd St
(74146)
Rates: $59-$79
(918) 254-1626
(800) 687-6667

MICROTEL INN
16518 E Admiral
Pl (74116)
Rates: $41-$65
(918) 234-9100
(888) 771-7171

MOTEL 6-EAST
1011 S Garnett Rd
(74128)
Rates: $31-$36
(918) 234-6200
(800) 466-8356

MOTEL 6-WEST
5828 W Skelly Dr
(74107)
Rates: $28-$33
(918) 445-0223
(800) 466-8356

RAMADA INN
3131 E 51st St
(74105)
Rates: $71
(918) 743-9811
(800) 272-6232

**RAMADA INN
DOWNTOWN**
17 W 7th St
(74119)
Rates: $59-$89
(918) 585-5898
(800) 272-6232

**SHERATON
HOTEL**
10918 E 41st St
(74105)
Rates: $119-$160
(918) 627-5000
(800) 325-3535

VINITA

**PARK HILLS
MOTEL**
Rt 4, Box 292
(74301)
Rates: $20-$28
(918) 256-5511

SUPER 8 MOTEL
30954 S Hwy 69
(74301)
Rates: $39-$48
(918) 783-5888
(800) 800-8000

WAGONOR

**INDIAN LODGE
MOTEL**
SH 51 E (74467)
Rates: $32-$70
(918) 485-3184

**WESTERN HILLS
GUEST RANCH**
SH 51 (74477)
Rates: $45-$98
(918) 772-2545

WATONGA

**ROMAN NOSE
RESORT**
Rt 1 (73772)
Rates: $45-$68
(580) 623-7281

WEATHERFORD

**BEST WESTERN
MARK
MOTOR HOTEL**
525 E Main St
(73096)
Rates: $45-$59
(580) 772-3325
(800) 528-1234
(800) 598-3089

DAYS INN
1019 E Main St
(73096)
Rates: $38-$60
(580) 772-5592
(800) 329-7466

SCOTTISH INNS

616 E Main St
(73096)
Rates: $26-$36
(580) 772-3349
(800) 251-1962

TRAVEL INN
3401 E Main St
(73096)
Rates: $21-$25
(580) 772-6238

WOODWARD

NORTHWEST INN
Hwy 270 & 1st St
(73801)
Rates: $54-$71
(580) 256-7600

**RED COUNTRY
INN**
2314 8th St (73801)
Rates: $30-$39
(580) 254-9147

SUPER 8 MOTEL
4120 Williams Ave
(73801)
Rates: $35-$52
(580) 254-2964
(800) 800-8000

WAYFARER INN
2901 Williams Ave
(73801)
Rates: $35-$52
(580) 256-5553

YUKON

**BEST WESTERN
INN & SUITES**
11440 W I-40
Service Rd (73099)
Rates: $45-$70
(800) 528-1234

**COMFORT INN-
WEST**
321 N Mustang
Rd (73099)
Rates: $52-$70
(405) 324-1000
(800) 228-5150
(800) 428-4577

HAMPTON INN
1351 Canadian Ct
(73099)
Rates: $65-$75
(405) 350-6400
(800) 426-7866

AREA CODES - If the local number doesn't connect, check for a new area code.

OREGON

AGNESS

LUCAS PIONEER RANCH & LODGE
03904 Cougar Ln
(97406)
Rates: $45-$60
(541) 247-7443

SINGING SPRINGS RESORT
34501 Agness
Illahe Rd (97406)
Rates: $30-$50
(541) 247-6162

ALBANY

BEST INN & SUITES
1100 Price Rd SE
(97321)
Rates: $70-$125
(541) 928-5050
(800) 237-8466

BEST WESTERN PONY SOLDIER INN
315 Airport Rd SE
(97321)
Rates: $82-$99
(541) 928-6322
(800) 528-1234
(800) 634-7669

BUDGET INN
2727 Pacific Blvd
SE (97321)
Rates: $36-$49
(541) 926-4246
(800) 527-0700

HAWTHORN INN & SUITES
251 Airport Rd SE
(97321)
Rates: $82-$95
(541) 928-0921
(800) 527-1133

MARCO POLO MOTEL
2410 Pacific Blvd
SE (97321)
Rates: $22-$40
(541) 926-4401

MOTEL ORLEANS
1212 Price Rd SE
(97321)
Rates: $38-$44
(541) 926-0170
(800) 626-1900

RELAX INN
1730 SE Pacific
Blvd (97321)
Rates: $32-$40
(541) 926-8442

STARDUST MOTEL
2735 E Pacific
Blvd (97321)
Rates: $38-$68
(541) 926-4233

VAL-U-INN MOTEL
3125 Santiam
Hwy SE (97321)
Rates: $40-$80
(541) 926-1538
(800) 547-0106

ARLINGTON

VILLAGE INN MOTEL
131 Beech St
(97812)
Rates: $48
(541) 454-2646

ASHLAND

ASHLAND GRANDE HISTORIC HOTEL
212 E Main St
(97520)
Rates: $99-$139
(541) 488-5400
(800) 426-0670

ASHLAND MOTEL
1145 Siskiyou
Blvd (97520)
Rates: $30-$43
(541) 482-2561
(800) 460-8858

ASHLAND PATTERSON HOUSE BED & BREAKFAST
639 N Main St
(97520)
Rates: $70-$105
(541) 482-9171
(888) 482-9171

BEST WESTERN BARD'S INN
132 N Main St
(97520)
Rates: $95-$175
(541) 482-0049
(800) 528-1234

BEST WESTERN WINDSOR INN
2520 Ashland St
(97520)
Rates: $85-$94
(541) 488-2330
(800) 528-1234

GREEN SPRINGS INN
11470 Hwy 66
(97520)
Rates: $40-$99
(541) 482-0614

GREEN SPRINGS BOX R RANCH
16799 Hwy 66
(97520)
Rates: $110-$150
(541) 482-1873

HAWTHORN INN & SUITES
434 Valley View
Rd (97520)
Rates: $51-$119
(541) 482-6932
(800) 527-1133

HILLSIDE INN
1520 Siskiyou
Blvd (97520)
Rates: $71-$79
(541) 482-2626
(800) 326-9903

KNIGHTS INN MOTEL
2359 Hwy 66
(97520)
Rates: $58-$66
(541) 482-5111
(800) 843-5644
(800) 547-4566

PHOENIX MOTEL
510 N Main St
(97520)
Rates: n/a
(541) 535-1555

RODEWAY INN
1193 Siskiyou
Blvd (97520)
Rates: $78-$88
(541) 482-2641
(800) 228-2000
(800) 547-6414

SUPER 8 MOTEL
2350 Ashland St
(97520)
Rates: $44-$59
(541) 482-8887
(800) 800-8000

VISTA MOTEL
535 Clover Ln
(97520)
Rates: $29-$42
(541) 482-4423
(888) 672-5290

WINDMILL'S ASHLAND HILLS INN & SUITES
2525 Ashland St
(97520)
Rates: $99-$250
(541) 482-8310
(800) 547-4747

ASTORIA

BAYSHORE MOTOR INN
555 Hamburg
(97103)
Rates: $65-$85
(503) 325-2205
(800) 621-0641

CLEMENTINE'S BED & BREAKFST
847 Exchange St
(97103)
Rates: $60-$100
(503) 325-2005
(800) 521-6801

CREST MOTEL
5366 Leif Erickson
Dr (97103)
Rates: $73-$96
(503) 325-3141
(800) 421-3141

LAMPLIGHTER MOTEL
131 W Marine Dr
(97103)
Rates: $45-$78
(503) 325-4051
(800) 845-0947

RED LION INN
400 Industry St
(97103)
Rates: $54-$124
(503) 325-7373
(800) 733-5466

BAKER CITY

BAKER CITY MOTEL
880 Elm St (97814)
Rates: $28-$37
(541) 523-6391
(800) 931-9229

BRIDGE STREET INN
134 Bridge St (97814)
Rates: $33-$44
(541) 523-6571
(800) 932-9220

EL DORADO INN
695 Campbell
(97814)
Rates: $40-$59
(541) 523-6494
(800) 537-5756

GEISER GRAND HISTORIC HOTEL
1996 Main St
(97814)
Rates: $79-$199
(541) 523-1889
(888) GEISERG

GREEN GABLES MOTEL
2533 10th St (97814)
Rates: $30+
(541) 523-5588

OREGON TRAIL MOTEL & RESORT
211 Bridge St (97814)
Rates: $36-$44
(541) 523-5844
(800) 628-3982

POWDER RIVER BED & BREAKFAST
HCR 87, Box 500
(97814)
Rates: $60-$65
(541) 523-7143
(800) 600-7143

QUALITY INN
810 Campbell
(97814)
Rates: $55-$84
(541) 523-2242
(800) 228-5151

TRAIL MOTEL
2815 10th St
(97814)
Rates: n/a
(541) 523-4646

WARNERS SLOUGH HOUSE BED & BREAKFAST
Rt 2, Box 135
(97814)
Rates: n/a
(541) 523-6196

WELCOME INN
175 Campbell St
(97814)
Rates: $47-$63
(541) 523-3431

THE WESTERN MOTEL
3055 10th St
(97814)
Rates: $28-$36
(541) 523-3700
(800) 481-3701

BANDON

BEST WESTERN INN AT FACE ROCK
3225 Beach Loop
Rd (97411)
Rates: $69-$205
(541) 347-9441
(800) 528-1234
(800) 638-3092

CAPRICE MOTEL
Rt 1, Box 530 (97411)
Rates: $34-$60
(541) 347-4494

DRIFTWOOD MOTEL
460 Hwy 101
(97411)
Rates: $55-$80
(541) 347-9022
(888) 374-3893

LA KRIS MOTEL
Hwy 101 S at 9th
St (97411)
Rates: $42-$85
(541) 347-3610
(888) 496-3610

PACIFIC HOUSE BED & BREAKFAST
2165 Beach Loop
Dr (97411)
Rates: $75-$90
(541) 347-9526

SUNSET OCEANFRONT
1755 Beach Loop
Rd (97411)
Rates: $53-$175
(541) 347-2453
(800) 842-2407

TABLE ROCK MOTEL
840 Beach Loop
Rd (97411)
Rates: $35-$90
(541) 347-2700

BEATTY

BEATTY MOTEL
Hwy 140, P.O.Box
335 (97621)
Rates: n/a
(541) 533-2689

BEAVERTON

ALOHA JUNCTION INN & GARDEN B&B
5085 SW 170th
Ave (97007)
Rates: $59-$75
(503) 642-7236
(888) 832-5251

GREENWOOD INN
10700 SW Allen
Blvd (97005)
Rates: $89-$133
(503) 643-7444
(800) 289-1300

HOMESTEAD VILLAGE GUEST STUDIOS
875 SW 158th Ave
(97006)
Rates: $59-$94
(503) 690-3600
(888) 782-9473

HOMEWOOD SUITES
15525 NW
Gateway Ct
(97006)
Rates: n/a
(503) 614-0900
(800) 225-5466

RAMADA INN
13455 SW Canyon
Rd (97005)
Rates: $90-$110
(503) 643-9100
(800) 272-6232

SHILO INNS
9900 SW Canyon
Rd (97225)
Rates: $79-$189
(503) 297-2551
(800) 222-2244

VAL-U-INN MOTEL
12255 SW Canyon
Rd (97005)
Rates: $49-$69
(503) 643-6621
(800) 443-7777

BEND

ARLINE MCDONALD'S VACATION HOMES
1530 NW
Jacksonville
(97701)
Rates: $150-$250
(541) 382-4534

BEND RIVERSIDE MOTEL & CONDO
1565 NW Hill St
(97702)
Rates: $58-$89
(541) 389-2363
(800) 284-2363

BEND RIVERSIDE MOTEL II
1565 NW ill St
(97701)
Rates: $52-$110
(541) 388-4000
(800) 228-4019

BEST INN & SUITES
61200 S Hwy 97
(97702)
Rates: $59-$135
(541) 388-2227
(800) 237-8466

BEST WESTERN ENTRADA LODGE
19221 Century Dr
(97702)
Rates: $59-$89
(541) 382-4080
(800) 528-1234

BEST WESTERN INN & SUITES
721 NE 3rd St
(97701)
Rates: $59-$89
(541) 382-1515
(800) 528-1234

BUDGET INN
1300 SE Hwy 97
(97702)
Rates: $35-$45
(541) 389-1448

CASCADE MOTEL LODGE
420 SE 3rd St
(97702)
Rates: $85
(541) 382-2612
(800) 852-6031

CASCADE VIEW RANCH GUEST HOUSE
60435 Tekampe
Rd (97702)
Rates: $150-$285
(541) 388-5658

CHALET MOTEL
510 SE 3rd St
(97702)
Rates: $29-$40
(541) 382-6124

CIMARRON MOTOR INN
201 NE 3rd St
(97701)
Rates: $44-$59
(541) 382-8282
(800) 304-4050

CIMARRON NORTH
437 NE 3rd St
(97701)
Rates: $39-$54
(541) 382-7711
(800) 304-4050

CULTUS LAKE RESORT
P.O. Box 262
(97709)
Rates: $52-$89
(541) 389-3230

ECONO LODGE
20600 Grandview
Dr (97701)
Rates: $39-$125
(541) 318-0848
(800) 553-2666

GUEST HOUSE BED & BREAKFAST
20020 Glen Vista
Rd (97702)
Rates: n/a
(541) 382-8565

HAMPTON INN
15 NE Butler
Market Rd (97701)
Rates: $69-$99
(541) 388-4114
(800) 426-7866

HOLIDAY INN EXPRESS
20615 Grand View
(97701)
Rates: $80-$89
(541) 317-8500
(800) 465-4329

HOLIDAY MOTEL
880 SE 3rd St
(97702)
Rates: $34-$38
(541) 382-4620
(800) 252-0121

MOTEL WEST
228 NE Irving
(97701)
Rates: $36-$50
(541) 389-5577
(800) 282-5577

PALMER'S MOTEL
645 NE
Greenwood Ave
(97701)
Rates: $30-$55
(541) 382-1197
(877) 655-8885

PLAZA MOTEL
1430 NW Hill St
(97702)
Rates: $28-$45
(541) 382-1621
(800) 300-1621

AREA CODES - If the local number doesn't connect, check for a new area code.

RED LION-NORTH
1415 NE 3rd St
(97701)
Rates: $64-$99
(541) 382-7011
(800) 733-5466

RED LION-SOUTH
849 NE 3rd St
(97701)
Rates: $84-$99
(541) 382-8384
(800) 733-5466

THE RIVERHOUSE RESORT
3075 N Hwy 97
(97701)
Rates: $79-$109
(541) 389-3111
(800) 547-3928

RODEWAY INN
3705 N Hwy 97
(97701)
Rates: $32-$75
(541) 382-2211
(800) 228-2000
(800) 507-2211

SCANDIA PINES LODGE
61405 S Hwy 97
(97702)
Rates: $39-$89
(541) 389-5910
(800) 500-5910

SHILO SUITES HOTEL
3105 O B Riley Rd
(97701)
Rates: $89-$199
(541) 389-9600
(800) 222-2244

SLEEP INN
600 NE Bellevue
(97701)
Rates: $54-$74
(541) 330-0050
(800) 753-3746

SONOMA LODGE
450 SE 3rd St
(97702)
Rates: $30-$49
(541) 382-4891

SUPER 8 MOTEL
1275 S Hwy 97
(97702)
Rates: $50-$68
(541) 388-6888
(800) 800-8000

SWALLOW RIDGE BED & BREAKFAST
65711 Twin
Bridges Rd (97701)
Rates: $45-$55
(541) 389-1913

WESTWARD HO MOTEL
904 SE 3rd St
(97702)
Rates: $34-$75
(541) 382-2111
(800) 999-8143

BIGGS JUNCTION

RIVIERA MOTEL
97484 Biggs-Rufus
Hwy (97065)
Rates: $55-$78
(541) 739-2501
(800) 944-4156

BLUE RIVER

HOLIDAY FARM RESORT B&B
54455 McKenzie
River Dr (97413)
Rates: $115-$375
(541) 822-3715
(800) 823-3715

MCKENZIE RIVER BED & BREAKFAST
55482 Delta Rd
(97413)
Rates: $70-$85
(541) 822-8232
(888) 355-2583

MCKENZIE RIVER CONFERENCE CENTER
54705 McKenzie
Hwy (97413)
Rates: $20-$40
(541) 431-4667
(800) 844-4947

BOARDMAN

DODGE CITY INN
1st & Front Sts
(97818)
Rates: $41-$45
(541) 481-2451
(800) 233-2368

ECONO LODGE
105 Front St SW
(97818)
Rates: $44-$79
(541) 481-2375
(800) 553-2666

RIVERVIEW MOTEL
200 Front St (97818)
Rates: $32-$42
(541) 481-2775

BROOKINGS

BEAVER STATE MOTEL
437 Chetco Ave
(97415)
Rates: $39-$55
(541) 469-5361

BONN MOTEL
1216 Chetco Ave
(97415)
Rates: $38-$48
(541) 469-2161

CHART HOUSE OUTFITTERS
15833 Pedrioli Rd
(97415)
Rates: $38-$75
(541) 469-3867
(800) 290-6208

HARBOR INN MOTEL
15991 Hwy 101 S
(97415)
Rates: $48-$62
(541) 469-3194
(800) 469-8884

LOWDEN'S BEACHFRONT B&B
14626 Wollam Rd
(97415)
Rates: $59-$160
(541) 469-7045
(800) 453-4768

PACIFIC SUNSET INN
1144 Chetco Ave
(97415)
Rates: $34-$58
(541) 469-2141
(800) 469-2141

SEA DREAMER INN B&B
15167 McVay Ln
(97415)
Rates: $38-$75
(541) 469-6629
(800) 408-4367

WESTWARD MOTEL
1026 Chetco Ave
(97415)
Rates: $38-$59
(541) 469-7471
(888) 521-6020

BURNS

BEST INN
999 Oregon Ave
(97720)
Rates: $44-$85
(541) 573-1700
(800) 237-8466

DAYS INN
577 W Monroe
(97720)
Rates: $42-$85
(541) 573-2047
(800) 329-7466

SILVER SPUR MOTEL
789 N Bdwy
(97720)
Rates: $41-$45
(541) 573-2077
(800) 400-2077

CAMP SHERMAN

BLACK BUTTE RESORT MOTEL
25635 SW Forest
Service Rd (97730)
Rates: $55-$65
(541) 595-6514

COLD SPRGS RESORT
25615 Cold
Springs Resort Ln
(97730)
Rates: $93-$112
(541) 595-6271

METOLIUS RIVER LODGES
12390 SW FS Rd
1419-700 (97730)
Rates: $70-$114
(541) 595-6290
(800) 595-6290

TWIN VIEW RESORT
13860 SW FS Rd
1419 (97730)
Rates: $66-$98
(541) 595-6125

CANNON BEACH

CANNON BEACH ECOLA CREEK LODGE
208 5th St (97110)
Rates: $99-$120
(503) 436-2776
(800) 873-2749

CANNON VILLAGE MOTEL
3163 S Hemlock St
(97110)
Rates: $40-$130
(503) 436-2317

HALLMARK RESORT
1400 S Hemlock St
(97110)
Rates: $59-$229
(503) 436-1566
(888) 448-4449

HAYSTACK RESORT MOTEL
3339 S Hemlock St
(97110)
Rates: $119-$189
(503) 436-1577
(800) 499-2220

MCBEE MOTEL COTTAGES
888 S Hemlock St
(97110)
Rates: $35-$135
(503) 436-2569
(800) 238-4107

QUIET CANNON LODGINGS
372 N Spruce St
(97110)
Rates: $95-$105
(503) 436-1405

SURF SAND RESORT
Ocean Front &
Gower Sts (97110)
Rates: $129-$319
(503) 436-2274
(800) 547-6100

TOLOVANA INN
3400 S Hemlock St
(97110)
Rates: $68-$150
(503) 436-2211
(800) 333-8890

CANYONVILLE

LEISURE INN
554 SW Pine St
(97417)
Rates: $31-$50
(541) 839-4278

TRAVELODGE SUITES
140 Creekside Rd
(97417)
Rates: $60-$68
(800) 578-7878

AREA CODES - If the local number doesn't connect, check for a new area code.

CASCADE LOCKS

BEST WESTERN COLUMBIA RIVER INN
735 Wanapa St (97014)
Rates: $89-$129
(541) 374-8777
(800) 528-1234
(800) 595-7108

SCANDIAN MOTOR LODGE
25 Oneonta St (97014)
Rates: $32-$48
(541) 374-8417

CAVE JUNCTION

COUNTRY HILLS RESORT
7901 Caves Hwy (97523)
Rates: $45-$60
(541) 592-3406
(800) 997-8464

RUSK RANCH COUNTRY COTTAGE
27742 Redwood Hwy, Box 270 (97523)
Rates: $48-$75
(541) 592-4658

CHARLESTON

CAPTAIN JOHN'S MOTEL
8061 Kingfisher Dr (97420)
Rates: $40-$70
(541) 888-4041

CHEMULT

CHEMULT MOTEL
Hwy 97 (97731)
Rates: $38-$44
(541) 365-2228

CRATER LAKE MOTEL & RV PARK
Hwy 97 (97731)
Rates: $27-$80
(541) 365-2241

DAWSON HOUSE LODGE
Hwy 97 & 1st St (97731)
Rates: $35-$70
(541) 365-2232

FEATHERBED INN
P.O. Box 128 (97731)
Rates: $27-$48
(541) 365-2235

HOLIDAY VILLAGE MOTEL & RV PARK
Hwy 97, Milepost 209 (97731)
Rates: $34-$36
(541) 365-2394

SINGING PINES RANCH MOTEL
Hwy 97, Box 117 (97731)
Rates: n/a
(541) 365-9909

CHILOQUIN

AGENCY LAKE RESORT
37000 Modoc Rd (97624)
Rates: $30-$45
(541) 783-2489

MELITA'S MOTEL
39500 Hwy 97 N (97624)
Rates: $26-$53
(541) 783-2401

THE SPORTSMAN'S MOTEL
27627 Hwy 97 N (97624)
Rates: $27-$45
(541) 783-2867
(888) 905-9074

SPRING CREEK RANCH MOTEL
47600 Hwy 97 N (97624)
Rates: $28-$34
(541) 783-2775
(800) 626-1292

WILLIAMSON RIVER RESORT
31900 Modoc Rd (97624)
Rates: $25-$50
(541) 783-2071

CLACKAMAS

CLACKAMAS INN
16010 SE 82nd Dr (97266)
Rates: $59-$99
(503) 650-5340
(800) 874-6560

COMFORT SUITES
15929 SE McKinley Ave (97015)
Rates: $60-$99
(503) 723-3450
(800) 228-5150

CLATSKANIE

NORTHWOODS INN
945 E Columbia River Hwy (97016)
Rates: n/a
(503) 728-4311

COLUMBIA RIVER GORGE

See Cascade Locks, Hood River, The Dalles, Portland and Troutdale for additional lodging.

CONDON

CONDON MOTEL
216 N Washington (97823)
Rates: $38
(541) 384-2181

COOS BAY

BEST WESTERN HOLIDAY MOTEL
411 N Bayshore Dr (97420)
Rates: $73-$98
(541) 269-5111
(800) 528-1234
(800) 228-8655

COOS BAY MANOR B&B
955 S 5th St (97420)
Rates: $65-$100
(541) 269-1224
(800) 269-1224

EDGEWATER INN
275 E Johnson St (97420)
Rates: $85-$99
(541) 267-0423
(800) 233-0423

LAZY J MOTEL
1143 Hill St (97420)
Rates: n/a
(541) 269-9666

MOTEL 6 PREMIER
1445 N Bayshore Dr (97420)
Rates: $52-$66
(541) 267-7171
(800) 466-8356

PLAINVIEW MOTEL
2760 Cape Arago Hwy (97420)
Rates: $40-$95
(541) 888-5166
(800) 962-2815

RED LION INN
1313 N Bayshore Dr (97420)
Rates: $89-$89
(541) 267-4141
(800) 733-5466

TIMBER LODGE MOTEL
1001 N Bayshore Dr (97420)
Rates: n/a
(541) 267-7066
(800) 782-7592

COQUILLE

MYRTLE LANE MOTEL
787 N Central Blvd (97423)
Rates: $34-$39
(541) 396-2102

CORVALLIS

ASHWOOD B&B
2940 NW Ashwood Dr (97330)
Rates: $60-$70
(541) 757-9772

BEST INN & SUITES
935 NW Garfield (97330)
Rates: $48-$64
(541) 758-9125
(800) 237-8466

BUDGET INN
1480 SW 3rd St (97330)
Rates: $28-$55
(541) 752-8756

ECONO LODGE
345 NW 2nd St (97330)
Rates: $40-$50
(541) 752-9601
(800) 553-2666

JASON INN
800 NW 9th St (97330)
Rates: $36-$48
(541) 753-7326
(800) 346-3291

SHANICO INN
1113 NW 9th St (97330)
Rates: $56-$80
(541) 754-7474
(800) 432-1233

SUPER 8 MOTEL
407 NW 2nd St (97330)
Rates: $50-$90
(541) 758-8088
(800) 800-8000

TOWNE HOUSE MOTOR INN
350 SW 4th St (97330)
Rates: $40-$48
(541) 753-4496
(800) 898-4496

COTTAGE GROVE

BEST WESTERN VILLAGE GREEN
725 Row River Rd (97424)
Rates: $59-$129
(541) 942-2491
(800) 528-1234
(800) 343-7666

CITY CENTER MOTEL
737 Hwy 99 S (97424)
Rates: $32-$35
(541) 942-8322

COMFORT INN
845 Gateway Blvd (97424)
Rates: $59-$134
(541) 942-9747
(800) 228-5150
(800) 944-0287

HOLIDAY INN EXPRESS
1601 Gateway Blvd (97424)
Rates: $58-$125
(541) 942-1000
(800) 465-4329

RELAX INN
1030 Pacific
Hwy 99 N (97424)
Rates: $32-$38
(541) 942-5132

RIVER COUNTRY INN
71864 London Rd
(97424)
Rates: $65
(541) 942-9334

CRATER LAKE

WHISPERING PINES MOTEL
Hwy 138 & 97
(97604)
Rates: $35-$55
(541) 365-2259

CRESCENT

WOODSMAN COUNTRY LODGE
136740 Hwy 97
(97733)
Rates: $35-$41
(541) 433-2710

CRESCENT LAKE JUNCTION

CRESCENT CREEK COTTAGES
Hwy 58, Milepost 71 (97425)
Rates: $30-$50
(541) 433-2324

CRESCENT LAKE LODGE & RESORT
P.O. Box 73 (97425)
Rates: $45-$120
(541) 433-2505

ODELL LAKE LODGE & RESORT
Hwy 58, Milepost 67 (97425)
Rates: $42-$95
(541) 433-2540

SHELTER COVE RESORT
W Odell Lake Rd,
Hwy 58 (97425)
Rates: $65-$85
(541) 433-2548

WILLAMETTE PASS INN
Hwy 58, Milepost 69 (97425)
Rates: $58-$88
(541) 433-2211

CRESWELL

MOTEL ORLEANS
345 E Oregon Ave
(97426)
Rates: $35-$55
(541) 895-3341
(800) 626-1900

CURTIN

STARDUST MOTEL
455 Bear Creek Rd
(97428)
Rates: $28-$38
(541) 942-5706
(888) 657-2527

DALLAS

BEST WESTERN DALLAS INN & SUITES
250 Orchard Dr
(97338)
Rates $59-$129
(503) 623-6000
(800) 528-1234

RIVERSIDE INN
517 Main St
(97338)
Rates: $40-$50
(503) 623-8163

DAYVILLE

FISH HOUSE INN B&B
110 Franklin
Hwy 26 (97825)
Rates: $40-$65
(541) 987-2124
(888) 256-FISH

DEADWOOD

CEDARHILL GETAWAY RENTAL
92201 W Fork Rd
(97430)
Rates: $20-$25
(per person)
(541) 345-1619
(877) 345-1633

DEPOE BAY

CROWN PACIFIC INN
50 NE Bechill St
(97341)
Rates: $70-$88
(541) 765-7773
(888) 845-5131

INN AT ARCH ROCK
70 NW Sunset St
(97341)
Rates: $79-$275
(541) 765-2560
(800) 767-1835

SURFRIDER RESORT
3115 NW Hwy 101
(97341)
Rates: $75-$130
(541) 764-2311
(800) 662-2378

DETROIT

ALL SEASONS MOTEL
130 Breitenbush
Rd (97342)
Rates: $40-$80
(503) 854-3421

DIAMOND LAKE

DIAMOND LAKE RESORT
Diamond Lake
(97601)
Rates: $56-$135
(541) 793-3333
(800) 733-7593

ELGIN

CITY CENTRE MOTEL
51 S 7th Ave
(97827)
Rates: $42-$44
(541) 437-2441

MINAM MOTEL
72601 Hwy 82
(97827)
Rates: $27-$48
(541) 437-4475

ELKTON

THE BIG K GUEST RANCH
20029 Hwy 138 W
(97436)
Rates: $130-$225
(541) 583-2295
(800) 390-2445

ENTERPRISE

BOUCHER GUEST COTTAGE
83162 W Dorrance
Ln (97828)
Rates: $55+
(541) 426-3209

PONDEROSA MOTEL
102 Greenwood
SE (97828)
Rates: $54-$64
(541) 426-3186

WILDERNESS INN
301 W North St
(97828)
Rates: $49-$59
(541) 426-4535
(800) 965-1205

EUGENE

BEST WESTERN GREENTREE INN
1759 Franklin
Blvd (97403)
Rates: $64-$86
(541) 485-2727
(800) 528-1234

BEST WESTERN NEW OREGON MOTEL
1655 Franklin
Blvd (97403)
Rates: $64-$86
(541) 683-3669
(800) 528-1234

CAMPUS INN
390 East Bdwy
(97401)
Rates: $58-$72
(541) 343-3376
(800) 888-6313

CLASSIC RESIDENCE INN
1140 W 6th Ave
(97402)
Rates: $30-$40
(541) 343-0730

COUNTRY SQUIRE INN
33100 Van Duyn
Rd (97401)
Rates: $39-$100
(541) 484-2000

COURTESY INN
345 W 6th Ave
(97401)
Rates: $35-$65
(541) 345-3391

HAWTHORN INN & SUITES
8 Club Rd (97401)
Rates: n/a
(800) 527-1133

HILTON HOTEL
66 E 6th & Oak Sts
(97401)
Rates: $120-$212
(541) 342-2000
(800) 445-8667
(800) 937-6660

MOTEL 6
3690 Glenwood
Dr (97403)
Rates: $44-$60
(541) 687-2395
(800) 466-8356

PINE KNOT MOTEL
1410 W 6th Ave
(97402)
Rates: $25-$55
(541) 485-0742

QUALITY INN & SUITES
2121 Franklin
Blvd (97403)
Rates: $65-$100
(541) 342-1243
(800) 228-5151

RAMADA INN
225 Coburg Rd
(97401)
Rates: $68-$100
(541) 342-5181
(800) 272-6232
(800) 917-5500

RED LION INN
205 Coburg Rd
(97401)
Rates: $65-$110
(541) 342-5201
(800) 733-5466

SIXTY-SIX MOTEL
755 E Bdwy
(97401)
Rates: $30-$45
(541) 342-5041

TRAVELODGE
1859 Franklin
Blvd (97403)
Rates: $65-$75
(541) 342-6383
(800) 578-7878

THE VALLEY RIVER INN
1000 Valley River
Way (97440)
Rates: $170-$300
(541) 687-0123
(800) 543-8266

FLORENCE

LIGHTHOUSE INN
155 Hwy 101
(97439)
Rates: $65-$75
(541) 997-3221

MERCER LAKE RESORT
88875 Bay Berry
Ln (97439)
Rates: $60-$70
(541) 997-3633
(800) 355-3633

MONEY SAVER MOTEL
170 Hwy 101
(97439)
Rates: $59-$69
(541) 997-7131

OCEAN BREEZE MOTEL
85165 Hwy 101 S
(97439)
Rates: $60-$83
(541) 997-2642
(800) 753-2642

PARK MOTEL
85034 Hwy 101 S
(97439)
Rates: $49-$129
(541) 997-2634
(800) 392-0441

VILLA WEST MOTEL
901 Hwy 101
(97439)
Rates: $50-$58
(541) 997-3457

FOREST GROVE

BUDGET INN
1925 C St (97116)
Rates: $38-$60
(503) 359-5766

HOLIDAY MOTEL
3224 Pacific Ave
(97116)
Rates: $45-$60
(503) 357-7411

FORT KLAMATH

CRATER LAKE RESORT & CABINS
50711 Hwy 62,
Milepost 92
(97626)
Rates: $35-$60
(541) 381-2349

SUN PASS RANCH BED & BREAKFST
52125 Hwy 62
(97626)
Rates: n/a
(541) 381-2259

WILSON'S COTTAGES
57997 Hwy 62
(97626)
Rates: $40-$75
(541) 381-2209

FOSSIL

BRIDGE CREEK FLORA INN B&B
828 Main St
B(97830)
Rates: $60-$75
(541) 763-2355

GARIBALDI

BAY SHORE INN
227 Garibaldi Ave
(97118)
Rates: $69-$110
(541) 322-2552

HARBOR VIEW INN
302 S 7th St (97118)
Rates: $30-$55
(541) 322-3251

TILLA-BAY MOTEL
805 Garibaldi Ave
(97118)
Rates: $39+
(541) 322-3405

GEARHART

GEARHART BY THE SEA RESORT
1157 N Marion
(97138)
Rates: $126-$178
(503) 738-8331
(800) 547-0115

SURFSIDE CONDOS ON THE BEACH
P.O. Box 2591
(97138)
Rates: $69-$145
(503) 738-6384

WINDJAMMER MOTEL
4253 Hwy 101 N
(97138)
Rates: $48-$117
(503) 738-3250
(800) 479-5191

GLADSTONE

BUDGET INN
19240 SE
McLaughlin Blvd
(97027)
Rates: $35-$85
(503) 656-1955
(800) 655-9368

GLENEDEN BEACH

BEACHCOMBERS HAVEN
7045 NW Glen
Ave (97388)
Rates: $125-$165
(541) 764-2252
(800) 428-5533

WESTIN SALISHAN LODGE & GOLF RESORT
7760 Hwy 101 N
(98388)
Rates: $249-$300
(541) 764-2371
(800) SALISHAN

GLIDE

STEELHEAD RUN B&B & FINE ART GALLERY
23049 N Umpqua
Hwy, Box 639
(97443)
Rates: $65-$105
(541) 496-0563
(800) 348-0563

GOLD BEACH

BEST WESTERN INN OF THE BEACHCOMBER
29266 Ellensburg
Ave (97444)
Rates: $89-$105
(541) 247-6691
(800) 528-1234
(888) 790-2378

CITY CENTER MOTEL
94200 Harlow St
(97444)
Rates: $40-$80
(541) 247-6675

DRIFT IN MOTEL
94260 Port Dr
(97444)
Rates: $25-$75
(541) 247-4547
(800) 424-3833

ECONO LODGE
29171 Ellensburg
Ave (97444)
Rates: $60-$99
(541) 247-6606
(800) 553-2666

IRELAND'S RUSTIC LODGES
29330 Ellensburg
Ave S (97444)
Rates: $50-$70
(541) 247-7718

JOT'S RESORT & CONDOS
94360 Wedderburn
Loop Rd (97444)
Rates: $85-$135
(541) 247-6676
(800) 367-5687

KIMBALL CREEK BEND RESORT
97136 N Bank
Rogue (97444)
Rates: $41-$70
(541) 247-7580

MOTEL 6
94433 Jerry's Flat
Rd (97444)
Rates: $30-$79
(541) 247-4533
(800) 466-8356
(800) 759-4533

NESIKA BEACH VACATION RENTAL
33026 Nesika Rd
(97444)
Rates: $75-$80
(541) 247-6434

OREGON TRAIL LODGE
29855 N
Ellensburg Ave
(97444)
Rates: $21-$70
(541) 247-6030

ROGUE LANDING
94749 Jerry's Flat
Rd (97444)
Rates: $20-$50
(541) 247-6105

SAND 'N SEA MOTEL
29362 S
Ellensburg Ave
(97444)
Rates: $59-$90
(541) 247-6658
(800) 808-7263

SHORE CLIFF INN
29346 Ellensburg
Ave (97444)
Rates: $60-$75
(541) 247-7091

WESTERN VILLAGE MOTEL
29399 S
Ellensburg Ave
(97444)
Rates: $40-$60
(541) 247-6611

WHIMSEY HOUSE VACATION RENTAL
94249 Third St
(97444)
Rates: $85
(541) 247-2661

GOVERNMENT CAMP

MT. HOOD INN
87450 E Govt
Camp Loop
(97028)
Rates: $134-$164
(503) 272-3205
(800) 443-7777

SUMMIT MEADOW CABINS
P.O. Box 235
(97028)
Rates: $90-$170
(503) 272-3494

GRANTS PASS

BEST WESTERN GRANTS PASS INN
111 NE Agness
Ave (97526)
Rates: $73-$85
(541) 476-1117
(800) 528-1234
(800) 553-7666

BEST WESTERN INN AT THE ROGUE
8959 Rogue River
Hwy (97527)
Rates: $85-$105
(541) 582-2200
(800) 528-1234
(800) 238-0700

CITY CENTER MOTEL
741 NE 6th St
(97526)
Rates: n/a
(541) 476-6134

COMFORT INN
1889 NE 6th St
(97526)
Rates: $39-$75
(541) 479-8301
(800) 228-5150

FLAMINGO INN
728 NW 6th St
(97526)
Rates: $30-$42
(541) 476-6601

HAWTHORN INN & SUITES
243 NE Morgan Ln (97526)
Rates: $64-$88
(541) 472-1808
(800) 527-1133

HOLIDAY INN EXP
105 NE Agness (97526)
Rates: $83-$94
(541) 471-6144
(800) 465-4329
(800) 838-7666

MOTEL 6
1800 NE 7th St (97526)
Rates: $45-$61
(541) 474-1331
(800) 466-8356

REDWOOD MOTEL
815 NE 6th St (97526)
Rates: $58-$92
(541) 476-0878

REGAL LODGE
1400 NW 6th St (97526)
Rates: $30-$35
(541) 479-3305

RIVERSIDE INN RESORT
971 SE 6th St (97526)
Rates: $65-$350
(541) 476-6873
(800) 334-4567

ROD & REEL MOTEL
7875 Rogue River Hwy (97527)
Rates: $40-$75
(541) 582-1516
(800) 516-5557

ROGUE RIVER INN
6285 Rogue River Hwy (97527)
Rates: $43-$79
(541) 582-1120

ROGUE VALLEY MOTEL
7799 Rogue River Hwy (97527)
Rates: $42-$72
(541) 582-3762

SHILO INN
1880 NW 6th St (97526)
Rates: $49-$109
(541) 479-8391
(800) 222-2244

SUPER 8 MOTEL
1949 NE 7th St (97526)
Rates: $49-$65
(541) 474-0888
(800) 800-8000

THRIFTLODGE
748 SE 7th St (97526)
Rates: $32-$50
(541) 476-7793
(800) 525-9055

TRAVELODGE
1950 NW Vine St (97526)
Rates: $50-$62
(541) 479-6611
(800) 578-7878

GRESHAM

BRIARWOOD INN
2572 NE Hogan Dr (97030)
Rates: $69-$129
(503) 907-1777
(877) 907-1777

HAWTHORN INN & SUITES
2323 NE 181st Ave (97230)
Rates: $75-$96
(503) 492-4000
(800) 527-1133

TRAVELERS INN & SUITES
121 NE 181st Ave (97230)
Rates: $49-$69
(503) 661-5100
(888) 599-5100

HALFWAY

CLEAR CREEK FARM BED & BREAKFAST
Rt 1, Box 138 (97834)
Rates: $55-$60
(541) 742-2238
(800) 742-4992

PINE VALLEY LODGE
163 N Main St (97834)
Rates: $65-$105
(541) 742-2027

HALSEY

PIONEER VILLA TRUCK PLAZA
33180 Hwy 228 (97348)
Rates: $45
(541) 369-2801

HARBOR

BEST WESTERN BEACHFRONT INN
16008 Boat Basin Rd (97415)
Rates: $69-$135
(541) 469-7779
(800) 528-1234
(800) 468-4081

HERMISTON

ECONOMY INN
835 N 1st St (97838)
Rates: $40-$45
(541) 567-5516
(888) 567-9521

OXFORD INN
655 N 1st St (97838)
Rates: $39-$59
(541) 567-7777
(888) 729-7848

OXFORD SUITES
1050 N 1st St (97838)
Rates: $69-$109
(541) 564-8000
(888) 545-7848

THE WAY INN
635 S Hwy 395 (97838)
Rates: $32-$34
(541) 567-5561
(888) 564-8767

HILLSBORO

BEST WESTERN CAVANAUGHS INN
3500 NE Cornell Rd (97124)
Rates: $90-$110
(503) 648-3500
(800) 528-1234

CANDLEWOOD SUITES
3133 NE Shute Rd (97124)
Rates: $69-$118
(503) 681-2121
(888) 226-3539

RESIDENCE INN PORTLAND WEST
18855 NW Tanasbourne Dr (97124)
Rates: $89-$169
(503) 531-3200
(800) 331-3131

WELLESLEY INN & SUITES
19311 NW Cornell Rd (97124)
Rates: $74-$94
(503) 439-0706
(800) 444-8888

HOOD RIVER

BERYL HOUSE BED & BREAKFST
4079 Barrett Dr (97031)
Rates: $60-$70
(541) 386-5567

BEST WESTERN HOOD RIVER INN
1108 E Marina Way (97031)
Rates: $79-$119
(541) 386-2200
(800) 528-1234
(800) 828-7873

COLUMBIA GORGE HOTEL
4000 Westcliff Dr (97031)
Rates: $150-$275
(541) 386-5566
(800) 345-1921

HACKETT HOUSE BED & BREAKFST
922 State St (97031)
Rates: $45-$75
(541) 386-1014

HOOD RIVER VACATION RENTALS
823 Cascade Ave (97031)
Rates: n/a
(541) 387-3113

LOST LAKE RESORT
Lost Lake Rd (97031)
Rates: $45-$95
(541) 386-6366

MEREDITH GORGE MOTEL
4300 Westcliff Dr (97031)
Rates: $49-$79
(541) 386-1515

VAGABOND LODGE
4070 Westcliff Dr (97031)
Rates: $44-$73
(541) 386-2992

IDLEYLD PARK

NORTH UMPQUA RESORT
23885 N Umpqua Hwy (97447)
Rates: $27-$39
(541) 496-0149

JACKSONVILLE

JACKSONVILLE INN HISTORIC HOTEL
175 E California St (97530)
Rates: $115-$245
(541) 899-1900
(800) 321-9344

THE STAGE LODGE
830 N 5th St (97530)
Rates: $72-$145
(431) 899-3953
(800) 253-8254

JOHN DAY

BEST WESTERN INN
315 W Main St (97845)
Rates: $58-$114
(541) 575-1700
(800) 528-1234
(800) 243-2628

AREA CODES - If the local number doesn't connect, check for a new area code.

BUDGET 8 MOTEL
711 W Main St
(97845)
Rates: $38-$52
(541) 575-2155

BUDGET INN
250 E Main St
(97845)
Rates: $38-$45
(541) 575-2100
(800) 854-4442

DREAMERS LODGE
144 N Canyon
Blvd (97845)
Rates: $44-$64
(541) 575-0526
(800) 654-2849

SONSHINE BED & BREAKFAST
210 NW Canton
(97845)
Rates: $55-$65
(541) 575-1827

SUNSET INN
390 W Main St
(97845)
Rates: $44-$58
(541) 575-1462
(800) 452-4899

TRAVELLER'S MOTEL
755 S Canyon
Blvd (97845)
Rates: $30+
(541) 575-2076

JORDAN VALLEY

SAHARA MOTEL
607 Main St
(97910)
Rates: $42-$44
(541) 586-2810
(800) 828-4432

JOSEPH

COLLETTS' CABINS & FINE ARTS
84681 Ponderosa
Lane (97846)
Rates: $60-$115
(541) 432-2391

DRAGON MEADOWS B&B
504 N Lake St
(97846)
Rates: $65+
(541) 432-1027

INDIAN LODGE MOTEL
201 S Main St
(97846)
Rates: $36-$57
(541) 432-2651

JUNCTION CITY

GUEST HOUSE MOTEL
1335 Ivy St (97448)
Rates: $44-$80
(541) 998-6524
(800) 835-5170

KEIZER

WITTENBERG INN
5188 Wittenberg
Ln (97303)
Rates: $59-$129
(503) 390-4733
(800) 299-7221

KENO

GREEN SPRINGS BOX R RANCH
16799 Hwy 66
(97627)
Rates: $110-$150
(541) 482-1873

KERBY

HOLIDAY MOTEL
24810 Redwood
Hwy (97531)
Rates: $47-$51
(503) 592-3003

KING CITY

BEST WESTERN NORTHWIND INN & SUITES
16105 SW Pacific
Hwy (97224)
Rates: $79-$104
(503) 431-2100
(800) 528-1234

KLAMATH FALLS

A-1 BUDGET MOTEL
3844 Hwy 97 N
(97601)
Rates: $38-$50
(541) 884-8104

BEST WESTERN KLAMATH INN
4061 S 6th St (97603)
Rates: $80-$123
(541) 882-1200
(800) 528-1234

CIMARRON MOTOR INN
3060 S 6th St
(97603)
Rates: $45-$65
(541) 882-4601
(800) 742-2648

ECONO LODGE
75 Main St (97601)
Rates: $31-$115
(541) 884-7735
(800) 553-2666

HARRIMAN SPRINGS RESORT
26661 Rocky Point
Rd (97601)
Rates: n/a
(541) 356-2331

HIGH CHAPARRAL MOTEL
5440 Hwy 97 N
(97601)
Rates: $22-$90
(541) 882-4675

HILL VIEW MOTEL
5543 S 6th St
(97601)
Rates: $38-$45
(541) 883-7771

LAKE OF THE WOODS RESORT
950 Harriman Rd
(97601)
Rates: $55-$80
(541) 949-8300

MAVERICK MOTEL
1220 Main St
(97601)
Rates: $39-$45
(541) 882-6688
(800) 404-6690

MOTEL 6
5136 S 6th St
(97601)
Rates: $45-$61
(541) 884-2110
(800) 466-8356

OLYMPIC LODGE
3006 Green
Springs Dr (97601)
Rates: $30-$57
(541) 883-8800

OREGON MOTEL 8
5225 Hwy 97 N
(97601)
Rates: $44-$48
(541) 883-3431

QUALITY INN
100 Main St
(97601)
Rates: $53-$99
(541) 882-4666
(800) 228-5151
(800) 732-4666

RED LION INN
3612 S 6th St
(97603)
Rates: $59-$84
(541) 882-8864
(800) 733-5466

ROCK-WOOD MOTEL
2005 Biehn St
(97601)
Rates: n/a
(541) 882-9992

ROCKY POINT RESORT
28121 Rocky Point
Rd (97601)
Rates: $48-$89
(541) 356-2287

SHILO SUITES HOTEL
2500 Almond St
(97601)
Rates: $89-$125
(541) 885-7980
(800) 222-2244

SOUTH ENTRANCE MOTEL
9339 Hwy 97 S
(97601)
Rates: n/a
(541) 883-1994

SUPER 8 MOTEL
3805 Hwy 97 N
(97601)
Rates: $47-$64
(541) 884-8880
(800) 800-8000

TRAVELODGE
11 Main St (97601)
Rates: $30-$52
(541) 882-4494
(800) 578-7878

LA GRANDE

GREENWELL MOTEL
305 Adams Ave
(97850)
Rates: $25-$30
(541) 963-4134
(800) 772-0991

HOWARD JOHNSON INN
2612 Island Ave
(97850)
Rates: $67-$87
(541) 963-7195
(800) 446-4656

MOON MOTEL
2116 Adams Ave
(97850)
Rates: n/a
(541) 963-2724

ORCHARD MOTEL
2206 Adams Ave
(97850)
Rates: $30-$39
(541) 963-6160

STARDUST LODGE
402 Adams Ave
(97850)
Rates: $27-$50
(541) 963-4166

TRAVELODGE
2215 Adams Ave
(97850)
Rates: $44-$74
(541) 963-7116
(800) 578-7878

LA PINE

BEST WESTERN NEWBERRY STATION
16515 Reed Rd &
Hwy 97 (97739)
Rates: $55-$155
(541) 536-5130
(800) 528-1234
(800) 210-8616

DIAMOND STONE GUEST LODGE BED & BREAKFST
16693 Sprague
Loop (97739)
Rates: $75-$120
(541) 536-6263
(800) 600-6263

EAST LAKE RESORT & MARKETPLACE
22430 East Lake
Rd (97739)
Rates: $35-$105
(541) 536-2230

HIGHLANDER MOTEL
51511 Hwy 97 S
(97739)
Rates: $30-$51
(541) 536-2131

AREA CODES - If the local number doesn't connect, check for a new area code.

LAMPLITER MOTEL
51526 Hwy 97 S
(97739)
Rates: $32-$36
(541) 536-2931

PAULINA LAKE RESORT
P.O. Box 7 (97739)
Rates: $65-$135
(541) 536-2240

TIMBERCREST INN
52560 Hwy 97 S
(97739)
Rates: $35-$45
(541) 536-1737

WEST VIEW MOTEL
51371 Hwy 97 S
(97739)
Rates: $36-$39
(541) 536-2115
(800) 440-2115

LAKE OSWEGO

BEST WESTERN SHERWOOD INN
15700 SW Upper
Boones Ferry Rd
(97034)
Rates: $55-$75
(503) 620-2980
(800) 528-1234

CROWNE PLAZA
14811 Kruse Oaks
Blvd (97035)
Rates: $159-$180
(503) 624-8400
(800) 227-6963

RESIDENCE INN PORTLAND SOUTH
15200 SW Bangy
Rd (97035)
Rates: $145-$165
(503) 684-2603
(800) 331-3131

LAKESIDE

LAKESHORE LODGE
290 S 8th St
(97449)
Rates: $34-$49
(541) 759-3161
(800) 759-3951

SEADRIFT MOTEL
11022 Coast Hwy
101 (97449)
Rates: $36-$44
(541) 759-3102

LAKEVIEW

BEST WESTERN SKYLINE MOTOR LODGE
414 North G St
(97630)
Rates: $70-$90
(541) 947-2194
(800) 528-1234

HUNTER'S HOT SPRINGS RESORT
Hwy 395 N (97630)
Rates: $45-$55
(541) 947-4800

INTERSTATE 8 MOTEL
354 North K St
(97630)
Rates: $34-$38
(541) 947-3341

LAKEVIEW LODGE MOTEL
301 North G St
(97630)
Rates: $40-$80
(541) 947-2181

RIM ROCK MOTEL
727 South F St
(97630)
Rates: $30-$32
(541) 947-2185

LEBANON

CASCADE CITY CENTER MOTEL
1296 Main St
(97355)
Rates: $32-$45
(541) 258-8154

SHANICO INN
1840 Main St
(97355)
Rates: $40-$46
(541) 259-2601

LINCOLN CITY

ANCHOR MOTEL AND LODGE
4417 SW Hwy 101
(97367)
Rates: $40-$60
(541) 996-3810
(800) 582-8611

BEL-AIRE MOTEL
2945 NW Hwy
101 (97367)
Rates: n/a
(541) 994-2984

BEST WESTERN LINCOLN SANDS INN
535 NW Inlet St
(97367)
Rates: $99-$399
(541) 994-4227
(800) 528-1234
(800) 445-3234

BLUE HERON LANDING MOTEL
4006 W Devils
Lake Rd (97367)
Rates: $59-$64
(541) 994-4708

BUDGET INN MOTEL
1713 NW 21st St
(97367)
Rates: $36-$54
(541) 994-5281

CITY CENTER MOTEL
1014 NE Hwy 101
(97367)
Rates: $35-$65
(541) 994-2612

COHO INN
1635 NW Harbor
(97367)
Rates: $109-$134
(541) 994-3684
(800) 848-7006

DOLPHIN MOTEL
1018 SE Hwy 101
(97367)
Rates: $35-$75
(541) 996-2124

EDGECLIFF MOTEL
3733 SW Hwy 101
(97367)
Rates: $50-$95
(541) 996-2055

ENCHANTED COTTAGE B&B
4507 SW Coast
(97367)
Rates: n/a
(541) 996-4101

ESTER LEE MOTEL
3803 SW Hwy 101
(97367)
Rates: $70-$90
(541) 996-3606
(888) 996-3606

HIDEAWAY OCEANFRONT MOTEL
810 SW 10th St
(97367)
Rates: n/a
(541) 994-8874

LINCOLN CITY INN
1091 SE 1st St
(97367)
Rates: $59-$99
(541) 996-4400

O'DYSIUS HOTEL
120 NW Inlet Ct
(97367)
Rates: $145-$289
(541) 994-4121
(800) 869-8069

OVERLOOK MOTEL
3521 SW Anchor
(97367)
Rates: $52-$115
(541) 996-3300

PACIFIC REST B&B
1611 NE 11th St
(97367)
Rates: n/a
(541) 994-2337

SAILOR JACK'S HIDDEN COVE
1035 NW Harbor
Ave (97367)
Rates: $59-$138
(541) 994-3696
(888) 432-8346

SEA ECHO MOTEL
3510 NE Hwy 101
(97367)
Rates: $45+
(541) 994-2575

SEA HORSE OCEANFRONT
2039 N Harbor Dr
(97367)
Rates: $50-$150
(541) 994-2101
(800) 662-2101

SEA REST MOTEL
1249 NW 15th St
(97367)
Rates: n/a
(541) 994-3053

SEAGULL BEACHFRONT MOTEL
1511 NW Harbor
Ave (97367)
Rates: $46-$199
(541) 994-2948
(800) 422-0219

SHILO OCEANFRONT RESORT
1501 NW 40th Pl
(97367)
Rates: $49-$259
(541) 994-3655
(800) 222-2244

SURFTIDES BEACH RESORT
2945 NW Jetty
Ave (97367)
Rates: $56-$101
(541) 994-2191
(800) 452-2159

WESTSHORE OCEANFRONT MOTEL
3127 SW Anchor
Ave (97367)
Rates: $79-$89
(541) 996-2091
(800) 621-3187

WHISTLING WINDS
3264 NW Jetty
Ave (97367)
Rates: n/a
(541) 994-6155

MADRAS

BEST WESTERN RAMA INN
12 SW 4th (97741)
Rates: $59-$99
(541) 475-6141
(800) 528-1234
(888) 726-2466

BUDGET INN
133 NE 5th St
(97741)
Rates: $35-$60
(541) 475-3831

HOFFY'S MOTEL
600 N Hwy 26
(97741)
Rates: $32-$125
(541) 475-4633
(800) 227-6865

JUNIPER MOTEL
414 N Hwy 26
(97741)
Rates: $35-$65
(541) 475-6186
(800) 244-1399

ROYAL DUTCH MOTEL
1101 SW Hwy 97
(97741)
Rates: $32+
(541) 475-2281

SONNY'S MOTEL
1539 SW Hwy 97
(97741)
Rates: $57-$110
(541) 475-7217
(800) 624-6137

MANZANITA

SUNSET SURF MOTEL
248 Ocean Rd
(97130)
Rates: $50-$119
(541) 368-5224
(800) 243-8035

MAUPIN

DESCHUTES MOTEL
616 Mill St (97037)
Rates: $45-$50
(541) 395-2626

THE OASIS RESORT
609 Hwy 197
(97037)
Rates: $50-$70
(541) 395-2611

McKENZIE BRIDGE

BELKNAP LODGE & HOT SPRINGS CABINS
59296 Belknap
Spgs Rd (97413)
Rates: n/a
(541) 822-3512

THE COUNTRY PLACE
56245 Delta Dr
(97413)
Rates: $75-$220
(541) 822-6008

McMINNVILLE

PARAGON MOTEL
2065 Hwy 99 W
(97128)
Rates: $39-$91
(503) 472-9493
(800) 525-5469

MEDFORD

BEST INN & SUITES
1015 S Riverside
Ave (97501)
Rates: $49-$65
(541) 773-8266
(800) 237-8466

BEST WESTERN HORIZON INN
1154 Barnett Rd
(97504)
Rates $71-$84
(541) 779-5085
(800) 528-1234
(800) 452-2255

BEST WESTERN PONY SOLDIER INN
2340 Crater Lake
Hwy (97504)
Rates: $82-$99
(541) 779-2011
(800) 528-1234
(800) 634-7669

CAPRI MOTEL
250 Barnett Rd
(97501)
Rates: $33-$42
(541) 773-7796

CEDAR LODGE MOTOR INN
518 N Riverside
Ave (97501)
Rates: $45-$62
(541) 773-7361
(800) 282-3419

HORIZON INN & SUITES
1154 E Barnett Rd
(97501)
Rates: $54-$125
(541) 779-5085
(800) 452-2255

MOTEL 6 NORTH
2400 Biddle Rd
(97504)
Rates: $48-$64
(541) 779-0550
(800) 466-8356

MOTEL 6 SOUTH
950 Alba Dr (97504)
Rates: $37-$49
(541) 773-4290
(800) 466-8356

PEAR TREE MOTEL
300 Pear Tree Lane
(97504)
Rates: $65-$73
(541) 535-4445
(800) 645-7332

RED LION HOTEL
200 N Riverside
Ave (97501)
Rates: $69-$79
(541) 779-5811
(800) 733-5466

RESTON HOTEL
2300 Crater Lake
Hwy (97504)
Rates: $69-$130
(541) 779-3141
(800) 779-7829

SHILO INN
2111 Biddle Rd
(97504)
Rates: $45-$99
(541) 770-5151
(800) 222-2244

WINDMILL INN
1950 Biddle Rd
(97504)
Rates: $84
(541) 779-0050
(800) 547-4747

MERLIN

DOUBLETREE RANCH
6000 Abegg Rd
(97523)
Rates: $65-$75
(541) 476-1686

MERRILL

MERRILL MOTEL
P.O. Box 323
(97633)
Rates: n/a
(541) 798-5598

MILTON-FREEWATER

MORGAN INN
104 N Columbia
(97862)
Rates: $41-$105
(541) 938-5547
(800) 553-4017

OUT WEST MOTEL
84040 Hwy 11
(97862)
Rates: $37-$44
(541) 938-6647
(800) 881-6647

MILWAUKIE

MILWAUKIE INN
14015 SE
McLoughlin Blvd
(97267)
Rates: $35-$65
(503) 659-2125
(800) 255-1553

OCEANVIEW VACATION RENTALS
9981 SE 32nd Ave
(97222)
Rates: $60-$70
(503) 653-8378

MOLALLA

STAGE COACH INN MOTEL
415 Grange St
(97038)
Rates: $49-$70
(503) 829-4382

MONMOUTH

COLLEGE INN MOTEL
235 S Pacific Ave
(97361)
Rates: $35-$58
(503) 838-1711

COURTESY INN
270 N Pacific Hwy
(97361)
Rates: $50-$65
(503) 838-4438

MOSIER

HEWETT'S BED & BREAKFAST
501 Third St
(97040)
Rates: $45-$75
(541) 478-3455

MOUNT HOOD

MT. HOOD INN
87450 E Govt
Camp Loop
(97028)
Rates: $130-$160
(503) 272-3205
(800) 443-7777

SHAMROCK FOREST INN
59550 E Hwy 26
(97028)
Rates: $38-$69
(503) 622-4003

MYRTLE CREEK

QUICK STOP MOTEL & MARKET
6453 Dole Rd
(97457)
Rates: $32-$55
(541) 863-7267

MYRTLE POINT

MYRTLE TREES MOTEL
1010 8th St (97458)
Rates: $36-$45
(541) 572-5811

NESIKA BEACH

BREAKER HOUSE AT NESIKA BEACH
32864 Nesika
Beach Rd (97444)
Rates: $80-$145
(541) 247-6670

NESKOWIN

THE BREAKERS CONDOMINUMS
48060 Breakers
Blvd (97149)
Rates: $100-$205
(503) 392-3417

NETARTS

EDGEWATER MOTEL
First St (97143)
Rates: $72-$82
(503) 842-1300

SAMS VACATION RENTALS
1035 5th St Loop
(97143)
Rates: $55
(503) 842-5814

TERIMORE LODGING BY THE SEA
5105 Crab Ave
(97143)
Rates: $35-$97
(503) 842-4623
(800) 635-1821

AREA CODES - If the local number doesn't connect, check for a new area code.

THREE CAPES INN
4800 Netarts Hwy
W (97143)
Rates: $45-$60
(503) 842-4003

NEWBERG

SHILO INN
501 Sitka Ave
(97132)
Rates: $65-$89
(503) 537-0303
(800) 222-2244

NEWPORT

**AGATE BEACH
OCEAN FRONT
MOTEL**
175 NW Gilbert
Way (97365)
Rates: $90-$100
(541) 265-8746
(800) 755-5674

THE ANCHORAGE
7743 N Coast
Hwy (97365)
Rates: $60-$66
(541) 265-5463

**CITY CENTER
MOTEL**
538 SW Coast
Hwy (97365)
Rates: $38-$65
(541) 265-7381
(800) 628-9665

**DRIFTWOOD
VILLAGE MOTEL**
7947 N Coast
Hwy (97365)
Rates: $55-$125
(541) 265-5738

**HALLMARK
RESORT**
744 SW Elizabeth
St (97365)
Rates: $129-$239
(541) 265-2600
(888) 448-4449

**HOLIDAY INN
NEWPORT AT
AGATE BEACH**
3019 N Coast
Hwy (97365)
Rates: $119-$149
(541) 265-9411
(800) 465-4329
(800) 547-3310

**MONEY SAVER
MOTEL**
861 SW Coast
Hwy 101 (97365)
Rates: $44-$85
(541) 265-2277

**NEWPORT
MOTOR INN**
1311 N Hwy 101
(97365)
Rates: $26-$48
(541) 265-8516

**PENNY SAVER
MOTEL**
710 N Hwy 101
(97365)
Rates: $30-$60
(541) 265-6631

**SANDS MOTOR
LODGE**
206 N Coast Hwy
(97365)
Rates: $36-$48
(541) 265-5321

**SHILO
OCEANFRONT
RESORT**
536 SW Elizabeth
(97365)
Rates: $99-$159
(541) 265-7701
(800) 222-2244

**STARFISH POINT
CONDOS**
140 NW 48th St
(97365)
Rates: $115-$175
(541) 265-3751

**SURF 'N SAND
MOTEL**
8143 N Hwy 101
(97365)
Rates: $58-$89
(541) 265-2215

TIDES INN MOTEL
715 SW Bay St
(97365)
Rates: $38-$55
(541) 265-7202

TRAVELERS INN
606 SW Coast
Hwy (97365)
Rates: $35-$75
(541) 265-7723
(800) 615-2627

VAL-U-INN MOTEL
531 SW Fall St
(97365)
Rates: $69-$150
(541) 265-6203
(800) 443-7777

**VIKINGS
COTTAGES**
729 NW Coast St
(97365)
Rates: $65-$80
(541) 265-2477
(800) 480-2477

**WEST WIND
MOTEL**
747 SW Coast St
(97365)
Rates: $40-$55
(541) 265-5388
(800) 305-5388

WILLER'S MOTEL
754 SW Coast
Hwy (97365)
Rates: $38-$80
(541) 265-2241
(800) 945-5377

NORTH BEND

**BAY BRIDGE
MOTEL**
33 US 101 (97459)
Rates: $45-$57
(541) 756-3151
(800) 557-3156

**CITY CENTER
MOTEL**
750 Connecticut
Ave (97459)
Rates: $28-$40
(541) 756-5118

**ITTY BITTY INN
BED & BREAKFST**
1504 Sherman Ave
(97459)
Rates: $40-$45
(541) 756-6398
(888) 276-9253

PARKSIDE INN
1480 Sherman Ave
(97459)
Rates: n/a
(541) 756-4124

**PONY VILLAGE
MOTOR LODGE**
Virginia Ave
(97459)
Rates: $45-$60
(541) 756-3191

NORTH
POWDER

**POWDER RIVER
MOTEL**
850 2nd St (97867)
Rates: $25-$38
(541) 898-2829

OAKLAND

RANCH MOTEL
581 John Long Rd
(97462)
Rates: $27-$75
(541) 849-2126

OAKRIDGE

ARBOR INN
48229 Hwy 58
(974632)
Rates: $27-$46
(541) 782-2611

**BEST WESTERN
OAKRIDGE INN**
47433 Hwy 58
(97463)
Rates: $55-$79
(541) 782-2212
(800) 528-1234

CASCADE MOTEL
47487 Hwy 58
(97463)
Rates: n/a
(541) 782-2602

**OAKRIDGE
MOTEL**
48197 Hwy 58 E
(97463)
Rates: $26-$30
(541) 782-2432

ODELL LAKE

**SHELTER COVE
RESORT**
Hwy 58, W Odell
Lake Rd (97044)
Rates: $60-$85
(541) 433-2548

OLALLIE LAKE
SCENIC AREA

**OLALLIE LAKE
RESORT CABINS**
Mt. Hood
National Forest
(97760)
Rates: $25-$75
(541) 504-1010

ONTARIO

BEST WESTERN INN
251 Goodfellow St
(97914)
Rates: $55-$155
(541) 889-2600
(800) 528-1234
(800) 828-0364

**BUDGET
COLONIAL INN**
1395 Tapadera
Ave (97914)
Rates: $27-$55
(541) 889-9615

BUDGET INN
1737 N Oregon St
(97914)
Rates: $35-$40
(541) 889-3101
(800) 905-0024

CARLILE MOTEL
589 N Oregon St
(97914)
Rates: $37-$65
(541) 889-8658
(800) 640-8658

HOLIDAY INN
1249 Tapadera
Ave (97914)
Rates: $72-$77
(541) 889-8621
(800) 465-4329

MOTEL 6
275 NE 12th St
(97914)
Rates: $31-$42
(541) 889-6617
(800) 466-8356

**OREGON TRAIL
MOTEL**
92 E Idaho Ave
(97914)
Rates: $25-$75
(541) 889-8633
(800) 895-7945

PLAZA MOTEL
1144 SW 4th Ave
(97914)
Rates: $25-$95
(541) 889-9641

SLEEP INN
1221 SE 1st Court
(97914)
Rates: $42-$65
(541) 881-0007
(800) 753-3746

STOCKMAN'S MOTEL
81 SW 1st St
(97914)
Rates: $35-$50
(541) 889-4446

SUPER 8 MOTEL
266 Goodfellow St
(97914)
Rates: $53-$115
(541) 889-8282
(800) 800-8000

OREGON CITY

RIVERSHORE HOTEL
1900 Clackamette
Dr (97045)
Rates: $72-$125
(503) 655-7141
(800) 443-7777

OTTER ROCK

ALPINE CHALETS
7045 Otter Crest
Loop (97369)
Rates: $80-$90
(541) 765-2572
(800) 825-5768

PACIFIC CITY

ANCHORAGE MOTEL
6585 Pacific Ave
(97135)
Rates: $44-$67
(503) 965-6773
(800) 941-6250

INN AT CAPE KIWANDA
33105 Cape
Kiwanda Dr
(97135)
Rates: $149-$159
(503) 965-7001
(888) 965-7001

INN AT PACIFIC CITY
35215 Brooten Rd
(97135)
Rates: $59-$69
(503) 965-6366
(888) 722-2489

PACIFIC CITY LODGING
35280 Brooten Rd
(97135)
Rates: $59-$79
(503) 965-6464
(888) 722-2489

SEA VIEW VACATION RENTALS
P.O. Box 1049
(97135)
Rates: $75-$235
(503) 965-7888

PENDLETON

BEST WESTERN PENDLETON INN
400 SE Nye Ave
(97801)
Rates: $59-$79
(541) 276-2135
(800) 528-1234

BUDGET INN
1807 SE Court Ave
(97801)
Rates: $30-$35
(541) 276-4521

CHAPARRAL MOTEL
620 SW Tutuilla
(97801)
Rates: $37-$57
(541) 276-8654

HOLIDAY INN EXPRESS
600 SE Nye Ave
(97801)
Rates: $45-$250
(541) 966-6520
(800) 465-4329

LET 'ER BUCK MOTEL
205 SE Dorion Ave
(97801)
Rates: $28-$42
(541) 276-3293

MOTEL 6
325 SE Nye Ave
(97801)
Rates: $32-$66
(541) 276-3160
(800) 466-8356

OXFORD SUITES
2400 SW Court Pl
(97801)
Rates: $79-$119
(541) 276-6000

RED LION INN
304 SE Nye Ave
(97801)
Rates: $55-$59
(541) 276-6141
(800) 733-5466

7 INN
I-84 exit 202
(97801)
Rates: $39-$60
(541) 276-4711
(800) REG7INN

SUPER 8 MOTEL
601 SE Nye Ave
(97801)
Rates: $47-$62
(541) 276-8881
(800) 800-8000

TRAVELODGE
411 SW Dorion
Ave (97801)
Rates: $49-$69
(541) 276-7531
(800) 578-7878

VAGABOND INN
210 SW Court Ave
(97801)
Rates: $28-$57
(541) 276-5252
(800) 522-1555

WILDHORSE RESORT HOTEL
72779 Hwy 331
(97801)
Rates: $63-$140
(541) 276-0355
(800) 654-WILD

PILOT ROCK

PILOT ROCK MOTEL
362 NE 4th St
(97868)
Rates: $30-$53
(541) 443-2851

PISTOL RIVER

ARCADIA ON THE OREGON COAST VACATION HOME
23154 Hwy 101
(97444)
Rates: n/a
(888) 227-1963

PORT ORFORD

CASTAWAY BY-THE-SEA MOTEL
545 W 5th St
(97465)
Rates: $45-$85
(541) 332-4502

SEA CREST MOTEL
44 Hwy 101
(97465)
Rates: $52-$71
(541) 332-3040
(888) 332-3040

SHORELINE MOTEL
206 6th St (97465)
Rates: $36-$46
(541) 332-2903

PORTLAND

ALADDIN MOTOR INN
8905 SW 30th Ave
(97219)
Rates: $39-$75
(503) 246-8241
(800) 292-4466

THE BENSON HOTEL
309 SW Broadway
at Oak (97205)
Rates: $190-$900
(503) 228-2000
(888) 5BENSON

BEST INN & SUITES
3828 NE 82nd Ave
(97220)
Rates: $63-$85
(503) 256-2550
(800) 237-8466

BEST VALUE INN
3310 SE 82nd Ave
(97266)
Rates: $33-$50
(503) 777-4786
(800) 358-5066

BEST WESTERN HISTORIC IMPERIAL HOTEL
400 SW Broadway
(97205)
Rates: $115-$140
(503) 228-7221
(800) 528-1234
(800) 452-2323

BEST WESTERN INN CONV CTR
420 NE Holladay
St (97232)
Rates: $75-$110
(503) 233-6331
(800) 528-1234
(800) 637-5958

BEST WESTERN INN AT THE MEADOWS
1215 N Hayden
Meadows Dr
(97217)
Rates: $89-$109
(503) 286-9600
(800) 528-1234

BUDGET VALUE VIKING MOTEL
6701 N Interstate
Ave (97217)
Rates: $38-$48
(503) 285-6687
(800) 308-5097

CYPRESS INN
809 SW King St
(97205)
Rates: $45-$80
(503) 226-6288
(800) 532-9543

DAYS INN NORTH
9930 N Whitaker
Rd (97217)
Rates: $60-$90
(503) 289-1800
(800) 329-7466
(800) 833-1800

DOUBLETREE HOTEL COLUMBIA RIVER
1401 N Hayden
Island Dr (97215)
Rates: $69-$89
(503) 283-2111
(800) 222-8733

DOUBLETREE HOTEL-DOWNTOWN
310 SW Lincoln
(97201)
Rates: $79-$160
(503) 221-0450
(800) 222-8733

DOUBLETREE HTL JANTZEN BEACH
909 N Hayden
Island Dr (97217)
Rates: $69-$89
(503) 283-4466
(800) 222-8733

DOUBLETREE HOTEL LLOYD CENTER
1000 NE
Multnomah St
(97232)
Rates: $89-$175
(503) 281-6111
(800) 222-8733

ECONO LODGE
18323 SE Stark St
(97233)
Rates: $40-$70
(503) 491-4444
(800) 553-2666

FIFTH AVENUE SUITES HISTORIC HOTEL
521 SW 5th Ave
(97204)
Rates: $150-$250
(503) 222-0001
(800) 711-2971

FOURTH AVENUE MOTEL
1889 SW 4th Ave
(97201)
Rates: $40-$45
(503) 226-7646

HAWTHORN INN & SUITES
431 NE Multnomah
(97232)
Rates: $69-$119
(503) 233-7933
(800) 527-1133

HAWTHORN INN & SUITES
4319 NW Yeon
(97210)
Rates: $81-$105
(503) 497-9044
(800) 527-1133

THE HEATHMAN HOTEL
1001 SW Broadway (97205)
Rates: $200-$650
(503) 241-4100
(800) 551-0011

HISTORIC HOTEL VINTAGE PLAZA
422 SW Broadway
(97205)
Rates: $160-$300
(503) 228-1212
(800) 243-0555

HOWARD JOHNSON AIRPORT HOTEL
7101 NE 82nd Ave
(97220)
Rates: $60-$98
(503) 255-6722
(800) 446-4656

MADISON SUITES
3620 NE 82nd Ave
(97220)
Rates: $40-$50
(503) 257-4981
(800) 945-4425

MALLORY HISTORIC HOTEL
729 SW 15th Ave
Rates: $85-$150
(503) 223-6311
(800) 228-8657

THE MARK SPENCER HOTEL
409 SW 11th Ave
(97205)
Rates: $85-$140
(503) 224-3293
(800) 548-3934

MARRIOTT HOTEL CITY CENTER
520 SW Broadway
(97205)
Rates: $139-$159
(503) 226-6300
(800) 228-9290

MARRIOTT HOTEL DOWNTOWN
1401 SW Front Ave (97201)
Rates: $137-$500
(503) 226-7600
(800) 228-9290

MOTEL 6 CENTRAL
3104 SE Powell Blvd (97202)
Rates: $42-$62
(503) 238-0600
(800) 466-8356

OLALLIE LAKE RESORT CABINS
21222 NW Cannes Dr (97229)
Rates: $70
(503) 557-1010

OXFORD SUITES
12226 N Jantzen Dr (97217)
Rates: $79-$189
(503) 283-3030

PORTLAND CENTER APARTMENTS
200 SW Harrison St (97201)
Rates: n/a
(503) 224-3030

QUALITY INN AIRPORT
8247 NE Sandy Blvd (97220)
Rates: $69-$119
(503) 256-4111
(800) 228-5151

RADISSON HOTEL
1441 NE 2nd Ave
(97232)
Rates: $97-$125
(503) 233-2401
(800) 333-3333

RANCH INN MOTEL
10138 SW Barbur Blvd (97219)
Rates: $33-$40
(503) 246-3375

RED LION INN COLISEUM
1224 N Thunderbird Way (97227)
Rates: $59-$89
(503) 235-8311
(800) 547-8010

RESIDENCE INN BY MARRIOTT AT LLOYD CENTER
1710 NE Multnomah St (97232)
Rates: $122-$195
(503) 288-1400
(800) 331-3131

RIVERPLACE HOTEL
1510 SW Harbor Way (97201)
Rates: $219-$769
(503) 228-3233
(800) 227-1333

ROSE MANOR INN
4546 SE McLoughlin Blvd (97202)
Rates: $30-$51
(503) 236-4175
(800) 252-8222

ROSE MOTEL
8920 SW Barbur (97219)
Rates: $35-$65
(503) 244-0107

SIXTH AVENUE AMERICAN HOSPITALITY INN
2221 SW 6th Ave (97201)
Rates: $45-$55
(503) 226-2979

SULLIVAN'S GULCH B&B
1744 NE Clackamas St (97232)
Rates: $70-$85
(503) 331-1104

SUPER 8 MOTEL AIRPORT
11011 NE Holman (97220)
Rates: $60-$79
(503) 257-8988
(800) 800-8000

TRAVELODGE AIRPORT
9727 NE Sandy Blvd (97220)
Rates: $59-$109
(503) 255-1400
(800) 578-7878

TRAVELODGE CONVENTION CENTER
1506 NE 2nd Ave (97232)
Rates: $71-$109
(503) 231-7665
(800) 578-7878

TRAVELODGE SUITES
7740 SE Powell Blvd (97206)
Rates: $75-$95
(503) 788-9394
(800) 578-7878

VAGABOND INN
518 NE Holladay St (97232)
Rates: n/a
(503) 234-4391
(800) 522-1555

VALUE INN DOWNTOWN
415 SW Montgomery St (97201)
Rates: $35-$60
(503) 226-4751

THE WESTIN PORTLAND
750 SW Alder (97205)
Rates: $115-$250
(502) 294-9000
(800) 228-3000

PRAIRIE CITY

STRAWBERRY MOUNTAIN INN BED & BREAKFST
940 Hwy 26 E
(97869)
Rates: $65-$125
(541) 820-4522
(800) 545-6913

PRINEVILLE

CITY CENTER MOTEL
509 E 3rd St
(97754)
Rates: $30-$40
(541) 447-5522

LITTLE PINE MOTEL
251 N Deer St
(97754)
Rates: $32-$55
(541) 447-3440

RUSTLERS INN
960 W 3rd St
(97754)
Rates: $39-$42
(541) 447-4185

PROSPECT

PROSPECT HISTORICAL HOTEL
391 Mill Creek Dr
(97536)
Rates: $70-$130
(541) 560-3664
(800) 994-6490

RAINIER

BUDGET INN
120 "A" St W
(97048)
Rates: $35-$85
(503) 556-4231
(800) 263-5658

REDMOND

HUB MOTEL SUPER VALUE INN
1128 N Hwy 97
(97756)
Rates: $35-$42
(541) 548-2101
(800) 784-3482

MOTEL 6
2247 S Hwy 97
(97756)
Rates: $40-$60
(541) 923-2100
(800) 466-8356

REDMOND INN
1545 Hwy 97 N
(97756)
Rates: $55-$65
(541) 548-1091
(800) 833-3259

SUPER 8 MOTEL
3629 21st Place
(97756)
Rates: $49-$68
(541) 548-8881
(800) 800-0000

REEDSPORT

ANCHOR BAY INN
1821 Winchester
Ave (97467)
Rates: $43-$67
(541) 271-2149
(800) 767-1821

BEST BUDGET INN
1894 Winchester
Ave (97467)
Rates: $28-$95
(541) 271-3686

**BEST WESTERN
SALBASGEON INN**
1400 Hwy Ave 101
(97467)
Rates: $73-$125
(541) 271-4831
(800) 528-1234

ECONOMY INN
1593 Highway
Ave (97467)
Rates: $35-$75
(541) 271-3671
(800) 799-9970

**FIR GROVE
MOTEL**
2178 Winchester
Ave (97467)
Rates: $346-$45
(541) 271-4848

**SALBASGEON
INN OF THE
UMPQUA**
45209 Hwy 38
(97467)
Rates: $68-$93
(541) 271-2025

**SALTY SEAGULL
MOTEL**
1806 Winchester
Ave (97467)
Rates: $29-$44
(541) 271-3729
(800) 476-8336

ROCKAWAY BEACH

**BROADWATER
VACATION RENTALS**
438 Hwy 101 N
(97136)
Rates: $59-$149
(503) 355-2248

**COASTAL
HIDEAWAYS**
216 Hwy 101 N
(97136)
Rates: $65-$125
(503) 355-2229

**GETAWAY MOTEL
ON THE BEACH**
621 S Pacific (97136)
Rates: $40-$110
(503) 355-2501
(800) 756-5552

**OCEAN LOCO-
MOTION MOTEL**
19130 Alder Ave
(97136)
Rates: $47-$90
(503) 355-2093

**OCEAN SPRAY
MOTEL**
505 N Pacific Ave
(97136)
Rates: $48-$75
(503) 355-2237

101 MOTEL
530 N Hwy 101
(97136)
Rates: $35-$55
(503) 355-2420
(888) 878-3973

**SAND DOLLAR
MOTEL**
105 NW 23rd Ave
(97136)
Rates: $45-$100
(503) 355-2301

**SEA TREASURES
INN**
301 N Miller St
(97136)
Rates: $50-$80
(503) 355-8220
(800) 444-1864

**SURFSIDE
OCEANFRONT
RESORT MOTEL**
101 NW 11th Ave
(97136)
Rates: $48-$149
(503) 355-2312
(800) 243-7786

**TRADEWINDS
MOTEL**
523 N Pacific St
(97136)
Rates: $55-$95
(503) 355-2112
(800) 824-0938

ROSEBURG

BEST INN & SUITES
427 NW Garden
Valley Blvd
(97470)
Rates: $49-$69
(541) 673-5561
(800) 237-8466

**BEST WESTERN
DOUGLAS INN**
511 SE Stephens St
(97470)
Rates: $47-$78
(541) 673-6625
(800) 528-1234
(877) 368-4466

**BEST WESTERN
GARDEN VILLA**
760 NW Garden
Valley Blvd
(97470)
Rates: $71-$91
(541) 672-1601
(800) 528-1234
(800) 547-3446

**BUDGET 16
MOTEL**
1067 NE Stephens
St (97470)
Rates: $30-$57
(541) 673-5556
(800) 414-1648

**CASA LOMA
MOTEL**
1107 NE Stephens
St (97470)
Rates: $27-$35
(541) 673-5569

**CITY CENTER
MOTEL**
1321 SE Stephens
St (97470)
Rates: $30-$40
(541) 673-6134

DUNES MOTEL
610 W Madrone St
(97470)
Rates: $43-$59
(541) 672-6684
(800) 260-9973

HOLIDAY INN EXP
375 W Harvard
Blvd (97470)
Rates: $89-$105
(541) 673-7517
(800) 465-4329
(800) 898-ROOM

HOLIDAY MOTEL
444 SE Oak st
(97470)
Rates: $30-$40
(541) 672-4457

**HOWARD
JOHNSON
EXPRESS INN**
978 NE Stephens
St (97470)
Rates: $68-$100
(541) 673-5082
(800) 446-4656

ROSE CITY MOTEL
1142 NE Stephens
St (97470)
Rates: $30-$50
(541) 673-8209

**SHADY OAKS
MOTEL**
2954 Old Hwy 99
S (97470)
Rates: $37-$46
(541) 672-2608

SUPER 8 MOTEL
3200 NW Aviation
Dr (97470)
Rates: $46-$62
(541) 672-8880
(800) 800-0000

**SYCAMORE MOTEL
NATIONAL 9**
1627 SE Stephens
St (97470)
Rates: n/a
(541) 672-3354
(800) 524-9999

VISTA MOTEL
1183 NE Stephens
St (97470)
Rates: $30-$40
(541) 673-2736

WINDMILL INN
1450 NW
Mulholland Dr
(97470)
Rates: $80-$102
(541) 673-0901
(800) 547-4747

RUFUS

**DINTY'S MOTOR
INN**
P.O. Box 136
(97050)
Rates: n/a
(541) 739-2596

TYEE MOTEL
304 1/2 E 1st St
(97050)
Rates: $40-$45
(541) 739-2310

ST. HELENS

**BEST WESTERN
OAK MEADOWS
INN**
585 S Columbia
River Hwy
(97501)
Rates: $79-$89
(503) 397-3000
(800) 528-1234

SALEM

**CITY CENTRE
MOTEL**
510 Liberty St SE
(97301)
Rates: $42-$52
(503) 364-0121
(800) 289-0121

COZZZY INN
1875 Fisher Rd NE
(97305)
Rates: $39-$49
(503) 588-5423

**EAGLE CREST BED
& BREAKFAST**
4401 Eagle Crest
NW (97301)
Rates: $55
(503) 364-3960

MAR DON MOTEL
3355 Portland Rd
NE (97301)
Rates: $30-$45
(503) 585-2089

AREA CODES - If the local number doesn't connect, check for a new area code.

MOTEL 6
1401 Hawthorne
Ave NE (97302)
Rates: $39-$55
(503) 371-8024
(800) 466-8356

**OREGON
CAPITAL INN**
745 Commercial St
SE (97308)
Rates: $34-$49
(503) 363-2451

**PHOENIX INN
SOUTH**
4370 Commercial
SE (97308)
Rates: $69-$89
(503) 588-9220
(800) 445-4498

QUALITY INN
3301 Market St NE
(97301)
Rates: $82-$105
(503) 370-7888
(800) 228-5151

SUPER 8 MOTEL
1288 Hawthorne
NE (97301)
Rates: $47-$70
(503) 370-8888
(800) 800-8000

TIKI LODGE MOTEL
3705 Market St NE
(97301)
Rates: $39-$59
(503) 581-4441
(800) 438-8458

**TRAVELODGE-
SALEM CAPITAL**
1555 State St
(97301)
Rates: $54-$84
(503) 581-2466
(800) 578-7878

SANDY

**BEST WESTERN
SANDY INN**
37465 Hwy 26
(97055)
Rates: $59-$78
(503) 668-7100
(800) 528-1234

**BROOKSIDE BED
& BREAKFAST**
45232 SE Paha
Loop (97055)
Rates: $50-$65
(503) 668-4766

SCAPPOOSE

**BARNSTORMER
B&B**
53758 W Lane Rd
(97056)
Rates: $55-$95
(503) 543-2740
(888) 875-1670

**MALARKEY
RANCH B&B**
55948 Columbia
River Hwy (97056)
Rates: n/a
(503) 543-5244

SEASIDE

**BEST WESTERN
OCEAN VIEW
RESORT**
414 N Promenade
(97138)
Rates: $149-$230
(503) 738-3334
(800) 528-1234
(800) 234-8439

CITY CENTER MOTEL
250 1st Ave
(97138)
Rates: $48-$149
(503) 738-6377
(800) 479-5191

**COMFORT INN
BOARDWALK**
545 Broadway
(97138)
Rates: $94-$180
(503) 738-3011
(800) 228-5150

**EDGEWATER INN
PROMENADE**
341 S Promenade
(97138)
Rates: $69-$159
(503) 738-4142
(800) 822-3170

**THE GUEST
HOUSE B&B**
486 Necanicum Dr
(97138)
Rates: $60-$95
(503) 717-0495
(800) 340-8150

**INN ON
THE PROMENADE**
361 S Promenade
(97138)
Rates: $50-$140
(503) 738-5241
(800) 654-2506

**THE LANAI
MOTEL**
3140 Sunset Blvd
(97138)
Rates: $45-$85
(503) 738-6343
(800) 738-2683

MOTEL 6
2369 S Holladay
Dr (97138)
Rates: $59-$70
(503) 738-6269
(800) 466-8356

**SEASIDE
CONVENTION
CENTER INN**
441 2nd Ave
(97138)
Rates: $99-$109
(503) 738-9581
(800) 699-5070

SEASIDER MOTEL
110 5th Ave
(97138)
Rates: $50-$75
(503) 738-7764
(800) 840-7764

**SEASIDER II
MOTEL**
210 N Downing St
(97138)
Rates: $45-$75
(503) 738-7622

SEAVIEW INN
120 9th Ave
(97138)
Rates: $54-$84
(503) 738-5371
(800) 479-5191

**SHILO INN
SEASIDE EAST**
900 S Holladay
(97138)
Rates: $45-$125
(503) 738-0549
(800) 222-2244

SILVER SANDS
65 9th Ave (97138)
Rates: n/a
(503) 738-5590

SHADY COVE

**THE EDGEWATER
INN ON THE
ROGUE RIVER**
7800 Rogue River
Dr (97539)
Rates: $74-$109
(541) 878-3171

SISTERS

**BEST WESTERN
PONDEROSA
LODGE**
500 Hwy 20 W
(97759)
Rates: $84+
(541) 549-1234
(800) 528-1234
(888) 549-4321

BLUE LAKE RESORT
Blue Lake Dr,
Hwy 20/126
(97759)
Rates: $68-$108
(541) 595-6671

COMFORT INN
540 Hwy 20 W
(97759)
Rates: $89-$109
(541) 549-7829
(800) 228-5150

**RAGS TO WALK-
ERS GUEST RANCH**
17045 Farthing Ln
(97759)
Rates: $95-$150
(541) 548-7000
(800) 422--5622

SQUAW CREEK B&B
68733 Junipine Ln
(97759)
Rates: $80-$90
(541) 549-4312
(800) 930-0055

SOUTH BEACH

**SOLACE BY THE
SEA B&B**
9602 S Coast Hwy
(97366)
Rates: $110-$175
(541) 867-3566
(800) 4-SOLACE

**THIEL SHORES
MOTEL**
9812 S Coast Hwy
(97366)
Rates: $55-$75
(541) 867-4305

SPRINGFIELD

**BEST INN &
SUITES**
3315 Gateway
(97477)
Rates: $49-$76
(541) 746-1314
(800) 237-8466

COMFORT SUITES
969 Kruse Way
(97477)
Rates: $88-$179
(541) 746-5359
(800) 228-5150

**DOUBLETREE
HOTEL**
3280 Gateway Rd
(97477)
Rates: $74-$130
(541) 726-8181
(800) 222-8733

MOTEL 6
3752 International
Ct (97477)
Rates: $36-$54
(541) 741-1105
(800) 466-8356

SHILO INN
3350 Gateway St
(97477)
Rates: $59-$109
(541) 747-0332
(800) 222-2244

**VILLAGE INN
MOTEL**
1875 Mohawk
Blvd (97477)
Rates: $56-$72
(541) 747-4546
(800) 327-6871

STAYTON

**GARDNER HOUSE
BED & BREAKFST**
633 N 3rd Ave
(97383)
Rates: $55-$67
(503) 769-5478

SUBLIMITY

**SILVER
MOUNTAIN B&B**
4672 Drift Creek
Rd SE (97385)
Rates: $60-$75
(503) 769-7127
(800) 952-3905

SUMMER LAKE

**THE LODGE AT
SUMMER LAKE**
36980 Hwy 31
(97640)
Rates: $39-$139
(541) 943-3993

SUMMER LAKE INN
D7 Ranch, 31501 Hwy 31 (97640)
Rates: $50-$230
(541) 943-3983
(800) 261-2778

SUMPTER

SUMPTER B&B
344 NE Columbia St (97877)
Rates: n/a
(541) 894-2229
(800) 640-3184

SUNNY VALLEY

SUNNY VALLEY MOTEL
352 Sunny Valley Loop (97497)
Rates: $30-$45
(541) 476-9217

SUNRIVER

SUNRAY PROPERTIES VACATION RENTALS
P.O. Box 4518 (97707)
Rates: n/a
(541) 593-3225
(800) 531-1130

TWIN LAKES RESORT
11200 S Century Dr (97707)
Rates: $72-$106
(541) 593-6526

VILLAGE PROPERTIES VACATION RENTALS
P.O. Box 3055 (97707)
Rates: $80-$350
(541) 593-1653
(800) 786-7483

SUTHERLIN

MICROTEL INN
1400 Hospitality Pl (97479)
Rates: $49+
(541) 459-2236
(888) 771-7171

PENNYWISE MOTEL
150 Myrtle St (97479)
Rates: $64-$69
(541) 459-1424

TOWN & COUNTRY MOTEL
1386 W Central Ave (97479)
Rates: $43-$52
(541) 459-9615
(800) 459-9615

SWEET HOME

THE SUN MOTEL
3026 Hwy 20 (97386)
Rates: $22-$40
(541) 367-2206

SWEET HOME INN
805 Long St (97386)
Rates: $45-$65
(541) 367-5137
(800) 595-8859

THE DALLES

AMERICAN HOSPITALITY INNS
200 W 2nd St (97058)
Rates: $39-$49
(541) 296-9111

BEST WESTERN RIVER CITY INN
112 W 2nd St (97058)
Rates: $69-$89
(541) 296-9107
(800) 528-1234
(800) 935-2378

CAPTAIN GRAY'S GUEST HOUSE
210 W 4th St (97058)
Rates: $60-$90
(541) 298-2222
(800) 448-4729

DAYS INN
2500 W 6th St (97058)
Rates: $55-$69
(541) 296-1191
(800) 329-7466

INN AT THE DALLES
3550 SE Frontage Rd (97058)
Rates: $35-$46
(541) 296-1167
(800) 982-3496

LONE PINE MOTEL
351 Ln Pine Dr (97058)
Rates: $59-$109
(541) 298-2800
(800) 955-9626

QUALITY INN
2114 W 6th (97058)
Rates: $49-$95
(541) 298-5161
(800) 228-5151

SHAMROCK MOTEL
118 W 4th St (97058)
Rates: $28-$38
(541) 296-5464

SHILO INN
3223 Bret Clodfelter Way (97058)
Rates: $69-$129
(541) 298-5502
(800) 222-2244

SUPER 8 MOTEL
609 Cherry Heights Rd (97058)
Rates: $47-$62
(541) 296-6888
(800) 800-8000

TIGARD

EMBASSY SUITES HOTEL
9000 SW Washington Sq Rd (97223)
Rates: $109-$159
(503) 644-4000
(800) 362-2779

HOMESTEAD VILLAGE GUEST STUDIOS
13009 SW 68th Pkwy (97223)
Rates: $56-$63
(503) 670-0555
(888) 782-9473

MOTEL 6 PREMIER
17950 SW McEwan Rd (97224)
Rates: $37-$58
(503) 620-2066
(800) 466-8356

MOTEL 6 PREMIER
17959 SW McEwan Rd (97224)
Rates: $36-$51
(503) 684-0760
(800) 466-8356

SHILO INN-WASHINGTON SQUARE
10830 SW Greenburg Rd (97223)
Rates: $65-$109
(503) 620-4320
(800) 222-2244

TILLAMOOK

MAR-CLAIR INN
11 Main Ave (97141)
Rates: $66-$84
(503) 842-7571
(800) 331-6857

SHILO INN
2515 N Main Ave (97141)
Rates: $59-$135
(503) 842-7971
(800) 222-2244

WESTERN ROYAL INN
1125 N Main (97141)
Rates: $50-$95
(503) 842-8844
(800) 624-2912

TRAIL

OBSTINATE J RANCH
29680 Hwy 62 (97541)
Rates: $80-$110
(541) 878-2718

TROUTDALE

MOTEL 6
1610 NW Frontage Rd (97060)
Rates: $40-$56
(503) 665-2254
(800) 466-8356

PHOENIX INN
477 NW Phoenix Dr (97060)
Rates: $66-$79
(503) 669-6500
(800) 824-6824

TUALATIN

SWEETBRIER INN
7125 SW Nyberg Rd (97062)
Rates: $75-$115
(503) 692-5800
(800) 551-9167

UMATILLA

DESERT RIVER INN
705 Willamette Ave (97882)
Rates: $41-$60
(541) 922-4871
(800) 447-7529

REST-A-BIT MOTEL
1370 6th St, Hwy 730 (97882)
Rates: $45-$49
(541) 922-3271
(800) 423-9913

UNION

ANGLE FARM COUNTRY INN BED & BREAKFST
1782 S Main St (97883)
Rates: n/a
(541) 562-5671

UNION CREEK

UNION CREEK RESORT
56484 Hwy 62 (97536)
Rates: $38-$80
(541) 560-3565

VALE

1900 SEARS & ROEBUCK HOME BED & BREAKFST
484 N 10th (97918)
Rates: $50-$95
(541) 889-9009

AREA CODES - If the local number doesn't connect, check for a new area code.

VIDA

WAYFARER RESORT COTTAGES
46725 Goodpasture Rd (97488)
Rates: $60-$200
(541) 896-3613
(800) 627-3613

WALDPORT

ALSEA MANOR MOTEL
190 SW Hwy 101 (97394)
Rates: $49-$65
(541) 563-3249
(888) 700-0503

BAYSHORE INN
902 NW Bayshore Dr (97394)
Rates: $45-$70
(541) 563-3202
(800) 526-9586

EDGEWATER COTTAGES
3978 SW Pacific Coast Hwy (97394)
Rates: $70-$130
(541) 563-2240

OCEAN ODYSSEY RENTALS
P.O. Box 491 (97394)
Rates: $65-$225
(541) 563-4504

SUNDOWN MOTEL
5050 SW Pacific Coast Hwy (97394)
Rates: $41-$95
(541) 563-3018
(800) 535-0192

TARRY-A-WHILE MOTEL
7160 SW Coast Hwy (97394)
Rates: $40-$90
(541) 563-3377

WALDPORT MOTEL
170 SW Arrow (97394)
Rates: $30-$50
(541) 563-3035

WALLOWA

CHEROKEE MINGO MOTEL
102 N Alder (97885)
Rates: $40+
(541) 886-2021

WARRENTON

RAY'S MOTEL
45 NE Skipanon Dr (97146)
Rates: $32-$43
(503) 861-2566
(800) 348-2566

SHILO INN
1609 E Harbor Dr (97146)
Rates: $65-$189
(503) 861-2181
(800) 222-2244

WELCHES

MT. HOOD VILLAGE
65000 E Hwy 26 (97067)
Rates: n/a
(503) 622-4011

OLD WELCHES INN B&B
26401 E Welches Rd (97067)
Rates: $95-$140
(503) 622-3574

OREGON ARK MOTEL
61700 E Hwy 26 (97067)
Rates: $30-$50
(503) 622-3121

WESTLAKE

SILTCOOS LAKE RESORT
82855 Fir St (97493)
Rates: $35-$65
(541) 997-3741

WESTPORT

WESTPORT MOTEL
Hwy 30, East of Astoria
Rates: $45-$85
(503) 455-2212

WHEELER

INNS AT WHEELER
495 Nehalem Blvd (97147)
Rates: $39-$175
(503) 368-3474
(888) 615-3474

WILSONVILLE

BEST INN & SUITES
8815 SW Sun Place (97070)
Rates: $43-$94
(503) 682-3184
(800) 237-8466

BURNS WEST MOTEL
8750 SW Elligsen Rd (97070)
Rates: n/a
(503) 682-2123
(800) 909-2876

COMFORT INN
8855 SW Citizen Dr (97070)
Rates: $64-$130
(503) 682-9000
(800) 228-5150

HOLIDAY INN SELECT
25425 SW 95th Ave (97070)
Rates: $71-$125
(503) 682-2211
(800) 465-4329

SNOOZ INN
30245 SW Parkway Ave (97070)
Rates: $36-$42
(503) 682-2333
(800) 343-1553

SUPER 8 MOTEL
25438 SW Parkway Ave (97070)
Rates: $45-$63
(503) 682-2088
(800) 800-8000

WOODBURN

BEST WESTERN WOODBURN INN
2887 Newberg Hwy (97071)
Rates: $69-$105
(503) 982-6515
(800) 528-1234
(800) 766-6433

FAIRWAY INN MOTEL
2450 Country Club Ct (97071)
Rates: $36-$42
(503) 981-3211
(800) 981-2466

HAWTHORN INN & SUITES
120 NE Arney Rd (97071)
Rates: $75-$125
(503) 982-1272
(800) 527-1133

SUPER 8 MOTEL
821 Evergreen Rd (97071)
Rates: $46-$67
(503) 981-8881
(800) 800-8000

YACHATS

THE ADOBE RESORT
1555 Hwy 101 (97498)
Rates: $60-$175
(541) 547-3141
(800) 522-3623

BEACHCOMBER'S MOTEL
95500 Hwy 101 S (97498)
Rates: $30-$100
(541) 547-3432

FIRESIDE RESORT MOTEL
1881 Hwy 101 N (97498)
Rates: $65-$120
(541) 547-3636
(800) 336-3573

GRACE COVE RENTAL
466 Ocean View Dr (97498)
Rates: $115
(541) 547-4111

HOLIDAY INN MARKET & MOTEL
5933 Hwy 101 N (97498)
Rates: $45-$65
(541) 547-3120

OCEAN COVE INN
Prospect & Hwy 101 (97498)
Rates: $60-$85
(541) 547-3900

RAVEN'S RETREAT RENTAL
228 Jennifer (97498)
Rates: $90-$120
(541) 547-4111

ROCK PARK COTTAGES
431 West 2nd St (97498)
Rates: $60-$115
(541) 547-3214

SEE VUE MOTEL
95590 Hwy 101 (97498)
Rates: $49-$65
(541) 547-3227

SHAMROCK LODGETTES RESORT & SPA
105 Hwy 101 S (97498)
Rates: $75-$118
(541) 547-3312
(800) 845-5028

SHORE PINES COTTAGE RENTAL
88 Trout St (97498)
Rates: $70
(541) 547-4111

SILVER SURF MOTEL
3767 Hwy 101 N (97498)
Rates: $79-$89
(541) 547-3175
(800) 281-5723

WILDWOOD LODGE VACATION RENTAL
1430 King St (97498)
Rates: $200-$350+
(541) 465-9010

YA-TEL MOTEL
640 Hwy 101 (97498)
Rates: $48-$69
(541) 547-3225

YACHATS INN
331 Hwy 101 S (97498)
Rates: $65-$92
(541) 547-3456

AREA CODES - If the local number doesn't connect, check for a new area code.

**YACHATS
VACATION
RENTAL HOME**
c/o Sweetland
Properties
P. O. Box 525
(Waldport 97394)
Rates: $100-$550
(541) 563-5913

**YACHATS
VILLAGE RENTALS**
P.O. Box 44
(97498)
Rates: n/a
(541) 547-3501

YAMHILL

**FLYING M GUEST
RANCH**
23029 NW Flying
M Rd (97148)
Rates: $60-$200
(503) 662-3222

PENNSYLVANIA

ABBOTTSTOWN

THE INN AT THE ALTLAND HOUSE
Center Sq Rt 30
(17901)
Rates: $89
(717) 259-9535

ADAMSTOWN

BLACK FOREST INN
500 Lancaster Ave
(19501)
Rates: $43-$119
(717) 484-4801

ALLENTOWN

ALLENWOOD MOTEL
1058 Hausman Rd
(18104)
Rates: $40-$45
(610) 395-3707

DAYS INN
1151 Bulldog Dr
(18104)
Rates: $65-$150
(610) 395-3731
(800) 329-7466
(888) 395-5200

ECONO LODGE
2115 Downeyflake Ln (18103)
Rates: $40-$125
(610) 797-2200
(800) 553-2666

HOLIDAY INN EXP
1715 Plaza Ln
(18104)
Rates: $54-$95
(610) 435-7880
(800) 465-4329

HOWARD JOHNSON INN
3220 Hamilton Blvd (18103)
Rates: $39-$139
(610) 439-4000
(800) 446-4656

MICROTEL INN
1880 Steelstone Rd
(18103)
Rates: $55-$65
(610) 266-9070
(888) 771-7171
(800) 647-7280

RED ROOF INN
1846 Catasauqua Rd (18103)
Rates: $61-$98
(610) 264-5404
(800) 843-7663

SHERATON INN-JETPORT
3400 Airport Rd
(18103)
Rates: $139-$169
(610) 266-1000
(800) 325-3535

ALTOONA

ECONO LODGE
2906 Pleasant Vly Blvd (16601)
Rates: $35-$58
(814) 944-3555
(800) 553-2666

HAMPTON INN
180 Charlotte Dr
(16601)
Rates: $84-$89
(814) 941-3500
(800) 426-7866

MOTEL 6
1500 Sterling St
(16601)
Rates: $42-$60
(814) 946-7601
(800) 466-8356

RAMADA INN
Rt 220, Plank Rd Exit (16601)
Rates: $97-$145
(814) 946-1631
(800) 272-6232

SUPER 8 MOTEL
3535 Fairway Dr
(16601)
Rates: $49-$60
(814) 942-5350
(800) 800-8000

ALUM BANK

WEST VU MOTEL
4158 Quaker Valley Rd (15521)
Rates: $32-$45
(814) 839-2632

BARTONSVILLE
(See Pocono Mountains Area)

BEAVER FALLS

BEAVER VALLEY MOTEL
SR 18 (15010)
Rates: $37-$52
(724) 843-0630

HOLIDAY INN
SR 18 (15010)
Rates: $89
(724) 841-3700
(800) 465-4329

BEDFORD

BEST WESTERN BEDFORD INN
4517 Bus Rt 220 N
(15522)
Rates: $48-$78
(814) 623-9006
(800) 528-1234
(800) 752-8592

BUDGET HOST MIDWAY INN
4378 Bus Rt 220
(15522)
Rates: $35-$65
(814) 623-8107
(800) 283-4678

ECONO LODGE
1411 Hillcrest
(15522)
Rates: $32-$90
(814) 623-5174
(800) 553-2666

HOST INN
Bus Rt 220 N
(15522)
Rates: $26-$37
(814) 623-9511

JANEY LYNN MOTEL
3567 Bus Rt 220 N
(15522)
Rates: $29-$75
(814) 623-9515

MOTEL TOWN HOUSE
200 S Richard St
(15522)
Rates: $302$65
(814) 623-5138
(800) 879-8696

QUALITY INN
4407 Bus Rt 220 N
(15522)
Rates: $60-$72
(814) 623-5188
(800) 228-5151

SUPER 8 MOTEL
Bus Rt 220 N
(15522)
Rates: $43-$58
(814) 623-5880
(800) 800-8000

BENSALEM

COMFORT INN
3660 Street Rd
(19020)
Rates: $109-$170
(215) 245-0100
(800) 228-5150

BENTON

THE RED POPPY HISTORIC B&B
RR 2, Box 82
(17814)
Rates: $55-$85
(570) 925-5823

BERWICK

RED MAPLE INN
RR 3, Rt 11 (18603)
Rates: $40-$70
(717) 752-6220

BERWYN

RESIDENCE INN BY MARRIOTT
600 W Swedesford Rd (19312)
Rates: $155-$199
(610) 640-9494
(800) 331-3131

BETHEL

COMFORT INN MIDWAY
I-78 Exit 5 (19507)
Rates: $62-$159
(717) 933-8888
(800) 228-5150

BETHEL PARK

HOLIDAY INN SOUTH HILLS
164 Ft. Couch Rd
(15241)
Rates: $82-$120
(412) 833-5300
(800) 465-4329

BETHLEHEM

COMFORT INN
3191 Highfield Dr
(18017)
Rates: $71-$110
(610) 865-6300
(800) 228-5150

COMFORT SUITES UNIVERSITY
120 W 3rd St
(18015)
Rates: $89-$119
(610) 882-9700
(800) 228-5150

HOTEL BETHLEHEM
437 Main St
(18017)
Rates: n/a
(610) 867-3711

RESIDENCE INN BY MARRIOTT
2180 Motel Dr
(18018)
Rates: $120-$129
(610) 317-2662
(800) 331-3131

BLAKESLEE

(See Pocono
Mountains Area)

BLOOMSBURG

ECONO LODGE
189 Columbia
Mall Dr (17815)
Rates: $50-$85
(570) 387-0490
(800) 553-2666

**THE INN AT
TURKEY HILL**
991 Central Rd
(17815)
Rates: $90-$185
(570) 387-1500

**MAGEE'S
MAIN STREET**
20 W Main St
(17815)
Rates: $55-$150
(800) 331-9815

BLUE BELL

**KORMANSUITES
EXTENDED STAY**
1707 Meadow Dr
(17506)
Rates: n/a
(610) 275-5265
(800) 567-6268

BLUE MOUNTAIN

KENMAR MOTEL
17788
Cumberland Hwy
(17240)
Rates: $45-$65
(717) 423-5915

BOYERTOWN

MEL-DOR MOTEL
494 Swamp Creek
Rd (19545)
Rates: $45-$49
(610) 367-2626

BRADDOCK HILLS

HOLIDAY INN
915 Brinton Rd
(15221)
Rates: $73
(412) 247-2700
(800) 465-4329

BRADFORD

**GLENDORN-
A LODGE IN
THE COUNTRY**
1032 W Coryden
(16701)
Rates: $375-$675
(814) 362-6511

**HOWARD
JOHNSON HOTEL**
100 S Davis St
(16701)
Rates: $62-$89
(814) 362-4501
(800) 446-4656

BREEZEWOOD

COMFORT INN
16550 Lincoln
Hwy (15533)
Rates: $50-$75
(814) 735-2200
(800) 228-5150

**PENN AIRE
MOTEL**
P. O. Box 156
(15533)
Rates: $36-$46
(814) 735-4351

WILTSHIRE MOTEL
140 S Breezewood
Rd (15533)
Rates: $33-$46
(814) 735-4361

BRIDGEVILLE

COMFORT INN
3053 Washington
Pike (15017)
Rates: $69-$109
(412) 914-2000
(800) 228-5150

KNIGHTS INN
111 Hickory Grade
Rd (15017)
Rates: $45-$52
(412) 221-8110
(800) 843-5644

BROOKVILLE

**BUDGET HOST
GOLD EAGLE INN**
250 W Main St
(15825)
Rates: $35-$58
(814) 849-7344
(800) 283-4678

DAYS INN
230 Allegheny
Blvd (15825)
Rates: $49-$96
(814) 849-8001
(800) 329-7466

**HOLIDAY INN
EXPRESS**
235 Allegheny
Blvd (15825)
Rates: $59-$79
(814) 849-8381
(800) 465-4329

**HOWARD
JOHNSON**
245 Allegheny
Blvd (15825)
Rates: $38-$49
(814) 849-3335
(800) 446-4656

SUPER 8 MOTEL
251 Allegheny
Blvd (15825)
Rates: $46-$65
(814) 849-8840
(800) 800-8000

BURNHAM

CLARION INN
13015 Ferguson
Valley Rd (17009)
Rates: $60-$87
(717) 248-4961
(800) 252-7466

BUTLER

COMFORT INN
1 Comfort Lane
(16001)
Rates: $64-$94
(724) 287-7177
(800) 228-5150

DAYS INN
139 Pittsburgh Rd
(16001)
Rates: $59-$89
(724) 287-6761
(800) 329-7466

SUPER 8 MOTEL
138 Pittsburgh Rd
(16001)
Rates: $46-$65
(724) 287-8888
(800) 800-8000

CAMP HILL

**RADISSON PENN
HARRIS HOTEL**
1150 Camp Hill
By-Pass (17011)
Rates: $79
(717) 763-7117
(800) 333-3333

CANONSBURG

SUPER 8 MOTEL
8 Curry Ave
(15317)
Rates: $47-$69
(724) 873-8808
(800) 800-8000

CARLISLE

ALBRIGHT MOTEL
1165 Harrisburg
Pike (17013)
Rates: $25-$28
(717) 249-4380

**BEST WESTERN
INN**
1245 Harrisburg
Pike (17013)
Rates: $40-$80
(717) 243-5411
(800) 528-1234
(800) 304-1082

CLARION HOTEL
1700 Harrisburg
Pike (17013)
Rates: $83-$159
(717) 243-1717
(800) 252-7466
(800) 293-4243

COMFORT SUITES
10 S Hanover St
(17013)
Rates: $74-$149
(717) 960-1000
(800) 228-5150

DAYS INN
101 Alexander
Springs Rd
(17013)
Rates: $65-$129
(717) 258-4147
(800) 329-7466

ECONO LODGE
1460 Harrisburg
Pike (17013)
Rates: $42-$85
(717) 249-7775
(800) 553-2666

HOLIDAY INN
1450 Harrisburg
Pike (17013)
Rates: $55-$104
(717) 245-2400
(800) 465-4329

MOTEL 6
1153 Harrisburg
Pike (17013)
Rates: $36-$66
(717) 249-7622
(800) 466-8356

QUALITY INN
1255 Harrisburg
Pike (17013)
Rates: $68-$129
(717) 243-6000
(800) 228-5151

RODEWAY INN
1239 Harrisburg
Pike (17013)
Rates: $49-$85
(717) 249-2800
(800) 228-2000

SLEEP INN
5 E Garland Dr
(17013)
Rates: $60-$145
(717) 249-8863
(800) 753-3746

TRAVELODGE
1252 Harrisburg
Pike (17013)
Rates: $45-$90
(717) 243-8585
(800) 578-7878

CHADDS FORD

**BRANDYWINE
RIVER HOTEL**
US 1 & SR 100
(19317)
Rates: $125-$169
(610) 388-1200

CHALK HILL

**LODGE AT
CHALK HILL**
Rt 40E, Box 240
(15421)
Rates: $65-$84
(724) 438-8880
(800) 833-4283

CHAMBERSBURG

COMFORT INN
3301 Black Gap
Rd (17201)
Rates: $59-$99
(717) 263-6655
(800) 228-5150

DAYS INN
30 Falling Springs
Rd (17201)
Rates: $60-$78
(717) 263-1288
(800) 329-7466

**QUALITY INN
& SUITES**
1095 Wayne Ave
(17201)65-$125
(717) 263-3400
(800) 228-5151

TRAVELODGE
565 Lincoln Way E
(17201)
Rates: $44-$74
(717) 264-4187
(800) 578-7878

CLARION

DAYS INN
Rt 68 & I-80 (16214)
Rates: $46-$120
(814) 226-8682
(800) 329-7466

HOLIDAY INN
Rt 68 & 1-80 (16214)
Rates: $95
(814) 226-8850
(800) 465-4329

SUPER 8 MOTEL
Rt 3 & Rt 68
(16214)
Rates: $55-$90
(814) 226-4550
(800) 800-8000

CLEARFIELD

**BEST WESTERN
INN**
Rt 879 (16830)
Rates: $56-$69
(814) 765-2441
(800) 528-1234
(800) 396-2441

BUDGET INN
Rt 322 E (16830)
Rates: $27-$42
(814) 765-2639

COMFORT INN
Industrial Park Rd
(16830)
Rates: $75-$115
(814) 768-6400
(800) 228-5150

DAYS INN
Rt 879 & I-80
(16830)
Rates: $45-$80
(814) 765-5381
(800) 329-7466

RODEWAY INN
US 322 E (16830)
Rates: $23-$74
(814) 765-7587
(800) 228-2000

SUPER 8 MOTEL
Rt 879 & I-80
(16830)
Rates: $43-$61
(814) 768-7580
(800) 800-8000

COOKSBURG

**FOREST VIEW
CABINS**
Box 105 (16217)
Rates: n/a
(814) 744-8413

COOPERSBURG

TRAVELODGE
321 S 3rd St
(18036)
Rates: $40-$105
(610) 282-1212
(800) 578-7878

CORAOPOLIS

EMBASSY SUITES
550 Cherrington
Pkwy (15108)
Rates: $119-$169
(412) 269-9070
(800) 362-2779

HAMPTON INN
1420 Beers School
Rd (15108)
Rates: $74-$84
(412) 264-0020
(800) 426-7866

**HOLIDAY INN
AIRPORT**
1406 Beers School
Rd (15108)
Rates: $119-$139
(412) 262-3600
(800) 465-4329

**LA QUINTA INN
AIRPORT**
1433 Beers School
Rd (15108)
Rates: $62-$75
(412) 269-0400
(800) 687-6667

**MARRIOTT
AIRPORT**
100 Aten Rd
(15108)
Rates: $72-$164
(412) 788-8800
(800) 228-9290

MOTEL 6
1170 Thorn Run
Rd (15108)
Rates: $39-$54
(412) 269-0990
(800) 466-8356

**RED ROOF INN
AIRPORT**
1454 Beers School
Rd (15108)
Rates: $50-$70
(412) 264-5678
(800) 843-7663

SLEEP INN
2500 Market Place
Blvd (15108)
Rates: $49-$79
(412) 859-4000
(800) 753-3746

SUPER 8 MOTEL
1465 Beers School
Rd (15108)
Rates: $42-$54
(412) 264-7888
(800) 800-8000

CRAFTON

DAYS INN
100 Kisow Dr
(15205)
Rates: n/a
(412) 922-0120
(800) 329-7466

**MOTEL 6
AIRPORT**
211 Beecham Dr
(15205)
Rates: $34-$42
(412) 922-9400
(800) 466-8356

CRANBERRY TOWNSHIP

AMERISUITES
136 Emeryville Dr
(16066)
Rates: $75-$125
(724) 779-7900
(800) 833-1516

DAYS INN
924 Sheraton Dr
(16066)
Rates: $62-$138
(724) 772-2700
(800) 329-7466

**HOLIDAY INN
EXPRESS**
20003 Rt 19
(16066)
Rates: $74-$79
(724) 772-1000
(800) 465-4329

RED ROOF INN
20009 Rt 19
(16066)
Rates: $55-$76
(724) 776-5670
(800) 843-7663

DANVILLE

RED ROOF INN
300 Red Roof Inn
Rd (17821)
Rates: $34-$53
(570) 275-7600
(800) 843-7663

DELMONT

SUPER 8 MOTEL
180 Sheffield Dr
(15626)
Rates: $44-$60
(724) 468-4888
(800) 800-8000

DENVER

**BLACK HORSE
LODGE & SUITES**
2180 N Reading
Rd (17517)
Rates: $79-$119
(717) 336-7563

COMFORT INN
2015 N Reading
Rd (17517)
Rates: $80-$140
(717) 336-4649
(800) 228-5150

**PENNSYLVANIA
DUTCH MOTEL**
2275 N Reading
Rd (17517)
Rates: $36-$50
(717) 336-5559

RED CARPET INN
2069 N Reading
Rd (17517)
Rates: n/a
(717) 336-5254
(800) 251-1962

DICKSON CITY

(See Pocono
Mountains Area)

DOUGLASSVILLE

ECONO LODGE
387 Ben Franklin
Hwy (19518)
Rates: $48-$85
(610) 385-3016
(800) 553-2666

DU BOIS

**DU BOIS MANOR
MOTEL**
525 Liberty Blvd
(15801)
Rates: $30-$45
(814) 371-5400
(800) 336-7701

HOLIDAY INN
US 219 & I-80
(15801)
Rates: $75
(814) 371-5100
(800) 959-3412

RAMADA INN
Rt 255 & I-80
(15801)
Rates: $55-$95
(814) 371-7070
(800) 272-6232

DUNCANNON

RED CARPET INN
RD 4, Box 4913
(17020)
Rates: n/a
(717) 834-3320
(800) 251-1962

AREA CODES - If the local number doesn't connect, check for a new area code.

DUNCANSVILLE

COMFORT INN
130 Patchway Rd
(16635)
Rates: $65-$129
(814) 693-1800
(800) 228-5150

DUNMORE

(See Pocono
Mountains Area)

EAST STROUDSBURG

(See Pocono
Mountains Area)

EASTON

BEST WESTERN EASTON INN
185 S 3rd St
(18042)
Rates: $75-$130
(610) 253-9131
(800) 528-1234
(800) 882-0113

DAYS INN
2555 Nazareth Rd
(18042)
Rates: $63-$130
(610) 253-0546
(800) 329-7466

EBENSBURG

COMFORT INN
111 Cook Rd
(15931)
Rates: $58-$150
(814) 472-6100
(800) 228-5150

THE COTTAGE RESTAURANT & INN
RD 4, Box 50 (15931)
Rates: $48-$64
(814) 472-8002

EMLENTON

WHIPPLE TREE INN & FARM B&B
Big Bend Rd (16373)
Rates: $50-$60
(724) 867-9543

ENTRIKEN

RAYSTOWN RESORT & LODGE
Rt 994 (16638)
Rates: n/a
(814) 658-3500

EPHRATA

SMITHTON COUNTRY INN HISTORIC B&B
900 W Main St
(17522)
Rates: $65-$175
(717) 733-6094

ERIE

DAYS INN
7415 Schultz Rd
(16509)
Rates: $70-$100
(814) 868-8521
(800) 329-7466

HAMPTON INN
8050 Old Oliver
Rd (16509)
Rates: $59-$79
(814) 866-6800
(800) 426-7866

HOLIDAY INN EXP
18 W 18th St (16501)
Rates: n/a
(814) 456-2961
(800) 465-4329

MICROTEL INN
8100 Peach St
(16509)
Rates: $37-$75
(814) 864-1010
(888) 771-7171
(800) 975-4400

MOTEL 6
7575 Peach St (16509)
Rates: $60-$100
(814) 864-4811
(800) 466-8356

QUALITY INN & SUITES
8040 Perry Hwy
(16509)
Rates: $79-$129
(814) 864-4911
(800) 28-5151

RED CARPET INN
7455 Schultz Rd
(16509)
Rates: n/a
(814) 868-0879
(800) 251-1962

RED ROOF INN
7865 Perry Hwy
(16509)
Rates: $60-$107
(814) 868-5246
(800) 843-7663

SUPER 8 MOTEL

8040 B Perry Hwy
(16506)
Rates: $69-$99
(814) 864-9200
(800) 800-8000

ERWINNA

HISTORIC GOLDEN PHEASANT COUNTRY INN
763 River Rd
(18920)
Rates: $75-$155
(610) 294-9595

ESSINGTON

COMFORT INN AIRPORT
53 Industrial Hwy
(19029)
Rates: $88-$150
(610) 521-9800
(800) 228-5150

HOLIDAY INN AIRPORT
45 Industrial Hwy
(19029)
Rates: $119-$129
(610) 521-2400
(800) 465-4329

MOTEL 6 AIRPORT
43 Industrial Hwy
(19029)
Rates: $49-$66
(215) 521-6650
(800) 466-8356

RAMADA INN AIRPORT
76 Industrial Hwy
(19029)
Rates: $95-$105
(610) 521-9600
(800) 272-6232

RED ROOF INN AIRPORT
49 Industrial Hwy
(19029)
Rates: $78-$95
(610) 521-5090
(800) 843-7663

EXTON

BEST WESTERN EXTON HOTEL & CONF CENTER
815 N Pottstown
Pike (19341)
Rates: $79-$129
(610) 363-1100
(800) 528-1234
(888) 253-6119

COMFORT INN
5 N Pottstown
Pike (19341)
Rates: $79-$130
(610) 524-8811
(800) 228-5150

HAMPTON INN
4 N Pottstown
Pike (19341)
Rates: $83-$89
(610) 363-5555
(800) 426-7866

HOLIDAY INN EXPRESS
120 N Pottstown
Pike (19341)
Rates: $72
(610) 524-9000
(800) 465-4329

FAYETTEVILLE

RITE SPOT MOTEL
5651 Lincoln Way
E (17222)
Rates: $41-$47
(717) 352-2144

FOGELSVILLE

CLOVERLEAF MOTEL
327 Star Rd
(18051)
Rates: $40-$50
(610) 395-3367

HOLIDAY INN CONF CENTER
7736 Adrienne Dr
(18051)
Rates: $139-$149
(610) 391-1000
(800) 465-4329

FRACKVILLE

ECONO LODGE
501 S Middle St
(17931)
Rates: $30-$94
(570) 874-3838
(800) 553-2666

GRANNY'S BUDGET HOST INN

115 W Coal St
(17931)
Rates: $38-$48
(570) 874-0408
(800) 283-4678

MOTEL 6
701 Altamont Blvd
(17931)
Rates: $39-$45
(570) 874-1223
(800) 466-8356

FRANKLIN

FRANKLIN MOTEL
1421 Liberty St
(16323)
Rates: n/a
(814) 437-3061

INN AT FRANKLIN
1411 Liberty St
(16323)
Rates: $60-$80
(814) 437-3031

SUPER 8 MOTEL
Rt 8 & 62 (16323)
Rates: $45-$61
(814) 432-2102
(800) 800-8000

FRYSTOWN

MOTEL OF FRYSTOWN
90 Fort Motel Dr
(17067)
Rates: $35-$45
(717) 933-4613

GALETON

OX YOKE INN
RD 1, Route 6
(16922)
Rates: n/a
(814) 435-6522

PINE LOG MOTEL
5156 US Rt 6 W
(16922)
Rates: $50-$75
(814) 435-6400

GETTYSBURG

BEST INN
301 Steinwher Ave
(17325)
Rates: $62-$90
(717) 334-1188
(800) 237-8466

COLTON MOTEL
232 Steinwehr Ave
(17325)
Rates: $29-$65
(717) 334-5514
(800) 262-0317

COMFORT INN
871 York Rd
(17325)
Rates: $55-$199
(717) 337-2400
(800) 228-5150

HERITAGE MOTOR INN
613 Baltimore St
(17325)
Rates: $81-$99
(717) 334-9281

HOLIDAY INN
516 Baltimore Pike
(17325)
Rates: $98-$200
(717) 334-6211
(800) 465-4329

HOWARD JOHNSON
301 Steinwehr Ave
(17325)
Rates: $37-$100
(717) 334-1188
(800) 446-4656

GIBSONIA

COMFORT INN
5137 SR 8 (15044)
Rates: $55-$81
(724) 444-8700
(800) 228-5150

GLEN MILLS

SWEETWATER FARM BED & BREAKFAST
50 Sweetwater Rd
(19342)
Rates: n/a
(610) 459-4711

GLEN ROCK

ROCKY RIDGE MOTEL
Rt 216, Steaks Run
Rd (17327)
Rates: $28-$38
(717) 235-5646

GRANTVILLE

COMFORT SUITES
I-81 & Station Rd
(17028)
Rates: $65-$225
(800) 228-5150

ECONO LODGE
252 Bow Creek Rd
(17028)
Rates: $40-$75
(717) 469-0631
(800) 553-2666

HOLIDAY INN
604 Station Rd
(17028)
Rates: $99-$199
(717) 469-0661
(800) 465-4329

GREEN TREE

HAMPTON INN
555 Trumbull Dr
(15205)
Rates: $75
(412) 922-0100
(800) 426-7866

HAWTHORNE SUITES
700 Marshfield
Ave (15205)
Rates: $99-$149
(412) 279-6300
(800) 527-1133

RADISSON HOTEL
101 Marriott Dr
(15205)
Rates: $99-$159
(412) 922-8400
(800) 333-3333

GREENCASTLE

ECONO LODGE
736 Buchanan
Trail E (17225)
Rates: $40-$65
(717) 597-5255
(800) 553-2666

HAMLIN

(See Pocono
Mountains Area)

HARRISBURG

BAYMONT INN
200 N Mountain
Rd (17112)
Rates: $60-$80
(717) 540-9339
(800) 301-0200

BAYMONT INN & SUITES
990 Eisenhower
Blvd (17111)
Rates: $64-$71
(717) 939-8000
(800) 301-0200

BEST WESTERN CAPITAL PLAZA
150 Nationwide
Dr (17110)
Rates: $61-$83
(717) 545-9089
(800) 528-1234
(800) 872-7776

BEST WESTERN COUNTRY OVEN
300 N Mountain
Rd (17112)
Rates: $75-$89
(717) 652-7180
(800) 528-1234

CLARION INN
5680 Allentown
Blvd (17109)
Rates: $65-$129
(717) 657-2200
(800) 252-7466

COMFORT INN
7744 Linglestown
Rd (17112)
Rates: $99-$179
(717) 540-8400
(800) 228-5150

COMFORT INN EAST
4021 Union
Deposit Rd
(17109)
Rates: $79-$119
(717) 561-8100
(800) 228-5150

COMFORT INN RIVERFRONT
525 S Front St
(17104)
Rates: $89-$139
(717) 233-1611
(800) 228-5150

HAWTHORN SUITES
770 E Park Dr
(17111)
Rates: n/a
(800) 527-1133

HOLIDAY INN
4751 Lindle Rd
(17111)
Rates: $102-$114
(717) 939-7841
(800) 465-4329

HOWARD JOHNSON
473 Eisenhower
Blvd (17111)
Rates: $79-$99
(717) 564-6300
(800) 446-4656

RED ROOF INN-N
400 Corporate Cir
(17110)
Rates: $49-$71
(717) 657-1445
(800) 843-7663

RED ROOF INN-S
950 Eisenhower
Blvd (17111)
Rates: $56-$76
(717) 939-1331
(800) 843-7663

RESIDENCE INN BY MARRIOTT
4480 Lewis Rd
(17111)
Rates: $139-$179
(717) 561-1900
(800) 331-3131

SHERATON INN
800 East Park Dr
(17111)
Rates: $75-$135
(717) 561-2800
(800) 325-3535

SLEEP INN
7930 Linglestown
Rd (17112)
Rates: $49-$179
(717) 540-9100
(800) 753-3746

SUPER 8 MOTEL-NORTH
4125 N Front St
(17110)
Rates: $60-$89
(717) 233-5891
(800) 800-8000

WYNDHAM GARDEN HOTEL
765 Eisenhower
Blvd (17111)
Rates: $89-$129
(717) 558-9500
(800) 996-3426
(800) 253-0238

HARRISVILLE

DAYS INN
I-80 & Rt 8 (16038)
Rates: $49-$64
(814) 786-7901
(800) 329-7466

HAWLEY

(See Pocono
Mountains Area)

HAZLETON

(See Pocono
Mountains Area)

HERMITAGE

HOLIDAY INN
3200 S Hermitage
Rd (16159)
Rates: $86
(724) 981-1530
(800) 465-4329

ROYAL MOTEL
301 S Hermitage
Rd (16148)
Rates: $33-$39
(724) 347-5546
(800) 831-8348

HERSHEY

COMFORT INN
1200 Mae St
(17036)
Rates: $75-$225
(717) 566-2050
(800) 228-5150

HAMPTON INN
749 E Chocolate
Ave (17033)
Rates: $169-$250
(800) 426-7866

HONESDALE

(See Pocono
Mountains Area)

HONEY BROOK

WAYNESBROOK INN HISTORIC B&B
Main St (19344)
Rates: $58-$205
(610) 273-2444

HORSHAM

DAYS INN
245 Easton Rd
(19044)
Rates: $89-$135
(215) 674-2500
(800) 329-7466

HOMESTEAD VILLAGE GUEST STUDIOS
537 Dresher Rd (19044)
Rates: n/a
(215) 956-9966
(888) 782-9473

RESIDENCE INN BY MARRIOTT
3 Walnut Grove Dr (19044)
Rates: $130-$160
(215) 443-7330
(800) 331-3131

HUNTINGDON

JENNY SPRINGS CABIN RENTAL
Rothrock State Forest (16652)
Rates: n/a
(814) 627-5311

HUNTINGDON MOTOR INN
Motor Inn Rd (16652)
Rates: $379$65
(814) 643-1133

INDIANA

BEST WESTERN UNIVERSITY INN
1545 Wayne Ave (15701)
Rates: $58-$90
(724) 349-9620
(800) 528-1234
(888) 299-9620

CHARBERT FARM BED & BRKFAST
2439 Laurel Rd (15701)
Rates: $55-$95
(724) 726-8264

COMFORT INN
1350 Indian Spgs Rd (15701)
Rates: $59-$105
(724) 465-7000
(800) 228-5150

HOLIDAY INN HOLIDOME
1395 Wayne Ave (15701)
Rates: $59-$89
(724) 463-3561
(800) 477-3561

SUPER 8 MOTEL
111 Plaza Dr (15701)
Rates: $42-$54
(724) 349-4600
(800) 800-8000

JOHNSTOWN

COMFORT INN
455 Theatre Dr (15904)
Rates: $55-$105
(814) 266-3678
(800) 228-5150

HOLIDAY INN
250 Market St (15901)
Rates: $84
(814) 535-7777
(800) 465-4329

HOLIDAY INN EXP
1440 Scalp Ave (15904)
Rates: $64-$79
(814) 266-8789
(800) 465-4329

MOTEL 6
430 Napoleon Place (15901)
Rates: $51-$63
(814) 536-1114
(800) 466-8356

SLEEP INN
453 Theatre Dr (15904)
Rates: $50-$65
(814) 262-9292
(800) 753-3746

SUPER 8 MOTEL
627 Solomon Run Rd (15904)
Rates: $40-$59
(814) 535-5600
(800) 800-8000

JONESTOWN

DAYS INN
3 Everest Lane (17038)
Rates: $68-$115
(717) 865-4064
(800) 329-7466

KANE

KANE VIEW MOTEL
Rt 6 (16735)
Rates: $38-$52
(814) 837-8600

KEMPTON

HAWK MTN INN BED & BREAKFST
RD 1, Box 186 (19529)
Rates: n/a
(215) 756-4224

KING OF PRUSSIA

HOMESTEAD VILLAGE GUEST STUDIOS
400 American Ave (19406)
Rates: n/a
(610) 962-9000
(888) 782-9473

MAINSTAY SUITES
440 American Ave (19406)
Rates: $59-$119
(800) 660-6246

MOTEL 6
815 W Dekaib Pike (19406)
Rates: $60-$73
(610) 265-7200
(800) 466-8356

SLEEP INN
440 American Ave (19406)
Rates: $69
(800) 753-3746

KINTNERSVILLE

LIGHTFARM HISTORIC B&B
2042 Berger Rd (18930)
Rates: $79-$150
(610) 847-3276

KITTANNING

COMFORT INN
422 W Belmont (16201)
Rates: $65-$95
(724) 543-5200
(800) 228-5150

QUALITY INN ROYLE
405 Butler Rd (16201)
Rates: $55-$85
(724) 543-1159
(800) 228-5151

RODEWAY INN
US 422 E (16201)
Rates: $50-$58
(724) 543-1100
(800) 228-2000

KULPSVILLE

HOLIDAY INN
1750 Sumneytown Pike (19443)
Rates: $85-$100
(215) 368-3800
(800) 465-4329

KUTZTOWN

CAMPUS INN
15080 Kutztown Rd (19530)
Rates: $50-$75
(610) 683-8721

LINCOLN MOTEL
Main St (19530)
Rates: $45-$70
(610) 683-3456

LAKE HARMONY
(See Pocono Mountains Area)

LAMAR

COMFORT INN
I-80 & SR 64 (16848)
Rates: $59-$100
(570) 726-4901
(800) 228-5150

LANCASTER

BEST WESTERN EDEN RESORT INN/CONF CTR
222 Eden Rd (17601)
Rates: $40-$169
(717) 569-6444
(800) 528-1234

COMFORT INN
500 Centerville Rd (17601)
Rates: $76-$109
(717) 898-2431
(800) 228-5150

HOTEL BRUNSWICK
Chestnut & Queen Sts (17603)
Rates: $89-$109
(717) 397-4801

LANCASTER HOST HOTEL & CONF CENTER
2300 E Lincoln Hwy (17602)
Rates: $139-$159
(717) 299-5500

SUPER 8 MOTEL
2129 E Lincoln Hwy (17602)
Rates: $39-$88
(717) 393-8888
(800) 800-8000

TRAVEL INN
2151 E Lincoln Hwy (17602)
Rates: $69-$79
(717) 299-8971

TRAVELODGE
2101 Columbia Ave (17603)
Rates: $58-$82
(717) 397-4201
(800) 578-7878

LANDENBERG

TIPTREE LODGE APT RENTALS
308 Buttonwood Rd (19350)
Rates: n/a
(302) 234-9872

LANGHORNE

RED ROOF INN
3100 Cabot Blvd W (19047)
Rates: $101-$121
(215) 750-6200
(800) 843-7663

LANSDALE

KORMANSUITES
1203 A Cross Hill Ct (19446)
Rates: n/a
(215) 542-1777
(800) 567-6268

LENHARTS-VILLE

TOP MOTEL
RD 1, Box 834 (19534)
Rates: n/a
(215) 756-6021

AREA CODES - If the local number doesn't connect, check for a new area code.

LEVITTOWN

COMFORT INN
6401 Bristol Pk
(19057)
Rates: $80-$105
(215) 547-5000
(800) 228-5150

LEWISBURG

BRYNWOOD INN
Rt 15 & 45 (17837)
Rates: $50-$73
(570) 524-2121

DAYS INN
Rt 15 (17837)
Rates: $61-$135
(570) 523-1171
(800) 329-7466

ECONO LODGE
Rt 15, Box 651
(17837)
Rates: $35-$85
(570) 523-1106
(800) 553-2666

LIGONIER

**LADY OF THE
LAKE B&B**
157 Rt 30 E (15658)
Rates: $85-$135
(724) 238-6955

LITITZ

**GENERAL
SUTTER HISTORIC
COUNTRY INN**
14 E Main St (17543)
Rates: $60-$105
(717) 626-2115

LOCK HAVEN

**BEST WESTERN
INN**
101 E Walnut St
(17745)
Rates: $65-$99
(570) 748-3297
(800) 528-1234

MALVERN

**HOMEWOOD
SUITES HOTEL**
12 E Swedesford
Rd (19355)
Rates: $95-$149
(610) 296-3500
(800) 225-5466

MAINSTAY SUITES
8 E Swedesford
Rd (19355)
Rates: $69-$129
(610) 695-9200
(800) 6606246

MANHEIM

RODEWAY INN
2931 Lebanon Rd
(17545)
Rates: $54-$58
(717) 665-2755
(800) 228-2000

MANSFIELD

COMFORT INN
300 Gateway Dr
(16933)
Rates: $77-$170
(570) 662-3000
(800) 228-5150
(800) 822-5470

MANSFIELD INN
26 S Main St
(16933)
Rates: $50-$75
(570) 662-2136

OASIS MOTEL
RD 1, Box 90
(16933)
Rates: $30-$40
(570) 659-5576

**WEST'S DELUXE
MOTEL**
RD 1, Box 97
(16933)
Rates: $36-$50
(570) 659-5141
(800) 995-9378

MARS

DAYS INN
909 Sheraton Dr
(16046)
Rates: $62-$72
(724) 772-2700
(800) 329-7466

MOTEL 6
Rt 19 S (16046)
Rates: $42-$48
(724) 776-4333
(800) 466-8356

OAK LEAF MOTEL
US Rt 19 (16046)
Rates: n/a
(724) 776-1551

MARSHALLS CREEK
(See Pocono
Mountains Area)

MATAMORAS
(See Pocono
Mountains Area)

MEADVILLE

DAVID MEAD INN
455 Chestnut St
(16335)
Rates: n/a
(814) 336-1692

DAYS INN
18360 Conneaut
Lake Rd (16335)
Rates: $56-$86
(814) 337-4264
(800) 329-7466

MOTEL 6
11237 Shaw Ave
(16335)
Rates: $55-$100
(814) 724-6366
(800) 466-8356

SUPER 8 MOTEL
17259 Conneaut
Lake Rd (16335)
Rates: $42-$65
(814) 333-8883
(800) 800-8000

MECHANICS-BURG

DAYS INN
1012 Wesley Dr
(17055)
Rates: $59-$129
(717) 766-3700
(800) 329-7466

HAMPTON INN
4950 Ritter Rd
(17055)
Rates: $86-$98
(717) 691-1300
(800) 426-7866

HOLIDAY INN
5401 Carlisle Pike
(17055)
Rates: $99
(717) 697-0321
(800) 465-4329

MERCER

**COLONIAL INN
MOTEL**
383 N Perry Hwy
(16137)
Rates: $24-$36
(412) 662-5600

**HOWARD
JOHNSON**
835 Perry Hwy
(16137)
Rates: $74-$83
(412) 748-3030
(800) 446-4656

MIDDLETOWN

DAYS INN
800 Eisenhower
Blvd (17057)
Rates: $49-$79
(717) 939-4147
(800) 329-7466

MIFFLINVILLE

SUPER 8 MOTEL
3rd Street (18631)
Rates: $66
(570) 759-6778
(800) 800-8000

MILESBURG

HOLIDAY INN
I-80 & Hwy 80,
Exit 23 (16853)
Rates: $75-$155
(814) 355-7521
(800) 465-4329

MILFORD
(See Pocono
Mountains Area)

MONROEVILLE

DAYS INN
2727 Mosside
Blvd (15146)
Rates: $48-$66
(412) 856-1610
(800) 329-7466

HAMPTON INN
3000 Mosside
Blvd (15146)
Rates: $99-$109
(412) 380-4000
(800) 426-7866

HOLIDAY INN
2750 Mosside
Blvd (15146)
Rates: $139
(412) 372-1022
(800) 465-4329

RED ROOF INN
2729 Mosside
Blvd (15146)
Rates: $56-$85
(412) 856-4738
(800) 843-7663

SUPER 8 MOTEL
1807 Rt 286
(15146)
Rates: $49-$55
(724) 733-8008
(800) 800-8000

MONTROSE
(See Pocono
Mountains Area

MOON RUN

**AMERISUITES
AIRPORT**
6011 Campbells
Run Rd (15205)
Rates: $115
(412) 494-0202
(800) 833-1516

**COMFORT INN
AIRPORT**
7011 Old
Steubenville Pkwy
(15205)
Rates: $53-$93
(412) 787-2600
(800) 228-5150

MAINSTAY SUITES
1000 Summit Park
Dr (15275)
Rates: $49-$109
(412) 490-7343
(800) 660-6246

**MARRIOTT
AIRPORT**
777 Aten Rd
(15108)
Rates: n/a
(412) 788-8800
(800) 328-9297

**RED ROOF INN
AIRPORT**
6404 Steubenville
Pike (15205)
Rates: $54-$78
(412) 787-7870
(800) 843-7663

RESIDENCE INN AIRPORT
1500 Park Lane Dr (15275)
Rates: $149
(412) 787-3300
(800) 331-3131

WYNDHAM GARDEN HOTEL AIRPORT
1 Wyndham Cir (15275)
Rates: $109
(724) 695-0002
(800) 996-3426

MORGAN-TOWN

CONESTOGA WAGON MOTEL
Rt 23 (19543)
Rates: n/a
(215) 286-5061

HOLIDAY INN
230 Cherry St (19543)
Rates: $89-$109
(610) 286-3000
(800) 465-4329

MORRISVILLE

HOLIDAY INN EXPRESS
Rt 1 & Pennsylvania Ave (19067)
Rates: n/a
(215) 428-2600
(800) 465-4329

NEW BERLINVILLE

MEL-DOR MOTEL
P. O. Box 349 (19545)
Rates: $35-$45
(610) 367-2626

NEW CASTLE

COMFORT INN
1740 New Butler Rd (16101)
Rates: $68-$150
(724) 658-7700
(800) 228-5150

NEW COLUMBIA

COMFORT INN
I-80 & US 15 (17856)
Rates: $67-$135
(520) 568-8000
(800) 228-5150

NEW CUMBERLAND

DAYS INN
353 Lewisberry Rd (17070)
Rates: $55-$105
(717) 774-4156
(800) 329-7466

HOLIDAY INN & CONF CENTER
148 Sheraton Dr (17070)
Rates: $129-$159
(717) 774-2721
(800) 465-4329

MOTEL 6
200 Commerce Dr (17070)
Rates: $31-$46
(717) 774-8910
(800) 466-8356

NEW HOLLAND

THE HOLLANDER MOTEL
320 E Main St (17557)
Rates: $52-$65
(717) 354-4377

NEW HOPE

AARON BURR HOUSE B&B
80 W Bridge St (18938)
Rates: $90-$255
(215) 862-2343

BEST WESTERN INN
6426 Lower York Rd (18938)
Rates: $89-$150
(215) 862-5221
(800) 528-1234
(800) 467-3202

THE FOX & HOUND B&B
246 W Bridge St (18938)
Rates: $70-$170
(215) 862-5082

NEW HOPE MOTEL IN THE WOODS
400 W Bridge St (18938)
Rates: $59-$109
(215) 862-2800

WEDGEWOOD INN B&B
111 W Bridge St (18938)
Rates: $90-$265
(215) 862-2520

NEW KENSINGTON

CLARION INN
300 Tarentum Bridge Rd (15068)
Rates: $64-$99
(724) 335-9171
(800) 252-7466

NEW STANTON

CARDINAL MOTEL
P. O. Drawer B (15672)
Rates: $30-$36
(724) 925-2162

RAMADA INN
110 N Main St (15672)
Rates: $58-$105
(724) 925-6755
(800) 272-6232

SUPER 8 MOTEL
103 Blair Blvd (15672)
Rates: $43-$57
(724) 925-8915
(800) 800-8000

NORTH EAST

RED CARPET INN
12264 E Main St (16428)
Rates: $36-$49
(814) 725-4554
(800) 251-1962

OAKDALE

COMFORT INN
7011 Old Stuebenville Pike (15071)
Rates: $52-$95
(412) 787-2600
(800) 228-5150

OAKLAND

HAMPTON INN
3315 Hamlet St (15213)
Rates: $98-$109
(412) 681-1000
(800) 426-7866

OIL CITY

HOLIDAY INN
1 Seneca St (16301)
Rates: $74-$100
(814) 677-1221
(800) 465-4329

PHILADELPHIA

BEST WESTERN CENTER CITY HOTEL
501 N 22nd St (19130)
Rates: $109-$139
(215) 568-8300
(800) 528-1234

BEST WESTERN INDEPENDENCE PARK INN
235 Chestnut St (19106)
Rates: $140-$190
(215) 922-4443
(800) 528-1234
(800) 624-2988

CLARION SUITES
1010 Race St (19107)
Rates: $85-$219
(215) 922-1730
(800) 252-7466

CROWNE PLAZA CITY CENTER
1800 Market St (19103)
Rates: $139-$229
(215) 561-7500
(800) 227-6963

FOUR SEASONS HOTEL
1 Logan Sq (19103)
Rates: $320-$425
(215) 963-1500
(800) 332-3442

HAWTHORN SUITES & CONV CENTER
1100 Vine St (19103)
Rates: $149-$159
(215) 829-8300
(800) 527-1133

HILTON-AIRPORT
4509 Island Ave (19153)
Rates: $115
(215) 365-4150
(800) 445-8667

MARRIOTT AIRPORT
1 Arrivals Rd (19153)
Rates: $199-$235
(215) 492-9000
(800) 228-9290

MARRIOTT HOTEL
1201 Market St (19107)
Rates: $230-$250
(215) 625-2900
(800) 228-9290

1011 CLINTON BED & BREAKFST
1011 Clinton St (19107)
Rates: $135-$200
(215) 923-8144

PARK HYATT HISTORIC HOTEL
1415 Chancellor Ct (19102)
Rates: $240-$265
(215) 893-1234

RESIDENCE INN BY MARRIOTT
4630 Island Ave (19153)
Rates: $199
(215) 492-1611
(800) 331-3131

RITTENHOUSE HOTEL & CONDO RESIDENCES
210 W Rittenhouse Sq (19103)
Rates: $335-$360
(215) 546-9000

WARWICK HOTEL & TOWERS
1701 Locust St (19103)
Rates: $169-$289
(215) 735-6000

PHILIPSBURG

HARBOR INN
Rts 322 & 53 N (16866)
Rates: $51-$61
(814) 342-0250

MAIN LINER MOTEL
US 322 (16866)
Rates: $31-$55
(814) 342-2004

PINE GROVE

COMFORT INN
I-81 & SR 443
(17963)
Rates: $49-$149
(570) 345-8031
(800) 228-5150

ECONO LODGE
RR 5, Box 15
(17963)
Rates: $40-$70
(570) 345-4099
(800) 553-2666

PITTSBURGH

BEST WESTERN UNIVERSITY CENTER
3401 Blvd of the Allies (15213)
Rates: $77-$102
(412) 683-6100
(800) 528-1234
(800) 254-4444

DAYS INN
100 Kisow Dr
(15205)
Rates: $41-$51
(412) 922-0120
(800) 329-7466

DOUBLETREE HOTEL
1000 Penn Ave
(15222)
Rates: $159-$199
(412) 281-3700
(800) 222-8733

ECONO LODGE
4800 Steubenville Pike (15205)
Rates: $35-$52
(412) 922-6900
(800) 553-2666

HAMPTON INN UNIVERSITY CTR
3315 Harriet St
(15213)
Rates: $99-$119
(412) 681-1000
(800) 426-7866

HILTON & TOWERS
Gateway Center
(15222)
Rates: $99-$179
(412) 391-4600
(800) 445-8667

HOLIDAY INN AIRPORT
401 Holiday Dr
(15220)
Rates: n/a
(412) 922-8100
(800) 465-4329

HOLIDAY INN UNIVERSITY CTR
100 Lytton Ave
(15213)
Rates: $135
(412) 682-6200
(800) 465-4329

THE WESTIN WILLIAM PENN
530 William Penn Pl (15219)
Rates: $204-$274
(412) 281-7100
(800) 228-3000

PITTSTON TOWNSHIP

BEST HOTEL
Rt 315 (18640)
Rates: $69-$169
(570) 655-1234
(800) 937-4667

HOLIDAY INN EXP
30 Concorde Dr
(18641)
Rates: n/a
(570) 654-3300
(800) 465-4329

HOWARD JOHNSON
307 Rt 315 (18640)
Rates: $55-$99
(570) 654-3301
(800) 446-4656

KNIGHTS INN
310 Rt 315 (18640)
Rates: $35-$50
(570) 654-6020
(800) 843-5644

POCONO MOUNTAINS AREA

BEST WESTERN INN
P O Box 413
(Blakeslee 18610)
Rates: $60-$140
(800) 528-1234

BEST WESTERN GENETTI MOTOR LODGE
32nd & N Church
(Hazleton 18201)
Rates: $59-$109
(570) 454-2494
(800) 528-1234

BEST WESTERN GENETTI HOTEL
77 E Market St
(Wilkes-Barre 18701)
Rates: $49-$89
(570) 823-6152
(800) 528-1234
(800) 833-6152

BEST WESTERN INN AT HUNT'S LANDING
120 Rt 6 & 209
(Matamoras 18336)
Rates: $62-$119
(570) 491-2400
(800) 528-1234
(800) 308-2378

BLUE BERRY MOUNTAIN INN BED & BREAKFAST
Edmund Dr
(Blakeslee 18610)
Rates: $110-$125
(717) 646-7144

BUDGET INN
1027 O'Neill Hwy
(Dunmore 18512)
Rates: $42-$95
(570) 346-8782

BUDGET MOTEL
I-80, Exit 51
(East Stroudsburg 18301)
Rates: $45-$80
(570) 424-5451
(800) 233-8144

CLIFF PARK INN & GOLF COURSE
155 Cliff Park Rd
(Milford 18337)
Rates: $90-$175
(570) 296-6491

COMFORT INN
I-84 & SR 191
(Hamlin 18436)
Rates: $49-$169
(570) 689-4148
(800) 228-5150

DAYS INN
1226 O'Neill Hwy
(Dunmore 18512)
Rates: $50-$77
(570) 348-6101
(800) 329-7466

DAYS INN
760 Kidder St
(Wilkes-Barre 18702)
Rates: $52-$61
(570) 826-0111
(800) 329-7466

DAYS INN & SUITES
SR 940
(White Haven 18661)
Rates: $55-$180
(570) 443-0391
(800) 329-7466

FALLS PORT INN
330 Main Ave
(Hawley 18428)
Rates: $55-$95
(570) 226-2609

FIFE & DRUM MOTOR INN
100 Terrace St
(Honesdale 18431)
Rates: $35-$79
(570) 253-1392

HAMPTON INN
114 S 8th St (East Stroudsburg 18360)
Rates: $85-$93
(570) 424-0400
(800) 426-7866

HAMPTON INN
1063 Hwy 315
(Wilkes-Barre 18702)
Rates: $58-$75
(570) 825-3838
(800) 426-7866

HAZELTON MOTOR INN
615 E Broad St
(Hazleton 18201)
Rates: $38-$42
(570) 459-1451

HOLIDAY INN
Rt 611 & I-80
(Bartonsville 18321)
Rates: $62-$125
(570) 424-6100
(800) 465-4329

HOLIDAY INN
200 Tigue St
(Dunmore 18512)
Rates: $135
(570) 343-4771
(800) 465-4329
(800) 959-3412

HOLIDAY INN
880 Kidder St
(Wilkes-Barre 18702)
Rates: $84
(570) 824-8901
(800) 465-4329

HOWARD JOHNSON HOTEL
Rt 447 & 209 N
& I-80 (East Stroudsburg 18360)
Rates: $39-$119
(800) 446-4656

MILFORD MOTEL
591 Rt 6 & 209
(Milford 18337)
Rates: $50-$80
(570) 296-6411

MOUNT LAUREL MOTEL
1039 S Church St
(Hazleton 18201)
Rates: $38-$55
(570) 455-6391

MYER MOTEL
600 Rt 6 & 209
(Milford 18337)
Rates: $50-$88
(570) 296-7223

POCONO MOUNTAIN LODGE
SR 940
(White Haven 18661)
Rates: $50-$68
(800) 443-4049

QUALITY HOTEL
1946 Scranton-
Carbondale Hwy
(Dickson City
18508)
Rates: $65-$95
(570) 383-9979
(800) 228-5151

RAMADA INN
Rt 940 (Lake
Harmony 18624)
Rates: $65-$175
(570) 443-8471
(800) 272-6232

RAMADA INN
Rt 309
(Hazleton 18201)
Rates: $69-$99
(570) 455-2061
(800) 272-6232

RED CARPET INN
400 Kidder St
(Wilkes-Barre
18702)
Rates: $33-$60
(570) 823-2171
(800) 251-1962

RED CARPET INN
240 Rt 6
(Milford 18337)
Rates: $55-$99
(570) 296-9444
(800) 251-1962

RED ROOF INN
1035 Hwy 315
(Wilkes-Barre
18702)
Rates: $46-$78
(570) 829-6422
(800) 843-7663

**RIDGE HOUSE
HISTORIC B&B**
6 Ridge St
(Montrose 18801)
Rates: $40-$55
(717) 278-4933

SUPER 8 MOTEL
340 Green Tree DrE
(East Stroudsburg
18301)
Rates: $62-$82
(570) 424-7411
(800) 800-8000

**TOURIST VILLAGE
MOTEL**
Pike US 6 & 209
(Milford 18337)
Rates: $48-$78
(570) 491-4414

TRAVELODGE
Box 184, Rt 611
(Bartonsville
18321)
Rates: $60-$162
(570) 476-1500
(800) 578-7878

VALUE INN
5219 Milford Rd
(Marshalls Creek
18335)
Rates: $49-$109
(570) 588-1100

POTTSTOWN

COMFORT INN
99 Robinson St
(19464)
Rates: $79-$92
(610) 326-5000
(800) 228-5150

DAYS INN
29 High St (19464)
Rates: $43-$69
(610) 970-1101
(800) 329-7466

**HOLIDAY INN
EXPRESS**
1600 Industrial
Hwy (19464)
Rates: $65
(610) 327-3300
(800) 465-4329

PUNXSU-
TAWNEY

**COUNTRY VILLA
MOTEL**
Rt 119 (15767)
Rates: $30-$44
(814) 938-8330

**PANTALL
HISTORIC HOTEL**
135 E Mahoning
(15767)
Rates: $59-$103
(814) 938-6600
(800) 872-6825

QUAKERTOWN

RODEWAY INN
1920 SR 663
(18951)
Rates: $59-$79
(215) 536-7600
(800) 228-2000

READING

**BEST WESTERN
DUTCH COLONY
INN**
4635 Perkiomen
Ave (19606)
Rates: $78-$108
(610) 779-2345
(800) 528-1234
(800) 828-2830

**ECONO LODGE
NORTHEAST**
2310 Fraver Dr
(19605)
Rates: $42-$68
(610) 378-1145
(800) 553-2666

WELLESLEY INN
910 Woodland
Ave (19610)
Rates: n/a
(610) 374-1500
(800) 444-8888

RIDGEWAY

ROYAL INN
Boot Jack Rd
(15853)
Rates: $39-$55
(814) 773-3153

ST. MARYS

COMFORT INN
976 S St. Mary's
Rd (15857)
Rates: $55-$95
(814) 834-2030
(800) 228-5150

SAXTON

**THE BRYAN
HOUSE VACA-
TION RENTAL**
1101A Church St
(16678)
Rates: n/a
(814) 635-2828

SCRANTON
(Endless
Mountain Area)

ECONO LODGE
1175 Kane St
(18505)
Rates: $35-$95
(570) 348-1000
(800) 553-2666

**HOWARD
JOHNSON
EXPRESS INN**
320 Franklin Ave
(18503)
Rates: $59-$95
(717) 346-7061
(800) 446-4656

SELINSGROVE

COMFORT INN
710 S US Hwy 11
& 15 (17870)
Rates: $69-$105
(570) 374-8880
(800) 228-5150

HAMPTON INN
Hwy 11 & 15
(17870)
Rates: $70-$110
(570) 743-2223
(800) 426-7866

SEWICKLEY

**SEWICKLEY
COUNTRY INN**
801 Ohio River
Blvd (15143)
Rates: $64-$80
(412) 741-4300
(800) 835-6072

SHAMOKIN
DAM

HAMPTON INN
3 Stettler Ave
(17876)
Rates: $70-$80
(570) 743-2223
(800) 426-7866

SHARTLESVILLE

DUTCH MOTEL
Motel Rd (19554)
Rates: $32-$47
(610) 488-1479

SHICKSHINNY

**THE BLUE HERON
BED & BREAKFST**
RR 2, Box 2212
(18655)
Rates: $60-$90
(570) 864-3740

SHIPPENS-
BURG

**BUDGET HOST
SHIPPENSBURG
INN**
10 Hershey Rd
(17257)
Rates: $33-$40
(717) 530-1234
(800) 283-4678

SLIPPERY ROCK

**EVENING STAR
MOTEL**
915 New Castle
Rd (16057)
Rates: $40-$49
(724) 794-3211

SOMERSET

**BEST WESTERN
EXECUTIVE INN**
165 Water Works
Rd (15501)
Rates: $45-$95
(814) 445-3996
(800) 528-1234
(888) 859-8609

**BUDGET HOST
INN**
799 N Central Ave
(15501)
Rates: $28-$75
(814) 445-7988
(800) 283-4678

BUDGET INN
736 N Center Ave
(15501)
Rates: $20-$55
(814) 443-6441

DAYS INN
220 Water Works
Rd (15501)
Rates: $44-$100
(814) 445-9200
(800) 329-7466

DOLLAR INN
1146 N Center Ave
(15501)
Rates: $25-$60
(814) 445-2977
(800) 250-1505

HOLIDAY INN
202 Harmon St
(15501)
Rates: $69-$109
(814) 445-9611
(800) 465-4329
(800) 354-7405

INN AT GEORGIAN PLACE B&B
800 Georgian Place Dr (15501)
Rates: $95-$185
(814) 443-1043

KNIGHTS INN
585 Ramada Rd (15501)
Rates: $39-$71
(814) 445-8933
(800) 843-5644

SUPER 8 MOTEL
125 Lewis Dr (15501)
Rates: $39-$59
(814) 445-8788
(800) 800-8000

SOUTH WILLIAMSPORT

KINGS INN
590 Montgomery Pike (17701)
Rates: $29-$52
(570) 322-4707

RIDGEMONT MOTEL
Montgomery Pike (17701)
Rates: $33-$37
(570) 321-5300

STATE COLLEGE

AUTOPORT MOTEL
1405 S Atherton St (16801)
Rates: $65-$89
(814) 237-7666

BEST WESTERN INN
1663 S Atherton St (16801)
Rates: $49-$155
(814) 237-8005
(800) 528-1234
(800) 635-1177

BREWMEISTER'S B&B MOTEL
2070 Cato Ave (16801)
Rates: $40-$70
(814) 238-0015

DAYS INN-PENN STATE
240 S Pugh St (16801)
Rates: $59-$90
(814) 238-8454
(800) 329-7466

HOLIDAY INN
1925 Waddle Rd (16803)
Rates: n/a
(800) 465-4329

MOTEL 6 PENN STATE UNIV
1274 NAtherton St (16801)
Rates: $53-$70
(814) 234-1600
(800) 466-8356

RAMADA INN
1450 S Atherton St (16801)
Rates: $95-$175
(814) 238-3001
(800) 272-6232

STRASBURG

HISTORIC STRASBURG INN
One Historic Dr (17579)
Rates: $139-$159
(717) 687-7691
(800) 872-0201

TOWANDA
(Endless Mountain Region)

TOWANDA MOTEL
383 York Ave (18848)
Rates: $39-$70
(717) 265-2178

TREVOSE

RED ROOF INN
3100 Lincoln Hwy (19053)
Rates: $56-$88
(215) 244-9422
(800) 843-7663

TURTLE CREEK

JAMES STREET BED & BREAKFAST
553 James St (15145)
Rates: $35-$55
(412) 372-8060

ULYSSES

PINE LOG MOTEL
Rt 1, Box 15 (16948)
Rates: $32-$38
(814) 435-6400

UNIONTOWN

HOLIDAY INN
700 W Main St (15401)
Rates: $99
(724) 437-2816
(800) 258-7238

MOUNT VERNON INN
180 W Main St (15401)
Rates: $33-$78
(724) 437-2704

WARREN

HOLIDAY INN
210 Ludlow St (16365)
Rates: $79
(814) 726-3000
(800) 465-4329

SUPER 8 MOTEL
204 Struthers St (16365)
Rates: $50-$62
(814) 723-8881
(800) 800-8000

WASHINGTON

HAMPTON INN
119 Murtland Ave (15301)
Rates: $63-$77
(724) 228-4100
(800) 426-7866

HOLIDAY INN MEADOW LANDS
340 Race Track Rd (15301)
Rates: $95
(724) 222-6200
(800) 465-4329

LONGSTRETCH HARBOUR HISTORIC B&B
951 National Pike E (15301)
Rates: $40-$75
(724) 223-8283

MOTEL 6
1283 Motel 6 Dr (15301)
Rates: $38-$54
(724) 223-8040
(800) 466-8356

RED ROOF INN
1399 W Chestnut St (15301)
Rates: $50-$69
(724) 228-5750
(800) 843-7663

WATSONTOWN

ALOHA MOTEL
16 W Brimmer Ave (17777)
Rates: $50-$60
(717) 538-5979

WAYNESBORO

BEST WESTERN INN
239 W Main St (17268)
Rates: $55-$72
(717) 762-9113
(800) 528-1234
(877) 333-1986

WAYNESBURG

COMFORT INN
1 Comfort Lane (15370)
Rates: $59-$150
(724) 627-3700
(800) 228-5150

ECONO LODGE
350 Miller Ln (15370)
Rates: $40-$77
(724) 627-5544
(800) 553-2666

SUPER 8 MOTEL
80 Miller Ln (15370)
Rates: $42-$62
(724) 627-8880
(800) 800-8000

WELLSBORO

CANYON MOTEL
18 East Ave (16901)
Rates: $30-$52
(570) 724-1681
(800) 255-2718

COLTON POINT MOTEL
US 6, Jct Rt 287 (16901)
Rates: $30-$55
(570) 724-2155

FOXFIRE B&B
RD 2, Box 439 (16901)
Rates: $36-$65
(570) 724-5175

WEST CHESTER

ABBEY GREEN MOTOR LODGE
1036 Wilmington Pike (19382)
Rates: $39-$57
(610) 692-3310

MICROTEL INN & SUITES
500 Willowbrook Ln (19382)
Rates: $49-$79
(610) 738-9111
(888) 771-7171
(888) 619-9292

WEST HAZELTON

COMFORT INN
SR 93 & Kiwanis Blvd (18201)
Rates: $85-$119
(570) 455-9300
(800) 228-5150

FOREST HILL INN
SR 93 (18201)
Rates: $47-$52
(570) 459-2730
(800) 736-2730

WEST MIDDLESEX

COMFORT INN-SHENANGO VLY
SR 18 & Wilson Rd (16159)
Rates: $55-$120
(724) 342-7200
(800) 228-5150

RADISSON HOTEL
Rt 18 & I-80 (16159)
Rates: $90-$110
(724) 528-2501
(800) 333-3333

WHITE HAVEN
(See Pocono
Mountains Area)

WILKES-BARRE
(See Pocono
Mountains Area)

WILLIAMSPORT

BING'S MOTEL
2961 Lycoming
Creek Rd (17701)
Rates: $28-$34
(570) 494-0601

CITY VIEW INN
RD 4, Box 550
(17701)
Rates: $42-$48
(570) 326-2601

ECONO LODGE
2401 E 3rd St
(17701)
Rates: $50-$135
(570) 326-1501
(800) 553-2666

**GENETTI
HISTORIC HOTEL**
200 W 4th St
(17701)
Rates: $95-$175
(570) 326-6600
(800) 321-1388

HOLIDAY INN
1840 E 3rd St
(17701)
Rates: $69-$79
(570) 326-1981
(800) 465-4329

RADISSON INN
100 Pine St (17701)
Rates: $79
(570) 327-8231
(800) 333-3333

WIND GAP

TRAVEL INN
499 E Moorestown
Rd (18091)
Rates: $45-$70
(610) 863-4146

WYOMISSING

CLARION HOTEL
1040 Park Rd
(19610)
Rates: $89-$149
(610) 372-7811
(800) 252-7466

ECONO LODGE
635 Spring St
(196109
Rates: $40-$120
(610) 378-5105
(800) 553-2666

**SHERATON
BERKSHIRE
HOTEL**
1741 W Papermill
Rd (19610)
Rates: $89-$199
(610) 376-3811
(800) 325-3535

WELLESLEY INN
910 Woodland
Ave (19610)
Rates: $55-$129
(610) 374-1500
(800) 444-8888

WYSOX

COMFORT INN
US 6, The Golden
Mile (18854)
Rates: $72-$127
(570) 265-5691
(800) 228-5150

YORK

DAYS INN
222 Arsenal Rd
(17402)
Rates: $45-$99
(717) 843-9971
(800) 329-7466

**HOLIDAY INN
HOLIDOME**
2000 Loucks Rd
(17402)
Rates: $102
(717) 846-9500
(800) 465-4329

MOTEL 6
125 Arsenal Rd
(17404)
Rates: $31-$48
(717) 846-6260
(800) 466-8356

RAMADA INN
2600 E Market St
(17402)
Rates: $69-$74
(717) 755-1966
(800) 272-6232

RED ROOF INN
323 Arsenal Rd
(17402)
Rates: $50-$68
(717) 843-8181
(800) 843-7663

SUPER 8 MOTEL
40 Arsenal Rd
(17404)
Rates: $48-$76
(717) 852-8686
(800) 800-8000

RHODE ISLAND

BLOCK ISLAND

BLUE DORY INN BED & BREAKFST
Dodge St (02807)
Rates: n/a
(401) 466-5891
(800) 992-7290

EASTGATE HOUSE BED & BREAKFAST
Spring St (02807)
Rates: n/a
(401) 465-2164

BRISTOL

JOSEPH REYNOLDS HOUSE INN BED &BREAKFAST
956 Hope St (02809)
Rates: n/a
(401) 254-0230
(800) 754-0230

CHARLES-TOWN

KRYSTAL PENGUIN MOTEL
5399 Post Rd (02813)
Rates: n/a
(401) 364-0062
(888) 879-8106

CRANSTON

DAYS INN
101 New London Ave (02920)
Rates: $55-$89
(401) 942-4200
(800) 329-7466

EAST PROVIDENCE

NEW YORKER MOTOR LODGE
400 Newport Ave (02916)
Rates: n/a
(401) 434-8000

MIDDLETOWN

BARTRAM'S BED &BREAKFAST
94 Kane Ave (02842)
Rates: n/a
(401) 846-2259

THE BAY WILLOWS INN
1225 Aquidneck Ave (02842)
Rates: $39-$169
(401) 847-8400
(800) 838-5642

HOWARD JOHNSON INN
351 W Main Rd (02842)
Rates: $99-$179
(401) 849-2000
(800) 654-2000

RAMADA INN
936 W Main Rd (02842)
Rates: $49-$199
(401) 846-7600
(800) 272-6232
(800) 846-8322

SEAVIEW INN MOTEL
240 Aquidneck Ave (02842)
Rates: $59-$189
(401) 846-5000
(800) 495-2046

TRAVELODGE
1185 W Main Rd (02842)
Rates: $40-$160
(401) 849-4700
(800) 578-7878

NEWPORT

ANNA'S VICTORIAN CONNECTION
5 Fowler Ave (02840)
Rates: n/a
(401) 849-2489

B&B INTERNATIONAL
21 Dearborn St (02840)
Rates: n/a
(401) 846-7716

BANNISTER'S WHARF MARINA & GUEST ROOMS
Bannister's Wharf (02840)
Rates: n/a
(401) 846-4500

HARBOR-BASE PINEAPPLE INN
372 Coddington Hwy (02840)
Rates: $25-$70
(401) 847-2600

INN ON BELLEVUE BED & BREAKFST
30 Bellevue Ave (02840)
Rates: n/a
(401) 848-6242

MOTEL 6
249 J T Connell Hwy (02840)
Rates: $60-$76
(401) 848-0600
(800) 466-8356

1 MURRAY HOUSE BED & BREAKFAST
Murray Pl (02840)
Rates: n/a
(401) 846-3337

SANFORD-COVELL VILLA MARINA B&B
72 Washington St (02840)
Rates: n/a
(401) 847-0206

1751 BANISTER HOUSE
P. O. Box 381 (02840)
Rates: n/a
(401) 846-0059

NORTH KINGSTOWN

COVE MOTEL
7825 Post Rd (02904)
Rates: n/a
(401) 294-4853

THE WICKFORD HOUSE BED & BREAKFAST
68 Main St (02904)
Rates: n/a
(401) 294-6479

PROVIDENCE

PROVIDENCE BILTMORE HOTEL-A GRAND HERITAGE HOTEL
Kennedy Plaza (02903)
Rates: n/a
(401) 421-0700
(800) 294-7799

PROVIDENCE MARRIOTT
1 Orms St (02903)
Rates: n/a
(401) 272-2400
(800) 937-PROV

THE WESTIN HOTEL
1 W Exchange St (02903)
Rates: $265-$315
(401) 598-8000
(800) 228-3000

SOUTH KINGSTOWN

CAPTAIN'S B&B
2 Heather Hollow Rd (02879)
Rates: n/a
(401) 782-3445

THE HOLLY HOUSE B&B
522 Main St (02879)
Rates: n/a
(401) 783-5454
(800) 275-5450

WARWICK

COMFORT INN
1940 Post Rd (02886)
Rates: $99-$149
(401) 732-0470
(800) 228-5150

CROWNE PLAZA HOTEL AT THE CROSSINGS
801 Greenwich Ave (02886)
Rates: $199-$209
(401) 732-6000
(800) 227-6963

MAINSTAY SUITES
268 Metro Center Blvd (02886)
Rates: $69-$129
(401) 732-6667
(800) 228-5151

MASTER HOSTS INNS
2138 Post Rd (02886)
Rates: $69-$160
(401) 737-7400
(800) 251-1962

MOTEL 6
20 Jefferson Blvd (02888)
Rates: $49-$72
(401) 467-9800
(800) 466-8356

REDWOOD LODGE MOTEL
2282 Post Rd (02886)
Rates: n/a
(401) 739-1150
(800) 874-4114

RESIDENCE INN BY MARRIOTT
500 Kilvert St (02886)
Rates: $143-$170
(401) 737-7100
(800) 331-3131

AREA CODES - If the local number doesn't connect, check for a new area code.

SHERATON
PROVIDENCE
AIRPORT HOTEL
1850 Post Rd
(02886)
Rates: $128-$250
(401) 738-4000
(800) 557-2050

WEST
WARWICK

LEPRECHAUN
MOTEL
325 Quaker Lane
(02893)
Rates: n/a
(401) 828-1509

WESTERLY

FRANKLIN
GARDENS MOTEL
129 Franklin St
(02891)
Rates: n/a
(401) 596-2705
(888) 596-2705

SANDPIPER
MOTEL
55 Winnapaug Rd
(02891)
Rates: n/a
(401) 596-7920

SEA SHELL MOTEL
19 Winnapaug Rd
(02891)
Rates: n/a
(401) 348-8337

THE VILLA INN
BED & BREAKFST
190 Shore Rd
(02891)
Rates: $85-$165
(401) 596-1054
(800) 722-9240

SOUTH CAROLINA

AIKEN

COMFORT INN
3608 Richland Ave
W (29801)
Rates: $45-$200
(803) 641-1100
(800) 228-5150

DAYS INN
1204 Richland Ave
W (29801)
Rates: $38-$45
(803) 649-5524
(800) 329-7466

DELUXE INN
1919 Edgefield
Hwy (29801)
Rates: $27-$44
(803) 642-2840

**HOWARD
JOHNSON
EXPRESS INN
& SUITES**
1936 Whiskey Rd
S (29803)
Rates: $34-$155
(803) 649-5000
(800) 446-4656

RAMADA LIMITED
1850 Richland Ave
W (29801)
Rates: $39-$54
(803) 648-6821
(800) 272-6232

**TOWN &
COUNTRY INN**
2340 Sizemore Cr
(29801)
Rates: $60-$95
(803) 642-0270

**THE WILLCOX
HISTORIC
COUNTRY INN**
100 Colleton Ave
SW (29801)
Rates: $69-$135
(803) 649-1377
(800) 368-1047

ANDERSON

DAYS INN
1007 Smith Mill
Rd (29625)
Rates: $58-$89
(864) 375-0375
(800) 329-7466

LA QUINTA INN
3430 Clemson
Blvd (29621)
Rates: $49-$79
(864) 225-3721
(800) 687-6667

QUALITY INN
3509 Clemson
Blvd (29621)
Rates: $69-$89
(864) 226-1000
(800) 228-5151

RAMADA INN
3025 N Main St
(29621)
Rates: $45-$150
(864) 226-6051
(800) 272-6232

**ROYAL AMERI-
CAN MOTOR INN**
4515 Clemson
Blvd (29621)
Rates: $33-$42
(864) 226-7236
(800) 524-9823

BEAUFORT

**BATTERY CREEK
INN**
102 B Marina Blvd
(29902)
Rates: $70+
(843) 521-1441

DAYS INN
1660 S Ribaut
(Port Royal 29902)
Rates: $56-$97
(843) 524-1551
(800) 329-7466

ECONO LODGE
2221 Boundary St
(29902)
Rates: $50-$125
(843) 521-1555
(800) 553-2666

HOLIDAY INN
2001 Boundary St
(29902)
Rates: $50-$60
(843) 524-2144
(800) 465-4329

**HOWARD JOHN-
SON EXPRESS**
3651 Trask Pkwy
(29902)
Rates: $65-$80
(843) 524-6020
(800) 446-4656

BISHOPVILLE

ECONO LODGE
1153 S Main St
(29010)
Rates: $34-$150
(805) 428-3200
(800) 553-2666

BLYTHEWOOD

COMFORT INN
436 McNulty Rd
(29016)
Rates: $65-$125
(803) 754-1441
(800) 228-5150

CAMDEN

COLONY INN
2020 W DeKalb St
(29020)
Rates: $49-$55
(803) 432-5508

GREENLEAF INN
1310 N Broad St
(29020)
Rates: $45-$70
(803) 425-1806
(800) 437-5874

**LORD CAMDEN
INN B&B**
1502 Broad St
(29020)
Rates: $70-$110
(803) 713-9050

PARKVIEW MOTEL
1039 W DeKalb St
(29020)
Rates: $21-$27
(803) 432-7687

CAYCE

KNIGHTS INN
1987 Airport Blvd
(29033)
Rates: $29-$47
(803) 794-0222
(800) 843-5644

**MASTERS
ECONOMY INN**
2125 Commerce
Dr (29033)
Rates: $24-$35
(803) 791-5850

CHARLESTON

**BEST WESTERN
INN**
1540 Savannah
Hwy (29407)
Rates: $89-$149
(843) 571-6100
(800) 528-1234

**DAYS INN-
AIRPORT**
2998 W Montague
Ave (29418)
Rates: $39-$89
(843) 747-4101
(800) 329-7466

**DOUBLETREE
GUEST SUITES**
181 Church St
(29401)
Rates: $139-$269
(843) 577-2644
(800) 222-8733

**HOLIDAY INN-
RIVERVIEW**
301 Savannah
Hwy (29407)
Rates: $99-$145
(843) 556-7100
(800) 465-4329

**INDIGO INN
HISTORIC B&B**
1 Maiden Ln
(29401)
Rates: $140-$236
(843) 577-5900
(800) 845-7639

MAINSTAY SUITES
5045 N Arco Lane
(29418)
Rates: $85-$99
(843) 740-3440
(800) 660-6246

MARRIOTT HOTEL
4770 Marriott Dr
(29406)
Rates: $94
(843) 747-1900
(800) 228-9290

**MASTERS
ECONOMY INN**
6100 Rivers Ave
(29406)
Rates: $39-$48
(800) 633-3434

MIDDLETON INN
Ashley River Rd
(29414)
Rates: $109-$139
(843) 556-0500
(800) 543-4774

MOTEL 6-NORTH
2551 Ashley
Phosphate Rd
(29418)
Rates: $34-$44
(843) 572-6590
(800) 466-8356

MOTEL 6-SOUTH
2058 Savannah
Hwy (29407)
Rates: $35-$48
(843) 556-5144
(800) 466-8356

ORCHARD INN
4725 Saul White
Blvd (29418)
Rates: $36-$57
(843) 747-3671

**RESIDENCE INN
BY MARRIOTT**
7645 Northwoods
Blvd (29406)
Rates: $90-$130
(843) 572-5757
(800) 331-3131

**SHERATON
CHARLESTON
HOTEL**
170 Lockwood Dr
(29401)
Rates: $127-$152
(843) 723-3000
(800) 325-3535

SUPER 8 MOTEL
4620 Dorchester
Rd (29405)
Rates: $49-$69
(843) 747-7500
(800) 800-8000

**TOWN &
COUNTRY INN**
2008 Savannah
Hwy (29407)
Rates: $69-$119
(843) 571-1000
(800) 334-6660

TRAVELODGE
6059 Fain St
(29406)
Rates: $50-$65
(843) 744-7388
(800) 578-7878

CHERAW

DAYS INN
820 Market St
(29520)
Rates: $40-$125
(843) 537-5554
(800) 329-7466

INN CHERAW
321 Second St
(29520)
Rates: $40-$70
(843) 537-2011
(800) 535-8709

CLEMSON

HOLIDAY INN
894 Tiger Blvd
(29633)
Rates: $65-$99
(864) 654-4450
(800) 465-4329

CLINTON

COMFORT INN
12785 Hwy 56 N
(29325)
Rates: $48-$70
(864) 833-5558
(800) 228-5150

DAYS INN
Jct I-26 & I-385
(29325)
Rates: $48-$85
(864) 833-6600
(800) 329-7466

RAMADA INN
Hwy 56 & I-26
(29325)
Rates: $59-$89
(864) 833-4900
(800) 272-6232

COLUMBIA

**ADAMS MARK
HOTEL**
1200 Hampton St
(29201)
Rates: $69-$134
(803) 771-7000
(800) 444-2326

AMERISUITES
7525 Two Notch
Rd (29223)
Rates: $48-$53
(803) 736-6666
(800) 833-1516

**BAYMONT INN
& SUITES EAST**
1538 Horseshoe
Dr (29204)
Rates: $50-$56
(803) 736-6400
(800) 301-0200

**BAYMONT INN
& SUITES WEST**
911 Bush River Rd
(29210)
Rates: $46
(803) 798-3222
(800) 301-0200

**COMFORT INN
NORTHEAST**
499 Piney Grove
Rd (29210)
Rates: $45-$99
(803) 798-0500
(800) 228-5150

COMFORT SUITES
7337 Garner's
Ferry Rd (29209)
Rates: $67-$114
(803) 695-5555
(800) 228-5150

DAYS INN
133 Plumbers Rd
(29203)
Rates: $35-$99
(803) 754-4408
(800) 329-7466

DAYS INN
7128 Parklane Rd
(29223)
Rates: $35-$44
(803) 736-0000
(800) 329-7466

DAYS INN
1144 Bush River
Rd (29210)
Rates: $40-$65
(803) 772-4910
(800) 329-7466

**HOLIDAY INN-
COLISEUM**
630 Assembly St
(29201)
Rates: $99-$113
(803) 779-7800
(800) 465-4329

HOLIDAY INN-NE
7510 Two Notch
Rd (29223)
Rates: $72-$88
(803) 736-3000
(800) 465-4329

**KNIGHTS INN
NORTHWEST**
1803 Bush River
Rd (29210)
Rates: $30-$75
(803) 772-0022
(800) 843-5644

**KNIGHTS INN
WEST**
2210 Bush River
Rd (29210)
Rates: $45-$75
(803) 798-9665
(800) 578-7878

LA QUINTA INN
1335 Garner Ln
(29210)
Rates: $49-$79
(803) 798-9590
(800) 687-6667

MICROTEL INN
1520 Barbara Dr
(29223)
Rates: $42-$56
(803) 736-3237
(888) 771-7171

MOTEL 6 EAST
7541 Nates Rd
(29223)
Rates: $34-$46
(803) 736-3900
(800) 466-8356

MOTEL 6 WEST
1776 Burning Tree
Rd (29210)
Rates: $37-$53
(803) 798-9210
(800) 466-8356

**RAMADA PLAZA
HOTEL**
8105 Two Notch
Rd (29223)
Rates: $79-$99
(803) 736-5600
(800) 272-6232

**RED ROOF INN-
EAST**
7580 Two Notch
Rd (29223)
Rates: $50-$64
(803) 736-0850
(800) 843-7663

**RED ROOF INN-
WEST**
10 Berryhill Rd
(29210)
Rates: $37-$64
(803) 798-9220
(800) 843-7663

**RESIDENCE INN
BY MARRIOTT**
150 Stoneridge Dr
(29210)
Rates: $130
(803) 779-7000
(800) 331-3131

**SHERATON
HOTEL & CONF
CENTER**
2100 Bush River
Rd (29210)
Rates: $135-$155
(803) 731-0300
(800) 325-3535

SUPER 8 MOTEL
5719 Fairfield Rd
(29203)
Rates: $39-$56
(803) 735-0008
(800) 800-8000

DILLON

COMFORT INN
810 Radford Blvd
(29536)
Rates: $53-$75
(843) 774-4137
(800) 424-6423

DAYS INN
818 Radford Blvd
(29536)
Rates: $25-$75
(843) 774-6041
(800) 329-7466

ECONO LODGE
1223 Radford Blvd
(29536)
Rates: $32-$125
(843) 774-4181
(800) 553-2666

**HOWARD
JOHNSON
EXPRESS INN**
904 Radford Blvd
(29536)
Rates: $35-$65
(843) 774-5111
(800) 446-4656

SUPER 8 MOTEL
1203 Radford Blvd
(29536)
Rates: $40-$99
(843) 774-4161
(800) 800-8000

EASLEY

DAYS INN
121 Days Inn Dr
(29640)
Rates: $48-$125
(864) 859-9902
(800) 329-7466

FLORENCE

DAYS INN NORTH
2111 W Lucas St
(29501)
Rates: $40-$90
(843) 665-4444
(800) 329-7466

DAYS INN SOUTH
3783 W Palmetto
St (29502)
Rates: $35-$63
(843) 665-8550
(800) 329-7466

**HOWARD
JOHNSON
EXPRESS**
3821 Bancroft Rd
(29503)
Rates: $145
(843) 664-9494
(800) 446-4656

AREA CODES - If the local number doesn't connect, check for a new area code.

MOTEL 6
1834 W Lucas Rd
(29501)
Rates: $35-$51
(843) 667-6100
(800) 466-8356

PARK INN INTERNATIONAL
831 S Irby St
(29501)
Rates: $36-$44
(843) 662-9421
(800) 437-7275

RAMADA INN
2038 W Lucas
(29501)
Rates: $79-$200
(843) 669-4241
(800) 272-6232

RED ROOF INN
2690 David McLeod
Blvd (29501)
Rates: $40-$72
(843) 678-9000
(800) 843-7663

RODEWAY INN I-95
3024 T.V. Rd
(29501)
Rates: $45-$100
(843) 669-1715
(800) 228-2000

SHONEY'S INN
I-95 & US 52
(29501)
Rates: $44-$54
(843) 669-1921
(800) 222-2222

THUNDERBIRD MOTOR INN
2004 W Lucas Rd
(29502)
Rates: $36-$47
(843) 669-1611
(800) 522-9552

YOUNG'S PLANTATION INN
Hwy 76 (29502)
Rates: $29-$35
(843) 669-4171
(800) 476-2299

FORT MILL

DAYS INN
3482 Carowinds
Blvd (29715)
Rates: $45-$90
(803) 548-8000
(800) 329-7466

MOTEL 6
255 Carowinds
Blvd (29715)
Rates: $39-$52
(803) 548-9656
(800) 466-8356

GAFFNEY

COMFORT INN
143 Corona Dr
(29341)
Rates: $65-$95
(864) 487-4200
(800) 228-5150

DAYS INN
136 Peachoid Rd
(29341)
Rates: $45-$50
(864) 489-7172
(800) 329-7466

HAMPTON INN
Hwy 105 & Nancy
Creek Rd (29341)
Rates: $65-$75
(864) 206-0011
(800) 426-7866

SLEEP INN
834 Windslow Ave
(29341)
Rates: $45-$150
(864) 487-5337
(800) 753-3746

GEORGETOWN

CLARION CARRIAGE HOUSE INN
706 Church St
(29440)
Rates: $54-$79
(843) 546-5191
(800) 252-7466

DEASONS MOTEL
412 St. James St
(29440)
Rates: n/a
(843) 546-4117

ECONO LODGE
600 Church St
(29440)
Rates: $48-$85
(843) 546-5111
(800) 553-2666

GOOSE CREEK

DAYS INN
1430 Redbank Rd
(29445)
Rates: $50-$75
(843) 797-6000
(800) 329-7466

GREENVILLE

AMERISUITES
40 W Orchard
Park Rd (29615)
Rates: $79-$125
(864) 232-3000
(800) 833-1516

COMFORT INN I-85
412 Mauldin Rd
(29605)
Rates: $54-$155
(864) 277-6730
(800) 228-5150

CROWNE PLAZA
851 Congaree Rd
(29607)
Rates: $59-$149
(864) 297-6300
(800) 227-6963

DAYS INN
831 Congaree Rd
(29607)
Rates: $59-$99
(864) 288-6221
(800) 329-7466

GUESTHOUSE SUITES PLUS
48 McPrice Ct
(29615)
Rates: $108
(864) 297-0099

HOLIDAY INN I-85
4295 Augusta Rd
(29605)
Rates: $84
(864) 277-8921
(800) 465-4329

LA QUINTA INN
31 Old Country
Rd (29607)
Rates: $49-$79
(864) 297-3500
(800) 687-6667

MICROTEL INN
20 Interstate Ct
(2915)
Rates: $52-$63
(864) 297-7866
(888) 771-7171
(888) 297-7866

MOTEL 6
224 Bruce Rd
(29605)
Rates: $35-$43
(864) 277-8630
(800) 466-8356

PHOENIX INN
246 N
Pleasantburg Dr
(29606)
Rates: $65-$130
(864) 233-4651
(800) 257-3529

RAMADA LIMITED SOUTH
1314 S
Pleasantburg Dr
(29605)
Rates: $46-$89
(864) 277-3734
(800) 272-6232

RED ROOF INN
2801 Laurens Rd
(29607)
Rates: $46-$58
(864) 297-4458
(800) 843-7663

RESIDENCE INN BY MARRIOTT
48 McPrice Ct
(29615)
Rates: $89-$109
(864) 297-0099
(800) 331-3131

GREENWOOD

RAMADA INN
1014 Montague
Ave (29649)
Rates: $65+
(864) 223-4231
(800) 272-6232

GREER

COMFORT SUITES
2681 Dry Pocket
Rd (29650)
Rates: $79-$179
(864) 213-9331
(800) 228-5150

MAINSTAY SUITES
2671 Dry Pocket
Rd (29650)
Rates: $49-$129
(864) 987-5566
(800) 660-6246

HARDEEVILLE

DAYS INN STATELINE
Hwy 17 & I-95
(29927)
Rates: $40-$65
(864) 784-2281
(800) 329-7466

ECONOMY INN
101 Frontage Rd
(29927)
Rates: $26-$33
(864) 784-2201

HOWARD JOHNSON LODGE
Hwy 17 & I-95
(29927)
Rates: $33-$69
(843) 784-2271
(800) 446-4656

KNIGHTS INN
Hwy 17 & I-95
(29927)
Rates: $35-$45
(843) 784-2196
(800) 843-5644

RAMADA LIMITED
Hwy 278 & I-95,
Exit 8 (29927)
Rates: $44-$99
(843) 784-3192
(800) 272-6232

SCOTTISH INNS
Hwy 17 & I-95
(29927)
Rates: n/a
(843) 784-2151
(800) 251-1962

HARTSVILLE

LANDMARK INN
1301 S 4th St
(29550)
Rates: $52-$68
(843) 332-2611
(800) 628-9108

HILTON HEAD ISLAND

BAYSHORE OF HILTON HEAD CONDOS
81 Pope Ave,
Heritage Plaza
(29938)
Rates: $500-$6000
(843) 842-9494

AREA CODES - If the local number doesn't connect, check for a new area code.

COMFORT INN
2 Tanglewood Dr
(29928)
Rates: $60-$159
(843) 842-6662
(800) 228-5150

MOTEL 6
830 Wm Hilton
Pkwy (29928)
Rates: $35-$56
(843) 785-2700
(800) 466-8356

**QUALITY INN
& SUITES**
200 Museum St
(29926)
Rates: $49-$169
(843) 681-3655
(800) 228-5151

RED ROOF INN
5 Regency Pkwy
(29928)
Rates: $66-$87
(843) 686-6808
(800) 843-7663

LAKE CITY

DAYS INN
170 S Ron McNair
Blvd (29560)
Rates: $49-$89
(843) 394-3269
(800) 329-7466

LANDRUM

**THE RED HORSE
INN COTTAGE**
310 N Campbell
Rd (29356)
Rates: $105-$125
(864) 895-4968

LATTA

**PATRICK HENRY
MOTOR LODGE**
203 N Richardson
St (29565)
Rates: $20-$35
(843) 752-5861

LEXINGTON

COMFORT INN
328 W Main St
(29072)
Rates: $52-$110
(803) 359-3099
(800) 228-5150

RAMADA LIMITED
1015 S Lake Dr
(29072)
Rates: $50-$60
(803) 356-6533
(800) 272-6232

LITTLE RIVER

DAYS INN
1564 Hwy 17 N
(29566)
Rates: $52-$95
(843) 249-3535
(800) 329-7466

LUGOFF

DAYS INN
529 Hwy 601 S
(29078)
Rates: $48-$125
(803) 438-6990
(800) 329-7466

HOLIDAY INN
Hwy 1 S (29078)
Rates: $49-$85
(803) 438-9441
(800) 465-4329

RAMADA LIMITED
542 Hwy 601 S
(29078)
Rates: $48-$65
(803) 438-1807
(800) 272-6232

MANNING

COMFORT INN
I-95 & SR 261
(29102)
Rates: $49-$120
(803) 473-7550
(800) 228-5150

DAYS INN
Rt 5, Box 448
(29102)
Rates: $44-$74
(803) 473-2913
(800) 329-7466

ECONOMY INN
Hwy 261 (29102)
Rates: $28-$44
(803) 473-4021

SUN SET INN
I-95 & US 301
(29102)
Rates: $21-$30
(803) 473-2561

SUPER 8 MOTEL
Rt 6 , Box 883
(29102)
Rates: $34-$49
(803) 473-4646
(800) 800-8000

MT PLEASANT

**COMFORT INN
EAST**
310 Hwy 17
Bypass (29464)
Rates: $69-$139
(843) 884-5853
(800) 228-5150

**GUILDS INN
HISTORIC B&B**
101 Pitt St (29464)
Rates: $85-$140
(843) 881-0510
(800) 331-0510

MAINSTAY SUITES
400 McGrath
Darby Blvd
(29464)
Rates: $49-$149
(843) 881-1722
(800) 660-9246

**MASTERS
ECONOMY INN**
300 Wingo Way
(29464)
Rates: $36-$64
(843) 884-2814
(800) 633-3434

RED ROOF INN
301 Johnnie
Dodds Blvd
(29464)
Rates: $53-$107
(843) 884-1411
(800) 843-7663

SLEEP INN
299 Wingo Way
(29646)
Rates: $39-$109
(843) 856-5000
(800) 753-3746

MYRTLE BEACH

**AZALEAS BEACH
HOUSES**
4302 Seaview St
(Ocean Drive
29582)
Rates: $400-$900
Weekly
(843) 361-9043

DAYS INN
3209 Hwy 17 S
(North Myrtle
Beach 29582)
Rates: $38-$159
(843) 272-6196
(800) 329-7466

**EL DORADO
MOTEL**
2800 S Ocean Blvd
(29577)
Rates: $59-$69
(843) 626-3559

**LA QUINTA INN
& SUITES**
1561 21st Ave N
(29577)
Rates: $85-$159
(843) 916-8801
(800) 687-6667

**MARINER
APARTMENT
MOTEL**
7003 N Ocean
Blvd (29572)
Rates: $31-$94
(843) 449-5281

RED ROOF INN
2801 S Kings Hwy
(29577)
Rates: n/a
(843) 626-4444
(800) 843-7663

ST JOHN'S INN
6803 N Ocean
Blvd (29572)
Rates: $79-$140
(843) 449-5251
(800) 845-0624

SEA MIST RESORT
1200 S Ocean Blvd
(29577)
Rates: $68-$295
(843) 448-1551
(800) 732-6478

**STAYBRIDGE
SUITES BY
HOLIDAY INN**
3163 Outlet Blvd
(29579)
Rates: n/a
(843) 903-4000
(800) 238-8000

WATERSIDE INN
2000 N Ocean
Blvd (29577)
Rates: $61-$154
(843) 448-5935
(800) 248-8286

NEWBERRY

**BEST WESTERN
INN**
11701 S Hwy 34
(29108)
Rates: $40-$55
(803) 276-5850
(800) 528-1234

DAYS INN
Rt 1, Box 407-B
(29108)
Rates: $36-$55
(803) 276-2294
(800) 329-7466

NORTH CHARLESTON

**COMFORT INN
COLISEUM**
5055 N Arco Ln
(29418)
Rates: $40-$109
(843) 554-6485
(800) 228-5150

LA QUINTA INN
2499 La Quinta Ln
(29418)
Rates: $59-$95
(843) 797-8181
(800) 687-6667

RED ROOF INN
7480 Northwoods
Blvd (29418)
Rates: $48-$58
(843) 572-9100
(800) 843-7663

SUPER 8 MOTEL
2311 Ashley
Phosphate Rd
(29406)
Rates: $50-$63
(843) 572-2228
(800) 800-8000

ORANGEBURG

DAYS INN
Rt 2, Box 215 (29115)
Rates: $40-$90
(803) 534-0500
(800) 329-7466

**HOWARD
JOHNSON
EXPRESS**
3608 Old St
Matthews Rd
(29115)
Rates: $35-$70
(803) 531-4900
(800) 446-4656

AREA CODES - If the local number doesn't connect, check for a new area code.

QUALITY INN & SUITES
1415 John C
Calhoun Dr
(29115)
Rates: $60-$90
(803) 531-4600
(800) 228-5151

RAMADA LIMITED
826 John C
Calhoun Dr
(29115)
Rates: $40-$65
(803) 534-7630
(800) 272-6232

SHONEY'S INN
Hwy 601 (29118)
Rates: n/a
(800) 222-2222

SUPER 8 MOTEL
610 John C.
Calhoun Dr
(29115)
Rates: $44-$58
(803) 531-1921
(800) 800-8000

RICHBURG

DAYS INN
3217 Lancaster
Hwy (29729)
Rates: $31-$85
(803) 789-5555
(800) 329-7466

ECONO LODGE
3190 Lancaster
Hwy (29729)
Rates: $36-$125
(803) 789-3000
(800) 553-2666

RELAX INN
I-77 & Hwy 9
(29729)
Rates: $25-$95
(803) 789-6363

SUPER 8 MOTEL
3085 Lancaster
Hwy (29729)
Rates: $44-$79
(803) 789-7888
(800) 800-8000

RIDGE SPRING

SOUTHWOOD MANOR B&B
100 E Main St
(29129)
Rates: $65-$75
(803) 685-5100

RIDGELAND

BEST WESTERN POINT SOUTH
I-95 & US 17
(29936)
Rates: $40-$58
(843) 726-8101
(800) 528-1234

COMFORT INN
I-95 & SR 336
(29936)
Rates: $50-$125
(843) 726-2121
(800) 228-5150

ECONO LODGE
516 E Main St
(29936)
Rates: $41-$125
(843) 726-5553
(800) 553-2666

PALMS MOTEL
Hwy 17 (29936)
Rates: $23-$30
(843) 726-5511

RAMADA LIMITED
Hwy 336 & I-95,
Exit 21 (29936)
Rates: $42-$55
(843) 717-9595
(800) 272-6232

RIDGEWAY

RIDGEWAY MOTEL
Hwy 34 (29130)
Rates: $26-$29
(803) 337-3238

ROCK HILL

BEST WESTERN INN
1106 Anderson Rd
(29730)
Rates: $60-$135
(803) 329-1330
(800) 528-1234

THE BOOK & THE SPINDLE B&B
626 Oakland Ave
(29730)
Rates: $65-$85
(803) 328-1913

ECONO LODGE
962 Riverview Rd
(29730)
Rates: $36-$125
(803) 329-3232
(800) 553-2666

HOLIDAY INN
2640 Cherry Rd
(29730)
Rates: $74-$89
(803) 329-1122
(800) 465-4329

ST. GEORGE

BEST WESTERN INN
I-95 & Hwy 78
(29477)
Rates: $45-$69
(843) 563-2277
(800) 528-1234

COMFORT INN
139 Motel Dr
(29477)
Rates: $50-$90
(843) 563-4180
(800) 228-5150

ECONOMY INN
5971 W Jim Bilton
Blvd (29477)
Rates: $30-$60
(843) 563-4195

ECONOMY MOTEL
125 Motel Dr
(29477)
Rates: $27-$45
(843) 563-2360

HOLIDAY INN
6014 W Jim Bilton
Blvd (29477)
Rates: $70-$95
(843) 563-4581
(800) 465-4329

ST. GEORGE MOTOR INN
215 S Parler Ave
(29477)
Rates: $16-$20
(843) 563-3029

SOUTHERN INN II
I-95 & US 78
(29477)
Rates: $20-$29
(843) 563-3775

SUPER 8 MOTEL
114 Winningham
Rd (29477)
Rates: $38-$65
(843) 563-5551
(800) 800-8000

ST. STEPHENS

ECONO LODGE
3986 Byrnes Dr
(29479)
Rates: $45-$60
(843) 567-7397
(800) 553-2666

SANTEE

COMFORT INN
265 Britain St
(29142)
Rates: $60-$125
(803) 854-3221
(800) 228-5150

DAYS INN
9078 Old Hwy 6
(29142)
Rates: $45-$74
(803) 854-2175
(800) 329-7466

ECONOMY INN
626 Bass Dr (29142)
Rates: $30-$42
(803) 854-2107

HAMPTON INN
9000 Old Hwy 6
(29142)
Rates: $65-$85
(803) 854-2444
(800) 426-7866

RAMADA INN
123 Mall Dr (29142)
Rates: $58
(803) 854-2191
(800) 272-6232

SUPER 8 MOTEL
9125 Old Hwy 6
(29142)
Rates: $32-$43
(803) 854-3456
(800) 800-8000

SIMPSONVILLE

COMFORT INN
600 Fairview Rd
(29680)
Rates: $55-$90
(864) 963-2777
(800) 228-5150

SPARTANBURG

DAYS INN
578 N Church St
(29303)
Rates: $30-$56
(864) 585-4311
(800) 329-7466

DAYS INN
1000 Hearon Cir
(29303)
Rates: $59-$125
(864) 503-9048
(800) 329-7466

ECONO LODGE
700 Sunbeam Rd
(29303)
Rates: $34-$105
(864) 578-9450
(800) 553-2666

HAMPTON INN
4930 College Dr
(29303)
Rates: $59-$64
(864) 576-6080
(800) 426-7866

HOWARD JOHNSON INN
6690 Pottery Rd
(29301)
Rates: $49-$79
(864) 576-0042
(800) 446-4656

MOTEL 6
105 Jones Rd
(29303)
Rates: $33-$42
(864) 573-6383
(800) 466-8356

QUALITY HOTEL
7136 Asheville
Hwy (29303)
Rates: $59-$69
(864) 503-0780
(800) 228-5151

RAMADA INN
200 International
Dr (29303)
Rates: $69-$99
(864) 576-5220
(800) 272-6232

RED ROOF INN
125 Sloane Garden
Rd (29316)
Rates: n/a
(864) 814-7663
(800) 843-7663

RESIDENCE INN BY MARRIOTT
9011 Fairforest Rd
(29301)
Rates: $49-$184
(864) 576-3333
(800) 331-3131

WILSON WORLD HOTEL
9027 Fairforest Rd (29301)
Rates: $69-$94
(864) 574-2111
(800) 945-7667

SUMMERTON

ECONO LODGE
I-95 & SR 102 (29148)
Rates: $34-$49
(803) 485-2865
(800) 553-2666

TRAVELODGE
Rd 1 or I-95, Exit 108 (29148)
Rates: $30-$50
(803) 485-2635
(800) 578-7878

SUMMERVILLE

ECONO LODGE
110 Holiday Inn Dr (29483)
Rates: $45-$70
(843) 875-3022
(800) 553-2666

HOLIDAY INN EXP
120 Holiday Inn Dr (29483)
Rates: $99
(843) 875-3300
(800) 465-4329

SUMTER

ECONOMY INN
1211 Camden Rd (29150)
Rates: $35-$39
(803) 469-4740

MAGNOLIA HOUSE B&B
230 Church St (29151)
Rates: $75-$85
(803) 775-6694

RAMADA INN
226 N Washington St (29151)
Rates: $59-$109
(803) 775-2323
(800) 272-6232

TRAVELERS REST

SLEEP INN
110 Hawkins Rd (29690)
Rates: $48-$70
(864) 834-7040
(800) 753-3746

TURBEVILLE

DAYS INN
I-95 & Hwy 378, Exit 135 (29162)
Rates: $30-$150
(843) 659-8060
(800) 329-7466

WALTERBORO

BEST WESTERN INN
1140 Snider's Hwy (29488)
Rates: $45-$79
(843) 538-3600
(800) 528-1234

COMFORT INN
1245 Snider's Hwy (29488)
Rates: $39-$89
(843) 538-5403
(800) 228-5150

ECONO LODGE
1145 Snider's Hwy (29488)
Rates: $40-$85
(843) 538-3830
(800) 553-2666

HOLIDAY INN
1120 Snider's Hwy (29488)
Rates: $75
(843) 538-5473
(800) 465-4329

RICE PLANTERS INN
97 Ladson St (29488)
Rates: $25-$40
(843) 538-8964
(800) 647-4831

SUPER 8 MOTEL
1972 Bells Hwy (29488)
Rates: $37-$65
(843) 538-5383
(800) 800-8000

THUNDERBIRD INN
1142 Snider's Hwy (29488)
Rates: $25-$36
(843) 538-2503
(800) 538-2473

WEST COLUMBIA

HOLIDAY INN AIRPORT
500 Chris Dr (29169)
Rates: $80
(803) 794-9440
(800) 465-4329

RAMADA INN
114 McSwain Dr (29169)
Rates: $66-$75
(803) 796-2700
(800) 272-6232

SUPER 8 MOTEL
2516 Augusta Rd (29169)
Rates: $40-$65
(803) 796-4833
(800) 800-8000

WINNSBORO

DAYS INN
1804 Hwy 321 Bypass (29180)
Rates: $36-$85
(803) 635-1447
(800) 329-7466

YEMASSEE

DAYS INN
Jct US 17 & I-95 (29945)
Rates: $40-$64
(843) 726-8156
(800) 329-7466

PALMETTO LODGE
12 Lane St (29945)
Rates: $20-$32
(843) 589-2361

SUPER 8 MOTEL
Hwy 68 & I-95 (29945)
Rates: $24-$46
(843) 589-2177
(800) 800-8000

YORK

DAYS INN
1568 Alexander Love Hwy (29745)
Rates: $43-$120
(803) 684-2525
(800) 329-7466

SOUTH DAKOTA

ABERDEEN

BEST WESTERN RAMKOTA INN
1400 8th Ave NW (57401)
Rates: $61-$79
(605) 229-4040
(800) 528-1234

BREEZE-INN MOTEL
1216 6th Ave SW (57401)
Rates: $25-$35
(605) 225-4222

BUDGET SAVER MOTEL
1409 6th Ave SE (57401)
Rates: n/a
(605) 225-5300

COMFORT INN
2923 6th Ave SE (57401)
Rates: $53-$100
(605) 226-0097
(800) 228-5150

RAMADA INN
2727 6th Ave SE (57401)
Rates: $61-$120
(605) 225-3600
(800) 272-6232

SUPER 8 MOTEL-EAST
2405 6th Ave SE (57401)
Rates: $41-$58
(605) 229-5005
(800) 800-8000

SUPER 8 MOTEL-NORTH
770 NW Hwy 281 (57401)
Rates: $35-$52
(605) 226-2288
(800) 800-8000

SUPER 8 MOTEL-WEST
714 S Hwy 281 (57401)
Rates: $35-$52
(605) 225-1711
(800) 800-8000

WHITE HOUSE INN
500 6th Ave SW (57401)
Rates: $36-$53
(605) 225-5000
(800) 225-6000

BELLE FOURCHE

ACE MOTEL
109 6th Ave (57717)
Rates: $25-$48
(605) 892-2612

MOTEL LARIAT
1033 Elkhorn (57717)
Rates: $39-$48
(605) 892-2601

MOTEL 6
1815 5th Ave (57717)
Rates: $34-$66
(605) 892-6663
(800) 466-8356

SUNSET MOTEL
HCR 30, Box 65 (57717)
Rates: $25-$55
(605) 892-2508

SUPER 8 MOTEL
501 National St (57717)
Rates: $35-$55
(605) 892-3361
(800) 800-8000

BERESFORD

CROSSROADS MOTEL
1409 W Cedar (57004)
Rates: $22-$32
(605) 763-2020

SUPER 8 MOTEL
1410 W Cedar (57004)
Rates: $39-$54
(605) 763-2001
(800) 800-8000

BRANDON

HOLIDAY INN EXPRESS
1105 N Spillrock Blvd (57005)
Rates: $95
(605) 582-2901
(800) 465-4329

BROOKINGS

STAR MOTEL
108 6th St (57006)
Rates: n/a
(605) 692-6345
(800) 884-2518

SUPER 8 MOTEL
3034 LeFevre Dr (57006)
Rates: $44-$56
(605) 692-6920
(800) 800-8000

WAYSIDE MOTEL
1430 6th St (57006)
Rates: $26-$30
(605) 692-4831
(800) 658-4577

BUFFALO

TIPPERARY LODGE
N Hwy 85 (57720)
Rates: $30-$38
(605) 375-3721

CANISTOTA

BEST WESTERN U-BAR MOTEL
130 Ash St (57012)
Rates: $33-$65
(605) 296-3466
(800) 528-1234
(800) 566-8227

CANOVA

SKOGLUND FARM BED & BRKFAST
Rt 1, Box 45 (57321)
Rates: n/a
(605) 247-3445

CHAMBERLAIN

ALEWEL'S LAKE SHORE MOTEL
115 N River St (57325)
Rates: $24-$56
(605) 734-5566

BEL AIRE MOTEL
312 E King St (57325)
Rates: $35-$64
(605) 734-5595

RADISSON RESORT AT CEDAR SHORE
101 Geo Mickleson Shoreline Dr (57325)
Rates: $69-$189
(605) 734-6376
(800) 333-3333
(888) 697-6363

CORSICA

PARKWAY MOTEL-IMA
Hwy 281 (57328)
Rates: $21-$35
(605) 946-5230
(800) 341-8000

CUSTER

AMERICAN PRESIDENTS CABINS, CAMPGROUND & RESORT
Hwy 16A, P O Box 446 (57730)
Rates: $49-$77
(605) 673-3373

AMERICAN PRESIDENTS MOTEL
Hwy 16A, P O Box 446 (57730)
Rates: $21-$59
(605) 673-3373

BAVARIAN INN MOTEL
1000 N 5th St (57730)
Rates: $72-$95
(605) 673-2802
(800) 657-4312

BLACK HILLS BALLOONS B&B
Rt 1, Box 10 (57730)
Rates: $65-$75
(605) 673-2520

BLUE BELL LODGE & RESORT
HCR 83, Box 63 (57730)
Rates: $75-$100
(605) 255-4531
(800) 265-4531

CHIEF MOTEL
120 Mt. Rushmore Rd (57730)
Rates: $59-$87
(605) 673-2318

COMFORT INN
401 Mt. Rushmore Rd W (57730)
Rates: $69-$139
(800) 228-5150

DAYS INN
532 Crook St (57730)
Rates: $29-$79
(605) 673-4500
(800) 329-7466

LEGION LAKE RESORT
HCR 83, Box 67 (57730)
Rates: $69-$110
(605) 255-4521
(800) 658-3530

AREA CODES - If the local number doesn't connect, check for a new area code.

ROCKET MOTEL
211 Mt. Rushmore
Rd (57730)
Rates: $30-$78
(605) 673-4401

**ROOST RESORT
COTTAGES**
HCR 83, Box 120
(57730)
Rates: $56-$68
(605) 673-2326
(800) 294-4603

VALLEY MOTEL
Hwy 16A (57730)
Rates: n/a
(605) 673-4819
(800) 252-2446

CUSTER STATE PARK

**DOUBLE L B&B
& HORSECAMP**
HC 83, Box 1041
(57730)
Rates: n/a
(605) 673-2558

DAKOTA DUNES

**COUNTRY INN
& SUITES**
151 Tower Rd
(57049)
Rates: $59-$79
(605) 232-3500
(800) 456-4000

DEADWOOD

**BUDGET HOST
JACKPOT INN**
Hwy 385 at S
city limits (57732)
Rates: $59-$80
(605) 578-7791
(800) 283-4678
(888) 886-6835

DAYS INN
12 Timm Lane
(57732)
Rates: $40-$140
(605) 578-1294
(800) 329-7466

**FIRST GOLD
HOTEL**
270 Main St
(57732)
Rates: $99-$139
(605) 578-3979
(800) 274-1876

EAGLE BUTTE

SUPER 8 MOTEL
P.O. Box 180
(57625)
Rates: $48-$66
(605) 964-8888
(800) 800-8000

EDGEMONT

RAINBOW MOTEL
Hwy 18 & 471
(57735)
Rates: n/a
(605) 662-7244

EUREKA

LAKEVIEW MOTEL
RR 1, Box 49
(57437)
Rates: $24-$35
(605) 284-2400
(888) 666-9306

FAITH

**PRAIRIE VISTA
INN**
Hwy 212 (57626)
Rates: $49-$65
(605) 967-2343
(800) 341-8000

FAULKTON

SUPER 8 MOTEL
700 Main St
(57438)
Rates: $36-$62
(605) 598-4567
(800) 800-8000

FORT PIERRE

**FORT PIERRE
MOTEL**
211 S First St
(57532)
Rates: $36-$48
(605) 223-3111
(800) 286-0895

**HOLIDAY INN
EXPRESS HOTEL &
SUITES**
110 E Stanley Rd
(57532)
Rates: $63
(605) 223-9045
(800) 465-4329

FREEMAN

FENSEL'S MOTEL
Hwy 81 (57029)
Rates: n/a
(605) 925-4204
(800) 658-3319

SUPER 8 MOTEL
1019 S Hwy 81
(57029)
Rates: $40-$53
(605) 925-4888
(800) 800-8000

GETTYSBURG

**HARER LODGE
BED & BREAKFST**
RR 1, Box 87A
(57442)
Rates: n/a
(605) 765-2167
(800) 283-3356

TRAIL MOTEL-IMA
211 E Garfield
(57442)
Rates: $23-$38
(605) 765-2482
(800) 341-8000

HERMOSA

**HERMOSA HILLS
BED & BRKFAST**
HCR 89, Box 62
(57744)
Rates: n/a
(605) 255-4278
(800) 247-4404

HILL CITY

**BEST WESTERN
GOLDEN SPIKE
INN**
106 Main St
(57745)
Rates: $39-$129
(605) 574-2577
(800) 528-1234

**LANTERN INN
MOTEL**
131 Main St
(57745)
Rates: $48-$96
(605) 574-2582
(800) 456-0520

**LODGE AT
PALMER GULCH**
12620 SR 244
(57745)
Rates: $105-$128
(605) 574-2525
(800) 562-8503

**ROBINS ROOST
CABINS**
12630 Robins
Roost Rd (57745)
Rates: n/a
(605) 574-2252

SUPER 8 MOTEL
209 Main St
(57745)
Rates: $35-$58
(605) 574-4141
(800) 800-8000

HOT SPRINGS

BISON MOTEL
646 S 5th St
(57747)
Rates: n/a
(605) 745-5191
(800) 456-5174

COMFORT INN
737 S 6th St
(57747)
Rates: $59-$149
(605) 745-7378
(800) 228-5150

HILLS INN
640 S 6th St
(57747)
Rates: n/a
(605) 745-3130
(888) 445-7546

**MUELLER HOUSE
BED & BREAKFAST**
201 S 6th St
(57747)
Rates: n/a
(888) 268-8259

SUPER 8 MOTEL
800 Mammoth St
(57747)
Rates: $73-$91
(605) 745-3888
(800) 800-8000

HURON

**BEST WESTERN
INN**
2000 Dakota Ave S
(57350)
Rates: $49-$69
(605) 352-2000
(800) 528-1234

**THE
CROSSROADS
HOTEL**
100 4th St SW
(57350)
Rates: $51-$61
(605) 352-3204
(800) 876-5858

**HOLIDAY INN
EXPRESS**
100 21st St SW
(57250)
Rates: n/a
(605) 352-6655
(800) 465-4329

TRAVELER MOTEL
241 Lincoln NW
(57350)
Rates: n/a
(605) 352-6401

INTERIOR

**BADLANDS
BUDGET HOST
MOTEL**
HC 54, Box 115
(57750)
Rates: $45-$50
(605) 433-5335
(800) 283-4678

**BADLANDS INN-
IMA**
I-90 Exit 131,
Hwy 377 (57750)
Rates: $28-$50
(605) 433-5401
(800) 341-8000

**CEDAR PASS
LODGE HISTORIC
COTTAGE**
1 Cedar St, Box 5
(57750)
Rates: $35-$45
(605) 433-5460

AREA CODES - If the local number doesn't connect, check for a new area code.

KADOKA

BEST WESTERN H & H EL CENTRO MOTEL
105 E Hwy 16 (57543)
Rates: $34-$94
(605) 837-2287
(800) 528-1234
(800) 837-8011

DAKOTA INN-IMA
I-90 Exit 150 (57543)
Rates: $40-$70
(605) 837-2151
(800) 341-8000

HILLTOP MOTEL
225 Hwy 16 E (57543)
Rates: $45-$70
(605) 837-2216
(800) 582-4356

WEST MOTEL
306 Hwy 16 W (57543)
Rates: $36-$60
(605) 837-2427
(800) 830-9378

KENNEBEC

KING'S MOTEL
HC 81, Box 30 (57544)
Rates: $25-$38
(605) 869-2270

KEYSTONE

BED & BREAKFST INN
208 1st St (57751)
Rates: $75-$84
(605) 666-4490
(888) 833-4490

BEST WESTERN FOUR PRESI-DENTS MOTEL
250 Winter St (57751)
Rates: $54-$94
(605) 666-4472
(800) 528-1234
(800) 732-9155

THE FIRST LADY INN
702 Hwy 16A (57751)
Rates: $89-$99
(605) 666-4990
(800) 252-2119

HILLSIDE HISTORIC COUNTRY COTTAGES
13315 S Hwy 16 (57701)
Rates: $34-$60
(605) 342-4121

KELLY INN
320 Old Cemetary Rd (57751)
Rates: $89-$99
(605) 666-4483
(800) 635-3559

MINER'S MOTEL
#522 Hwy 16A, PO Bx 157 (57751)
Rates: $35-$109
(605) 666-4638
(800) 727-2421

MT. RUSHMORES WHITE HOUSE RESORT
115 Swanzey St (57751)
Rates: $55-$125
(605) 666-4443
(800) 456-1878

POWDER HOUSE LODGE
Hwy16 A (57751)
Rates: $53-$135
(605) 666-4646

TRIPLE R RANCH
Hwy 16A (57751)
Rates: n/a
(605) 666-4605
(888) RRRANCH

LEAD

BEST WESTERN GOLDEN HILLS RESORT
900 Miners Ave (57754)
Rates: $59-$129
(605) 584-1800
(800) 528-1234
(888) 465-3080

WHITE HOUSE INN
395 Glendale Dr (57754)
Rates: $40-$115
(605) 584-2000
(800) 654-5323

LEMMON

PRAIRIE MOTEL
115 E 10th (57638)
Rates: $25-$32
(605) 374-3304
(800) 619-0030

LOWER BRULE

GOLDEN BUFFALO RESORT-IMA
120 Crazy Horse St (57548)
Rates: $40-$60
(605) 473-5506
(800) 341-8000

MADISON

LAKE PARK MOTEL
1515 NW 2nd St (57042)
Rates: $40-$52
(605) 256-3524

SUPER 8 MOTEL
Jct Hwy 34 & 81 (57042)
Rates: $36-$47
(605) 256-6931
(800) 800-8000

MILBANK

LANTERN MOTEL
S Hwy 15 (57252)
Rates: $28-$42
(605) 432-4591
(800) 627-6075

MANOR MOTEL-IMA
E Hwy 12 (57252)
Rates: $39-$49
(605) 432-4527
(800) 341-8000

MILLER

DEW DROP INN
HC 64, Bx 140, N Hwy14/45 (57362)
Rates: $27-$50
(605) 853-2431
(888) DEWDROP

MITCHELL

BEST WESTERN INN
1001 S Burr (57301)
Rates: $32-$89
(605) 996-5536
(800) 528-1234
(800) 996-2376

COACHLIGHT MOTEL
1000 W Havens St (57301)
Rates: $37-$48
(605) 996-5686

ECONO LODGE
1313 S Ohlman St (57301)
Rates: $45-$75
(605) 996-6647
(800) 553-2666

HOLIDAY INN
1525 W Havens St (57301)
Rates: $100-$110
(605) 996-6501
(800) 465-4329

MOTEL 6
1309 S Ohlman St (57301)
Rates: $31-$42
(605) 996-0530
(800) 466-8356

SIESTA MOTEL
1210 W Havens St (57301)
Rates: $35-$60
(605) 996-5544
(800) 424-0537

MOBRIDGE

SUPER 8 MOTEL
12 W Hwy (57601)
Rates: $32-$55
(605) 845-7215
(800) 800-800

WRANGLER MOTOR INN-IMA
820 West Grand Cir (57601)
Rates: $51-$71
(605) 845-3641
(800) 341-8000

MURDO

ANDERSON MOTEL
408 Lincoln (57559)
Rates: n/a
(605) 669-2448

BEST WESTERN GRAHAM'S
301 W 5th St (57559)
Rates: $44-$79
(605) 669-2441
(800) 528-1234

SUPER 8 MOTEL
604 E 5th (57559)
Rates: $34-$79
(605) 669-2437
(800) 800-8000

NORTH SIOUX CITY

COMFORT INN
1311 River Dr (57049)
Rates: $45-$100
(605) 232-3366
(800) 228-5150

ECONO LODGE
110 Sodrac Dr (57049)
Rates: $35-$95
(605) 232-9600
(800) 553-2666

HAMPTON INN
101 S Sodrac Dr (57049)
Rates: $62-$99
(605) 232-9739
(800) 426-7866

SUPER 8 MOTEL
1300 River Dr (57049)
Rates: $48-$116
(605) 232-4716
(800) 800-8000

OACOMA

COMFORT INN
W Hwy SR 16 (57365)
Rates: $45-$129
(605) 734-4222
(800) 228-5150

AREA CODES - If the local number doesn't connect, check for a new area code.

DAYS INN
I-90, Exit 260
(57365)
Rates: $35-$90
(605) 734-4100
(800) 329-7466

ECONO LODGE
SR 16 W (57365)
Rates: $34-$99
(605) 734-5593
(800) 553-2666

OASIS INN-IMA
I-90, Exit 260
(57365)
Rates: $36-$70
(605) 734-6061
(800) 341-8000

PICKSTOWN

FORT RANDALL INN
US 18/281 (57367)
Rates: $40-$57
(605) 487-7801
(800) 340-7801

PIEDMONT

ELK CREEK RESORT & LODGE
Elk Creek Rd
(57769)
Rates: $99-$119
(605) 787-4884
(800) 846-2267

PIERRE

BEST WESTERN KINGS INN
200 S Pierre
(57501)
Rates: $47-$70
(605) 224-5951
(800) 528-1234
(800) 232-1112

BEST WESTERN RAMKOTA INN
920 W Sioux
(57501)
Rates: $65-$78
(605) 224-6877
(800) 528-1234

BUDGET HOST STATE MOTEL
640 N Euclid Ave
(57501)
Rates: $38-$50
(605) 224-5896
(800) 283-4678

CAPITOL INN MOTEL
815 Wells Ave
(57501)
Rates: $28-$35
(800) 658-3055

COMFORT INN
410 W Sioux
(57501)
Rates: $57-$105
(605) 224-0377
(800) 228-5150

DAYS INN
520 W Sioux
(57501)
Rates: $45-$55
(605) 224-0411
(800) 329-7466

GOVERNOR'S INN
700 W Sioux
(57501)
Rates: $45-$101
(605) 224-4200
(800) 341-8000

KELLY INN
713 W Sioux
(57501)
Rates: $47-$62
(605) 224-4140
(800) 635-3559

SUPER 8 MOTEL
320 W Sioux
(57501)
Rates: $38-$58
(605) 224-1617
(800) 800-8000

PLANKINTON

SUPER 8 MOTEL
801 S Main,
RR 3 (57368)
Rates: $65-$80
(605) 942-7722
(800) 800-8000

PLATTE

KINGS INN MOTEL
Hwy 44 (57369)
Rates: $22-$34
(605) 337-3385
(800) 337-7756

PRESHO

HUTCH'S MOTEL-IMA
930 E 9th St
(57568)
Rates: $26-$60
(605) 895-2591
(800) 341-8000

RAPID CITY

A ROSEMARY FOR REMEMBRANCE COUNTRY INN
815 Main St
(57701)
Rates: n/a
(800) 577-3952

BIG SKY MOTEL
4080 Tower Rd
(57701)
Rates: $43-$48
(605) 348-3200
(800) 318-3208

CASTLE INN
15 E North St
(57701)
Rates: $29-$90
(603) 348-4120
(800) 658-5464

DAYS INN
1901 W Main St
(57702)
Rates: $39-$59
(605) 343-6040
(800) 329-7466

ECONO LODGE
625 E Disk Dr
(57701)
Rates: $49-$250
(605) 342-6400
(800) 553-2666

FAIR VALUE INN
1607 La Crosse St
(57701)
Rates: $55-$65
(605) 342-8118
(800) 954-8118

FAMILY INN
3737 Sturgis Rd
(57702)
Rates: n/a
(605) 342-2892
(800) 349-2892

FOOTHILLS INN
1625 La Crosse St
(57701)
Rates: $30-$120
(605) 348-5640
(800) 348-5640

GOLD STAR MOTEL
801 E North
(57701)
Rates: $55-$68
(605) 341-7051

HOLIDAY INN EXPRESS HOTEL & SUITES
645 E Disk Dr
(57701)
Rates: n/a
(605) 355-9090
(800) 465-4329

KNIGHTS INN
2401 Mt. Rushmore Rd
(57701)
Rates: $36-$89
(605) 348-1453
(800) 843-5644

MOTEL 6
620 E Latrobe St
(57701)
Rates: $70-$86
(605) 343-3687
(800) 466-8356

QUALITY INN
1902 La Crosse St
(57701)
Rates: $49-$119
(605) 342-3322
(800) 228-5151

RAMADA INN
1721 La Crosse St
(57701)
Rates: $100-$150
(605) 342-1300
(800) 272-6232

RODEWAY INN
2208 Mt. Rushmore Rd
(577091
Rates: $95-$159
(605) 342-1303
(800) 228-2000

SUPER 8 MOTEL
2124 La Crosse St
(57701)
Rates: $31-$57
(605) 348-8070
(800) 800-8000

THRIFTY MOTOR INN
1303 La Crosse St
(57701)
Rates: $55-$65
(605) 342-0551
(800) 318-0551

TIP-TOP MOTEL-SUMMIT INN/IMA
405 St Joseph St
(57701)
Rates: $30-$111
(605) 343-3901
(800) 341-8000

ROCKERVILLE

ROCKERVILLE TRADING POST & MOTEL
13525 Main St
(57701)
Rates: $45-$75
(605) 341-4880
(800) 450-0496

SIOUX FALLS

BAYMONT INN
3200 Meadow Ave
(57106)
Rates: $62-$106
(605) 362-0835
(800) 301-0200

BEST WESTERN RAMKOTA INN
2400 N Louise Ave
(57107)
Rates: $89-$109
(605) 336-0650
(800) 528-1234

BRIMARK INN
3200 W Russell St
(57101)
Rates: $39-$58
(605) 332-2000
(800) 658-4508

BUDGET HOST INN
2620 E 10th St
(57103)
Rates: $34-$49
(605) 336-1550
(800) 283-4678

COMFORT INN-NORTH
5100 N Cliff Ave
(57104)
Rates: $55-$89
(605) 331-4490
(800) 228-5150

AREA CODES - If the local number doesn't connect, check for a new area code.

COMFORT INN-SOUTH
3216 S Carolyn Ave (57106)
Rates: $55-$89
(605) 361-2822
(800) 228-5150

COMFORT SUITES
3208 S Carolyn Ave (57106)
Rates: $65-$99
(605) 362-9711
(800) 228-5150

DAYS INN
5001 N Cliff Ave (57104)
Rates: $50-$100
(605) 331-5959
(800) 329-7466

EXEL INN
1300 W Russell St (57104)
Rates: $37-$62
(605) 331-5800
(800) 367-3935

KELLY INN
3101 W Russell St (57107)
Rates: $62-$79
(605) 338-6242
(800) 635-3559

MAINSTAY SUITES
4545 W Homefield Dr (57106)
Rates: $79-$124
(605) 361-2626
(800) 660-6246

MOTEL 6
3009 W Russell St (57107)
Rates: $31-$44
(605) 336-7800
(800) 466-8356

RAMADA LIMITED
407 South Lyons Ave (57106)
Rates: $65-$85
(605) 330-0000
(800) 272-6232

SELECT INN
3500 S Gateway Blvd (57106)
Rates: $33-$53
(605) 361-1864
(800) 641-1000

SLEEP INN
1500 N Kiwanis Ave (57104)
Rates: $75-$65
(605) 339-3992
(800) 753-3746

SUPER 8 MOTEL
1508 W Russell St (57104)
Rates: $31-$53
(605) 339-9330
(800) 800-8000

SISSETON

HOLIDAY MOTEL
E of Jct US 127 (57262)
Rates: $22-$30
(605) 698-7644
(888) 460-9548

VIKING MOTEL
West Hwy 10 (57262)
Rates: n/a
(605) 698-7663
(800) 823-7669

SPEARFISH

BEST WESTERN INN
346 W Kansas (57783)
Rates: $75-$85
(605) 642-4676
(800) 528-1234
(800) 843-6358

HOLIDAY INN
I-90 & Exit 14 (57783)
Rates: $90
(605) 642-4683
(800) 465-4329
(800) 999-3541

KELLY INN
540 E Jackson Blvd (57783)
Rates: $75-$99
(605) 642-7795
(800) 635-3559

QUEEN'S MOTEL
305 Main St (57783)
Rates: $25-$49
(605) 642-2631

ROYAL REST MOTEL
444 Main St (57783)
Rates: $40-$50
(605) 642-3842

SHADY PINES CABINS
514 Mason St (57783)
Rates: n/a
(800) 551-8920

SHERWOOD LODGE
231 West Jackson Blvd (57783)
Rates: n/a
(605) 642-4688
(800) 234-2032

SUPER 8 MOTEL
440 Heritage Dr (57783)
Rates: $36-$54
(605) 642-4721
(800) 800-8000

STURGIS

BEST WESTERN INN
2431 S Junction Ave (57785)
Rates: $69-$94
(605) 347-3604
(800) 528-1234
(800) 611-3569

DAYS INN
I-90 Exit 30 & Hwy 14 (57785)
Rates: $65-$105
(605) 347-3027
(800) 329-7466

JUNCTION INN
1802 S Junction Ave (57785)
Rates: $29-$69
(605) 347-5675

NATIONAL 9 INN POKER ALICE HOUSE
2426 Junction Ave (57785)
Rates: $29-$63
(605) 347-2506
(800) 658-3695

SUPER 8 MOTEL
HC 55, Box 306 (57785)
Rates: $36-$44
(605) 347-4447
(800) 800-8000

VERMILLION

BUDGET HOST TOMAHAWK MOTEL
1313 W Cherry (57069)
Rates: $30-$50
(605) 624-2601
(800) 283-4678

COMFORT INN
701 W Cherry St (57069)
Rates: $42-$105
(605) 624-8333
(800) 228-5150

SUPER 8 MOTEL
1208 E Cherry St (57069)
Rates: $34-$52
(605) 624-8005
(800) 800-8000

TRAVELODGE
916 N Dakota St (57069)
Rates: $46-$51
(605) 624-2824
(800) 578-7878

WALL

BEST WESTERN PLAINS MOTEL
712 Glenn St (57790)
Rates: $69-$115
(605) 279-2145
(800) 528-1234

ECONO LODGE
804 Glenn St (57790)
Rates: $79-$139
(605) 279-2121
(800) 553-2666

HITCHING POST MOTEL
211 10th Ave (57790)
Rates: $27-$63
(605) 279-2133
(888) 279-2233

KINGS INN MOTEL
608 Main St (57790)
Rates: $63-$75
(605) 279-2178
(800) 782-2613

KNIGHTS INN
I-90, Exit 110 on South Blvd (57790)
Rates: $35-$95
(605) 279-2127
(800) 843-5644

WATERTOWN

BEST WESTERN RAMKOTA INN
1901 9th Ave SW (57201)
Rates: $54-$67
(605) 886-8011
(800) 528-1234

BUDGET HOST INN
309 8th Ave SE (57201)
Rates: $30-$45
(605) 886-8455
(800) 283-4678

COMFORT INN
800 35th St Cir (57201)
Rates: $59-$120
(605) 886-3010
(800) 228-5150

COUNTRY INN & SUITES
3400 8th Ave SE (57201)
Rates: $59-$129
(605) 886-8900
(800) 456-4000

DRAKE MOTOR INN
Jct 212 & 81 (57201)
Rates: $27-$37
(605) 886-8411
(800) 252-4532

GUEST HOUSE MOTOR INN
101 N Broadway (57201)
Rates: $32-$37
(605) 886-8061
(800) 356-7979

STONES INN-IMA
3900 9th Ave SE
(57201)
Rates: $40-$53
(605) 882-3630
(800) 341-8000

**TRAVEL HOST
MOTEL**
1714 9th Ave SW
(57201)
Rates: $32-$44
(605) 886-6120
(800) 658-5512

WEBSTER

SUPER 8 MOTEL
P. O. Box 592
(57274)
Rates: $34-$49
(605) 345-4701
(800) 800-8000

WINNER

**BUFFALO TRAIL
MOTEL**
950 W 1st St
(57580)
Rates: $111-$120
(605) 842-2212

SUPER 8 MOTEL
902 E Hwy 44
(57580)
Rates: $29-$98
(605) 842-0991
(800) 800-8000

**WARRIOR INN
MOTEL**
Hwys 44 & 118
(57580)
Rates: $34-$70
(605) 842-3121
(800) 658-4705

YANKTON

**BEST WESTERN
KELLY INN**
1607 E Hwy 50
(57078)
Rates: $89-$155
(605) 665-2906
(800) 528-1234

**BROADWAY
MOTEL**
1210 Broadway
(57078)
Rates: $25-$33
(605) 665-7805

COMFORT INN
2118 Broadway
(57078)
Rates: $56-$95
(605) 665-8053
(800) 228-5150

**LEWIS & CLARK
RESORT
& CABINS**
43496 Lake Shore
Dr (57078)
Rates: $84-$199
(605) 665-2680

**MULBERRY INN
BED & BREAKFST**
512 Mulberry St
(57078)
Rates: $25-$48
(605) 665-7116

SUPER 8 MOTEL
1603 E Hwy 50
(57078)
Rates: $37-$48
(605) 665-6510
(800) 800-8000

AREA CODES - If the local number doesn't connect, check for a new area code.

TENNESSEE

ALCOA

EXECUTIVE LODGE MOTEL
215 Hall Rd (37701)
Rates: n/a
(865) 984-9958

MAINSTAY SUITES
361 Fountain View Circle (37701)
Rates: $59-$159
(865) 379-7799
(800) 660-6246

RAMADA INN
2962 Alcoa Hwy (37701)
Rates: $30-$61
(865) 970-3060
(800) 272-6232

ALTAMONT

THE 1885 MANOR BED & BREAKFAST
1830 Courthouse Cabin (37301)
Rates: n/a
(931) 692-3153

THE WOODLEE HOUSE BED & BREAKFAST
10 Cumberland St (37301)
Rates: n/a
(931) 692-2368

ANTIOCH

DAYS INN
501 Collins Park Dr (37013)
Rates: $42-$54
(615) 731-7800
(800) 329-7466

HOLIDAY INN- THE CROSSINGS
201 Crossings Pl (37013)
Rates: $75-$78
(615) 731-2361
(800) 465-4329
(888) 683-8883

ASHLAND CITY

BIRD SONG COUNTRY INN BED & BREAKFST
1306 Hwy 49 E (37015)
Rates: n/a
(615) 792-4005

ATHENS

DAYS INNS
2541 Decatur Pike (37302)
Rates: $36-$47
(423) 745-5800
(800) 329-7466

HOMESTEAD INN EAST
1827 Holiday Dr (37303)
Rates: $36-$40
(423) 745-9002

KNIGHTS INN
2620 Decatur Pike (37303)
Rates: $30-$48
(423) 744-8200
(800) 843-5644

MOTEL 6
2002 Whitaker Rd (37307)
Rates: n/a
(423) 745-4441
(800) 466-8356

RAMADA INN
115 County Rd 247 (37303)
Rates: $59-$99
(423) 745-1212
(800) 272-6232

SCOTTISH INNS
712 Congress Pkwy (37303)
Rates: n/a
(423) 745-4880
(800) 251-1962

SUPER 8 MOTEL
2541 Decatur Pike (37303)
Rates: $36-$55
(423) 745-4500
(800) 800-8000

BELLS

MOTEL 6
9730 Hwy 70 E (38006)
Rates: $30-$40
(901) 772-9500
(800) 466-8356

BENTON

LAKE OCOEE INN & MARINA
Rt 1, Box 347 (37307)
Rates: n/a
(423) 338-2064
(800) 272-7238

BIG SANDY

GRANNY'S BRANCH RESORT CABINS
10385 Lick Creek Rd (38221)
Rates: n/a
(901) 593-5328

STUMPWATER CAMP CABINS
1259 Sandy's Camp Rd (38221)
Rates: n/a
(901) 593-3200

BLOUNTVILLE

ROCKY TOP CAMPGROUND CABINS
496 Pearl Ln (37617)
Rates: n/a
(423) 323-2535
(800) 452-6456

SMITH HAVEN BED & BREAKFAST
2357 St Rt 37 (37617)
Rates: n/a
(423) 323-0174
(800) 606-4833

BOLIVAR

THE BOLIVAR INN
626 W Market St (38008)
Rates: $25-$45
(901) 658-3372

SUPER 8 MOTEL
916 W Market St (38008)
Rates: $50-$60
(901) 658-7888
(800) 800-8000

BON AQUA

MORNING STAR STABLES B&B
11375 Back Piney Rd (37025)
Rates: n/a
(931) 670-5052

BRENTWOOD

AMERISUITES
202 Summit View Dr (37027)
Rates: $120+
(615) 661-9477
(800) 833-1516

BAYMONT INN & SUITES
108 Westpark Dr (37027)
Rates: $65-$74
(615) 376-4666
(800) 301-0200

ENGLISH MANOR BED & BREAKFST
6304 Murray Ln (37027)
Rates: n/a
(615) 373-4627
(800) 332-4640

HILTON SUITES
9000 Overlook Blvd (37027)
Rates: $115-$189
(615) 370-0111
(800) 445-8667

MAINSTAY SUITES
107 Brentwood Blvd (37027)
Rates: $72-$89
(615) 371-8477
(800) 660-6246

RESIDENCE INN BY MARRIOTT
206 Ward Cir (37027)
Rates: $109-$139
(615) 371-0100
(800) 331-3131

SLEEP INN
1611 Service Merchandise Blvd (37027)
Rates: $64-$85
(615) 376-2122
(800) 753-3746

BRISTOL

BEST WESTERN I-81 BRISTOL
111 Holiday Dr (37620)
Rates: $59-$200
(540) 968-1101
(800) 528-1234
(877) 968-1101

DAYS INN
3281 W State St (37620)
Rates: $48-$165
(540) 968-9119
(800) 329-7466

HAMPTON INN
3299 W State St (37620)
Rates: $69-$80
(540) 764-3600
(800) 426-7866

REGENCY INN
975 Volunteer Pkwy (37620)
Rates: $38-$135
(540) 968-9474

BROWNSVILLE

DAYS INN
2530 Anderson
Ave (38012)
Rates: $55-$70
(901) 772-3297
(800) 329-7466

SKYLIT MOTEL
105 S Grand
(38012)
Rates: n/a
(901) 772-3605

BUCHANAN

**CYPRESS BAY
RESORT**
110 Cypress
Resort Loop
(38222)
Rates: n/a
(901) 232-8221

**SHAMROCK
RESORT**
220 Shamrock Rd
(38222)
Rates: n/a
(901) 232-8211
(800) 852-7885

BUCKSNORT

**COUNTRY INN
MOTEL**
111 E Rt 1 (37140)
Rates: $30-$49
(615) 729-5450

BUTLER

**HEAD FOR THE
HILLS RESORT**
631 Cowan Town
Rd (37640)
Rates: n/a
(423) 768-3346
(800) 705-7724

CAMDEN

**BIRDSONG
RESORT/
MARINA &
CAMPGROUND
CABINS**
255 Marina Rd
(38320)
Rates: n/a
(901) 584-7880
(800) 225-7469

DAYS INN
Rt 2, Box 320
(38320)
Rates: $39-$51
(901) 584-3111
(800) 329-7466

**GUEST HOUSE
INN-MAGIC
VALLEY**
170 Hwy 641 N
(38320)
Rates: $50-$64
(901) 584-2222
(800) 21-GUEST

CARTHAGE

**DEFEATED CREEK
MARINA**
156 Marina Ln
(37030)
Rates: n/a
(615) 774-3131

CARYVILLE

**BUDGET HOST
INN**
115 Woods Ave
(37714)
Rates: $27-$36
(423) 562-9595
(800) 283-4678

**LAKE VIEW INN
HOTEL**
276 John McGhee
Blvd (37714)
Rates: n/a
(423) 562-9456
(800) 431-6887

SUPER 8 MOTEL
200 John McGhee
Blvd (37714)
Rates: $44-$54
(423) 562-8476
(800) 800-8000

CELINA

**CEDAR HILL
RESORT**
2371 Cedar Hill
Rd (38551)
Rates: $35-$110
(931) 243-3201
(800) 872-8393

**DALE HOLLOW
MARINA**
99 Arlon Webb Dr
(38551)
Rates: n/a
(931) 243-2211

**HUNTER'S LODGE
CABINS**
970 Bill Hunter Rd
(38551)
Rates: n/a
(931) 243-3459

CENTERVILLE

**BUCKSNORT
MOTEL**
I-40 Exit 152
(37033)
Rates: n/a
(931) 729-5450
(800) 841-5813

DAYS INN
634 David St
(37033)
Rates: $45-$99
(931) 729-5600
(800) 329-7466

CHATTANOOGA

**ALPINE LODGE
MOTEL**
4328 Cummings
Hwy (37419)
Rates: n/a
(423) 821-2546

**BAYMONT INN
& SUITES**
3540 Cummings
Hwy (37419)
Rates: $42-$106
(423) 821-1090
(800) 301-0200

**BEST INN &
SUITES**
7717 Lee Hwy
(37421)
Rates: $48-$89
(423) 894-5454
(800) 237-8466

**BEST WESTERN
AIRPORT INN**
6650 Ringgold Rd
(37412)
Rates: $42-$109
(423) 894-1860
(800) 528-1234

**BEST WESTERN
ROYAL INN**
3644 Cummings
Hwy (37419)
Rates: $60-$90
(423) 821-6840
(800) 528-1234

COMFORT SUITES
2431 Williams St
(37408)
Rates: $59-$129
(423) 265-0008
(800) 228-5150

DAYS INN
101 E 20th St
(37408)
Rates: $34-$75
(423) 267-9761
(800) 329-7466

DAYS INN
7725 Lee Hwy
(37421)
Rates: $44-$74
(423) 899-2288
(800) 329-7466

DAYS INN
5435 Alabama
Hwy (Ringgold
GA 30736)
Rates: $39-$100
(706) 965-5730
(800) 329-7466

**DAYS INN
LOOKOUT MT**
3801 Cummings
Hwy (37419)
Rates: $43-$83
(423) 821-6044
(800) 329-7466

ECONO LODGE
1417 St.Thomas St
(37412)
Rates: $29-$59
(423) 894-1417
(800) 553-2666

**EXTENDED STAY
AMERICA**
6240 Airpark Dr
(37421)
Rates: n/a
(423) 892-1315
(800) 482-1254

**HOLIDAY INN
EXPRESS**
7024 McCutcheon
Rd (37421)
Rates: $75-$96
(423) 490-8560
(800) 465-4329

**HOLIDAY INN
I-75 AIRPORT**
2345 Shallowford
Village Dr (37421)
Rates: $79-$96
(423) 855-2898
(800) 465-4329

**HOSPITALITY
INNS OF
AMERICA**
6616 Ringgold Rd
(37412)
Rates: n/a
(423) 499-4432

**KINGS LODGE
MOTEL**
2400 Westside Dr
(37404)
Rates: $40-$50
(423) 698-8944
(800) 251-7702

LA QUINTA INN
7015 Shallowford
Rd (37421)
Rates: $65-$89
(423) 855-0011
(800) 687-6667

**LOOKOUT LAKE
BED & BREAKFAST**
3408 Elder Mtn Rd
(37419)
Rates: n/a
(423) 821-8088

MICROTEL INN
7014 McCutcheon
Rd (37421)
Rates: $35-$54
(423) 510-0761
(888) 771-7171
(800) 874-8507

MOTEL 6
7707 Lee Hwy
(37421)
Rates: $34-$44
(423) 892-7707
(800) 466-8356

QUALITY INN
2000 E 23rd St
(37404)
Rates: $57-$90
(423) 622-8353
(800) 228-5151

**RAMADA INN
SOUTH**
6639 Capehart Ln
(37412)
Rates: $39-$88
(423) 894-6110
(800) 272-6232

RED ROOF INN
7014 Shallowford
Rd (37421)
Rates: $50-$80
(423) 899-0143
(800) 843-7663

AREA CODES - If the local number doesn't connect, check for a new area code.

RED ROOF INN AIRPORT SOUTH
6521 Ringgold Rd (37412)
Rates: n/a
(423) 894-6720
(800) 843-7663

SKY HARBOR BAVARIAN INN
2159 Old Wauhatchie Pike (37409)
Rates: n/a
(423) 821-8619

SUPER 8 MOTEL-AQUARIUM
20 Birmingham Rd (37419)
Rates: $50-$67
(423) 821-8880
(800) 800-8000

SUPER 8 MOTEL
1401 Mack Smith Rd (37412)
Rates: $40-$50
(423) 892-3888
(800) 800-8000

CLARKSVILLE

COMFORT INN
1112 SR 76 (37043)
Rates: $40-$65
(931) 358-2020
(800) 228-5150

DAYS INN
1100 Hwy 76 (37043)
Rates: $40-$80
(931) 358-3194
(800) 329-7466

HACHLAND HILL INN & CORP. RETREAT
1601 Madison St (37043)
Rates: n/a
(931) 647-4084

HOLIDAY INN I-24
3095 Wilma Rudolph Blvd (37040)
Rates: $63-$75
(931) 648-4848
(800) 465-4329

MICROTEL INN & SUITES
241 Holiday Dr (37040)
Rates: $39-$59
(931) 905-1505
(888) 771-7171

MID TOWN INN
890 Kraft St (37040)
Rates: n/a
(931) 647-6536

MOTEL 6
254 Holiday Dr (37040)
Rates: $33-$45
(931) 920-6666
(800) 466-8356

QUALITY INN
803 N 2nd St (37040)
Rates: $42-$70
(931) 645-9084
(800) 228-5151

RAMADA LIMITED
3100 Wilma Rudolph Blvd (37040)
Rates: $35-$60
(931) 552-0098
(800) 272-6232

RED ROOF INN
197 Holiday Dr (37040)
Rates: n/a
(931) 905-1555
(800) 843-7663

ROYAL INN
I-24 & US 79 (37040)
Rates: n/a
(931) 648-8800
(800) 446-4656

SKYWAY MOTEL
2581 Ft. Campbell Blvd (37042)
Rates: $23-$35
(931) 431-5225

SOUTHERN PINES BED & BREAKFAST
52 Taylor Rd (37042)
Rates: n/a
(931) 647-0399

SUPER 8 MOTEL
3065 Wilma Rudolph Blvd (37040)
Rates: $42-$56
(931) 647-2002
(800) 800-8000

TRAVELODGE
3075 Wilma Rudolph Blvd (37040)
Rates: $44-$60
(931) 645-1400
(800) 578-7878

VACATION HOTEL
650 Providence Blvd (37042)
Rates: n/a
(931) 645-6483

CLEVELAND

BAYMONT SUITES
107 Interstate Dr NW (37312)
Rates: $70
(423) 339-1000
(800) 301-0200

BEST WESTERN CLEVELAND INN
156 James Asberry Dr (37311)
Rates: $50-$75
(423) 472-5566
(800) 528-1234

COLONIAL INN
1555 25th St (37311)
Rates: $22-$32
(423) 472-6845

COMFORT INN
153 James Asbury Dr (37312)
Rates: $45-$80
(423) 478-5265
(800) 228-5150

DAYS INN
2550 Georgetown Rd (37311)
Rates: $30-$75
(423) 476-2112
(800) 329-7466

HOLIDAY INN NORTH
2400 Executive Park Dr (37320)
Rates: $110
(423) 472-1504
(800) 465-4329

HOSPITALITY INN
172 Pleasant Grove (37353)
Rates: $40-$50
(423) 479-4531

LINCOLN INN
2589 Georgetown Rd (37312)
Rates: n/a
(423) 479-3720

QUALITY INN-CHALET
2595 Georgetown Rd (37311)
Rates: $54-$80
(423) 476-8511
(800) 228-5151

TRAVEL INN
3000 Valley Hills Tr NW (37311)
Rates: $26-$42
(615) 472-2185
(800) 838-9998

COKER CREEK

SHADY PINES COTTAGES
12135 Hwy 68 S (37314)
Rates: n/a
(423) 261-2242

COLLEGE GROVE

PEACOCK HILL COUNTRY INN BED & BREAKFAST
6994 Giles Hill Rd (37046)
Rates: $125-$225
(615) 368-7727
(800) 327-6663

COLLIERVILLE

COMFORT INN
1230 W Poplar (38017)
Rates: $69-$89
(901) 853-1235
(800) 228-5150

COLUMBIA

COMFORT INN
1544 Bear Creek Pkwy (38401)
Rates: $50-$80
(931) 388-2500
(800) 228-5150

DAYS INN
1504 Nashville Hwy (38401)
Rates: $40-$46
(931) 381-3297
(800) 329-7466

ECONO LODGE
1548 Bear Creek Pkwy (38401)
Rates: $50-$55
(931) 381-1410
(800) 553-2666

JAMES K POLK MOTEL
1111 Nashville Hwy (38401)
Rates: $35-$40
(931) 388-4913

OAK SPRINGS INN & GALLERY
1512 Williamsport Pike (38401)
Rates: n/a
(931) 388-7539
(800) 542-7698

RAMADA INN
1208 Nashville Hwy (38401)
Rates: $48-$75
(931) 388-2720
(800) 272-6232

COOKEVILLE

ALPINE LODGE & SUITES
2021 E Spring St (38506)
Rates: $36-$52
(931) 526-3333
(800) 213-2016

BEST WESTERN THUNDERBIRD MOTEL
900 S Jefferson Ave (38501)
Rates: $39-$150
(931) 526-7115
(800) 528-1234

COMFORT SUITES
1035 Interstate Dr (38501)
Rates: $54-$80
(931) 372-1881
(800) 228-5150

DAYS INN
1292 Bunker Hill Rd (38501)
Rates: $40-$55
(931) 528-1511
(800) 329-7466

AREA CODES - If the local number doesn't connect, check for a new area code.

EASTWOOD INN
1646 E Spring St
(38506)
Rates: n/a
(931) 526-6158
(800) 325-2525

ECONO LODGE
1100 S Jefferson
Ave (38506)
Rates: $50-$75
(931) 528-1040
(800) 553-2666

HAMPTON INN
1025 Interstate Dr
(38501)
Rates: $60-$70
(931) 520-1117
(800) 426-7866

HOLIDAY INN
970 S Jefferson
Ave (38501)
Rates: $69-$75
(931) 526-7125
(800) 465-4329

KEY WEST INN
663 S Willow Ave
(38501)
Rates: n/a
(931) 525-1110
(800) 833-0555

STAR MOTOR INN
1115 S Willow Ave
(38501)
Rates: n/a
(931) 526-9511
(800) 842-1685

CORDOVA

BEST SUITES
8166 Varnavas Dr
(38018)
Rates: $70-$124
(901) 386-4600
(800) 237-8466

CORNERSVILLE

ECONO LODGE
3731 Pulaski Hwy
(37047)
Rates: $50-$55
(931) 293-2111
(800) 553-2666

COSBY

CUB MOTEL
4344 Cosby Hwy
(37722)
Rates: n/a
(423) 487-4344

**GARDEN OF
EDEN CABINS**
467 Laurel Springs
Rd (37722)
Rates: n/a
(423) 487-2617

**LITTLE CREEK
CABINS**
173 Stonebrook Dr
(37722)
Rates: n/a
(423) 908-7147

**SERENITY FALLS
CABIN RENTALS**
4555 Redwood
Way (37722)
Rates: n/a
(423) 487-2900

COUNCE

COUNTRY CABINS
1095 YMCA Ln
(38326)
Rates: n/a
(901) 925-5500
(800) 848-8177

COVINGTON

**BEST WESTERN
INN**
873 Hwy 51 N
(38019)
Rates: $50-$60
(901) 476-8561
(800) 528-1234

BUDGET INN
8563 Hwy 22
(38225)
Rates: n/a
(901) 364-3151

CROSSVILLE

**BEAN POT
HOLIDAY
TRAVL-L-PARK
CABINS**
23 Bean Pot
Campgrnd Loop
(38558)
Rates: n/a
(931) 484-7671
(877) 848-7958

DAYS INN
305 Executive Dr
(38556)
Rates: $44-$70
(931) 484-9691
(800) 329-7466

FAIRFIELD GLADE
3670 Peavine Rd
(38558)
Rates: n/a
(931) 456-6320
(800) 354-1404

HERITAGE INN
2900 N Main St
(38555)
Rates: n/a
(931) 484-9505
(800) 762-7065

SCOTTISH INNS
2906 N Main St
(38555)
Rates: $30-$60
(931) 484-8122
(800) 251-1962

VILLAGER LODGE
714 N Main St
(38555)
Rates: n/a
(931) 484-7561
(800) 972-4061

CUMBERLAND GAP

**CUMBERLAND
GAP INN**
630 Brooklyn St
(37724)
Rates: $65-$75
(423) 869-9172
(888) 408-0127

RAMADA INN
US Hwy 58
(37724)
Rates: $65-$71
(423) 869-3631
(800) 272-6232

DANDRIDGE

**BEST WESTERN
JEFFERSON
LODGING**
119 Sharon Dr
(37725)
Rates: $35-$140
(865) 397-1910
(800) 528-1234
(877) 397-1910

**D & D MCARTHUR
COTTAGE**
2515 Hills Chapel
Rd (37225)
Rates: n/a
(865) 397-5207

**INDIAN CREEK
BOAT DOCK
CABINS**
2321 Norman Way
(37225)
Rates: n/a
(865) 397-7286

**THE MARTHA
BED & BREAKFAST**
314 E Meeting St
(37225)
Rates: n/a
(865) 397-6192

**MOUNTAIN
HARBOR INN BED
& BREAKFAST**
1199 Hwy 139
(37725)
Rates: $60-$135
(865) 397-3345

**TENNESSEE
MOUNTAIN INN**
531 Patriot Dr
(37725)
Rates: $40-$100
(865) 397-9437
(800) 235-9440

DAYTON

**BEST WESTERN
DAYTON INN**
7835 Rhea County
Hwy (37321)
Rates: $55-$100
(423) 775-6560
(800) 528-1234
(800) 437-9604

DAYS INN
3914 Rhea County
Hwy (37321)
Rates: $45-$85
(423) 775-9718
(800) 329-7466

**THE MAGNOLIA
HOUSE B&B**
656 Market St
(37321)
Rates: n/a
(423) 775-9288
(888) 775-9288

DECATUR

**COTTON PORT
FISH 'N' CAMP
MOTEL**
County Rd 235
(37322)
Rates: n/a
(423) 334-4999

DEL RIO

**BEAR'S DEN LOG
CABIN RENTAL**
651 Odyssey Rd
(37727)
Rates: n/a
(423) 487-4419

**GANNON'S
FRENCH BROAD
OUTPOST RANCH
CABINS**
461 Old River Rd
(37727)
Rates: n/a
(423) 487-3120
(800) 995-POST

DENMARK

ECONO LODGE
196 Providence Rd
(38391)
Rates: $48-$85
(901) 427-2778
(800) 553-2666

DICKSON

COMFORT INN
2325 Hwy 46 S
(37055)
Rates: $46-$79
(615) 446-2423
(800) 228-5150

DAYS INN
Hwy 46 & I-40,
Exit 172 (37055)
Rates: $39-$50
(615) 446-7561
(800) 329-7466

**DICKSON
STATION INN**
1025 E Christi Dr
(37055)
Rates: n/a
(615) 441-5252
(888) 375-5522

HOLIDAY INN
2420 Hwy 46 S
(37055)
Rates: $59-$84
(615) 446-9081
(800) 465-4329

**INN ON MAIN
STREET B&B**
112 S Main St
(37055)
Rates: n/a
(615) 441-6879

AREA CODES - If the local number doesn't connect, check for a new area code.

SUPER 8 MOTEL
150 Suzanne Dr
(37055)
Rates: $46-$69
(615) 446-1923
(800) 800-8000

DOVER

**LEATHERWOOD
RESORT
& MARINA**
751 Leatherwood
Bay Rd (37058)
Rates: n/a
(931) 232-5137
(888) 453-3434

**SUNSET MOTOR
INN**
314 Hwy 79
(37058)
Rates: n/a
(931) 232-5102

DRESDEN

**DRESDEN MOTOR
INN**
8563 Hwy 22
(83225)
Rates: n/a
(901) 364-3151

ELIZABETHTON

DAYS INN
505 W Elk Ave
(37643)
Rates: $40-$70
(423) 543-3344
(800) 329-7466

ELKTON

ECONOMY INN
I-65 & Bryson Rd
(38455)
Rates: n/a
(615) 468-2594

ERWIN

HOLIDAY INN EXP
2002 Temple Hill
Rd (37650)
Rates: n/a
(423) 743-4100
(800) 465-4329

ETOWAH

ETOWAH MOTEL
330 N Tennessee
Ave (37331)
Rates: n/a
(423) 263-7618

**HOLIDAY
TERRACE MOTEL**
324 N Tennessee
Ave (37331)
Rates: n/a
(423) 263-7618

FAIRVIEW

**SWEET ANNIE'S
BED, BREAKFAST
& BARN**
7201 Cumberland
Dr (37062)
Rates: n/a
(615) 799-8833

FAYETTEVILLE

**BEST WESTERN
FAYETTEVILLE INN**
3021 Thornton
Taylor Pkwy
(37334)
Rates: $51-$85
(931) 433-0100
(800) 528-1234

DAYS INN
1651 Huntsville
Hwy (37334)
Rates: $37-$59
(931) 433-6121
(800) 329-7466

FRANKLIN

**AMERISUITES-
COOL SPRINGS**
650 Bakers Bridge
Rd (37067)
Rates: $79-$97
(615) 771-8900
(800) 834-1516

**BAYMONT INN
& SUITES**
4207 Franklin
Commons Ct
(37064)
Rates: $60-$65
(615) 791-7700
(800) 301-0200

**BEST WESTERN
FRANKLIN INN**
1308
Murfreesboro Rd
(37064)
Rates: $65-$90
(615) 790-0570
(800) 528-1234
(800) 251-3200

DAYS INN
4217 S Carothers
Rd (37064)
Rates: $59-$200
(615) 790-1140
(800) 329-7466

**GOOSECREEK
INN**
2404 Goose Creek
Bypass (37064)
Rates: n/a
(615) 794-7200

**HOMESTEAD
VILLAGE**
680 Bakers Bridge
Ave (37067)
Rates: n/a
(615) 771-7600
(888) 782-9473

**NAMASTE ACRES
BARN B&B**
5436 Leipers
Creek (37064)
Rates: $75-$85
(615) 791-0333

RED CARPET INN
2406 Goose Creek
Bypass (37064)
Rates: n/a
(615) 794-7200
(800) 251-1962

SUPER 8 MOTEL
1307
Murfreesboro Rd
(37064)
Rates: $52-$85
(615) 794-7591
(800) 800-8000

FRANKWING

**HOLLOW POND
FARM BED, BARN
& BREAKFAST**
P O Box 775, Tight
Bark Hollow Rd
(38459)
Rates: n/a
(931) 424-8535
(800) 463-0154
(Horses allowed
only)

**OUTBACK
HIDEAWAY
CABINS**
64 Endsley Rd
(38459)
Rates: n/a
(931) 732-4297

GALLATIN

SHONEY'S INN
221 W Main St
(37066)
Rates: n/a
(615) 452-5433
(800) 222-2222

GATLINBURG

**AFFORDABLE
DISCOUNT
CABINS**
P. O. Box 1093
(37738)
Rates: n/a
(865) 430-8512
(800) 221-2871

ALTO MOTEL
P. O. Box 1277
(37738)
Rates: $60-$70
(865) 436-5175

**BON AIR
MOUNTAIN INN**
950 Parkway
(37738)
Rates: $43-$95
(865) 436-4857
(800) 848-4857

**CHERRY HILL
CABIN**
302 Newman Rd
(37738)
Rates: n/a
(865) 436-5881
(888) 737-4295

**CREEKSTONE
MOTEL**
104 Oglewood Ln
(37738)
Rates: $32-$54
(800) 572-7770

**DUDLEY CREEK
MOTEL & CABINS**
844 E Parkway
(37738)
Rates: n/a
(865) 436-4347
(888) 430-5867

**ECONO LODGE
DOWNTOWN**
247 Newton Lane
(37738)
Rates: $39-$78
(865) 436-6626
(800) 553-2666

**FAMILY INNS OF
AMERICA SUITES**
218 Ski Mountain
Rd (37738)
Rates: n/a
(865) 436-3300
(800) 468-6326

**GRANDVIEW
CABIN &
COTTAGES**
335 E Holly Ridge
Rd (37738)
Rates: $80-$100
(865) 436-3161
(800) 578-4330

**GREENBRIER
VALLEY RESORTS
CABIN RENTALS**
3629 E Parkway
(37738)
Rates: n/a
(865) 436-2015
(800) 546-1144

**HIGHLAND
MOTOR INN**
131 Parkway
(37738)
Rates: $50-$88
(865) 436-4110
(800) 635-8874

**HOLIDAY INN
SUNSPREE
RESORT**
520 Airport Rd
(37738)
Rates: $79-$139
(865) 436-9201
(800) 465-4329

**JACKSON
MOUNTAIN
HOMES RENTALS**
466 Brookside
Village Way, #3
(37738)
Rates: n/a
(865) 436-8876
(800) 473-3163

**LAURELWOOD
MOTEL**
115 Willow Lane
(37738)
Rates: n/a
(865) 436-4155

**MAPLES PREMIER
CHALETS**
1670 E Parkway
(37738)
Rates: n/a
(865) 430-3985
(800) 878-8981

MARGIE'S CHALETS
P.O. Box 288
(37738)
Rates: n/a
(865) 436-9475
(800) 264-9475

MICROTEL INN
211 Airport Rd
(37738)
Rates: $59-$94
(865) 436-0107
(888) 771-7171
(800) 266-3500

MOUNTAIN HERITAGE INN HOTEL
575 River Rd
(37738)
Rates: n/a
(865) 436-3474
(800) 343-7953

MOUNTAIN VIEW CHALETS
General Delivery
(37738)
Rates: n/a
(865) 436-0983
(800) 548-3872

RAMADA INN FOUR SEASONS
756 Parkway
(37738)
Rates: $54-$139
(865) 436-7881
(800) 272-6232

REAGAN INN
135 Reagan Dr
(37738)
Rates: n/a
(865) 436-7991
(800) 834-0434

RED CARPET INN
349 E Parkway
(37738)
Rates: n/a
(865) 436-5179
(800) 251-1962

RIVER TERRACE RESORT & CONVENTION CENTER
240 River Rd
(37728)
Rates: $59-$109
(865) 436-5161

ROCKY RIVER MOTEL
544 E Parkway
(37738)
Rates: n/a
(865) 430-3918
(800) 643-3138

SMOKY TOP CABIN RENTALS
P O Box 1566
(37738)
Rates: n/a
(865) 436-5749
(800) 468-6813

TERRACE MOTEL
396 Parkway
(37738)
Rates: n/a
(865) 436-4965

TRENT MOTOR LODGE
919 Parkway
(37738)
Rates: n/a
(865) 436-4807
(800) 468-6326

WATSON'S MOTEL
426 Ski Mountain
Rd (37738)
Rates: n/a
(865) 436-4747
(800) 621-8249

GERMANTOWN

BEST INNS OF AMERICA
7787 Wolf River
Blvd (38138)
Rates: $49-$80
(901) 757-7800
(800) 237-8466

HOMEWOOD SUITES
7855 Wolf River
Blvd (38138)
Rates: $129
(901) 751-2500
(800) 225-5466

GOODLETTS-VILLE

BAYMONT INN
120 Cartwright Ct
(37072)
Rates: $55-$120
(615) 851-1891
(800) 301-0200

MOTEL 6
323 Cartwright St
(37072)
Rates: $33-$46
(615) 859-9674
(800) 466-8356

RED ROOF INN
110 Northgate Dr
(37072)
Rates: $40-$77
(615) 859-2537
(800) 843-7663

RODEWAY INN
650 Wade Cir
(37072)
Rates: $32-$50
(615) 859-1416
(800) 228-2000

SHONEY'S INN
100 Northcreek
Blvd (37072)
Rates: n/a
(615) 851-1067
(800) 222-2222

GREENEVILLE

DAYS INN
935 E Andrew
Johnson Hwy
(37743)
Rates: $44-$120
(423) 639-2156
(800) 329-7466

GENERAL MORGAN INN & CONFERENCE CENTER
111 N Main St
(37743)
Rates: $89-$129
(423) 787-1000
(800) 223-2679

HARRIMAN

BEST WESTERN SUNDANCER MOTOR LODGE
120 Childs Rd
(37748)
Rates: $42-$59
(865) 882-6200
(800) 528-1234

HOLIDAY INN EXPRESS
1145 S Roane St
(37748)
Rates: $59-$69
(865) 882-5340
(800) 465-4329

HENDERSON-VILLE

MORNING STAR BED & BRKFAST
460 Jones Ln
(37075)
Rates: n/a
(615) 264-2614

HERMITAGE

COMFORT INN
5768 Old Hickory
Blvd (37076)
Rates: $50-$75
(615) 889-5060
(800) 228-5150

HERMITAGE INN
4144 Lebanon Rd
(37076)
Rates: $48-$73
(615) 883-7444

RAMADA LIMITED
5770 Old Hickory
Blvd (37076)
Rates: $55-$70
(615) 889-8940
(800) 272-6232

HOHENWALD

RIDGETOP B&B
2141 Columbia
Hwy (Hampshire
38461)
Rates: n/a
(931) 285-2777
(800) 377-2770

HOLLADAY

DAYS INN
13845 Hwy 641 N
(38341)
Rates: $40-$60
(901) 847-2278
(800) 329-7466

HORNBEAK

BOARDMAN RESORT
813 Lake Dr
(38232)
Rates: n/a
(901) 538-2112

HAMILTON'S RESORT
4992 Hamilton Rd
(38232)
Rates: n/a
(901) 538-2325

HUNTSVILLE

HOLIDAY INN EXPRESS
11597 Scott Hwy
(37756)
Rates: $62-$69
(423) 663-4100
(800) 465-4329

HURRICANE MILLS

BEST WESTERN INN
15542 Hwy 13 S
(37078)
Rates: $49-$80
(931) 296-4251
(800) 528-1234

BUFFALO RIVER KOA CABINS
473 Barren Hollow
Rd (37078)
Rates: n/a
(931) 296-1306
(800) KOA-0832

DAYS INN
15415 Hwy 13 S
(37078)
Rates: $40-$60
(931) 296-7647
(800) 329-7466

HOLIDAY INN EXPRESS
Hwy 13, Exit 143
(37078)
Rates: $54-$65
(931) 296-2999
(800) 465-4329

SUPER 8 MOTEL
15470 Hwy 13 S
(37078)
Rates: $34-$48
(931) 296-2432
(800) 800-8000

JACKSON

AMERIHOST INN
465 Vann Dr
(38301)
Rates: $69-$79
(901) 661-9995
(800) 434-5800

BAYMONT INN
2370 N Highland
Ave (38305)
Rates: $49-$54
(901) 664-1800
(800) 301-0200

BEST WESTERN OLD HICKORY INN
1849 Hwy 45
Bypass (38305)
Rates: $45-$69
(901) 668-4222
(800) 528-1234

DAYS INN
1919 Hwy 45
Bypass (38305)
Rates: $38-$55
(901) 688-3444
(800) 329-7466

DAYS INN-WEST
2239 N
Hollywood Dr
(38305)
Rates: $38-$55
(901) 668-4840
(800) 329-7466

GARDEN PLAZA HOTEL
1770 Hwy 45
Bypass (38305)
Rates: $79-$109
(901) 664-6900
(800) 3GARDEN

SUPER 8 MOTEL
2295 N Highland
Ave (38305)
Rates: $34-$52
(901) 668-1145
(800) 800-8000

TRAVELERS MOTEL
2247 N Highland
Ave (38305)
Rates: $26-$66
(901) 668-0542

JAMESTOWN

JORDAN MOTEL
Rt 1, Box 32
(38556)
Rates: n/a
(931) 879-8129

LAUREL FORK RUSTIC RETREAT CABINS
1364 Oby Blevins
Rd (37841)
Rates: n/a
(865) 281-7495

JASPER

ACUFF COUNTRY INN MOTEL
1156 Hwy 28
(37347)
Rates: n/a
(423) 942-6370
(800) 782-7217

DAYS INN
Hwy 72 Dixie Lee
Junction (37347)
Rates: $30-$54
(423) 837-7933
(800) 329-7466

JEFFERSON CITY

APPLE VALLEY CHALET RESORT
1850 Paul Dr
(37760)
Rates: n/a
(865) 475-3745
(800) 545-8106

JELLICO

BEST WESTERN HOLIDAY PLAZA MOTEL
133 Holiday Dr
(37762)
Rates: $36-$80
(423) 784-7241
(800) 528-1234

DAYS INN
I-75 & 25 W,
Exit 160 (37762)
Rates: $46-$51
(423) 784-7281
(800) 329-7466

JELLICO MOTEL
I-75 & 25 W,
Exit 160 (37762)
Rates: n/a
(423) 784-7211
(800) 251-9498

JOELTON

DAYS INN
201 Gifford Pl
(37080)
Rates: $45-$65
(615) 876-3261
(800) 329-7466

JOHNSON CITY

COMFORT INN
1900 S Roan St
(37604)
Rates: $49-$159
(423) 928-9600
(800) 228-5150

DAYS INN
2312 Brown's Mill
Rd (37601)
Rates: $55-$150
(423) 282-3211
(800) 329-7466

GARDEN PLAZA HOTEL
211 Mockingbird
Ln (37604)
Rates: $79-$89
(423) 929-2000
(800) 342-7336

HART HOUSE BED & BREAKFAST
207 E Holston Ave
(37601)
Rates: n/a
(423) 926-3147

HOLIDAY INN
101 W
Springbrook Dr
(37604)
Rates: $81-$87
(423) 282-4611
(800) 465-4329

JOHNSON INN
2700 W Market St
(37604)
Rates: n/a
(423) 926-8145

RED ROOF INN
210 Broyles Dr
(37601)
Rates: $47-$74
(423) 282-3040
(800) 843-7663

SUPER 8 MOTEL
108 Wesley St
(37601)
Rates: $44-$53
(423) 282-8818
(800) 800-8000

KINGSPORT

COMFORT INN
100 Indian Center
Ct (37660)
Rates: $75-$200
(423) 378-4418
(800) 228-5150

ECONO LODGE
1704 E Stone Dr
(37660)
Rates: $40-$56
(423) 245-0286
(800) 553-2666

KINGSPORT INN
700 Lynn Garden
Dr (37660)
Rates: $42-$50
(423) 247-3133

LA QUINTA INN
10150 Airport
Pkwy (37663)
Rates: $53-$73
(423) 323-0500
(800) 687-6667

MICROTEL INN
1708 E Stone Dr
(37660)
Rates: $35-$54
(423) 378-9220
(888) 771-7171
(800) 965-4400

RED CARPET INN
9980 Airport
Pkwy (37663)
Rates: n/a
(423) 279-7111
(800) 251-1962

WESTSIDE INN
1017 W Stone Dr
(37660)
Rates: n/a
(423) 247-2176
(888) 882-2176

KINGSTON

DAYS INN
495 Gallaher Rd
(37763)
Rates: $35-$81
(865) 376-2069
(800) 329-7466

KINGSTON SPRINGS

BEST WESTERN HARPETH INN
116 Luyben Hills
Rd (37082)
Rates: $65-$100
(615) 952-3961
(800) 528-1234

ECONO LODGE
123 Luyben Hills
Rd (37082)
Rates: $55-$75
(615) 952-2900
(800) 553-2666

KNOXVILLE

BAYMONT INN & SUITES WEST
11341 Campbell
Lakes Dr (37922)
Rates: $47-$71
(865) 671-1010
(800) 301-0200

BEST WESTERN HIGHWAY HOST
118 Merchant Dr
(37912)
Rates: $50-$114
(865) 688-3141
(800) 528-1234
(800) 826-4360

BEST WESTERN WEST
500 Lovell Rd
(37932)
Rates: $40-$80
(865) 675-7666
(800) 528-1234
(800) 658-8666

DAYS INN
1706 W
Cumberland Ave
(37916)
Rates: $39-$180
(865) 521-5000
(800) 329-7466

DAYS INN CONFERENCE CTR
5335 Central Ave
(37912)
Rates: $65-$90
(865) 687-5800
(800) 329-7466

DAYS INN WEST
326 Lovell Rd
(37922)
Rates: $42-$83
(865) 966-5801
(800) 329-7466

ECONO LODGE
9340 Park West
Blvd (37923)
Rates: $32-$89
(865) 693-6061
(800) 553-2666

FAMILY INNS OF AMERICA
300 Merchants Dr (37912)
Rates: n/a
(865) 689-2200
(800) 303-0089

FAMILY INNS OF AMERICA
4625 Asheville Hwy (37914)
Rates: n/a
(865) 637-0001
(800) 932-1177

FAMILY INNS OF AMERICA
4300 Rutledge Pike (37914)
Rates: n/a
(865) 546-3910
(800) 362-8383

HAMPTON INN-W
9128 Executive Park Blvd (37923)
Rates: $74-$84
(865) 693-1011
(800) 426-7866

HILTON HOTEL
501 W Church St (37902)
Rates: $84
(865) 523-2300
(800) 445-8667

HOLIDAY INN-W
1315 Kirby Rd (37909)
Rates: $99-$189
(865) 584-3911
(800) 465-4329

HOWARD JOHNSON PLAZA HOTEL
7621 Kingston Pike (37919)
Rates: $109
(865) 693-8111
(800) 446-4656

HYATT REGENCY HOTEL
500 Hill Ave SE (37915)
Rates: $129-$154
(865) 637-1234
(800) 233-1234

LA QUINTA INN
258 N Peters Rd (37923)
Rates: $59-$76
(865) 690-9777
(800) 687-6667

LA QUINTA INN NORTH
5634 Merchants Center Blvd (37912)
Rates: $56-$75
(865) 687-8989
(800) 687-6667

MICROTEL INN
309 N Peters Rd (37922)
Rates: $37-$69
(865) 531-8041
(888) 771-7171
(800) 579-1683

MOTEL 6
402 Lovell Rd (37922)
Rates: $35-$51
(865) 675-7200
(800) 466-8356

QUALITY INN NORTH
6712 Central Ave Pike (37912)
Rates: $69-$89
(865) 689-6600
(800) 228-5151

RAMADA LIMITED EAST
722 Brakebill Rd (37924)
Rates: $49-$110
(865) 546-7271
(800) 272-6232

RED CARPET INN
1500 Cherry St (37917)
Rates: n/a
(865) 546-7110
(800) 251-1962

RED ROOF INN-N
5640 Merchants Center Blvd (37912)
Rates: $30-$70
(865) 689-7100
(800) 843-7663

RED ROOF INN-W
209 Advantage Pl (37922)
Rates: $36-$70
(865) 691-1664
(800) 843-7663

RESIDENCE INN BY MARRIOTT
Langley Place at North Peters Rd (37922)
Rates: n/a
(865) 539-5339
(800) 331-3131

RODEWAY INN
6730 Central Ave Pike (37918)
Rates: $29-$69
(865) 687-3500
(800) 228-2000

SLEEP INN
214 Prosperity Dr (37922)
Rates: $65-$95
(865) 531-5900
(800) 753-3746

SUPER 8 MOTEL DOWNTOWN
6200 Papermill Rd (37919)
Rates: $44-$70
(865) 584-8511
(800) 800-8000

SUPER 8 MOTEL-W
11748 Snyder Rd (37932)
Rates: $39-$59
(865) 675-5566
(800) 800-8000

TRAVELODGE
608 Lovell Rd (37932)
Rates: $43-$50
(865) 966-6781
(800) 578-7878

KODAK

BEST WESTERN DUMPLIN VALLEY INN
3426 Winfield Dunn Pkwy (37764)
Rates: $40-$95
(865) 933-3467
(800) 528-1234

LA FOLLETTE

SHANGHAI RESORT CAMPGROUND CABINS
1042 Shanghai Rd (37766)
Rates: n/a
(423) 562-8650
(800) 245-7651

LA VERGNE

COMFORT INN
107 Enterprise Blvd (37086)
Rates: $45-$89
(615) 793-3600
(800) 228-5150

LAKE CITY

THE LAMB'S INN
620 N Main (37769)
Rates: $29-$53
(865) 426-2171

MOUNTAIN LAKE MARINA & CAMPGROUND CABINS
136 Campground Rd (37769)
Rates: n/a
(865) 426-6510

LAKELAND

SUPER 8 MOTEL
9779 Huff & Puff Rd (38002)
Rates: $45-$72
(901) 372-4575
(800) 800-8000

LAWRENCE-BURG

BEST WESTERN VILLA INN
2126 N Locust Ave (38464)
Rates: $49-$69
(931) 762-4448
(800) 528-1234
(800) 838-4552

LEBANON

BEST WESTERN EXECUTIVE INN
631 S Cumberland St (37087)
Rates: $69-$89
(615) 444-0505
(800) 528-1234

COMFORT INN
829 S Cumberland St (37087)
Rates: $44-$55
(615) 444-1001
(800) 228-5150

DAYS INN
Hwy 231 Murfreesboro Rd (37087)
Rates: $35-$80
(615) 444-5635
(800) 329-7466

HAMPTON INN
704 S Cumberland St (37087)
Rates: $69-$85
(615) 444-7400
(800) 426-7866

SUPER 8 MOTEL
914 Murfreesboro Rd (37090)
Rates: $45-$65
(615) 444-5637
(800) 800-8000

LENOIR CITY

ECONO LODGE
1211 US 321 N (37771)
Rates: $43-$79
(865) 986-0295
(800) 553-2666

INN OF LENOIR MOTOR LODGE
503 Hwy 321 N (37771)
Rates: n/a
(865) 986-8043
(888) 471-0042

RAMADA LIMITED
400 Interchange Park Dr (37772)
Rates: $40-$89
(865) 986-9000
(800) 272-6232

LIMESTONE

SNAPP INN BED & BREAKFAST
1990 Davy Crockett Park Rd (37681)
Rates: n/a
(423) 257-2482

LINDEN

AVALEEN SPRINGS BED & BREAKFAST
161 Hwy 412, Rt 3 (37096)
Rates: n/a
(931) 589-2857
(877) 474-3055

AREA CODES - If the local number doesn't connect, check for a new area code.

LOUDON

HOLIDAY INN EXPRESS
12452 Hwy 72N (37774)
Rates: $79-$89
(423) 458-5668
(800) 465-4329

KNIGHTS INN
15100 Hwy 72 (37774)
Rates: $40-$60
(423) 458-5855
(800) 843-5644

MADISON

RODEWAY INN
625 N Gallatin Rd (37115)
Rates: $30-$50
(615) 865-2323
(800) 228-2000

MANCHESTER

ECONO LODGE
890 Interstate Dr (37355)
Rates: $29-$53
(931) 728-6023
(800) 553-2666

HAMPTON INN
33 Paradise St (37355)
Rates: $59-$73
(931) 728-3300
(800) 426-7866

RAMADA INN
2314 Hillsboro Blvd (37355)
Rates: $33-$89
(931) 728-0800
(800) 272-6232

RED ROOF INN
95 Expressway Dr (37355)
Rates: n/a
(931) 728-8968
(800) 843-7663

SCOTTISH INNS
2457 Hillsboro Blvd (37355)
Rates: $29-$69
(931) 728-0506
(800) 251-1962
(800) 765-4936

SUPER 8 MOTEL
2430 Hillsboro Blvd (37355)
Rates: $45-$65
(931) 728-9720
(800) 800-8000

MARTIN

UNIVERSITY LODGE
800 University St (38237)
Rates: $38-$45
(901) 587-9577
(800) 748-9480

MARYVILLE

411 MOTEL
2651 Hwy 411 S (37801)
Rates: n/a
(865) 982-5361

HIDEAWAY COTTAGES & LOG CABIN RENTALS
102 Oriole Lane (37803)
Rates: n/a
(865) 984-1700

THE OWL'S HOOT CHALET
102 Oriole Lane (37803)
Rates: n/a
(865) 984-1700

MCKENZIE

MCKENZIE MOTOR INN
121 Highland Dr (38201)
Rates: n/a
(901) 352-3325

MCMINNVILLE

BEST WESTERN MCMINNVILLE INN
2545 Sparta Hwy (37110)
Rates: $33-$62
(931) 473-7338
(800) 528-1234

COMFORT INN
508 Sunnyside Heights (37110)
Rates: $42-$110
(931) 473-4446
(800) 228-5150

SCOTTISH INNS
1105 Sparta St (37110)
Rates: $23-$34
(931) 473-2181
(800) 251-1962

SHONEY'S INN
508 Sunnyside Hts (37110)
Rates: $48-$79
(931) 473-4446
(800) 222-2222

MEMPHIS

AMERISUITES
7905 Giacosa Pl (38133)
Rates: $119-$139
(901) 371-0010
(800) 833-1516

AMERISUITES
1220 Primacy Pkwy (38119)
Rates: $89-$109
(901) 680-9700
(800) 833-1516
(800) 434-5800

BAYMONT INN & SUITES
6020 Shelby Oaks Dr (38134)
Rates: $64-$72
(901) 377-2233
(800) 301-0200

BAYMONT INN & SUITES-MEMPHIS AIRPORT
3005 Millbranch Rd (38116)
Rates: $61-$66
(901) 396-5411
(800) 301-0200

BEST SUITES
2575 Thousand Oaks Cove (38118)
Rates: $69-$124
(901) 365-2575
(800) 237-8466

BEST WESTERN TRAVELERS INN
5024 Hwy 78 (38118)
Rates: $50-$120
(901) 363-8430
(800) 528-1234

BROWNESTONE HOTEL
300 N 2nd (38105)
Rates: $75-$275
(901) 525-2511
(800) 468-3515

COMFORT INN
2889 Austin Peay Hwy (38128)
Rates: $50-$150
(901) 386-0033
(800) 228-5150

COMFORT INN
1300 Ingram Blvd (W Memphis, AR 72301)
Rates: $60-$85
(870) 732-0044
(800) 228-5150

COMFORT INN AIRPORT / GRACELAND
1581 E Brooks Rd (38116)
Rates: $65-$98
(901) 345-3344
(800) 228-5150

COUNTRY SUITES BY CARLSON
4300 American Way (38118)
Rates: $69-$79
(901) 366-9333
(800) 456-4000

DAYS INN
340 W Illinois Ave (38106)
Rates: $45-$75
(901) 948-9005
(800) 329-7466

DAYS INN-GRACELAND
3839 Elvis Presley Blvd (38116)
Rates: $65-$90
(901) 346-5500
(800) 329-7466

DRURY INN
1556 Sycamore View (38134)
Rates: $66-$89
(901) 373-8200
(800) 378-7946

ECONO LODGE
2315 S Service Rd (W Memphis, AR 72303)
Rates: $40-$59
(870) 732-2830
(800) 553-2666

HAMPTON INN AIRPORT/ GRACELAND
2979 Millbranch Rd (38116)
Rates: $59-$79
(901) 396-2200
(800) 426-7866

HOLIDAY INN EAST
5795 Poplar Ave (38119)
Rates: $109-$159
(901) 682-7881
(800) 465-4329

HOLIDAY INN MEDICAL CENTER
1837 Union Ave (38104)
Rates: $65-$75
(901) 278-4100
(800) 465-4329

HOMEWOOD SUITES
5811 Poplar Ave (38119)
Rates: $89-$149
(901) 763-0500
(800) 225-5466

HOWARD JOHNSON PLAZA HOTEL
1441 E Brooks Rd (38116)
Rates: $59-$69
(901) 398-9211
(800) 446-4656

LA QUINTA INN
1236 Primacy Pkwy (38119)
Rates: $69-$99
(901) 374-0330
(800) 687-6667

LA QUINTA INN-AIRPORT
2745 Airways Blvd (38132)
Rates: $58-$72
(901) 396-1000
(800) 687-6667

AREA CODES - If the local number doesn't connect, check for a new area code.

LA QUINTA INN-E
6068 Macon Cove
(38134)
Rates: $65-$82
(901) 382-2323
(800) 687-6667

LA QUINTA INN-MEDICAL CENTER
42 S Camilla St
(38104)
Rates: $69-$89
(901) 526-1050
(800) 687-6667

MEMPHIS AIRPORT HOTEL
2240 Democrat Rd
(38132)
Rates: $50-$275
(901) 332-1130

MEMPHIS INN EAST
6050 Macon Cove
(38134)
Rates: $35-$61
(901) 373-9898
(800) 770-4667

MEMPHIS MARRIOTT
2625 Thousand
Oaks Blvd (38118)
Rates: $139-$174
(901) 362-6200
(800) 582-1601

MOTEL 6-EAST
1321 Sycamore
View Rd (38134)
Rates: $42-$58
(901) 382-8572
(800) 466-8356

MOTEL 6-GRACELAND EAST
1117 E Brooks Rd
(38116)
Rates: $35-$46
(901) 346-0992
(800) 466-8356

RAMADA INN
5225 Summer Ave
(38122)
Rates: $49-$79
(901) 685-0704
(800) 272-6232

RED ROOF INN-E
6055 Shelby Oaks
Dr (38134)
Rates: $50-$60
(901) 388-6111
(800) 843-7663

RED ROOF INN MEDICAL CENTER
210 S Pauline
(38104)
Rates: $54-$70
(901) 528-0650
(800) 843-7663

RED ROOF INN-S
3875 American
Way (38118)
Rates: $46-$72
(901) 363-2335
(800) 843-7663

RESIDENCE INN BY MARRIOTT
6141 Old Poplar
Pike (38119)
Rates: $115-$159
(901) 685-9595
(800) 331-3131

WELLESLEY INN & SUITES
2520 Horizon
Lake Dr (38119)
Rates: $66
(901) 380-1525
(800) 444-8888

MILAN

RAMADA LIMITED
US Hwy 70/79 &
45 (38358)
Rates: $47-$67
(901) 686-3345
(800) 272-6232

MILLINGTON

BEST WESTERN INN
7726 Hwy 51 N
(38053)
Rates: $54-$79
(901) 873-2222
(800) 528-1234
(800) 400-2686

MAGNOLIA INN
8193 Hwy 51 N
(38053)
Rates: $46-$50
(901) 873-4400

MONTEAGLE

ADAMS EDGEWORTH COUNTRY INN
Monteagle
Assembly (37356)
Rates: $70-$195
(931) 924-4000
(877) 352-9466

BEST WESTERN SMOKE HOUSE LODGE
850 W Main St
(37356)
Rates: $49-$189
(931) 924-2091
(800) 528-1234
(800) 489-2091

BUDGET HOST INN
Rt 1, Box 1126
(37356)
Rates: $25-$65
(931) 924-2221
(800) 283-4678

DAYS INN
742 Dixie Lee Ave
(37356)
Rates: $30-$65
(931) 924-2900
(800) 329-7466

MOORESBURG

CHEROKEE LAKE CAMPGROUND CABINS
9617 Hwy 11 W
(37811)
Rates: n/a
(423) 272-3333

MORRISTOWN

RAMADA INN & CONFERENCE CENTER
5435 S Davy
Crockett Pkwy
(37813)
Rates: $59-$120
(423) 587-2400
(800) 272-6232

SUPER 8 MOTEL
5400 S Davy
Crockett Pkwy
(37813)
Rates: $44-$59
(423) 318-8888
(800) 800-8000

MT. JULIET

NATUREVIEW INN BED & BREAKFAST
3354 Old Lebanon
Dirt Rd (37122)
Rates: n/a
(615) 758-4439
(800) 758-7972

MOUNTAIN CITY

CREEK SIDE GUEST HOUSE
4923 Hwy 421 S
(37683)
Rates: n/a
(423) 727-6853

MURFREESBORO

BAYMONT INN & SUITES
2135 S Church St
(37129)
Rates: $60-$116
(615) 890-1006
(800) 301-0200
(888) 889-2226

BEST WESTERN CHAFFIN INN
168 Chaffin Pl
(37129)
Rates: $65-$85
(615) 895-3818
(800) 528-1234

DAYS INN
2036 S Church St
(37130)
Rates: $35-$50
(615) 893-1090
(800) 329-7466

GARDEN PLAZA HOTEL
1850 Old Fort
Pkwy (37129)
Rates: $79-$119
(615) 895-5555
(800) 342-7336

HAMPTON INN
2230 Old Fort
Pkwy (37129)
Rates: $66-$70
(615) 896-1172
(800) 426-7866

HOLIDAY INN HOLIDOME
2227 Old Fort
Pkwy (37129)
Rates: $69-$89
(615) 896-2420
(800) 465-4329

HOWARD JOHNSON EXPRESS INN
2424 S Church St
(37130)
Rates: $30-$85
(615) 896-5522
(800) 446-4656

MOTEL 6
114 Chaffin Pl
(37129)
Rates: $32-$40
(615) 890-8524
(800) 466-8356

MURFREESBORO MOTEL
1150 NW Broad St
(37129)
Rates: $25-$38
(615) 893-2100

QUALITY INN
118 Westgate
(37130)
Rates: $49-$99
(615) 848-9030
(800) 228-5151

QUALITY INN HALL OF FAME
1407 Division St
(37203)
Rates: $49-$150
(615) 242-1631
(800) 228-5151

RAMADA LIMITED
1855 S Church St
(37130)
Rates: $40-$100
(615) 896-5080
(800) 272-6232

RED ROOF INN
2282 Old Fort
Pkwy (37130)
Rates: n/a
(615) 893-0104
(800) 843-7663

SCOTTISH INNS
2029 S Church St
(37130)
Rates: $25-$58
(615) 896-3210
(800) 251-1962

SHONEY'S INN
1954 S Church St
(37130)
Rates: $51-$69
(615) 896-6030
(800) 222-2222

NASHVILLE

AMERISUITES
220 Rudy's Circle
Dr (37214)
Rates: $99-$129
(615) 872-0422
(800) 833-1516

AREA CODES - If the local number doesn't connect, check for a new area code.

APPLE BROOK BED, BREAKFAST & BARN
9127 Hwy 100 (37221)
Rates: n/a
(615) 646-5082
(877) 646-5082
(Horses allowed only)

BAYMONT INN/ OPRYLAND/ AIRPORT
531 Donelson Pike (37214)
Rates: $66-$76
(615) 885-3100
(800) 301-0200

BAYMONT INN
5612 Lenox Ave (37209)
Rates: $58-$75
(615) 353-0700
(800) 301-0200

BEST SUITES OF AMERICA
2521 Elm Hill Pike (37214)
Rates: $69-$139
(615) 391-3919
(800) 237-8466

BEST WESTERN CALUMENT INN
701 Stewarts Ferry Pike (37214)
Rates: $45-$175
(615) 889-9199
(800) 528-1234

DAYS INN
1400 Brick Church Pike (37207)
Rates: $36-$87
(615) 228-5977
(800) 329-7466

DRURY INN-AIRPORT
837 Briley Pkwy (37217)
Rates: $56-$75
(615) 361-6999
(800) 325-8300

DRURY INN-SOUTH
341 Harding Pl (37211)
Rates: $60-$80
(615) 834-7170
(800) 325-8300

ECONO LODGE
2403 Brick Church Pike (37207)
Rates: $29-$89
(615) 226-9805
(800) 553-2666

ECONO LODGE OPRYLAND AREA
2460 Music Valley Dr (37214)
Rates: $49-$81
(615) 889-0090
(800) 553-2666

EMBASSY SUITES
10 Century Blvd (37214)
Rates: $129-$169
(615) 871-0033
(800) 362-2779

FAMILY INNS OF AMERICA
3430 Percy Priest Dr (37214)
Rates: n/a
(615) 889-5090
(800) 457-2299

GUEST HOUSE INN & SUITES
1909 Hayes St (37203)
Rates: $70-$84
(615) 329-1000
(800) 777-4904

HAMPTON INN
2350 Elm Hill Pike (37214)
Rates: $75-$91
(615) 871-0222
(800) 426-7866

HILLSBORO HOUSE B&B
1933 20th Ave S (37212)
Rates: $85-$95
(615) 292-5501
(800) 228-7851

HOLIDAY INN EXP
2516 Music Valley Dr (37214)
Rates: $80-$99
(615) 889-0086
(800) 465-4329

HOLIDAY INN EXPRESS
2401 Brick Church Pike (37207)
Rates: $61
(615) 226-4600
(800) 465-4329

HOLIDAY INN SELECT-OPRYLAND/ AIRPORT
2200 Elm Hill Pike (37214)
Rates: $69-$139
(615) 883-9770
(800) 465-4329

HOLIDAY INN SELECT-MUSIC ROW
2613 West End Ave (37203)
Rates: $129-$179
(615) 327-4707
(800) 465-4329

HOMESTEAD VILLAGE GUEST STUDIOS
727 McGavock Pike (37214)
Rates: $65-$100
(615) 316-9020
(888) 782-9473

HOMEWOOD SUITES
2640 Elm Hill Pike (37210)
Rates: n/a
(615) 884-8111
(800) 225-5466

HOWARD JOHNSON INN
6834 Charlotte Pike (37209)
Rates: $48-$70
(615) 352-7080
(800) 446-4656

LA QUINTA INN-AIRPORT
2345 Atrium Way (37214)
Rates: $68-$94
(615) 885-3000
(800) 687-6667

LA QUINTA INN-METRO CENTER
2001 Metro Center Blvd (37228)
Rates: $59-$82
(615) 259-2130
(800) 687-6667

LA QUINTA INN-SOUTH
4311 Sidco Dr (37204)
Rates: $55-$82
(615) 834-6900
(800) 687-6667

LOEWS VANDERBILT PLAZA HOTEL
2100 W End Ave (37203)
Rates: $119-$159
(615) 320-1700
(800) 235-6397

MOTEL 6-AIRPORT
420 Metroplex Dr (37211)
Rates: $36-$46
(615) 833-8887
(800) 466-8356

MOTEL 6-NORTH
311 W Trinity Ln (37207)
Rates: $34-$50
(615) 227-9696
(800) 466-8356

MOTEL 6-SOUTH
95 Wallace Rd (37211)
Rates: $33-$55
(615) 333-9933
(800) 466-8356

PEAR TREE INN SOUTH
343 Harding Pl (37211)
Rates: $50-$65
(615) 834-4242
(800) 282-8733

QUARTERS MOTOR INN
1100 Bell Rd (37013)
Rates: $50-$85
(615) 731-5990

RAMADA INN
1001 Bell Rd (37013)
Rates: $49-$89
(615) 731-8540
(800) 272-6232

RED ROOF INN
510 Claridge Dr (37214)
Rates: $46-$68
(615) 872-0735
(800) 843-7663

RED ROOF INN SOUTH
4271 Sidco Dr (37204)
Rates: $46-$68
(615) 832-0093
(800) 843-7663

SHERATON MUSIC CITY HOTEL
777 McGavock Pike (37214)
Rates: $149-$169
(615) 885-2200
(800) 325-3535

SHONEY'S INN MUSIC ROW DOWNTOWN
1501 Demonbreun St (37203)
Rates: $65-$72
(615) 255-9977
(800) 222-2222

SHONEY'S INN MUSIC VALLEY
2420 Music Valley Dr (37214)
Rates: $98-$133
(615) 885-4030
(800) 222-2222

SUPER 8 MOTEL
412 Robertson Rd (37209)
Rates: $50-$67
(615) 356-0888
(800) 800-8000

TRAVEL PARK HOLIDAY
2572 Music Valley Dr (37214)
Rates: $24-$28
(615) 889-4225

TWELVE OAKS MOTEL
656 W Iris Dr (37204)
Rates: n/a
(615) 385-1323

UNION STATION-A WYNDHAM GRAND HERITAGE HOTEL
1001 Broadway (37203)
Rates: $99-$169
(615) 726-1001
(800) 331-2123

WILSON INN & SUITES
600 Ermac Dr (37214)
Rates: n/a
(615) 889-4466
(800) WILSONS

AREA CODES - If the local number doesn't connect, check for a new area code.

NEWPORT

BEST WESTERN INN
1015 Cosby Hwy (37822)
Rates: $48-$139
(423) 623-8713
(800) 528-1234
(800) 251-4022

BRYANT TOWN MOTEL
766 Cosby Hwy (37861)
Rates: n/a
(423) 623-6006

COMFORT INN
1149 Smokey Mtn Ln (37821)
Rates: $42-$169
(423) 623-5355
(800) 228-5150

FAMILY INNS OF AMERICA
1311 Hwy 25/70 W (37821)
Rates: n/a
(423) 623-2626
(800) 362-8282

FAMILY INNS OF AMERICA
1025 Cosby Hwy (37821)
Rates: n/a
(423) 623-6033
(800) 452-8282

HOLIDAY INN
1010 Cosby Rd (37821)
Rates: $90
(423) 623-8622
(800) 465-4329

MOTEL 6
255 Heritage Blvd (37821)
Rates: $37-$53
(423) 623-1850
(800) 466-8356

RELAX INN
1848 W Knoxville Hwy (37821)
Rates: $24-$85
(423) 625-1521

NORMANDY

PARIS PATCH FARM & INN
625 Cortner Rd (37360)
Rates: n/a
(931) 857-3017
(800) 876-3017

OAK RIDGE

COMFORT INN
433 S Rutgers Ave (37830)
Rates: $64-$104
(865) 481-8200
(800) 228-5150

DAYS INN
206 S Illinois (37830)
Rates: $44-$66
(865) 483-5615
(800) 329-7466

GARDEN PLAZA HOTEL
215 S Illinois (37830)
Rates: $89-$109
(865) 481-2468
(800) 342-7336

SUPER 8 MOTEL
1590 Oak Ridge Tpk (37830)
Rates: $44-$69
(865) 483-1200
(800) 800-8000

OAKLAND

DAYS INN
6805 Hwy 64 (38060)
Rates: $40-$90
(800) 329-7466

ONEIDA

BIG SOUTH FORK WILDNERESS RESORTS
4800 Station Camp Rd (37841)
Rates: n/a
(423) 569-9847

GALLOWAY INN
299 Galloway Dr (37841)
Rates: $28-$36
(423) 569-8835

TOBE'S MOTEL & RESTAURANT
20151 Alberta St (37841)
Rates n/a
(423) 569-8581

ONLY

BUDGET HOST INN AT BUCKSNORT
Rt 1 (37140)
Rates: $30-$49
(800) 283-4678

TRAVELODGE
5032 Hwy 230 W (37140)
Rates: $27-$67
(931) 729-5450
(800) 578-7878

OOLTEWAH

SUPER 8 MOTEL
5111 Hunter Rd (37363)
Rates: $39-$49
(423) 238-5951
(800) 800-8000

PARIS

AVALON MOTEL
1315 Wood St (38242)
Rates: n/a
(901) 642-4121

BEST WESTERN TRAVELERS INN
1297 E Wood St (38242)
Rates: $40-$52
(901) 642-8881
(800) 528-1234

PARIS LANDING MOTEL
15515 Hwy 79 N (Buchanan 38222)
Rates: n/a
(901) 642-0217

PARROTTS-VILLE

MEADOW CREEK MTN FARMS & RIDING STABLES CABINS
959 Browns Chapel Rd (37843)
Rates: n/a
(423) 623-7543

PARSONS

DEERFIELD INN
863 Tennessee Ave N (38363)
Rates: n/a
(901) 847-4700

PIGEON FORGE

BAYMONT INN
2179 Parkway (37863)
Rates: $60-$100
(865) 428-7305
(800) 301-0200

BRENTWOOD RIDGE RESORT CHALETS
3103 Conrad Way (37863)
Rates: n/a
(865) 428-6067
(800) 428-8067

FAMILY INNS OF AMERICA EAST
3785 Parkway (37863)
Rates: n/a
(865) 453-5573
(800) 452-1177

FAMILY INNS OF AMERICA NORTH
3239 Parkway (37863)
Rates: n/a
(865) 453-7151
(800) 732-8181

FAMILY INNS OF AMERICA SOUTH
4112 Parkway (37863)
Rates: n/a
(865) 453-5549
(800) 582-1177

FAMILY INNS OF AMERICA WEST
3144 Parkway (37863)
Rates: n/a
(865) 453-4905
(800) 272-1177

GRAND INNS OF AMERICA
3206 Parkway (37863)
Rates: n/a
(4865) 453-0056
(800) 247-8282

GRAND RESORT HOTEL & CONVENTION CENTER
3171 Parkway (37863)
Rates: $70-$130
(865) 453-1000
(800) 251-4444

HEARTLANDER COUNTRY STAR RESORT
2385 Parkway (37863)
Rates: $30-$125
(865) 453-4106
(800) 843-6686

MICROTEL
202 Emert St (37863)
Rates: $59-$94
(865) 429-0150
(888) 771-7171
(800) 431-7666

MOTEL 6
336 Henderson Chapel Rd (37863)
Rates: $39-$86
(865) 908-1244
(800) 466-8356

MOUNTAIN MIST CABIN RENTALS
2225 Parkway, #1 (37863)
Rates: n/a
(865) 428-5428
(800) 634-5814

MOUNTAIN VALLEY PROPERTIES
513 Wears Valley Rd, #2 (37863)
Rates: n/a
(865) 429-5205
(800) 644-4859

RIVIERA MOTEL
4035 Parkway (37863)
Rates: n/a
(865) 453-4677
(800) 251-9752

SMOKY SHADOWS MOTEL & CONFERENCE CENTER
4215 Parkway (37863)
Rates: n/a
(865) 453-7155
(800) 282-2121

AREA CODES - If the local number doesn't connect, check for a new area code.

SUNSET COTTAGE & CABIN RENTALS
115 Corner Heights Rd (37863)
Rates: $65-$300
(865) 429-8478
(800) 211-4599

TIMBERS LOG MOTEL
134 Davis Rd (37863)
Rates: n/a
(865) 428-5216
(800) 445-1803

PORTLAND

BUDGET HOST INN
5339 Long Rd (37148)
Rates: $30-$35
(615) 325-2005
(800) 283-4678

POWELL

BAYMONT INN
7534 Prime Time Rd (37849)
Rates: $59-$80
(423) 947-7500
(800) 301-0200

COMFORT INN
323 E Emory Rd (37849)
Rates: $69-$89
(423) 938-5500
(800) 228-5150

PULASKI

BUDGET INN
1025 Columbia Hwy (38478)
Rates: n/a
(931) 363-5571

STAR MOTEL
1749 Elkton Pk (38478)
Rates: n/a
(931) 363-3185

SUPER 8 MOTEL
2400 Hwy 64 (38478)
Rates: $40-$70
(931) 363-4501
(800) 800-8000

RICEVILLE

RELAX INN
3803 Hwy 39 W (37370)
Rates: $20-$25
(615) 745-5893

SAMBURG

BILL NATION'S CAMP
244 W Lakeview Dr (38232)
Rates: n/a
(901) 538-2177

BOARDMAN'S RESORT
813 Lake Dr (38232)
Rates: n/a
(901) 538-2112

DUCK INN
218 Church (38254)
Rates: n/a
(901) 538-2364

HAMILTON'S RESORT
4992 Hamilton Rd (38232)
Rates: n/a
(901) 538-2325

SAMBURG MOTEL
100 Lakeview St (38254)
Rates: n/a
(901) 538-2467
(800) 742-0385

SAVANNAH

SAVANNAH MOTEL
105 Adams St (38372)
Rates: n/a
(901) 925-3392

SHAWS KOMFORT MOTEL
2302 Wayne Rd (38372)
Rates: n/a
(901) 925-3977

WHARF RESTAURANT & RV PARK CABINS
120 Wharf Ln (38372)
Rates: n/a
(901) 925-9469

SELMER

SUPER 8 MOTEL
644 Mulberry Ave (38375)
Rates: $50-$60
(901) 645-8880
(800) 800-8000

SEVIERVILLE

CABINS OF TIMBER TOPS
1976 Timber Top Way (37862)
Rates: n/a
(865) 429-0831
(800) 266-1066

CAMELOT BED & BREAKFAST
2659 Boyd's Creek Hwy (37876)
Rates: $75-$125
(865) 429-2070

CHARIS CREEK LODGE
250 Apple Valley Rd (37862)
Rates: n/a
(865) 429-5704

ENGLISH MOUNTAIN CONDO RESORT
1081 Cove Rd (37876)
Rates: n/a
(865) 453-1071
(800) 842-6415

HIGH VALLEY RENTALS
630 Thomas Loop Rd (37876)
Rates: $85-$95
(865) 428-0608

LITTLE ROUND TOP CABINS
3310 Mountain Lakes Way (37862)
Rates: n/a
(865) 428-5984

SMOKY MOUNTAIN HOSTEL
3248 Manis Rd (37862)
Rates: n/a
(865) 429-8563
(800) 357-1857

SPRING GAP LOG CABINS
3054 Kulpan Way (37862)
Rates: $85-$105
(865) 453-0829

SEYMOUR

BAYS MOUNTAIN GOLF COURSE & COUNTRY INN
701 Chris-Haven Dr (37865)
Rates: n/a
(423) 577-8172

WAY-OMA MOTEL
10240 Chapman Hwy (37865)
Rates: n/a
(423) 577-7995

SHELBYVILLE

BEST WESTERN CELEBRATION INN
724 Madison St (37160)
Rates: $55-$195
(931) 684-2378
(800) 528-1234

OLDE GORE HOUSE BED & BREAKFAST
410 Belmont Ave (37160)
Rates: n/a
(931) 685-0636

SUPER 8 MOTEL
317 N Cannon Blvd (37160)
Rates: $49-$60
(931) 684-6050
(800) 800-8000

SILVER POINT

HIDEAWAYS AT CENTER HILL LAKE
337 Hurricane Ln (38582)
Rates: n/a
(931) 858-3687

SMITHVILLE

LAKESIDE RESORT CABINS
358 Relax Dr (37166)
Rates: n/a
(615) 597-4298

SMYRNA

DAYS INN
1300 Plaza Dr (37167)
Rates: $55-$150
(615) 355-6161
(800) 329-7466

SOMERVILLE

PLEASANT RETREAT
420 Hotel St (38076)
Rates: n/a
(901) 465-4599
(901) 465-3916

SPRING CITY

ARROWHEAD RESORT
261 Bennet Dr (37381)
Rates: n/a
(423) 365-6484

RHEA HARBOR RESORT & MARINA
385 Lake Shire Dr (37381)
Rates: n/a
(423) 365-6851
(800) 382-6851

TERRACE VIEW RESORT & MARINA
3367 Euchee Chapel Rd (37381)
Rates: n/a
(423) 365-5238
(888) 666-6333

SPRING HILL

HOLIDAY INN EXPRESS
104 Kedron Rd (37174)
Rates: $60-$100
(931) 486-1234
(800) 465-4329

SPRINGFIELD

BEST WESTERN SPRINGFIELD
2001 Memorial Blvd (37172)
Rates: $55-$125
(615) 384-1234
(800) 528-1234

SPRINGVILLE

HILL TOP LODGE
Rt 3, Antioch Rd
(38256)
Rates: n/a
(931) 644-2049

**HOWELL'S
RESORT**
Rt 1 Box 409A
(38256)
Rates: n/a
(931) 642-7442

**MANSARD
ISLAND RESORT
& MARINA**
60 Mansard Island
Dr (38256)
Rates: n/a
(901) 642-5590
(800) 533-5590

**PLEASANT VIEW
RESORT CABINS**
289 Pleasant View
Resort Rd (38256)
Rates: n/a
(901) 593-5511
(877) 593-5511

STEWART

**SOUTHERNAIRE
MOTEL**
Rt 1,Box 63
(37175)
Rates: n/a
(931) 721-3321

SWEETWATER

**BEST WESTERN
SWEETWATER INN**
1421 Murray's
Chapel Rd (37874)
Rates: $65-$85
(423) 337-3541
(800) 528-1234
(800) 647-3529

**BUDGET HOST
INN**
207 Hwy 68
(37874)
Rates: $29-$79
(423) 337-9357
(800) 283-4678

COMFORT INN
731 S Main St
(37874)
Rates: $40-$70
(423) 337-6646
(800) 228-5150

**COMFORT INN-
WEST**
248 Hwy 68
(37874)
Rates: $45-$75
(423) 337-3353
(800) 228-5150

DAYS INN
229 Hwy 68
(37874)
Rates: $38-$69
(423) 337-4200
(800) 329-7466

**SWEETWATER
HOTEL
TRAVELODGE
& CONVENTION
CENTER**
180 Hwy 68,
Exit 60 (37874)
Rates: 45+
(423) 337-3511
(800) 523-5727

TEN MILE

**BAYSIDE MARINA
& RESORT**
134 Bayside Dr
(37880)
Rates: n/a
(865) 376-7031

TIPTONVILLE

**BACKYARD BIRDS
LODGE BED
& BREAKFAST**
Air Park Rd
(38079)
Rates: n/a
(901) 253-9064

**BLUE BANK
RESORT**
Rt 1, Box 970,
Hwy 21 (38079)
Rates: n/a
(901) 253-6878
(877) 258-3226

**BOYETTE'S
RESORT CABINS**
Rt 1, Box 1230
(38079)
Rates: n/a
(901) 253-6523

**CYPRESS POINT
RESORT CABINS**
Rt 1, Box 1225,
Hwy 21 (38079)
Rates: n/a
(901) 253-6654
(800) 394-1886

GRAY'S CAMP
Rt 1 Box 280
(38079)
Rates: n/a
(901) 253-7813

RAY'S CAMP
Rt 1 Box 5B-1
(38079)
Rates: n/a
(901) 253-7765

TOWNSEND

**APPALACHIAN
CABIN RENTALS**
140 Black Mash
Hollow Rd
(37882)
Rates: n/a
(865) 448-0832

**BEST WESTERN
VALLEY VIEW
LODGE**
7726 E Lamar
Alexander Pkwy
(37882)
Rates: $41-$129
(865) 448-2237
(800) 292-4844
(800) 528-1234

**BLUE SMOKE
MOUNTAIN
CABINS**
11233 Carrs Creek
Rd (37882)
Rates: n/a
(865) 448-3068

**DOGWOOD
CABINS**
7016 E Lamar
Alexander Pkwy
(37882)
Rates: n/a
(865) 448-9054
(888) 448-9054

**GARDEN WALK
CABIN RENTALS**
139 Bear Lodge Dr
(37882)
Rates: n/a
(865) 448-8897
(800) 750-8659

**GILBERTSON'S
LAZY HORSE
RETREAT**
938 Schoolhouse
Gap Rd (37882)
Rates: n/a
(865) 448-6810

**GOODE NIGHT
VACATION
RENTALS**
608 Rudd Hollow
Rd (37882)
Rates: n/a
(865) 448-6842

**HIDEAWAY
COTTAGES &
LOG CABINS**
Black Mash
Hollow Rd
(37882)
Rates: n/a
(865) 984-1700

**HILLBILLY HILTON
CABINS**
8430 Hwy 73
(37882)
Rates: n/a
(865) 448-6463

**HILLSIDE RETREAT
CABIN RENTALS**
7459 Old
Tuckaleechee Rd
(37882)
Rates: n/a
(865) 448-2276

**LITTLE ROUND
TOP CABINS**
Little Round Top
Ln (37882)
Rates: n/a
(865) 428-5984

**MOUNTAIN
LAUREL CABINS**
146 Black Mash
Hollow Rd
(37882)
Rates: n/a
(865) 448-9657

**THE OWL'S HOOT
CABIN RENTAL**
139 Black Mash
Hollow (37882)
Rates: n/a
(865) 984-1700

**PEARLS OF THE
MOUNTAINS
CABIN RENTALS**
7717 E Lamar
Alexander Pkwy
(37882)
Rates: n/a
(865) 448-8001
(800) 324-8415

**PILGRIM CABIN
RENTAL**
7207 Old
Tuckaleechee Rd
(37882)
Rates: n/a
(865) 448-6878

**ROAD'S EDGE
CABIN RENTAL**
333 Black Mash
Hollow Rd
(37882)
Rates: n/a
(865) 982-9975

**ROCKY RIVER
CABINS**
8113 Old Hwy 73
(37882)
Rates: n/a
(865) 448-6001

**STRAWBERRY
PATCH INN**
7509 Old Hwy 73
(37882)
Rates: n/a
(865) 448-6306

**WEAR'S MOTEL
& COTTAGES**
8270 Hwy 73
(37882)
Rates: $45-$80
(865) 448-2296

**THE WRIGHT
CABINS**
136 Black Mash
Hollow Rd
(37882)
Rates: n/a
(865) 448-9090

TULLAHOMA

**HOLIDAY
LANDING MOTEL**
912 Old Awalt Rd
(37388)
Rates: n/a
(931) 455-3151
(800) 856-4703

**STEEPLECHASE
INN**
1410 N Jackson St
(37388)
Rates: n/a
(931) 455-4501

AREA CODES - If the local number doesn't connect, check for a new area code.

UNICOI

FAMILY INNS OF AMERICA
100 Country Club Dr (37692)
Rates: n/a
(423) 743-9181
(800) 545-3311

UNION CITY

CULTRA MOTOR INN
1221 Reelfoot Ave (38261)
Rates: n/a
(901) 885-6610

SUPER 8 MOTEL
1400 Vaden Ave (38261)
Rates: $41-$53
(901) 885-4444
(800) 800-8000

WALLAND

TWIN VALLEY B&B HORSE RANCH
2848 Old Chillhowee Rd (37886)
Rates: n/a
(423) 984-0980
(800) 872-2235

WAVERLY

CLYDETON BOAT DOCK RESORT CABINS
10669 Clydeton Rd (37185)
Rates: n/a
(931) 296-2211

MASON'S BOAT DOCK & CAMP-GRND/CABINS
10275 Clydeton Rd (37185)
Rates: n/a
(931) 296-9165

NOLAN HOUSE BED & BREAKFAST
375 Hwy 13 N (37185)
Rates: n/a
(931) 296-2511

TURKEY CREEK MARINA & RESORT
6565 Turkey Creek Rd (37185)
Rates: n/a
(931) 296-2992

WHITE HOUSE

COMFORT INN
340 Hester Lane (37188)
Rates: $40-$60
(615) 672-8850
(800) 228-5150

HOLIDAY INN EXPRESS
354 Hester Lane (37188)
Rates: $54-$65
(615) 672-7200
(800) 465-4329

WHITE PINE

DAYS INN
3670 Roy Messer Hwy (37890)
Rates: $51-$129
(865) 674-2573
(800) 329-7466

WHITEVILLE

SUPER 8 MOTEL
2040 Hwy 65 (38075)
Rates: $50-$60
(901) 254-8884
(800) 800-8000

WILDERSVILLE

BEST WESTERN CROSSROADS INN
21045 Hwy 22 N (38388)
Rates: $34-$56
(901) 968-2532
(800) 528-1234

WINCHESTER

BEST WESTERN INN
1602 Dinah Shore Blvd (37398)
Rates: $45-$85
(931) 967-9444
(800) 528-1234

WINCHESTER INN MOTEL
700 S College St (37398)
Rates: $24-$50
(931) 967-3846

TEXAS

ABILENE

ANTILLEY INN
6550 S Hwy 83
(70606)
Rates: $33-$38
(915) 695-3330

BEST WESTERN MALL SOUTH
3950 Ridgemont
Dr (79606)
Rates: $61-$68
(915) 695-1262
(800) 528-1234
(800) 346-1574

BUDGETHOST COLONIAL INN
3210 Pine St (79601)
Rates: $42-$50
(915) 677-2683
(800) 283-4678

CLARION HOTEL
5403 S 1st (79605)
Rates: $64-$75
(915) 695-2150
(800) 592-4466

COMFORT INN
1758 E I-20 (79601)
Rates: $59-$120
(915) 676-0203
(800) 228-5150

COMFORT SUITES
3165 S Danville Dr
(79606)
Rates: $74-$120
(915) 795-8500
(800) 228-5150

DAYS INN
1702 I-20 E (79601)
Rates: $45-$56
(915) 672-6433
(800) 329-7466

EXECUTIVE INN
1650 I-10 E (79601)
Rates: $35-$55
(915) 677-2200

HAMPTON INN
3917 Ridgemont
Dr (79606)
Rates: $55-$69
(915) 695-0044
(800) 426-7866

HOLIDAY INN EXPRESS
1625 SR 351
(79601)
Rates: $55-$70
(915) 673-5271
(800) 465-4329

LA QUINTA INN
3501 W Lake Rd
(79601)
Rates: $65-$85
(915) 676-1676
(800) 687-6777

MOTEL 6
4951 W Stamford
(79603)
Rates: $33-$43
(915) 672-8462
(800) 466-8356

QUALITY INN
505 Pine St (79601)
Rates: $59-$64
(915) 676-0222
(800) 228-5151
(800) 588-0222 (TX)

ROYAL INN
5695 S 1st St
(79605)
Rates: $25-$48
(915) 692-3022
(800) 588-4386

SUPER 8 MOTEL
1525 E I-20 (79601)
Rates: $43-$55
(915) 673-5251
(800) 800-8000

TRAVELODGE
840 E Hwy 80
(79601)
Rates: $45-$59
(915) 677-8100
(800) 578-7878

ADDISON

CROWNE PLAZA GALLERIA
14315 Midway Rd
(75244)
Rates: $69-$119
(972) 980-8877
(800) 227-6963

HAMPTON INN
4505 Beltway Dr
(75244)
Rates: $80-$100
(972) 991-2800
(800) 426-7866

HOMEWOOD SUITES
4451 Beltline Rd
(75244)
Rates: $139
(972) 788-1342
(800) 225-5466

LA QUINTA INN & SUITES
14925 Landmark
Blvd (75244)
Rates: $99-$109
(800) 687-6777

MOTEL 6
4325 Beltline Rd
(75244)
Rates: $46-$61
(972) 386-4577
(800) 466-8356

SUMMERFIELD SUITES HOTEL
4900 Edwin Lewis
Dr (75244)
Rates: $88-$148
(972) 661-3113
(800) 833-4353

ALBANY

ALBANY MOTOR INN
Hwy 180 @ 283 N
(76430)
Rates: $40-$65
(888) 525-2269

ALICE

DAYS INN
555 N Johnson St
(78332)
Rates: $45-$55
(361) 664-6616
(800) 329-7466

KINGS INN MOTEL
815 Hwy 281 S
(78332)
Rates: $30-$35
(361) 664-4351

ALLEN

AMERIHOST INN
407 S Central
Expwy (75013)
Rates: $50-$60
(972) 396-9494
(800) 434-5800

ALPINE

ANTELOPE LODGE
2310 W Hwy 90
(79830)
Rates: $34-$62
(800) 880-8106

BEST WESTERN ALPINE CLASSIC INN
2401 E Hwy 90
(79830)
Rates: $59-$67
(915) 837-1530
(800) 528-1234

THE CORNER HOUSE B&B
801 E Avenue
(79830)
Rates: $27-$65
(915) 837-7161
(800) 585-7795

HIGHLAND INN
1404 E Hwy 90
(79830)
Rates: $40-$66
(915) 837-5811

HISTORIC HOLLAND HOTEL
209 W Holland
Ave (79830)
Rates: $40-$75
(800) 535-8040

LONGHORN RANCH MOTEL
HC 65, PO Box
267 (79830)
Rates: $45-$55
(915) 371-2541

RAMADA LIMITED
2800 W Hwy 90
(79830)
Rates: $70-$85
(915) 837-1100
(800) 272-6232

ALVIN

COMFORT INN
SR 35 Bypass
(77511)
Rates: $54-$69
(800) 228-5150

COUNTRY HEARTH INN
1588 S Hwy 35
Bypass (77511)
Rates: $52-$70
(281) 331-0335
(888) 325-7815

DAYS INN
110 E Hwy 6
(77511)
Rates: $39-$64
(281) 331-5227
(800) 329-7466

AMARILLO

BEST WESTERN AMARILLO INN
1610 Coulter Dr
(79106)
Rates: $72-$92
(806) 358-7861
(800) 528-1234

BEST WESTERN SANTA FE INN
4600 I-40 E (79120)
Rates: $75-$85
(806) 372-1885
(800) 528-1234

BIG TEXAN INN
7701 I-40 E (79120)
Rates: $40-$65
(806) 372-5000
(800) 657-7177

SUNDAY HOUSE INN MOTEL
P. O. Box 578 (79830)
Rates: $34-$42
(915) 837-3363
(800) 510-3363

TERLINGUA RANCH LODGE
HC 65, Box 220
(79830)
Rates: $30-$42
(915) 371-2416

AREA CODES - If the local number doesn't connect, check for a new area code.

BRONCO MOTEL
6005 Amarillo
Blvd W (79106)
Rates: $32-$39
(806) 355-3321

COACHLIGHT INN #3
2115 I-40 E (79102)
Rates: $32-$46
(806) 376-5911

COACHLIGHT INN #4
6810 I-40 E (79104)
Rates: $33-$47
(806) 373-6871

COMFORT INN AIRPORT
1515 I-40 E (79102)
Rates: $44-$94
(806) 376-9993
(800) 228-5150

ECONO LODGE
2915 I-40 E (79104)
Rates: $40-$70
(806) 372-8101
(800) 553-2666

HAMPTON INN
1700 I-40E (79103)
Rates: $69-$99
(806) 372-1425
(800) 426-7866

HOLIDAY INN I-40
1911 I-40 at Ross-
Osage (79102)
Rates: $75-$85
(806) 372-8741
(800) 465-4329

HOMEGATE STUDIOS & SUITES
6800 I-40 W
(79103)
Rates: $99-$109
(806) 358-7943

LA QUINTA INN-AIRPORT
1708 I-40 E (79103)
Rates: $69-$89
(806) 373-7486
(800) 687-6667

LA QUINTA INN MEDICAL CENTER
2108 S Coulter St
(79106)
Rates: $69-$89
(806) 352-6311
(800) 687-6667

MOTEL 6-AIRPORT
4301 I-40 E (79104)
Rates: $30-$38
(806) 373-3045
(800) 466-8356

MOTEL 6-CENTRAL
2032 Paramount
Blvd (79109)
Rates: $33-$45
(806) 355-6554
(800) 466-8356

MOTEL 6-EAST
3930 I-40 E (79103)
Rates: $29-$38
(806) 374-6444
(800) 466-8356

MOTEL 6-WEST
6040 I-40 W
(79106)
Rates: $31-$341
(806) 359-7651
(800) 466-8356

QUALITY INN
1803 Lakeside Dr
(79120)
Rates: $79-$139
(806) 335-1561
(800) 228-5151
(800) 847-6556 (TX)

RADISSON INN AIRPORT
7090 I-40 E (79104)
Rates: $104-$124
(806) 373-3303
(800) 333-3333

RAMADA INN EAST
2501 I-40 E (79104)
Rates: $79-$89
(806) 379-6555
(800) 272-6232

RED ROOF INN
1620 I-40 E (79103)
Rates: n/a
(806) 374-2020
(800) 843-7663

RESIDENCE INN BY MARRIOTT
6700 I-40 W
(79106)
Rates: $189
(806) 354-2978
(800) 331-3131

TRAVELODGE-EAST
3205 I-40 E, Tee
Anchor Blvd
(79104)
Rates: $40-$60
(806) 372-8171
(800) 578-7878

TRAVELODGE-WEST
2035 Paramount
Blvd (79109)
Rates: $50-$62
(806) 353-3541
(800) 578-7878

ANGLETON

COUNTRY HEARTH INN
1235 N Velasco
(77515)
Rates: $50-$63
(409) 849-2465
(888) 325-7816

ANTHONY

SUPER 8 MOTEL WEST
100 Park North Dr
(79821)
Rates: $41-$60
(915) 886-2888
(800) 800-8000

ARANSAS PASS

HOMEPORT INN
1515 W Wheeler
Ave (78336)
Rates: $30-$36
(361) 758-3213

TRAVELODGE
545 N Commercial
(78336)
Rates: $35-$65
(361) 758-53-5
(800) 578-7878

ARLINGTON

AMERISUITES
2380 E Road to Six
Flags Dr (76011)
Rates: $59-$129
(800) 833-1516

BAYMONT INN & SUITES
2401 Diplomacy
Dr (76011)
Rates: $76-$86
(817) 633-2400
(800) 301-0200

BEST WESTERN GREAT SOUTH-WEST INN
3501 E Division St
(76011)
Rates: $49-$89
(817) 640-7722
(800) 528-1234
(800) 346-2378

DAYS INN
1901 Pleasant
Ridge (76011)
Rates: $55-$65
(800) 329-7466

DAYS INN AIRPORT SOUTH-BALLPARK/ SIX FLAGS
1195 N Watson Rd
(76011)
Rates: $59-$68
(817) 649-8881
(800) 329-7466

DAYS INN BALLPARK AT ARLINGTON-SIX FLAGS
910 N Collins St
(76011)
Rates: $66-$95
(817) 261-8444
(800) 329-7466

HAWTHORN SUITES HOTEL
2401 Brookhollow
Plaza Dr (76011)
Rates: $110-$160
(817) 640-1188
(800) 225-5466
(800) 527-1133 (TX)

HOMESTEAD VILLAGE
1980 W Pleasant
Ridge Rd (76011)
Rates: n/a
(817) 465-8500
(888) 782-9473

HOMESTEAD VILLAGE GUEST STUDIOS
1221 N Watson Rd
(76011)
Rates: $40-$45
(817) 633-7588
(888) 782-9473

HOWARD JOHNSON
117 S Watson Rd
(76011)
Rates: $64-$79
(817) 633-4000
(800) 446-4656

LA QUINTA INN
825 N Watson Rd
(76011)
Rates: $79-$109
(817) 640-4142
(800) 687-6667

LA QUINTA INN & SUITES
4001 Scott's
Legacy (76011)
Rates: $99-$109
(817) 467-7756
(800) 687-6667

LESTER MOTOR INN
2725 W Division
St (76012)
Rates: $20-$35
(817) 275-5496

MICROTEL INN
1740 Oak Village
Blvd (76013)
Rates: $50-$85
(817) 557-8400
(888) 771-7171

MOTEL 6
2626 E Randol
Mill Rd (76011)
Rates: $42-$58
(817) 649-0147
(800) 466-8356

OASIS MOTEL
818 W Division St
(76011)
Rates: $23-$40
(817) 274-1616

PARK INN LIMITED
703 Benge Dr
(76013)
Rates: $50-$60
(817) 860-2323
(800) 437-7275

RAMADA INN
1601 E Division St
(76011)
Rates: $39-$94
(817) 261-2300
(800) 272-6232

AREA CODES - If the local number doesn't connect, check for a new area code.

RESIDENCE INN BY MARRIOTT
1050 Brookhollow Plaza Dr (76006)
Rates: $66+
(817) 649-7300
(800) 331-3131

SLEEP INN
750 Six Flags Dr (76004)
Rates: $69-$95
(817) 649-1010
(800) 753-3746

STADIUM INN
2001 E Copeland Rd (76011)
Rates: $38-$69
(817) 461-1122

ATHENS

BUDGET INN
305 Dallas Hwy (75751)
Rates: $30-$35
(903) 675-5194

MOTEL 6
205 Dallas Hwy 175 (75751)
Rates: $33-$41
(903) 675-7511
(800) 446-8356

SPANISH TRACE INN MOTEL
716 E Tyler St (75751)
Rates: $38-$95
(903) 675-5173
(800) 488-5173

VICTORIAN INN
1803 E Hwy 31 (75751)
Rates: $32-$55
(903) 677-1470

ATLANTA

THE BUTLER'S INN
1100 W Main t (75551)
Rates: $38-$65
(903) 796-8235

AUBREY

THE GUEST HOUSE B&B
Rt 1, Box 203 (76227)
Rates: $55-$75
(817) 440-2076

AUSTIN

AMERISUITES-ARBORETUM
3612 Tudor Blvd (78759)
Rates: $89-$149
(512) 231-8491
(800) 833-1516

BALCOR SUITES
11215 Research Blvd (78759)
Rates: $55-$75
(512) 343-0584

BAYMONT INN & SUITES
150 Parker Dr (78728)
Rates: $67-$72
(512) 246-2800
(800) 301-0200

BEL-AIR MOTEL
3400 S Congress (78704)
Rates: $20-$38
(512) 444-5973

BEST WESTERN ATRIUM NORTH
7928 Gessner Dr (78753)
Rates: $69-$89
(512) 339-7311
(800) 528-1234
(800) 468-3708 (TX)

BEST WESTERN SEVILLE PLAZA INN
4323 I-35 S (78744)
Rates: $60-$80
(512) 447-5511
(800) 528-1234

THE BROOK HOUSE B&B
609 W 33rd St (78705)
Rates: $69-$109
(512) 459-0534

CAPITOL MOTOR INN
2525 I-35 S (78741)
Rates: $40-$45
(512) 441-0143

CLARION INN & SUITES CONF CTR
2200 S I-35 (78704)
Rates: $55-$135
(512) 444-0561
(800) 252-7466

COMFORT INN
700 Delmar Ave (78752)
Rates: $65-$129
(512) 302-5576
(800) 228-5150

CORPORATE SUITES
4815 W Braker (78759)
Rates: $79-$139
(512) 345-8822
(800) 845-6343

COUNTRY COTTAGE
2008 Travis Hghts Blvd (78765)
Rates: $100-$400
(512) 479-0073

DAYS INN UNIVERSITY-DOWNTOWN
3105 N I-35 (78722)
Rates: $59-$99
(512) 478-1631
(800) 329-7466

DOUBLETREE GUEST SUITES
303 W 15th St (78701)
Rates: $109-$179
(512) 478-7000
(800) 222-8733

DOUBLETREE HOTEL
6505 I-35 N (78752)
Rates: $99-$119
(512) 454-3737
(800) 222-8733

DRURY INN HIGHLAND MALL
919 E Koenig Ln (78751)
Rates: $67-$91
(512) 454-1144
(800) 378-7946

DRURY INN & SUITES NORTH
6511 I-35 N (78752)
Rates: $68-$92
(512) 467-9500
(800) 378-7946

EXEL INN
2711 I-35 S (78741)
Rates: $42-$79
(512) 462-9201
(800) 367-3935

FOUR POINTS HOTEL BY SHERATON
7800 N I-35 (78753)
Rates: $103-$122
(512) 836-8520
(800) 325-3535

FOUR SEASONS HOTEL
98 San Jacinto Blvd (78701)
Rates: $260-$1185
(512) 478-4500
(800) 332-3442

GOVERNOR'S INN BED & BRKFAST
611 W 22nd St (78705)
Rates: $59-$119
(512) 477-0711
(800) 871-8908

GREENSHORES ON LAKE AUSTIN
6900 Greenshores Rd (78730)
Rates: $65-$125
(512) 346-0011

HABITAT SUITES HOTEL
500 Highland Mall Blvd (78752)
Rates: $127-$137
(512) 467-6000
(800) 535-4663

HAWTHORN SUITES CENTRAL
935 La Posada Dr (78752)
Rates: $129-$159
(512) 459-3335
(800) 527-1133

HAWTHORN SUITES SOUTH
4020 I-35 S (78704)
Rates: $98-$108
(512) 440-7722
(800) 527-1133

HEART OF TEXAS MOTEL
5303 US 290 W (78735)
Rates: $50-$65
(512) 892-0644

HILTON & TOWERS NORTH
6000 Middle Fiskville Rd (78752)
Rates: $95-$250
(512) 451-5757
(800) 445-8667

HOLIDAY INN AIRPORT HIGHLAND MALL
6911 I-35 N (78752)
Rates: $70-$110
(512) 459-4251
(800) 465-4329

HOLIDAY INN AUSTIN SOUTH
3401 I-35 S (78741)
Rates: $89
(512) 448-2444
(800) 465-4329

HOLIDAY INN NORTHWEST PLAZA
8901 Business Park Dr (78759)
Rates: $119
(512) 343-0888
(800) 465-4329

HOLIDAY INN TOWN LAKE
20 N I-35 (78701)
Rates: $99-$149
(512) 472-8211
(800) 465-4329

HOMESTEAD GUEST STUDIOS
507 S 1st St (78701)
Rates: n/a
(512) 476-1818
(888) 782-9473

HOMESTEAD VILLAGE
937 Camino La Costa (78752)
Rates: n/a
(512) 458-5453
(888) 782-9473

HOMESTEAD VILLAGE GUEST STUDIOS-NW
11901 Pavillon Blvd (78701)
Rates: n/a
(512) 258-3556
(888) 782-9473

HOMEWOOD SUITES
10925 Stonelake Blvd (78759)
Rates: n/a
(512) 349-9966
(800) 225-5466

LA QUINTA INN-BEN WHITE
4200 I-35 S (78745)
Rates: $69-$85
(512) 443-1774
(800) 687-6667

LA QUINTA INN-CAPITOL
300 E 11th St (78701)
Rates: $89-$109
(512) 476-1166
(800) 687-6667

LA QUINTA INN-HIGHLAND MALL/AIRPORT
5812 I-35 N (78751)
Rates: $69-$85
(512) 459-4381
(800) 687-6667

LA QUINTA INN-NORTH
7100 I-35 N (78752)
Rates: $69-$89
(512) 452-9401
(800) 687-6667

LA QUINTA INN-OLTORF
1603 E Oltorf Blvd (78741)
Rates: $57-$99
(512) 447-6661
(800) 687-6667

LA QUINTA INN & SUITES
11901 N Mopac Expy (78701)
Rates: $79-$109
(512) 832-2121
(800) 687-6667

LA QUINTA INN & SUITES-AIRPORT
7625 E Ben White Blvd (78704)
Rates: n/a
(512) 386-6800
(800) 687-6667

LA QUINTA INN SOUTH WEST
4525 Gaines Ranch Lp (78745)
Rates: $89-$119
(512) 899-3000
(800) 687-6667

LAKE AUSTIN SPA RESORT
1705 Quinlan Park Rd (78732)
Rates: $425-$3450
(512) 266-2444
(800) 847-5637

MARRIOTT HOTEL AT THE CAPITOL
701 E 11th St (78701)
Rates: $225
(512) 478-1111

MASTER HOSTS-CHARIOT INN
7300 I-35 N (78752)
Rates: $38-$51
(512) 452-9371
(800) 251-1962

MOTEL 6-CENTRAL NORTH
8010 I-35 N (78753)
Rates: $33-$51
(512) 837-9890
(800) 466-8356

MOTEL 6 CENTRAL SOUTH
5330 I-35 N(78751)
Rates: $44-$60
(512) 467-9111
(800) 466-8356

MOTEL 6-NORTH
9420 I-35 N (78753)
Rates: $40-$56
(512) 339-6161
(800) 466-8356

MOTEL 6-SOUTH AIRPORT
2707 I-35 S (78741)
Rates: $42-$58
(512) 444-5882
(800) 466-8356

NEW AUSTIN MOTEL
2607 I-35 S (78741)
Rates: $26-$34
(512) 443-4242

QUALITY INN AIRPORT
909 E Koenig Ln (78751)
Rates: $52-$69
(512) 452-4200
(800) 228-5151

QUALITY SUITES
14620 N IH-35 (78728)
Rates: $85-$149
(512) 251-9110
(800) 228-5151

RAMADA INN SOUTH
1212 W Ben White Blvd (787046)
Rates: $70-$88
(512) 447-0151
(800) 272-6232

RED LION HOTEL AIRPORT
6121 I-35 N (78752)
Rates: $79-$99
(512) 323-5466
(800) 733-5466

RED ROOF INN-N
8210 N I-35 (78753)
Rates: $46-$60
(512) 835-2200
(800) 843-7663

RED ROOF INN-S
4701 S I-35 (78744)
Rates: $40-$50
(512) 448-00091
(800) 843-7663

RENAISSANCE AUSTIN HOTEL
9721 Arboretum Blvd (78759)
Rates: $179-$217
(512) 343-2626
(800) 468-3571

RESIDENCE INN BY MARRIOTT
3713 Tudor Blvd (78759)
Rates: $139-$169
(512) 502-8200
(800) 331-3131

RESIDENCE INN BY MARRIOTT
4537 S I-35 (78744)
Rates: $99-$149
(512) 912-1100
(800) 331-3131

SHERATON AUSTIN HOTEL
500 N I-35 (78753)
Rates: n/a
(512) 480-8181
(800) 325-3535

STARS PASSPORT INN UNIVERSITY
3105 I-35 N (78722)
Rates: $28-$49
(512) 478-1631
(800) 725-7666

SUPER 8 MOTEL
6000 Middle Fiskville Rd (78752)
Rates: $39-$74
(512) 467-8163
(800) 800-8000

SUPER 8 MOTEL CENTRAL
1201 N I-35 (78702)
Rates: $52-$79
(512) 472-8331
(800) 800-8000

TOWN LAKE MOTOR INN
2915 I-35 S (78741)
Rates: $30-$36
(512) 444-8432

WALNUT FOREST MOTEL
11506 I-35 N (78753)
Rates: $22-$28
(512) 835-0864

WELLESLEY INN & SUITES
12424 Research Blvd (78759)
Rates: $89-$107
(512) 219-6500
(888) 444-8888

WELLESLEY INN & SUITES
8221 N I-45 (78753)
Rates: $79-$149
(512) 339-6005
(888) 444-8888

WELLESLEY INN & SUITES
1001 S I0-35 (78744)
Rates: $75-$115
(512) 326-0100
(888) 444-8888

BAIRD

BAIRD MOTOR INN
500 I-20 E (79504)
Rates: $40-$55
(915) 854-2527

BALLINGER

BALLINGER CLASSIC MOTEL
1005 Hutchings (76821)
Rates: $34-$40
(915) 365-5717

DESERT INN MOTEL
Hwy 67 W (76821)
Rates: $28-$40
(915) 365-2518

STONEWALL MOTEL
201 N Broadway (76821)
Rates: $26-$36
(915) 895-7760

BANDERA

BANDERA LODGE
700 Hwy 16S (78003)
Rates: $55-$73
(830) 796-3093
(800) 796-3514

COOL WATER ACRES B&B
Rt 1, Box 785 (78003)
Rates: $70-$90
(830) 796-4866

RIVER FRONT MOTEL
Main St (78003)
Rates: $49-$69
(830) 460-3690
(800) 870-5671

RIVER OAK INN & RESTAURANT
1203 Main St (78003)
Rates: $39-$109
(830) 796-7751

BASTROP

BASTROP INN MOTEL
102 Childers Dr (78602)
Rates: $30-$35
(512) 321-3949

AREA CODES - If the local number doesn't connect, check for a new area code.

DAYS INN
4102 Hwy 71 E
(78602)
Rates: $40-$85
(512) 321-1157
(800) 329-7466

PECAN STREET INN B&B
1010 Pecan St
(78602)
Rates: $60-$100
(512) 321-3315

BAY CITY

ECONO LODGE
3712 7th St (77414)
Rates: $39-$59
(409) 245-5115
(800) 553-2666

BAYTOWN

BAYMONT INN & SUITES
5215 I-10 E (77521)
Rates: $61-$66
(281) 421-7300
(800) 301-0200

HOLIDAY INN EXPRESS
5222 I-10 E (77521)
Rates: $59-$75
(281) 421-7200
(800) 465-4329

LA QUINTA INN
4911 I-10 E (77521)
Rates: $55-$99
(281) 421-5566
(800) 687-6667

MOTEL 6
8911 Hwy 146
(77520)
Rates: $37-$53
(281) 576-5777
(800) 466-8356

QUALITY INN
300 S Hwy 146
(77520)
Rates: $55-$104
(281) 427-7481
(800) 228-5151

BEAUMONT

BEST WESTERN BEAUMONT INN
2155 N 11th St
(77703)
Rates: $55-$71
(409) 898-8150
(800) 528-1234

BEST WESTERN JEFFERSON INN
1610 I-10 S (77707)
Rates: $55-$71
(409) 842-0037
(800) 528-1234

DAYS INN
30 I-10 N (77702)
Rates: $32-$42
(409) 838-0581
(800) 329-7466

GRAND DUERR BED & BREAKFAST
2298 McFaddin at
7th (77701)
Rates: $99-$159
(409) 833-9600

HILTON HOTEL
2355 I-10 S (77705)
Rates: $79-$159
(409) 842-3600
(800) 445-8667

HOLIDAY INN BEAUMONT PLAZA
3950 I-10 S (77705)
Rates: $95-$125
(409) 842-5995
(800) 465-4329

HOLIDAY INN I-10 MIDTOWN
2095 N 11th St
(77703)
Rates: $70-$100
(409) 892-2222
(800) 465-4329

J & J MOTEL
6675 Eastex Frwy
(77705)
Rates: $24+
(409) 892-4241

LA QUINTA INN
220 I-10 N (77703)
Rates: $59-$76
(409) 838-9991
(800) 687-6667

MOTEL 6
1155 I-10 S (77701)
Rates: $36-$45
(409) 835-5913
(800) 466-8356

RAMADA INN
1295 N 11th St
(77702)
Rates: $45-$65
(409) 892-7722
(800) 272-6232

RAMADA LIMITED
4085 IH 10 South
(77705)
Rates: $45-$60
(409) 842-1111
(800) 272-6232

ROAD RUNNER MOTEL
3985 College St
(77707)
Rates: $28-$36
(409) 842-4420

SCOTTISH INNS
2640 I-10 E (77703)
Rates: $26-$31
(409) 899-3152
(800) 251-1962

BEDFORD

COMFORT INN
2904 Crystal Spgs
St (76095)
Rates: $54-$99
(817) 545-2555
(800) 228-5150

LA QUINTA INN
1450 W Airport
Frwy (76022)
Rates: $59-$79
(817) 267-5200
(800) 687-6667

BEEVILLE

DAYS INN
400 S US 181
Bypass (78102)
Rates: $52-$66
(361) 358-4000
(800) 329-7466

EL CAMINO MOTEL
1500 N
Washington
(78102)
Rates: $27-$35
(361) 358-2141

EXECUTIVE INN
1601 N St. Mary
(78102)
Rates: $36-$40
(361) 358-0022

BELLMEAD

MOTEL 6
1509 Hogan Ln
(76705)
Rates: $33-$42
(254) 799-4957
(800) 466-8356

BELTON

BEST WESTERN RIVER FOREST MOTEL
1414 E 6th Ave
(76513)
Rates: $40-$80
(254) 939-5711
(800) 528-1234

BUDGET HOST-THE BELTON INN
1520 I-35 S (76513)
Rates: $39-$55
(254) 939-0744
(800) 283-4678

RAMADA LIMITED
1102 E 2nd Ave
(76513)
Rates: $45-$65
(254) 939-3745
(800) 272-6232

BENBROOK

MOTEL 6
8603 Hwy 377 S
(76126)
Rates: $39-$48
(800) 466-8356

BIG BEND NATIONAL PARK

CHISOS MOUNTAINS LODGE
Basin Rural
Station (79834)
Rates: $31-$71
(915) 477-2291

BIG SPRING

BEST WESTERN BIG SPRING INN
700 W I-20 St
(79720)
Rates: $48-$64
(915) 267-1601
(800) 528-1234

DAYS INN
2701 S Gregg St
(79720)
Rates: $35-$55
(915) 267-5237
(800) 329-7466

ECONO LODGE
804 I-20 W (79720)
Rates: $40-$69
(915) 263-5200
(800) 553-2666

MOTEL 6
600 I-20 W (79720)
Rates: $29-$34
(915) 267-1695
(800) 466-8356

BLANCO

CREEKWOOD COUNTRY INN BED & BREAKFAST
P. O. Box 1357
(78606)
Rates: $75-$85
(210) 833-2248

BOERNE

BEST WESTERN TEXAS COUNTRY INN
35150 I-10 W
(78006)
Rates: $59-$90
(830) 249-9791
(800) 528-1234
(800) 299-9791

BOERNE LAKE LODGE B&B RESORT
310 Lakeview Dr
(78006)
Rates: $150-$250
(830) 816-6060
(800) 809-5050

KEY TO THE HILLS MOTEL
1228 S Main St
(78006)
Rates: $48-$60
(830) 249-3562
(800) 690-5763

BONHAM

DAYS INN
1515 Old Ector Rd
(75418)
Rates: $45-$55
(903) 583-3121
(800) 329-7466

BORGER

NENDELS INN
100 Bulldog Blvd
(79007)
Rates: $29-$51
(806) 273-9556

AREA CODES - If the local number doesn't connect, check for a new area code.

BOWIE

DAYS INN
Hwy 287 & 59
(76230)
Rates: $42-$65
(817) 872-5426
(800) 329-7466

PARK'S INN
708 Park Ave
(76230)
Rates: $30-$41
(817) 872-1111

BRADY

**BEST WESTERN
BRADY INN**
2200 S Bridge St
(76825)
Rates: $41-$75
(915) 597-3997
(800) 528-1234

DAYS INN
2108 S Bridge St
(76825)
Rates: $40-$95
(915) 597-0789
(800) 329-7466

PLATEAU MOTEL
2023 S Bridge St
(76825)
Rates: $27-$38
(915) 597-2185

BRECKENRIDGE

RIDGE MOTEL
Hwy 180,
P. O. Box 312
(76424)
Rates: $28-$40
(817) 559-2244
(800) 462-5308

BRENHAM

**BEST WESTERN
INN**
1503 Hwy 290 E
(77833)
Rates: $59-$79
(409) 251-7791
(800) 5218-1234

**BRENHAM HOUSE
BED & BREAKFAST**
705 Clinton St
(77833)
Rates: $75
(800) 259-8367

DAYS INN
201 Hwy 290
Loop East (77833)
Rates: $40-$80
(409) 830-1110
(800) 329-7466

RAMADA LIMITED
2217 S Market St
(77833)
Rates: $45-$69
(409) 836-1300
(800) 272-6232

BROADDUS

**COUNTRY INN
"A MOTEL"**
P. O. Box 428,
Hwy 147 (75929)
Rates: $35-$70
(409) 872-3691

BROOKSHIRE

**BRAZOS VALLEY
INN**
217 Waller Ave
(77423)
Rates: $36-$49
(281) 934-3122

BROWNFIELD

**BEST WESTERN
CAPROCK INN**
321 Lubbock Rd
(79316)
Rates: $45-$59
(806) 637-9471
(800) 528-1234

BROWNSVILLE

**FOUR POINTS
BY SHERATON**
3777 N Expwy
(78520)
Rates: $89-$109
(956) 350-9191
(800) 325-7385

LA QUINTA INN
55 Sam Perl Blvd
(78520)
Rates: $43-109
(956) 546-0381
(800) 687-6667

MOTEL CITRUS
2043 Central Blvd
(78520)
Rates: $35-$80
(956) 550-9077

MOTEL 6
2255 N Expwy
(78521)
Rates: $34-$41
(956) 546-4699
(800) 466-8356

RED ROOF INN
2377 N Expwy 83
(78520)
Rates: n/a
(956) 504-2300
(800) 843-7663

BROWNWOOD

**BEST WESTERN
BROWNWOOD**
410 E Commerce
(76801)
Rates: $49-$65
(915) 646-3511
(800) 528-1234
(877) 646-3513

**GATE I MOTOR
INN**
4410 Hwy 377 S
(76801)
Rates: $34
(915) 643-5463

**GOLD KEY INN
MOTEL**
515 E Commerce
(76801)
Rates: $29-$44
(915) 646-2551
(800) 646-0912

**LAKE
BROWNWOOD
BED & BREAKFST**
9321 CR 558
(76801)
Rates: $75-$95
(915) 784-7729

BRYAN

PREFERENCE INN
1601 S Texas Ave
(77802)
Rates: $40-$79
(409) 822-6196

BUFFALO

**BEST WESTERN
CRAIG'S INN**
I-45 & US 79
(75831)
Rates: $44-$55
(903) 322-5831
(800) 528-1234

BURLESON

COMFORT SUITES
321 S Burleson
Blvd (76028)
Rates: $89-$185
(817) 426-6666
(800) 228-5150

DAYS INN
329 S Burleson
Blvd (76028)
Rates: $59-$69
(817) 447-1111
(800) 329-7466

BURNET

**ROCKY REST
COUNTRY INN**
404 S Water St
(78611)
Rates: $55-$60
(512) 756-2600

CALDWELL

THE SURREY INN
403 E Hwy 21
(77836)
Rates: $37-$40
(409) 567-3221

**VARSITY INN
CALDWELL**
705 Hwy 36 N
(77836)
Rates: $33-$49
(409) 567-4661

CAMERON

VARSITY MOTEL
1004 E 1st St
(76520)
Rates: $34-$40
(817) 697-6446

CANTON

**BEST WESTERN
CANTON INN**
2251 N Trade
Days Blvd (75103)
Rates: $57-$69
(903) 567-6591
(800) 528-1234

DAYS INN
109 S at I-20
(75103)
Rates: $42-$110
(903) 567-6588
(800) 329-7466

SUPER 8 MOTEL
110 N I-20 (75103)
Rates: $45-$63
(903) 567-6567
(800) 800-8000

CANYON

**COUNTRY HOME
BED & BREAKFST**
Rt 1, Box 447 (79015)
Rates: $55-$85
(800) 664-7636

CANYON LAKE

**MARICOPA
RANCH RESORT**
12381 FM 306
(78130)
Rates: $45-$105
(830) 964-3731
(800) 460-8891

CARROLLTON

**HOWARD
JOHNSON INN**
1735 S I-35 E
(75006)
Rates: $42-$62
(972) 446-8366
(800) 446-4656

RED ROOF INN
1720 S Broadway
(75006)
Rates: $36-$61
(972) 245-1700
(800) 843-7663

CARTHAGE

CARTHAGE MOTEL
321 S Shelby (75633)
Rates: $28-$35
(903) 693-3814

CENTER

**BEST WESTERN
CENTER INN**
1005 Hurst St
(75935)
Rates: $43-$67
(409) 598-3384
(800) 528-1234

CENTER POINT

**MARIANNE'S
COUNTRY B&B**
Rt 1, Box 527
(78010)
Rates: $80-$95
(830) 634-7489
(800) 634-7489

AREA CODES - If the local number doesn't connect, check for a new area code.

CENTERVILLE

DAYS INN
Hwy 7 & I-45
(75833)
Rates: $44-$75
(903) 536-7175
(800) 329-7466

CHANNELVIEW

BEST WESTERN HOUSTON EAST
15919 I-10 E
(77530)
Rates: $40-$80
(281) 452-1000
(800) 528-1234

ECONO LODGE
17011 I-10 E (77530)
Rates: $44-$165
(281) 457-2966
(800) 553-2666

TRAVELODGE
15831 Second St
(77520)
Rates: 50+
(281) 862-0222
(800) 578-7878

CHILDRESS

BEST WESTERN CLASSIC INN
1805 Ave F NW
(79201)
Rates: $48-$62
(940) 937-6353
(800) 528-1234
(800) 346-1576

COMFORT INN
1804 Ave F NW
(79201)
Rates: $69-$129
(940) 937-6363
(800) 228-5150

ECONO LODGE
1612 Ave F NW
(79201)
Rates: $38-$65
(940) 937-3695
(800) 553-2666

CISCO

BEST WESTERN INN
1898 Hwy 206 W
(76437)
Rates: $54-$64
(254) 442-3735
(800) 528-1234
(800) 621-2457

CISCO MOTOR INN
204 I-20 W (76437)
Rates: $30-$50
(254) 442-3040

OAK MOTEL
300 I-20 E (76437)
Rates: $20-$29
(254) 442-2100

CLARENDON

BAR H WORKING DUDE RANCH
P O Box 1191
(79226)
(800) 627-9871

WESTERN SKIES MOTEL
800 W 2nd St
(79226)
Rates: $35-$45
(806) 874-3501

CLAUDE

L A MOTEL
200 E 1st St
(79019)
Rates: $28-$45
(806) 226-4981

CLEBURNE

BUDGET HOST SAGAMAR INN
2107 N Main
(76031)
Rates: $44-$60
(817) 556-3631
(800) 283-4678

DAYS INN
101 N Ridgeway
Dr (76031)
Rates: $50-$80
(817) 645-8836
(800) 329-7466

CLIFTON

THE RIVER'S BEND BED & BREAKFAST
P. O. Box 228
(76634)
Rates: $75-$150
(817) 675-4936

CLUTE

LA QUINTA INN
1126 Hwy 332 W
(77531)
Rates: $55-$99
(409) 265-7461
(800) 687-6667

MAINSTAY SUITES
Hwy 332 (77531)
Rates: $65-$125
(800) 660-6246

MOTEL 6
1000 Hwy 332 W
(77531)
Rates: $31-$36
(409) 265-4764
(800) 466-8356

COLDSPRING

SAN JACINTO INN
13815 Hwy 150 W
(77331)
Rates: $40-$43
(409) 653-3008

COLEMAN

BEST WESTERN INN
1401 Hwy 84
Bypass (76834)
Rates: $45-$65
(915) 625-4176
(800) 528-1234

COLLEGE STATION

COMFORT INN
104 Texas Ave S
(77840)
Rates: $59-$119
(409) 846-7333
(800) 228-5150

HILTON HOTEL & CONF CENTER
801 University Dr
E (77840)
Rates: $73-$205
(409) 693-7500
(800) 445-8667

HOLIDAY INN
1503 Texas Ave S
(77840)
Rates: $49-$61
(409) 693-1736
(800) 465-4329

LA QUINTA INN
607 Texas Ave S
(77840)
Rates: $69-$129
(409) 696-7777
(800) 687-6667

MANOR HOUSE MOTOR INN
2504 Texas Ave S
(77840)
Rates: $65-$76
(409) 764-9540
(800) 231-4100

MOTEL 6
2327 Texas Ave S
(77840)
Rates: $35-$40
(409) 696-3379
(800) 466-8356

RAMADA INN
1502 Texas Ave S
(77840)
Rates: $69-$125
(409) 693-9891
(800) 272-6232

COLORADO CITY

VILLA INN MOTEL
2310 Hickory St
(79512)
Rates: $32-$44
(915) 728-5217

COLUMBUS

COLUMBUS INN
2208 Hwy 71 S
(78934)
Rates: $50-$65
(409) 732-5723

HOLIDAY INN EXPRESS HOTEL & SUITES
4321 I-10 (78934)
Rates: n/a
(800) 465-4329

COMANCHE

GUEST HOUSE-HERITAGE HILL BED & BREAKFAST
Hwy 36 E, Rt 3
Box 221 (76442)
Rates: $70-$100
(915) 356-3397

COMFORT

MOTOR INN AT COMFORT
32 Hwy 87 & I-10
(78013)
Rates: $50+
(830) 995-3822

IDLEWILDE BED & BREAKFAST
115 Hwy 473
(78013)
Rates: $63-$93
(830) 995-3844

KLEINA HIMMUL BED & BREAKFAST
Rt 1, Box 127-B
(78013)
Rates: $75-$85
(830) 995-2003

CONCAN

NEAL'S LODGES
P O Box 165
(78838)
Rates: $50-$175
(830) 232-6118

CONROE

BAYMONT INN
1506 I-45 S (77301)
Rates: $60-$72
(409) 539-5100
(800) 301-0200

HEATHER'S GLEN-BED & BREAKFAST
200 E Phillips
(77301)
Rates: $75-$95
(409) 441-6611
(800) 665-2643

HOLIDAY INN
1601 I-45 S (77301)
Rates: $59-$65
(409) 756-8941
(800) 465-4329

MOTEL 6
820 I-45 S (77304)
Rates: $31-$40
(409) 760-4003
(800) 466-8356

RAMADA LIMITED
1520 S Frazier
(77301)
Rates: $49-$79
(409) 756-8939
(800) 272-6232

CONWAY

BUDGET HOST INN S&S MOTEL
I-40 & Hwy 207
(79068)
Rates: $35-$47
(806) 537-5111
(800) 283-4678

AREA CODES - If the local number doesn't connect, check for a new area code.

CORPUS CHRISTI

ANCHOR RESORT CONDOMINIUMS
14300 S Padre
Island Dr (78418)
Rates: $69-$129
(800) 460-8770

BAYFRONT INN
601 N Shoreline
(78401)
Rates: $49-$99
(361) 883-7271
(800) 456-2293

BEST WESTERN CORPUS CHRISTI INN
2838 S Padre
Island Dr (78415)
Rates: $69-$99
(361) 854-0005
(800) 528-1234
(800) 445-9463

BEST WESTERN GARDEN INN
11217 I-37 (78410)
Rates: $64-$99
(361) 241-6675
(800) 528-1234

CHRISTY ESTATE SUITES
3942 Holly Rd
(78415)
Rates: $129-$189
(361) 854-1091
(800) 6-SUITE

DAYS INN
901 Navigation
Blvd (78408)
Rates: $62-$90
(361) 888-8599
(800) 329-7466

DRURY INN
2021 N Padre
Island Dr (78408)
Rates: $59-$77
(361) 289-8200
(800) 378-7946

GULF BEACH-II LUXURY MOTOR INN
3500 Surfside Blvd
(78402)
Rates: $45-$70
(361) 882-3500

HAMPTON INN-AIRPORT NORTH
5501 I-37 at
McBride (78408)
Rates: $79-$89
(361) 289-5861
(800) 426-7866

HOLIDAY INN EMERALD BEACH
1102 S Shoreline
Blvd (78401)
Rates: $140
(361) 883-5731
(800) 465-4329

HOLIDAY INN-PADRE IS. DRIVE
5549 Leopard St
(78408)
Rates: $89-$99
(361) 289-5100
(800) 465-4329

HOLIDAY INN SUN SPREE GULF BEACH RESORT
15202 Windward
Dr (78418)
Rates: $129-$250
(361) 949-8041
(800) 465-4329

HOWARD JOHNSON EXPRESS INN
224 I-37 N (78408)
Rates: $30-$80
(361) 883-2951
(800) 446-4656

LA QUINTA INN-N
5155 I-37 N (78408)
Rates: $69-$129
(361) 888-5721
(800) 687-6667

LA QUINTA INN-S
6225 S Padre
Island Dr (78412)
Rates: $79-$129
(361) 991-5730
(800) 687-6667

MOTEL 6-EAST
8202 S Padre
Island Dr (78412)
Rates: $42-$68
(361) 991-8858
(800) 466-8356

MOTEL 6-NW
845 Lantana St
(78408)
Rates: $33-$49
(361) 289-9397
(800) 466-8356

RACETRACK HOTEL & SUITES
6255 I-37, Corn
Products Rd
(78409)
Rates: $45-$199
(800) 723-2738

RED ROOF INN AIRPORT
6301 I-37 (78409)
Rates: $40-$56
(361) 289-6925
(800) 843-7663

RED ROOF INN SOUTH
6805 S Padre
Island Dr (78412)
Rates: n/a
(361) 992-9222
(800) 843-7663

RESIDENCE INN BY MARRIOTT
5229 Blanche
Moore Dr (78411)
Rates: $89-$139
(361) 985-1113
(800) 331-3131

SHONEY'S INN
6255 IH-37 (78409)
Rates: n/a
(512) 299-5644
(800) 222-2222

SURFSIDE CONDOMINIUM APARTMENTS
15005 Windward
Dr (78418)
Rates: $110-$120
(361) 949-8128
(800) 548-4585

CORSICANA

DAYS INN
2018 Hwy 287 S
(75110)
Rates: $39-$90
(903) 872-0659
(800) 329-7466

RAMADA INN
2000 S Hwy 287
(75110)
Rates: $49-$69
(903) 874-7413
(800) 272-6232

CROCKETT

CROCKETT FAMILY RESORT & MARINA
Rt 3, Box 460
(75835)
Rates: $40-$60
(877) 544-8466

CROCKETT INN
1600 Loop 304 E
(75835)
Rates: $35+
(409) 544-5611
(800) 633-9518

EMBERS MOTOR INN
1401 Loop 304 E
(75835)
Rates: $25-$36
(409) 544-5681

CUERO

SANDS MOTEL & RV PARK
2117 N Esplanade
(77954)
Rates: $32-$38
(512) 275-3437

DALHART

BEST WESTERN NURSANICKEL MOTEL
Hwy 87 S (79022)
Rates: $39-$69
(806) 249-5637
(800) 528-1234
(800) 309-2399

BUDGET INN
415 Liberal St
(79022)
Rates: $39-$59
(806) 244-4557

ECONO LODGE
123 Liberal St
(79022)
Rates: $29-$79
(806) 249-6464
(800) 553-2666

SANDS MOTEL
301 Liberal St
(79022)
Rates: $34-$59
(806) 244-4568

SUPER 8 MOTEL
301 Liberal St
(79022)
Rates: $41-$56
(806) 249-8526
(800) 800-8000

DALLAS

ADAMS MARK HOTEL
400 N Olive St
(75201)
Rates: $79-$99
(972) 922-8000
(800) 444-ADAM

AMERISUITES PARK CENTRAL
12411 N Central
Expy (75243)
Rates: $59-$119
(972) 456-1224
(800) 833-1516

AMERISUITES WEST END
1907 N Lamar St
(75202)
Rates: $98-$152
(214) 999-0500
(800) 833-1516

BRISTOL HOUSE RESIDENTIAL SUITES
7880 Alpha Rd
(75240)
Rates: $126-$136
(972) 391-0000

CANDLEWOOD SUITES
7930 N Stemmons
(75247)
Rates: $60-$129
(214) 631-3333

COMFORT INN GALLERIA
14975 Landmark
Blvd (75240)
Rates: $69-$125
(972) 701-0881
(800) 228-5150

COMFORT INN SOUTH
8541 S Hampton
Rd (75232)
Rates: $54-$72
(972) 572-1020
(800) 228-5150

CRESCENT COURT HOTEL
400 Crescent
Court (75210)
Rates: $230-$320
(972) 871-3200
(800) 654-6541

AREA CODES - If the local number doesn't connect, check for a new area code.

CROWNE PLAZA MARKET CENTER
7050 Stemmons Frwy (75247)
Rates: $69-$119
(214) 630-8500
(800) 227-6963

CROWNE PLAZA SUITES DALLAS
7800 Alpha Rd (75240)
Rates: $69-$129
(972) 233-7600
(800) 227-6963

DOUBLETREE HOTEL AT CAMPBELL CENTRE
8250 N Central Expwy (75206)
Rates: $120-$134
(214) 691-8700
(800) 222-8733

DRURY INN- DALLAS NORTH
2421 Walnut Hill Ln (75229)
Rates: $62-$82
(972) 484-3330
(800) 378-7946

ECONO LODGE
2275 Valley View Lane (75234)
Rates: $45-$65
(972) 243-5500
(800) 553-2666

EMBASSY SUITES HOTEL-DALLAS/ PARK CENTRAL
13131 N Central Expwy (75243)
Rates: $160
(972) 234-3300
(800) 362-2779

EXECUTIVE INN
3232 W Mockingbird Ln (75235)
Rates: $36-$72
(972) 357-5601

EXEL INN OF DALLAS EAST
8510 East R L Thornton Frwy (75228)
Rates: $38-$75
(972) 328-8500
(800) 356-8013

GRAND HOTEL
1914 Commerce St (75201)
Rates: $149-$550
(972) 747-7000
(800) 421-0011

HAMPTON INN CONV CENTER
1015 Elm (75202)
Rates: $94-$119
(212) 742-5678
(800) 426-7866

HARVEY HOTEL
7815 LBJ Frwy at Colt Rd (75240)
Rates: $59-$110
(972) 960-7000
(800) 922-9222

HAWTHORN SUITES
7900 Brookriver Dr (75247)
Rates: $135-$155
(214) 688-1010
(800) 527-1133

HOLIDAY INN ARISTOCRAT HOTEL
1933 Main St (75201)
Rates: n/a
(214) 741-7700
(800) 465-4329

HOLIDAY INN EXPRESS
13185 N Central Expwy & I-635 (75243)
Rates: n/a
(972) 907-9500
(800) 465-4329

HOLIDAY INN EXPRESS LOVE FIELD
2370 W Northwest Hwy (75220)
Rates: $69-$75
(214) 350-5577
(800) 465-4329

HOLIDAY INN SELECT
2645 LBJ Frwy (75234)
Rates: n/a
(972) 243-3363
(800) 465-4329

HOMESTEAD VILLAGE
9801 Adela Ct (75243)
Rates: n/a
(214) 342-5400
(888) 782-9473

HOMEWOOD SUITES MARKET CENTER
2747 N Stemmons Frwy (75207)
Rates: n/a
(214) 819-9700
(800) 225-5466

HOMEWOOD SUITES PARK CENTRAL AREA
9169 Markville Dr (75243)
Rates: $89-$109
(972) 437-6966
(800) 225-5466

HOTEL CRESCENT COURT
400 Crescent Court (75201)
Rates: $320-$1950
(214) 871-3200

HOTEL ST. GERMAIN
2516 Maple Ave (75201)
Rates: $265-$650
(214) 871-2516

HYATT REGENCY DALLAS AT REUNION
300 Reunion Blvd (75207)
Rates: $94-$150
(972) 651-1234
(800) 233-1234

LA MERIDIEN DALLAS HOTEL
650 N Pearl St (75201)
Rates: $129-$188
(214) 979-9000

LA QUINTA INN
13685 N Central Expwy (75206)
Rates: $59-$79
(972) 234-1016
(800) 687-6667

LA QUINTA INN- CENTRAL
4440 N Central Expwy (75206)
Rates: $69-$89
(214) 821-4220
(800) 687-6667

LA QUINTA INN-E
8303 E Thornton Frwy (75228)
Rates: $69-$99
(214) 324-3731
(800) 687-6667

LA QUINTA INN LOVE FIELD
1625 Regal Row (75247)
Rates: $59-$79
(214) 630-5701
(800) 687-6667

LA QUINTA INN NORTHPARK
10001 N Central Expwy (75231)
Rates: $69-$89
(214) 361-8200
(800) 687-6667

THE MANSION ON TURTLE CREEK
2821 Turtle Creek Blvd (75219)
Rates: $360-$490
(214) 559-2100
(800) 527-5432

MARRIOTT PARK CENTRAL
7750 LBJ Frwy (75251)
Rates: $70-$104
(972) 233-4421
(800) 228-9290

MOTEL 6 NORTH
2753 Forest Ln (75234)
Rates: $39-$46
(972) 620-2828
(800) 466-8356

MOTEL 6 SOUTH
2660 Forest Ln (75234)
Rates: $40-$56
(972) 484-9111
(800) 466-8356

MOTEL 6-SE
4220 Indepen-dence Dr (75237)
Rates: $35-$42
(972) 296-3331
(800) 466-8356

QUALITY SUITES
2380 W Northwest Hwy (75220)
Rates: $79-$135
(214) 904-9955
(800) 228-5151

RADISSON HOTEL & SUITES DALLAS
2330 W Northwest Hwy (75220)
Rates: $89-$179
(214) 351-4477
(800) 333-3333

RADISSON MOCKINGBIRD WEST
1893 W Mockingbird Ln (75235)
Rates: $77-$129
(214) 634-8850
(800) 333-3333

RED ROOF INN DOWNTOWN
4500 Harry Hines Blvd (75219)
Rates: n/a
(214) 522-6650
(800) 843-7663

RED ROOF INN DALLAS EAST
8108 E.Thornton Frwy (75228)
Rates: $41-$61
(214) 388-8741
(800) 843-7663

RED ROOF INN MARKET CENTER
1550 Empire Central Dr (75235)
Rates: $46-$59
(214) 638-5151
(800) 843-7663

RED ROOF INN- NORTHWEST
10335 Gardner Rd (75220)
Rates: $45-$58
(972) 506-8100
(800) 843-7663

RENAISSANCE HOTEL MARKET CENTER
2222 Stemmons Frwy (75207)
Rates: $139-$199
(972) 631-2222
(800) 228-9898

AREA CODES - If the local number doesn't connect, check for a new area code.

RESIDENCE INN BY MARRIOTT
14975 Quorum Dr (75240)
Rates: 89-$179
(800) 331-3131

RESIDENCE INN BY MARRIOTT/CENTRAL-N.PARK
10333 N Central Expwy (75231)
Rates: $121-$159
(214) 750-8220
(800) 331-3131

RESIDENCE INN BY MARRIOTT-MARKET CENTER
6950 N Stemmons Frwy (75247)
Rates: $129
(214) 631-2472
(800) 331-3131

RESIDENCE INN BY MARRIOTT-NORTH
13636 Goldmark Dr (75240)
Rates: $103-$130
(972) 669-0478
(800) 331-3131

SHERATON BROOKHOLLOW HOTEL
12720 Merit Dr (75251)
Rates: $77
(214) 630-7000
(800) 325-3535

WELLESLEY INN & SUITES PARK CENTRAL
9019 Vantage Point Rd (75243)
Rates: $59-$129
(888) 444-8888

WESTIN HOTEL GALLERIA DALLAS
13340 Dallas Pkwy (75240)
Rates: $249
(972) 934-9494
(800) 228-3000

WILSON WORLD HOTEL & SUITES
2324 N Stemmons Frwy (75207)
Rates: $69-$129
(800) 945-7667

DE SOTO

RED ROOF INN
1401 N Beckley Ave (75115)
Rates: $40-$48
(972) 224-7100
(800) 843-7663

DECATUR

BEST WESTERN INN
1801 Hwy 287 S (76234)
Rates: $53-$85
(940) 627-5982
(800) 528-1234
(800) 399-1553

COMFORT INN
1709 Hwy 287 S (76234)
Rates: $49-$120
(940) 627-6919
(800) 228-5150

DECATUR MANOR GUEST HOUSE
500 W Walnut St (76234)
Rates: $59-$99
(940) 627-3079

PAINTED VALLEY RANCH B&B
1724 W Preskitt Rd (76234)
Rates: $89-$129
(888) 817-6377

DEL RIO

AMISTAD LODGE MOTEL
Hwy 90 W, HCR 3, Box 25 (78840)
Rates: $31+
(830) 775-8591

ANGLER'S LODGE MOTEL
Hwy 90 W, HCR 3, Box 25 (78840)
Rates: $27+
(830) 775-1586

BEST WESTERN INN OF DEL RIO
810 Ave F (78840)
Rates: $79-$99
(830) 775-7511
(800) 528-1234
(800) 336-3537 (TX)

BEST WESTERN LA SIESTA
2000 Ave F (78840)
Rates: $49-$115
(830) 775-6323
(800) 528-1234
(877) 574-3782

DAYS INN & SUITES
3808 Hwy 90 W (78840)
Rates: $43-$175
(830) 775-0585
(800) 329-7466

DEL RIO MOTOR LODGE
1300 Ave F (78840)
Rates: $20+
(830) 775-2486
(800) 882-9826

DESERT HILLS MOTEL
1912 Ave F (78840)
Rates: $20-$28
(830) 775-3548

HOLIDAY INN EXPRESS
3616 Ave F (78840)
Rates: $42-$67
(830) 775-2933
(800) 465-4329

LA QUINTA INN
2005 Ave F (78840)
Rates: $59-$79
(830) 775-7591
(800) 687-6667

LAKEVIEW INN DIABLO EAST
Hwy 90 W, HCR 3, Box 38 (78840)
Rates: $27-$45
(830) 775-9521
(800) 344-0109

MOTEL 6
2115 Ave F (78840)
Rates: $31-$36
(830) 774-2115
(800) 466-8356

ROUGH CANYON INN MOTEL
Hwy 277 N, RR 2 (78840)
Rates: $27+
(830) 774-6266

WESTERN MOTEL
1203 Ave F (78840)
Rates: $24-$56
(830) 774-4661

DENISON

MOTEL 6
615 N Hwy 75 (75020)
Rates: $37-$44
(903) 465-4446
(800) 466-8356

RAMADA INN
1600 S Austin Ave (75021)
Rates: $35-$60
(903) 465-6800
(800) 272-6232

DENTON

DENTON INN
820 S I-35 E (76205)
Rates: $46-$49
(940) 387-0591

DESERT SANDS MOTOR INN
611 S I-35 E (76205)
Rates: $28-$50
(940) 387-6181

EXEL INN
4211 N I-35 E (76201)
Rates: $39-$64
(940) 383 1471
(800) 367-3935

HOLIDAY LODGE
1112 E University (76205)
Rates: $25-$31
(940) 382-9688

HOWARD JOHNSON EXPRESS INN
3116 Bandera Dr (76207)
Rates: n/a
(940) 383-1681
(800) 446-4656

LA QUINTA INN
700 Fort Worth Dr (76201)
Rates: $69-$89
(940) 387-5840
(800) 687-6667

MOTEL 6
4125 N I-35 (76207)
Rates: $35-$45
(940) 566-4798
(800) 466-8356

RADISSON HOTEL & EAGLE POINT GOLF CLUB
2211 I-35E N (76205)
Rates: $99
(940) 565-8499
(800) 333-3333

WESTERN INN
3116 Bandera Dr (76207)
Rates: $28-$34
(940) 383-1681

DIBOLL

BEST WESTERN INN
910 N Temple Dr (75941)
Rates: $45-$48
(800) 528-1234

DONNA

HOWARD JOHNSON EXPRESS INN
602 N Victoria Rd (78537)
Rates: $55-$79
(956) 464-7801
(800) 446-4656

SUPER 8 MOTEL
2005 E Expwy 83 (78537)
Rates: $45-$74
(956) 461-2226
(800) 800-8000

DUMAS

ECONO LODGE OLD TOWN INN
1719 S Dumas Ave (79029)
Rates: $35-$100
(806) 935-9098
(800) 553-2666

HOLIDAY INN EXP
1525 S Dumas Ave (79029)
Rates: $55
(806) 935-4000
(800) 465-4329

KONA KAI DUMAS INN MOTEL
1701 S Dumas Ave (79029)
Rates: $67-$80
(806) 935-6441

PHILLIPS MANOR MOTEL
18721 S Dumas Ave (79029)
Rates: $28-$44
(806) 935-9281

SUPER 8 MOTEL
119 W 17th (79029)
Rates: $50-$79
(806) 935-6222
(800) 800-8000

DUNCANVILLE

HOLIDAY INN-DALLAS SW
711 E Camp Wisdom Rd (75116)
Rates: $71-$99
(972) 298-8911
(800) 465-4329

MOTEL 6
202 Jellison Rd (75116)
Rates: $37-$44
(972) 296-0345
(800) 466-8356

EAGLE LAKE

THE FARRIS 1912 INN
201 N McCarty St (77434)
Rates: $40-$95
(409) 234-2546

EAGLE PASS

BEST WESTERN EAGLE PASS
1923 Loop 431 (78852)
Rates: $72-$84
(830) 758-1234
(800) 528-1234
(800) 992-3245

HOLLY INN
2421 E Main St (78852)
Rates: $39-$44
(830) 773-9261
(800) 424-8125

LA QUINTA INN
2525 E Main St (78852)
Rates: $59-$79
(830) 773-7000
(800) 687-6667

SUPER 8 MOTEL
2150 Del Rio Blvd (78852)
Rates: $50-$65
(830) 773-9531
(800) 272-9786

EARLY

POST OAK INN
606 Early Blvd (76802)
Rates: $40-$50
(915) 643-5621)

EASTLAND

THE EASTLAND B&B
112 N Lamar St (76448)
Rates: $65-$85
(254) 629-8397

ECONO LODGE
2001 I-20 W (76448)
Rates: $38-$50
(254) 629-3324
(800) 553-2666

RAMADA INN
2501 I-20 East (76448)
Rates: $45-$65
(254) 629-2655
(800) 272-6232

SUPER 8 MOTEL & RV PARK
3900 I-20 E (76448)
Rates: $40-$52
(254) 629-3336
(800) 800-8000

EDINBURG

ECHO HOTEL & CONF CENTER
1903 S Closner Blvd (78359)
Rates: $47-$91
(800) 422-0336

EL CAMPO

BEST WESTERN EXECUTIVE INN
US Hwy 59 S (77437)
Rates: $55-$120
(800) 528-1234

EL CAMPO INN
210 W Hwy 59 (77437)
Rates: $34-$48
(409) 543-1110

EL PASO

AMERICANA INN
14387 Gateway Blvd W (79927)
Rates: $34-$48
(915) 852-3025

BAYMONT INN & SUITES
7620 N Mesa St (79912)
Rates: $45-$75
(915) 585-2999
(800) 301-0200

BAYMONT INN & SUITES
7944 Gateway Blvd E (79915)
Rates: $46-$57
(915) 591-3300
(800) 301-0200

BEST WESTERN AIRPORT INN
7144 Gateway Blvd E (79915)
Rates: $50-$64
(915) 779-7700
(800) 528-1234
(800) 295-7276 (TX)

BEST WESTERN SUNLAND PARK INN
1045 Sunland Park Dr (79922)
Rates: $49-$69
(915) 587-4900
(800) 528-1234

BUDGET LODGE MOTEL
1301 N Mesa St (79902)
Rates: $23-$37
(915) 533-6821

CAMINO REAL HOTEL
202 S El Paso St (79901)
Rates: $140-$165
(915) 534-3099
(800) 722-6466

CHASE SUITE HOTEL BY WOODFIN
6791 Montana Ave (79925)
Rates: $67-$170
(915) 772-8000
(800) 237-8811

CLARION HOTEL AIRPORT
6789 Boeing St (79925)
Rates: $49-$125
(915) 778-6789
(800) 252-7466

COMFORT INN
7651 N Mesa St (79915)
Rates: $45-$80
(915) 845-1906
(800) 228-5150

COMFORT INN AIRPORT EAST
900 N Yarborough St (79915)
Rates: $40-$89
(915) 594-9111
(800) 228-5150
(800) 497-1347 (TX)

COMFORT SUITES
949 Sunland Park Dr (79922)
Rates: $65-$99
(915) 587-5300
(800) 228-5150

DAYS INN
10635 Gateway W (79935)
Rates: $35-$41
(915) 595-1913
(800) 329-7466

ECONO LODGE
6363 Montana St (79925)
Rates: $45-$60
(915) 778-3311
(800) 553-2666

EMBASSY SUITES HOTEL
6100 Gateway Blvd E (79905)
Rates: $89-$99
(915) 779-6222
(800) 362-2779

HILTON-EL PASO AIRPORT
2027 Airway Blvd (79925)
Rates: $114-$147
(915) 778-4241
(800) 445-8667
(800) 742-7248 (TX)

HOMEGATE STUDIOS & SUITES
8250 Gateway Blvd E (79907)
Rates: $45-$75
(888) 456-4283

HOWARD JOHNSON LODGE
8887 Gateway Blvd W (79925)
Rates: $57-$74
(915) 591-9471
(800) 446-4656

INTERNATIONAL HOTEL
113 W Missouri (79901)
Rates: $55-$130
(915) 544-3300
(800) 228-2828

LA QUINTA INN-AIRPORT
6140 Gateway Blvd E (79905)
Rates: $59-$79
(915) 778-9321
(800) 687-6667

LA QUINTA INN CIELO VISTA
9125 Gateway Blvd W (79925)
Rates: $69-$89
(915) 593-8400
(800) 687-6667

LA QUINTA INN-LOMALAND
11033 Gateway Blvd W (79935)
Rates: $55-$75
(915) 591-2244
(800) 687-6667

LA QUINTA INN-WEST
7550 Remcon Cir (79912)
Rates: $55-$75
(915) 833-2522
(800) 687-6667

MARRIOTT-EL PASO
1600 Airway Blvd (79925)
Rates: $124-$154
(915) 779-3300
(800) 228-9290

MICROTEL INN & SUITES AIRPORT
2001 Airway Blvd (79925)
Rates: $42-$64
(915) 772-3650
(888) 771-7171

AREA CODES - If the local number doesn't connect, check for a new area code.

MOTEL 6
1330 Lomaland Dr (79935)
Rates: $32-$44
(915) 592-6386
(800) 466-8356

MOTEL 6-CENTRAL
4800 Gateway Blvd E (79905)
Rates: $32-$39
(915) 533-7521
(800) 466-8356

MOTEL STUDIO 6 EAST
11049 Gateway Blvd W (79935)
Rates: n/a
(915) 594-8533
(800) 466-8356

PEAR TREE APARTMENTS
222 Bartlett (79912)
Rates: $44-$77
(915) 833-7327

QUALITY INN
6201 Gateway Blvd W (79925)
Rates: $45-$95
(915) 778-6611
(800) 228-5151

RAMADA INN
500 Executive Center Blvd (79902)
Rates: $45-$78
(915) 532-8981
(800) 272-6232

RED ROOF INN EAST
11400 Chito Samaniego (79936)
Rates: $35-$45
(915) 599-8877
(800) 843-7663

RED ROOF INN WEST
7530 Remcon Cir (79912)
Rates: $45-$56
(915) 587-9977
(800) 843-7663

RESIDENCE INN BY MARRIOTT
6791 Montana St (79925)
Rates: $109-$139
(915) 772-8000
(800) 331-3131

SLEEP INN
953 Sunland Park Dr (79922)
Rates: $55-$94
(915) 585-7577
(800) 753-3746

ELGIN

RAGTIME RANCH BED & BREAKFAST
P. O. Box 575 (78621)
Rates: $95-$125
(800) 800-9743

ENNIS

QUALITY INN
107 Chamber of Commerce Dr (75119)
Rates: $59-$79
(972)875-9641
(800) 228-5151

EULESS

LA QUINTA INN-DFW AIRPORT WEST
1001 W Airport Frwy (76040)
Rates: $65-$85
(817) 540-0233
(800) 687-6667

MOTEL 6
110 W Airport Frwy (76039)
Rates: $35-$50
(817) 545-0141
(800) 466-8356

FARMERS BRANCH

BEST WESTERN DALLAS NORTH
13333 N Stemmons Frwy (75234)
Rates: $49-$99
(972) 241-8521
(800) 528-1234
(800) 308-4593

DAYS INN DALLAS NORTH
13313 N Stemmons Frwy (75234)
Rates: $59-$69
(972) 488-0800
(800) 329-7466

DOUBLETREE AT PARK WEST
1590 LBJ Frwy (75234)
Rates: $68-$99
(972) 869-4300
(800) 222-8733

LA QUINTA INN NORTHWEST
13235 N Stemmons Frwy (75234)
Rates: $49-$79
(972) 620-7333
(800) 687-6667

FORNEY

SUPER 8 MOTEL
103 W Hwy 80 (75126)
Rates: $50-$65
(972) 552-3888
(800) 800-8000

FORT DAVIS

FORT DAVIS MOTOR INN
Hwy 17 N (79734)
Rates: $55-$65
(800) 80-DAVIS

HISTORIC LIMPIA HOTEL
P. O. Box 822
On the Town Square (79734)
Rates: $59-$160
(915) 426-3237
(800) 662-5517

FORT HANCOCK

FORT HANCOCK MOTEL
I-20, Exit 72 (79839)
Rates: $38-$52
(915) 769-3981
(800) 553-4654

FORT STOCKTON

ATRIUM WEST INN HOTEL & SUITES
1305 N Hwy 285 (79735)
Rates: $50-$100
(915) 336-6666

BEST WESTERN SWISS CLOCK INN
3201 W Dickinson Blvd (79735)
Rates: $59-$99
(915) 336-8521
(800) 528-1234

COMFORT INN
3200 W Dickinson Blvd (79735)
Rates: $52-$85
(915) 336-8531
(800) 228-5150

COMMANCHE MOTEL & RV PARK
1301 E Dickinson Blvd (79735)
Rates: $25-$39
(800) 530-3793

HOLIDAY INN EXPRESS
1308 N Hwy 285 (79735)
Rates: $53-$69
(915) 336-5955
(800) 465-4329

LA QUINTA INN
2601 I-10 W (79735)
Rates: $49-$69
(915) 336-9781
(800) 687-6667

MOTEL 6
3001 W Dickinson Blvd (79735)
Rates: $27-$32
(915) 336-9737
(800) 466-8356

SANDS MOTEL
1801 W Dickinson Blvd (79735)
Rates: $26-$30
(915) 336-2274

SUPER 8 MOTEL
800 E Dickinson Blvd (79735)
Rates: $42-$54
(915) 336-9711
(800) 800-8000

TOWN & COUNTRY MOTEL
1505 W Dickinson Blvd (97935)
Rates: $21-$30
(915) 336-2651

FORT WORTH

AMERISUITES CITY VIEW
5900 City View Blvd (76132)
Rates: $89-$114
(817) 361-9797
(800) 833-1516

BEST WESTERN WEST BRANCH INN
7301 W Frwy (76116)
Rates: $50-$99
(817) 244-7444
(800) 528-1234
(888) 474-9566

BEST WESTERN INN
6700 Fossil Bluff Dr (76137)
Rates: $59-$89
(817) 847-8484
(800) 528-1234

CARAVAN MOTOR HOTEL
P. O. Box 10128 (76114)
Rates: $28-$42
(817) 626-1951

DAYS INN
42131-35 W South Fwy (76115)
Rates: $40-$65
(817) 923-1987
(800) 329-7466

DAYS INN
1551 University Dr (76107)
Rates: $45-$65
(817) 336-9823
(800) 329-7466

DAYS INN WEST
8500 I-30 W & Las Vegas Tr (76108)
Rates: $32-$59
(817) 246-4961
(800) 329-7466

GREEN OAKS INN & CONF CENTER
6901 W Frwy (76116)
Rates: $61-$98
(817) 738-7311
(800) 433-2174
(800) 772-7341 (TX)

AREA CODES - If the local number doesn't connect, check for a new area code.

HAMPTON INN
2700 Cherry Ln
(76116)
Rates: $69-$74
(817) 560-4180
(800) 426-7866

**HOLIDAY INN
& CONF CENTER**
100 Altamesa Blvd
E (76134)
Rates: $69-$85
(817) 293-3088
(800) 465-4329

**HOLIDAY INN
EXPRESS HOTEL
& SUITES**
4609 City Lake
Blvd W (76109)
Rates: n/a
(817) 292-4900
(800) 465-4329

**HOMESTEAD
VILLAGE**
1601 River Run
(76137)
Rates: $70
(817) 338-4808
(888) 782-9473

**LA QUINTA INN
& SUITES NORTH**
4700 North Frwy
(76137)
Rates: $69-$129
(817) 222-2888
(800) 687-6667

LA QUINTA INN-NE
7920 Bedford
Euless Rd (76118)
Rates: $49-$99
(800) 687-6667

**LA QUINTA INN
& SUITES -SW**
4900 Bryant Irvin
Rd (76132)
Rates: $85-$129
(817) 370-2700
(800) 687-6667

LA QUINTA INN-W
7888 I-30 W
(76108)
Rates: $45-$99
(817) 246-5511
(800) 687-6667

LEXINGTON INN
8709 Airport Frwy
(76180)
Rates: $49-$99
(817) 656-8881

**MICROTEL INN &
SUITES**
3740 Tanacross Dr
(76117)
Rates: n/a
(817) 759-9999
(888) 771-7171

MOTEL 6-EAST
1236 Oakland
Blvd (76103)
Rates: $38-$56
(817) 834-7361
(800) 466-8356

MOTEL 6-NORTH
3271 I-35 W
(76106)
Rates: $38-$56
(817) 625-4359
(800) 466-8356

MOTEL 6-SOUTH
6600 S Frwy
(76134)
Rates: $38-$56
(817) 293-8595
(800) 466-8356

MOTEL 6-WEST
8701 I-30 W
(76116)
Rates: $35-$46
(817) 244-9740
(800) 466-8356

**RADISSON PLAZA
HOTEL**
815 Main St
(76102)
Rates: $79-$107
(817) 870-2100
(800) 333-3333

**RAMADA INN-
MIDTOWN**
1401 S University
Dr (76107)
Rates: $57-$80
(817) 336-9311
(800) 272-6232

**RESIDENCE INN
BY MARRIOTT**
1701 S University
Dr (76107)
Rates: $110
(817) 870-1011
(800) 331-3131

**ROYAL WESTERN
SUITES**
8401 I-30 W
(76116)
Rates: $46-$52
(817) 560-0060

**STOCKYARDS
HOTEL**
109 E Exchange
Ave (76106)
Rates: $84-$350
(800) 423-8471

TRAVELODGE
4201 South Frwy
(76115)
Rates: $45-$80
(817) 923-8281
(800) 578-7878

**WORTHINGTON
HOTEL**
200 Main St
(76102)
Rates: $170-$225
(817) 870-1000
(800) 433-5677

FREDERICKS-
BURG

**ALFRED HAUS
BED & BREAKFAST**
231 W Main St
(78624)
Rates: $74+
(830) 997-5612

**ALLEGANI'S
LITTLE HORSE
INN**
307 S Creek
(78624)
Rates: $75-$95
(830) 997-7448

**BE MY GUEST
LODGING
SERVICE**
110 N Milam
(78624)
Rates: $61-$135
(800) 314-8555

**BECKERS BED &
BREAKFAST &
BICYCLES**
404 W Hackberry
St (78624)
Rates: $75-$85
(830) 990-9157

**BEST WESTERN
SUNDAY HOUSE
INN**
501 E Main St
(78624)
Rates: $55-$125
(830) 997-4484
(800) 528-1234
(800) 274-3762

**BUDGET HOST
DELUXE INN**
901 E Main St
(78624)
Rates: $34-$75
(830) 997-3344
(800) 283-4678

COMFORT INN
908 S Adams St
(78624)
Rates: $64-$89
(830) 997-9811
(800) 228-5150

**COUNTRY INN
MOTEL**
Hwy 290 W
(78624)
Rates: $35-$58
(830) 997-2185

DIETZEL MOTEL
909 W Main St
(78624)
Rates: $35-$62
(830) 997-3330

ECONO LODGE
810 S Adams St
(78624)
Rates: $49-$104
(830) 997-3437
(800) 553-2666

**FREDERICKSBURG
INN & SUITES**
201 S Washington
(78624)
Rates: $59-$81
(830) 977-0202
(800) 446-0202

**FRONTIER INN
MOTEL &RV PARK**
Rt 2, Box 99
(78624)
Rates: $36-$75
(830) 997-4389

**THE GARDEN
HOUSE BED &
BREAKFAST**
104 N Adams St
(78624)
Rates: $69
(830) 990-8455
(800) 745-3591

**HEIDIS RIVER
VIEW GUEST
RANCH**
110 N Milam
(78624)
Rates: $60-$100
(830) 997-8555

**MILLERS INN
MOTEL**
910 E Main St
(78624)
Rates: $32-$80
(830) 997-2244

**MISS TOODLES
INN BED &
BREAKFAST**
104 N Adams St
(78624)
Rates: $115+
(830) 990-8455
(800) 745-3591

PEACH TREE INN
401 S Washington
(78624)
Rates: $35-$100
(830) 997-2117
(800) 843-4666

**ROCK HOUSE
ON ACORN
BED & BREAKFAST**
231 W Main St
(78624)
Rates: $85+
(830) 997-5612

**ROCKY TOP
BED & BREAKFAST**
RR 965,
Enchanted Rock
Rd (78624)
Rates: $70
(830) 997-8145

**SCHMIDT BARN
BED & BREAKFAST**
231 W Main St
(78624)
Rates: $65-$140
(830) 997-5612

**SETTLERS
CROSSING
HISTORIC GUEST
HOUSES**
Rt 1, Box 315
(78624)
Rates: $85-$119
(830) 997-2722
(800) 874-1020

**STONEWALL
VALLEY
RANCH HOUSE**
104 N Adams St
(78624)
Rates: $85
(830) 990-8455
(800) 745-3591

STRACKBEIN-ROEDER SUNDAY HAUS BED & BREAKFAST
231 W Main St (78624)
Rates: $100+
(830) 997-5612

SUNSET INN
900 S Adams St (78624)
Rates: $45-$52
(830) 997-9581

WATKINS HILL-FREDERICKS-BURG'S GUEST HOUSE
608 E Creek St (78624)
Rates: $100-$225
(830) 997-6739
(800) 899-1672

WEST MAIN HAUS BED & BREAKFAST
231 W Main St (78624)
Rates: $75+
(830) 997-5612

WOLF CREEK BARN B&B
231 W Main St (78624)
Rates: $98+
(830) 997-5612

FREEPORT

COUNTRY HEARTH INN
1015 W 2nd at Velasco (77541)
Rates: $52-$70
(409) 239-1602
(888) 443-2784

FULTON

BAY FRONT COTTAGES
309 S Fulton Beach Rd (78382)
Rates: $45-$54
(361) 729-6693

BEST WESTERN INN BY THE BAY
3902 I-35 N (78358)
Rates: $58-$72
(361) 729-8351
(800) 528-1234
(800) 235-6076

HARBOR LIGHTS COTTAGES
108 Laurel (78358)
Rates: $41+
(361) 729-6770

KONTIKI BEACH RESORT MOTEL
2290 Fulton Beach Rd (78358)
Rates: $60-$65
(361) 729-4975
(800) 242-3407

REEF MOTEL
3rd & Broadway (78358)
Rates: $40+
(361) 729-6955

SPORTSMAN MANOR
4170 I-35 N (78358)
Rates: $36-$44
(361) 729-5331
(800) 224-6684

GAINESVILLE

BEST WESTERN SOUTH WINDS MOTEL
2103 I-35 N (76240)
Rates: $39-$81
(940) 665-7737
(800) 528-1234
(800) 731-1501

BUDGET HOST
Rt 2, Box 120 (76240)
Rates: $36-$45
(940) 665-2856
(800) 283-4678

DAYS INN
498 A-B Wichita Falls Ex (76240)
Rates: $35-$45
(8940) 665-5555
(800) 329-7466

GALVESTON

HILLTOP MOTEL
8828 Seawall Blvd (77554)
Rates: $35-$75
(409) 744-4423

HOTEL GALVEZ
2024 Seawall Blvd (77550)
Rates: $110-$199
(800) 392-4285

LA QUINTA INN
1402 Seawall Blvd (77550)
Rates: $85-$149
(409) 763-1224
(800) 687-6667

MOTEL 6
7404 Ave J Broadway (77554)
Rates: $33-$56
(409) 740-3794
(800) 466-8356

GARLAND

COMFORT INN
3536 W Kingsley Rd (75041)
Rates: $52-$100
(214) 340-3501
(800) 228-5150

DAYS INN
6222 Beltline Rd (75043)
Rates: $40-$49
(972) 226-7621
(800) 329-7466

LA QUINTA INN
12721 I-635 (75041)
Rates: $55-$75
(972) 271-7581
(800) 687-6667

MOTEL 6
436 W I-30 & Beltline (75043)
Rates: $35-$40
(972) 226-7140
(800) 466-8356

RAMADA LIMITED
1821 NW Hwy & 635 (75041)
Rates: $49-$74
(972) 278-5070
(800) 272-6232

RED ROOF INN
13700 LBJ Frwy (75041)
Rates: $36-$64
(972) 686-0202
(800) 843-7663

GATESVILLE

BEST WESTERN CHATEAU VILLE MOTOR INN
2501 E Main St (76528)
Rates: $37-$59
(254) 865-2281
(800) 528-1234
(888) 451-4521

GEORGE WEST

BEST WESTERN EXECUTIVE INN
208 N Nueces, Hwy 281 N (78022)
Rates: $50-$90
(361) 449-3300
(800) 528-1234

GEORGETOWN

COMFORT INN
1005 Leander Rd (78628)
Rates: $54-$89
(817) 863-7504
(800) 228-5150

DAYS INN
209 I-35 N (78628)
Rates: $47-$75
(817) 863-5572
(800) 329-7466

HOLIDAY INN EXPRESS HOTEL & SUITES
200 I-35 (78628)
Rates: n/a
(817) 552-1811
(800) 465-4329

LA QUINTA INN
333 I-35 N (78628)
Rates: $69-$89
(817) 869-2541
(800) 687-6667

GIDDINGS

BEST WESTERN CLASSIC INN
3556 E Austin (78942)
Rates: $39-$61
(409) 542-5791
(800) 528-1234

GIDDINGS SANDS MOTEL
1600 E Austin (78942)
Rates: $34-$46
(409) 542-3111

GILMER

RAMADA LIMITED
1200 Hwy 271 S (75644)
Rates: $50-$75
(903) 843-6099
(800) 272-6232

GLADEWATER

BEST WESTERN INN
1009 E Broadway (75647)
Rates: $46-$65
(903) 845-8003
(800) 528-1234

GLEN ROSE

BEST WESTERN DINOSAUR VALLEY INN & SUITES
1311 NE Big Bend Trail (76043)
Rates: $50-$140
(800) 528-1234

COUNTRY WOODS INN B&B
420 Grand Ave (76043)
Rates: $90-$125
(888) 84-WOODS

GLEN HOTEL
201 Barnard St (76043)
Rates: $35-$60
(254) 897-2420

GLEN ROSE INN & SUITES
Hwy 67 & FM 56 (76043)
Rates: $45-$64
(800) 577-2540

HIDEAWAY COUNTRY LOG CABIN BED & BREAKFAST
P. O. Box 430 (76043)
Rates: $70-$93
(254) 823-6606

ROUGH CREEK LODGE EXECUTIVE RETREAT/RESORT
P O Box 2400 (76043)
Rates: $229-$1200
(800) 864-4705

TRES RIOS RV MOTEL
2322 CR 312 (76043)
Rates: $45-$160
(888) 4-CAMPRV

AREA CODES - If the local number doesn't connect, check for a new area code.

GRAHAM

GATEWAY INN
1401 Hwy 16 S
(76450)
Rates: $35-$45
(940) 549-0222

GRANBURY

COMFORT INN
1201 Plaza Dr N
(76048)
Rates: $55-$150
(817) 573-2611
(800) 228-5150

DAYS INN
1339 N Plaza Dr
(76048)
Rates: $59-$99
(817) 573-2691
(800) 329-7466
(800) 858-8607 (TX)

**PLANTATION INN
ON THE LAKE**
1451 E Pearl St
(76048)
Rates: $60-$90
(817) 573-8846
(800) 422-2402

GRAND PRAIRIE

DAYS INN
2615 Sara Jane
Pkwy (75050)
Rates: $45-$135
(972) 623-1998
(800) 329-7466

**LA QUINTA INN
SIX FLAGS**
1410 NW 19th St
(75050)
Rates: $75-$95
(972) 641-3021
(800) 687-6667

**MOTEL 6
EXTENDED STAY**
406 E Safari Blvd
(75050)
Rates: $40-$51
(972) 642-9424
(800) 466-8356

RAMADA INN
402 E Safari Blvd
(75050)
Rates: $49-$65
(972) 263-4421
(800) 272-6232

GRAPEVINE

**MAINSTAY SUITES
DFW AIRPORT**
2040 N SR 121
(76051)
Rates: $60-$120
(800) 660-6246

SLEEP INN
2040 121 Access
Rd N (76051)
Rates: $45-$85
(800) 753-3746

GREENVILLE

**BUDGET HOST
INN**
5118 I-30 & US 69
(75401)
Rates: $27-$42
(903) 455-8462
(800) 283-4678

GOLD KEY INN
1215 E I-30 (75402)
Rates: $69
(903) 454-7000

MOTEL 6
5109 I-30 & US 69
(75402)
Rates: $25-$32
(903) 455-0515
(800) 466-8356

ROYAL INN
I-30 & US 69
(75401)
Rates: $27-$40
(903) 455-9600

SUPER 8 MOTEL
5010 Hwy 69 S
(75402)
Rates: $44-$62
(903) 454-3736
(800) 800-8000

GROVES

MOTEL 6
5201 E Pkwy
(77619)
Rates: $27-$32
(409) 962-6611
(800) 466-8356

HALLETTSVILLE

**AUNT CAROL'S
BED & BREAKFST**
Rt 2, Box 212C
(77964)
Rates: $65-$75
(888) 556-6582

HAMILTON

**HAMILTON
GUEST HOTEL B&B**
109 N Rice (76351)
Rates: $49-$79
(254) 386-8977
(800) 876-2502

**VALUE LODGE
INN MOTEL**
Rt 3, Box 319
(76351)
Rates: $25-$40
(254) 386-8959

WESTERN MOTEL
1208 S Rice St
(76351)
Rates: $31-$37
(254) 386-3141

HARLINGEN

**BEST WESTERN
HARLINGEN INN**
6779 US 83 W
Expwy (78552)
Rates: $49-$66
(956) 425-7070
(800) 528-1234
(800) 425-7080

COMFORT INN
406 N Expwy 77
(78552)
Rates: $56-$99
(956) 412-7771
(800) 228-5150

DAYS INN
1901 W Tyler St
(78550)
Rates: $49-$79
(956) 425-1810
(800) 329-7466

LA QUINTA INN
1002 US 83 S
Expwy (78552)
Rates: $69-$89
(956) 428-6888
(800) 687-6667

MOTEL 6
224 US 77 S
Expwy (78550)
Rates: $30-$36
(956) 421-4200
(800) 466-8356

SUPER 8 MOTEL
1115 US 77 & 83 S
Expwy (78550)
Rates: $45-$69
(956) 412-8873
(800) 800-8000

HASKELL

**BEVERS HOUSE
ON BRICK ST
BED & BREAKFAST**
311 N Ave F
(79521)
Rates: $60-$75
(940) 864-3284
(800) 580-3284

HEARNE

EXECUTIVE INN
Hwy 6 at FM 485
(77859)
Rates: $40-$69
(409) 279-5345

OAK TREE INN
1051 N Market St
(77859)
Rates: $54-$79
(409) 279-5599

HEBBRONVILLE

**TEXAS EXECUTIVE
INN**
1302 N Smith
(78361)
Rates: $36-$52
(512) 527-4082
(800) 870-7689

HENDERSON

**BEST WESTERN
INN OF
HENDERSON**
1500 Hwy 259 S
(75652)
Rates: $59-$79
(903) 657-9561
(800) 528-1234

HEREFORD

**BEST WESTERN
RED CARPET INN**
830 W 1st St
(79045)
Rates: $42-$56
(806) 364-0540
(800) 528-1234

HILLSBORO

**BEST WESTERN
HILLSBORO INN**
307 I-35 (76645)
Rates: $52-$66
(254) 582-8465
(800) 528-1234

RAMADA INN
I-35 & Hwy 22
(76645)
Rates: $39-$59
(254) 582-3493
(800) 272-6232

HONDO

WHITETAIL LODGE
US 90 & Hwy 173
(78861)
Rates: $42-$56
(830) 426-3031
(800) 375-4065

HOUSTON

AMERISUITES
300 Ronan Park Pl
(77060)
Rates: $64-$159
(281) 820-6060
(800) 833-1516

**BAYMONT INN
& SUITES**
12701 N Freeway
(77060)
Rates: $62
(281) 875-2000
(800) 301-0200

**BAYMONT INN
& SUITES**
11130 NW Frwy
(77092)
Rates: $58-$64
(713) 680-8282
(800) 301-0200

**BAYMONT INN
& SUITES**
6790 SW Frwy
(77074)
Rates: $57-$62
(713) 784-3838
(800) 301-0200

**BEST WESTERN
GREENWAY
PLAZA INN
& SUITES**
2929 SW Freeway
(77098)
Rates: $55-$70
(713) 528-6161
(800) 528-1234

**BRAESWOOD
HOTEL & CONV
CENTER**
2100 S Braeswood
(77030)
Rates: $58-$69
(254) 797-9000
(800) 722-1368

AREA CODES - If the local number doesn't connect, check for a new area code.

COMFORT SUITES GALLERIA
6221 Richmond Ave (77057)
Rates: $89-$195
(713)-787-0004
(800) 228-5150

DAYS INN
4640 S Main St (77002)
Rates: $59-$79
(713) 523-3777
(800) 329-7466

DAYS INN
9535 Katy Frwy (77024)
Rates: $39-$89
(713) 467-4411
(800) 329-7466

DAYS INN-ASTRODOME
8500 Kirby Dr (77054)
Rates: $59-$129
(713) 796-8383
(800) 329-7466

DAYS INN
9025 N Frwy (77037)
Rates: $44-$55
(281) 820-1500
(800) 329-7466

DAYS INN & SUITES
9041 Westheimer Rd (77063)
Rates: $63-$69
(713) 783-1400
(800) 329-7466

DOUBLETREE GUEST SUITES
5353 Westheimer Rd (77056)
Rates: $169
(713) 961-9000
(800) 222-8733
(800) 772-7666 (TX)

DOUBLETREE HOTEL AT ALLEN CENTER
400 Dallas St (77002)
Rates: $195-$235
(713) 759-0202
(800) 222-8733
(800) 772-7666 (TX)

DRURY INN-GALLERIA
1615 W Loop 610 S (77027)
Rates: $83-$103
(713) 963-0700
(800) 378-7946

DRURY INN HOUSTON HOBBY
7902 Mosley Rd (77017)
Rates: $65-$85
(713) 941-4300
(800) 378-7946

DRURY INN I-10 WEST
1000 N Hwy 6 (77079)
Rates: $62-$78
(713) 558-7007
(800) 378-7946

FAIRWIND CORPORATE LODGING
15900 Space Ctr Blvd (77062)
Rates: $30-$95
(888) 833-2677

FOUR SEASONS HOTEL
1300 Lamar St (77010)
Rates: $260-$380
(713) 650-1300
(800) 332-3442

THE GRANT MOTOR INN
8200 S Main St (77025)
Rates: $42-$66
(713) 668-8000

HAMPTON INN I-10 EAST
828 Mercury Dr (77013)
Rates: $59-$79
(713) 673-4200
(800) 426-7866

HAWTHORN SUITES HOTEL
6910 Southwest Frwy (77074)
Rates: $139-$159
(713) 785-3415
(800) 527-1133

HILTON HOBBY AIRPORT
8181 Airport Blvd (77061)
Rates: $80-$134
(713) 645-3000
(800) 445-8667
(800) 695-2740 (TX)

HILTON & TOWERS-WESTCHASE
9999 Westheimer Rd (77042)
Rates: $82-$127
(713) 974-1000
(800) 445-8667

HILTON-UNIVERSITY CONF CTR
4800 Calhoun Rd (77004)
Rates: $79-$89
(713) 743-2610
(800) 445-8667

HOLIDAY INN-GALLERIA
7787 Katy Frwy (77024)
Rates: $101-$121
(713) 681-5000
(800) 465-4329

HOLIDAY INN HOUSTON AIRPORT
15222 JFK Blvd (77032)
Rates: $80-$150
(281) 449-2311
(800) 465-4329

HOLIDAY INN SELECT GREENWAY PLAZA
2712 Southwest Frwy (77098)
Rates: $90-$160
(713) 523-8488
(800) 465-4329

HOLIDAY INN SELECT WEST
14703 Park Row (77079)
Rates: $96-$190
(281) 558-5580
(800) 465-4329

HOMESTEAD VILLAGE-PARK 10
1255 Hwy 6 N (77084)
Rates: n/a
(281) 579-6959
(888) 782-9473

HOMESTEAD VILLAGE GUEST STUDIOS
7979 Fannin St (77054)
Rates: $50-$65
(713) 797-0000
(888) 782-9473

HOMESTEAD VILLAGE GUEST STUDIOS
3030 W Sam Houston Pkwy (77085)
Rates: n/a
(713) 785-8550
(888) 782-9473

HOMESTEAD VILLAGE GUEST STUDIOS
14255 Northwest Frwy (77040)
Rates: n/a
(713) 895-2900
(888) 782-9473

HOMESTEAD VILLAGE GUEST STUDIOS
220 Bammel-Westfield Rd (77090)
Rates: $49-$54
(281) 580-2221
(888) 782-9473

HOMESTEAD VILLAGE GUEST STUDIOS
2300 W Loop S (77092)
Rates: n/a
(713) 960-9660
(888) 782-9473

HOMESTEAD VILLAGE GUEST STUDIOS
12700 Featherwood (77034)
Rates: $29-$59
(281) 929-5400
(888) 782-9473

HOMESTEAD VILLAGE GUEST SUITES
13223 Champions Center Dr (77069)
Rates: $259
(281) 397-9922
(888) 782-9473

HOTEL SOFITEL
425 N Sam Houston Pkwy E (77060)
Rates: $79-$109
(281) 445-9000

HOWARD JOHNSON
4225 N Freeway (77022)
Rates: $39-$65
(713) 695-6011
(800) 446-4656

HOWARD JOHNSON EXPRESS
4602 Katy Frwy (77007)
Rates: $42-$55
(713) 861-9000
(800) 446-4656

HOWARD JOHNSON EXPRESS INN
13611 Rankin Circle W (77073)
Rates: n/a
(281) 821-0410
(800) 446-4656

HOWARD JOHNSON HOBBY AIRPORT
7777 Airport Blvd (77061)
Rates: $56+
(713) 644-1261
(800) 446-4656

HOWARD JOHNSON INN
17607 Eastex Fwy & Will Clayton Fwy (77396)
Rates: $45-$65
(281) 446-4611
(800) 446-4656

HYATT REGENCY HOUSTON
1200 Louisiana St (77002)
Rates: $150-$206
(713) 654-1234
(800) 233-1234

INTERSTATE MOTOR LODGE
13213 I-10 E (77015)
Rates: $40-$45
(713) 453-6353

AREA CODES - If the local number doesn't connect, check for a new area code.

J W MARRIOTT HOUSTON
5150 Westheimer Rd (77056)
Rates: $139-$189
(713) 961-1500
(800) 231-6058

LA QUINTA INN-ASTRODOME
9911 Buffalo Speedway (77054)
Rates: $69-$109
(713) 668-8082
(800) 687-6667

LA QUINTA INN-AIRPORT
6 N Belt E (77060)
Rates: $59-$89
(281) 447-6888
(800) 687-6667

LA QUINTA INN-BROOKHOLLOW
11002 Northwest Frwy (77092)
Rates: $49-$99
(713) 688-2581
(800) 687-6667

LA QUINTA INN-COUNTY FAIR
13290 FM 1960W (77065)
Rates: $59-$84
(281) 469-4018
(800) 687-6667

LA QUINTA INN GREENWAY PLAZA
4015 Southwest Frwy (77027)
Rates: $59-$92
(713) 623-4750
(800) 687-6667

LA QUINTA INN HOBBY AIRPORT
9902 Gulf Frwy (77034)
Rates: $59-$82
(713) 941-0900
(800) 687-6667

LA QUINTA INN-EAST
11999 E Frwy (77029)
Rates: $55-$84
(713) 453-5425
(800) 687-6667

LA QUINTA INN-LOOP 1960
17111 N Frwy (77090)
Rates: $59-$79
(281) 444-7500
(800) 687-6667

LA QUINTA INN SHARPSTOWN
8201 Southwest Frwy (77074)
Rates: $52-$76
(713) 772-3626
(800) 687-6667

LA QUINTA INN-SOUTHWEST FRWY/BELTWAY
10552 Southwest Frwy (77074)
Rates: $45-$79
(713) 270-9559
(800) 687-6667

LA QUINTA INN & SUITES-BUSH AIRPORT
15510 JFK Blvd (77032)
Rates: $75-$115
(281) 219-2000
(800) 687-6667

LA QUINTA INN & SUITES-GALLERIA
1625 W Loop S (77027)
Rates: $69-$129
(713) 355-3440
(800) 687-6667

LA QUINTA INN & SUITES-PARK 10
15225 Katy Frwy (77094)
Rates: $59-$102
(281) 646-9200
(800) 687-6667

LA QUINTA INN-WEST
11113 Katy Frwy (77079)
Rates: $59-$82
(713) 932-0808
(800) 687-6667

LA QUINTA INN-WIRT RD
8017 Katy Frwy (77024)
Rates: $59-$89
(713) 688-8941
(800) 687-6667

LANCASTER HISTORIC HOTEL
701 Texas at Louisiana (77002)
Rates: $200-$350
(713) 228-9500
(800) 231-0336

LOVETT INN HISTORIC B&B
501 Lovett Blvd (77006)
Rates: $85-$250
(713) 522-5224
(800) 779-5224

MARRIOTT-BY THE GALLERIA
1750 W Loop S (77027)
Rates: $69-$159
(713) 960-0111
(800) 228-9290

MARRIOTT HOTEL-HOUSTON MEDICAL CENTER
6580 Fannin St (77030)
Rates: $179
(713) 796-0080
(800) 228-9290

MARRIOTT WESTSIDE
13210 Katy Frwy (77079)
Rates: $99-$164
(281) 558-8338
(800) 228-9290

MEDALLION HOTEL HOUSTON
3000 N Loop W (77092)
Rates: $105-$115
(713) 688-0100
(800) 688-3000

MOTEL 6
16884 Northwest Frwy (77040)
Rates: $40-$56
(713) 937-7056
(800) 466-8356

MOTEL 6
14833 Katy Frwy (77094)
Rates: $37-$43
(713) 497-5000
(800) 466-8356

MOTEL 6
5555 W 34th St (77092)
Rates: $38-$44
(713) 682-8588
(800) 466-8356

MOTEL 6-ASTRODOME
3223 S Loop W (77025)
Rates: $39-$54
(713) 664-6425
(800) 466-8356

MOTEL 6 HOBBY AIRPORT
8800 Airport Blvd (77061)
Rates: $37-$42
(713) 941-0990
(800) 466-8356

MOTEL 6
9638 Plainfield Rd (77036)
Rates: $38-$54
(713) 778-0008
(800) 466-8356

MOTEL 6 WEST
2900 W Sam Houston Pkwy (77042)
Rates: $46-$62
(713) 334-9188
(800) 466-8356

OMNI HOUSTON
4 Riverway (77056)
Rates: $130-$150
(713) 871-8181
(800) 843-6664

QUALITY INN-AIRPORT
6115 Will Clayton Pkwy (77205)
Rates: $64-$89
(281) 446-9131
(800) 228-5151
(800) 231-6134 (TX)

RADISSON HOTEL & CONF CENTER
9100 Gulf Frwy (77017)
Rates: $124-$145
(713) 943-7979
(800) 333-3333

RADISSON SUITE HOTEL HOUSTON
1400 Old Spanish Trail (77054)
Rates: $139
(713) 796-1000
(800) 333-3333

RAMADA LIMITED
9000 S Main (77085)
Rates: $45-$70
(713) 666-4151
(800) 272-6232

RAMADA LIMITED 1960
15725 Bammel Village Dr (77014)
Rates: $45-$62
(281) 893-5224
(800) 272-6232
(800) 201-3201 (TX)

RAMADA LIMITED
4723 W Alabama (77027)
Rates: $79-$179
(713) 621-2797
(800) 272-6232

RAMADA PLAZA HOTEL/GALLERIA
7611 Katy Frwy, Hwy 10 W (77024)
Rates: $69-$121
(713) 688-2222
(800) 272-6232

RED LION HOTEL/GALLERIA AREA
2525 W Loop S (77027)
Rates: $80
(713) 961-3000
(800) 733-5466

RED ROOF INN HOBBY AIRPORT
9005 Airport Blvd (77061)
Rates: $36-$61
(713) 943-3300
(800) 843-7663

RED ROOF INN NORTHWEST
12929 Northwest Frwy (77040)
Rates: $36-$61
(713) 939-0800
(800) 843-7663

RED ROOF INN WEST
15701 Park Ten Place (77084)
Rates: $38-$50
(281) 579-7200
(800) 843-7663

AREA CODES - If the local number doesn't connect, check for a new area code.

RED ROOF INN WESTCHASE
2960 W Sam Houston Pkwy S (77042)
Rates: $47-$63
(713) 785-9909
(80) 843-7663

RENAISSANCE HOUSTON HOTEL
6 Greenway Plaza E (77046)
Rates: $169-$179
(713) 629-1200

RESIDENCE INN BY MARRIOTT
9965 Westheimer (77042)
Rates: $89-$149
(713) 974-5454
(800) 331-3131

RESIDENCE INN BY MARRIOTT-ASTRODOME
7710 S Main St (77030)
Rates: $89-$160
(713) 660-7993
(800) 331-3131

RESIDENCE INN HOUSTON CLEAR LAKE
525 Bay Area Blvd (77058)
Rates: $85-$124
(281) 486-2424
(800) 331-3131

ROBIN'S NEST B&B INN
4104 Greeley (77006)
Rates: $75-$120
(713) 528-5821
(800) 622-8343

RODEWAY INN-SW FREEWAY
3135 Southwest Frwy (77098)
Rates: $49-$69
(713) 526-1071
(800) 228-2000

SHERATON HOUSTON BROOKHOLLOW
3000 N Loop W (77092)
Rates: $58-$89
(713) 688-0100
(800) 325-3535

SHONEY'S INN-ASTRODOME
2364 SouthLoop W (77054)
Rates: $68-$93
(713) 799-2436
(800) 222-2222

SHONEY'S INN
12323 Katy Frwy (77079)
Rates: $75
(281) 493-5626
(800) 222-2222

SHONEY'S INN
6687 SW Freeway (77074)
Rates: $64-$105
(713) 776-2633
(800) 222-2222

SLEEP INN HOUSTON INTL AIRPORT
15675 John F Kennedy Blvd (77032)
Rates: $49-$89
(281) 442-7770
(800) 753-3746

SUPER 8 MOTEL
4045 North Frwy (77022)
Rates: $33-$45
(713) 691-6671
(800) 800-8000

SUPER 8 MOTEL BELTWAY
9799 B Katy Frwy (77024)
Rates: $39-$55
(713) 468-7801
(800) 800-8000

SUPER 8 MOTEL HOBBY AIRPORT
6711 Telephone Rd (77061)
Rates: $42-$55
(713) 645-7666
(800) 800-8000

SUPER 8 MOTEL NASA
18103 Kingsrow Ln (77058)
Rates: $50-$125
(281) 333-5385
(800) 800-8000

TOWNPLACE SUITES
15155 Katy Frwy (77024)
Rates: $59-$89
(281) 646-0058

TOWNEPLACE SUITES BY MARRIOTT
1050 Bay Area Blvd (77058)
Rates: $59-$129
(800) 257-3000

TRAVELODGE
4726 FM 1960 W (77069)
Rates: $45-$70
(281) 587-9171
(800) 578-7878

WELLESLEY INN & SUITES-MEDICAL CENTER
1301 S Braeswood (77030)
Rates: $69-$109
(888) 444-8888

WELLESLEY INN & SUITES-MEMORIAL
7855 Katy Frwy (77024)
Rates: $65-$109
(888) 444-8888

HUNTSVILLE

HOLIDAY INN EXPRESS
201 W Hill Park Circle (77340)
Rates: n/a
(409) 293-8800
(800) 465-4329

LA QUINTA INN
124 I-45 N (77340)
Rates: $62-$79
(409) 295-6454
(800) 687-6667

MOTEL 6
122 I-45 N (77340)
Rates: $33-$38
(409) 291-6927
(800) 466-8356

PARK INN INTERNATIONAL
1407 I-45 N (77340)
Rates: $42-$57
(409) 295-6454
(800) 437-7275

SAM HOUSTON INN
3296 I-45 S, Exit 114 (77340)
Rates: $44-$54
(409) 295-9151
(800) 395-9151

HURST

AMERISUITES
1601 Hurst Town Center Dr (76054)
Rates: $70-$119
(817) 577-3003
(800) 833-1516

INGLESIDE

COMFORT INN
2800 Hwy 361 (78362)
Rates: $54-$89
(361) 775-2700
(800) 228-5150

INGRAM

HUNTER HOUSE MOTOR INN
310 Hwy 39 W (78025)
Rates: $44-$99
(210) 367-2377
(800) 655-2377

IRVING

AMERISUITES LAS COLINAS
333 W John Carpenter Frwy (75039)
Rates: $69-$139
(972) 910-0302
(800) 833-1516

DRURY INN-DFW AIRPORT
4210 W Airport Frwy (75062)
Rates: $72-$90
(972) 986-1200
(800) 378-7946

ECONO LODGE
3135 E Airport Frwy (75062)
Rates: $40-$70
(800) 553-2666

FOUR SEASONS RESORT & CLUB
4150 N Mac-Arthur Blvd (75038)
Rates: $315-$425
(972) 717-0700
(800) 332-3442

HAMPTON INN-DFW AIRPORT
4340 W Airport Frwy (75061)
Rates: $72-$90
(972) 986-3606
(800) 426-7866

HARVEY HOTEL-DFW AIRPORT
4545 W John Carpenter Frwy (75063)
Rates: $59-$183
(972) 929-4500
(800) 922-9222

HARVEY SUITES
4550 W John Carpenter Frwy (75063)
Rates: $59-$170
(972) 929-4499
(800) 922-9222

HOMEGATE STUDIOS & SUITES
3950 W Airport Frwy (75062)
Rates: $49-$79
(888) 456-4283

HOMEWOOD SUITES LAS COLINAS
4300 Wingren Rd (75039)
Rates: $69-$150
(972) 556-0665
(800) 225-5466

IRVING INN SUITES
909 W Airport Frwy (75062)
Rates: $30-$50
(972) 255-7108

LA QUINTA INN DFW AIRPORT
4105 W Airport Frwy (75062)
Rates: $59-$79
(972) 252-6546
(800) 687-6667

MOTEL 6
510 S Loop 12 (75060)
Rates: $28-$34
(972) 438-4227
(800) 466-8356

MOTEL 6
7800 Heathrow Dr (75063)
Rates: $42-$58
(972) 915-3993
(800) 466-8356

OMNI MANDALAY LAS COLINAS
221 E Las Colinas Blvd (75039)
Rates: $89-$210
(972) 556-0800
(800) 843-6664

RED ROOF INN-DFW AIRPORT
8150 Esters Blvd (75063)
Rates: $53-$92
(972) 929-0020
(800) 843-7663

RED ROOF INN-DFW SOUTH
2611 W Airport Frwy (75062)
Rates: $50-$64
(972) 570-7500
(800) 843-7663

RESIDENCE INN BY MARRIOTT
950 Walnut Hill Ln (75038)
Rates: $75-$160
(972) 580-7773
(800) 331-3131

SHERATON GRAND HOTEL
4440 W Carpenter Frwy (75261)
Rates: $118-$140
(972) 929-8400
(800) 325-3535
(800) 345-5251 (TX)

SHONEY'S INN
4770 W Carpenter Fwy (75261)
Rates: n/a
(800) 222-2222

STAYBRIDGE SUITES BY HOLIDAY INN
1201 Executive Circle (75038)
Rates: n/a
(972) 465-9400
(800) 465-4329
(800) 238-8000

SUITES INN
1701 W Airport Frwy (75062)
Rates: $30-$50
(972) 255-1133

WELLESLEY INN & SUITES
5401 Green Park Dr (75038)
Rates: $62-$99
(888) 444-8888

WELLESLEY INN & SUITES-DFW
3950 W Airport Frwy (75062)
Rates: $59-$99
(972) 790-1950
(888) 444-8888

WILSON WORLD MOTOR HOTEL
4600 W Airport Frwy (75062)
Rates: $89-$130
(972) 513-0800
(800) 333-9457

JACKSBORO

JACKSBORO INN
704 S Main St (76458)
Rates: $34-$43
(940) 567-3751

JASPER

BEST WESTERN INN
205 W Gibson (75951)
Rates: $48-$59
(409) 384-7767
(800) 528-1234

DAYS INN
1730 S Wheeler (75951)
Rates: $38-$46
(409) 384-6816
(800) 329-7466

RAMADA INN
239 E Gibson (75951)
Rates: $59-$62
(409) 384-9021
(800) 272-6232

JEFFERSON

BEST WESTERN INN
400 S Walcott (75657)
Rates: $63-$73
(903) 665-3983
(800) 528-1234

BUDGET INN
Hwy 59 S (75657)
Rates: $28-$50
(903) 665-2581

JOHNSON CITY

DREAM CATCHER BED & BREAKFAST
Rt 1, Box 345 (78636)
Rates: $60-$85
(830) 868-4875

SAVE INN MOTEL
107 Hwy 281 & 290 S (78636)
Rates: $36-$56
(830) 868-4044

JUNCTION

CAROUSEL INN
1908 Main St (76849)
Rates: $24-$38
(915) 446-3301

DAYS INN
111 St. Martinez St (768495)
Rates: $45-$65
(915) 446-3730
(800) 329-7466

THE HILLS MOTEL
1520 Main St (76849)
Rates: $32-$40
(915) 446-2567

LA VISTA MOTEL
2040 N Main St (76849)
Rates: $27-$36
(915) 446-2191

KATY

BEST WESTERN HOUSTON WEST INN
22455 I-10 W (77450)
Rates: $53-$67
(281) 392-9800
(800) 528-1234

HOLIDAY INN EXPRESS
22108 Katy Fwy (77450)
Rates: $59-$64
(281) 395-4800
(800) 465-4329

SUPER 8 MOTEL
22157 Katy Frwy (77450)
Rates: $45-$55
(281) 395-5757
(800) 800-8000

KENEDY

DAYS INN
453 N Sunset Strip (78119)
Rates: $35-$85
(830) 583-2521
(800) 329-7466

KERRVILLE

BEST WESTERN SUNDAY HOUSE INN
2124 Sidney Baker St (78028)
Rates: $65-$105
(830) 896-1313
(800) 528-1234
(800) 677-9477 (TX)

BUDGET INN MOTEL
1804 Sidney Baker St (78028)
Rates: $40-$60
(830) 896-8200

DIETERT HAUS B&B
710 Mockingbird (78028)
Rates: $80
(830) 895-2235

ECONO LODGE
2145 Sidney Baker St (78028)
Rates: $39-$79
(830) 896-1711
(800) 553-2666

FLAGSTAFF INN
906 Junction Hwy (78028)
Rates: $40+
(830) 792-4449

HILLCREST INN
1508 Sidney Baker St (78028)
Rates: $36-$80
(830) 896-7400
(800) 221-0251

HOLIDAY INN-Y.O. RANCH HOTEL & CONF CENTER
2033 Sidney Baker St (78028)
Rates: $101-$325
(830) 257-4440
(800) 465-4329
(800) 531-2800 (TX)

INN OF THE HILLS RIVER RESORT
1001 Junction Hwy (78028)
Rates: $65-$175
(830) 895-5000
(800) 292-5690

LA REATA RANCH BED & BREAKFAST
225 Junction Hwy (78028)
Rates: $75
(830) 896-5503

MOTEL 6
1810 Sidney Baker Rd (78028)
Rates: $39-$56
(830) 257-1500
(800) 466-8356

TURTLE CREEK LODGE
1520 Upper Turtle Creek (78028)
Rates: $150-$250
(830) 828-0377

KILGORE

HOLIDAY INN EXPRESS HOTEL & SUITES
3298 Hwy 259 N (75662)
Rates: n/a
(800) 465-4329

RAMADA INN
3501 Hwy 259 N (75662)
Rates: $48-$66
(903) 983-3456
(800) 272-6232

KILLEEN

LA QUINTA INN
1112 S Ft Hood St (76541)
Rates: $65-$85
(254) 526-8331
(800) 687-6667

RAMADA INN
1100 S Ft Hood St
(76541)
Rates: $52-$74
(254) 634-3101
(800) 272-6232

KINGSVILLE

**BEST WESTERN
KINGSVILLE INN**
2402 E King Ave
(78363)
Rates: $53-$71
(361) 595-5656
(800) 528-1234

HOLIDAY INN
3430 Hwy 77 S
(78363)
Rates: $49-$59
(361) 595-5753
(800) 465-4329

**HOWARD
JOHNSON**
105 Hwy 77 (78363)
Rates: $47-$79
(361) 592-6471
(800) 446-4656

MOTEL CARBY
1415 S 14th St
(78363)
Rates: $24-$30
(361) 592-5214

MOTEL 6
101 Hwy 77 N
(78363)
Rates: $32-$36
(361) 592-5106
(800) 466-8356

MOTEL 77
716 S 14th St
(78363)
Rates: $23-$30
(361) 592-4322

KOUNTZE

**LITTLE HOUSE
ON TIMBER RIDGE**
Hwy 92 & 1943
(77625)
Rates: $75+
(409) 246-3107

LA GRANGE

**NORTHPOINTE
EXECUTIVE SUITES**
202 Northpointe
Ave (78945)
Rates: $42-$55
(630) 968-6406

LA MARQUE

RAMADA INN
5201 Gulf Frwy
(77568)
Rates: $48-$108
(409) 986-9777
(800) 272-6232

LA PORTE

LA QUINTA INN
1105 Hwy 146 S
(77571)
Rates: $59-$89
(281) 470-0760
(800) 687-6667

LAGUNA VISTA

**BUDGET HOST
INN**
1411 E Hwy 100
(78578)
Rates: $40-$60
(956) 943-7866
(800) 283-4678

LAKE JACKSON

**BEST WESTERN
LAKE JACKSON
INN**
915 Hwy 332 W
(77566)
Rates: $50-$60
(409) 297-3031
(800) 528-1234
(800) 722-5094

RAMADA INN
925 Hwy 332 W
(77566)
Rates: $117-$155
(409) 297-1161
(800) 272-6232
(800) 544-2119 (TX)

LAKE LBJ

**TROPICAL
HIDEAWAY BEACH
RESORT**
604 Highcrest Dr
(78654)
Rates: $85-$250
(210) 598-9896
(800) 662-4431

**VALENTINE
LAKESIDE RESORT**
P O Box 31
(Kingsland 78639)
Rates: $55-$165
(915) 388-4418

LAMAR

SEA GUN RESORT
5868 I-35 N
(77710)
Rates: $40-$82
(512) 729-3292
(800) 224-2232

LAMESA

**BUDGET HOST
INN**
901 S Dallas Ave
(79331)
Rates: $30-$41
(806) 872-2118
(800) 283-4678

SHILOH INN
1707 Lubbock
Hwy (79331)
Rates: $37-$240
(806) 872-6721

LAMPASAS

CIRCLE MOTEL
1502 S Key Ave
(76550)
Rates: $40-$52
(512) 556-6201
(800) 521-5417

**SARATOGA
MOTEL**
1408 S Key Ave
(76550)
Rates: $30-$60
(512) 556-6244

LAREDO

**BEST WESTERN
FIESTA INN**
5240 San Bernardo
Ave (78040)
Rates: $62-$69
(956) 723-3603
(800) 528-1234

**FAMILY GARDENS
INN**
5830 San Bernardo
Ave (78041)
Rates: $57-$64
(956) 723-5300
(800) 292-4053

HAMPTON INN
7903 San Dario
(78041)
Rates: $73-$79
(956) 717-8888
(800) 426-7866

**HOLIDAY INN
CIVIC CENTER**
800 Garden St
(78040)
Rates: $89
(956) 727-5800
(800) 465-4329

LA QUINTA INN
3610 Santa Ursula
Ave (78041)
Rates: $69-$89
(956) 722-0511
(800) 687-6667

MOTEL 6-NORTH
5920 San Bernardo
Ave (78041)
Rates: $40-$56
(956) 722-8133
(800) 466-8356

MOTEL 6-SOUTH
5310 San Bernardo
Ave (78041)
Rates: $39-$55
(956) 725-8187
(800) 466-8356

RED ROOF INN
1006 W Calton Rd
(78041)
Rates: $41-$66
(956) 712-0733
(800) 843-7663

**RIO GRANDE
PLAZA HOTEL
BY HOWARD
JOHNSON**
1 S Main Ave
(78040)
Rates: $62-$125
(956) 722-2411
(800) 446-4656

LEAKEY

**WHISKEY
MOUNTAIN INN
BED & BREAKFAST**
HCR 1, Box 555
(78873)
Rates: $50-$80
(830) 232-6797
(800) 370-6797

LEWISVILLE

LA QUINTA INN
1657 N Stemmons
Frwy (75067)
Rates: $59-$79
(972) 221-7525
(800) 687-6667

**MICROTEL INN
& SUITES**
881 S Stemmons
Frwy (75067)
Rates: $39-$79
(972) 434-0447
(888) 642-7685
(888) 771-7171

MOTEL 6
1705 Lakepointe
Dr (75057)
Rates: $39-$50
(972) 436-5008
(800) 466-8356

**RAMADA LIMITED
AIRPORT**
1102 Texas St (75057)
Rates: $48-$80
(972) 221-2121
(800) 272-6232

**RESIDENCE INN
BY MARRIOTT**
755 C Vista Ridge
Blvd (75067)
Rates: $120-$130
(972) 315-3777
(800) 331-3131

LINDALE

DAYS INN
13307 CR 472 E
(75771)
Rates: $40-$70
(903) 882-7800
(800) 329-7466

LITTLEFIELD

**CRESCENT PARK
MOTEL**
2000 Hall Ave
(79339)
Rates: $35-$55
(806) 385-4464
(800) 658-9960

LIVE OAK

LA QUINTA INN
12822 I-35 N
(78233)
Rates: $59-$79
(210) 657-5500
(800) 687-6667

LIVINGSTON

**PARK INN
INTERNATIONAL**
2500 Hwy 59 S
(77351)
Rates: $34-$40
(409) 327-2525
(800) 437-7275

RAMADA INN
1200 N
Washington
(77351)
Rates: $39-$62
(409) 327-3366
(800) 272-6232

LLANO

**THE BADU HOUSE
HISTORIC B&B**
601 Bessemer St
(78643)
Rates: $55-$65
(915) 247-4304

**BEST WESTERN
CLASSIC INN**
901 W Young St
(78643)
Rates: $47-$72
(915) 247-4101
(800) 528-1234
(800) 346-1578

TRAVELODGE
700 W Young
(78643)
Rates: $35-$60
(915) 247-4111
(800) 578-7878

LOCKHART

**BEST WESTERN
PLUM CREEK**
2001 Hwy 183 S
(78644)
Rates: $45-$80
(512) 398-4911
(800) 528-1234

LOCKHART INN
1207 Hwy 183 S
(78644)
Rates: $25-$34
(512) 398-5201

LONGVIEW

HAMPTON INN
112 S Access Rd
(75603)
Rates: $68-$80
(903) 758-0959
(800) 426-7866

LA QUINTA INN
502 S Access Rd
(75602)
Rates: $59-$79
(903) 757-3663
(800) 687-6667

LONGVIEW INN
605 Access Rd
(75602)
Rates: $40-$80
(903) 753-0350
(800) 933-1139

MOTEL 6
110 S Access Rd
(75603)
Rates: $33-$38
(903) 758-5256
(800) 466-8356

TRAVELODGE
3304 S Eastman
Rd (75602)
Rates: $42-$50
(903) 758-0711
(800) 578-7878

LUBBOCK

**CIRCUS INN
MOTEL**
150 Slaton Hwy
I-27 (79404)
Rates: $26-$39
(888) 745-5677

DAYS INN
2401 4th St (79415)
Rates: $45-$70
(806) 747-7111
(800) 329-7466

ECONO LODGE
910 Ave Q (79401)
Rates: $45-$65
(806) 765-6307
(800) 553-2666

**HOLIDAY INN
CIVIC CENTER**
801 Ave Q (79401)
Rates: $70-$95
(806) 763-1200
(800) 465-4329

**HOLIDAY INN-
LUBBOCK PLAZA
HOTEL**
3201 Loop 289 S
(79423)
Rates: $86
(806) 797-3241
(800) 465-4329

**HOWARD
JOHNSON
EXPRESS INN**
4801 Ave Q
(79412)
Rates: $35-$75
(806) 747-1671
(800) 446-4656

LA QUINTA INN
601 Ave Q (79412)
Rates: $65-$86
(806) 763-9441
(800) 687-6667

MOTEL 6
909 66th St (79412)
Rates: $32-$39
(806) 745-5541
(800) 466-8356

**RAMADA
REGENCY HOTEL
& CONF CENTER**
6624 I-27 (79404)
Rates: $59-$148
(806) 745-2208
(800) 272-6232

**RESIDENCE INN
BY MARRIOTT**
2551 S Loop 289
(79423)
Rates: $82
(806) 745-1963
(800) 331-3131

**SHERATON FOUR
POINTS HOTEL**
505 Ave Q (79401)
Rates: $80-$109
(806) 747-0171
(800) 325-3535

SUPER 8 MOTEL
5410 I-27 (79412)
Rates: $50-$80
(806) 762-8400
(800) 800-8000

SUPER 8 MOTEL
501 Ave Q (79401)
Rates: $40-$60
(806) 762-8726
(800) 800-8000

VILLA INN
5401 Ave Q
(79412)
Rates: $45-$90
(800) 448-0073

LUCKENBACH

**THE LUCKENBACH
INN B&B**
HC 13, Box 9
(78624)
Rates: $95-$125
(210) 997-2205
(800) 997-1124

LUFKIN

**BEST WESTERN
EXPO INN**
4200 N Medford
Dr (75901)
Rates: $45-$60
(409) 632-7300
(800) 528-1234

COMFORT SUITES
4402 S 1st St (75901)
Rates: $66-$103
(409) 632-4949
(800) 228-5150

DAYS INN
2130 S 1st St
(75901)
Rates: $51-$61
(409) 639-3301
(800) 329-7466

**HOLIDAY HOUSE
MOTEL**
308 N Timberland
Dr (75901)
Rates: $22-$28
(409) 634-6626

HOLIDAY INN
4306 S 1st St
(75901)
Rates: $40-$65
(409) 639-3333
(800) 465-4329

LA QUINTA INN
2119 S 1st St
(75901)
Rates: $59-$86
(409) 634-3351
(800) 687-6667

MOTEL 6
1110 S Timberland
Dr (75901)
Rates: $29-$34
(409) 637-7850
(800) 466-8356

LULING

COACHWAY INN
1908 E Pierce St
(78648)
Rates: $32-$48
(830) 875-5635

LYTLE

DAYS INN
19525 McDonald
St (78052)
Rates: $34-$59
(830) 772-4777
(800) 329-7466

MARATHON

THE GAGE HOTEL
102 Hwy 90 W
(79842)
Rates: $40-$60
(915) 386-4205
(800) 884-4243

MARBLE FALLS

**BEST WESTERN
MARBLE FALLS
INN**
1403 Hwy 281
(78654)
Rates: $55-$89
(830) 693-5122
(800) 528-1234

MARFA

RIATA INN
Hwy 90 E (79843)
Rates: $40-$70
(915) 729-3800

MARLIN

RELAX INN
Hwy G Bypass,
FM 147 (76661)
Rates: $34-$45
(254) 883-2581

MARSHALL

**BEST WESTERN
OF MARSHALL**
5555 E End Blvd S
(75670)
Rates: $59-$69
(903) 935-1941
(800) 528-1234

DAYS INN
101 W I-20 (75672)
Rates: $59-$150
(903) 927-1718
(800) 329-7466

**ECONOMY INN
EXPRESS**
5201 E End Blvd
(75672)
Rates: $45-$69
(903) 935-0707

HAMPTON INN
5100 S East End
Blvd (75672)
Rates: $59-$89
(903) 927-0079
(800) 426-7866

LA MAISON MALFACON COUNTRY INN
700 E Rusk St (75670)
Rates: $45-$60
(903) 938-3600

MEREDITH HOUSE BED & BREAKFAST
410 E Meredith St (75670)
Rates: $40-$80
(903) 935-7147

MOTEL 6
300 I-20 E (75670)
Rates: $31-$36
(903) 935-4393
(800) 466-8356

RAMADA INN
5301 E End Blvd S (75670)
Rates: $59-$80
(903) 938-9261
(800) 272-6232

MASON

HILL COUNTRY INN
Box 123 (76856)
Rates: $34-$73
(915) 347-6317

MATHIS

MATHIS MOTOR INN
1223 N Front St (78368)
Rates: $27-$36
(512) 547-3272
(800) 251-7531

MCALLEN

CASA DE PALMAS DOUBLETREE
101 Main St (78501)
Rates: $62-$99
(956) 653-1101
(800) 274-1102

DRURY INN
612 W Expwy 83 (78501)
Rates: $69-$93
(956) 687-5100
(800) 378-7946

HAMPTON INN
300 W Expwy 83 (78501)
Rates: $68-$93
(956) 682-4900
(800) 426-7866

LA QUINTA INN
1100 S 10th St (78501)
Rates: $74-$86
(956) 687-1101
(800) 687-6667

MOTEL 6
700 Expwy 83 (78501)
Rates: $38-$45
(956) 687-3700
(800) 466-8356

RAMADA LIMITED
1505 S 9th St (78501)
Rates: $55-$65
(956) 686-4401
(800) 272-6232

RESIDENCE INN BY MARRIOTT
220 W Expwy 83 (78501)
Rates: $70-$104
(956) 994-8626
(800) 331-3131

THRIFTY INN
620 Expwy 83 (78501)
Rates: $39-$65
(956) 631-6700

MCKINNEY

DAYS INN
2104 N Central Expwy (75070)
Rates: $60-$75
(972) 548-8888
(800) 329-7466

WOODS MOTEL
1431 N Tennessee St (75070)
Rates: $30-$41
(972) 542-4469

MCLEAN

CACTUS INN MOTEL
101 Pine St (79057)
Rates: $30-$49
(806) 779-2346

MERCEDES

DAYS INN
Mile 2 W & Expwy 83 (78570)
Rates: $43-$75
(956) 565-3121
(800) 329-7466

MESQUITE

DAYS INN
3601 Hwy 80 E (75150)
Rates: $40-$55
(214) 279-6561
(800) 329-7466

HAMPTON INN
1700 Rodeo Dr (75145)
Rates: $79-$119
(972) 329-3100
(800) 426-7866

MOTEL 6
3629 Hwy 80 E (75150)
Rates: $26-$30
(214) 613-1662
(800) 466-8356

MIDLAND

BEST WESTERN INN
3100 W Wall St (79701)
Rates: $54-$69
(915) 699-4144
(800) 528-1234

CLAYDESTA INN
4108 N Big Spring (79705)
Rates: $49-$89
(800) 365-3222

DAYS INN
1003 S Midkiff Rd (79701)
Rates: $44-$86
(915) 697-3155
(800) 329-7466

HAMPTON INN
3904 W Wall St (79703)
Rates: $55+
(915) 694-7774
(800) 426-7866

HILTON/TOWERS
117 W Wall St (79701)
Rates: $69-$129
(915) 683-6131
(800) 445-8667
(800) 722-6131 (TX)

HOLIDAY INN COUNTRY VILLA
4300 W Wall St (79703)
Rates: $54-$159
(915) 697-3181
(800) 465-4329

LA QUINTA INN
4130 W Wall St (79703)
Rates: $55-$75
(915) 697-9900
(800) 687-6667

LEXINGTON HOTEL SUITES
1003 S Midkiff Rd (79701)
Rates: $44-$60
(915) 697-3155

MOTEL 6
1000 S Midkiff Rd (79701)
Rates: $25-$30
(915) 697-3197
(800) 466-8356

SLEEP INN
3828 W Wall St (79703)
Rates: $45-$69
(915) 689-6822
(800) 753-3746

SUPER 8 MOTEL
1000 I-20 W (79701)
Rates: $34-$51
(915) 684-8888
(800) 800-8000

TRAVELODGE
2500 Commerce Dr (79703)
Rates: $35-$60
(915) 694-1300
(800) 578-7878

MIDLOTHIAN

BEST WESTERN MIDLOTHIAN INN
220 N Hwy 67 (76065)
Rates: $55-$69
(972) 775-1891
(800) 528-1234

MINERAL WELLS

BUDGET HOST INN MESA HOTEL
3601 E Hwy 180 (76067)
Rates: $39-$56
(940) 325-3377
(800) 283-4678

DAYS INN
3701 E Hubbard (76067)
Rates: $45-$85
(940) 325-6961
(800) 329-7466

HOWARD JOHNSON EXPRESS
2809 Hwy 180 W (76067)
Rates: $42-$55
(940) 328-1111
(800) 446-4656

12 OAKS INN MOTEL
4103 Hwy 180 E (76067)
Rates: $38-$42
(940) 325-6956

MISSION

MISSION INN
1786 W Hwy 83 (78572)
Rates: $46
(210) 581-7451

MONAHANS

BEST WESTERN COLONIAL INN
702 I-20 W (79756)
Rates: $39-$56
(915) 943-4345
(800) 528-1234

MOUNT PLEASANT

BEST WESTERN INN & SUITES
102 E Burton St (75455)
Rates: $59-$89
(903) 577-7377
(800) 528-1234

DAYS INN
2501 W Ferguson (75455)
Rates: $50-$72
(903) 577-0152
(800) 329-7466

SUPER 8 MOTEL
204 Lakewood Dr (75455)
Rates: $45-$69
(903) 572-9808
(800) 800-8000

TANKERSLEY GARDENS B&B
Rt 7, Box 696 (75455)
Rates: $45-$110
(903) 572-0567

AREA CODES - If the local number doesn't connect, check for a new area code.

MOUNT VERNON

SUPER 8 MOTEL
I-30 & Hwy 37
(75457)
Rates: $42-$53
(903) 588-2882
(800) 800-8000

MOUNTAIN HOME

Y. O. RANCH
Hwy 41 W (78058)
Rates: $65-$95
(210) 640-3222
(800) 967-2624

MULESHOE

HERITAGE HOUSE INN
2301 W American
Blvd (79347)
Rates: $44-$75
(806) 272-7575
(800) 253-5896

NACOGDOCHES

EAGLE'S AERIE B&B
12 E Lake Estates,
Rt 3 (75964)
Rates: $55+
(409) 564-7995
(800) 754-3906

THE FREDONIA HISTORIC HOTEL
200 N Fredonia St
(75961)
Rates: $59-$99
(409) 564-1234
(800) 594-5323

HARDEMAN GUEST HOUSE-HISTORIC B& B
316 N Church St
(75961)
Rates: $65-$80
(409) 569-1947
(800) 884-1947

LA QUINTA INN
3215 South St (75961)
Rates: $59-$86
(409) 560-5453
(800) 687-6667

STRATFORD HOUSE INN
2612 North St
(75961)
Rates: $35-$50
(800) 935-0676

NAVASOTA

BEST WESTERN INN
8965 Hwy 6
(77868)
Rates: $59-$89
(800) 528-1234

SUPER 8 MOTEL
818 Hwy 6 Loop S
(77868)
Rates: $49-$79
(409) 825-7775
(800) 800-8000

NEDERLAND

BEST WESTERN
200 Memorial
Hwy 69 (77627)
Rates: $44-$59
(409) 727-1631
(800) 528-1234

NEW BOSTON

BEST WESTERN INN
1024 N Center
(75570)
Rates: $56-$63
(903) 628-6999
(800) 528-1234

NEW BRAUNFELS

CAMP HUACO SPRINGS CABINS
1405 Gruene Rd
(78130)
Rates: $25-$95
(830) 625-5411
(800) 553-5628

ECONO LODGE
815 I-35 W (78130)
Rates: $40-$65
(830) 620-7766
(800) 553-2666

EDELWEISS INN
1063 I-35 N
(78130)
Rates: $39-$99
(830) 629-6967

HOLIDAY INN
1051 I-35 E (78130)
Rates: $99
(830) 625-8017
(800) 465-4329

KUEBLER-WALDRIP HAUS BED & BREAKFAST
1620 Hueco
Springs Loop
(78132)
Rates: $89-$200
(830) 625-8372
(800) 299-8372

MOTEL 6
1275 I-35 (78130)
Rates: $38-$75
(800) 466-8356

OAKWOOD INN
375 Hwy 46 S
(78130)
Rates: $30-$150
(830) 625-6282

RODEWAY INN
1209 I-35 S (78130)
Rates: $79-$89
(830) 629-6991
(800) 228-2000
(800) 967-1168 (TX)

SUPER 8 MOTEL
510 Hwy 46 S
(78130)
Rates: $59-$95
(830) 629-1155
(800) 800-8000

NOCONA

NOCONA HILLS MOTEL & RESORT
100 E Huron
Circle (76255)
Rates: $32-$44
(940) 825-3161

NORTH PADRE ISLAND

MOTEL 6
8202 S Padre
Island Dr (78412)
Rates: $36-$56
(361) 991-8858
(800) 466-8356

NORTH RICHLAND HILLS

HOMESTEAD VILLAGE GUEST STUDIOS
7450 NE Loop 820
(76180)
Rates: n/a
(817) 788-6000
(888) 782-9473

LA QUINTA INN
7920 Bedford-Euless Rd (76180)
Rates: $59-$69
(817) 485-2750
(800) 687-6667

LEXINGTON INN-DFW WEST
8709 Airport Frwy
(76180)
Rates: $62-$85
(817) 656-8881
(800) 656-8886

MOTEL 6
7804 Bedford-Euless Rd (76180)
Rates: $38-$54
(817) 485-3000
(800) 466-8356

ODEM

DAYS INN
1505 Voss (78370)
Rates: $49-$90
(361) 368-2166
(800) 329-7466

ODESSA

BEST WESTERN GARDEN OASIS
110 I-20 W (79761)
Rates: $58-$78
(915) 337-3006
(800) 528-1234
(877) 524-9231

CLASSIC SUITES
3031 I-20 E
Business (79761)
Rates: $27-$32
(915) 333-9678

DAYS INN
3075 E Hwy 80
(79761)
Rates: $50-$60
(915) 335-8000
(800) 329-7466

HOLIDAY INN EXPRESS HOTEL & SUITES
3001 E Business
Loop I-20 (79760)
Rates: n/a
(915) 333-3931
(800) 465-4329

HOLIDAY INN HOTEL & SUITES
6201 Hwy 80 E
(79760)
Rates: $58-$160
(915) 362-2311
(800) 465-4329

LA QUINTA INN
5001 Hwy 80 E
(79761)
Rates: $55-$75
(915) 333-2820
(800) 687-6667

MOTEL ONE
2925 E Hwy 80
(79761)
Rates: $24-$28
(915) 332-4500

MOTEL 6
200 E I-20 Service
Rd (79766)
Rates: $27-$32
(915) 333-4025
(800) 466-8356

PARKWAY INN
3071 Hwy 80 E
(79761)
Rates: $28-$33
(915) 332-4224
(800) 926-6760

RELAX INN
1518 S Grant
(79761)
Rates: n/a
(915) 333-1486

SUPER 8 MOTEL
6713 E Hwy 80
(79762)
Rates: $36-$53
(915) 363-8281
(800) 800-8000

VILLA WEST INN
300 W Pool Road
(79760)
Rates: $24-$35
(915) 335-5055

ORANGE

BEST WESTERN INN OF ORANGE
2630 I-10 (77630)
Rates: $51-$65
(409) 883-6616
(800) 528-1234

DAYS INN
2900 IH-10 (77632)
Rates: $35-$60
(409) 883-9981
(800) 329-7466

HOLIDAY INN EXPRESS
2900 I-10 (77632)
Rates: $50-$70
(409) 988-0110
(800) 465-4329

KING'S INN MOTEL
2208 I-10 W (77630)
Rates: $36+
(409) 883-6701

MOTEL 6
4407 27th St (77630)
Rates: $29-$34
(409) 883-4891
(800) 466-8356

RAMADA INN
2610 I-10 W (77630)
Rates: $65-$150
(409) 883-0231
(800) 272-6232

OZONA

DAYSTOP
820 Loop 466 W (76943)
Rates: $38-$60
(915) 392-2631
(800) 329-7466

TRAVELODGE
8 11th St (76943)
Rates: $35-$45
(915) 392-2656
(800) 578-7878

PADUCAH

HUNTERS LODGE MOTEL
902 11th St (79248)
Rates: $40-$55
(806) 492-2167

PALESTINE

BEST WESTERN INN
1601 W Palestine Ave (75801)
Rates: $45-$70
(903) 723-4655
(800) 528-1234
(800) 523-0121

DAYS INN
1100 E Palestine Ave (75801)
Rates: $35-$135
(903) 729-3151
(800) 329-7466
(800) 944-1143 (TX)

RAMADA INN
1101 E Palestine Ave (75801)
Rates: $59-$85
(903) 723-7300
(800) 272-6232

PANHANDLE

S & S MOTOR INN
I-40 & SR 207 (79068)
Rates: $35-$47
(806) 537-5111

PARIS

BEST WESTERN INN OF PARIS
3755 NE Loop US 286 (75460)
Rates: $49-$60
(903) 785-5566
(800) 528-1234

COMFORT INN
3505 NE Loop US 286 (75460)
Rates: $60-$72
(903) 784-7481
(800) 228-5150

VICTORIAN INNS
425 NE 35th St (75460)
Rates: $42-$60
(903) 785-3871
(800) 935-0863

PASADENA

RAMADA INN
114 S Richy (77506)
Rates: $55-$85
(713) 477-6871
(800) 272-6232

PEARLAND

BEST WESTERN INN
1855 N Main St (77581)
Rates: $51-$69
(281) 997-2000
(800) 528-1234

PEARSALL

EXECUTIVE INN
613 North Oak (78061)
Rates: $36-$50
(830) 334-3693

PECOS

BEST WESTERN SWISS CLOCK INN
900 W Palmer (79772)
Rates: $59-$86
(915) 447-2215
(800) 528-1234

LAURA LODGE
1000 E Business 20 (79772)
Rates: $28-$40
(915) 445-4924

MOTEL 6
3002 S Cedar St (79772)
Rates: $29-$34
(915) 445-9034
(800) 466-8356

QUALITY INN
4002 S Cedar St (79772)
Rates: $71-$101
(915) 445-5404
(800) 228-5151

PHARR

RAMADA LIMITED SUITES
1130 E Expy 83 (78577)
Rates: $50-$75
(956) 702-3330
(800) 272-6232

SUPER 8 MOTEL
Hwy 271 & Nolana (78577)
Rates: $65-$82
(956) 782-8880
(800) 800-8000

PITTSBURG

CARSON HOUSE INN & GRILLE
302 Mt Pleasant St (75686)
Rates: $69-$79
(903) 856-2468

PLAINVIEW

BEST WESTERN CONESTOGA INN
600 I-27 N (79072)
Rates: $60-$99
(806) 293-9454
(800) 528-1234

BUDGET INN
2001 W 5th St (79072)
Rates: $24-$35
(806) 293-2578

DAYS INN
3600 Olton Rd (79072)
Rates: $40-$65
(806) 293-2561
(800) 329-7466

WARRICK INN
800 Broadway (79072)
Rates: $29-$45
(806) 293-4266

PLANO

AMERISUITES
3100 Dallas Pkwy (75093)
Rates: $109-$119
(972) 378-3997
(800) 833-1516

BEST WESTERN PARK SUITES HOTEL
640 Park Blvd E (75074)
Rates: $85-$120
(972) 578-2243
(800) 528-1234

COMFORT INN
621 Central Pkwy E (75074)
Rates: $55-$110
(972) 424-5568
(800) 228-5150

HARVEY HOTEL
1600 N Central Expwy (75074)
Rates: $59-$120
(972) 578-8555
(800) 922-9222

HOLIDAY INN
700 Central Pkwy E (75074)
Rates: $69-$89
(972) 881-1881
(800) 465-4329

HOMEWOOD SUITES
4705 Old Shepard Pl (75093)
Rates: $109-$169
(972) 758-8800
(800) 225-5466

LA QUINTA INN
1820 N Central Expwy (75074)
Rates: $65-$85
(972) 423-1300
(800) 687-6667

LA QUINTA INN & SUITES
4800 W Plano Pkwy (75091)
Rates: $69-$89
(972) 599-0700
(800) 687-6667

MAINSTAY SUITES
4709 W Plano Pkwy (75091)
Rates: $60-$100
(972) 596-9966
(800) 660-6246

MOTEL 6
2550 N Central Expwy (75074)
Rates: $39-$61
(972) 578-1626
(800) 466-8356

RED ROOF INN
301 Ruisseau Dr (75032)
Rates: $44-$70
(972) 881-8191
(800) 843-7663

SLEEP INN
4801 W Plano Pkwy (75093)
Rates: $60-$89
(972) 867-1111
(800) 753-3746

WELLESLEY INN & SUITES
2900 Dallas Pkwy (75093)
Rates: $79-$109
(972) 378-9978
(888) 444-8888

PORT ARANSAS

BEACH HOUSE RENTALS
2122 On The Beach (78373)
Rates: $125-$300
(361) 749-5434

AREA CODES - If the local number doesn't connect, check for a new area code.

BEACHGATE CONDOSUITES
2000 On The Beach (78373)
Rates: $50-$265
(361) 749-5900

BELLE'S INN MOTEL
710 Station at Ave G (78373)
Rates: $35-$65
(361) 749-6138

EXECUTIVE KEYS APARTMENT MOTEL
820 Access Rd 1A (78373)
Rates: $38-$172
(361) 749-6272
(800) 248-1095

HARBOR VIEW MOTEL
121 W Cotter (78373)
Rates: $35
(361) 749-6391

LONE PALM MOTEL
306 S Alister (78373)
Rates: $28-$80
(361) 749-5450

PARADISE ISLE MOTEL
314 Cutoff Rd (78373)
Rates: $40
(361) 749-6993

ROCK COTTAGES
603 E Ave G (78373)
Rates: $39-$45
(361) 749-6360

SEA HORSE LODGE
503 E Ave G (78373)
Rates: $65-$95
(361) 749-5513

SEA & SANDS COTTAGES
410 10th St (78373)
Rates: $65-$110
(361) 749-5191

SEASIDE MOTEL
500 Sandcastle Dr (78373)
Rates: $39-$180
(361) 749-4105
(800) 765-3101

SUNDAY VILLAS
1900 S 11th St (78373)
Rates: $70
(361) 749-6480

TROPIC ISLAND MOTEL
315 Cutoff Rd (78373)
Rates: $55-$105
(361) 749-6128

PORT ISABEL

SOUTHWIND INN
600 Davis St (78578)
Rates: $50-$120
(956) 943-3392

WHITE SANDS MOTEL
418 W Hwy 100 (78578)
Rates: $32-$52
(956) 943-2414

YACHT CLUB HOTEL
700 Yturria St (78578)
Rates: $35-$99
(956) 943-1301

PORT LAVACA

DAYS INN
2100 N Bypass 35 (77979)
Rates: $45-$80
(512) 552-4511
(800) 329-7466

PORTLAND

COMFORT INN
1703 N Hwy 181 (78374)
Rates: $59-$94
(361) 643-2222
(800) 228-5150

QUANAH

QUANAH PARKER INN
1405 W 11th St (79252)
Rates: $27-$40
(817) 663-6366
(800) 441-7971

QUEEN CITY

TRAVELODGE
301 Hwy 59 (75572)
Rates: $33-$51
(903) 796-7191
(800) 578-7878

RAINBOW

RAINBOW'S END BED & BREAKFST
County Road 312 (76077)
Rates: $90+
(817) 897-2238

RANGER

DAYS INN
I-20 Ex 349, Box 160-C (76470)
Rates: $40-$53
(254) 647-1176
(800) 329-7466

RANKIN

RIATA INN
509 E Hwy 67 (79778)
Rates: $40-$70
(915) 693-2300

RICHARDSON

CLARION HOTEL
1981 N Central Expwy (75080)
Rates: $95-$155
(972) 444-4000
(800) 285-3434

HAMPTON INN
1577 Gateway Blvd (75080)
Rates: $79-$89
(972) 234-5400
(800) 426-7866

LA QUINTA INN
13685 N Central Expwy (75243)
Rates: $49-$99
(972) 234-0682
(800) 687-6667

RESIDENCE INN BY MARRIOTT
1040 Waterwood Dr (75081)
Rates: $69-$145
(972) 669-5888
(800) 331-3131

SLEEP INN
2458 N Central Expwy (75080)
Rates: $56-$95
(972) 470-9440
(800) 626-5337

WYNDHAM GARDEN HOTEL
901 E Campbell Rd (75080)
Rates: $109
(972) 479-0500
(800) 996-3426

RICHMOND

EXECUTIVE INN
26035 Southwest Frwy (77469)
Rates: $31-$40
(281) 342-5387

RIPE CREEK

LIGHTNING DUDE RANCH
818 FM 1283 (78063)
Rates: $85-$120
(830) 535-4096

ROANOKE

COMFORT SUITES
US 114 & Cannon Pkwy (79262)
Rates: $99-$159
(800) 228-5150

ROBSTOWN

DAYS INN
320 Hwy 77 S (78380)
Rates: $50-$95
(361) 387-9416
(800) 329-7466

ROCKDALE

REGENCY INN
2 N Hwy 77/79 (76567)
Rates: $44-$57
(512) 446-7555

ROCKPORT

ANCHOR MOTEL
1204 E Market (78382)
Rates: $40-$60
(361) 729-3249

ANTHONY'S BY THE SEA B&B
732 S Pearl St (78382)
Rates: $75-$95
(800) 460-2557

BIG TREE TRAILER INN & COTTAGES
HC 04, Box 146 (77710)
Rates: $20-$40
(361) 729-8708

DEL CAMINO APARTMENT MOTEL
1009 I-35 N (78382)
Rates: $65
(361) 729-2510

HOLIDAY LODGE MOTEL
1406 I-35 N (78382)
Rates: $34-$40
(361) 729-3433

HUNT'S CASTLE MOTEL - WATERFRONT
725 S Water St (78382)
Rates: $49-$149
(361) 729-2273
(888) 345-4868

KEY ALLEGRO RENTALS
1798 Bayshore (78382)
Rates: $110
(361) 729-2333
(800) 348-1627

KONTIKI BEACH RESORT
2290 N Fulton Beach Rd (78382)
Rates: $55-$205
(800) 388-0649

LAGUNA REEF APARTMENT MOTEL
1021 Water St (78382)
Rates: $75-$250
(361) 729-1742
(800) 248-1057

OCEAN VIEW MOTEL
1131 S Water St (78382)
Rates: $35-$65
(361) 729-3326

AREA CODES - If the local number doesn't connect, check for a new area code.

PELICAN MOTEL
1011 E Market St
(78382)
Rates: $40-$55
(361) 729-3837
(800) 248-1057

ROCKPORTER INN
813 S Church St
(78382)
Rates: $40
(361) 729-9591

ROD AND REEL MOTEL
1105 E Market St
(78382)
Rates: $31-$54
(361) 729-2028
(888) 729-2028

SANDOLLAR RESORT MOTEL
HC O1, Box 30
(78382)
Rates: $44-$59
(361) 729-2381

SANDRA BAY COTTAGES
1801 Broadway
(78382)
Rates: $45+
(361) 729-6257

SEAVIEW MOTEL
1155 I-35 N (78382)
Rates: $35-$55
(361) 729-9112

SUN TAN MOTEL
1805 Broadway
(78382)
Rates: $39-$60
(361) 729-2179

SUNSET INN
800 S Church St
(78382)
Rates: $26-$35
(361) 729-4792

VILLAGE INN MOTEL
503 N Austin St
(78382)
Rates: $48-$55
(361) 729-6370
(800) 338-7539

ROCKWALL

SUPER 8 MOTEL
1130 I-30 (75087)
Rates: $44-$55
(972) 722-9922
(800) 800-8000

ROSENBERG

BEST WESTERN SUNDOWNER MOTOR INN
28382 SW
Freeway (77471)
Rates: n/a
(281) 342-6000
(800) 528-1234

HOLIDAY INN EXPRESS HOTEL & SUITES
27927 SW
Freeway (77471)
Rates: n/a
(800) 465-4329

ROUND ROCK

BEST WESTERN EXECUTIVE INN
1851 N I-35
(78664)
Rates: $59-$79
(512) 255-3222
(800) 528-1234

HILTON GARDEN INN
2310 N I-35
(78681)
Rates: $69-$139
(512) 341-8200
(800) 445-8667

LA QUINTA INN
2004 I-35 N (78681)
Rates: $65-$85
(512) 255-6666
(800) 687-6667

RAMADA LIMITED
1400 I-35 N (78681)
Rates: $58-$75
(512) 255-4437
(800) 272-6232

RESIDENCE INN BY MARRIOTT
2505 S I-35 (78664)
Rates: $108-$149
(800) 331-3131

RODEWAY INN & SUITES
1802 I-35 S (78681)
Rates: $49-$99
(512) 246-0055
(800) 228-2000

SLEEP INN
1990 N I-35 (78681)
Rates: $59-$79
(512) 310-1111
(800) 753-3746

ROUND TOP

ROUND TOP INN BED & BREAKFST
102 Bauer
Rummell (78954)
Rates: $95-$125
(409) 249-5294
(888) 356-8946

SAN ANGELO

BEST WESTERN INN OF THE WEST
415 W Beauregard
St (76901)
Rates: $49-$59
(915) 653-2995
(800) 528-1234
(800) 582-9668

DAYS INN
4613 S Jackson
(76903)
Rates: $45-$55
(915) 658-6594
(800) 329-7466

EL PATIO MOTEL
1901 W
Beauregard St
(76901)
Rates: $20-$35
(915) 655-5711
(800) 677-7735

HOLIDAY INN CONVENTION CENTER HOTEL
441 Rio Concho
Dr (76903)
Rates: $99-$107
(915) 658-2828
(800) 465-4329

INN OF THE CONCHOS
2021 N Bryant
Blvd (76903)
Rates: $59-$89
(915) 658-2811
(800) 621-6041

LA QUINTA INN
2307 Loop 306
(76904)
Rates: $59-$79
(915) 949-0515
(800) 687-6667

MOTEL 6
311 N Bryant Blvd
(76903)
Rates: $31-$36
(915) 658-8061
(800) 466-8356

QUALITY INN
4205 S Bryant
Blvd (76903)
Rates: $44-$70
(915) 653-6966
(800) 228-5151

RAMADA LIMITED
2201 N Bryant
Blvd (76903)
Rates: $49-$79
(915) 653-8442
(800) 272-6232

SANTA FE JCT MOTOR INN
410 W Ave L
(76903)
Rates: $26-$55
(915) 655-8101
(800) 634-2599

SUPER 8 MOTEL
1601 S Bryant
Blvd (76903)
Rates: $41-$57
(915) 653-1323
(800) 800-8000

TRAVELODGE
333 Rio Concho
Dr (76903)
Rates: $39-$48
(915) 659-0747
(800) 578-7878

SAN ANTONIO

A BLANSETT BARN GUEST HOUSE
206 Madison
(78204)
Rates: $125-$300
(800) 221-1412

ALOHA INN
1435 Austin Hwy
(78209)
Rates: $40-$50
(210) 828-0933
(800) 752-6354

AMERISUITES
7615 Jones
Maltsberger Rd
(78216)
Rates: $95-$135
(210) 930-2333
(800) 833-1516

AMERISUITES
4325 AmeriSuites
Dr (78230)
Rates: $62-$129
(800) 833-1516

ARBOR HOUSE INN & SUITES BED & BREAKFAST
540 S St. Mary's
Sreet (78205)
Rates: $95-$175
(210) 472-2005
(888) 272-6700

BEST WESTERN FIESTA INN
13535 I-10 W
(78249)
Rates: $45-$119
(210) 697-9761
(800) 528-1234

BEST WESTERN INGRAM PARK INN
6855 NW Loop
410 (78238)
Rates: $39-$109
(210) 520-8080
(800) 528-1234

BEST WESTERN LACKLAND INN & SUITES
6815 Hwy 90 W
(78227)
Rates: $59-$120
(210) 675-9690
(800) 528-1234
(888) 227-2313

BEST WESTERN TOWN HOUSE AIRPORT
942 NE Loop 410
(78209)
Rates: $49-$89
(210) 826-6311
(800) 528-1234

CANDLEWOOD SUITES HOTEL
9350 I-10 W
(78230)
Rates: $59-$84
(210) 615-0550

CLARION SUITES HOTEL
13101 E Loop
1604 N ((78233)
Rates: $59-$149
(210) 655-9491
(800) 252-7466

COACHMAN INN BROOKS FIELD
3180 Gollard Rd
(78223)
Rates: $36-$52
(210) 337-7171

AREA CODES - If the local number doesn't connect, check for a new area code.

COMFORT INN-SEA WORLD
4 Plano Pl (78229)
Rates: $55-$275
(210) 684-8606
(800) 228-5150

COUNTRY HEARTH INN
7500 Louis
Pasteur (78229)
Rates: $53-$69
(210) 616-0030
(888) 325-7821

DAYS INN
1500 S Laredo St
(78204)
Rates: $49-$129
(210) 271-3334
(800) 329-7466

DAYS INN-NE
3443 I-35 N (78219)
Rates: $34-$79
(210) 225-4521
(800) 329-7466
(800) 548-2626 (TX)

DAYS INN WINDCREST
9401 IH-35 N (78233)
Rates: $49-$74
(210) 650-9779
(800) 329-7466

DRURY INN EAST
8300 I-35 N
(78239)
Rates: $54-$81
(210) 654-1144
(800) 378-7946

DRURY SUITES
95 NE Loop 410
(78216)
Rates: $68-$93
(210) 308-8100
(800) 378-7946

EMBASSY SUITES HOTEL-AIRPORT
10110 Hwy 281 N
(78216)
Rates: $109-$169
(210) 525-9999
(800) 362-2779

EXECUTIVE GUESTHOUSE HOTEL
12828 Hwy 281 N
(78216)
Rates: $89-$170
(210) 494-7600
(800) 362-8700

HAMPTON INN AIRPORT
8818 Jones
Maltsberger
(78216)
Rates: $70-$92
(210) 366-1800
(800) 426-7866

HAWTHORN SUITES
4041 Bluemel Rd
(78240)
Rates: $79-$175
(210) 561-9660
(800) 527-1133

HAWTHORN SUITES AIRPORT
2383 NE Loop 10
(78217)
Rates: $70
(210) 599-4204
(800) 527-1133

HAWTHORN SUITES RIVERWALK
830 N St. Marys
Street (78205)
Rates: $98
(210) 527-1900
(800) 527-1133

HILTON HOTEL & CONFERENCE CENTER-AIRPORT
611 NW Loop 410
(78216)
Rates: $121-$185
(210) 340-6060
(800) 445-8667

HILTON PALACIO DEL RIO
200 S Alamo St
(78205)
Rates: $169-$219
(210) 222-1400
(800) 445-8667

HOLIDAY INN-CROCKETT HOTEL
320 Bonham (78205)
Rates: $89-$149
(210) 225-6500
(800) 465-4329
(800) 292-1050

HOLIDAY INN-DOWNTOWN-MARKET SQUARE
318 W Durango
(78204)
Rates: $139
(210) 225-3211
(800) 465-4329

HOLIDAY INN EXPRESS
11939 N I-35
(78233)
Rates: n/a
(210) 599-0999
(800) 465-4329

HOLIDAY INN EXPRESS AIRPORT
91 NE Loop 410
(78216)
Rates: $69-$94
(210) 308-6700
(800) 465-4329

HOLIDAY INN NORTHEAST
3855 I-35 N
(78219)
Rates: $69-$99
(210) 226-4361
(800) 465-4329

HOLIDAY INN RIVERWALK
217 N St. Mary's
Street (78205)
Rates: $116-$143
(210) 224-2500
(800) 465-4329

HOLIDAY INN SELECT
77 NE Loop 410
(78216)
Rates: $99-$125
(210) 349-9900
(800) 465-4329

HOMEGATE STUDIOS & SUITES-AIRPORT
11221 San Pedro
Ave (78216)
Rates: $57-$89
(888) 456-4283

HOMEGATE STUDIOS & SUITES-FIESTA PARK
10950 Laureate Dr
(78249)
Rates: $59-$79
(888) 456-4283

HOMESTEAD VILLAGE GUEST STUDIOS
7719 Louis
Pasteur Ct (78229)
Rates: $40-$55
(210) 349-3100
(888) 782-9473

HOMESTEAD VILLAGE GUEST STUIODS
1015 Central Pkwy
S Loop 410 (78232)
Rates: $50-$70
(210) 491-9009
(888) 782-9473

HOMESTEAD VILLAGE-SIX FLAGS
11802 I-10 W (78230)
Rates: n/a
(210) 691-0121
(888) 782-9473

HOWARD JOHNSON
9603 I-35 N (78233)
Rates: $36-$75
(210) 655-2120
(800) 446-4656

HOWARD JOHNSON EXPRESS INN
2755 N Pan Am
Expwy (78208)
Rates: $30-$109
(210) 229-9220
(800) 446-4656

HOWARD JOHNSON EXPRESS INN
13279 IH-10 W
(78249)
Rates: $59-$79
(210) 558-7152
(800) 446-4656

HOWARD JOHNSON RIVERWALK PLAZA HOTEL & RESORT
100 Villita (78205)
Rates: $89-$299
(210) 226-2271
(800) 446-4656

KNIGHTS INN
6370 I-35 N
(78218)
Rates: $44-$79
(210) 646-6336
(800) 843-5644

LA MANSION DEL RIO HOTEL
112 College St
(78205)
Rates: $199-$1900
(210) 518-1000
(800) 531-7208
(800) 292-7300 (TX)

LA QUINTA INN-AIRPORT EAST
333 NE Loop 410
(78216)
Rates: $79-$119
(210) 828-0781
(800) 687-6667

LA QUINTA INN-AIRPORT WEST
219 NE Loop 410
(78216)
Rates: $79-$119
(210) 342-4291
(800) 687-6667

LA QUINTA INN CONVENTION CENTER
1001 E Commerce
St (78205)
Rates: $89-$119
(210) 222-9181
(800) 687-6667

LA QUINTA INN INGRAM PARK
7134 NW Loop
410 (78238)
Rates: $79-$119
(210) 680-8883
(800) 687-6667

LA QUINTA INN-LACKLAND
6511 Military Dr
W (78227)
Rates: $69-$89
(210) 674-3200
(800) 687-6667

LA QUINTA INN MARKET SQUARE
900 Dolorosa St
(78207)
Rates: $79-$119
(210) 271-0001
(800) 687-6667

LA QUINTA INN-SOUTH
7202 S Pan Am
Expwy (78224)
Rates: $49-$119
(210) 922-2111
(800) 687-6667

LA QUINTA INN TOEPPERWEIN
12822 I-35 N
(78233)
Rates: $49-$119
(210) 657-5500
(800) 687-6667

AREA CODES - If the local number doesn't connect, check for a new area code.

LA QUINTA INN VANCE JACKSON
5922 NW Expwy (78201)
Rates: $59-$79
(210) 734-7931
(800) 687-6667

LA QUINTA INN WINDSOR PARK
6410 I-35 N (78218)
Rates: $59-$79
(210) 653-6619
(800) 687-6667

LA QUINTA INN-WURZBACH
9542 I-10 W (78230)
Rates: $79-$119
(210) 593-0338
(800) 687-6667

MARRIOTT PLAZA
555 S Alamo (78205)
Rates: $99-$264
(800) 727-3239

MARRIOTT RIVERCENTER
101 Bowie St (78205)
Rates: $209-$259
(210) 223-1000
(800) 228-9290
(800) 648-4462 (TX)

MARRIOTT RIVERWALK
711 E Riverwalk (78205)
Rates: $209-$259
(210) 224-4555
(800) 228-9290
(800) 648-4462 (TX)

MOTEL 6-EAST
138 N WW White Rd (78219)
Rates: $37-$53
(210) 333-1850
(800) 466-8356

MOTEL 6-FIESTA
16500 I-10 W (78257)
Rates: $48-$64
(210) 697-0731
(800) 466-8356

MOTEL 6 NORTHEAST
4621 E Rittiman Rd (78218)
Rates: $31-$46
(210) 665-8088
(800) 466-8356

MOTEL 6 -FT. SAM HOUSTON
5522 N Pan Am Expwy (78218)
Rates: $31-$46
(210) 661-8791
(800) 466-8356

MOTEL 6-NORTH
9503 I-35 N (78233)
Rates: $33-$51
(210) 650-4419
(800) 466-8356

MOTEL 6-NW MEDICAL CENTER
9400 Wurzbach Rd (78240)
Rates: $37-$56
(210) 593-0013
(800) 466-8356

MOTEL 6-RIVERWALK
211 N Pecos St (78207)
Rates: $50-$71
(210) 225-1111
(800) 466-8356

MOTEL 6 SOUTH
7950 I-35 S (78224)
Rates: $33-$54
(210) 928-2866
(800) 466-8356

MOTEL 6-WEST SEA WORLD
2185 SW Loop 410 (78227)
Rates: $42-$58
(210) 673-9020
(800) 466-8356

O'CASEYS BED & BREAKFAST
225 W Craig Place (78212)
Rates: $69-$115
(800) 738-1378

OAK MOTOR LODGE
150 Humphreys Ave (78209)
Rates: $29-$75
(210) 826-6368
(800) 385-9568

PAINTED LADY INN ON BROADWAY B&B
620 Broadway (78215)
Rates: $79-$189
(210) 220-1092

PARK INN SUITES
2131 N I-35 (78208)
Rates: $49-$150
(210) 354-2998

PEAR TREE INN
143 NE Loop 410 (78216)
Rates: $66-$83
(210) 366-4300
(800) 282-8733

PLAZA SAN ANTONIO HOTEL
555 S Alamo St (78205)
Rates: $244-$500
(210) 229-1000
(800) 421-1172
(800) 727-3239

QUALITY INN & SUITES
222 South W W White Rd (78219)
Rates: $79-$99
(210) 359-7200
(800) 228-5151

QUALITY INN NW MEDICAL CENTER
6023 I-10 W (78201)
Rates: $49-$94
(210) 736-1900
(800) 228-5151

RADFORD INN
13575 I-10 W (78201)
Rates: n/a
(210) 690-5500

RAMADA LIMITED EAST
3939 E Houston St (78220)
Rates: $37-$99
(210) 359-1111
(800) 272-6232

RED ROOF INN
6880 NW Loop 410 (78238)
Rates: $43-$70
(210) 509-3434
(800) 843-7663

RED ROOF INN AIRPORT
333 Wolf Rd & US 281 (78216)
Rates: $48-$73
(210) 340-4055
(800) 843-7663

RED ROOF INN ALAMO DOWNS
6880 NW Loop 410 (78238)
Rates: $46-$66
(210) 509-3434
(800) 843-7663

RED ROOF INN DOWNTOWN
1011 E Houston St (78205)
Rates: $70-$90
(210) 229-9973
(800) 843-7663

RED ROOF INN LACKLAND
6861 Hwy 90 W (78227)
Rates: n/a
(210) 675-4120
(800) 843-7663

RELAY STATION MOTEL
5530 I-10 E (78219)
Rates: $32-$47
(210) 662-6691
(800) 735-2981

RESIDENCE INN BY MARRIOTT
1014 NE Loop 410 (78209)
Rates: $99-$139
(210) 805-8118
(800) 331-3131

RESIDENCE INN BY MARRIOTT
628 S Santa Rosa Blvd (78204)
Rates: $89-$219
(210) 231-6000
(800) 331-3131

RESIDENCE INN BY MARRIOTT
425 Bonham St (78205)
Rates: n/a
(210) 212-5555
(800) 331-3131

RODEWAY INN
900 N Main Ave (78212)
Rates: $44-$120
(210) 223-2951
(800) 228-2000

RODEWAY INN CROSSROADS
6804 NW Expwy (78201)
Rates: $40-$65
(210) 734-7111
(800) 228-2000

RODEWAY INN SIX FLAGS
19793 I-10 W (78257)
Rates: $58-$99
(210) 698-3991
(800) 228-2000

RUBY INN MOTEL
9903 I-35 N (78233)
Rates: $39-$50
(210) 650-0087

ST. ANTHONY HOTEL
300 E Travis St (78205)
Rates: $125-$190
(210) 227-4392
(800) 338-1338

7 OAKS RESORT
1400 Austin Hwy (78209)
Rates: $50-$65
(210) 824-5371
(800) 346-5866

SLEEP INN NW MEDICAL CENTER
8318 I-10 W (78230)
Rates: $45-$95
(210) 344-5400
(800) 753-3746

STAYBRIDGE SUITES BY HOLIDAY INN NW COLONNADE
4320 Spectrum One (78230)
Rates: n/a
(210) 558-9009
(800) 238-8000

SUPER 8 MOTEL
11027 I-35 N (78233)
Rates: $35-$85
(210) 637-1033
(800) 800-8000

SUPER 8 MOTEL
5336 Wurzbach Rd (78238)
Rates: $41-$62
(210) 520-0888
(800) 800-8000

SUPER 8 MOTEL DOWNTOWN
3617 N Pan Am
Expwy (78219)
Rates: $42-$88
(210) 227-8888
(800) 800-8000

SUPER 8 MOTEL FIESTA TEXAS
5319 Casa Bella
(78249)
Rates: $54-$94
(210) 696-6916
(800) 800-8000

THRIFTY INN -NW
9806 I-10 W (78230)
Rates: $41-$80
(210) 696-0810

WOODFIELD SUITES
100 W Durango
Blvd (78204)
Rates: $109-$169
(800) 338-0008

SAN AUGUSTINE

SAN AUGUSTINE INN
1009 Hwy 21 W
(75972)
Rates: $32-$40
(409) 275-3452

SAN BENITO

DAYS INN
1451 W Expwy 83
& 77 (78586)
Rates: $40-$85
(956) 399-3891
(800) 329-7466

VIEH'S B&B
Rt 4, Box 75A
(78586)
Rates: $65+
(956) 425-4651

SAN MARCOS

AMERIHOST INN
4210 I-35 S (78666)
Rates: $67-$77
(512) 392-6800
(800) 434-5800

DAYS INN
1005 I-35 N
(78666)
Rates: $40-$95
(512) 353-5050
(800) 329-7466

EXECUTIVE HOUSE HOTEL
1433 I-35 N
(78666)
Rates: $30-$65
(512) 353-7770

HOWARD JOHNSON EXPRESS INN
1635 Aquarena
Spgs Dr (78666)
Rates: $39-$65
(512) 353-8011
(800) 446-4656

LA QUINTA INN
1619 I-35 N
(78666)
Rates: $69-$99
(512) 392-8800
(800) 687-6667

LONESOME DOVE BED & BREAKFAST
407 Oakwood
Loop (78666)
Rates: $65-$85
(512) 392-2921

MOTEL 6
1321 I-35 N
(78666)
Rates: $33-$44
(512) 396-8705
(800) 466-8356

RAMADA LIMITED
1701 IH-35 North
(78667)
Rates: $39-$125
(512) 395-8000
(800) 272-6232

RODEWAY INN
801 I-35 N (78666)
Rates: $35-$115
(512) 353-1303
(800) 228-2000

STRATFORD INN
1601 I-35 N
(78666)
Rates: $39-$79
(512) 396-3700

SUPER 8 MOTEL
1429 I-35 N
(78666)
Rates: $40-$55
(512) 396-0400
(800) 800-8000

SANDERSON

DESERT AIR MOTEL
P. O. Box 326
(79848)
Rates: $30-$39
(915) 345-2572

SCHULENBURG

OAKRIDGE MOTOR INN
P. O. Box 43 (78956)
Rates: $42-$64
(409) 743-4192

SEALY

RODEWAY INN
2021 Meyers St
(77474)
Rates: $35-$54
(409) 885-7407
(800) 228-2000

SEGOVIA

BEST WESTERN RIVER VALLEY INN
HC 10, Box 138
(76849)
Rates: $50-$79
(915) 446-3331
(800) 528-1234

SEGUIN

BEST WESTERN INN
1603 I-10, Hwy 46
(78155)
Rates: $69-$99
(830) 379-9631
(800) 528-1234

HOLIDAY INN
2950 N Hwy 123
Bypass (78155)
Rates: $78-$92
(830) 372-0860
(800) 465-4329

SUPER 8 MOTEL
1525 N Hwy 46
(78155)
Rates: $50-$65
(830) 379-6888
(800) 800-8000

SEMINOLE

RAYMOND MOTOR INN
301 W Ave A
(79360)
Rates: $37-$45
(915) 758-3653

SEMINOLE INN
2200 Hobbs Hwy
(79360)
Rates: $40-$45
(915) 758-9881
(800) 658-9985

SEYMOUR

SAGAMAR INN
1101 N Main St
(76380)
Rates: $40-$65
(940) 888-5507

SHAMROCK

BEST WESTERN IRISH INN
301 I-40 E (79079)
Rates: $49-$75
(806) 256-2106
(800) 528-1234
(800) 538-6747

BUDGET HOST BLARNEY INN
402 E 12th St
(79079)
Rates: $23-$45
(806) 956-2101
(800) 283-4678

ECONO LODGE
1006 E 12th St
(79079)
Rates: $35-$65
(806) 256-2111
(800) 553-2666

THE WESTERN MOTEL
104 E 12th St
(79079)
Rates: $35-$55
(806) 256-3244

SHERMAN

CROSSROADS INN
2424 Texoma
Pkwy (75090)
Rates: $26+
(903) 893-0184

DAYS INN
1831 Texoma
Pkwy (75090)
Rates: $45-$66
(903) 892-0433
(800) 329-7466

ECONOMY INN
1530 Texoma
Pkwy (75090)
Rates: $30-$35
(903) 893-7666
(800) 826-0778

GRAYSON HOUSE INN
2105 Texoma
Pkwy (75090)
Rates: $49-$77
(903) 892-2161
(800) 723-4194

HOLIDAY INN
3605 Hwy 75 S
(75090)
Rates: $56-$69
(903) 868-0555
(800) 465-4329

LA QUINTA INN
2912 Hwy 75 N
(75090)
Rates: $69-$89
(903) 870-1122
(800) 687-6667

SHERWOOD INN
401 S Sam
Rayburn Frwy
(75090)
Rates: $38
(903) 893-6581

SUPER 8 MOTEL
111 E Hwy 1417
(75090)
Rates: $40-$50
(903) 868-9325
(800) 800-8000

SINTON

BEST WESTERN INN
8108 Hwy 77
(78387)
Rates: $60-$65
(361) 364-2882
(800) 528-1234

SMITHVILLE

THE KATY HOUSE BED & BREAKFAST
201 Ramona St
(78957)
Rates: $65-$85
(512) 237-4262
(800) 843-5289

AREA CODES - If the local number doesn't connect, check for a new area code.

SNYDER

BEACON LODGE
1900 E Hwy 80
(79549)
Rates: $39-$47
(915) 573-8526

BEST WESTERN INN
Hwy 84 & 180
(79550)
Rates: $47-$67
(800) 528-1234

DAYS INN
800 E Coliseum Dr
(79549)
Rates: $40-$75
(915) 573-1166
(800) 329-7466

WILLOW PARK INN
1137 E Hwy 180
& 84 (79549)
Rates: $45-$75
(915) 573-1961
(800) 854-6818

SONORA

DAYS INN
1312 N Service Rd
(76950)
Rates: $40-$60
(915) 387-3516
(800) 329-7466

HOLIDAY HOST MOTEL
Hwy 290 E (76950)
Rates: $31-$39
(915) 387-2532

TWIN OAKS MOTEL
907 N Crockett
Ave (76950)
Rates: $35-$52
(915) 387-2551

SOUTH PADRE ISLAND

BAHIA MAR RESORT
6300 Padre Blvd
(78597)
Rates: $165-$170
(956) 761-1343

BEST WESTERN FIESTA ISLES
5701 Padre Blvd
(78597)
Rates: $99-$249
(956) 761-4913
(800) 528-1234

CASTAWAYS
3700 Gulf Blvd
(78597)
Rates: $95+
(956) 761-1903

CONTINENTAL CONDOMINIUMS
4908 Gulf Blvd
(78597)
Rates: $84+
(956) 761-1306

DAYS INN
3913 Padre Blvd
(78597)
Rates: $59-$189
(956) 761-7831
(800) 329-7466

ECONO LODGE
Padre Blvd (78597)
Rates: $35-$189
(800) 553-2666

LA INTERNATIONAL
5008 Gulf Blvd
(78597)
Rates: $75+
(956) 761-1306

MOTEL 6
4013 Padre Blvd
(78597)
Rates: $37-$60
(956) 761-7911
(800) 466-8356

PALMS RESORT
3616 Gulf Blvd
(78597)
Rates: $44+
(956) 761-1316

RADISSON RESORT
500 Padre Blvd
(78597)
Rates: $89-$330
(956) 761-6511
(800) 333-3333

RAMADA LIMITED
3109 Padre Blvd S
(78597)
Rates: $65-$200
(956) 761-4097
(800) 272-6232

SAND CASTLE MOTEL
200 W Kingfish
(78597)
Rates: $46-$64
(956) 761-1321

THE TIKI APARTMENT HOTEL
6608 Padre Blvd
(78597)
Rates: $115-$235
(956) 761-2694

SPRING

MOTEL 6
19606
Cypresswood Ct
(77388)
Rates: $37-$46
(281) 350-6400
(800) 466-8356

STAFFORD

BEST WESTERN FORT BEND INN & SUITES
11206 W Airport
Blvd (77477)
Rates: $59-$69
(281) 575-6060
(800) 528-1234

HOMESTEAD VILLAGE GUEST STUDIOS
12827 Southwest
Frwy (77477)
Rates: $29-$74
(888) 782-9473

LA QUINTA INN
12727 Southwest
Frwy (77477)
Rates: $65-$9
(281) 240-2300
(800) 687-6667

MICROTEL INN
4630 Techniplex
Dr (77477)
Rates: $46-$58
(281) 240-8100
(888) 771-7171

RESIDENCE INN BY MARRIOTT
12703 Southwest
Frwy (77477)
Rates: n/a
(800) 331-3131

WELLESLEY INN & SUITES
4726 Sugar Grove
Blvd (77477)
Rates: $69-$99
(888) 444-8888

STEPHENVILLE

BEST WESTERN CROSS TIMBERS
1625 S Loop (76401)
Rates: $50-$70
(254) 968-2114
(800) 528-1234

COMFORT INN
2925 W Wash-ington
(76401)
Rates: $50-$70
(254) 965-7162
(800) 228-5150

HOLIDAY INN
2865 W
Washington (76401)
Rates: $62-$98
(254) 968-5256
(800) 465-4329

TEXAN INN
3030 W
Washington (76401)
Rates: $36-$46
(254) 968-5003

SUGAR LAND

DRURY INN & SUITES
13770 SW Frwy
(77478)
Rates: $67-$87
(281) 277-9700
(800) 378-7946

SHONEY'S INN & SUITES
14444 SW Frwy
(77478)
Rates: $56-$63
(281) 565-6655
(800) 222-2222

SULPHUR SPRINGS

BEST WESTERN TRAIL DUST INN
1521 Shannon Rd
(75482)
Rates: $54-$99
(903) 885-7515
(800) 528-1234
(800) 980-2378

COMFORT SUITES
1521 E Industrial
(75483)
Rates: $59-$84
(903) 438-0918
(800) 228-5150

HOLIDAY INN
1495 E Industrial
(75482)
Rates: $59-$69
(903) 885-0562
(800) 465-4329

SURFSIDE BEACH

ANCHOR MOTEL
1302 Bluewater
Hwy (77541)
Rates: $35-$55
(409) 239-3543

SWEETWATER

MOTEL 6
510 NW Georgia
St (79556)
Rates: $31-$36
(915) 235-4387
(800) 466-8356

MULBERRY MANSION B&B
1400 Sam Houston
(79556)
Rates: $65-$225
(915) 235-3811
(800) 235-3911

RAMADA INN SUNDAY HOUSE
701 SW Georgia
St (79556)
Rates: $46-$56
(915) 235-4853
(800) 272-6232

RANCH HOUSE MOTEL
301 SW Georgia St
(79556)
Rates: $37-$57
(915) 236-6341
(800) 622-5361

TAYLOR

REGENCY INN
2007 N Main
(76574)
Rates: $40-$49
(512) 352-2666

AREA CODES - If the local number doesn't connect, check for a new area code.

TEMPLE

BEST WESTERN INN AT SCOTT & WHITE
2625 S 31st St (765604)
Rates: $56-$72
(254) 778-5511
(800) 528-1234
(800) 749-0318

DAYS INN
I-35 Ex Nugent (76504)
Rates: $39-$59
(254) 774-9223
(800) 329-7466

ECONO LODGE
1001 N General Bruce Dr (76504)
Rates: $35-$72
(254) 771-1688
(800) 553-2666

HOWARD JOHNSON EXPRESS INN
1912 S 31st St (76504)
Rates: $30-$55
(254) 778-5521
(800) 446-4656

LA QUINTA INN
1604 W Barton Ave (76504)
Rates: $65-$85
(254) 771-2980
(800) 687-6667

MOTEL 6
1100 N General Bruce Dr (76504)
Rates: $34-$50
(254) 778-0272
(800) 466-8356

RAMADA INN
802 N General Bruce Dr (76504)
Rates: $44-$54
(254) 778-4411
(800) 272-6232

STRATFORD HOUSE INN
1602 N General Bruce Dr (76502)
Rates: $43-$58
(254) 771-1495

SUPER 8 MOTEL
5505 S General Bruce Dr (76502)
Rates: $39-$53
(254) 778-0962
(800) 800-8000

TERLINGUA

BIG BEND MOTOR INN
Hwy 118 & 170 (79852)
Rates: $65-$77
(915) 371-2218
(800) 848-2363

CHISOS MINING COMPANY MOTEL
Box 228, Hwy 170 (79852)
Rates: $31-$49
(915) 371-2254

LAJITAS ON THE RIO GRANDE
Star Rt 70, Box 400 (79852)
Rates: $48-$65
(915) 424-3471

TERRELL

BEST WESTERN LA PIEDRA INN
309 I-20 E (75160)
Rates: $45-$65
(972) 563-2676
(800) 528-1234

MOTEL 6
101 Mira Place (75160)
Rates: $37-$44
(972) 524-6066
(800) 466-8356

SUPER 8 MOTEL
1705 Hwy 34 S (75160)
Rates: $50-$65
(972) 563-1511
(800) 800-8000

TEXARKANA

BAYMONT INN & SUITES
5102 N State Line Ave (71854)
Rates: $42-$89
(800) 301-0200

BEST WESTERN NORTHGATE MOTOR LODGE
400 W 53rd St (75502)
Rates: $46-$55
(903) 793-6565
(800) 528-1234
(800) 262-0048 (TX)

COMFORT INN
5105 State Line Ave (75501)
Rates: $41-$51
(903) 792-6688
(800) 228-5150

FOUR POINTS HOTEL SHERATON
5301 N State Line Ave (75503)
Rates: n/a
(903) 792-3222
(800) 325-3535

HOLIDAY INN EXPRESS
5401 N State Line Ave (75503)
Rates: $69
(903) 792-3366
(800) 465-4329

HOUSE OF WADLEY
618 Pecan (71854)
Rates: $99-$129
(870) 773-7093

LA QUINTA INN
5201 N State Line Ave (75503)
Rates: $59-$79
(903) 794-1900
(800) 687-6667

MOTEL 6-EAST
900 Realtor Ave (75502)
Rates: $27-$34
(501) 772-0678
(800) 466-8356

MOTEL 6-WEST
1924 Hampton Rd (75503)
Rates: $31-$41
(903) 793-1413
(800) 466-8356

RAMADA INN
I-30 at Summerhill Rd (75501)
Rates: $40-$56
(903) 794-3131
(800) 272-6232

TEXAS CITY

LA QUINTA INN
1121 Hwy 146 N (77590)
Rates: $49-$79
(409) 948-3101
(800) 687-6667

THE COLONY

COMFORT SUITES
4796 Memorial Dr (75056)
Rates: $69-$160
(972) 668-5555
(800) 228-5150

THE WOODLANDS

DRURY INN & SUITES
28099 I-45 N (77381)
Rates: $69-$89
(281) 362-7222
(800) 378-7946

LA QUINTA INN
28673 I-45 N (77381)
Rates: $65-$85
(281) 367-7722
(800) 687-6667

RED ROOF INN
24903 I-45 N (77380)
Rates: $45-$60
(281) 367-5040
(800) 843-7663

RESIDENCE INN BY MARRIOTT
1040 Lake Front Cr (77380)
Rates: $116
(281) 292-3252
(800) 331-3131

THREE RIVERS

NOLAN RYAN'S BASS INN
Hwy 72 W (78071)
Rates: $37-$99
(361) 786-3521
(800) 803-3340

TYLER

BEST WESTERN INN & SUITES
2828 W NW Loop 323 (75702)
Rates: $49-$84
(903) 595-2681
(800) 528-1234
(800) 298-9537

DAYS INN
3300 Mineola Hwy (75702)
Rates: $45-$125
(903) 595-2451
(800) 329-7466

DAYS INN
12732 Hwy 155 N (75708)
Rates: $38-$65
(903) 877-9227
(800) 329-7466

ECONO LODGE
2739 WMW Loop 323 (75702)
Rates: $39-$69
(903) 531-9513
(800) 553-2666

HOLIDAY INN SOUTHEAST CROSSING
3310 Troup Hwy (75701)
Rates: $79
(903) 593-3600
(800) 465-4329

LA QUINTA INN
1601 W SW Loop 323 (75701)
Rates: $62-$99
(903) 561-2223
(800) 687-6667

MOTEL 6
3236 Gentry Pkwy (75702)
Rates: $30-$38
(903) 595-6691
(800) 466-8356

RAMADA INN
2701 WNW Loop 323 (75702)
Rates: $44-$60
(903) 593-7391
(800) 272-6232

AREA CODES - If the local number doesn't connect, check for a new area code.

RESIDENCE INN BY MARRIOTT
3303 Troup Hwy (75701)
Rates: $72-$125
(903) 595-5188
(800) 331-3131

SHERATON TYLER HOTEL
5701 S Broadway (75702)
Rates: $87-$99
(903) 561-5800
(800) 325-3535

STRATFORD HOUSE INN MOTEL
2600 W NW Loop 323 (75702)
Rates: $31-$35
(903) 597-2756

SUPER 8 MOTEL
2616 N NW Loop 323 (75702)
Rates: $46-$69
(903) 593-8361
(800) 800-8000

UNCERTAIN

MOSSY BRAKE LODGE B&B
151 Mossy Brake Dr S (75661)
Rates: $65
(903) 789-3440
(800) 607-6002

SPATTERDOCK GUEST HOUSE
Rt 2, Box 66-B (75661)
Rates: $100
(903) 789-3268

UVALDE

BEST WESTERN CONTINENTAL INN
701 E Main St (78801)
Rates: $45-$85
(830) 278-5671
(800) 528-1234

FRIDAY RANCH
P O Box 1 (78802)
Rates: $110-$225
(830) 597-2257
(Working ranch)

HOLIDAY INN
920 E Main St (78801)
Rates: $60-$75
(830) 278-4511
(800) 465-4329

VAN HORN

BEST WESTERN AMERICAN INN
1309 W Broadway (79855)
Rates: $42-$70
(915) 283-2030
(800) 528-1234
(800) 621-2478

BEST WESTERN INN VAN HORN
1705 W Broadway (79855)
Rates: $39-$89
(915) 283-2410
(800) 528-1234
(800) 367-7589 (TX)

COMFORT INN
1601 W Broadway (79855)
Rates: $45-$79
(915) 283-2211
(800) 228-5150

DAYS INN
600 E Broadway St (79855)
Rates: $40-$60
(915) 283-2401
(800) 329-7466

ECONOMY INN
1500 W Broadway St (79855)
Rates: $25-$38
(915) 283-2754
(800) 826-0778

FREEWAY INN MOTEL
505 Van Horn Dr (79855)
Rates: $21-$29
(915) 283-2939

HOLIDAY INN EXPRESS
1905 SW Frontage Rd (79855)
Rates: $54-$64
(915) 283-7444
(800) 465-4329

MOTEL 6
1805 Broadway (79855)
Rates: $35-$42
(915) 283-2992
(800) 466-8356

RAMADA LIMITED
200 Golf Course Dr (79855)
Rates: $48-$88
(915) 283-2780
(800) 272-6232

SUPER 8 MOTEL
1807 E Service Rd (79855)
Rates: $38-$52
(915) 283-2282
(800) 800-8000

VEGA

BEST WESTERN COUNTRY INN
1800 Vega Blvd (79092)
Rates: $49-$69
(806) 267-2131
(800) 528-1234

VERNON

BEST WESTERN VILLAGE INN
1615 Expressway (76384)
Rates: $46-$59
(940) 552-5417
(800) 528-1234
(800) 600-5417 (TX)

DAYS INN
3110 Frontage Rd (76384)
Rates: $38-$55
(940) 552-9982
(800) 329-7466

ECONO LODGE
4100 Hwy 287 NW (76384)
Rates: $30-$69
(940) 553-3384
(800) 553-2666

GREENTREE INN
3029 Morton (76384)
Rates: $39
(940) 552-5421
(800) 600-5421

SUPER 8 MOTEL
1829 Exp Hwy 287 (76384)
Rates: $33-$48
(940) 552-9321
(800) 800-8000

WESTERN MOTEL
715 Wilbarger St (76384)
Rates: $25-$40
(940) 552- 2531

VICTORIA

HOLIDAY INN HOLIDOME
2705 E Houston Hwy (77901)
Rates: $63-$145
(361) 575-0251
(800) 465-4329

LA QUINTA INN
7603 N Navarro St (77904)
Rates: $59-$79
(361) 572-3585
(800) 687-6667

MOTEL 6
3716 E Houston Hwy (77901)
Rates: $35-$40
(361) 573-1273
(800) 466-8356

WACO

BEST WESTERN OLD MAIN LODGE
I-35 & 4th St, Box 174 (76703)
Rates: $58-$71
(254) 753-0316
(800) 528-1234
(800) 299-9226 (TX)

BEST WESTERN WACO MALL
6624 Hwy 84 W (76712)
Rates: $56-$70
(254) 776-3194
(800) 528-1234
(800) 346-1581

DAYS INN
1504 I-35 N (76705)
Rates: $59-$89
(254) 799-8585
(800) 329-7466

ECONO LODGE
500 I-35 E (76704)
Rates: $40-$70
(254) 756-5371
(800) 553-2666

HILTON INN
113 S University Parks Dr (76701)
Rates: $79-$109
(254) 754-8484
(800) 445-8667
(800) 234-5244

HOLIDAY INN
1001 Martin Luker King Blvd (76704)
Rates: $72
(254) 753-0261
(800) 465-4329

KNIGHTS INN
1510 I-35 W (76705)
Rates: $35-$65
(254) 799-0244
(800) 843-5644

LA QUINTA INN
1110 S 9th St (76706)
Rates: $79-$99
(254) 752-9741
(800) 687-6667

MOTEL 6 PREMIER
3120 Jack Kultgen Frwy (76706)
Rates: $36-$46
(254) 662-4622
(800) 466-8356

RESIDENCE INN BY MARRIOTT
501 Univeristy Park Dr (76706)
Rates: n/a
(254) 714-1386
(800) 331-3131

WAXAHACHIE

BEST WESTERN
200 I-35 E (75165)
Rates: $52-$68
(972) 937-4202
(800) 528-1234

BONNYNOOK INN B&B
414 W Main (75165)
Rates: $75-$105
(972) 938-7207
(800) 486-5936

RAMADA LIMITED
795 S I-35 E (75165)
Rates: $34-$149
(972) 937-4982
(800) 272-6232

WEATHERFORD

**BEST WESTERN
SANTA FE INN**
1927 Santa Fe Dr
(76086)
Rates: $54-$69
(817) 594-7401
(800) 528-1234
(800) 229-3400

COMFORT INN
809 Palo Pinto St
(76086)
Rates: $50-$95
(817) 599-8683
(800) 228-5150

SUPER 8 MOTEL
111 I-20 W (76087)
Rates: $37-$48
(817) 594-8702
(800) 800-8000

WEBSTER

MOTEL 6
1001 W NASA Rd
One (77598)
Rates: $40-$55
(281) 332-4581
(800) 466-8356

**WELLESLEY INN
& SUITES**
720 W Bay Area
Blvd (77598)
Rates: $99-$129
(281) 338-7711
(888) 444-8888

WELLINGTON

**CHEROKEE INN
& RESTAURANT**
1105 Houston
(79095)
Rates: $28-$27
(806) 447-2508

WESLACO

**BEST WESTERN
PALM AIRE
MOTOR INN
& SUITES**
415 S Int'l Blvd
(78596)
Rates: $51-$111
(956) 969-2411
(800) 528-1234
(800) 248-6511

**HOLIDAY INN
EXPRESS**
1702 E Expwy 83
(78596)
Rates: $89-$110
(956) 969-9920
(800) 465-4329

WEST
COLUMBIA

**COUNTRY
HEARTH INN**
714 Columbia Dr
(77486)
Rates: $50-$62
(409) 345-2399
(888) 325-7819

WESTLAKE

**MARRIOTT
SOLANA
DALLAS/FW**
5 Village Cir
(76262)
Rates: $79-$179
(817) 430-3848
(800) 228-9290

WHARTON

**COUNTRY
HEARTH INN**
1808 FM 102
(77488)
Rates: $45-$57
(409) 532-1152
(888) 325-7820

WICHITA FALLS

**BEST WESTERN
TOWNE CREST INN**
1601 8th St (76301)
Rates: $37-$44
(940) 322-1182
(800) 528-1234

COMFORT INN
1750 Maurine St
(76304)
Rates: $57-$75
(940) 322-2477
(800) 228-5150

DAYS INN
1211 Central
Expwy (76305)
Rates: $33-$48
(940) 723-5541
(800) 329-7466

ECONO LODGE
1700 Fifth St
(76301)
Rates: $55-$70
(940) 761-1889
(800) 553-2666

LA QUINTA INN
1128 Central Frwy
(76305)
Rates: $45-$79
(940) 322-6971
(800) 687-6667

MOTEL 6
1812 Maurine St
(76304)
Rates: $39-$46
(940) 322-8817
(800) 466-8356

**NEW
TRADEWINDS
MOTOR HOTEL**
1212 Broad St
(76301)
Rates: $30-$55
(800) 678-8885

RAMADA LIMITED
3209 Hwy 287 @
Beverly Dr Exit
(76305)
Rates: $55-$64
(940) 855-0085
(800) 272-6232

RED ROOF INN
1032 Central Frwy
(76305)
Rates: n/a
(940) 766-6881
(800) 843-7663

SHERATON INN
100 Central Frwy
(76305)
Rates: $59-$72
(940) 761-6000
(800) 325-3535

WIMBERLEY

**HILL COUNTRY
ACCOMMODA-
TIONS**
14015 Ranch Rd
12 (78676)
Rates: $75-$650
(800) 926-5028

**HOMESTEAD
COTTAGES
BED & BREAKFAST**
RR 2 at Scudder
Ln (78676)
Rates: $85-$99
(512) 847-8788
(800) 918-8788

**LONESOME DOVE
RIVER INN AT
CLIFFSIDE B&B**
600 River Rd
(78676)
Rates: $85+
(800) 690-3683

**7A RANCH
RESORT**
333 Wayside Dr
(78676)
Rates: $50-$86
(512) 847-2517

**SINGING CYPRESS
GARDENS**
P O Box 824
(78676)
Rates: $75-$150
(800) 827-1913

**SOUTHWIND B&B
INN AND CABINS**
2701 FM 3237
(78676)
Rates: $75-$90
(800) 508-5277

WINNIE

**BEST WESTERN
GULF COAST INN**
46318 I-10 East
(77665)
Rates: $47-$62
(409) 296-9292
(800) 528-1234

WINNSBORO

**THEE HUBBELL
HOUSE
BED & BREAKFAST**
307 West Elm
(75494)
Rates: $75-$175
(800) 227-0639

WOODVILLE

WOODVILLE INN
201 N Magnolia
(75979)
Rates: $34-$42
(409) 283-3741

YOAKUM

**BUDGET HOST
LA MANCHA INN**
606 S Hwy 77A
(77995)
Rates: $40-$75
(361) 293-5211
(800) 283-4678

ZAPATA

**BASS LAKE
SUNDOME MOTEL**
Rt 1, Box 200
(78076)
Rates: $25-$49
(956) 765-4961

**BEST WESTERN
INN BY THE LAKE**
Star Rt 1, Box 252
(78076)
Rates: $54-$70
(956) 765-8403
(800) 528-1234
(800) 399-1558

**FALCON
EXECUTIVE INN**
Hwy 83 S (78076)
Rates: $40-$65
(956) 765-6982

AREA CODES - If the local number doesn't connect, check for a new area code.

UTAH

ALTAMONT

MOON LAKE RESORT
P.O. Box 70
(Mountain Home 84001)
Rates: $50-$75
(801) 454-3475

AMERICAN FORK

AMERICAN FORK BED & BREAKFAST
1021 N 150 W
(84003)
Rates: $49-$75
(801) 756-9459

QUALITY INN & SUITES
712 S Utah Valley Dr (84003)
Rates: $54-$129
(801) 763-8383
(800) 228-5151

BEAVER

BEAVER LODGE
355 Main St,
Box 406 (84713)
Rates: n/a
(435) 438-2462

BEST WESTERN BUTCH CASSIDY INN
161 S Main St
(84713)
Rates: $59-$69
(435) 438-2438
(800) 528-1234

BEST WESTERN PARADISE INN
1451 N 300 (84713)
Rates: $53-$78
(435) 438-2455
(800) 528-1234

COUNTRY INN
1450 N 300 W
(84713)
Rates: $40-$49
(435) 438-2484
(800) 754-2484

DELANO MOTEL
480 N Main St
(84713)
Rates: $39-$49
(435) 438-2418
(800) 537-2165

GRANADA INN
75 S Main St
(84713)
Rates: $40-$49
(435) 438-2292

QUALITY INN
1540 S 450 W
(84713)
Rates: $45-$64
(435) 438-5426
(800) 228-5151

STAG MOTEL
370 N Main St
(84713)
Rates: $39-$49
(435) 438-2411

BICKNELL

AQUARIUS MOTEL
240 W Main St
(84715)
Rates: $30-$48
(435) 425-3835
(800) 833-5379

SUNGLOW MOTEL
63 E Main St
(84715)
Rates: $27-$37
(435) 425-3821

BIG WATER

CLIFF PALACE MOTEL
132 S Main (84741)
Rates: $50-$75
(435) 678-2264
(800) 553-8093

HIGHWAY HOST MOTEL
Hwy 89, Box 4
(84741)
Rates: $50-$75
(435) 675-3731
(800) 748-5034

WARM CREEK MOTEL
Hwy 89, Box 410004 (84741)
Rates: $50-$75
(435) 675-9199
(800) 748-5065

BLANDING

BEST WESTERN GATEWAY INN
88 E Center St
(84511)
Rates: $36-$75
(435) 678-2278
(800) 528-1234

FOUR CORNERS INN
131 E Center St
(84511)
Rates: $50-$60
(435) 678-3257
(800) 574-3150

SUNSET INN
88 W Center St
(84512)
Rates: $40-$49
(435) 678-3323

BLUFF

KOKOPELLI INN
Hwy 191 (84512)
Rates: $50-$75
(435) 672-2322
(800) 541-8854

RECAPTURE LODGE
220 E Main St
(84512)
Rates: $44-$75
(435) 672-2281

BOULDER

BOULDER MOUNTAIN LODGE
20 N Hwy 12
(84716)
Rates: $79-$150
(435) 335-7460
(800) 556-3446

BOULDER MOUNTAIN RANCH
Hell's Backbone Rd Box 1373
(84716)
Rates: $50-$75
(435) 335-7480

CIRCLE CLIFFS MOTEL
95 N Hwy 12
(84716)
Rates: $40-$49
(435) 335-7353

BRIAN HEAD

BRIAN HEAD CONDO RESERVATIONS
385 S Hwy 143
(84719)
Rates: $75+
(435) 677-2045
(800) 722-4742

LODGE AT BRIAN HEAD
314 Hunter Ridge Rd (84719)
Rates: $65-$250
(435) 677-3222
(800) 386-5634

BRIGHAM CITY

BUSHNELL LODGE
115 E 700 S (84302)
Rates: $50-$75
(435) 723-8575
(800) 586-2605

CRYSTAL INN
480 Westland Dr
(84302)
Rates: $75-$150
(435) 723-0440
(800) 408-0440

HOWARD JOHNSON
1167 S Main St
(84302)
Rates: $48-$58
(435) 723-8511
(800) 446-4656

BRYCE CANYON NATIONAL PARK

BEST WESTERN RUBY'S INN
Hwy 63 (84764)
Rates: $90-$120
(435) 834-5341
(800) 528-1234
(800) 468-8660

BRYCE COUNTRY CABINS
320 N Main St
(Tropic 84776)
Rates: $50-$75
(435) 679-8643
(888) 679-8643

BRYCE CANYON RESORTS
13500 E Hwy 12
(84717)
Rates: $65-$75
(435) 834-5351
(800) 834-0043

BRYCE JUNCTION INN
3068 E Hwy 12
(84764)
Rates: $39-$70
(435) 676-2221

BRYCE PIONEER VILLAGE
80 S Main
(Tropic 84776)
Rates: $50-$125
(435) 679-8654
(800) 222-0381

BRYCE VIEW LODGE
UT Hwy 63
(84764)
Rates: $55-$65
(435) 834-5180

HAROLDS PLACE CABINS
3066 Hwy 12
(84764)
Rates: $60
(435) 676-2350

WORLD HOST BRYCE VALLEY INN
199 N Main St
(Tropic 84776)
Rates: $47-$89
(435) 679-8811

CANNONDALE

GALLOPING TORTOISE B&B
250 N Hwy 12
(84718)
Rates: $50-$75
(435) 679-8664

CANNONVILLE

GRAND STAIRCASE INN
105 N
Kodachrome Dr
(84718)
Rates: $55-$79
(435) 679-8400

CASTLE DALE

VILLAGE INN MOTEL
375 E Main St
(84513)
Rates: $40-$49
(435) 381-2309

CEDAR BREAKS NATIONAL MONUMENT

ASPEN WHISPERING PINES LODGE
P. O. Box 1001
(84762)
Rates: $85-$135
(801) 682-2378

CEDAR CITY

ASTRO BUDGET INN
323 S Main St
(84720)
Rates: $49-$75
(435) 586-6557

CEDAR REST MOTEL
479 S Main St
(84720)
Rates: $30-$55
(435) 586-9471

COMFORT INN
250 N 1100 W
(84720)
Rates: $64-$92
(435) 586-2082
(800) 228-5150

DAYS INN
1204 S Main St
(84720)
Rates: $55-$89
(435) 867-8877
(800) 329-7466

ECONOMY MOTEL
443 S Main St
(84720)
Rates: $21-$42
(435) 586-4461

HOLIDAY INN & CONVENTION CENTER
1575 W 200 N
(84720)
Rates: $75-$125
(435) 586-8888
(800) 465-4329

MOTEL 6
1620 W 200 N
(84720)
Rates: $40-$54
(435) 586-9200
(800) 466-8356

QUALITY INN DOWNTOWN
18 S Main St
(84720)
Rates: $44-$99
(435) 586-2433
(800) 228-5151

RODEWAY INN
281 S Main St
(84720)
Rates: $62-$76
(435) 586-9916
(800) 228-2000

SUPER 8 MOTEL
145 N 1550 W
(84720)
Rates: $50-$57
(435) 586-8880
(800) 800-8000

TRAVELODGE
2555 N Main St
(84720)
Rates: $52-$85
(435) 586-7435
(800) 578-7878

VALU INN
344 S Main St
(84720)
Rates: $25-$55
(435) 586-9114

CENTRAL

DIXIE DEER LODGE
148 E Center Rd
(84722)
Rates: $39-$49
(435) 574-2650

CIRCLEVILLE

THE BUNKHOUSE
400 S 303 W, Box 85 (84723)
Rates: $40-$75
(435) 577-2522

BUTCH CASSIDY'S HIDEOUT MOTEL
339 S Hwy 89
(84723)
Rates: $48-$52
(435) 577-2008
(888) 577-2008

CLEARFIELD

SUPER 8 MOTEL
572 N Main
(84015)
Rates: $40-$65
(801) 825-8000
(800) 800-8000

COALVILLE

A COUNTRY PLACE
99 S Main (84017)
Rates: $40-$75
(435) 336-2451
(800) 371-2451

DELTA

BEST WESTERN MOTOR INN
527 E Topaz Blvd
(84624)
Rates: $42-$68
(435) 864-3882
(800) 528-1234
(800) 354-9378

BUDGET MOTEL
75 South 350 E
(84624)
Rates: $25-$45
(435) 864-4533

DIAMOND "D" MOTOR LODGE
234 W Main
(84624)
Rates: $29-$49
(435) 864-2041

DRAPER

RAMADA LIMITED
12605 S Minuteman Dr (84020)
Rates: $45-$75
(801) 571-1122
(800) 272-6232

DUCHESNE

RIO DAMIAN MOTEL
23 W Main St,
Box 166 (84021)
Rates: $50-$75
(435) 738-2217

DUCK CREEK VILLAGE

DUCK CREEK VILLAGE INN
Hwy 14, Box 1149
(84762)
Rates: $50-$75
(435) 682-2565

FALCON'S NEST CABINS
60 Movie Ranch
Rd (84762)
Rates: $50-$75
(435) 682-2556
(800) 240-4930

INN AT CEDAR MOUNTAIN
116 Color Country
Rd (84762)
Rates: $79-$125
(435) 682-2378
(800) 897-4995

MEADEAU VIEW LODGE
Movie Ranch Rd
Box 1331 (84762)
Rates: $50-$75
(435) 682-2495
(800) 332-0568

PINEWOODS RESORT
125 Color Country
Rd (84762)
Rates: $79-$125
(435) 682-2512
(800) 848-2525

WHISPERING PINES LODGE
116 Color Country
Rd (84762)
Rates: $75-$150
(435) 682-2378

DUTCH JOHN

RED CANYON LODGE
790 Red Canyon
Rd (84023)
Rates: $40-$150
(435) 889-3759

ECHO

KOZY CAFE & MOTEL
24 Echo Main St
(84024)
Rates: $30-$49
(435) 336-5641

EDEN

SNOWBERRY INN BED & BREAKFAST
1315 N Hwy 158,
Box 795 (84310)
Rates: $75-$150
(801) 745-2634

EPHRAIM

IRON HORSE MOTEL
670 N Main
(84627)
Rates: $50-$125
(435) 283-4223
(800) 339-4201

ESCALANTE

CIRCLE D MOTEL
475 W Main St,
Box 305 (84726)
Rates: $40-$75
(435) 826-4297

QUIET FALLS MOTEL
75 S 100 W (84726)
Rates: $40-$49
(435) 826-4250

RAINBOW COUNTRY B&B
585 E 300 S
(84726)
Rates: $50-$75
(435) 826-4567
(800) 252-8824

FAIRVIEW

SKYLINE MOTEL
236 N State St
(84629)
Rates: $40-$49
(801) 427-3312

FILLMORE

BEST INN & SUITES
940 S Hwy 99
(84631)
Rates: $49-$75
(435) 743-4334
(800) 237-8466

BEST WESTERN PARADISE INN
1025 N Main St
(84631)
Rates: $51-$71
(435) 743-6895
(800) 528-1234

FILLMORE MOTEL
61 N Main St (84631)
Rates: $32-$43
(435) 743-5454

SPINNING WHEEL MOTEL
65 S Main St (84631)
Rates: $25-$36
(435) 743-6260

FRY CANYON

FRY CANYON LODGE
90 W Hwy 95
(84533)
Rates: $74-$89
(435) 259-5334

GARDEN CITY

BEAR LAKE MOTOR LODGE
50 S Bear Lake Blvd (84028)
Rates: $50-$75
(435) 946-3271

BLUE WATER RESORT
2126 S Bear Lake Blvd (84028)
Rates: $75-$150
(435) 946-3333

EAGLE FEATHER INN B&B
135 S Bear Lake Blvd (84028)
Rates: $50-$75
(435) 946-2846

HARBOR VILLAGE RESORT
900 N Bear Lake Blvd (84028)
Rates: $75-$300
(435) 946-3448
(800) 324-6840

GREEN RIVER

BOOK CLIFF LODGE
395 E Main
(84525)
Rates: $30-$125
(435) 564-3406

BUDGET INN MOTEL
60 E Main (84525)
Rates: $30-$75
(435) 564-3441

MANCOS ROSE MOTEL
20 W Main (84525)
Rates: $40-$49
(435) 564-9660
(800) 626-2671

MOTEL 6
946 E Main (84525)
Rates: $46-$61
(435) 564-3436
(800) 466-8356

NATIONAL 9 INN
456 W Main (84525)
Rates: $40-$49
(435) 564-8237
(800) 474-3304

OASIS MOTEL
118 W Main (84525)
Rates: $29-$49
(435) 564-3690

ROBBER'S ROOST MOTEL
225 W Main (84525)
Rates: $29-$49
(435) 564-3452

SUPER 8 MOTEL
1248 E Main (84525)
Rates: $60-$65
(435) 564-8888
(800) 800-8000

HANKSVILLE

BEST VALUE INN MOTEL
322 E 100 N
(84734)
Rates: $40-$49
(435) 542-3471

HATCH

GALAXY MOTEL
216 N Main (84735)
Rates: $49-$76
(435) 735-4327

MTN RIDGE MOTEL & RV PARK
106 S Main (84735)
Rates: $50-$75
(435) 735-4258
(800) 870-4258

NEW BRYCE MOTEL
227 W Main
(84735)
Rates: $37-$47
(435) 735-4265
(800) 370-5272

RIVERSIDE MOTEL
594 Hwy 98
(84735)
Rates: $42-$52
(435) 735-4223
(800) 824-5651

HEBER CITY

DANISH VIKING LODGE
989 S Main (84032)
Rates: $39-$250
(435) 654-2202
(800) 544-4066

HEBER VALLEY RV PARK & RESORT
7000 N Old Hwy 40 (80432)
Rates: $50-$75
(435) 654-4049

HY LANDER MOTEL
425 S Main (84032)
Rates: $30-$48
(435) 654-2150
(800) 932-0355

NATIONAL 9 HIGH COUNTRY INN
1000 S Main (84032)
Rates: n/a
(435) 654-0201

HUNTINGTON

VILLAGE INN MOTEL
307 S Main (84528)
Rates: $40-$49
(801) 687-9888

HUNTSVILLE

JACKSON FORK INN
7345 E 900 S
(84317)
Rates: $75-$150
(435) 745-0051
(800) 255-0672

HURRICANE

BEST WESTERN WESTON'S LAMPLIGHTER
280 W State
(84737)
Rates: $47-$169
(435) 635-4647
(800) 528-1234

MOTEL 6
650 W State
(84737)
Rates: $49-$89
(435) 635-4010
(800) 466-8356

PAH TEMPE HOT SPRINGS RESORT B&B
825 N 800 E
(84737)
Rates: $50-$75
(435) 635-2353

WESTONS INN
65 S 700 W (84737)
Rates: n/a
(435) 635-0808

JUNCTION

JUNCTION MOTEL
300 S Main (84740)
Rates: $40-$49
(435) 577-2629

KANAB

AIKENS LODGE-NATIONAL 9
9 W Center St
(84741)
Rates: $38-$51
(435) 644-2625
(800) 524-9999

BON-BON INN
236 Hwy 89 N
(84741)
Rates: $40-$57
(435) 644-5094

BRANDON MOTEL BED & BREAKFST
223 West Center St
(84741)
Rates: $50-$75
(435) 644-2631
(800) 839-2631

BUDGET HOST K MOTEL
300 S 100 E
(84741)
Rates: $40-$150
(435) 644-2611
(800) 283-4678

COLOR COUNTRY INN
1550 S Hwy 89A
(84741)
Rates: $50-$75
(435) 644-2164
(800) 473-2164

CORAL SANDS MOTEL
60 S 100 E (84741)
Rates: $40-$75
(435) 644-2616
(800) 654-0805

FOUR SEASONS MOTEL
36 North 300 W
(84741)
Rates: $65-$74
(435) 644-2635

HOLIDAY INN EXPRESS
815 E Hwy 89
(84741)
Rates: $80-$89
(435) 644-8888
(800) 465-4329

K MOTEL
300 S 100 E
(84741)
Rates: $37-$59
(435) 644-2611

PARRY LODGE
89 E Center St
(84741)
Rates: $48-$75
(435) 644-2601
(800) 748-4101

QUAIL PARK LODGE
125 Hwy 89 N
(84741)
Rates: $32-$52
(435) 644-5094
(800) 644-8115

SHILO INN
296 W 100 N
(84741)
Rates: $49-$149
(435) 644-2562
(800) 222-2244

SUN-N-SAND MOTEL
347 S 100 E
(84741)
Rates: $34-$75
(435) 644-5050
(800) 654-1868

TREASURE TRAIL MOTEL
150 W Center St
(84741)
Rates: $40-$58
(435) 644-2687
(800) 603-2687

KOOSHAREM

GRASS VALLEY GUEST RANCH MOTEL & CAFE
138 N Main St
(84744)
Rates: $40-$49
(435) 638-7322

LAKE POWELL

CITY CENTER MOTEL
Hwy 276 (84533)
Rates: $89-$149
(435) 684-7000

HALLS CROSSING FAMILY UNITS
Halls Crossing
Marina (84533)
Rates: $76-$125
(435) 684-7000
(800) 528-6154

HITE MARINA FAMILY UNITS
Hite Marina
(84533)
Rates: $76-$125
(435) 684-2278
(800) 528-6154

LAYTON

HAMPTON INN
1702 N Woodland
Park Dr (84041)
Rates: $79-$89
(801) 775-8800
(800) 426-7866

HOLIDAY INN EXPRESS
1695 Woodland
Park Dr (84041)
Rates: $75-$105
(801) 773-3773
(800) 465-4329

LA QUINTA INN
1965 N 1200 West
(84041)
Rates: $65-$125
(801) 776-6700
(800) 687-6667

TOWN PLACE SUITES
1743 Woodland
Park Blvd (84041)
Rates: n/a
(801) 779-2422

VALLEY VIEW MOTEL
1560 N Main St
(84041)
Rates: $40-$49
(801) 825-1632

LEHI

BEST WESTERN TIMPANOGOS INN
195 S 850 E (84043)
Rates: $63-$125
(801) 768-1400
(800) 528-1234

MOTEL 6
210 S 1200 E (84043)
Rates: $42-$48
(801) 768-2668
(800) 466-8356

SUPER 8 MOTEL
125 S 850 E (84043)
Rates: $60-$79
(801) 768-8800
(800) 800-8000

LOGAN

BEST WESTERN WESTON INN
250 N Main
(84321)
Rates: $49-$109
(435) 752-5700
(800) 528-1234
(800) 532-5055

DAYS INN
364 S Main (84321)
Rates: $36-$62
(435) 753-5623
(800) 329-7466

MANILA

NIKI'S INN
Hwy 43 (84046)
Rates: $35-$47
(435) 784-3117

VACATION INN
Hwy 43 (84046)
Rates: $43-$59
(435) 784-3259
(800) 662-4327

MANTI

MANTI COUNTRY VILLAGE
145 N Main St
(84642)
Rates: $37-$48
(435) 835-9300
(800) 452-0787

MANTI MOTEL
445 N Main St
(84642)
Rates: $50-$75
(435) 835-8533

MARYSVALE

BIG ROCK CANDY MOUNTAIN RESORT
Hwy 89 Sevier
River Cyn (84750)
Rates: $39-$89
(435) 326-2000
(888) 560-7625

LIZZY & CHARLIE'S RV PARK CABINS
300 E Rio Grande
Ave (84750)
Rates: $29-$49
(435) 326-4213

MARYSVALE MINERS LODGE
315 N Main St
(84750)
Rates: $40-$75
(435) 326-4258

MEXICAN HAT

BURCH'S TRADING CO. & MOTEL
Main St (84531)
Rates: $50-$125
(8435) 683-2221

SAN JUAN INN
Hwy 163 & San
Juan River (84531)
Rates: $68-$70
(435) 683-2220
(800) 447-2022

VALLEY OF THE GODS B&B
P. O. Box 310307
(84531)
Rates: $76-$125
(970) 749-1164

MIDVALE

BEST WESTERN EXECUTIVE INN
280 W 7200 South
(84047)
Rates: $69-$99
(801) 566-4141
(800) 528-1234
(800) 253-0512

DISCOVERY INN
380 W 7200 South
(84047)
Rates: $57-$69
(801) 561-2256

HOMEWOOD SUITES
844 E N Union
(84047)
Rates: $107-$139
(801) 561-5999
(800) 225-5466

LA QUINTA INN
530 Catalpa Rd
(84047)
Rates: $75-$150
(801) 566-3291
(800) 687-6667

MOTEL 6
496 N Catalpa Rd
(84047)
Rates: $40-$56
(801) 561-0058
(800) 466-8356

MILFORD

THE STATION MOTEL
485 S 100 W (84751)
Rates: $50-$75
(435) 387-2481

MOAB

APACHE MOTEL
166 S 400 E (84532)
Rates: $39-$85
(435) 259-5727
(800) 228-6882

ARCHES INN
41 W 100 N
(84532)
Rates: $50-$150
(435) 259-5191

BIG HORN LODGE
550 S Main St
(84532)
Rates $75-$80
(435) 259-6171

BOWEN MOTEL
169 N Main St
(84532)
Rates: $365$125
(435) 259-7132
(800) 874-5439

CEDAR BREAKS CONDOS
10 S 400 E (84532)
Rates: $90-$130
(435) 259-7830

COMFORT SUITES
800 S Main St
(84532)
Rates: $89-$110
(435) 259-5252
(800) 228-5150

ENTRADA RANCH
Mile 9 Entrada
Ridge Rd (84532)
Rates: $50-$150
(435) 259-5796

THE GONZO INN
100 W 200 S
(84532)
Rates: $120-$250+
(435) 359-2515
(800) 791-4044

HEATHER LANE BED & BREAKFAST
4381 Heather Lane
(84532)
Rates: $49-$75
(435) 259-5928

HOTEL OFF CENTER
96 E Center
(84532)
Rates: $50-$75
(801) 259-4244

KOKOPELLI LODGE
72 S 100 E (84532)
Rates: $54-$75
(435) 259-7615
(888) 530-3134

AREA CODES - If the local number doesn't connect, check for a new area code.

MOAB VALLEY INN
711 S Main St (84532)
Rates: $80-$150
(435) 259-4419
(800) 831-6622

PACK CREEK RANCH
La Sal Mtn Loop Rd (84532)
Rates: $90-$200
(435) 259-5505

PIONEER SPRINGS B&B
1275 S Boulder (84532)
Rates: $50-$125
(435) 259-4663

RAMADA INN
182 S Main St (84532)
Rates: $32-$99
(435) 259-7141
(800) 272-6232

RED ROCK LODGE
51 N 100 W (84532)
Rates: $55-$65
(435) 259-5431

RED STONE INN
535 S Main St (84532)
Rates: $65-$75
(435) 259-3500
(800) 772-1972

ROSE TREE INN
481 Rose Tree Ln (84532)
Rates: $50-$75
(435) 259-5125
(800) 748-4386

RUSTIC INN MOTEL
120 E 100 S (84532)
Rates: $45-$75
(435) 259-6177
(800) 231-8184

SILVER SAGE INN
840 S Main St (84532)
Rates: $39-$75
(435) 259-4420

SLEEP INN
1051 S Main St (84532)
Rates: $70-$95
(435) 259-4655
(800) 753-3746

SLICKROCK CABINS
1301 1/2 N Hwy 191 (84532)
Rates: $30-$45
(435) 259-7660
(800) 488-8873

SUNSET MOTEL
41 W 100 N (84532)
Rates: $50-$150
(801) 259-5191
(800) 421-5614

VIRGINIAN MOTEL
70 E 200 S (84532)
Rates: $53-$75
(435) 259-5951
(800) 261-2063

MONTICELLO

BEST WESTERN WAYSIDE MOTOR INN
197 E Central (84535)
Rates: $35-$74
(435) 587-2261
(800) 528-1234
(800) 633-9700

CANYONLANDS MOTOR INN
97 N Main (84535)
Rates: $50-$75
(435) 587-2266
(800) 952-6212

SUPER 8 MOTEL
649 N Main (84535)
Rates: $35-$64
(435) 587-2489
(800) 800-8000

MOUNT CARMEL JUNCTION

BEST WESTERN THUNDERBIRD RESORT
Hwy 9 & 89 (84755)
Rates: $46-$93
(435) 648-2203
(800) 528-1234
(888) 848-6358

GOLDEN HILLS MOTEL
125 E State St (84755)
Rates: $28-$43
(435) 648-2268
(800) 648-2268

MT. CARMEL MOTEL & TRAILER PARK
Hwy 89 Muddy Creek Bridge (84755)
Rates: $29-$49
(435) 648-2323

MURRAY

HOMESTEAD VILLAGE
975 E 6600 S (84123)
Rates: $59-$84
(801) 685-2102
(888) 782-9473

RESTON HOTEL
5335 College Dr (84123)
Rates: $62-$74
(801) 264-1054
(800) 231-9710

NEPHI

BEST WESTERN PARADISE INN
1025 S Main (84648)
Rates: $51-$78
(435) 623-0624
(800) 528-1234

MOTEL 6
2195 S Main St (84648)
Rates: $43-$49
(435) 623-0666
(800) 466-8356

SAFARI MOTEL
413 S Main (84648)
Rates: $32-$49
(435) 623-1071

STARLITE MOTEL
675 S Main (84648)
Rates: $40-$49
(435) 623-4000

TEMPLE VIEW LODGE
260 E Main (84642)
Rates: $50-$75
(801) 835-6663

NORTH SALT LAKE

BEST WESTERN COTTONTREE INN
1030 N 400 E (84054)
Rates: $69-$89
(801) 292-7666
(800) 528-1234
(800) 662-6886

OAKLEY

GRAYSTONE LODGE & GUESTHOUSE
40 W Boulderville Rd (84055)
Rates: $76-$125
(435) 783-5744
(800) 675-8397

PEOA VACATION COTTAGE
5880 N Hwy 32 (Peoa 84061)
Rates: $76-$125
(435) 783-5339

OGDEN

BEST REST INN
1206 W 21st St (84401)
Rates: $66
(801) 393-8644
(800) 343-8644

BEST WESTERN HIGH COUNTRY INN
1335 W 12th St (84404)
Rates: $59-$75
(801) 394-9474
(800) 528-1234
(800) 594-8979

BIG Z MOTEL
1123 W 2150 S (84401)
Rates: $32-$37
(801) 394-6632

COLONIAL MOTEL
1269 Washington Blvd (84404)
Rates: $40-$49
(801) 399-5851

COMFORT SUITES
1150 W 2150 S (84404)
Rates: $83-$150
(801) 621-2545
(800) 228-5150

FLYING J INN
1206 W 21st St (84401)
Rates: $45-$49
(801) 393-8644
(800) 343-8644

HISTORIC RADISSON SUITE & HOTEL
2510 Washington Blvd (84404)
Rates: $119-$250
(801) 627-1900
(800) 333-3333

MILLSTREAM MOTEL
1450 Washington Blvd (84404)
Rates: $50-$75
(801) 394-9425

MOTEL 6-DOWNTOWN
1455 Washington Blvd (84404)
Rates: $32-$46
(801) 627-4560
(800) 466-8356

MOTEL 6-RIVERDALE
1500 W Riverdale Rd (84405)
Rates: $35-$52
(801) 627-2880
(800) 466-8356

MT. LOMOND MOTEL
755 N Harrisville Rd (84401)
Rates: $39-$49
(801) 782-7477

SLEEP INN
1155 S 1700 W (84404)
Rates: $48-$95
(801) 731-6500
(800) 753-3746

SUPER 8 MOTEL
1508 W 2100 S (84401)
Rates: $40-$54
(801) 731-7100
(800) 800-8000

WESTERN COLONY INN
234 24th St (84401)
Rates: $50-$75
(801) 627-1332

ORDERVILLE

PARKWAY MOTEL
74 E State St
(84758)
Rates: $40-$49
(435) 648-2380

OREM

**BEST INN
& SUITES**
1100 W 780 N
(84058)
Rates: $49-$129
(801) 235-9555
(800) 237-8466

**LA QUINTA INN
& SUITES**
521 W 1300
(84058)
Rates: $75-$95
(801) 226-0440
(800) 687-6667

PANGUITCH

**ADOBE SANDS
MOTEL**
390 N Main
(84759)
Rates: $49-$125
(435) 676-8874
(800) 497-9261

**BRYCE WAY
MOTEL**
429 N Main St
(84759)
Rates: $49-$250
(435) 676-2400
(800) 225-6534

CAMERON MOTEL
78 W Center St
(84759)
Rates: $50-$75
(435) 676-8840
(800) 537-9212

**COLOR COUNTRY
MOTEL**
180 W 400 South
(84759)
Rates: $25-$53
(435) 676-2386
(800) 225-6518

**JOLLY HOUSE
BED & BREAKFAST**
81 E 900 S (84759)
Rates: n/a
(435) 676-8151

**MARIANNA INN
MOTEL**
699 N Main
(84759)
Rates: $50-$75
(435) 676-8844
(800) 331-7407

NELSON MOTEL
308 Main (84759)
Rates: $29-$75
(435) 676-8441

**OUTDOORSMAN
INN**
413 N Main
(84759)
Rates: $40-$125
(435) 676-2782

**PATRIARCHS
MOTEL & CABINS**
12120 W Hwy 9
(84759)
Rates: $29-$49
(435) 648-2154

**PURPLE SAGE
MOTEL**
104 E Center St
(84759)
Rates: $50-$125
(435) 241-6889
(800) 676-8533

**ROCKING HORSE
INN**
2762 N Hwy 89
(84759)
Rates: $29-$49
(435) 676-2287

**SPORTSMAN'S
PARADISE CABINS**
2153 Hwy (84759)
Rates: $29-$59
(435) 676-8348
(888) 678-8348

PANGUITCH LAKE

**BEAR PAW LAKE
VIEW RESORT**
905 S Hwy 143
(84759)
Rates: $50-$75
(435) 676-2650
(888) 553-8439

**PANGUITCH LAKE
RESORT**
796 S Lake Shore
Dr (84759)
Rates: $50-$125
(435) 676-2657

PARK CITY

**AFFORDABLE
LUXURY & DIS-
COUNT LODGING
OF UTAH**
1375 Deer Valley
Dr (84060)
Rates: $76-$125
(435) 649-1592
(800) 255-6451

**BEST WESTERN
LANDMARK INN**
6560 N Landmark
Dr (84060)
Rates: $139-$169
(435) 649-7300
(800) 528-1234
(800) 548-8824

**HOLIDAY INN
EXPRESS HOTEL
& SUITES**
1501 W Ute Blvd
(84098)
Rates: $164-$210
(435) 658-1600
(800) 465-4329

MARRIOTT HOTEL
1895 Sidewinder
Dr (84060)
Rates: $76-$250
(435) 649-2900
(800) 228-9290
(800) 234-9003

RADISSON INN
2121 Park Ave
(84060)
Rates: $199-$219
(435) 649-5000
(800) 333-3333

PAROWAN

ACE MOTEL
82 N Main (84761)
Rates: n/a
(435) 477-3384

**BEST WESTERN
SWISS VILLAGE INN**
580 N Main St
(84761)
Rates: $54-$69
(435) 477-3391
(800) 528-1234
(800) 793-7401

**CRIMSON HILLS
MOTEL**
400 S Hwy 91
(84761)
Rates: $39-$49
(435) 477-8662

DAYS INN
625 W 200 S
(84761)
Rates: $42-$70
(435) 477-3326
(800) 329-7466

PAYSON

COMFORT INN
830 N Main
(84651)
Rates: $66-$110
(801) 465-4861
(800) 228-5150

PINE VALLEY

**PINE VALLEY
LODGE**
960 E Main St
(84722)
Rates: $50-$75
(435) 574-2544

PRICE

BUDGET HOST
145 N Carbonville
Rd (84501)
Rates: $37-$47
(435) 637-2424
(800) 283-4678

GREENWELL INN
655 E Main
(84501)
Rates: $39-$125
(435) 637-3520
(800) 666-3520

**PRICE RIVER INN-
NATIONAL 9**
641 W Price River
Dr (84501)
Rates: $34-$75
(435) 637-7000
(800) 524-9999

SHAMAN LODGE
3769 W Garden
Creek Rd (84501)
Rates: $75-$300
(435) 637-7489
(800) 710-7842

PROVO

**BEST INN
& SUITES**
1555 N Canyon
Rd (84604)
Rates: $65-$129
(801) 374-6020
(800) 237-8466

COLONY
INN SUITES-
NATIONAL 9
1380 S University
Ave (84601)
Rates: $39-$75
(801) 374-6800
(800) 524-9999

DAYS INN
1675 North 200 W
(84604)
Rates: $54-$74
(801) 375-8600
(800) 329-7466

**ECONO LODGE
AIRPORT**
1625 W Center St
(84601)
Rates: $39-$65
(801) 373-0099
(800) 552-2666

HAMPTON INN
1511 S 40 E (84601)
Rates: $69-$89
(801) 377-6396
(800) 426-7866

MOTEL 6
1600 S University
Ave (84601)
Rates: $31-$46
(801) 375-5064
(800) 466-8356

**RESIDENCE INN
BY MARRIOTT**
252 W 2230 N
(84604)
Rates: $79-$250
(801) 374-1000
(800) 331-3131

SLEEP INN
1505 S 40th E
(84601)
Rates: $49-$89
(801) 377-6597
(800) 753-3746

UPTOWN MOTEL
469 W Center St
(84601)
Rates: $28-$70
(801) 373-8248

**VALLEY INN
MOTEL**
1425 S State St
(84606)
Rates: $40-$49
(801) 377-3804

RICHFIELD

BEST WESTERN APPLE TREE INN
145 S Main St (84701)
Rates: $69
(435) 896-5481
(800) 528-1234

BUDGET HOST NIGHTS INN
69 S Main St (84701)
Rates: $36-$60
(435) 896-8228
(800) 525-9024

DAYS INN
333 N Main St (84701)
Rates: $40-$65
(435) 896-6476
(800) 329-7466

JENSEN MOTEL
290 S Main St (84701)
Rates: $40-$49
(435) 896-5447

MONTAIR MOTEL
190 S Main St (84701)
Rates: $40-$49
(435) 896-4415

NEW WEST MOTEL
447 S Main St (84701)
Rates: $49-$75
(435) 896-4076
(800) 278-4076

QUALITY INN
540 S Main St (84701)
Rates: $39-$79
(435) 896-5465
(800) 228-5151

ROMANICO INN
1170 S Main St (84701)
Rates: $34-$46
(435) 896-8471
(800) 948-0001

WESTON INN
647 S Main St (84701)
Rates: $50-$75
(435) 896-9271
(800) 255-9840

RIVERDALE

MOTEL 6
1500 W Riverdale Rd (84405)
Rates: $29-$49
(801) 627-2880
(800) 466-8356

ROCKVILLE

BLUE HOUSE B&B
125 E Main (84763)
Rates: $50-$75
(435) 772-3912
(800) 869-3912

ROOSEVELT

BEST WESTERN INN
E Hwy 40 (84066)
Rates: $49-$79
(435) 722-4644
(800) 528-1234

FRONTIER MOTEL
75 S 200 E (84066)
Rates: $36-$55
(435) 722-2201
(800) 248-1014

WESTERN HILLS MOTEL
737 E 200 S (84066)
Rates: $40-$49
(435) 722-5115

ST. GEORGE

AMBASSADOR INN
1481 S Sunland Dr (84770)
Rates: $40-$70
(435) 673-7900

AN OLDE PENNY FARTHING INN BED & BREAKFAST
278 N 100 W (84770)
Rates: $50-$150
(435) 673-7755

ANCESTOR INN
60 W St. George Blvd (84770)
Rates: $49-$125
(435) 673-4666
(800) 866-6882

ATKIN'S SINGLETREE INN
260 E St. George Blvd (84770)
Rates: $58-$72
(435) 673-6161

BLOOMINGTON TOWNHOMES
144 Brigham Rd, Ste A (84770)
Rates: $76-$125
(435) 673-6172

THE BLUFFS MOTEL
1140 S Bluff (84770)
Rates: $49-$125
(435) 628-6699
(800) 832-5833

BUDGET INN & SUITES
1221 S Main (84770)
Rates: $40-$75
(435) 673-6661
(800) 929-0790

THE COYOTE INN AT GREEN VALLEY SPA
1871 W Canyon View Dr (94770)
Rates: $430-$480
(435) 628-8060
(800) 237-1068

DAYS INN & THUNDERBIRD ART GALLERY
150 N 1000 E (84770)
Rates: $46-$85
(435) 673-6123
(800) 329-7466

DESERT EDGE INN
525 E St. George Blvd (84770)
Rates: $35-$49
(435) 673-6137

ECONO LODGE
460 E St. George Blvd (84770)
Rates: $35-$69
(435) 673-4861
(800) 553-2666

HOLIDAY INN-HOLIDOME
850 S Bluff St (84770)
Rates: $75-$150
(435) 628-4235
(800) 465-4329

MOTEL 6
205 N 1000 E St (84770)
Rates: $31-$46
(435) 628-7979
(800) 466-8356

RED CLIFFS INN
912 Red Cliffs Dr (84780)
Rates: $33-$68
(435) 673-3537
(888) 733-2543

SANDS MOTEL
581 E St. George Blvd (84770)
Rates: $50-$150
(435) 673-3501

SHERATON FOUR POINTS HOTEL
1450 S Hilton Dr (84770)
Rates: $84-$104
(435) 628-0463
(800) 325-3535

SOUTHSIDE INN
750 E St. George Blvd (84770)
Rates: $40-$49
(435) 628-9000
(888) 628-9081

SUN TIME INN
420 E St. George Blvd (84770)
Rates: $50-$75
(435) 673-6181
(800) 237-6253

TRAVELODGE
175 N 1000 E (84770)
Rates: $36-$99
(435) 673-4621
(800) 578-7878

SALINA

BUDGET HOST SCENIC HILLS MOTEL
75 East 1500 S (84654)
Rates: $42-$55
(435) 529-7483
(800) 283-4678

HENRY'S HIDEAWAY
60 N State St (84654)
Rates: $48-$60
(435) 529-7467
(800) 354-6468

RANCH MOTEL
80 N State St (84654)
Rates: $33-$42
(435) 529-7789

SAFARI MOTEL
1425 S State St (84654)
Rates: $35-$75
(435) 529-7447

SALT LAKE CITY

ALL-STAR
754 W North Temple (84116)
Rates: $40-$49
(801) 531-7300

ALPINE EXECUTIVE SUITES
150 S 900 E (84102)
Rates: $99-$149
(801) 533-8184

BEST INN& SUITES
1009 S Main (84111)
Rates: $60-$99
(801) 355-4567
(800) 237-8466

BEST WESTERN SALT LAKE PLAZA
122 W So Temple (84101)
Rates: $99-$119
(801) 521-0130
(800) 528-1234
(800) 366-3684

CHASE SUITE HOTEL
765 E 400 S (84102)
Rates: $135
(801) 532-5511

COLONIAL VILLAGE
1530 S Main (84115)
Rates: $40-$49
(801) 486-8171

COMFORT INN AIRPORT
200 N Admiral Byrd Rd (84116)
Rates: $78-$179
(801) 537-7444
(800) 228-5150

CONTINENTAL MOTEL
819 W North Temple (84116)
Rates: $40-$49
(801) 363-4546

COVERED WAGON MOTEL
230 W N Temple (84103)
Rates: $40-$75
(801) 533-9100

DAYS INN AIRPORT
1900 W N Temple St (84116)
Rates: $63-$110
(801) 539-8538
(800) 329-7466

DAYS INN CENTRAL
315 W 33rd South (South Salt Lake City 84115)
Rates: $49-$95
(801) 486-8780
(800) 329-7466

DOUBLETREE INN
255 S W Temple (84101)
Rates: $126-$250
(801) 328-2000
(800) 222-8733

ECONO LODGE
715 W N Temple (84116)
Rates: $49-$69
(801) 363-0062
(800) 553-2666

HILTON AIRPORT
5151 Wiley Post Way (84116)
Rates: $126-$250
(801) 539-1515
(800) 999-3736

HILTON HOTEL DOWNTOWN
150 W 5th S (84101)
Rates: $139-$165
(801) 532-3344
(800) 445-8667

HOMESTEAD GUEST STUDIOS
1220 E 2100 S (84116)
Rates: $54-$125
(801) 474-0771
(888) 782-9374

HOMESTEAD VILLAGE
5683 S Redwood Rd (84116)
Rates: $59-$125
(801) 269-9292
(888) 782-9473

HOTEL MONACO
15 W 200 S (84116)
Rates: $139-$149
(801) 595-0000

HOWARD JOHNSON EXP INN
121 N 300 W (84103)
Rates: $59-$99
(801) 521-3450
(800) 446-4656

LA QUINTA INN & SUITES AIRPORT
4905 W Wiley Post Way (84116)
Rates: $85-$105
(801) 366-4444
(800) 687-6667

LOG CABIN ON THE HILL B&B
2275 E 6200 S (84121)
Rates: $50-$150
(801) 272-2969
(888) 639-2969

MICROTEL INN & SUITES
61 N Tommy Thompson Rd (84116)
Rates: $45-$60
(801) 236-2800
(888) 771-7171

MOTEL 6 AIRPORT WEST
1990 W North Temple St (84116)
Rates: $40-$56
(801) 364-1053
(800) 466-8356

MOTEL 6 DOWNTOWN
176 W 6th South St (84101)
Rates: $39-$58
(801) 531-1252
(800) 466-8356

QUALITY INN CITY CENTER
154 West 600 S (84101)
Rates: $59-$104
(801) 521-2930
(800) 228-5151

QUALITY INN MIDVALLEY
4465 Century Dr (84123)
Rates: $49-$105
(801) 268-2533
(800) 228-5151

RAMADA INN DOWNTOWN
230 W 600 S (84101)
Rates: $59-$79
(801) 364-5200
(800) 272-6232

RAMADA LIMITED & SUITES
315 N Admiral Byrd Rd (84116)
Rates: $75-$250
(801) 539-5005
(800) 272-6232

RED BRICK INN BED & BREAKFST
1030 E 100 S (84116)
Rates: $60-$120
(801) 322-4917

RESTON HOTEL
5335 College Dr (84123)
Rates: $62-$71
(801) 264-1054

SKYLINE INN
2475 E 1700 S (84108)
Rates: $57-$69
(801) 582-5350

SUGARHOUSE VILLAGE-ALL SUITES INN
1339 E 2100 S (84116)
Rates: $76-$125
(801) 486-9976
(888) 577-8483

SUPER 8 MOTEL AIRPORT
223 N Jimmy Doolittle Rd (84116)
Rates: $65-$76
(801) 533-8878
(800) 800-8000

TRAVELODGE
144 W N Temple St (84103)
Rates: $58-$99
(801) 533-8200
(800) 578-7878

TRAVELODGE CITY CENTER
524 S W Temple St (84101)
Rates: $49-$75
(801) 531-7100
(800) 578-7878

WASATCH FRONT SKI CONDOS
2020 E 3300 S, #23 (84109)
Rates: $76-$125+
(801) 486-4296
(800) 762-7606

SANDY

BEST WESTERN COTTON TREE
10695 S Auto Mall Dr (84054)
Rates: $69-$79
(801) 523-8484
(800) 528-1234
(800) 662-6886

COMFORT INN
8955 S 255 W (84070)
Rates: $54-$149
(801) 255-4919
(800) 228-5150

HAMPTON INN
10690 S Holiday Park Dr (84070)
Rates: $78-$88
(801) 571-0800
(800) 426-7866

MAJESTIC ROCKIES MOTEL
8901 S State (84111)
Rates: $40-$49
(801) 255-2313

QUALITY INN & SUITES
10680 Auto Mall Dr (84070)
Rates: $70-$129
(801) 495-1317
(800) 221-5151

RESIDENCE INN BY MARRIOTT
270 W 10000 South (84070)
Rates: $126-$250
(801) 561-5005
(800) 331-3131

SCIPIO

HOTEL SCIPIO
195 N State, Box 75 (84656)
Rates: $40-$49
(801) 758-2450

SOUTH JORDAN

SUPER 8 MOTEL
10722 S 300 W (84095)
Rates: $59-$110
(801) 553-8888
(800) 800-8000

SPANISH FORK

IDEAL MOTEL
150 S Main St (84660)
Rates: $40-$49
(801) 798-1900

WESTERN INN
632 Kirby Ln (84660)
Rates: $83-$97
(801) 798-9400

SPRING CITY

HORSESHOE MOUNTAIN B&B
310 S Main, Box 84 (84662)
Rates: $50-$75
(435) 462-2871
(888) 242-2871

SPRINGDALE

BEST WESTERN ZION PARK INN
1215 Zion Park Blvd (84767)
Rates: $58-$99
(435) 772-3200
(800) 528-1234
(800) 934 7275

CANYON RANCH MOTEL
668 Zion Park Blvd (84767)
Rates: $58-$88
(435) 772-3357

CANYON VISTA BED & BREAKFST
2175 Zion Park Blvd (84767)
Rates: $76-$125
(435) 772-3801

CLIFFROSE LODGE
281 Zion Park Blvd (84767)
Rates: $45-$145
(435) 772-3234
(800) 243-8824

AREA CODES - If the local number doesn't connect, check for a new area code.

DRIFTWOOD LODGE
1515 Zion Park Blvd (84767)
Rates: $72-$102
(435) 772-3262

EL RIO LODGE IN ZION CANYON
995 Zion Park Blvd (84767)
Rates: $50-$75
(435) 772-3205
(888) 772-3205

FLANIGAN'S INN & CAFE
428 Zion Park Blvd (84767)
Rates: $79-$99
(435) 772-3244

SPRINGVILLE

BEST WESTERN COTTONTREE INN
1455 N 1750 W (84663)
Rates: $64-$99
(801) 489-3641
(800) 528-1234
(800) 662-6886

DAYS INN
520 S 2000 W (84663)
Rates: $39-$69
(801) 491-0300
(800) 329-7466

TOOELE

OQUIRRH MOTOR INN
8740 N State Hwy 36 (84074)
Rates: $29-$49
(801) 250-0118

TOQUERVILLE

YOUR INN B&B
650 Spring Dr (84774)
Rates: $40-$150
(435) 635-9964

TORREY

CACTUS HILL MOTEL
830 S 1000 E (84744)
Rates: $38-$45
(435) 425-3578

CAPITOL REEF INN & CAFE
360 W Main St (84744)
Rates: $35-$75
(435) 425-3271

LUNA MESA OASIS
P.O. Box 140 (84774)
Rates: $40-$49
(435) 456-9122

RIM ROCK INN
2523 E Hwy 24 (84774)
Rates: $50-$75
(435) 425-3398
(888) 447-4676

TORREY TRADING POST
75 W Main St (84774)
Rates: $40-$49
(435) 425-3716

TREMONTON

MARBLE MOTEL
116 N Tremonton St (84337)
Rates: $49-$75
(435) 257-3524

SANDMAN MOTEL
585 W Main St (84337)
Rates: $42-$50
(435) 257-7149

TROPIC

DOUGS COUNTRY INN MOTEL
141 N Main St (84776)
Rates: $50
(435) 679-8600

VERNAL

ECONO LODGE DOWNTOWN
311 E Main (84078)
Rates: $51-$83
(435) 789-2000
(800) 553-2666

RODEWAY INN
590 W Main (84078)
Rates: $48-$65
(435) 789-8172
(800) 228-2000

SAGE MOTEL & RESTAURANT
54 W Main (84078)
Rates: $39-$75
(435) 789-1442
(800) 760-1442

SUPER 8 MOTEL
1624 W Hwy 40 (84078)
Rates: $50-$65
(435) 789-4326
(800) 800-8000

WASHINGTON

RED CLIFF INN
912 Red Cliff Dr (84780)
Rates: $50-$75
(435) 673-3537
(800) 438-6465

WELLINGTON

NATIONAL 9 INN
50 S 700 E (84542)
Rates: $34-$75
(435) 637-7980
(800) 524-9999

WENDOVER

HERITAGE MOTEL
505 E Wendover Blvd (84083)
Rates: $50-$75
(435) 665-7744
(800) 457-5927

MOTEL 6
561 E. Wendover Blvd (84083)
Rates: $30-$46
(435) 665-2267
(800) 466-8356

STATE LINE INN
295 E Wendover Bvd (84083)
Rates: n/a
(435) 665-2226

WESTERN MOTEL
645 E Wendover Blvd (84083)
Rates: $50-$75
(435) 665-2215
(800) 556-2215

WEST VALLEY

PARKWAY SUITES
3580 W Parkway Blvd (84119)
Rates: $40-$99
(801) 977-0800

SLEEP INN
3440 S 2200 W (84119)
Rates: $55-$155
(435) 975-1888
(800) 753-3746

WEST VALLEY CITY

BAYMONT INN & SUITES
2229 W City Center Ct (84119)
Rates: $66-$71
(801) 886-1300
(800) 307-0200

HAWTHORNE INN & SUITES
3540 S 220 W (84119)
Rates: $80
(801) 954-9292
(800) 527-1133

WOODS CROSS

HAMPTON INN
2393 South 800 West (84087)
Rates: $69-$80
(801) 296-1211
(800) 426-7866

MOTEL 6
2433 S 800 W (84087)
Rates: $38-$75
(801) 298-0289
(800) 466-8356

TRAVEL NOTES

VERMONT

ADDISON

WHITFORD HOUSE INN
912 Grandey Rd
(05491)
Rates: $110-$175
(802) 758-2704
(800) 746-2704

ALBURG

AUBERGE ALBURG
54 S Main St (05440)
Rates: $20-$75
(802) 796-3169

HENRY'S SPORTSMAN'S COTTAGES
218 Poor Farm Rd
(05440)
Rates: $380-$460
(802) 796-3616

YE OLDE GRAYSTONE B&B
RFD 1, Box 76
(05440)
Rates: $50-$55
(802) 796-3911

ANDOVER

INN AT HIGH VIEW
753 East Hill Rd
(05143)
Rates: $105-$175
(802) 875-2724

ARLINGTON
(Also see Sunderland)

CUTLEAF MAPLES MOTEL & LODGE
3420 Rt 7A (05250)
Rates: $40-$80
(802) 375-2725

ROARING BRANCH HOUSKEEPING CABINS
Sunderland Hill Rd (05250)
Rates: $600-$700 Weekly
(802) 375-6401

VALHALLA MOTEL
Historic Rt 7A
(05250)
Rates: $38-$70
(802) 375-2212
(800) 258-2212

AVERILL

QUIMBY COUNTRY COTTAGES & LODGE
Rt 114 Forest Lake Rd (05901)
Rates: $99-$133
(802) 822-5533

BARNET

INN AT MAPLEMONT FARM
2742 Rt 5 S (05821)
Rates: $75-$100
(802) 633-4880
(800) 230-1617

BARRE

BUDGET INN
573 N Main St
(05641)
Rates: $39-$89
(802) 479-3333
(800) 446-4656

HOLLOW INN & MOTEL
278 S Main St
(05641)
Rates: $95-$105
(802) 479-9313
(800) 998-9444

BARTON

PINE CREST MOTEL & CABINS
RR 1, Box 279
(05822)
Rates: $35-$50
(802) 525-3472

BELLOWS FALLS

WHIPPOWIL COTTAGES
US Rt 5 (05101)
Rates: n/a
(802) 463-3442

BENNINGTON

APPLEY VALLEY INN & CAFE
Rt 7 (05201)
Rates: $59-$85
(802) 442-6588

BENNINGTON MOTOR INN
143 W Main St
(05201)
Rates: $78-$86
(802) 442-5479
(800) 359-9900

DARLING KELLY'S MOTEL
357 Rt 7 S (05201)
Rates: $79-$85
(802) 442-2322
(877) 447-1364

KNOTTY PINE MOTEL
130 Northside Dr
(05201)
Rates: $70-$84
(802) 442-5487

PLEASANT VALLEY MOTEL
Pleasant Valley Rd
(05201)
Rates: $40-$48
(802) 442-6222

SOUTH GATE MOTEL
124 Elm St (05201)
Rates: $54-$89
(802) 447-7525

VERMONTER MOTOR LODGE
RR 1, Box 2377
(05201)
Rates: $45-$90
(802) 442-2529
(800) 382-3175

BETHEL

GREENHURST HISTORICAL INN
River St, RD 2
Box 60 (05032)
Rates: $50-$100
(802) 234-9474
(800) 510-2553

POPLAR MANOR BED & BRKFAST
Rt 107 & 12
(05032)
Rates: $42-$44
(802) 234-5426

BOLTON VALLEY

TRAILSIDE CONDOS
HC 33, Box 751
(05477)
Rates: $190-$454
(802) 434-2769
(800) 451-5025

BONDVILLE

BROMLEY VIEW INN
Rt 30, Box 161
(05340)
Rates: $60-$90
(802) 297-1459
(800) 297-1459

BRADFORD

BRADFORD MOTEL
Rt 5 (05033)
Rates: $48-$70
(802) 222-4467

BRANDON

BRANDON MOTOR LODGE
Rt 7 South (05733)
Rates: $38-$70
(802) 247-9594
(800) 675-7614

GINGERBREAD HOUSE FINE ARTS BED & BRKFAST
RR 3, Rt 73 E
Box 3241 (05733)
Rates: $60-$150
(802) 247-3380

HIVUE B&B TREE FARM
Highpond Rd
(05733)
Rates: $50+
(802) 247-3042
(800) 880-3042

BRATTLEBORO

COLONIAL MOTEL & SPA
889 Putney Rd
(05301)
Rates: $60-$95
(802) 257-7733
(800) 239-0032

40 PUTNEY ROAD BED & BREAKFST
40 Putney Rd
(05301)
Rates: $90-$160
(802) 254-6268
(800) 941-2413

MOTEL 6
1254 Putney Rd
(05301)
Rates: $39-$54
(802) 254-6007
(800) 466-8356

QUALITY INN & SUITES
1380 Putney Rd
(05301)
Rates: $59-$109
(802) 254-8701
(800) 228-5151

BRIDGEWATER CORNERS

THE CORNERS INN & RESTAURANT
Rt 4 & Upper Rd
(05035)
Rates: $45-$85
(802) 672-9968

BRIDPORT

CHAMPLAIN VALLEY ALPACAS & FARMSTAY
326 Fiddlers Lane
(05734)
Rates: $35-$200
(802) 758-3276

AREA CODES - If the local number doesn't connect, check for a new area code.

BRISTOL

BRISTOL COMMONS INN
Jct 17 & 116
(05443)
Rates: $39-$68
(802) 453-2326

FIREFLY RANCH BED & BRKFAST
P. O. Box 152
(05443)
Rates: $75-$150
(802) 453-2223

BROWNSVILLE

BURTON FARM LODGE B&B
RFD 1, Box 558
(05089)
Rates: $60-$70
(802) 484-3300

MILLBROOK B&B
Rt 44 (05037)
Rates: $67-$117
(802) 484-7283

THE POND HOUSE AT SHATTUCK HILL FARM B&B
P. O. Box 234
(05037)
Rates: $135-$150
(802) 484-0011

BURKE

(Also see
East Burke)

OLD TIME B&B
P. O. Box 244
(05871)
Rates: $30-$50
(800) 507-9873

BURLINGTON

(Also see South
Burlington)

BEL-AIRE MOTEL
111 Shelburne Rd
(05401)
Rates: $36-$85
(802) 863-3116

HO HUM MOTEL-ROUTE 2
1660 Williston Rd
(05401)
Rates: $32-$96
(802) 863-4551

HOWARD JOHNSON
1 Dorset St (05402)
Rates: $55-$110
(802) 863-5541
(800) 446-4656

SHERATON HOTEL & CONF CENTER
870 Williston Rd
(05403)
Rates: $145-$200
(802) 865-6600
(800) 325-3535

TOWN & COUNTRY MOTEL
490 Shelburne Rd
(05401)
Rates: $32-$75
(802) 862-5786

CANAAN

LAKE WALLACE MOTEL
Rt 114 (05903)
Rates: n/a
(802) 266-3311

CAVENDISH

CAVENDISH POINTE HOTEL
Rt 103 (05142)
Rates: $139-$209
(802) 226-7688
(800) 438-7908

COLCHESTER

DAYS INN
23 College Pkwy
(05446)
Rates: $40-$109
(802) 655-0900
(800) 329-7466

HAMPTON INN
8 Mountain View
Dr (05446)
Rates: $99-$114
(802) 655-6177
(800) 426-7866

MOTEL 6
74 South Park Dr
(05446)
Rates: $42-$72
(802) 654-6860
(800) 466-8356

CRAFTSBURY COMMON

THE INN ON THE COMMON
Main St (05827)
Rates: $245-$290
(802) 586-9619
(800) 521-2233

DERBY

THE BORDER MOTEL
135 N Main (05829)
Rates: $42-$49
(802) 766-2088
(800) 280-1898

DORSET

BARROWS HOUSE
Rt 30 (05251)
Rates: $155-$250
(802) 867-4455
(800) 639-1620

EAST BURKE
(Also see Burke)

THE OLD CUTTER INN
143 Pinkham Rd
(05832)
Rates: $54+
(802) 626-5152
(800) 295-1943

THE VILLAGE INN
Rt 114 (05832)
Rates: $60-$75
(802) 626-3161

EAST DUMMERSTON

BRATTLEBORO NORTH KOA/ COOLIDGE GIFT SHOP & MOTEL COTTAGES
1238 Rt 5 (05346)
Rates: 40-$65
(802) 254-5908
(800) 562-5909

ENOSBURG FALLS

BERKSON FARMS LODGING
1205 W Berkshire
Rd, Rt 108 N
(05450)
Rates: $55-$65
(802) 933-2522

ESSEX JUNCTION

THE WILSON INN
10 Kellog Rd
(05452)
Rates: $94-$138
(802) 879-1515
(800) 879-1515

FAIRLEE

SILVER MAPLE LODGE & COTTAGES B&B
Rt 5 (05045)
Rates: $56-$86
(802) 333-4326
(800) 666-1946

FRANKLIN

FAIR MEADOWS FARM B&B
Box 430, Rt 235
(05457)
Rates: n/a
(802) 285-2132

GRAFTON

THE HAYES HOUSE
Bear Hill Rd
(05146)
Rates: n/a
(802) 843-2461

ISLAND POND

LAKEFRONT MOTEL
Cross St (05846)
Rates: $59-$84
(802) 723-6507

JAMAICA

THREE MOUNTAIN INN
Rt 30 (05343)
Rates: $115-$295
(802) 874-4140
(800) 532-9399

JEFFERSON-VILLE

DEER RUN MOTOR INN
SR 15 (05464)
Rates: $55-$85
(802) 644-8866
(800) 354-2728

THE HIGHLANDER MOTEL
RR 1, Box 436
(05464)
Rates: $42-$64
(802) 644-2725
(800) 367-6471

THE JEFFERSON HOUSE
Main St, Box 288
(05464)
Rates: $55-$75
(802) 644-2030

JERICHO

HOMEPLACE B&B
Old Pump Rd
(05465)
Rates: $55-$75
(802) 899-4694

KILLINGTON

BUTTERNUT ON THE MOUNTAIN
Box 306,
Killington Rd
(05751)
Rates: $65-$250
(802) 422-2000
(800) 524-7654

CEDARBROOK MOTOR INN/SUITES
US 4 & SR 100 S
(05751)
Rates: $34-$114
(802) 422-9666
(800) 446-1088

VAL ROCK MOTEL
8006 Rt 4 (05751)
Rates: $64-$120
(802) 422-3881
(800) 238-8762

LONDON-DERRY

FROG'S LEAP INN
RR 1, Box 107, Rt
100 (05148)
Rates: $120-$275
(802) 824-3019
(877) 376-4753

WHITE PINE LODGE
Rt 11 West (05148)
Rates: $50-$110
(802) 824-3909

AREA CODES - If the local number doesn't connect, check for a new area code.

LUDLOW

THE COMBES FAMILY INN
953 E Lake Rd (05149)
Rates: $60-$134
(802) 228-8799
(800) 822-8799

HAPPY TRAILS MOTEL
321 Rt 103 S (05149)
Rates: $100-$200
(802) 228-8888
(800) 228-9984

OKEMO MTN VACATION CENTER RENTALS
44 Pond St (05149)
Rates: n/a
(802) 228-8255
(800) 829-8205

TIMBER INN MOTEL
Main St (05149)
Rates: $59-$149
(802) 228-8666

MANCHESTER

AVALANCHE MOTOR LODGE
Rt 11 & 30 (05254)
Rates: $55-$75
(802) 362-2622
(800) 592-2622

BRITTANY INN MOTEL
Rt 7A, Box 760 (05255)
Rates: $51-$72
(802) 362-1033
(800) 298-4650

MARLBORO

WHETSTONE INN
Off Hwy 9 (05344)
Rates: $30-$85
(802) 254-2500

MENDON

CORTINA INN & RESORT
103 US Rt 4 (05701)
Rates: $104-$199
(802) 773-3333
(800) 451-6108

ECONO LODGE PICO
51 Rt 4 E (05701)
Rates: $56-$125
(802) 773-6644
(800) 553-2666
(800) 992-9067

EDELWEISS MOTEL & CHALETS
119 US Rt 4 (05751)
Rates: $54-$115
(802) 775-5577
(800) 479-2863

MENDON MTN ORCHARDS MOTEL
16 US Rt 4 (05701)
Rates: $42-$47
(802) 775-5477

MENDON MOUNTAINVIEW RESORT/LODGE
78 US 4 (05751)
Rates: $39-$139
(802) 773-4311
(800) 368-4311

RED CLOVER HISTORIC COUNTRY INN
7 Woodward Rd (05701)
Rates: $185-$450
(802) 775-2290
(800) 752-0571

MIDDLEBURY

FAIRHILL B&B
Rd 3, Box 2300 (05753)
Rates: n/a
(802) 388-3044

MIDDLEBURY B&B
Washington St (05753)
Rates: $55-$85
(802) 388-4851

MIDDLEBURY COUNTRY INN
14 Courthouse Square (05753)
Rates: $76-$355
(802) 388-4961
(800) 842-4666

SUGARHOUSE MOTOR INN
Rt 7 (05753)
Rates: $50-$60
(802) 388-2770
(800) 784-2746

MONTPELIER

ECONO LODGE
101 Northfield St (05602)
Rates: $49-$99
(802) 223-5258
(800) 553-2666

MOUNT TABOR

MOUNT TABOR INN & TAVERN
217 Troll Hill Rd (05739)
Rates: $75-$125
(802) 293-5907

NEWFANE

FOUR COLUMNS INN
22 West St (05345)
Rates: $140-$280
(802) 365-7713

WEST RIVER LODGE & STABLES
117 Hill Rd (05345)
Rates: $60-$95
(802) 365-7745

NEWPORT

TOP O' THE HILLS MOTEL & INN
HCR 61, Box 14 (05855)
Rates: $75-$95
(802) 334-2452
(800) 258-6748

WATER'S EDGE BED & BREAKFST
324 Wishing Well Ave (05855)
Rates: $70-$120
(802) 334-7726

NORTH HERO

SHORE ACRES INN
237 Shore Acres Dr (05475)
Rates: $90-$155
(802) 372-8722

NORTH SPRINGFIELD

THE ABBY-LYN MOTEL
RD 1, Box 80 (05150)
Rates: $60-$75
(802) 886-2223

ORLEANS

GREEN ACRES CABINS
1051 Rt 5A (05860)
Rates: n/a
(802) 525-3722

WILLOUGHVALE INN
793 Rt 5A (05860)
Rates: $89-$225
(802) 525-4123
(800) 594-9102

ORWELL

BUCKSWOOD B&B
633 Rt 73E (05760)
Rates: $55-$65
(802) 948-2054

PERKINSVILLE

GWENDOLYN'S B&B INN
Rt 106 (05151)
Rates: $55-$92
(802) 263-5248

PERU

JOHNNY SEESAW'S LODGE
SR 11 (05152)
Rates: $75-$200
(802) 824-5533
(800) 424-2729

PITTSFIELD

CLEAR RIVER INN & TAVERN
Rt 100 (05762)
Rates: $38-$85
(802) 746-7916
(800) 746-7916

POULTNEY

STONEBRIDGE INN B&B
3 Beaunau St (05764)
Rates: $60-$84
(802) 287-9849
(800) 308-7001

PUTNEY

PUTNEY INN
Depot Rd (05346)
Rates: $98-$158
(802) 387-5517
(800) 653-5517

QUECHEE

QUALITY INN AT QUECHEE GORGE
US 4 (05059)
Rates: $60-$140
(802) 295-7600
(800) 228-5151
(800) 732-4376

READING

BAILEY'S MILL BED & BRKFAST
Bailey's Mill Rd (05062)
Rates: $70-$135
(802) 484-7809
(800) 639-3437

RICHMOND

MAMA BOWER'S BED & BREAKFAST
P O Box 22 (05477)
Rates: $40-$65
(802) 434-2632

ROCHESTER

HARVEY'S MTN VIEW INN & FARM
RR 1, Box 53 (05767)
Rates: $35-$75
(802) 767-4273

RUTLAND

BEST WESTERN INN & SUITES
Rt 4 E (05702)
Rates: $69-$189
(802) 773-3200
(800) 528-1234
(800) 828-3334

ECONO LODGE
238 S Main St (05701)
Rates: $49-$159
(802) 773-2784
(800) 553-2666

GREEN-MONT MOTEL
138 N Main St (05701)
Rates: $57-$110
(802) 775-2575
(800) 774-2575

AREA CODES - If the local number doesn't connect, check for a new area code.

HIGHLANDER MOTEL
203 N Main St (05701)
Rates: $50-$100
(802) 773-6069
(800) 884-6069

HOLIDAY INN
476 SR 7 S (05701)
Rates: $140-$218
(802) 775-1911
(800) 465-4329
(800) 462-4810

HOWARD JOHNSON
401 SR 7 S (05701)
Rates: $109-$159
(802) 775-4303
(800) 446-4656

RAMADA LIMITED
253 S Main St (05701)
Rates: $69-$151
(802) 773-3361
(800) 272-6232

ROYAL MOTEL
115 Woodstock Ave (05701)
Rates: $37-$109
(802) 773-9176

TYROL MOTOR INN
RR 2, Box 7602 (05701)
Rates: $40-$106
(802) 773-7485

ST. ALBANS

CADILLAC MOTEL
213 Main St (05478)
Rates: $43-$70
(802) 524-2191

ECONO LODGE
287 S Main St (05478)
Rates: $70-$95
(802) 524-5956
(800) 553-2666

OLD MILL RIVER PLACE B&B
6206 Georgia Shore Rd (05478)
Rates: $55-$65
(802) 524-7211

ST. JOHNSBURY

AIME'S MOTEL
46 VT Rt 18 (05819)
Rates: $55-$70
(802) 748-3194
(800) 504-6663

COMFORT SUITES
I-91 & US 5, S Main St (05819)
Rates: $59-$300
(800) 228-5150

FAIRBANKS INN
401 Western Ave (05819)
Rates: $95-$125
(802) 748-5666

HOLIDAY MOTEL
222 Hastings St (05819)
Rates: $45-$95
(802) 748-8192

MAPLE CENTER MOTEL
20 Hastings St (05819)
Rates: $42-$85
(802) 748-2393

SAXTONS RIVER

THE INN AT SAXTONS RIVER
27 Main St (05154)
Rates: $98-$108
(802) 869-2110

SHAFTSBURY

BAYBERRY MOTEL
Rt 7A, Box 137 (05262)
Rates: $38-$75
(802) 447-7180

HILLBROOK MOTEL
Historic SR 7A (05262)
Rates: $40-$70
(802) 447-7201

KIMBERLY COTTAGE
Myers Rd, Box 345 (05262)
Rates: $85-$185
(802) 442-4354

SERENITY MOTEL
4379 RI 7A (05262)
Rates: $55-$80
(802) 442-6490
(800) 644-6490

SHARON

COLUMNS MOTOR LODGE
Rt 14 (05065)
Rates: $38-$46
(802) 763-7040

SHELBURNE

ECONO LODGE
3164 Shelburne Rd (05482)
Rates: $39-$125
(802) 985-3377
(800) 553-2666

SHOREHAM

INDIAN TRAIL FARM B&B
Box 49, Smith St (05770)
Rates: $50+
(802) 897-5292

SOUTH BURLINGTON
(Also see Burlington)

ANCHORAGE INN
108 Dorset St (05403)
Rates: $68-$100
(802) 863-7000
(800) 336-1869

BEST WESTERN WINDJAMMER INN & CONF CTR
1076 Williston Rd (05403)
Rates: $89-$179
(802) 853-1125
(800) 528-1234
(800) 371-1125

HARBOR SUNSET MOTEL
1700 Shelburne Rd (05403)
Rates: $25-$45
(802) 864-5080

HAWTHORN SUITES HOTEL
401 Dorset St (05403)
Rates: $99-$229
(802) 860-1212
(800) 527-1133

HOLIDAY INN
1068 Williston Rd (05403)
Rates: $115-$146
(802) 863-6363
(800) 465-4329

HOWARD JOHNSON HOTEL
1720 Shelburne Rd (05403)
Rates: $65-$111
(802) 860-6000
(800) 446-4656

SHERATON HOTEL & CONF CENTER
870 Williston Rd (05403)
Rates: $200-$240
(802) 865-6600
(800) 325-3535

SUPER 8 MOTEL
1016 Shelburne Rd (05403)
Rates: $39-$94
(802) 862-6421
(800) 800-8000

SOUTH HERO

SANDBAR MOTOR INN
US Rt 2 (05486)
Rates: $48-$85
(802) 372-6911

SOUTH WOODSTOCK

KEDRON VALLEY HISTORIC INN
Rt 106 (05071)
Rates: $186-$309
(802) 457-1473
(800) 836-1193

SPRINGFIELD

HOLIDAY INN EXPRESS
818 Charlestown Rd (05156)
Rates: $99
(802) 885-4516
(800) 465-4329

PA-LO-MAR MOTEL
2 Linhale Dr (05156)
Rates: $30-$56
(802) 885-4142

STARKSBORO

MILLHOUSE B&B
394 State Prison Hollow Rd (05487)
Rates: $35-$40
(802) 453-2008
(800) 859-5758

STOCKBRIDGE

CHASE INN B&B
Rt 100 (05772)
Rates: $20-$40
(802) 746-8972
(800) 746-8972

STOWE

ANDERSEN LODGE-AN AUSTRIAN INN
3430 Mountain Rd (05672)
Rates: $78-$248
(802) 253-7336
(800) 336-7336

BURGUNDY ROSE MOTOR INN
Rt 100 (05672)
Rates: $45-$79
(802) 253-7768
(800) 989-7768

COMMODORES INN
231 Main St (05672)
Rates: $78-$248
(802) 253-7131
(800) 447-8693

DISTINCTIVE RENTAL HOMES OF STOWE
804 S Main St (05672)
Rates: $250-$1700
(802) 253-5646

EDSON HILL VIEW BED & BREAKFST
903 Edson Hill Rd (05672)
Rates: $65-$110
(802) 253-4337
(800) 559-4337

1860 HOUSE B&B
P.O. Box 276 (05672)
Rates: n/a
(802) 253-7351
(800) 248-1860

AREA CODES - If the local number doesn't connect, check for a new area code.

GREEN MOUNTAIN COUNTRY INN
18 S Main St
(05672)
Rates: $89-$335
(802) 253-7301
(800) 253-7302

HOB KNOB INN
2364 Mountain Rd
(05672)
Rates: $85-$150
(802) 253-8549
(800) 245-8540

HONEYWOOD COUNTRY LODGE & INN
4527 Mountain Rd
(05672)
Rates: $109-$199
(802) 253-4124
(800) 659-6289

INN AT TURNER MILL B&B
56 Turner Mill Ln
(05672)
Rates: $50-$85
(802) 253-2062
(800) 992-0016

INNSBRUCK INN
4361 Mountain Rd
(05672)
Rates: $69-$169
(802) 253-8582
(800) 225-8582

MIGUEL'S STOWE AWAY B&B INN
3148 Mountain Rd
(05672)
Rates: $35-$120
(802) 253-7574
(800) 245-1240

THE MOUNTAIN ROAD RESORT
1007 Mountain Rd
(05672)
Rates: $90-$225
(802) 253-4566
(800) 367-6873

MOUNTAINEER INN
3343 Mountain Rd
(05672)
Rates: $59-$105
(802) 253-7525

NOTCH BROOK CONDOMINIUMS
1229 Notch Brook Rd (05672)
Rates: $66-$275
(802) 253-4882
(800) 253-4882

RASPEBERRY PATCH B&B
606 Randolph Rd
(05672)
Rates: $50-$95
(802) 253-4145
(800) 624-0639

RENTALS OF STOWE
35 S Main St
(05672)
Rates: n/a
(802) 253-9786
(800) 848-9120

RIVERSIDE INN
1965 Mountain Rd
(05672)
Rates: $19-$50
(802) 253-4217
(800) 966-4217

SALZBURG INN
Mountain Rd,
Rt 108 (05672)
Rates: $58-$78
(802) 253-8541
(800) 448-4554

SEASON'S PASS INN
613 S Main St
(05672)
Rates: $62-$105
(802) 253-7244

SKI INN
Rt 108 (05672)
Rates: $20-$30
(802) 253-4050

STOWE INN AT LITTLE RIVER
123 Mountain Rd
(05672)
Rates: $55-$350
(802) 253-4836
(800) 227-1108

TEN ACRES LODGE COUNTRY INN
14 Barrows Rd
(05672)
Rates: $200-$260
(802) 253-7638
(800) 327-7357

TOPNOTCH AT STOWE RESORT & SPA
4000 Mountain Rd
(05672)
Rates: $230-$900
(802) 253-8585
(800) 451-8686

WALKABOUT CREEK LODGE B&B
199 Edson Hill Rd
(05672)
Rates: $70-$150
(802) 253-7354
(800) 426-6697

YE OLDE ENGLAND INNE
433 Mountain Rd
(05672)
Rates: $99-$455
(802) 253-7558
(800) 477-3771

STRATTON MOUNTAIN

LIFTLINE LODGE RESORT HOTEL
Stratton Mtn Rd
(05155)
Rates: $59-$145
(802) 297-2600
(800) 597-5438

SUNDERLAND

ARCADY AT THE SUNDERLAND RESORT
6249 Rt 7A
(Arlington/ Sunderland 05250)
Rates: $70-$130
(802) 362-1176
(800) 362-1151

SWANTON

BLUE FORD MOTEL
325 N River Rd
(05488)
Rates: $35-$75
(802) 868-4147

COUNTRY ESSENCE B&B
641 Rt 7 N (05488)
Rates: $60+
(802) 868-4247

TAFTSVILLE

APPLEBUTTER INN BED & BRKFAST
Happy Valley Rd
(05073)
Rates: $40-$65
(802) 457-4158

TOWNSHEND

BOARDMAN HOUSE B&B
On the Green
(05353)
Rates: $65-$85
(802) 365-4086

UNDERHILL

4 PAUSE B&B
354 Pleasant Valley Rd (05489)
Rates: $55-$70
(802) 899-3927

VERGENNES

BASIN HARBOR CLUB RESORT
Basin Harbor Rd
(05491)
Rates: $110-$250
(802) 475-2311
(800) 622-4000

HILLCREST CAMPGROUND & COTTAGES
686 Basin Harbor Rd (05491)
Rates: $45
(802) 475-2343

WAITSFIELD

THE GARRISON HOTEL
Box 539-C, Rt 17
(05673)
Rates: $29-$450
(802) 496-2352
(800) 766-7829

HYDE AWAY INN
RR 1, Box 65, Rt 17
(05673)
Rates: $49-$95
(802) 496-2322
(800) 777-4933

MILLBROOK INN
533 McCullough
(05673)
Rates: $39-$70
(802) 496-2405
(800) 477-2809

SUGARBUSH RESORT
RR 1, Box 35
(05674)
Rates: $30+
(802) 583-3333
(800) 537-8427

SUGARBUSH VILLAGE CONDOS
RR 1, Box 68-12
(05674)
Rates: $20-$42
(802) 583-3000
(800) 451-4326

TUCKER HILL LODGE
Rt 17, Box 147
(05673)
Rates: $40-$55
(802) 496-3984
(800) 543-7841

WARREN

GOLDEN LION RIVERSIDE INN
Sugarbush Access Rd, Rt 100 (05674)
Rates: $26-$44
(802) 496-3084

POWDERHOUND INN & CONDOS
203 Powderhound Rd (05674)
Rates: $80-$145
(802) 496-5100
(800) 548-4022

THE SUPER LODGE
Sugarbush Access Rd, Rt 100 (05674)
Rates: $79-$99
(802) 583-3300

WATERBURY

HOLIDAY INN
45 Blush Hill Rd
(05676)
Rates: $139-$179
(802) 244-7822
(800) 465-4329

1836 CABINS
Box 128-T, Rt 100,
Stowe Rd (05677)
Rates: $89-$119
(802) 244-8533

THE OLD STAGECOACH INN B&B
18 N Main St (05676)
Rates: $55-$200
(802) 244-5056
(800) 262-2206

WELLS RIVER

BIRCHWOOD MOTOR INN
RR 1, Box 2 (45081)
Rates: n/a
(802) 757-2274
(800) 895-2277

WEST BRATTLEBORO

MOLLY STARK MOTEL
829 Marlboro Rd (05301)
Rates: $48-$80
(802) 254-2440

WEST DANVILLE

INDIAN JOE COURT CABINS & COTTAGES
US Rt 2, Box 126 (05873)
Rates: $40-$75
(802) 684-3430

WEST DOVER

MOUNTAIN RESORT RENTALS
N. Comm. Ctr, Rt 100 (05356)
Rates: n/a
(802) 464-1445
(888) 336-1445

SNOW GOOSE INN
259 Rt 100 (05356)
Rates: $105-$300
(802) 464-3984
(888) 604-7964

SUPER 8 MOTEL
Rt 100 (05356)
Rates: $54-$149
(802) 464-5112
(800) 800-8000

WESTON

THE DARLING FAMILY INN
815 Rt 100 (05161)
Rates: $80-$125
(802) 824-3223

WHITE RIVER JUNCTION

BEST WESTERN AT THE JUNCTION
I-89 & I-91 (05001)
Rates: $99-$139
(802) 295-3015
(800) 528-1234
(800) 370-4656

COMFORT INN
8 Sykes Ave (05001)
Rates: $59-$149
(802) 295-3051
(800) 228-5150
(800) 628-7727

HOTEL COOLIDGE
17 S Main St (05001)
Rates: $39-$99
(802) 295-3118
(800) 622-1124

WILDER

WILDER MOTEL
319 Hartford Ave (05088)
Rates: $45-$65
(802) 295-9793

WILLIAMSTOWN

AUTUMN CREST INN
RFD 1, Box 1540 (05679)
Rates: $88-$148
(802) 433-6627
(800) 339-6627

AUTUMN HARVEST COUNTRY INN
118 Clark Rd (05679)
Rates: $59-$139
(802) 433-1355

WILLISTON

RESIDENCE INN BY MARRIOTT
35 Hurricane Ln (05495)
Rates: $105-$145
(802) 878-2001
(800) 331-3131

WILMINGTON

INN AT QUAIL RUN B&B
106 Smith Rd (05363)
Rates: $105-$220
(802) 464-3362
(800) 343-7227

THE VINTAGE MOTEL
195 Rt 9 W (05363)
Rates: $55-$90
(802) 464-8824
(800) 899-9660

WOODSTOCK

BRAESIDE MOTEL
Rt 4 E (05091)
Rates: $88-$108
(802) 457-1366
(800) 303-1366

THREE CHURCH STREET B&B
3 Church St (05091)
Rates: $70-$105
(802) 457-1925
(800) 457-1925

THE WINSLOW HOUSE B&B
492 Woodstock Rd (05091)
Rates: $95-$150
(802) 457-1820

AREA CODES - If the local number doesn't connect, check for a new area code.

VIRGINIA

ABINGDON

COMFORT INN
170 Jonesboro Rd
(24210)
Rates: $55-$200
(540) 676-2222
(800) 228-5150

ALDIE

THE CASTLE
Rt 15, Box 28K
Rates: n/a
(703) 327-4113

ALEXANDRIA

**ALEXANDRIA
SUITES HOTEL**
420 N Van Dorn St
(22303)
Rates: $99-$119
(703) 370-1000

CLASSIC B&B
6216 Saddle Tree
Dr (22340)
Rates: $100
(703) 922-7836

**COMFORT INN
MOUNT VERNON**
7212 Richmond
Hwy (22306)
Rates: $50-$85
(703) 765-9000
(800) 228-5150

DAYS INN
6100 Richmond
Hwy (22303)
Rates: $45-$70
(703) 329-0500
(800) 329-7466

DAYS INN
110 S Bragg St
(22312)
Rates: $66-$94
(703) 354-4950
(800) 329-7466

**DOUBLETREE
GUEST SUITES**
100 S Reynolds St
(22304)
Rates: $119-$159
(703) 370-9600
(800) 424-2900

ECONO LODGE
8849 Richmond
Hwy (22309)
Rates: $50-$70
(703) 780-0300
(800) 553-2666

**EXECUTIVE CLUB
SUITES**
610 Bashford Ln
(22314)
Rates: $110-$130
(703) 739-2582
(800) 535-2582

**HILTON MARK
CENTER**
5000 Seminary Rd
(22309)
Rates: $119-$239
(703) 845-1010
(800) 445-8667

**HOLIDAY INN-
OLD TOWN**
480 King St
(22314)
Rates: $161-$171
(703) 549-6080
(800) 465-4329

**HOLIDAY INN
EISENHOWER
METRO**
2460 Eisenhower
Ave (22314)
Rates: $99-$139
(703) 960-3400
(800) 465-4329

**HOMESTAD
VILLAGE GUEST
STUDIOS**
200 Blue Stone Rd
(22309)
Rates: $89-$94
(703) 329-3399
(888) 782-9473

**HOWARD
JOHNSON**
5821 Richmond
Hwy (22303)
Rates: $59-$109
(703) 329-1400
(800) 446-4656

**RADISSON
HOTEL-
OLD TOWN**
901 Fairfax St
(22314)
Rates: $89
(703) 683-6000
(800) 333-3333

RED ROOF INN
5975 Richmond
Hwy (22303)
Rates: $49-$62
(703) 960-5200
(800) 843-7663

**SHERATON
SUITES**
801 N St. Asaph St
(22314)
Rates: $139-$155
(703) 836-4700
(800) 325-3535

ALTAVISTA

**COMFORT SUITES
HOTEL**
1558 Main St
(24517)
Rates: $69-$149
(804) 369-4000
(800) 228-5150

AMHERST

**CRUMPS MTN
COTTAGE**
2150 Indian Creek
Rd (24521)
Rates: n/a
(804) 277-5563

FAIRVIEW B&B
Rt 4, Box 117
(25421)
Rates: $65-$70
(804) 277-8500

APPOMATTOX

BUDGET INN
714 W
Confederate Blvd
(24522)
Rates: $40-$50
(804) 352-7451

SUPER 8 MOTEL
Rt 4, Box 100 (24522)
Rates: $45-$65
(804) 352-2339
(800) 800-8000

ARLINGTON

**BEST WESTERN
ROSSLYN-KEY
BRIDGE HOTEL**
1850 N Fort Myer
Dr (22209)
Rates: $129-$169
(703) 522-0400
(800) 528-1234
(800) 539-2743

**CROWNE PLAZA
AIRPORT**
1489 Jefferson
Davis Hwy
(22202)
Rates: n/a
(703) 416-1600
(800) 227-6963

**DOUBLETREE
HOTEL NATIONAL
AIRPORT**
300 Army Navy
Dr (22202)
Rates: $65-$155
(703) 416-4100
(800) 222-8733

**EXECUTIVE CLUB
SUITES**
108 S Courthouse
Rd (22204)
Rates: $110
(703) 522-2582
(800) 535-2582

**HOLIDAY INN
ROSSLYN**
1900 N Ft Myer Dr
(22209)
Rates: $120
(703) 807-2000
(800) 465-4329

**HOMESTEAD
VILLAGE GUEST
STUDIOS**
4504 Brookfield
Corp Dr (22309)
Rates: (89-$134
(703) 263-3361
(888) 782-9473

**HOWARD
JOHNSON
PLAZA HOTEL**
2650 Jefferson
Davis Hwy (22202)
Rates: $69-$189
(703) 684-7200
(800) 446-4656

**HYATT
ARLINGTON
AT KEY BRIDGE**
1325 Wilson Blvd
(22209)
Rates: $69-$181
(703) 525-1234
(800) 525-1234

**MARRIOTT
CRYSTAL
GATEWAY HOTEL**
1700 Jefferson
Davis Hwy
(22202)
Rates: $105-$192
(703) 920-3230
(800) 228-9290

**MARRIOTT
KEY BRIDGE**
1401 Lee Hwy
(22209)
Rates: $164-$184
(703) 524-6400
(800) 228-9290
(800) 327-9789

**QUALITY HOTEL
COURTHOUSE
PLAZA**
1200 N
Courthouse Rd
(22201)
Rates: $79-$169
(703) 524-4000
(800) 228-5151

**QUALITY INN
IWO JIMA**
1501 Arlington
Blvd (22203)
Rates: $90-$109
(703) 524-5000
(800) 228-5151

STOUFFER CONCOURSE HOTEL
2399 Jefferson
Davis Hwy
(22202)
Rates: $89-$240
(703) 418-6800

BASYE

SKY CHALET COUNTRY INN
P O Box 300
(22810)
Rates: n/a
(504) 856-2147

BEDFORD

BEST WESTERN TERRACE HOUSE
921 Blue Ridge
Ave (24523)
Rates: $44-$63
(540) 586-8266
(800) 528-1234

BERRYVILLE

BLUE RIDGE B&B RESERVATIONS
Rt 2, Box 3895
(22611)
Rates: n/a
(703) 955-1246
(800) 296-1246

BIG STONE GAP

COUNTRY INN MOTEL
627 Gilley Ave
(24219)
Rates: $42-$48
(540) 523-0374

BLACKSBURG

BEST WESTERN RED LION INN
900 Plantation Rd
(24060)
Rates: $64-$92
(540) 552-7770
(800) 528-1234

BRUSH MOUNTAIN INN
3030 Mt. Tabor Rd
(24062)
Rates: n/a
(703) 951-7530

BUDGET HOST INN
3333 S Main St
(24060)
Rates: $32-$48
(540) 951-4242
(800) 446-4656

COMFORT INN
3705 S Main St
(24060)
Rates: $65-$145
(540) 951-1500
(800) 228-5150

DONALDSON BROWN RESORT & CONF CENTER
201 Otey St
(24061)
Rates: n/a
(540) 231-9485
(877) 200-3360

FOUR POINTS BY SHERATON
900 Prices Fork Rd
(24060)
Rates: $89-$149
(540) 552-7001
(800) 325-3535

RAMADA LIMITED
3503 Holiday
Lane (24060)
Rates: $50-$110
(540) 951-1330
(800) 272-6232

BLACKSTONE

EPES HOUSE BED & BREAKFST
210 College Ave
(23824)
Rates: n/a
(804) 292-7941

BLAND

BIG WALKER MOTEL
P. O. Box 155
(24315)
Rates: $34-$48
(540) 688-3331

BOWLING GREEN

MANSION VIEW BED & BREAKFAST
P. O. Box 787
(22427)
Rates: n/a
(804) 633-2202
(800) 251-9335

WEBB'S MOTEL
18080 A.P. Hill
Blvd (22427)
Rates: n/a
(804) 633-6755

BOYDTON

SOUTHERN HERITAGE BED & BREAKFAST
1100 Jefferson St
(23917)
Rates: n/a
(804) 738-0167

BRACEY

DAYS INN
2850 Hwy 903
(23919)
Rates: $49-$75
(804) 689-2000
(800) 329-7466

BRANDY STATION

BLUE HAVEN BED & BREAKFAST
14648 Carrico
Mills Rd (22714)
Rates: $65-$85
(540) -825-0716

BRISTOL

ECONO LODGE
912 Commonwealth
Ave (24201)
Rates: $33-$130
(540) 466-2112
(800) 553-2666

LA QUINTA INN
1014 Old Airport
Rd (24201)
Rates: $49-$69
(540) 669-9353
(800) 687-6667

RED CARPET INN
15589 Lee Hwy
(24202)
Rates: n/a
(540) 669-1151
(800) 251-1962
(800) 948-6257

SKYLAND MOTEL
15545 Lee Hwy
(24201)
Rates: $20-$45
(540) 669-0166

SUPER 8 MOTEL
2139 Lee Hwy
(24201)
Rates: $65-$95
(540) 466-8800
(800) 800-8000

BUCHANAN

WATTSTULL INN
Rt 1, Box 21
(24066)
Rates: $42-$45
(703) 254-1551

BUENA VISTA

BUENA VISTA MOTEL
477 E 29th St
(24416)
Rates: $36-$59
(540) 261-2138

BUFFALO JUNCTION

THE LITTLE RETREAT
877 Riverview Ave
(24592)
Rates: n/a
(800) 843-0633

BURGESS

BAILEY-COCKRELL HOUSE B&B
P O Box 296
(22432)
Rates: n/a
(804) 453-5900

CALLAO

STRANGERS IN GOOD COMPANY BED & BREAKFAST
170 Bell's Cove Rd
(22435)
Rates: n/a
(804) 529-5132

CAPE CHARLES

DAYS INN
29106 Lankford
Hwy (23310)
Rates: $59-$99
(757) 331-1000
(800) 329-7466

SUNSET BEACH INN
Rt 13 (23310)
Rates: n/a
(757) 331-4786

CARMEL CHURCH

DAYS INN
24320 Rogers
Clark Blvd (22546)
Rates: $65-$99
(804) 448-2011
(800) 328-7466

RAMADA INN
23500 Welcome
Way Dr (22546)
Rates: $69-$89
(804) 448-2828
(800) 272-6232

CHAMPLAIN

LINDEN HOUSE B&B PLANTATION
11770 Tidewater
Trail (22438)
Rates: $95
(804) 443-1170

CHANTILLY

HOMESTEAD VILLAGE GUEST STUDIOS
4504 Brookfield
Corporate Dr
(20151)
Rates: n/a
(703) 263-3361
(888) 782-9473

MARRIOTT TOWNE PLACE SUITES
14036 Tunderbolt
Place (20151)
Rates: n/a
(703) 709-0453
(800) 228-3830

MARRIOTT WASHINGTON DULLES AIRPORT
333 W Service Rd
(22021)
Rates: $59-$110
(703) 471-9500
(800) 228-9290

CHARLES CITY

RIVER'S REST MOTEL & MARINA
9100 Willcox Neck
Rd (23030)
Rates: $49-$69
(804) 829-2753

AREA CODES - If the local number doesn't connect, check for a new area code.

CHARLOTTES-VILLE

BEST WESTERN CAVALIER INN
105 Emmet St
(22905)
Rates: $49-$99
(804) 296-8111
(800) 528-1234

BEST WESTERN MOUNT VERNON
1613 Emmet St
(22906)
Rates: $55-$68
(804) 296-5501
(800) 528-1234

CAMPS & COTTAGES OF CHARLOTTESVILLE
Rt 6, Box 260A
(22902)
Rates: n/a
(804) 293-2529

COMFORT INN
1807 Emmet St
(22901)
Rates: $64-$135
(804) 293-6188
(800) 228-5150

DAYS INN
1600 Emmet St
(22901)
Rates: $54-$129
(804) 293-9111
(800) 329-7466

ECONO LODGE
400 Emmet St
(22903)
Rates: $45-$100
(804) 296-2104
(800) 553-2666

ENGLISH INN
2000 Morton Dr
(22901)
Rates: n/a
(804) 971-9900

HOLIDAY INN
1200 5th St (22902)
Rates: n/a
(804) 977-5100
(800) 465-4329

KNIGHTS INN
1300 Seminole Tr
(22901)
Rates: $41-$78
(804) 973-8133
(800) 843-5644

OMNI HOTEL
235 W Main St
(22901)
Rates: n/a
(804) 971-5500
(800) 843-6664

THE QUARTERS
611 Preston Pl
(22903)
Rates: n/a
(804) 979-7264

RED ROOF INN
1309 W Main St
(22903)
Rates: n/a
(804) 295-4333
(800) 843-7663

RESIDENCE INN BY MARRIOTT
1111 Millmont St
(22903)
Rates: n/a
(804) 923-0300
(800) 331-3131

SUPER 8 MOTEL
390 Greenbrier Dr
(22901)
Rates: $49-$70
(804) 973-0888
(800) 800-8000

CHESAPEAKE

DAYS INN
1439 N George Washington Hwy
(23323)
Rates: $45-$65
(757) 487-8861
(800) 329-7466

ECONO LODGE
4725 Military Hwy W (23321)
Rates: $35-$80
(757) 488-4963
(800) 553-2666

MOTEL 6
701 Woodlake Dr
(23320)
Rates: $42-$58
(757) 420-2976
(800) 466-8356

RED ROOF INN
724 Woodlake Dr
(23320)
Rates: $54-$67
(757) 523-0123
(800) 843-7663

SUPER 8 MOTEL
100 Red Cedar Ct
(23320)
Rates: $45-$65
(757) 547-8880
(800) 800-8000

SUPER 8 MOTEL
3216 Churchland Blvd (23320)
Rates: $52-$66
(757) 686-8888
(800) 800-8000

TOWNPLACE SUITES BY MARRIOTT
2000 Old Greenbriar Rd
(23320)
Rates: $79-$109
(757) 523-5004
(800) 257-3000

WELLESLEY INN
1750 Sara Dr
(23320)
Rates: $60-$170
(757) 366-0100
(800) 444-8888

CHESTER

DAYS INN
2410 W Hundred Rd (23831)
Rates: $58-$89
(804) 748-5871
(800) 329-7466

HOWARD JOHNSON
2401 W Hundred Rd (23831)
Rates: $68-$95
(804) 748-6321
(800) 446-4656

CHILHOWIE

KNIGHTS INN
108 River Rd
(24319)
Rates: $38-$69
(540) 646-8981
(800) 843-5644

CHINCO-TEAGUE

BAY COMPANY RENTALS
6207 Maddox Blvd (23336)
Rates: n/a
(800) 221-5059

BAYSIDE RETREAT
4215 Main St (23336)
Rates: n/a
(757) 336-6798

EAST SIDE RENTALS
7462 East Side Rd
(23336)
Rates: n/a
(757) 336-6861

ISLAND PROPERTY ENTERPRISES
4065 Main St
(23336)
Rates: n/a
(800) 346-2559

MAIN STREET HOUSE B&B
4356 MainSt
(23336)
Rates: n/a
(757) 336-6030

SEA BREEZE RENTALS
6755 Maddox Blvd (23336)
Rates: n/a
(800) 795-3931

SEA TAG LODGE
7486 E Side Dr
(23336)
Rates: n/a
(757) 336-5555

CHISWELL

SUPER 8 MOTEL
199 Ft. Chiswell Rd (24360)
Rates: $49-$65
(540) 637-4027
(800) 800-8000

CHRISTIANS-BURG

DAYS INN
P. O. Box 768
(24073)
Rates: $45-$84
(540) 382-0261
(800) 329-7466

HOWARD JOHNSON EXPRESS
100 Bristol Dr
(24073)
Rates: $39-$75
(540) 381-0150
(800) 446-4656

SUPER 8 MOTEL
55 Laurel St NE
(24073)
Rates: $48-$84
(540) 382-5813
(800) 800-8000

SUPER 8 MOTEL
2780 Roanoke St
(24073)
Rates: $44-$60
(540) 382-7421
(800) 800-8000

CLARKSVILLE

BAYVIEW EFFICIENCIES
405 4th St (23927)
Rates: n/a
(804) 374-9216

CLIFTON FORGE

LONGDALE INN
6209 Longdale Furnace Rd
(24422)
Rates: n/a
(540) 862-0892
(800) 862-0386

COLLINSVILLE

DUTCH INN MOTEL
2360 Virginia Ave
(24078)
Rates: $62-$90
(540) 647-3721

FAIRYSTONE MOTEL
626 Virginia Ave
(24078)
Rates: $37-$48
(540) 647-3941

KNIGHTS INN
2357 Virginia Ave
(24078)
Rates: $44-$52
(540) 647-3716
(800) 843-5644

COLONIAL BEACH

DAYS INN
30 Colonial Ave
(22443)
Rates: $46-$85
(804) 224-0404
(800) 329-7466

COLONIAL HEIGHTS

COMFORT SUITES
931 South Ave
(23834)
Rates: $69-$155
(800) 228-5150

DAYS INN
2310 Indian Hill
Rd (23834)
Rates: $70-$96
(804) 520-1010
(800) 329-7466

TRAVELODGE-NORTH
2201 Ruffinmill
Rd (23834)
Rates: $38-$55
(804) 526-4611
(800) 578-7878

COVINGTON

BEST WESTERN MOUNTAINVIEW
820 E Madison St
(24426)
Rates: $70-$91
(540) 962-4951
(800) 528-1234

BUDGET INN MOTEL
Monroe &
Riverside Sts
(24426)
Rates: n/a
(540) 962-3966

COMFORT INN
203 Interstate Dr
(24426)
Rates: $63-$84
(540) 962-2141
(800) 228-5150

HIGHLAND MOTEL
720 S Highland
Ave (24426)
Rates: n/a
(540) 962-3901

KNIGHTS COURT
908 Valley Ridge
Rd (24426)
Rates: $53-$73
(540) 962-7600
(800) 843-5644

MILTON HALL B&B INN
207 Thorny Ln
(24426)
Rates: n/a
(540) 965-0196

CROZET

YANCY MILLS BED & BREAKFAST
6334 Hillsboro
Lane (22932)
Rates: n/a
(804) 823-4839

CULPEPER

COMFORT INN
890 Willis Lane
(22701)
Rates: $75-$99
(540) 825-4900
(800) 228-5150

HOLIDAY INN
Rt 29 S Business
(22701)
Rates: $99
(540) 825-1253
(800) 465-4329

SUPER 8 MOTEL
889 Willis Lane
(22701)
Rates: $46-$64
(540) 825-8088
(800) 800-8000

CUMBERLAND

RT. 60 MOTEL
Rt 60, Box 162
(23040)
Rates: n/a
(804) 492-4119

DALEVILLE

BEST WESTERN COACHMAN INN
437 Roanoke Rd
(24083)
Rates: $58-$72
(540) 992-1234
(800) 528-1234
(800) 628-1958

DANVILLE

DAYS INN
1390 Piney Forest
Dr (24540)
Rates: $45-$75
(804) 836-6745
(800) 329-7466

STRATFORD INN
2500 Riverside Dr
(24540)
Rates: $61-$75
(804) 793-2500

DOSWELL

BEST WESTERN-KINGS QUARTERS
I-95 & Rt 30
(23047)
Rates: $29-$189
(804) 876-3321
(800) 528-1234

DULLES

TOWNPLACE SUITES BY MARRIOTT
22744 Holiday
Park Dr (20101)
Rates: n/a
(703) 707-2017
(800) 257-3000

DUMFRIES

HOLIDAY INN EXPRESS
17133 Dumfries
Rd (22026)
Rates: $65-$85
(703) 221-1141
(800) 465-4329

EMPORIA

BEST WESTERN EMPORIA INN
1100 W Atlantic St
(23847)
Rates: $55-$77
(804) 634-3200
(800) 528-1234

COMFORT INN
1411 Skippers Rd
(23847)
Rates: $45-$69
(804) 348-3282
(800) 228-5150

DAYS INN
921 W Atlantic St
(23847)
Rates: $53-$83
(804) 634-9481
(800) 329-7466

HAMPTON INN
1207 W Atlantic St
(23847)
Rates: $60-$75
(804) 634-9200
(800) 426-7866

HOLIDAY INN
311 Florida Ave
(23847)
Rates: $70
(804) 634-4191
(800) 465-4329

KNIGHTS INN
3173 Sussex Dr
(23847)
Rates: $30-$64
(804) 535-8535
(800) 843-5644

RED CARPET INN
1586 Skippers Rd
(23847)
Rates: $29-$37
(804) 634-4181
(800) 251-1962

RESTÉ MOTEL
3190 Sussex Dr
(23847)
Rates: $30-$50
(804) 535-8505

ETLAN

DULLANEY HOLLOW /OLD RAG MTN
Rt 6, Box 214
(22719)
Rates: n/a
(540) 923-4470

FAIRFAX

HOLIDAY INN FAIR OAKS
11787 Lee Jackson
Hwy (22033)
Rates: $134
(703) 352-2525
(800) 465-4329

HOMESTEAD VILLAGE GUEST STUDIOS
8281 Willow Oaks
Corporate Dr
(22031)
Rates: n/a
(703) 204-0088
(888) 782-9473

HOMESTEAD VILLAGEGUEST STUDIOS
12104 Monument
Dr (22033)
Rates: $75-$105
(703) 274-3444
(888) 782-9473

HYATT FAIR LAKES
12777 Fair Lakes
Cir (22033)
Rates: $190+
(703) 818-1234
(800) 233-1234

RESIDENCE INN BY MARRIOTT
Fairfax Cty Pkwy
/Fair Lakes
(22033)
Rates: n/a
(703) 266-4900
(800) 331-3131

WELLESLEY INN
10327 Lee Hwy
(22030)
Rates: $80-$155
(703) 359-2888
(800) 444-8888

FAIRFIELD

FOX HILL ORDINARY
4383 Borden Grant
Trail (24435)
Rates: n/a
(888) 440-4383

FALLS CHURCH

MARRIOTT HOTEL
3111 Fairview
Park Dr (22042)
Rates: $79-$145
(703) 849-9400
(800) 228-9290

FANCY GAP

CASCADE MOUNTAIN INN
96 Cascade Trail
(24328)
Rates: $50-$85
(540) 728-2300

FARMVILLE

SUPER 8 MOTEL
Hwy 15 S (23901)
Rates: $45-$65
(804) 392-8196
(800) 800-8000

FERRUM

OLD SPRING FARM B&B
7629 Charity Hwy
(24088)
Rates: n/a
(540) 930-3404

AREA CODES - If the local number doesn't connect, check for a new area code.

FORT HAYWOOD

INN AT TABB'S CREEK LANDING
P.O. Box 219 (23138)
Rates: n/a
(804) 725-5136

FORT MONROE

CHAMBERLIN HOTEL
General Delivery
(23651)
Rates: n/a
(757) 723-6511
(800) 582-8975

FRANKLIN

BEST WESTERN FRANKLIN INN
Hwy 58 S (23851)
Rates: $45-$70
(757) 562-4100
(800) 528-1234

COMFORT INN
1620 Armory Dr
(23851)
Rates: $48-$75
(757) 569-0018
(800) 228-5150

DAYS INN
1660 Armory Dr
(23851)
Rates: $60-$80
(757) 562-2225
(800) 328-7466

FREDERICKS-BURG

BEST WESTERN INN
2205 William St
(22401)
Rates: $50-$72
(540) 371-5050
(800) 528-1234

BEST WESTERN CENTRAL PARK
3000 Plank Rd
(22401)
Rates: $46-$65
(540) 786-7404
(800) 528-1234

CENTRAL PARK HOTEL
2801 Plank Rd
(22401)
Rates: $89
(540) 786-8321

DAYS INN-NORTH
14 Simpson Rd
(22405)
Rates: $29-$56
(540) 373-5340
(800) 329-7466

DAYS INN-SOUTH
5316 Jefferson
Davis Hwy
(22401)
Rates: $50-$55
(540) 898-6800
(800) 329-7466

DUNNING MILLS INN
2305-C Jefferson
Davis Hwy
(22401)
Rates: $55-$90
(540) 373-1256

ECONO LODGE
5321 Jefferson
Davis Hwy
(22408)
Rates: $39-$85
(540) 898-5440
(800) 553-2666

ECONO LODGE
I-95, Exit 130-B
(22404)
Rates: $35-$55
(540) 786-8374
(800) 553-2666

HAMPTON INN
2310 Plank Rd
(22401)
Rates: $64-$86
(540) 371-0330
(800) 426-7866

HERITAGE INN
5308 Jefferson
Davis Hwy
(22402)
Rates: $30-$59
(540) 898-1000

HOLIDAY INN-S
5324 Jefferson
Davis Hwy
(22401)
Rates: $75-$85
(540) 898-1102
(800) 465-4329

HOLIDAY INN-N
564 Warrenton Rd
(22405)
Rates: $67-$82
(540) 371-5550
(800) 465-4329

HOWARD JOHNSON
5327 Jefferson
Davis Hwy
(22408)
Rates: $75-$85
(540) 898-1800
(800) 446-4656

MOTEL 6
401 Warrenton Rd
(22405)
Rates: $32-$44
(540) 371-5443
(800) 466-8356

QUALITY INN
543 Warrenton Rd
(22406)
Rates: $65-$95
(540) 373-0000
(800) 228-5151

RAMADA INN
2802 Plank Rd
(22404)
Rates: $50-$85
(540) 786-8361
(800) 272-6232

SHERATON INN
2801 Plank Rd
(22404)
Rates: $59-$99
(540) 786-8321
(800) 325-3535

SUPER 8 MOTEL
3002 Mall Court
(22401)
Rates: $45-$65
(540) 786-8881
(800) 800-8000

FRONT ROYAL

BLUEMONT INN
1525 N
Shenandoah Ave
(22630)
Rates: $45-$65
(540) 635-9447
(800) 461-1720

BUDGET INN
1122 N Royal St
(22630)
Rates: $35-$75
(540) 635-2196
(800) 766-6748

CENTER CITY MOTEL
416 S Royal Ave
(22630)
Rates: $25-$45
(540) 635-4050

PIONEER MOTEL
541 S Royal Ave
(22630)
Rates: n/a
(540) 635-4784

RELAX INN
1801 N
Shenandoah Ave
(22630)
Rates: $29-$65
(540) 635-4101
(877) 487-3529

SCOTTISH INNS
533 S Royal Ave
(22630)
Rates: $39-$79
(540) 636-6168
(800) 251-1962

SUPER 8 MOTEL
111 South St
(22630)
Rates: $46-$62
(540) 636-4888
(800) 800-8000

TWI-LITE MOTEL
53 W 14th St
(22630)
Rates: $59-$85
(540) 635-4148
(800) 230-7349

GALAX

CREST HAVEN FARM
114 Deerfield Rd
(24333)
Rates: n/a
(540) 236-4436

GLADE SPRING

ECONOMY INN
P. O. Box 453
(24340)
Rates: $30-$42
(703) 429-5131
(800) 826-0778

GLEN ALLEN

AMERISUITES
4100 Cox Rd
(23060)
Rates: $82-$92
(804) 747-9644
(800) 833-1516

HOMESTEAD VILLAGE-INNSBROOK
10961 W Broad St
(23060)
Rates: $59-$99
(804) 747-8898
(888) 782-9473

HOMEWOOD SUITES
4100 Innslake Dr
(23060)
Rates: n/a
(804) 217-8000
(800) 225-5466

RESIDENCE INN BY MARRIOTT
3940 Westerre
Pkwy (23060)
Rates: $114-$179
(804) 762-9852
(800) 331-3131

TOWNPLACE SUITES BY MARRIOTT
4231 Park Place Ct
(23060)
Rates: n/a
(804) 747-5253
(800) 257-3000

THE VIRGINIA CLIFFE INN
2900 Mountain Rd
(23060)
Rates: n/a
(804) 266-1661

GLOUCESTER POINT

TIDEWATER MOTEL
Rt 17 (23072)
Rates: n/a
(804) 642-2155

GORDONS-VILLE

NORFIELDS FARM BED & BREAKFAST
1982 James Madison
Hwy (22942)
Rates: n/a
(540) 832-2952
(800) 754-0105

ROCKLANDS B&B
17439 Rocklands
Dr (22942)
Rates: n/a
(540) 832-7176

AREA CODES - If the local number doesn't connect, check for a new area code.

SLEEPY HOLLOW FARM B&B
16280 Blue Ridge Turnpike (22942)
Rates: $85
(540) 832-5555
(800) 215-4804

GOSHEN

BIG RIVER GUEST LODGE
1800 Big River Rd (24439)
Rates: n/a
(800) 997-2745

HUMMINGBIRD INN
30 Wood Lane (24439)
Rates: $95-$155
(540) 997-9065
(800) 397-3214

GREENVILLE

HESSIAN ECONO LODGE
Jct US 11/340 (24440)
Rates: $45-$75
(540) 337-1231
(800) 553-2666

GRUNDY

COMFORT INN
US 460 & Main St (24614)
Rates: $60-$89
(540) 935-5050
(800) 228-5150
(800) 561-2291

HAMPTON

ARROW INN
7 Semple Farm Rd (23666)
Rates: $46-$67
(757) 865-0300
(800) 833-2520

CANDLEWOOD SUITES
401 Butler Farm Rd (23666)
Rates: $89
(757) 766-8976

CHAMBERLIN HOTEL
2 Fenwick Rd (23651)
Rates: n/a
(757) 723-6511

COLISEUM INTERSTATE INN
2000 W Mercury Blvd (23666)
Rates: n/a
(757) 838-7070

DAYS INN
1918 Coliseum Dr (23666)
Rates: $49-$90
(757) 826-4810
(800) 329-7466

ECONO LODGE-COLISEUM
2708 W Mercury Blvd (23666)
Rates: $34-$100
(757) 826-8970
(800) 553-2666

HAMPTON INN
1813 W Mercury Blvd (23666)
Rates: $74-$99
(757) 838-8484
(800) 426-7866

HOLIDAY INN
1815 W Mercury Blvd (23666)
Rates: $99-$129
(757) 838-0200
(800) 465-4329

LA QUINTA INN
2138 W Mercury Blvd (23666)
Rates: $69-$89
(757) 827-8680
(800) 687-6667

QUALITY INN & SUITES CONF CTR
1215 W Mercury Blvd (23666)
Rates: $89-$129
(757) 838-5011
(800) 228-5151

RED ROOF INN
1925 Coliseum Dr (23666)
Rates: $41-$91
(757) 838-1870
(800) 843-7663

SHERATON INN-COLISEUM
1215 W Mercury Blvd (23666)
Rates: $59-$99
(757) 838-5011
(800) 325-3535

SUPER 8 MOTEL
1330 Thomas St (23669)
Rates: $44-$64
(757) 723-2888
(800) 800-8000

HARDYSVILLE

RIVER'S RISE B&BS
Rte 652,
PO Box 18 (23070)
Rates: n/a
(804) 776-7521

HARRISON-BURG

COMFORT INN
1440 E Market St (22801)
Rates: $72-$99
(540) 433-6066
(800) 228-5150

DAYS INN
1131 Forest Hill Rd (22801)
Rates: $49-$130
(540) 433-9353
(800) 329-7466

ECONO LODGE
US 33 & I-81 (22801)
Rates: $45-$89
(540) 433-2576
(800) 553-2666

HOWARD JOHNSON INN
605 Port Republic Rd (22801)
Rates: $44-$69
(540) 434-6771
(800) 446-4656

MOTEL 6
10 Linda Ln (22801)
Rates: $32-$42
(540) 433-6939
(800) 466-8356

RAMADA INN
1 Pleasant Valley Rd (22801)
Rates: $45-$85
(540) 434-9981
(800) 272-6232

RED CARPET INN
3210 S Main St (22801)
Rates: $25-$38
(540) 434-6704
(800) 251-1962

ROCKINGHAM MOTEL
4035 S Main St (22801)
Rates: $33-$39
(540) 433-2538

SHERATON FOUR POINTS HOTEL
1400 E Market St (22801)
Rates: $99-$109
(540) 433-2521
(800) 325-3535

SUPER 8 MOTEL
3330 S Main (22801)
Rates: $47-$64
(540) 433-8888
(800) 800-8000

VILLAGE INN
4979 S Valley Pike (22801)
Rates: $50-$60
(540) 434-7355
(800) 736-7355

HERNDON

HILTON HOTEL WASH/DULLES
13869 Park Center Rd (22071)
Rates: $95-$167
(703) 478-2900
(800) 445-8677

HOLIDAY INN EXPRESS-WASH/DULLES
485 Elden St (22070)
Rates: $104
(703) 478-9777
(800) 465-4329

RESIDENCE INN BY MARRIOTT
315 Elden St (22070)
Rates: $65-$155
(703) 435-0044
(800) 331-3131

SUMMERFIELD SUITES HOTEL
13700 Coopermine Rd (22071)
Rates: $99-$178
(703) 713-6800
(800) 833-4353

HILLSVILLE

BEST WESTERN FOUR SEASONS SOUTH
57 Airport Rd (24343)
Rates: $53-$69
(540) 728-4136
(800) 528-1234

DOE RUN AT GROUNDHOG MOUNTAIN
MP 189, Blue Ridge Pkwy (24343)
Rates: $109-$275
(540) 398-2212

ECONO LODGE
I-77 & US 58 (24343)
Rates: $61-$71
(540) 728-9118
(800) 553-2666

HOLIDAY INN EXPRESS
85 Airport Rd (24343)
Rates: $69-$150
(540) 728-2120
(800) 465-4329

HOPEWELL

COMFORT INN
5380 Oaklawn Blvd (23860)
Rates: $55-$85
(804) 452-0022
(800) 228-5150

INNKEEPER
3852 Courthouse Rd (23860)
Rates: n/a
(804) 458-2600

HOT SPRINGS

ROSELOE MOTEL
590 US 220 N (24445)
Rates: $38-$55
(540) 839-5373

VINE COTTAGE INN
General Delivery (24445)
Rates: n/a
(540) 839-2422

AREA CODES - If the local number doesn't connect, check for a new area code.

HUME

CANTERBURY COTTAGE ON PENDRAGON LAKE
12055 Crest Hill Rd (22639)
Rates: n/a
(540) 364-3970

INDEPENDENCE

BLUE RIDGE VIEWS VACATION RENTALS
751 Mtn View Rd (24348)
Rates: n/a
(540) 773-2496

CLIFFHANGER
288 Tarnywood Rd (24348)
Rates: n/a
(757) 868-7948
(336) 372-2293

THE FARMHOUSE ON ELK CREEK
6957 Peach Bottom Rd (24348)
Rates: n/a
(540) 655-4413

NEW RIVER RETREAT CABIN
538 Old River Lane (24348)
Rates: n/a
(540) 773-3946

IRVINGTON

HOPE AND GLORY INN
634 King Carter Dr (22480)
Rates: n/a
(804) 438-6053

TIDES INN
480 King Center Dr (22480)
Rates: $130-$450
(804) 438-5000

TIDES LODGE
#1 St. Andrews Lane (22480)
Rates: $105-$325
(804) 438-6000

KEYSVILLE

SHELDON'S MOTEL
1450 Four Locust Hwy (23947)
Rates: $48-$54
(804) 736-8434

LEESBURG

COLONIAL INN
21 S King St (22075)
Rates: n/a
(703) 777-5000

DAYS INN
721 E Market St (22075)
Rates: $59-$89
(703) 777-6622
(800) 329-7466

HOLIDAY INN AT CARRADOC HALL
1500 E Market St (22076)
Rates: $109-$159
(703) 771-9200
(800) 465-4329

LAUREL BRIGADE INN
20 W Market St (22075)
Rates: n/a
(703) 777-1010

LEESBURG WEST-PARK HOTEL
59 Club House Dr SW (22075)
Rates: n/a
(703) 777-1910

LITTLE ROCK MOTEL
Rt 4, Box 608 (22075)
Rates: n/a
(703) 777-3499

NORRIS HOUSE INN
108 Loudoun St SW (20175)
Rates: n/a
(703) 777-1806
(800) 644-1806

PIEDMONT MOTEL
Rt 2, Box 230 (22075)
Rates: n/a
(703) 777-3361

LEXINGTON

APPLEWOOD INN & LLAMA TREKKING
242 Tarn Beck Lane (24450)
Rates: n/a
(540) 463-1962
(800) 463-1902

BEST WESTERN AT HUNT RIDGE
25 Willow Springs Rd (24450)
Rates: $80-$99
(540) 464-1500
(800) 528-1234
(800) 464-1501

COMFORT INN-VIRGINIA HORSE CENTER
62 Comfort Way (24450)
Rates: $50-$82
(540) 463-7311
(800) 228-5150

DAYS INN-KEYDET GENERAL
325 W Midland Trail (24450)
Rates: $48-$70
(540) 463-2143
(800) 329-7466

ECONO LODGE
66 Econo Lane (24450)
Rates: $38-$80
(540) 463-7371
(800) 553-2666

GREYSTONE CABIN
1288 Collierstown Rd (24450)
Rates: n/a
(540) 463-5906

HOLIDAY INN EXPRESS
I-64, Exit 55 (24450)
Rates: $65-$104
(540) 463-7351
(800) 465-4329

HOWARD JOHNSON
2836 N Lee Hwy (24450)
Rates: $60-$75
(540) 463-9181
(800) 446-4656

RAMADA INN
2814 N Lee Hwy (24450)
Rates: $52-$68
(540) 463-6400
(800) 272-6232

SUPER 8 MOTEL
Rt 7, Box 99 (24450)
Rates: $50-$65
(540) 463-7858
(800) 800-8000

THE KEEP
116 Lee Ave (24450)
Rates: n/a
(540) 463-3560

THRIFTY INN
820 S Main St (24450)
Rates: $29-$49
(540) 463-2151

LIGHTFOOT

ECONO LODGE
7051 Richmond Rd (23090)
Rates: $30-$130
(757) 564-3341
(800) 553-2666

LINCOLN

CREEK CROSSING FARM
37768 Chappelle Hill Rd (22078)
Rates: n/a
(540) 338-4548

LOCUST DALE

INN AT MEANDER PLANTATION
HC 5, Box 460 (22948)
Rates: n/a
(540) 672-4912
(800) 385-4936

LORTON

COMFORT INN GUNSTON CORNER
8180 Silverbrook Rd (22079)
Rates: $59-$129
(703) 643-3100
(800) 228-5150

LOUISA

GINGER HILL B&B
47 Holly Springs Dr (23093)
Rates: $75-$130
(703) 967-3260

LURAY

BEST WESTERN INTOWN OF LURAY
410 W Main St (22835)
Rates: $69-$95
(540) 743-6511
(800) 528-1234

CARDINAL MOTEL
US Bus 211 (22835)
Rates: n/a
(540) 743-5010

DAYS INN
138 Whispering Hill Rd (22835)
Rates: $59-$150
(540) 743-4521
(800) 329-7466

DEERLANE COTTAGES
P O Box 188 (22835)
Rates: n/a
(540) 743-3344
(800) 696-3337

INTOWN MOTEL
410 W Main St (22835)
Rates: $38-$85
(540) 743-6511

LION & CROW LODGE & CABINS
244 Forest Rd (22835)
Rates: n/a
(540) 743-6605
(877) 833-6515

LURAY CAVERNS MOTEL WEST
US 211 Bypass (22835)
Rates: n/a
(540) 743-4536

MIMSLYN INN
401 W Main St (22835)
Rates: n/a
(540) 743-5105
(800) 296-5105

RAMADA INN
US 211 Bypass E
(22835)
Rates: $69-$150
(540) 743-4521
(800) 272-6232

**STONE
MOUNTAIN
CABIN**
1680 Egypt Bend
Rd (22835)
Rates: n/a
(540) 843-4944

LYNCHBURG

COMFORT INN
3125 Albert
Lankford Dr
(24506)
Rates: $73-$120
(804) 847-9041
(800) 228-5150

ECONO LODGE
2400 Stadium Rd
(24501)
Rates: $55-$70
(804) 847-1045
(800) 553-2666

**HOLIDAY INN
SELECT**
601 Main St
(24504)
Rates: $69-$89
(804) 528-2500
(800) 465-4329

**HOWARD
JOHNSON**
US 29 N (24506)
Rates: $48-$69
(804) 845-7041
(800) 446-4656

LYNDHURST

**CABIN
CREEKWOOD**
Rt 1, Box 444-J
(22952)
Rates: n/a
(540) 943-8552

MADISON

**DULANEY
HOLLOW AT OLD
RAG MOUNTAIN
COTTAGES**
Rt 6, Box 215
(22727)
Rates: n/a
(540) 923-4470

MADISONVILLE

**MADISONVILLE
FARM INN**
HC 1, Box 35
(23958)
Rates: n/a
(804) 248-9020

MANASSAS

**BEST WESTERN
BATTLEFIELD INN**
10820 Bals Ford
(22109)
Rates: $59-$105
(703) 361-8000
(800) 528-1234

RED ROOF INN
10610 Automotive
Dr (22110)
Rates: $55-$82
(703) 335-9333
(800) 843-7663

**SUNRISE HILL
FARM BED &
BREAKFAST**
5590 Old Farm
Lane (20109)
Rates: n/a
(703) 754-8309

MARION

BEST WESTERN
1424 N Main St
(24354)
Rates: $60-$73
(540) 783-3193
(800) 528-1234

**BUDGET HOST
MARION MOTEL**
435 S Main St
(24354)
Rates: $28-$85
(540) 783-8511
(800) 283-4678

**HUNGRY MOTHER
STATE PARK
CABINS**
2854 Park Blvd
(24354)
Rates: n/a
(540) 782-9032
(800) 933-7275

**VIRGINIA HOUSE
MOTOR INN**
1419 N Main St
(24354)
Rates: $44-$49
(540) 783-5112

MARTINSVILLE

BEST LODGE
1985 Virginia Ave
(24114)
Rates: $40-$65
(540) 647-3941

**BEST WESTERN
INN**
1755 Virginia Ave
(24114)
Rates: $55-$85
(540) 632-5611
(800) 528-1234
(800) 388-3934

SUPER 8 MOTEL
1044 N Memorial
Blvd (24114)
Rates: n/a
(540) 666-8888
(800) 800-8000

MAX
MEADOWS

GATEWAY MOTEL
Rt 3, Box 488
(24360)
Rates: $25-$36
(540) 637-3119

SUPER 8 MOTEL
I-77 & I-81, Exit 80
(24360)
Rates: $55-$140
(540) 637-4027
(800) 800-8000

MCLEAN

**BEST WESTERN
TYSONS
WESTPARK**
8401 Westpark Dr
(22102)
Rates: $79-$149
(703) 734-2800
(800) 528-1234
(800) 533-3301

**HILTON TYSONS
CORNER**
7920 Jones Branch
Dr (22102)
Rates: n/a
(703) 847-5000
(800) 445-8667

MEADOWS
OF DAN

**PRIMELAND
RESORT/STABLES
& KENNELS**
4621 Busted Rock
Rd (24120)
Rates: n/a
(540) 251-8012

WOODBERRY INN
MP 908, Blue
Ridge Pky (24120)
Rates: n/a
(540) 593-2567

MELFA

**CAPT'S QUARTERS
MOTEL**
Rt 13, Box D (23410)
Rates: n/a
(757) 787-4545

MIDDLEBURG

**MIDDLEBURG
COUNTRY INN
& HORSE
BOARDING**
209 E Washington
St (22117)
Rates: n/a
(800) 262-6082

RED FOX INN
2 E Washington St
(22117)
Rates: n/a
(540) 687-6301

MILLBORO

**DOUTHAT STATE
PARK CABINS**
Rt 1, Box 212
(24460)
Rates: n/a
(540) 862-8100

**FORT LEWIS
LODGE**
HCR 3, Box 21A
(24460)
Rates: n/a
(703) 925-2314

MINT SPRING

**ARMSTRONG
FAMILY MOTEL**
I-81, Exit 217
(24463)
Rates: $48
(540) 337-261

DAYS INN
I-81, Exit 217
(24463)
Rates: $59-$119
(540) 337-3031
(800) 329-7466

MONTEREY

BOBBIE'S B&B
HC-02, Box 5
(24465)
Rates: n/a
(540) 468-2308

**MONTVALLEE
MOTEL**
P O Box 25 (24465)
Rates: n/a
(540) 468-2500

MONTROSS

**THE INN
AT MONTROSS**
P. O. Box 908,
Courthouse Sq
(22520)
Rates: $65-$125
(804) 493-0573
(800) 321-0979

MOUNT
JACKSON

**BEST WESTERN
INN**
250 Conickville
Rd (22842)
Rates: $60-$85
(540) 477-2911
(800) 528-1234

**THE WIDOW KIP'S
COUNTRY INN**
335 Orchard Dr
(22842)
Rates: $100
(540) 477-2400
(800) 478-8714

MOUTH OF
WILSON

**CABIN ON THE
RIDGE**
548 York Ridge Rd
(24363)
Rates: n/a
(540) 579-4452

**WILSON CREEK
DELIGHT**
61 Red Fox Lane
(24363)
Rates: n/a
(540) 579-6763

AREA CODES - If the local number doesn't connect, check for a new area code.

NASSAWADOX

ANCHOR MOTEL
7120 Lankford
Hwy (23413)
Rates: $60-$77
(757) 442-6363

NATURAL BRIDGE

BUDGET INN
4331 S Lee Hwy
(24578)
Rates: $32-$68
(540) 291-2896

FANCY HILL MOTEL
US 11 & I-81
(24578)
Rates: n/a
(540) 291-2143

NATURAL BRIDGE INN & CONF CTR
US 11 & Rt 130
(24578)
Rates: n/a
(540) 291-2121

WATTSTULL INN
Blue Ridge Pkwy
Exit Rt 43 (24578)
Rates: n/a
(540) 254-1551

NELLYSFORD

ACORN INN
P. O. Box 431
(22958)
Rates: n/a
(804) 361-9357

NEW CHURCH

THE GARDEN & THE SEA INN
4188 Nelson Rd
(23415)
Rates: $75-$175
(757) 824-0672
(800) 824-0672

NEW MARKET

BUDGET INN
2192 Old Valley
Pike (22844)
Rates: $29-$65
(540) 740-3105
(800) 296-6835

DAYS INN
9360 George C
Collins Pkwy
(22844)
Rates: $39-$80
(540) 740-4100
(800) 329-7466

THE SHENVALEE
US 11, P O Box
930 (22844)
Rates: n/a
(540) 740-3181

NEWPORT NEWS

AMERICAN TUDOR INN
15540 Warwick
Blvd (23602)
Rates: n/a
(757) 887-0180

CAPRI COUNTRY INN
12880 Jefferson
Ave (23608)
Rates: n/a
(757) 877-7000
(877) 622-9901

COMFORT INN
12330 Jefferson
Ave (23602)
Rates: $89-$99
(757) 249-0200
(800) 228-5150

DAYS INN-OYSTER POINT
11829 Fishing Pt
Dr (23606)
Rates: $85-$150
(757) 873-6700
(800) 329-7466

DAYS INN
14747 Warwick
Blvd (23602)
Rates: $53-$65
(757) 874-0201
(800) 329-7466

ECONO LODGE FORT EUSTIS
15237 Warwick
Blvd (23602)
Rates: $39-$78
(757) 874-9244
(800) 553-2666

HOST INN
985 J. Clyde Morris
Blvd (23601)
Rates: $40-$77
(757) 599-3303
(888) 599-3303

KING JAMES MOTOR HOTEL
6045 Jefferson Ave
(23605)
Rates: $30-$50
(757) 245-2801

MOTEL 6
797 J. Clyde Morris
Blvd (23601)
Rates: $36-$48
(757) 595-6336
(800) 466-8356

NEWPORT NEWS INN
6128 Jefferson Ave
(23605)
Rates: $39-$60
(757) 826-4500

RAMADA INN OYSTER POINT
950 J. Clyde Morris
Blvd (23601)
Rates: $65-$89
(757) 599-4460
(800) 841-1112
(800) 272-6232

SUPER 8 MOTEL
945 J. Clyde Morris
Blvd (23605)
Rates: $44-$64
(757) 595-8888
(800) 800-8000

TDY INN
15910 Warwick
Blvd (23608)
Rates: n/a
(757) 888-6667
(800) 282-8849

THE-RIFT INN
6129 Jefferson Ave
(23605)
Rates: n/a
(757) 838-6852

TOWNPLACE SUITES BY MARRIOTT
200 Cybemetics
Way (23605)
Rates: n/a
(757) 874-8884
(800) 257-3000

NORFOLK

ANCHORAGE INN
929 E Ocean View
Ave (23503)
Rates: n/a
(757) 583-2605

BEACHCOMBER MOTEL
2090 E Ocean
View Ave (23503)
Rates: n/a
(757) 583-2605

CLARION HOTEL
700 Monticello
Ave (23510)
Rates: $99-$119
(757) 627-5555
(800) 252-7466

DAYS INN
1631 Bayville St
(23503)
Rates: $85-$95
(757) 583-4521
(800) 329-7466

DAYS INN MILITARY CIRCLE
5701 Chambers St
(23502)
Rates: $48-$78
(757) 461-0100
(800) 329-7466

ECONO LODGE
3343 N Military
Hwy (23518)
Rates: $55-$128
(757) 855-3116
(800) 553-2666

ECONO LODGE
865 N Military
Hwy (23502)
Rates: $36-$85
(757) 461-4865
(800) 553-2666

ECONO LODGE
9601 4th View St
(23503)
Rates: $34-$89
(757) 480-9611
(800) 553-2666

ECONO LODGE AZALEA GARDENS
1850 E Little
Creek (23518)
Rates: $32-$99
(757) 588-8888
(800) 553-2666

HILTON HOTEL
1500 N Military
Hwy (23502)
Rates: n/a
(757) 466-8000
(800) 445-8667

HOWARD JOHNSON EXPRESS INN
930 E Virginia
Beach Blvd
(23504)
Rates: $35-$90
(757) 622-4488
(800) 446-4656

JAMES MADISON HOTEL
345 Granby St
(23504)
Rates: $99-$139
(757) 622-6682

LAFAYETTE HOTEL
4233 Granby St
(23504)
Rates: n/a
(757) 622-5383

MARRIOTT HOTEL WATERSIDE
235 E Main St
(23510)
Rates: $139
(757) 627-4200
(800) 228-9290

MOTEL 6
853 N Military
Hwy (23502)
Rates: $36-$48
(757) 461-2380
(800) 466-8356

QUALITY INN
6280
Northampton
Blvd (23502)
Rates: $79-$150
(757) 461-6251
(800) 228-5151

QUALITY INN BAYVIEW/NAVAL BASE
1010 W Ocean
View Ave (23503)
Rates: $49-$102
(757) 587-8761
(800) 228-5151

SHERATON WATERSIDE HOTEL
777 Waterside Dr (23510)
Rates: n/a
(757) 622-6664
(800) 325-3535

NORTON

HOLIDAY INN
551 Hwy 58 E (24273)
Rates: $79-$115
(540) 679-7000
(800) 465-4329

SUPER 8 MOTEL
425 Wharton Lane (24273)
Rates: $49-$67
(540) 679-0893
(800) 800-8000

ONLEY

ANCHOR MOTEL
P.O. Box 69 (23418)
Rates: $42-$58
(757) 787-8000

ORANGE

WILLOW GROVE INN
14079 Plantation Way (22960)
Rates: n/a
(540) 672-5982
(800) 949-1778

PETERSBURG

AMERICAN INN
2209 County Dr (23803)
Rates: $31-$37
(804) 733-2800

BEST WESTERN INN
405 E Washington St (23803)
Rates: $40-$116
(804) 733-1776
(800) 528-1234
(800) 796-8327

CALIFORNIA INN
2214 Country Dr (23803)
Rates: n/a
(804) 732-5500

COMFORT INN
11974 S Crater Rd (23805)
Rates: $50-$99
(804) 732-2900
(800) 228-5150

DAYS INN
12208 S Crater Rd (23805)
Rates: $57-$80
(804) 733-4400
(800) 329-7466

ECONO LODGE-SOUTH
16905 Parkdale Rd (23805)
Rates: $34-$85
(804) 862-2717
(800) 553-2666

FLAGSHIP INN
815 S Crater Rd (23803)
Rates: $32-$52
(804) 861-3470

THE HIGH STREET INN B&B
405 High St (23803)
Rates: $75-$110
(804) 733-0505
(888) 733-0505

HOWARD JOHNSON HOTEL
501 E Wythe St (23803)
Rates: $38-$75
(804) 732-5950
(800) 446-4656

QUALITY INN
12205 S Crater Rd (23805)
Rates: $50-$79
(804) 733-0600
(800) 228-5151

RAMADA INN
501 E Washington St (23803)
Rates: $48-$69
(804) 733-0730
(800) 272-6232

STAR MOTEL
39 S Crater Rd (23803)
Rates: n/a
(804) 733-3600

PORT HAYWOOD

INN AT TABB'S CREEK LNDNG
Rt 14, P. O. Box 219 (23138)
Rates: n/a
(804) 725-5136

PORT ROYAL

BROWN'S MOTEL
25550 A.P. Hill Blvd (22535)
Rates: n/a
(804) 742-5523

PORTSMOUTH

DAYS INN
1031 London Blvd (23704)
Rates: $45-$110
(757) 399-4414
(800) 329-7466

HOLIDAY INN-WATERFRONT
8 Crawford Pkwy (23704)
Rates: $92-$113
(757) 393-2573
(800) 465-4329

HARBOR TOWER APARTMENTS
One Harbor Ct (23704)
Rates: n/a
(757) 393-1600
(800) 897-1601

POUNDING MILL

SUPER 8 MOTEL
Rt 2, Box 565 (24637)
Rates: $50-$68
(540) 964-9888
(800) 800-8000

PRINCE GEORGE

COMFORT INN
5380 Oaklawn Blvd (23875)
Rates: $55-$100
(804) 452-0022
(800) 553-2666

PULASKI

RED CARPET INN
I-81, Exit 94 (24301)
Rates: $28-$46
(540) 980-2230
(800) 251-1962

PUNGOTEAGUE

PUNGOTEAGUE JUNCTION BED & BREAKFAST
General Delivery (23422)
Rates: n/a
(757) 442-3581

RADFORD

THE ALLEGHANY INN
1123 Grove Ave (24141)
Rates: $65-$95
(540) 731-4466

BEST WESTERN INN
1501 Tyler Ave (24141)
Rates: $75-$92
(540) 639-3000
(800) 528-1234
(800) 628-1955

DOGWOOD LODGE
7073 Lee Hwy (24141)
Rates: $30-$38
(540) 639-9338

SUPER 8 MOTEL
1600 Tyler Ave (24141)
Rates: $47-$65
(540) 731-9355
(800) 800-8000

RAPHINE

DAYS INN
544 Oakland Cr (24472)
Rates: $54-$109
(540) 377-2604
(800) 329-7466

REEDVILLE

MORRIS HOUSE
Main St (22539)
Rates: n/a
(804) 453-7016

RESTON

HOMESTEAD GUEST STUDIOS
12190 Sunset Hills Rd (20191)
Rates: n/a
(703) 707-9700
(888) 782-9473

RICHMOND

AMERISUITES-ARBORETUM
201 Arboretum Place (23236)
Rates: $67-$129
(804) 560-1566
(800) 833-1516

BEST WESTERN EXECUTIVE HOTEL
7007 W Broad St (23294)
Rates: $49-$79
(804) 672-7007
(800) 528-1234

DAYS INN
1600 Robin Hood Rd (23220)
Rates: $35-$70
(804) 353-1287
(800) 329-7466

DAYS INN
2100 Dickens Rd (23230)
Rates: $58-$105
(804) 282-3300
(800) 329-7466

ECONO LODGE-SOUTH
2125 Willis Rd (23237)
Rates: $39-$100
(804) 271-6031
(800) 553-2666

ECONO LODGE-WEST
6523 Midlothian Tpk (23225)
Rates: $36-$85
(804) 276-8241
(800) 553-2666

ECONOMY HOUSE MOTEL
2302 Willis Rd (23237)
Rates: n/a
(804) 275-1412

HOLIDAY INN CENTRAL
3207 N Boulevard (23230)
Rates: $89-$119
(804) 359-9441
(800) 465-4329

HOLIDAY INN AT PHILIP MORRIS
4303 Commerce Rd (23234)
Rates: $49-$109
(804) 275-7891
(800) 465-4329

HOMESTEAD VILLAGE GUEST STUDIOS
241 Arboretum Place (23236)
Rates: $49
(804) 272-1800
(888) 782-9473

THE JEFFERSON HOTEL
Franklin & Adams Sts (23220)
Rates: $150-$265
(804) 788-8000

LA QUINTA MOTOR INN
6910 Midlothian Tpk (23225)
Rates: $45-$59
(804) 745-7100
(800) 687-6667

PARK SUITES HOTEL
9th & Bank St (23219)
Rates: n/a
(804) 343-7300

QUALITY INN WEST END
8008 W Broad St (23294)
Rates: $75-$159
(804) 346-0000
(800) 228-5151

RAMADA INN - SOUTH
2126 Willis Rd (23237)
Rates: $59-$85
(804) 271-1281
(800) 272-6232

RAMADA LIMITED
5221 Brook Rd (23227)
Rates: $48-$73
(804) 266-7603
(800) 272-6232

RED ROOF INN
4350 Commerce Rd (23234)
Rates: $49-$81
(804) 271-7240
(800) 843-7663

RED ROOF INN
100 Greshamwood Pl (23225)
Rates: $56-$62
(804) 745-0600
(800) 843-7663

RESIDENCE INN BY MARRIOTT
2121 Dickens Rd (23230)
Rates: $67-$162
(804) 285-8200
(800) 331-3131

RICHMOND HOTEL & CONF CENTER
6531 W Broad St (23234)
Rates: $89-$139
(804) 285-9951

SHERATON AIRPORT INN
4700 S Laburnom Ave (23231)
Rates: $59-$105
(804) 226-4300
(800) 325-3535

SLEEP INN
950 E Parham Rd (23228)
Rates: $74-$165
(804) 515-7800
(800) 753-3746

SUPER 8 MOTEL
8260 Midlothian Tpke (23235)
Rates: $44-$64
(804) 320-2823
(800) 800-8000

TRAVELODGE
5221 Brook Rd (23227)
Rates: $39-$59
(804) 261-6887
(800) 578-7878

VIRGINIA STATE PARK CABINS
Rt 203 Governor St, Ste 302 (23219)
Rates: $50-$130
(804) 786-1712
(800) 933-7275

RINER

RIVER'S EDGE B%B
6208 Little Camp Rd (24149)
Rates: n/a
(540) 381-4147
(888) 786-9413

ROANOKE

AMERISUITES
5040 Valley View Blvd (24012)
Rates: $69-$119
(540) 366-4700
(800) 833-1516

CLARION HOTEL-AIRPORT
2727 Ferndale Dr NW (24017)
Rates: $69-$139
(540) 372-4500
(800) 252-7466

DAYS INN CIVIC CENTER
535 Orange Ave NE (24016)
Rates: $60-$100
(540) 342-4551
(800) 329-7466

HOLIDAY INN TANGLEWOOD
4468 Starkey Rd SW (24014)
Rates: $75-$85
(540) 774-4400
(800) 465-4329

HOWARD JOHNSON EXPRESS
320 Kimball Ave NE (24016)
Rates: $50-$80
(540) 344-0981
(800) 446-4656

HOWARD JOHNSON EXPRESS INN
3695 Thirlane Rd (23019)
Rates: $45-$65
(540) 563-0229
(800) 446-4656

PATRICK HENRY HOTEL
617 S Jefferson St (24016)
Rates: n/a
(540) 345-8811

RAMADA INN-RIVER'S EDGE
1927 Franklin Rd SW (24014)
Rates: $45-$85
(540) 343-0121
(800) 272-6232

RAMADA LIMITED
6520 Thirlane Rd (24014)
Rates: $48-$70
(540) 563-2871
(800) 272-6232

RED CARPET INN
7645 Williamson Rd (24019)
Rates: $33-$47
(540) 362-3344
(800) 251-1962

RODEWAY INN-CIVIC CENTER
526 Orange Ave NE (24016)
Rates: $32-$80
(540) 981-9341
(800) 228-2000

SUPER 8 MOTEL
6616 Thirlane Rd (24019)
Rates: $45-$65
(540) 563-8888
(800) 800-8000

VILLAGER LODGE
6510 Thirlane Rd (24019)
Rates: $35-$60
(540) 265-7600

WYNDHAM ROANOKE AIRPORT
2801 Hershberger Rd (24017)
Rates: $69-$229
(540) 563-9300
(800) 996-3426

ROCKY MOUNT

BUDGET HOST INN
Hwy 220 N (24151)
Rates: $35-$44
(540) 483-9757
(800) 283-4678

FRANKLIN MOTEL
20281 Virgil H. Goode Hwy (24151)
Rates: $33-$50
(540) 483-9962
(800) 775-3506

ROSSLYN

EXECUTIVE CLUB SUITES
1730 Arlington Blvd (22209)
Rates: n/a
(703) 525-2582
(800) 535-2582

RUTHER GLEN

HOLIDAY INN EXPRESS
24011 Ruther Glen Rd (22546)
Rates: n/a
(804) 448-2608
(800) 465-4329

HOWARD JOHNSON EXPRESS
23786 Rogers Clark Blvd (22546)
Rates: $85-$118
(804) 448-2499
(800) 446-4656

TRAVELODGE
24368 Rogers Clark Blvd (22546)
Rates: $49-$65
(804) 448-9694
(800) 578-7878

SALEM

BAYMONT INN
140 Sheraton Dr (24153)
Rates: $50-$80
(540) 562-2717
(800) 301-0200

BUDGET HOST INN
5399 W Main St (24153)
Rates: $38-$69
(540) 380-2080
(800) 283-4678

HOLIDAY INN
1671 Skyview Rd (24153)
Rates: $59-$89
(540) 389-7061
(800) 465-4329

KNIGHTS INN
301 Wildwood Rd
(24153)
Rates: $39-$60
(540) 389-0280
(800) 843-5644

QUALITY INN
179 Sheraton Dr
(24153)
Rates: $52-$77
(540) 562-1912
(800) 228-5151

SUPER 8 MOTEL
300 Wildwood Rd
(24153)
Rates: $41-$61
(540) 389-0297
(800) 800-0000

SANDSTON

**DAYS INN-
AIRPORT**
5500 Williamsburg
Rd (23150)
Rates: $45-$85
(804) 222-2041
(800) 329-7566

**ECONO LODGE-
AIRPORT**
5408 Williamsburg
Rd (23150)
Rates: $36-$125
(804) 222-1020
(800) 553-2666

**HOLIDAY INN
AIRPORT**
5203 Williamsburg
Rd (23150)
Rates: n/a
(804) 222-6450
(800) 465-4329

LEGACY INN
5252 Airport
Square Ln (23150)
Rates: $30-$46
(804) 226-4519

**MICROTEL INN
& SUITES**
6000 Audubon Dr
(23150)
Rates: $49-$80
(804) 737-3322
(888) 771-7171

MOTEL 6
5704 US Hwy 60
(23150)
Rates: $33-$46
(804) 222-7600
(800) 466-8356

SCOTTSVILLE

CHESTER INN
Rt 4, Box 57
(24590)
Rates: n/a
(804) 286-2218

**HIGH MEADOWS
VINEYARD &
MOUNTAIN
SUNSET INN**
High Meadows
Ln (24590)
Rates: $82-$285
(804) 286-2218
(800) 232-1832

SKIPPERS

ECONO LODGE
I-95 S & SR 629
(23879)
Rates: $34-$65
(804) 634-6124
(800) 553-2666

SMITHFIELD

**FOUR SQUARE
PLANTATION
BED & BREAKFAST**
13357 Four Square
Rd (23430)
Rates: n/a
(757) 365-0749

**MANSION ON
MAIN BED
& BREAKFAST**
36 Main St (23430)
Rates: n/a
(757) 357-0006

SOUTH
BOSTON

**BEST WESTERN
HOWARD HOUSE
INN**
2001 Seymour Dr
(24592)
Rates: $60-$83
(804) 572-4311
(800) 528-1234

SUPER 8 MOTEL
1040 Bill Tuck
Hwy (24592)
Rates: $54-$65
(804) 572-8868
(800) 800-8000

SOUTH HILL

**BEST WESTERN
SOUTH HILL**
Hwy 58 & I-85
(23970)
Rates: $56-$80
(804) 447-3123
(800) 528-1234

COMFORT INN
918 E Atlantic St
(23970)
Rates: $39-$89
(804) 447-2600
(800) 228-5150

ECONO LODGE
623 E Atlantic St
(23970)
Rates: $40-$80
(804) 447-7116
(800) 553-2666

SPERRYVILLE

**THE CONYERS
HOUSE B&B**
Rt 1, Box 157
(22740)
Rates: $90-$195
(703) 987-8025

SPRINGFIELD

COMFORT INN
6560 Loisdale Ct
(22150)
Rates: $79-$99
(703) 922-9000
(800) 228-5150

HAMPTON INN
6550 Loisdale Ct
(22150)
Rates: $89-$129
(703) 924-9444
(800) 426-7866

MOTEL 6
6868 Springfield
Blvd (22150)
Rates: $51-$62
(703) 644-5311
(800) 466-8356

SPOTSYLVANIA

**ROXBURY MILL
BED & BREAKFST**
6908 Roxbury Mill
Rd (22553)
Rates: n/a
(540) 582-6611

STANARDSVILLE

**THE LAFAYETTE
HOTEL**
146 Main St
(22973)
Rates: n/a
(804) 985-6345

STANLEY

**JORDAN
HOLLOW
FARM INN**
Rt 2, Box 375
(22851)
Rates: n/a
(703) 778-2209

STAUNTON

**ARMSTRONG
MOTEL**
Rt 2, Box 412-B
(24401)
Rates: n/a
(540) 337-2611

**ASHTON
COUNTRY
HOUSE B&B**
1205 Middlebrook
Ave (24401)
Rates: $65-$125
(540) 885-7819

COMFORT INN
1302 Richmond
(24401)
Rates: $69-$119
(540) 886-5000
(800) 228-5150

DAYS INN
Rt 2, Box 414
(24401)
Rates: $45-$74
(540) 337-3031
(800) 329-7466

DAYS INN
273-D Bells Lane
(24402)
Rates: $44-$104
(540) 248-0888
(800) 329-7466

ECONO LODGE
Rt 2, Box 364
(24401)
Rates: $32-$85
(540) 337-1231
(800) 553-2666

ECONO LODGE
1031 Richmond
(24401)
Rates: $54-$78
(540) 885-5158
(800) 553-2666

**INGLESIDE
RESORT & CONF
CENTER**
US 11 (24401)
Rates: n/a
(540) 248-1201

QUALITY INN
96 Baker Lane
(24402)
Rates: $59-$89
(540) 248-5111
(800) 228-5151

SUPER 8 MOTEL
1015 Richmond
Rd (24401)
Rates: $54-$78
(540) 886-2888
(800) 800-8000

STEPHENS CITY

COMFORT INN
167 Town Run
Lane (22655)
Rates: $65-$85
(540) 869-6500
(800) 228-5150

STERLING

**HAMPTON INN
DULLES AIRPORT**
45440 Holiday Dr
(22170)
Rates: $59-$115
(703) 471-4300
(800) 426-7866

**HOLIDAY INN
WASH/DULLES**
1000 Sully Rd
(22170)
Rates: $189
(703) 471-7411
(800) 465-4329

**TOWNPLACE
SUITES BY
MARRIOTT**
22744 Holiday
Park Dr (22170)
Rates: $89-$99
(703) 707-2017
(800) 257-3000

AREA CODES - If the local number doesn't connect, check for a new area code.

STRASBURG

BUDGET INN
28999 Old Valley
Pike (22657)
Rates: n/a
(540) 465-5298

**HOTEL
STRASBURG**
201 Holliday St
(22657)
Rates: $79-$149
(540) 465-9191
(800) 348-8327

**VALLEY VIEW
MOTEL**
29156 Old Valley
Pike (22657)
Rates: n/a
(540) 465-8510

SUFFOLK

DAYS INN
1526 Holland Rd
(23434)
Rates: $59-$195
(757) 539-5111
(800) 329-7466

HOLIDAY INN
2864 Pruden Blvd
(23434)
Rates: $64-$72
(757) 934-2311
(800) 465-4329

SYRIA

**GRAVES
MOUNTAIN
LODGE
GUEST RANCH**
Hwy 670 (22743)
Rates: $75-$200
(540) 923-4231

THORNBURG

**HOLIDAY INN
EXPRESS**
6409 Dan Bell
Lane (22565)
Rates: $69-$89
(540) 582-1097
(800) 465-4329

TRIANGLE

**RAMADA INN
QUANTICO**
4316 Inn St (22172)
Rates: $50-$75
(703) 221-1181
(800) 272-6232

US INN
4502 Inn St (22172)
Rates: n/a
(703) 221-1115

TROUTDALE

**FOX HILL INN BED
& BREAKFAST**
Rt 2, Box 1A1
(24378)
Rates: n/a
(703) 677-3313
(800) 874-3313

**HIDDEN HOLLOW
HIDEAWAY**
670 Grange Hall
Rd (24378)
Rates: n/a
(888) 698-9907

TROUTVILLE

COMFORT INN
2654 Lee Hwy S
(24175)
Rates: $67-$88
(540) 992-5600
(800) 228-5150

DAYSTOP
US 220 (24175)
Rates: $49-$75
(540) 992-3100
(800) 329-7466

TRAVELODGE
2444 Lee Hwy S
(24175)
Rates: $55-$65
(540) 992-6700
(800) 578-7878

VERONA

RAMADA LIMITED
70 Lodge Lane
(24482)
Rates: $50-$85
(540) 248-8981
(800) 272-6232

VIENNA

**COMFORT INN
TYSONS CORNER**
1587 Springhill Rd
(22182)
Rates: $89-$189
(703) 448-8020
(800) 228-5150

**HOMESTEAD
GUEST STUDIOS**
8210 Old
Courthouse Rd
(22182)
Rates: n/a
(703) 356-6300
(888) 782-9473

**MARRIOTT HOTEL
TYSONS CORNER**
8028 Leesburg
Pike (22182)
Rates: $136-$172
(703) 734-3200
(800) 228-9290

**RESIDENCE INN
BY MARRIOTT
TYSONS CORNER**
8616 Westwood
Center Dr (22182)
Rates: $129-$169
(703) 893-0120
(800) 331-3131

**VIENNA
WOLFTRAP
MOTEL**
430 Maple Ave W
(22180)
Rates: n/a
(703) 281-2330

VIRGINIA BEACH

**ANGIE'S GUEST
COTTAGE**
302 24th St (23451)
Rates: n/a
(757) 428-4690

**CORAL SAND
MOTEL**
23rd & Pacific
(23451)
Rates: n/a
(757) 425-0872

**DAYS INN
EXPRESSWAY**
4600 Bonney Rd
(23462)
Rates: $42-$110
(757) 473-9745
(800) 329-7466

**DAYS INN
OCEANFRONT**
Oceanfront &
32nd St (23451)
Rates: $145-$225
(757) 428-7233
(800) 329-7466

ECONO LODGE
3637 Bonney Rd
(23452)
Rates: $35-$125
(757) 486-5711
(800) 553-2666

EXECUTIVE INN
717 S Military
Hwy (23464)
Rates: $29-$69
(757) 420-2120
(800) 678-3466

FLAGSHIP MOTEL
512 Atlantic Ave
(23451)
Rates: $60-$175
(757) 425-6422

**HOLLY KOVE
EFFICIENCIES**
395 Norfolk Ave
(23451)
Rates: n/a
(757) 425-8374

**LA COQUILLE
MOTEL
APARTMENTS**
314 16th St (23451)
Rates: $45-$88
(757) 422-3889

LA QUINTA INN
192 Newtown Rd
(23462)
Rates: $75-$102
(757) 497-6620
(800) 687-6667

LAKESIDE MOTEL
2572 Virginia
Beach Blvd (23452)
Rates: n/a
(757) 340-3211

LOTUS POND B&B
1324 Sandbridge
Rd (23456)
Rates: n/a
(757) 426-7164

**MARDI GRAS
MOTEL**
28th & Atlantic
(23451)
Rates: n/a
(757) 428-3434

**OCEAN HOLIDAY
HOTEL**
2417 Atlantic Ave
(23451)
Rates: $95-$195
(757) 425-6920
(800) 345-7263

**RAMADA INN
AIRPORT SOUTH**
5725
Northampton
Blvd (23455)
Rates: $62-$140
(757) 464-9351
(800) 272-6232

RED ROOF INN
196 Ballard Ct
(23462)
Rates: $60-$75
(757) 490-0225
(800) 843-7663

**SANDPIPER
MOTEL**
1112 Pacific Ave
(23451)
Rates: n/a
(757) 422-0001

SEA MIST MOTEL
27th & Pacific Ave
(23451)
Rates: n/a
(757) 428-4926

**STARGATE
ATLANTIC**
28th & Atlantic
(23451)
Rates: n/a
(757) 428-3434

**STARGATE
OCEANFRONT
MOTEL**
1909 Atlantic Ave
(23451)
Rates: n/a
(757) 425-0650

**SUNDOWNER
MOTEL**
27th & Pacific Ave
(23451)
Rates: n/a
(757) 428-3011

SUNTIDE MOTEL
6607 Atlantic Ave
(23451)
Rates: n/a
(757) 428-6404

**THUNDERBIRD
MOTOR LODGE**
3410 Atlantic Ave
(23451)
Rates: $65-$135
(757) 428-3024
(800) 633-6669

TOWNPLACE SUITES BY MARRIOTT
5757 Cleveland St (23451)
Rates: $64-$119
(757) 490-9367
(800) 257-3000

WACHA-PREAGUE

WACHAPREAGUE MOTEL & MARINA
General Delivery (23480)
Rates: n/a
(757) 787-2105

WARM SPRINGS

ANDERSON COTTAGE B&B
B7B Old Germantown Rd (24484)
Rates: n/a
(540) 839-2975

MEADOW LANE LODGE
Star Rt A, Box 110 (24484)
Rates: n/a
(703) 839-5959

THREE HILLS INN
Rt 220, P.O. Box 9 (24484)
Rates: $49-$149
(540) 839-5381

WARRENTON

CHESWICK MOTEL
394 Broadview Ave (22186)
Rates: n/a
(540) 349-1901

COMFORT INN
7379 Comfort Inn Dr (22186)
Rates: $65-$85
(540) 349-8900
(800) 228-5150

HAMPTON INN
501 Blackwell Rd (22186)
Rates: $63-$79
(540) 349-4200
(800) 426-7866

HOWARD JOHNSON INN
6 Broadview Ave (22186)
Rates: $45-$85
(540) 347-4141
(800) 446-4656

WARSAW

BEST WESTERN WARSAW
4522 Richmond Rd (22572)
Rates: $54-$78
(804) 333-1700
(800) 528-1234

SIMONSON HOUSE & COTTAGE
2883 Simonson Rd (22572)
Rates: n/a
(804) 333-3347

WASHINGTON

GAY STREET INN
160 Gay St (22747)
Rates: n/a
(540) 675-3288

WATERFORD

MILLTOWN FARMS INN
14163 Milltown Rd (22190)
Rates: n/a
(540) 882-4470

WAYNESBORO

BEST WESTERN INN
15 Windigrove Dr (22960)
Rates: $60-$104
(540) 932-3060
(800) 528-1234

DAYS INN
2060 Rosser Ave (22980)
Rates: $39-$95
(540) 942-1171
(800) 329-7466

DELUXE BUDGET MOTEL
2112 W Main St (22980)
Rates: $25-$55
(540) 949-8253

SUPER 8 MOTEL
2045 Rosser Ave (22980)
Rates: $45-$65
(540) 943-3888
(800) 800-8000

WHITETOP

BLUFF MOUNTAIN CABIN
634 Bluff Mtn Rd (24292)
Rates: n/a
(540) 388-3838

ENCHANTED LODGE
420 Old Park Rd (24292)
Rates: n/a
(540) 466-4044

WILLIAMSBURG

BEST WESTERN
7411 Pocahantas Trail (23187)
Rates: $89-$119
(757) 229-3003
(800) 528-1234
(800) 446-9228

BEST WESTERN-COLONIAL CAPITOL INN
111 Penniman Rd (23187)
Rates: $89-$109
(757) 253-1222
(800) 528-1234
(800) 446-9228

BEST WESTERN-PATRICK HENRY INN
249 E York St (23187)
Rates: $109-$169
(757) 229-9540
(800) 528-1234
(800) 446-9228

BEST WESTERN WILIAMSBURG WESTPARK HOTEL
1600 Richmond Rd (23185)
Rates: $69-$99
(757) 229-1134
(800) 528-1234
(800) 446-1062

DAYS INN
902 Richmond Rd (23185)
Rates: $35-$79
(757) 229-5060
(800) 329-7466

ECONO LODGE POTTERY
7051 Richmond Rd (23188)
Rates: $29-$129
(757) 564-3341
(800) 553-2666

FAMILY INN OF AMERICA
5413 Airport Rd (23188)
Rates: n/a
(757) 565-1900
(800) 521-3377

GOVERNOR'S INN
504 N Henry St (23185)
Rates: $45-$100
(757) 229-1000
(800) 447-4329

HERITAGE INN
1324 Richmond Rd (23185)
Rates: $80
(757) 229-6220
(800) 782-3800

HOLIDAY INN PATRIOT
3032 Richmond Rd (23185)
Rates: $79-$129
(757) 565-2600
(800) 446-6001

HOTEL COLONIAL AMERICA
6483 Richmond Rd (23185)
Rates: n/a
(757) 565-1000

HOWARD JOHNSON INN
300 By Pass Rd (23185)
Rates: $29-$89
(757) 229-6270
(800) 446-4656

INN AT 802
802 Jamestown Rd (23185)
Rates: $125-$145
(757) 564-0845
(800) 672-4086

MOTEL 6
3030 Richmond Rd (23185)
Rates: $32-$56
(757) 565-3433
(800) 466-8356

QUARTERPATH INN
620 York St (23185)
Rates: $65-$85
(757) 220-0960
(800) 446-9222

RAMADA INN CENTRAL
5351 Richmond Rd (23185)
Rates: $32-$92
(757) 565-2000
(800) 272-6232

RAMADA INN & CONF CENTER-HISTORIC DISTRICT
500 Merrimac Trail (23185)
Rates: $79-$114
(757) 220-1410
(800) 272-6232
(800) 666-8888

RESIDENCE INN BY MARRIOTT
1648 Richmond Rd (23185)
Rates: n/a
(757) 941-2000
(800) 331-3131
(888) 259-9222

SHERATON HOTEL
351 York St (23185)
Rates: $45-$198
(757) 229-4100
(800) 272-6232

SUPER 8 MOTEL
1233 Richmond Rd (23185)
Rates: $39-$81
(757) 253-1087
(800) 800-8000

THOMAS JEFFERSON INN
7247 Pocahontas Trail (23185)
Rates: n/a
(757) 220-2000

AREA CODES - If the local number doesn't connect, check for a new area code.

WILLIAMSBURG CENTER HOTEL
600 Bypass Rd
(23185)
Rates: n/a
(757) 220-2800
(800) 492-2855

WILLIS WHARF

BALLARD HOUSE BED & BREAKFST
12527 Ballard Dr
(23486)
Rates: $50
(757) 442-2206

WINCHESTER

BAYMONT INN & SUITES
800 Millwood Ave
(22601)
Rates: $59-$64
(540) 678-0800
(800) 301-0200

BEST WESTERN LEE-JACKSON
711 Millwood Ave
(22601)
Rates: $53-$58
(540) 662-4154
(800) 528-1234

DAYS INN
2951 Valley Ave
(22601)
Rates: $46-$69
(540) 667-1200
(800) 329-7466

ECHO VILLAGE MOTEL
US Rt 11 (22603)
Rates: n/a
(703) 869-1900

HAMPTON INN
1204 Berryville Ave (22601)
Rates: $52-$85
(540) 678-4000
(800) 426-7866

HOWARD JOHNSON EXPRESS
2549 Valley Ave
(22601)
Rates: $35-$60
(540) 662-2521
(800) 446-4656

MOHAWK MOTEL
2754 Northwestern Pike (22603)
Rates: $34-$38
(540) 667-1410

QUALITY INN EAST
603 Millwood Ave
(22601)
Rates: $62-$77
(540) 667-2250
(800) 228-5151

TOURIST CITY MOTEL
214 Millwood Ave
(22601)
Rates: $29-$38
(540) 662-9011

TRAVELODGE
160 Front Royal Pike (22602)
Rates: $53-$71
(540) 665-0685
(800) 578-7878

WOODBRIDGE

DAYS INN
14619 Potomac Mills Rd (22192)
Rates: $67-$96
(703) 494-4433
(800) 329-7466

ECONO LODGE
13317 Gordon Blvd (22191)
Rates: $46-$85
(703) 491-5196
(800) 553-2666

FRIENDSHIP INN
13964 Jefferson Davis Hwy (22191)
Rates: $44-$80
(703) 494-4144
(800) 453-4511

QUALITY INN
1109 Horner Rd
(22191)
Rates: $49-$95
(703) 494-0300
(800) 228-5151

WOODSTOCK

BUDGET HOST INN
1290 S Main St
(22664)
Rates: $36-$48
(540) 459-4086
(800) 283-4678

COMFORT INN
1011 Motel Dr
(22664)
Rates: $60-$99
(540) 459-7600
(800) 228-5150

RAMADA INN
1130 Motel Dr
(22664)
Rates: $52-$75
(540) 459-5000
(800) 272-6232

WYTHEVILLE

DAYS INN
150 Malin Dr
(24382)
Rates: $45-$75
(540) 228-5500
(800) 329-7466

ECONO LODGE
1190 E Main St
(24382)
Rates: $33-$100
(540) 228-5517
(800) 553-2666

HOLIDAY INN
1800 E Main St
(24382)
Rates: $89
(540) 228-5483
(800) 465-4329

INTERSTATE MOTOR LODGE
705 Chapman Rd
(24382)
Rates: $25-$52
(540) 228-8618

MOTEL 6
220 Lithia Rd
(24382)
Rates: $30-$42
(540) 228-7988
(800) 466-8356

RAMADA INN
955 Pepper's Ferry Rd (24382)
Rates: $49-$95
(540) 228-6000
(800) 272-6232

RED CARPET INN
280 Lithia Rd
(24382)
Rates: $45-$115
(540) 228-5525
(800) 251-1962

SUPER 8 MOTEL
130 Nye Cir
(24382)
Rates: $40-$49
(540) 228-6620
(800) 800-8000

WYTHEVILLE INN
355 Nye Rd
(24382)
Rates: 59-$79
(540) 228-7300

YORKTOWN

MARL INN BED & BREAKFAST
220 Church St
(23690)
Rates: n/a
(757) 898-9268

WASHINGTON

ABERDEEN

CENTRAL PARK MOTEL
6504 Olympic
Hwy (98520)
Rates: $30-$45
(360) 533-1210

NORDIC INN
1700 S Boone St
(98520)
Rates: $35-$64
(360) 533-0100
(800) 442-1010

OLYMPIC INN
616 W Heron St
(98520)
Rates: $45-$95
(360) 533-4200
(800) 562-8618

RED LION INN
521 W Wishkah St
(98520)
Rates: $74-$99
(360) 532-5210
(800) 547-8010

THUNDERBIRD MOTEL
410 W Wishkah St
(98520)
Rates: $46-$64
(360) 532-3153

TOWNE MOTEL
712 W Wishkah St
(98520)
Rates: n/a
(360) 533-2340

TRAVELURE MOTEL
623 W Wishkah St
(98520)
Rates: $37-$62
(360) 532-3280

AIRWAY HEIGHTS

HEIGHTS MOTEL
13504 W Hwy 2
(99001)
Rates: $25
(509) 244-2072

LANTERN PARK MOTEL
13820 W Sunset
Hwy (99001)
Rates: $29-$57
(509) 244-3653

MICROTEL INN & SUITES
1215 S Garfield Rd
(99001)
Rates: $36-$70
(509) 928-8644
(888) 771-7171

AMANDA PARK

AMANDA PARK MOTEL
8 River Dr (98526)
Rates: $35
(360) 288-2237
(800) 410-2237

ANACORTES

ANACORTES INN
3006 Commercial
Ave (98221)
Rates: $65-$125
(360) 293-3153
(800) 327-7976

FIDALGO COUNTRY INN
1250 Hwy 20
(98221)
Rates: $79-$169
(360) 293-3494
(800) 244-4179

ISLANDS INN
3401 Commercial
Ave (98221)
Rates: $60-$100
(360) 293-4644

OLD BROOK INN BED & BREAKFAST
530 Old Brook Ln
(98221)
Rates: $80-$90
(360) 293-4768
(800) 503-4768

SAN JUAN MOTEL
1103 6th St (98221)
Rates: $35-$56
(360) 293-5105
(800) 533-8009

SHIP HARBOR INN
5316 Ferry
Terminal Rd
(98221)
Rates: $50-$105
(360) 293-5177
(800) 852-8568

ARLINGTON

ARLINGTON MOTOR INN
2214 SR 530
(98223)
Rates: $47-$59
(360) 652-9595

CROSSROADS INN MOTEL
5200 172nd St NE
(98223)
Rates: $59-$120
(360) 403-7222

SMOKEY POINT MOTOR INN
17329 Smokey
Point Dr (98223)
Rates: $45-$75
(360) 659-8561

ASHFORD

CABINS AT THE BERRY
37221 SR 706 E
(98304)
Rates: $65-$125
(360) 569-2628

GATEWAY INN RESORT
38820 SR 706 E
(98304)
Rates: $30-$60
(360) 569-2506

ASOTIN

ASOTIN MOTEL
P.O. Box 188
(99402)
Rates: $34-$40
(509) 243-4888

AUBURN

COMFORT INN
One 16th St NE
(98071)
Rates: $59-$85
(253) 833-1222
(800) 228-5150

HOWARD JOHNSON INN
1521 D St NE
(98002)
Rates: $72-$85
(253) 939-5950
(800) 446-4656

MICROTEL INN & SUITES
Nine 16th St W
(98001)
Rates: $50-$87
(253) 833-7171
(888) 771-7171

NENDEL'S VALU INN
102 15th St NE
(98802)
Rates: $45-$65
(253) 833-8007

VAL-U INN
Nine 14th Ave
NW (98001)
Rates: $54-$89
(253) 735-9600
(800) 443-7777

BAINBRIDGE ISLAND

BAINBRIDGE INN BED & BREAKFAST
9200 Hemlock Ave
NE (98110)
Rates: n/a
(206) 842-7564

FROG ROCK INN BED & BREAKFAST
15576 Washington
Ave NE (98110)
Rates: $60-$75
(206) 842-2761

MONARCH MANOR B&B
7656 Yeomalt Pt
Dr NE (98110)
Rates: $75-$250
(206) 780-0112

BEAVER

EAGLE POINT INN
MP 202, Hwy 101
W (98305)
Rates $42-$48
(360) 327-3660

BELFAIR

BELFAIR MOTEL
23322 Hwy 3 NE
(98528)
Rates: $50-$60
(360) 275-4485

BELLEVUE

CANDLEWOOD SUITES HOTEL
15805 SE 37th St
(98006)
Rates: $79-$135
(425) 373-1212

DOUBLETREE HOTEL
300 112th Ave SE
(98004)
Rates: $195+
(425) 455-1300
(800) 222-8733

DOUBLETREE HOTEL-BELLEVUE CENTER
818 112th Ave NE
(98004)
Rates: $139-$150
(425) 455-1515
(800) 222-8733

HOMESTEAD VILLAGE GUEST STUDIOS
3700 132nd Ave SE
(98006)
Rates: $84-$94
(425) 865-8680
(888) 782-9473

HOMESTEAD VILLAGE GUEST STUDIOS
15805 NE 28th St (98008)
Rates: $89-$109
(425) 885-6675
(888) 782-9473

LA RESIDENCE SUITE HOTEL
475 100th Ave NE (98004)
Rates: $70-$120
(425) 455-1475

RESIDENCE INN BY MARRIOTT
14455 NE 29th Pl (98007)
Rates: $139-$189
(425) 882-1222
(800) 331-3131

WEST COAST BELLEVUE HOTEL
625 116th Ave NE (98004)
Rates: $104-$135
(425) 455-9444
(800) 426-0670

BELLINGHAM

BEST WESTERN LAKEWAY INN
714 Lakerway Dr (98226)
Rates: $69-$129
(360) 671-1011
(800) 528-1234
(888) 671-1011

CASCADE INN
208 N Samish Way (98225)
Rates: n/a
(360) 733-2520

COACHMAN INN
120 N Samish Way (98225)
Rates: $45-$70
(360) 671-9000
(800) 962-6641

DAYS INN
125 E Kellogg Rd (98226)
Rates: $59-$129
(360) 671-6200
(800) 329-7466

LIONS INN MOTEL
2419 Elm St (98225)
Rates: $44-$48
(360) 733-2330

MAC'S MOTEL
1215 E Maple (98225)
Rates: n/a
(360) 734-7570

MOTEL 6
3701 Byron (98225)
Rates: $42-$58
(360) 671-4494
(800) 466-8356

QUALITY INN BARON SUITES
100 E Kellogg Rd (98226)
Rates: $74-$114
(360) 647-8000
(800) 228-5151

RODEWAY INN
3710 Meridian St (98225)
Rates: $40-$95
(360) 738-6000
(800) 228-2000

SHAMROCK MOTEL
4133 W Maplewood Ave (98226)
Rates: n/a
(360) 676-1050

SHANGRI-LA DOWNTOWN MOTEL
611 E Holly St (98225)
Rates: $38-$48
(360) 733-7050

TRAVEL HOUSE INN
3750 Meridian St (98225)
Rates: $44-$60
(360) 671-4600

VAL-U INN
805 Lakeway Dr (98226)
Rates: $50-$84
(360) 671-9600
(800) 443-7777

BINGEN

CITY CENTER MOTEL
208 W Steuben (98605)
Rates: $32-$53
(509) 493-2445

BIRCH BAY

BEV'S BEACH RESORT
8126 Birch Bay Dr (98230)
Rates: $75-$125
(360) 371-2756

BIRCH BAY BUNGALOWS
8226 Birch Bay Dr (98230)
Rates: $60-$70
(360) 371-2851

BLAINE

THE INN AT SEMI-AH-MOOA WYNDHAM RESORT
9565 Semiahmoo Pkwy (98230)
Rates: $99-$275
(360) 371-2000
(800) 770-7992

MOTEL INTNL
758 Peace Portal Dr (98231)
Rates: n/a
(360) 332-8222

WESTVIEW MOTEL
1300 Peace Portal Dr (98230)
Rates: n/a
(360) 332-5501

BOTHELL

RESIDENCE INN BY MARRIOTT
11920 NE 195th St (98011)
Rates: $108-$162
(425) 485-3030
(800) 331-3131

BREMERTON

BEST WESTERN BREMERTON INN
4303 Kitsap Way (98312)
Rates: $71-$169
(360) 405-1111
(800) 528-1234
(800) 776-2291

THE CHIEFTAN MOTEL
600 National Ave N (98312)
Rates: $35-$45
(360) 479-3111

DUNES MOTEL
3400 11th St (98312)
Rates: $45-$65
(360) 377-0093
(800) 828-8238

FLAGSHIP INN
4320 Kitsap Way (98312)
Rates: $59-$99
(360) 479-6566

HOWARD JOHNSON BAYVIEW HOTEL
5640 Kitsap Way (98312)
Rates: $79-$109
(360) 373-7349
(800) 446-4656

MIDWAY INN
2909 Wheaton Way (98310)
Rates: $59-$74
(360) 479-2909
(800) 231-0575

OYSTER BAY INN
4412 Kitsap Way (98312)
Rates: $69-$80
(360) 377-5510
(800) 393-3862

SUPER 8 MOTEL
5068 Kitsap Way (98310)
Rates: $46-$63
(360) 377-8881
(800) 800-8000

BREWSTER

BREWSTER MOTEL
801 S Bridge St (98812)
Rates: $32-$60
(509) 689-2625

BRIDGEPORT

BRIDGEPORT Y MOTEL
2138 Columbia (98813)
Rates: $35-$38
(509) 686-2002

BUCKLEY

MOUNTAIN VIEW INN
29405 Hwy 410 (98321)
Rates: $58-$68
(360) 829-1100
(800) 582-4111

WEST MAIN MOTOR INN
466 W Main (98321)
Rates: n/a
(360) 829-2400

CARSON

CARSON MINERAL HOT SPRINGS
372 St. Martin Rd (98610)
Rates: $30-$100
(509) 427-8292
(800) 607-3678

CASHMERE

VILLAGE INN MOTEL
229 Cottage Ave (98815)
Rates: $37-$65
(509) 782-3522

CASTLE ROCK

MOUNT ST. HELENS MOTEL
1340 Mt. St. Helens Way NE (98611)
Rates: $30-$48
(360) 274-7721

7 WEST MOTEL
864 Walsh Ave NE (98611)
Rates: $38-$51
(360) 274-7526

TIMBERLAND INN & SUITES
1271 Mt. St. Helens Way (98611)
Rates: $59-$110
(360) 274-6002

CATHLAMET

NASSA POINT MOTEL
851 E Hwy 4 (98612)
Rates: $28-$45
(360) 795-3941

AREA CODES - If the local number doesn't connect, check for a new area code.

CENTRALIA

DAYS INN
702 Harrison Ave
(98531)
Rates: $54-$109
(360) 736-2875
(800) 329-7466

FERRYMAN'S INN
1003 Eckerson Rd
(98531)
Rates: $45-$52
(360) 330-2094

MOTEL 6
1310 Belmont Ave
(98531)
Rates: $35-$56
(360) 330-2057
(800) 466-8356

PARK MOTEL
1011 Belmont Ave
(98531)
Rates: $29-$38
(360) 736-9333

PEPPERTREE WEST MOTOR INN
1208 Alder St
(98531)
Rates: $35-$46
(360) 736-1124
(800) 795-1124

TRAVELODGE
1325 Lakeshore Dr
(98531)
Rates: $60-$70
(360) 736-9344
(800) 578-7878

CHEHALIS

RELAX INN
550 SW Parkland
Dr (98532)
Rates: $35-$75
(360) 748-8608
(800) 843-6916

CHELAN

BEST WESTERN LAKESIDE LODGE & SUITES
2312 W Woodin
Ave (98816)
Rates: $129-$229
(509) 682-4396
(800) 528-1234
(800) 468-2781

BRICKHOUSE INN BED & BREAKFAST
304 Wapato St
(98816)
Rates: n/a
(509) 682-4791
(800) 799-2332

CABANA MOTEL
420 Manson Rd
(98816)
Rates: $68-$117
(509) 682-2233
(800) 799-2332

CLOUD BASE VACATION RENTAL
17 S Butte Rd
(98816)
Rates: n/a
(509) 682-2349

KELLY'S RESORT
12801 S Lakeshore
Rd (98816)
Rates: $80-$160
(509) 687-3220
(800) 561-8978

LAKE CHELAN MOTEL
2044 W Woodin
Ave (98816)
Rates: $35+
(509) 682-2742

MIDTOWNER MOTEL
721 E Woodin Ave
(98816)
Rates: n/a
(509) 682-4051

CHENEY

BUNKERS RESORT AT WILLIAMS LAKE
S 36402 Bunker
Landing Rd
(99004)
Rates: $45-$55
(509) 235-5212

ROSEBROOK INN
304 W 1st (99004)
Rates: $34-$51
(509) 235-6538

WILLOW SPRINGS MOTEL
5 B St (99004)
Rates: $37-$45
(509) 235-5138

CHEWELAH

NORDLIG MOTEL
101 W Grant St
(99109)
Rates: $44-$50
(509) 935-6704

49ER MOTEL & RV PARK
311 S Park St
(99109)
Rates: n/a
(509) 935-8613

CLALLAM BAY

WINTER'S SUMMER INN BED & BREAKFAST
16651 Hwy 112
(98326)
Rates: $46-$75
(360) 963-2264

CLARKSTON

ASTOR MOTEL
1201 Bridge St
(99403)
Rates: n/a
(509) 758-2509

GOLDEN KEY MOTEL
1376 Bridge St
(99403)
Rates: n/a
(509) 758-5566

HACIENDA LODGE MOTEL
812 Bridge St
(99403)
Rates: n/a
(509) 758-8853
(800) 600-5583

HIGHLAND HOUSE BED & BREAKFAST
707 Highland
(99403)
Rates $40-$85
(509) 758-3126

MOTEL 6
222 Bridge St
(99403)
Rates: $35-$48
(509) 758-1631
(800) 466-8356

CLE ELUM

ASTER INN & ANTIQUES
521 E 1st St
(98922)
Rates: $32-$65
(509) 674-2551
(888) 616-9722

CHALET MOTEL
800 E First St
(98922)
Rates: $35-$55
(509) 674-2320

STEWART LODGE
805 W First St
(98922)
Rates: $51-$73
(509) 674-4548

TIMBER LODGE INN
301 W First St
(98922)
Rates: $50-$75
(509) 674-5966
(800) 589-1133

TRAVELERS INN
1001 E First St
(98922)
Rates: $34-$100
(509) 674-5535

WIND BLEW INN
811 Hwy 970
(98922)
Rates: $43-$53
(509) 674-2294

CLINTON

(See Whidbey
Island for lodging)

COLVILLE

BEAVER LODGE RESORT
2430 Hwy 20 East
(99114)
Rates: n/a
(509) 684-5657

BENNY'S COLVILLE INN
915 S Main St
(99114)
Rates: $40-$105
(509) 684-2517
(800) 680-2517

COMFORT INN
166 NE Canning
Dr (99114)
Rates: $52-$150
(509) 684-2010
(800) 228-5150

DOWNTOWN MOTEL
369 S Main St
(99114)
Rates: $28-$48
(509) 684-2565

MAPLE AT SIXTH BED & BREAKFAST
407 E 6th (99114)
Rates: $45-$55
(800) 446-2750

CONCONULLY

CONCONULLY LAKE RESORT
102 Sinlahekin Rd
(98819)
Rates: $25-$48
(509) 826-0813
(800) 850-0813

CONCONULLY MOTEL
P.O. Box 181
(98819)
Rates: n/a
(509) 826-1610

GIBSON'S NORTH FORK LODGE
100 W Boone
(98819)
Rates: n/a
(509) 826-1475

JACK'S MOTEL
116 A Ave (98819)
Rates: n/a
(509) 826-0132
(800) 893-5668

KOZY CABINS
111 E Broadway
(98819)
Rates: $35-$42
(509) 862-6780

LIAR'S COVE RESORT
1835 A
Conconully Rd
(98819)
Rates: $40-$50
(509) 826-1288
(800) 830-1288

MAPLE FLATS RV PARK & RESORT
310 A Ave (98819)
Rates: n/a
(509) 826-4231
(800) 683-1180

SHADY PINES RESORT
125 W Fork Salmon Cr Rd (98819)
Rates: $54-$60
(800) 552-2287

CONNELL

M & M MOTEL
730 S Columbia Ave (99326)
Rates: $30+
(509) 234-8811

TUMBLEWOOD MOTEL
433 S Columbia Ave (99326)
Rates: $23-$38
(509) 234-2081

COPALIS BEACH

BEACHWOOD RESORT
SR 109, PO Box 116 (98535)
Rates: n/a
(360) 289-2177

ECHOES OF THE SEA MOTEL
3208 SR 109 (98535)
Rates: $38-$78
(360) 289-3358
(800) 578-ECHO

IRON SPRINGS RESORT
3707 Hwy 109 (98535)
Rates: n/a
(360) 276-4230

LINDA'S LOW TIDE MOTEL
14 McCullough Rd (98535)
Rates: $30-$60
(360) 289-3450

ROD'S BEACH RESORT
2961 SR 109 (98535)
Rates: n/a
(360) 289-2222

TIDELANDS RESORT
2991 Hwy 109 (98535)
Rates: n/a
(360) 289-8963

COULEE CITY

ALA COZY MOTEL
9988 Hwy 2 E (99115)
Rates: $38-$58
(509) 632-5703

BLUE TOP MOTEL
109 N 6th St (99115)
Rates: $27-$48
(509) 632-5596

COULEE LODGE RESORT
33017 Park Lake Rd NE (99115)
Rates: $27-$53
(509) 632-5565

LAKEVIEW MOTEL
HCR 1, Box 11 (99115)
Rates: n/a
(509) 632-5792

LAUREN'T SUN VILLAGE RESORT
33575 Park Lake Rd NE (99115)
Rates: $42-$95
(509) 632-5664

SUN LAKES PARK RESORT
34228 Park Lake Rd NE (99115)
Rates: $58-$91
(509) 632-5291

COULEE DAM

COULEE HOUSE MOTEL
110 Roosevelt Way (99116)
Rates: $64-$100
(509) 633-1101
(800) 715-7767

COUPEVILLE
(See Whidbey Island for lodging)

CURLEW

BLUE COUGAR MOTEL
18081 Hwy 21 N (99118)
Rates: n/a
(509) 779-4817

CUSICK

BLUESLIDE RESORT
40041 Hwy 20 (99119)
Rates: $35-$44
(509) 445-1327

THE OUTPOST RESORT/RV PARK
405351 Hwy 20 (99119)
Rates: $40-$60
(509) 445-1317

DARRINGTON

STAGE COACH INN
1100 Seeman St (98241)
Rates: $60-$75
(360) 436-1776

DAYTON

BLUE MOUNTAIN MOTEL
414 W Main St (99328)
Rates: n/a
(509) 382-3040

THE PURPLE HOUSE B&B
415 E Clay St (99328)
Rates: $85-$125
(509) 382-3159
(800) 486-2574

THE WEINHARD HISTORIC HOTEL
235 E Main St (99328)
Rates: $70-$125
(509) 382-4032

DEER PARK

LOVE'S VICTORIAN B&B
North 31317 Cedar Rd (99006)
Rates: $74-$98
(509) 276-6939

DEMING

THE GUEST HOUSE B&B
5723 Schombush Rd (98244)
Rates: $45-$60
(360) 592-2343

THE LOGS RESORT
9002 Mt. Baker Hwy (98244)
Rates: $75+
(360) 599-2711

DES MOINES

KING'S ARMS MOTEL APARTMENT
23226 30th Ave S (98198)
Rates: $27-$59
(253) 824-0300

EAST WENATCHEE

CEDARS INN
80 Ninth St NE (98802)
Rates: $64-$87
(509) 886-8000

EATONVILLE

HENLEY'S SILVER LAKE RESORT CABINS
40718 S Silver Lake Rd E (98328)
Rates: n/a
(360) 832-3580

MOUNTAIN VIEW CEDAR LODGE
36203 Pulford Rd E (98328)
Rates: $85-$115
(360) 832-8080
(800) 903-5636

EDMONDS

EDMONDS HARBOR INN
130 W Dayton St (98020)
Rates: $79-$109
(425) 771-5021
(800) 441-8033

HUDGENS HAVEN BED & BREAKFAST
9313 190th St SW (98020)
Rates: $60-$65
(425) 776-2202

K & E MOTOR INN
23921 Hwy 99 (98020)
Rates: $49-$64
(425) 778-2181
(800) 787-2181

TRAVELODGE
23825 Hwy 99 (98026)
Rates: $54-$99
(425) 771-8008
(800) 578-7878

ELBE

HOBO INN
54104 Mountain Hwy E (98330)
Rates: $70-$85
(360) 569-2500

ELK

JERRY'S LANDING RESORT
N 41114 Lakeshore (99009)
Rates: n/a
(509) 292-2337

ELLENSBURG

BEST WESTERN ELLENSBURG INN
1700 Canyon Rd (98926)
Rates: $63-$78
(509) 925-9801
(800) 528-1234
(800) 321-8791

COMFORT INN
1722 Canyon Rd (98926)
Rates: $77-$141
(509) 925-7037
(800) 228-5150

HAROLDS MOTEL
601 N Water (98926)
Rates: $28-$48
(509) 925-4141

I-90 INN MOTEL
1390 Dollar Way Rd N (98926)
Rates: $46-$68
(509) 925-9844

NITES INN MOTEL
1200 S Ruby (98926)
Rates: $45-$53
(509) 962-9600

SUPER 8 MOTEL
1500 Canyon Rd
(98926)
Rates: $48-$68
(509) 962-6888
(800) 800-8000

ENUMCLAW

**BEST WESTERN
PARK CENTER
HOTEL**
1000 Griffin Ave
(98022)
Rates: $75-$93
(360) 825-4490
(800) 528-1234

KING'S MOTEL
1334 Roosevelt
Ave E (98022)
Rates: $45-$54
(360) 825-1626

EPHRATA

**COLUMBIA
MOTEL**
1257 Basin St SW
(98823)
Rates: $35-$60
(509) 754-5226

LARIAT MOTEL
1639 Basin St SW
(98823)
Rates: n/a
(509) 754-2437

EVERETT

EVERETT INN
12619 4th Ave W
(98204)
Rates: $40-$105
(425) 347-9099

**HOLIDAY INN
HOTEL &
CONF CENTER**
101 128th St SE
(98208)
Rates: $79-$119
(425) 337-2900
(800) 465-4329

MOTEL 6 NORTH
10006 Everett Way
(98204)
Rates: $40-$53
(425) 347-2060
(800) 466-8356

MOTEL 6 SOUTH
224 128th St SW
(98204)
Rates: $42-$56
(425) 353-8120
(800) 466-8356

**ROYAL MOTOR
INN**
952 N Broadway
(98201)
Rates: $44+
(425) 259-5177

TRAVELODGE
3030 Broadway
(98201)
Rates: $49-$89
(425) 259-6141
(800) 578-7878

FEDERAL WAY

**BEST WESTERN
EXECUTEL**
31611 20th Ave S
(98003)
Rates: $129-$149
(253) 941-6000
(800) 528-1234
(800) 648-3311

COMFORT IN
31622 Pacific Hwy
S (98003)
Rates: $89-$139
(253) 529-0101
(800) 225-5150

**ROADRUNNER
MOTEL**
1501 350th St S
(98003)
Rates: $30-$38
(800) 828-7202

**STEVENSON
MOTEL**
33330 Pacific Hwy
S (98003)
Rates: n/a
(253) 927-2500

SUPER 8 MOTEL
1688 348th St S
(98003)
Rates: $49-$68
(253) 838-8808
(800) 800-8000

FERNDALE

EXECUTIVE INN EXP
5370 Barrett Rd
(98248)
Rates: $99-$139
(360) 380-4600

**SCOTTISH LODGE
MOTEL**
5671 Riverside Dr
(98248)
Rates: $30
(360) 384-4040

SUPER 8 MOTEL
5788 Barrett Ave
(98248)
Rates: $47-$63
(360) 384-8881
(800) 800-8000

FIFE

**BEST WESTERN
EXECUTIVE INN**
5700 Pacific Hwy
E (98424)
Rates $84-$135
(253) 922-0080
(800) 528-1234

COMFORT INN
5601 Pacific Hwy
E (98424)
Rates: $59-$89
(253) 926-2301
(800) 228-5150

DAYS INN
3021 Pacific Hwy
E (98424)
Rates: $45-$90
(253) 922-3500
(800) 329-7466

ECONO LODGE
3518 Pacific Hwy
E (98424)
Rates: $40-$62
(253) 922-0550
(800) 553-2666

HOMETEL INN
3520 Pacific Hwy
E (98424)
Rates: $40-$60
(253) 922-0555
(800) 258-3520

**KINGS MOTOR
INN**
5115 Pacific Hwy
E (98424)
Rates: $36
(253) 922-3636
(800) 929-3509

MOTEL 6
5201 20th St E
(98424)
Rates: $35-$49
(253) 922-1270
(800) 466-8356

PARADISE MOTEL
1618 59th Ave
Court E (98424)
Rates: n/a
(253) 922-5158

**ROYAL
COACHMAN INN**
5805 Pacific Hwy
E (98424)
Rates: $69-$81
(253) 922-2500
(800) 422-3051

FIR ISLAND

**SOUTH FORK
MOORAGE BED
& BREAKFAST**
2187 Mann Rd
(98238)
Rates: $95-$115
(360) 445-4803

FORKS

**BAGBY'S TOWN
MOTEL**
1080 Forks Ave S
(98331)
Rates: $30-$45
(360) 374-6231
(800) 742-2429

FORKS MOTEL
351 Forks Ave S
(98331)
Rates: $50-$90
(360) 374-6243
(800) 544-3416

**HOH HUMM
RANCH BED
& BREAKFAST**
171763 Hwy 101
(98331)
Rates: $39-$76
(360) 374-5337

**HOH RIVER
RESORT**
Rain Forest
(98331)
Rates: $40
(360) 374-5566

**MANITOU LODGE
BED & BREAKFST**
813 Kilmer Rd
(98331)
Rates: $90-$120
(360) 374-6295

**MILL CREEK INN
BED & BREAKFAST**
Hwy 101 S (98331)
Rates: n/a
(360) 374-5873

**MILLER TREE INN
BED & BREAKFAST**
654 E Division St
(98331)
Rates: $55-$125
(360) 374-6806

**THREE RIVERS
RESORT CABINS**
7764 LaPush Rd
(98331)
Rates: $35-$45
(360) 374-5300

TOWN MOTEL
HC 80, Box 350
(98331)
Rates: n/a
(360) 374-6231

**WESTWARD HOH
RESORT**
Rain Forest
(98331)
Rates: $35
(360) 374-6657

FREELAND
(See Whidbey
Island for lodging)

FRIDAY HARBOR
(See San Juan
Island for lodging)

GIG HARBOR

**BEST WESTERN
WELSLEY INN**
6575 Kimball
(98335)
Rates: $99-$169
(253) 858-9690
(800) 528-1234
(888) 462-0002

**HARBORSIDE
BED & BREAKFAST**
8708 Goodman Dr
NW (98332)
Rates: $115
(253) 851-1795

**THE INN AT
GIG HARBOR**
3211 56th St NW
(98335)
Rates: $105-$115
(253) 858-1111

AREA CODES - If the local number doesn't connect, check for a new area code.

NO CABBAGES BED & BREAKFST
10319 Sunrise Beach Dr NW (98332)
Rates: $55
(253) 858-7797

WESTWYND MOTEL & SUITES
6703 144 St NW (98332)
Rates: $44-$72
(253) 857-4047
(800) 468-9963

GLACIER

GLACIER CREEK LODGE
10036 Mt. Baker Hwy (98244)
Rates: $40-$135
(360) 599-2991

MT. BAKER CHALET RESORT
9857 Mt. Baker Hwy (98244)
Rates: $50-$180
(360) 599-2405

GOLDENDALE

BARCHRIS MOTEL
128 N Academy (98620)
Rates: n/a
(509) 773-4325

PONDEROSA MOTEL
775 E Broadway St (98620)
Rates: $40-$70
(509) 773-5842

GRAND COULEE

TRAIL WEST MOTEL
108 Spokane Way (99133)
Rates: $32-$70
(509) 633-3155

GRANDVIEW

GRANDVIEW MOTEL
522 E Wine Country Rd (98930)
Rates: $26-$39
(509) 882-1323

GRANITE FALLS

MOUNTAIN VIEW INN MOTEL
32005 Mt. Loop Hwy (98252)
Rates: $35-$60
(360) 691-6668

GRAYLAND

GRAYLAND MOTEL & COTTAGES
2013 SR 105 S (98547)
Rates: n/a
(360) 267-2395
(800) 292-0845

OCEAN GATE RESORT
1939 SR 105 S (98547)
Rates: n/a
(360) 267-1956
(800) 473-1956

OCEAN SPRAY MOTEL
1757 SR 105 S (98547)
Rates: $45-$70
(360) 267-2205

SURF MOTEL & COTTAGES
2029 SR 105 S (98547)
Rates: $56-$67
(360) 267-2244

WALSH MOTEL
1593 SR 105 S (98547)
Rates: $40+
(360) 267-2191

GREEN ACRES

ALPINE MOTEL & RV PARK
18815 E Cataldo (99016)
Rates: $40-$66
(509) 928-2700

GREENWATER

ALTA CRYSTAL RESORT/MT. RAINIER
68317 SR 410 E (98022)
Rates: $69-$159
(360) 663-2500
(800) 277-6475

THE INN AT THE RANCH CABIN
16423 Mountainside Dr (98022)
Rates: $75-$150
(360) 663-2667

HANSVILLE

GUEST HOUSE AT TWIN SPITS BED & BREAKFAST
2570 NE Twin Spits Rd (98340)
Rates: $60-$75
(360) 638-1001

HOME VALLEY

HOME VALLEY BED & BREAKFAST
P.O. Box 377 (98648)
Rates: n/a
(509) 427-7070

HOODSPORT

CANAL CREEK MOTEL
N 27131 Hwy 101 (98548)
Rates: $38-$52
(360) 877-6770

SUNRISE MOTEL & RESORT
N 24520 Hwy 101 (98548)
Rates: n/a
(360) 877-5301

HOQUIAM

SNORE & WHISKER MOTEL
3031 Simpson Ave (98550)
Rates: $35-$65
(360) 532-5060

TIMBERLINE INN
415 Perry Ave (98550)
Rates: $35-$75
(360) 533-8048

WESTWOOD INN
910 Simpson Ave (98550)
Rates: $42-$85
(360) 532-8161
(800) 562-0994

ILWACO

A-CO-HO MOTEL & CHARTERS
Port of Ilwaco, P.O. Box 268 (98624)
Rates: n/a
(360) 642-3333
(800) 339-2646

COL-PACIFIC MOTEL
P.O. Box 34 (98624)
Rates: n/a
(360) 642-3177

HEIDI'S INN MOTEL
126 Spruce St (98624)
Rates: $30-$70
(360) 642-2387
(800) 576-1032

INCHELIUM

HARTMAN'S LOG CABIN RESORT
5744 S Twin Lakes Access Rd (99138)
Rates: $36-$50
(509) 722-3543

RAINBOW BEACH RESORT
HC1, Box 146, Twin Lakes Rd (99138)
Rates: n/a
(509) 722-5901

INDEX

THE CABIN AT INDEX BED & BREAKFAST
52525 Riverside Rd (98256)
Rates: $80-$95
(360) 827-2102

IONE

PEND OREILLE INN
107 Riverside (99139)
Rates: n/a
(509) 442-3418

PLAZA MOTEL
103 S 2nd Ave (99139)
Rates: $30-$40
(509) 442-3534

ISSAQUAH

MOTEL 6
1885 15th Pl NW (98027)
Rates: $56-$72
(425) 392-8405
(800) 466-8356

MOUNTAINS & PLAINS BED & BREAKFAST
100 Big Bear Place NW (98027)
Rates: $38-$80
(800) 231-8068

KALALOCH

KALALOCH LODGE
157151 Hwy 101 (98331)
Rates: $55-$225
(360) 962-2271

KALAMA

KALAMA RIVER INN
602 NE Frontage Rd (98625)
Rates: $30-$39
(360) 673-2855

KELSO

BEST WESTERN ALADDIN MOTOR INN
310 Long Ave (98626)
Rates: $72-$97
(360) 425-9660
(800) 528-1234
(800) 764-7378

BUDGET INN
505 N Pacific Ave (98626)
Rates: $35-$53
(360) 636-4610

GUESTHOUSE INN & SUITES
501 Three Rivers Dr (98626)
Rates: $125-$130
(360) 414-5953

MOTEL 6
106 Minor Rd (98626)
Rates: $44-$60
(360) 425-3229
(800) 466-8356

AREA CODES - If the local number doesn't connect, check for a new area code.

RED LION INN
510 Kelso Dr
(98626)
Rates: $84-$134
(360) 636-4400
(800) 733-5466

SUPER 8 MOTEL
250 Kelso Dr
(98626)
Rates: $48-$66
(360) 423-8880
(800) 800-8000

KENNEWICK

BEST WESTERN INN
4001 W 27th St
(99336)
Rates: $69-$79
(509) 586-1332
(800) 528-1234

CASABLANCA BED & BREAKFAST
94806 E Granada
Ct (99337)
Rates: $85-$115
(888) 627-0676

CAVANAUGH'S COLUMBIA CENTER
1101 N Columbia
Center Blvd
(99336)
Rates: $109-$280
(509) 783-0611
(800) 843-4667

CLEARWATER INN
5616 W
Clearwater Ave
(99336)
Rates: $59+
(509) 735-2242
(800) 424-1145

COMFORT INN
7801 W Quinault
Ave (99336)
Rates: $56-$99
(509) 783-8396
(800) 228-5150

GREEN GABLE MOTEL
515 W Columbia
Dr (99336)
Rates: n/a
(509) 582-5811

HAWTHORN INN & SUITES
4220 W 27th Pl
(99337)
Rates: $79-$93
(509) 736-3326
(800) 527-1133

MOTEL 6
1751 Fowler St
(99352)
Rates: $33-$44
(509) 783-1250
(800) 466-8356

RAMADA INN CLOVER ISLAND
435 Clover Island
(99336)
Rates: $80-$110
(509) 586-0541
(800) 272-6232

SUPER 8 MOTEL
626 N Columbia
Center Blvd
(99336)
Rates: $50
(509) 736-6888
(800) 800-8000

TAPADERA INN
300A N Ely St
(99336)
Rates: $38-$60
(509) 783-6191
(800) 722-8277

TRAVELODGE INN & SUITES
321 N Johnson St
(99336)
Rates: $46-$74
(509) 735-6385
(800) 578-7878

KENT

BEST INN & SUITES
25100 74th Ave S
(98032)
Rates: $89-$149
(800) 804-1539
(800) 237-8466

CYPRESS INN
22218 84th Ave S
(98032)
Rates: $67-$89
(253) 395-0219
(800) 752-9991

DAYS INN SOUTH
1711 W Meeker St
(98032)
Rates: $79-$98
(253) 854-1950
(800) 329-7466

GOLDEN KENT MOTEL
22203 84th Ave S
(98032)
Rates: $40-$55
(253) 872-8372

HOWARD JOHNSON INN
1233 N Central
(98032)
Rates: $69-$129
(253) 852-7224
(800) 446-4656

ROYAL SKIES APARTMENTS
25907 27th Pl S
(98032)
Rates: n/a
(253) 941-7788

VAL-U INN
22420 84th Ave S
(98032)
Rates $69-$89
(253) 872-5525
(800) 443-7777

KETTLE FALLS

BARNEY'S CAFE & MOTEL
395 & 20 Jct
(99141)
Rates: n/a
(509) 738-6546

BULL HILL RANCH & RESORT
3738 Bull Hill Rd
(99141)
Rates: $85-$140
(509) 732-4355

GRANDVIEW INN MOTEL & RV PARK
978 Hwy 395 N
(99141)
Rates: n/a
(509) 738-6733

KETTLE FALLS INN
205 E 3rd St,
Hwy 395 (99141)
Rates: $43-$59
(509) 738-6514
(888) 315-2378

KINGSTON

KINGSTON HOUSE B&B
26117 Ohio Ave
NE (98346)
Rates: $85-$180
(360) 297-8818

SMILEY'S COLONIAL MOTEL
11067 Hwy 104
(98346)
Rates: $30-$59
(360) 297-3622

KIRKLAND

BEST WESTERN KIRKLAND INN
12223 116th NE
(98034)
Rates: $86-$97
(425) 822-2300
(800) 528-1234
(800) 332-4200

LA QUINTA INN
10530 NE
Northup Way
(98033)
Rates: $99-$119
(425) 828-6585
(800) 687-6667

MOTEL 6
12010 120th Place
NE (98034)
Rates: $58-$74
(425) 821-5618
(800) 466-8356

THE WOODMARK HOTEL ON LAKE WASHINGTON
1200 Carillon
Point (98033)
Rates: $155-$165
(425) 822-3700

LA CONNER

ART'S PLACE B&B
511 Talbott St
(98257)
Rates: $60
(360) 466-3033

LA CONNER COUNTRY INN
107 S 2nd St
(98257)
Rates: $95-$120
(360) 466-3101

KINGSTON

KINGSTON HOUSE B&B
26117 Ohio Ave
NE (98346)
Rates: $85-$180
(360) 297-8818

LACEY

SUPER 8 MOTEL
4615 Martin Way
(98503)
Rates: $51-$68
(360) 459-8888
(800) 800-8000

LAKE BAY

RANSOM'S POND OSTRICH FARM BED & BREAKFAST
3915 Mahnke Rd
KPS (98351)
Rates: $75-$95
(206) 884-5666

LAKE CRESCENT

HISTORIC LAKE CRESCENT LODGE RESORT
416 Lake Crescent
Rd (Port Angeles
98362)
Rates: $64-$114
(360) 928-3211

LAKEWOOD

BEST WESTERN INN
6125 Motor Ave
SW (98499)
Rates: $65-$110
(253) 584-2212
(800) 528-1234

MADIGAN MOTEL
12039 Pacific Hwy
SW (98499)
Rates: $30-$60
(253) 588-8697

NIGHTS INN
9325 S Tacoma
Way (98499)
Rates: $32-$44
(253) 582-7550

QUALITY INN
9920 S Tacoma
Way (98499)
Rates: $56-$129
(253) 588-5241
(800) 228-5151

LANGLEY

(See Whidbey
Island for lodging)

LEAVENWORTH

ALPEN INN
405 W Hwy 2
(98826)
Rates: $49-$109
(509) 548-4326
(800) 423-9380

ALPINE CHALETS
3601 Allen Ln
(98826)
Rates: $82-$125
(509) 548-5674
(800) 548-5011

BAYERN ON THE RIVER
1505 Alpensee
Strasse (98826)
Rates: $50-$79
(509) 548-5875
(800) 873-3960

BEDFINDERS
305 8th St (98826)
Rates: $95-$195
(509) 548-4410
(800) 323-2920

BINDLESTIFFS RIVERSIDE CABINS
1600 Hwy 2
(98826)
Rates: $55-$65
(509) 548-5015

DER RITTERHOF MOTOR INN
190 Hwy 2, Box 307 (98826)
Rates: $80-$170
(509) 548-5845
(800) 255-5845

EVERGREEN INN
1117 Front St
(98826)
Rates: $45-$125
(509) 548-5515
(800) 327-7212

LAKE WENATCHEE HIDE-A-WAYS
19944 Hwy 207
(98826)
Rates: $95-$135
(509) 548-9074
(800) 883-2611

NATAPOC LODGING
12338 Bretz Rd
(98826)
Rates: $140+
(509) 763-3313
(888) 628-2762

OBERTAL MOTOR INN
922 Commercial St
(98826)
Rates: $69-$109
(509) 548-5204
(800) 537-9382

PHIPPEN'S BED & BREAKFAST
10285 Ski Hill Dr
(98826)
Rates: $70-$90
(800) 666-9806

RIVER'S EDGE MOTEL
8401 Hwy 2
(98826)
Rates: $62-$77
(509) 548-7612
(800) 451-5285

RODEWAY INN & SUITES
185 Hwy 2 (98826)
Rates: $59-$169
(509) 548-7992
(800) 228-2000

SAIMON'S HIDE-A-WAYS
16408 River Rd
(98826)
Rates: $95-$145
(509) 763-3213
(800) 845-8638

SQUIRREL TREE INN
15251 Hwy 2
(98826)
Rates: $50
(509) 763-3157

TYROLEAN RITZ HOTEL
633 Front St
(98826)
Rates: $68-$135
(509) 548-5455
(800) 854-6365

LILLIWAUP

MIKE'S BEACH RESORT
N 38470 Hwy 101
(98555)
Rates: $45-$95
(360) 877-5324
(800) 231-5324

LONG BEACH PENINSULA

ANCHORAGE COTTAGES
2209 N Blvd
(98631)
Rates: $59-$103
(360) 642-2351
(800) 646-2351

ARCADIA COURT MOTEL
401 N Ocean
Beach Blvd
(98631)
Rates: $41-$85
(360) 642-2613

BOULEVARD MOTEL
301 N Ocean Blvd
(98631)
Rates: $35-$75
(360) 642-2434

BREAKERS MOTEL
26th St & Hwy 103
(98631)
Rates: $54-$160
(800) 219-9833

CHAUTAUQUA LODGE
304 N 14th (98631)
Rates: $40-$160
(360) 665-6238
(800) 869-8401

EDGEWATER INN MOTEL
409 10th St (98631)
Rates: $94
(360) 642-2311
(800) 561-2456

LIGHTHOUSE MOTEL
12415 Pacific Way
(98631)
Rates: $47-$59
(360) 642-3622

LONG BEACH MOTEL
1200 Pacific Hwy
S (98631)
Rates: n/a
(360) 642-3500

OCEAN LODGE
101 Bolstad Ave
(98631)
Rates: $50-$150
(360) 642-2777

OUR PLACE AT THE BEACH
1309 S Blvd
(98631)
Rates: $34-$80
(360) 642-3793
(800) 538-5107

PACIFIC VIEW MOTEL
203 Bolstad St
(98631)
Rates: $38-$90
(360) 642-2415
(800) 238-0859

SAND LO MOTEL
1910 N Pacific
Hwy (98631)
Rates: n/a
(360) 642-2600
(800) 676-2601

THE SANDS MOTEL
12211 Pacific Way
(98631)
Rates: $33-$50
(360) 642-2100

SHAMAN MOTEL
115 3rd St SW
(98631)
Rates: $79-$89
(360) 642-3714
(800) 753-3750

THUNDERBIRD MOTEL
201 N Blvd
(98631)
Rates: $30-$80
(360) 642-2412

LONGVIEW

HOLIDAY INN EXPRESS
723 7th Ave
(98632)
Rates: $79-$160
(360) 414-1000
(800) 465-4329

HUDSON MANOR INN
1616 Hudson St
(98632)
Rates: $38-$46
(360) 425-1100

TOWN CHALET MOTOR HOTEL
1822 Washington
Way (98632)
Rates: $31-$46
(360) 423-2020

TOWNHOUSE MOTEL
744 Washington
Way (98632)
Rates: $326$50
(360) 423-7200

LOPEZ ISLAND

LOPEZ ISLANDER RESORT & MARINA
P.O. Box 459,
Fisherman Bay Rd
(Lopez, 98261)
Rates: n/a
(800) 736-3434

LYNDEN

WINDMILL INN MOTEL
8022 Guide
Meridian Rd
(98264)
Rates: $45-$62
(360) 354-3424

LYNNWOOD

BEST WESTERN LYNWOOD / SEATTLE NORTH
4300 200th St SW
(98036)
Rates: $79-$109
(425) 775-7447
(800) 528-1234
(800) 775-0805

RESIDENCE INN BY MARRIOTT
18200 Alderwood
Mall Pkwy (98037)
Rates: $150-$210
(425) 771-1100
(800) 331-3131

ROSE MOTEL
20222 Hwy 99
(98036)
Rates: n/a
(425) 744-5616

AREA CODES - If the local number doesn't connect, check for a new area code.

SILVER CLOUD INN
19332 36th Ave W
(98036)
Rates: $72-$107
(425) 775-7600
(800) 205-6935

MAPLE FALLS

YODELER INN BED & BREAKFAST
7485 Mt. Baker
Hwy (98266)
Rates: $65
(800) 642-9033

MARYSVILLE

BEST WESTERN TULALIP INN
8128 33rd Ave NE
(98271)
Rates: $59-$109
(360) 659-4488
(800) 528-1234
(800) 481-4804

THE VILLAGE MOTOR INN
235 Beach St
(98270)
Rates: $60-$65
(360) 659-0005

METALINE FALLS

CIRCLE MOTEL
HC2, Box 616,
Hwy 31 (99153)
Rates: $30-$45
(509) 446-4343

MOCLIPS

BARNACLE MOTEL
4816 Pacific Ave
(98562)
Rates: $45-$65
(360) 276-4318

HI-TIDE OCEAN BEACH RESORT CONDOS
4890 Railroad Ave
(98562)
Rates: $95-$169
(360) 276-4142
(800) 662-5477

MOCLIPS MOTEL
4852 Pacific Ave
(98562)
Rates: n/a
(360) 276-4228

MOONSTONE BEACH MOTEL
4849 Pacific Ave
(98562)
Rates: $50-$64
(360) 276-4346
(888) 888-9063

OCEAN CREST RESORT
4651 SR 109 N,
Sunset Beach
(98562)
Rates: $60-$175
(360) 276-4465
(800) 684-8439

THE SPINDRIFT
4807 Pacific Ave
(98562)
Rates: $105-$155
(800) 645-8443

MONROE

BEST WESTERN BARON INN
19233 Hwy 2
(98272)
Rates: $49-$99
(360) 794-3111
(800) 528-1234

BROOKSIDE MOTEL
19930 Hwy 2
(98272)
Rates: n/a
(360) 794-8832

FAIRGROUNDS INN MOTEL
18950 Hwy 2
(98272)
Rates: $35-$60
(360) 794-5401

MONTESANO

THE ABEL HOUSE
117 Fleet St S
(98563)
Rates: $65-$85
(360) 249-6002
(800) 235-ABEL

MONTE SQUARE MOTEL
518 1/2 South 1st
St (98563)
Rates: $35-$45
(360) 249-4424

MORTON

EVERGREEN MOTEL
121 Front St
(98356)
Rates: $27-$45
(360) 496-5407

RESORT OF THE MOUNTAINS
1130 SR 7 (98356)
Rates: n/a
(360) 496-5885

SEASONS MOTEL
200 A Westlake
(98356)
Rates: $50-$70
(360) 496-6835

STILTNER MOTEL
250 Morton Rd
(98356)
Rates: n/a
(360) 496-5103

MOSES LAKE

BEST WESTERN HALLMARK INN
3000 Marina Dr
(98837)
Rates: $84-$109
(509) 765-9211
(800) 528-1234
(888) 448-4449

EL RANCHO MOTEL
1214 S Pioneer
Way (98837)
Rates: $30-$44
(509) 765-9173
(888) 315-2378

HOLIDAY INN EXPRESS
1745 E Kittleson
(98837)
Rates: $79-$105
(509) 766-2000
(800) 465-4329

INTERSTATE INN
2801 W Broadway
(98837)
Rates: $36-$54
(509) 765-1777
(800) 777-5889

LAKESHORE MOTEL
3206 W Lakeshore
Dr (98837)
Rates: $34+
(509) 765-9201

MAPLES MOTEL
1006 W 3rd
(98837)
Rates: n/a
(509) 765-5665

MOTEL 6
2822 Wapato Dr
(98837)
Rates: $33-$46
(509) 766-0250
(800) 466-8356

OASIS INN
466 Melva Ln
(98837)
Rates: n/a
(509) 765-8636

SAGE "N" SAND MOTEL
1011 S Pioneer
Way (98837)
Rates: $32-$52
(509) 765-1755

SHILO INN
1819 E Kittleson
(98837)
Rates: $69-$99
(509) 765-9317
(800) 222-2244

SUNLAND MOTOR INN
309 E Third Ave
(98837)
Rates: $34-$52
(509) 765-1170
(800) 220-4403

SUPER 8 MOTEL
449 Melva Lane
(98837)
Rates: $47-$63
(509) 765-8886
(800) 800-8000

TRAVELODGE
316 S Pioneer Way
(98837)
Rates: $49-$89
(509) 765-8631
(800) 578-7878

MOSSYROCK

MOSSYROCK INN
118 E State St
(98564)
Rates: n/a
(360) 983-8641

MOUNT VERNON

BEST WESTERN COLLEGE WAY INN
300 W College
Way (98273)
Rates: $55-$87
(360) 424-4287
(800) 528-1234
(800) 793-4024

BEST WESTERN COTTONTREE INN
2300 Market St
(98273)
Rates: $60-$90
(360) 428-5678
(800) 528-1234
(800) 662-6886

COMFORT INN
1910 Freeway Dr
(98273)
Rates: $69-$89
(360) 428-7020
(800) 228-5150

DAYS INN
2009 Riverside Dr
(98273)
Rates: $60-$125
(360) 424-4141
(800) 329-7466

HILLSIDE MOTEL
2300 Bonnie View
Rd (98273)
Rates: n/a
(360) 445-3252

WEST WINDS MOTEL
2020 Riverside Dr
(98273)
Rates: $32-$50
(360) 424-4224

WHISPERING FIRS BED & BREAKFAST
1957 Kanako Ln
(98273)
Rates: $65-$95
(360) 428-1990
(800) 428-1992

MOUNTLAKE TERRACE

HOMESTEAD VILLAGE GUEST STUDIOS
6017 244th St SW (98043)
Rates: $59-$64
(425) 771-3139
(888) 782-9473

NACHES

APPLE COUNTRY BED & BREAKFAST
4561 Old Naches Hwy (98937)
Rates: $65+
(509) 965-0344

SILVER BEACH RESORT
40380 Hwy 12 (98937)
Rates: n/a
(509) 672-2500

SQUAW ROCK RESORT
15070 SR 410 (98937)
Rates: $65-$79
(509) 658-2926

TROUT LODGE
27090 Hwy 12 (98937)
Rates: $40-$55
(509) 672-2211

NAHCOTTA

MOBY DICK HOTEL & OYSTER FARM
25814 Sundridge Rd (98637)
Rates: $65-$95
(360) 665-4543

OUR HOUSE IN NAHCOTTA / OYSTERVILLE B&B
P.O. Box 33 (98637)
Rates: $85-$95
(360) 665-6667

NASELLE

SLEEPY HOLLOW MOTEL
1032 SR 4 (98638)
Rates: $35-$40
(360) 484-3232

NEAH BAY

THE CAPE MOTEL & RV PARK
1500 Bay View Ave (98357)
Rates: $45-$74
(360) 645-2250

SILVER SALMON RESORT
Bayview & Roosevelt (98357)
Rates: $35+
(360) 645-2388

SNOW CREEK RESORT
Marker 691, Hwy 112 (98357)
Rates: $45-$74
(360) 645-2284

TYEE MOTEL & RV PARK
Bayview Ave (98357)
Rates: $40-$95
(360) 645-2233

NEWPORT

GOLDEN SPUR MOTOR INN
924 W Hwy 2 (99156)
Rates: $38-$54
(509) 447-3823

THE LAZY J HIDEAWAY
3792 Deer Valley Rd (99156)
Rates: $60
(509) 447-2535
(800) 898-3412

NEWPORT CITY INN
220 N Washington (99156)
Rates: $38-$60
(509) 447-3463

OAK HARBOR

(See Whidbey Island for lodging)

OCEAN CITY

NORTH BEACH MOTEL
2601 SR 109 (98569)
Rates: $30-$55
(360) 289-4116
(800) 640-8053

PACIFIC SANDS MOTEL & RESORT
2687 SR 109 (98569)
Rates: $40-$56
(360) 289-3588

WEST WINDS RESORT MOTEL
2537 SR 109 (98569)
Rates: $36-$66
(360) 289-3448
(800) 867-3448

OCEAN PARK

COASTAL COTTAGES OF OCEAN PARK
P.O. Box 888 (98640)
Rates: $50-$69
(360) 665-4658
(800) 200-0424

HARBOR VIEW MOTEL
3306 281st St (98640)
Rates: $40-$60
(360) 665-4959

OCEAN PARK RESORT
25904 "R" St (98640)
Rates: $65-$100
(360) 665-4585
(800) 835-4634

SHAKTI COVE COTTAGES
253rd Place (98640)
Rates: $60-$75
(360) 665-4000

SUNSET VIEW RESORT
25517 Park Ave (98640)
Rates: $64-$159
(360) 665-4494

WESTGATE MOTEL & TRAILER COURT
20803 Pacific Hwy (98640)
Rates: $42-$55
(360) 665-4211

OCEAN SHORES

BEACH FRONT VACATION RENTALS
759 Ocean Shores Blvd (98569)
Rates: $65-$225
(800) 544-8887

CASA DEL ORO MOTEL
667 Point Brown Ave NW (98569)
Rates: $85-$120
(360) 289-2281
(800) 291-2281

CHALET VILLAGE CABINS
659 Ocean Shores Blvd (98569)
Rates: $85-$95
(360) 289-4297
(800) 303-4297 (WA)

DISCOVERY INN
1031 Discovery Ave SE (98569)
Rates: $52-$78
(360) 289-3371
(800) 882-8821

GREY GULL CONDO MOTEL
651 Ocean Shores Blvd SW (98569)
Rates: $120-$325
(360) 289-3381
(800) 562-9712 (WA)

NAUTILUS CONDO HOTEL
835 Ocean Shores Blvd (98569)
Rates: $80-$135
(360) 289-2722
(800) 221-4541

OCEAN SHORES MOTEL
681 Ocean Shores Blvd N (98569)
Rates: $40-$125
(360) 289-3351
(800) 464-2526 (WA)

POLYNESIAN CONDO RESORT
615 Ocean Shores Blvd (98569)
Rates: $89-$119
(360) 289-3361
(800) 562-4836

THE SANDS RESORT
801 Ocean Shores Blvd (98569)
Rates: $49-$125
(360) 289-2444
(800) 841-4001

SANDS ROYAL PACIFIC MOTEL
801 Ocean Shores Blvd NW (98569)
Rates: $39-$129
(360) 289-3306
(800) 562-9748

SILVER KING MOTEL
1070 Discovery Ave SE (98569)
Rates: $35-$90
(360) 289-3386
(800) 562-6001 (WA)

SURFVIEW CONDOS
757 Ocean Court NW (98569)
Rates: $65-$85
(360) 289-3077
(800) 544-8887 (WA)

WESTERLY MOTEL
870 Ocean Shores Blvd NW (98569)
Rates: $30-$50
(360) 289-3711

ODESSA

ODESSA MOTEL
601 E First Ave (99159)
Rates: $35-$47
(509) 982-2412

OKANOGAN

CEDARS INN
One Apple Way (98840)
Rates: $45-$57
(509) 422-6431

PONDEROSA MOTOR LODGE
1034 S 2nd Ave (98840)
Rates: $39-$45
(509) 422-0400
(800) 732-6702

U & I RIVERS EDGE MOTEL
838 2nd St N (98840)
Rates: $28-$35
(509) 422-2920

AREA CODES - If the local number doesn't connect, check for a new area code.

OLALLA

**OLALLA
ORCHARD B&B**
12530 Orchard
Ave SE (98359)
Rates: $95
(253) 857-5915

OLYMPIA

**BAILEY
MOTOR INN**
3333 Martin Way
(98506)
Rates: n/a
(360) 491-7515

**BEST WESTERN
ALADDIN
MOTOR INN**
900 S Capitol Way
(98501)
Rates: $72-$125
(360) 352-7200
(800) 528-1234
(800) 367-7771

**CAVANAUGHS AT
CAPITOL LAKE**
2300 Evergreen
Park Dr SW
(98502)
Rates: $108-$118
(360) 943-4000

**THE CINNAMON
RABBIT B&B**
1304 7th Ave W
(98502)
Rates: $60-$75
(360) 357-5520

**DEEP LAKE
RESORT**
12405 Tilley Rd S
(98512)
Rates: $53-$85
(360) 352-7388

**LEE STREET
SUITES**
348 Lee St SW
(98501)
Rates: n/a
(360) 943-8391

**RAMADA INN
GOVERNOR
HOUSE**
621 S Capitol Way
(98501)
Rates: $130-$160
(360) 352-7700
(800) 272-6232

SHALIMAR SUITES
5895 Capital Blvd
S (98501)
Rates: $26-$48
(360) 943-8391

TYEE HOTEL
500 Tyee Dr
(98502)
Rates: $70-$78
(360) 352-0511
(800) 648-6440
(800) 386-8933

OLYMPIC NATIONAL PARK

**LOG CABIN
RESORT**
3183 E Beach Rd
(Port Angeles
98363)
Rates: $75-$120
(360) 928-3325

OMAK

**LEISURE VILLAGE
MOTEL**
630 Okoma Dr
(98841)
Rates: $36-$47
(509) 826-4442
(800) 427-4495 (WA)

MOTEL NICHOLAS
527 E Grape St
(98841)
Rates: $37-$46
(509) 826-4611

OMAK INN
912 Koala Dr
(98841)
Rates: $53-$58
(509) 826-3822

**RODEWAY INN
& SUITES**
122 Main St
(98841)
Rates: $49-$69
(509) 826-0400
(800) 228-2000

ROYAL MOTEL
514 E Riverside Dr
(98841)
Rates: $28-$44
(509) 826-5715

STAMPEDE MOTEL
215 W 4th St
(98841)
Rates: n/a
(800) 639-1161

ORCAS ISLAND

**BARTWOOD
LODGE**
178 Fossil Bay Dr
(Eastsound 98245)
Rates: $39
(360) 376-2242

**DOE BAY VILLAGE
RESORT**
P.O. Box 437
(Olga 98279)
Rates: $40+
(360) 376-2291

**NORTH SHORE
COTTAGES**
P.O. Box 1273
(Eastsound 98245)
Rates: $120
(360) 376-5131

**SMALL ISLAND
FARM & INN**
Rt 1, Box 76
(Eastsound 98245)
Rates: $70-$95
(360) 376-4292

**WEST BEACH
RESORT**
Rt 1, Box 510
(Eastsound 98245)
Rates: $105-$150
(360) 376-2240

OROVILLE

CAMARY MOTEL
1815 Main St
(98844)
Rates: $36-$55
(509) 476-3694

OTHELLO

**BEST WESTERN
LINCOLN INN**
1020 E Cedar St
(99344)
Rates: $49-$109
(509) 488-5671
(800) 528-1234
(800) 240-7865

MAR DON RESORT
8198 Hwy 262 E
(99344)
Rates: $38-$55
(509) 346-2651

THE RAMA INN
1450 E Main St
(99344)
Rates: n/a
(509) 488-6612

PACIFIC BEACH

**SAND DOLLAR
MOTEL**
53 Central (98571)
Rates: $43-$100
(360) 276-4525

**SANDPIPER
BEACH RESORT
CONDOS**
4159 SR 109 (98571)
Rates: $55-$195
(360) 276-4580
(800) 567-4737

**SHORELINE
MOTEL**
12 1st St South
(98571)
Rates: $45-$75
(360) 276-4433

PACKWOOD

**MOUNTAIN VIEW
LODGE MOTEL**
13163 Hwy 12
(98361)
Rates: $45-$75
(360) 494-5555

**TATOOSH
MEADOWS
RESORT**
102 E Main (98361)
Rates: $100-$300
(800) 294-2311

**WOODLAND
MOTEL**
11890 Hwy 12
(98361)
Rates: $40-$50
(360) 494-6766

PASCO

AIRPORT MOTEL
2532 N 4th St
(99301)
Rates: $27-$38
(509) 545-1460

DOUBLETREE INN
2525 N 20th Ave
(99301)
Rates: $89-$109
(509) 547-0701
(800) 222-8733

**KING CITY TRUCK
STOP MOTEL**
2100 E Hillsboro
Rd (99301)
Rates: $38-$48
(509) 547-8511

MOTEL 6
1520 N Oregon St
(99301)
Rates: $32-$40
(509) 546-2010
(800) 466-8356

**SAGE 'N SUN
MOTEL**
1232 S 10th St
(99301)
Rates: $28-$48
(800) 391-9188

SLEEP INN
9930 Bedford St
(99301)
Rates: $50-$90
(509) 545-9554
(800) 753-3746

**THUNDERBIRD
MOTEL**
414 W Columbia
(99301)
Rates: n/a
(509) 547-9506

TRI-MARK MOTEL
720 W Lewis St
(99301)
Rates: n/a
(509) 547-7766

**THE VINEYARD
INN**
1800 W Lewis
(99301)
Rates: $39-$55
(509) 547-0791
(800) 824-5457

PATEROS

**LAKE PATEROS
MOTOR INN**
115 Lakeshore Dr
(98846)
Rates: $51-$59
(509) 923-2207
(800) 444-1985

PESHASTIN

**TIMBERLINE
HOTEL**
8284 Hwy 2
(98847)
Rates: n/a
(509) 548-7415

POINT ROBERTS

CEDAR HOUSE INN B&B
1534 Gulf Rd (98281)
Rates: $36-$49
(360) 945-0284

POMEROY

PIONEER MOTEL
1201 Main St, Box 579 (99347)
Rates: $35-$50
(509) 843-1559

PORT ANGELES

AGGIE'S INN
602 E Front St (98362)
Rates: $46-$68
(360) 457-0471

CHINOOK MOTEL
1414 E 1st St (98362)
Rates: $45-$80
(360) 452-2336

ELWHA RANCH BED & BREAKFAST
905 Herrick Rd (98363)
Rates: $75+
(360) 457-6540

FLAGSTONE MOTEL
415 E 1st St (98362)
Rates: $52-$68
(360) 457-9494

LAKE CRESCENT LODGE
416 Lake Crescent Rd (98362)
Rates: $64-$114
(360) 928-3211

LOG CABIN RESORT & RV PARK
3183 E Beach Rd (98363)
Rates: $62-$100
(360) 928-3325

MAPLE ROSE INN BED & BREAKFAST
115 Reservoir Rd (98363)
Rates: $79-$157
(360) 457-7673
(800) 570-2007

THE POND MOTEL
1425 W Hwy 101 (98362)
Rates: $25-$62
(360) 452-8422

PORTSIDE INN
1510 E Front St (98362)
Rates: $79-$99
(360) 452-4015

RED LION HOTEL
221 N Lincoln St (98362)
Rates: $95-$139
(360) 452-9215
(800) 733-5466

RIVIERA INN MOTEL
535 E Front St (98362)
Rates: $49-$77
(360) 417-3955

RUFFLES MOTEL
812 E 1st St (98363)
Rates: n/a
(360) 457-7788

SUPER 8 MOTEL
2104 E 1st St (98362)
Rates: $45-$61
(360) 452-8401
(800) 800-8000

UPTOWN INN
101 E 2nd St (98362)
Rates: $40-$129
(360) 457-9434
(800) 858-3812

PORT HADLOCK

PORT HADLOCK INN
201 Alcohol Loop Rd (98339)
Rates: n/a
(360) 385-5801

THE OLD ALCOHOL PLANT
310 Alcohol Loop Rd (98339)
Rates: $59-$250
(360) 385-7030
(800) 785-7030

VALLEY VIEW CABINS
12775 Hwy 30 (98339)
Rates: $45-$50
(360) 385-1666
(800) 280-1666

PORT LUDLOW

HERON BEACH INN
1 Heron Rd (98365)
Rates: $135-$450
(360) 437-0411

PORT ORCHARD

CEDAR HOLLOW GUEST HOUSE B&B
3875 Locker Rd (98366)
Rates: $75
(360) 871-1527

GUESTHOUSE INN
220 Bravo Terrace (98366)
Rates: $84-$99
(360) 895-7818

VISTA MOTEL
1090 Bethel (98366)
Rates: $30-$59
(360) 876-8046

PORT TOWNSEND

ALADDIN MOTOR INN
2333 Washington St (98368)
Rates: $50-$99
(360) 385-3747
(800) 281-3747

ANNAPURNA INN BED & BREAKFAST
538 Adams St (98368)
Rates: $65-$115
(360) 385-2909
(800) 868-2662

BISHOP VICTORIAN GUEST SUITES HISTORIC HOTEL
714 Washington St (98368)
Rates: $94-$199
(360) 385-6122
(800) 824-4738

CABIN VACATION RENTAL
839 Jacob Miller (98368)
Rates: $95
(360) 385-5571

COMMANDER'S HOUSE GETAWAY
Point House (98368)
Rates: $49-$125
(360) 385-2828
(800) 826-3854

FT. WORDEN STATE PARK CONF CENTER
200 Battery Way (98368)
Rates: $45-$80
(360) 385-4730

GALA'S GETAWAY RENTAL
4343 Haines St (98368)
Rates: $60-$80
(360) 385-1194

HARBORSIDE INN
330 Benedict St (98368)
Rates: $72-$102
(360) 385-7909
(800) 942-5960

NORTH BEACH RETREAT RENTAL
510 56th St (98368)
Rates: $50+
(360) 385-1621

THE HISTORIC PALACE HOTEL
1004 Water St (98368)
Rates: $69-$159
(360) 385-0733
(800) 962-0741

PILOT HOUSE VACATION RENTAL
327 Jackson St (98368)
Rates: $60-$95
(360) 379-0811

POINT HUDSON RESORT & MARINA
103 Hudson St (98368)
Rates: $45-$90
(360) 385-2828
(800) 826-3854

PORT TOWNSEND INN
2020 Washington St (98368)
Rates: $68-$175
(360) 385-2211
(800) 216-4985

PUFFIN & GULL APARTMENT MOTEL
825 Washington St (98368)
Rates: n/a
(360) 385-1475

THE SWAN HOTEL
222 Monroe St (98368)
Rates: $115-$250
(360) 385-1718
(800) 776-1718

TIDES INN
1807 Water St (98368)
Rates: $58-$124
(360) 385-0595
(800) 822-8696

VALLEY VIEW MOTEL
162 Hwy 20 (98368)
Rates: $35-$50
(360) 385-1666
(800) 280-1666

WATER STREET HOTEL
635 Water St (98368)
Rates: $50-$120
(360) 385-5467
(800) 735-9810

POULSBO

POULSBO INN
18680 Hwy 305 (98370)
Rates: $70-$105
(360) 779-3921
(800) 597-5151

SANDY HOOK BEACH SHACK
14532 Sandy Hook Rd. NE, cabin #2 (98370)
Rates: $50.00 -$70
(206)842-4260 or (360)394-3632

AREA CODES - If the local number doesn't connect, check for a new area code.

PROSSER

**BEST WESTERN
PROSSER INN**
225 Merlot Dr
(99350)
Rates: $69-$99
(509) 786-7977
(800) 528-1234
(800) 688-2192

PROSSER MOTEL
1206 Wine
Country Rd
(99350)
Rates: $40-$50
(509) 786-2555

PULLMAN

**AMERICAN
TRAVEL INN**
515 S Grand Ave
(99163)
Rates: $47-$64
(509) 334-3500

**HAWTHORN INN
& SUITES**
928 NW Olsen St
(99163)
Rates: $72-$119
(509) 332-0928
(800) 527-1133

**HOLIDAY INN
EXPRESS**
SE 1190 Bishop
Blvd (99163)
Rates: $79-$109
(509) 334-4437
(800) 465-4329

**MANOR LODGE
MOTEL**
SE 455 Paradise
(99163)
Rates: $39-$59
(509) 334-2511

**QUALITY INN
PARADISE CREEK**
SE 1400 Bishop
(99163)
Rates: $64-$84
(509) 332-0500
(800) 228-5151

PUYALLUP

MOTEL PUYALLUP
1412 S Meridian St
(98371)
Rates: $39-$64
(253) 845-8825

**NORTHWEST
MOTOR INN**
1409 S Meridian St
(98371)
Rates: $60-$73
(253) 841-2600
(800) 845-9490

QUILCENE

**MAPLE GROVE
MOTEL**
61 Maple Grove
Rd (98376)
Rates: $40-$50
(360) 765-3410

QUINAULT

**LAKE QUINAULT
LODGE**
345 S Shore Rd
(98575)
Rates: $65-$130
(360) 288-2900
(800) 562-6672
(WA)

QUINCY

**THE SUNDOWNER
MOTEL**
414 F St SE (98848)
Rates: n/a
(509) 787-3587

**TRADITIONAL
INNS**
500 F St SW (98848)
Rates: $38-$90
(509) 787-3525

RAINIER

**7 C'S GUEST
RANCH**
11123 128th St SE
(98576)
Rates: $30-$100
(360) 446-7957

RANDLE

MEDICI MOTEL
471 Cispus Rd
(98377)
Rates: $45
(360) 497-7700
(800) 697-7750

**WOODLAND
MOTEL**
11890 US 12
(98377)
Rates: $40-$50
(360) 494-6766

RAYMOND

**MAUNU'S
MOUNTCASTLE
MOTEL**
524 3rd St (98577)
Rates: $40-$55
(360) 942-5571

WILLIS MOTEL
425 3rd St (98577)
Rates: $40+
(360) 942-5313

RENTON

**BED & BREAKFAST
ASSOCIATION
OF SUBURBAN
SEATTLE**
908 Grant Ave S
(98055)
Rates: $65-$120
(425) 277-4747

**MICROTEL INN
& SUITES**
I-405 @ Exit 7
(98056)
Rates: n/a
(425) 277-7700
(888) 771-7171

TRAVELODGE
3700 E Valley Rd
(98055)
Rates: $59-$78
(425) 251-9591
(800) 578-7878

REPUBLIC

**THE NORTHERN
INN**
852 S Clark Ave
(99166)
Rates: $28-$33
(509) 775-3371

**FISHERMAN'S
COVE RESORT**
15 Fisherman's
Cove Rd (99166)
Rates: $25-$85
(509) 775-3641

**FRONTIER INN
MOTEL**
979 S Clark Ave
(99166)
Rates: $34-$57
(509) 775-3361

**K-DIAMOND-K
CATTLE & GUEST
RANCH**
15661 Hwy 21 S
(99166)
Rates: $60-$100
(509) 775-3536

KLONDIKE MOTEL
150 N Clark Ave
(99166)
Rates: $36-$44
(509) 775-3555

TIFFANYS RESORT
1026 Tiffany Rd
(99166)
Rates: $43-$115
(509) 775-3152

RICHLAND

BALI HI MOTEL
1201 George
Washington Way
(99352)
Rates: $39-$45
(509) 943-3101

**BEST WESTERN
TOWER INN &
CONF CENTER**
1515 W George
WashingtonWay
(99352)
Rates: $79-$129
(509) 946-4121
(800) 528-1234
(800) 635-3980

ELK CITY HOTEL
1426 Potter Ave
(99352)
Rates: $25-$48
(208) 842-2452

**RED LION INN
HANFORD HOUSE**
802 George
Washington Way
(99352)
Rates: $55-$65
(509) 946-7611
(800) 733-5466

**ROBERT YOUNG
SUITES LODGING
SERVICE**
2455 George
Washington Way,
Suite O-177
(99352)
Rates: $46-$105
(509) 946-5002

SHILO INN
50 Comstock St
(99352)
Rates: $69-$199
(509) 946-4661
(800) 222-2244

VAGABOND INN
515 George
Washington Way
(99352)
Rates: $40-$80
(509) 946-6117
(800) 552-1555

RIMROCK

**GAME RIDGE
MOTEL-LODGE**
27350 Hwy 12
(98937)
Rates: $39-$115
(509) 672-2212
(800) 301-9354

RITZVILLE

**BEST INN
& SUITES**
1513 Smitty's Blvd
(99169)
Rates: $59-$89
(509) 659-1007
(800) 237-8466

**COLWELL
MOTOR INN**
501 W 1st St
(99169)
Rates: $44-$66
(509) 659-1620
(888) 315-2378

COTTAGE MOTEL
508 E 1st Ave
(99169)
Rates: n/a
(509) 659-0721

EMPIRE MOTEL
101 W 1st Ave
(99169)
Rates: $27-$47
(509) 659-1030

TOP HAT MOTEL
210 E 1st St
(99169)
Rates: $35-$42
(509) 659-1100

AREA CODES - If the local number doesn't connect, check for a new area code.

ROCKPORT

CLARK'S SKAGIT RIVER CABINS
5675 Hwy 20 (98283)
Rates: $56-$140
(360) 386-4437
(800) 273-2606

TOTEM TRAIL MOTEL
5551 Hwy 20 (98283)
Rates: $35-$50
(360) 873-4535

ROSLYN

THE LITTLE ROSLYN INN
106 5th St (98941)
Rates: $38-$90
(509) 649-2936

THE ORIGINAL ROSLYN INN
102 5th St (98941)
Rates: $190
(509) 649-2936

THE ROSLYN "INN BETWEEN"
104 5th St (98941)
Rates: $390
(509) 649-2936

SAN JUAN ISLAND

BLAIR HOUSE B&B
345 Blair Ave (98250)
Rates: $75-$125
(360) 378-5907
(800) 899-3030

FRIDAY HARBOR HOUSE MOTEL
130 West St (98250)
Rates: $167-$325
(360) 378-8455

HALVORSEN HOUSE B&B
216 Halvorsen Rd (98250)
Rates: $104-$155
(360) 378-2707

HARRISON HOUSE SUITES
235 C St (98250)
Rates: $125-$195
(360) 378-3587
(800) 407-7933

INN AT FRIDAY HARBOR
410 Spring St (98250)
Rates: $145-$195
(360) 378-4000
(800) 752-5752

SAN JUAN INN
50 Spring St (98250)
Rates: $70-$175
(360) 378-2070
(800) 742-8210

SAN JUAN ISLAND PRIVATE VACATION RENTALS
P O Box 1133 (98250)
Rates: $110-$200
(360) 378-3190
(888) 367-5211

SNUG HARBOR RESORT & MARINA
1997 Mitchell Bay Rd (98250)
Rates: $30-$200
(360) 378-4762

TUCKER HOUSE BED & BREAKFAST
260 B St (98250)
Rates: $70-$135
(360) 378-2783
(800) 965-0123

WESTWINDS B&B
4909 H-Hannah Rd (98250)
Rates: $165-$245
(360) 378-5283

WHARFSIDE B&B ON THE JACQUELINE
Slip K-13 (98250)
Rates: $80-$95
(360) 378-5661

SAN JUAN ISLANDS

For lodging, see individual island listings - Lopez Island, San Juan Island, Shaw Island and Orcas Island

SEABECK

SUMMER SONG BED & BREAKFAST
P.O. Box 82 (98380)
Rates: n/a
(360) 830-5089

SEATAC

AIRPORT PLAZA HOTEL
18601 Pacific Hwy S (98188)
Rates: $60-$65
(206) 433-0400

CLARION HOTEL SEATTLE AIRPORT
3000 S 176th St (98188)
Rates: $89-$109
(206) 242-0200
(800) 252-7466

DOUBLETREE AIRPORT HOTEL
18740 Int'l Blvd (98188)
Rates: $69-$119
(206) 246-8600
(800) 222-8733

HILTON HOTEL SEATTLE AIRPORT
17620 Pacific Hwy S (98188)
Rates: $129-$169
(206) 244-4800
(800) 445-8667

HOLIDAY INN SEA-TAC
17338 Intl' Blvd (98188)
Rates: $129-$159
(206) 248-1000
(800) 465-4329

LA QUINTA INN SEA TAC INTL
2824 S 188th St (98188)
Rates: $89-$109
(206) 241-5211
(800) 687-6667

MARRIOTT SEA-TAC AIRPORT
3201 S 176th St (98188)
Rates: $160-$183
(206) 241-2000
(800) 228-9290

MOTEL 6 SEA-TAC AIRPORT
16500 Pacific Hwy S (98188)
Rates: $50-$66
(206) 246-4101
(800) 466-8356

MOTEL 6 SEA-TAC AIRPORT SOUTH
18900 47th Ave S (98188)
Rates: $47-$63
(206) 241-1648
(800) 466-8356

SEA-TAC CREST MOTOR INN
18845 Int'l Blvd (98188)
Rates: $42-$59
(206) 433-0999
(800) 554-0300

SHADOW MOTEL
2930 S 176th St (98188)
Rates: n/a
(206) 246-9300

SUPER 8 MOTEL
3100 S 192nd (98188)
Rates: $65-$89
(206) 433-8188
(800) 800-8000

SEATTLE

For additional lodging in the Seattle area, see listings under: Bellevue, Bainbridge Island, Bothel, Bremerton, Camano Island, Issaquah, Mercer Island, Redmond, Renton, SeaTac, Shoreline, Whidbey Island.

THE ALEXIS HISTORIC HOTEL
1007 First Ave (98104)
Rates: $230-$370
(206) 624-4844
(800) 426-7033

AURORA SEAFAIR INN
9100 Aurora Ave N (98103)
Rates: $70-$100
(206) 524-3600
(800) 445-9297

B&B ON BROADWAY
722 Broadway Ave E (98102)
Rates: $85-$115
(206) 329-8933
(888) 329-8933

BEECH TREE MANOR INN B&B
1405 Queen Anne Ave N (98109)
Rates: $45-$79
(206) 281-7037

BELLEVUE PLACE BED & BREAKFAST
1111 Bellevue Place E (98102)
Rates: $85-$95
(206) 325-9253
(800) 325-9253

BEST WESTERN AIRPORT EXECUTEL
20717 Int'l Blvd S (98198)
Rates: $69-$129
(206) 878-3300
(800) 528-1234
(800) 648-3311

BEST WESTERN EXECUTIVE INN
200 Taylor Ave N (98109)
Rates: $79-$175
(206) 448-9444
(800) 528-1234
(800) 351-9444

CAVANAUGH'S ON FIFTH AVE
1415 Fifth Ave (98101)
Rates: $245-$260
(206) 971-8000
(800) 843-4667

CROWNE PLAZA
1113 6th Ave (98101)
Rates: n/a
(206) 464-1980
(800) 227-6963

EASTLAKE INN
2215 Eastlake E
(98102)
Rates: n/a
(206) 322-7726

**FOUR SEASONS
OLYMPIC HOTEL**
411 University St
(98101)
Rates: $295-$550
(206) 621-1700
(800) 332-3442

**GEISHA
MOTOR INN**
9613 Aurora Ave
N (98103)
Rates: n/a
(206) 524-8880

**HAWTHORN INN
& SUITES**
2224 8th Ave
(98121)
Rates: $110-$185
(206) 624-6820
(800) 527-1133

HOTEL MONACO
1101 Fourth Ave
(98101)
Rates: $230-$295
(206) 621-1770
(800) 945-2240

LEGEND MOTEL
22204 Pacific Hwy
S (98198)
Rates: n/a
(206) 878-0366

MOTEL 6-SOUTH
20651 Military Rd
(98188)
Rates: $48-$68
(206) 824-9902
(800) 466-8356

**PARGARDENS
BED & BREAKFAST**
14716 26th Ave
NE (98155)
Rates: $60-$75
(206) 367-1437
(888) 742-2632

**PENSIONE
NICHOLAS BED
& BREAKFAST**
1923 First Ave
(98101)
Rates: $60-$80
(206) 441-7125
(800) 440-7125

**RAMADA INN
NORTHGATE**
2140 N Northgate
Way (98133)
Rates: $109-$129
(206) 365-0700
(800) 272-6232

**RESIDENCE INN
BY MARRIOTT**
800 Fairview Ave
N (98109)
Rates: $115-$350
(206) 624-6000
(800) 331-3131

RODEWAY INN
2930 S 176th St
(98188)
Rates: $39-$89
(206) 246-9300
(800) 228-2000

**SANDPIPER CORP
SUITES**
11000 1st Ave SW
(98146)
Rates: $39-$59
(206) 242-8883

SHADOW MOTEL
2930 S 176th
(98188)
Rates: $32-$50
(206) 246-9300

SUN HILL MOTEL
8517 Aurora Ave
N (98103)
Rates: n/a
(206) 525-1205

**TRAVELODGE
SPACE NEEDLE**
200 6th Ave N
(98109)
Rates: $119-$279
(206) 441-7878
(800) 578-7878

**VAGABOND INN
SPACE NEEDLE**
325 Aurora Ave N
(98109)
Rates: $90-$98
(206) 441-0400
(800) 522-1555

**W SEATTLE
HOTEL**
1112 4th Ave
(98101)
Rates: $239-$315
(206) 264-6000

**THE WESTIN
HOTEL**
1900 5th Ave
(98101)
Rates: $149-$295
(206) 728-1000
(800) 228-3000

SEAVIEW

**SEAVIEW COHO
MOTEL**
3701 Pacific Way
(98644)
Rates: $55-$110
(360) 642-2531
(800) 681-8153

**SOU'WESTER
LODGE & CABINS**
Beach Access Rd-
38th Pl (98644)
Rates: $39-$109
(360) 642-2542

*SEDRO
WOOLLEY*

SKAGIT MOTEL
1977 Hwy 20
(98284)
Rates: n/a
(360) 856-6001

**THREE RIVERS
INN MOTEL**
210 Ball St (98284)
Rates: $63-$77
(360) 855-2626
(800) 221-5122

SEKIU

**BAY MOTEL
& MARINA**
15562 Hwy 112 W
(98381)
Rates: $34-$65
(360) 963-2444

**CURLEY'S RESORT
& DIVE CENTER**
291 Front St
(98381)
Rates: $46-$75
(360) 963-2281
(800) 542-9680

**HERB'S MOTEL &
CHARTERS**
411 Front St
(98381)
Rates: $45-$74
(360) 963-2346

**OLSON'S RESORT
& MARINA**
444 Front St
(98381)
Rates: $50-$85
(360) 963-2311

**STRAITSIDE
RESORT CABINS**
241 Front St
(98381)
Rates: $45-$74
(360) 963-2100

**VAN RIPER'S
RESORT**
280 Front St
(98381)
Rates: n/a
(360) 963-2334

SEQUIM

**BEST WESTERN
SEQUIM BAY
LODGE**
268522 Hwy 101 E
(98382)
Rates: $81-$91
(360) 683-0691
(800) 528-1234
(800) 622-0691

**COFFEL'S
SUNDOWNER
MOTEL**
364 W
Washington St
(98382)
Rates: $69-$79
(360) 683-5532

ECONO LODGE
801 E Washington
St (98382)
Rates: $69-$125
(360) 683-7113
(800) 553-2666

**GROVELAND
COTTAGE B&B**
4861 Sequim-
Dungeness Way
(98382)
Rates: $60-$110
(360) 683-3565
(800) 879-8859

**JUAN DE FUCA
COTTAGES**
182 Marine Dr
(98382)
Rates: $125-$150
(360) 683-4433

**RANCHO LAMRO
BED & BREAKFAST**
1734 Woodcock
Rd (98382)
Rates: n/a
(360) 683-8133

RED RANCH INN
830 W
Washington St
(98382)
Rates: $50-$100
(360) 683-4195
(800) 777-4195

SHELTON

**CANAL SIDE
RESORT MOTEL**
N 21660 Hwy 101
(98584)
Rates: $38-$48
(360) 877-9422

**CITY CENTER BEST
RATES MOTEL**
128 E Alder
(98584)
Rates: $36-$54
(360) 426-3397

**LAKE
NAHWATZEL
RESORT**
W 12900 Shelton-
Matlock Rd
(98584)
Rates: $30-$50
(360) 426-8323

**RESTFULL
FARM B&B**
W 2230 Shelton
Valley Rd (98584)
Rates: $60-$70
(360) 426-8774

SHELTON INN
628 Railroad Ave
(98584)
Rates: $48-$68
(360) 426-4468
(800) 451-4560

SUPER 8 MOTEL
2943 Northview
Circle (98584)
Rates: $51-$69
(360) 426-1654
(800) 800-8000

AREA CODES - If the local number doesn't connect, check for a new area code.

SILVER CREEK

LAKE MAYFIELD MOTEL
2911 US Hwy 12 (98585)
Rates: n/a
(360) 985-2484

SILVER LAKE

SILVER LAKE MOTEL & RESORT
3201 Spirit Lake Hwy (98645)
Rates: $30-$80
(360) 274-6141

SILVERDALE

CIMARRON MOTEL
9734 NW Silverdale Way (98315)
Rates: $56-$66
(360) 692-7777
(800) 273-5076

SEABREEZE COTTAGES & SPA
16609 Olympic View Rd NW (98315)
Rates: $76-$169
(360) 692-4648

SKYKOMISH

SKYKOMISH HOTEL
102 Railroad Ave (98288)
Rates: n/a
(360) 677-8105

SKYRIVER INN
333 River Dr E (98288)
Rates: $65-$100
(360) 677-2261
(800) 367-8194 (WA)

SNOHOMISH

SNOHOMISH GRAND HOTEL BED & BREAKFAST
901 1/2 1st St (98290)
Rates: $60-$75
(360) 568-8854

SNOHOMISH GRAND VALLEY INN
11910 Springetti Rd (98290)
Rates: n/a
(360) 568-8854

SNOQUALMIE

SALISH LODGE & SPA
6501 Railroad Ave SE (98065)
Rates: $229-$575
(425) 888-2556
(800) 826-6124

SNOQUALMIE PASS

BEST WESTERN SUMMITT INN
603 SR 906 (98068)
Rates: $79-$299
(425) 434-6300
(800) 557-7829

SOAP LAKE

NOTARAS LODGE
236 E Main Ave (98851)
Rates: $58-$250
(509) 246-0462

ROYAL VIEW MOTEL
Hwy 17 & 4th Sts (98851)
Rates: n/a
(509) 246-1831

TOLO VISTA COTTAGE
22 N Daisy (98851)
Rates: n/a
(509) 246-1512

SOUTH BEND

H & H MOTEL
Hwy 101, PO Box 613 (98586)
Rates: $34-$49
(360) 875-5523

THE RUSSELL HOUSE HISTORIC BED & BREAKFST
902 E Water St (98586)
Rates: $60-$200
(360) 875-6487

SPOKANE

ALPINE MOTEL & RV PARK
18815 E Cataldo (99201)
Rates: $50-$60
(509) 928-2700

APPLE TREE INN
9508 N Division St (99218)
Rates: $50-$55
(509) 466-3020
(800) 323-5796

BEL AIR MOTEL 7
1303 E Sprague Ave (99202)
Rates: $33-$49
(509) 535-1677

BELL MOTEL
9030 W Sunset Hwy (99204)
Rates: $30-$43
(800) 223-1388

BEST INN & SUITES
6309 E Broadway (99212)
Rates: $49-$149
(509) 535-7185
(800) 237-8466

BEST WESTERN PEPPER TREE AIRPORT INN
3711 S Geiger (99204)
Rates: $65-$150
(509) 624-4655
(800) 528-1234
(800) 799-3933

BEST WESTERN THUNDERBIRD INN
120 W Third Ave (99204)
Rates: $69-$89
(509) 747-2011
(800) 528-1234
(800) 578-2473

BEST WESTERN TRADE WINDS
3033 N Division St (99207)
Rates: $59-$95
(509) 326-5500
(800) 528-1234
(800) 621-8593

BROADWAY MOTEL
6317 E Broadway (99212)
Rates: $66-$74
(509) 535-2442

BUDGET SAVER MOTEL
1234 E Sprague Ave (99202)
Rates: $26-$59
(509) 534-0669

CAVANAUGH'S RESIDENT COURT
1203 W Fifth Ave (99204)
Rates: $34-$68
(509) 624-4142
(800) 325-4000

CAVANAUGH'S RIDPATH HOTEL
515 W Sprague Ave (99201)
Rates: $105-$135
(509) 838-2711
(800) 325-4000

CAVANAUGH'S RIVER INN
700 N Division St (99202)
Rates: $89-$126
(509) 326-5577
(800) 325-4000

CLINIC CENTER MOTEL
702 S McClellan (99204)
Rates: n/a
(509) 747-6081

COMFORT INN NORTH
7111 N Division St (98208)
Rates: $39-$150
(509) 467-7111
(800) 228-5150

COUNTRY INN & SUITES
3808 N Sullivan Rd (99216)
Rates: $69-$79
(509) 893-0955
(800) 456-4000

DAYS INN
4212 W Sunset Blvd (99204)
Rates: $50-$65
(509) 747-2021
(800) 329-7466

DOUBLETREE SPOKANE CITY CENTER
322 N Spokane Falls Ct (99201)
Rates: $79-$109
(509) 455-9600
(800) 222-8733

DOUBLETREE SPOKANE VALLEY
1100 N Sullivan Rd (99220)
Rates: $79-$109
(509) 524-9000
(800) 222-8733

HAMPTON INN
2010 S Assembly Rd (99224)
Rates: $74-$93
(509) 747-1100
(800) 426-7866

HAWTHORN INN & SUITES
3808 N Sullivan Rd (99216)
Rates: $69-$79
(509) 893-0955
(800) 528-1133

HOWARD JOHNSON INN
211 S Division St (99202)
Rates: $60-$75
(509) 838-6630
(800) 446-4656

LIBERTY MOTEL
6801 N Division St (99208)
Rates: $38-$60
(509) 467-6000

MAPLETREE MOTEL
4824 E Sprague Ave (99212)
Rates: $26-$48
(509) 535-5810

MOTEL 6
1508 S Rustle St (99204)
Rates: $39-$52
(509) 459-6120
(800) 466-8356

MOTEL 6
1919 N Hutchinson Rd (99212)
Rates: $35-$54
(509) 926-5399
(800) 466-8356

PARK LANE MOTEL & SUITES
4412 E Sprague Ave (99212)
Rates: $57-$62
(509) 535-1626
(800) 533-1626

QUALITY INN OAKWOOD
7919 N Division St (98208)
Rates: $69-$89
(509) 467-4900
(800) 228-5151

QUALITY INN VALLEY SUITES
8923 E Mission Ave (99212)
Rates: $79-$91
(509) 928-5218
(800) 228-5151

RAMADA INN AIRPORT
Airport Rd (99219)
Rates: $83-$97
(509) 838-5211
(800) 272-6232

RAMADA INN & SUITES
9601 N Newport Hwy (99218)
Rates: $59-$89
(509) 468-4201
(800) 272-6232

RAMADA LIMITED
123 S Post St (99204)
Rates: $44-$64
(509) 838-8504
(800) 272-6232

RANCH MOTEL
1609 S Lewis St (99204)
Rates: $25-$32
(509) 456-8919
(800) 871-8919

RED TOP MOTEL
7217 E Trent Ave (99212)
Rates: $42-$105
(509) 926-5728

ROYAL SCOT MOTEL
20 W Houston (99208)
Rates: n/a
(509) 467-6672
(888) 467-7268

SELECT INN
1420 W 2nd Ave (99204)
Rates: $36-$62
(509) 838-2026
(800) 246-6835

SHANGRI-LA MOTEL
2922 W Government Way (99204)
Rates: $47-$76
(509) 747-2066
(800) 234-4941

SHILO HOTEL
923 E 3rd Ave (99202)
Rates: $79-$119
(509) 535-9000
(800) 222-2244

THE SPOKANE HOUSE HOTEL
4301 W Sunset Blvd (99224)
Rates: $64-$69
(509) 838-1471

SUPER 8 MOTEL
2020 N Argonne Rd (99212)
Rates: $54-$76
(509) 928-4888
(800) 800-8000

SUPER 8 MOTEL WEST
11102 W Westbow Blvd (99204)
Rates: $49-$79
(509) 838-8800
(800) 800-8000

TRADE WINDS MOTEL
907 W 3rd Ave (99204)
Rates: $50-$70
(509) 838-2091
(800) 586-5397

TRAVELODGE
33 W Spokane Falls Blvd (99201)
Rates: $83-$180
(509) 623-9727
(800) 578-7878

SPRAGUE

LAST ROUNDUP MOTEL & RV PARK
312 E First (99032)
Rates: $36-$54
(509) 257-2583

PURPLE SAGE MOTEL
405-9 First (99032)
Rates: $28-$42
(509) 257-2507

SULTAN

DUTCH CUP MOTEL
918 Main St (98294)
Rates: $57-$70
(360) 793-2215
(800) 844-0488

SUMAS

BB BORDER INN MOTEL
121 Cleveland (98295)
Rates: n/a
(360) 988-5800

SUMNER

SUMNER MOTOR INN
15506 E Main St (98380)
Rates: $50-$66
(253) 863-3250

SUNNYSIDE

RODEWAY INN
3209 Picard Pl (98944)
Rates: $69-$84
(509) 837-5781
(800) 228-2000

SUN VALLEY INN
724 Valley Hwy (98944)
Rates: $25-$75
(509) 837-4721

TOWN HOUSE MOTEL
509 Yakima Valley Hwy (98944)
Rates: $38-$52
(509) 837-5500
(800) 342-4435

TRAVELODGE
408 Yakima Valley Hwy (98944)
Rates: $48-$52
(509) 837-7878
(800) 578-7878

TACOMA

BEST WESTERN TACOMA INN
8726 S Hosmer St (98444)
Rates: $69-$97
(253) 535-2880
(800) 528-1234
(800) 305-2888

BLUE SPRUCE MOTEL
12715 Pacific Ave (98444)
Rates: n/a
(253) 531-6111

BUDGET INN-SOUTH TACOMA
9915 S Tacoma Way (98499)
Rates: $36+
(253) 588-6615

CORPORATE SUITES
219 Division Ct E (98404)
Rates: n/a
(800) 255-6058

DAYS INN
6802 Tacoma Mall Blvd (98409)
Rates: $69-$150
(253) 475-5900
(800) 329-7466

HIDDEN MAPLE BED & BREAKFAST
4616 N 46th (98407)
Rates: $75-$95
(253) 756-2094

LA QUINTA INN
1425 E 27th St (98421)
Rates: $89-$109
(253) 383-0146
(800) 687-6667

MOTEL 6 SOUTH
1811 S 76th St (98408)
Rates: $48-$68
(253) 473-7100
(800) 466-8356

RAMADA INN TACOMA DOME
2611 East E St (98421)
Rates: $62-$110
(253) 572-7272
(800) 272-6232

ROYAL COACHMAN INN
5805 Pacific Hwy E (98424)
Rates: $73-$84
(253) 922-2500
(800) 422-3051

SHERATON TACOMA HOTEL
1320 Broadway Plaza (98402)
Rates: $120-$146
(253) 572-3200
(800) 325-3535

SHILO INN
7414 S Hosmer St (98408)
Rates: $79-$109
(253) 475-4020
(800) 222-2244

VALLEY MOTEL
1220 Puyallup Ave (98421)
Rates: n/a
(253) 272-7720

VICTORY MOTEL
10801 Pacific Hwy SW (98499)
Rates: $23-$50
(253) 588-9107

TENINO

OFFUT LAKE RESORT
4005 120th Ave SE (98589)
Rates: $27-$45
(360) 264-2438

THORP

CIRCLE H HOLIDAY RANCH RESORT
810 Watt Canyon Rd (98946)
Rates: n/a
(509) 964-2000

TOKELAND

TRADEWINDS ON THE BAY MOTEL
4305 Pomeroy Ave (98590)
Rates: n/a
(360) 267-7500

AREA CODES - If the local number doesn't connect, check for a new area code.

TOLEDO

COWLITZ MOTEL
162 Cowlitz Loop
Rd (98591)
Rates: n/a
(360) 864-6611

TONASKET

**BONAPARTE
LAKE RESORT**
615 Bonaparte
Lake Rd (98855)
Rates: n/a
(509) 486-2491

**RAINBOW
RESORT**
761 Loomis Hwy
(98855)
Rates: $26-$60
(509) 223-3700
(800) 347-4375

RED APPLE INN
Hwy 97 & 1st St
(98855)
Rates: $37-$47
(509) 486-2119

**SPECTACLE LAKE
RESORT**
10 McCammon Rd
(98855)
Rates: $30-$105
(509) 223-3433

TOPPENISH

**EL CORRAL
MOTEL**
61731 Hwy 97
(98948)
Rates: $34-$39
(509) 865-2365

**OXBOW
MOTOR INN**
511 S Elm St
(98948)
Rates: $31-$49
(509) 865-5800
(800) 222-3161

**TOPPENISH INN
MOTEL**
515 S Elm St
(98948)
Rates: $60-$102
(509) 865-7444

TUKWILA

**HOMESTEAD
VILLAGE GUEST
STUDIOS**
15635 W Valley
Hwy (98188)
Rates: n/a
(425) 235-7160
(888) 782-9473

**HOMEWOOD
SUITES HOTEL**
6955 Fort Dent
Way (98188)
Rates: $129-$199
(425) 433-8000
(800) 225-5466

**RESIDENCE INN
BY MARRIOTT**
16201 W Valley
Hwy (98188)
Rates: $150-$200
(425) 226-5500
(800) 331-3131

**SOUTH CITY
MOTEL**
14242 S Pacific
Hwy (98168)
Rates: n/a
(425) 243-0222

TUMWATER

**BEST WESTERN
TUMWATER INN**
5188 Capitol Blvd
(98501)
Rates: $70-$83
(360) 956-1235
(800) 528-1234
(800) 848-4992

**GUESTHOUSE
INN & SUITES**
1600 74th Ave SW
(98512)
Rates: $78-$135
(360) 943-5040

MOTEL 6
400 W Lee St
(98501)
Rates: $40-$56
(360) 754-7320
(800) 466-8356

TWISP

**IDLE-A-WHILE
MOTEL**
505 N Hwy 20
(98856)
Rates: $45-$72
(509) 997-3222

**SPORTSMAN
MOTEL**
1010 E Hwy 20
(98856)
Rates: $29-$45
(509) 997-2911

**WAGON WHEEL
MOTEL**
HCR 73, Box 57
(98856)
Rates: n/a
(509) 997-4671

UNION

**ALDERBROOK
RESORT**
E 7101 Hwy 106
(98592)
Rates: $69-$105
(360) 898-2200
(800) 622-9370

**ROBIN HOOD
VILLAGE**
E 6780 Hwy 106
(98592)
Rates: $75-$85
(360) 898-2163

UNION GAP

**BEST WESTERN
AHTANUM INN**
2408 Rudkin Rd
(98903)
Rates: $61-$79
(509) 248-9700
(800) 528-1234
(800) 348-9701

**QUALITY INN
YAKIMA VALLEY**
12 E Valley Mall
Blvd (98903)
Rates: $49-$99
(509) 248-6924
(800) 228-5151

SUPER 8 MOTEL
2605 Rudkin Rd
(98903)
Rates: $49-$65
(509) 248-8880
(800) 800-8000

USK

THE HOTEL USK
410 River Rd
(99180)
Rates: $25-$57
(509) 445-1526

VALLEY

**TEAL'S WAITTS
LAKE RESORT**
3365 Waitts Lake
Rd (99181)
Rates: n/a
(509) 937-2400

VANCOUVER

**BEST INN &
SUITES-CASCADE
PARK**
221 NE Chkalov
Dr (98684)
Rates: 627-$130
(360) 256-7044
(800) 237-8466

**BEST INN &
SUITES**
7001 NE Hwy 99
(98665)
Rates: $68-$82
(360) 696-0516
(888) 696-0516

COMFORT INN
13207 NE 20th
Ave (98686)
Rates: $49-$74
(360) 574-6000
(800) 228-5150

FERRYMAN'S INN
7901 NE 6th Ave
(98665)
Rates: $54-$68
(360) 574-2151

**HOMEWOOD
SUITES**
701 SE Columbia
Shores Blvd
(98661)
Rates: n/a
(360) 750-1100
(800) 225-5466

QUALITY INN
7001 NE Hwy 99
(98665)
Rates: $67-$85
(360) 696-0516
(800) 228-5151

**RED LION HOTEL
AT THE QUAY**
100 Columbia St
(98660)
Rates: $69-$89
(360) 694-8341
(800) 733-5466

**RESIDENCE INN
BY MARRIOTT**
8005 NE Parkway
Dr (98662)
Rates: $139-$189
(360) 253-4800
(800) 331-3131

RIVERSIDE MOTEL
4400 Columbia
House Blvd (98661)
Rates: n/a
(360) 693-3677

**SHILO INN
DOWNTOWN**
401 E 13th St
(98686)
Rates: $65-$95
(360) 696-0411
(800) 222-2244

**SHILO INN
HAZEL DELL**
13206 Hwy 99
(98686)
Rates: $59-$99
(360) 573-0511
(800) 222-2244

**SUNNYSIDE
MOTEL**
12200 NE Hwy 99
(98686)
Rates: n/a
(360) 573-4141

VALUE MOTEL
708 NE 78th St
(98665)
Rates: n/a
(360) 574-2345

**VANCOUVER
LODGE**
601 Broadway
(98660)
Rates: $40-$75
(360) 693-3668

VASHON
ISLAND

**ANGELS OF THE
SEA B&B**
26431 99th Ave
SW (98070)
Rates: $65-$85
(206) 463-6980
(800) 798-9249

CASTLE HILL B&B
26734 94th Ave
SW (98070)
Rates: $65+
(206) 463-5491

SWALLOW'S NEST GUEST COTTAGES
6030 248th St SW (98070)
Rates: $75-$180
(206) 463-2646
(800) 269-6378

VERADALE

COMFORT INN VALLEY
905 N Sullivan Rd (99037)
Rates: $39-$150
(509) 924-3838
(800) 228-5150

WALLA WALLA

A & H MOTEL
2599 Isaacs (99362)
Rates: n/a
(509) 529-0560

BEST WESTERN WALLA WALLA SUITES INN
7 E Oak St (99362)
Rates: $79-$115
(509) 525-4700
(800) 528-1234

BUDGET INN
305 N 2nd Ave (99362)
Rates: $40-$75
(509) 529-4410

CAPRI MOTEL
2003 Melrose St (99362)
Rates: $32-$65
(509) 525-1130

CITY CENTER MOTEL
627 W Main St (99362)
Rates: $32-$50
(509) 529-2660
(800) 453-3160

COLONIAL MOTEL
2279 E Isaacs (99362)
Rates: $32-$55
(509) 529-1220

HAWTHORN INN & SUITES
520 N 2nd St (99362)
Rates: $69-$109
(509) 525-2522
(800) 527-1133

HOWARD JOHNSON EXP
325 E Main St (99362)
Rates: $74-$124
(509) 529-4360
(800) 446-4656

SICYON GALLERY BED & BREAKFAST
1283 Star (99362)
Rates: n/a
(509) 525-2964

SUPER 8 MOTEL
2315 Eastgate St N (99362)
Rates: $52-$68
(509) 525-8800
(800) 800-8000

TRAVELODGE
421 E Main St (99362)
Rates: $48-$75
(509) 529-4940
(800) 578-7878

WHITMAN MOTOR INN
107 N 2nd St (99362)
Rates: $39-$115
(509) 525-2200
(800) 237-4436

WENATCHEE

AVENUE MOTEL
720 N Wenatchee Ave (98801)
Rates: $43-$65
(509) 663-7161
(800) 733-8981

COMFORT INN
815 N Wenatchee Ave (98801)
Rates: $80-$90
(509) 662-1700
(800) 228-5150

FORGET ME NOT BED & BREAKFAST
1133 Washington St (98801)
Rates: n/a
(509) 663-6114

HAWTHORN INN & SUITES
1905 N Wenatchee Ave (98801)
Rates: $64-$99
(509) 664-6565
(800) 527-1133

HILL CREST MOTEL
2921 School St (98801)
Rates: $25-$40
(509) 663-5157

HOLIDAY LODGE
610 N Wenatchee Ave (98801)
Rates: $38-$75
(509) 663-8167
(800) 722-0852

LYLE'S MOTEL
924 N Wenatchee Ave (98801)
Rates: $30-$75
(509) 663-5155
(800) 582-3788

ORCHARD INN
1401 N Miller Ave (98801)
Rates: $49-$77
(509) 662-3443
(800) 368-4571

RED LION HOTEL
1225 N Wenatchee Ave (98801)
Rates: $79-$89
(509) 663-0711
(800) 733-5466

STARLITE MOTEL
1640 N Wenatchee Ave (98801)
Rates: $35-$55
(509) 663-8115
(800) 668-1862

UPTOWNER MOTEL
101 N Mission St (98801)
Rates: $40-$55
(509) 663-8516
(800) 288-5279

VAGABOND INN
700 N Wenatchee Ave (98801)
Rates: $40-$70
(509) 663-8133
(800) 522-1555

WELCOME INN
232 N Wenatchee Ave (98801)
Rates: $40-$55
(509) 663-7121
(800) 561-8856

WEST COAST WENATCHEE CENTER HOTEL
201 N Wenatchee Ave (98801)
Rates: $79-$89
(509) 662-1234
(800) 426-0670

WESTPORT

ALASKAN MOTEL & APARTMENTS
708 N First (98595)
Rates: n/a
(360) 268-9133

BREAKERS MOTEL
971 N Montesano St (98595)
Rates: $52-$70
(360) 268-0848

CHINOOK MOTEL
707 N Montesano St (98595)
Rates: n/a
(360) 268-9623

CRANBERRY MOTEL
920 S Montesano St (98595)
Rates: $30+
(360) 268-0807

FRANK L. AQUATIC GARDENS RESORT
725 S Montesano St (98595)
Rates: $42-$108
(360) 268-9200

GLENACRES INN BED & BREAKFAST
222 N Montesano St (98595)
Rates: n/a
(360) 268-9391

HARBOR RESORT
871 Neddie Rose Dr (98595)
Rates: n/a
(360) 268-0169

ISLANDER MOTEL & CHARTERS
421 Westhaven & Neddie Rose (98595)
Rates: $50
(360) 268-9166
(800) 322-1740

MARINERS COVE INN
303 Ocean Ave (98595)
Rates: $49-$60
(360) 268-0531

OCEAN AVENUE INN
275 W Ocean Ave (98595)
Rates: $50-$145
(360) 268-9278
(888) 692-5262

SHIPWRECK MOTEL
2653 Nyhus St (98595)
Rates: n/a
(360) 268-9151

WHIDBEY ISLAND

(Clinton)

HOME BY THE SEA COTTAGES
2388 E Sunlight Beach Rd (98236)
Rates: $155-$175
(360) 321-2964

NORTHWEST VACATION HOMES
6497 E Hunziker Ln (98236)
Rates: $100-$275
(360) 341-5005
(800) 544-4304

(Coupeville)

THE VICTORIAN HISTORIC BED & BREAKFAST
602 N Main St (98239)
Rates: $65-$100
(360) 678-5305

(Freeland)

HARBOUR INN MOTEL
1606 E Main St (98249)
Rates: $58-$88
(360) 331-6900

(Langley)

DRAKE'S LANDING B&B
203 Wharf St (98260)
Rates: $65+
(360) 221-3999

ISLAND TYME B&B
4940 S Bayview Rd (98260)
Rates: $95-$140
(360) 221-5078
(800) 898-8963

(Oak Harbor)

ACORN MOTOR INN
3150 Hwy 20 (98277)
Rates: $52-$78
(360) 675-6646
(800) 280-6646

BEST WESTERN HARBOR PLAZA
33175 SR 20 (98277)
Rates: $109-$119
(360) 679-4567
(800) 528-1234
(800) 927-5478

WHITE PASS

GAME RIDGE MOTEL & LODGE
27350 Hwy 12 (98937)
Rates: $39-$82
(509) 672-2212

WHITE SALMON

INN OF THE WHITE SALMON BED & BREAKFAST
172 W Jewett (98672)
Rates: $75-$115
(509) 493-2335
(800) 972-5226

WILBUR

EIGHT BAR B MOTEL
718 E Main (99185)
Rates: $30-$65
(509) 647-2400

SETTLE INN
303 NE Main (99185)
Rates: $34-$45
(509) 647-2100

WINLOCK

SUNRISE MOTEL
663 SR 505 (98596)
Rates: $38
(360) 785-4343

WINTHROP

BEST WESTERN CASCADE INN
960 Hwy 20, Box 813 (98862)
Rates: $67-$150
(509) 996-3100
(800) 528-1234
(800) 468-6754

PINE-NEAR MOTEL
350 Castle Ave (98862)
Rates: n/a
(509) 996-2391

RIVER RUN INN & RESORT
27 Rader Rd (98862)
Rates: $60-$89
(509) 996-2173
(800) 757-2709

THE VIRGINIAN RESORT
808 N Cascade Hwy (98862)
Rates: $75-$95
(509) 996-2535
(800) 854-2834

WINTHROP INN
950 Hwy 20 (98862)
Rates: $60-$85
(509) 996-2217
(800) 444-1972

WOLFRIDGE RESORT COTTAGES
412B Wolf Creek Rd (98862)
Rates: $44-$149
(509) 996-2828

WOODLAND

LEWIS RIVER INN
1100 Lewis River Rd (98674)
Rates: $48-$71
(360) 225-6257
(800) 543-4344

SCANDIA MOTEL
1123 Hoffman St (98674)
Rates: $32-$42
(360) 225-8006

WOODLANDER INN
1500 Atlantic St (98674)
Rates: $47-$55
(360) 225-6548
(800) 444-9667

YAKIMA

ALL STAR MOTEL
1900 N 1st St (98901)
Rates: n/a
(509) 452-7111

BALI HAI MOTEL
710 N 1st St (98901)
Rates: $23-$43
(509) 452-7178

BEST WESTERN PEPPERTREE INN
1614 N 1st St (98901)
Rates: $65-$125
(509) 453) 8898
(800) 528-1234
(800) 834-1649

CAVANAUGH'S AT YAKIMA CENTER
607 E Yakima Ave (98901)
Rates: $72-$91
(509) 248-5900
(800) 843-4667

CAVANAUGH'S GATEWAY HOTEL
9 N 9th St (98901)
Rates: $72-$91
(509) 452-6511
(800) 843-4667

COMFORT SUITES
3702 Fruitvale Blvd (98902)
Rates: $94-$104
(509) 249-1900
(800) 228-5150

DOUBLETREE INN YAKIMA VALLEY
1507 N 1st St (98901)
Rates: $59-$99
(509) 248-7850
(800) 222-8733

HOLIDAY INN EXPRESS
1001 East A St (98901)
Rates: $74-$98
(509) 249-1000
(800) 465-4329

MOTEL 6
1104 N 1st St (98901)
Rates: $32-$46
(509) 454-0080
(800) 466-8356

NENDEL'S INN
1405 N 1st St (98901)
Rates: $32-$66
(509) 453-8981
(800) 547-0106

NISKA'S INNS OF AMERICA
1022 N 1st St (98901)
Rates: $35+
(509) 453-5615

OXFORD SUITES
1701 Terrace Hghts Dr (98801)
Rates: $75-$105
(509) 457-9000

RED APPLE MOTEL
416 N 1st St (98901)
Rates: n/a
(509) 248-7150

RED CARPET MOTOR INN
1608 Fruitvale Blvd (98902)
Rates: $34-$65
(509) 457-1131
(800) 457-5090

RED LION INN
818 N 1st St (98901)
Rates: $46-$69
(509) 453-0391
(800) 547-8010

SUN COUNTRY INN
1700 N 1st St (98901)
Rates: $48-$58
(509) 248-5650

VAGABOND INN
510 N 1st St (98901)
Rates: $42-$57
(509) 457-6155
(800) 522-1555

YELM

LOG HOUSE BED & BREAKFAST
11249 Bald Hill Rd (98597)
Rates: $95-$150
(360) 458-4385

PRAIRIE MOTEL
700 Prairie Park Ln (98597)
Rates: $55-$100
(360) 458-8300

ZILLAH

COMFORT INN
911 Vintage Valley Pkwy (98953)
Rates: $76-$130
(509) 829-3399
(800) 228-5150

AREA CODES - If the local number doesn't connect, check for a new area code.

WEST VIRGINIA

BARBOURSVILLE

COMFORT INN
249 Mall Rd
(25504)
Rates: $53-$150
(304) 733-2122
(800) 228-5150

BECKLEY

BECKLEY HOTEL
1940 Harper Rd
(25801)
Rates: $65-$200
(800) 274-6010

BEST WESTERN FOUR SEASONS INN
1939 Harper Rd
(25801)
Rates: $54-$80
(304) 252-0671
(800) 528-1234

CHARLES HOUSE MOTEL
223 S Heber St
(25801)
Rates: n/a
(304) 253-8318

COMFORT INN
1909 Harper Rd
(25801)
Rates: $61-$113
(304) 255-2161
(800) 228-5150

COUNTRY INN & SUITES
2120 Harper Rd
(25801)
Rates: $75-$85
(3040 252-5100
(800) 458-4000

HOWARD JOHNSON
1907 Harper Rd
(25801)
Rates: $49-$109
(304) 255-5900
(800) 446-4656

SUPER 8 MOTEL
2014 Harper Rd
(25801)
Rates: $45-$64
(304) 253-0802
(800) 800-8000

BERKELEY SPRINGS

THE GATEHOUSE VACATION RENTAL AT SLEEPY CREEK
126 Camp Harmison Dr
(25411)
Rates: n/a
(304) 258-9282

PARK HAVEN MOTOR LODGE
Rt 1, Box 298,
Rt 522 S (25411)
Rates: n/a
(304) 258-1734

BLUEFIELD

ECONO LODGE
3400 Cumberland Rd (24701)
Rates: $36-$85
(304) 327-8171
(800) 553-2666

HOLIDAY INN ON THE HILL
US 460 (24701)
Rates: $100
(304) 325-6170
(800) 465-4329

RAMADA INN-EAST RIVER MTN
3175 E Cumberland Rd
(24701)
Rates: $67-$77
(304) 325-5421
(800) 272-6232

BRIDGEPORT

HEDGES MOTEL
Rt 50 East (26330)
Rates: n/a
(304) 842-2811

HOLIDAY INN
100 Lodgeville Rd
(26330)
Rates: $79-$90
(304) 842-5411
(800) 465-4329

KNIGHTS INN
1235 W Main St
(26330)
Rates: $42-$80
(304) 842-7115
(800) 843-5644

SLEEP INN
115 Tolley Rd
(26330)
Rates: $59-$99
(304) 842-1919
(800) 753-3746

SUPER 8 MOTEL
168 Barnett Run Rd (26330)
Rates: $44-$65
(304) 842-7381
(800) 800-8000

BUCKHANNON

BAXA HOTEL-MOTEL
21 N Kanawha St
(26201)
Rates: $29-$38
(304) 472-2500

COLONIAL MOTEL
24 N Kanawha St
(26201)
Rates: n/a
(304) 472-3000

BURNSVILLE

BURNSVILLE MOTEL
5th & Main
(26335)
Rates: $26-$31
(304) 853-2918

CHAPMANVILLE

RODEWAY INN
SR 10 & US 119
(25508)
Rates: $45-$85
(304) 855-7182
(800) 228-2000

CHARLESTON

DAYS INN
6400 MacCorkle Ave (25304)
Rates: $45-$85
(304) 925-1010
(800) 329-7466

HOLIDAY INN CIVIC CENTER
100 Civic Center Dr (25301)
Rates: $99
(304) 345-0600
(800) 465-4329

HOLIDAY INN DOWNTOWN
600 Kanawha Blvd E (25301)
Rates: $99
(304) 344-4092
(800) 465-4329

KNIGHTS INN
6401 MacCorkle Ave SE (25304)
Rates: $35-$45
(304) 925-0451
(800) 843-5644

MOTEL 6
6311 MacCorkle Ave SE (25304)
Rates: $34-$49
(304) 925-0471
(800) 466-8356

RED ROOF INN
6305 MacCorkle Ave SE (25304)
Rates: $43-$67
(304) 925-6953
(800) 843-7663

CLARKSBURG

TERRACE MOTEL
1202 E Pike St
(26301)
Rates: n/a
(304) 622-6161

CROSS LANES

COMFORT INN
102 Racer Dr
(25313)
Rates: $59-$104
(304) 776-8070
(800) 228-5150

MOTEL 6
330 Goff Mountain Rd
(25313)
Rates: $34-$46
(304) 776-5911
(800) 466-8356

DAVIS

DEERFIELD VILLAGE RESORT
Cortland Lane
(26260)
Rates: $140
(304) 866-4698
(800) 342-3217

DUNBAR

SUPER 8 MOTEL
911 Dunbar Ave
(25064)
Rates: $47-$65
(304) 768-6888
(800) 800-8000

ELKINS

BUDGET HOST INN
Rt 219 & 250 S
(26241)
Rates: $45-$62
(304) 636-7711
(800) 283-4678

CHEAT RIVER LODGE
Rt 1, Box 115
(26241)
Rates: n/a
(304) 636-2301

AREA CODES - If the local number doesn't connect, check for a new area code.

DAYS INN
1200 Harrison Ave
(26241)
Rates: $53-$74
(304) 637-4667
(800) 329-7466

ECONO LODGE
US 33 E (26241)
Rates: $40-$70
(304) 636-5311
(800) 553-2666

MOUNTAIN SPLENDOR INN
P. O. Box 1802
(26241)
Rates: n/a
(304) 636-8111

SUPER 8 MOTEL
350 Beverly Pike
(26241)
Rates: $44-$62
(304) 636-6500
(800) 800-8000

FAIRMONT

COUNTRY CLUB MOTOR LODGE
1499 Locust Ave
(26554)
Rates: $23-$30
(304) 366-4141

DAYS INN
228 Middletown Rd (26554)
Rates: $44-$77
(304) 366-5995
(800) 329-7466

HOLIDAY INN
930 E Grafton Rd
(26554)
Rates: $72-$109
(304) 366-5500
(800) 465-4329

RED ROOF INN
50 Middletown Rd (26554)
Rates: $45-$61
(304) 366-6800
(800) 843-7663

SUPER 8 MOTEL
2208 Pleasant Valley Rd (26554)
Rates: $48-$69
(304) 363-1488
(800) 800-8000

FAYETTEVILLE

COMFORT INN-NEW RIVER
US 19 & Laurel Creek Rd (25840)
Rates: $30-$200
(304) 574-3443
(800) 228-5150

WHITE HOUSE BED & BREAKFST
120 Fayette Ave
(25840)
Rates: $70-$110
(304) 574-1400

FRANKLIN

MT. STATE MOTEL
Rt 220 North
(26807)
Rates: n/a
(304) 358-2084

HARPERS FERRY

CLIFFSIDE INN
US Rt 340 (25425)
Rates: $45-$71
(800) 786-9437

HILLSBORO

THE CURRENT
Denmar Rd
(24946)
Rates: n/a
(304) 653-4722

HUNTINGTON

DAYS INN
5196 US 60 E
(25705)
Rates: $50-$64
(304) 733-4477
(800) 329-7466

ECONO LODGE
3325 US 60 E
(25705)
Rates: $39-$70
(304) 529-1331
(800) 553-2666

HOLIDAY INN HOTEL & SUITES
800 3rd Ave
(25701)
Rates: $89-$95
(304) 523-8880
(800) 465-4329

RADISSON HOTEL
1001 3rd Ave
(25701)
Rates: $78-$88
(304) 525-1001
(800) 333-3333

RED ROOF INN
5190 US 60 E
(25705)
Rates: $47-$74
(304) 733-3737
(800) 843-7663

TRAVELODGE
1415 3rd Ave
(25701)
Rates: $45-$95
(304) 525-7741
(800) 578-7878

HURRICANE

RAMADA LIMITED
419 Hurricane Creek Rd (25526)
Rates: $52
(304) 562-3346
(800) 272-6232

RED ROOF INN
SR 34 & I-64
(25526)
Rates: $54-$64
(304) 757-6392
(800) 843-7663

JANE LEW

WILDERNESS PLANTATION INN
Rt 7, Berlin Rd
(26378)
Rates: $46-$63
(304) 884-7806

KEYSER

ECONO LODGE
Rt 220 S (26726)
Rates: $55-$85
(304) 788-0913
(800) 553-2666

LEWISBURG

BRIER INN
540 N Jefferson St
(24901)
Rates: $46-$51
(304) 645-7722

BUDGET HOST FORT SAVANNAH INN
204 N Jefferson St
(24901)
Rates: $34-$75
(304) 645-3055
(800) 678-3055

DAYS INN
635 N Jefferson St
(24901)
Rates: $48-$110
(304) 645-2345
(800) 329-7466

GENERAL LEWIS INN
301 E Washington St (24901)
Rates: $54-$92
(304) 645-2600

SUPER 8 MOTEL
550 N Jefferson St
(24901)
Rates: $48-$84
(304) 647-3188
(800) 800-8000

LOGAN

SUPER 8 MOTEL
316 Riverview Ave
(25601)
Rates: $49-$70
(304) 752-8787
(800) 800-8000

MARLINTON

MARLINTON MOTOR INN
US 219 N (24954)
Rates: $38+
(304) 799-4711

MARTINSBURG

DAYS INN
209 Viking Way
(25401)
Rates: $59-$70
(304) 263-1800
(800) 329-7466

ECONO LODGE
I-81 & Spring Mills Rd (25401)
Rates: $44-$61
(304) 274-2181
(800) 553-2666

ECONOMY INN
1193 Winchester
(25401)
Rates: $32-$40
(304) 267-2994

HAMPTON INN
975 Foxcroft Ave
(25401)
Rates: $59-$75
(304) 267-2900
(800) 426-7866

HOLIDAY INN
301 Foxcroft Ave
(25401)
Rates: $69-$89
(304) 267-5500
(800) 465-4329

KNIGHTS INN
1599 Edwin Miller Blvd (25401)
Rates: $45-$70
(304) 267-2211
(800) 843-5644

KRISTA LITE MOTEL
Rt 1 (25401)
Rates: $35-$39
(304) 263-0906

PIKESIDE MOTEL
2138 Winchester Ave (25401)
Rates: n/a
(304) 263-5189

RELAX INN
1022 Winchester
(25401)
Rates: $28-$59
(304) 263-0831

SCOTTISH INNS
1024 Winchester Ave (25401)
Rates: $30-$50
(304) 267-2935
(800) 251-1962

TRAVELODGE
1700 Edwin Miller Blvd (25401)
Rates: $65-$79
(304) 263-8811
(800) 578-7878

MINERAL WELLS

MICROTEL INN
104 Old Nicolette Rd (26150)
Rates: $43-$65
(304) 489-3892
(888) 771-7171

MORGANTOWN

ECONO LODGE COLISEUM
3506 Monongahela Blvd (26505)
Rates: $66-$79
(304) 599-8181
(800) 553-2666

FRIENDSHIP INN-MOUNTAINEER
452 Country Club Rd (26505)
Rates: $35-$46
(304) 599-4850
(800) 453-4511

HOLIDAY INN
1400 Saratoga Ave (26505)
Rates: $79-$95
(304) 599-1680
(800) 465-4329

RAMADA INN
US Rt 119 (26505)
Rates: $75-$115
(304) 296-3431
(800) 272-6232

MOUNT NEBO

DAYS INN
Rt 19 S (26679)
Rates: $31-$95
(304) 872-5151
(800) 329-7466

NEW CREEK

TOLL GATE MOTEL
HC 72, Box 121 (26743)
Rates: $27-$34
(304) 788-5100

NITRO

BEST WESTERN MOTOR INN
4115 1st Ave (25143)
Rates: $60-$75
(304) 755-8341
(800) 528-1234

OCEANA

OCEANA MOTEL
Cook Parkway (24870)
Rates: n/a
(304) 682-6186

PARKERSBURG

BEST WESTERN INN
US 50 (26101)
Rates: $36-$69
(304) 485-6551
(800) 528-1234

ECONO LODGE
US 50 (26101)
Rates: $30-$145
(304) 428-7500
(800) 553-2666

EXPRESSWAY MOTOR INN
6333 Emerson Ave (26101)
Rates: $38-$50
(304) 385-1851

MOTEL 6
3604 7th St (26101)
Rates: $37-$54
(304) 424-5100
(800) 466-8356

RED ROOF INN
3714 E 7th St (26101)
Rates: $50-$66
(304) 485-1741
(800) 843-7663

THE STABLES LODGE
3604 7th St (26101)
Rates: n/a
(304) 424-5100

PENCE SPRINGS

PENCE SPRINGS HOTEL
P. O. Box 90 (24962)
Rates: $45-$300
(304) 445-2606

PHILIPPI

SUPER 8 MOTEL
Rt 250 (26416)
Rates: $64-$70
(304) 457-5888
(800) 800-8000

PRINCETON

DAYS INN
347 Meadowfield Lane (24740)
Rates: $55-$82
(304) 425-8100
(800) 329-7466

RAMADA LIMITED
1115 Oakvale Rd (24740)
Rates: $43-$68
(304) 425-8711
(800) 272-6232

SLEEP INN
1015 Oakvale Rd (24740)
Rates: $45-$110
(304) 431-2800
(800) 753-3746

TOWN-N-COUNTRY MOTEL
805 Oakvale Rd (24740)
Rates: $33-$55
(304) 425-8156

RAVENSWOOD

SCOTTISH INNS
Rt 2, Box 33 (20164)
Rates: $28-$35
(304) 273-2830
(800) 251-1962

RICHWOOD

FOUR SEASONS LODGE
39-55 Rt Marlinton Rd (26261)
Rates: n/a
(304) 846-4605

RIPLEY

BEST WESTERN MCCOYS INN & CONF CENTER
701 W Main St (25271)
Rates: $69-$149
(304) 372-9122
(800) 528-1234
(800) 288-9122

SUPER 8 MOTEL
102 Duke Dr (25271)
Rates: $41-$62
(304) 372-8880
(800) 800-8000

SEEBERT

GREENBRIER RIVER CABINS
Greenbrier River Bike Trail (24946)
Rates: n/a
(304) 653-4646
(800) 225-5982

SHEPHERDSTOWN

DAYS INN
Maddex Square Shopping Ctr (25443)
Rates: $55-$65
(800) 329-7466

SOUTH CHARLESTON

RAMADA PLAZA HOTEL
400 Second Ave (25309)
Rates: $99-$140
(304) 744-4641
(800) 272-6232

RED ROOF INN
4006 MacCorkle Ave SW (25309)
Rates: $49-$84
(304) 744-1500
(800) 843-7663

SUMMERSVILLE

BEST WESTERN INN LAKE MOTOR LODGE
1203 S Broad St (26651)
Rates: $45-$54
(304) 872-6900
(800) 528-1234
(800) 214-9551

COMFORT INN
903 Industrial Dr N (26651)
Rates: $50-$119
(304) 872-6500
(800) 228-5150

SLEEP INN
701 Professional Park Dr (26651)
Rates: $45-$81
(304) 872-4500
(800) 753-3746

SUPER 8 MOTEL
306 Merchants Walk (26651)
Rates: $42-$62
(304) 872-4888
(800) 800-8000

SUTTON

ELK MOTOR CT
35 Camden Ave (26601)
Rates: n/a
(304) 765-7173

TRIADELPHIA

DAYS INN
I-70 & Dallas Pike (26059)
Rates: $45-$125
(304) 547-0610
(800) 329-7466

HOLIDAY INN EXP
I-70 Exit 11 Dallas Pike (26059)
Rates: $53-$63
(304) 547-1380
(800) 465-4329

WEIRTON

BEST WESTERN INN AT WEIRTON
350 Three Springs Dr (26062)
Rates: $79-$139
(304) 723-5522
(800) 528-1234

WESTON

COMFORT INN
I-79 & US 33 (26452)
Rates: $59-$69
(304) 269-7000
(800) 228-5150

SUPER 8 MOTEL
12 Market Pl (26452)
Rates: $48-$66
(304) 269-1086
(800) 800-8000

WHITE SULPHUR SPRINGS

BUDGET INN
830 E Main St (24986)
Rates: $28-$60
(304) 536-2121

THE HISTORIC JAMES WYLIE HOUSE
208 E Main St (24986)
Rates: n/a
(304) 536-9444
(800) 870-1613

OLD WHITE MOTEL
865 E Main St (24986)
Rates: $30-$65
(304) 536-2441

AREA CODES - If the local number doesn't connect, check for a new area code.

WISCONSIN

ABBOTSFORD

CEDAR CREST MOTEL
207 N 4th St
(54405)
Rates: $24-$38
(715) 223-3661

HOME MOTEL
412 N 4th St
(54405)
Rates: $34-$45
(715) 223-6343

ABRAMS

FOSTER FARM HOUSE VACATION HOME
4991-Hwy 41
(54101)
Rates: $50-$75
(414) 826-7570

ALGOMA

ALGOMA BEACH MOTEL & CONDOS
1500 Lake St
(54201)
Rates: $50-$185/
$300-1110 Wkly
(920) 487-2828
(888) 254-6621

BARBIE ANN MOTEL
533 4th St (54201)
Rates: $30-$45
(920) 487-5561

RIVER HILLS MOTEL
820 N Water St
(54201)
Rates: $45-$70
(920) 487-3451
(800) 236-3451

SCENIC SHORE INN MOTEL
2221 Lake St
(54201)
Rates: $40-$52
(920) 487-3214

WEST WIND SHORES COTTAGES
N6870 Hwy 42
(54201)
Rates: $52-$87
(920) 487-5867

ALLENTON

ADDISON HOUSE BED & BREAKFAST
6373 Hwy 175
(53002)
Rates: $45-$85
(262) 629-9993

ALMA

TRITSCH HOUSE BED & BREAKFAST
601 S 2nd St
(54610)
Rates: $65-$115
(608) 685-4090

AMBERG

ITALIAN INN
N14835 Hwy 141
(54104)
Rates: $35-$45
(715) 759-5231

AMERY

AMERY'S CAMELOT MOTEL
359 S Keller Ave
(54001)
Rates: $35-$55
(715) 268-8194
(800) 899-7014

APPLETON

BAYMONT INN
3920 W College
Ave (54914)
Rates: $54-$71
(920) 734-6070
(800) 301-0200

BEST WESTERN MIDWAY HOTEL
3033 W College
Ave (54914)
Rates: $89-$122
(920) 731-4141
(800) 528-1234

COMFORT SUITES-COMFORT DOME
3809 W Wisconsin
Ave (54914)
Rates: $89-$140
(920) 730-3800
(800) 228-5150

COUNTRY INN & SUITES
355 Fox River Dr
(54915)
Rates: $72-$99
(920) 830-3240
(800) 456-4000

EXEL INN
210 N Westhill
Blvd (54914)
Rates: $38-$110
(920) 733-5551
(800) 367-3935

MICROTEL INN & SUITES
321 Metro Dr
(54915)
Rates: $39-$70
(920) 997-3121
(888) 771-7171

NORTHLAND MOTEL
138 E Northland
Ave (54911)
Rates: $27-$65
(920) 739-8847

RESIDENCE INN BY MARRIOTT
310 Metro Dr
(54915)
Rates: $76-$199
(920) 954-0570
(800) 331-3131

ROADSTAR INN
3623 W College
Ave (54914)
Rates: $37-$85
(920) 731-5271

SNUG INN MOTEL
3437 N Richmond
(54914)
Rates: $40-$70
(920) 739-7316
(800) 236-4444

WOODFIELD SUITES
3730 W College
Ave (54914)
Rates: $90-$180
(920) 734-7777
(800) 338-0008

ARBOR VITAE

BUCKHORN LODGE & MOTEL
1720 Buckhorn Rd
(54568)
Rates: $50-$150/
$330-$830 Wkly
(715) 356-5090

ARCADIA

RKD MOTEL
915 E Main St
(54612)
Rates: $40-$60
(608) 323-3338
(888) 812-3338

ASHLAND

AMERICINN MOTEL & SUITES
3009 E Lakeshore
Dr (54806)
Rates: $68-$140
(715) 682-9950
(800) 634-3444

ANDERSON'S CHEQUAMEGON MOTEL
2200 W Lakeshore
Dr (54806)
Rates: $39-$59
(715) 682-4658
(800) 727-2776

ASHLAND MOTEL
2300 W Lakeshore
Dr (54806)
Rates: $33-$73
(715) 682-5503
(877) 682-5503

BAYVIEW MOTEL
2419 E Lakeshore
Dr (54806)
Rates: $25-$45
(715) 682-5253
(800) 249-3200

CREST MOTEL
115 Sanborn Ave
(54806)
Rates: $35-$65
(715) 682-6603
(800) 657-1329

HOTEL CHEQUAMEGON
101 W Lakeshore
Dr (54806)
Rates: $60-$145
(715) 682-9095
(800) 946-5555

LAKE AIRE MOTOR INN
101 E Lakeshore
Dr (54806)
Rates: $45-$95
(715) 682-4551

LAKESIDE MOTEL
1706 W Lakeshore
Dr (54806)
Rates: $20-$60
(715) 682-4575

SUPER 8 MOTEL
1610 W Lakeshore
Dr (54806)
Rates: $46-
$791(715) 682-9377
(800) 800-8000

TOWN MOTEL
920 W Lakeshore
Dr (54806)
Rates: $39-$59
(715) 682-5555

BAILEYS HARBOR

BAKER'S SUNSET MOTEL & COTTAGES
8404 Hwy 57
(54202)
Rates: $70-$128
(920) 839-2218

JOURNEY'S END MOTEL
8271 Journey's
End Lane (54202)
Rates: $35-$65
(920) 839-2887
(800) 944-3582

**PARENT MOTEL
& COTTAGES**
8404 Hwy 57
(54202)
Rates: $50-$68
(920) 839-2218

**RIDGES RESORT
& GUEST HOUSE
LAKESIDE GOLF
ACADEMY**
8252 Hwy 57
(54202)
Rates: $43-$165
(920) 839-2127
(800) 328-1710

**SANDS RESORT
MOTEL**
2371 Ridges Dr
(54202)
Rates: $50-$110
(414) 839-2401

BALDWIN

**COLONIAL
MOTEL**
I-94 & US 63
(54002)
Rates: $30-$50
(715) 684-3351

SUPER 8 MOTEL
2110 10th Ave
(54002)
Rates: $53-$72
(715) 684-2700
(800) 800-8000

BALSAM LAKE

**BALSAM LAKE
MOTEL**
501 W Main St
(54810)
Rates: $34-$45
(715) 485-3501

**FOX DEN
MOTEL & RESORT**
101 County Rd 1
(54810)
Rates: $35-$80
(715) 485-3400

**SUNSET VIEW
RESORT**
701 Pearson Rd
(54810)
Rates: $55-$75
(715) 485-3178

BARABOO

**BARABOO HILLS
CAMPGROUND
COTTAGES**
E10545 Terrytown
Rd (53913)
Rates: $20-$60
(608) 356-8505
(800) 226-7242

**CAMPUS INN
MOTEL**
750 W Pine St
(53913)
Rates: $39-$200
(608) 356-8366
(800) 421-4748

**DEVIL'S LAKE
RESORT**
S 5798 Old Lake
Rd (53913)
Rates: $70-$150/
$350-$690 Wkly
(608) 356-6757

4 WINDS MOTEL
S 4090 A Hwy 12
(53913)
Rates: $35-$100
(608) 356-9481

**GARDEN GATE
BED & BREAKFAST**
220 8th St (53913)
Rates: $65-$120
(608) 356-0963

**LOG LODGE
MOTEL**
830 W Pine St
(53913)
Rates: $40-$140
(608) 356-6552

**SILVER DALE
RESORT**
E11878 Hwy DL
(53913)
Rates: $67-$97/
$300-$485 Wkly
(608) 356-4004

**SPINNING WHEEL
MOTEL**
809 8th St (53913)
Rates: $53-$85
(608) 356-3933

**SUNSET RESORT
BED & BRKFAST**
HCR 61 Box 6325
(54873)
Rates: $55-$65
(608) 795-2449

**SWANSON'S
DOWNTOWN
MOTOR COURT**
414 8th Ave
(53913)
Rates: $29-$60
(608) 356-4005

**THUNDERBIRD
MOTOR INN**
1013 8th St (53913)
Rates: $38-$95
(608) 356-7757
(800) 233-0827

BAYFIELD

**APPLE TREE INN
BED & BREAKFST**
Rt 1, Box 251
(54814)
Rates: $85-$95
(715) 779-5572
(800) 400-6532

BAY VILLA MOTEL
Rte 1 Box 33
(54814)
Rates: $48-$84
(715) 779-3252

**HARBOR'S EDGE
MOTEL**
33 N Front St
(54814)
Rates: $50-$105
(715) 779-3962

**JBL SHORELINE
CONDOMINIUMS**
P. O. Box 898
(54814)
Rates: $50-$88
(715) 779-5489

**MORNING GLORY
BED & BRKFAST**
119 S 6th St
(54814)
Rates: $60-$77
(715) 779-5621

**SEAGULL BAY
MOTEL**
325 S 7th St
(54814)
Rates: $35-$70
(715) 779-5558

WINFIELD INN
100 Lynde Ave
(54814)
Rates: $39-$145
(715) 779-3252

BEAVER DAM

**GRAND VIEW
MOTEL**
1510 N Center
(53916)
Rates: $24-$40
(920) 885-9208

SUPER 8 MOTEL
711 Park Ave
(53916)
Rates: $43-$63
(920) 887-8880
(800) 800-8000

BELGIUM

**QUARRY INN
MOTEL**
690 Hwy D
(53004)
Rates: $29-$57
(414) 285-3475

BELOIT

COMFORT INN
2786 Milwaukee
Rd (53511)
Rates: $54-$89
(608) 362-2666
(800) 228-5150

**DRIFTWOOD
MOTEL**
1826 Riverside Dr
(53511)
Rates: $26-$36
(608) 364-4081

ECONO LODGE
2956 Milwaukee
Rd (53511)
Rates: $39-$49
(608) 364-4000
(800) 553-2666

IKE'S MOTEL
114 Dearborn Ave
(53511)
Rates: $30-$60
(608) 362-3423

SUPER 8 MOTEL
3002 Milwaukee
Rd (53511)
Rates: $46-$68
(608) 365-8680
(800) 800-8000

BERLIN

**TRAVELER'S REST
MOTEL**
227 Ripon Rd
(54923)
Rates: $40-$47
(920) 361-4441
(800) 555-7954

BIRCHWOOD

**LINCOLNWOOD
RESORT**
N 1075 Eastside
Rd (54817)
Rates: $70-$120/
$390-$635 Wkly
(715) 354-3533

**BLACK RIVER
FALLS**

**BEST WESTERN-
ARROWHEAD
LODGE**
600 Oasis Rd
(54615)
Rates: $56-$199
(715) 284-9471
(800) 528-1234
(800) 284-9471

DAYS INN
919 Hwy 54
(54615)
Rates: $61-$90
(715) 284-4333
(800) 329-7466

**FALLS ECONOMY
MOTEL**
512 E 2nd St
(54615)
Rates: $34-$52
(715) 284-9919

**PINES
MOTOR LODGE**
I-94 & Hwy 12 N
(54615)
Rates: $35-$50
(715) 284-5311
(800) 345-7463

**RIVER CREST
RESORT**
N 6978 Hwy 12
(54615)
Rates: $59-$79/
$285-$385 Wkly
(715) 284-4763
(800) 863-4764

AREA CODES - If the local number doesn't connect, check for a new area code.

BLOOMER

BLOOMER INN & SUITES
Hwy 53 & 40
(54724)
Rates: $40-$105
(715) 568-3234
(800) 322-7995

OASIDE MOTEL
2407 Woodard Dr
(54724)
Rates: $36-$75
(715) 568-3234
(800) 322-7995

TWI-LITE MOTEL
18981 Hwy 40
(54724)
Rates: $25-$40
(715) 568-5200

BOSCOBEL

HUBL'S MOTEL
41120 Hwy 60
(53805)
Rates: $27-$75
(608) 375-4277

BOULDER JUNCTION

OUTDOORSMAN RESTAURANT & INN
Main St (54512)
Rates: n/a
(715) 385-2826

WHITE BIRCH VILLAGE RESORT COTTAGES
8746 Hwy K East
(54512)
Rates: $642-$1019
Weekly
(715) 385-2182

WILDCAT LODGE RESORT COTTAGES
P 6500 Hwy M
(54512)
Rates: $68-$125/
$475-$1310 Wkly
(715) 385-2421

ZASTROWS LYNX LAKE LODGE
P. O. Box 277
(54512)
Rates: $249
(715) 686-2249
(800) 882-5969

BRANTWOOD

PALMQUIST'S FARM
Rt 1, Box 134
(54513)
Rates: $49-$59
(715) 564-2558

BRILLION

SANDMAN MOTEL
550 W Ryan St
(54110)
Rates: $35-$55
(920) 756-2106

BROOKFIELD

HOMESTEAD GUEST STUDIOS
325 N Brookfield
Rd (53005)
Rates: $59-$79
(262) 782-9300
(888) 782-9473

MARRIOTT HOTEL
375 S Moorland
Rd (53005)
Rates: $85-$119
(262) 786-1100
(800) 228-9290

MOTEL 6
20300 W
Bluemound Rd
(53045)
Rates: $35-$48
(262) 786-7337
(800) 466-8356

RESIDENCE INN BY MARRIOTT
950 S Pinehurst Ct
(53005)
Rates: $179
(262) 782-5990
(800) 331-3131

CABLE

LAKEWOODS RESORT & GOLF
HC 73, Box 715
(54821)
Rates: $70-$500
(715) 794-2561
(800) 255-5937

MOGASHEEN RESORT
Off Country Rd D
(54821)
Rates: $75-$165
(715) 794-2113

PILOT FISH INN MOTEL
Hwy M & Telemark
Rd (54821)
Rates: n/a
(715) 798-3474
(877) 798-3474

CAMBRIDGE

BISON TRAIL BED & BREAKFAST
W9443 E Kroghville
Rd (53523)
Rates: $55-$75
(920) 648-5433

CAMERON

VIKING MOTEL
201 S 1st St (54822)
Rates: $40-$65
(715) 458-2111

CAMP DOUGLAS

K & K MOTEL
219 Hwy 12 & 16
(54618)
Rates: $45-$60
(608) 427-3100

CAMPBELLS-PORT

MIELKE-MAUK HOUSE B&B
W 977 Hwy F
(53010)
Rates: $65-$95
(920) 533-8602

NEWCASTLE PINES
N1499 Hwy 45
(53010)
Rates: $75-$95
(920) 533-5252

CASCADE

FOUR SEASONS RESORT
W9029 Crooked
Lake Dr (53011)
Rates: $65
(262) 626-2934

TIMBERLAKE INN BED & BREAKFST
311 Madison Ave
(53011)
Rates: $75-$100
(920) 528-8481
(888) 528-8481

CASSVILLE

SAND BAR MOTEL
1115 E Bluff St
(53806)
Rates: $40-$60
(608) 725-5300

CECIL

FIRESIDE INN
400 Lake St
(54111)
Rates: $30-$119
(715) 745-6444
(800) 325-5289

CHETEK

RED LODGE RESORT
400 Russell St
(54728)
Rates: $65-$120
(715) 924-4113

WILDWOOD RESORT
865 - 23 3/4 St
(54728)
Rates: $40-$175
(715) 924-3259

CHILTON

THUNDERBIRD MOTEL
121 E Chestnut
(53014)
Rates: $35-$65
(920) 849-4216

CHIPPEWA FALLS

AMERICINN MOTEL & SUITES
11 W South Ave
(54729)
Rates: $57-$115
(715) 723-5711
(800) 634-3444

COUNTRY VILLA MOTEL
Rt 3 Box 40
(54729)
Rates: $26-$40
(715) 288-6376

INDIANHEAD MOTEL
501 Summit Ave
(54729)
Rates: $42-$48
(715) 723-9171

LAKE AIRE MOTEL & MICRO MART
5732 Sandburst Ln
(54729)
Rates: $30-$50
(715) 723-2231
(800) 236-2231

PARK INN INTERNATIONAL
1009 W Park Ave
(54729)
Rates: $72-$119
(715) 723-2281
(800) 446-9320

CLEAR LAKE

ATHLETIC CLUB MOTEL
200 Digital Dr
(54005)
Rates: $35-$65
(715) 263-3111

CLINTONVILLE

CLINTONVILLE MOTEL
297 S Main St
(54929)
Rates: $32-$48
(715) 823-6565

LANDMARK MOTEL
5 N Main St
(54929)
Rates: $43-$70
(715) 823-7899
(800) 223-5503

CRANDON

LAKELAND MOTEL
400 S Lake Ave
(54520)
Rates: $28-$40
(715) 478-2423

RUSTIC HAVEN RESORT
3675 Lake Lucerne
Dr (54520)
Rates: $65-$80
(715) 478-2255

CRIVITZ

BONNIE BELL MOTEL
1450 US Hwy 141
(54114)
Rates: $31-$63
(715) 854-7395

THE PINES MOTEL
N 7968 Hwy 141
(54114)
Rates: $30-$60
(715) 854-7987

SHAFFER PARK MOTEL
N 7217 Shaffer Rd
(54114)
Rates: $64-$120
(715) 854-2186

CROSS PLAINS

BBB FARM BED & BREAKFAST
3883 Observatory
Rd (53528)
Rates: $80-$95
(608) 798-1123

CUMBERLAND

ISLAND INN MOTEL
Hwy 63 N (54829)
Rates: $42-$90
(715) 822-8540

DANBURY

DES MOINES LAKE CABINS
3119 Cherry Ln
(54830)
Rates: $65-$85
(715) 259-7931

DARLINGTON

TOWNE MOTEL
245 W Harriet St
(53530)
Rates: n/a
(608) 776-2661

DE FOREST

HOLIDAY INN EXPRESS
7184 Morrisonville
Rd (53532)
Rates: $69-$99
(608) 846-8686
(800) 465-4329

DELAFIELD

BAYMONT INN & SUITES
2801 Kettle Ct W
(53018)
Rates: $574$125
(262) 646-8500
(800) 301-0200

HOLIDAY INN EXPRESS HOTEL & SUITES
3030 Golf Rd
(53018)
Rates: $89-$109
(414) 646-7077
(800) 465-4329

DICKEYVILLE

PLAZA MOTEL
203 S Main (53808)
Rates: $22-$50
(608) 568-7562
(800) 545-4061

DODGEVILLE

BEST WESTERN QUIET HOUSE
1130 N Johns St
(53533)
Rates: $83-$145
(608) 935-7739
(800) 528-1234

PINE RIDGE MOTEL
405 Hwy YZ
(53533)
Rates: $39-$55
(608) 935-3386

SUPER 8 MOTEL
1308 Johns St
(53533)
Rates: $73-$83
(608) 935-3888
(800) 800-8000

DRESSER

VALLEY MOTEL
211 State Rd 35
(54009)
Rates: $35-$85
(715) 755-2781
(800) 545-6107

DUNBAR

RICHARDS' MOTEL
11466 W Hwy 8
(54119)
Rates: $28-$38
(715) 324-5444

DURAND

DURAND MOTEL
610-11th Ave
(54736)
Rates: $22-$35
(715) 755-2781
(800) 545-6107

DYCKESVILLE

HIAWATHA MOTOR INN
1982 N Hwy 45
(54217)
Rates: $30-$80
(920) 479-6431
(800) 645-4370

PINE-AIRE RESORT & CAMPGROUND
4443 Chain
O'Lakes Rd
(54217)
Rates: $75-$200
(920) 479-9208
(800) 597-6777

SUNSET BEACH MOTEL & CONDO
8931 N Hwy 57
(54217)
Rates: $39-$129
(920) 866-2978

EAGLE RIVER

BEST WESTERN DERBY INN
Hwy 45 N (54521)
Rates: $60-$170
(715) 479-1600
(800) 528-1234
(888) 499-0403

DAYS INN
844 N Railroad St
(54521)
Rates: $70-$99
(715) 479-5151
(800) 329-7466
(800) 356-8018

THE EDGEWATER INN & RESORT
5054 Hwy 70 W
(54521)
Rates: $40-$77
(715) 479-4011
(888) 334-3987

GYPSY VILLA RESORT
950 Circle Dr
(54217)
Rates: $59-$376
(715) 479-8644
(800 232-9714

PINE-AIRE RESORT & CAMPGROUND COTTAGES
4443 Chain
O'Lakes Rd
(54521)
Rates: $88-$260
(715) 479-9208
(800) 597-6777

RIVERSIDE MOTEL RESORT
5012 Hwy 70
(54521)
Rates: n/a
(800) 530-0019

7 MILE PINECREST RESORT
11899 Knapp Rd
(54521)
Rates: $60-$200
(715) 479-8118
(800) 358-4467

SUPER 8 MOTEL
200 W Pine St
(54521)
Rates: $48-$80
(715) 477-0888
(800) 800-8000

WHITE EAGLE MOTEL
4948 Hwy 70 W
(54521)
Rates: $40-$60
(715) 479-4426
(800) 782-6488

EAST TROY

MITTEN FARM BED & BREAKFAST
W2452 County Rd
J (53120)
Rates: $60
(262) 642-5530

EAU CLAIRE

AMERICINN MOTEL & SUITES
620 Texaco Dr
(54703)
Rates: $69-$139
(715) 874-4900
(800) 634-3444

ANTLERS MOTEL
2245 S Hastings
Way (54703)
Rates: $38-$65
(715) 834-5313
(800) 423-4526

BEST WESTERN WHITE HOUSE INN
1828 S Hastings
Way (54701)
Rates: $49-$125
(715) 832-8356
(800) 528-1234
(877) 213-1600

COMFORT INN
3117 Craig Rd
(54701)
Rates: $54-$119
(715) 833-9798
(800) 228-5150

COUNTRY INN & SUITES BY CARLSON
3614 Gateway Dr
(54701)
Rates: $69-$99
(715) 832-7289
(800) 456-4000

DAYS INN-WEST
6319 Traux Ln
(54703)
Rates: $55-$119
(715) 874-5550
(800) 329-7466

EAU CLAIRE MOTEL
3210 E Clairemont
Ave (54701)
Rates: $27-$41
(715) 835-5148
(800) 624-3763

ECONO LODGE
4608 Royal Dr
(54701)
Rates: $54-$109
(715) 833-8818
(800) 533-2666

EXEL INN
2305 Craig Rd
(54701)
Rates: $38-$110
(715) 834-3193
(800) 367-3935

HIGHLANDER INN
1135 W MacArthur
Ave (54701)
Rates: $27-$35
(715) 835-2261

HOLIDAY INN CAMPUS AREA
2703 Craig Rd
(54701)
Rates: $70-$85
(715) 835-2211
(800) 465-4329

AREA CODES - If the local number doesn't connect, check for a new area code.

HOLIDAY INN CONVENTION CENTER
205 S Barstow St
(54701)
Rates: $64-$99
(715) 835-6121
(800) 465-4329

MAPLE MANOR MOTEL
2507 S Hastings Way (54701)
Rates: $35-$45
(715) 834-2618
(800) 624-3763

PARK INN & SUITES INT'L
3340 Mondovi Rd (54701)
Rates: $59-$149
(715) 838-9989
(888) 634-5330

QUALITY INN
809 W Clairmont Ave (54701)
Rates: $59-$139
(715) 834-6611
(800) 228-5151

ROADSTAR INN
1151 W MacArthur Ave (54701)
Rates: $30-$40
(715) 832-9731

SUPER 8 MOTEL
6260 Texaco Dr (54703)
Rates: $35-$59
(715) 874-6868
(800) 800-8000

EDGERTON

COMFORT INN
11102 Goede Rd (53534)
Rates: $69-$149
(608) 884-2118
(800) 228-5150

TOWNE EDGE MOTEL
1104 N Main St (53534)
Rates: $30-$60
(608) 884-9328

EGG HARBOR

THE ALPINE INN & COTTAGES
7715 Alpine Rd (54209)
Rates: $76-$163
(920) 868-3000

THE SHALLOWS RESORT
7353 Horseshoe Bay Rd (54209)
Rates: $65-$300
(920) 868-3458
(800) 257-1560

ELCHO

KATCH'S PINE POINT RESORT
545 Seymour St (Seymour 54428)
Rates: $70
(920) 833-2903

ELLISON BAY

ANDERSON'S RETREAT COTTAGES
12621 Woodland Dr (54210)
Rates: $65-$90/ $425-$465 Wkly
(920) 854-2746

ELM GROVE

SLEEPY HOLLOW MOTEL
12600 W Bluemound Rd (53122)
Rates: $39-$110
(414) 782-8333
(800) 341-8000

ELROY

ELROY VALLEY INN
Hwy 80 & 82 (53929)
Rates: $30-$50
(608) 462-8251

EPHRAIM

SOMERSET INN & SUITES
10401 N Water St (54211)
Rates: 69-$159
(920) 854-1819
(800) 809-1819

FENNIMORE

FENMORE HILLS MOTEL
5814 Hwy 18 W (53809)
Rates: $52-$125
(608) 822-3281

NAPPS MOTEL
645 12th St (53809)
Rates: $30-$50
(608) 822-3226
(888) 806-3226

FERRRYVILLE

GRANDVIEW MOTEL
RR 1 Box 280 (54628)
Rates: $38-$65
(608) 734-3235

MISSISSIPPI HUMBLE BUSH BED & BRAKFAST
Hwy 35, Main St (54628)
Rates: $65-$85
(608) 734-3022

FIFIELD

BOYD'S MASON LAKE RESORT
N12351 Boyd's Rd (54524)
Rates: $62-$85
(715) 762-3469

FISH CREEK

JULIE'S PARK CAFE & MOTEL
4020 Hwy 42 (54212)
Rates: $75-$102
(920) 868-2999

FOND DU LAC

BAYMONT INN & SUITES
77 Holiday Lane (54935)
Rates: $55-$250
(920) 921-4000
(800) 301-0200

DAYS INN
107 N Pioneer Rd (54937)
Rates: $35-$60
(920) 923-6790
(800) 329-7466

ECONOMY INN
77 N Pioneer Rd (54935)
Rates: $30-$70
(920) 922-6030
(888) 291-3681

FOND DU LAC KOA CMPGRND COTTAGES
W 5099 Hwy B (54935)
Rates: $38
(920) 477-2300
(800) KOA-3912

HOLIDAY INN
625 W Rolling Meadows Dr (54935)
Rates: $120-$140
(920) 923-1440
(800) 465-4329

KNIGHTS INN
738 W Johnson St (54935)
Rates: $33-$80
(920) 923-6990
(800) 843-5644

THE LITTLE LAKE HOUSE
N7903 Lakeshore Dr (54935)
Rates: $100-$250/ $500-$1850 Wkly
(920) 923-9636

MICROTEL INN & SUITES
US 41 & 151 (54935)
Rates: $39-$64
(920) 929-4000
(888) 771-7171

NORTHWAY MOTEL
301 S Pioneer Rd (54935)
Rates: $50-$70
(920) 921-7975
(888) 276-1580

PIONEER MOTEL
195 N Pioneer Rd (54935)
Rates: $29-$65
(920) 921-2181

STRETCH, EAT & SLEEP MOTEL
Hwy 41 & 100 (54935)
Rates: $26-$36
(920) 923-3131

SUPER 8 MOTEL
391 N Pioneer Rd (54935)
Rates: $51-$63
(920) 922-1088
(800) 800-8000

FONTANA

FONTANA COUNTRY INN & SUITES
W 5869 Brick Church Rd (53125)
Rates: $95-$150
(262) 275-2878

FORT ATKINSON

SUPER 8 MOTEL
225 S Water St E (53538)
Rates: $50-$80
(920) 563-8444
(800) 800-8000

VILLA INN HOTEL
1255 Whitewater Ave (53538)
Rates: $39-$99
(920) 568-4552

FRIENDSHIP

DUCK CREEK LODGE MOTEL
1870 Duck Creek Dr (53934)
Rates: $28-$48
(608) 339-3502
(800) 311-3502

ISLAND RESORT COTTAGES
306 Hillwood Lane (53934)
Rates: $35-$75
(608) 339-6725

GAYS MILLS

UPPER PLACE VACATION COTTAGE
RR 2 (54631)
Rates: $120-$200/ $525-$565 Wkly
(608) 588-7187

GERMANTOWN

HOLIDAY INN EXPRESS
W 177 N 9675
Rivers Bend Ln
(53022)
Rates: $109
(262) 255-01100
(800) 465-4329

SUPER 8 MOTEL
N96 W17490
County Line Rd
(53022)
Rates: $52-$64
(262) 255-0880
(800) 800-8000

GILLETT

SLEEPY HOLLOW MOTEL
5 Hwy 22 E
(54124)
Rates: $40-$58
(920) 855-2727

GILLS ROCK

HARBOR HOUSE INN B&B
12666 Hwy 42
(54210)
Rates: $60-$159
(920) 854-5196

MAPLE GROVE MOTEL
809 State Rd 42
(54210)
Rates: $50-$70
(920) 854-2587
(877) 448-4484

WINDSIDE COTTAGES
12714 Hwy 42
(54210)
Rates: $60-$100
(920) 854-4871

GLENDALE

BAYMONT INN NE
5110 N Port
Washington Rd
(53217)
Rates: $66-$100
(414) 964-8484
(800) 301-0200

EXEL INN NORTHEAST
5485 N Port
Washington Rd
(53217)
Rates: $47-$82
(414) 961-7272
(800) 367-3935

RESIDENCE INN BY MARRIOTT
7275 N Port
Washington Rd
(53217)
Rates: $149-$184
(414) 352-0070
(800) 331-3131

WOODFIELD SUITES
5423 N Port
Washington Rd
(53217)
Rates: $100-$160
(414) 962-6767
(800) 338-0008

GORDON

STRONG'S RESORT & RV CAMPGROUND
13933 S Resort Rd
(54838)
Rates: $80-$120
(715) 376-2382

GRAFTON

PORT MOTEL OF GRAFTON
2340 E Sauk Rd
(53024)
Rates: $30-$55
(262) 284-9964

GRANTSBURG

CEDAR POINT RESORT & CAMPGROUND
12480 Cedar Point
Ln (54840)
Rates: $70-$80
(715) 488-2224

WOOD RIVER INN MOTEL
703 W SR 70
(54840)
Rates: $42-$50
(715) 463-2541

GREEN BAY

A-1 TOWER MOTEL
2625 Humboldt
Rd (54311)
Rates: $45-$90
(920) 468-1242

AMERICINN
2032 Velp Ave
(54303)
Rates: $75-$95
(920) 434-9790
(800) 634-3444

ARENA MOTEL
871 Lombardi Ave
(54311)
Rates: $40-$54
(920) 494-5636

BAY MOTEL
1301 S Military
Ave (54304)
Rates: $39-$70
(920) 494-3441
(877) 229-7799

BAYMONT INN
2840 S Oneida
(54304)
Rates: $63-$88
(920) 494-7887
(800) 301-0200

BEST WESTERN WASHINGTON STREET INN
321 S Washington
St (54301)
Rates: $75-$129
(920) 437-8771
(800) 528-1234
(800) 252-2952

DAYS INN-CITY CENTER
406 N Washington
St (54301)
Rates: $65-$120
(920) 435-4484
(800) 329-7466

DAYS INN-LAMBEAU FIELD
1978 Holmgren
Way (54304)
Rates: $49-$99
(920) 498-8088
(800) 329-7466

EXEL INN
2870 Ramada Way
(54304)
Rates: $50-$110
(920) 499-3599
(800) 367-3935

HOLIDAY INN-CITY CENTRE
200 Main St
(54301)
Rates: $92-$119
(920) 437-5900
(800) 465-4329

MOTEL 6
1614 Shawano Ave
(54303)
Rates: $33-$40
(920) 494-6730
(800) 466-8356

RESIDENCE INN BY MARRIOTT
335 W St. Joseph
St (54301)
Rates: $159
(920) 435-2222
(800) 331-3131

SUPER 8 MOTEL
2868 S Oneida St
(54304)
Rates: $60-$77
(920) 494-2042
(800) 800-8000

VALLEY MOTEL
116 N Military
Ave (54303)
Rates: $35-$44
(920) 494-3455

GREEN LAKE

DARTFORD INN
N 6264 Lawson Dr
(54941)
Rates: $35-$70
(920) 294-6546

HARSHAW

SMITTY'S IDLEWILD RESORT
5320 Lakewood
Rd (54529)
Rates: $50-$65
(715) 277-2314

HARTFORD

SUPER 8 MOTEL
1539 E Sumner St
(53027)
Rates: $41-$59
(262) 673-7431
(800) 800-8000

HAYWARD

AMERICINN
15601 Hwy 63 N
(54843)
Rates: $52-$160
(715) 634-2700
(800) 634-3444

BEST WESTERN NORTHERN PINE INN
9966 N State Rd 27
(54843)
Rates: $69-$99
(715) 634-4959
(800) 528-1234
(800) 777-7996

COMFORT SUITES
15586 County Rd
B (54843)
Rates: $69-$199
(715) 634-0700
(800) 228-5150

COUNTRY INN & SUITES
SR 27, PO Box
1010 (54843)
Rates: $58-$68
(715) 634-4100
(800) 456-4000

EMPIRE LODGE
13180 N Empire
Rd (54843)
Rates: $80-$125
(715) 462-3772

GHOST LAKE LODGE
Rt 7, Box 74501
(54843)
Rates: $75-$225
(715) 462-3939

HERMAN'S LANDING COTTAGES
8255 N Cty Rd CC
(54843)
Rates: $90-$190/
$400-$940 Wkly
(715) 462-3626

KW NELSON LAKE LANDING
13045 N Dam Rd
(54843)
Rates: $52-$89
(715) 634-4175

MUSKY RUN RESORT
12503 N Town Hall Rd (54843)
Rates: $65-$160
(715) 462-3445

NELSON LAKE LODGE
12980 N Lodge Rd (54843)
Rates: $80-$170
(715) 634-3750

NORTHLAND LODGE
9181 W Brandt Rd (54843)
Rates: $96-$300
(715) 462-3379

NORTHWOODS MOTEL
Rt 6, Box 6453 (54843)
Rates: $43-$48
(715) 634-8088
(800) 232-9202

PARK ISLAND RESORT & MOTEL
Hwy 27 to Cty T (54843)
Rates: $45-$130
(715) 634-2591

PINE CREST RESORT COTTAGES
12459 N Town Hall Rd (54843)
Rates: $65-$105
(715) 462-3297

ROSS' TEAL LAKE LODGE
12425 N Ross Rd (54843)
Rates: $110-$520
(715) 462-3631

SUNSET LODGE- TEAL LAKE
Rt 7, Box 7405 (54843)
Rates: $65-$165
(715) 462-3757

SUPER 8 MOTEL
317 S Hwy 27 (54843)
Rates: $52-$73
(715) 634-2646
(800) 800-8000

TOTEM POLE LODGE & RESORT
9216 W Brandt Rd W (54843)
Rates: $90-$140
(715) 462-3757

VIRGIN TIMBER RESORT COTTAGES
10820 N Moose Lake Rd (54843)
Rates: $75-$162
(715) 462-3269

WHIPLASH LAKE RESORT & CORPORATE RETREAT
12721 N Upper "A" Rd (54843)
Rates: n/a
(715) 462-4302

WILDERNESS HAVEN RESORT COTTAGES
Rt 9, Box 9442 (54843)
Rates: $55-$85
(715) 634-1060

HAZELHURST

HAZELHURST INN
6941 Hwy 51 (54531)
Rates: $49-$60
(715) 356-6571

HILES

LITTLE PINE MOTEL & RESORT
RR 2, Box 655, Hwy 32 (54511)
Rates: $32-$75
(715) 649-3431

HILLSBORO

TIGER INN
629 High Ave (54634)
Rates: $49-$62
(608) 489-2918

HIXTON

MOTEL 95 & CAMPGROUND
I-94 & Hwy 95 (54635)
Rates: $28-$50
(715) 963-4311
(888) 668-3595

HUDSON

BAKER BREWSTER VICTORIAN INN
904 Vine St (54016)
Rates: $89-$149
(715) 381-2895
(877) 381-2895

COMFORT INN
811 Dominion Dr (54016)
Rates: $44-$104
(715) 386-6355
(800) 228-5150

ESCAPE BY THE LAKE B&B
922 Sally's Alley N (54016)
Rates: $129
(715) 381-2871

J.R. RANCH MOTEL
736 Hwy 12 (54016)
Rates: $30-$95
(715) 386-6190
(800) 386-6190

JEFFERSON-DAY HOUSE B&B
1109 3rd St (54016)
Rates: $99-$179
(715) 386-7111

ROYAL INN MOTEL
1509 Coulee Rd (54016)
Rates: $40-$70
(715) 386-2366

SUPER 8 MOTEL
808 Dominion Dr (54016)
Rates: $68-$160
(715) 386-8800
(800) 800-8000

HURLEY

DAYS INN
850 N 10th Ave (54534)
Rates: $59-$95
(715) 561-3500
(800) 329-7466

EAGLE BLUFF CONDO RENTALS
990 10th Ave N (54534)
Rates: $45-$235
(715) 561-2787
(800) 336-0973

HAVEN NORTH CONDOMINUMS
1075 LaRue Ct (54534)
Rates: $49-$259/ $239-$329 Wkly
(715) 561-5626
(888) 404-2836

WHITECAP MOUNTAINS RECREATION
Cty Trunk E on Webster Lake (54534)
Rates: $45-$125/ $250+ Wkly
(715) 561-2227
(800) 933-7669

IOLA

NORSEMAN HOUSE MOTEL
410 N Main St (54945)
Rates: $29-$60
(715) 445-3300

IRON RIVER

DELTA LODGE COTTAGES
Rt 2, Box 161 (54847)
Rates: $50-$100
(715) 372-4299

HERMITAGE SUPPER CLUB & RESORT
Rt 2, Box 48 (54847)
Rates: $55-$75
(715) 372-4580

JANESVILLE

BAYMONT INN & SUITES
616 Midland Rd (53546)
Rates: $45-$85
(608) 758-4545
(800) 301-0200

BEST WESTERN OF JANESVILLE
3900 Milton Ave (53546)
Rates: $59-$159
(608) 756-4511
(800) 528-1234
(800) 334-4271

MICROTEL INN
3121 Wellington Pl (53546)
Rates: $39-$58
(608) 752-3121
(888) 771-7171
(800) 597-5221

MOTEL 6
3907 Milton Ave (53546)
Rates: $35-$51
(608) 756-1742
(800) 466-8356

SELECT INN
3520 Milton Ave (53545)
Rates: $38-$52
(608) 754-0251
(800) 641-1000

SUPER 8 MOTEL
3430 Milton Ave (53545)
Rates: $41-$57
(608) 756-2040
(800) 800-8000

JEFFERSON

RODEWAY INN
1456 S Ryan Ave (53549)
Rates: $55-$160
(920) 674-4404
(800) 228-2000

JOHNSON CREEK

COLONIAL INN MOTEL
Hwy 26 & B (53038)
Rates: $24-$50
(414) 699-3518

DAYS INN
W 4545 Linmar Ln (53038)
Rates: $52-$180
(920) 699-8000
(800) 329-7466

KING ARTHUR'S INN
1 Hartwig Dr (53038)
Rates: $51-$99
(920) 699-4141

KAUKAUNA

SETTLE INN
1201 Maloney Dr
(54130)
Rates: $40-$80
(920) 766-0088
(800) 831-4785

KENOSHA

BAYMONT INN
7540 118th Ave
(53142)
Rates: $69-$80
(262) 857-7911
(800) 301-0200

HOLIDAY INN EXPRESS
5125 6th Ave
(53140)
Rates: $89-$110
(262) 658-3281
(800) 465-4329

KNIGHTS INN WEST
7221 122nd Ave
(53142)
Rates: $45-$90
(262) 857-2622
(800) 843-5644

KEWASKUM

COUNTRY RIDGE INN B&B
4134 Ridge Rd
(53040)
Rates: $55-$70
(262) 626-4853

THE DOCTORS INN B&B
1121 Fond du Lac
Ave (53040)
Rates: $55-$75
(262) 626-2666

KEWAUNEE

COHO MOTEL
705 Main St
(54216)
Rates: $35-$75
(920) 388-3565

LA CROSSE

BLUFF VIEW INN
3715 Mormon
Coulee Rd (54601)
Rates: $27-$75
(608) 788-0600

DAYS INN
101 Sky Harbour
Dr (54603)
Rates: $49-$149
(608) 783-1000
(800) 329-7466

EAGLE BLUFF MOTEL
2344 State Rd 16
(54603)
Rates: $39-$55
(608) 781-7381

EDGEWATER MOTEL
N5326 Hilltop Dr
(54603)
Rates: $25-$60
(608) 783-2286

EXEL INN
2150 Rose St
(54603)
Rates: $39-$100
(608) 781-0400
(800) 367-3935

HEROLD'S MOTEL
3827 Mormon
Coulee Rd (54603)
Rates: $30-$42
(608) 788-1065

HOWARD JOHNSON EXPRESS INN
529 Park Plaza Dr
(54603)
Rates: $42-$67
(608) 784-9500
(800) 446-4656

MEDARY MOTEL
2344 SR 16 (54601)
Rates: $35-$42
(608) 781-7381

RADISSON HOTEL
200 Harborview
Plaza (54601)
Rates: $115-$139
(608) 784-6680
(800) 333-3333

ROADSTAR INN
2622 Rose St
(54603)
Rates: $36-$54
(608) 781-3070

SUPER 8 MOTEL
1625 Rose St
(54603)
Rates: $68-$85
(608) 781-8880
(800) 800-8000

LA POINTE

WOODS MANOR BED & BREAKFST
933 Nebraska
Row (54850)
Rates: $125-$230
(715) 747-3102
(800) 966-3756

LAC DU FLAMBEAU

DILLMAN'S SAND LAKE LODGE
3305 Sand Lake
Ln (54538)
Rates: $55-$400
(715) 588-3143

SANDY POINT RESORT & DISC GOLF RANCH
1230 Sandy Point
Ln (54538)
Rates: n/a
(715) 588-3233
(888) 588-3233

TY-BACH B&B
3104 Simpson Ln
(54538)
Rates: $65-$75
(715) 588-7851

LADYSMITH

BEST WESTERN EL RANCHO MOTEL
8500 W Flambeau
Ave (54848)
Rates: $48-$64
(715) 532-6666
(800) 528-1234

DAVIS MOTEL
820 Miner Ave W
& Hwy 7 (54848)
Rates: $34-$80
(715) 532-5576

HI-WAY 8 MOTEL
420 E Edgewood
Ave (54848)
Rates: $32-$60
(715) 532-3346
(877) 444-9298

LAKE DELTON

HO-CHUNK LODGE
131 Canyon Rd
(53940)
Rates: $79-$149
(608) 254-2584
(800) 303-0265

MOTEL 6
S 2275A Hwy 12
(53940)
Rates: $33-$59
(608) 254-5000
(800) 466-8356

PLAYDAY MOTEL
1781 Wisconsin
Dells Pky (53940)
Rates: $59-$135
(608) 253-3961
(888) 339-3063

LAKE GENEVA

ALPINE MOTEL
682 Wells St (53147)
Rates: $35-$125
(262) 248-4264

BOULEVARD MOTEL
722 Wells St (53147)
Rates: $40-$110
(262) 248-8374

ELEVEN GABLES INN ON THE LAKE
493 Wrigley Dr
(53147)
Rates: $89-$255
(262) 248-8393
(800) 362-0395

GENERAL BOYD'S BED & BRKFAST
W2915 Country
Trunk BB (53147)
Rates: $90-$130
(262) 248-3543

LAKE GENEVA MOTEL
524 Wells St (53147)
Rates: $45-$120
(262) 248-3464

PINE TREE MOTEL
903 Wells St (53147)
Rates: n/a
(262) 248-4988

PLAZA MOTEL
304 Wells St
(53147)
Rates: $40-$100
(262) 248-3049

ROSES BED & BREAKFAST
429 S Lake Shore
Dr (53147)
Rates: $95-$155
(262) 248-4344
(888) 767-3262

T C SMITH HISTORIC INN BED & BREAKFST
865 Main St (53147)
Rates: $125-$365
(262) 248-1097
(800) 423-0233

LAKEWOOD

NORTH STAR MOTEL
15698 Hwy 32
(54138)
Rates: $38-$90
(715) 276-6351
(800) 326-6351

LANCASTER

MARTHA'S B&B
7867 University
Farm Rd (53813)
Rates: $60
(608) 723-4711

LAND O' LAKES

SUNRISE LODGE
5894 W Shore Dr
(54540)
Rates: $65-$187
(715) 547-3684
(800) 221-9689

WHISPERING PINES RESORT
5932 W Shore Rd
(54540)
Rates: $60-$105
(715) 547-3600

LODI

LODI VALLEY SUITES MOTEL
N 1440 Hwy 113
(53555)
Rates: $59-$125
(608) 592-7452

PRAIRIE GARDEN BED & BRKFAST
W13172 Hwy 188
(53555)
Rates: $55-$115
(608) 592-5187
(800) 380-8427

SUNSET RESORT COTTAGES
N2849 Lake Point
Dr (53555)
Rates: $65-$85
(608) 592-4880

LUBLIN

DEER TRAIL CABINS
W1030 County Hwy A (54447)
Rates: $35-$75
(715) 669-3464

LUCK

LUCK COUNTRY INN MOTEL
10 Robertson St (54853)
Rates: $51-$86
(715) 472-2000
(800) 544-7396

LYNDON STATION

CROCKETT'S RESORT COTTAGES
N2884 28th Ave (53944)
Rates: $16-$48
(608) 666-2040
(888) 621-4711

MADELINE ISLAND

MADELINE ISLAND VACATION RENTALS
E 256 Middle Rd, La Pointe (54850)
Rates: $90-$195/ $540-$1200 Wkly
(715) 747-5775
(888) 747-5775

MADISON

AMERICINN
101 W Broadway (53716)
Rates: $64-$125
(608) 222-8601
(800) 634-3444

BAYMONT INN & SUITES
8102 Excelsior Dr (53717)
Rates: $783$129
(608) 831-7711
(800) 301-0200

BEST WESTERN WEST TOWNE SUITES
650 Grand Canyon Dr (53719)
Rates: $99-$149
(608) 833-4200
(800) 528-1234
(800) 847-7919

COLLINS HOUSE BED & BRKFAST
704 E Gorham St (53703)
Rates: $85-$160
(608) 255-4230

COMFORT SUITES
1253 John Q Hammons Dr (53704)
Rates: $89-$260
(608) 836-3033
(800) 228-5150

CROWNE PLAZA HOTEL
4402 E Washington Ave (53704)
Rates: $79-$179
(608) 244-4703
(800) 227-6963
(800) 404-7630

DAYS INN
4402 E Broadway Svc Rd (53704)
Rates: $75-$175
(608) 223-1800
(800) 329-7466

EAST TOWNE SUITES
4801 Annamark Dr (53704)
Rates: $64-$149
(608) 244-2020
(800) 950-1919

EDGEWATER HOTEL
666 Wisconsin Ave (53703)
Rates: $98-$395
(608) 256-9071
(800) 922-5512

EXEL INN
4202 E Towne Blvd (53704)
Rates: $42-$115
(608) 241-3861
(800) 367-3935

EXPO INN MOTEL
910 Ann St (53713)
Rates: $35-$47
(608) 251-6555

HOLIDAY INN EXPRESS
722 John Nolen Dr (53713)
Rates: $74-$130
(608) 255-7400
(800) 465-4329

IVY INN HOTEL
2355 University Ave (53705)
Rates: $68-$89
(608) 233-9717
(877) 489-4661

MERRILL SPRINGS INN MOTEL
5117 University Ave (53704)
Rates: $34-$62
(608) 233-5357

MICROTEL INN & SUITES
2139 E Springs Dr (53704)
Rates: $39-$84
(608) 242-9000
(888) 771-7171
(888) 258-1283

MOTEL 6-NORTH
1754 Thierer Rd (53704)
Rates: $34-$42
(608) 241-8101
(800) 466-8356

MOTEL 6-SOUTH
6402 E Broadway (53704)
Rates: $32-$41
(608) 221-0415
(800) 466-8356

QUALITY INN-SOUTH
4916 E Broadway (53716)
Rates: $63-$100
(608) 222-5501
(800) 228-5151

RED ROOF INN
4830 Hayes Rd (53704)
Rates: $53-$72
(608) 241-1787
(800) 843-7663

RESIDENCE INN BY MARRIOTT
4862 Hayes Rd (53704)
Rates: $129
(608) 244-5047
(800) 331-3131

RESIDENCE INN BY MARRIOTT
501 D'Onofrio Dr (53719)
Rates: $160
(608) 833-8333
(800) 225-5466

ROADSTAR-WEST TOWNE
6900 Seybold Rd (53719)
Rates: $44-$76
(608) 274-6900

SELECT INN
4845 Hayes Rd (53704)
Rates: $44-$89
(608) 249-1815
(800) 641-1000

SUPER 8 MOTEL
1602 W Beltline Hwy (53713)
Rates: $64-$76
(608) 258-8882
(800) 800-8000

WINGATE INN
3510 Mill Pond Rd (53704)
Rates: $75-$95
(608) 224-1500

WOODFIELD SUITES HOTEL
5217 Terrace Dr (53704)
Rates: $90-$165
(608) 245-0123
(800) 338-0008

MANITOWISH WATERS

BUTLER'S FOUR SEASONS RESORT
535 Alder Cir (54545)
Rates: $70-$85
(715) 543-2955

CHIPPEWA RETREAT
37 Deer Park Rd (54545)
Rates: n/a
(715) 543-8111

SLEIGHT'S WILDWOOD MOTEL
HC 2, Box 166 Wildwood Rd (54545)
Rates: $25-$100
(715) 543-2140

VOSS' BIRCHWOOD LODGE
P. O. Box 456 (54545)
Rates: $52-$79
(715) 543-8441

MANITOWOC

BIRCH CREEK INN
4626 Calumet Ave (54220)
Rates: $36-$250
(920) 684-3374
(800) 424-6126

COMFORT INN
2200 S 44th St (54220)
Rates: $84-$109
(920) 683-0220
(800) 228-5150

DAYS INN
908 Washington St (54220)
Rates: $35-$125
(920) 682-8271
(800) 329-7466

HOLIDAY INN
4601 Calumet Ave (54220)
Rates: $140-$160
(920) 682-6000
(800) 465-4329

INN ON MARITIME BAY
101 Maritime Dr (54220)
Rates: $95-$135
(920) 682-7000
(800) 654-5353

SUPER 8 MOTEL
4004 Calumet Ave (54220)
Rates: $45-$65
(920) 684-7841
(800) 800-8000

MARINETTE

CHALET MOTEL
1301 Marinette
Ave (54143)
Rates: $34-$44
(715) 735-6687
(800) 341-8000

**THE DOME
RESORT**
751 University Dr
(54143)
Rates: n/a
(715) 735-0533

MARQUETTE

**CAHOON'S
RESORT**
N Dodges Ave,
Box 13 (53947)
Rates: $65-$85
(920) 394-3107

MARSHFIELD

**BEST WESTERN
MARSHFIELD
INNKEEPER**
2700 S Roddis Ave
(54449)
Rates: $54-$70
(715) 387-1761
(800) 528-1234
(800) 227-1761

**DOWNTOWN
MOTEL**
750 S Central Ave
(54449)
Rates: $30-$56
(715) 387-1111

KNIGHTS INN
2121 W Arnold St
(54449)
Rates: $34-$120
(715) 387-2511
(888) 387-5255

MARSHFIELD INN
116 W Ives (54449)
Rates: $42-$62
(715) 387-6381
(800) 851-8669

MAUSTON

**ALASKAN
MOTOR INN**
I-90/94 &
Hwy 82 (53948)
Rates: $27-$63
(608) 847-5609
(800) 835-8268

**CITY CENTER
MOTEL**
315 E State St
(53948)
Rates: $26-$48
(608) 847-5634

**COUNTRY INN
BY CARLSON**
1001 SR 82 (53948)
Rates: $75-$96
(608) 847-5959
(800) 456-4000

SUPER 8 MOTEL
1001 A Hwy 82 E
(53948)
Rates: $72-$61
(608) 847-2300
(800) 800-8000

WILLOWS MOTEL
1035 E state St
(53948)
Rates: $38-$51
(608) 847-6800

**WOODSIDE
RANCH RESORT**
W 4015 Hwy 82
(53948)
Rates: $130-$150
(608) 847-4275
(800) 626-4275

MAYVILLE

**THE AUDUBON
INN**
45 N Main St
(53050)
Rates: $100-$130
(920) 387-5858

MAZOMANIE

BEL AIRE MOTEL
10291 Hwy 14
(53560)
Rates: $30-$50
(608) 795-2806

MEDFORD

AMERICINN
435 S 8th St
(54451)
Rates: $60-$100
(715) 748-2330
(800) 634-3444

MEDFORD INN
321 N 8th St
(54451)
Rates: $32-$42
(715) 748-4420

MENOMONEE FALLS

**BEST WESTERN
MENOMONEE
FALLS INN**
N88 W 14776
Main St (53051)
Rates: $50-$80
(414) 255-1700
(800) 528-1234

MENOMONIE

**BEST WESTERN
HOLIDAY MANOR**
1815 N Broadway
(54751)
Rates: $49-$135
(715) 235-9651
(800) 528-1234
(800) 622-0504

**BOLO COUNTRY
INN B&B**
207 Pine Ave W
(54751)
Rates: $55-$85
(715) 235-5596
(800) 553-2656

**CEDAR TRAIL
GUESTHOUSE**
E4761 County Rd
C (54751)
Rates: $50-$70
(715) 664-8828

MOTEL 6
2100 Stout St
(54751)
Rates: $37-$51
(715) 235-6901
(800) 466-8356

MEQUON

**BEST WESTERN
QUIET HOUSE
& SUITES**
10330 N Port
Washington Rd
(53092)
Rates: $101-$200
(262) 241-3677
(800) 528-1234

**BREEZE INN
TO THE CHALET
MOTEL**
10401 N Port
Washington Rd
(53092)
Rates: $59-$85
(262) 241-4510
(800) 343-4510

**PORT ZEDLER
MOTEL**
10036 N Port
Washington Rd
(53092)
Rates: $40-$90
(262) 241-5850

MERCER

**GREAT
NORTHERN
MOTEL**
Hwy 51S (54547)
Rates: $39-$59
(715) 476-2440

**PINE NOEL
RESORT**
3307 Goettsche Rd
(54547)
Rates: $440-$490
Weekly
(715) 476-2539

**VOYAGEUR INN
TAVERN &
LODGING**
4514 Lake of the
Falls Rd (54547)
Rates: $40-$100
(715) 476-0013

MERRILL

**BEST WESTERN
PINE RIDGE**
200 S Pine Ridge
Ave (54452)
Rates: $45-$70
(715) 536-9526
(800) 528-1234
(888) 220-5160

**BRICK HOUSE
BED & BREAKFAST**
108 S Cleveland St
(54452)
Rates: $40-$60
(715) 536-3230

**MERRILL VIEW
MOTEL**
703 S Center Ave
(54452)
Rates: $32-$52
(715) 536-5555

SUPER 8 MOTEL
3209 E Main St
(54452)
Rates: $55-$70
(715) 536-6880
(800) 800-8000

MILTON

**CHASE ON THE
HILL B&B**
11624 State Rd 26
(53563)
Rates: $45-$60
(608) 868-6646

MILWAUKEE

**THE ACANTHUS
INN B&B**
3009 W Highland
Blvd (53208)
Rates: $85-$120
(414) 342-9788

**AMBASSADOR
HOTEL**
2308 W Wisconsin
Ave (53233)
Rates: $59-$109
(414) 342-8400

**BAYMONT INN
& SUITES**
5442 N Lovers Ln
(53225)
Rates: $75-$93
(414) 535-1300
(800) 301-0200

**BEST WESTERN
INN TOWNE**
710 N Old World
Third St (53203)
Rates: $89-$119
(414) 224-8400
(800) 528-1234

BILLER HOTEL
725 N 22nd St
(53233)
Rates: $42-$69
(414) 933-6000

THE EXECUTIVE INN
2301 W Wisconsin
Ave (53203)
Rates: $69-$109
(414) 342-0000

EXEL INN - NE
5485 N Port
Washington Rd
(53217)
Rates: $46-$125
(414) 961-7272
(800) 367-3935

EXEL INN SOUTH
1201 W College
Ave (53154)
Rates: $46-$125
(414) 764-1776
(800) 367-3935

HOTEL METRO
411 E Mason St
(53202)
Rates: $185-$285
(414) 272-1937
(877) 638-7620

HOWARD JOHNSON
1716 W Layton
Ave (53221)
Rates: $59-$85
(414) 282-7000
(800) 446-4656

HOWARD JOHNSON EXPRESS INN
176 W Wisconsin
Ave (53203)
Rates: $59-$99
(800) 446-4656

MOTEL 6
5037 S Howell Ave
(53207)
Rates: $37-$50
(414) 482-4414
(800) 466-8356

PORT MOTEL
9717 W Appleton
Ave (53225)
Rates: $33-$46
(414) 466-4728

SUPER 8 MOTEL-AIRPORT
5253 S Howell Ave
(53207)
Rates: $66-$92
(414) 481-8488
(800) 800-8000

MINERAL POINT

COMFORT INN
1345 Business
Park Rd (53565)
Rates: $54-$149
(608) 987-4747
(800) 228-5150

MINOCQUA

AMERICINN
700 Hwy 51
(54548)
Rates: $85-$163
(715) 356-3730
(800) 634-3444

AQUA AIRE MOTEL
806 Hwy 51 N
(54548)
Rates: $36-$79
(715) 356-3433

BEST WESTERN LAKEVIEW MOTOR LODGE
311 Park St &
Hwy 51 (54548)
Rates: $78-$116
(715) 356-5208
(800) 528-1234
(800) 852-1021

CLOUDNINE BAR & RESORT
5678 Lakewood
Rd (54548)
Rates: $400-$500
Weekly
(715) 277-2662

COMFORT INN
8729 Hwy 51 N
(54548)
Rates: $53-$100
(715) 358-2588
(800) 228-5150
(800) 876-8422

CROSS TRAILS MOTOR LODGE
8644 Hwy 51 N
(54548)
Rates: $30-$69
(715) 356-5202
(800) 841-5261

MOTEL MINOCQUA
7528 Hwy 51 S
(54548)
Rates: $30-$70
(715) 356-3090
(888) 218-9650

SUPER 8 MOTEL
8730 Hwy 51 N
(54548)
Rates: $65-$100
(715) 356-9541
(800) 800-8000

MINONG

TRAVELER'S INN
N12871
Greenwood Rd
(54859)
Rates: $31-$84
(715) 466-2293

MONONA

COUNTRY INN & SUITES
400 River Place
(53716)
Rates: $79-$111
(608) 221-0055
(800) 456-4000

MONROE

KNIGHTS INN
250 N 18th Ave
(53577)
Rates: $30-$125
(608) 325-4138
(800) 325-1178

LUDLOW MANSION BED & BREAKFAST
1421 Mansion Dr
(53577)
Rates: $90-$140
(608) 325-1219

MONTELLO

HILLTOP MOTEL
131 Church St
(53949)
Rates: $34-$50
(608) 297-2090
(800) 760-9960

SUNDOWNER MOTEL
510 Underwood
Ave (53949)
Rates: $31-$59
(608) 297-2121

TNT HORSE RANCH BED & BREAKFAST
N4649 18th Rd
(53949)
Rates: n/a
(608) 297-2056

MOSINEE

AMERIHOST INN
400 Orbiting Dr
(54455)
Rates: $65-$75
(715) 693-9000
(800) 434-5800

HOLIDAY INN HOTEL & SUITES
1000 Imperial Ave
(54455)
Rates: $80-$180
(715) 355-1111
(800) 465-4329

LAKEVIEW LOG CABIN RESORT
2391 County Hwy
DB (54455)
Rates: $100-$125
(715) 693-2595
(800) 545-9388

NEENAH

FOX VALLEY INN
2000 Holly Rd
(54956)
Rates: $24-$65
(920) 734-9872

NEILLSVILLE

FANNIES MOTEL & SUPPER CLUB
W3741 US Hwy 10
(54456)
Rates: $30-$45
(715) 743-2169

HEARTLAND MOTEL
7 S Hewett St
(54456)
Rates: $40-$60
(715) 743-4004

NEKOOSA

SHERMALOT MOTEL
1148 Queens Way
(54457)
Rates: $45-$52
(715) 325-2626

NEW GLARUS

SWISS-AIRE MOTEL
1200 Hwy 69
(53574)
Rates: $61-$105
(608) 527-2138
(800) 798-4391

NEW HOLSTEIN

STARLITE MOTEL
1321 Milwaukee
Dr (53061)
Rates: $36-$51
(920) 898-4265

NEW LISBON

EDGE O' THE WOOD MOTEL
W 7396 Frontage
Rd (53950)
Rates: $37-$55
(608) 562-3705
(800) 638-4929

TRAVELODGE
1700 E Bridge St
(53950)
Rates: $55-$100
(608) 562-5141
(800) 578-7878
(888) 895-6200

NEW LONDON

RAINBOW MOTEL
1140 N Shawano
St (54961)
Rates: $36-$60
(920) 982-4550
(888) 588-9147

NEW RICHMOND

AMERICINN MOTEL
1020 S Knowles
Ave (54017)
Rates: $53-$109
(715) 246-3993
(800) 634-3444

RIVERFRONT INN MOTEL
814 N Knowles
Ave (54017)
Rates: $49-$100
(715) 246-4606

SUPER 8 MOTEL
Hwy 65 S (54017)
Rates: $53-$79
(715) 246-7829
(800) 800-8000

NORTHFIELD

TRIPLE R RESORT
N11818 Hixton-
Levis Rd (54635)
Rates: 41-$112
(715) 964-8777
(888) 963-8777

OAK CREEK

BAYMONT INN & SUITES
7141 S 13th St
(53154)
Rates: $70-$87
(414) 762-2266
(800) 301-0200

COMFORT SUITES
6362 13th St
(53154)
Rates: $79-$160
(414) 570-1111
(800) 228-5150

EXEL INN
1201 W College
Ave (53154)
Rates: $45-$75
(414) 764-1776
(800) 367-3935

AREA CODES - If the local number doesn't connect, check for a new area code.

KNIGHTS INN SOUTH
9420 S 20th
(53154)
Rates: $45-$90
(414) 761-3807
(800) 843-5644

RED ROOF INN
6360 S 13th St
(53154)
Rates: $49-$71
(414) 764-3500
(800) 843-7663

OCONOMOWOC

HOLIDAY INN SUNSPREE RESORT
1350 Royale Mile Rd (53066)
Rates: n/a
(414) 567-5934
(800) 465-4329

INN AT PINE TERRACE
351 E Lisbon Rd (53066)
Rates: $69-$129
(414) 567-7463

OLYMPIA RESORT & SPA
1350 Royale Mile Rd (53066)
Rates: $89-$229
(414) 567-0311
(800) 558-9573

OCONTO

OCONTO MOTEL
5680 Hwy 41 S
(54153)
Rates: $33-$42
(920) 834-2000

OGEMA

HIGH POINT VILLAGE INN
W3075 Cnty RR
(54459)
Rates: $60-$150
(715) 767-5287

ONALASKA

BAYMONT INN & SUITES
5377 N Kinney Coulee Rd (54650)
Rates: $69-$140
(608) 783-7191
(800) 301-0200

CLEAR WATER CABINS
W7605 CTH ZB
(54650)
Rates: $50-$110
(608) 781-1716

COMFORT INN
1223 Crossing Meadows Dr
(54650)
Rates: $69-$129
(608) 781-7500
(800) 228-5150

COZY CORNER COTTAGES
W8071 CTH ZB
(54650)
Rates: $58
(608) 781-3792

HOLIDAY INN EXPRESS
9409 Hwy 16
(54650)
Rates: n/a
(608) 783-6555
(800) 465-4329

MICROTEL INN
3240 N Kinney Coulee Rd (54650)
Rates: $45-$80
(608) 783-0833
(888) 771-7171
(888) 818-2359

ONALASKA INN
651 2nd Ave S
(54650)
Rates: $25-$45
(608) 783-2270
(800) 341-8000

SHADOW RUN LODGE
710 2nd Ave N
(54650)
Rates: $32-$70
(608) 783-0020
(800) 657-4749

ONTARIO

THE INN AT WILDCAT MOUNTAIN
Hwy 33,
P.O. Box 112
Rates: $50-$75
(608) 337-4352

OSCEOLA

RIVER VALLEY INN & SUITES
1030 Cascade St
(54020)
Rates: $72-$105
(715) 294-4060
(888) 791-2200

OSHKOSH

BAYMONT INN
1950 Omro Rd
(54901)
Rates: $60-$77
(920) 233-4190
(800) 301-0200

HOLIDAY INN EXPRESS HOTEL & SUITES
2251 Westowne Ave (54901)
Rates: $109-$185
(920) 303-1300
(800) 465-4329

HOWARD JOHNSON
1919 Omro Rd
(54901)
Rates: $45-$120
(920) 233-1200
(800) 446-4656

OSHKOSH LODGE
1015 S Washburn St (54409)
Rates: $32-$48
(920) 233-4300

PARK PLAZA INTL HOTEL & CONF CENTER
1 N Main St
(54901)
Rates: $109-$145
(920) 231-5000
(800) 365-4458

RAMADA INN
500 S Koeller
(54901)
Rates: $59-$89
(920) 233-1511
(800) 272-6232

SUPER 8 MOTEL
1581 W South Park Ave (54903)
Rates: $42-$54
(920) 426-2885
(800) 800-8000

OSSEO

BUDGET HOST TEN SEVEN INN
12554 Gunderson Rd (54758)
Rates: $35-$60
(715) 597-3114
(800) 888-2199

RODEWAY INN
I-94 & US 10
(54758)
Rates: $42-$68
(715) 597-3175
(800) 228-2000

OXFORD

CROSSROADS MOTEL
W6330 Hwy 23
(53952)
Rates: $40-$66
(608) 589-5151

PARK FALLS

BUCKHORN RETREAT
344 Division St
(54552)
Rates: n/a
(715) 762-2086

MASON MOTEL
798 S 4th Ave
(54552)
Rates: $30-$45
(715) 762-3780

NORTHWAY MOTOR LODGE
1113 Hwy 13S
(54552)
Rates: $55-$75
(715) 762-2406
(800) 844-7144

SUPER 8 MOTEL
1212 Hwy 13S
(54552)
Rates: $50-$71
(715) 762-3383
(800) 800-8000

WESTPHALS' EDGE O' TOWN MOTEL
900 4th Ave N
(54552)
Rates: $33-$65
(715) 762-4110

PELICAN LAKE

WEAVER'S RESORT & CAMPGROUND
1001 Weaver Rd
(54463)
Rates: $80-$85
(715) 487-5217

PEMBINE

GRAND MOTEL
N18379 Hwy 141
(54156)
Rates: $30-$58
(715) 324-5417

PESHTIGO

DREES MOTEL
French St,
Hwy 41 S (54157)
Rates: $25-$43
(715) 582-4559
(800) 245-0402

PHELPS

AFTERGLOW LAKE RESORT
5050 Sugar Maple Rd (54554)
Rates: $88-$215/ $410-$1240 Wkly
(715) 545-2560

PHILLIPS

HIDDEN VALLEY INN & RESORT
W7724 Co. Hwy W (54555)
Rates: $46-$125
(715) 339-2757

RED PINE MOTEL/RESORT
850 Elk Lake Dr
(54555)
Rates: $44-$232
(715) 339-4333
(800) 651-4333

SKYLINE MOTEL
804 N Lake Ave
(54555)
Rates: $39-$63
(715) 339-3086
(800) 596-0407

SUPER 8 MOTEL
Hwy 13 S (54555)
Rates: $45-$66
(715) 339-2898
(800) 800-8000

AREA CODES - If the local number doesn't connect, check for a new area code.

TIMBER INN
606 N Lake Ave
(54555)
Rates: $43-$49
(715) 339-3071
(800) 844-4521

PLATTEVILLE

**BEST WESTERN
GOVERNOR
DODGE MOTOR
INN**
W Hwy 151
(53818)
Rates: $64-$79
(608) 348-2301
(800) 528-1234

MOUND VIEW INN
1755 E Hwy 151
(53818)
Rates: $40-$75
(608) 348-9518

SUPER 8 MOTEL
100 Hwy 80-81 S
(53818)
Rates: $41-$70
(608) 348-8800
(800) 800-8000

PLOVER

DAYS INN
5253 Harding Ave
(54467)
Rates: $32-$75
(715) 341-7300
(800) 329-7466

ELIZABETH INN
5246 Harding Ave
(54467)
Rates: $44-$72
(715) 341-3131
(800) 472-8322

PLYMOUTH

**BEVERLY'S LOG
GUEST HOUSE**
W6926 Stoney
Ridge Ln (53073)
Rates: $65-$75
(920) 892-6064

**52 STAFFORD
AN IRISH GUEST
HOUSE B&B**
52 Stafford St
(53073)
Rates: $80-$130
(920) 893-0552
(800) 421-4667

**HARMONY HILLS
IN THE HOLOW
BED & BREAKFST**
W7625 Cty Rd N
(53073)
Rates: $70-$90
(920) 528-8233

**PLYMOUTH INN
HOTEL**
606 E Mill St
(53073)
Rates: $45-$130
(920) 893-5623
(888) 779-5623

PORT WASHINGTON

**BEST WESTERN
HARBORSIDE
MOTOR INN**
135 E Grand Ave
(53024)
Rates: $79-$199
(262) 284-9461
(800) 528-1234

**DRIFTWOOD
MOTEL**
3415 N Green Bay
Rd (53024)
Rates: $32-$54
(262) 284-4413

**THE GRAND INN
BED & BRKFAST**
832 W Grand Ave
(53024)
Rates: $100-$125
(262) 284-6719

PORTAGE

LAMP-LITE MOTEL
Hwy 51/16
(53901)
Rates: $30-$45
(608) 742-6365

**PORTERHOUSE
MOTEL**
1721 New Pinery
Rd (53901)
Rates: $26-$69
(608) 742-2186

**RIDGE MOTOR
INN**
2900 New Pinery
Rd (53901)
Rates: $55-$160
(608) 742-5306
(877) 742-5306

POYNETTE

**BAYVIEW LODGE
RESORT**
N3135 County
Hwy V (53955)
Rates: $60
(608) 635-4089
(800) 369-6333

**FAMILY TIME
RESORT ON LAKE
WISCONSIN**
W10941 Corning
Rd (53955)
Rates: $65-$155
(608) 635-7291

**HAPPY HOLLOW
RESORT**
N3769 Tipperary
Rd (53955)
Rates: $80-$95
(608) 635-4032

**JAMIESON
HOUSE INN**
407 N Franklin St
(53955)
Rates: $70-$155
(608) 635-4100
(888) 462-3216

PRAIRIE DU CHIEN

**BEST WESTERN
QUIET HOUSE
SUITES**
Hwy 18/35 & 61 S
(53821)
Rates: $93-$150
(608) 326-4777
(800) 528-1234

**HIDDEN VALLEY
LODGE MOTEL**
1833 S Marquette
Rd (53821)
Rates: $35-$95
(608) 326-8476
(800) 349-8476

PRAIRIE MOTEL
1616 S Marquette
Rd (53821)
Rates: $30-$65
(608) 326-6461

SUPER 8 MOTEL
Hwys 18/35 & 60
S (53821)
Rates: $60-$102
(608) 326-8777
(800) 800-8000

**WINDSOR PLACE
INN MOTEL**
Hwy 18 & 35 S
(53821)
Rates: $65-$100
(608) 326-7799

PRENTICE

**COUNTRYSIDE
MOTEL**
W5370 E
Greenberg Rd
(54556)
Rates: $38-$49
(715) 428-2333

RACINE

KNIGHTS INN
1149 Oakes Rd
(53406)
Rates: $60-$95
(262) 886-6667
(800) 843-5644

MARRIOTT HOTEL
7111 Washington
Ave (53406)
Rates: $150
(262) 886-6100
(800) 228-9290

**MICROTEL INN
& SUITES**
5455 Durand Ave
(53406)
Rates: n/a
(888) 881-7171

**QUALITY INN-
RIVERSIDE**
3700
Northwestern Ave
(53405)
Rates: $65-$99
(262) 637-9311
(800) 228-5151

SUPER 8 MOTEL
7141 Kinzie Ave
(53406)
Rates: $55-$95
(262) 884-0486
(800) 800-8000

REEDSBURG

**BEST VALUE
COPPER SPRINGS
MOTEL**
E7278 Hwy 23
& 33 (53959)
Rates: $39-$58
(608) 524-4312
(800) 341-8000

COMFORT INN
12115 E Main St
(53959)
Rates: $80-$98
(608) 524-8535
(800) 228-5150

**MOTEL
REEDSBURG**
1133 E Main St
(53959)
Rates: $29-$68
(608) 524-2306
(800) 526-6835

RHINELANDER

AMERICINN
648 W Kemp St
(54501)
Rates: $58-$71
(715) 369-9600
(800) 634-3444

**BEST WESTERN
CLARIDGE
MOTOR INN**
70 N Stevens St
(54501)
Rates: $564$120
(715) 362-7100
(800) 528-1234
(800) 427-1377

**BUCK HAVEN
RESORT**
4743 Wilderness
Ln (54529)
Rates: $60-$90
(715) 277-2341

COMFORT INN
1490 Lincoln St
(54501)
Rates: $47-$129
(715) 369-1100
(800) 228-5150

**HOLIDAY ACRES
RESORT ON LAKE
THOMPSON**
4060 S Shore Dr
(54501)
Rates: $79-$264
(715) 369-1500
(800) 261-1500

HOLIDAY INN
668 W Kemp St
(54501)
Rates: $69
(715) 369-3600
(800) 465-4329

KAFKA'S RESORT
4281 W Lake
George Rd (54501)
Rates: $80-$130
(715) 369-2929
(800) 426-6674

MERRY DALE RESORT
4150 Satuit Ln,
Lake George
(54501)
Rates: $60-$135
(715) 362-3794
(800) 315-3990

SUPER 8 MOTEL
667 W Kemp St
(54501)
Rates: $37-$60
(715) 369-5880
(800) 800-8000

RIB LAKE

LAKEVIEW RESORT
N9503 Spirit Lake
Rd (54470)
Rates: n/a
(715) 427-3344

RICE LAKE

CURRIER'S LAKEVIEW RESORT MOTEL
2010 E Sawyer St
(54868)
Rates: $47-$87
(715) 234-7474
(800) 433-5253

PULLMAN MOTEL
903 Hammond
Ave (54868)
Rates: $30-$60
(715) 234-7919

STARLIGHT MOTEL
1710 S Main St
(54868)
Rates: $35-$58
(715) 234-4444
(800) 992-1669

SUPER 8 MOTEL
2401 S Main St
(54868)
Rates: $47-$68
(715) 234-6956
(800) 800-8000

RICHLAND CENTER

LITTLEDALE B&B
21925 County
Hwy ZZ (53581)
Rates: $45-$55
(608) 647-7118

STARLITE MOTEL
2000 Hwy 14 East
(53581)
Rates: $27-$36
(608) 647-6158

SUPER 8 MOTEL
100 Foundry Dr
(53581)
Rates: $44-$74
(608) 647-8988
(800) 800-8000

TRAVELODGE
1450 Veteran's Dr
(53581)
Rates: $55-$90
(608) 647-8869
(800) 578-7878

RIPON

AMERICINN
1219 W Fond du
Lac St (54971)
Rates: $50-$125
(920) 748-7578
(800) 634-3444

RIVER FALLS

SUPER 8 MOTEL
1207 St. Croix St
(54022)
Rates: $68-$88
(715) 425-8388
(800) 800-8000

ROTHSCHILD

BUDGE INN MOTEL
1106 E Grand Ave
(54474)
Rates: $29-$50
(715) 359-5986

ST. CROIX FALLS

DALLES HOUSE MOTEL-IMA
726 Vincent
(54024)
Rates: $51-$129
(715) 483-3206
(800) 341-8000

ST. GERMAIN

ELBERT RESORT CONDOS
1056 Elbert Rd
(54558)
Rates: $80-$300
(715) 479-1034
(800) 545-8293

NORTH WOODS REST MOTEL
8083 Hwy 70
(54558)
Rates: $37-$47
(715) 479-8770

PARK COTTAGES
8079 Paton Rd
(54558)
Rates: $70-$100
(715) 479-2346

ST. GERMAIN BED & BREAKFAST
6255 Hwy 70 E
(54558)
Rates: $80-$85
(715) 479-8007
(888) 479-8007

ST. GERMAIN MOTEL
170 Hwy 70
(54558)
Rates: $36-$76
(715) 542-3535

TWIN WATERS RESORT
8560 Inlet Rd
(54558)
Rates: $65-$125
(715) 542-3486

SAUK CITY

RAY'S RIVERSIDE RESORT
7554 Hwy 12
(53583)
Rates: $30-$60
(608) 643-3243

SAYNER

FROELICH'S SAYNER LODGE
P. O. Box 100
(54560)
Rates: $60-$100
(715) 542-3261
(800) 553-9695

WOODLANDS RESORT ON PLUM LAKE
8553 Camp
Highland Rd
(54560)
Rates: $75-$125
(715) 542-2474

SCHOFIELD

NITE INN/INTERIM LODGING
425 Grand Ave
(54476)
Rates: $29-$55
(715) 355-1641

SHAWANO

SUPER 8 MOTEL
211 Waukechon St
(54166)
Rates: $49-$75
(715) 526-6688
(800) 800-8000

SHEBOYGAN

AMERICINN MOTEL & SUITES
3664 S Taylor Dr
(53081)
Rates: $75-$135
(920) 208-8130
(800) 634-3444

BAYMONT INN
2932 Kohler
Memorial Dr
(53081)
Rates: $59-$76
(920) 457-2321
(800) 301-0200

COMFORT INN
4332 N 40th St
(53083)
Rates: $58-$110
(920) 457-7724
(800) 228-5150

PARKWAY MOTEL
3900 Motel Rd
(53081)
Rates: $42-$64
(920) 458-8338
(800) 341-8000

SELECT INN
930 N 8th St
(53081)
Rates: $32-$57
(920) 458-4641
(800) 641-1000

SUPER 8 MOTEL
3402 Wilgus Rd
(53081)
Rates: $49-$66
(920) 458-8080
(800) 800-8000

SHELL LAKE

AQUA VISTA RESORT & MOTEL
412 E Hwy B
(54871)
Rates: $345$98
(715) 468-2256
(800) 889-2256

SIREN

THE LODGE AT CROOKED LAKE HOTEL
24271 SR 35 N
(54872)
Rates: $65-$250
(715) 349-2500
(877) 843-5634

PINE WOOD MOTEL
23862 Hwy 35
(54872)
Rates: $34-$52
(715) 349-5225

SISTER BAY

EDGE OF TOWN MOTEL
11092 Hwy 42
(54234)
Rates: $58-$70
(920) 854-2012

SCANDIA COTTAGES
11062 Beach Rd
(54234)
Rates: $60-$150
(920) 854-2447

SPARTA

BEST NIGHTS INN
303 W Wisconsin
St (54656)
Rates: $28-$89
(608) 269-3066

COUNTRY INN BY CARLSON
737 Avon Rd
(54656)
Rates: $71-$119
(608) 269-3110
(800) 456-4000

AREA CODES - If the local number doesn't connect, check for a new area code.

DOWNTOWN MOTEL
509 S Water St
(54656)
Rates: $28-$48
(608) 269-3138

HERITAGE MOTEL
704 W Wisconsin St (54656)
Rates: $30-$50
(608) 269-6991

JUSTIN TRAILS COUNTRY INN & NORDIC SKI CENTER
7452 Kathryn Ave (54656)
Rates: $80-$300
(608) 269-4522
(800) 488-4521

SPARTAN MOTEL
1900 W Wisconsin St (54656)
Rates: $28-$40
(608) 269-2770

SUPER 8 MOTEL
716 Avon Rd
(54656)
Rates: $61-$76
(608) 269-8489
(800) 800-8000

SPOONER

AMERICAN HERITAGE INN
101 Maple St
(54801)
Rates: $64-$135
(715) 635-9770
(800) 356-8018

COUNTRY HOUSE LODGING & RV
717 S Hwy 63 S
(54801)
Rates: $42-$89
(715) 635-8721

GREEN ACRES MOTEL
N 4809 Hwy 63 S & 253 (54801)
Rates: $49-$79
(715) 635-2177

TREGO INN MOTEL
Hwy 53 & 63
(54801)
Rates: $40-$70
(715) 635-3204
(800) 681-5939

SPRING GREEN

THE SILVER STAR B&B COUNTRY INN
3852 Limmex Hill Rd (53588)
Rates: $95-$135
(608) 935-7297

SPRING GREEN MOTEL
Hwy 14 (53577)
Rates: $28-$70
(608) 588-2141
(888) 647-4410

STAR LAKE

RISMON'S LODGE
Hwy K 8080
(54561)
Rates: $36
(715) 542-3682

STEVENS POINT

BAYMONT INN & SUITES
4917 Main St
(54481)
Rates: $57-$95
(715) 344-1900
(800) 301-0200

HOLIDAY INN
1501 N Point Dr
(54481)
Rates: $99-$119
(715) 341-1340
(800) 465-4329

POINT MOTEL
209 Division St
(54481)
Rates: $33-$56
(715) 344-8312
(800) 344-3093

SUPER 8 MOTEL
247 N Division St
(54481)
Rates: $46-$66
(715) 341-8888
(800) 800-8000

TRAVELER MOTEL
3350 Church St
(54481)
Rates: $32-$50
(715) 344-6455
(888) 315-2378

STOCKHOLM

PINE CREEK LODGE
N447 244th St
(54769)
Rates: $85
(715) 448-3203

STODDARD

WATER'S EDGE MOTEL
201 N Pearl St
(54658)
Rates: n/a
(608) 457-2126

STURGEON BAY

CARL'S OLD BRIDGE MOTEL
114 N Madison Ave (54235)
Rates: $30-$70
(920) 743-1245

CHAL-A MOTEL
3910 SR 42 & 57
(54235)
Rates: $49-$59
(920) 743-6788

CHERRYLAND MOTEL & COTTAGES
1309 Green Bay Rd (54235)
Rates: $45-$105
(920) 743-3289

COMFORT INN
923 Greenbay
(54235)
Rates: $46-$150
(920) 743-7846
(800) 228-5150

HOLIDAY MOTEL
29 N 2nd Ave
(54235)
Rates: $26-$79
(920) 743-5571

NAUTICAL INN B&B
234 Kentucky St
(54235)
Rates: $55
(920) 743-3399

NIGHTENGALE MOTEL
1547 Egg Harbor Rd (54235)
Rates: $27-$62
(920) 743-7633

PEMBROKE INN BED & BREAKFAST
410 N 4th Ave
(54235)
Rates: $80-$120
(920) 746-9776

QUIET COTTAGE
4608 Glidden Dr
(54235)
Rates: $160-$185
(920) 743-4526

SNUG HARBOR INN & MARINA
1627 Memorial Dr
(54235)
Rates: $50-$149
(920) 743-2337
(800) 231-5767

STURTEVANT

HOLIDAY INN EXPRESS
13339 Hospitality Ct (53177)
Rates: $74-$94
(262) 884-0200
(800) 465-4329

SUN PRAIRIE

AMERIHOST INN
105 Business Park Dr (53590)
Rates: $65-$90
(608) 834-9889
(800) 434-5800

MCGOVERN'S MOTEL & SUITES
820 W Main St
(53590)
Rates: $47-$85
(608) 837-7321
(888) 837-7321

SUPERIOR

BAY MOTEL
306 E 3rd St
(54880)
Rates: $20-$150
(715) 392-5166
(888) 668-5229

BEST WESTERN BAY WALK INN
1405 Susquehanna Ave (54880)
Rates: $55-$99
(715) 392-7600
(800) 528-1234

BEST WESTERN BRIDGEVIEW MOTOR INN
415 Hammond Ave (54880)
Rates: $65-$110
(715) 392-8174
(800) 777-5572

DRIFTWOOD INN
2200 E 2nd St
(54880)
Rates: $30-$75
(715) 398-6661

PRIME RATE INN
110 Harborview Pkwy (54880)
Rates: $99-$139
(715) 392-4783

STOCKADE MOTEL
1610 E 2nd St
(54880)
Rates: $24-$75
(715) 398-3585

SUNSHINE MOTEL
1807 N 58th St
(54880)
Rates: $20-$150
(715) 394-7055
(888) 786-8355

SUPERIOR INN
525 Hammond Ave (54880)
Rates: $75-$119
(715) 394-7706

THREE LAKES

MAPLE SHORES RESORT
1660 Superior St
(54562)
Rates: $45-$115
(715) 546-3111

TOMAH

AMERICINN
750 Vandervort St
(54660)
Rates: $70-$150
(608) 372-4100
(800) 634-3444

BRENTWOOD INN
24318 Gopher Ave
(54660)
Rates: $50-$75
(608) 372-4500

BUDGET HOST DAYBREAK INN
215 E Clifton
(54660)
Rates: $55-$65
(608) 372-5946
(800) 999-7088

COMFORT INN
305 Wittig Rd
(54660)
Rates: $64-$99
(608) 372-6600
(800) 228-5150

CRANBERRY SUITES
319 Wittig Rd
(54660)
Rates: $77-$100
(608) 374-2801

HOLIDAY INN
1017 E McCoy
Blvd (54660)
Rates: $69
(608) 372-3211
(800) 465-4329

LARK INN
229 N Superior
Ave (54660)
Rates: $49-$74
(608) 372-5981
(800) 447-5275

PARK MOTEL
1515 Kilbourne
Ave (54660)
Rates: $42-$62
(608) 372-4655

SUPER 8 MOTEL
1008 E McCoy
Blvd (54660)
Rates: $60-$79
(608) 372-3901
(800) 800-8000

TOMAHAWK

FOUR SEASONS MOTEL
833 N 4th St
(54487)
Rates: $36-$60
(715) 453-5345
(800) 373-1056

PINE CONE RANCH RESORT
N11668 Lamer Rd
(54487)
Rates: $99-$165
(715) 453-3991
(800) 657-4891

PINE POINT RESORT COTTAGES
W4249 Sandy
Lane (54487)
Rates: $70
(715) 453-4930

SUPER 8 MOTEL
108 W Mohawk
Dr (54487)
Rates: $55-$79
(715) 453-5210
(800) 800-8000

TOMAHAWK LODGE & RESORT
N10985 County
CC (54487)
Rates: $60-$80
(715) 453-3452

TREMPEALEAU

RIVERVIEW MOTEL
11321 Main St
(54661)
Rates: $30-$90
(608) 534-7784

TREVOR

STATE LINE MOTEL
23610 128th St
(53179)
Rates: n/a
(414) 396-9561

TWO RIVERS

COOL CITY MOTEL
3009 Lincoln Ave
(54241)
Rates: $21-$51
(920) 793-2244
(800) 729-1520

VILLAGE INN MOTEL
3310 Memorial Dr
(54241)
Rates: $50-$175
(920) 794-8818
(800) 551-4795

VERONA

RODEWAY INN
131 Horizon Dr
(53593)
Rates: $60-$109
(608) 848-7829
(800) 228-2000

VIROQUA

DOUCETTE'S HICKORY HILL MOTEL
SR 27 & 82 (54665)
Rates: $40-$65
(608) 637-3104

MIDWAY MOTEL
850 N Main
(54665)
Rates: $40-$139
(608) 637-2929

WABENO

SAFARI MOTEL
4454 N Branch St
(54566)
Rates: $28-$36
(715) 473-3521

WASHBURN

REDWOOD MOTEL & CHALETS
26 W Bayfield St
(54891)
Rates: $50-$78
(715) 373-5512

SUPER 8 MOTEL
Harbor View Dr
(54891)
Rates: $70-$90
(715) 373-5671
(800) 800-8000

WASHINGTON ISLAND

DOR-CROS CHALET MOTEL COTTAGES
Box 259, Lobdell
Point Rd (54246)
Rates: $45-$69
(920) 847-2126

FINDLAY'S HOLIDAY INN
Detroit Harbor
(54246)
Rates: $60-$100
(414) 847-2526

JACKSON HARBOR INN
RR 1, Box 119
(54246)
Rates: $50-$85
(920) 847-2454

VIKING VILLAGE MOTEL
P. O. Box 135
(54246)
Rates: $48-$85
(414) 847-2551

WATERTOWN

CANDLE-GLO MOTEL
1200 N 4th St
(53098)
Rates: $27-$42
(920) 261-2281

FLAGS INN MOTEL
N627 Hwy 26
(53094)
Rates: $35-$65
(920) 261-9400
(800) 288-5875

HERITAGE INN
700 E Main St
(53094)
Rates: $44-$49
(414) 261-9010

HOLIDAY INN EXPRESS
101 Aviation Way
(43095)
Rates: $80-$99
(920) 262-1910
(800) 465-4329

KARLSHUEGEL INN
749 N Church St
(53098)
Rates: $60-$85
(920) 261-3980

SUPER 8 MOTEL
1730 S Church St
(53094)
Rates: $54-$89
(920) 261-1188
(800) 800-8000

WAUKESHA

EXEL GRAND HOTEL
2840 N
Grandview Blvd
(53072)
Rates: $65-$125
(262) 524-9300
(800) 574-3935

SELECT INN
2510 Plaza Ct
(53072)
Rates: $46-$70
(262) 786-6015
(800) 641-1000

SUPER 8 MOTEL
2501 Plaza Ct
(53186)
Rates: $37-$56
(262) 785-1590
(800) 800-8000

WAUPACA

BAYMONT INN & SUITES
110 Grand Seasons
Dr (54981)
Rates: $75-$229
(715) 258-9212
(800) 301-0200
(877) 880-1054

PARK MOTEL & LIBRARY LOUNGE
E 3621 Hwy 10/49
(54981)
Rates: $34-$99
(715) 258-3225

VILLAGE INN MOTEL
1060 W Fulton St
(54981)
Rates: $46-$110
(715) 258-6526
(800) 626-6391

WINDMILL MANOR BED & BREAKFAST
N2919 Hwy QQ
(54981)
Rates: $85-$135
(715) 256-1770

WAUPUN

AMERICINN
5 Gateway Dr
(53963)
Rates: $53-$80
(920) 324-2500
(800) 634-3444

INN TOWN MOTEL
27 S State St
(53963)
Rates: $35-$51
(920) 324-4211
(800) 433-6231

WAUSAU

ACE MOTEL
2211 Stewart Ave
(54401)
Rates: n/a
(715) 845-4261

BAYMONT INN
1910 Stewart Ave
(54401)
Rates: $54-$66
(715) 842-0421
(800) 301-0200

BEST WESTERN MIDWAY HOTEL
2901 Martin Ave
(54401)
Rates: $75-$95
(715) 842-1616
(800) 528-1234

DAYS INN
4700 Rib Mtn Rd
(54401)
Rates: $54-$100
(715) 355-5501
(800) 329-7466

EXEL INN
116 S 17th Ave
(54401)
Rates: $39-$65
(715) 842-0641
(800) 367-3935

MARLENE MOTEL
2010 Stewart Ave
(54401)
Rates: $32-$39
(715) 845-6248
(800) 835-0180

PARK INN INTERNATIONAL
2101 N Mountain
Rd (54401)
(715) 842-0711
(800) 928-7281

SKI INN HOTEL & CONF CENTER
201 N 17th Ave
(54401)
Rates: $39-$61
(715) 845-4341

SUPER 8 MOTEL
2006 Stewart Ave
(54401)
Rates: $45-$65
(715) 848-2888
(800) 800-8000

WAUSAU INN & CONF CENTER
2001 N Mountain
Rd (54401)
Rates: $65-$73
(715) 842-0711
(800) 928-7281

WAUSAUKEE

BEAR POINT MOTEL
Hwy 180 (54177)
Rates: $30-$45
(715) 856-5921

HOTEL WAUSAUKEE B&B
P. O. Box 254
(54177)
Rates: $45-$50
(715) 856-5316

WAUTOMA

SUPER 8 MOTEL
Hwy 21 & 73E
(54982)
Rates: $58-$93
(920) 787-4811
(800) 800-8000

WAUWATOSA

EXEL INN WEST
115 N Mayfair Rd
(53226)
Rates: $46-$125
(414) 257-0140
(800) 367-3935

WEBSTER

WAGNER'S PORT SAND RESORT & CAMPGROUND
4904 State Hwy 70
(54893)
Rates: $50
(715) 349-2395

WEBSTER MOTEL
Hwy 25 & Main St
(54893)
Rates: $24-$44
(715) 866-8951

WEST BEND

SUPER 8 MOTEL
2433 W
Washington St
(53095)
Rates: $49-$67
(414) 335-6788
(800) 800-8000

WEST SALEM

AMERICINN
125 Boul Rd (54669)
Rates: $80-$100
(608) 786-3340
(800) 634-3444

WESTBY

CENTRAL EXPRESS INN
Hwy 27 & 14
(54667)
Rates: $45-$50
(608) 634-2950

OLD TOWNE MOTEL
Hwy 27 & 14 &
61 S (54667)
Rates: $35-$50
(608) 634-2111
(800) 605-0276

WESTFIELD

MARTHA'S ETHNIC B&B
259 2nd St (53964)
Rates: $45-$65
(608) 296-3361

SANDMAN MOTEL
N6820 Harris Ct
(53964)
Rates: $35-$70
(608) 296-2565

WEYER-HAEUSER

COUNTRY VIEW MOTEL
W14691 Hwy 8
(54895)
Rates: $24-$30
(715) 353-2780

WHITE LAKE

JESSE'S HISTORIC WOLF RIVER LODGE
W2119 Taylor Rd
(54491)
Rates: $80-$160
(715) 882-2182

WHITEWATER

BLACK STALLION INN
Rt 1 US Hwy 12
(53190)
Rates: n/a
(414) 473-7700

WHITE HORSE INN MOTEL
W4890 Tri County
Line Rd (53190)
Rates: $40-$50
(414) 473-4777

WILLARD

THE BARN OF CLARK COUNTY
N7890 Bachelors
Ave (54493)
Rates: $59-$79
(715) 267-3215

WINDSOR

DAYS INN
6311 Rostad Dr
(53598)
Rates: $89-$165
(608) 846-7473
(800) 329-7466

SUPER 8 MOTEL
4506 Lake Cir
(53598)
Rates: $50-$75
(608) 846-3971
(800) 800-8000

WINTER

HOWE'S NORTHERN HIDEAWAY
W5284 Log Lodge
Rd (54896)
Rates: $44-$125
(715) 266-5953

WISCONSIN DELLS

BAKERS SUNSET BAY RESORT
921 Canyon Rd
(53965)
Rates: $95-$205
(608) 254-8406
(800) 435-6515

BRIDGE VIEW MOTEL
1020 River Rd
(53965)
Rates: $55-$88
(608) 254-6114

DAY'S END MOTEL
N604 Hwy 12-16,
Exit 85 (53965)
Rates: $33-$114
(608) 254-8171
(800) 341-8000

DELTON OAKS MOTEL RESORT
730 E Hiawatha
Dr (53965)
Rates: $60-$200
(608) 253-4092
(888) 374-6257

INTERNATIONAL MOTEL
1311 E Broadway
(53965)
Rates: $30-$140
(608) 254-2431

LAKE AIRE MOTEL
436 Dells Pkwy
(53965)
Rates: $35-$120
(608) 253-5351

PINE AIR MOTEL & SUITES
511 Wisconsin
Dells Pky (53965)
Rates: $48-$275
(608) 254-2131
(800) 635-8627

SANDS MOTEL
124 Wisc Dells
Pkwy S (53965)
Rates: n/a
(608) 254-7447

STAR MOTEL-RESORT
1531 Wisc Dells
Pkwy (53965)
Rates: $40-$150
(608) 254-2051

SUPER 8 MOTEL
800 County Hwy
H (53965)
Rates: $57-$88
(608) 254-6464
(800) 800-8000

SURFSIDE MOTEL
231 Wisc Dells
Pkwy (53965)
Rates: $39-$180
(608) 254-7594

THUNDER VALLEY INN B&B
W15344 Waubeek
Rd (53965)
Rates: $45-$95
(608) 254-4145

TWI-LITE MOTEL
111 Wisc Dells
Pkwy S (53965)
Rates: $28-$150
(608) 253-1911

AREA CODES - If the local number doesn't connect, check for a new area code.

WISCONSIN RAPIDS

BEST WESTERN-RAPIDS MOTOR INN
911 Huntington Ave (54494)
Rates: $48-$70
(715) 423-3211
(800) 528-1234

CAMELOT MOTEL
9210 Hwy 13 S (54494)
Rates: $35-$48
(715) 325-5111

HOTEL MEAD
451 E Grand Ave (54494)
Rates: $83-$129
(715) 423-1500
(800) 843-6323

SUPER 8 MOTEL
3410 8th St S (54494)
Rates: $49-$66
(715) 423-8080
(800) 800-8000

WOODRUFF

ARBOR VITAE MOTEL
1431 Hwy 51 N (54568)
Rates: $38-$59
(715) 356-3393
(800) 967-9609

SKYLARK MOTEL
Hwy 51 (54568)
Rates: $35-$66
(715) 356-5558

WYOMING

AFTON

BEST WESTERN HI COUNTRY INN
689 S Washington (83110)
Rates: $45-$90
(307) 885-3856
(800) 528-1234

THE CORRAL COTTAGES
161 S Washington (83110)
Rates: $30-$45
(307) 886-5424

LAZY B MOTEL
219 Washington (83110)
Rates: $30-$80
(307) 886-3187

MOUNTAIN INN
83542 Hwy 89 (83110)
Rates: $47-$72
(307) 886-3156

THE ROCKING P BED & BREAKFST
Box 127
(Smoot 83126)
Rates: n/a
(307) 886-0455
(Horses allowed only)

ALPINE

ALPINE INN
Box 263 (83128)
Rates: $35-$99
(307) 654-7644

BEST WESTERN FLYING SADDLE LODGE
Hwy 89 & 26 (83128)
Rates: $75-$160
(307) 654-7561
(800) 528-1234

LAKESIDE MOTEL
Box 238 (83128)
Rates: $30-$50
(307) 654-7507

ROYAL RESORT
Hwy 89 & 26 (83128)
Rates: $70-$100
(307) 654-7545
(800) 343-6755

THREE RIVERS MOTEL
US Hwy 89 (83128)
Rates: $26-$50
(307) 654-7551

ATLANTIC CITY

ATLANTIC CITY MERCHANTILE
100 Main St (82520)
Rates: $25-$50
(307) 332-5143
(888) 257-0215

MINER'S DELIGHT BED & BREAKFST
290 Atlantic Rd (82520)
Rates: n/a
(307) 332-0248
(888) 292-0248

BAGGS

DRIFTERS INN
Hwy 789 (82321)
Rates: $25-$49
(307) 383-2015

BASIN

LILAC MOTEL
710 W C St (82410)
Rates: $26-$45
(307) 568-3355

BEULAH

WINDY ACRES RANCH B&B
5480 Hwy 14 (82712)
Rates: n/a
(307) 283-2664

BIG HORN

BOZEMAN TRAIL B&B
304 Hwy 335 (82833)
Rates: $75-$99
(307) 672-2381

BONDURANT

HOBACK VILLAGE MOTEL
14272 Hwy 189-191 (82922)
Rates: $30-$60
(307) 733-3631

SMILING S MOTEL
33 Mi S of Jackson, Box 171 (82922)
Rates: $25-$50
(307) 733-3457

BUFFALO

ARROWHEAD MOTEL
749 Fort St (82834)
Rates: $32-$60
(307) 684-9453
(800) 824-1719

BLUE GABLES MOTEL
662 N Main St (82834)
Rates: $26-$100
(307) 684-7822
(800) 684-2574

BUFFALO MOTEL
370 N Main St (82834)
Rates: $37-$59
(307) 684-0753
(888) 684-0753

CANYON MOTEL
997 Fort St (82834)
Rates: $36-$55
(307) 684-2957
(800) 231-0742

COWBOY TOWN MOTEL
181 Hwy 16 E (82834)
Rates: $37-$99
(307) 684-0603
(888) 323-2865

CROSSROADS INN
75 N Bypass (82834)
Rates: $45-$94
(307) 684-2256
(800) 852-2302

ECONO LODGE
333 Hart St (82834)
Rates: $34-$87
(307) 684-2219
(800) 553-2666

MOTEL 6
100 Flat Iron Dr (82834)
Rates: $39-$65
(307) 684-7000
(800) 466-8356

MOUNTAIN VIEW MOTEL
585 Fort St (82834)
Rates: $26-$44
(307) 684-2881

SOUTH FORK INN
Hwy US 16 (82834)
Rates: $26-$45
(307) 684-9609

SUPER 8 MOTEL
655 E Hart St (82834)
Rates: $69-$75
(307) 684-2531
(800) 800-8000

WYOMING MOTEL
610 E Hart St (82834)
Rates: $62-$88
(307) 684-5505
(800) 666-5505

Z-BAR MOTEL
626 Fort St (82834)
Rates: $48-$63
(307) 684-5535
(888) 313-1227

CASPER

ALL AMERICAN INN
5755 Cy Ave (82601)
Rates: $25-$50
(307) 235-6688

BEST WESTERN CASPER INN
2325 E Yellowstone Hwy (82602)
Rates: $54-$84
(307) 234-3541
(800) 528-1234
(800) 675-4242

DAYS INN
301 East E St (82601)
Rates: $57-$67
(307) 234-1159
(800) 329-7466

ELK VALLEY INN
3256 N Fork Hwy (82601)
Rates: $51-$85
(307) 587-4149

FIRST INTERSTATE INN
205 E Wyoming Blvd (82601)
Rates: $29-$45
(307) 234-9125

HAMPTON INN
400 West F St (82601)
Rates: $75-$95
(307) 235-6668
(800) 426-7866

HOLIDAY INN
300 W F St (82601)
Rates: $79-$129
(307) 235-2531
(800) 465-4329

MOTEL 6
1150 Wilkins Cir (82601)
Rates: $29-$38
(307) 234-3903
(800) 466-8356

NATIONAL 9 INN
100 West F St
(82601)
Rates: $23-$56
(307) 235-2711
(800) 524-9999

PARKWAY PLAZA
123 W East St
(82601)
Rates: $55
(307) 235-1777
(800) 270-7829

RADISSON HOTEL
800 N Poplar
(82601)
Rates: $85
(307) 266-6000
(800) 333-3333

**RANCH HOUSE
MOTEL**
1130 E F St (82601)
Rates: $25-$50
(307) 266-4044

ROYAL INN
440 East A St
(82601)
Rates: $20-$36
(307) 234-3501
(800) 967-6925

SUPER 8 MOTEL
3838 Cy Ave
(82604)
Rates: $53-$69
(307) 266-3480
(800) 800-8000
(888) 266-0497

TOPPER MOTEL
728 E A St (82601)
Rates: $25-$50
(307) 237-8407

**VIRGINIAN
MOTEL**
830 E A St (82601)
Rates: $25-$50
(307) 266-9731

**WESTRIDGE
MOTEL**
955 Cy Ave (82601)
Rates: $38-$58
(307) 234-8911
(800) 341-8000

**YELLOWSTONE
MOTEL**
1610 E Yellowstone
(82601)
Rates: $25-$49
(307) 234-9174
(800) 531-9257

CENTENNIAL

**CENTENNIAL
VALLEY
TRADING POST**
2755 Hwy 130
(82055)
Rates: $26-$49
(307) 721-5074

**FRIENDLY FLY
STORE & MOTEL**
Hwy 130, Box 195
(82055)
Rates: $51-$100
(307) 742-6033

**THE OLD CORRAL
MOUNTAIN
LODGE**
Main St (82055)
Rates: $51-$100
(307) 745-5918

**SARAH ROSE
HOTEL**
2747 Hwy 130
(82055)
Rates: $61-$100
(307) 742-5476
(888) 400-9953

**SNOWY
MOUNTAIN
LODGE**
3474 Hwy 130
(82055)
Rates: n/a
(307) 742-7669

CHEYENNE

**A DRUMMOND'S
RANCH B&B**
399 Happy Jack
Rd (82007)
Rates: $65-$175
(307) 634-6042

**ADVENTURERS
COUNTRY B&B**
3803 I-80 S Service
Rd (82001)
Rates: n/a
(307) 632-4087

ATLAS MOTEL
1524 W
Lincolnway
(82001)
Rates: $25-$50
(307) 632-9214

**BEST WESTERN
HITCHING POST**
1700 W Lincolnway
(82001)
Rates: $89-$200
(307) 638-3301
(800) 528-1234
(800) 221-0125

**BIT-O-WYO
RANCH B&B**
470 Happy Jack
Rd (82001)
Rates: n/a
(307) 638-8340
(Horses allowed
only)

**CHEYENNE
MOTEL**
1601 E
Lincolnway
(82001)
Rates: $25-$50
(307) 778-7664

COMFORT INN
2245 Etchepare Dr
(82007)
Rates: $79-$145
(307) 638-7202
(800) 228-5150

DAYS INN
2360 W
Lincolnway
(82003)
Rates: $69-$84
(307) 778-8877
(800) 329-7466

FIREBIRD MOTEL
1905 E
Lincolnway
(82001)
Rates: $25-$50
(307) 632-5505

**FLEETWOOD
MOTEL**
3800 E
Lincolnway
(82001)
Rates: $40-$50
(307) 638-8908
(800) 634-7763

FRONTIER MOTEL
1400 W
Lincolnway
(82001)
Rates: $26-$48
(307) 634-7961

**HOME RANCH
MOTEL**
2414 E Lincolnway
(82001)
Rates: $27-$47
(307) 634-3575

**HOWDY
PARDNER B&B**
1920 Tranquility
Rd (82009)
Rates: n/a
(406) 259-7993
(307) 634-6493

LA QUINTA INN
2410 W
Lincolnway
(82001)
Rates: $75-$95
(307) 632-7117
(800) 687-6667

LINCOLN COURT
1700 W
Lincolnway
(82001)
Rates: $55-$85
(307) 638-3302
(800) 221-0125

MOTEL 6
1735 Westland Rd
(82001)
Rates: $33-$52
(307) 635-6806
(800) 466-8356

**NAGLE WARREN
MANSION B&B**
222 E 17th St
(82001)
Rates: n/a
(307) 637-3333
(800) 811-2610

OAK TREE INN
1625 Stillwater
Ave (82001)
Rates: $35-$60
(307) 778-6620

**PORCH SWING
BED & BRKFAST**
712 E 20th St
(82001)
Rates: $50-$80
(307) 778-7182

QUALITY INN
5401 Walker Rd
(82001)
Rates: $35-$175
(307) 632-8901
(800) 228-5151
(800) 876-8901

**RAINSFORD INN
BED & BREAKFST**
219 E 18th St
(82001)
Rates: n/a
(307) 638-2337

RANGER MOTEL
909 W 16th St
(82001)
Rates: $27-$48
(307) 634-7995

RODEO INN
3839 E
Lincolnway
(82001)
Rates: $35-$60
307) 634-2171

ROUNDUP MOTEL
403 S Greeley
Hwy (82001)
Rates: $25-$50
(307) 634-7741

**SAPP BROS.
BIG C**
I-80 & Archer
(82001)
Rates: $24-$50
(307) 632-6000
(800) 788-4671

SUPER 8 MOTEL
1900 W
Lincolnway
(82001)
Rates: $38-$125
(307) 635-8741
(800) 800-8000

**TWIN CHIMNEYS
MOTEL**
2405 E
Lincolnway
(82001)
Rates: $27-$48
(307) 632-8921

**WINDY HILLS
GUEST HOUSE
BED & BREAKFAST**
393 Happy Jack
Rd (82007)
Rates: $70-$168
(307) 632-6423

WYOMING MOTEL
1401 W
Lincolnway
(82001)
Rates: $25-$50
(307) 632-8104

AREA CODES - If the local number doesn't connect, check for a new area code.

CHUGWATER

SUPER 8 MOTEL
100 Buffalo Dr
(82210)
Rates: $55-$64
(307) 422-3248
(800) 800-8000

CLEARMONT

RBL BISON GUEST RANCH B&B
4355 US Hwy 14-16 E (82835)
Rates: $48-$78
(307) 758-4387
(800) 597-0109

CODY

BEST BET INN
1701 17th St
(82414)
Rates: $24-$46
(307) 587-9009

BEST WESTERN SUNRISE MOTOR INN
1407 8th St (82414)
Rates: $79-$99
(307) 587-5566
(800) 528-1234

BEST WESTERN SUNSET MOTOR INN
1601 8th St (82414)
Rates: $85-$139
(307) 587-4265
(800) 528-1234
(800) 624-2727

BIG BEAR MOTEL
139 W Yellowstone Hwy
(82414)
Rates: $70
(307) 587-3117
(800) 325-7163

CARTER MOUNTAIN MOTEL
1701 Central
(82414)
Rates: $25-$50
(307) 587-4295

ELK VALLEY INN & CAMPGROUND
3256 Yellowstone Hwy (82414)
Rates: $30-$45
(307) 587-4149

GATEWAY MOTEL
203 Yellowstone Ave (82414)
Rates: $25-$50
(307) 587-2561

HIGH COUNTRY MOTOR INN
405 Yellowstone Ave (82414)
Rates: $52-$98
(307) 587-5960
(800) 835-7427

HOUSE OF BURGESS B&B
1508 Alger Ave
(82414)
Rates: n/a
(307) 527-7208

KELLY INN
2513 Greybull Hwy (82414)
Rates: $92-$112
(307) 527-5505
(800) 635-3559

MOUNTAIN VIEW INN
N Fork Star Rt
(82414)
Rates: $45-$100
(307) 587-2081

PARKWAY INN
720 Yellowstone Ave (82414)
Rates: $88-$98
(307) 587-4208

QUESTION CREEK BED & BRKFAST
311 Lane 17 (82414)
Rates: n/a
(307) 754-3249

SEVEN K'S MOTEL
232 W Yellowstone Ave (82414)
Rates: $23-$45
(307) 587-5890
(800) 223-9204

SKYLINE MOTOR INN
1919 17th St
(82414)
Rates: $48-$62
(307) 587-4201
(800) 843-8809

STAGE STOP
502 Yellowstone Ave (82414)
Rates: $52-$97
(307) 527-5065

STREAMSIDE INN
Yellowstone Hwy 14, 16 & 20 (82414)
Rates: $61-$100
(307) 587-8242
(800) 285-1282

SUPER 8 MOTEL
730 Yellowstone Ave (82414)
Rates: $85-$135
(307) 527-6214
(800) 800-8000

TRAIL INN & MOTEL
2750 N Fork Hwy
(82414)
Rates: $25-$50
(307) 587-3741

TROUT CREEK INN
Yellowstone Hwy W (82414)
Rates: $28-$64
(307) 587-6288
(800) 341-8000

UPTOWN MOTEL
1562 Sheridan Ave
(82414)
Rates: $25-$50
(307) 587-4245

WESTERN 6 GUN MOTEL
423 Yellowstone Ave (82414)
Rates: $54-$99
(307) 587-4835

WISE CHOICE INN
2908 N Fork Hwy
(82414)
Rates: $66-$75
(307) 587-5004

YELLOWSTONE VALLEY INN
3324 N Fork Hwy
(82414)
Rates: $52-$97
(307) 587-3961
(888) 705-7703

COKEVILLE

HIDEOUT MOTEL
245 S Hwy 30 N
(83114)
Rates: $23-$44
(307) 279-3281

VALLEY HI MOTEL
Hwy 30 & 89
(83114)
Rates: $25-$48
(307) 279-3251

DAYTON

FOOTHILLS MOTEL
101 N Main
(82836)
Rates: $25-$50
(307) 655-2547

DIAMONDVILLE

ENERGY INN
US 30 & 189
(83116)
Rates: $51-$100
(307) 877-6901

DOUGLAS

ALPINE INN
2310 E Richards
(82633)
Rates: $40-$60
(307) 358-4780

BEST WESTERN DOUGLAS INN
1450 Riverbend Dr (82633)
Rates: $69-$99
(307) 358-9790
(800) 528-1234
(800) 344-2113

CARRIAGE HOUSE B&B
413 Center St
(82633)
Rates: n/a
(307) 358-2752

CHIEFTAIN MOTEL
815 Richards
(82633)
Rates: $29-$43
(307) 358-2673

FIRST INTERSTATE INN
2349 E Richards
(82633)
Rates: $27-$44
(307) 358-2833
(800) 992-9026

4 WINDS MOTEL
615 E Richards
(82633)
Rates: $25-$50
(307) 358-2322

PLAINS MOTEL
628 Richards E
(82633)
Rates: $25-$49
(307) 358-4484

SUPER 8 MOTEL
314 Russell Ave
(82633)
Rates: $37-$61
(307) 358-6800
(800) 800-8000

VAGABOND MOTEL
430 E Richards
(82633)
Rates: $25-$50
(307) 358-9414

DUBOIS

BALD MOUNTAIN INN
1349 W Ramshorn
(82513)
Rates: $38-$100
(307) 455-2844
(800) 682-9323

BLACK BEAR COUNTRY INN
505 N Ramshorn St (82513)
Rates: $30-$60
(307) 455-2344
(800) 873-2327

BRANDING IRON INN-IMA
401 N Ramshorn St (82513)
Rates: $48-$59
(307) 455-2893
(800) 341-8000

CHINOOK WINDS MTN LODGE
640 S 1st St
(82513)
Rates: $40-$120
(307) 455-2987

PINNACLE BUTTES LODGE
3577 Hwy 26 W
(82513)
Rates: $50-$160
(307) 455-2506

RIVERSIDE INN
5810 Hwy 26
(82513)
Rates: $30-$50
(307) 455-2337

AREA CODES - If the local number doesn't connect, check for a new area code.

STAGECOACH MOTOR INN
103 E Ramshorn St (82513)
Rates: $38-$64
(307) 455-2303
(800) 455-5090

SUPER 8 MOTEL
1414 Warm Springs Dr (82513)
Rates: $45-$57
(307) 455-3694
(800) 800-8000

TRAILS END MOTEL
511 Ramshorn St (82513)
Rates: $35-$100
(307) 455-2540
(888) 455-6660

WIND RIVER MOTEL
519 W Ramshorn St (82513)
Rates: $25-$50
(307) 455-2611
(877) 455-2621

EDGERTON

TEAPOT MOTOR LODGE
727 Hwy 387 (82635)
Rates: $25-$48
(307) 437-6541

ENCAMPMENT

RIVERSIDE CABINS
Star Rt, Box 15 (82325)
Rates: $25-$50
(307) 327-5361

RUSTIC MOUNTAIN LODGE B&B
Star Rt, Box 49 (82325)
Rates: $45-$65
(307) 327-5539

VACHER'S BIGHORN LODGE
508 McCaffrey Ave (82325)
Rates: $25-$50
(307) 327-5110
(888) 327-5110

EVANSTON

ALEXANDER MOTEL
Box 181 (82930)
Rates: $25-$50
(307) 789-2346

DAYS INN
339 Wasatch Rd (82930)
Rates: $55-$85
(307) 789-2220
(800) 329-7466

ECONOMY INN
1710 Harrison Dr (82930)
Rates: $30-$49
(307) 789-2777

HILLCREST DX MOTEL
1725 Harrison Dr (82930)
Rates: $25-$50
(307) 789-1111

MOTEL 6
261 Bear River Dr (82930)
Rates: $34-$42
(307) 789-0791
(800) 466-8356

NATIONAL 9 INN
1724 Harrison Dr (82930)
Rates: $25-$50
(307) 789-9610
(800) 524-9999

PRAIRIE INN MOTEL
264 Bear River Dr (82930)
Rates: $35-$60
(307) 789-2920

SUPER 8 MOTEL
70 Bear River Dr (82930)
Rates: $34-$47
(307) 789-7510
(800) 800-8000

WESTON PLAZA HOTEL
1983 Harrison Dr (82930)
Rates: $44-$49
(307) 789-0783
(800) 255-9840

WESTON SUPER BUDGET INN
1936 Harrison Dr (82930)
Rates: $25-$50
(307) 789-2810
(800) 255-9840

EVANSVILLE

COMFORT INN
480 Lathrop (82601)
Rates: $66-$89
(307) 235-3038
(800) 228-5150

SHILO INN
739 Luker Ln, I-25 & Curtis Rd (82636)
Rates: $49-$99
(307) 237-1335
(800) 222-2244

FARSON

SITZMAN'S MOTEL
Box 25 (82932)
Rates: $25-$50
(307) 273-9241

FORT BRIDGER

WAGON WHEEL MOTEL
270 N Main (82933)
Rates: $25-$50
(307) 782-6361

GILLETTE

ARROWHEAD MOTEL
202 Emerson (82716)
Rates: $24-$47
(307) 686-0909

BEST WESTERN TOWER WEST LODGE
109 N Hwy 14-16 (82716)
Rates: $52-$97
(307) 686-2210
(800) 528-1234
(800) 762-7375

CIRCLE L MOTEL
410 E 2nd (82716)
Rates: $25-$46
(307) 682-9375

DAYS INN
910 E Boxelder Rd (82716)
Rates: $30-$150
(307) 682-3999
(800) 329-7466

ECONO LODGE
400 Butler-Spaeth Rd (92716)
Rates: $30-$120
(307) 682-4757
(800) 553-2666

HOLIDAY INN
2009 S Douglas Hwy 59 (82716)
Rates: $125
(307) 686-3000
(800) 686-3368

MOTEL 6
2105 Rodgers Dr (82716)
Rates: $29-$46
(307) 686-8600
(800) 466-8356

MUSTANG MOTEL
922 E 3rd St (82716)
Rates: $25-$50
(307) 682-4784

NATIONAL 9 INN
1020 Hwy 51 E (82716)
Rates: $36-$56
(307) 682-5111
(800) 524-9999

RAMADA LIMITED
608 E 2nd St (82716)
Rates: $40-$95
(307) 682-9341
(800) 272-6232

RODEWAY INN
3011 Rodgers Dr (72616)
Rates: $35-$95
(307) 686-1989
(800) 228-2000

SUPER 8 MOTEL
208 S Decker Ct (82716)
Rates: $30-$72
(307) 682-8078
(800) 800-800

THRIFTY INN
1004 E Hwy 14-16 (82716)
Rates: $25-$50
(307) 621-2616
(800) 621-2182

GLENDO

GLENDO MARINA MOTEL
383 Glendo Park Rd (82213)
Rates: $35-$58
(307) 735-4216

GLENROCK

ALL AMERICAN INN
500 W Aspen (82637)
Rates: $29-$39
(307) 436-2772

GLENROCK MOTEL
108 S 3rd St (82637)
Rates: $25-$50
(307) 436-2772

GRAND TETON NATIONAL PARK

COLTER BAY VILLAGE/CABINS
US 89 & 287, P O Box 240 (Moran 83013)
Rates: $58-$104
(307) 543-2811
(800) 628-9988

FLAGG RANCH VILLAGE
Hwy 89 & US 191, P O Box 187 (Moran 83013)
Rates: $131-$140
(307) 543-2861
(800) 443-2311

HATCHEL RESORT
US 26 & 287 (Moran 83013)
Rates: $90-$180
(307) 543-2413

JACKSON LAKE LODGE
US 89 & 287 P O Box 240 (Moran 83013)
Rates: $115-$198
(307) 543-2855
(307) 543-2811
(800) 628-9988

AREA CODES - If the local number doesn't connect, check for a new area code.

SIGNAL MOUNTAIN LODGE
US 89, 191 & 287,
P O Box 50
(Moran 83013)
Rates: $75-$170
(307) 543-2831
(800) 672-6012

GREEN RIVER

COACHMAN INN
470 E Flaming
Gorge (82935)
Rates: $30-$49
(307) 875-3681

DESMOND MOTEL
140 N 7th W
(82935)
Rates: $26-$36
(307) 875-3701

FLAMING GORGE MOTEL
316 E Flaming
Gorge Way
(82935)
Rates: $25-$50
(307) 875-4190

OAK TREE INN
1170 W Flaming
Gorge Way
(82935)
Rates: $55-$60
(307) 875-3500

SUPER 8 MOTEL
280 W Flaming
Gorge Way (82935)
Rates: $42-$56
(307) 875-9330
(800) 800-8000

WESTERN MOTEL
890 Flaming
Gorge Way
(82935)
Rates: $33-$40
(307) 875-2840

GREYBULL

ANTLER MOTEL
1116 N 6th St
(82426)
Rates: $40-$53
(307) 765-4404

K-BAR MOTEL
300 Greybull Ave
(82426)
Rates: $24-$54
(307) 765-4426
(877) 765-4426

SAGE MOTEL
1009 N 6th St
(82426)
Rates: $36-$48
(307) 765-4443

YELLOWSTONE MOTEL
247 Greybull Ave
(82426)
Rates: $50-$65
(307) 765-4456

GUERNSEY

ANNETTE'S B&B
Box 31 (82214)
Rates: n/a
(307) 836-2148

BUNKHOUSE MOTEL
350 W Whalen
(82214)
Rates: $32-$37
(307) 836-2356

HANNA

GOLDEN RULE MOTEL
305 S Adams
(82327)
Rates: $25-$50
(307) 325-6525

HELL'S HALF ACRE

HELL'S HALF ACRE MOTEL
Hwys 20 & 26
(82648)
Rates: n/a
(307) 472-0018

HULETT

DIAMOND L GUEST RANCH
Box 70 (82720)
Rates: $90+
(307) 467-5236
(800) 851-5909

HULETT MOTEL
202 Main St (82720)
Rates: $45-$60
(307) 467-5220
(800) 451-4332

MOTEL PIONEER
119 Hunter
(82720)
Rates: $24-$39
(307) 467-5656
(800) 231-6335

PINE RIDGE RANCH B&B
979 New Haven
Rd (82720)
Rates: n/a
(307) 467-5519

JACKSON HOLE

ALPINE MOTEL
70 Jean St (83001)
Rates: $24-$38
(307) 739-3200

CACHE CREEK MOTEL
390 N Glenwood
(83001)
Rates: $51-$100
(307) 733-7781
(800) 843-4788

COTTAGE AT SNOW KING
470 King St (83001)
Rates: $25-$50
(307) 733-3480

DON'T FENCE ME INN
2350 N Moose-Wilson Rd (83001)
Rates: n/a
(307) 733-7979

ELK COUNTRY INN
480 W Pearl St
(83001)
Rates: $51-$150
(307) 733-2364

FLAT CREEK MOTEL
1935 N US 89
(83001)
Rates: $65-$95
(307) 733-5276
(800) 438-9338

FRIENDSHIP INN ANTLER MOTEL
43 W Pearl St
(83001)
Rates: $62-$125
(307) 733-2535
(800) 453-4511

JACKSON HOLE RACQUET CLUB RESORT
Star Rt 362A
(83001)
Rates: $51-$100
(307) 733-3990
(800) 443-8616

MAD DOG RANCH
6 mi NW of Jackson,
Box 7737 (83001)
Rates: $51-$100
(307) 733-3729

MOTEL 6
600 S Hwy 89
(83001)
Rates: $76-$92
(307) 733-1620
(800) 466-8356

PAINTED BUFFALO INN
400 W Broadway
(83001)
Rates: $95-$139
(307) 733-5430
(800) 288-3866

PROSPECTOR MOTEL
155 N Jackson St
(83001)
Rates: $45-$125
(307) 733-4858
(800) 851-0070

QUALITY 49'ER INN & SUITES
330 W Pearl St
(83001)
Rates: $84-$200
(307) 733-7550
(800) 228-5151

RANCH INN
45 E Pearl St
(83001)
Rates: $40-$250
(307) 733-6363
(800) 348-5599

RAWHIDE MOTEL
75 S Millward
(93001)
Rates: $51-$150
(307) 733-1216
(800) 835-2999

RED LION WYOMING INN
930 Broadway
(83001)
Rates: $189-$225
(307) 734-0035
(800) 844-0035

SNOW KING RESORT
400 E Snow King
Ave (83001)
Rates: $200-$430
(307) 733-5200
(800) 522-5464

TETON GABLES MOTEL
Jct 191-189-22
(83001)
Rates: $51-$99
(307) 733-3723

TWIN MOUNTAIN RIVER RANCH BED & BREAKFST
Star Rt 40 (83001)
Rates: n/a
(307) 733-1168

VIRGINIAN LODGE
750 W Broadway
(83001)
Rates: $51-$150
(307) 733-2792
(800) 262-4999

WESTERN MOTEL
225 S Glenwood
(83001)
Rates: $51-$98
(307) 733-3291
(800) 845-7999

JELM

WOODS LANDING
9 State Hwy 10
(82063)
Rates: $25-$50
(307) 745-9638

KAYCEE

CASSIDY INN MOTEL
346 Nolan Ave
(82426)
Rates: $25-$50
(307) 738-2250

GRAVES B&B COWBOY BUNKHOUSES
1729 Barnum Rd
(82639)
Rates: n/a
(307) 738-2319

RIVERSIDE INN
120 2nd St (82639)
Rates: $35-$55
(307) 738-2659

SIESTA MOTEL
255 Nolan Ave
(82639)
Rates: $25-$48
(307) 738-2291

KEMMERER

ANTLER MOTEL
419 Coral St
(83101)
Rates: $30-$50
(307) 877-4461

BON RICO MOTEL
Hwy 189, Box 150
(83101)
Rates: $25-$50
(307) 877-4503

FAIRVIEW MOTEL
61 Hwy N 30 at
189 (83101)
Rates: $30-$44
(307) 877-3938
(800) 247-3938

**FOSSIL BUTTE
MOTEL**
1424 Central Ave
(83101)
Rates: $27-$48
(307) 877-3996

**LAKE VIVA
NAUGHTON
MARINA MOTEL**
Hwy 233 (83101)
Rates: n/a
(307) 877-9669

**RAILWAY INN
MOTEL**
1427 W 5th Ave
(83101)
Rates: $25-$50
(307) 877-3544

LANDER

**BEST WESTERN
THE INN
AT LANDER**
260 Grand View
Dr (82520)
Rates: $56-$95
(307) 332-2847
(800) 528-1234

**BUDGET HOST
PRONGHORN
LODGE**
150 E Main St
(82520)
Rates: $56-$74
(307) 332-3940
(800) 283-4678

**THE BUNK HOUSE
BED & BREAKFAST**
2024 Mortimore
Ln (82520)
Rates: n/a
(307) 332-5624
(800) 582-5262

**COTTAGE HOUSE
AT SQUAW CREEK
BED & BREAKFAST**
72 Squaw Creek
Ct (82520)
Rates: n/a
(307) 332-5003

**DOWNTOWN
MOTEL**
569 Main St
(82520)
Rates: $25-$50
(307) 332-3171

HOLIDAY LODGE
210 McFarlane Dr
(82520)
Rates: $37-$47
(307) 332-2511
(800) 624-1974

MAVERICK MOTEL
808 Main St
(82520)
Rates: $25-$47
(307) 332-2300
(877) 622-2300

**PIECE OF CAKE
BED & BREAKFST**
2343 Baldwin Crk
Rd (82520)
Rates: $70-$90
(307) 332-7608

ROCK SHOP INN
4260 Hwy 28
(82520)
Rates: $35-$80
(307) 332-7396

**SILVER SPUR
MOTEL**
1240 Main St
(82520)
Rates: $40-$90
(307) 332-5189
(800) 922-7831

TETON MOTEL
586 W Main St
(82520)
Rates: $26-$48
(307) 332-3582

LARAMIE

**BEST WESTERN
FOSTER'S
COUNTRY INN**
1561 Snowy
Range Rd (82070)
Rates: $52-$101
(307) 742-8371
(800) 528-1234

**BEST WESTERN
GAS LITE MOTEL**
960 N 3rd St
(82070)
Rates: $45-$85
(307) 742-6616
(800) 528-1234

ECONO LODGE
1370 McCue St
(82070)
Rates: $49-$150
(307) 745-8900
(800) 553-2666

1ST INN GOLD
421 Boswell
(82070)
Rates: $78-$91
(307) 742-3721
(800) 642-4212

HOLIDAY INN
2313 Soldier
Springs (82070)
Rates: $85-$107
(307) 742-6611
(800) 526-5245

MOTEL 6
621 Plaza Ln
(82070)
Rates: $31-$42
(307) 742-2307
(800) 466-8356

MOTEL 8
501 Boswell Dr
(82070)
Rates: $25-$49
(307) 745-4856

**NORMAN HOUSE
BED & BREAKFST**
100 S 8th St
(82070)
Rates: n/a
(307) 742-2899

**PRAIRIE BREEZE
BED & BREAKFAST**
718 Ivinson Ave
(82070)
Rates: n/a
(307) 745-5482
(800) 840-2170

RANGER MOTEL
453 N 3rd (82070)
Rates: $25-$50
(307) 742-6677

SUNSET INN
1104 S 3rd St
(82070)
Rates: $46-$85
(307) 742-3741

**THUNDERBIRD
LODGE**
1369 N 3rd (82070)
Rates: $25-$48
(307) 745-4871

TRAVELODGE
165 N 3rd St
(82070)
Rates: $60-$85
(307) 742-6671
(800) 578-7878

UNIVERSITY INN
1720 Grand Ave
(82070)
Rates: $35-$69
(307) 721-8855
(800) 869-9466

WYCOTO LODGE
4039 Hwy 230
(82070)
Rates: $25-$50
(307) 742-4230

LOVELL

**CATTLEMAN
MOTEL**
470 Montana Ave
(82431)
Rates: $38-$52
(307) 548-2296

**HORSESHOE
BEND MOTEL**
375 E Main St
(82431)
Rates: $36-$58
(307) 548-2221

SUPER 8 MOTEL
595 E Main St
(82431)
Rates: $34-$57
(307) 548-2725
(800) 800-8000

WESTERN MOTEL
180 W Main St
(82431)
Rates: $35-$250
(307) 548-2781

LUSK

RAWHIDE MOTEL
805 S Main St
(82225)
Rates: $26-$49
(307) 334-2440
(888) 679-2558

**SAGE & CACTUS
VILLAGE TEPEE B&B**
Box 158, Star Rt 1
(82225)
Rates: n/a
(307) 663-7653

**TOWN HOUSE
MOTEL**
525 S Main St
(82225)
Rates: $32-$64
(307) 334-2376

TRAIL MOTEL
305 W 8th St
(82225)
Rates: $52-$62
(307) 334-2530

LYMAN

**VALLEY WEST
MOTEL**
Main St (82937)
Rates: $25-$50
(307) 787-3700

LYSITE

**DEER CREEK
GUEST RANCH**
Box 3 (82642)
Rates: n/a
(307) 457-2451

MANDERSON

**HARMONY
RANCH COTTAGE
BED & BREAKFAST**
182 Hwy 31 (82432)
Rates: n/a
(307) 568-2514

MEDICINE BOW

TRAMPAS LODGE
Box 66 (82329)
Rates: $25-$50
(307) 379-2280

**VIRGINIAN
HOTEL**
404 Lincoln Hwy,
Box 127 (82329)
Rates: $25-$50
(307) 379-2377

MEETEETSE

OASIS MOTEL
1702 State St
(82433)
Rates: $51-$99
(307) 868-2551

VISION QUEST MOTEL
2207 State St
(82433)
Rates: $25-$50
(307) 868-2512
(888) 281-9866

MILLS

RED ARROW MOTEL
West Yellowstone
& Wyoming Blvd
(82644)
Rates: $25-$50
(307) 234-5293

MOORCROFT

COZY MOTEL
219 W Converse St
(82721)
Rates: $35-$99
(307) 756-3486

KEYHOLE MARINA & MOTEL
215 McKean Rd
(82721)
Rates: $23-$38
(307) 756-9529

MOORCOURT MOTEL
Hwy 14 & Devils
Tower Rd (82721)
Rates: $35-$65
(307) 756-3411

WYOMING MOTEL & CAMPING PARK
112 E Converse St
(82721)
Rates: $35-$58
(307) 756-3452

NEWCASTLE

AUTO INN MOTEL
2503 W Main
(82701)
Rates: $40-$64
(307) 746-2734
(877) 228-8646

FLYING V CAMBRIA INN
23726 Hwy 85
(82701)
Rates: $52-$99
(307) 746-2096

FOUNTAIN MOTOR INN
2 Fountain Plaza
(82701)
Rates: $42-$62
(307) 746-4426
(800) 882-8858

FOUR CORNERS STORE, DINER & INN
24713 US Hwy 85
N (82701)
Rates: $35-$100
(307) 746-4776

HILLTOP MOTEL
1121 S Summit
(82701)
Rates: $25-$50
(307) 746-4494

MORGAN MOTEL
205 S Spokane
(82701)
Rates: $25-$50
(307) 746-2715

PINES MOTEL
248 E Wentworth
(82701)
Rates: $42-$75
(307) 746-4334
(800) 946-4334

SAGE MOTEL
1227 S Summit
Ave (82701)
Rates: $36-$58
(307) 746-2724

SUNDOWNER INN
451 W Main
(82701)
Rates: $23-$37
(307) 746-2796

PAINTER

HUNTER PEAK RANCH
4027 Crandall Rd
(82414)
Rates: $90-$120
(307) 587-3711

PINE BLUFFS

GATOR'S TRAVELYN MOTEL
515 W 7th St
(82082)
Rates: $25-$50
(307) 245-3226

SUNSET MOTEL
316 W 3rd (82082)
Rates: $25-$50
(307) 245-3591

PINEDALE

BEST WESTERN PINEDALE INN
850 W Pine St
(82941)
Rates: $60-$119
(307) 367-6869
(800) 528-1234

BOULDER LAKE LODGE
Box 1100 (82941)
Rates: n/a
(307) 537-4300

CAMP O'THE PINES MOTEL
38 N Fremont
(82941)
Rates: $23-$45
(307) 367-4536

THE CHAMBERS HOUSE B&B
111 W Magnolia St
(82041)
Rates: n/a
(307) 367-2168
(800) 567-2168

HALF MOON LODGE MOTEL
46 N Sublett Ave
(82941)
Rates: $51-$100
(307) 367-2851

LAKESIDE LODGE RESORT MARINA
99 FS 111 on
Fremont Lake
(82941)
Rates: $52-$98
(307) 367-2221

LOG CABIN MOTEL
49 E Magnolia
(82941)
Rates: $50-$65
(307) 367-4579

PINE CREEK INN
650 W Pine St
(82941)
Rates: $25-$47
(307) 367-2191

POLE CREEK RANCH B&B
244 Pole Creek Rd
(82941)
Rates: $50-$55
(307) 367-4433

RIVERA LODGE
442 W Marilyn
(82941)
Rates: $52-$97
(307) 367-2424

SUNDANCE MOTEL
148 E Pine (82941)
Rates: $35-$65
(307) 367-4336

TETON COURT MOTEL
123 E Magnolia St
(82941)
Rates: $27-$47
(307) 367-4317

WINDOW ON THE WINDS B&B
10151 Hwy 191
(82941)
Rates: $60-$95
(307) 367-2600
(888) 367-1345

POWDER RIVER

HELL'S HALF ACRE MOTEL & CAMPGROUND
Hell's Half Acre
(82648)
Rates: $24-$36
(307) 472-0018

POWELL

BEST CHOICE MOTEL
337 E 2nd St
(82435)
Rates: $25-$50
(307) 754-2243
(800) 308-8447

BEST WESTERN KINGS INN
777 E 2nd St
(82435)
Rates: $68-$90
(307) 754-5117
(800) 528-1234
(800) 441-7778

THE JOANN RANCH B&B
137 Rd 8VE
(82435)
Rates: n/a
(307) 645-3109

PARK MOTEL
737 E 2nd St
(82435)
Rates: $25-$50
(307) 754-2233
(800) 506-7378

SUPER 8 MOTEL
845 E Coulter
(82435)
Rates: $34-$46
(307) 754-7231
(800) 800-8000

RANCHESTER

HISTORIC OLD STONE HOUSE BED & BREAKFAST
135 Wolf Creek Rd
(82839)
Rates: $50-$100
(307) 655-9239

WESTERN MOTEL
350 Dayton St
(82839)
Rates: $45-$65
(307) 655-2212

RAWLINS

BEST WESTERN-COTTONTREE INN
2221 W Spruce St
(82301)
Rates: $69-$89
(307) 324-2737
(800) 528-1234
(800) 662-6886

BRIDGER INN
1904 E Cedar St
(82301)
Rates: $26-$34
(307) 328-1401

DAYS INN
2222 E Cedar St
(82301)
Rates: $44-$100
(307) 324-6615
(800) 329-7466

RAWLINS MOTEL
905 W Spruce St
(82301)
Rates: $28-$42
(307) 324-3456

SLEEP INN
1400 Higley Blvd
(82301)
Rates: $59-$71
(307) 328-1732
(800) 753-3746

WESTON INN
1801 E Cedar St
(82301)
Rates: $25-$49
(307) 324-2783
(800) 255-9840

RIVERSIDE

**BEAR TRAP BAR,
CAFE & CABINS**
120 E Riverside
Ave (82325)
Rates: $25-$45
(307) 327-5277

**LAZY ACRES
CAMPGROUND
& MOTEL**
Hwy 230 (82325)
Rates: $25-$35
(307) 327-5968

**RIVERSIDE
CABINS**
Star Rt, Box 15
(82325)
Rates: $61-$100
(307) 327-5361

RIVERTON

**COTTONWOOD
RANCH B&B**
951 Missouri
Valley Rd (82501)
Rates: n/a
(307) 856-3064

DAYS INN
909 W Main St
(82501)
Rates: $50-$70
(307) 856-9677
(800) 329-7466

DRIFTWOOD INN
611 W Main St
(82501)
Rates: $30-$40
(307) 856-4811

HI-LO MOTEL
414 N Federal
Blvd (82501)
Rates: $24-$33
(307) 856-9223

INN EL RANCHO
221 S Federal Blvd
(82501)
Rates: $30-$45
(307) 856-7455

**MOUNTAIN VIEW
MOTEL**
720 W Main St
(82501)
Rates: $27-$47
(307) 856-2418

**ROOMER'S
MOTEL**
319 N Federal
(82501)
Rates: $35-$50
(307) 857-1735
(800) 857-4097

**SUNDOWNER
STATION MOTEL**
1616 N Federal
Blvd (82501)
Rates: $50-$65
(307) 856-6503
(800) 874-1116

SUPER 8 MOTEL
1040 N Federal
Blvd (82501)
Rates: $47-$62
(307) 857-2400
(800) 800-8000

**THUNDERBIRD
MOTEL**
302 E Fremont
(82501)
Rates: $36-$46
(307) 856-9201

ROCK RIVER

**LONGHORN
LODGE**
Rt 287 (82083)
Rates: $25-$50
(307) 378-2555

ROCK SPRINGS

COMFORT INN
1670 Sunset Dr
(82901)
Rates: $56-$75
(307) 382-9490
(800) 228-5150

DAYS INN
1545 Elk St (82901)
Rates: $51-$60
(307) 362-5646
(800) 329-7466

HOLIDAY INN
1675 Sunset Dr
(82901)
Rates: $68-$79
(307) 382-9200
(800) 465-4329

**THE INN
AT ROCK SPRGS**
2518 Foothill Blvd
(82901)
Rates: $44-$80
(307) 362-9600
(800) 442-9692

MOTEL 6
2615 Commercial
Way (82901)
Rates: $40-$56
(307) 362-1850
(800) 466-8356

MOTEL 8
108 Gateway Blvd
(82901)
Rates: $25-$50
(307) 362-8200
(888) 362-8200

RODEWAY INN
1004 Dewar Dr
(82901)
Rates: $44-$76
(307) 362-6673
(800) 228-2000

SPRINGS MOTEL
1525 9th St (82901)
Rates: $40-$50
(307) 362-6683

**THUNDERBIRD
MOTEL**
1556 9th St (82901)
Rates: $35-$55
(307) 362-3739

SARATOGA

**BROOKSONG
BED & BREAKFST**
HC 63, Box 9L
(82331)
Rates: n/a
(307) 326-8744

**CARY'S SAGE
& SAND MOTEL**
311 S 1st (82331)
Rates: $25-$50
(307) 326-8339

HACIENDA MOTEL
1116 S 1st St
(82331)
Rates: $54-$74
(307) 326-5751

RIVIERA LODGE
303 N 1st (82331)
Rates: $25-$50
(307) 326-5651

SILVER MOON
412 E Bridge
(82331)
Rates: $25-$50
(307) 326-5974

SHELL

**HAP'S TRAPPER
CREEK B&B**
4046 Trapper Crk
Rd (82441)
Rates: n/a
(307) 765-9685

**MAYLAND RANCH
LODGE & CABINS**
P. O. Box 215
(82441)
Rates: $50-$75
(307) 765-2669

**TRAPPER'S REST
BED & BREAKFAST**
4351 Trapper Crk
Rd (82441)
Rates: $50-$90
(307) 765-9239
(800) 826-8872

**WAGON WHEEL
LODGE**
Hwy 14 (82441)
Rates: $23-$38
(307) 765-2561

SHERIDAN

ALAMO MOTEL
1326 N Main
(82801)
Rates: $25-$37
(307) 672-2455

APPLE TREE INN
1552 Coffeen Ave
(82801)
Rates: $32-$45
(307) 672-2428
(800) 670-2428

ASPEN INN
1744 N Main St
(82801)
Rates: $35-$58
(307) 672-9064

**BEST WESTERN
SHERIDAN
CENTER MOTOR
INN**
612 N Main
(82801)
Rates: $70-$90
(307) 674-7421
(800) 528-1234

BRAMBLE MOTEL
2366 N Main
(82801)
Rates: $24-$38
(307) 674-4902

EVERGREEN INN
580 E 5th St
(82801)
Rates: $25-$40
(307) 672-9757
(800) 771-4761

**FOOTHILLS
RANCH B&B**
521 Pass Creek Rd
(Parkman 82838)
Rates: n/a
(307) 655-9362

**GUEST HOUSE
MOTEL**
2007 N Main
(82801)
Rates: $45-$55
(307) 674-7496
(800) 226-9405
(800) 341-8000

HOLIDAY INN
1809 Sugarland Dr
(82801)
Rates: $72-$125
(307) 672-8931
(800) 465-4329

HOLIDAY LODGE
625 Coffeen Ave
(82801)
Rates: $25-$50
(307) 672-2407

LARIAT MOTEL
2068 Coffeen Ave
(82801)
Rates: $35-$60
(307) 672-6475

MILL INN
2161 Coffeen Ave
(82801)
Rates: $35-$59
(307) 672-6401

AREA CODES - If the local number doesn't connect, check for a new area code.

PARKWAY MOTEL
2112 Coffeen Ave
(82801)
Rates: $24-$47
(307) 674-7259

**RANCH WILLOW
BED & BREAKFST**
501 Hwy 14 E
(82801)
Rates: n/a
(307) 674-1510
(800) 354-2830

**ROCK TRIM
MOTEL**
449 Coffeen Ave
(82801)
Rates: $40-$60
(307) 672-2464

**STAGE STOP
MOTEL**
2167 N Main
(82801)
Rates: 35-$50
(307) 672-3459

SUPER 8 MOTEL
2435 N Main St
(82801)
Rates: $36-$70
(307) 672-9725
(800) 800-8000

SUPER SAVER INN
1789 N Main
(82801)
Rates: $23-$35
(307) 672-0471

**TRAILS END
MOTEL**
2125 N Main St
(82801)
Rates: $34-$52
(307) 672-2477

TRIANGLE MOTEL
540 CoffeenAve
(82801)
Rates: $34-$49
(307) 674-8031

XL MOTEL
907 N Broadway
(82801)
Rates: $24-$30
(307) 674-6458

SHOSHONI

**DESERT INN
MOTEL**
605 W 2nd (82649)
Rates: $30-$100
(307) 876-2273

SHOSHONI MOTEL
503 W 2nd (82649)
Rates: $35-$60
(307) 876-2216

STORY

STORY PINES INN
46 N Piney Rd
(82842)
Rates: $61-$100
(307) 683-2120
(800) 596-6297

**WAGON BOX
SUPPER CLUB INN**
Box 248 (82842)
Rates: $30-$48
(307) 683-2444
(800) 308-2444

SUNDANCE

**BEAR LODGE
MOTEL-IMA**
218 Cleveland Ave
(82729)
Rates: $48-$64
(307) 283-1611
(800) 341-8000

**BEST WESTERN
INN/SUNDANCE**
26 Hwy 585
(82729)
Rates: $64-$109
(307) 283-2800
(800) 528-1234
(800) 238-0965

**DEAN'S PINEVIEW
MOTEL**
117 N 8th St
(82729)
Rates: $28-$34
(307) 283-2262

SUNDANCE INN
2719 E Cleveland
(82729)
Rates: $44-$99
(307) 283-1100

**SUNDANCE
MOUNTAIN INN**
26 Hwy 585
(82729)
Rates: $59-$99
(307) 283-3737

TEN SLEEP

**FLAGSTAFF
MOTEL**
Box 376 (82442)
Rates: $25-$32
(307) 366-2745

**LOG CABIN
MOTEL**
Box 50 (82442)
Rates: $24-$30
(307) 366-2320

**MEADOWLARK
LAKE RESORT**
26 mi E on Hwy
16, Box 86 (82442)
Rates: n/a
(307) 366-2424
(800) 858-5672

TETON VILLAGE

**CRYSTAL SPRINGS
INN**
3285 W
McCollister Dr
(83025)
Rates: $46-$84
(307) 733-4423

THE HOSTEL
Box 546 (83025)
Rates: $25-$50
(307) 733-3415

**SASSY MOOSE
INN B&B**
3859 Miles Rd
(83014)
Rates: $129-$149
(307) 733-1277
(800) 356-1277

THAYNE

**SWISS MOUNTAIN
MOTEL**
119 Wright St
(83127)
Rates: $35-$50
(307) 883-2227

THERMOPOLIS

**BROADWAY INN
BED & BRKFAST**
342 Broadway
(82443)
Rates: n/a
(307) 864-2636
(888) 821-9759

**CACTUS INN
MOTEL**
605 S 6th (82443)
Rates: $26-$32
(307) 864-3155

COACHMAN INN
112 Hwy 20, South
Yellowstone
(82443)
Rates: $27-$40
(307) 864-3141
(888) 864-3854

**EL RANCHO
MOTEL**
924 Shoshoni Rd
(82443)
Rates: $25-$42
(307) 864-2341
(800) 283-2777

**HOLIDAY INN
OF THE WATERS**
115 E Park (82443)
Rates: $68-$110
(307) 864-3131
(800) 465-4329

JURASSIC INN
501 S 6th (82443)
Rates: $29-$38
(307) 864-2325

RAINBOW MOTEL
408 Park St
(82443)
Rates: $24-$33
(307) 864-2129
(800) 544-8815

**ROUNDTOP
MOUNTAIN
MOTEL**
412 N 6th (82443)
Rates: $28-$33
(307) 864-3126

SUPER 8 MOTEL
Lane 5, Hwy 20 S
(82443)
Rates: $47-$58
(307) 864-5515
(800) 800-8000

**WIND RIVER
MOTEL**
501 S 6th St
(82443)
Rates: $24-$34
(307) 864-2325

TORRINGTON

**BLUE LANTERN
MOTEL**
1402 S Main
(82240)
Rates: $25-$49
(307) 532-8999

KING'S INN
1555 S Main
(82240)
Rates: $65-$85
(307) 532-4011

MAVERICK MOTEL
US 26 & 85 (82240)
Rates: $36-$38
(307) 532-4064

**OREGON TRAIL
LODGE**
710 East Valley
Blvd (82240)
Rates: $26-$47
(307) 532-2101

UPTON

UPTON MOTEL
440 1st St (82730)
Rates: $32-$45
(307) 468-9282

**WESTON INN
MOTEL**
1601 Hwy 16
(82730)
Rates: $35-$46
(307) 468-2401

WAPITI

**ABSAROKA
MOUNTAIN
LODGE**
1231 E
Yellowstone Hwy
(82450)
Rates: $66-$110
(307) 587-3963

**ELEPHANT HEAD
LODGE**
1170 E
Yellowstone Hwy
(82450)
Rates: $75-$110
(307) 587-3980

**GOFF CREEK
LODGE**
995 E Yellowstone
Hwy (82414)
Rates: $95-$115
(307) 587-3753
(800) 859-3985

**SHOSHONE
LODGE RANCH**
349 Yellowstone
Hwy (82414)
Rates: $99-$189
(307) 587-4044

AREA CODES - If the local number doesn't connect, check for a new area code.

WISE CHOICE INN
2908 Yellowstone
Hwy (82450)
Rates: $50-$70
(307) 587-5004
(888) 673-2637

WHEATLAND

**BEST WESTERN
TORCHLIGHT
MOTOR INN**
1809 N 16th St
(82201)
Rates: $75-$80
(307) 322-4070
(800) 528-1234
(800) 662-3968

**BLACKBIRD INN
BED & BREAKFST**
1101 11th St
(82201)
Rates: n/a
(307) 322-4540

**HOMESTEAD BED
& BREAKFAST**
431 E Havely Rd
(82201)
Rates: $50-$74
(307) 322-3316

MOTEL 6
95 16th St (82201)
Rates: $34-$46
(307) 322-1800
(800) 466-8356

**MOTEL WEST
WINDS**
1756 South Rd
(82201)
Rates: $35-$64
(307) 322-2705

PLAINS MOTEL
208 16th St (82201)
Rates: $25-$50
(307) 322-3416

VIMBO'S MOTEL
203 16th St (82201)
Rates: $69-$77
(307) 322-3842

WYOMING MOTEL
1101 9th St (82201)
Rates: $25-$49
(307) 322-5383

WORLAND

**BEST WESTERN
SETTLERS INN**
2200 Big Horn Ave
(82401)
Rates: $44-$58
(307) 347-8201
(800) 528-1234

COMFORT INN
100 North Rd 11
(82401)
Rates: $59-$99
(307) 347-9898
(800) 228-5150

DAYS INN
500 N 10th (82401)
Rates: $48-$68
(307) 347-4251
(800) 329-7466

SUPER 8 MOTEL
2500 Big Horn Ave
(82401)
Rates: $42-$55
(307) 347-9236
(800) 800-8000

**TOWN &
COUNTRY MOTEL**
1021 Russell Ave
(82401)
Rates: $24-$36
(307) 347-3249

**TOWN HOUSE
MOTOR INN**
119 N 10th (82401)
Rates: $28-$32
(307) 347-2426

YELLOWSTONE NATIONAL PARK

The following
accommodations
are located near
the park entrances:

**CANYON VILLAGE
LODGE & CABINS**
Box 165 (82190)
Rates: $60-$80
(307) 344-7311

**LAKE LODGE &
CABINS**
Box 165 (82190)
Rates: $60-$80
(307) 344-7311

**LAKE
YELLOWSTONE
HOTEL & CABINS**
Box 165 (82190)
Rates: $80+
(307) 344-7311

**MAMMOTH HOT
SPRINGS &
HOTEL**
Box 165 (82190)
Rates: $60-$80
(307) 344-7311

**OLD FAITHFUL
LODGE CABINS**
Box 165 (82190)
Rates: $40-$80
(307) 344-7311

**OLD FAITHFUL
SNOW LODGE**
Yellowstone Natl
Park (82190)
Rates: $51-$100
(307) 344-7311

**ROOSEVELT
LODGE & CABINS**
Box 165 (82190)
Rates: $51-$100
(307) 344-7311

STATE DEPARTMENTS OF TOURISM

ALABAMA	**KENTUCKY**	**NORTH DAKOTA**
800-252-2262	800-225-8747	800-435-5663
ALASKA	**LOUISIANA**	**OHIO**
907-929-2200	800-334-8626	800-282-5393
ARIZONA	**MAINE**	**OKLAHOMA**
888-520-3434	88-624-6345	800-652-6552
ARKANSAS	**MARYLAND**	**OREGON**
800-628-8725	800-543-1036	800-547-7842
CALIFORNIA	**MASSACHUSETTS**	**PENNSYLVANIA**
800-862-2543	800-447-6277	800-847-4872
COLORADO	**MICHIGAN**	**RHODE ISLAND**
800-265-6723	800-543-2937	800-556-2484
CONNECTICUT	**MINNESOTA**	**SOUTH CAROLINA**
800-282-6863	800-657-3700	803-734-0122
DELAWARE	**MISSISSIPPI**	**SOUTH DAKOTA**
800-441-8846	800-927-6378	800-732-5682
DIST. OF COLUMBIA	**MISSOURI**	**TENNESSEE**
202-789-7000	800-877-1234	800-836-6200
FLORIDA	**MONTANA**	**TEXAS**
888-735-2872	800-847-4868	800-452-9292
GEORGIA	**NEBRASKA**	**UTAH**
800-847-4842	800-228-4307	801-538-1030
HAWAII	**NEVADA**	**VERMONT**
800-464-2924	800-638-2328	800-837-6668
IDAHO	**NEW HAMPSHIRE**	**VIRGINIA**
800-635-7820	800-386-4664	800-847-4882
ILLINOIS	**NEW JERSEY**	**WASHINGTON**
800-223-0121	800-537-7397	360-586-2088
INDIANA	**NEW MEXICO**	**WEST VIRGINIA**
800-289-6646	800-545-2040	800-225-5982
IOWA	**NEW YORK**	**WISCONSIN**
800-345-4692	800-225-5697	800-432-8747
KANSAS	**NORTH CAROLINA**	**WYOMING**
800-252-6727	800-847-4862	800-225-5996

TRAVEL NOTES

HOTEL/MOTEL 800 NUMBERS

ADAMS MARK HOTELS
800-444-2326

AMERICINN
800-634-3444

AMERIHOST INNS
800-434-5800

AMERISUITES
800-833-1516

AUBERGES WANDLYN INNS
800-561-0000

BAYMONT INN
800-301-0200

BEST INNS OF AMERICA
800-237-8466

BEST WESTERN
800-528-1234

BUDGET HOST
800-283-4678

CANADIAN PACIFIC HOTELS
800-441-1414

CLARION INNS
800-252-7466

COMFORT INNS
800-228-5150

COUNTRY INN & SUITES
800-456-4000

COURTYARD BY MARRIOTT
800-321-2211

CROWNE PLAZA
800-227-6963

DAYS INN
800-329-7466

DELTA PACIFIC
800-268-1133

DOUBLETREE
800-222-8733

DOWNTOWNER INNS
800-251-1962

DRURY INNS
800-378-7946

ECONO LODGE
800-553-2666

EMBASSY SUITES
800-362-2779

EXEL INNS
800-367-3935

FAIRFIELD INN BY MARRIOTT
800-228-2800

FAIRMONT HOTELS
800-527-4727

FORTE/MERIDIEN
800-225-5843

FOUR SEASONS
800-332-3442

GOOD NITE INNS
800-648-3466

GUESTHOUSE INN & SUITES
800-214-8378

HAMPTON INNS
800-426-7866

HARLEY HOTELS
800-321-2323

HARVEY HOTELS
800-922-9222

HAWTHORN SUITES
800-527-1133

HEARTLAND INNS
800-334-3277

HELMSLEY HOTELS
800-221-4982

HILTON HOTELS
800-445-8667

HOLIDAY INNS
800-465-4329

HOMESTEAD VILLAGE
888-782-9473

HOMEWOOD SUITES
800-225-5466

HOWARD JOHNSON
800-446-4656

HYATT HOTELS
800-233-1234

IMA HOTELS
800-341-8000

INN SUITES
800-842-4242

INNS OF AMERICA
800-826-0778

INTER-CONTINENTAL
800-327-0200

KELLY INNS
800-635-3559

KNIGHTS INNS
800-843-5644

L-K INNS
800-282-5711

LA QUINTA INNS
800-687-6667

LEES INN
800-733-5337

LEXINGTON SUITES
800-537-8483

LOEWS HOTEL
800-235-6397

MAINSTAY SUITES
800-660-6246

MARRIOTT HOTEL
800-228-9290

MASTER HOST INNS
800-251-1962

MICROTEL INNS
888-771-7171

MOTEL 6
800-466-8356

NIKKO INTERNATIONAL
800-645-5687

NOVOTEL
800-668-6835

OMNI HOTELS
800-843-6664

PARKS INNS INTERNATIONAL
800-670-7275

PASSPORT INN
800-251-1962

PEAR TREE INNS
800-282-8733

PRINCESS RESORTS
800-441-1414

QUALITY INNS
800-228-5151

RADISSON SUITES
800-333-3333

RAMADA INNS
800-272-6232

RED CARPET INNS
800-251-1962

RED LION INNS
800-733-5466

RED ROOF INNS
800-843-7663

RENAISSANCE HOTELS
800-468-3571

RESIDENCE INN BY MARRIOTT
800-331-3131

RITZ-CARLTON
800-241-3333

RODD SIGNATURE
800-565-7633

RODEWAY INNS
800-228-2000

SANDMAN INNS
800-726-3626

SCOTTISH INNS
800-251-1962

SHERATON/ITT & ALL-SUITES
800-325-3535

SHILO INNS
800-222-2244

SHONEY'S INN
800-222-2222

SIGNATURE INNS
800-822-5252

SILVER CLOUD INNS
800-551-7207

SLEEP INNS
800-753-3746

STAYBRIDGE SUITES
800-238-8000

SUMMERFIELD SUITES
800-833-4353

SUPER 8 MOTELS
800-800-8000

SUSSE CHALET
800-524-2538

THRIFTLODGE
800-525-9055

TOWNPLACE SUITES
800-257-3000

TRAVELODGE
800-578-7878

VAGABOND INNS
800-522-1555

VALUE INNS
800-443-7777

WELLESLEY INNS
800-444-8888

WESTIN HOTELS
800-228-3000

WINDMILL INNS OF AMERICA
800-547-4747

WOODFIN SUITES
800-237-8811

WYNDHAM HOTELS
800-996-3426

Quick Guide

to Pet-Friendly B&Bs,

Historic Lodging &

Luxury Hotels

TRAVEL NOTES

_____

_____

_____

_____

_____

_____

_____

_____

_____

_____

_____

_____

_____

_____

_____

_____

_____

_____

_____

_____

_____

_____

_____

_____

_____

_____

ALABAMA

BIRMINGHAM
The Tutwiler Hotel

EUTAW

FAIRHOPE
Marcella's Tea Room
& Inn B&B

MONTGOMERY
Colonel's Rest B&B

SELMA
Grace Hall B&B

THOMASVILLE

ALASKA

ANCHORAGE
A Comfort B&B
Adams Place B&B
Alaska Auntie's B&B
Aurora Winds B&B Resort
Bear Den B&B
Fernbrook B&B
Poppy Seed B&B
Qupquigiaq B&B
6 Bar Ranch B&B
Sixth & B B&B
12th & L B&B
Valarian Visit B&B

DENALI NATIONAL PARK
Valley Vista B&B

EAGLE RIVER
Mountain Air B&B
Shooting Star B&B

FAIRBANKS
AAAA Care B&B
A Pioneer B&B
Chena River B&B
Fox Creek B&B
Hillside B&B
Sourdough B&B
Such A Deal B&B

GUSTAVIS
A Puffin's B&B
Tri Bed B&B

HAINES
Fort Wm. H. Seward B&B

HOMER
Brigitte's Bavarian B&B
Home B&B/Seekins
Patchwork Farm B&B
Sundmarks B&B

INDIAN
Cabin Comfort B&B

JUNEAU
Jan's View B&B

KETCHIKAN
Ingersoll Hotel
Millar Street House B&B

KING SALMON
King Salmon Guides B&B

KODIAK
Kodiak B&B

PALMER
Hatcher Pass B&B

SEWARD
"The Farm" B&B

SOLDOTNA
B&B Cottages
Raven Mt. Farm B&B

TALKEETNA
Alaska Log Cabin B&B

TOK
Cleft of the Rock B&B
Stage Stop B&B

TRAPPER CREEK
McKinley Foothills B&B

ARIZONA

BISBEE
The Bisbee Inn B&B
Park Place B&B

CAREFREE
The Boulders Resort

CLARKDALE
Birds Eye View
B&B/Guest Cottages

DRAGOON
Kelly's Whistlestop B&B

FLAGSTAFF
Haley's Hideaway B&B

FOUNTAIN HILLS
Arizona Trails B&B
Reservation Service

GRAND CANYON
(South Rim)
El Tovar Historic Hotel

JEROME
The Surgeon's House B&B

LITCHFIELD PARK
The Wigwam Resort

ORACLE
Villa Cardinale B&B

PARADISE VALLEY
Marriott's Camelback Inn
Marriott's Mountain
Shadows Resort

PHOENIX
Arizona Biltmore
Royal Palms Hotel & Casitas
Uptown B&B

PRESCOTT
Lynx Creek Farm B&B

SCOTTSDALE
Four Seasons Resort
at Troon North
Gainey Suites Hotel
Inn at the Citadel
The Phoenician Resort
Scottsdale Princess

SEDONA
Courthouse Butte Villa B&B
Greyfire Farm B&B

SELIGMAN
Historic Rte 66 Motel

STAR VALLEY
Opal Ranch Inn B&B

TEMPE
The Buttes-
A Wyndham Resort

TUCSON
The Cat & The Whistle B&B
The Cove B&B
The Golf Villas at Oro Valley
Loews Ventana
Canyon Resort
Mountain Views B&B
Sheraton El Conquistador
Tillinghast Place B&B
Westward Look Resort

WINSLOW
La Posada Historic Hotel

ARKANSAS

DEVALLS BLUFF
Palaver Place B&B

EUREKA SPRINGS
A Cliff Cottage, The Place
Next Door, A B&B Inn
Basin Park Hotel
Cottage Inn B&B
Harvest House B&B
Hillside Cottage B&B
Rogue's Manor at
Sweet Springs B&B
Scandia Inn B&B
Taylor Page Inn B&B
White Dover Manor B&B

ARKANSAS
(CONTINUED)

EVENING SHADE
The Turman House B&B

HARRISON
Merry Otter B&B

HOT SPRINGS
Woodbine Hollow B&B

MENA
Aerie B&B

WOOSTER
Patton House B&B

CALIFORNIA

AHWAHNEE
Silver Spur B&B

APTOS
Apple Lane Inn B&B
Mangels House B&B

ATASCADERO
Lakeview B&B

BASS LAKE
The Lakehouse B&B

BEN LOMOND
Chateau Des Fleaurs B&B

BENICIA
The Painted Lady B&B

BERRY CREEK
Lake Oroville B&B

BEVERLY HILLS
Beverly Hilton
Four Seasons Beverly Hills
L'Ermitage Beverly Hills
The Regent Beverly Wilshire

BIG BEAR LAKE
Eagle's Nest B&B

BOONVILLE
Anderson Creek Inn B&B

CAPITOLA
El Salto by the Sea B&B
Summer House B&B

CARLSBAD
Four Seasons Resorr Aviara

CARMEL
Carmel Country Inn B&B
Carmel Garden Court B&B
Cypress Inn
Forest Lodge B&B
Highlands Inn
Sunset House B&B
Vagabond House Inn B&B
Wayside Inn

CARMEL VALLEY
Carmel Valley Ranch
Quail Lodge Resort & Golf

CHICO
The Esplanade B&B
O'Flaherty House B&B

CLIO
White Sulphur Springs
Ranch B&B

CLOVERDALE
Abramas House Inn B&B

CORONADO
Loews Coronado Bay Resort

DESERT HOT SPRINGS
Royal Palms Inn B&B

DUNSMUIR
Riverwalk Inn B&B

EUREKA
A Weaver's Inn B&B
Eureka Inn Historic Hotel

FORT BRAGG
Old Stewart House Inn

FREMONT
Lord Bradley's Inn B&B

GARDEN GROVE
Hidden Village B&B

GEORGETOWN
American River Inn B&B

GLEN ELLEN
Big Dog Inn B&B

GREEN VALLEY LAKE
Lodge at Green Valley B&B

GROVELAND
Groveland Hotel Country Inn

HALF MOON BAY
Zaballa House Inn B&B

INDIAN WELLS
Miramonte Resort Hotel

INVERNESS
Rosemary Cottage B&B

JAMESTOWN
Historic National Hotel B&B

JENNER
Jenner Inn & Cottages

JOSHUA TREE
Joshua Tree Inn B&B

KENWOOD
The Little House B&B

LA QUINTA
La Quinta Hotel

LAKE ARROWHEAD
Arrowhead Saddleback
Historic Country Inn
Prophets' Paradise B&B

LAKE TAHOE AREA
Inn at Heavenly Valley B&B
Norfolk Woods Country Inn

LEWISTON
Old Lewiston Inn B&B

LITTLE RIVER
The Inn At Schoolhouse
Creek B&B

LOS ANGELES
Century Plaza Hotel & Tower
Chateau Marmont Hotel

LOTUS
Golden Lotus B&B Inn

MARIPOSA
The Clubb's B&B
The Pelennor B&B

MARKLEEVILLE
The Mountain &
Garden B&B

MCCLOUD
Stoney Brook B&B

MENDOCINO
Blair House B&B
Seaside Cottage B&B

MONTARA
Farallone Inn B&B

MONTE RIO
Highland Dell Inn B&B

MONTECITO
Four Seasons Biltmore Hotel
San Ysidro Ranch

MORRO BAY
Coffey Break B&B

MOUNT SHASTA
Wagon Creek Inn B&B

NEEDLES
Old Trails Inn B&B

NEWPORT BEACH
Four Seasons Hotel

NICE
Gingerbread Cottages B&B

NIPINNAWASSEE
Deer Valey Inn B&B

NIPOMO
Kaleidoscope Inn B&B

OAKHURST
Pine Rose Inn B&B

OAKLAND
Clarion Suites Lake Merritt
    Historic Hotel

OJAI
Ojai Valley Inn & Spa

OLEMA
Roundstone Farm B&B

PALM SPRINGS
Casa Cody Country Inn

PASO ROBLES
Shamrock Inn B&B

PEBBLE BEACH
Lodge at Pebble Beach

POINT REYES STATION
Berry Patch Cottage B&B
The Tree House B&B
Thirty Nine Cypress B&B

RANCHO MIRAGE
Westin Mission Hills Resort

RANCHO SANTA FE
Inn at Rancho Santa Fe
Rancho Valencia Resort

RED MOUNTAIN
Old Owl Cottages Inn B&B

REDDING
Palisades Paraside B&B
Tiffany House B&B Inn

REDWOOD CITY
Hotel Sofitel
    San Francisco Bay

SAN ANDREAS
Courtyard B&B Inn

SAN DIEGO
Hanalei Hotel
Horton Grand Hotel
Lawrence Welk Resort
San Diego Paradise
    Point Resort
U. S. Grant Hotel

SAN FRANCISCO
Campton Place Hotel
Golden Gate Hotel B&B
Haus Kleebauer B&B
Hotel Monaco
Hotel Palomar
Hotel Triton
The Inn San Francisco B&B
Serrano Hotel
The Steinhart
The Westin St. Francis Hotel

SAN LUIS OBISPO
Heritage Inn B&B

SANTA BARBARA
Four Seasons Biltmore Hotel

SANTA CRUZ
Cliff Crest B&B
Laguna Creek Inn B&B
Redwood Croft B&B

SANTA MARIA
Historic Santa Maria Inn

SANTA MONICA
The Georgian
Loews Santa Monica Beach

SANTA ROSA
Coopers Grove Ranch B&B

SKY FOREST
Storybook Inn B&B

SONOMA
Martha's Cottage B&B
Sparrow's Nest Inn B&B
Stone Grove B&B
Tree House B&B
Villa Castillo B&B

SONORA
Hammons House Inn B&B
Mountain View B&B

SOQUEL
Blue Spruce Inn B&B

TWENTYNINE PALMS
Roughley Manor B&B

VALLEY SPRINGS
10th Green Inn B&B

WATSONVILLE
Country Sunrise B&B

WEST HOLLYWOOD
The Argyle Historic Hotel

WESTPORT
Howard Creek Ranch B&B

WILLITS
Etta Place B&B Inn

YOSEMITE NAT'L PARK
Yosemite's Four Seasons

COLORADO

ASPEN
Historic Hotel Jerome
The Little Nell Resort Hotel

COLLBRAN
Hill's Summer Chuckwagon
    & B&B

CRAWFORD
Black Canyon Ranch B&B

DENVER
Holiday Chalet B&B Hotel
Loews Giorgio Hotel

DILLON
Annabelle's B&B

DURANGO
Leland House B&B Suites
Rochester Historic B&B Hotel

EDWARDS
Lazy Ranch B&B

GLENWOOD SPRINGS
Historic Hotel Colorado

HOT SULPHUR SPRINGS
Bridges Stagecoach
    Country Inn B&B

MANCOS
Ryter House B&B

MANITOU SPRINGS
Red Eagle Mountain B&B

MARBLE
Ute Meadows Inn B&B

MONTROSE
Uncompahgre B&B

MOSCA
Inn at Historical Zapata Ranch

NORWOOD
Annie's Country B&B
Lone Cone Elk Ranch B&B

PAGOSA SPRINGS
Be Our Guest B&B

SALIDA
Piñon & Sage B&B Inn
The Tudor Rose B&B

SILVERTON
Alma House B&B
Villa Dallavalle B&B
Wyman Hotel & Inn B&B

SOUTH FORK
Spruce Lodge B&B & Cabins

STRASBURG
Strasburg Inn B&B

TELLURIDE
The Peaks at Telluride

TRINIDAD
Chicosa Canyon B&B

VICTOR
Historic Victor Hotel

CONNECTICUT

COVENTRY
Mill Brook Farm B&B

ESSEX
Griswold Historic Country Inn

GUILFORD
B&B at B

Complete listing information is located in the main directory section.

CONNECTICUT
(CONTINUED)

LEDYARD
Applewood Farms B&B

LITCHFIELD
Historic Tollgate Hill Inn

NEW MILFORD
The Heritage Inn of
Litchfield County

NORFOLK
Blackberry River Inn B&B

NORTH STONINGTON
The John York
House 1741 B&B

NORWALK
Silver Mine Tavern B&B

OLD LYME
Old Lyme Inn

SIMSBURY
The Simsbury 1820 House

WATERBURY
House on the Hill B&B

DELAWARE

BRIDGEVILLE
Teddy Bear B&B

LEWES
Country Lane B&B

DISTRICT OF COLUMBIA

(DOWNTOWN & VICINITY)
The Carlton Historic Hotel
Four Seasons Hotel
Hotel Washington
The Jefferson Hotel
The Luxury Collection
Historic Hotel
Park Hyatt Washington. D.C.
Renaissance Mayflower Hotel
The Willard
Inter-Continental

FLORIDA

AMELIA ISLAND
Florida House Inn B&B

APALACHICOLA
The Gibson Country Inn

BRANDON
Behind the Fence B&B

CEDAR KEY
Cedar Key B&B

CLERMONT
Mulberry Inn B&B

DELAND
Deland Country Inn B&B

DELRAY BEACH
Colony Hotel & Cabana Club

HIGH SPRINGS
The Rustic Inn B&B

HOMESTEAD
Katy's Place B&B

INVERNESS
The Crown Hotel

ISLAMADORA
Bed & Breakfast Islamadora

KEY WEST
Casa Alante Guest
Cottages B&B
Center Court Historic Inn &
Cottages B&B
Chelsea House Historic B&B
Courtney's Place Cottages
Curry Mansion Inn B&B
Frances St. Bottle Inn B&B
The Palms Hotel Historic B&B
Whispers B&B Inn

LAKE WALES
Chalet Suzanne Inn

MIAMI BEACH
Historic Breakwater Hotel
Brigham Gardens B&B
Fontainebleau Hilton Resort
Loews Miami Beach Hotel

MICAPONY
Shady Oak B&B

ORLANDO
Veranda B&B Inn

PALM BEACH
Four Seasons
Ocean Grand
Plaza Inn

PALM BEACH GARDENS
Heron Cay B&B

PALMETTO
Sea Inn B&B

QUINCY
Allison House B&B

RUSKIN
Southern Comfort B&B

WEST PALM BEACH
Hibiscus House Historic B&B

GEORGIA

AMERICUS
Pathway Inn B&B

ATLANTA
Angus & Agatha's Luxury B&B
Bed & Breakfast Atlanta
Reservation Service
Beverly Hills Inn B&B
Four Seasons Hotel
Granada Suite Hotel

BLACKSHEAR
Pond View Inn B&B

BLAIRSVILLE
Misty Mountain Inn
& Cottages
Nottley Dam
Guest House B&B

CLERMONT
Historic Clermont Hotel

LAWRENCEVILLE
A Touch of Home B&B

MADISON
Brady Inn B&B

MT. AIRY
Mt. Airy B&B

PAVO
Fast Turtle Inn B&B

PLAINS
Plains B&B Inn

ST. MARYS
Goodbread House B&B

SAUTEE
Royal Windsor
Cottage B&B

SAVANNAH
Bed & Breakfast Inn
East Bay Country Inn
Joan's On Jones B&B
Olde Harbour Inn B&B
St. Julian Street B&B

SENOIA
Culpepper House B&B

STATESBORO
Statesboro Country Inn

THOMASVILLE
Susina Plantation Inn B&B

VILLA RICA
Ahava Plantation B&B
Twin Oaks B&B

WATKINSVILLE
Ashford Manor B&B

YOUNG HARRIS
Creekside Hideaway
B&B & Cabin

Complete listing information is located in the main directory section.

IDAHO

ALBION
Mountain Manor B&B

ASHTON
Jensen's RV/B&B

BLACKFOOT
Alder Inn B&B

BOISE
Owyhee Plaza Historic Hotel

CAMBRIDGE
Cambridge House B&B

COEUR D'ALENE
Coeur d'Alene B&B
Country Ranch B&B
O'Neill's B&B
Summer House by the
    Lake B&B

ELK CITY
Canterbury House Inn B&B

GOODING
Gooding Hotel B&B

HARRISON
Peg's Bed N' Breakfast Place

KETCHUM
River Street Inn

KINGSTON
Kingston's Ranch B&B

KOOSKIA
Bear Hollow B&B

LAVA HOT SPRINGS
Riverside Inn & Hot Springs
White Wolf B&B

NORTH FORK
100 Acre Wood B&B

PLUMMER
Bonnie's B&B

POCATELLO
Back O'Beyond B&B

POTLATCH
Rollings Hills B&B

RIGGINS
The Lodge B&B

SALMON
Syringa Lodge

SHOUP
Smith House B&B

SUN VALLEY
Elkhorn Resort

WINCHESTER
Winchester Country Inn

ILLINOIS

CHICAGO
Ambassador West
    Grand Heritage
Chicago Hilton & Towers
City Suites Historic Hotel
Four Seasons Hotel
Palmer House Hilton
Regal Knickerbocker Hotel
Ritz-Carlton
Tremont Hotel

COBDEN
Shawnee Hill B&B

COLLINSVILLE
Maggie's B&B

ELIZABETH
Ridgeview B&B

EVANSTON
A Sommer Place B&B

GALENA
Cloran Mansion B&B
Country Gardens B&B

GREENVILLE
Prairie House Country Inn

KANKAKEE
Norma's B&B

METROPOLIS
Isle of View B&B

MINONK
Victorian Oaks B&B

MOUNT CARROLL
The Captains Quarters B&B

PEORIA
Pere Marquette Hotel

PRINCETON
Prairie Hill Barn B&B

RUSHVILLE
The Bottenberg B&B

WINDSOR
The Deerfield B&B

INDIANA

CRAWFORDSVILLE
Davis House B&B

FISHERS
Frederick Talbot Inn

GOSHEN
Country B&B

LAFAYETTE
Loeb House Historic Inn

LINGONIER
Minuette B&B

METAMORA
Thorpe House Country Inn

MONTICELLO
Quiet Water B&B

NEW HARMONY
Wright Place B&B

RISING SUN
Jelly House Country Inn B&B

WALKERTON
Hesters Cabin B&B

IOWA

CLEAR LAKE
Pheasant Country Inn B&B

CRESTON
Carol's B&B

GRINNELL
Clayton Farms B&B

SIOUX RAPIDS
Hansen House B&B Inn

KANSAS

ABILENE
Balfour's House B&B

ASHLAND
Rolling Hills B&B

BALDWIN CITY
Grove House B&B

BELVUE
In The Country Inn

BERN
Lear Acres B&B

BONNER SPRINGS
Carol's Candelight Cottage

COTTONWOOD FALLS
1874 Stone House
    on Mulberry Hill
Grand Central Hotel

COUNCIL GROVE
The Cottage House Hotel

DOVER
Historic Sage Inn

ENTERPRISE
Ehrsam Place B&B

FORT SCOTT
The Lyons House B&B

GLASCO
Rustic Remembrances B&B

GREAT BEND
Peaceful Acres B&B

Complete listing information is located in the main directory section.

KANSAS
(CONTINUED)

HILL CITY
Pheasant Run B&B

LAKIN
Windy Heights B&B

LAWRENCE
Grove House B&B

LIBERAL
Boles Ranch B&B

ROSE HILL
Queen Anne's Lake B&B

SALINA
Hunters Leigh B&B

TOPEKA
Lippincotts Fyshe House B&B
Ravenwood Mission Creek
    Lodge B&B

UDALL
Imprint Horse Farm B&B

WALDO
Covert Creek Lodge B&B

KENTUCKY

BEATTYVILLE
The Old School House B&B

BEREA
Cabin Fever B&B

BOWLING GREEN
Alpine Lodge B&B

CORBIN
Mom & Dad's Place B&B

COVINGTON
Carneal House Inn B&B
Sandford House B&B

GEORGETOWN
Homewood B&B
Log Cabin B&B

LAWRENCEBURG
Dowling Hall B&B

LEXINGTON
Halifax Lane Farm B&B

LOUISVILLE
Aleksander House B&B
Old Louisville Inn B&B
Seelbach Grand Hotel
Woodhaven B&B

PADUCAH
Farley Place B&B
Trinity Hills Farm B&B

RUSSELL SPRINGS
White Pillars B&B

SPRINGFIELD
Glenmar Plantation B&B

SULPHUR
Sulphur Trace Farm B&B

VERSAILLES
1823 Historic Rose Hill
    Inn B&B
Tyrone Pike B&B

LOUISIANA

AMITE
Blythewood Plantation B&B

BOSCO
Boscobel Cottage B&B

CHENEYVILLE
Loyd Hall Plantation B&B

DARROW
Tezcuco Plantation B&B

EUNICE
Seale Guesthouse B&B

HOUMA
Crochet House B&B

JENNINGS
Creole Rose Manor B&B

KROTZ SPRINGS
Country Store B&B Inn

LAFAYETTE
Bois Des Chenes Inn B&B

MONROE
Boscobel Cottage B&B

NATCHITOCHES
Cloutier Townhouse B&B

NEW IBERIA
La Maison B&B
Maison Marceline B&B

NEW ORLEANS
Maison Esplanade
    Guest House B&B
The Oliver Estate, A B&B
Rathbone Inn B&B
Robert Gordy House B&B
Windsor Court Hotel

NEW ROADS
River Blossom Inn B&B

ST. FRANCISVILLE
Butler Greenwood B&B
Green Springs B&B
Lake Rosemound Inn B&B

ST. MARTINVILLE
Maison Bleue B&B

SHREVEPORT
2439 Fairfield-A B&B

THIBODAUX
Oakes B&B

MAINE

BANGOR
The Phenix Inn B&B

BAR HARBOR
Balance Rock Inn B&B
Ledgelawn Inn Historic B&B

BELFAST
Belfast Bay Meadows Inn

BETHEL
The Briar Lea B&B
L'Auberge Country Inn

BOOTHBAY HARBOR
Welch House Inn B&B

BROWNFIELD
Foothills Farm B&B

CAMDEN
Blue Harbor House
    Country Inn

CASTINE
Pentagot Inn Historic B&B

FREEPORT
Isaac Randall House B&B

KITTERY
Enchanted Nights B&B

LIMERICK
Jeremiah Mason House B&B

NAPLES
Augustus Bove House B&B

PORTLAND
Andrews Lodging B&B
Black Cove Inn B&B

SEBASCO ESTATES
Small Point B&B

MARYLAND

ANNAPOLIS
American Heritage B&B
Loews Annapolis Hotel

BUCKEYSTOWN
Catoctin Inn & Conference
    Center B&B

CAMBRIDGE
Commodores Cottage
Sarke Plantation B&B

CENTREVILLE
Rose Tree B&B

CHESTERTOWN
The Parker House B&B

CLEAR SPRINGS
Cedar Crest Cottage B&B

Complete listing information is located in the main directory section.

ELKTON
Garden Cottage at Sinking
  Springs Farm

GRANTSVILLE
Walnut Ridge B&B

GRASONVILLE
Lands End Manor
  on the Bay B&B

HAGERSTOWN
Sunday's B&B

MECHANICSVILLE
Wide Bay Cottage at
  Dameron B&B

OCEAN CITY
Sheraton Fontainebleau Hotel

ROCK HALL
Bay Breeze Inn B&B
Huntingfield Manor B&B

ROYAL OAK
The Oaks, A Country Inn

ST. MICHAELS
Cygnet House B&B
Fox Run Farm B&B
Kemp House Inn

SHARPSBURG
Clipp's Mill & Log Cabin B&B

SILVER SPRING
Little House at
  Wind Swept B&B
The Park Crest Home B&B

SNOW HILL
River House Inn B&B

SOLOMONS
Locust Inn Rooms B&B

TAYLORS ISLAND
Becky Phipp's Inn B&B

TILGHMAN ISLAND
Harrison's Country Inn

WHITEHAVEN
Whitehaven B&B

MASSACHUSETTS

ANDOVER
Andover Country Inn

BARRE
Jenkins Inn

BLANDFORD
Pleasure Horse
  Paso Fino Farm B&B

BOSTON
Boston Harbor Hotel
Fairmont Copley Plaza Hotel
Four Seasons Hotel

Le Meridien Hotel
The Westin-Copley Place

BREWSTER
Greylin House

FALMOUTH
Bayberry Inn B&B

GREAT BARRINGTON
Chez Gabrielle B&B

GREENFIELD
The Brandt House B&B
Old Tavern Farm B&B

HOUSATONIC
Christine's B&B
  Carriage House

HYANNIS PORT
Simmons Homestead Inn B&B

LEE
Devonfield B&B

LENOX
Seven Hills Country Inn
Walker House Inn B&B

LEXINGTON
Mary Van & Jims
  "This Old House" B&B

LYNN
Diamond District B&B Inn

MARION
Village Landing B&B

MARTHA'S VINEYARD
Mill Hill B&B (Edgartown)
Point Way Inn B&B
  (Edgartown)
Tivoli Inn B&B (Oak Bluffs)
The Victorian Inn (Edgartown)

MARBLEHEAD
The Nesting Place B&B
Seagull Inn B&B

MIDDLEFIELD
Strawberry Banke Farm B&B

NEWBURYPORT
The Windsor House B&B

ORLEANS
Orleans B&B Association

PROVINCETOWN
White Wind Inn

REHOBOTH
Five Bridge Farm Inn B&B

RICHMOND
A B&B in the Berkshires
Middlerise B&B

ROCKPORT
Beach Knoll B&B
The Blueberry B&B

Carlson's B&B

SALEM
The Salem Inn Historic B&B

SHEFFIELD
Ivanhoe Country House B&B
Race Brook Lodge B&B
Stagecoach Hill Inn

STURBRIDGE
Publick House Historic Resort

TYRINGHAM
Sunset Farm B&B

WELLFLEET
Pine Moorings
  Cottages & B&B

WEST BARNSTABLE
Cozy Nest B&B

WEST HARWICH
Cape Cod Claddagh Inn

YARMOUTHPORT
Village Inn B&B

MICHIGAN

ALGONAC
Linda's Lighthouse Inn B&B

CLIO
Cinnamon Stick B&B

FENNVILLE
J. Paules Fenn Inn B&B
Spruce Cutters Cottage B&B

FRANKFORT
Hotel Frankfort B&B

HARRISVILLE
Widow's Watch B&B

LAKESIDE
White Rabbit Inn B&B

LUDINGTON
Ludington House B&B

NEW BUFFALO
Sans Souci B&B

SAUGATUCK
The Kirby House B&B

MINNESOTA

ALEXANDRIA
Carrington House B&B

ANNANDALE
Thayer's Historic B&B

BACKUS
Pine Mountain Inn B&B

DULUTH
Manor on the Creek B&B

Complete listing information is located in the main directory section.

MINNESOTA
(CONTINUED)

ELY
Blue Heron B&B

GLENCOE
Glencoe Castle B&B

HENDRICKS
Triple L Farm B&B

HERMAN
Lawndale Farm Wildlife
   Gallery B&B

HIBBING
Adams House B&B

NEVIS
Park Street Inn Historical B&B

NORTHFIELD
Archer House of Northfield
   Historic Country Inn

PARK RAPIDS
Loon Song B&B

PETERSON
Lilian's House of
   ISeven Gables B&B

PRESTON
The Jailhouse Historic Inn

PRIOR LAKE
Nature's Inn B&B Suites

RANIER
Sandbay B&B at Tara's Wharf

ROUND LAKE
The Prairie House on
   Round Lake B&B

RUSHFORD
Meadows Inn B&B

TAYLORS FALLS
The Springs Country Inn

WALKER
Tianna Farms B&B

WARROAD
Hospital Bay B&B

WATERTOWN
Wander Inn B&B

MISSISSIPPI

BILOXI
Broadwater Beach Resort
Lofty Oaks Inn B&B

LONG BEACH
Red Creek Colonial Inn

NATCHEZ
Cedar Grove Plantation B&B
The Guest House Hotel B&B

PASS CHRISTIAN
Inn at the Pass Historic B&B

TUNICA
Historic Hotel Marie

TUPELO
Mockingbird Inn B&B

VICKSBURG
Belle of the Bends B&B
The Corners B&B
Duff Green Mansion Inn B&B

MISSOURI

BRANSON
Welk Resort Center

HERMAN
Harbor House Inn

KANSAS CITY
Historic Suites of
   America Motel
Radisson Suite Historic Hotel
Ritz-Carlton

ST. LOUIS
Drury Inn Union Station
   Historic Motor Inn

MONTANA

BIG TIMBER
Big Timber Inn B&B

BOZEMAN
Bridger Mtns Highland
   House B&B

DE BORGIA
Hotel Albert B&B

DEER LODGE
Coleman Fee Mansion B&B

EMIGRANT
Querenica B&B

GALLATIN GATEWAY
Millers of Montana B&B

HAMILTON
Deer Crossing B&B
Ranch B&B

HELENA
Appleton Inn B&B
Barrister B&B
Birdseye B&B

KALISPELL
Kalispell Historic Grand Hotel

POLSON
Swan Hill B&B

ST. IGNATIUS
Stoneheart Inn B&B

SEELEY LAKE
The Emily A B&B

THREE FORKS
Sacajawea Historic
   Country Inn

TOWNSEND
Bedford Inn B&B

WHITEFISH
Crenshaw House B&B
Eagle's Roost B&B

NEBRASKA

AINSWORTH
Ainsworth Inn B&B
The Upper Room B&B

BATTLE CREEK
Bit 'O' Country Inn B&B

BREWSTER
Uncle Buck's Lodge

CALLAWAY
Chesley's Lodge
Travelers Inn
   Callaway House

CENTRAL CITY
The Popcorn Palace B&B

CHADRON
The Olde Main Street Inn B&B

DIXON
The Georges B&B

FARWELL
The Farwell Arms B&B

FUNK
Uncle Sam's Hilltop Lodge

GORDON
Meadow View Ranch B&B

HARRISON
Harrison House B&B

HOLDREGE
The Crow's Nest Inn B&B

HOWELLS
Beran B&B

MERNA
The Country Nest B&B

MURDOCK
Farm House B&B

NEWMAN GROVE
Crystal Key Inn B&B

OMAHA
Offutt House B&B

O'NEILL
Historic Golden Hotel

Complete listing information is located in the main directory section.

PIERCE
Willow Rose B&B

SPRINGVIEW
Larrington's Guest
Cottage B&B

STEINAUER
Convent House B&B

VALENTINE
Niobrara Inn B&B

WEST POINT
Von Schweigert Haus B&B

NEVADA

ELKO
Once Upon A Time B&B

GARDNERVILLE
The Nenzel Mansion B&B

GENOA
Genoa House Inn B&B

LAMOILLE
Breitenstein House B&B

SILVER CITY
Hardwicke House B&B

SILVER SPRINGS
A Secret Garden B&B

STATELINE
Harrah's Lake Tahoe
Hotel & Casino

UNIONVILLE
Old Pioneer Garden B&B

VIRGINIA CITY
Spargo House B&B

NEW HAMPSHIRE

CENTER HARBOR
Watch Hill B&B

CHESTERFIELD
Chesterfield Country Inn

DURHAM
Hickory Pond Inn Historic B&B

EAST SULLIVAN
Post & Beam B&B

EAST WAKEFIELD
Lake Ivanhoe
Camping & B&B Inn

FRANCONIA
Lovett's Inn by
Lafayette Brook

GILMANTON
Temperance Tavern B&B

HAMPTON
Lamie's Country Inn & Tavern

HOLDERNESS
Manor on Golden Pond
Country Inn

JACKSON
Dana Place Inn
Mountainside Farm B&B
The Village House Inn
Whitneys Inn

JEFFERSON
Applebrook B&B

KEARSARGE
Isaac. E. Merrill
House Inn B&B

LANCASTER
The Old Morse Lodge B&B

LOUDON
Lovejoy Farm B&B

NEWPORT
Historic Eagle Inn at
Coit Mountain

NORTH CONWAY
Isaac E. Merrill House Inn B&B
Oxen Yoke B&B
Stonehurst Manor
Historic Country Inn

PITTSFIELD
Apple Mountain Lodge

RINDGE
Woodbound Country Inn

SUGAR HILL
The Hilltop Inn B&B
Homestead Country Inn

SUNAPEE
Seven Hearths Inn B&B

SWANZEY
Loafer Inn at the 1792
Whitecomb House B&B

TAMWORTH
The Tamworth Country Inn

TILTON
Tilton Manor

WENTWORTH
Hilltop Acres B&B

WILTON CENTER
Auk's Nest B&B
Stepping Stones B&B

NEW JERSEY

BELMAR
Down The Shore B&B

CAPE MAY
The Moffett House B&B

HOPE
The Inn at Millrace Pond B&B

NEW MEXICO

ALBUQUERUQE
111 BnB Jazz Inn
Brittania & W.E. Mauger
Estate Historic B&B
Casita Chamisa B&B
Maggie's Raspberry
Ranch B&B

ARROYO SECO
Adobe & Stars B&B

GLENWOOD
Los Olmos Guest Ranch
Historic Cottage

HERNANDEZ
Casa Del Rio B&B

LAS CRUCES
Hilltop Hacienda B&B
Lundeen Inn
of the Arts B&B
The Smith B&B

LAS VEGAS
Historic Plaza Hotel

MESILLA
Happy Trails B&B

PLACITAS
Hacienda de Placitas Inn
of the Arts B&B

SANTA FE
Alexander's Inn B&B
Casapueblo Inn B&B
El Dorado Hotel
El Paradero Historic B&B
Hacienda Nicholas B&B
Hotel Santa Fe
Inn of the Anasazi
Inn on the Alameda
Las Palomas Historic Motel
The Madeleine Historic B&B
Open Sky B&B

TAOS
El Rincon B&B
Fechin Inn
Sagebrush Historic Inn
Touchstone Historic B&B

THOREAU
Zuni Mountain Lodge
Country Inn

Complete listing information is located in the main directory section.

NEW YORK

ALBANY
Mansion Hill Inn B&B

ANGELICA
Angelica Inn B&B

AUBURN
The Irish Rose B&B

BELLPORT
The Great South Bay Inn B&B

BRISTOL CENTER
The Acorn Inn B&B

CAMBRIDGE
Cambridge Inn B&B

CLINTON
The Hedges B&B

DEPOSIT
Alexander's Inn on
    Oquaga Lake B&B

DOVER PLAINS
Old Drovers Country Inn

DURHAM
Golden Harvest B&B

ELLICOTTVILLE
Jefferson Inn B&B

FARMINGTON
Sunrise Hill Country Inn

FLEISCHMANNS
River Run B&B

GENEVA
99 William Street B&B

GILBERTSVILLE
Signature Quilt B&B

HAMLIN
Sandy Creek
    Manor House B&B

HUDSON
St. Charles Historic Hotel

ITHACA
La Tourelle Country Inn

LIVINGSTON MANOR
The Magical Land of OZ B&B

LYONS
Kreiss Farm B&B

MOUNT TREMPER
La Duchesse Anne
    Historical B&B

NAPLES
Landmark Retreat B&B

NEW YORK CITY
The Carlyle
Four Seasons Hotel
Hotel Pierre-
    A Four Seasons Hotel
Hotel Plaza Athenee
Hotel Westbury
New York Palace Hotel
The Lowell
The Peninsula
The Stanhope
Waldorf Towers

NIAGARA FALLS
Boyles House B&B

NORTH CREEK
The Inn on Gore Mountain

PORT JEFFERSON
Danfords Inn

PULASKI
1880 House B&B

SARANAC LAKE
Hotel Saranac of
    Paul Smith's College
The Point

SARATOGA SPRINGS
Union Gables B&B

SOUTH WORCESTER
Charlotte Valley Inn B&B

SOUTHAMPTON
Oak Tree Inn B&B

WALLKILL
Audrey's Farm House B&B

WATKINS GLEN
Farm Sanctuary B&B

WILSON
Fisherman's Choice B&B

NORTH CAROLINA

ABERDEEN
Inn at the Bryant House B&B

APEX
Pearson Place B&B

ASHEVILLE
Hill House B&B

BANNER ELK
Banner Elk Inn B&B

BEAUFORT
Carteret County Home B&B

BOONE
The Lion's Den B&B & Chalet

BRYSON CITY
West Oak B&B & Cottages

COLUMBUS
Ly Navd Hills
    Guest House B&B

COROLLA
B&B on the Beach

FAISON
Magnolia Hall B&B

HATTERAS
Seaside Inn at Hatteras B&B

LAUREL SPRINGS
Doughton Hall B&B Inn

MARSHALL
Marshall House B&B Inn

MOCKSVILLE
Old Mocks Field B&B

MURPHY
Park Place B&B

OAK CITY
Southern Comfort B&B

PINEBLUFF
Pine Cone Manor B&B

PLEASANT GARDEN
Walnut Lane B&B

ROCKY MOUNT
Sunset Inn B&B

RUTHERFORDTON
Carrier Houses B&B

SMITHFIELD
Waverly's B&B

SOUTHERN PINES
Jefferson Inn

SOUTHPORT
Cape Fear Inn

SWANSBORO
Sunrise Lane B&B

TARBORO
Lady Ann of
    Historic Tarboro B&B

TRYON
Fence Bed & Barn B&B
Historic Block House
    Farm Inn
The Melrose Country Inn

WAYNESVILLE
Mountain Creek B&B

WILMINGTON
Anderson Guest House B&B
Blue Heaven B&B
Camellia Cottage B&B
Live Oaks B&B
219 S. 5th B&B

WINSTON-SALEM
Augustus Zevely Inn B&B

NORTH DAKOTA

DICKINSON
Hartfiel Inn Historic B&B

GRAFTON
Irlene Shirley's Gingerbread
House B&B

OHIO

CAMBRIDGE
Colonel Taylor Inn B&B

CLEVELAND
Ritz-Carlton Hotel

COLUMBUS
Victorian B&B
The Westin Great
Southern Columbus

FREDERICKTOWN
Heartland Country Resort
B&B

MIDDLETOWN
Manchester Inn & Conf.
Center Historic Hotel

SIDNEY
Greatstone Castle B&B

WARREN
Historic Park Hotel

WAYNESVILLE
The Apple Barn B&B

WESTERVILLE
Cornelia's Corner B&B

OKLAHOMA

CHECOTAH
Sharpe House B&B

GUTHRIE
Harrison House Inn B&B

KETCHUM
Summerside Inn B&B

OREGON

ASHLAND
Ashland Grande Hotel
Ashland Patterson House
B&B

ASTORIA
Clementine's B&B

BAKER CITY
Geiser Grand Historic Hotel
Powder River B&B
Warners Slough House B&B

BANDON
Pacific House B&B

BEAVERTON
Aloha Junction Inn
& Garden B&B

BEND
Guest House B&B
Swallow Ridge B&B

BLUE RIVER
Holiday Farm Resort B&B
McKenzie River B&B

BROOKINGS
Lowden's Beachfront B&B
Sea Dreamer Inn B&B

CAVE JUNCTION
Rusk Ranch Country Cottage

COOS BAY
Coos Bay Manor B&B

CORVALLIS
Ashwood B&B

DAYVILLE
Fish House Inn B&B

EUGENE
The Valley River Inn

FORT KLAMATH
Sun Pass Ranch B&B

FOSSIL
Bridge Creek Flora Inn B&B

GLENEDEN BEACH
Westin Salishan Lodge

GLIDE
Steelhead Run B&B

HALFWAY
Clear Creek Farm B&B

HOOD RIVER
Beryl House B&B
Hackett House B&B

JACKSONVILLE
Jacksonville Inn Hotel

JOHN DAY
Sonshine B&B

JOSEPH
Dragon Meadows B&B

LA PINE
Diamond Stone
Guest Lodge B&B

LINCOLN CITY
Enchanted Cottage B&B
Pacific Rest B&B

MOSIER
Hewett's B&B

NORTH BEND
Itty Bitty Inn B&B

PORTLAND
The Benson Hotel
Best Western Imperial Hotel
Fifth Avenue Suites Hotel
The Heathman Hotel
Historic Hotel Vintage Plaza
Mallory Historic Hotel
Sullivan's Gulch B&B

PRAIRIE CITY
Strawberry Mtn Inn B&B

PROSPECT
Prospect Historical Hotel

SALEM
Eagle Crest B&B

SANDY
Brookside B&B

SCAPPOOSE
Barnstormer B&B
Malarkey Ranch B&B

SEASIDE
The Guest House B&B

SISTERS
Rags to Walkers
Guest Ranch
Squaw Creek B&B

SOUTH BEACH
Solace by the Sea B&B

STAYTON
Gardner House B&B

SUBLIMITY
Silver Mountain B&B

SUMMER LAKE
Summer Lake Inn

SUMPTER
Sumpter B&B

THE DALLES
Captain Gray's Guest House

UNION
Angle Farm
Country Inn B&B

VALE
1900 Sears &
Roebuck Home

WELCHES
Old Welches Inn B&B

Complete listing information is located in the main directory section.

PENNSYLVANIA

ABBOTTSTOWN
The Inn at the
    Altland House

BENTON
The Red Poppy B&B

BLOOMSBURG
The Inn at Turkey Hill

EMLENTON
Whipple Tree
    Inn & Farm B&B

EPHRATA
Smithton Country Inn B&B

ERWINNA
Historic Golden Pheasant
    Country Inn

GLEN MILLS
Sweetwater Farm B&B

HONEY BROOK
Waynesbrook Inn B&B

INDIANA
Charbert Farm B&B

KEMPTON
Hawk Mt. Inn B&B

KINTNERSVILLE
Lightfarm Historic B&B

LIGONIER
Lady of the Lake B&B

LITITZ
General Sutter Country Inn

NEW HOPE
Aaron Burr House B&B
The Fox & Hound B&B
Wedgewood Inn B&B

PHILADELPHIA
Best Western
    Independence Park Inn
Four Seasons Hotel
1011 Clinton B&B
Park Hyatt Historic Hotel
The Rittenhouse Hotel

**POCONO
MOUNTAINS AREA**
Blue Berry Mountain
    Inn B&B (Blakeslee)
Falls Port Inn (Hawley)
Ridge House Historic
    B&B (Montrose)

PUNSUTAWNEY
Pantall Historic Hotel

SHICKSHINNY
The Blue Heron B&B

SOMERSET
Inn at Georgian Place B&B

STATE COLLEGE
Brewmeister's B&B Motel

STRASBURG
Historic Strasburg Inn

TURTLE CREEK
James Street B&B

WASHINGTON
Longstretch Harbour B&B

WELLSBORO
Foxfire B&B

WILLIAMSPORT
Genetti Historic Hotel

RHODE ISLAND

BLOCK ISLAND
Blue Dory Inn V&B
Eastgate House B&B

BRISTOL
Joseph Reynolds
    House Inn B&B

MIDDLETOWN
Bartram's B&B

NEWPORT
B&B International
Inn on Bellvue B&B
1 Murray House B&B
Sanford-Covell Villa
    Marina B&B
1751 Banister House

NORTH KINGSTOWN
The Wickford House B&B

PROVIDENCE
Providence Biltmore Hotel-
    A Grand Heritage Hotel

SOUTH KINGSTOWN
Captain's B&B
The Holly House B&B

WARWICK
Crowne Plaza Hotel
    at the Crossings

WESTERLY
The Villa Inn B&B

SOUTH CAROLINA

AIKEN
The Willcox Country Inn

CAMDEN
Lord Camden Inn B&B

CHARLESTON
Indigo Inn Historic B&B

LANDRUM
The Red Horse Inn Cottage

MT. PLEASANT
Guilds Inn Historic B&B

RIDGE SPRING
Southwood Manor B&B

ROCK HILL
Book & Spindle B&B

SOUTH DAKOTA

CANOVA
Skoglund Farm B&B

CUSTER
Black Hills Balloons B&B

CUSTER STATE PARK
Double L B&B & Horsecamp

GETTYSBURG
Harer Lodge B&B

HERMOSA
Hermosa Hills B&B

HOT SPRINGS
Mueller House B&B

INTERIOR
Cedar Pass Lodge Cottage

KEYSTONE
Bed & Breakfast Inn
Hillside Country Cottages

RAPID CITY
A Rose for Remembrance
    Country Inn

YANKTON
Mulberry Inn B&B

TENNESSEE

ALTAMONT
The Manor B&B
The Woodlee House B&B

ASHLAND CITY
Bird Song Country Inn & B&B

BLOUNTVILLE
Smith Haven B&B

BON AQUA
Morning Star Stables B&B

BRENTWOOD
English Manor B&B

CHATTANOOGA
Lookout Lake B&B

CLARKSVILLE
Southern Pines B&B

Complete listing information is located in the main directory section.

COLLEGE GROVE
Peacock Hill Country Inn B&B

DANDRIDGE
The Martha B&B
Mountain Harbor Inn B&B

DAYTON
The Magnolia House B&B

DICKSON
Inn on Main Street B&B

FAIRVIEW
Sweet Annie's
    Bed, Breakfast & Barn

FRANKLIN
Namaste Acres Barn B&B

FRANKWING
Hollow Pond Farm Bed, Barn
    & Breakfast (horses only)

GREENEVILLE
General Morgan Inn &
    Conference Center

HENDERSONVILLE
Morning Star B&B

HOHENWALD
Ridgetop B&B

JOHNSON CITY
Hart House B&B

LIMESTONE
Snapp Inn B&B

LINDEN
Avaleen Springs B&B

MONTEAGLE
Adams Edgeworth Inn

MT. JULIET
Natureview Inn B&B

NASHVILLE
Apple Brook Bed, Breakfast
    & Barn (horses only)
Hillsboro House B&B
Union Station Hotel

SEVIERVILLE
Camelot B&B

SHELBYVILLE
Olde Gore House B&B

TIPTONVILLE
Backyard Birds Lodge B&B

WALLAND
Twin Valley B&B Horse Ranch

WAVERLY
Nolan House B&B

TEXAS

ALPINE
The Corner House B&B
Historic Holland Hotel

AUBREY
The Guest House B&B

AUSTIN
The Brook House B&B
Four Seasons Hotel
Governor's Inn B&B

BANDERA
Cool Water Acres B&B

BASTROP
Pecan Street Inn B&B

BEAUMONT
Grand Duerr B&B

BLANCO
Creekwood Country Inn B&B

BOERNE
Boerne Lake
    Lodge B&B Resort

BRENHAM
Brenham House B&B

BROWNWOOD
Lake Brownwood B&B

CANYON
Country Home B&B

CENTER POINT
Marianne's B&B

CLIFTON
The River's Bend B&B

COMANCHE
Guest House-Heritage
    Hill B&B

COMFORT
Idlewilde B&B
Kleina Himmul B&B

CONROE
Heather's Glen B&B

DALLAS
Crescent Court Hotel
Grand Hotel
Hotel Crescent Court

DECATUR
Painted Valley Ranch B&B

EAGLE LAKE
The Farris 1912 Inn

EASTLAND
The Eastland B&B

ELGIN
Ragtime Ranch B&B

FORT DAVIS
Historic Limpia Hotel

FREDERICKSBURG
Alfred Haus B&B
Beckers Bed & Breakfast
    & Bicycles
The Garden House B&B
Miss Toodles Inn B&B
Rock House on Acorn B&B
Rocky Top B&B
Schmidt Barn B&B
Settlers Crossing
    Historic Guest Houses
Strackbein-Roeder
    Sunday Haus B&B
Watkins Hill-Fredericksburg
    Guest House
West Main Haus B&B
Wolf Creek Barn B&B

GLEN ROSE
Country Woods Inn B&B
Hideaway Country
    Log Cabin B&B

HALLETTSVILLE
Aunt Carol's B&B

HAMILTON
Hamilton Guest Hotel B&B

HASKELL
Bevers House on Brick St B&B

HOUSTON
Four Seasos Hotel-
    Houston Center
The Lancaster Hotel
The Lovett Inn-B&B
Robin's Nest B&B Inn

IRVING
Four Seasons Resort & Club

JOHNSON CITY
Dream Catcher B&B

KERRVILLE
Dietert Haus B&B
La Reata Ranch B&B
Turtle Creek Lodge

LEAKEY
Whiskey Mountain Inn B&B

LLANO
The Badu House Historic B&B

LUCKENBACH
The Luckenbach Inn B&B

MARSHALL
La Maison Malfacon
    Country Inn
Meredith House B&B

MOUNT PLEASANT
Tankersley Gardens B&B

Complete listing information is located in the main directory section.

TEXAS
(CONTINUED)

NACOGDOCHES
Eagle's Aerie B&B
The Fredonia Hotel
Hardeman Guest House-B&B

NEW BRAUNFELS
Kuebler-Waldrip Haus B&B

RAINBOW
Rainbow's End B&B

ROCKPORT
Anthony's by the Sea B&B

ROUND TOP
Round Top Inn B&B

SAN ANTONIO
A Blansett Barn Guest House
Arbor House Inn & Suites B&B
Hyatt Regency
   Hill Country Resort
O'Caseys B&B
Painted Lady Inn on
   Broadway B&B
Plaza San Antonio Hotel

SAN BENITO
Vieh's B&B

SAN MARCOS
Lonesome Dove B&B

SMITHVILLE
The Katy House B&B

SWEETWATER
Mulberry Mansion B&B

TEXARKANA
House of Wadley

UNCERTAIN
Mossy Brake Lodge B&B
Spatterdock Guest House

WAXAHACHIE
Bonnynook Inn B&B

WIMBERLEY
Homestead B&B
Lonesome Dove River
   Inn at Cliffside B&B
Singing Cypress Gardens
Southwind B&B Inn & Cabins

WINNSBORO
Thee Hubbel House B&B

UTAH

AMERICAN FORK
American Fork B&B

CANNONDALE
Galloping Tortoise B&B

EDEN
Snowberry Inn B&B

ESCALANTE
Rainbow Country B&B

GARDEN CITY
Eagle Feather Inn B&B

HURRICANE
Pah Tempe Hot Springs
   Resort B&B

KANAB
Brandon Motel B&B

MEXICAN HAT
Valley of the Gods B&B

MOAB
Heather Lane B&B
Pioneer Springs B&B

OGDEN
Historic Radisson Suite
   & Hotel

PANGUITCH
Jolly House B&B

ROCKVILLE
Blue House B&B

ST. GEORGE
An Olde Penny Farthing
   Inn B&B
Coyote Inn at
   Green Valley Spa

SALT LAKE CITY
Red Brick Inn B&B
Log Cabin on the Hill B&B

SPRING CITY
Horseshoe Mountain B&B

SPRINGDALE
Canyon Vista B&B

TOQUERVILLE
Your Inn B&B

VERMONT

ADDISON
Whitford House Inn

ALBURG
Ye Olde Graystone B&B

ANDOVER
The Inn at High View

BETHEL
Greenhurst Historical Inn
Poplar Manor B&B

BRANDON
Gingerbread House
   Fine Arts B&B
Hivue B&B Tree Farm

BRATTLEBORO
40 Putney Road B&B

BRISTOL
Firefly Ranch B&B

BROWNSVILLE
Burton Farm Lodge B&B
Millbrook B&B
The Pond House at
   Shattuck Hill Farm B&B

BURKE
Old Time B&B

BURLINGTON
Sheraton Hotel & Conf Ctr

CRAFTSBURY COMMON
The Inn on the Common

FAIRLEE
Silver Maple Lodge
   & Cottages B&B

FRANKLIN
Fair Meadows Farm B&B

JAMAICA
Three Mountain Inn

JERICHO
Homeplace B&B

LONDONDERRY
Frog's Leap Inn

LUDLOW
The Combes Family Inn

MENDON
Red Clover Country Inn

MIDDLEBURY
Fairhill B&B
Middlebury B&B
Middlebury Country Inn

NEWFANE
Four Columns Inn
West River Lodge & Stables

ORLEANS
WilloughVale Inn

ORWELL
Buckswood B&B

PERKINSVILLE
Gwendolyn's B&B Inn

POULTNEY
Stonebridge Inn B&B

PUTNEY
Putney Inn

READING
Bailey's Mill B&B

RICHMOND
Mama Bowers B&B

ROCHESTER
Harvey's Mtn. View
   Inn & Farm

Complete listing information is located in the main directory section.

ST. ALBANS
Old Mill River Place B&B

SHOREHAM
Indian Trail Farm B&B

SOUTH WOODSTOCK
Kedron Valley Historic Inn

STARKSBORO
Millhouse B&B

STOCKBRIDGE
Chase Inn B&B

STOWE
Andersen Lodge
    An Austrian Inn
Edson Hill View B&B
1860 House B&B
Green Mountain Country Inn
Honeywood Country
    Lodge & Inn
Inn at Turner Mill B&B
Miguel's Stowe Away B&B Inn
Raspberry Patch B&B
Ski Inn
Ten Acres Lodge Country Inn
Topnotch at Stowe Resort
Walkabout Creek Lodge B&B

SWANTON
Country Essence B&B

TAFTSVILLE
Applebutter Inn B&B

TOWNSEND
Boardman House B&B

UNDERHILL
4 Pause B&B

WAITSFIELD
Millbrook Inn

WATERBURY
The Old Stagecoach Inn B&B

WESTON
Darling Family Inn

WILLIAMSTOWN
Autumn Harvest Country Inn

WILLISTON
Old Time B&B

WILMINGTON
Inn at Quail Run B&B

WOODSTOCK
Three Church Street B&B
The Winslow House B&B

VIRGINIA

ALEXANDRIA
Classic B&B

AMHERST
Fairview B&B

BERRYVILLE
Blue Ridge B&B Reservations

BLACKSTONE
Epes House B&B

BOWLING GREEN
Mansion View B&B

BOYDTON
Southern Heritage B&B

BRANDY STATION
Blue Haven B&B

BURGESS
Bailey-Cockrell House B&B

CALLAO
Strangers In Good
    Company B&B

CHAMPLAIN
Linden House B&B Plantation

CHINCOTEAGUE
Main Street House B&B

COVINGTON
Milton Hall B&B Inn

CROZET
Yancy Mills B&B

FERRUM
Old Spring Farm B&B

GORDONSVILLE
Norfields Farm B&B
Rocklands B&B
Sleepy Hollow Farm B&B

GOSHEN
The Hummingbird Inn

HARDYSVILLE
River's Rise B&B

LOUISA
Ginger Hill B&B

MANASSAS
Sunrise Hill Farm B&B

MONTEREY
Bobbie's B&B

MOUNT JACKSON
The Widow Kip's Country Inn

NEW CHURCH
The Garden & The Sea B&B

PETERSBURG
The High Street Inn B&B

PUNGOTEAGUE
Pungoteague Jct B&B

RINER
River's Edge B&B

SCOTTSVILLE
High Meadows Vineyard &
    Mountain Sunset Inn

SMITHFIELD
Four Square Plantation B&B
Mansion on Main B&B

SPERRYVILLE
The Conyers House B&B

SPOTSYLVANIA
Roxbury Mill B&B

STAUNTON
Ashton Country House B&B

STRASBURG
Hotel Strasburg

TROUTDALE
Fox Hill Inn B&B

VIRGINIA BEACH
Lotus Pond B&B

WARM SPRINGS
Anderson Cottage B&B

WILLIS WHARF
Ballard House B&B

YORKTOWN
Marl Inn B&B

WASHINGTON

ANACORTES
Old Brook Inn B&B

BAINBRIDGE ISLAND
Bainbridge Inn B&B
Frog Rock Inn B&B
Monarch Manor B&B

BLAINE
The Inn at Semi-Ah-Moo

CHELAN
Brickhouse Inn B&B

CLALLAM BAY
Winter's Summer Inn B&B

CLARKSTON
Highland House B&B

COLVILLE
Maple at Sixth B&B

DAYTON
The Purple House B&B
The Weinhard Historic Hotel

DEER PARK
Love's Victorian B&B

Complete listing information is located in the main directory section.

WASHINGTON
(CONTINUED)

DEMING
The Guest House B&B

EDMONDS
Hudgens Haven B&B

FIR ISLAND
South Fork Moorage B&B

FORKS
Hoh Humm Ranch B&B
Manitou Lodge B&B
Mill Creek Inn B&B
Miller Tree Inn B&B

GIG HARBOR
Harborside B&B
No Cabbages B&B

HANSVILLE
Guest House at
Twin Spits B&B

HOME VALLEY
Home Valley B&B

INDEX
The Cabin at Index B&B

ISSAQUAH
Mountains & Plains B&B

KENNEWICK
Casablanca B&B

KINGSTON
Kingston House B&B

LA CONNER
Art's Place B&B

LAKE BAY
Ransom's Pond
Ostrich Farm B&B

LAKE CRESCENT
Lake Crescent Lodge Resort

LEAVENWORTH
Phippen's B&B

MAPLE FALLS
Yodeler Inn B&B

MOUNT VERNON
Whispering Firs B&B

NACHES
Apple Country B&B

NAHCOTTA
Our House in Nahcotta/
Oysterville B&B

OLALLA
Olalla Orchard B&B

OLYMPIA
The Cinnamon Rabbit B&B

POINT ROBERTS
Cedar House Inn B&B

PORT ANGELES
Elwha Ranch B&B
Maple Rose Inn B&B

PORT ORCHARD
Cedar Hollow
Guest House B&B

PORT TOWNSEND
Annapurna Inn B&B
Bishop Victorian
Guest Suites
The Palace Hotel
Water Street Hotel

RENTON
B&B Association of
Suburban Seattle

SAN JUAN ISLAND
Blair House B&B
Halvorsen House B&B
Tucker House B&B
Westwinds B&B
Wharfside B&B on the
Jacqueline

SEABECK
Summer Song B&B

SEATTLE
The Alexis Hotel
B&B on Broadway
Beech Tree
Manor Inn B&B
Bellevue Place B&B
Four Seasons
Olympic Hotel
Pargardens B&B
Pensione Nicholas B&B

SEQUIM
Groveland Cottage B&B
Rancho Lamro B&B

SHELTON
Restfull Farm B&B

SNOHOMISH
Snohomish
Grand Hotel B&B

SNOQUALMIE
Salish Lodge & Spa

SOUTH BEND
The Russell House B&B

TACOMA
Hidden Maple B&B

VASHON ISLAND
Angels of the Sea B&B
Castle Hill B&B

WALLA WALLA
Sicyon Gallery B&B

WENATCHEE
Forget Me Not B&B

WESTPORT
Glenacres Inn B&B

WHIDBEY ISLAND
The Victorian   B&B
(Coupeville)
Drake's Landing B&B (Langley)
Island Tyme B&B (Langley)

WHITE SALMON
Inn of the
White Salmon B&B

YELM
Log House B&B

WEST VIRGINIA

FAYETTEVILLE

White House B&B

LEWISBURG
General Lewis Inn

WHITE SULPHUR SPRINGS
The James Wylie House

WISCONSIN

ALLENTON
Addison House B&B

ALMA
Tritsch House B&B

BARABOO
Garden Gate B&B
Sunset Resort B&B

BAYFIELD
Apple Tree Inn B&B
Morning Glory B&B

CAMBRIDGE
Bison Trail B&B

CAMPBELLS-PORT
Mielke-Mauk House B&B

CASCADE
Timberlake Inn B&B

CROSS PLAINS
BBB Farm B&B

EAST TROY
Mitten Farm B&B

FERRYVILLE
Missississpi
Humble Bush B&B

GILLS ROCK
Harbor House Inn

HUDSON
Escape by the Lake B&B
Jefferson Day House B&B

KEWASKUM
Country Ridge Inn B&B
The Doctors Inn B&B

LA POINTE
Woods Manor B&B

LAC DU FLAMBEAU
Ty-Bach B&B

LAKE GENEVA
General Boyd's B&B
Roses B&B
T C Smith Historic Inn B&B

LANCASTER
Martha's B&B

LODI
Prairie Garden B&B

MADISON
Collins House B&B

MENOMONIE
Bolo Country Inn B&B

MERRILL
Brick House B&B

MILTON
Chase on the Hill B&B

MILWAUKIE
The Acanthus Inn B&B

MONROE
Ludlow Mansion B&B

MONTELLO
TNT Horse Ranch B&B

PLYMOUTH
52 Stafford An Irish
   Guest House B&B
Harmony Hills In The
   Hollow B&B

**PORT
WASHINGTON**
The Grand Inn B&B

RICHLAND CENTER
Littledale B&B

ST. GERMAIN
St. Germain B&B

SPRING GREEN
The Silver Star B&B
   Country Inn

STURGEON BAY
Nautical Inn B&B
Pembroke Inn B&B

WAUPACA
Windmill Manor B&B

WAUSAUKEE
Hotel Wausaukee B&B

WESTFIELD
Martha's Ethnic B&B

WHITE LAKE
Jesse's Historic
   Wolf River Lodge

WISCONSIN DELLS
Thunder Valley Inn B&B

WYOMING

AFTON
The Rocking P B&B

ATLANTIC CITY
Miner's Delight B&B

BEULAH
Windy Acres Ranch B&B

BIG HORN
Bozeman Trail B&B

CHEYENNE
A Drummond's Ranch B&B
Adventurers Country B&B
Bit-O-Wyo Ranch B&B
   (horses only)
Howdy Pardners B&B
Nagle Warren Mansion B&B
Porch Swing B&B
Rainsford Inn B&B
Windy Hills Guest House B&B

CLEARMONT
RBL Bison Ranch B&B

CODY
House of Burgess B&B
Question Creek B&B

DOUGLAS
Carriage House B&B

ENCAMPMENT
Rustic Mountain Lodge B&B

GUERNSEY
Annette's B&B

HULETT
Pine Ridge Ranch B&B

JACKSON
Twin Mountain River Ranch
B&B

KAYCEE
Graves B&B

LANDER
Bunk House B&B
Cottage House at
   Squaw Creek B&B
Piece of Cake B&B

LARAMIE
Norman House B&B
Prairie Breeze B&B

LUSK
Sage & Cactus Village
   Tepee B&B

MANDERSON
Harmony Ranch Cottage B&B

PINEDALE
The Chambers House B&B
Pole Creek Ranch B&B
Window on the Winds B&B

RANCHESTER
Historic Old Stone House B&B

RIVERTON
Cottonwood Ranch B&B

SARATOGA
Brooksong B&B

SHELL
Hap's Trapper Creek B&B
Trapper's Rest B&B

SHERIDAN
Foothills Ranch B&B
Ranch Willow B&B

**TETON
VILLAGE**
Sassy Moose Inn B&B

THERMOPOLIS
Broadway Inn B&B

WHEATLAND
Blackbird Inn B&B
Homestead B&B

Complete listing information is located in the main directory section.

TRAVEL NOTES

CANADIAN DIRECTORY OF PET-FRIENDLY LODGING

TRAVELING BETWEEN THE UNITED STATES AND CANADA

Dogs and cats

If you intend to travel into Canada with either a dog or a cat, your animal must have a certificate signed by a licensed veterinarian. This certificate must clearly describe the animal and validate that the animal has been vaccinated against rabies within the past 36 months. The certificate will also be needed for your animal's re-entry into the United States. Make certain that the rabies vaccination does not expire while you're touring Canada. Exemptions from this rule: Seeing eye dogs, puppies and kittens under three months, provided they are healthy at the time of importation.

Passports and proof of citizenship

United States citizens are not required to have a passport to enter Canada or return to the United States. Proof of citizenship in the form of a birth certificate, voter's certificate or baptismal certificate are normally all you'll need. If you're a naturalized citizen, carry your naturalization papers. U.S. resident aliens must have an Alien Registration Receipt Card. If minors are traveling with you, or on their own, they must present a notarized letter of consent signed by both parents or guardians in addition to providing proof of citizenship.

You should know that Canadian customs can stop a person traveling with a minor from entering Canada if customs has been advised that a divorced or separated parent is attempting to cross the border with a minor child without the written permission of the absent parent.

The Canadian GST

Beginning January 1, 1991, the Canadian government established a 7% Goods and Services Tax (GST) which is levied on most items sold and most services rendered. Non-Canadians may apply for a rebate on many items, among them short-term accommodations. There is a minimum rebate claim of $7 and evidence of purchase is required. Penalties apply and vary by province and territory. Be prepared and avoid penalties and delays.

Brochures explaining the GST and containing a rebate form are available in Canada at the land border as well as in airport duty-free shops, information centers, custom offices and many individual hotels. For additional information, write: Revenue Canada, Visitor Rebate Program, Summerside Tax Centre, Summerside, PE, Canada C1N 6C6; phone (902) 432-5608 or call (800) 668-4748 toll-free in Canada.

Personal baggage may be brought into Canada on a temporary basis without payment of duties and taxes. Infrequently, a refundable security deposit may be required by customs at the time of your entry. All items brought into the country must accompany you on your departure.

Personal baggage can include clothing, personal effects, sporting goods, cars, vessels, aircraft, snowmobiles, cameras, food products and those items that would be considered appropriate for the purpose and length of your stay.

There are some limitations as follows: Tobacco products are limited to 50 cigars, 200 cigarettes and 400 grams (14 oz.) of tobacco per person. Alcoholic beverages are limited to 1.14 litres (40 oz.) of liquor or wine or 8.5 litres (300 oz.) of beer or ale, (the equivalent of 24 bottles/cans). A minimum stay of 24 hours is normally required when transporting liquor or tobacco products into Canada.

Liquor and tobacco products exceeding the allowable quantities are subject to federal duty and taxes as well as provincial liquor fees. In addition, you must be 18 or 19 (depending on the province or territory) to bring alcohol into Canada and be at least 16 to import tobacco and related products.

Gifts

With the exception of tobacco, alcoholic beverages and advertising matter, gifts taken into or mailed to Canada are allowed free entry as long as the value of the gift doesn't exceed $60 (Canadian currency). Gifts with a higher value are subject to duty and taxes on the excess amount.

Plants and fruits

House plants may be admitted into Canada. Other plants and plant material need a permit from Agriculture Canada and a state or federal phytosanitary certificate obtained from the plant health authority of origin.

Fresh fruits and vegetables not typically grown in Canada, i.e., tropical and subtropical items, may be imported. However, they may be inspected by a plant health inspector at the time of entry. Fresh fruit and vegetables commonly grown in Canada, may be refused entry, depending on the original and final destination of the fruits or vegetables. For further information, contact the Plant Health Division, Food Production and Inspection Branch, Agriculture Canada, Ottawa, ON, Canada K1A 0C6.

Employment of visitors

Without employment authorization prior to entry into Canada, employment of visitors is not permitted. In order to secure employment, a permit for a specific job for a specific period of time must be obtained from the Canadian Department of Manpower and Immigration. You will be denied entry into Canada if it is your intention to finance your visit by seeking a paying job.

U.S. Customs regulations

Exemptions granted to returning residents of the United States include a $400 exemption if not used within the prior 30 days for residents who have been in Canada no less than 48 hours. Based on retail value, the exemptions apply only to goods acquired for personal or household use or as gifts - not intended for resale. Exemptions for a family can be combined, i.e. a family of four would be entitled to a $1,600 duty-free exemption on one declaration even if the articles declared by one member of the family exceeded that individual's $400 exemption.

Evidence of retail value will be needed. Keep all sales slips. The goods for which the exemption is claimed must be with you at the time of re-entry.

You can also send gifts to friends and relatives in the United States free of duty and taxes. However, the retail value of any one gift may not exceed more than $40. Only one gift per day can be received by any one recipient. Tobacco products, alcoholic beverages and perfume containing alcohol with a value of more than $5 retail are excluded from this provision. The package containing the gift must be marked "Unsolicited Gift" and include the contents and retail value on the outside of the package. These gifts are not considered part of your $400 exemption. You do not have to declare them upon your return to the United States.

If you qualify for the $400 exemption, you may include 100 cigars and 200 cigarettes duty free. Cigarettes may be subject to state or local tax. If you're over 21, you may include 1 litre in your $400 exemption from tax and duty. In all cases, state liquor laws are enforced by customs.

When your stay in Canada has been less than 48 hours, you may return with duty and tax free merchandise that has a maximum value of $25. This exemption must not include more than 50 cigarettes, 10 cigars, 150 millilitres of alcohol or 150 millilitres of perfume containing alcohol. Members of a family unit may NOT combine their purchases under this exemption. All goods must be declared.

National Park entrance fees

Daily or annual permits are available for visiting Canada's National Parks. The entrance fees vary according to the park and the age of the visitor. The annual permit admits a vehicle and all occupants to all national parks. The daily permit is valid only on the date of purchase.

The main number for Canadian National Park information is (888) 773-8888. The PARKS CANADA NATIONAL OFFICE address is 25 Eddy Street, Hull, Quebec, Canada K1A 0M5 . The website for the Canadian National Parks is very informative and gives rates for all the parks. You can access it at http://www.parkscanada.gc.ca.

FOR YOUR INFORMATION:

Seat Belts: The use of seat belts is mandatory in all vehicles traveling in or through Canada.

Radar Detectors: The possession and use of radar detection devices is illegal in Manitoba, Newfoundland, Northwest Territories, Ontario, Prince Edward Island, Quebec and Yukon Territory.

Currency: Prices and admission fees are in Canadian dollars. It is financially advantageous to use Canadian currency when traveling in Canada. You can obtain the official exchange rate of U.S. funds at a bank in Canada or purchase traveler's checks in Canadian currency.

Legal Questions: Persons with felony convictions, DWI's or other offenses may be denied entry into Canada. For further info, contact the Department of Citizenship and Immigration at (613) 995-6486 or call (888) 242-2100 toll-free inside Canada. For additional information refer to: http://www.cic.gc.ca.

ALBERTA

AIRDRIE

SUPER 8 MOTEL
815 E Lake Blvd
(T4B 2A2)
(403) 948-4188
(800) 800-8000

ATHABASCA

**BEST WESTERN
ATHABASCA INN**
5211 41 Ave
(T9S 1A5)
(780) 675-2294
(800) 528-1234
(800) 567-5718

BANFF

**BEST WESTERN
SIDING 29 LODGE**
453 Marten St
(T0L 0C0)
(403) 762-5575
(800) 528-1234

**CANADIAN
PACIFIC BANFF
SPRINGS HOTEL**
405 Spray Ave
(403) 762-2211
(800) 441-1414

**CASTLE MTN
VILLAGE**
Box 1655 (T0L
0C0)
(403) 762-3868

**JOHNSTON
CANYON RESORT**
Hwy 1A
(403) 762-2971

PTARMIGAN INN
337 Banff Ave
(403) 762-2207

RED CARPET INN
425 Banff Ave
(T0L 0C0)
(403) 762-4184

**ROCKY
MOUNTAIN
RESORT**
1029 Banff Ave
(403) 762-5531

BROOKS

**THE DOUGLAS
COUNTRY INN**
Hwy 873 (T0J 0J0)
(403) 362-2873

HERITAGE INN
1303 2nd St W
(403) 362-6666

SUPER 8 MOTEL
1240 Cassils Rd E
(T1R 1B6)
(403) 362-8000
(800) 800-8000

CALGARY

**BEST WESTERN
AIRPORT INN**
1947 18th Ave NE
(T2E 7T8)
(403) 250-5015
(800) 528-1234

**BEST WESTERN
HOSPITALITY
INN**
135 Southland Dr
SE (T2J 5X5)
(403) 278-5050
(800) 528-1234
(877) 278-5050

**BEST WESTERN
SUITES
DOWNTOWN**
1330 8 St SW
(T2R 1B6)
(403) 228-6900
(800) 528-1234
(800) 981-2555

**BEST WESTERN
VILLAGE PARK
INN**
1804 Crowchild
Trail NW (T2M
3Y7)
(403) 289-0241
(800) 528-1234
(888) 774-7716

BLACKFOOT INN
5940 Blackfoot
Trail
SE (T2H 2B5)
(403) 252-2253
(800) 661-1151

**CALGARY
WESTWAYS
GUEST HOUSE**
216 25th Ave SW
(403) 229-1758

**CARRIAGE
HOUSE INN**
9030 MacLeod
Trail
S (T2H 0M4)
(403) 253-1101
(800) 661-9566

**THE COAST
PLAZA HOTEL**
1316 33rd St NE
(403) 248-8888

DAYS INN WEST
1818 16th Ave
NW (T2M 0L8)
(403) 289-1961
(800) 329-7466

**DELTA BOW
VALLEY HOTEL**
209 4th Ave SE
(T2G 0C6)
(403) 266-1980
(800) 268-1133

ECONO LODGE
2231 Banff Trail
(T2M 4L2)
(403) 289-1921
(800) 553-2666

**ECONO LODGE
WEST**
101 St & Trans-
Canada Hwy 1
W (T2M 4N3)
(403) 288-4436
(800) 553-2666

**ELBOW RIVER
INN & CASINO**
1919 Macleod
Trail SE
(403) 269-6771

**GREENWOOD
INN HOTEL**
3515 26th St NE
(403) 250-8855

**HOLIDAY INN
AIRPORT**
1250 McKinnon
Dr NE (T2E 7T7)
(403) 230-1999
(800) 465-4329

**HOLIDAY INN
DOWNTOWN**
119 12th Ave SW
(T2R 2G8)
(403) 266-4611
(800) 465-4329

**HOLIDAY INN
EXPRESS
UNIVERSITY**
2227 Banff Trail
NW
(T2M 4L2)
(403) 289-6600
(800) 465-4329

**THE PALLISER
FAIRMONT
HOTEL/RESORT**
133 9th Ave SW
(403) 262-1234
(800) 527-4727

**QUALITY HOTEL
& CONF CENTRE**
3828 Macleod
Trail (T2G 2R2)
(403) 243-5531
(800) 228-5151

**QUALITY INN
AIRPORT**
4804 Edmonton
Tr
NE (T2E 3V2)
(403) 276-3391
(800) 228-5151

**QUALITY INN
MOTEL VILLAGE**
2359 Banff Trail
NW
(T2M 4L2)
(403) 289-1973
(800) 228-5151

**RADISSON
HOTEL AIRPORT**
2120 16th Ave NE
(403) 291-4666
(800) 333-3333

RAMADA HOTEL
708 8th Ave SW
(T2P 1H2)
(403) 263-7600
(800) 272-6232
(800) 661-8684

**RAMADA
CROWCHILD INN**
5353 Crowchild
Tr NW (T3A
1W9)
(403) 288-5353
(800) 272-6232

**SUPER 8 MOTEL
AIRPORT**
3030 BarlowTrail
NE
(T1Y 1A2)
(403) 291-9888
(800) 800-8000

**SUPER 8 MOTEL
NORTHWEST**
1904 Crowchild
Tr NW (T2M
3Y7)
(403) 289-9211
(800) 800-8000

SUPER 8 MOTEL
60 Shawville
SE (T2R 1J4)
(403) 254-8878
(800) 800-8000

TRAVELODGE
2750 Sunridge
Blvd NE
(T1Y3C2)
(403) 291-1260
(800) 578-7878

TRAVELODGE
9206 MacLeod
Trail S
(T2J 0P5)
(403) 253-7070
(800) 578-7878

WESTIN HOTEL
320 4th Ave SW
(T2P 2S6)
(403) 266-1611
(800) 228-3000

CAMROSE

TRAVELODGE
6216 48th Ave
(T4V 0K6)
(780) 672-3377
(800) 578-7878

CANMORE

**BANFF
BOUNDARY
LODGE**
1000 Harvie Hgts
Rd
(403) 678-9555

**BEST WESTERN
GREEN GABLES
INN**
1602 2nd Ave
(T1W 1M8)
(403) 678-5488
(800) 528-1234
(800) 661-2133

**BEST WESTERN
POCATERRA INN**
1725 Mountain
Ave
(T1W 2W1)
(403) 678-4334
(800) 528-1234
(888) 678-6786

**HOWARD
JOHNSON**
1402 Bow Valley
Trail (T1W 1N5)
(403) 609-4656
(800) 446-4656

**RADISSON
HOTEL
& CONF CENTRE**
511 Bow Valley Tr
(403) 678-3625
(800) 333-3333

**RUNDLE MTN
MTL/GUESTHAUS**
1723 Bow Valley
Trail
(403) 678-5322

**RUNDLE RIDGE
CHALETS**
1100 Harvie
Hghts Rd
(403) 678-5387

**THE STOCKADE
LOG CABINS**
1050 Harvie
Hghts Rd
(403) 678-5212

CARDSTON

**FLAMINGO
MOTEL**
848 Main St S
(403) 653-3952

**HOWARD
JOHNSON
EXPRESS INN**
37 8th Ave W
(T0K 0K0)
(403) 653-4481
(800) 446-4656

CLARESHOLM

BLUEBIRD MOTEL
5505 Main St S
(T0L 0T0)
(403) 625-3395
(800) 661-4891

COCHRANE

BOW RIVER INN
3 Westside Dr
(403) 932-7900

COLD LAKE

**NEW FRONTIER
MOTEL**
1002 8th Ave
(780) 639-3030

DEAD MAN'S FLATS

**PIGEON MTN
MOTEL**
250 1st Ave
(403) 678-5756

DIDSBURY

SUPER 8 MOTEL
1714 20th Ave
(T0M 0W0)
(403) 335-8088
(800) 800-8000

DRAYTON VALLEY

SUPER 8 MOTEL
3727 50th St
(T7A 1S4)
(780) 542-9122
(800) 800-8000

DRUMHELLER

**BEST WESTERN
JURASSIC INN**
1103 Hwy 9 S
(T0J 0Y0)
(403) 823-7700
(800) 528-1234
(888) 823-3466

SUPER 8 MOTEL
600 - 680 2nd St
SE (T0J 0Y0)
(403) 823-8887
(800) 800-8000
(888) 823-8882

EDMONTON

**ALBERTA PLAZA
SUITE HOTEL**
10049 103rd St
(780) 423-1565

**ARGYLL
PLAZA HOTEL**
9933 63rd Ave
(T6E 6C9)
(780) 438-5876
(800) 661-6454

**BEST WESTERN
CEDAR PARK INN**
5116 Calgary Tr
N (T6H 2H4)
(780) 434-7411
(800) 528-1234
(800) 661-9461

**BEST WESTERN
CITY CENTRE INN**
11310 - 109 St
(T5G 2T7)
(780) 479-2042
(800) 666-5026

**CHATEAU LOUIS
HTL & CONF CTR**
11727 Kingsway
(T5G 3A1)
(780) 452-7770
(800) 661-9843

COMFORT INN
17610 100th Ave
(T5S 1S9)
(780) 484-4415
(800) 228-5150

**CROWNE PLAZA
CHATEAU
LACOMBE**
10111 Bellamy Hill
(T5J 1N7)
(780) 428-6611
(800) 227-6963

DAYS INN
10041 106 St
(T5J 1G3)
(780) 423-1925
(800) 329-7466

**DELTA
EDMONTON
CENTRE SUITE
HOTEL**
10222 102nd St
(780) 429-3900

**DELTA
EDMONTON
SOUTH HOTEL
& CONF CENTRE**
4404 Calgary Tr
(780) 434-6415

ECONO LODGE
4009 Calgary
Trail N (T6J 5H2)
(780) 435-4877
(800) 553-2666

ECONO LODGE
10209 100th Ave
(T5J 0A1)
(780) 428-6442
(800) 553-2666

EDMONTON INN
11830 Kingsway
Ave
(780) 454-9521

**HOLIDAY INN
& CONV CENTRE**
4520 76th Ave
(T6B 0A5)
(780) 468-5400
(800) 465-4329

**HOLIDAY INN
EXPRESS**
10017 179A St
(T5S 2L7)
(780) 483-4000
(800) 465-4329

**HOLIDAY INN
THE PALACE**
4235 Calgary Tr N
(T6J 5H2)
(780) 438-1222
(800) 465-4329

**HOTEL
MACDONALD**
10065 100th St
(780) 424-5181

**HOWARD
JOHNSON
PLAZA HOTEL**
10010-104 St
(T5J 0Z1)
(780) 423-2450
(800) 446-4656

**MAYFIELD INN
& SUITES**
16615 109 Ave
(T5P 4K8)
(780) 484-0821

**RAMADA INN
& CONF CENTRE**
11834 Kingsway
Ave (T56 3J5)
(780) 454-5454
(800) 272-6232

RODEWAY INN
10425 100th Ave
(T5J 0A3)
(780) 423-5611
(800) 228-2000

TRAVELODGE
10320 45th Ave S
(T6H 5K3)
(780) 436-9770
(800) 578-7878

**TRAVELODGE
BEVERLY CREST**
3414 118th Ave
(T5W 0Z4)
(780) 474-0456
(800) 578-7878

**TRAVELODGE-
WEST**
18320 Stony Plain
Rd (T5S 1A7)
(780) 483-6031
(800) 661-9563

WESTIN HOTEL
10135 100th St
(T5J 0N7)
(780) 426-3636
(800) 228-3000

EDSON

**BEST WESTERN
HIGH ROAD INN**
300 52nd St
(T7V 1E8)
(780) 712-2378
(800) 528-1234
(888) 895-1444

FORT MACLEOD

SUNSET MOTEL
104 Hwy 3W
(403) 553-4448

FORT MCMURRAY

BEST WESTERN NOMAD INN
10006 MacDonald Ave (T9H 1S8)
(800) 528-1234

TRAVELODGE HOTEL
9713 Hardin St (T9H 1L2)
(780) 743-3301
(800) 578-7878

FORT SASKATCHEWAN

BEST WESTERN FORT INN & SUITES
10115 88th Ave (T8L 2T3)
(780) 998-7888
(800) 528-1234
(877) 998-7493

GRAND PRAIRIE

SERVICE PLUS INNS & SUITES
10810 107th A Ave
(780) 538-3900

STANFORD INN
11401 100th Ave
(780) 539-5678

SUPER 8 MOTEL
10050 116th Ave (T8V 4K5)
(780) 532-8288
(800) 800-8000

HANNA

BEST WESTERN HANA INN
113 Palleser Tr (T0J 1P0)
(403) 854-2400
(800) 528-1234
(888) 854-2401

HINTON

CRESTWOOD HOTEL
678 Carmichael Lane
(780) 865-4001

HOLIDAY INN
393 Gregg Ave (T7V 1N1)
(780) 865-3321
(800) 465-4329

PINES MOTEL
709 Gregg Ave (T7X 1X6)
(780) 865-2624

RAMADA LIMITED SUITES
500 Smith St (T7V 2A1)
(780) 865-2575
(800) 272-6232

SUPER 8 MOTEL
284 Smith St (T7V 2A1)
(780) 817-2228
(800) 800-8000

JASPER

JASPER INN
98 Geikie St
(780) 852-4461

JASPER PARK LODGE
Lodge Road
(780) 852-3301

LOBSTICK LODGE
94 Geikie St (T0E 1E0)
(780) 852-4431
(800) 661-9317

MARMOT LODGE
86 Connaught Dr (T0E 1E0)
(780) 852-4471
(800) 661-6521

PATRICIA LAKE BUNGALOWS
Pyramid Lake Rd
(780) 852-3560

SUNWAPTA FALLS RESORT
Hwy 93
(780) 852-4852

TEKARRA LODGE
Hwy 93 A
(780) 852-3058

KANANASKIS

DELTA LODGE
Kananaskis Village
(403) 591-7711

LAKE LOUISE

CHATEAUX LAKE LOUISE
111 Lake Louise Dr (T0L 1E0)
(403) 522-3511
(800) 441-1414

LAKE LOUISE INN
P. O. Box 209 (T0L 1E0)
(800) 661-9237

LEDUC

SUPER 8 MOTEL
8004 Sparrow Crescent
(780) 986-8898
(800) 800-8000

TRAVELODGE
5704 50th St (T9E 6J4)
(780) 986-2264
(800) 578-7878

LETHBRIDGE

DAYS INN
100 3rd Ave S (T1J 4L2)
(403) 327-6000
(800) 329-7466

ECONO LODGE
1124 Mayor McGrath Dr S (T1K 2P8)
(403) 328-5591
(800) 553-2666

EL RANCHO TRAVELODGE MOTOR HOTEL
526 Mayor Magrath Dr (T1J 3M2)
(403) 327-5701
(800) 578-7878

LETHBRIDGE LODGE
320 Scenic Dr
(403) 328-1123

PEPPER TREE INN
1142 Mayor Magrath Dr (T1K 2P8)
(403) 328-4436

QUALITY INN
1030 Mayor Magrath Dr (T1K 2P8)
(403) 328-6636
(800) 228-5151

RAMADA HOTEL & SUITES
2375 Mayor Magrath Dr (T1K 7M1)
(403) 380-5050
(800) 272-6232

SUPER 8 MOTEL
2210 7th Ave S (T1J 1M7)
(403) 329-0100
(800) 800-8000

LLOYD-MINSTER

TROPICAL INN
5621 44th St (T9V 0B2)
(780) 875-7000

WAYSIDE INN
5411 44th St
(780) 875-4404

WEST HARVEST INN
5620 44th St (T9V 0B6)
(780) 875-6113

MEDICINE HAT

BEST WESTERN INN
722 Redcliff Dr (T1A 5E3)
(403) 527-3700
(800) 528-1234

DAYS INN
3216 13th Ave SE (T1B 1H8)
(403) 526-7487
(800) 329-7466

IMPERIAL INN
3282 13th Ave SE (T1B 1H8)
(403) 527-8811

MEDICINE HAT LODGE HOTEL & CONV CENTRE
1051 Ross Glen Dr SE (T1B 3T8)
(403) 529-2222
(800) 661-8095

RANCHMAN MOTEL
1617 Bomford Crescent SW
(403) 527-2263

SUPER 8 MOTEL
1280 Trans-Canada Way (T1B 1J5)
(403) 528-8888
(800) 800-8000

NISKU

INTERNATIONAL INN
501 11th Ave
(780) 955-3001

NISKU INN & CONF CENTER
1103 4th St
(780) 955-7744

OKOTOKS

OKOTOKS COUNTRY INN
59 River Side Gate
(403) 938-1999

OLDS

BEST WESTERN
Hwy 27 & Hwy 2A (T4H 1P7)
(403) 556-5900
(800) 528-1234
(888) 908-5900

PEACE RIVER

TRAVELLER'S MOTOR HOTEL
9510 100th St
(780) 624-3621

PINCHER CREEK

HERITAGE INN
919 Waterton Ave
(403) 627-5000

SUPER 8 MOTEL
1307 Freebam
Ave (T0K 1W0)
(403) 627-5671
(800) 800-8000

RED DEER

HOLIDAY INN
6500 67th Ave
(T4P 1A2)
(403) 342-6567
(800) 465-4329

**SERVICE PLUS
INN & SUITES**
6853 66th St
(403) 342-4445

SUPER 8 MOTEL
7474 Gaetz Ave
(T4P 1X7)
(403) 343-1102
(800) 800-8000

TRAVELODGE
2807 50th Ave
(T4R 1H6)
(403) 346-2011
(800) 578-7878

SHERWOOD PARK

**FIRST CANADA
INNS**
26 Strathmoor Dr
(780) 464-1000

FRANKLIN'S INN
2016 Sherwood
Dr (T8A 3X3)
(780) 467-1234

**RAMADA LTD
EAST**
30 Broadway
Blvd
(780) 467-6727
(800) 272-6232

STETTLER

**BEST WESTERN
CRUSADER INN**
6020 50th Ave
(T0C 2L0)
(403) 742-3371
(800) 528-1234
(888) 742-5808

SUPER 8 MOTEL
5720 44th Ave
(T0C 2L0)
(403) 742-3391
(800) 800-8000
(888) 742-8008

STONY PLAIN

**RAMADA INN
& SUITES**
3301 43rd Ave
(T7Z 1L1)
(780) 963-9222
(800) 272-6232

**STONY MOTOR
INN**
4801 48 St
(T0E 2G0)
(780) 963-3444

STRATHMORE

**BEST WESTERN
STRATHMORE
INN**
550 Hwy 1
(T1P 1M6)
(403) 934-5777
(800) 528-1234

SUPER 8 MOTEL
450 Westlake Rd
(T1P 1H8)
(403) 934-1808
(800) 800-8000

TABER

HERITAGE INN
4830 46th Ave
(T0K 2G0)
(403) 223-4424

THREE HILLS

SUPER 8 MOTEL
208 18th Ave N
(T0M 2A0)
(403) 443-8888
(800) 800-8000

VALLEYVIEW

**RAVEN
MOTOR INN**
4606 50th St
(T0H 2N0)
(780) 524-3383

VERMILION

SUPER 8 MOTEL
5108 47th Ave
(T9X 1J6)
(403) 853-4741
(800) 800-8000

WATERTON PARK

BAYSHORE INN
111 Waterton Ave
(403) 859-2211

**THE LODGE AT
WATERTON LAKE**
101 Clematis Ave
(403) 859-2151

WESTLOCK

**HIGHWAY
MOTOR INN**
East Service Rd
(T0G 2L0)
(780) 349-3138

WETASKIWIN

**FORT ETHIER
LODGE**
3802 56th St
(T9A 2B2)
(780) 352-9161

SUPER 8 MOTEL
3820 56th St
(T9A 2B2)
(780) 361-3808
(800) 800-8000

WAYSIDE INN
4103 56th St
(780) 352-6681

WHITECOURT

QUALITY INN
5420 47th Ave
(T7S 1P3)
(780) 778-5477
(800) 228-5151

SUPER 8 MOTEL
4121 Kepler St
(T7S 1P6)
(780) 778-8908
(800) 800-8000

**TRAVELODGE
HOTEL**
5003 50th St
(T7S 1N3)
(780) 778-2216
(800) 578-7878

BRITISH COLUMBIA

ABBOTSFORD

ALPINE MOTOR INN
32111 Marshall Rd (V2T 1A3)
(604) 859-3171

BEST WESTERN BAKERVIEW INN
1821 Sumas Way (V2S 4L5)
(604) 859-1341
(800) 528-1234

BEST WESTERN REGENCY INN
32110 Marshall Rd (V2T 1A1)
(604) 853-3111
(800) 528-1234
(800) 771-3077

HOLIDAY INN EXPRESS
2073 Clearbrook Rd
(V2T 2X1)
(604) 859-6211
(800) 465-4329

RAMADA INN
36035 N Parallel Rd
(V3G 2C6)
(604) 870-1050
(800) 272-6232

WELCOME INN
1881 Sumas Way (V2S 4L5)
(604) 853-1141

BARRIERE

MOUNTAIN SPRINGS MOTEL
4253 Yellowhead Hwy
(250) 672-0090

BLUE RIVER

GLACIER MOUNTAIN LODGE
Hwy 5 & Shell Rd
(250) 673-2393

MIKE WIEGELE HELI-SKIING
Harrwood Dr, Hwy 5
(250) 673-8381

BOSWELL

DESTINY BAY RESORT
11935 Hwy 3A
(250) 223-8234

MOUNTAIN SHORES RESORT & MARINA
13485 Hwy 3A
(V0B 1A0)
(250) 223-8258

BURNABY

BEST WESTERN KINGS INN & CONF CENTRE
5411 Kingsway (V5H 2G1)
(604) 438-1383
(800) 528-1234
(800) 211-1122

LAKE CITY MOTOR INN
5415 Lougheed Hwy
(V5H 2B3)
(604) 294-5331

STAY'N SAVE INN
3777 Henning Dr
(V5H 2B3)
(604) 473-500
(800) 663-0298

CACHE CREEK

BONAPARTE MOTEL
1395 Hwy 97 N
(V0K 1H0)
(250) 457-9693

TUMBLEWEED MOTEL
1221 Quartz Rd
(V0K 1H0)
(250) 457-6522

CAMPBELL RIVER

BEST WESTERN AUSTRIAN CHALET
462 S Island Hwy
(V9W 1A5)
(250) 923-4231
(800) 528-1234
(800) 6677207

CAMPBELL RIVER LODGE FISHING & ADVENTURE RESORT
1760 Island Hwy
(250) 287-7446

SUPER 8 MOTEL
340 S Island Hwy
(V9W 1A5)
(250) 286-6622
(800) 800-8000

CASTLEGAR

BEST WESTERN FIRESIDE INN
1810 8th Ave
(V1N 2Y2)
(250) 365-2128
(800) 528-1234
(800) 499-6399

DAYS INN
651 18th St
(V1N 2N1)
(250) 365-2700
(800) 329-7466

CHASE

CHASE COUNTRY INN MOTEL
576 Coburn St
(V0E 1M0)
(250) 679-3333

QUAAOUT LODGE RESORT
Trans Canada Hwy 1
(250) 679-3090

CHEMAINUS

FULLER LAKE MOTEL
9300 Trans Canada Hwy
(250) 246-3282

CHILLIWAC

BEST WESTERN RAINBOW COUNTRY INN
43971 Industrial Way (V2R 3A4)
(604) 795-3828
(800) 528-1234
(800) 665-1030

COMFORT INN
45405 Luckakuck Way (V2R 3C7)
(604) 858-0636
(800) 228-5150

ECONO LODGE
8600 Young Rd
(V2P 4P4)
(604) 795-9155
(800) 553-2666

HOLIDAY INN
45920 1st Ave
(V2P 7K1)
(604) 795-4788
(800) 465-4329

RAINBOW MOTOR INN
45620 Yale Rd W
(V2P 2N2)
(604) 792-6412

TRAVELODGE
45466 Yale Rd W
(V2R 1A9)
(604) 792-4240
(800) 578-7878

CHRISTINA LAKE

NEW HORIZON MOTEL
2037 Hwy 3
(V0H 1E0)
(250) 447-9312

CLEARWATER

JASPER WAY INN
57 E Old N Thompson Hwy
(V0E 1N0)
(250) 674-3345

COURTENAY

BEST WESTERN COLLINGWOOD INN
1675 Cliffe Ave (V9N 2K6)
(250) 338-1464
(800) 528-1234
(800) 663-7922

THE COAST WESTERLY HOTEL
1590 Cliffe Ave
(250) 338-7741

KINGFISHER OCEANSIDE RESORT & SPA
4330 S Island Hwy
(V9N 8H9)
(250) 338-1323

TRAVELODGE
2605 S Island Hwy
(V9N 2L8)
(250) 334-4491
(800) 578-7878

COWICHAN BAY

HOWARD JOHNSON RESORT HOTEL
1681 Cowichan Bay Rd (V0R 1N0)
(250) 748-6222
(800) 446-4656

CRANBROOK

BEST WESTERN COACH HOUSE MOTOR INN
1417 Cranbrook St N (V1C 3S7)
(250) 426-7236
(800) 528-1234

HERITAGE INN OF THE SOUTH
803 Cranbrook St N (V1C 3S2)
(250) 489-4301

MODEL A INN
1908 Cranbrook
St N
(250) 489-4600

PONDEROSA MOTEL
500 Van Horne St
S (V1C 4H3)
(250) 426-6114

SUPER 8 MOTEL
2370 Cranbrook
St N (V1C 3T2)
(250) 489-8028
(800) 800-8000

CRESTON

CITY CENTRE MOTEL
220 15th Ave N
(V0B 1G0)
(250) 428-2257

DOWNTOWNER MOTOR INN
1218 Canyon St
(V0B 1G0)
(250) 428-2238
(800) 665-9904

SUNSET MOTEL
2705 Hwy 3
(V0B 1G0)
(250) 428-2229

DAWSON CREEK

THE GEORGE DAWSON INN
11705 8th St
(V1G 4N9)
(250) 782-9151

SUPER 8 MOTEL
1440 Alaska Ave
(V1G 1Z5)
(250) 782-8899
(800) 800-8000

TRAIL INN MOTEL
1748 Alaska Ave
(V1G 4H7)
(250) 782-8595
(800) 663-2749

DELTA

BEST WESTERN TSAWWASSEN INN
1665 56th St
(V4L 2B2)
(604) 943-8221
(800) 528-1234
(800) 943-8221

DELTA TOWN & COUNTRY INN
6005 Hwy 17
(V4K 4E2)
(604) 946-4404

DUNCAN

BEST WESTERN COWICHAN VALLEY INN
6464 Trans
Canada Hwy
(V9L 6C6)
(250) 748-2722
(800) 528-1234
(800) 927-6199

DAYS INN
5325 Trans
Canada Hwy
(V9L 3X5)
(250) 748-0661
(800) 329-7466

FALCON NEST MOTEL
5867 Trans
Canada Hwy
(250) 748-8188

SILVER BRIDGE INN & CONF CENTRE
140 Trans Canada
Hwy (V9L 3P7)
(250) 748-4311

ENDERBY

HOWARD JOHNSON FORTUNES LANDING
1902 George St
(V0E 1V0)
(250) 838-6825
(800) 446-4656

FERNIE

CEDAR LODGE
1101 7th Ave
(V0B 1M0)
(250) 423-4622

PARK PLACE LODGE
742 Hwy 3
(250) 423-6871

SUPER 8 MOTEL
2021 Hwy #3
(V0B 1M1)
(250) 423-6788
(800) 800-8000

FIELD

KICKING HORSE LODGE
100 Centre St
(250) 343-6303

FORT NELSON

TRAVELODGE
4711 50th Ave
(V0E 1R0)
(250) 774-3911
(800) 578-7878

FORT ST. JOHN

BEST WESTERN COACHMAN INN
8540 Alaska Rd
(V1T 5L6)
(250) 787-0651
(800) 528-1234
(888) 388-9408

RAMADA LIMITED
10103 98 Ave
(V1J 1P8)
(250) 787-0779
(800) 272-6232

GIBSONS

CEDAR'S INN
895 Sunshine Coast
Hwy (V0N 1V0)
(604) 886-3008

GOLDEN

BEST WESTERN MOUNTAINVIEW INN
1024 - 11th St N
(V0A 1H0)
(250) 344-2333
(800) 528-1234

GOLDEN RIM MOTOR INN
1416 Golden View
Rd (V0A 1H0)
(250) 344-2216

HILLSIDE LODGE & CHALETS
1740 Seward
Frontage Rd
(250) 344-7281

GRAND FORKS

IMPERIAL MOTEL
7389 Riverside,
Box 2558
(V0H 1H0)
(250) 442-8236

WESTERN TRAVELLER MOTEL
1591 Central Ave
(V0H 1H0)
(250) 442-5566

HARRISON HOT SPRINGS

HARRISON HOT SPRINGS RESORT
100 Esplanade
(V0M 1K0)
(604) 796-2244
(800) 663-2266

QUALITY HOTEL
190 Lillooet Ave
(V0M 1K0)
(604) 796-5555
(800) 228-5151

HOPE

ALPINE MOTEL
505 Old Hope-
Princeton Hwy
(604) 869-9931

INN-TOWNE MOTEL
510 Trans Canada
Hwy 1 (V0X 1L0)
(604) 869-7276

QUALITY INN
350 Old Hope-
Princeton Hwy
(V0X 1L0)
(604) 869-9951
(800) 228-5151

SWISS CHALETS MOTEL
456 Trans Canada
Hwy (V0X 1L0)
(604) 869-9020

WINDSOR MOTEL
778 3rd Ave
(V0X 1L0)
(604) 869-9944

KAMLOOPS

A SUPER VIEW MOTEL
1200 Rogers Way
(250) 374-8100

CASA MARQUIS MOTOR INN
530 Columbia St
(V2C 2V1)
(250) 372-7761

COURTESY MOTEL
1773 E Trans
Canada Hwy
(250) 372-8533

DAYS INN
1285 W Trans
Canada Hwy
(V2E 2J7)
(250) 374-5911
(800) 329-7466

DREAM LODGE
1855 Rogers
Place
(250) 314-9889

FOUNTAIN MOTEL
506 Columbia St
(V2C 2V1)
(250) 374-4451

GRANDVIEW MOTEL
463 Grandview
Terr (V2C 3Z3)
(250) 372-1312

HOSPITALITY INN
500 W Columbia
St (V2C 1K6)
(250) 374-4164

HOWARD JOHNSON EXPRESS INN
610 Columbia St
(V2C 1L1)
(250) 374-1515
(800) 446-4656

LAMPLIGHTER MOTEL
1901 Trans
Canada Hwy E
(V2C 3Z9)
(250) 372-3386

RANCHLAND MOTEL
2357 Trans
Canada Hwy E
(V2C 4A8)
(250) 828-8787
(800) 663-4902

STAY'N SAVE INNS
1325 Columbia St
W
(250) 374-8877
(800) 663-0298

SUPER 8 MOTEL
1521 Hugh Allan
Dr (V1S 1P4)
(250) 374-8688
(800) 800-8000

THOMSPON HOTEL & CONF CENTRE
650 Victoria St
(250) 374-1999

THRIFT INN
2459 Trans Canada
Hwy E (V2C 4A9)
(250) 374-2488

TRAVELODGE
430 Columbia St
(V2C 2T5)
(250) 372-8202
(800) 578-7878

KELOWNA

BEST WESTERN INN
2402 Hwy 97 N
(V1X 4J1)
(250) 860-1212
(800) 528-1234
(888) 860-1212

BIG WHITE MOTOR LODGE
1891 Parkinson
Way (V1Y 7V6)
(250) 860-3982
(800) 663-8603

PANDOSY INN
3327 Lakeshore Rd
(250) 762-5858

RAMADA LODGE HOTEL
2170 Harvey Ave
(V1Y 6G8)
(250) 860-9711
(800) 272-6232

SAFARI INN
1651 Powick Rd
(V1X 4L1)
(250) 860-8122

SIESTA MOTOR INN
3152 Lakeshore
Rd
(250) 763-5013

STAY'N SAVE INN
1140 Harvey Ave
(250) 862-8888
(800) 663-0298

SUPER 8 MOTEL
2592 Hwy 97 N
(V1X 4J4)
(250) 762-8222
(800) 800-8000

TOWN & COUNTRY MOTEL
2629 Hwy 97 N
(V1X 4J6)
(250) 860-7121

KIMBERLEY

QUALITY INN
300 Wallinger
Ave (V1A1Z4)
(250) 427-2266
(800) 228--5151

LADYSMITH

SEAVIEW MARINE RESORT
11111 Chemainus
Rd
(250) 245-3768

LANGLEY

HOLIDAY INN EXPRESS HOTEL & SUITES
8750 204th St
(V1M 2Y5)
(604) 882-2000
(604) 859-6211
(800) 465-4329

TRAVELODGE-LANGLEY MOTOR INN
20470 88th Ave
(V1M 2Y6)
(604) 888-4891
(800) 578-7878

WESTWARD INN
19650 Fraser Hwy
(V3A 4C7)
(604) 534-9238

LOGAN LAKE

LOGAN LAKE LODGE
111 Chartrand
Ave (V0K 1W)
(250) 523-9466

MADEIRA PARK

SUNSHINE COAST RESORT
12695 Sunshine
Coast Hwy (V0N
2H0)
(640) 883-9177

MALAHAT

MALAHAT BUNGALOWS MOTEL
Malahat Dr (V0R
2L0)
(250) 478-3011

MANNING PARK

MANNING PARK RESORT
Hwy 3, Crowsnest
(250) 840-8822

MAPLE RIDGE

TRAVELODGE
21650 Lougheed
Hwy (V2X 2S1)
(604) 467-1511
(800) 578-7878

MCBRIDE

NORTH COUNTRY LODGE
868 N Frontage
Rd
(V0J 2E0)
(250) 560-0001

MERRITT

BEST WESTERN NICOLA INN
4025 Walters St
(V1K 1K1)
(250) 378-4253
(800) 528-1234
(888) 663-2830

DAYS INN
3350 Voght St
(V1K 1C7)
(250) 378-2292
(800) 329-7466

MERRITT MOTOR INN
3561 Voght St
(V0K 2B0)
(250) 378-9422

TRAVELODGE
3581 Voght St
(V1K 1C5)
(250) 378-8830
(800) 578-7878

MISSION

BEST WESTERN MISSION CITY LODGE
32281 Lougheed
Hwy
(V2V 6B2)
(604) 820-5500
(800) 528-1234
(888) 552-5542

NAKUSP

THE SELKIRK INN
210 6th Ave W
(V0G 1R0)
(250) 265-3666

NANAIMO

BEST WESTERN DORCHESTER HOTEL
70 Church St
(V9R 5H4)
(250) 754-6835
(800) 528-1234
(800) 661-2449

BEST WESTERN NORTH GATE
6450 Metral Dr
(V9T 2L8)
(250) 390-2222
(800) 528-1234

DAYS INN-HARBORVIEW
809 Island Hwy S
(V9R 5K1)
(250) 754-8171
(800) 329-7466

TRAVELODGE
96 Terminal Ave
N (V9S 4J2)
(250) 754-6355
(800) 578-7878

NARAMATA

THE VILLAGE MOTEL
244 Robinson Dr
(250) 496-5535

NELSON

BEST WESTERN BAKER STREET INN
153 Baker St
(V1L 4H1)
(250) 352-3525
(800) 528-1234
(888) 255-3525

NORTH VANCOUVER

OLD ENGLISH B&B REGISTRY
1226 Silverwood
Crescent
(V7P 1J3)
(604) 986-5069

OLIVER

SOUTHWIND MOTOR INN
34017 Hwy 97S
(V0H 1T0)
(250) 498-3442

100 MILE HOUSE

RED COACH INN
170 N Cariboo
Hwy (V0K 2E0)
(250) 295-2266
(800) 663-8422

SUPER 8 MOTEL
989 Alder Ave
(V0K 2E0)
(250) 395-8888
(800) 800-8000

ONE HUNDRED EIGHT MILE RANCH

BEST WESTERN 108 RESORT
4816 Telqua Dr
(V0K 2Z0)
(250) 791-5211
(800) 528-1234
(800) 667-5233

OSOYOOS

WESTRIDGE MOTOR INN
9913 Hwy 3
(V0H 1V0)
(250) 495-7322

PARKSVILLE

BEST WESTERN BAYSIDE INN
240 Dogwood St (V9P 2H5)
(250) 248-8333
(800) 528-1234
(800) 663-4232

OCEANSIDE INN
424 W Island Hwy (V9P 2G3)
(250) 248-2232

TIGH NA MARA RESORT HOTEL
1095 E Island Hwy (V9P 2G5)
(250) 248-2072

V.I.P. MOTEL
414 W Island Hwy (V9P 2G3)
(250) 248-3244
(800) 663-7300

PARSON

TIMBER INN-CHALET & RESTAURANT
3483 Hwy 95
(250) 348-2228

PEACHLAND

HATHEUME LAKE RESORT
P. O. Box 490 (V0H 1X0)
(250) 767-2642

PENTICTON

BEST WESTERN INN AT PENTICTON
3180 Skaha Lake Rd (V2A 6G4)
(250) 493-0311
(800) 528-1234
(800) 668-6746

GOLDEN SANDS RESORT
1028 Lakeshore Dr (V2A 1C1)
(250) 492-4210

PENTICTON LAKESIDE RESORT & CONF CENTRE
21 Lakeshore Dr W (V2A 7M5)
(250) 493-8221
(800) 663-1144

PENTICTON SLUMBER LODGE
274 Lakeshore Dr W (V2A 7M5)
(250) 492-4008

RAMADA INN & SUITES
1050 Eckhardt Ave W (V2A 2C3)
(250) 492-8926
(800) 272-6232

SPANISH VILLA RESORT
890 Lakeshore Dr W (V2A 1C1)
(250) 492-2922

WATERFRONT INN
3688 Parkview St (V2A 6H1)
(250) 492-8228
(800) 563-6006

PORT ALBERNI

BEST WESTERN BARCLAY HOTEL
4277 Stamp Ave (V9Y 7X8)
(250) 724-7171
(800) 528-1234

COAST HOSPITALITY INN
3835 Redford St (V9Y 3S2)
(250) 723-8111
(800) 663-6677

TIMBERLODGE & RV CAMPGROUND
Site 210, Comp 12, Hwy 4 (V9Y 7L6)
(250) 723-9415

PORT COQUITLAM

BEST WESTERN POCO INN
1545 Lougheed Hwy (V3B 1A5)
(604) 941-6216
(800) 528-1234
(800) 930-2235

PORT HARDY

PIONEER INN
4965 Byng Rd, Box 699 (V0N 2P0)
(250) 949-7271

PRINCE GEORGE

BEST WESTERN CITY CENTRE
910 Victoria Dr (V2L 2K8)
(250) 563-1267
(800) 528-1234

CONNAUGHT MOTOR INN
1550 Victoria St (V2L 2L3)
(250) 562-4441
(800) 663-6620

PRINCE RUPERT

ALEEDA MOTEL
900 3rd Ave W (V8J 1M8)
(250) 627-1367

PRINCETON

BEST WESTERN PRINCETON INN
169 Hwy 3 (V0X 1W0)
(250) 295-3537
(800) 528-1234
(888) 295-3537

QUADRA ISLAND

TAKU RESORT
616 Taku Rd
(250) 285-3031

QUALICUM BEACH

OLD DUTCH INN BY THE SEA
2690 Island Hwy (V9K 1T3)
(250) 752-6914

QUESNEL

TALISMAN INN
753 Front St (V2J 2Y2)
(250) 992-7247

RADIUM HOT SPRINGS

CEDAR MOTEL
7593 Main St W (V0A 1M0)
(250) 347-9463

THE CHALET EUROPE
5063 Madsen Rd (V0A 1M0)
(250) 347-9305

LIDO MOTEL
4876 McKay St (V0A 1M0)
(250) 347-9533

SUNRISE SUITE MOTEL
7371 Prospector Ave (V0A 1M0)
(250) 347-0008

SUNSET MOTEL
4883 McKay St (V0A 1M0)
(250) 347-9863

REVELSTOKE

BEST WESTERN WAYSIDE INN
1901 Laforme Blvd (V0E 2S0)
(250) 837-6161
(800) 528-1234
(800) 663-5307

THE REGENT INN
112 First St E (V0E 2S0)
(250) 837-2107

SUPER 8 MOTEL
1700 W Victoria (V0E 2S0)
(250) 837-0888
(800) 800-8000

SWISS CHALET MOTEL
1101 Victoria Rd (V0E 2S0)
(250) 837-4650

RICHMOND

BEST WESTERN RICHMOND INN
7551 Westminster Hwy (V6X 1A3)
(604) 273-7878
(800) 528-1234
(800) 663-0299

COMFORT INN AIRPORT
3031 #3 Rd & Sea Island Way (V6X 2B6)
(604) 278-5161
(800) 228-5150

DELTA PACIFIC RESORT & CONF CENTRE
1021 St. Edwards Dr (V6X 2M9)
(604) 278-9611
(800) 268-1133

DELTA VANCOU-VER AIRPORT
3500 Cessna Dr (V7B 1C7)
(604) 278-1241
(800) 268-1133

HOWARD JOHNSON HOTEL
9020 Bridgeport Rd (V6X 1S1)
(604) 270-6030
(800) 446-4656

MARRIOTT HOTEL AIRPORT
7571 Westminster Hwy
(604) 276-2112
(800) 228-9290

RADISSON PRESIDENT HOTEL & SUITES
8181 Cambie Rd
(604) 276-8181
(800) 333-3333

RAMADA INN AIRPORT
7188 Westminster Hwy (V6X 1A1)
(604) 207-9000
(800) 272-6232

STAY'N SAVE INNS
10551 St. Edwards Dr
(604) 273-3311
(800) 663-0298

ROSSLAND

SWISS ALPS INN
1199 Nancy Green Hwy (V0G 1Y0)
(250) 362-7364

SAANICHTON

**QUALITY INN-
WADDLING DOG**
2476 Mt. Newton
Cross Rd
(V8M 2B8)
(250) 652-1146
(800) 228-5151

SUPER 8 MOTEL
2477 Mt. Newton
Cross Rd
(V8M 2B7)
(250) 652-6888
(800) 800-8000

SALMON ARM

**BEST WESTERN
VILLAGER WEST
MOTOR INN**
61 10th St SW
(V1E 4M2)
(250) 832-9793
(800) 528-1234

**THE COAST
SHUSWAP
LODGE**
200 Trans Canada
Hwy W (V1E
4P6)
(250) 832-7081
(800) 661-4355

SUPER 8 MOTEL
2901 10th Ave NE
(V1E 4N1)
(250) 832-8812
(800) 800-8000

TRAVELODGE
2401 Trans
Canada Hwy W
(V1E 4P7)
(250) 832-9721
(800) 578-7878

SALTSPRING ISLAND

**SEABREEZE
INN MOTEL**
101 Bittancourt
Rd
(250) 537-4145

SAVONA

**LAKESIDE
COUNTRY INN**
7001 Savona
Acces Rd
(250) 373-2528

SECHELT

**BELLA BEACH
MOTOR INN**
4748 Hwy 101
(V0N 3A0)
(604) 885-7191

SICAMOUS

SUPER 8 MOTEL
1122 Riverside
Ave (V0E 2V0)
(250) 836-4988
(800) 800-8000

SIDNEY

**BEST WESTERN
EMERALD ISLE INN**
2306 Beacon Ave
(V8L 1X2)
(250) 656-4441
(800) 315-3377

**CEDARWOOD
INN & SUITES**
9522 Lochside Dr
(V8L 1N8)
(250) 656-5551

**TRAVELODGE-
VICTORIA
AIRPORT**
2280 Beacon Ave
(V8L 1X1)
(250) 656-1176
(800) 578-7878

SILVERTON

**WILLIAM
HUNTER CABINS**
303 Lake Ave
(250) 358-2844

SMITHERS

**ASPEN MOTOR
INN**
4268 Yellowhead
Hwy (V0J 2N0)
(250) 847-4551
(800) 663-7676

SOOKE

**OCEAN
WILDERNESS
COUNTRY INN**
109 W Coast Rd
(V0S 1N0)
(250) 646-2116
(800) 323-2116

SOOKE HARBOUR HOUSE

1528 Whiffen Spit
Rd (V0S 1N0)
(250) 642-3421

SUMMERLAND

**SUMMERLAND
MOTEL**
2107 Tait St
(V0H 1Z0)
(250) 494-4444

SURREY

**DAYS HOTEL-
SURREY CENTRE**
9850 King George
Hwy (V3T 4Y3)
(604) 588-9511

RAMADA LTD
19225 Hwy 10
(V3S 8V9)
(604) 576-8388
(800) 272-6232

**SHERATON
GUILDFORD
HOTEL**
15269 104th Ave
(604) 582-9288
(800) 325-3535

**SUPER 8 MOTEL
AT SKY TRAIN
STATION**
13893 Fraser
Hwy (V3T 4E6)
(604) 581-7122
(800) 800-8000

TERRACE

**BEST WESTERN
TERRACE INN &
CONF CENTRE**
4553 Greig Ave
(V8G 1M7)
(250) 635-0083
(800) 528-1234
(800) 488-1898

**COAST INN
OF THE WEST**
4620 Lakelse Ave
(V8G 1R1)
(250) 638-8141
(800) 772-5555

TOFINO

**CRYSTAL COVE
BEACH RESORT**
1165 Cedarwood
Place (V0R 2Z0)
(250) 725-4213

**WICKANINNISH
INN**
Osprey Lane at
Chesterman Beach
(V0R 2Z0)
(250) 725-3100

VALEMOUNT

**BEST WESTERN
CANADIAN
LODGE**
1501 5th Ave
(V0E 2Z0)
(250) 566-8222
(800) 528-1234
(800) 811-5808

VANCOUVER

**BEST WESTERN
EXHIBITION PARK**
3475 W Hastings
St (V5K 2A5)
(604) 294-4751
(800) 528-1234

**BEST WESTERN
SANDS**
1755 Davie St
(V6G 1W5)
(604) 682-1831
(800) 528-1234
(800) 661-7887

**BOSMAN'S
MOTOR HOTEL**
1060 Howe St
(V6Z 1P5)
(604) 682-3171
(800) 663-7840

**CANADIAN
PACIFIC HOTEL
VANCOUVER**
900 W Georgia St
(V6C 2W6)
(604) 684-3131
(800) 441-1414

**CANADIAN
PACIFIC
WATERFRONT
CENTRE HOTEL**
900 Canada Place
Way
(604) 691-1991
(800) 441-1414

DELTA VANCOUVER SUITES

550 W Hastings
St
(604) 689-8188
(800) 268-1133

**FOUR SEASONS
HOTEL**
791 W Georgia St
(V6C 2T4)
(604) 689-9333
(800) 332-3442

**THE GEORGIAN
COURT HOTEL**
773 Beatty St
(V6B 2M4)
(604) 682-5555
(800) 663-1155

**GRANVILLE
ISLAND HOTEL**
1253 Johnston St
(604) 683-7373

**HOLIDAY INN
HOTEL & SUITES**
1110 Howe St
(V6Z 1R2)
(604) 684-2151
(800) 465-4329

**HOLIDAY INN
VANCOUVER
CENTRE**
711 W Broadway
Ave (V5Z 3Y2)
(604) 879-0511
(800) 465-4329

**THE LONDON
GUARD MOTEL**
2227 Kingsway
(V5N 2T6)
(604) 430-4646

**METROPOLITAN
HOTEL**
645 Howe St
(V6C 2Y9)
(604) 687-1122

**PACIFIC
PALISADES
HOTEL**
1277 Robson St
(V6G 1C1)
(604) 688-0461

**THE PAN PACIFIC
VANCOUVER
HOTEL**
999 Canada Place
(V6C 3B5)
(604) 662-8111
(800) 663-1515

QUALITY INN-INN AT FALSE CREEK
1335 Howe St
(V6Z 1R7)
(604) 682-0229
(800) 228-5151

RENAISSANCE HOTEL HARBOURSIDE
1133 W Hastings St
(604) 689-9211
(800) 468-3571

RESIDENCE INN BY MARRIOTT
1234 Hornby St
(604) 688-1234
(800) 331-3131

SYLVIA HOTEL
1154 Gilford St
(V6G 2P6)
(604) 681-9321

2400 MOTEL
2400 Kingsway
(V5R 5G9)
(604) 434-2464

VERNON

BEST WESTERN LODGE & CONF CENTRE
3914 32 St
(V1T 5P1)
(250) 545-3385
(800) 528-1234
(800) 663-4422

BEST WESTERN VILLAGER INN
5121 26th St
(V1T 8G4)
(250) 549-2224
(800) 528-1234
(800) 549-2270

COMFORT INN
4204 32nd St
(V1T 5P4)
(250) 542-4434
(800) 228-5150

THE MARIA ROSE B&B
8083 Aspen Rd
(250) 549-4773

SCHELL MOTEL
2810 35th St
(V1T 6B5)
(250) 545-1351

TRAVELODGE
3000 28th Ave
(V1T 1W1)
(250) 545-2101
(800) 578-7878

VICTORIA

ADMIRAL MOTEL
257 Belleville St
(V8V 1X1)
(250) 388-6267

BLUE RIDGE INNS
3110 Douglas St
(250) 388-4345

DASHWOOD SEASIDE MANOR
1 Cook St
V8V 3W6)
(250) 385-5517

DUTCHMAN INN
2828 Rock Bay
Ave (V8T 4S1)
(250) 386-7557

THE EMPRESS
721 Government
St (V8W 1W5)
(250) 384-8111
(800) 268-9411

EXECUTIVE HOUSE HOTEL
777 Douglas St
(V8W 2B5)
(250) 388-5111
(800) 663-7001

HARBOUR TOWERS HOTEL
345 Quebec St
(V8V 1W4)
(250) 385-2405
(800) 663-5896

HOWARD JOHNSON INN
310 Gorge Rd
(V8T 2W2)
(250) 382-2151
(800) 446-4656

OCEAN POINTE RESORT HOTEL & SPA
45 Songhees Rd
(250) 360-2999

OXFORD CASTLE INN
133 Gorge Rd E
(V9A 1L4)
(250) 388-6431

QUALITY INN HARBOURVIEW
455 Belleville St
(V8V 1X3)
(250) 386-2421
(800) 228-5151

ROBIN HOOD MOTEL
136 Gorge Rd E
(V9A 1L4)
(250) 388-4302

RYAN'S BED & BREAKFAST
224 Superior St
(250) 389-0012

SHAMROCK MOTEL
675 Superior St
(V8V 1V1)
(240) 385-8768

STAY 'N SAVE INN
3233 Maple St
(V8X 4Y9)
(250) 475-7500
(800) 663-0298

TALLY-HO MOTOR INN
3020 Douglas St
(V8T 4N4)
(250) 386-6141
(800) 663-5660

TRAVELLER'S INN-IN TOWN
3025 Douglas St
(250) 978-1000

WESTBANK

HOLIDAY INN
2569 Dobbin Rd
(V4T 2J6)
(250) 768-8879
(800) 465-4329

WHISTLER

BEST WESTERN LISTEL WHISTLER HOTEL
4121 Village
Green (V0N 1B4)
(604) 932-1133
(800) 528-1234
(800) 663-5472

CANADIAN PACIFIC CHATEAU WHISTLER RESORT
4599 Chateau
Blvd, Box 100
(V0N 1B0)
(604) 938-8000
(800) 268-9411
(800) 441-1414

DELTA WHISTLER RESORT
4050 Whistler
Way (V0N 1B0)
(604) 932-1982
(800) 268-1133

DELTA WHISTLER VILLAGE SUITES
4308 Main St
(604) 905-3987
(800) 268-1133

EDGEWATER LODGE
8841 Hwy 99
(604) 932-0688

RESIDENCE INN BY MARRIOTT
4899 Painted
Cliff Rd
(604) 905-3400
(800) 331-3131

SUMMIT LODGE
4359 Main St
(604) 932-2778

TANTALUS RESORT CONDO LODGE
4200 Whistler
Way
(604) 932-4146

WILLIAMS LAKE

DRUMMOND LODGE MOTEL
1405 Cariboo
Hwy
(V2G 2W3)
(250) 392-5334
(800) 667-4555

SUPER 8 MOTEL
1712 Broadway
Ave S
(V2G 2W4)
(250) 398-8884
(800) 800-8000

YALE

FORT YALE MOTEL
31265 Trans
Canada Hwy
(V0K 2S0)
(604) 863-2216

MANITOBA

BRANDON

COMFORT INN
925 Middleton
Ave
(R7C 1A8)
(204) 727-6232
(800) 228-5150

RODEWAY INN
300 18th St N
(R7A 6Z2)
(204) 728-7230
(800) 228-2000

ROYAL OAK INN
3130 Victoria Ave
(R7A 5Z7)
(204) 728-5775

SUPER 8 MOTEL
1570 Highland Ave
(R7C 1A7)
(204) 729-8024
(800) 800-8000

VICTORIA INN
3550 Victoria Ave
W (R7A 5Z4)
(204) 725-1532

CHURCHILL

POLAR INN
15 Franklin St
(R0B 0E0)
(204) 675-8878

DAUPHIN

RODEWAY INN
Hwy 5 & 10 S
(R7N 2V4)
(204) 638-5102
(800) 228-2000

SUPER 8 MOTEL
1457 Main St S
(R7N 3B3)
(204) 638-0800
(800) 800-8000

FLIN FLON

**VICTORIA INN
NORTH**
10 Hwy N
(R8A 1M9)
(204) 687-7555

GIMLI

**LAKEVIEW
RESORT**
10 Centre St (R0C
1B0)
(204) 642-8565

HECLA VILLAGE

**SOLMUNDSON
GESTA HUS**
Hwy 8, Hecla
Provincial Park
(204) 279-2088

MORRIS

SUPER 8 MOTEL
400 Main St
(R0G 1K0)
(204) 746-6879
(800) 800-8000

NEEPAWA

SUPER 8 MOTEL
160 Main St W
(R0J 1H0)
(204) 476-8888
(800) 800-8000

PORTAGE LA PRAIRIE

**MANITOBAH
INN**
Trans Canada
Hwy 1, Box 867
(R1N 3C3)
(204) 857-9791

**WESTGATE INN
MOTEL**
1010
Saskatchewan
Ave E (R1N 0K1)
(204) 239-5200

RUSSELL

**RUSSELL INN
HOTEL & CONF
CENTER**
Hwy 16 & 83
(R0J 1W0)
(204) 773-2186

THE PAS

KILIWAK INN
Hwy 10 N
(204) 623-1800

WESCANA INN
439 Fischer Ave
(204) 623-5446

THOMPSON

**COUNTRY INN
& SUITES**
70 Thompson Dr
N
(R8N 0C3)
(204) 778-8879
(800) 456-4000

WINKLER

WINKLER INN
851 Main St N
(204) 325-4381

WINNIPEG

**BEST WESTERN
CARLTON INN**
220 Carlton St
(R3C 1P5)
(204) 942-0881
(800) 528-1234

**BEST WESTERN
INTERNATIONAL
INN**
1808 Wellington
Ave
(R3H 0G3)
(204) 786-4801
(800) 528-1234

**CANAD INNS
EXPRESS
FORT GARRY**
1792 Pembina
Hwy
(R3T 2G2)
(204) 269-6955

**CANAD INNS
WINDSOR PARK**
1034 Elizabeth
Rd
(204) 253-2641

**CANADIAN
PACIFIC-THE
LOMBARD**
2 Lombard Pl
(R3B 0Y3)
(204) 957-1350
(800) 441-1414

COMFORT INN
3109 Pembina
Hwy
(R3T 4R6)
(204) 269-7390
(800) 228-5150

**COMFORT INN-
AIRPORT**
1770 Sargent Ave
(R3H 0C8)
(204) 783-5627
(800) 228-5150

**COUNTRY INN
& SUITES**
730 King Edward
St
(R3H 1B4)
(204) 783-6900
(800) 456-4000

**CROWNE PLAZA
DOWNTOWN**
350 St. Mary's
Ave
(R3C 3J2)
(204) 942-0551
(800) 227-6963

DAYS INN
550 McPhillips St
(R2X 2H2)
(204) 586-8525
(800) 329-7466

**GORDON
DOWNTOWNER
MOTOR HOTEL**
330 Kennedy St
(204) 943-5581

**HOLIDAY INN
WINNIPEG
SOUTH**
1330 Pembina
Hwy
(R3T 2B4)
(204) 452-4747
(800) 465-4329

**HOWARD
JOHNSON
HOTEL**
1740 Ellice Ave
(R3H 0B3)
(204) 775-7131
(800) 446-4656

**PLACE LOUIS
RIEL ALL-SUITE
HOTEL**
190 Smith St
(204) 947-6961

QUALITY INN
635 Pembina
Hwy (R3M 2L4)
(204) 453-8247
(800) 228-5151

**RADISSON
HOTEL
WINNIPEG
DOWNTOWN**
288 Portage Ave
(R3C 0B8)
(204) 956-0410
(800) 333-3333

**RAMADA
MARLBOROUGH
HOTEL**
331 Smith St
(R3B 2G9)
(204) 942-6411
(800) 272-6232

SUPER 8 MOTEL
1485 Niakwa Rd
E (R2J 3T3)
(204) 253-1935
(800) 800-8000

**TWIN PILLARS
BED & BREAK-
FAST**
235 Oakwood
Ave
(204) 284-7590

**VISCOUNT
GORT HOTEL**
1670 Portage Ave
(204) 775-0451

NEW BRUNSWICK

BATHURST

ATLANTIC HOST HOTEL
1450 Vanier Blvd
(506) 548-3335

BEST WESTERN DANNY'S INN & CONF CENTRE
St. Peter Ave W
(E2A 3Z2)
(506) 546-6621
(800) 528-1234
(800) 200-1350

COMFORT INN
1170 St. Peter Ave
(E2A 2Z9)
(506) 547-8000
(800) 228-5150

COUNTRY INN & SUITES
777 St. Peter Ave
(E2A 1Y9)
(506) 548-4949
(800) 456-4000

KEDDY'S LE CHATEAU BATHURST
80 Main St
(506) 546-6691

CAMPBELL-TON

COMFORT INN
111 Val D'Amour
Rd
(E3N 3G9)
(506) 753-4121
(800) 228-5150

HOWARD JOHNSON HOTEL
157 Water St
(E3N 3H2)
(506) 753-4133
(800) 446-4656

COCAGNE

COCAGNE MOTEL
Hwy 11
(506) 576-6657

DALHOUSIE

BEST WESTERN MANOIR ADE-LAIDE
385 Adelaide
(E8C 1B4)
(506) 684-5681
(800) 528-1234
(800) 934-5444

EDMUND-STON

COMFORT INN
5 Bateman Ave
(E3V 3L1)
(506) 739-8361
(800) 228-5150

HOWARD JOHNSON PLAZA HOTEL
100 Rice St
(E3V 1T4)
(506) 739-7321
(800) 446-4656

FLORENCE-VILLE

FLORENCEVILLE MOTOR INN
239 Burnham Rd
(R0J 1K0)
(506) 392-6053

FREDERICTON

CARRIAGE HOUSE INN
230 University
Ave (506) 452-9924

COMFORT INN
255 Prospect St
W
(E3B 5Y4)
(506) 453-0800
(800) 228-5150

COUNTRY INN & SUITES
665 Prospect St
(506) 459-0035
(800) 456-4000

HOLIDAY INN
35 Mactaquac Rd
(French Village
E3E 1L2)
(506) 363-5111
(800) 465-4329

HOWARD JOHNSON HOTEL
Lower St. Mary's,
Trans Canada Hwy
#2 (E3B 5E3)
(506) 460-5500
(800) 446-4656

KEDDY'S INN
368 Forest Hill
Rd (E3B 5G2)
(506) 454-4461
(800) 561-7666

LORD BEAVERBROOK HOTEL
659 Queen St
(506) 455-3371

GRAND FALLS

AUBERGE PRES-DU-LAC INN
Trans Canada
Hwy #2
(E0J 1M0)
(506) 473-1300

MIRAMICHI

COMFORT INN
201 Edward St
(506) 622-1215
(800) 228-5150

COUNTRY INN & SUITES
333 King George
Hwy
(506) 627-1999
(800) 456-4000

RODD MIRAMICHI RIVER-A RODD SIGNATURE HOTEL
1809 Water St
(506) 773-3111
(800) 565-7633

MONCTON

BEACON LIGHT MOTEL
1062 Mountain
Rd
(506) 384-1734

BEST WESTERN CRYSTAL PALACE HOTEL
499 Paul St
(Montcon/Dieppe
E1A 6S5)
(506) 858-8584
(800) 528-1234
(800) 561-7108

BRUNSWICK HOTEL
1005 Main St
(506) 854-6340

COLONIAL INNS
42 Highfield St
(E1C 8T6)
(506) 382-3395
(800) 561-4667

COMFORT INN EAST
20 Maplewood
Dr (E1A 6P9)
(506) 859-6868
(800) 228-5150

COMFORT INN MAGNETIC HILL
2495 Mountain
Rd
(E1C 8K2)
(506) 384-3175
(800) 228-5150

COUNTRY INN & SUITES
2475 Mountain
Rd
(E1C 8J3)
(506) 852-7000
(800) 456-4000

ECONO LODGE
1905 W Main St
(E1E 1H9)
(506) 382-2587
(800) 553-2666

HOLIDAY INN EXPRESS

2515 Mountain
Rd
(E1C BR7)
(506) 384-1050
(800) 465-4329

KEDDY'S MOTOR INN
1510 Shediac Rd
(E1C 8K1)
(506) 854-2210
(800) 561-7666

NOR-WEST MOTEL
1325 Mountain
Rd
(506) 384-1222

RODD PARK HOUSE INN
434 Main St
(506) 382-1664
(800) 565-7633

TRAVELODGE
434 Main St
(E1C 1B9)
(506) 382-1664
(800) 578-7878

NEWCASTLE

COMFORT INN
201 Edward St
(E1V 2Y7)
(506) 622-1215
(800) 228-5150

SACKVILLE

MARSHLANDS INN
55 Bridge St
(E0A 3C0)
(506) 536-0170

SAINT JOHN

COLONIAL INNS
175 City Rd
(E2L 3T5)
(506) 652-3000
(800) 561-4667

COMFORT INN
1155 Fairville
Blvd
(E2M 5T9)
(506) 674-1873
(800) 228-5150

**COUNTRY INN
& SUITES**
1011 Fairville
Blvd
(E2M 4Y2)
(506) 635-0400
(800) 456-4000

**DELTA
BRUNSWICK**
39 King St
(E2L 4W3)
(506) 648-1981
(800) 268-1133

**FORT HOWE
HOTEL**
10 Portland St
at Main St
(506) 657-7320

**HOWARD
JOHNSON
HOTEL**
400 Main St,
Chelsey Dr
(E2K 4N5)
(506) 642-2622
(800) 446-4656

**ISLAND VIEW
MOTEL**
1726
Manawagonish
Rd (E2M 3Y5)
(506) 672-1381

REGENT MOTEL
2121 Ocean West
Way
(E2M 5H6)
(506) 672-8273

**SAINT JOHN
HILTON**
1 Market Square
(506) 693-8484
(800) 445-8667

**SHADOW LAWN
COUNTRY INN**
3180 Rothesay Rd
(506) 847-7539

SAINT-LEONARD

DAIGLE'S MOTEL
68 rue DuPont
(E0L 1M0)
(506) 423-6351

ST. ANDREWS

**CANADIAN
PACIFIC THE
ALGONQUIN**
184 Adolphus St,
Off Hwy 127
(506) 529-8823
(800) 441-1414

**KINGSBRAE
ARMS HOTEL**
219 King St
(E5B 1Y1)
(506) 529-1897
(877) 529-1897

ST. GEORGE

**GRANITE
TOWN HOTEL &
COUNTRY INN**
79 Main St
(506) 755-6415

**LAKE
DIGDEGUASH
FOUR SEASONS
CHALETS**
148 Pleasant St
(E3L 2X2)
(506) 755-2737

ST. STEPHEN

**LEON BAY
LODGE**
Rt 3
(506) 466-1240

ST. STEPHEN INN
99 King St (E3L
2C6)
(506) 466-1814

SUSSEX

ECONO LODGE
1015 Main St
(E4E 2M6)
(506) 433-2220
(800) 553-2666

**PINE CONE
MOTEL**
Hwy 114 (E0E
1P0)
(506) 433-3958

**QUALITY INN
FAIRWAY**
Trans Canada
Hwy #2
(E4E 5L6)
(506) 433-3470
(800) 228-5151

WOODSTOCK

**AUBERGE
WANDLYN INN**
Trans Canada
Hwy #2 (E0J 2B0)
(506) 328-8876
(800) 561-0000

**PANORAMA
MOTEL**
Trans Canada
Hwy #2
(E0J 2B0)
(506) 328-3315

**STILES MOTEL
HILLVIEW**
827 Main St
(E0J 2B0)
(506) 328-6671

*YOUNGS
COVE ROAD*

**MCCREADY'S
MOTEL**
Young's Cove
Rd, Centre (E0E
1S0)
(506) 362-2916

NEWFOUNDLAND

CORNER BROOK

BEST WESTERN MAMATEEK INN
Maple Valley Rd
Box 787 (A1H 6G7)
(709) 639-8901
(800) 528-1234
(800) 563-8600

COMFORT INN
41 Maple Valley Rd
(A2H 6P2)
(709) 639-1980
(800) 228-5150

HOLIDAY INN
48 West St
(A2H 2Z2)
(709) 634-5381
(800) 465-4329

GANDER

ALBATROSS MOTEL
Trans Canada Hwy #1
(A1V 1W8)
(709) 256-3956

COMFORT INN
112 Trans Canada Hwy #1 (A1V 1P8)
(709) 256-3535
(800) 228-5150

HOTEL GANDER
100 Trans Canada Hwy (A1V 1P5)
(709) 256-3931

SINBAD'S HOTEL & SUITES
Bennett Dr
(A1V 1W8)
(709) 651-2678
(800) 563-4900

GRAND FALLS

MOUNT PETYON MOTOR HOTEL
214 Lincoln Rd
(A2A 1P8)
(709) 489-2251
(800) 563-4900

ST. JOHN'S

THE BATTERY HOTEL & SUITES
100 Signal Hill Rd
(709) 576-0040

BEST WESTERN TRAVELLERS INN
199 Kenmount Rd (A1B 3P9)
(709) 722-5540
(800) 528-1234
(800) 261-5540

DELTA ST. JOHNS HOTEL
120 New Gower St
(A1C 6K4)
(709) 739-6404
(800) 268-1133

HOLIDAY INN GOVERNMENT CENTRE
180 Portugal Cove Rd (A1B 2N2)
(702) 722-0506
(800) 465-4329

STEPHENVILLE

HOLIDAY INN
44 Queen St
(A2N 2M5)
(709) 643-6666
(800) 465-4329

NORTHWEST TERRITORIES

BAKER LAKE

IGLU HOTEL
Box 179 (X0C 0A0)
(867) 793-2801

FORT PROVIDENCE

SNOWSHOE INN
(X0E 0L0)
(867) 699-3511

HAY RIVER

MACKENZIE PLACE
Box 1880 (X0E 0R0)
(867) 874-2535

MIGRATOR MOTEL
Box 1847 (X0E 0R0)
(867) 874-6792

PTARMIGAN INN
Box 1000 (X0E 0R0)
(867) 874-6781

HOLMAN

ARCTIC CHAR INN
General Delivery
(X0E 0S0)
(867) 396-3531

IQALUIT

NAVIGATOR INN
P. O. Box 158
(X0A 0H0)
(867) 979-6201

NORMAN WELLS

RAYUKA INN
Box 308 (X0E 0V0)
(867) 587-2354

YELLOWKNIFE

YELLOWKNIFE INN
P. O. Box 490
(X1A 2N4)
(867) 873-2601

NOVA SCOTIA

AMHERST

AUBERGE WANDLYN INN
Box 275, Hwy 104
(B4H 3Z2)
(902) 667-3331
(800) 561-0000

COMFORT INN
143 S Albion St
(B4H 2X2)
(902) 667-0404
(800) 228-5150

ANTIGONISH

MARITIME INN
158 Main St
(B2G 2B7)
(902) 863-4001

AULDS COVE

COVE MOTEL & MARINER DINING ROOM
Hwy 104
(902) 747-2700

BADDECK

MCINTYRE'S HOUSEKEEPING COTTAGES
8908 Hwy 105
(B0E 1B0)
(902) 295-1133

SILVER DART LODGE
259 Hwy 205
(B0E 1B0)
(902) 295-2340

BEDORD

ESQUIRE MOTEL
771 Bedford Hwy
(902) 835-3367

TRAVELERS MOTEL
773 Bedford Hwy
(B4A 1A4)
(902) 835-3394

BLACK POINT

GRAND VIEW MOTEL
Hwy 3 (B0J 1B0)
(902) 857-9776

BRIDGETOWN

BRIDGETOWN MOTOR HOTEL
396 Granville St E
(B0S 1C0)
(902) 665-4403

BRIDGEWATER

AUBERGE WANDLYN INN
50 North St, Box 40
(B4V 2W6)
(902) 543-7131
(800) 561-0000

COMFORT INN
49 North St
(B4V 2V7)
(902) 543-1498
(800) 228-5150

CHESTER

WINDJAMMER MOTEL
4070 Rt 3 (B0J 1J0)
(902) 275-3567

CHETICAMP

CABOT TRAIL SEA & GOLF CHALETS
71 Fraser Doucet Ln
(902) 224-1777

LAURIE'S MOTOR INN
15456 Main St
(902) 224-2400

CHURCH POINT

LA MANOIR SAMSON INN
1768 Rt 1
(902) 769-2526

DARTMOUTH

BEST WESTERN MIC MAC HOTEL
313 Prince Albert Rd (B2Y 1N3)
(902) 469-5850
(800) 528-1234
(800) 565-1275

COMFORT INN
456 Windmill Rd
(B3A 1J7)
(902) 463-9900
(800) 228-5150

COUNTRY INN & SUITES
101 Yorkshire Ave
(B2Y 3Y2)
(902) 465-4000
(800) 456-4000

FUTURE INNS
20 Highfield Park Dr
(B3A 4S8)
(902) 465-6555

HOLIDAY INN HARBOURVIEW
99 Wyse Rd
(B3A 1L9)
(902) 463-1100
(800) 465-4329

KEDDY'S DARTMOUTH INN
9 Braemer Dr
(B2H 3H6)
(902) 469-0331
(800) 561-7666

RAMADA PARK PLACE PLAZA HOTEL
240 Brownlow Ave (B3B 1X6)
(902) 468-8888
(800) 272-6232

DIGBY

ADMIRAL DIGBY INN
441 Shore Rd
(B0V 1A0)
(902) 245-2531

DINGWALL

MARKLAND COASTAL RESORT
802 Dingwall Rd
(902) 383-2246

HALIFAX

AUBERGE WANDLYN INN
50 Bedford Hwy
(B3M 2J2)
(902) 443-0416
(800) 561-0000

CHEBUCTO INN
6151 Lady Hammond Rd
(902) 453-4330

CITADEL HOTEL
1960 Brunswick St
(B3J 2G7)
(902) 422-1391
(800) 565-7162

DELTA BARRINGTON HOTEL
1875 Barrington St
(B3J 3L6)
(902) 429-7410
(800) 268-1133

DELTA HALIFAX
1990 Barrington St
(B3J 1P2)
(902) 425-6700
(800) 268-1133
(800) 828-7447

ECONO LODGE
560 Bedford Hwy
(B3M 2L8)
(902) 443-0303
(800) 553-2666

HOLIDAY INN EXPRESS
133 Kearney Lake Rd
(B3M 4P3)
(902) 445-1100
(800) 465-4329

HOLIDAY INN SELECT HALIFAX CENTRE
1980 Robie St
(B3H 3G5)
(902) 423-1161
(800) 465-4329

KEDDY'S HALIFAX HOTEL
20 St. Margarets Bay Rd (B3N 1J4)
(902) 477-5611
(800) 561-7666

THE LORD NELSON HOTEL
1515 S Park St, Box 700 (B3J 2T3)
(800) 565-2020

THE PRINCE GEORGE HOTEL
1725 Market St
(B3J 3N9)
(902) 425-1986
(800) 565-1567

SHERATON HALIFAX HOTEL
1919 Upper Water St
(902) 421-1700
(800) 325-3535

TRAVELODGE
374 Bedford Hwy,
(B3M 2L1)
(902) 443-1576
(800) 578-7878

THE WESTIN NOVA SCOTIAN
1181 Hollis St
(B3H 2P6)
(902) 421-1000
(800) 228-3000

INGONISH BEACH

KELTIC LODGE
Middle Head Peninsula
(B0C 1L0)
(902) 285-2880

KENTVILLE

ALLEN'S MOTEL
384 Park St
(B4N 1M9)
(902) 678-2683

AUBERGE WANDLYN INN
3230 Hwy 1
(B4N 1M9)
(902) 678-8311
(800) 561-0000

SUN VALLEY MOTEL
905 Park St
(B4N 1M9)
(902) 678-7368

LISCOMB

LISCOMB LODGE
Hwy 7,
Guysborough
Cnty
(902) 779-2307

LUNENBURG

BOSCAWEN INN
150 Cumberland St
(B0J 2C0)
(902) 634-3325

HOMEPORT MOTEL & INN
167 Victoria Rd
(B0J 2C0)
(902) 634-8234

MAHONE BAY

BAYVIEW PINES COUNTRY INN
678 Oakland Rd
(902) 624-9970

THE MANSE AT MAHONE BAY COUNTRY INN
88 Orchard St
(902) 624-1121

MARGAREE VALLEY

THE NORMAWAY INN
691 Egypt Rd
(902) 248-2987

MAVILLETTE

CAPE VIEW MOTEL & COTTAGES
Rt 1
(902) 645-2258

NEW GLASGOW

COMFORT INN
740 Westville Rd
(B2H 2J8)
(902) 755-6450
(800) 228-5150

COUNTRY INN & SUITES
700 Westville Rd
(B2H 2J8)
(902) 928-1333
(800) 456-4000

NORTH SYDNEY

BEST WESTERN NORTH STAR INN
39 Forrest St
(B2A 3M3)
(902) 794-8581
(800) 528-1234
(800) 561-8585

CLANSMAN MOTEL
Peppett St
(B2A 3M3)
(902) 794-7226

PORT HASTINGS

KEDDY'S INN
Trans Canada
Hwy 105
(902) 625-0460
(800) 561-7666

MACPUFFIN MOTEL
Hwy 4
(902) 625-0621

SKYE LODGE
353 Port Hastings
(B0E 2T0)
(902) 625-1300

PORT HAWKESBURY

MARITIME INN
717 Reeves St,
Box 759 (B0E 2V0)
(902) 625-0320

SCOTSBURN

STONEHAME CHALETS
Trans Canada
Hwy 104
(902) 485-3468

SHELBURNE

MACKENZIE'S MOTEL & COTTAGES
260 Water St
(B0T 1W0)
(902) 875-2842

SMITHS COVE

HEDLEY HOUSE MOTEL
RR 1
(902) 245-2500

MOUNTAIN GAP INN
Hwy 101
(902) 245-5841

SYDNEY

COMFORT INN
368 Kings Rd
(B1S 1A8)
(902) 562-0200
(800) 228-5150

DAYS INN
480 Kings Rd
(B1S 1A8)
(902) 539-6750
(800) 329-7466

DELTA SYDNEY HOTEL
300 Esplanade
(902) 562-7500
(800) 268-1133

SYDNEY MINES

GOWRIE HOUSE COUNTRY INN
139 Shore Rd
(B1V 1A6)
(902) 544-1050

TRURO

BEST WESTERN GLENGARRY TRADE & CONV CENTRE
150 Willow St
(B2N 4Z6)
(902) 893-4311
(800) 528-1234
(800) 567-4276

COMFORT INN
12 Meadow Dr
(B2N 5V4)
(902) 893-0330
(800) 228-5150

KEDDY'S INN
437 Prince St
(B2N 1E6)
(902) 895-1651
(800) 561-7666

PALLISER RESORT
Tidal Bore Rd
(902) 893-8951

WESTERN SHORE

OAK ISLAND INN & MARINA
55 Vaughn Rd
(B0J 3M0)
(902) 627-2600
(800) 565-5075

WHITE POINT

WHITE POINT BEACH RESORT
White Point
Beach,
Hwy 103
(902) 354-2711

YARMOUTH

BEST WESTERN MERMAID MOTEL
545 Main St
(B5A 1J6)
(902) 742-7821
(800) 528-1234
(800) 772-2774

CAPRI MOTEL
8-12 Herbert St
(B5A 1J6)
(902) 742-7168

COMFORT INN
96 Starrs Rd
(B5A 2T5)
(902) 742-1119
(800) 228-5150

LAKELAWN MOTEL
641 Main St
(902) 742-3588

RODD COLONY HARBOUR INN
6 Forrest St
(B5A 3K7)
(902) 742-9194
(800) 565-7633

RODD GRAND YARMOUTH-A RODD SIGNATURE HOTEL
417 Main St
(B5A 4B2)
(902) 742-2446
(800) 565-7633

ONTARIO

AURORA

**HOWARD JOHN-
SON**
15520 Yonge St
(L4G 1P2)
(905) 727-1312
(800) 446-4656

BANCROFT

**BEST WESTERN
SWORD MOTOR
INN**
146 Hastings St
(K0L 1C0)
(613) 332-2474
(800) 528-1234

BARRIE

**BEST WESTERN
ROYAL OAK INN**
35 Hart Dr
(L4N 5M3)
(705) 721-4848
(800) 528-1234

COMFORT INN
75 Hart Dr
(L4N 5M3)
(705) 722-3600
(800) 228-5150

HOLIDAY INN
20 Fairview Rd
(L4M 6E7)
(705) 728-6191
(800) 465-4329

TRAVELODGE
55 Hart Dr
(L4N 5M3)
(705) 734-9500
(800) 578-7878

TRAVELODGE
300 Bayfield St
(L4M 3B9)
(705) 722-4466
(800) 578-7878

BARRY'S BAY

**MOUNTAIN
VIEW MOTEL**
Box 101, RR 2
(K0J 1B0)
(613) 756-2757

BAYFIELD

**THE LITTLE INN
OF BAYFIELD**
Main St
(519) 565-2611

BELLEVILLE

**BEST WESTERN
INN**
387 Front St N
(K8P 3C8)
(613) 969-1112
(800) 528-1234

COMFORT INN
200 Park St N
(K8P 2Y9)
(613) 966-7703
(800) 228-5150

QUALITY INN
407 Front St N
(K8P 3C8)
(613) 962-9211
(800) 228-5151

**RAMADA INN
ON THE BAY**
11 Bay Bridge Rd,
Hwy 62 (K8N
4Z1
(613) 968-3411
(800) 272-6232

BLENHEIM

QUEEN'S MOTEL
Hwy 3, Talbots
Trail
(519) 676-5477

BOWMANVILLE

**HOWARD
JOHNSON
CLARINGTON
HOTEL**
143 Duke St
(L1C 2W4)
(905) 623-3373
(800) 446-4656

BRACEBRIDGE

**BELLWOOD
MOTEL**
133 Manitoba St
(705) 645-4424

ISLANDER INN
320 Taylor Rd
(705) 645-2235

BRAMPTON

COMFORT INN
5 Rutherford Rd
(L6W 3J3)
(905) 452-0600
(800) 228-5150

HOLIDAY INN
30 Peel Centre Dr
(L6T 4G3)
(905) 792-9900
(800) 465-4329

BRANTFORD

COMFORT INN
58 King George
Rd
(N3R 5K4)
(519) 753-3100
(800) 228-5150

DAYS INN
460 Fairview Dr
(N3R 7A9)
(519) 759-2700
(800) 329-7466

RAMADA INN
664 Colborne St
(N3S 3P8)
(519) 758-9999
(800) 272-6232

BRIGHTON

**PRESQUILE
BEACH MOTEL**
243 Main St W,
RR 4 (K0K 1H0)
(613) 475-1010

BROCKVILLE

**BEST WESTERN
WHITE HOUSE
MOTEL**
1843 Hwy 2 E
(K6V 5T1)
(613) 345-1622
(800) 528-1234

COMFORT INN
7777 Kent Blvd
(K6V 6N7)
(613) 345-0042
(800) 228-5150

SUPER 8 MOTEL
7789 Kent Blvd
(K6V 6N7)
(613) 345-3900
(800) 800-8000

BURLINGTON

COMFORT INN
3290 S Service Rd
(L7N 3M6)
(905) 639-1700
(800) 228-5150

HOLIDAY INN
3063 S Service Rd
(L7N 3E9)
(905) 639-4443
(800) 465-4329

**TOWN & COUN-
TRY MOTEL**
517 Plains Rd E
(L7T 2E2)
(905) 634-2383

**TRAVELODGE
HOTEL**
2020 Lakeshore
Rd
(L7S 1Y2)
(905) 681-0762
(800) 578-7878

CAMBRIDGE

**BEST WESTERN
CAMBRIDGE
HOTEL**
730 Hespeler Rd
(519) 623-4600
(800) 528-1234

COMFORT INN
220 Holiday Inn
Dr (N3C 1Z4)
(519) 658-1100
(800) 228-5150

GATEWAY INN
650 Hespeler Rd
(N1R 6J8)
(519) 622-1070

HOLIDAY INN
200 Holiday Inn
Dr (N3C 1Z4)
(519) 658-4601
(800) 465-4329

**LANGDON HALL
COUNTRY HOUSE
HOTEL & SPA**
RR 3
(519) 740-2100

CHAPLEAU

**RIVERSIDE
MOTEL**
116 Cherry St,
Box 699 (P0M
1K0)
(705) 864-0440

CHATHAM

COMFORT INN
1100 Richmond
St (N7M 5J5)
(519) 352-5500
(800) 228-5150

LUXURY INN
25 Michener Rd
(N7L 4B8)
(519) 354-3366

TRAVELODGE
555 Bloomfield
Rd(N7M 5J5)
(519) 436-1200
(800) 578-7878

CHATSWORTH

KEY MOTEL
RR 3, Hwy 6 & 10
(N0H 1G0)
(519) 794-2350

COBOURG

**BEST WESTERN
COBOURG INN
& CONV CENTRE**
930 Burnham St
(K3A 2X9)
(905) 372-2105
(800) 528-1234

COMFORT INN
121 Densmore Rd
(K9A 4J9)
(905) 372-7007
(800) 228-5150

CORNWALL

BEST WESTERN PARKWAY INN & CONV CENTRE
1515 Vincent
Massey Dr
(K6H 5R6)
(613) 932-0451
(800) 528-1234
(800) 874-2595

DAYS INN
1541 Vincent
Massey Dr
(K6J 5K6)
(613) 937-3535
(800) 329-7466

ECONO LODGE
1142 Brookdale
Ave (K61 4P4)
(613) 936-1996
(800) 553-2666

HOLIDAY INN
1625 Vincent
Massey Dr
(K6H 5R6)
(613) 937-0111
(800) 465-4329

RAMADA INN & CONF CENTRE
805 Brookdale
Ave (K6J 4P3)
(613) 933-8000
(800) 272-6232

DOWNSVIEW

MONTECASSINO HOTEL & BANQUET HALLS
3710 Chesswood
Dr
(416) 630-8100

DRYDEN

BEST WESTERN MOTOR INN
349 Government
Rd (P8N 2Z5)
(807) 223-3201
(800) 528-1234
(888) 394-2378

COMFORT INN
522 Government
Rd
(P8N 2P5)
(807) 223-3893
(800) 228-5150

ELLIOT LAKE

DUNLOP LAKE LODGE
75 Dunlop Lake
Rd (P5A 2J7)
(705) 848-8090

ELMSDALE

FERN GLEN INN BED & BREAKFAST
RR 1
(705) 636-1391

ETOBICOKE

HOLIDAY INN TORONTO AIRPORT
970 Dixon Rd
(M9W 1J9)
(416) 675-7611
(800) 465-4329

QUALITY SUITES-AIRPORT
262 Carlingview
Dr (M9W 5G1)
(416) 674-8442
(800) 228-5151

QUALITY HOTEL & SUITES-AIRPORT EAST
2180 Islington
Ave (M9P 3P1)
(416) 240-9090
(800) 228-5151

RAMADA HOTEL - TORONTO AIRPORT
2 Holiday Dr
(M9C 2Z7)
(416) 621-2121
(800) 272-6232

TRAVELODGE HOTEL
445 Rexdale Blvd
(M9W 6K5)
(416) 740-9500
(800) 578-7878

TRAVELODGE HOTEL
925 Dixon Rd
(M9W 1J8)
(416) 674-2222
(800) 578-7878

FONTHILL

HIPWELL'S MOTEL
299 Hwy 10 W,
Box 253 (L0S 1E0)
(905) 892-3588

FORT ERIE

COMFORT INN
1 Hospitality Dr
(L2A 6G1)
(905) 871-8500
(800) 228-5150

GANANOQUE

COUNTRY SQUIRE RESORT
715 King St E
(K7G 1H4)
(613) 382-3511

GLOUCESTER

COMFORT INN
1252 Michael St
(613) 744-2900
(800) 228-5150

TRAVELODGE
1486 Innes Rd
(K1B 3V5)
(613) 745-1133
(800) 578-7878

GRAVEN-HURST

HOWARD JOHNSON INN
1165 Muskoka Rd
S (P1P 1K6)
(705) 687-7707
(800) 446-4656

GRIMSBY

HOWARD JOHNSON INN
2 Windward Dr
(905) 309-7171
(800) 446-4656

GUELPH

BEST WESTERN EMERALD INN
106 Carden St
(N1H 3A3)
(519) 836-1331
(800) 528-1234

COMFORT INN
480 Silvercreek
Pkwy (N1H 7R5)
(519) 763-1900
(800) 228-5150

HOLIDAY INN
601 Scottsdale Dr
(N1G 3E7)
(519) 836-0231
(800) 465-4329

SUPER 8 MOTEL
281 Woodlawn
Rd (N1H 7K7)
(519) 836-5850
(800) 800-8000

HAMILTON

COMFORT INN
183 Centennial
Pkwy N (L8E 1H8)
(905) 560-4500
(800) 228-5150

HOWARD JOHNSON PLAZA HOTEL
112 King St E
(L8N 1A8)
(905) 546-8111
(800) 446-4656

RAMADA PLAZA HOTEL
150 King St E
(L8N 1B2)
(905) 528-3451
(800) 272-6232

SHERATON HAMILTON HOTEL
116 King St W
(L8P 4V3)
(905) 529-5515
(800) 325-3535

HAWKES-BURY

BEST WESTERN MOTEL L'HER-ITAGE
1575 Tupper St
(K6A 3E1)
(613) 632-5941
(800) 528-1234

HILTON BEACH

HILTON HARBOR RESORT
3117 Marks St
(705) 246-0063
(800) 445-8667

HUNTSVILLE

COMFORT INN
86 King William
St
(P0A 1K0)
(705) 789-1701
(800) 228-5150

HIGHLAND COURT MOTEL
208 W Main St
(P0A 1K0)
(705) 789-4424

TULIP MOTOR INN
1661 Muskoka
Rd 3 N (P0A 1K0)
(705) 789-4001
(800) 565-4001

INGERSOLL

TRAVELODGE
20 Samnah Cres
(N5C 3J7)
(519) 425-1100
(800) 578-7878

IRON BRIDGE

RED TOP MOTOR INN
Hwy 17 (P0R 1H0)
(705) 843-2100

JORDAN

**BEST WESTERN
BEACON
HARBORSIDE
RESORT &
CONF CENTRE**
2793 Beacon Blvd
(905) 562-4155
(800) 528-1234
(888) 823-2266

KAPUSKAS-ING

COMFORT INN
172 Government
Rd E (P5N 2W9)
(705) 335-8583
(800) 228-5150

KENORA

**BEST WESTERN
LAKESIDE INN &
CONV CENTRE**
470 1st Ave S
(P9N 1W5)
(807) 468-5521
(800) 528-1234
(800) 465-1120

COMFORT INN
1230 Hwy 17 E
(P9N 1L9)
(807) 468-8845
(807) 228-5150

DAYS INN
920 Hwy 17 E
(P9N 3X1)
(807) 468-2003
(800) 329-7466

SUPER 8 MOTEL
240 Lakeview Dr
(P9N 3W7)
(807) 468-8016
(800) 800-8000

TRAVELODGE
800 Sunset Strip
(P9N 1N9)
(807) 468-3155
(800) 578-7878

**WHISPERING
PINES MOTEL**
Hwy 17 E
(P0X 1H0)
(807) 548-4025

KINGSTON

COMFORT INN
55 Warne Crescent
(K7L 4V4)
(613) 546-0500
(800) 228-5150

**COMFORT INN
MIDTOWN**
1454 Princess St
(K7M 3E5)
(613) 549-5550
(800) 228-5150

ECONO LODGE
2327 Princess St
(K7M 3G1)
(613) 531-8929
(800) 553-2666

**EXECUTIVE
MOTEL**
794 Hwy 2 E
(K7L 4V1)
(613) 549-1620

**HOLIDAY INN
KINGSTON
WATERFRONT**
1 Princess St
(K7L 1A1)
(613) 549-8400
(800) 465-4329

**HOWARD
JOHNSON
CONFEDERATION
PLACE HOTEL**
237 Ontario St
(K7L 2Z4)
(613) 549-6300
(800) 446-4656

**THE NORTH
NOOK B&B**
83 Earl St
(613) 547-8061

PEACHTREE INN
1187 Princess St
(613) 546-4411

SUPER 8 MOTEL
720 Princess St
(K7L 1G2)
(613) 542-7395
(800) 800-8000

KIRKLAND LAKE

COMFORT INN
455 Government
Rd W (P0K 1A0)
(705) 567-4909
(800) 228-5150

SUPER 8 MOTEL
50 Government
Rd E
(P2N 1A5)
(705) 567-3241
(800) 800-8000

KITCHENER

**ARAM'S "ROOTS
& WINGS" B&B**
11 Sunbridge
Cres
(519) 743-4557

COMFORT INN
2899 King St E
(N2A 1A6)
(519) 894-3500
(800) 228-5150

**THE CONESTOGA
HOWARD
JOHNSON
HOTEL**
1333 E Weber St
(N2A 1C2)
(519) 893-1234
(800) 446-4656

**FOUR POINTS
HOTEL
SHERATON**
105 King St E
(N2G 3W9)
(519) 744-4141
(800) 325-3535

HOLIDAY INN
30 Fairway Rd S
(N2A 2N2)
(519) 893-1211
(800) 465-4329

**RADISSON
HOTEL**
2960 King St E
(N2A 1A9)
(519) 849-9500
(800) 333-3333

**RODEWAY
SUITES
CONESTOGA**
55 New Dundee
Rd (N2G 3W5)
(519) 895-2272
(800) 228-2000

LEAMINGTON

COMFORT INN
279 Erie St S
(N8H 3C4)
(519) 326-9071
(800) 228-5150

DAYS INN
Hwy 18 S,RR 1
(N8H 3V4)
(519) 326-8646
(800) 329-7466

LINDSAY

**RAMADA INN &
CONV CENTRE**
1754 Hwy 7 W
(K9V 4R2)
(705) 328-1743
(800) 272-6232

LONDON

**BEST WESTERN
LAMPLIGHTER INN**
591 Wellington
Rd S (N6C 4R3)
(519) 681-7151
(800) 528-1234
(888) 232-6747

**DELTA LONDON
ARMOURIES
HOTEL**
325 Dundas St
(N6B 1T9)
(519) 679-6111
(800) 268-1133

**HOWARD
JOHNSON INN**
1150 Wellington
Rd S (N6E 1M3)
(519) 681-1550
(800) 446-4656

QUALITY INN
1156 Wellington
Rd (N6E 1M3)
(519) 685-9300
(800) 228-5151

QUALITY SUITES
1120 Dearness Dr
(N6E 1N9)
(519) 680-1024
(800) 228-5151

**STATIONPARK
ALL SUITE HOTEL**
242 Pall Mall St
(N6A 5P6)
(519) 642-4444

SUPER 8 MOTEL
636 York St
(N5W 2S7)
(519) 433-8161
(800) 800-8000

MARATHON

PENINSULA INN
Hwy 17 (P0T
2E0)
(807) 229-0651

MARKHAM

COMFORT INN
8330 Woodbine
Ave
(L3R 2N8)
(905) 477-6077
(800) 228-5150

MIDLAND

COMFORT INN
980 King St
(L4R 4K5)
(705) 526-2090
(800) 228-5150

MILTON

QUALITY INN
161 Chisholm Dr
(L9T 4A6)
(905) 875-3818
(800) 228-5151

MISSISSAUGA

**BEST WESTERN
ADMIRAL HOTEL
& SUITES**
40 Admiral Blvd
& Hwy 10 (L5T
2W1)
(800) 528-1234

COMFORT INN
1500 Matheson
Blvd (L4W 3Z4)
(905) 624-6900
(800) 228-5150

**DELTA MEADOW-
VALE RESORT &
CONF CENTRE**
6750 Mississauga
Rd
(905) 821-1981
(800) 268-1133

**FOUR POINTS
HOTEL
SHERATON
TORONTO
AIRPORT**
5444 Dixie Rd
(905) 624-1144
(800) 325-3535

HAMPTON INN
7040 Edward
Blvd (L2S 1Z1)
(905) 564-2122
(800) 426-7866

**HILTON HOTEL
TORONTO
AIRPORT**
5875 Airport Rd
(905) 677-9900
(800) 445-8667

**HOLIDAY INN
TORONTO WEST**
100 Britannia Rd
(L4Z 2G1)
(905) 890-5700
(800) 465-4329

**HOWARD
JOHNSON
EXPRESS INN**
2420 Surveyor Rd
(L5N 4E6)
(905) 858-8600
(800) 446-4656

**NOVOTEL
HOTEL**
3670 Hurontario
St (L5B 1P3)
(905) 896-1000
(800) 668-6835

**RADISSON
HOTEL**
2501 Argentia Rd
(L5N 4G8)
(905) 858-2424
(800) 333-3333

**SANDALWOOD
HOTEL & SUITES**
5050 Orbitor Dr
(905) 238-9600

**SHERATON
GATEWAY
HOTEL
TORONTO
INT'L AIRPORT**
Box 3000
(905) 672-7000
(800) 325-3535

MONTEVILLE

**MEMQUISIT
LODGE**
Hwy 64 &
Memquisit Lodge
Rd
(705) 898-2355

MOUNT HOPE

**SUPER 8 MOTEL
HAMILTON
AIRPORT**
2975 Homestead
Dr (L0R 1W0)
(905) 679-3355
(800) 800-8000

NEPEAN

**MONTEREY INN
RESORT**
2259 Hwy 16
(K2E 6Z8)
(613) 226-5813

**RIDEAU HEIGHTS
MOTOR INN**
72 Rideau
Heights Rd
(613) 226-4152

NEW LISKEARD

ECONO LODGE
Hwy 11 N
(P0J 1P0)
(705) 647-6705
(800) 553-2666

QUALITY INN
Hwy 11 N
(P0J 1P0)
(705) 647-7357
(800) 228-5151

NEWMARKET

COMFORT INN
1230 Journey's
End Cir (L3Y
7V1)
(905) 895-3355
(800) 228-5150

NIAGARA FALLS

**BEST WESTERN
FALLSVIEW
MOTOR HOTEL**
5551 Murray St
(L2G 2J4)
(905) 356-0551
(800) 528-1234
(800) 263-2580

CAMELOT INN
5640 Stanley Ave
(L2G 3X5)
(905) 354-3754

**FLAMINGO
MOTOR INN**
7701 Lundy's Ln
(L2H 1H3)
(905) 356-4646
(800) 738-7701

GLENGATE MOTEL
5534 Stanley Ave
(L2G 3X2)
(905) 357-1333

**HOLIDAY INN
BY THE FALLS**
5339 Murray Hill
(905) 356-1333
(800) 465-4329

**HOWARD
JOHNSON
PLAZA HOTEL**
5905 Victoria Ave
(L2G 3L8)
(905) 357-4040
(800) 446-4656

**INN ON THE
NIAGARA PARK-
WAY**
7857 Niagara
River Pkwy
(905) 295-4371

**NIAGARA
PARKWAY
COURT MOTEL**
3708 Main St
(L2G 6B1)
(905) 295-3331

**PENINSULA INN
& RESORT**
7373 Niagara
Square Dr
(905) 354-8812

SHERATON INN
6045 Stanley Ave
(L2G 3Y3)
(905) 374-4142
(800) 325-3535
(800) 267-5439

**STANLEY
MOTOR INN**
6220 Stanley Ave
(905) 358-92138

SUNSET INN
5803 Stanley Ave
(L2G 3X8)
(905) 354-7513

THRIFTLODGE
6000 Stanley Ave
(L2G 3Y1)
(905) 358-6243
(800) 578-7878

*NIAGARA-
ON-THE-LAKE*

**COUNTRYSIDE
BED&BREAKFAST**
RR 2, Line 1 Rd
(L0S 1J0)
(905) 884-6218

**GATE HOUSE
HOTEL**
142 Queen St
(905) 468-3263

NORTH BAY

**BEST WESTERN
NORTH BAY INN**
700 Lakeshore Dr
(P1A 2G4)
(705) 474-5800
(800) 528-1234
(800) 461-6199

COMFORT INN
676 Lakeshore Dr
(P1A 2G4)
(705) 494-9444
(800) 228-5150

COMFORT INN
1200 O'Brien St
(P1B 9B3)
(705) 476-5400
(800) 228-5150

TRAVELODGE
800 Sunset Strip
(P9N 1L9)
(705) 468-3155
(800) 578-7878

TRAVELODGE
718 Lakeshore Dr
(P1A 2G4)
(705) 472-7171
(800) 578-7878

OAKVILLE

**QUALITY HOTEL
& EXEC SUITES**
754 Bronte Rd
(L6J 4Z3)
(905) 847-6667
(800) 228-5151

**RAMADA INN &
CONV CENTRE**
360 Oakville
Place
Dr (L6H 6K8)
(905) 845-7561
(800) 272-6232

ORILLIA

COMFORT INN
75 Progress Dr
(L3V 6V7)
(705) 327-7744
(800) 228-5150

**TRAVELODGE
HOTEL**
600 Sundial Dr
(L3V 6H3)
(705) 325-2233
(800) 578-7878

OSHAWA

COMFORT INN
605 Bloor St W
(L1J 5Y6)
(905) 434-5000
(800) 228-5150

HOLIDAY INN
1011 Bloor St E
(L1H 7K6)
(906) 576-5101
(800) 465-4329

OTTAWA

**ALBERT HOUSE
INN BED &
BREAKFAST**
478 Albert St
(613) 236-4479

COMFORT INN
1252 Michael St
(K1J 7T1)
(613) 744-2900
(800) 228-5150

**DAYS INN
DOWNTOWN**
319 Rideau St
(K1N 5Y4)
(613) 789-5555
(800) 329-7466

**DELTA OTTAWA
HOTEL & SUITES**
361 Queen St
(K1R 7S9)
(613) 238-6000
(800) 268-1133

**HOWARD
JOHNSON
HOTEL**
140 Slater St
(K1P 5H6)
(613) 238-2888
(800) 446-4656

LES SUITES HOTEL
130 Besserer St
(613) 232-2000

LORD ELGIN HOTEL
100 Elgin St
(K1P 5K8)
(613) 235-3333
(800) 267-4298

MARRIOTT HOTEL
100 Kent St
(K1P 5R7)
(613) 238-1122
(800) 228-9290

NOVOTEL HOTEL OTTAWA
33 Nicholas St
(K1N 9M7)
(613) 230-3033
(800) 668-6835

QUALITY HOTEL DOWNTOWN
290 Rideau St
(K1N 5Y3)
(613) 789-7511
(800) 228-5151

RAMADA HOTEL & SUITES
111 Cooper St
(K2P 2E3)
(613) 238-1331
(800) 272-6232

SHERATON HOTEL
150 Albert St
(K1P 5G2)
(613) 238-1500
(800) 325-3535

SOUTHWAY INN
2431 Bank St
(K1V 8R9)
(613) 737-0811

TRAVELODGE
2098 Montreal Rd
(K1J 6M8)
(613) 745-1531
(800) 578-7878

TRAVELODGE HOTEL
402 Queen St
(K1R 5A7)
(613) 236-1133
(800) 578-7878

TRAVELODGE HOTEL
1376 Carling Ave
(K1Z 7L5)
(613) 722-7600
(800) 578-7878

WEBB'S MOTEL
1705 Carling Ave
(K2A 1C8)
(613) 728-1881

WESTIN HOTEL
11 Colonel By Dr
(K1N 9H4)
(613) 560-7000
(800) 228-3000

OWEN SOUND

COMFORT INN
955 9th Ave E
(N4K 6N4)
(519) 371-5500
(800) 228-5150

CRYSTAL MOTEL
672 10th St W
(519) 372-2929

OWEN SOUND MOTOR INN
485 9th Ave E
(N4K 3E2)
(519) 371-3011

TRAVELODGE
880 10th St E
(N4K 1T4)
(519) 371-9297
(800) 578-7878

PARRY SOUND

BEST WESTERN GEORGIAN INN
48 Joseph St
(P2A 2G5)
(705) 746-5837
(800) 528-1234

COMFORT INN
120 Bowes St
(P2A 2L7)
(705) 746-6221
(800) 228-5150

JOLLY ROGER INN
Hwy 69
(705) 378-2461

SUNNY POINT COTTAGES & INN
Box P, Rosseau
Rd (P0C 1K0)
(705) 378-2505
(800) 265-0432

PEMBROKE

BEST WESTERN PEMBROKE INN & CONF CENTRE
1 International
Dr (K8A 6X9)
(613) 735-0131
(800) 528-1234
(800) 567-2378

COLONIAL FIRESIDE INN
1350 Pembroke St
W (K8A 7A3)
(613) 732-3623

COMFORT INN
959 Pembroke St
E (K8A 3M3)
(613) 735-1057
(800) 228-5150

PETER-BOROUGH

COMFORT INN
1209 Landsdowne
St (K9J 7M2)
(705) 740-7000
(800) 228-5150

HOLIDAY INN WATERFRONT
150 George St N
(K9J 3G5)
(705) 743-1144
(800) 465-4329

KING BETHUNE HOUSE B&B
270 King St
(705) 743-4101

QUALITY INN
1074 Landsdowne
St (K9J 1Z9)
(705) 748-6801
(800) 228-5151

ROBYN'S MOTEL
1136 Hwy 7E
(705) 745-3225

PICKERING

COMFORT INN
533 Kingston Rd
(L1V 3N7)
(905) 831-6200
(800) 228-5150

PLANTAGENET

MOTEL DE CHAMPLAIN
200 Hwy 17
(K0B 1L0)
(613) 673-5220

PORT ELGIN

SUPER 8 MOTEL
Hwy 21 S
(N0H 2C0)
(519) 832-2058
(800) 800-8000

PORT HOPE

THE CARLYLE INN
86 John St
(L1A 3V9)
(905) 885-8686

COMFORT INN
Hwy 401 & 28
(L1A 3V9)
(905) 885-7000
(800) 228-5150

THE HILL & DALE MANOR B&B
47 Pine St S
(L1A 3V9)
(905) 885-8686

PROVIDENCE BAY

HURON SANDS MOTEL
5216 Hwy 551,
General Delivery
(P0P 1T0)
(705) 377-4616

RICHARDS LANDING

THE CLANSMEN MOTEL
Hwy 548
(705) 246-2581

RICHMOND HILL

BEST WESTERN PARKWAY INN
600 Hwy 7 E
(L4B 1B2)
(905) 881-2600
(800) 528-1234
(800) 668-0101

ROSSPORT

THE WILLOWS INN BED & BREAKFAST
1 Main St
(807) 824-3389

ST. CATHARINES

COMFORT INN
2 Dunlop Dr
(L2R 1A2)
(905) 687-8890
(800) 228-5150

HOLIDAY INN
2 N Service Rd
(L2N 4G9)
(905) 934-8000
(800) 465-4329

HOWARD JOHNSON HOTEL & CONF CTR
89 Meadowvale
Dr (L2N 3Z8)
(905) 934-5400
(800) 446-4656

RAMADA PARK-WAY INN & CONV CTR
327 Ontario St
(L2R 5L3)
(905) 688-2324
(800) 272-6232

ST. THOMAS

COMFORT INN
100 Centennial
Ave
(N5R 5B2)
(519) 633-4082
(800) 228-5150

SARNIA

BEST WESTERN GUILDWOOD INN
1400 Venetian Blvd (N7T 7W6)
(519) 337-7577
(800) 528-1234

DRAWBRIDGE INN
283 N Christina St
(519) 337-7571

HOLIDAY INN
1498 Venetian Blvd (N7T 7W6)
(519) 336-4130
(800) 465-4329

SAULT STE. MARIE

AMBASSADOR MOTEL
1275 Great Northern Rd (P6A 5K7)
(705) 759-6199

BEL-AIR MOTEL
398 Pim St (P6B 2V1)
(705) 945-7950

COMFORT INN
333 Great Northern Rd (P6B 4Z8)
(705) 759-8000
(800) 228-5150

GLENVIEW VACATION COTTAGES
2611 Great Northern Rd
(705) 759-3436

HOLIDAY INN WATERFRONT
208 St. Mary's River Dr (P6A 5V4)
(705) 949-0611
(800) 465-4329

NORTHLANDER MOTEL
243 Great Northern Rd
(705) 254-6452

RAMADA INN & CONV CENTER
229 Great Northern Rd (P6B 4Z2)
(705) 942-2500
(800) 262-6232

SATELITE MOTEL
248 Great Northern Rd (P6B 4Z6)
(705) 759-2897

SLEEP INN
727 Bay St (P6A 1X6)
(705) 253-7533
(800) 753-3746

TRAVELODGE SUITES
332 Bay St, (P6A 1X1)
(705) 759-1400
(800) 578-7878

SIMCOE

BEST WESTERN LITTLE RIVER INN
203 Queensway W (N3Y 2M9)
(519) 426-2125
(800) 528-1234

COMFORT INN
85 The Queensway E (N3Y 4M5)
(519) 426-2611
(800) 228-5150

SUDBURY

BEST WESTERN DOWNTOWN SUDBURY CENTRE-VILLE
151 Larch St (P3E 1C3)
(705) 673-7801
(800) 528-1234
(800) 387-0697

COMFORT INN
440 2nd Ave N (P3A 4S9)
(705) 560-4502
(800) 228-5150

COMFORT INN
2171 Regent St S (P3E 5V3)
(705) 522-1101
(800) 228-5150

DAYS INN
117 Elm St (P3C 1T3)
(705) 674-7517
(800) 329-7466

HOWARD JOHNSON HOTEL
390 Elgin St S (P3B 1B4)
(705) 675-1273
(800) 446-4656

RAMADA INN CITY CENTRE
85 Ste. Anne Rd (P3E 4S4)
(705) 675-1123
(800) 272-6232

SUPER 8 MOTEL
1956 Regent St S (P3E 3Z9)
(705) 522-7600
(800) 800-8000

TRAVELODGE
1401 Paris St (P3E 3B6)
(705) 522-1100
(800) 578-7878

THESSALON

CAROLYN BEACH MOTEL
1 Lakeside Dr (P0R 1L0)
(705) 842-3330

THOROLD

NIAGARA SUITES HOTEL
3530 Schmon Pkwy
(905) 984-8484

THUNDER BAY

BEST WESTERN CROSSROADS MOTOR INN
655 W Arthur St (P7E 5R6)
(807) 577-4241
(800) 528-1234
(800) 265-3253

BEST WESTERN NOR'WESTER RESORT HOTEL
2080 Hwy 61 (P7J 1B8)
(807) 473-9123
(800) 528-1234
(888) 473-2378

COMFORT INN
660 W Arthur St (P7E 5R8)
(807) 475-3155
(800) 228-5150

PINEBROOK BED & BREAKFAST
134 Mitchell Rd
(807) 683-6114

RITZ MOTEL
2600 Arthur St E
(807) 623-8189

SUPER 8 MOTEL
439 Memorial Ave (P7B 3Y6)
(807) 344-2612
(800) 800-8000

TRAVELODGE
450 Memorial Ave (P7B 3Y7)
(807) 345-2343
(800) 578-7878

TRAVELODGE HOTEL
698 W Arthur St (P7E 5R8)
(807) 473-1600
(800) 578-7878

TILLSON-BURG

SUPER 8 MOTEL
92 Simcoe St (N4G 2J1)
(519) 842-7366
(800) 800-8000

TIMMINS

BEST WESTERN HOTEL & CONF CENTRE
1800 Riverside Dr (P4N 7J5)
(705) 267-6241
(800) 528-1234

COMFORT INN BY JOURNEY'S END
939 Algonquin Blvd E (P4N 7J5)
(705) 264-9474
(800) 228-5150

SUPER 8 MOTEL
730 Algonquin Blvd E (P4N 7G2)
(705) 268-7171
(800) 800-8000

TRAVELODGE
1136 Riverside Dr (P4R 1A2)
(705) 360-1122
(800) 578-7878

TORONTO
(Metro Area)

BEST WESTERN CARLTON PLACE HOTEL-AIRPORT
33 Carlston Crt (M9W 6H5)
(416) 675-1234
(800) 528-1234

BEST WESTERN ROSEHAMPTON HOTEL & SUITES
808 Mt. Pleasant Rd (M4P 2L2)
(416) 487-5101
(800) 528-1234
(800) 387-8899

CANADIAN PACIFIC HOTEL-ROYAL YORK
100 Front St W (M5J 1E3)
(416) 368-2511
(800) 441-1414

CANADIAN PACIFIC SKY-DOME HOTEL
1 Blue Jays Way (M5V 3B4)
(416) 341-7100
(800) 441-1414

CARLINGVIEW AIRPORT INN
221 Carlingview Dr (M9W 5E8)
(416) 675-3303

COLONY HOTEL
89 Chestnut St
(M5G 1R1)
(416) 977-0707

COMFORT INN
66 Norfinch Dr
(M3N 1X1)
(416) 736-4700
(800) 228-5150

DAYS INN DOWNTOWN
30 Carlton St
(M5B 2E9)
(416) 977-6655
(800) 329-7466

DELTA CHELSEA HOTEL
33 Gerrard St W
(M5G 1Z4)
(416) 595-1975
(800) 268-1133

DELTA TORONTO AIRPORT
801 Dixon Rd
(M9W 1J5)
(416) 675-6100
(800) 268-1133

DELTA TORONTO EAST
2035 Kennedy Rd
(M1T 3G2)
(416) 299-1500
(800) 268-1133

FOUR SEASONS HOTEL
21 Avenue Rd
(M5R 2G1)
(416) 964-0411
(800) 332-3442

HILTON TORONTO
145 Richmond St W
(416) 869-3456
(800) 445-8667

HOLIDAY INN ON KING
370 King St W
(M5V 1J9)
(416) 599-4000
(800) 465-4329

HOTEL INTER-CONTINENTAL
220 Bloor St W
(M5S 1T8)
(416) 960-5200

HOWARD JOHNSON PLAZA HOTE NORTH YORK
2737 Keele St
(M2M 2E9)
(416) 636-4656
(800) 446-4656

LE ROYAL MERIDIEN KING EDWARD HOTEL
37 King St E
(M5C 1E9)
(416) 863-3131

METROPOLITAN HOTEL
108 Chestnut St
(416) 977-5000

NOVOTEL NORTH YORK HOTEL
3 Park Home Ave
(M2N 6L3)
(416) 733-2929
(800) 221-4542

NOVOTEL-TORONTO AIRPORT
135 Carlingview Dr (M9W 5E7)
(416) 798-9800
(800) 221-4542

NOVOTEL-TORONTO CENTRE
45 The Esplanade
(M5E 1W2)
(416) 367-8900
(800) 221-4542

PARK HYATT HOTEL
4 Avenue Rd
(M5R 2E8)
(416) 924-1234

QUALITY HOTEL-DOWNTOWN
111 Lombard St
(M5C 2T9)
(416) 367-5555
(800) 228-5151

QUALITY HOTEL-MIDTOWN
280 Bloor St W
(M5S 1V8)
(416) 968-0010
(800) 228-5151

RADISSON PLAZA HOTEL ADMIRAL HARBOURFRONT
249 Queen's Quay W
(416) 203-3333
(800) 333-3333

RADISSON SUITE HOTEL AIRPORT
640 Dixon Rd
(416) 242-7400
(800) 333-3333

RAMADA HOTEL AIRPORT EAST
1677 Wilson Ave
(M3L 1A5)
(416) 249-8171
(800) 272-6232

VALHALLA INN
1 Valhalla Inn Rd
(M9B 1S9)
(416) 239-2391

THE WESTIN HARBOUR CASTLE
One Harbour Square (M5J 1A6)
(416) 869-1600
(800) 228-3000

TRENTON

COMFORT INN
68 Monogram Pl
(K8V 6S3)
(613) 965-6660
(800) 228-5150

DAYS INN
10 Trenton St
(K8V 4M9)
(613) 392-9291
(800) 329-7466

HOLIDAY INN
99 Glen Miller Rd
(K8V 5R1)
(613) 394-4855
(800) 465-4329

TWEED

PARK PLACE MOTEL
43 Victoria St
(K0K 3J0)
(613) 478-3134

WALLACE-BURG

SUPER 8 MOTEL
76 McNaughton Ave (N8A 1R9)
(519) 627-0781
(800) 800-8000

WASAGA BEACH

BON AIR MOTEL
268 Main St (L0L 2P0)
(705) 429-6364

KINGSBRIDGE INN
268 Main St (L0L 2P0)
(705) 429-6364

WATERLOO

COMFORT INN
190 Weber St N
(N2J 3H4)
(519) 747-9400
(800) 228-5150

WATERLOO INN
475 King St N
(519) 884-0220

WAWA

KINNIWABI PINES MOTEL/COTTAGES
Hwy 17
(P0S 1K0)
(705) 856-7302

PARKWAY MOTEL
Box 784, Hwy 17
(P0S 1K0)
(705) 856-7020

SPORTSMAN'S MOTEL
45 Mission Rd, Box 219
(P0S 1K0)
(705) 856-2272

WAWA NORTHERN LIGHTS MOTEL
Box 124, Hwy 17 N (P0S 1K0)
(705) 856-1900

WELLAND

BEST WESTERN ROSE CITY SUITES
300 Prince Charles Dr (L3C 7B3)
(905) 732-0922
(800) 528-1234
(800) 387-8186

COMFORT INN
870 Niagara St
(L3C 1M3)
(905) 732-4811
(800) 228-5150

WHITBY

QUALITY SUITES
1700 Champlain Ave (L1N 6A7)
(905) 432-8800
(800) 228-5151

WHITEFISH FALLS

THE ISLAND LODGE
Box 87, Hwy 6
(705) 285-4343
(Phone for boat)

WINDSOR

COMFORT INN
2955 Dougall Ave
(N9E 1S1)
(519) 966-7800
(800) 228-5150

HILTON WINDSOR
277 Riverview Dr W (N9A 5K4)
(519) 973-5555
(800) 445-8667

HOLIDAY INN SELECT
1855 Huron Church Rd
(N9C 2L6)
(519) 966-1200
(800) 465-4329

HOWARD JOHNSON PLAZA HOTEL
430 Ouellette Ave
(N9A 1B2)
(519) 256-4656
(800) 446-4656

**IVY ROSE
MOTOR INN**
2885 Howard
Ave
(519) 966-1700

**QUALITY SUITES-
DOWNTOWN**
250 Dougall Ave
(N9A 7C6)
(519) 977-9707
(800) 228-5151

**RADISSON
RIVERFRONT
HOTEL**
333 Riverside
Drive W
(519) 977-9777
(800) 333-3333

WOODSTOCK

**QUALITY INN &
CONV CENTRE**
580 Bruin Blvd
(N4V 1E5)
(519) 537-5586
(800) 228-5151

SUPER 8 MOTEL
560 Norwich Ave
(N4V 1C6)
(519) 421-4588
(800) 800-8000

WYOMING

**COUNTRY VIEW
MOTEL & RV
PARK CAMPING
RESORT**
Hwy 22
(519) 845-3394

PRINCE EDWARD ISLAND

CAVENDISH

BAY VISTA MOTOR INN
RR 1 (C0A 1N0)
(902) 963-2225

CAVENDISH BOSOM BUDDIES COTTAGES
RR 1 (C0A 1N0)
(902) 963-3449

CAVENDISH MAPLES COTTAGES
(Rt 6 & 13 (C0A 1N0)
(902) 963-2818

CHARLOTTETOWN

BEST WESTERN CHARLOTTETOWN
238 Grafton St
(C1A 1L5)
(902) 892-2461
(800) 528-1234

COMFORT INN
112 Trans Canada Hwy (C1E 1E7)
(902) 566-4424
(800) 228-5150

DELTA PRINCE EDWARD HOTEL
18 Queen St
(C1A 8B9)
(902) 566-2222
(800) 268-1133

HOLIDAY INN EXPRESS HOTEL & SUITES
Trans Canada Hwy 1
(902) 892-1201
(800) 465-4329

QUALITY INN ON THE HILL
150 Euston St
(C1A 1W5)
(902) 894-8572
(800) 228-5151

RODD CHARLOTTETOWN A RODD SIGNATURE HOTEL
Kent & Pownal Sts
(902) 894-7371
(800) 565-7633

RODD CONFEDERATION INN & SUITES
Trans Canada Hwy (C1A 7L3)
(902) 892-2481
(800) 565-7633

RODD ROYALTY INN & CONF CENTER
Intersection of Hwys 1 & 2
(C1A 8C2)
(902) 894-8566
(800) 565-7633

THRIFTLODGE
Highway 1
(C1A 7L3)
(902) 892-2481
(800) 578-7878

CORNWALL

SUNNY KING MOTEL
Centre on Hwy 1
(C0A 1H0)
(902) 566-2209

MAYFIELD

QUALITY INN
Rt 13 (C0A 1N0)
(902) 963-2213
(800) 228-5151

MONTAGUE

RODD MARINA INN & SUITES
115 Sackville st
(C0A 1R0)
(902) 838-4075
(800) 565-7633

NORTH RUSTICO

ST. LAWRENCE MOTEL
PEI National Park on Gulf Shore Road
(902) 963-2053

ROSENEATH

RODD BRUDENELL RIVER A RODD SIGNATURE RESORT
Rt 4 & 3
(902) 652-2332
(800) 565-7633

STRATFORD

ANNE'S OCEAN VIEW HAVEN B&B
Kinloch R
(902) 569-4644

SUMMERSIDE

QUALITY INN GARDEN OF THE GULF
618 Water St E
(C1N 2V5)
(902) 436-2295
(800) 228-5151

WOODSTOCK

RODD MILL RIVER- A RODD SIGNATURE HOTEL
Rt 136 (C0B 1V0)
(902) 859-3555
(800) 565-7633

QUEBEC

ALMA

COMFORT INN
870 Ave du Pont
Sud (G8B 2V8)
(418) 668-9221
(800) 228-5150

ANCIENNE LORETTE

COMFORT INN-WEST
1255 Boul
Duplessis
(G2G 2B4)
(418) 872-5900
(800) 228-5150

AYLMER

CHATEAU CARTIER RESORT
1170 Chemin
Aylmer
(819) 778-0000

BAIE-ST-PAUL

HOTEL BAIE-SAINT-PAUL
911 Boul Mgr
Laval
(418) 435-3683

BEAUPORT

COMFORT INN-EAST
240 Boul Sainte-Anne (G1E 3L7)
(418) 666-1226
(800) 228-5150

BOUCHERVILLE

COMFORT INN-SOUTH SHORE
96 Boul de
Mortagne
(J4B 5M7)
(450) 641-2880
(800) 228-5150

BROSSARD

COMFORT INN SOUTH
7863 Boul
Taschereau
(J4Y 1A4)
(450) 678-9350
(800) 228-5150

CHICOUTIMI

COMFORT INN
1595 Boul Talbot
(G7H 4C3)
(418) 693-8686
(800) 228-5150

LE NOUVEL HOTEL LA SAGUE-NEENNE
250 des
Saguenéens
(G7H 3A4)
(418) 545-8326

DORVAL

COMFORT INN-AEROPORT
340 Ave Michel-Jasmin (H9P 1C1)
(514) 636-3391
(800) 228-5150

QUALITY HOTEL-DORVAL AEROPORT
7700 Cote de
Liesse
(H4T 1E7)
(514) 731-7821
(800) 228-5151

TRAVELODGE DORVAL AIR-PORT
1010 Herron Rd
(H9S 1B3)
(514) 631-4537
(800) 578-7878

DRUMMOND-VILLE

COMFORT INN
1055 Rue Hains
(J2C 6G6)
(819) 477-4000
(800) 228-5150

GASPE

MOTEL ADAMS
20 Rue Adams
(G0C 1R0)
(418) 368-2244

QUALITY INN DES COMMANDANTS
178 Rue De La
Reine(G0C 1R0)
(418) 368-3355
(800) 228-5151

GATINEAU

COMFORT INN
630 Boul la
Gappe
(J8T 9Z6)
(819) 243-6010
(800) 228-5150

GRANBY

HOTEL LA CASTEL
901 Rue
Principale
(450) 378-9071

HULL

HOLIDAY INN
2 Montcalm St,
(J8X 4B4)
(819) 778-3880
(800) 465-4329

L'ANCIENNE LORETTE

COMFORT INN
1255 Boul
Duplessis
(G2G 2B4)
(418) 872-5900
(800) 228-5150

LA MALBAIE POINTE AU PIC

ECONO LODGE
250 Boul de
Comporte
(G5A 1T1)
(418) 665-3733
(800) 553-2666

LA MANOIR REICHELIEU
181 Rue
Richelieu
(418) 665-3703

LA POCATIERE

MOTEL LA POCATOIS
235 Rt 132
(G0R 1Z0)
(418) 856-1688

LAC-BROME (KNOWLTON)

AUBERGE LAKEVIEW INN
50 Rue Victoria
(450) 243-6183

LAVAL

COMFORT INN
2055 Autoroute
des Laurentides
(H7S 1Z6)
(450) 686-0600
(800) 228-5150

ECONO LODGE
1981 Blvd Cure
Labelle (H7T
1L4)
(450) 681-6411
(800) 553-2666

HOTEL PRESIDENT LAVAL
2225 Autoroute
des Laurentides
(450) 682-2225

QUALITY SUITES

2035 Autoroute
des Laurentides
(H7S 1Z6)
(450) 686-6777
(800) 228-5151

TRAVELODGE HOTEL
2900 Boul le
Carrefour
(H7T 2K9)
(450) 682-9000
(800) 578-7878

LEBEL SUR LENNOXVILLE

LA PAYSANNE MOTEL
42 Queen
(J1M 1H9)
(819) 569-5585

LEVIS

COMFORT INN
10 du Vallon est
(G6V 9J3)
(418) 835-5605
(800) 228-5150

LONGUEUIL

DAYS INN
2800 Boul Marie
Victorian
(J4G 1P5)
(450) 677-8911
(800) 329-7466

HOLIDAY INN
900 Rue St-Charles
(J4K 2T1)
(450) 646-8100
(800) 465-4329

LOUISVILLE

GITE DU CAR-REFOUR AND MAISON HISTORIQUE J.L.L. HAMELIN
11 Ave St-Laurent
Ouest
(819) 228-4932

MARIA

QUALITY INN HONGUEDO
546 Boul Perron
(60C 1Y0)
(418) 759-3488
(800) 228-5151

MATANE

MOTEL LA MARINA
1032 Ave Du Phare Ouest
(418) 562-3234

QUALITY INN INTER-RIVES MATANE
1550 Ave Du Phare Ouest
(G4W 3M6)
(418) 562-6433
(800) 228-5151

MONT LAURIER

COMFORT INN
700 Blvd Paquette
(J9L 1L4)
(819) 623-6465
(800) 228-5150

MONTEBELLO

LE CHATEAU MONTEBELLO
392 Rue Notre-Dame
(819) 423-6341

MONTREAL

(Metro Area)

BEST WESTERN EUROPA DOWNTOWN
1240 Rue Drummond
(H3G 1V7)
(514) 866-6492
(800) 528-1234
(800) 361-3000

CHATEAU VERSAILLES HOTEL
1659 Rue Sherbrooke Ouest
(514) 933-3611

CROWNE PLAZA-METRO CENTRE
505 Rue Sherbrooke East
(H2L 1K2)
(514) 842-8581
(800) 227-6963

DELTA MONTREAL
475 Ave President Kennedy (H3A 2T4)
(514) 286-1986
(800) 268-1133

HILTON MONTREAL BONAVENTURE
1 Place Bonaventure
(514) 878-2332
(800) 445-8667

HOLIDAY INN MIDTOWN
420 Rue Sherbrooke Ouest (H3A 1B4)
(514) 842-6111
(800) 465-4329

HOTEL AUBERGE UNIVERSAL
5000 Rue Sherbrooke E
(514) 253-3365

HOTEL INTER-CONTINENTAL
360 Rue St-Antoine Ouest
(514) 987-9900

HOTEL LORD BERRI
11 Rue Berri
(514) 845-9236

HOTEL OMNI MONTREAL
1050 Rue Sherbrooke Ouest
(H3A 2R6)
(514) 284-1110
(800) 843-6664

LA CENTRE SHERATON
1201 Boul Rene-Levesque Ouest
(514) 878-2000
(800) 325-3535

LOEWS HOTEL VOGUE
1425 Rue de la Montagne
(514) 285-5555
(800) 235-6397

NOVOTEL
1180 Rue de la Montagne
(H3G 1Z1)
(514) 861-6000
(800) 668-6835

QUALITY HOTEL
3440 Ave Du Parc
(H2X 2H5)
(514) 849-1413
(800) 228-5151

RENAISSANCE HOTEL DU PARC
3625 Ave du Parc
(H2X 3P8)
(514) 288-6666
(800) 468-3571

RESIDENCE INN BY MARRIOTT
2056 Rue Peel
(514) 982-6064
(800) 331-3131

SHERATON FOUR POINTS MONTREAL
475 Rue Sherbrooke Ouest (H3A 2L9)
(514) 842-3961
(800) 325-3535

TRAVELODGE HOTEL
50 Boul René-Lévesque Ouest
(H2Z 1A2))
(514) 874-9090
(800) 578-7878

NEW RICHMOND

HOTEL MOTEL FRANCIS
210 Pandiac
(G0C 2B0)
(418) 392-4485

PASPEBIAC

MOTEL CAROL
127 Boul Gerard D Levesque CP1035
(418) 752-3158

PERCE

AU PIC DE L'AURORE
1 Rt 132
(418) 782-2166

BONAVENTURE PAVILLON COTE SURPRISE
367 Rt 132
(418) 782-2166

HOTEL MOTEL MANOIR DE PERCE
212 Rt 132
(418) 782-2022

PINE HILL

HOTEL DU LAC CARLING
2255 Rt 327
(450) 533-9211

POINTE CLAIRE

COMFORT INN-WEST ISLAND
700 Boul Saint-Jean (H9R 3K2)
(514) 697-6210
(800) 228-5150

HOLIDAY INN
6700 Trans Canada Hwy (H9R 1C2)
(514) 697-7110
(800) 465-4329

QUALITY SUITES-WEST ISLAND
6300 Trans Canada Hwy (H9R 1B9)
(514) 426-5060
(800) 228-5151

QUEBEC CITY

(Metro Area)

CHATEAU GRANDE-ALLEE
601 Grande-Allee E
(418) 647-4433

HILTON QUEBEC
1100 Boul Rene-Levesque E
(418) 647-2411
(800) 445-8667

HOTEL CHATEAU BELLEVUE
16 Rue de La Porte
(418) 692-2573

HOTEL CHATEAU LAURIER
1220 George V W
(418) 522-8108

HOTEL LA MANOIR LAFAYETTE
661 Rue Grande Allee
(418) 522-2652

L'HOTEL DU VIEUX QUEBEC
1190 Rue St-Jean
(418) 692-1850

LOEWS LE CONCORDE
1225 Place Montcalm
(G1R 4W6)
(418) 647-2222
(800) 235-6397

QUALITY HOTEL DOWNTOWN
330 rue de la Couronne
(G1K 6E6)
(418) 649-1919
(800) 228-5151

QUALITY SUITES
1600 Rue Bouvier
(G2K 1N8)
(418) 622-4244
(800) 228-5151

RAMADA HOTEL DOWNTOWN
395 Rue De La Couronne
(G1K 7X4)
(418) 647-2611
(800) 272-6232

RIMOUSKI

COMFORT INN
455 Boul St-Germain Ouest
(G5L 3P2)
(418) 724-2500
(800) 228-5150

HOTEL L'EMPRESS
360 Monte Industrielle
(418) 723-6944

RIVIERE DU-LOUP

COMFORT INN
85 Boul Cartier
(G5R 4X4)
(418) 867-4162
(800) 228-5150

DAYS INN
182 Rue Fraser
(G2R 1C8)
(418) 862-6354
(800) 329-7466

ROBERVAL

HOTEL CHATEAU ROBERVAL
1225 Boul
St-Dominique
(418) 275-7511

ROCK FOREST

COMFORT INN
4295 Boul
Bourque (J1N 1C3
(819) 564-4400
(800) 228-5150

ROUYN-NORANDA

COMFORT INN
1295 Rue
Lariviere
(J9X 6M6)
(819) 797-1313
(800) 228-5150

SALABERRY DE VALLEYFIELD

HOTEL VALLEY-FIELD BY DELTA
40 Ave du
Centenaire
(450) 373-1990
(800) 268-1133

ST.-ANTOINE-DE-TILLY

MANOIR DE TILLY COUNTRY INN
3854 Chemin de
Tilly
(418) 886-2407

ST-FAUSTIN-LAC CARRE

MOTEL SUR LA COLLINE
357 Rt 117
(819) 688-2102

ST-FELICIEN

HOTEL DU JARDIN
1400 Boul du
Jardin
(418) 679-8422

ST. GEORGES DE BEAUCE

ECONO LODGE
16525 Boul
Lacroix (G5V 2G2)
(418) 227-1227
(800) 553-2666

ST-HYACINTHE

HOTEL GOUVERNEUR ST-HYACINTHE
1200 Johnson
(450) 774-3810

ST-JEAN-PORT-JOLI

AUBERGE DU FAUBOURG
280 Ave de Gaspe
Ouest
(418) 598-6455

ST. JEAN-SUR RICHELIEU

COMFORT INN
700 Rue Gadbois
(J3A 1V1)
(450) 359-4466
(800) 228-5150

HOTEL GOUVERNEUR
725 Boul du
Seminaire nord
(450) 348-7376

ST. LAURENT

HOLIDAY INN AEORPORT
6500 Cote de
Liesse (H4T 1E3)
(514) 739-3391
(800) 465-4329

QUALITY HOTEL DORVAL

7700 Cote de
Liesse
(514) 731-7821
(800) 228-5151

RAMADA HOTEL MONTREAL AIRPORT
7300 Cote de
Liesse (H4T 1E7)
(514) 733-8818
(800) 272-6232

ST. LEONARD

ECONO LODGE
4645 Metropolitan
E (H1R 1Z4)
(514) 725-3671
(800) 553-2666

ST. LIBOIRE

ECONO LODGE
110 Charlotte
(J0H 1R0)
(450) 793-4444
(800) 553-2666

STE-AGATHE-NORD

AUBERGE DE LA SAUVAGINE
1592 Rt 329 Nord
(819) 326-7673

STE-ANNE-DES-MONTS

MOTEL BEAURIVAGE
245 1 Ere Ave
Ouest
(418) 763-2291

STE. FOY

COMFORT INN WEST
7320 Boul
Wilfred-Hamel
(G2G 1C1)
(418) 872-5038
(800) 228-5150

HOLIDAY INN
3125 Boul
Hochelaga (G1V
4A8)
(418) 653-4901
(800) 465-4329

MOTEL L'ABITATION

2828 Boul Laurier
(G1V 2M1)
(418) 653-7267
(800) 567-7267

MOTEL ONCLE SAM
7025 Boul
Wilfred-Hamel
(G2G 1B6)
(418) 872-1488

STE. HELENE DE BAGOT

DAYS INN
410 Couture
(J0H 1M0)
(450) 791-2580
(800) 329-7466

STE-MARTHE

AUBERGE DES GALLANT
1171 Chemin St-Henri
(450) 459-4241

SEPT-ILES

COMFORT INN
854 Boul Laure
(G4R 1Y7)
(418) 968-6005
(800) 228-5150

SHAWINIGAN

AUBERGE ESCAPADE
3383 Rue Garnier
(819) 539-6911

SHAWINIGAN SUD

MOTEL SAFARI
4500 12e Ave
(G9N 6T5)
(819) 536-2664

SHERBROOKE

DELTA SHER-BROOKE HOTEL & CONF CENTRE
2685 Rue King
Ouest
(819) 822-1989
(800) 268-1133

MOTEL LA RESERVE

4235 Rue King
Ouest
(819) 566-6464

THETFORD MINES

COMFORT INN
123 Boul Smith S
(G6G 7S7)
(418) 338-0171
(800) 228-5150

TRACY

HOTEL LE DAUPIN
8200 Rue
Industrielle
(450) 743-2791

TROIS-RIVIERES

DELTA TROIS-RIVIERES HOTEL & CONF CENTRE
1620 Rue Notre-Dame
(819) 376-1991
(800) 268-1133

TROIS-RIV-IERES OUEST

BEST WESTERN TROIS-RIVIERES
3600 Boul Royal
(G9A 4M3)
(819) 379-3232
(800) 528-1234
(800) 463-4620

COMFORT INN
6255 Rue Corbeil
(G8Z 4P9)
(819) 371-3566
(800) 228-5150

DAYS INN
3155 Boul St. Jean
(G9A 5E1)
(819) 377-4444
(800) 329-7466

VAL D'OR

COMFORT INN
1665 3 Ieme Ave
(J9P 1V9)
(819) 825-9360
(800) 228-5150

SASKATCHEWAN

CARONPORT

THE PILGRIM INN
310 College Dr
(306) 756-5002

ELBOW

LAKEVIEW LODGE MOTEL
447 Saskatchewan St (S0H 1J0)
(306) 854-4444

FOAM LAKE

LA VISTA MOTEL
Hwy 16 & 310
(S0A 1A0)
(306) 272-3341

KINDERSLEY

BEST WESTERN WESTRIDGE MOTOR INN
100 12 Ave NW
(S0L 1S0)
(306) 463-4687
(800) 528-1234

LLOYD MINSTER

IMPERIAL 400 MOTEL
4320 44th St, Box 2070 (S9V 1R5)
(306) 825-4400

MOOSE JAW

COMFORT INN
155 Thatcher Dr W (L8P 1J1)
(306) 692-2100
(800) 228-5150

HERITAGE INN
1590 Main St N
(S6H 7N7)
(306) 693-7550

PRAIRIE OASIS MOTEL
955 Thatcher Dr E (S6H 4N9)
(306) 693-8888

SUPER 8 MOTEL
1706 Main St N
(S6H 4P1)
(306) 692-8888
(800) 800-8000

NORTH BATTLEFORD

RODEWAY INN
971 Hwy 16
(S9A 3W2)
(306) 445-7747
(800) 228-2000

SUPER 8 MOTEL
1006 Hwy 16 Bypass (S9A 3W2)
(306) 446-8888
(800) 800-8000

TROPICAL INN
1001 Hwy 16 Bypass (S9A 2W3)
(306) 446-4700

PRINCE ALBERT

COMFORT INN
3863 2nd Ave W
(S6W 1A1)
(306) 763-4466
(800) 228-5150

IMPERIAL 400 MOTEL
3580 2nd Ave W
(S6V 5G2)
(306) 764-6881

TRAVELODGE
3551 2nd Ave W
(S6V 5G1)
(306) 764-6441
(800) 578-7878

REGINA

BEST WESTERN SEVEN OAKS INN
777 Albert St
(S4R 2P6)
(306) 757-0121
(800) 528-1234
(800) 667-8063

CHELTON SUITES HOTEL
1907 11th Ave
(S4P 0J2)
(306) 569-4600
(800) 667-9922

COMFORT INN
3221 E Eastgate Dr (S4Z 1A4)
(306) 789-5522
(800) 228-5150

COUNTRY INNS & SUITES
3321 E Eastgate Bay (S4Z 1A4)
(306) 789-9117
(800) 456-4000

RAMADA HOTEL & CONV CENTRE
1818 Victoria Ave
(S4P 0R1)
(306) 569-1666
(800) 272-6232

SUPER 8 MOTEL
2730 Victoria Ave E (S4N 6M5)
(306) 789-8833
(800) 800-8000

TRAVELODGE
1110 E Victoria Ave (S4N 7A9)
(306) 565-0455
(800) 578-7878

SASKATOON

BEST WESTERN INN & SUITES
1715 Idylwyld Dr N
(S7L 1B4)
(306) 244-5552
(800) 528-1234
(888) 244-5552

COMFORT INN
2155 Northridge Dr (S7L 6X6)
(306) 934-1122
(800) 228-5150

COUNTRY INNS & SUITES
617 Cynthia St
(S7L 6B7)
(306) 934-3900
(800) 456-4000

DELTA BESSBOROUGH
601 Spadina Cres E (S7K 3G8)
(306) 244-5521
(800) 268-1133

RAMADA HOTEL SASKATOON
90 - 22nd St E
(S7K 3X6)
(306) 244-2311
(800) 272-6232

SUPER 8 MOTEL
705 Circle Dr
(S7K 3T7)
(306) 384-8989
(800) 800-8000

SWIFT CURRENT

BEST WESTERN INN
105 George St W
(S9H 0K4)
(306) 773-4660
(800) 528-1234

CARAVEL MOTEL
705 N Service Rd
(S9H 3X6)
(306) 773-8385

COMFORT INN
1510 S Service Rd E (S9H 3X6)
(306) 778-3994
(800) 228-5150

IMPERIAL 400 MOTEL
1150 Begg St E
(S9H 3X6)
(306) 773-2033

RODEWAY INN
1200 S Service Rd
(S9H 3X6)
(306) 773-4664
(800) 228-2000

SAFARI MOTEL
810 Begg St E
(S9H 3X6)
(306) 773-4608

SUPER 8 MOTEL
405 N Service Rd E (S9H 3X6)
(306) 778-6088
(800) 800-8000

WESTWIND MOTEL
155 Begg St W
(S9H 3S8)
(306) 773-1441

WEYBURN

PERFECT INNS
238 Sims Ave
(S4H 2J8)
(306) 842-2691

WEYBURN INN
5 Government Rd
(S4H 0N8)
(306) 842-6543

YORKTON

HOLIDAY INN
100 Broadway E (S3N 2V6)
(306) 783-9781
(800) 465-4329

IMPERIAL 400 MOTEL
207 Broadway E (S3N 2V6)
(306) 783-6581

TRAVELODGE
345 Broadway W
(S3N 0N8)
(306) 783-6571
(800) 578-7878

YUKON

BEAVER CREEK

WESTMARK INN
Alaska Hwy,
MP 1202
(867) 862-7501

DAWSON CITY

BONANZA GOLD MOTEL
Hwy 2 (Y0B 1G0)
(867) 993-6789

WESTMARK INN
5th & Harper Sts
(Y0B 1G0)
(867) 993-5542

WHITE RAM MANOR BED & BREAKFAST
7th & Harper Sts
(Y0B 1G0)
(867) 993-5772

HAINES JUNCTION

GATEWAY MOTEL
Box 5460
(867) 634-2371

WHITEHORSE

BEST WESTERN GOLD RUSH INN
411 Main St
(Y1A 2B6)
(867) 668-4500
(800) 528-1234

HIGH COUNTRY INN
4051 4th Ave
(867) 667-4471

TOWN & MOUNTAIN HOTEL
401 Main St
(Y1A 2B6)
(867) 668-7644

TRAILS NORTH
Mile 922, Alaska
Hwy (Y1A 3Y8)
(867) 633-2327

WESTMARK KLONDIKE INN
2288 Second Ave
(Y1A 1C8)
(867) 668-4747

WESTMARK WHITEHORSE HOTEL & CONF CENTRE
201 Wood St
(867) 393-4700